CONTEMPORARY ISSUES IN BIOETHICS

SEVENTH EDITION

Edited by

Tom L. Beauchamp
Kennedy Institute of Ethics and Department of Philosophy
Georgetown University

LeRoy Walters
Kennedy Institute of Ethics and Department of Philosophy
Georgetown University

Jeffrey P. Kahn
Center for Bioethics
University of Minnesota

Anna C. Mastroianni
School of Law and Institute for Public Health Genetics
University of Washington

THOMSON

WADSWORTH

Australia • Brazil • Canada • Mexico • Singapore • Spain • United Kingdom • United States

THOMSON

WADSWORTH

Philosophy Editor: Worth Hawes
Assistant Editor: Patrick Stockstill
Editorial Assistant: Kamilah S. Lee
Technology Project Manager: Julie Aguilar
Marketing Manager: Christina Shea
Marketing Assistant: Mary Anne Payumo
Marketing Communications Manager: Darlene
    Amidon-Brent
Creative Director: Rob Hugel

Art Director: Maria Epes
Print Buyer: Karen Hunt
Permissions Editor: Mardell Glinski Schultz
Production Service: Matrix Productions Inc.
Copy Editor: Cheryl Smith
Cover Designer: Yvo Riezebos Design/
    Hatty Lee
Compositor: International Typesetting
and Composition

For more information about our products,
contact us at:
**Thomson Learning Academic Resource
Center
1-800-423-0563**
For permission to use material from this text
or product, submit a request online at
http://www.thomsonrights.com.
Any additional questions about permissions
can be submitted by e-mail to
thomsonrights@thomson.com.

Library of Congress Control Number:
2007929153

ISBN-13: 978-0-495-00673-2
ISBN-10: 0-495-00673-4

Thomson Higher Education
10 Davis Drive
Belmont, CA 94002-3098
USA

Wadsworth—Thomson Learning
10 Davis Drive
Belmont, CA 94002-3098
USA

Asia
Thomson Learning
60 Albert Street, #15-01
Albert Complex
Singapore 189969

Australia
Nelson Thomson Learning
102 Dodds Street
South Melbourne, Victoria 3205
Australia

Canada
Nelson Thomson Learning
1120 Birchmont Road
Toronto, Ontario M1K 5G4
Canada

Europe/Middle East/Africa
Thomson Learning
Berkshire House
168-173 High Holborn
London WC1V 7AA
United Kingdom

Latin America
Thomson Learning
Seneca, 53
Colonia Polanco
11560 Mexico D.F.
Mexico

Spain
Paraninfo Thomson Learning
Calle/Magallanes, 25
28015 Madrid, Spain

CONTENTS

CHAPTER 3: THE PATIENT–PROFESSIONAL RELATIONSHIP   129

CHAPTER 4: EUGENICS AND HUMAN GENETICS   199

CHAPTER 5: REPRODUCTION   299

PREFACE

This seventh edition of *Contemporary Issues in Bioethics* differs significantly from the sixth and earlier editions. The most important change is that two new coeditors, Jeffrey Kahn and Anna Mastroianni, have joined the coeditors of the first six editions, Tom Beauchamp and LeRoy Walters. This enlarged and enhanced group of coeditors has allowed us to review the contents of the book in a fresh way and has permitted each coeditor to focus on a limited number of topics in greater depth.

Users of this edition and past editions will note several major improvements over the sixth edition. The seventh edition includes new chapters on Organ Transplantation (Chapter 7) and Biotechnology and Bioscience (Chapter 10). The selections on Public Health (Chapter 9) are entirely new for this edition. The discussion of Justice and Health Care (Chapter 8) has also been substantially revised to take account of recent philosophical and public policy debates. All reproductive questions are now united in a single chapter—Chapter 5— that considers both assisted reproduction and moral and legal arguments about abortion. The coeditors have also been able to include up-to-the-last-minute information from U.S. Supreme Court decisions. Finally, a new essay by a Japanese scholar reviews medical atrocities committed by Imperial Japanese armies during the occupation of China. In the book as a whole, 60 of the 112 selections are new to this edition.

The first chapter provides a brief survey of developments in moral philosophy that are directly relevant to bioethical debates. In each succeeding chapter we have tried to give students and faculty members a sense of the cutting-edge of contemporary ethical discussion. We have sought balance in our selections, providing readers with the facts and the best arguments used to support diverse viewpoints. In our view, students should be encouraged to think critically about the issues raised in this book. Easy answers to complex ethical and public-policy questions are not likely to be intellectually satisfying or practically useful in the long run.

This book has been a collaborative effort from start to finish. Tom and Jeffrey shared editorial responsibility for Chapter 1, while Tom assumed primary responsibility for Chapters 6 and 8, Jeffrey for Chapters 7 and 10, Anna for Chapters 3, 5, and 9, and LeRoy for Chapters 2 and 4. In our editorial efforts we have been ably assisted and supported by Barton Moffatt, Erica Eggerston, Patrick Connolly, and Stacylyn Dewey—our graduate and undergraduate research assistants. These able students worked tirelessly to help us identify pertinent literature by searching online databases, gathering candidate documents, tracking elusive references, and compiling bibliographies. Our lists of suggested readings give but a small indication of the many authors, committees, and commissions whose work we would like to have included in this anthology. Tom and LeRoy are grateful to Moheba Hanif, Sally Schofield, and Linda Powell for their administrative support, Anna appreciates the administrative support of Victoria Parker, and Jeff would like to thank Debra Carter and Barton Moffatt for their help in managing the complex permissions process.

We have again been fortunate to be assisted by the finest library and information-retrieval colleagues in the world. In particular, we acknowledge the exceptional work of Doris M. Goldstein, Director of Library and Information Services, and her dedicated colleagues, Frances Abramson, Richard Anderson, Laura Bishop, Mark Clemente, Martina Darragh, Roxie France-Nuriddin, Jeanne Furcron, Harriet Gray, Lucinda Huttlinger, Ted Jackson, Tamar Joy Kahn, Patricia Martin, Hannelore Ninomiya, Anita Nolen, Leslie Pendley, Susan Poland, Kathy Schroeder, and Mara Snyder.

Our faculty colleagues at our three home institutions have been sources of constant support and inspiration in all of our academic endeavors. Madison Powers stands out for his contribution to our thinking about Chapter 8 (Justice and Health).

At Wadsworth Publishing Company, we thank our editors, Patrick Stockstill and Worth Hawes, for their helpful suggestions, and Jerry Holloway and Matt Ballantyne for coordinating the publishing process. We also appreciate the help of Christina Shea in providing advance publicity for our book. Mardell Glinski-Schultz has provided expert assistance on copyright and permission questions. At Matrix Productions in Tucson, Aaron Downey has efficiently overseen the copyediting process and the conversion of our text into pages. At International Typesetting and Composition, multiple typesetters with whom we have not spoken directly have done a superb job of accurately keying the pages that follow. We also appreciate the work of our copyeditor, Cheryl Smith, and our proofreader, Diane Jones.

We are grateful to the reviewers who have used previous editions of CIB in their teaching and who suggested numerous ways to improve this seventh edition: Faith Bjalobok, Duquesne University; William H. Bruening, Indiana University-Purdue University, Fort Wayne; Patrick G. Derr, Clark University; Jacqueline Fox, University of South Carolina; Mary S. Gregory, Northern Virginia Community College; Sandra Shapshay, Indiana University, Bloomington; Paul D. Simmons, University of Louisville; Andrew Trew, John Carroll University; and Gladys B. White, Georgetown University.

Finally, we want to acknowledge the patience and support of our spouses, Ruth, Sue, Orlee, and Greg, and of our children—Karine and Zachary, David and Robert, Ben and Danny, and Ryan and Ella—throughout the always-arduous process of reading, selecting, editing, introducing, and proofreading.

We hope that this book will stimulate discussion in academic settings and make a modest contribution to the development of more enlightened public policies on these important biomedical topics.

June 2007

Tom L. Beauchamp
Kennedy Institute of Ethics and Department of Philosophy
Georgetown University

LeRoy Walters
Kennedy Institute of Ethics and Department of Philosophy
Georgetown University

Jeffrey P. Kahn
Center for Bioethics
University of Minnesota

Anna C. Mastroianni
School of Law and Institute for Public Health Genetics
University of Washington

Chapter 1
Ethical Theory and Bioethics

The moral problems discussed in this book have emerged from professional practice in the fields of clinical medicine, biomedical and biotechnology research, nursing, public health, and the social and behavioral sciences. The goal of this first chapter is to provide a basis in language, norms, and theory sufficient for reading and critiquing the selections in the later chapters.

Everyone is aware that ethics in the biomedical professions has had a distinguished history. Among the most influential sources of medical and nursing ethics, in particular, are its traditions: the concepts, practices, and norms that have long guided conduct in these fields. The history and precise character of these traditions may be the logical starting point in reflecting on professional ethics, but great traditions such as Hippocratic ethics often fail to provide a comprehensive, unbiased, and adequately justified ethics. Indeed, the history of medical ethics over the last two thousand years is a disappointing history from the perspective of today's concerns in bioethics about the rights of patients and research subjects.

Prior to the early 1970s, there was no firm ground in which a commitment to principles outside of Hippocratic medical ethics could flourish. Particular ethical codes written for the medical, nursing, and research professions had always been written by their own members to govern their own conduct. To consult persons outside the profession was thought not only unnecessary, but dangerous. This conception has collapsed in the face of the pressures of the modern world. Such a professional morality has been judged inadequately comprehensive, at least somewhat incoherent, not nimble enough to address fast-changing issues, and insensitive to conflicts of interest. The birth of bioethics occurred as a result of an increasing awareness that this older ethic had become obsolete.

Ethical theory has helped supply new concepts and forms of reasoning not found previously in the ethics of the health professions. But ethical theory is not the only source of ongoing reform in bioethics, as we will see.

FUNDAMENTAL PROBLEMS

THE STUDY OF MORALITY

Some Basic Concepts and Definitions. The field of ethics includes the study of social morality as well as philosophical reflection on its norms and practices. The terms *ethical theory* and *moral philosophy* refer, in their most common usage, to philosophical reflection on morality. The term *morality*, by contrast, refers to traditions of belief about right and wrong human conduct. Morality is a social institution with a history and a code of learnable rules and conventions. Like natural languages and political constitutions, core parts of morality exist before we become instructed in the relevant rules and regulations. As we develop and mature, we learn moral responsibilities together with other social obligations, such as duties to abide by laws. Eventually we learn to distinguish general social rules of law and morals from rules binding only on members of special groups, such as those rules that bind only members of the veterinary profession. That is, we learn to distinguish general *social morality* from *professional moralities, institutional codes, traditional cultural moralities*, and the like.

We learn moral rules alongside other important social rules, making it difficult to distinguish between the two. For example, we are constantly reminded in our early years that we must observe social rules of etiquette, such as saying "Please" when we want something and "Thank you" when we receive it, as well as more specific rules such as "A judge is addressed as 'Judge'." We are also taught rules of prudence, such as "Don't touch a hot stove," together with rules of housekeeping, dressing, and the like.

Morality enters the picture when certain actions ought or ought not to be performed because of the considerable impact these actions can be expected to have on the interests of other people. We first learn maxims such as "It is better to give than to receive" and "Respect the rights of others." These are elementary instructions in morality; they express what society expects of us and of everyone in terms of taking the interests of other people into account. We thus learn about moral instructions and expectations, and gradually we come to understand morality as a set of normative standards about doing good, avoiding harm, respecting others, keeping promises, and acting fairly. We are also taught standards of character and moral excellence.

All persons living a moral life grasp the core dimensions of morality. They know not to lie, not to steal others' property, to keep promises, to respect the rights of others, not to kill or cause harm to innocent persons, and the like. All persons committed to morality are comfortable with these rules and do not doubt their relevance and importance. They know that to violate these norms is unethical and will likely generate feelings of remorse as well as subject violators to moral blame by others. Individuals do not create these moral norms, and morality therefore cannot be purely a personal policy or code.

The Common Morality. The set of norms shared by all persons committed to morality constitutes what will here be called "the common morality."[1] The common morality is not merely *a* morality, among *other* moralities. The common morality applies to everyone, and all persons are rightly judged by its standards. The following are examples of standards of action (rules of obligation) found in the common morality: Do not lie to others; keep promises; do not cause harm to others; and take account of the well-being of others. This background of shared rules in the common morality is the raw data for theory and is why we can speak of the origins of moral principles as in the common morality that we all already share.

In recent years, the favored language to express the idea of universal morality has been "human rights," but standards of obligation and virtue are no less important. It would of course be absurd to suppose that all persons do, in fact, accept the norms of the common morality. Many amoral, immoral, or selectively moral persons do not care about or identify with moral demands. Nonetheless, all persons in all cultures who are committed to *moral conduct* do accept the demands of the common morality.

The problem is that there are also many distinct moralities comprised of moral norms and positions that spring from particular cultural, philosophical, and religious sources. One reason that well-developed codes of medical ethics vary from society to society, and even from person to person, is that rules in these codes are not a part of universal morality. That is, no part of common morality has a specific focus on what doctors should and should not do. Universal common morality only supplies the core moral concepts and principles on the basis of which we can and should *reflect on* the more specific problems that arise in the health professions. For example, while everyone is obligated to tell the truth, there may be occasions on which a doctor should not make a full disclosure to a patient or to a family.

Whereas the common morality contains general moral norms that are abstract, universal, and content-thin, particular moralities present concrete, nonuniversal, and content-rich norms. These moralities include the many responsibilities, aspirations, ideals, sympathies, attitudes, and sensitivities found in diverse cultural traditions, religious traditions, professional traditions, and institutional expectations.

Sometimes persons who suppose that they speak with an authoritative moral voice operate under the false belief that they have the force of the common morality (that is, universal morality) behind them. The particular moral viewpoints that such persons represent may be acceptable and even praiseworthy, but they also may not bind other persons or communities. For example, persons who believe that scarce medical resources such as transplantable organs should be allocated by lottery rather than by medical need or waiting time may have very good moral reasons for their views, but they cannot claim the force of the common morality for those views.

A theory of common morality does not hold that all *customary* moralities qualify as part of the *common* morality; and use of the common morality in moral reasoning need not lead to conclusions that are socially received. An important function of the general norms in the common morality is to provide a basis for the evaluation and criticism of groups or communities whose customary moral viewpoints are in some respects deficient. Critical reflection may ultimately vindicate moral judgments that at the outset were not widely shared.

Four Approaches to the Study of Ethics. Morality can be studied and developed in a variety of ways. In particular, four ways appear prominently in the literature of ethics. Two of these approaches describe and analyze morality without taking moral positions, and these approaches are therefore called *nonnormative.* Two other approaches do involve taking moral positions and are therefore called *normative* or *prescriptive.* These four approaches can be grouped as follows:

A. *Nonnormative approaches*
   1. Descriptive ethics
   2. Metaethics
B. *Normative approaches*
   3. General normative ethics
   4. Practical normative ethics

It would be a mistake to regard these categories as expressing rigid, sharply differentiated approaches. They are often undertaken at the same time, and they overlap in goal and content. Nonetheless, when understood as broad polar contrasts exemplifying models of inquiry, these distinctions are important.

First among the two nonnormative fields of inquiry into morality is *descriptive ethics,* or the factual description and explanation of moral behavior and beliefs. Anthropologists, sociologists, and historians who study moral behavior employ this approach when they explore how moral attitudes, codes, and beliefs differ from person to person and from society to society. Their works often dwell in detail on matters such as professional codes and practices, codes of honor, and rules governing permissible killing in a society. Although philosophers do not typically engage in descriptive ethics in their work, some have combined descriptive ethics with philosophical ethics—for example, by analyzing the ethical practices of Native American tribes, or researching Nazi experimentation during World War II, and by writing case studies. In the broad field of bioethics, scholars and researchers may engage in either descriptive or normative ethics in their work, and some engage in both.

The second nonnormative field, *metaethics*, involves analysis of the meanings of central terms in ethics, such as *right, obligation, good, virtue,* and *responsibility.* The proper analysis of the term *morality* and the distinction between the moral and the nonmoral are common metaethical problems. Crucial terms in bioethics, including *physician-assisted suicide, informed consent, allocation of organs,* and *universal access* to health care, can be and should be given careful conceptual attention, and they are so treated in various chapters in this volume. (Descriptive ethics and metaethics may not be the only forms of nonnormative inquiry. In recent years there has been an active discussion of the biological bases of moral behavior and of the ways in which humans do and do not differ from animals.)

General normative ethics attempts to formulate and defend basic principles and virtues governing the moral life. Ideally, any ethical theory will provide a system of moral principles or virtues and reasons for adopting them and will defend claims about the range of their applicability. In the course of this chapter the most prominent of these theories will be examined, as will various principles of respect for autonomy, justice, and beneficence that have played a major role in some of these theories.

General normative theories are sometimes used to justify positions on particular moral problems such as abortion, euthanasia, the distribution of health care, research involving human subjects, human embryonic stem cell research, and policies governing organ procurement and allocation. Usually, however, no direct move can be made from moral theory and principles to particular judgments and actions, and theory and principles therefore typically only *facilitate* the development of policies, action guides, or judgments. In general, the attempts to delineate practical action guides are referred to as *practical ethics* (B.4 in the preceding outline).

Substantially the same general ethical theories and principles apply to problems across different professional fields and in areas beyond professional ethics as well. One might appeal to principles of justice, for example, in order to illuminate and resolve issues of taxation, health care distribution, criminal punishment, and affirmative action in hiring. Similarly, principles of veracity (truthfulness) are invoked to discuss secrecy and deception in international politics, misleading advertisements in business ethics, balanced reporting in journalistic ethics, and the disclosure of the nature and extent of an illness to a patient in medical ethics.

MORAL DILEMMAS AND DISAGREEMENTS

In the teaching of ethics, moral problems are often examined through cases—in particular, law cases, clinical cases, and public policy cases. These cases, which appear in virtually every chapter in this book, vividly display dilemmas and disagreements that require students to identify and grapple with real moral problems.

Moral Dilemmas. In a case presented in Chapter 3, two judges on an appeals court became entangled in apparent moral disagreement when ruling in a murder trial. A woman named Tarasoff had been killed by a man who previously had confided to a therapist his intention to kill her as soon as she returned home from a summer vacation. Owing to obligations of confidentiality between patient and physician, a psychologist and a consulting psychiatrist did not report the threat to the woman or to her family, though they did make one unsuccessful attempt to commit the man to a mental hospital.

One judge held that the therapist could not escape liability: "When a therapist determines, or pursuant to the standards of his profession should determine, that his patient presents a serious danger of violence to another, he incurs an obligation to use reasonable care to protect the intended victim against such danger." Notification of police and direct warnings to the family were mentioned as possible instances of due care. The judge argued that although medical confidentiality must generally be observed by physicians, it was overridden in this case by an obligation to the possible victim and to the "public interest in safety from violent assault."

In the minority opinion, a second judge stated his firm disagreement. He argued that a patient's rights are violated when rules of confidentiality are not observed, that psychiatric treatment would be frustrated by any failure to respect confidentiality, and that patients would subsequently lose confidence in psychiatrists and would fail to provide full disclosures. He also suggested that violent assaults would actually increase because mentally ill persons would be discouraged from seeking psychiatric aid.[2]

The Tarasoff case is an instance of a moral dilemma because strong moral reasons support the rival conclusions of the two judges. The most difficult and recalcitrant moral controversies that we encounter in this volume generally have at least some dilemmatic features. They may even involve what Guido Calabresi has called "tragic choices." Everyone who has been faced with a difficult decision—such as whether to have an abortion, to have a pet "put to sleep," to commit a family member to a mental institution, or to withdraw life support from a loved one—knows through deep anguish what is meant by a personal dilemma.

Dilemmas occur whenever one has good reasons for mutually exclusive alternatives; if one set of reasons is acted upon, events will result that are desirable in some respects but undesirable in others. Here it appears that an agent morally ought to do one thing and also morally ought to do another thing, but the agent is precluded by circumstances from doing both. Although the moral reasons behind each alternative are good reasons, neither set of reasons clearly outweighs the other. Parties on both sides of dilemmatic disagreements thus can *correctly* present moral reasons in support of their competing conclusions. The reasons behind each alternative are good and weighty, and neither set of reasons is obviously best. Most moral dilemmas therefore present a need to balance rival claims in untidy circumstances.

One possible response to the problem of public moral dilemmas and disputes is that we do not have and are not likely ever to have a single theory or method for resolving public disagreements. In any pluralistic culture there may be many sources of moral value and consequently a pluralism of moral points of view on many issues: bluffing in business deals, providing national health insurance to all citizens, involuntary isolation of patients during infectious disease outbreaks, the use of human embryos in research, civil disobedience in pursuit of justice, and so on. If this response is correct, we can understand why there seem to be intractable moral dilemmas and controversies. However, there also are ways to alleviate at least some dilemmas and disagreements, as we shall now see.

The Resolution of Moral Disagreements. No single set of considerations is an entirely reliable method for resolving disagreement and controversy, but several methods for dealing constructively with moral disagreements have been employed in the past. Each deserves recognition as a method of constructively contending with disagreement.

1. *Obtaining Objective Information.* First, many moral disagreements can be at least facilitated by obtaining factual information concerning points of moral controversy. It has often been assumed that moral disputes are produced solely by differences over moral principles or their interpretation and application, rather than by a lack of information. However, disputes over what morally ought or ought not to be done often have nonmoral elements as central ingredients. For example, debates about the justice of government allocation of health dollars to preventive and educational strategies have often bogged down over factual issues of whether these strategies actually do function to prevent illness and promote health.

In some cases new information facilitates negotiation and compromise. New information about the alleged dangers involved in certain kinds of scientific research, for instance, have turned public controversies regarding the risks of science and the rights of scientific researchers in unanticipated directions. In several controversies over research with a high level of uncertainty, it has been feared that the research might create an irreversible and dangerous situation—for example, by releasing a pathogen for which the population has no immunity and for which there is no effective treatment.

Controversies about sweetening agents for drinks, toxic substances in the workplace, pesticides in agriculture, radiation therapies, and vaccine dissemination, among others, have been laced with issues of both values and facts. The arguments used by disagreeing parties in these cases sometimes turn on a dispute about liberty or justice and therefore sometimes are primarily normative, but they may also rest on purely factual disagreements. The problem is that rarely, if ever, is all the information obtained that would be sufficient to settle such disagreements.

2. *Providing Definitional Clarity.* Second, controversies have been calmed by reaching conceptual or definitional agreement over the language used by disputing parties. Controversies about "euthanasia," "rationing" health care, "informed consent," and "mental health," for example, are often needlessly entangled because disputing parties use different senses of the terms and have invested heavily in their particular definitions. For example, it may be that one party equates "euthanasia" with mercy killing and another party equates it with voluntarily elected natural death. Some even hold that euthanasia is by definition *nonvoluntary* mercy killing. Any resulting moral controversy over the concept of euthanasia will then be ensnared in terminological problems, rendering it doubtful that the parties are even discussing the same concepts and problems. Accordingly, careful conceptual analysis may be essential to facilitate discussion of issues. Many essays in this volume dwell at some length on conceptual analysis.

3. *Adopting a Code.* Third, resolution of moral problems can be facilitated if disputing parties can come to agreement on a common set of specific moral guidelines, such as rules that define "conflict of interest," and then state obligations to avoid such conflicts. If this method requires a complete shift from one starkly different moral point of view to another, disputes will virtually never be eased. Differences that divide persons at the level of their most cherished views are deep divisions, and conversions are infrequent. Nonetheless, carefully articulated codes reached by discussion and negotiation can lead to the adoption of a new or changed moral framework that can serve as a common basis for evaluation of conduct.

Virtually every professional association in medicine and nursing has a code of ethics, and the reason for the existence of these codes is to give guidance in a circumstance of uncertainty or dispute. Their rules apply to all persons in the relevant professional roles in medicine, nursing, and research and often help resolve charges of unprofessional or unethical conduct. These codes contain general rules and cannot be expected to cover every possible case, but agreed-upon rules do provide an important starting point.

4. *Using Examples and Counterexamples.* Fourth, resolution of moral controversies can be aided by a constructive method of example and opposed counterexample. Cases or examples favorable to one point of view are brought forward, and counterexamples to these cases are thrown up against the examples and claims of the first. This form of debate occurred when a national commission once considered the level of risk that can justifiably be permitted in scientific research involving children as subjects, where no therapeutic benefit is offered

to the child. On the basis of principles of acceptable risk used in their own previous deliberations, commissioners were at first inclined to accept the view that only low-risk or minimal-risk procedures could be justified in the case of children (where *minimal risk* refers analogically to the level of risk present in standard medical examinations of patients). Examples from the history of medicine were cited that revealed how certain significant diagnostic, therapeutic, and preventive advances in medicine would have been unlikely, or at least slowed, unless procedures that posed a higher level of risk had been employed. Counterexamples of overzealous researchers who placed children at too much risk were then thrown up against these examples, and the debate continued in this way for several months.

Eventually a majority of commissioners abandoned their original view that nontherapeutic research involving more than minimal risk was unjustified. The majority accepted the position that a somewhat higher level of risk can be justified by the benefits provided to other children, as when some terminally ill children become subjects of research in the hope that something will be learned about their disease that can be applied to other children. Once a consensus on this issue crystallized, resolution was achieved on the primary moral controversy about the involvement of children as research subjects in so-called nontherapeutic research (although two commissioners never agreed).

5. *Analyzing Arguments.* Fifth and finally, one of the most important methods of philosophical inquiry is the exposing of inadequacies, gaps, fallacies, and unexpected consequences of an argument. If an argument rests on accepting two incoherent points of view, then pointing out the incoherence will require a change in the argument. There are many subtle ways of attacking an argument. For example, in Chapters 5 and 6 there are discussions of the nature of "persons"—whether, for example, fetuses are persons and whether the irreversibly comatose are persons. Some writers on topics of abortion and the right to die have not appreciated that their arguments about persons were so broad that they carried important but unnoticed implications for other groups, such as infants and animals. Their arguments implicitly provided reasons they had not noticed for denying rights to infants (rights that adults have), or for granting (or denying) the same rights to fetuses that infants have, and in some cases for granting (or denying) the same rights to animals that infants have.

It may, of course, be correct to hold that infants have fewer rights than adults, or that fetuses and animals should be granted the same rights as infants. The present point is simply that if a moral argument leads to conclusions that a proponent is not prepared to defend and did not previously anticipate, the argument will probably have to be changed, and this process may reduce the distance between the parties who were initially in disagreement. This style of argument may be supplemented by one or more of the other four ways of reducing moral disagreement. Much of the work published in journals takes the form of attacking arguments, using counterexamples, and proposing alternative principles.

The moral life will of course always be plagued by forms of conflict and incoherence. Our pragmatic goal should be methods that help alleviate and overcome disagreement, not methods that will always eradicate problems. We need not claim that moral disagreements can always be resolved, or even that every rational person must accept the same method for approaching problems. However, if something is to be done to alleviate disagreement, a resolution is more likely to occur if the methods outlined in this section are used.

THE PROBLEM OF RELATIVISM

The fact of moral disagreement and the idea of a universal common morality raise questions about whether moral judgments can be reached impartially and hold for everyone, or instead lead to an inescapable relativism of moral belief.

Cultural Relativism. Relativists have often appealed to anthropological data indicating that moral rightness and wrongness vary from place to place and that there are no absolute or universal moral standards that could apply to all persons at all times. They maintain that rightness is contingent on cultural beliefs and that the concepts of rightness and wrongness are meaningless apart from the specific cultural and historical contexts in which they arise. The claim is that patterns of culture can only be understood as unique wholes and that moral beliefs are closely connected in a culture.

Although it is true that many cultural practices and individual beliefs vary, it does not follow that morally committed people in various parts of the world disagree about the moral standards that were described earlier in this chapter as norms in the common morality. Two cultures may agree about these norms and yet disagree about how to apply them in particular situations or practices. The two cultures may even agree on all the basic principles of morality yet disagree about how to live by these principles in particular circumstances.

For example, if personal payments for special services are common in one culture and punishable as bribery in another, then it is undeniable that these customs are different, but it does not follow that the moral principles underlying the customs are relative. One culture may exhibit a belief that practices of payments to "grease" the process produce a social good by eliminating government interference and by lowering the salaries paid to functionaries, while the people of another culture may believe that the overall social good is best promoted by eliminating all special favors. Both justifications rest on an appraisal of the overall social good, but the people of the two cultures apply this principle in disparate and apparently competing ways.

This possibility suggests that a basic or fundamental conflict between cultural values can only occur if apparent cultural disagreements about proper principles or rules occur at the level of ultimate moral principles. Otherwise, the apparent disagreements can be understood in terms of, and perhaps be arbitrated by, appeal to deeper shared values. If a moral conflict were truly fundamental, then the conflict could not be removed even if there were perfect agreement about the facts of a case, about the concepts involved, and about background beliefs.

We need, then, to distinguish *relativism of judgments* from *relativism of standards:* Judgments that differ across cultures and individuals may rely upon the same general standards for their justification. Relativism of judgment is so pervasive in human social life that it would be foolish to deny it. When people differ about whether one policy for keeping hospital information confidential is more acceptable than another, they differ in their judgments, but they need not have different moral standards about the importance of maintaining medical confidentiality. They may hold the same moral standard but differ over how to implement that standard.

Showing that a relativism of standards is morally incorrect is more than we can hope to achieve here, but we might make some headway in this direction. First, we can recall the earlier discussion of common morality, by contrast to other moralities such as cultural moralities, professional moralities, and individual moralities. The common morality, by definition (or by its very nature) is not relative; it applies to all equally. Second, we can show how difficult it would be to demonstrate that a relativism of standards is true. Suppose, for the sake of argument, that disagreement exists at the deepest level of moral belief; that is, suppose that two cultures disagree on one or more fundamental moral norms. It does not follow even from this cultural relativity of *standards* that there is no ultimate norm or set of norms in which everyone *ought* to believe. Consider an analogy to religious disagreement: From the fact that people have incompatible religious or atheistic beliefs, it does not follow that there is no single correct set of religious or atheistic propositions. Nothing more than skepticism is justified by the facts about religion that are adduced by anthropology; and, similarly, nothing more than this skepticism would be justified if fundamental conflicts of social belief were discovered in ethics.

Normative Relativism. Consider now a second type of relativism. Some relativists interpret "What is right at one place or time may be wrong at another" to mean that *it is right* in one context to act in a way that *it is wrong* to act in another. This thesis is normative, because it makes a value judgment; it delineates *which standards or norms correctly determine right and wrong behavior.* One form of this normative relativism asserts that one ought to do what one's society determines to be right (a group or social form of normative relativism), and a second form holds that one ought to do what one personally believes is right (an individual form of normative relativism).

This normative position has sometimes crudely been translated as "Anything is right or wrong whenever some individual or some group judges that it is right or wrong." However, less crude formulations of the position can be given, and more or less plausible examples can be adduced. One can hold the view, for example, that in order to be right something must be conscientiously and not merely customarily believed. Alternatively, it might be formulated as the view that whatever is believed to be right is right if it is part of a well-formed traditional moral code of rules in a society—for example, a medical code of ethics developed by a professional society.

However, this theory is very difficult to defend. The evident inconsistency of this form of relativism with many of our most cherished moral beliefs is a strong reason to be doubtful of it. No general theory of normative relativism is likely to convince us that a belief is acceptable merely because others believe it in a certain way, although that is exactly the commitment of this theory. At least some moral views seem relatively more enlightened, no matter how great the variability of beliefs. The idea that practices such as slavery, sexual exploitation under severe threat, quarantining persons while not treating their contagious diseases, and banning women from attending medical school, cannot be evaluated across cultures by some common standard seems morally unacceptable, not morally enlightened. It is one thing to suggest that such beliefs might be *excused* (and persons found not culpable for holding those beliefs), still another to suggest that they are *right.*

We can also evaluate this second form of relativism by focusing on (1) the objectivity of morals within cultures, and (2) the stultifying consequences of a consistent commitment to moral relativism. (The first focus provides an argument against *individual* relativism, and the second provides an argument against a *cultural* source of relativism.)

We noted previously that the common morality provides one set of standards of objectivity that cuts across all cultures. In addition, we also said that particular moralities are concerned with practices of right and wrong transmitted within cultures from one generation to another. The terms of social life are set by these practices, whose rules are pervasively acknowledged and shared in that culture. Within the culture, then, there is both universal morality and a significant measure of moral agreement (objectivity) in the culture itself. Neither the common morality nor the culture's morality can be modified through a person's individual preferences.

For example, a hospital corporation cannot develop its professional ethics in any way it wishes. No hospital chain can draw up a code that brushes aside the need for confidentiality of patient information or that permits surgeons to proceed without adequate consents from patients, and a physician cannot make up his or her individual "code" of medical ethics. If codes deviate significantly from standard or accepted rules, they will rightly be rejected as subjective and mistaken.

Room for invention or alteration in morality is therefore restricted. Beliefs cannot become *moral* standards simply because an individual so labels them. Because individual (normative) relativism claims that moral standards can be invented or labeled, the theory seems *factually* mistaken. This critique of *individual* relativism does not count against *cultural* relativism, of course, because a cultural relativist could easily accept this critique. Our focus needs to shift, then, to a second argument, which is directed at cultural forms of normative relativism.

The problem is this: In circumstances of disagreement, moral reflection is needed to resolve moral issues, whether or not people accept different norms. When two parties argue about a serious, divisive, and contested moral issue—for example, conflicts of interest—most of us think that some fair and justified compromise may be reached despite the differences of belief causing the dispute. People seldom infer from the mere fact of a conflict between beliefs that there is no way to judge one view as correct or as better argued or fairer minded than the other. The more implausible the position advanced by one party, the more convinced others become that some views are mistaken or require supplementation.

People seldom conclude, then, that there is not a better and worse ethical perspective and body of argument. If cultural normative relativists deny this claim, they seem to deny one of our most cherished moral outlooks.

THE ACCEPTABILITY OF MORAL DIVERSITY AND MORAL DISAGREEMENT

Even conscientious and reasonable moral agents who work diligently at moral reasoning sometimes disagree with other equally conscientious persons. They may disagree about whether disclosure to a fragile patient is appropriate, whether religious values about brain death have a central place in secular ethics, whether physician-assisted suicide should be legalized, and hundreds of other issues in bioethics. Such disagreement does not indicate moral ignorance or moral defect. We simply lack a single, entirely reliable way to resolve all disagreements.

This fact returns us to the questions about the common morality by contrast to particular moralities with which we opened this chapter. Neither the common morality nor ethical theory has the resources to provide a single solution to every moral problem. So-called "moral" disagreement can emerge for many reasons, including (1) factual disagreements (for example, about the level of suffering that an action will cause), (2) scope disagreements about who should be protected by a moral norm (for example, whether fetuses or animals are protected), (3) disagreements about which norms are relevant in the circumstances, (4) disagreements about appropriate specifications, (5) disagreements about the weight of the relevant norms in the circumstances, (6) disagreements about appropriate forms of balancing, (7) the presence of a genuine moral dilemma, and (8) insufficient information or evidence.

Different parties may emphasize different principles or assign different weights to principles even when they do not disagree over which principles are relevant. Such disagreement may persist among morally committed persons who conform to all the demands that morality makes upon them. In the face of this problem, when evidence is incomplete and different sets of evidence are available to different parties, one individual or group may be justified in reaching a conclusion that another individual or group is justified in rejecting. Even when both parties have incorrect beliefs, each party may be justified in holding those beliefs. We cannot hold persons to a higher standard in practice than to make judgments conscientiously in light of the relevant norms and the available and relevant evidence.

These facts about the moral life sometimes discourage those who must deal with practical problems, but the phenomenon of reasoned moral disagreement provides no basis for skepticism about morality or about moral thinking. Indeed, it offers a reason for taking morality seriously and using the best tools that we have to carry our moral projects as far as we can. After all, we frequently obtain near complete agreement in our moral judgments, and we always have the universal basis for morality (the common morality) considered earlier in this chapter.

When disagreements arise, a moral agent can—and often should—defend his or her decision without disparaging or reproaching others who reach different decisions. Recognition of legitimate diversity (by contrast to moral violations that call for criticism) is exceedingly important when we evaluate the actions of others. What one person does may not be what other persons should do when they face the same problem. Similarly, what one institution or government should do may not be what another institution or government should do. From this perspective, individuals and societies legitimately construct different requirements that comprise part of the moral life (consistent with what we have called morality in the broad sense), and we may not be able to judge one as better than another.[3]

MORAL JUSTIFICATION

Typically we have no difficulty in deciding whether to act morally. We make moral judgments through a mix of appeals to rules, paradigm cases, role models, and the like. These moral beacons work well as long as we are not asked to deliberate about or justify our judgments. However, when we experience moral doubt or uncertainty, we are led to moral deliberation, and often from there to a need to justify our beliefs. As we deliberate, we usually consider which among the possible courses of action is morally justified—that is, which has the strongest moral reasons behind it. The reasons we finally accept express the conditions under which we believe some course of action is morally justified.

The objective of justification is to establish one's case by presenting a sufficient set of reasons for belief and action. Not all reasons, however, are good reasons, and even good reasons are not always sufficient for justification. There is, then, a need to distinguish a reason's *relevance* to a moral judgment from its final *adequacy* for that judgment; and also to distinguish an *attempted* justification from a *successful* justification. For example, a good reason for involuntarily committing certain mentally ill persons to institutions is that they present a clear and present danger to other persons. By contrast, a reason for commitment that is sometimes offered as a good reason, but that many people consider a bad reason (because it involves a deprivation of liberty), is that some mentally ill persons present a clear and present danger to themselves or that they require treatment for a serious mental disorder.

If someone holds that involuntary commitment on grounds of danger to self is a good reason and is solely sufficient to justify commitment, that person should be able to give some account of why this reason is good and sufficient. That is, the person should be able to give further justifying reasons for the belief that the reason offered is good and sufficient. The person might refer, for example, to the dire consequences for the mentally ill that will occur if no one intervenes. The person might also invoke certain principles about the moral importance of caring for the needs of the mentally ill. In short, the person is expected to give a set of reasons that amounts to an argued defense of his or her perspective. These appeals are usually either to a coherent group of moral principles or to consequences of actions, and they form the substantive basis of justification.

Many philosophers now defend the view that the relationship between general moral norms and particular moral judgments is bilateral (neither a unilateral "application" of general norms nor a unilateral abstraction from particular case judgments). John Rawls's celebrated account of *reflective equilibrium* has been the most influential model in this literature. In developing and refining a system of ethics, he argues, it is appropriate to start with the broadest possible set of *considered judgments* (see following) about a subject and to erect a provisional set of principles that reflects them. Reflective equilibrium views investigation in ethics (and theory construction) as a reflective testing of moral principles, theoretical postulates, and other relevant moral beliefs to render them as coherent as possible. Starting with paradigms of what is morally right or wrong, one searches for principles that are consistent with these paradigms as well as one another. Such principles and considered judgments are taken, as Rawls puts it, "provisionally as fixed points," but also as "liable to revision."

Considered judgments is a technical term referring to judgments in which moral beliefs and capacities are most likely to be presented without a distorting bias. Examples are judgments about the wrongness of racial discrimination, religious intolerance, and predatory sexual behavior. The goal of reflective equilibrium is to match, prune, and adjust considered judgments and principles so that they form a coherent moral outlook. This model demands the best approximation to full coherence under the assumption of a never-ending search for consistency and unanticipated situations. From this perspective, ethical theories and individual moral outlooks are never complete, always stand to be informed by practical contexts, and must be tested for adequacy by their practical implications.

Although the justification of particular moral *judgments* is often the issue, philosophers are as often concerned with the justification of general ethical *theories*. Which theory, we can now ask, is the best theory? Or do all theories fail tests for considered judgments and coherence?

TYPES OF ETHICAL THEORY

Many writers in bioethics believe that we would justifiably have more confidence in our individual and communal moral judgments if only we could justify them on the basis of a comprehensive ethical theory. The ambition of an ethical theory is to provide an adequate normative framework for processing, and ideally resolving, moral problems. However, our objective in this section is not to show how ethical theory actually can *resolve* problems, but only to present influential types of ethical theory.

These theories fall under the category that we earlier called general normative ethics. We will concentrate on utilitarianism, Kantianism, virtue (or character) ethics, the ethics of care, and casuistry. Some knowledge of these theories is indispensable for reflective study in bioethics because a sizable part of the field's literature draws on methods and conclusions found in these theories.

UTILITARIAN THEORIES

Utilitarianism is rooted in the thesis that an action or practice is right (when compared to any alternative action or practice) if it leads to the greatest possible balance of good consequences or to the least possible balance of bad consequences in the world as a whole. Utilitarians hold that there is one and only one basic principle of ethics: the principle of utility. This principle asserts that we ought always to produce the maximal balance of good consequences over bad consequences. The classical origins of this theory are found in the writings of Jeremy Bentham (1748–1832) and John Stuart Mill (1806–1873).

Utilitarians invite us to consider the larger objective or function of morality as a social institution, where *morality* is understood to include our shared rules of justice and other principles of the moral life. The point of the institution of morality, they insist, is to promote human welfare by minimizing harms and maximizing benefits: There would be no point to moral codes unless they served this purpose. Utilitarians thus see moral rules as the means to the fulfillment of individual needs as well as to the achievement of broad social goals.

Mill's Utilitarianism. In several types of ethical theory, classic works of enduring influence form the basis for development of the theory. The most influential presentation of utilitarianism is John Stuart Mill's book *Utilitarianism* (1863). In this work Mill refers to the principle of utility as the Greatest Happiness Principle: "Actions are right in proportion as they tend to promote happiness, wrong as they tend to produce the reverse of happiness, i.e., pleasure or absence of pain." Mill's view seems to be that the purpose of morality is to tap natural human sympathies to benefit others while at the same time controlling unsympathetic attitudes that cause harm to others. The principle of utility is conceived as the best means to these basic human goals.

For Mill and other utilitarians, moral theory is grounded in a theory of the general goals of life, which they conceive as the pursuit of pleasure and the avoidance of pain. The production of pleasure and pain assumes moral and not merely personal significance when the consequences of our actions affect the pleasurable or painful states of others. Moral rules and moral and legal institutions, as they see it, must be grounded in a general theory of good or value, and morally good actions are alone determined by these final values.

Essential Features of Utilitarianism. Several essential features of utilitarianism are found in the theories of Mill and all other utilitarians. In particular, four conditions must be satisfied in order to qualify as a utilitarian theory.

1. *The Principle of Utility: Maximize the Good.* First, actors are obliged to maximize the good: We ought always to produce the greatest possible balance of value over disvalue (or the least possible balance of disvalue, if only bad results can be achieved), whatever that balance is and however it is distributed. For example, we ought to maximize the public benefits of scientific research, clinical medicine, public health measures, and so forth. But what is the good or the valuable? This question takes us to the second condition.

2. *A Theory of Value: The Standard of Goodness.* The goodness or badness of consequences is to be measured by items that count as the primary goods or utilities. Various theories of value (or theories of the good) held by utilitarians elevate the following goods to prominence: (1) happiness, (2) the satisfaction of desires and aims, and (3) the attainment of such conditions or states of affairs as autonomy, understanding, various kinds of functioning, achievement, and deep personal relationships. Put another way, utilitarians think of what is good or valuable in terms of basic conditions of well-being such as happiness, health, security, freedom, and companionship and attachment.

Many utilitarians agree that ultimately we ought to look to the production of *agent-neutral* or intrinsic values, those that do not vary from person to person. That is, we should look to the production of what is good in itself, not merely what is good as a means to something else. Bentham and Mill are hedonists; they believe that only pleasure or happiness (synonymous terms in this context) can be intrinsically good. Pluralistic utilitarian philosophers, by contrast, believe that no single goal or state constitutes the good and that many values besides happiness possess intrinsic worth—for example, the values of friendship, knowledge, love, personal achievement, culture, freedom, and liberties might all qualify in a utilitarian theory.

Both the hedonistic and the pluralistic approaches have seemed to some recent philosophers relatively problematic for purposes of objectively aggregating widely different interests in order to determine where maximal value, and therefore right action, lies. Many utilitarians interpret the good as that which is *subjectively* desired or wanted. The satisfaction of desires or wants is seen as the goal of our moral actions. To maximize an individual's utility, under this conception, is to maximize what he or she has chosen or would choose from the available alternatives.

3. *Consequentialism.* Whatever its precise value theory, any utilitarian theory decides which actions are right entirely by reference to the *consequences* of the actions, rather than by reference to any intrinsic moral features the actions may have, such as truthfulness or fidelity. Here the utilitarian need not demand that all future consequences or even all avoidable consequences be anticipated. A utilitarian demands only that we take account of what can reasonably be expected to produce the greatest balance of good or least balance of harm. In judging the *agent* of the action, we should assess whether the agent conscientiously attempts to produce the best utilitarian outcome.

4. *Impartiality (Universalism).* Finally, in the utilitarian approach all parties affected by an action must receive *impartial consideration.* Utilitarianism here stands in sharp contrast to egoism, which proposes maximizing consequences for oneself rather than for all parties affected by an action. In seeking a blinded impartiality, utilitarianism aligns good and mature moral judgment with moral distance from the choices to be made. A moral point of view is *impartial* in the sense that a moral judgment is formed without regard to personal preference and interest and also without regard to the particular fortuitous advantages or disadvantages of persons such as special talents or handicaps, because these properties are morally arbitrary. The ideal, then, is unbiased evaluation without regard to a person's race, sex, nationality, and economic circumstances, none of which can be regarded as legitimate bases for treating persons differently from other persons.

Act and Rule Utilitarianism. Utilitarian moral philosophers are conventionally divided into several types, and it is best to think of "utilitarianism" as a label designating a family of theories that use a consequentialist, maximizing principle. A significant dispute has arisen among utilitarians over whether the principle of utility is to be applied to *particular acts* in particular circumstances or to *rules of conduct* that determine which acts are right and wrong. For the *rule utilitarian,* actions are justified by appeal to rules such as "Don't deceive" and "Don't break promises." These rules, in turn, are justified by appeal to the principle of utility. An *act utilitarian* simply justifies actions directly by appeal to the principle of utility. Act utilitarianism is thus characterized as a "direct" or "extreme" theory because the act utilitarian directly asks, "What good and evil consequences will result *directly* from this action in this circumstance?"—not "What good and evil consequences will result *generally* from this sort of action?"

Consider the following case, which occurred in the state of Kansas and which anticipates some issues about euthanasia encountered in Chapter 6. An elderly woman lay ill and dying. Her suffering came to be too much for her and her faithful husband of fifty-four years to endure, so she requested that he kill her. Stricken with grief and unable to bring himself to perform the act, the husband hired another man to kill his wife. An act utilitarian might reason that *in this case* hiring another person to kill the woman was justified, although *in general* we would not permit persons to perform such actions. After all, only this woman and her husband were directly affected, and relief of her pain was the main issue. It would be unfortunate, the act utilitarian might reason, if our "rules" against killing failed to allow for selective killings in extenuating circumstances, because it is extremely difficult to generalize from case to case. The jury, as it turned out, convicted not only the third party but also the husband of murder, and he was sentenced to twenty-five years in prison. An act utilitarian might maintain that a *rigid* application of rules inevitably leads to injustices and that rule utilitarianism cannot escape this problem of an undue rigidity of rules.

Many philosophers reject act utilitarianism, charging its exponents with basing morality on mere expediency. On act-utilitarian grounds, they say, it is desirable for a physician to kill babies with many kinds of birth defects if the death of the child would relieve the family and society of a burden and inconvenience and would lead to the greatest good for the greatest number. Many opponents of act utilitarianism have thus argued that strict rules, which cannot be set aside for the sake of convenience, must be maintained. Many of these apparently desirable rules can be justified by the principle of utility, so utilitarianism need not be abandoned if act utilitarianism is judged unworthy.

Rule utilitarians hold that rules have a central position in morality and cannot be compromised in particular situations. Compromise threatens the rules themselves. The rules' effectiveness is judged by determining whether the observance of a given rule would maximize social utility better than would any substitute rule (or having no rule). Utilitarian rules are, in theory, firm and protective of all classes of individuals, just as human rights firmly protect all individuals regardless of social convenience and momentary need.

Nonetheless, we can ask whether rule-utilitarian theories offer anything more than act utilitarianism. Dilemmas often arise that involve conflicts among moral rules—for example, rules of confidentiality conflict with rules protecting individual welfare, as in the Tarasoff case. If there are no rules to resolve these conflicts, perhaps the rule utilitarian cannot be distinguished from the act utilitarian.

KANTIAN THEORIES

We have seen that utilitarianism conceives the moral life in terms of producing what is valuable. A second type of theory departs significantly from this approach. Often called *deontological* (i.e., a theory that some features of actions other than or in addition to consequences make actions obligatory), this type is now increasingly called *Kantian*, because of its origins in the theory of Immanuel Kant (1724–1804).

Duty from Rules of Reason. Kant believed that an act is morally praiseworthy only if done neither for self-interested reasons nor as the result of a natural disposition, but rather from *duty*. That is, the person's motive for acting must be a recognition of the act as resting on duty. It is not good enough, in Kant's view, that one merely performs the morally correct action, because one could perform one's duty for self-interested reasons having nothing to do with morality. For example, if an employer discloses a health hazard to an employee only because he or she fears a lawsuit, and not because of a belief in the importance of truth telling, then this employer acts rightly but deserves no moral credit for the action.

Kant tries to establish the ultimate basis for the validity of moral rules in pure reason, not in intuition, conscience, or utility. He thinks all considerations of utility and self-interest morally unimportant, because the moral worth of an agent's action depends exclusively on the moral acceptability of the rule on the basis of which the person is acting. An action has moral worth only when performed by an agent who possesses a good will, and a person has a good will only if moral duty based on a universally valid rule is the sole motive for the action. Morality, then, provides a rational framework of principles and rules that constrain and guide everyone, without regard to their personal goals and interests.

Kant's supreme principle, *the categorical imperative*, also called *the moral law*, is expressed in several ways in his writings. His first formulation may be roughly paraphrased in this way: "Always act in such a way that you can will that everyone act in the same manner in similar situations." Kant's view is that wrongful practices, such as lying, theft, cheating, and failure to help someone in distress when you can easily do so, involve a kind of contradiction. Consider the example of cheating on exams. If everyone behaved as the cheater did, exams would not serve their essential function of testing mastery of relevant material, in which case there would effectively be no such thing as an exam. But cheating presupposes the background institution of taking exams, so the cheater cannot consistently will that everyone act as he or she does.

The categorical imperative is categorical, Kant says, because it admits of no exceptions and is absolutely binding. It is imperative because it gives instruction about how one must act. Kant draws a distinction between a *categorical imperative* and a *hypothetical imperative*. A hypothetical imperative takes the form, "If I want to achieve such and such a valued end, then I must do so and so." These prescriptions—so reminiscent of utilitarian and pragmatic thinking—tell us what we must do, provided that we already have certain desires, interests, or goals. An example is "If you want to regain your health, then you must take this medication," or "If you want to improve infant mortality rates, then you must improve your hospital facilities." These imperatives are not commanded for their own sake. They are commanded as means to an end that has already been willed or accepted. Hypothetical imperatives are not moral imperatives in Kant's philosophy because moral imperatives tell us what must be done independently of our goals or desires.

Kant emphasizes the notion of *rule as universal law*. Rules that determine duty are made correct by their universality, that is, the fact that they apply to everyone. This criterion of universality offers some worthwhile lessons for bioethics. Some of the clearest cases of immoral behavior involve a person's trying to make a unique exception of himself or herself purely for personal reasons. This conduct could not be made universal, because the rules presupposed by the idea of "being an exception" would be destroyed. If carried out consistently by others, this conduct would violate the rules presupposed by the system of morality, thereby rendering the system inconsistent—that is, having inconsistent rules of operation.

Kant's view is that wrongful practices, including invasion of privacy, lying, theft, and manipulative suppression of information, are "contradictory"; that is, they are not consistent with the very duties and institutions they presuppose. In cases of lying, for example, the universalization of rules that allow lying would entitle everyone to lie to you, just as you would be entitled to lie to them. Such rules are inconsistent with the practice of truth telling that they presuppose. Similarly, fraud in research is inconsistent with the practice of publishing the truth. All such practices are inconsistent with a rule or practice that they presuppose.

The Requirement to Never Treat Persons as Means. A second formulation of Kant's categorical imperative—one more frequently invoked in medical ethics—may be paraphrased in this way: "Treat every person as an end and never solely as a means."[4] This principle requires us to treat persons as having their own established goals. Deceiving prospective subjects in order to get them to consent to participate in nontherapeutic research is one example of a violation of this principle.

It has commonly been said that Kant is here arguing that we can never treat another as a means to our ends. This interpretation, however, misrepresents his views. He argues only that we must not treat another *exclusively* as a means to our own ends. When adult human research subjects are asked to volunteer, for example, they are treated as a means to a researcher's ends. However, they are not exclusively used for others' purposes, because they do not become mere servants or objects. Their consent justifies using them as means to the end of research.

Kant's imperative demands only that persons in such situations be treated with the respect and moral dignity to which all persons are always entitled, including the times when they are used as means to the ends of others. To treat persons merely as a means, strictly speaking, is to disregard their personhood by exploiting or otherwise using them without regard to their own thoughts, interests, and needs. It involves a failure to acknowledge that every person has a worth and dignity equal to that of every other person and that this worth and dignity cannot be compromised for utilitarian or any other reasons.

CONTEMPORARY CHALLENGES TO THE TRADITIONAL THEORIES

Thus far we have treated only two types of theory: utilitarianism and Kantianism. These theories combine a variety of moral considerations into a surprisingly systematized framework, centered around a single major principle. Much is attractive in these theories, and they were the dominant models in ethical theory throughout much of the twentieth century. During the 1970s and 1980s, utilitarian and deontological approaches also dominated the theoretical literature and discourse of bioethics.

Although utilitarian and deontological arguments or patterns of reasoning are still common today, the theories themselves no longer dominate the field of bioethics. The reasons for the demotion of utilitarian and single-principle deontological theories concern the disadvantages of any approach that attempts to characterize the entire domain of morality with one supreme principle. Three disadvantages are especially worthy of note. First, there is a problem of authority. Despite myriad attempts by philosophers in recent centuries to justify the claim that some principle is morally authoritative—that is, correctly regarded as the supreme moral principle—no such effort at justification has persuaded a majority of philosophers or other thoughtful people that either the principle or the moral system is as authoritative as the common morality that supplies its roots. Thus to attempt to illuminate problems in bioethics with a single-principle theory has struck many as misguided and, at times, presumptuous or dogmatic.

Second, even if an individual working in this field is convinced that some such theory is correct (authoritative), he or she needs to deal responsibly with the fact that many other morally serious individuals do not share this theory and give it little or no authority. Thus, problems of how to communicate and negotiate in the midst of disagreement do not favor appeals to rigid theories or inflexible principles, which can generate a gridlock of conflicting principled positions, rendering moral discussion hostile and alienating.

Third, there is the problem that a highly general principle is indeterminate in many contexts in which one might try to apply it. That is, the content of the principle itself does not always identify a unique course of action as right. It has increasingly become apparent that single-principle theories are significantly incomplete, frequently depending on independent moral considerations with the help of which the theories can serve as effective guides to action.

Much recent philosophical writing has focused on weaknesses in utilitarian and Kantian theories and on ways in which the two types of theory actually affirm some broader and less controversial conception of the moral life. Critics of utilitarian and Kantian models believe that these two types of theory need to be replaced with a better theory. Three accounts have been popular in bioethics as replacements for, or perhaps supplements to, utilitarian and Kantian theories: (1) virtue theory (which is character based), (2) the ethics of care (which is relationship based), and (3) casuistry (which is case based). These are the topics of the next three sections.

VIRTUE ETHICS

In discussing utilitarian and Kantian theories, we have looked chiefly at obligations and rights. Beyond obligations and rights, we often reflect on the agents who perform actions, have motives, and follow principles. Here we commonly make judgments about good and evil character in persons. Virtue ethics gives good character a preeminent place.

Virtue ethics descends from the classical Hellenistic tradition represented by Plato and Aristotle. Here the cultivation of virtuous traits of character is viewed as morality's primary function. Moral virtues are understood as morally praiseworthy character traits, such as courage, compassion, sincerity, reliability, and industry. In virtue ethics, the primary concern is with what sort of person is ideal, while action is considered to have secondary importance. People are viewed as acquiring virtues much as they do skills such as carpentry, playing an instrument, or cooking. They become just by performing just actions and become temperate by performing temperate actions. Virtuous character is cultivated and made a part of the individual, much like a language or tradition.

However, an ethics of virtue is more than habitual training. One must also have a correct *motivational structure*. A conscientious person, for example, not only has a disposition to act conscientiously, but a morally appropriate desire to be conscientious. The person characteristically has a moral concern and reservation about acting in a way that would not be conscientious.

Imagine a person who always performs his or her obligation because it is an obligation but intensely dislikes having to allow the interests of others to be of importance. Such a person does not cherish, feel congenial toward, or think fondly of others, and respects them only because obligation requires it. This person can, on a theory of moral obligation such as Kant's or Mill's, perform a morally right action, have an ingrained disposition to perform that action, and act with obligation as the foremost motive. It is possible (1) to be disposed to do what is right, (2) to intend to do it, and (3) to do it, while also (4) yearning to be able to avoid doing it. If the motive is improper, a vital moral ingredient is missing and if a person *characteristically* lacks this motivational structure, a necessary condition of virtuous character is absent.

Consider a physician who meets his moral obligations because they are his obligations and yet has underlying motives that raise questions of character. This physician detests his job and hates having to spend time with every patient who comes through the door. He cares not about being of service to people or creating a better environment in the office. All he wants to do is make money, avoid malpractice suits, and meet his obligations. Although this man never acts immorally from the perspective of duty, something in his character is deeply defective morally. The admirable compassion and dedication guiding the lives of many health professionals is absent in this person, who merely engages in rule-following behavior.

Virtue ethics may seem only of intellectual interest, but it has practical value in that a morally good person with right desires or motives is more likely to understand what should be done, to perform required acts, and to form moral ideals than is a morally bad or indifferent person. A trusted person has an ingrained motivation and desire to do what is right and to care about whether it is done. Whenever the feelings, concerns, and attitudes of others are the morally relevant matters, rules and principles are not as likely as human warmth and sensitivity to lead a person to notice what should be done. From this perspective, virtue ethics is at least as fundamental in the moral life as principles of basic obligation.

We also often morally evaluate a person's emotional responses—which tend to reflect one's character—even where no particular action is called for. One might admire a social worker's genuine sorrow at the news that another social worker's patient committed suicide; her expression of sorrow reflects her caring and sympathy. Moreover, in practice, well-established virtues may prove at least as important as mastery of principles, rules, and other action guides. For example, it may be the case that being truthful, compassionate, perceptive, diligent, and so forth is a more reliable basis for good medical practice than knowledge of the principles and rules of bioethics.

A proponent of character ethics need not claim that analysis of the virtues subverts or discredits ethical principles, rules, or theories. It is enough to argue that ethical theory is more complete if the virtues are included and that moral motives deserve to be at center stage in a way some leading traditional theories have inadequately appreciated. It is not difficult to see the compatibility of virtue ethics and duty ethics.

Indeed, it is doubtful that virtue can be adequately conceptualized without some background assumptions about right action. For example, seeing truthfulness as a virtue seems inseparable from seeing truth telling as a prima facie obligation. If we ask why one should generally be truthful, it seems evasive to say, "Because virtuous people are that way." A more adequate response would show how truthfulness displays respect for people's autonomy, tends to promote certain benefits, and ordinarily avoids certain kinds of harm.

THE ETHICS OF CARE

Related to virtue ethics in vital respects is a relatively new body of moral reflection often called the "ethics of care." This theory develops some of the themes in virtue ethics about the centrality of character, but the ethics of care focuses on a set of character traits that people all deeply value in close personal relationships: sympathy, compassion, fidelity, love, friendship, and the like. Noticeably absent are universal moral rules and impartial utilitarian calculations such as those espoused by Kant and Mill.

To understand this approach, consider the traditional theories' criterion of impartiality in moral judgment. This criterion of distanced fairness and treating similar cases similarly makes eminently good sense for courts, but does it make good sense of intimate moral relationships? The care perspective views this criterion as cutting away too much of morality in order to get to a standpoint of detached fairness. Lost in the traditional *detachment* of impartiality is *attachment*—that which we care about most and which is closest to us. In seeking blindness, we may be made blind and indifferent to the special needs of others. So, although impartiality is a moral virtue in some contexts, it may be a moral vice in others. The care perspective is especially important for roles such as parent, friend, physician, and nurse, where contextual response, attentiveness to subtle clues, and discernment are likely to be more important morally than impartial treatment.

Being cautious about abstract principles of obligation—the instruments of impartiality—is also characteristic of the ethics of care. Defenders of the ethics of care find principles often to be irrelevant, vacuous, or ineffectual in the moral life. A defender of principles could say that principles of care, compassion, and kindness structure our understanding of when it is appropriate to respond in caring, compassionate, and kind ways, but there is something hollow about this claim. It seems to best capture our moral experience to say that we rely on our emotions, our capacity for sympathy, our sense of friendship, and our knowledge of how caring people behave.

Exponents of the ethics of care have also criticized the autonomous, unified, rational beings that typify both the Kantian and the utilitarian conception of the moral self. They argue that moral decisions often require a sensitivity to the situation as well as an awareness of the beliefs, feelings, attitudes, and concerns of each of the individuals involved and of the relationships of those individuals to one another.

Additional reasons exist for thinking that a morality centered on care and concern cannot be squeezed into a morality of rules. For example, it seems difficult to express the responsibilities of a health care professional adequately through principles and rules. We can generalize about how caring physicians and nurses respond in encounters with patients, but these generalizations do not amount to principles, nor will such generalizations be subtle enough to give sound guidance for the next patient. Each situation calls for a different set of responses, and behavior that in one context is caring seems to intrude on privacy or be offensive in another context.

A morality centered on care and concern can potentially serve health care ethics in a constructive and balanced fashion, because it is close to the processes of reason and feeling exhibited in clinical contexts. Disclosures, discussions, and decision making in health care typically become a family affair, with support from a health care team. The ethics of care maintains that many human relationships in health care and research involve persons who are vulnerable, dependent, ill, and frail and that the desirable moral response is attached attentiveness to needs, not detached respect for rights. Feeling for and being immersed in the other person establish vital aspects of the moral relationship. Accordingly, this approach features responsibilities and forms of empathy that a rights-based account may ignore in the attempt to protect persons from invasion by others.

CASUISTRY

A third alternative to classic theories has been labeled casuistry. It focuses on decision making using particular cases, where the judgments reached rely on judgments reached in prior cases. Casuists are skeptical of the power of principles and theory to resolve problems in specific cases. They think that many forms of moral thinking and judgment do not involve appeals to general guidelines, but rather to narratives, paradigm cases, and precedents established by previous cases.[5]

Casuists concentrate our attention on practical decision making in particular cases and on the implications of those cases for other cases. Here we proceed by identifying the specific features of, and problems present in, the case. We may attempt to identify the relevant precedents and prior experiences we have had with related cases, attempting to determine how similar and how different the present case is from other cases. For example, if the case involves a problem of medical confidentiality, analogous cases would be considered in which breaches of confidentiality were justified or unjustified in order to see whether such a breach is justified in the present case.

Consider the way a physician thinks in making a judgment and then a recommendation to a patient. Many individual factors, including the patient's medical history, the physician's successes with other similar patients, paradigms of expected outcomes, and the like will play a role in formulating a judgment and recommendation to this patient, which may be very different from the recommendation made to the next patient with the same malady. The casuist views moral judgments and recommendations similarly. One can make successful moral judgments of agents, actions, and policies, casuists say, only when one has an intimate understanding of particular situations and an appreciation of treating similar cases similarly.

An analogy to case law is helpful in understanding the casuist's point. In case law, the normative judgments made by courts of law become authoritative, and it is reasonable to hold that these judgments are primary for later judges who assess other cases—even though the particular features of each new case will be different. Matters are similar in ethics, say casuists. Normative judgments about certain cases emerge through case comparisons. A case currently being considered is placed in the context of a set of cases that shows a family resemblance, and the similarities and differences are assessed. The relative weight of competing values is presumably determined by the comparisons to analogous cases. Moral guidance is provided by an accumulated mass of influential cases, which represent a consensus in society and in institutions reached by reflection on cases. That consensus then becomes authoritative and is extended to new cases.[6]

Cases like the Tarasoff case have been enormously influential in bioethics. Writers have used it as a form of authority for decisions in new cases. Features of their analyses have then been discussed throughout the literature of bioethics, and they become integral to the way we think and draw conclusions in the field. The leading cases become enduring and authoritative sources for reflection and decision making. Cases such as the so-called Tuskegee syphilis study (in which a group of men had treatment for syphilis withheld from them in order to follow the course of the disease, but were told they were being treated) are constantly invoked to illustrate *unjustified* biomedical experimentation. Decisions reached about moral wrongs in this case serve as a form of authority for decisions in new cases. These cases profoundly influence our standards of fairness, negligence, paternalism, and the like. Just as case law (legal rules) develops incrementally from legal decisions in cases, so the moral law (moral rules) develops incrementally. From this perspective, principles are less important for moral reasoning than cases.

At first sight, casuistry seems strongly opposed to the frameworks of principles in traditional duty-based theory. However, closer inspection of casuistry shows that its primary concern (like the ethics of care) is with an excessive reliance in recent philosophy on impartial, universal action guides. Two casuists, Albert Jonsen and Stephen Toulmin, write that "*good* casuistry . . . applies general principles to particular cases with discernment." As a history of similar cases and similar judgments mounts, we become more confident in our general judgments. A "locus of moral certitude" arises in the judgments, and the stable elements crystallize into tentative principles. As confidence in these generalizations increases, they are accepted less tentatively and moral knowledge develops.[7]

Today's casuists have resourcefully argued for the importance of analogical reasoning, paradigm cases, and practical judgment. Bioethics, like ethical theory, has sometimes unduly minimized this avenue to moral knowledge. Casuists also have rightly pointed out that generalizations are often best learned, accommodated, and implemented by using cases, case discussion, and case methods. These insights can be utilized by connecting them to an appropriate set of concepts, principles, and theories that control the judgments we make about cases.

Nonetheless, casuists' emphases can be misleading. Casuists sometimes write as if cases lead to moral paradigms, analogies, or judgments entirely by their facts alone—or perhaps by appeal only to a few salient features of the cases. This premise is suspect. No matter how many facts are stacked up, we will still need some *value* premises in order to draw out moral conclusions from the case. The properties that we observe to be of moral importance in cases are picked out by the values that we have already accepted as being morally important. In short, the paradigm cases of the casuists are inherently value-laden.

The best way to understand this idea of paradigm cases is as a combination of (1) *facts* that can be generalized to other cases—for example, "The patient refused the recommended treatment"—and (2) *settled values*—for example, "Competent patients have a right to refuse treatment." In a principle-based system, these settled values are called principles, rules, rights claims, and the like; and they are analytically distinguished from the facts of particular cases. In casuistical appeals to cases, rather than keeping values distinct from facts, the two are bound together in the paradigm case; the central values are generalizable and therefore preserved from one case to the next.

ETHICAL PRINCIPLES

Various basic principles are accepted in classical ethical theories and also seem to be presupposed in traditional codes of ethics. There is an "overlapping consensus" about the validity of these principles. But what is a principle, and which ones overlap the different theories?

A *principle* is a fundamental standard of conduct from which many other moral standards and judgments draw support for their defense and standing. For example, universal moral rights and basic professional duties can be delineated on the basis of moral principles. Ideally, a set of general principles will serve as an analytical framework of basic principles that expresses the general values underlying rules in the common morality and guidelines in professional ethics.

Three general moral principles have proved to be serviceable as a framework of principles for bioethics: respect for autonomy, beneficence, and justice. These three principles should not be construed as jointly forming a complete moral system or theory, but they can provide the beginnings of a framework through which we can begin to reason about problems in bioethics. Each is treated in a separate subsequent section.

One caution is in order about the nature and use of such principles. Moral thinking and judgment must take account of many considerations besides ethical principles and rules, and principles do not contain sufficient content to determine judgments in a great many cases. Often the most prudent course is to search for more information about cases and policies rather than trying to decide prematurely on the basis of either principles or some general theoretical commitments. More information sometimes will resolve problems and in other cases will help fix the principles that are most important in the circumstances.

Principles provide a starting point for moral judgment and policy evaluation, but, as we saw in the previous section and will see in the section on public policy, more content is needed than that supplied by principles alone. They are tested and reliable starting points, but they rarely are sufficient for moral thinking.

RESPECT FOR AUTONOMY

One principle at the center of modern bioethics is *respect for autonomy*. It is rooted in the liberal moral and political tradition of the importance of individual freedom and choice. In moral philosophy *personal autonomy* refers to personal self-governance: personal rule of the self by adequate understanding while remaining free from controlling interferences by others and from personal limitations that prevent choice. *Autonomy* thus means freedom from external constraint and the presence of critical mental capacities such as understanding, intending, and voluntary decision-making capacity.[8]

To *respect* an autonomous agent is to recognize with due appreciation that person's capacities and perspective, including his or her right to hold certain views, to make certain choices, and to take certain actions based on personal values and beliefs. The moral demand that we respect the autonomy of persons can be expressed as a principle of respect for autonomy: Autonomy of action should not be subjected to control by others. The principle provides the basis for the right to make decisions, which in turn takes the form of specific autonomy-related rights.

For example, in the debate over whether autonomous, informed patients have the right to refuse self-regarding, life-sustaining medical interventions, the principle of respect for autonomy suggests a morally appropriate response. But the principle covers even simple exchanges in the medical world, such as listening carefully to patients' questions, answering the questions in the detail that respectfulness would demand, and not treating patients in a patronizing fashion.

Respect for autonomy has historically been connected to the idea that persons possess an intrinsic value independent of special circumstances that confer value. As expressed in Kantian ethics, autonomous persons are ends in themselves, determining their own destiny, and are not to be treated merely as means to the ends of others. Thus, the burden of moral justification rests on those who would restrict or prevent a person's exercise of autonomy.

To respect the autonomy of self-determining agents is to recognize them as *entitled* to determine their own destiny, with due regard to their considered evaluations and view of the world. They must be accorded the moral right to have their own opinions and to act on them (as long as those actions produce no moral violation). Thus, in evaluating the self-regarding actions of others, we are obligated to respect those people as persons with the same right to their judgments as we possess to our own, and they in turn are obligated to treat us in the same way.

Medical and nursing codes have begun in recent years to include rules that are explicitly based on this principle. For example, the first principle of the American Nurses' Association Code reads as follows:

> The nurse, in all professional relationships, practices with compassion and respect for the inherent dignity, worth and uniqueness of every individual, unrestricted by considerations of social or economic status, personal attributes, or the nature of health problems.[9]

The controversial problems with the noble-sounding principle of respect for autonomy, as with all moral principles, arise when we must interpret its significance for particular contexts and determine precise limits on its application and how to handle situations when it conflicts with such other moral principles as beneficence and justice. Some of the best-known problems of conflict are found in cases of overriding refusals of treatment by patients, as in Jehovah's Witnesses' refusals of blood transfusions.

Many controversies involve questions about the conditions under which a person's right to autonomous expression demands actions by others and also questions about the restrictions society may rightfully place on choices by patients or subjects when these choices conflict with other values. If an individual's choices endanger the public health, potentially harm another party, or involve a scarce resource for which a patient cannot pay, it may be justifiable to restrict exercises of autonomy. If restriction is in order, the justification will rest on some competing moral principle such as beneficence or justice. This issue of both specifying and balancing the demands made by conflicting moral principles can now be seen to apply to each of these principles.

BENEFICENCE

The welfare of patients is the goal of health care. This welfare objective is medicine's context and justification: Clinical therapies are aimed at the promotion of health by cure or prevention of disease. This value has long been treated as a foundational value—and sometimes as *the* foundational value—in medical and nursing ethics. Among the most quoted principles in the history of codes of medical ethics is the maxim *primum non nocere:*

"Above all, do no harm." Although the origins of this abstract principle are obscure and its implications often unclear, it has appeared in many medical writings and codes, and was present in nursing codes as early as Florence Nightingale's Pledge for Nurses. Many current medical and nursing codes assert that the health professional's "primary commitment" is to protect the patient from harm and to promote the patient's welfare.

Other duties in medicine, nursing, public health, and research are expressed in terms of a *more positive* obligation to come to the assistance of those in need of treatment or in danger of injury. In the International Code of Nursing Ethics, for example, it is said that "[T]he nurse shares with other citizens the responsibility for initiating and supporting action to meet the health and social needs of the public."[10] Various sections of the *Principles of Medical Ethics* of the American Medical Association express a virtually identical point of view.

The range of duties requiring abstention from harm and positive assistance may be conveniently clustered under the single heading of *beneficence*. This term has a broad set of meanings, including the doing of good and the active promotion of good, kindness, and charity. But in the present context the principle of beneficence has a narrower meaning: It requires us to abstain from injuring others and to help others further their important and legitimate interests, largely by preventing or removing possible harms. Presumably such acts are required when they can be performed with minimal risk to the actors; one is not under an obligation of beneficence in all circumstances of risk.

According to William Frankena, the principle of beneficence can be expressed as including the following four elements: (1) One ought not to inflict evil or harm (a principle of nonmaleficence). (2) One ought to prevent evil or harm. (3) One ought to remove evil or harm. (4) One ought to do or promote good.[11] Frankena suggests that the fourth element may not be an obligation at all (being an act of benevolence that is over and above obligation) and contends that these elements appear in a hierarchical arrangement so that the first takes precedence over the second, the second over the third, and the third over the fourth.

There are philosophical reasons for separating passive nonmaleficence (as expressed in element 1) and active beneficence (as expressed in elements 2–4). Ordinary moral thinking often suggests that certain duties not to injure others are more compelling than duties to benefit them. For example, we do not consider it justifiable to kill a dying patient in order to use the patient's organs to save two others. Similarly, the obligation not to injure a patient by abandonment seems intuitively stronger than the obligation to prevent injury to a patient who has been abandoned by another (under the assumption that both are moral duties).

Despite the attractiveness of this hierarchical ordering rule, it is not firmly sanctioned by either morality or ethical theory. The obligation expressed in element 1 may not *always* outweigh those expressed in 2–4. For example, the harm inflicted in element 1 may be negligible or trivial, whereas the harm to be prevented in element 2 may be substantial: Saving a person's life by a blood transfusion clearly justifies the inflicted harm of venipuncture on the blood donor. One of the motivations for separating nonmaleficence from beneficence is that they themselves conflict when one must *either* avoid harm *or* bring aid. In such cases, one needs a decision procedure for choosing one alternative rather than another. But if the weights of the two principles can vary, as they can, there can be no mechanical decision rule asserting that one obligation must always outweigh the other.

One of the most vexing problems in ethical theory is the extent to which the principle of beneficence generates *general moral duties* that are incumbent on everyone—not because of a professional role but because morality itself makes a general demand of beneficence. Any analysis of beneficence, in the broad sense just delineated, would potentially demand severe sacrifice and extreme generosity in the moral life—giving a kidney for transplantation or donating bone marrow, for example. As a result, some philosophers have argued that this form of beneficent action is virtuous and a moral *ideal*, but not an obligation. We are not *required* by the general canons of morality to promote the good of persons, even if we are in a position to do so and the action is morally *justified*.

Several proposals have been offered in moral philosophy to resolve this problem by showing that beneficence *is* a principle of obligation, but these theoretical ventures are extraneous to our concerns here. The scope or range of acts required by the obligation of beneficence is an undecided issue, and perhaps an undecidable one. Fortunately, we do not need a resolution in the present context. That we are morally obligated on *some* occasions to assist others—at least in professional roles such as nursing, medicine, and research—is hardly a matter of moral controversy. Beneficent acts are demanded by the roles involved in fiduciary relationships between health care professionals and patients, lawyers and clients, researchers and subjects (at least in therapeutic research), bankers and customers, and so on.

We can treat the basic roles and concepts that give substance to the principle of beneficence in medicine as follows: The positive benefits that the physician and nurse are obligated to seek all involve the alleviation of disease and injury, if there is a reasonable hope of cure. The harms to be prevented, removed, or minimized are the pain, suffering, and disability of injury and disease. In addition, the physician and nurse are enjoined from *doing* harm if interventions inflict unnecessary pain and suffering on patients.

Those engaged in both medical practice and biomedical research know that risks of harm presented by interventions must be weighed against possible benefits for patients, subjects, and the public. The physician who professes to "do no harm" is not pledging never to cause harm, but rather to strive to create a positive balance of goods over inflicted harms. This is recognized in the Nuremberg Code, which enjoins: "The degree of risk to be taken should never exceed that determined by the humanitarian importance of the problem to be solved by the experiment."

JUSTICE

Every civilized society is a cooperative venture structured by moral, legal, and cultural principles that define the terms of social cooperation. Beneficence and respect for autonomy are principles in this fabric of social order, but *justice* has been the subject of more treatises on the terms of social cooperation than any other principle. A person has been treated justly if treated according to what is fair, due, or owed. For example, if equal political rights are due all citizens, then justice is done when those rights are accorded.

The term *distributive justice* refers to fair, equitable, and appropriate distribution in society determined by justified norms of distribution that structure part of the terms of social cooperation. Usually this term refers to the distribution of primary social goods, such as economic goods and fundamental political rights. But burdens are also within its scope. Paying for forms of national health insurance is a distributed burden; Medicare checks and grants to do research are distributed benefits.[12]

Recent literature on distributive justice has tended to focus on considerations of fair economic distribution, especially unjust distributions in the form of inequalities of income between different classes of persons and unfair tax burdens on certain classes. But many problems of distributive justice exist besides issues about income and wealth, including the issues raised in prominent contemporary debates over health care distribution, as discussed in Chapter 8.

There is no single principle of justice. Somewhat like principles under the heading of beneficence, there are several *principles* of justice, each requiring specification in particular contexts. But common to almost all theories of justice is a minimal, beginning principle: Like cases should be treated alike, or, to use the language of equality, equals ought to be treated equally and unequals unequally. This elementary principle is referred to as the *formal principle of justice*, or sometimes as the *formal principle of equality*—formal because it states no particular respects in which people ought to be treated. It merely asserts that whatever respects are under consideration, if persons are equal in those respects, they should be treated alike. Thus, the formal principle of justice does not tell us how to determine equality or proportion in these matters, and it therefore lacks substance as a specific guide to conduct. Equality must here be understood as "equality in the relevant respects." Many controversies about justice arise over what should be considered the relevant characteristics for equal treatment. Principles that specify these relevant characteristics are often said to be *material* because they identify relevant properties for distribution.

The following is a sample list of major candidates for the position of valid material principles of distributive justice (though longer lists have been proposed): (1) to each person an equal share; (2) to each person according to individual need; (3) to each person according to acquisition in a free market; (4) to each person according to individual effort; (5) to each person according to societal contribution; (6) to each person according to merit. There is no obvious barrier to acceptance of more than one of these principles, and some theories of justice accept all six as valid. Most societies use several principles in the belief that different rules are appropriate to different situations.

Because the formal and material principles leave space for differences in the interpretation of how justice applies to particular situations, philosophers have developed diverse *theories* of justice that provide material principles, specify the principles, and defend the choice of principles. These theories attempt to be more specific than the formal principle by elaborating how people are to be compared and what it means to give people their due. Egalitarian theories of justice emphasize equal access to primary goods; libertarian theories emphasize rights to social and economic liberty; and utilitarian theories emphasize a mixed use of such criteria so that public and private utility are maximized.

The *utilitarian theory* follows the main lines of the explanation of utilitarianism provided earlier, and thus economic justice is viewed as one among a number of problems concerning how to maximize value. The ideal economic distribution, utilitarians argue, is any arrangement that would have this maximizing effect.

Egalitarianism holds that distributions of burdens and benefits in a society are just to the extent they are equal, and deviations from equality in distribution are unjust. Most egalitarian accounts of justice are guardedly formulated, so that only *some* basic equalities among individuals take priority over their differences. In recent years an egalitarian theory discussed in the section on Kantian theories has enjoyed wide currency: John Rawls's *A Theory of Justice*. This book has as its central contention that we should distribute all economic goods and services equally except in those cases in which an unequal distribution would actually work to everyone's advantage, or at least would benefit the worst off in society.

Sharply opposed to egalitarianism is the *libertarian* theory of justice. What makes libertarian theories libertarian is the priority afforded to distinctive processes, procedures, or mechanisms for ensuring that liberty rights are recognized in economic practice—typically the rules and procedures governing social liberty and economic acquisition and exchange in free market systems. Because free choice is the pivotal goal, libertarians place a premium on the principle of respect for autonomy. In some libertarian systems, this principle is the sole basic moral principle, and there thus are no other principles of justice.

We will see in Chapter 8 that many philosophers believe that this approach is fundamentally wrong because economic value is generated through an essentially communal process that our health policies must reflect if justice is to be done.

Libertarian theorists, however, explicitly reject the conclusion that egalitarian patterns of distribution represent a normative ideal. People may be equal in a host of morally significant respects (for example, entitled to equal treatment under the law and equally valued as ends in themselves), but the libertarian contends that it would be a basic violation of *justice* to regard people as deserving of equal economic returns. In particular, people are seen as having a fundamental right to own and dispense with the products of their labor as they choose, even if the exercise of this right leads to large inequalities of wealth in society. Equality and utility principles, from this libertarian perspective, sacrifice basic liberty rights to the larger public interest by coercively extracting financial resources through taxation.

These three theories of justice all capture some of our intuitive convictions about justice, and each exhibits strengths as a theory of justice. Perhaps, then, there are several equally valid, or at least equally defensible, theories of justice and just taxation. This problem will be studied further in Chapter 8.

The Prima Facie Nature of Principles. W. D. Ross, a prominent twentieth-century British philosopher, developed a theory intended to assist us in resolving problems of a conflict between principles. Ross's views are based on an account of what he calls prima facie duties, which he contrasts with actual duties. A *prima facie duty* is a duty that is always to be acted upon unless it conflicts on a particular occasion with an equal or stronger duty. A prima facie duty, then, is always right and binding, all other things being equal; it is conditional on not being overridden or outweighed by competing moral demands. One's *actual duty*, by contrast, is determined by an examination of the respective weights of competing prima facie duties.

Ross argues that several valid principles, all of which can conflict, express moral duties (that is, obligations). These principles do not, Ross argues, derive from either the principle of utility or Kant's categorical imperative. For example, our promises create duties of fidelity, wrongful actions create duties of reparation, and the generous gifts of our friends create duties of gratitude. Ross defends several additional duties, such as duties of self-improvement, nonmaleficence, beneficence, and justice. Unlike Kant's system and the utilitarian system, Ross's list of duties is not based on any overarching principle. He defends it simply as a reflection of our ordinary moral conventions and beliefs.

The idea that moral principles are absolute values that cannot be overridden has had a long, but troubled, history. It seems beyond serious dispute that all moral norms can be justifiably overridden in some circumstances. For example, we might withhold the truth in order to prevent someone from killing another person; and we might disclose confidential information about one person in order to protect the rights of another person. Principles, duties, and rights are not absolute or unconditional merely because they are universal. Both utilitarians and Kantians have defended their basic rule (the principle of utility and the categorical imperative) as absolute, but this claim to absoluteness is dubious. For Ross's reasons, among others, many moral philosophers have with increasing frequency come to regard principles, duties, and rights not as unbending standards but rather as strong prima facie moral demands that may be validly overridden in circumstances of competition with other moral claims.

Although no philosopher or professional code has successfully presented a system of moral rules that is free of conflicts and exceptions, this fact is no cause for either scepticism or alarm. Prima facie duties reflect the complexity of the moral life, in which a hierarchy of rules and principles is impossible. The problem of how to weight different moral principles remains unresolved, as does the best set of moral principles to form the framework of bioethics. Nonetheless, the general categories of prima facie principles discussed here have proven serviceable as a basic starting point and source for reflection on cases and problems. The main difficulty with these principles is that in most difficult contexts they must be specified.

The Specification of Principles. Practical moral problems often cannot, as we noticed earlier, be resolved by appeal to highly general principles. Practical problems typically require that we make our general norms suitably specific.[13] Universal norms are mere starting points that almost always must be transformed into a more specific and relevant form in order to create policies, bring controversial cases to closure, resolve conflicts, and the like. The implementation of the principles must take account of feasibility, efficiency, cultural pluralism, political procedures, uncertainty about risk, noncompliance by patients, moral dilemmas, and the like. In short, the principles must be specified for a context.

Specification is not a process of producing general norms; it assumes that they are already available. It is the process of making these norms concrete so that they can meaningfully guide conduct. This requires reducing the indeterminateness of the general norms to give them increased action-guiding capacity while retaining the moral commitments in the original norm. Filling out the commitments of the norms with which one starts is accomplished by narrowing the scope of the norms, not merely by explaining what the general norms mean. For example, without further specification the principle *respect the autonomy of competent persons* is too spare to handle complicated problems of what to say or ask for in clinical medicine and research involving human subjects. A mere definition of *respect for autonomy* (as, say, "allowing competent persons to exercise their liberty rights") might clarify one's meaning, but would not narrow the general norm or render it more specific. Specification is a different kind of spelling out than analysis of meaning. It adds content. For example, one possible specification of *respect the autonomy of competent persons* is "respect the autonomy of competent patients after they become incompetent by following their advance directives."

After this specification, when one subsequently encounters difficult cases of vague advance directives and must decide whether to observe them, one could further specify as follows: "Respect the autonomy of competent patients (after they become incompetent) by following their advance directives if and only if the directives are clear and relevant." As other problems and conflicts of norms emerge, the process of specification must continue. That is, already specified rules, guidelines, policies, and codes must be further specified to handle new or more complex circumstances. Such progressive specification is the way we do and should handle problems that arise in devising internal standards of medical morality.

A specification, by definition, must retain the initial norm while adding content to it. In the case of progressive specification, there must remain a transparent connection to the initial norm that gives moral authority to the string of norms that develop over time. Of course, there is always the possibility that more than one line of specification will issue from one or more initial norms. That is, different persons may offer different specifications. In this process of specification, overconfidence in one's specifications can lead to a dogmatic certainty of the sort found in the authoritative pronouncements of professional medical associations. Moral disagreement in the course of formulating specifications is inevitable and may not be eliminated by even the most conscientious specifications. In any given problematic or dilemmatic case, several competing specifications are virtually certain to be offered by reasonable parties. Alternative specifications are no more a matter of regret than are other contexts in which reflective persons offer alternative solutions to practical problems.

LAW AND POLICY

Moral principles are often already embedded in public morality, public policies, and institutional practices, but if these values are already in place, how can moral reflection on philosophical theory assist us in the complicated task of forming and criticizing institutional policies, public policies, and laws?

ETHICS AND PUBLIC AFFAIRS

Institutional and public policies are almost always motivated by and incorporate moral considerations. Policies such as those that fund health care for the indigent and those that protect subjects of biomedical research are examples. Moral analysis is part of good policy formation, not merely a method for evaluating already formed policy. A *policy*, in the relevant sense, is composed of a set of normative, enforceable guidelines that govern a particular area of conduct and that have been accepted by an official body, such as an institutional board of trustees, an agency of government, or a legislature. The policies of corporations, hospitals, trade groups, and professional societies are private rather than public, but the discussion that follows is directed at all forms of policy.

Many articles in this volume are concerned with the use of ethical theory for the formulation of public affairs. Joel Feinberg has made a suggestive comment about one way in which the problems raised in these essays might be viewed from an ideal vantage point:

> It is convenient to think of these problems as questions for some hypothetical and abstract political body. An answer to the question of when liberty should be limited or how wealth ideally should be distributed, for example, could be used to guide not only moralists, but also legislators and judges toward reasonable decisions in particular cases where interests, rules, or the liberties of different parties appear to conflict. . . . We must think of an ideal legislator as somewhat abstracted from the full legislative context, in that he is free to appeal directly to the public interest unencumbered by the need to please voters, to make "deals" with colleagues, or any other merely "political" considerations. . . . The principles of the ideal legislator. . . . are still of the first practical importance, since they provide a target for our aspirations and a standard for judging our successes and failures.[14]

However, policy formation and criticism usually involve complex interactions between moral values and cultural and political values. A policy will be shaped by empirical data and information in relevant fields such as medicine, economics, law, and the like. By taking into consideration factors such as efficiency and clientele acceptance, we interpret principles so that they provide a practical strategy for real-world problems that incorporate the demands of political procedures, legal constraints, uncertainty about risk, and the like.[15] For example, in this book we will consider policies pertaining to physician-assisted suicide, ethics committees in hospitals, public allocations for health care, regulation of risk in the workplace, protection of animal and human subjects of research, legislative definitions of death, liability for failures of disclosure and confidentiality, policies to control developments in genetics, the control of epidemics, and a host of other moral problems of institutional and public policy.

A specific example of ethics at work in the formulation of policy is found in the work of the National Commission for the Protection of Human Subjects of Biomedical and

Behavioral Research, which was established by a federal law. Its mandate was to develop ethical guidelines for the conduct of research involving human subjects and to make recommendations to the Department of Health and Human Services (DHHS). To discharge its duties, the commission studied the nature and extent of various forms of research, its purposes, the ethical issues surrounding the research, present federal regulations, and the views of representatives of professional societies and federal agencies. The commission engaged in extensive public deliberations on these subjects, a process in which moral reasoning played as central a role as the information and methods supplied from other fields.

Subsequent government regulations regarding research issued by the relevant agency (DHHS) were developed on the basis of work provided by the commission. These public laws show the imprint of the commission in virtually every clause. The regulations cannot be regarded as exclusively ethical in orientation, but much distinctive ethical material is found in the commission documents, and ethical analysis provided the framework for its deliberations and recommendations. The commission also issued one exclusively philosophical volume, which sets forth the moral framework that underlies the various policy recommendations it made. It is among the best examples of the use of moral frameworks for actual (not merely theoretical or programmatic) policy development and of a philosophical publication issued through a government-sponsored body.

Several U.S. federal branches, agencies, and courts regularly use ethical premises in the development of their health policies, rules, or decisions. These include the Centers for Disease Control (CDC), the National Institutes of Health (NIH), the Agency for Healthcare Research and Quality (AHRQ), and the U.S. Supreme Court. Ethical analysis also often plays a prominent role in policy formation in bioethics. Examples include the widely examined work of the Oregon legislature on rationing in health care, the New York Task Force on Life and the Law, the New Jersey Bioethics Commission, the National Bioethics Advisory Commission, and the like. Their reports and legislative actions raise vital questions explored at various points in this book about the proper relation between government and professional groups in formulating standards of practice.

MORALITY AND LAW

The "morality" of many actions that have a public impact is commonly gauged by whether the law prohibits that form of conduct. Law is the public's agent for translating morality into explicit social guidelines and practices and for determining punishments for offenses. Case law (judge-made law expressed in court decisions), statutory law (federal and state statutes and their accompanying administrative regulations), and international law (law from treaties and agreements among nations) set standards for science, medicine, and health care, and these sources have deeply influenced bioethics.

In these forms law has placed many issues before the public. Case law, in particular, has established influential precedents that provide material for reflection on both legal and moral questions. Prominent examples include judicial decisions about informed consent and terminating life-sustaining treatment. The line of court decisions since the Karen Ann Quinlan case in the mid-1970s, for example, constitutes an important body of material for moral reflection. Many of the chapters in this book contain selections from case law, and selections in the chapters frequently mention actual or proposed statutory law.

Moral evaluation is, nonetheless, very different from *legal* evaluation. Issues of legal liability, costs to the system, practicability within the litigation process, and questions of compensation demand that legal requirements be different from moral requirements. The law is not the repository of our moral standards and values, even when the law is directly concerned with moral problems. A law-abiding person is not necessarily morally sensitive or virtuous, and from the fact that an act is legally acceptable it does not follow that the act is morally acceptable. For example, when women and slaves were denied rights, including the right to make medical decisions, in the United States, these acts were morally unjust, despite whatever law supported them. Currently in the United States, the doctrine of employment at will permits employers such as hospitals to fire employees for unjust reasons and is (within certain limits) legal, though such dismissals are often morally unjustifiable. In short, many actions that are not illegal are morally unsustainable.

The judgment that an act is morally acceptable also does not imply that the law should permit it. For example, the moral position that various forms of euthanasia are morally justified is consistent with the thesis that the government should legally prohibit these acts, on grounds that it would not be possible to control potential abuses.

Bioethics in many countries is currently involved in a complex and mutually stimulating relationship with the law. The law often appeals to moral duties and rights, places sanctions on violators, and in general strengthens the social importance of moral beliefs. Morality and law share concerns over matters of basic social importance and often acknowledge the same principles, obligations, and criteria of evidence. Nevertheless, the law rightly backs away from attempting to legislate against everything that is morally wrong.

LEGAL AND MORAL RIGHTS

Much of the modern ethical discussion that we encounter throughout this volume turns on ideas about rights, and many public policy issues concern rights or attempts to secure what are now generally called "human rights." Our political tradition itself has developed from various conceptions of natural rights or human rights. However, until the seventeenth and eighteenth centuries, problems of social and political philosophy were rarely discussed in terms of rights. New political views took root at this point in history, including the notion of universal rights. Rights came to be understood as powerful assertions of claims that demand respect and status.

Substantial differences exist between *moral* (or *human* or *natural*) *rights* and *legal rights*, because legal systems do not formally require reference to moral systems for their understanding or grounding, nor do moral systems formally require reference to legal systems. One may have a legal right to do something patently immoral or have a moral right without any corresponding legal guarantee. Legal rights are derived from political constitutions, legislative enactments, case law, and the executive orders of the highest state official. Moral rights, by contrast, exist independently of, and form a basis for, criticizing or justifying legal rights.

Philosophers have often drawn a distinction between positive and negative rights. A right to well-being—that is, a right to receive goods and services—is a *positive right*, and a right to liberty—a right not to be interfered with—is a *negative right*. The right to liberty is a negative right because no one has to do anything to honor it. Presumably all that must be done to honor negative rights is to leave people alone. The same is not true of positive rights. To honor those rights, someone has to provide something. For example, if a person has a human right to well-being and is starving, then someone has an obligation to provide that person with food.

This important distinction between positive and negative rights appears in Chapter 8 in a discussion of various rights pertaining to health and health care. Positive rights place an obligation to provide something on others, who can respond that this requirement interferes with their rights to use their resources for their chosen ends. This point has recently become a major issue in bioethics in light of the rise of theories of justice that address global poverty and that seek to restructure the global order. Assuming, as the United Nations does, that humans have a human right to have access to basic goods including housing, food, and health care, it can be argued that ensuring these rights to basic goods requires that coercive institutions such as governments, the World Health Organization, and the World Bank be designed to guarantee these positive rights to everyone.

Because negative rights are rights of noninterference, their direct connection to individual self-determination is apparent. Because general positive rights require that all members of the community yield some of their resources to advance the welfare of others by providing social goods and services, there is a natural connection in theories that emphasize positive rights to a sense of *the commons* that limits the scope of individualism. The broader the scope of positive rights in a theory, the more likely that theory is to emphasize a scheme of social justice that confers positive rights to redistributions of resources. Several authors in this volume propose such a view, again most prominently in Chapter 8.

Accordingly, a moral system composed of a powerful set of negative obligations and rights is antithetical to a moral system composed of a powerful set of positive obligations and rights, just as a strong individualism is opposed to a strong communitarianism. Many of the conflicts that we encounter throughout this book spring from these basic differences over the existence and scope of negative and positive rights and obligations, especially regarding the number, types, and weight of positive rights and obligations.

LAW, AUTHORITY, AND AUTONOMY

As important as autonomy rights are, no autonomy right is strong enough to entail a right to unrestricted exercises of autonomy. Acceptable liberty must be distinguished from unacceptable, but how are we to do so?

Liberty-Limiting Principles. Various principles have been advanced in the attempt to establish valid grounds for the limitation of autonomy. The following four "liberty-limiting principles" have all been defended.

1. *The Harm Principle:* A person's liberty is justifiably restricted to prevent harm to others caused by that person.
2. *The Principle of Paternalism:* A person's liberty is justifiably restricted to prevent harm to self caused by that person.
3. *The Principle of Legal Moralism:* A person's liberty is justifiably restricted to prevent that person's immoral behavior.
4. *The Offense Principle:* A person's liberty is justifiably restricted to prevent offense to others caused by that person.

Each of these four principles represents an attempt to balance liberty and other values. The harm principle is universally accepted as a valid liberty-limiting principle, but the other three principles are highly controversial. Only one of these controversial principles is pertinent to the controversies that arise in this volume: paternalism. Here the central problem is whether this form of justification for a restriction of liberty may ever validly be invoked, and, if so, how the principle is to be formulated.

Paternalism. The word *paternalism* refers to treating individuals in the way that a parent treats his or her child. Paternalism is the intentional limitation of the autonomy of one person by another, where the person who limits autonomy appeals exclusively to grounds of benefit for the person whose autonomy is limited. The essence of paternalism is an overriding of a person's autonomy on grounds of providing that person with a benefit—in medicine, a medical benefit.

Examples in medicine include involuntary commitment to institutions for treatment, intervention to stop "rational" suicides, resuscitating patients who have asked not to be resuscitated, withholding medical information that patients have requested, compulsory care, denial of an innovative therapy to patients who wish to try it, and some government efforts to promote health. Other health-related examples include laws requiring motorcyclists to wear helmets and motorists to wear seat belts and the regulations of governmental agencies such as the Food and Drug Administration that prevent people from purchasing possibly harmful or inefficacious drugs. In all cases the motivation is the beneficent promotion of individuals' health and welfare.

Paternalism has been under attack in recent years, especially by defenders of the autonomy rights of patients. The latter hold that physicians and government officials intervene too often and assume too much paternalistic control over patients' choices. Philosophers and lawyers have generally supported the view that the autonomy of patients is the decisive factor in the patient–physician relationship and that interventions can be valid only when patients are in some measure unable to make voluntary choices or to perform autonomous actions. The point is that patients can be so ill that their judgments or voluntary abilities are significantly affected, or they may be incapable of grasping important information about their case, thus being in no position to reach carefully reasoned decisions about their medical treatment or their purchase of drugs. Beyond this form of intervention, many have argued, paternalism is not warranted.

However, paternalism also has defenders, even under some conditions in which autonomous choice is overridden. Any careful proponent of a principle of paternalism will specify precisely which goods and needs deserve paternalistic protection and the conditions under which intervention is warranted. Some writers have argued that one is justified in interfering with a person's autonomy only if the interference protects the person against his or her own actions where those actions are extremely and unreasonably risky (for example, refusing a life-saving therapy in nonterminal situations) or are potentially dangerous and irreversible in effect (as are some drugs). According to this position, paternalism is justified if and only if the harms prevented from occurring to the person are greater than the harms or indignities (if any) caused by interference with his or her liberty and if it can be universally justified, under relevantly similar circumstances, always to treat persons in this way.

This moderate formulation of paternalism still leaves many critics resolutely opposed to all possible uses of this principle. Their arguments against paternalism turn on some defense of the importance of the principle of respect for autonomy. We will many times encounter such appeals in this volume, especially as applied to rightful state intervention in order to benefit patients or subjects without their authorization.

T.L.B.

NOTES

1. See, for example, Tom L. Beauchamp and James F. Childress, *Principles of Biomedical Ethics*, 6th ed (New York: Oxford University Press, 2008), especially chap. 10; Bernard Gert, Charles M. Culver, and Danner K. Clouser, *Bioethics: A Return to Fundamentals* (New York: Oxford University Press, 1997); Sissela Bok, *Common Values* (Columbia, MO: University of Missouri Press, 1995), 13–23, 50–59; Leigh Turner, "Zones of Consensus and Zones of Conflict: Questioning the 'Common Morality' Presumption in Bioethics," *Kennedy Institute of Ethics Journal* 13, no. 3 (2003): 193–218.

2. *Tarasoff v. Regents of the University of California*, California Supreme Court (17 California Reports, 3d Series, 425. Decided July 1, 1976).

3. Cf. Walter Sinnott-Armstrong, *Moral Dilemmas* (Basil Blackwell, 1988), 216–27; D. D. Raphael, *Moral Philosophy* (Oxford: Oxford University Press, 1981), 64–65; Daniel Statman, "Hard Cases and Moral Dilemmas," *Law and Philosophy* 15 (1996): 117–48.

4. Immanuel Kant, *Foundations of the Metaphysics of Morals*, 2nd ed., trans. Lewis White Beck (New York: Macmillan, 1990), 46.

5. Albert R. Jonsen, "Casuistry as Methodology in Clinical Ethics," *Theoretical Medicine* 12 (December 1991); Jonsen and S. Toulmin, *Abuse of Casuistry* (Berkeley: University of California Press, 1988); Jonsen, "Casuistry: An Alternative or Complement to Principles?" *Kennedy Institute of Ethics Journal* 5 (1995): 237–51.

6. John D. Arras, "Principles and Particularity: The Role of Cases in Bioethics," *Indiana Law Journal* 69 (Fall 1994): 983–1014 (with two replies); and "Getting Down to Cases: The Revival of Casuistry in Bioethics," *Journal of Medicine and Philosophy* 16 (1991): 29–51.

7. Jonsen and Toulmin, *Abuse of Casuistry*, 16–19, 66–67; Jonsen, "Casuistry and Clinical Ethics," 67, 71.

8. For strikingly different autonomy-based theories, see H. Tristram Engelhardt, Jr., *The Foundations of Bioethics*, 2nd ed. (New York: Oxford University Press, 1996); Joel Feinberg, *The Moral Limits of the Criminal Law* (New York: Oxford University Press, 1984–87); Jay Katz, *The Silent World of Doctor and Patient* (New York: The Free Press, 1984); and various essays in James S. Taylor, ed., *Personal Autonomy* (New York: Cambridge University Press, 2005).

9. American Nurses Association, *Code of Ethics for Nurses with Interpretive Statements* (Silver Spring, MD: American Nurses Publishing, 2001), quoted from the statement at http://nursingworld.org/ethics/chcode.htm (as posted Feb. 15, 2007).

10. 1953 and 1973 International Codes of Nursing Ethics of the International Council of Nurses.

11. William Frankena, *Ethics*, 2nd ed. (Englewood Cliffs, NJ: Prentice-Hall, 1973), 47.

12. For accounts of justice that have influenced contemporary bioethics, see John Rawls, *A Theory of Justice* (Cambridge: Harvard University Press, 1971); Norman Daniels, "Equity and Population Health: Toward a Broader Bioethics Agenda," *Hastings Center Report* 36, no. 4 (2006): 22–35; Madison Powers and Ruth Faden, *Social Justice: The Moral Foundations of Public Health and Health Policy* (New York: Oxford University Press, 2006); Thomas W. Pogge, *Freedom from Poverty as a Human Right: Who Owes What to the Very Poor?* (Oxford: Oxford University Press, 2007).

13. Henry S. Richardson, "Specifying Norms as a Way to Resolve Concrete Ethical Problems," *Philosophy and Public Affairs* 19 (Fall 1990): 279–310; and "Specifying, Balancing, and Interpreting Bioethical Principles," *Journal of Medicine and Philosophy* 25 (2000): 285–307.

14. Joel Feinberg, *Social Philosophy* (Englewood Cliffs, NJ: Prentice-Hall, 1973), 2–3.

15. Dennis Thompson, "Philosophy and Policy," *Philosophy and Public Affairs* 14 (Spring 1985): 205–18.

Chapter 2
Research Involving Humans and Animals

Introduction

Since the early 1990s there has been a renaissance of interest in research ethics. This new interest has been sparked in part by recent historical research on past abuses of human research subjects, especially the (often unwitting) subjects of U.S. radiation experiments. However, the field of bioethics has also devoted substantial attention to international research ethics and to the new questions that arise as the locus of much research moves from academic to commercial, or at least semicommercial, settings. While there is widespread agreement on the general ethical guidelines that should govern human research, there are lingering disagreements about the best oversight system for such research, compensation for research-related injuries, and research in Third World settings.

Meanwhile, on a parallel track, bioethicists, policy makers, and the public have also focused renewed attention on the welfare of animals in research. Here there is much less consensus than in the realm of human research, with at least two polar positions being argued vigorously by their advocates and with thoughtful scholars attempting to articulate new positions that mediate between the extremes.

CONCEPTUAL QUESTIONS

The definition of *research* can perhaps be best approached by way of considering the concepts of *therapy* and *research*. In the biomedical and behavioral fields, *therapy* refers to a class of activities designed solely to benefit an individual or the members of a group. Therapy may take several forms: It may be a treatment for a disease, or it may consist of diagnostic procedures or even preventive measures. In contrast, *research* refers to a class of scientific activities designed to develop or contribute to generalizable knowledge. Examples of research are a study of alternative methods for training pigeons, a comparison of two drugs for treating AIDS, and a review of patient charts in an effort to detect a correlation between smoking and lung cancer.

Two subtypes of research involving human or animal subjects can be identified. On one hand, research can be combined with the diagnosis, treatment, or prevention of illness in the subjects themselves; that is, it can be aimed directly toward discovering better methods of diagnosing or treating the condition from which human or animal patients are suffering or toward preventing disease in susceptible humans or animals. A study of a new polio vaccine in children at risk for contracting polio would be an example of such research. This kind of inquiry is often designated as *clinical research*. Randomized clinical trials are an important subtype of clinical research. On the other hand, research can be unrelated (or at least not directly related) to an illness or susceptibility of the subjects involved. For example, healthy human volunteers can be involved in studies that examine how long a new drug remains in the bodies of people who receive a certain dose of the drug. Similarly, healthy nonhuman animals are frequently involved in research that aims to understand disease processes in human beings. Thus, coronary arteries may be obstructed in canine subjects so that researchers can better understand what happens to the human heart in a myocardial infraction (heart attack). There is no simple or widely accepted term that applies to all the various kinds of nonclinical research.

There is one category of research that, at first glance, seems to straddle the line between clinical and nonclinical research. It is research on human patients that is unrelated to diagnosing or treating the patients' illnesses. This type of research deserves special mention because it was a prominent feature in the Tuskegee syphilis study and in the human radiation experiments conducted by the U.S. Atomic Energy Commission. In terms of the distinctions developed in the preceding paragraph, this kind of research should be categorized as nonclinical because it is not designed to benefit the patients being studied—even though the research may be conducted in a clinic.

Because of the ambiguities that have surrounded notions like *clinical* and especially *nontherapeutic* in connection with research, some commentators have recommended that these and similar terms be applied only to specific *procedures* or *interventions* rather than to research protocols as a whole. For example, in a clinical trial that compares a standard drug with an investigational new drug, the administration of each drug can reasonably be described as *therapeutic* in intent. The researchers also hope that both drugs will be therapeutic in their outcome for the subjects participating in the study. However, the study protocol will also require types of monitoring for the subjects and, in most cases, additional diagnostic tests that would not be required of patients receiving the standard drug in the typical clinical setting. In addition, subjects in a research protocol may be asked to begin their participation in a study by going through a washout period during which some or all current medications are stopped. These procedures, which differ from the usual practice of administering therapy to patients, can be designated as nontherapeutic procedures.

A BRIEF HISTORY OF ANIMAL AND HUMAN RESEARCH

Systematic research on living animals is a relatively recent phenomenon in the history of science. The first important results of animal research were achieved in the seventeenth century when William Harvey demonstrated the circulation of the blood and Robert Hooke explored the mechanism of respiration.[1] Both researchers employed living animals in their work. Similar physiological research continued during the eighteenth century but achieved special prominence in nineteenth-century France, especially in the pioneering studies of François Magendie and his student, Claude Bernard.[2] Late in life Bernard wrote an extended defense of animal research, often called *vivisection* by its critics, in the book entitled *An Introduction to the Study of Experimental Medicine*.[3] During the twentieth century basic physiological research involving animals continued, even as new modes of applied research in animals were developed—for example, innovations in surgical technique and the preclinical testing of drugs and biological agents such as vaccines.

Systematic research in human beings is also a relatively recent phenomenon. One of the earliest well-documented studies was Dr. Zabdiel Boylston's attempt, during the early years of the eighteenth century, to protect Boston's children against smallpox through inoculation. Boylston's feasibility study, conducted in 1703, involved inoculating his son and two of his slaves with small doses of infectious material.[4] At mid-century a Scottish-born physician, James Lind, demonstrated in a small clinical trial that citrus fruits prevented scurvy in sailors.[5] Toward the end of the eighteenth century, in 1789, Edward Jenner attempted to immunize several children against smallpox by using swinepox and cowpox injections. His own son and several orphan children were among the first subjects.[6]

The involvement of human subjects in research has increased steadily since 1800. During the nineteenth century the French physiological approach that had produced such striking results in animal studies was also applied to human beings. Once again, Claude Bernard was a pioneer.[7] Bernard's countrymen, Pierre Louis and Louis Pasteur, also made important contributions to biomedical knowledge.[8] At the turn of the century U.S. Army Major Walter Reed recruited more than a dozen human volunteers in his effort to demonstrate that yellow fever was transmitted through the bites of mosquitoes.[9] Large-scale clinical trials are primarily a post–World War II phenomenon, with Sir Bradford Hill's 1948 randomized study of streptomycin in the treatment of pulmonary tuberculosis being one of the first clear examples.[10]

CURRENT ETHICAL ISSUES IN HUMAN RESEARCH

THE MORAL JUSTIFICATION

The general justification for human research is that a human organism responds to biomedical interventions or other stimuli in ways that could not be predicted on the basis of studies with human cells or nonhuman animals. In other words, human physiology involves complex interactions among genes, cells, and organs that cannot be modeled by computer simulations or in other biological systems. In some research—for example, psychological research on reaction times or the capacity to recall words—the goal of the research is simply the acquisition of new knowledge about how human beings function. In much of biomedical research the aim is to find new ways to diagnose or treat disease.

In the literature on human research, including codes of research ethics, surprisingly little attention is paid to the general justification for involving human subjects in biomedical research. This silence at the most general level of justification is particularly striking when one considers that the traditional ethic of medicine has been exclusively a patient-benefit ethic. The motto *primum non nocere* (do no harm) has generally been interpreted to mean, "Do nothing that is not intended for the direct benefit of the patient." One must ask, then, whether good reasons can be given for deviating in any way from therapy, as that term was defined earlier.

The primary argument in favor of human research appeals to the principle of beneficence (as described in Chapter 1). It asserts that the social benefits to be gained from such research are substantial and that the harms resulting from the cessation of such investigations would be exceedingly grave. Proponents of carefully controlled human research have argued that the therapeutic value of many reputed "therapies" is in fact unknown; indeed, these treatments may be no more useful than the bloodletting technique so much in vogue during the eighteenth and nineteenth centuries. On this view, the only alternative to a perpetual plague of medically induced illness is the vigorous pursuit of biomedical research, including research involving human subjects.[11]

A second approach to the justification of human research is based on a joint appeal to the principles of beneficence and justice. According to this view, beneficence requires that each of us make at least a modest positive contribution to the good of our fellow citizens or the society as a whole. If our participation in research promises significant benefit to others, at little or no risk to ourselves, then such participation may be a duty of beneficence. In addition, if we fail to fulfill this modest duty while most of our contemporaries perform it, we may be acting unjustly, since we are not performing our fair share of a communal task.

The justice argument can be further elaborated by reference to the past. Every person currently alive is the beneficiary of earlier human subjects' involvement in research. To be more specific, the willingness of past human volunteers to take part in studies of antibiotics (such as penicillin) and vaccines (such as polio vaccine) has contributed to the health of us all. Accordingly, it seems unfair for us to reap the benefits of already performed research without making a similar contribution to the alleviation of disability and disease for future generations.

Several commentators on the moral justification of research involving human subjects have vigorously contested both of these approaches to the general justification of human research. In answer to the consequential argument, they assert that while human research generally contributes to medical progress, most research involving human subjects is not essential to the well-being or survival of the human species. These critics, most notably Hans Jonas,[12] have also rejected the thesis that there is a general moral duty to participate in biomedical research. On this view, there is no injustice involved in people's not volunteering to take part in the production of generalizable knowledge. Nonparticipants in research are simply being less altruistic than their fellow citizens who volunteer for this type of community service.[13]

Within the past 15 years, a paradigm shift has occurred in the debate about the moral justification of research involving human subjects. The view that participation in clinical research entails a sacrifice for human subjects has been replaced, or at least complemented, by the notion that participation in many kinds of clinical trials is, on balance, beneficial to the subjects themselves. The development of new therapies for AIDS and HIV infection was the first context in which this new emphasis appeared. More recently, commentators on the ethics of human research have called for expanded access by women, including pregnant women, and children to clinical trials.[14] The essay by Mastroianni and Kahn in this chapter devotes particular attention to this recent trend. Patricia King's article highlights the complexities involved in seeking to include members of ethnic minorities in clinical trials—especially in the wake of past abuses.

GENERAL CRITERIA FOR THE ETHICAL CONDUCT OF HUMAN RESEARCH

The codes and guidelines that have been developed for research involving human subjects can be construed as efforts to identify what philosophers term *necessary and sufficient conditions* for proper conduct. These guidelines can also be viewed as examples of what was identified in Chapter 1 as the common morality. That is, there is little disagreement about the general principles and rules that should govern human research, although there may be differences of opinion on the interpretation of some guidelines and uncertainties about how to apply the guidelines in particular circumstances.

The two central conditions identified by the U.S. National Bioethics Advisory Commission for ethical conduct in research are (1) independent review of proposed research to assess its potential benefits and harms for research subjects, and (2) the opportunity for potential subjects to decide freely whether to become participants in the proposed research.

Other commentators have proposed more extensive lists of conditions. For example, in an influential article that is not reprinted here, Ezekiel Emanuel, David Wendler, and Christine Grady have suggested seven conditions that make clinical research ethical:

1. Social or scientific value
2. Scientific validity
3. Fair subject selection
4. A favorable risk-benefit ratio (involving either a risk-benefit or a risk-knowledge calculus)
5. Independent review
6. Informed consent by subjects or their proxies
7. Respect for potential and enrolled subjects.[15]

According to the authors, "Fulfilling all 7 requirements is necessary and sufficient to make clinical research ethical."[16]

ETHICAL ISSUES IN ADVANCED INDUSTRIALIZED SOCIETIES

At the conclusion of its five-year existence, the U.S. National Bioethics Advisory Commission (NBAC) performed an audit of the oversight system for human research conducted in the United States. A summary of this audit is included in this chapter under the title "Protecting Research Participants—A Time for Change." While expressing appreciation for progress that has been made since the 1960s and 1970s, the members of NBAC suggest that major, perhaps even radical, changes are required to protect participants in human research. According to the commission, the guidelines for the conduct of research in the United States present a confusing patchwork of sometimes conflicting rules, depending on whether the research is funded by federal government agencies or by commercial firms. In response, the commission proposes the establishment of a new national office—perhaps analogous to the Federal Trade Commission—to oversee all human research in the United States, without regard to funding source. This new agency should, in the commission's view, enforce a uniform set of standards for the ethical conduct of research. NBAC also suggests ways to enhance the work of local research review committees because such committees are, in many ways, the linchpin of the current system for protecting human subjects.

ETHICAL ISSUES IN INTERNATIONAL SETTINGS

The essay by Solomon Benatar asks readers to expand their focus to problems in research that is sponsored by developed countries but conducted in less-developed countries. From his Third World perspective in Cape Town, South Africa, Benatar formulates a radical critique of spending priorities in the wealthiest nations. In his view, the developed countries are guilty of gross moral negligence, if not criminal neglect, in ignoring the health needs of Third World countries. Citing statistics published in 1990, Benatar notes that in the United States 90 percent of spending for health-related research is dedicated to diseases that cause only 10 percent of the global disease burden. Benatar's proposed solutions would go far beyond the revision of spending priorities in biomedical research and would include a fundamental restructuring of the relationship between the developed and less developed worlds.

PAST ABUSES OF HUMAN RESEARCH SUBJECTS

The current chapter includes four accounts of gross abuses committed against human subjects during the course of the twentieth century. The Nazi medical experiments and the Nuremberg Code that was developed in response to those horrendous abuses of human beings have become paradigmatic for the history of research ethics. The second example—the Tuskegee syphilis study—was more a study in the natural history of disease in African-American men than an experiment in the strict sense. President William Clinton formally apologized for the U.S. government's sponsorship of this study in 1997. A third example of unethical research is much less well known. During the 1930s and 1940s, Japanese soldiers who occupied China—in collaboration with physicians and scientists—deliberately exposed hapless civilians from the occupied country to a panoply of infectious diseases. The fact that the selection describing these atrocities was written by a Japanese scholar is, in itself, highly significant—especially when the Japanese government has been reluctant to acknowledge the full extent of Imperial Japan's involvement in the experiments. Finally, the United States government also sponsored several thousand human radiation experiments, many of them performed on unsuspecting human subjects, during the years between 1944 and 1974. These studies were first described in detail by a presidential advisory committee in 1995.

CODES AND GUIDELINES FOR HUMAN RESEARCH

The codes and guidelines reprinted in this chapter illustrate a gradual evolution in standards for the proper conduct of research involving human subjects. The central affirmation of the Nuremberg Code,[17] that the voluntary consent of every human subject is a *sine qua non* for the subject's participation, has gradually been supplemented by other important emphases. For example, the Declaration of Helsinki adds to Nuremberg's accent on consent the distinction between research involving patients and research involving healthy volunteers. Helsinki also advocates prior review of research protocols by an "independent committee," as well as making explicit provision for participation in research by legally incompetent persons. In the most recent revision of the Helsinki Declaration, adopted in 2000, the appropriate setting for the use of placebo-controlled trials was a hotly contested topic. The formulation contained in Article 29 was clarified in a supplementary statement issued a year later. Similarly, the stipulation in Article 30 about research participants being provided access to the "best proven . . . methods identified in [a] study" has been clarified—and relaxed somewhat—in a 2004 supplement to the 2000 version of the Declaration.

The CIOMS guidelines for human research illustrate the global character of such research and the substantial international consensus that exists in this arena—both at the level of ethical principles and in specific rules of practice. Like the earlier 1993 CIOMS guidelines, the 2002 guidelines are attentive to the issues that may arise when human research is conducted in Third World settings. What is new in the 2002 guidelines is the priority given to the moral justification for, and the scientific validity of, any proposed research involving human subjects. The question of external, culturally sensitive ethical review is also discussed in early guidelines. Individual informed consent is considered only after these essential prior questions have been resolved. In a sense, the 2002 CIOMS guidelines reflect an evolution of research ethics beyond the question that was so central in the Nuremberg Code—namely, the requirement that each human subject's participation in research be totally voluntary. By 2002, the issues of excellence in research design and prior external review had achieved parity with the question of (informed) consent.

ETHICAL ISSUES IN, AND GUIDELINES FOR, ANIMAL RESEARCH

The first question to be clarified in any discussion of animal research is: Which animals are to be included within the scope of consideration? Books and articles on the ethics of animal research have devoted surprisingly little attention to this question. One can usually infer from these writings that nonhuman mammals—such as monkeys, dogs, and rats—are to be included in the protected group. Indeed, in his influential book, *The Case for Animal Rights*, philosopher Tom Regan explicitly limited his argument to "all species of mammalian animals."[18] A somewhat broader class would be all vertebrates—that is, mammals plus birds, reptiles, amphibians, and fish. In the discussion that follows, it is assumed that the term animals refers to nonhuman vertebrates.

Statistics from two countries that closely monitor the use of animals in research may serve to make the notion of animal research more concrete. In the United Kingdom, approximately 2.7 million research procedures involving animals were performed in the year 2000. Approximately 21 percent of the procedures were performed in genetically modified animals. Rodents were the research subjects in 82 percent of the cases; fish, amphibians, reptiles, and birds comprised another 14 percent of the subjects.[19] Data from Canada indicate that 1,746,606 animals were used in scientific research, testing, and education in 1999. This number represents a 17.5 percent reduction from the number used in 1992, which was 2,115,006. Of the animals used in 1999, approximately 917,200, or 52.5 percent were rats and mice. Scientific research accounted for 83 percent of the total use of animals.[20]

The European Biomedical Research Association annually reports comprehensive statistics on the numbers of animals used for research in France, the United Kingdom, Germany, the Netherlands, Spain, Denmark, Portugal, Greece, and Ireland.[21] In contrast, U.S. reporting on animal research is grossly deficient. Current regulations adopted pursuant to the Animal Welfare Act do not require public reporting on the number of mice, rats, and birds used in research each year. Thus, a recent report from the Department of Agriculture indicates that in fiscal year 2000, 1,416,643 animals were used in research. It seems reasonable, as animal welfare advocate Barbara Orlans has suggested, to multiply this number by 10 to achieve numbers that are comparable to those of Canada and many European countries.[22] Thus, the number of animals used in U.S. research in fiscal year 2001 is likely to have been approximately 14 million. Even these figures are probably underestimates. Harvard Medical School alone estimated in 1999 that it would likely double its annual use of mice within the next five years to 1 million mice per year.[23]

The authors whose essays are reprinted in this chapter all represent mediating, or intermediate, positions in the debate about animal research. That is, none of the authors agrees with the abolitionists, on one hand, or with research proponents who deny that our treatment of animals raises moral questions, on the other. The essay by David DeGrazia argues that nonhuman animals and their interests deserve equal consideration to human beings and their interests. DeGrazia speaks of a "sliding scale" that can be used in evaluating animal interests—a scale that is based on the animals' "cognitive, affective, and social complexity." The author also complains about a "party line" among biomedical researchers, a position and a rhetorical style that attempt to depict animal welfare advocates as extremists.

Raymond Frey also adopts a moderate position on the ethics of research involving nonhuman animals. Frey accents the continuities between humans and especially the nonhuman animals that have the most highly developed cognitive and social capacities. He flatly rejects the view that the utility of research for humans and/or other animals alone provides a sufficient justification for every conceivable kind of animal research. For Frey, the capacity of nonhuman animals for a rich and complex quality of life should also be taken into account. The author acknowledges that there are problems with his position and, in particular, that some healthy nonhuman animals have a richer quality of life than some humans who have severely disabling conditions. Frey does not propose involving such humans in research. His principal recommendation is that animal researchers proposing to perform invasive or painful procedures always seek to involve only the species of animals that have a meager or poorly developed quality of life.

A specific case that deserves further ethical analysis is what is called "unrelieved pain and distress" in laboratory animals. Animal welfare advocates are deeply concerned about research that causes such animal pain and distress.[24] U.S. Department of Agriculture regulations require that all procedures that inflict unrelieved pain and distress on animals be reported to the Department annually. In fiscal year 2000, such procedures occurred in more than seven percent of reported animals and affected 104,202 animals.[25] However, as noted earlier, current regulations exclude bird and purpose-bred rats and mice. Thus, it is likely that the total number of laboratory animals experiencing unrelieved pain and distress is approximately one million per year in the United States alone.[26]

The concluding essay by Gillies Demers and his co-authors represents an important international effort to confront the dual problems of animal pain in research and the humane administration of euthanasia to animals that have been involved in research. Canadian and European advocates for animal welfare have taken the lead in proposing guidelines for the selection of what they call "humane end points" in research that involves pain for sentient nonhuman animals. The co-authors also suggest ways to minimize the pain and suffering of animals when they are killed after having been involved in research.

L.W.

NOTES

1. Baruch A. Brody. *The Ethics of Biomedical Research: An International Perspective.* New York: Oxford University Press, 1998, 12.

2. *Ibid.*

3. Claude Bernard. *An Introduction to the Study of Experimental Medicine.* Trans. H. C. Greene. New York: Dover, 1957.

4. Gert H. Brieger. "Human Experimentation: History." In Warren T. Reich, ed. *Encyclopedia of Bioethics.* New York: Free Press, 1978, 686.

5. *Ibid.*

6. Albert R. Jonsen. The *Birth of Bioethics.* New York: Oxford University Press, 1998, 126.

7. *Ibid.*, 127.

8. Leon Eisenberg. "The Social Imperatives of Medical Research." *Science* 198 (December 16, 1977), 1105–10.

9. Brieger. "Human Experimentation," 687–88.

10. Brody. *Ethics of Biomedical Research*, 140.

11. For a classic statement of this argument, see Eisenberg, "The Social Imperatives of Medical Research."

12. Hans Jonas. "Philosophical Reflections on Experimenting with Human Subjects." *Daedalus* 98 (Spring 1969), 219–47.

13. *Ibid.*, 223–24, 231–33.

14. See, for example, Anna C. Mastroianni, Ruth Faden, and Daniel Federman, eds. *Women and Health Research: Ethical and Legal Issues of Including Women in Clinical Studies*, 2 vols. Washington, DC: National Academy Press, 1994.

15. Ezekiel J. Emanuel, David Wendler, and Christine Grady. "What Makes Clinical Research Ethical?" *Journal of the American Medical Association* 283, (2000), 2701–11.

16. *Ibid.*, 2701.

17. For a careful and illuminating analysis of the joint authorship of the Nuremberg Code, see Ulf Schmidt. *Justice at Nuremberg: Leo Alexander and the Nazi Doctors' Trial.* Houndmills: Palgrave Macmillan, 2004, 203–05, 222–26, 243–53.

18. Tom Regan. *The Case for Animal Rights.* Berkeley: University of California Press, 1983.

19. U.K. Home Office. *Statistics of Scientific Procedures on Living Animals—Great Britain, 2000.* London: Her Majesty's Stationery Office, July 2001, 24–37. [http://www.archive.official-documents.co.uk/document/cm52/5244/524401.htm]

20. Canadian Council on Animal Care, Animal Use Survey for 1999. "Facts & Figures." online report. [http://www.ccac.ca/english/survey/aus99.htm]

21. European Biomedical Research Association. "European Statistics," primarily from the year 1991. [hhtp://www.ebra.org/stats/index.html]

22. F. Barbara Orlans. "Research on Animals, Law, Legislative, and Welfare Issues in the Use of Animals for Genetic Engineering and Xenotransplantation." In Thomas H. Murray and Maxwell J. Mehlman, eds. *Encyclopedia of Ethical, Legal, and Policy Issues in Biotechnology*, 2 vols. New York: John Wiley and Sons, 2000, 1024–25.

23. John F. Lauerman. "Animal Research," *Harvard Magazine* 101 (January–February 1999), 48–57. [http://www.harvardmagazine.com/issues/jf99/mice.html]

24. See for example, William S. Stokes. "Introduction: Reducing Unrelieved Pain and Distress in Laboratory Animals Using Humane Endpoints." *ILAR Journal* 41 (2000), 59–61. [http://www4.nationalacademies.org/ijhome.nsf/web/ilar_journal_online?OpenDocument]

25. U.S. Department of Agriculture. Animal Welfare Report: Fiscal Year 2002. Washington, DC: USDA, July 2001, 38–39. [http://www.aphis.usda.gov/ac/publications.html]

26. *Ibid.*

Past Abuses of Human Research Subjects

THE NUREMBERG MEDICAL TRIAL

War Crimes and Crimes Against Humanity

The United States of America, by the undersigned Telford Taylor, Chief of Counsel for War Crimes, duly appointed to represent said Government in the prosecution of war criminals, charges that the defendants herein participated in a common design or conspiracy to commit and did commit war crimes and crimes against humanity. . . .

COUNT TWO—WAR CRIMES

[1] Between September 1939 and April 1945 all of the defendants herein unlawfully, willfully, and knowingly committed war crimes, . . . in that they were principals in, accessories to, ordered, abetted, took a consenting part in, and were connected with plans and enterprises involving medical experiments without the subjects' consent, upon civilians and members of the armed forces of nations then at war with the German Reich and who were in the custody of the German Reich in exercise of belligerent control, in the course

From *Trials of War Criminals before the Nuernberg Military Tribunals under Control Council Law No. 10* (Nuernberg, October 1946–April 1949) (Washington, DC: U.S. Government Printing Office, 1949), I, 8, 11–15. Footnotes omitted.

of which experiments the defendants committed murders, brutalities, cruelties, tortures, atrocities, and other inhuman acts. Such experiments included, but were not limited to, the following:

(A) High-Altitude Experiments. From about March 1942 to about August 1942 experiments were conducted at the Dachau concentration camp, for the benefit of the German Air Force, to investigate the limits of human endurance and existence at extremely high altitudes. The experiments were carried out in a low-pressure chamber in which the atmospheric conditions and pressures prevailing at high altitude (up to 68,000 feet) could be duplicated. The experimental subjects were placed in the low-pressure chamber and thereafter the simulated altitude therein was raised. Many victims died as a result of these experiments and others suffered grave injury, torture, and ill-treatment. . . .

(B) Freezing Experiments. From about August 1942 to about May 1943 experiments were conducted at the Dachau concentration camp, primarily for the benefit of the German Air Force, to investigate the

most effective means of treating persons who had been severely chilled or frozen. In one series of experiments the subjects were forced to remain in a tank of ice water for periods up to 3 hours. Extreme rigor developed in a short time. Numerous victims died in the course of these experiments. After the survivors were severely chilled, rewarming was attempted by various means. In another series of experiments, the subjects were kept naked outdoors for many hours at temperatures below freezing. The victims screamed with pain as parts of their bodies froze. . . .

(C) Malaria Experiments. From about February 1942 to about April 1945 experiments were conducted at the Dachau concentration camp in order to investigate immunization for and treatment of malaria. Healthy concentration-camp inmates were infected by mosquitoes or by injections of extracts of the mucous glands of mosquitoes. After having contracted malaria the subjects were treated with various drugs to test their relative efficacy. Over 1,000 involuntary subjects were used in these experiments. Many of the victims died and others suffered severe pain and permanent disability. . . .

(D) Lost (Mustard) Gas Experiments. At various times between September 1939 and April 1945 experiments were conducted at Sachsenhausen, Natzweiler, and other concentration camps for the benefit of the German Armed Forces to investigate the most effective treatment of wounds caused by Lost gas. Lost is a poison gas which is commonly known as mustard gas. Wounds deliberately inflicted on the subjects were infected with Lost. Some of the subjects died as a result of these experiments and others suffered intense pain and injury. . . .

(E) Sulfanilamide Experiments. From about July 1942 to about September 1943 experiments to investigate the effectiveness of sulfanilamide were conducted at the Ravensbrueck concentration camp for the benefit of the German Armed Forces. Wounds deliberately inflicted on the experimental subjects were infected with bacteria such as streptococcus, gas gangrene, and tetanus. Circulation of blood was interrupted by tying off blood vessels at both ends of the wound to create a condition similar to that of a battlefield wound. Infection was aggravated by forcing wood shavings and ground glass into the wounds.

The infection was treated with sulfanilamide and other drugs to determine their effectiveness. Some subjects died as a result of these experiments and others suffered serious injury and intense agony. . . .

(F) Bone, Muscle, and Nerve Regeneration and Bone Transplantation Experiments. From about September 1942 to about December 1943 experiments were conducted at the Ravensbrueck concentration camp, for the benefit of the German Armed Forces, to study bone, muscle, and nerve regeneration, and bone transplantation from one person to another. Sections of bones, muscles, and nerves were removed from the subjects. As a result of these operations, many victims suffered intense agony, mutilation, and permanent disability. . . .

(G) Sea-Water Experiments. From about July 1944 to about September 1944 experiments were conducted at the Dachau concentration camp, for the benefit of the German Air Force and Navy, to study various methods of making sea water drinkable. The subjects were deprived of all food and given only chemically processed sea water. Such experiments caused great pain and suffering and resulted in serious bodily injury to the victims. . . .

(H) Epidemic Jaundice Experiments. From about June 1943 to about January 1945 experiments were conducted at the Sachsenhausen and Natzweiler concentration camps, for the benefit of the German Armed Forces, to investigate the causes of, and inoculations against, epidemic jaundice. Experimental subjects were deliberately infected with epidemic jaundice, some of whom died as a result, and others were caused great pain and suffering. . . .

(I) Sterilization Experiments. From about March 1941 to about January 1945 sterilization experiments were conducted at the Auschwitz and Ravensbrueck concentration camps, and other places. The purpose of these experiments was to develop a method of sterilization which would be suitable for sterilizing millions of people with a minimum of time and effort. These experiments were conducted by means of X-ray, surgery, and various drugs. Thousands of victims were sterilized and thereby suffered great mental and physical anguish. . . .

(J) Spotted Fever [Typhus] Experiments. From about December 1941 to about February 1945 experiments were conducted at the Buchenwald and

Natzweiler concentration camps, for the benefit of the German Armed Forces, to investigate the effectiveness of spotted fever and other vaccines. At Buchenwald numerous healthy inmates were deliberately infected with spotted fever virus in order to keep the virus alive; over 90 percent of the victims died as a result. Other healthy inmates were used to determine the effectiveness of different spotted fever vaccines and of various chemical substances. In the course of these experiments 75 percent of the selected number of inmates were vaccinated with one of the vaccines or nourished with one of the chemical substances and, after a period of 3 to 4 weeks, were infected with spotted fever germs. The remaining 25 percent were infected without any previous protection in order to compare the effectiveness of the vaccines and the chemical substances. As a result, hundreds of the persons experimented upon died. Experiments with yellow fever, smallpox, typhus, paratyphoid A (*Salmonella*), cholera, and diphtheria were also conducted. Similar experiments with like results were conducted at Natzweiler concentration camp. . . .

(K) Experiments with Poison. In or about December 1943, and in or about October 1944, experiments were conducted at the Buchenwald concentration camp to investigate the effect of various poisons upon human beings. The poisons were secretly administered to experimental subjects in their food. The victims died as a result of the poison or were killed immediately in order to permit autopsies. In or about September 1944 experimental subjects were shot with poison bullets and suffered torture and death. . . .

(L) Incendiary Bomb Experiments. From about November 1943 to about January 1944 experiments were conducted at the Buchenwald concentration camp to test the effect of various pharmaceutical preparations on phosphorous burns. These burns were inflicted on experimental subjects with phosphorous matter taken from incendiary bombs, and caused severe pain, suffering, and serious bodily injury . . . .

[2] Between June 1943 and September 1944 the defendants Rudolf Brandt and Wolfram Sievers unlawfully, willfully, and knowingly committed war crimes, . . . in that they were principals in, accessories to, ordered, abetted, took a consenting part in, and were connected with plans and enterprises involving the murder of civilians and members of the armed forces of

nations then at war with the German Reich and who were in the custody of the German Reich in exercise of belligerent control. One hundred twelve Jews were selected for the purpose of completing a skeleton collection for the Reich University of Strasbourg. Their photographs and anthropological measurements were taken. Then they were killed. Thereafter, comparison tests, anatomical research, studies regarding race, pathological features of the body, form and size of the brain, and other tests, were made. The bodies were sent to Strasbourg and defleshed.

[3] Between May 1942 and January 1944 the defendants Kurt Blome and Rudolf Brandt unlawfully, willfully, and knowingly committed war crimes, . . . in that they were principals in, accessories to, ordered, abetted, took a consenting part in, and were connected with plans and enterprises involving the murder and mistreatment of tens of thousands of Polish nationals who were civilians and members of the armed forces of a nation then at war with the German Reich and who were in the custody of the German Reich in exercise of belligerent control. These people were alleged to be infected with incurable tuberculosis. On the ground of insuring the health and welfare of Germans in Poland, many tubercular Poles were ruthlessly exterminated while others were isolated in death camps with inadequate medical facilities.

[4] Between September 1939 and April 1945 the defendants Karl Brandt, Blome, Viktor Brack, and Waldemar Hoven unlawfully, willfully, and knowingly committed war crimes, . . . in that they were principals in, accessories to, ordered, abetted, took a consenting part in, and were connected with plans and enterprises involving the execution of the so-called "euthanasia" program of the German Reich in the course of which the defendants herein murdered hundreds of thousands of human beings, including nationals of German-occupied countries. This program involved the systematic and secret execution of the aged, insane, incurably ill, of deformed children, and other persons, by gas, lethal injections, and diverse other means in nursing homes, hospitals, and asylums. Such persons were regarded as "useless eaters" and a burden to the German war machine. The relatives of these victims were informed that they died from natural causes, such as heart failure. German doctors involved in the "euthanasia" program were also sent to Eastern occupied countries to assist in the mass extermination of Jews.

GREGORY E. PENCE

The Tuskegee Study

Gregory E. Pence has taught for 31 years at the University of Alabama at Birmingham, where he holds appointments in the Philosophy Department and the School of Medicine. He is author of *The Elements of Bioethics; Re-Creating Medicine: Ethical Issues at the Frontiers of Medicine; Classic Cases in Medical Ethics* (4th ed., 2004); and *Who's Afraid of Human Cloning?* He has also edited an anthology entitled *Brave New Bioethics.*

The Tuskegee study of syphilis began during the great depression—around 1930—and lasted for 42 years. Because of its long time span . . . some historical background is important for understanding the many issues raised by the Tuskegee research.

THE MEDICAL ENVIRONMENT: SYPHILIS

Syphilis is a chronic, contagious bacterial disease, often venereal and sometimes congenital. Its first symptom is a chancre; after this chancre subsides, the disease spreads silently for a time but then produces an outbreak of secondary symptoms such as fever, rash, and swollen lymph glands. Then the disease becomes latent for many years, after which it may reappear with a variety of symptoms in the nervous or circulatory systems. Today, syphilis is treated with penicillin or other antibiotics; but this treatment has been possible only since about 1946, when penicillin first became widely available.

Until relatively recently, then, the common fate of victims of syphilis—kings and queens, peasants and slaves—was simply to suffer the sequelae once the first symptoms had appeared. Victims who suffered this inevitable progress included Cleopatra, King Herod of Judea, Charlemagne, Henry VIII of England, Napoleon Bonaparte, Frederick the Great, Pope Sixtus IV, Pope Alexander VI, Pope Julius II, Catherine the Great, Christopher Columbus, Paul Gauguin, Franz

Schubert, Albrecht Dürer, Johann Wolfgang von Goethe, Friedrich Nietzsche, John Keats, and James Joyce.[1]

It is generally believed that syphilis was brought to Europe from the new world during the 1490s, by Christopher Columbus's crews, but the disease may have appeared in Europe before that time. In any case, advances in transportation contributed greatly to the spread of syphilis. . . . For hundreds of years, syphilis was attributed to sin and was associated with prostitutes, though attempts to check its spread by expelling prostitutes failed because their customers were disregarded. Efforts to eradicate it by quarantine also failed.

In the eighteenth century, standing professional armies began to be established, and with them came a general acceptance of high rates of venereal disease. It is estimated, for instance, that around the year 1900, one-fifth of the British army had syphilis or gonorrhea.

Between 1900 and 1948, and especially during the two world wars, American reformers mounted what was called a *syphilophobia* campaign: the Social Hygiene Movement or Purity Crusade. Members of the campaign emphasized that syphilis was spread by prostitutes, and held that it was rapidly fatal; as an alternative to visiting a prostitute, they advocated clean, active sports (in today's terms, "Just say no"). According to the medical historian Allan Brandt, there were two splits resulting from disagreements within this reform movement: once during World War I, when giving out condoms was controversial; and later during World War II, when giving out penicillin was at issue.

In each of these conflicts, reformers whose basic intention was to reduce the physical harm of syphilis were on one side, whereas those who wanted to reduce illicit behavior were on the other side.[2]

The armed services during the world wars took a pragmatic position. Commanders who needed healthy troops overruled the moralists and ordered the release of condoms in the first war and penicillin in the second—and these continued to be used by returning troops after each war.

The spirochete (bacterium) which causes syphilis was discovered by Fritz Schaudinn in 1906. Syphilis is, classically, described in three stages:

- *Primary syphilis*—In this first stage, spirochetes mass and produce a primary lesion causing a *chancre* (pronounced "SHANK-er"). During the primary stage, syphilis is highly infectious.
- *Secondary syphilis*—In the second stage, spirochetes disseminate from the primary lesion throughout the body, producing systemic and widespread lesions, usually in internal organs and other internal sites. Externally, however—after the initial chancre subsides—syphilis spreads silently during a "latent" period lasting from 1 to 30 years, although secondary symptoms such as fever, rash, and swollen glands may appear. During the secondary stage, the symptoms of syphilis vary so widely that it is known as the "great imitator."
- *Tertiary syphilis*—In the third stage, chronic destructive lesions cause major damage to the cardiac system, the neurological system, or both, partly because immune responses decrease with age. During the tertiary stage, syphilis may produce paresis (slight or incomplete paralysis), gummas (gummy or rubbery tumors), altered gait, blindness, or lethal narrowing of the aorta.

Beginning in the sixteenth century, mercury—a heavy metal—was the common treatment for syphilis; it was applied to the back as a paste and absorbed through the skin. During the nineteenth century, this treatment alternated with bismuth, another heavy metal administered the same way. Neither mercury nor bismuth killed the spirochetes, though either could ameliorate symptoms.

In 1909, after the spirochete of syphilis had been identified, two researchers—a German, Paul Ehrlich, and a Japanese, S. Hata—tried 605 forms of arsenic and finally discovered what seemed to be a "magic bullet" against it: combination 606 of heavy metals including arsenic. Ehrlich called this *salvarsan* and patented it; the generic name is arsphenamine.[3] Salvarsan was administered as an intramuscular injection. After finding that it cured syphilis in rabbits, Ehrlich injected it into men with syphilis. (According to common practice, none of the men was asked to consent.)

At first, salvarsan seemed to work wonders, and during 1910 Ehrlich was receiving standing ovations at medical meetings. Later, however, syphilis recurred, fatally, in some patients who had been treated with salvarsan; furthermore, salvarsan itself apparently killed some patients. Ehrlich maintained that the drug had not been given correctly, but he also developed another form, neosalvarsan, which was less toxic and could be given more easily. Neosalvarsan also was injected intramuscularly—ideally, in 20 to 40 dosages given over 1 year.

Though better than salvarsan, neosalvarsan was (as described by a physician of the time) used erratically, and "generally without rhyme or reason—an injection now and then, possibly for a symptom, [for] some skin lesion, or when the patient had a ten-dollar bill."[4] It was also expensive. Moreover, neither salvarsan nor neosalvarsan was a "magic bullet" for patients with tertiary syphilis.

Another researcher, Caesar Boeck in Norway, took a different approach: from 1891 to 1910, he studied the natural course of untreated syphilis in 1,978 subjects. Boeck, a professor of dermatology at the University of Oslo, believed that heavy metals removed only the symptoms of syphilis rather than its underlying cause; he also thought that these metals suppressed what is today recognized as the immune system. He therefore decided that not treating patients at all might be an improvement over treatment with heavy metals.

In 1929, Boeck's student and successor, J. E. Bruusgaard, selected 473 of Boeck's subjects for further evaluation, in many cases examining their hospital charts.[5] This method had an obvious bias, since the more severely affected of Boeck's subjects would be most likely to have hospital records. Despite this bias, however, Bruusgaard was surprised to find that in 65 percent of these cases, either the subjects were externally symptom-free or there was no mention in their charts of the classic symptoms of syphilis. Of the subjects who had had syphilis for more than 20 years, 73 percent were asymptomatic.

Bruusgaard's findings contradicted the message of the syphilophobia campaign: they indicated that syphilis was not universally fatal, much less rapidly so. These results also suggested the possibility that some people with syphilis spirochetes would never develop any symptoms of the disease.

When the Tuskegee study began in 1932, Boeck's and Bruusgaard's work was the only existing study of the natural course of untreated syphilis.

THE RACIAL ENVIRONMENT

In the 1930s, American medicine was, and had long been, widely racist—certainly by our present standards and to some extent even by the standards of the time. For at least a century before the Tuskegee study began, most physicians condescended to African American patients, held stereotypes about them, and sometimes used them as subjects of nontherapeutic experiments.

The historian Todd Savitt, for example, has described how in the 1800s, J. Marion Sims, a pioneer in American gynecology, practiced techniques for closing vesical-vaginal fistulas on slave women.[6] John Brown, a former slave who wrote a book about his life under slavery, described how a physician in Georgia kept him in an open-pit oven to produce sunburns and to try out different remedies.

The best known account of the racial background of the Tuskegee study is James Jones's *Bad Blood* (1981; the significance of the title will become apparent below).[7] In the late nineteenth century, the United States was swept by social Darwinism, a popular corruption of Darwin's theory of evolution by natural selection. . . . Some whites predicted on this basis that the Negro race (to use the term then current) would be extinct by 1900: their idea was that Darwin's "survival of the fittest" implied a competition which Negroes would lose. (It bears repeating that this is a misconception and misapplication of Darwin's actual theory.) According to Jones, this popular belief was shared by white physicians, who thought that it was confirmed by defects in African Americans' anatomy and therefore became obsessed with the details of such presumed defects. Although comparable defects in white patients went unreported, defects in black patients were described in great detail in medical journals and became the basis for sweeping conclusions; to take one example, genital development and brain development were said to vary inversely.

In addition to social Darwinism, physicians shared many of the popular stereotypes of African Americans; well into the twentieth century, physicians often simply advanced such stereotypes as "facts." The following example appeared in *Journal of the American Medical Association* in 1914:

The negro springs from a southern race, and as such his sexual appetite is strong; all of his environments stimulate this appetite, and as a general rule his emotional type of religion certainly does not decrease it.[8]

African Americans were also seen as dirty, shiftless, promiscuous, and incapable of practicing personal hygiene. Around the turn of the century, a physician in rural Georgia wrote, "Virtue in the negro race is like 'angels' visits'—few and far between. In a practice of sixteen years in the South, I have never examined a virgin over fourteen years of age."[9] In 1919, a medical professor in Chicago wrote that African American men were like bulls or elephants in *furor sexualis,* unable to refrain from copulation when in the presence of females.[10]

Ideas about syphilis reflected this racial environment. For white physicians at the time when the Tuskegee study began, syphilis was a natural consequence of the innately low character of African Americans, who were described by one white physician as a "notoriously syphilis-soaked race."[11] Moreover, it was simply assumed that African American men would not seek treatment for venereal disease.

The historian Allan Brandt has suggested that in the United States during the early 1900s, it was a rare white physician who was not a racist—and that this would have remained the case throughout many years of the Tuskegee study. He writes, "There can be little doubt that the Tuskegee researchers regarded their subjects as less than human."[12]

DEVELOPMENT OF THE TUSKEGEE CASE

A "STUDY IN NATURE" BEGINS

Studies in nature were distinguished from experiments in 1865 by a famous experimenter and physiologist, Claude Bernard: in an experiment, some factor is manipulated, whereas a *study in nature* merely observes what would happen anyway. For a century before the Tuskegee study, medicine considered it crucially important to discover the natural history of a disease and therefore relied extensively on studies in nature.

The great physician William Osler had said, "Know syphilis in all its manifestations and relations, and all others things clinical will be added unto you."[13] As late as 1932, however, the natural history of syphilis had not been conclusively documented (the only existing study, as noted above, was that of Boeck and Bruusgaard), and there was uncertainty about the inexorability of its course. The United States Public Health Service (USPHS) believed that a study in nature of syphilis was necessary because physicians needed to know its natural sequence of symptoms and final outcomes in order to recognize key changes during its course. This perceived need was one factor in the Tuskegee research.

A second factor was simply that USPHS found what it considered an opportunity for such a study. Around 1929, there were several counties in the United States where venereal disease was extraordinarily prevalent, and a philanthropical organization—the Julius Rosenwald Foundation in Philadelphia—started a project to eradicate it. With help from USPHS, the foundation originally intended to treat with neosalvarsan all syphilitics in six counties with rates of syphilis above 20 percent. In 1930, the foundation surveyed African American men in Macon County, Alabama, which was then 82 percent black; this was the home of the famous Tuskegee Institute. The survey found the highest rate of syphilis in the nation: 36 percent. The foundation planned a demonstration study in which these African American syphilitics would be treated with neosalvarsan, and it did treat or partially treat some of the 3,694 men who had been identified as having syphilis (estimates of how many received treatment or partial treatment range from less than half to 95 percent). However, 1929 was the year when the great depression began; as it ground on, funds for philanthropy plummeted, and the Rosenwald Foundation pulled out of Tuskegee, hoping that USPHS would continue the treatment program. (Funds available for public health were also dropping, though: USPHS would soon see its budget lowered from over $1 million before the depression to less than $60,000 in 1935.)

In 1931, USPHS repeated the foundation's survey in Macon County, testing 4,400 African American residents; USPHS found a 22 percent rate of syphilis in men, and a 62 percent rate of congenital syphilis. In this survey, 399 African American men were identified who had syphilis of several years' duration but had never been treated by the Rosenwald Foundation or in any other way. It was the identification of these 399 untreated men that USPHS saw as an ideal opportunity for a study in nature of syphilis. The surgeon general suggested that they should be merely observed rather than treated: this decision would become a moral crux of the study.

It is important to reemphasize that the USPHS research—it was undertaken in cooperation with the Tuskegee Institute and is called the *Tuskegee study* for that reason—was a study in nature. The Tuskegee physicians saw themselves as ecological biologists, simply observing what occurred regularly and naturally. In 1936, a paper in *Journal of the American Medical Association* by the surgeon general and his top assistants described the 1932–1933 phase of the Tuskegee study as "an unusual opportunity to study the untreated syphilitic patient from the beginning of the disease to the death of the infected person." It noted specifically that the study consisted of "399 syphilitic Negro males who had never received treatment."[14]

There are also two important points to emphasize about the subjects of the Tuskegee study. First, at the outset the 399 syphilitic subjects had *latent syphilis,* that is, secondary syphilis; most of them were probably in the early latent stage. During this stage, syphilis is largely noninfectious during sexual intercourse, although it can be passed easily through a blood transfusion (or, in a pregnant woman, through the placenta). However, latent or secondary syphilis (as noted above) has extremely variable symptoms and outcomes; and external lesions, which can be a source of infection during sex, do sometimes appear.

Second, these 399 syphilitic subjects were not divided into the typical experimental and control or "treatment" and "not treatment" groups: they were all simply to be observed. There was, however, another group of "controls," consisting of about 200 age-matched men who did not have syphilis. (Originally, there was also a third group, consisting of 275 syphilitic men who had been treated with small amounts of arsphenamine; these subjects were followed for a while but were dropped from the study in 1936—perhaps because funds were lacking, or perhaps because the researchers were by then interested only in the "study in nature" group.)

THE MIDDLE PHASE: "BAD BLOOD"

The Tuskegee study was hardly a model of scientific research or scientific method; and even on its own terms, as a study in nature, it was carried out rather haphazardly. Except for an African American nurse, Eunice Rivers, who was permanently assigned to the study, there was no continuity of medical personnel. There was no central supervision; there were no written protocols; no physician was in charge.

Names of the subjects were not housed at any one location or facility. Most worked as sharecroppers or as small farmers and simply came into the town of Tuskegee when Eunice Rivers told them to do so (she would drive them into town in her car, a ride that several subjects described as making them feel important).

There were large gaps in the study. The "federal doctors," as the subjects called them, returned only every few years. Visits are documented in 1939 and then not again until 1948; 7 years passed between visits in 1963 and 1970. Only the nurse, Eunice Rivers, remained to hold the shaky study together. When the physicians did return to Tuskegee after a gap, they found it difficult to answer their own questions because the records were so poor.

Still, there were some rudimentary procedures. The physicians wanted to know, first, if they had a subject in the study group; and second, if so, how far his syphilis had progressed. To determine the progress of the disease, spinal punctures (called *taps*) were given to 271 of the 399 syphilitic subjects. In a spinal tap, a 10-inch needle is inserted between two vertebrae into the cerebrospinal fluid and a small amount of fluid is withdrawn—a delicate and uncomfortable process. The subjects were warned to lie very still, lest the needle swerve and puncture the fluid sac, causing infection and other complications.

Subjects were understandably reluctant to leave their farms, travel for miles over back roads to meet the physicians, and then undergo these painful taps, especially when they had no pressing medical problem. For this reason, the physicians offered inducements: free transportation, free hot lunches, free medicine for any disease other than syphilis, and free burials. (The free burials were important to poor subjects, who often died without enough money for even a pauper's grave; but USPHS couldn't keep this promise itself after its budget was reduced and had to be rescued by the Milbank Memorial Fund.) In return for these "benefits," the physicians got not only the spinal taps but, later, autopsies to see what damage syphilis had or had not done.

There seems no doubt that the researchers also resorted to deception. Subjects were told that they had "bad blood" and that the spinal taps were "treatment" for it; moreover, the researchers sensationalized the effects of untreated "bad blood." USPHS sent the subjects the following letter, under the imposing letterhead

"Macon County Health Department," with the subheading "Alabama State Board of Health and U.S. Public Health Service Cooperating with Tuskegee Institute" (all of which participated in the study):

> Dear Sir:
> Some time ago you were given a thorough examination and since that time we hope you have gotten a great deal of treatment for bad blood. You will now be given your last chance to get a second examination. This examination is a very special one and after it is finished you will be given a special treatment if it is believed you are in a condition to stand it.[15]

The "special treatment" mentioned was simply the spinal tap for neurosyphilis, a diagnostic test. The subjects were instructed to meet the public health nurse for transportation to "Tuskegee Institute Hospital for this free treatment." The letter closed in capitals:

REMEMBER THIS IS YOUR LAST CHANCE
FOR SPECIAL FREE TREATMENT.
BE SURE TO MEET THE NURSE.

To repeat, the researchers never treated the subjects for syphilis. In fact, during World War II, the researchers contacted the local draft board and prevented any eligible subject from being drafted—and hence from being treated for syphilis by the armed services. Although penicillin was developed around 1941–1943 and was widely available by 1946, the subjects in the Tuskegee study never received it, even during the 1960s or 1970s. However, as will be discussed below, it is not clear how much the subjects with late noninfectious syphilis were harmed by not getting penicillin.

THE FIRST INVESTIGATIONS

In 1966, Peter Buxtun, a recent college graduate, had just been hired by USPHS as a venereal disease investigator in San Francisco. After a few months, he learned of the Tuskegee study and began to question and criticize the USPHS officials who were still running it.[16] By this time, the physicians supervising the study and its data collection had been moved to the newly created Centers for Disease Control (CDC) in Atlanta. CDC officials were annoyed by Buxtun's questions about the morality of the study; later in 1966, having invited him to Atlanta for a conference on syphilis, they harangued him and tried to get him to be silent. He expected to be fired from USPHS; he was not, though, and he continued to press CDC for 2 more years.

By 1969, Buxtun's inquiries and protests led to a meeting of a small group of physicians at CDC to consider the Tuskegee study. The group consisted of William J. Brown (Director of Venereal Diseases at CDC), David Sencer (Director of CDC), Ira Meyers (Alabama's State Health Officer from 1951 to 1986), Sidney Olansky (a physician at Emory Hospital who was knowledgeable about the early years of the study and had been in charge of it in 1951), Lawton Smith (an ophthalmologist from the University of Miami), and Gene Stollerman (chairman of medicine at the University of Tennessee). In general, this group avoided Buxtun's questions about the morality of the study and focused on whether continuing the study would harm the subjects. Meyers said of the Tuskegee subjects, "I haven't seen this group, but I don't think they would submit to treatment" if they were told what was going on.[17] Smith (the ophthalmologist) pressed hardest for continuing the study; only Stollerman repeatedly opposed continuing it, on both moral and therapeutic grounds. At the end, the committee overrode Stollerman and voted to continue the study.

Also in 1969, Ira Meyers told the physicians in the Macon County Medical Society about the Tuskegee study. These physicians did not object to the study; in fact, they were given a list of all the subjects and agreed not to give antibiotics to any subjects for any condition, if a subject came to one of their offices. It should be noted that although this medical society had been all-white in the 1930s, during the 1960s its membership was almost entirely African American.

In 1970, a monograph on syphilis was published, sponsored by the American Public Health Association, to give useful information to public health officials and venereal disease (VD) control officers. This monograph stated that treatment for late benign syphilis should consist of "6.0 to 9.0 million units of benzathine pencillin G given 3.0 million units at sessions seven days apart."[18] The first author listed on the monograph is William J. Brown, head of CDC's Tuskegee section from 1957 to 1971. Brown had been on the CDC panel in 1969 (when the monograph was probably written) and had argued for continuing the Tuskegee study, in which, of course, subjects with late benign syphilis received *no* penicillin.

THE STORY BREAKS

In July of 1972, Peter Buxtun, who had then been criticizing the Tuskegee research for 6 years and was disappointed by CDC's refusal to stop it, mentioned the Tuskegee study to a friend who was a reporter for the Associated Press (AP) on the west coast. Another AP reporter—Jean Heller, on the east coast—was assigned to the story, and on the morning of July 26, 1972, her report appeared on front pages of newspapers nationwide.[19]

Heller's story described a medical study run by the federal government in Tuskegee, Alabama, in which poor, uneducated African American men had been used as "guinea pigs." After noting the terrible effects of tertiary syphilis, the story said that in 1969 a CDC study of 276 of the untreated subjects had proved that at least 7 subjects died "as a direct result of syphilis."

Heller's story had an immediate effect. (It might have made even more of an impact, but it was competing with a political story which broke the same day—a report that the Democratic candidate for vice president, Thomas Eagleton, had received shock therapy for depression.) Some members of Congress were amazed to learn of the Tuskegee study, and Senator William Proxmire called it a "moral and ethical nightmare."

CDC, of course, responded. J. D. Millar, chief of Venereal Disease Control, said that the study "was never clandestine," pointing to 15 published articles in medical and scientific journals over a 30-years span. Millar also maintained that the subjects had been informed that they could get treatment for syphilis at any time. "Patients were not denied drugs," he said; "rather, they were not offered drugs." He also tried to emphasize that "the study began when attitudes were much different on treatment and experimentation."[20]

The public and the press, however, scorned Millar's explanations. One political cartoon, for instance, showed a frail African American man being studied under a huge microscope by a white man in a white coat with a sign in the background: "This is a NO-TREATMENT study by your Public Health Service."[21] Another cartoon showed ragged African American men walking past tombstones; the caption read: "Secret Tuskegee Study— free autopsy, free burial, plus $100 bonus." Another showed a white physician standing near the body of an African American man, partially covered by a sheet; the chart at the foot of the hospital bed on which the body lay read "Ignore this syphilis patient (experiment in progress)"; in the background, a skeptical nurse holding a syringe asked, "*Now* can we give him penicillin?"

CDC and USPHS had always feared a "public relations problem" if the Tuskegee study became generally known, and now they had one. So did the Macon County Medical Society: when its president told the

Montgomery Advertiser that the members had voted to identify remaining subjects and given them "appropriate therapy," USPHS in Atlanta flatly contradicted him, retorting that the local physicians—African American physicians—had accepted the Tuskegee study. The society then acknowledged that it had agreed to continuation of the study but had not agreed to withhold treatment from subjects who came to the offices of its members, whereupon USPHS documented the physicians' agreement to do exactly that.

THE AFTERMATH

Almost immediately after Heller's story appeared, Congress commissioned a special panel to investigate the Tuskegee study and issue a report. (The report was supposed to be ready by December 31, 1972; as we will see, however, it was late.)

Also almost at once, senators Sparkman and Allen of Alabama (both Democrats) sponsored a federal bill to give each of the Tuskegee subjects $25,000 in compensation. The southern African American electorate had been instrumental in electing these two senators and many southern members of Congress in the 1960s and 1970s, as well as presidents Kennedy and Johnson.

On November 16, 1972, Casper Weinberger, Secretary of Health, Education, and Welfare (HEW), officially terminated the Tuskegee study. At that time, CDC estimated that 28 of the original syphilitic group had died of syphilis during the study; after the study was ended, the remaining subjects received penicillin.

In February and March 1973, Senator Edward Kennedy's Subcommittee on Health of the Committee on Labor and Public Welfare held hearings on the Tuskegee study. Two of the Tuskegee subjects, Charles Pollard and Lester Scott, testified; one of them appeared to have been blinded by late-stage syphilis. These two men revealed more about the study: Pollard said they had not been told that they had syphilis; both said they thought "bad blood" meant something like low energy. Kennedy strongly condemned the study and proposed new regulations for medical experimentation.

In April 1973, the investigatory panel that had been commissioned when the Tuskegee story broke finally issued its report, which did not prove to be very useful. Moreover, for some reason this panel had met behind closed doors, and thus reporters had not been able to cover it.[22]

On July 23, 1973, Fred Gray, representing some of the Tuskegee subjects, filed a class-action suit against the federal government. Gray, a former Alabama legislator (in 1970, he had become the first African American Democrat elected in Alabama since Reconstruction), had been threatening to sue for compensation since Heller's story first broke, hoping for a settlement. He presented the suit as an issue of race, suing only the federal government and omitting the Tuskegee Institute, Rivers, the Tuskegee hospitals, and the Macon County Medical Society.

Eventually, the Justice Department decided that it couldn't win the suit in federal court, since the trail would have been held in nearby Montgomery, in the court of Frank Johnson, a liberal Alabama judge who had desegregated southern schools and upgraded mental institutions. Therefore, in December 1974 the government settled out of court.

According to the settlement, "living syphilitics" (subjects alive on July 23, 1973) received $37,500 each; "heirs of deceased syphilitics," $15,000 (since some children might have congenital syphilis); "living controls," $16,000; heirs of "deceased controls," $5,000. (Controls and their descendants were compensated because they had been prevented from getting antibiotics during the years of the study.) Also, the federal government agreed to provide free lifetime medical care for Tuskegee subjects, their wives, and their children. By September 1988, the government had paid $7.5 million for medical care for Tuskegee subjects. At that time, 21 of the original syphilitic subjects were still alive—each of whom had had syphilis for at least 57 years.[23] In addition, 41 wives and 19 children had evidence of syphilis and were receiving free medical care.

By the time this settlement was reached, more than 18 months had passed since Jean Heller's first story, and the Tuskegee issue was no longer front-page news: even the *New York Times* was giving it only an occasional short paragraph or two on inside pages. The issue was, after all, complicated; ethical standards had changed over the long course of the Tuskegee research; and, as noted above, the special panel commissioned to evaluate the study had met in secret. The public, therefore, had more or less forgotten about the Tuskegee study.

NOTES

1. Molly Selvin, "Changing Medical and Societal Attitudes toward Sexually Transmitted Diseases: A Historical Overview," in King K. Holmes et al., eds., *Sexually Transmitted Diseases*, McGraw-Hill, New York, 1984, pp. 3–19.

2. Allan Brandt, "Racism and Research: The Case of the Tuskegee Syphilis Study," *Hastings Center Report*, vol. 8, no. 6, December 1978, pp. 21–29.

3. Paul de Kruif, *Microbe Hunters*, Harcourt Brace, New York, 1926, p. 323.

4. R. H. Kampmeier, "The Tuskegee Study of Untreated Syphilis" (editorial), *Southern Medical Journal*, vol. 65, no. 10, October 1972, pp. 1247–51.

5. J. E. Bruusgaard, "Über das Schicksal der nicht spezifisch behandelten Luetiker" ("Fate of Syphilitics Who Are Not Given Specific Treatment") *Archives of Dermatology of Syphilis*, vol. 157, April 1929, pp. 309–32.

6. Todd Savitt, *Medicine and Slavery: The Disease and Health of Blacks in Antebellum Virginia*, University of Illinois Press, Champaign, 1978.

7. James Jones, *Bad Blood*, Free Press, New York, 1981.

8. H. H. Hazen, "Syphilis in the American Negro," *Journal of the American Medical Association*, vol. 63, August 8, 1914, p. 463.

9. Jones, op. cit., p. 74

10. Ibid.

11. Ibid.

12. Brandt, op. cit.

13. Quoted in E. Ramont, "Syphilis in the AIDS Era," *New England Journal of Medicine*, vol. 316, no. 25, June 18, 1987, pp. 600–601.

14. R. A. Vonderlehr, T. Clark, and J. R. Heller, "Untreated Syphilis in the Male Negro," *Journal of the American Medical Association*, pp. 107, no. 11, September 12, 1936.

15. Archives of National Library of Medicine; quoted in Jones, op. cit., p. 127.

16. Jones, op. cit., pp. 190–93.

17. Quoted ibid., p. 196.

18. W. J. Brown et al., *Syphilis and Other Venereal Diseases*, Harvard University Press, Cambridge, Mass., 1970, p. 34.

19. Jean Heller, "Syphilis Victims in the United States Study Went Untreated for 40 Years," *New York Times*, July 26, 1972, pp. 1, 8.

20. Ibid., p. 8.

21. Jones, op. cit., insert following, p. 48.

22. Tuskegee Syphilis Study Ad Hoc Panel to Department of Health, Education, and Welfare, *Final Report*, Superintendent of Documents, Washington, D.C., 1973.

23. David Tase, "Tuskegee Syphilis Victims, Kin May Get $1.7 Million in Fiscal 1989," Associated Press, September 11, 1988.

WILLIAM J. CLINTON

In Apology for the Study Done in Tuskegee

William J. Clinton was elected Arkansas Attorney General in 1976 and won the governorship in 1978. He was elected the 42nd President of the United States in 1992 and served until 2001. More information can be found at www.whitehouse.gov/history/presidents.

. . . The eight men who are survivors of the syphilis study at Tuskegee are a living link to a time not so very long ago that many Americans would prefer not to remember, but we dare not forget. It was a time when our nation failed to live up to its ideals, when our nation broke the trust with our people that is the very foundation of our democracy. It is not only in remembering that shameful past that we can make amends and repair our nation, but it is in remembering that past that we can build a better present and a better future. And without remembering it, we cannot make amends and we cannot go forward.

Washington, DC: The White House, Office of the Press Secretary, 1997 May 16; 3p. (Online). Available: http://clinton4.nara.gov/textonly/New/Remarks/Fri/19970516-898.html.

So today America does remember the hundreds of men used in research without their knowledge and consent. We remember them and their family members. Men who were poor and African American, without resources and with few alternatives, they believed they had found hope when they were offered free medical care by the United States Public Health Service. They were betrayed.

Medical people are supposed to help when we need care, but even once a cure was discovered, they were denied help, and they were lied to by their government. Our government is supposed to protect the rights of its citizens; their rights were trampled upon. Forty years, hundreds of men betrayed, along with their wives and children, along with the community in Macon County, Alabama, the City of Tuskegee, the fine university there, and the larger African American community.

The United States government did something that was wrong—deeply, profoundly, morally wrong. It was an outrage to our commitment to integrity and equality for all our citizens.

To the survivors, to the wives and family members, the children and the grandchildren, I say what you know: No power on Earth can give you back the lives lost, the pain suffered, the years of internal torment and anguish. What was done cannot be undone. But we can end the silence. We can stop turning our heads away. We can look at you in the eye and finally say on behalf of the American people, what the United States government did was shameful, and I am sorry.

The American people are sorry—for the loss, for the years of hurt. You did nothing wrong, but you were grievously wronged. I apologize and I am sorry that this apology has been so long in coming.

To Macon County, to Tuskegee, to the doctors who have been wrongly associated with the events there, you have our apology, as well. To our African American citizens, I am sorry that your federal government orchestrated a study so clearly racist. That can never be allowed to happen again. It is against everything our country stands for and what we must stand against is what it was.

So let us resolve to hold forever in our hearts and minds the memory of a time not long ago in Macon County, Alabama, so that we can always see how adrift we can become when the rights of any citizens are neglected, ignored and betrayed. And let us resolve here and now to move forward together.

The legacy of the study at Tuskegee has reached far and deep, in ways that hurt our progress and divide our nation. We cannot be one America when a whole segment of our nation has no trust in America. An apology is the first step, and we take it with a commitment to rebuild that broken trust. We can begin by making sure there is never again another episode like this one. We need to do more to ensure that medical research practices are sound and ethical, and that researchers work more closely with communities.

Today I would like to announce several steps to help us achieve these goals. First, we will help to build that lasting memorial at Tuskegee. The school founded by Booker T. Washington, distinguished by the renowned scientist George Washington Carver and so many others who advanced the health and well-being of African Americans and all Americans, is a fitting site. The Department of Health and Human Services will award a planning grant so the school can pursue establishing a center for bioethics in research and health care. The center will serve as a museum of the study and support efforts to address its legacy and strengthen bioethics training.

Second, we commit to increase our community involvement so that we may begin restoring lost trust. The study at Tuskegee served to sow distrust of our medical institutions, especially where research is involved. Since the study was halted, abuses have been checked by making informed consent and local review mandatory in federally-funded and mandated research.

Still, 25 years later, many medical studies have little African American participation and African American organ donors are few. This impedes efforts to conduct promising research and to provide the best health care to all our people, including African Americans. So today, I'm directing the Secretary of Health and Human Services, Donna Shalala, to issue a report in 180 days about how we can best involve communities, especially minority communities, in research and health care. You must—every American group must be involved in medical research in ways that are positive. We have put the curse behind us; now we must bring the benefits to all Americans.

Third, we commit to strengthen researchers' training in bioethics. We are constantly working on making breakthroughs in protecting the health of our people and in vanquishing diseases. But all our people must be assured that their rights and dignity will be respected as new drugs, treatments and therapies are tested and used. So I am directing Secretary Shalala to work in partnership with higher education to prepare training materials for medical researchers. They will be available in a year. They will help researchers build on core ethical principles of respect for individuals, justice and informed consent, and advise them on how to use these principles effectively in diverse populations.

Fourth, to increase and broaden our understanding of ethical issues and clinical research, we commit to providing postgraduate fellowships to train bioethicists especially among African Americans and other minority groups. HHS will offer these fellowships beginning is September of 1998 to promising students enrolled in bioethics graduate programs.

And, finally, by executive order I am also today extending the charter of the National Bioethics

Advisory Commission to October of 1999. The need for this commission is clear. We must be able to call on the thoughtful, collective wisdom of experts and community representatives to find ways to further strengthen our protections for subjects in human research.

We face a challenge in our time. Science and technology are rapidly changing our lives with the promise of making us much healthier, much more productive and more prosperous. But with these changes we must work harder to see that as we advance we don't leave behind our conscience. No ground is gained and, indeed, much is lost if we lose our moral bearings in the name of progress.

The people who ran the study at Tuskegee diminished the stature of man by abandoning the most

basic ethical precepts. They forgot their pledge to heal and repair. They had the power to heal the survivors and all the others and they did not. Today, all we can do is apologize. But you have the power, for only you—Mr. Shaw, the others who are here, the family members who are with us in Tuskegee—only you have the power to forgive. Your presence here shows us that you have chosen a better path than your government did so long ago. You have not withheld the power to forgive. I hope today and tomorrow every American will remember your lesson and live by it.

Thank you, and God bless you.

TAKASHI TSUCHIYA

Imperial Japanese Medical Atrocities and Their Enduring Legacy in Japanese Research Ethics

Takashi Tsuchiya is Associate Professor in the Department of Philosophy, Faculty of Literature and Human Sciences, Osaka City University, Osaka, Japan. His research interests are the ethics of human experimentation based on a comparison of historical backgrounds in Japan, Germany, and the United States and cross-cultural studies of bioethics.

Editor's note: An earlier version of the following essay was presented to a plenary session of the Eighth World Congress of Bioethics in Beijing, China, in August 2006. A somewhat longer version of the essay will be published in the *Oxford Textbook of Clinical Research Ethics*, edited by Ezekiel Emanuel, et al., under the title "The Imperial Japanese Experiments in China."

During the years 1932 to 1945, Japanese researchers killed thousands of human beings in medical and public-health experiments. The experiments studied the progression of deliberately caused disease, surgical techniques, and infectious agents that could potentially be used in biological warfare. Most of the studies were conducted in China while that nation was under Japanese occupation, and most involved people of Chinese ancestry. However, Allied prisoners of war—including U.S. flyers who had been shot down during bombing raids on Japan—were also among the victims.

After the conclusion of the Pacific war, the U.S. government sought access to the data from the Japanese experiments. In conjunction with their quest for data, U.S. authorities granted immunity to most of the physicians and scientists who had participated in these medical crimes. There was thus no Japanese analog to the Nuremberg Medical Trial that is discussed elsewhere in this chapter. One consequence of American post-war policies is that, until now, Japanese political leaders have been reluctant to acknowledge that these crimes against humanity occurred.

The symbolic significance of this candid account's having been presented in Beijing, China, by a Japanese scholar can hardly be overstated.

This essay has four parts. First, I will explain the background of Imperial Japanese medical atrocities 1932–45. Second, their outline will be described with several examples. Third, the story of their post-war concealment will be told. Finally, I will analyze their enduring legacy in contemporary Japanese society.

PART I. BACKGROUND

Shiro Ishii, the founder and leader of Japan's network of human experimentation facilities, entered the Army in 1920 upon graduation from Kyoto Imperial University Faculty of Medicine. In 1925, Ishii began to lobby his superiors for research on biological warfare. In 1930, after a two-year trip to Europe and the United States, he became a professor in the Department of Epidemic Prevention of the Army Medical College in Tokyo. In this position he performed bacteriological studies, conducted research on and development of vaccines, and trained army surgeons. He wanted to improve the prestige of medical officers in the Japanese Army by developing a powerful biological weapons program—even though biological and chemical weapons had been prohibited by the Geneva Convention in 1920. Using the Army's authority and prestige in 1930s Japan, he also envisaged a national network for medical research that would be much more powerful and effective than the existing academic infrastructure, and that would be furnished with state-of-the-art laboratories that could freely use humans for research and development of military medicine.

The takeover of northeastern China—Imperial Japan called it "Manchuria"—by Japan's Kwantung Army in 1931 gave Ishii his opportunity. The following year, he established a large new department specializing in biological warfare in the Army Medical College, and deceptively named it the Epidemic Prevention Laboratory. This laboratory became the headquarters of his network. Simultaneously, he built a secret facility called the Togo Unit in Beiyinhe, a small town in Manchuria about 70 km southeast of Harbin. This was Ishii's first prison-laboratory, where deadly human experimentation probably began in the fall of 1933. The subjects were mainly Chinese but included some Soviets, Mongolians, and Koreans who were arrested by the Kwantung Army Military Police as spies and resisters and who were scheduled to be executed without trial. Ishii and his colleagues thought it was better to use them as human guinea pigs than merely to execute them.

The facilities of Beiyinhe were insufficient for Ishii's project. The buildings were not strong enough to serve as a prison; in fact, in September 1934, 16 captives revolted and escaped. So Ishii and the army built a much larger, stronger prison laboratory-factory in Pingfang (sometimes written as Ping Fan), about 20 km southeast of downtown Harbin.

Construction at Pingfang began in 1935; residents of four nearby villages were forced to evacuate, and the huge complex was completed around 1938. The Togo Unit became an official unit of the Japanese army in 1936, even before construction was completed. This means that the Japanese Emperor, Hirohito, formally acknowledged Ishii's project, though it seems he was unaware of its details.

The Togo Unit was now known as the Epidemic Prevention Department of the Kwantung Army, and as Unit 731. In addition to medical experimentation, Ishii's units were responsible for water purification

for Japanese troops in China from 1937 on, and so the unit was soon renamed the Epidemic Prevention and Water Supply Department (EPWSD). Ishii had invented a water purification machine that could be easily carried to the battlefield. During the battles for Beijing and Shanghai, he sent teams to the front to operate it—garnering even more support from army leaders. In 1938, the Japanese army adopted Ishii's machine as standard equipment and organized 18 divisional EPWSDs, whose directors were officers of Unit 731. By 1939, Ishii's network included some field water purification units, 18 divisional EPWSDs, and five permanent Epidemic Prevention Departments—in Harbin (Unit 731), Beijing (Unit 1855), Nanjing (Unit 1644), Guangzhou (Unit 8604), and Tokyo (The Epidemic Prevention Laboratory). Altogether, Ishii commanded more than 10,000 people. When the Japanese army occupied Singapore in 1942, another permanent EPWSD was added to the network (Unit 9420). Unit 731 itself had a proving ground in Anda (about 150 km northwest of Harbin) and five branches in Mudanjiang, Linkou, Sunwu, Hailar, and Dalian.

In addition, as a leader of army surgeons, Ishii had power over army hospitals in occupied cities in China. His network had also close connections with other biological warfare departments such as the Military Animals Epidemic Prevention Department in Changchun, Manchuria (Unit 100), and institutions for chemical warfare such as the Army Sixth Technology Institute in Tokyo, the Army Narashino School in the Tokyo suburb of Narashino, the Army Ninth Technology Institute (Noborito Institute) in Noborito, also a Tokyo suburb, and the Kwantung Army Chemical Department in Qiqihar in Manchuria (Unit 516).

Unit 731 probably moved to the new base in Pingfang in 1938. It was a 6-square-kilometer complex of secret laboratory-factories surrounded by trenches and high voltage electric wires. The whole district became a special military area, which meant anyone approaching without permission was to be shot by the guards. The main building had two special prisons in its inner yard, so that escapees could never get outside. The captives were called "maruta," which means "logs" in Japanese, and were identified only by numbers.

At a little-noted war crimes trial conducted by Soviet authorities at Khabarovsk in 1949, Surgeon Major General Kiyoshi Kawashima, who was chief of a division of Unit 731, testified that the prisons usually held 200 to 300 captives, including some women and children, but that their maximum capacity was said to be 400 (*Materials* 1950, p. 257). The Military Police sent 400 to 600 captives to Unit 731 every year under the Special Transfer Procedure, a system the Japanese army developed to supply human subjects. This system for procuring subjects marks a difference from that of Nazi Germany. The Nazi transfer system was not for procuring subjects but for genocide. But in the case of the Japanese medical experiments, victims were purposely selected and sent to Ishii's network to be subjects of experiments.

At least 3,000 people were tortured to death at Unit 731 from 1940 to 1945 (*Materials* 1950, p. 117). But this number does not include victims before 1940 or at other medical experimentation sites. Allied prisoners of war (POWs) may have been subjected to experiments by Unit 731 researchers at the camp in Mukden (now Shengyang) (Williams and Wallace 1989, Chap. 5; Harris 2002, Chap. 9).

In fact, the activities of Unit 731 researchers were only a part of the medical atrocities committed by Imperial Japan. According to a large body of testimony, deadly experiments also were performed in other permanent EPWSDs such as Units 1644 in Nanjing and 1855 in Beijing. American, Australian, and New Zealander POWs were forced to participate in experiments by Surgeon Captain Einosuke Hirano of the 24th Field EPWSD in Rabaul, Papua, New Guinea (Tanaka 1996), and eight U.S. airmen were killed in surgical experiments in Fukuoka, on the Japanese home islands (SCAP: Legal Section 1940–48).

PART II. MEDICAL ATROCITIES

Medical atrocities performed by Imperial Japanese doctors can be classified into three categories:

1. Training of Army Surgeons
2. Biological Warfare Maneuvers
3. Research with Humans

Here I can only describe outlines and a few examples. . . .

1. TRAINING OF ARMY SURGEONS

Surgeons at army hospitals performed many vivisections on Chinese captives, with anesthesia. For example, these doctors performed appendectomies and tracheostomies on the prisoners, shot them and took bullets from their bodies, cut open their arms and legs

and sewed up the skin around the wounds, and finally killed them. This was purportedly part of training newly assigned army surgeons to treat wounded soldiers at the front lines.

Confessions by many of the surgeons involved are on record (Yoshikai 1981; Chinese Central Archive et al., 1989). At Datong Army Hospital in Datong, Shanxi, in June probably of 1941, Surgeon Major Kazuharu Tanimura and Surgeon Lieutenant Rihei Miura conducted a three-day training program that involved lectures on military surgery and exercise surgeries such as suturing of blood vessels and nerves, thoracotomy, celiotomy, craniotomy, blood transfusion, various anesthetizations, appendectomy, and nephrectomy, performed serially on "six bodies of prepared materials" (Daido Rikugun Byoin 1941). The trainees were army surgeon officers of the Army Medical College. Judging from confessions about similar cases, the "materials" probably were arrested Chinese resisters who probably were killed in these exercises.

2. BIOLOGICAL WARFARE MANEUVERS

Hundreds of confessions testify to Imperial Japanese research into the use of biological warfare. According to testimonies of former junior assistants of Unit 731, when a war between Manchukuo-Japan and Mongol-the-Soviets broke in 1939 . . . Unit 731 performed biological warfare against the troops of Mongol-the-Soviets (Takidani 1989, pp. 187–188, 208; 731 Kenkyukai 1996, pp. 64–67). Moreover, Japanese army officers themselves wrote about biological warfare against China in their official records. According to these notes, at least three major attacks on Chinese citizens were carried out. (Imoto)

3. RESEARCH WITH HUMANS

The research by Japanese doctors falls into three categories: (A) Explaining Diseases, (B) Development of Therapies, and (C) Development of Biological and Chemical Weapons.

(A) Explaining Diseases. Doctors in Ishii's network performed lethal experiments on captives in order to gain new scientific knowledge. There were two major kinds of research programs. One group of experiments involved bacteriological studies, including intentional infection in order to observe how the disease occurs and progresses and to search for its pathogen. Another group involved physiological studies, which were similar to the experiments Nazi doctors performed, including observation of the body's

reaction to conditions such as extremely low temperature, low pressure such as that experienced at high altitudes, salt overdose, drinking only distilled water, and intravenous air injection.

Bacteriological Studies. Shiro Kasahara, a researcher at Kitasato Institute in Tokyo, worked for Unit 731 for several years. In 1944, Kasahara, Surgeon General Masaji Kitano, Commander of Unit 731 from August 1942 to March 1945, and others published a paper concerning the identification of the pathogen of epidemic hemorrhagic fever, the etiology of which was then still unknown. It reads:

We made an emulsion with 203 ground-up North Manchuria mites and salt water, and injected it into the thigh of an ape hypodermically. This first ape became feverish with a temperature of 39.4 degrees Celsius on the 19th day after the injection and became moderately infected. Then we took blood of this feverish ape and injected it into the second ape, which became feverish and produced protein in its urine. Typical epidemic hemorrhagic kidney was found at its autopsy . . . Epidemic hemorrhagic kidney was never found at autopsy in the most feverish period . . . But the kidney, liver, and spleen of this period are most infective. (Kasahara et al., 1944, p. 3)

This means they vivisected the "ape," because in order for surgeons to "autopsy in the most feverish period," the subject needed to be alive. Moreover, "the ape" must have been a human being, because the normal temperature of an ape is higher than that of a human being, 39.4 degrees Celsius is normal for an ape. In another paper, Kasahara and his colleagues noted that apes do not become feverish from this disease. So it seems probable that they infected humans and vivisected them (Tsuneishi 1981). Kasahara himself confessed later that he and his colleagues performed deadly experiments (Williams and Wallace 1989, pp. 39–40).

Extensive data regarding the dose at which 50% of those exposed would develop various diseases, the so-called minimum infectious dose for 50% (MID50), were described in a U.S. investigator's report (Fell 1947). A determination of the MID50 was thought to be very important for the development of biological weapons. Japanese researchers infected humans to learn the MID50 of anthrax, plague, typhoid, paratyphoid A and B, dysentery, cholera, and glanders. Experiments were performed to determine the MID50 for a variety of pathogens that were introduced into humans subcutaneously, orally, and through respiration of infected air samples. Some of the infections were not fatal, but many of those exposed died.

Physiological Studies. Hisato Yoshimura was a lecturer at Kyoto Imperial University Faculty of Medicine when his head professor ordered him to go to Unit 731 in 1938. He stayed there until Unit 731 collapsed in 1945, and he used captives in studies of frostbite. At the Khabarovsk Trial, many officers and soldiers testified about the cruelty of Yoshimura's experiments. Yoshimura himself gave a lecture on his frostbite studies in Harbin in 1941, although he said nothing about cruel experiments (Yoshimura 1941). After the war, he and his colleagues published three papers in Japanese medical journals—in English—reporting part of the studies (Yoshimura and Iida 1950–51; Yoshimura and Iida 1951–52, Yoshimura, Iida and Koishi 1951–52). We know that these English papers concern their studies at Unit 731, because they themselves wrote that outlines of the papers were read at the 21st and 22nd annual meetings of Japanese Physiological Society in 1942–43. They wrote, "The experiments were made on about 100 male subjects (laboratory workers, students, soldiers and laborers)" (Yoshimura and Iida 1950–51, p. 149). Women, children, and even an infant were included in the experiments:

The temperature reaction in ice water was examined on about 100 Chinese coolies from 15 to 74 years old and on about 20 Chinese pupils of 7 to 14 years . . . Though detailed studies could not be attained on children below 6 years of age, some observations were carried out on a baby . . . [T]he reaction was detected even on the third day after birth, and it increased rapidly with the lapse of days until at last it was nearly fixed after a month or so.

As to sexual difference of the reactivity, only an outlining aspect was obtained from the observation on the Orochon subjects . . . The reactivity of the female subject was a little lower than the male's in adult age, while they were nearly the same with each other in childhood. (Yoshimura and Iida 1951–52, pp. 178–179)

Frostbite experiments with Chinese captives were also performed elsewhere. Surgeon Major Kazuharu Tanimura of Datong Army Hospital organized a detachment and went on an expedition into Inner Mongolia from January 31 to February 11, 1941, to study frostbite, field surgeries, hemostatis, blood transfusion, and other procedures (Toki Eisei Kenkyuhan 1941). He took eight "living bodies"—male Chinese captives—as "material" for experiments. At dawn on February 6, researchers performed frostbite experiments on six people in various conditions such as wearing wet socks or gloves, drunk, hungry, and after the administration of atropine. Their report, reprinted in 1995, describes the results precisely with sketches and photographs. (ibid.) The eight captives were also used in other experiments and operations, and finally were shot or vivisected to death. The report includes the names of the subjects, direction for their confinement, a log of their killing, the program of their memorial service, and Tanimura's condolences.

(B) Development of Therapies. The second category of imperial Japanese human experiments was for development of therapies, including vaccines, surgical techniques both in hospital and on the battlefield, hemostasis, and transfusion of blood or its substitute.

Vaccine Experiments. Yoshio Shinozuka, a former junior assistant of Unit 731 whose birth name was Yoshio Tamura, wrote in 2004:

Unit 731 was developing an envelope vaccine of plague. . . . The Karasawa Division, to which I belonged, also performed human experimentation and vivisection on five Chinese under the pretext of a virulence test of the germ. First we collected blood from them and measured their immunity. On the next day, we injected four kinds of plague vaccines to each of four subjects. No vaccine was given to one subject as control. A week later, vaccines were given again. A month later, we injected 1.0 cc liquid with the same number of plague germs into every subject. All five were infected with plague . . . The man that had no vaccine was infected first. Two or three days later he became feverish and pale. On the next day he was dying and his face grew darker. He was still alive but the members of the Special Division, which administered the special prison of "Maruta" ["logs"] brought him naked on the stretcher to the dissection room where we awaited him. . . . Lieutenant Hosoda ausculated his heartbeat on his chest. At the moment the auscultation finished, Surgeon Colonel Ohyama ordered "Let's begin!" (Shinozuka and Takayanagi 2004, pp. 78–82)

Shinozuka's superiors vivisected the subject and took organs as specimens. Shinozuka testifies that even his friend, junior assistant Mitsuo Hirakawa, was detained in the special prison and vivisected when infected with plague. (ibid., pp. 88–96)

Surgical Innovation. Deadly experimental surgeries were performed on captives to develop new surgical methods, not to train beginning surgeons. At least two studies are documented. One set of experiments aimed at developing hospital techniques was performed on U.S. Army Air Corps crews in mainland Japan. The other experiments, to develop field surgical procedures, were performed on Chinese captives in Inner Mongolia.

From May to June 1945, Professor Fukujiro Ishiyama of the First Department of Surgery, Apprentice Army Surgeon Taku Komori, and other Ishiyama subordinates performed experimental surgeries on eight U.S. crewmen at Kyushu Imperial University Faculty of Medicine. The American airmen were captured when their B-29s were downed. The Japanese Western District Army decided to execute them and handed them over to Komori and Ishiyama. On May 17, 1945, Ishiyama removed a lung from two POWs. On May 22, Ishiyama and his team performed total gastric resection and heart surgery on a POW, and removed the gall bladder and half of the liver of another POW. On May 25, they performed trigeminal rhizotomy (severing the facial nerve roots) on a POW. Finally, on June 2, Ishiyama performed surgery on the mediastinum and removed the gall bladders of two of the three POWs. All eight American POWs died during these operations (SCAP: Legal Section 1940–48).

After the war, GHQ/SCAP brought this case to the military tribunal in Yokohama. Komori had already died; he had been badly injured in a U.S. air raid on Fukuoka in July 1945. Ishiyama hanged himself in prison in July 1946. On August 28, 1948, the Yokohama tribunal condemned two army officers and three university doctors to death by hanging, and sentenced another officer and two doctors to life imprisonment. Five other officers, eight doctors, and a head nurse were ordered to hard labor. (SCAP: Legal Section 1940–48) However, their sentences were reduced in 1950 when the Korean War broke out, and none among the convicted was executed.

Surgeon Major Kazuharu Tanimura and his colleagues experimented with field surgery during their expedition to Inner Mongolia. They wrote in their log that on February 4, 1941, they performed enteroanastomosis (intestinal bypass) on "living material No. 1." On the next day, "In order to follow up wounds, using living material No. 3, we amputated the left thigh, cut and sewed right thigh skin, and cut open the skin of the left hypogastrium. Treatments of dummy perforate gunshot wounds were performed on the left arm and right thigh of living material No. 7, and on the left waist and left chest of No. 6." On February 6, they shot No. 8 to make perforate wounds, then performed transfusion and tracheostomy on him (Toki Eisei Kenkyuhan 1941).

Transfusion Experiments. Tanimura's detachment performed various transfusion experiments, also to develop battlefield treatments. On February 5 1941, they wrote that subjects No. 1 and No. 3 had transfusions of blood and Ringer solution at room temperature. On February 7 they transfused blood kept in a thermos bottle, blood that had been frozen and then thawed, and sheep blood. On February 8 they transfused blood taken from the heart of a corpse (Toki Eisei Kenkyuhan 1941, pp. 25–29).

At the Kyushu Imperial University Faculty of Medicine, sterilized and diluted brine was transfused into U.S. airmen as a blood substitute in the experimental operations described above. On May 17, 1945, Professor Ishiyama and his aides transfused 2,000 cc of blood substitute into the POW whose lung was removed. On June 2, they drew about 500 cc of blood from the right thigh artery of another POW and transfused 300 cc of blood substitute (SCAP: Legal Section 1940–48).

(C) Development of Biological and Chemical Weapons. The third research category related to weapons development. The aim of those engaged in this kind of research was to find ways to kill people more effectively and efficiently. Doctors in Ishii's medical network performed both biological and chemical weapon experiments on humans.

Biological Weapon Experiments. U.S. investigator N.H. Fell described many biological weapon trials in his report. Regarding anthrax bomb trials he noted:

> In most cases the human subjects were tied to stakes and protected with helmets and body armor. The bombs of various types were exploded either statically, or with time fuses after being dropped from aircraft . . . The Japanese were not satisfied with the field trials with anthrax. However, in one trial with 15 subjects, 8 were killed as a result of wounds from the bombs, and 4 were infected by bomb fragments (3 of these 4 subjects died). In another trial with a more efficient bomb ("Uji"), 6 of 10 subjects developed a definite bacteremia, and 4 of these were considered to have been infected by the respiratory route; all four of these latter subjects died. However, these four subjects were only 25 meters from the nearest of the 9 bombs that were exploded in a volley. (Fell 1947)

Fell's description coincides with testimony by Japanese officers and soldiers at the Khabarovsk Trial and the Chinese investigation. Fell also reported of plague and glanders trials precisely (Fell 1947).

Chemical Weapon Experiments. A report authored by an unknown researcher in the Kamo Unit [Unit 731] describes a large human experiment of yperite gas (mustard gas) on September 7–10, 1940. Twenty subjects were divided into three groups and placed in combat emplacements, trenches, gazebos, and observatories. One group was clothed with Chinese underwear, no hat, and no mask, and was subjected to as much as 1,800 field gun rounds of yperite gas over 25 minutes. Another group was clothed in summer military uniform and shoes; three had masks and another three had no masks. They also were exposed to as much as 1,800 rounds of yperite gas. A third group was clothed in summer military uniform, three with masks and two without masks, and were exposed to as much as 4,800 rounds. Then their general symptoms and damage to skin, eye, respiratory organs, and digestive organs were observed at 4 hours, 24 hours, 2, 3, and 5 days after the shots. Injections of the blister fluid from one subject into another subject and analyses of blood and soil were also performed. Five subjects were forced to drink a solution of yperite and lewisite gas in water, with or without decontamination. The report describes the condition of every subject precisely without mentioning what happened to the subject in the long run (Kamo Butai).

Poison experiments were also performed at other EPWSDs. Engineer Major Shigeo Ban of the Army Ninth Technology Institute (Noborito Institute) confessed to performing poison experiments at Unit 1644 in Nanjing. Early in May 1941, the Army General Staff Corps ordered Ban and his eight colleagues to visit Unit 1644 to test the toxicity of a newly developed poison, acetone cyanhydrin, in humans (Ban 2001, pp. 81–82).

PART III. COVER-UP

Ishii's medical network suddenly collapsed in August 1945 when the Soviet Union declared war on Japan and advanced into Manchuria. The Japanese Army immediately decided to withdraw all human experimentation units from China and to destroy the evidence of medical atrocities. At Unit 731, all the surviving captives were killed, cremated, and cast into the Songhuajiang River. The main building with its special prisons was totally destroyed by artillery. Its surgeon officers, researchers, workers, and soldiers were hurriedly evacuated in specially chartered trains and ships. Most succeeded in escaping and returned to Japan. In Tokyo, the Epidemic Prevention Laboratory, headquarters of Ishii's network, had already been destroyed by U.S. air raids in March and May of 1945. But Ishii and his colleagues held onto their biological warfare data.

Although the United States occupied Japan after Japan's surrender on August 15, 1945, General Headquarters/Supreme Command for the Allied Powers (GHQ/SCAP) did not investigate medical crimes. Instead, investigators from the U.S. Army Chemical Corps in Camp Detrick, Maryland, which oversaw U.S. chemical and biological warfare efforts, sought the biological warfare data that Ishii and his colleagues had accumulated—so that the United States could catch up with the Soviet Union and other countries in biowar research and development (Ohta 1999; Tsuneishi 1994; Harris 1994; Regis 1999). The Soviets had begun research in biological warfare in 1928, but the United States had not started it until 1942. The Cold War had already begun to emerge, and U.S. officials were under pressure to surpass Soviet capabilities in all fields.

In return for the Japanese data, Lieutenant Colonel Murray Sanders, the first Chemical Corps investigator, asked General Douglas MacArthur and General Charles Willoughby, a close MacArthur aide, to promise Ishii and his researchers immunity from war crimes charges in September 1945. Ishii and his colleagues gave up some data, but they concealed from Sanders and his successor, Lieutenant Colonel Arvo T. Thompson, that the data were from experiments with humans. The United States did not obtain evidence of deadly human experiments until 1947.

Early in January 1947, the Soviet Union sought the extradition of Ishii and his researchers for investigation of their experiments, which the Soviets had learned about from captured officers and soldiers of Ishii's network. The Soviets also wanted the biowar data and threatened to reveal the Japanese medical atrocities at the International Military Tribunal for the Far East—the Tokyo Tribunal, which conducted the war crimes trials of top Japanese leaders from 1946 to 1948—if the United States did not share the information. U.S. officials dismissed this threat—the United States controlled the Tokyo Tribunal—but then began to investigate the Japanese researchers more closely.

At this point, U.S. officials recognized that human experiments had occurred, and the immunity that they had granted to Ishii and others now became a problem. In Nuremberg, the United States was prosecuting Nazi doctors for their human experiments. MacArthur's headquarters discussed the dilemma repeatedly with officials in Washington, and an interagency task force in the U.S. capital finally concluded;

Information of Japanese BW [biological warfare] experiments will be of great value to the U.S. research program . . . The value to the U.S. of Japanese BW data is of such importance to national security as to far outweigh the value accruing from "war crimes" prosecution . . . The BW information obtained from Japanese sources should be retained in Intelligence channels and should not be employed as "war crimes" evidence. (State-War-Navy Coordinating Subcommittee for the Far East 1947)

This conclusion was based on a close examination of the data that was finally provided by Ishii and his colleagues. The last investigator, Edwin V. Hill, reported to the Chief of the U.S. Army Chemical Corps:

Evidence gathered in this investigation has greatly supplemented and amplified previous aspects of this field. It represents data which have been obtained by Japanese scientists at the expenditure of many millions of dollars and years of work. Information has accrued with respect to human susceptibility to these diseases as indicated by specific infectious doses of bacteria. Such information could not be obtained in our own laboratories because of scruples attached to human experimentation. These data were secured with a total outlay of 250,000 yen to date, a mere pittance by comparison with the actual cost of the studies. (Hill 1947)

Thus, most officers and researchers involved in Japan's human experimentation program, including Ishii himself, never faced war crimes charges. Ishii died of laryngeal cancer in 1959, at the age of 67. Many army surgeon officers and researchers gained positions in medical schools, national institutes, or hospitals. Some practiced in their own clinics; some others established pharmaceutical companies (Williams and Wallace 1989, Chap. 17).

Although failing to get custody of Ishii or access to his data, the Soviet Union brought 12 captured officers and soldiers to trial before an open military tribunal at Khabarovsk in December 1949, commonly called the Khabarovsk Trial (*Materials* 1950). The accused included the Captain General of the Kwantung Army, Otozo Yamada, six army surgeon officers, and two veterinarian officers. Six of the accused were from

Unit 731 and two from Unit 100. They were all sentenced to confinement in a labor correction camp for sentences that ranged from two to 25 years, but they returned to Japan by 1956 when the Soviet Union and Japan resumed diplomatic relations.

The Soviets had intended to spread the news of the medical atrocities worldwide, but because the prosecutors, lawyers, and judges were all Russian, and there were no reporters from abroad, the proceedings drew little attention. The United States succeeded in branding the trial as communist propaganda.

The People's Republic of China also tried Japanese war criminals before military tribunals in 1956, but only one surgeon officer of Ishii's network was included. None of these defendants received a death sentence, and all returned to Japan by 1964 (Arai and Fujiwara 1999, p. 278).

PART IV. ENDURING LEGACY

In cooperation with the United States, Japan hid the medical atrocities from both the international and domestic public for decades. Testimony from the Khabarovsk trial was regarded as false communist propaganda. Former soldiers and junior assistants who bravely confessed to conducting such experiments in China were considered to have been brainwashed and neglected. But in 1981, popular writer Seiichi Morimura published a bestselling book about Unit 731 that included anonymous testimony by many of its soldiers (Morimura 1981). In the same year, historian Keiichi Tsuneishi published his first extensive study of Unit 731 (Tsuneishi 1981). Because of this, in Japan the word "Unit 731 (731 Butai)" became widely known with a dire impression, and historical studies have advanced greatly since then as significant documents have been found in Japan, the United States, China, and the former Soviet Union.

Outside Japan, the Imperial Japanese medical atrocities did not become widely known until the 1990s. But today, more than 60 years after the end of World War II, the U.S. government can no longer be closing its eyes to the record of human experimentation. Now it has refused to allow former employees of Unit 731 into the country on the ground that they are war criminals. In 1998 Yoshio Shinozuka, a former junior assistant of Unit 731 mentioned above, was denied entry, and deported to Japan from Chicago's O'Hare International Airport (Nishisato 2002, p. 251). However, this attitude of U.S. government is superficial and hypocritical, since the United States itself must share in the responsibility for keeping these experiments secret. Until the 1980s it had allowed free entrance of Ishii's researchers such as Ryoichi Naito, who had been Ishii's right-hand man and became president of a pharmaceutical company after the war. Now the United States denies entry of Shinozuka, the most courageous person who continues to publish his experience at Unit 731 and had been invited to confess his crimes in public symposia.

On the other hand, the Japanese government is still keeping silent on this issue. It acknowledged in the Diet in 1982 that Unit 731 surely existed, but has never explained what was done there. The government and conservative nationalists in Japan are still hiding the historical truth. Moreover, it seems they wish the truth would be forgotten. One of the most enduring legacies of these experiments is therefore the silence that continues to surround them.

Within the Japanese medical profession, the subject of "Jintai Jikken" (human experimentation) became taboo after the end of World War II. Many of the researchers who performed these experiments became prominent figures in academia. If junior researchers speak of human experimentation, they might touch on their head professors' "secret of secrets" and wreck their own academic careers. Therefore, not only Ishii's researchers themselves but also their disciples have hardly mentioned this issue publicly.

On the other hand, most of the public has thought it unnecessary to discuss human experimentation seriously. Because the Japanese and U.S. governments have been fairly successful in covering up the experiments, even today most people find it hard to believe that medical doctors, who devote themselves to saving lives, really treated human beings like guinea pigs. Those who found the historical documents to be credible and who appealed for public inquiry were often sneered at.

This failure to examine history publicly permits most Japanese citizens to regard human experimentation as a barbarism performed by mad doctors—totally different from typical medical procedures carried out by normal doctors. As a matter of fact, many cases of abuse of humans in research have been reported in newspapers, journals, and TV in postwar Japan (Tsuchiya 2003). However, these were presumed to be exceptional deviations. The Japanese public has avoided reflection on human experimentation in both military and civil medicine.

These circumstances are reflected in the field of medical ethics. The failure to confront reality means that Japanese medical ethics lack a framework for critically discussing and evaluating human experimentation. Medical ethicists have seldom tried to draw from historical cases of abuse the guiding principles that should regulate medical research. There has been little discussion, publication, or teaching about the protection of humans in research. Even in postwar cases of abuse, journalists and ethicists have focused discussion on a case-by-case basis and failed to derive general principles. Consequently, politicians have never proposed a blanket law to govern medical research, and the government has never articulated a general policy for the protection of humans in research. So far, Japanese guidelines for medical research are only patchworks of articles transferred from international guidelines such as the Declaration of Helsinki. They have not been derived from the lessons of history, especially of the past medical massacres performed by our own doctors.

This is a poor ethical state for a country boasting of its economic development and trying to lead world medical science. Looking into and evaluating one's own past is one of the prime imperatives of ethics. In order to be acknowledged as an ethical country, Japan must admit its past deeds, inquire into the truth, apologize to and compensate the victims for their suffering. This will surely lead to the establishment of true clinical research ethics in Japan.

REFERENCES

731 Kenkyukai (Society for the Investigation of Unit 731) ed. *Saikinsen Butai* (Germ Warfare Units). Tokyo: Bansei Sha 1996.

Arai T, Fujiwara A eds. Shinryaku no Shogen—Chugoku niokeru Nihonjin Senpan Jihitsu Kyojutsu Sho (Testimonies of Invasion: Japanese War Criminals' Autograph Confessions). Tokyo: Iwanami Shoten 1999.

Ban S. *Rikugun Noborito Kenkyujo no Shinjitsu* (The Truth about Noborito Institute). Tokyo: Fuyo Shobo Shuppan 2001.

Chinese Central Archive et al. eds. *Seitai Kaibo* (Vivisection), *Jintai Jikken* (Human Experimentation), and *Saikin Sakusen* (Germ Warfare). Tokyo: Dobunkan 1991–1992. These three volumes are [a] Japanese translation of *Xijunzhan yu Duqizhan* (Biological and Chemical Warfare). Beijing: Zhonghua Shuju (Chinese Printing Office) 1989.

Daido Rikugun Byoin (Datong Army Hopital). *Chumogun Gun'i Shoko Gunjin Gekagaku Syugo Kyoiku Katei Hyo* (A Program of a Group Education on Military Surgery for Army Surgeon Officers of the Occupation Forces in Mongolia). June 5–7 probably of 1941. Reprinted in Toki Eisei Kenkyuhan: Appendix.

Fell NH. *Brief Summary of New Information about Japanese B. W. Activities.* HHF/ars/3, 20 June 1947. Utah: Dugway Proving Ground, File No. 005. Reprinted in Kondo 2003: Disc 3.

Harris SH. *Factories of Death: Japanese Biological Warfare, 1932–45, and the American Cover-Up.* New York: Routledge 1994 (revised edition 2002).

Hill EV. *Summary Report on B. W. Investigations.* 12 December 1947. Utah: Dugway Proving Ground, APO 500. Reprinted in Kondo 2003: Disc 6.

Imoto K. *Gyomu Nisshi* (Operation Log). Collection of the Military Archives, Japan Defense Agency. Cited by Yoshimi and Iko 1993 & 1995.

Kamo Butai (Kamo Unit). *Kiidan Shageki ni yoru Hifu Shogai narabini Ippan Rinshoteki Shojo Kansatsu* (An Observation of Skin Injuries and General Clinical Symptoms [caused] by Shots of Yperite Shell). Date unknown. Reprinted in Tanaka and Matsumura 1991: 1–42.

Kasahara S, Kitano M et al. Ryukosei Syukketsunetsu no Byogentai no Kettei (Identification of the Pathogen of Epidemic Hemorrhagic Fever). *Nihon Byori Gakkai Kaishi* (Japanese Journal of Pathology) 1944; 34(1-2): 3–5.

Kondo S, ed. *731 Butai Saikinsen Shiryo Shusei (Japanese Biological Warfare; Unit 731: Official Declassified Records).* CD-ROM. 8 Vols. Tokyo: Kashiwa Shobo 2003.

Materials on the Trial of Former Servicemen of the Japanese Army Charged with Manufacturing and Employing Bacteriological Weapons the Khabarovsk Trial. Moscow: Foreign Languages Publishing House 1950.

Morimura S. *Akuma no Hoshoku* (Devils' Gluttony). Tokyo: Kobunsha 1981 (new edition Tokyo: Kadokawa Shoten 1983).

Nishisato F. Seibutsusen Butai 731 (Biological Warfare Unit 731). Tokyo: Kusanone Shuppankai 2002.

Ohta M. *731 Menseki no Keifu* (The Pedigree of 731 Immunity). Tokyo: Nihon Hyoronsha 1999.

Regis E. *The Biology of Doom: The History of America's Secret Germ Warfare Project.* New York: Henry Holt and Company 1999.

State-War-Navy Coordinating Subcommittee for the Far East. *Interrogation of Certain Japanese by Russian Prosecutor.* Enclosure. SFE 188/2, 1 August 1947. Reference: SWNCC 351/2/D. NARA, Record Group 165, Entry 468, Box 428. Reprinted in Kondo 2003: Disc 3.

SCAP [Supreme Command for the Allied Powers]: Legal Section: ADM. DIV. MISC. File *Trial Case #394: Record of Trial in the Case of United States vs. Kajuro Aihara.* 1940–1948. NARA, Record Group 331, Stack Area 290, Row 11, Compartment 34, Shelf 4, Boxes 1331–1332.

Shinozuka Y, Takayanagi M. *Nihon nimo Senso ga Atta: 731 Butai Moto Shonen Taiin no Kokuhaku* (There Was a War in Japan: A Confession of a Former Junior Assistant of Unit 731). Tokyo: Shin Nihon Shuppansha 2004.

Takidani J. *Satsuriku Kosho—731 Butai* (Murderous Factory Unit 731). Tokyo: Niimori Shobo 1989.

Tanaka A, Matsumura T. eds. *731 Butai Sakusei Shiryo* (Documents Made by Unit 731). Tokyo: Fuji Shuppan 1991.

Tanaka Y. Japanese Biological Warfare Plans and Experiments on POWs. In: Tanaka Y. *Hidden Horrors: Japanese War Crimes in World War II.* Boulder, Colorado: Westview Press 1996: 135–165.

Toki Eisei Kenkyuhan (The Detachment for Hygiene Studies in Winter). *Chumogun Toki Eisei Kenkyu Seiseki* (The Report of Hygiene Studies in Winter by the Occupation Forces in Mongolia). March 1941. Reprinted Tokyo: Gendai Syokan 1995.

Tsuchiya T. In the Shadow of the Past Atrocities: Research Ethics with Human Subjects in Contemporary Japan. *Eubios Journal of Asian and International Bioethics* 2003; 13(3): 100–101.

Tsuneishi K. *Kieta Saikinsen Butai* (The Germ Warfare Unit Disappeard). Tokyo: Kaimeisha 1981 (expanded version 1989) (pocket edition Tokyo: Chikuma Shobo 1993).

Tsuneishi K. *Igakusha Tachi no Soshiki Hanzai* (The Conspiracy of Medical Researchers). Tokyo: Asahi Shimbun Sha 1994 (reprinted in Asahi Bunko 1999).

Williams P, Wallace D. *Unit 731: Japan's Secret Biological Warfare in World War II.* New York: Free Press 1989.

Yoshikai N. *Kesenai Kioku: Yuasa Gun'i Seitaikaibo no Kiroku* (Unforgettable Memory: A Document of Army Surgeon Yuasa's Vivisection). Tokyo: Nitchu Shuppan 1981 (new expanded edition 1996).

Yoshimi Y, Iko T. *Nihon No Saikinsen* (Japanese Biological Warfare). *Senso Sekinin Kenkyu* (Studies in Responsibility for War) December 1993; 2: 8–29.

Yoshimi Y, Iko T. *731 Butai To Tenno-Rikugun Chuo* (Unit 731 and the Emperor-Army Leaders). Tokyo: Iwanami Syoten 1995.

Yoshimura H. *Tosho ni Tsuite* (On Frostbite). The manuscript of the special lecture at the 15th Meeting of the Harbin Branch of Manchu Medical Society, October 26, 1941. Reprinted in Tanaka and Matsumura 1991: 225–288.

Yoshimura H, Iida T. Studies on the Reactivity of Skin Vessels to Extreme Cold. Part 1. A Point Test on the Resistance against Frost Bite [*sic*]. *Japanese Journal of Physiology* 1950–1951; 1: 147–159.

Yoshimura H, Iida T. Studies on the Reactivity of Skin Vessels to Extreme Cold. Part 2. Factors Governing the Individual Difference of the Reactivity, or the Resistance against Frost Bite [*sic*]. *Japanese Journal of Physiology* 1951–1952; 2: 177–185.

Yoshimura H, Iida T, Koishi H. Studies on the Reactivity of Skin Vessels to Extreme Cold. Part 3. Effects of Diets on the Reactivity of Skin Vessels to Cold. *Japanese Journal of Physiology* 1951–1952; 2: 310–315.

ADVISORY COMMITTEE ON HUMAN RADIATION EXPERIMENTS

Final Report

THE CREATION OF THE ADVISORY COMMITTEE

On January 15, 1994, President Clinton appointed the Advisory Committee on Human Radiation Experiments. The President created the Committee to investigate reports of possible unethical experiments funded by the government decades ago.

The members of the Advisory Committee were fourteen private citizens from around the country: a representative of the general public and thirteen experts in bioethics, radiation oncology and biology, nuclear medicine, epidemiology and biostatistics, public health, history of science and medicine, and law. . . .

From United States Advisory Committee on Human Radiation Experiments, *Final Report: Executive Summary and Guide to Final Report* (Washington, DC: U.S. Government Printing Office, 1995), pp. 3–19.

The controversy surrounding the plutonium experiments and others like them brought basic questions to the fore: How many experiments were conducted or sponsored by the government, and why? How many were secret? Was anyone harmed? What was disclosed to those subjected to risk, and what opportunity did they have for consent? By what rules should the past be judged? What remedies are due those who were wronged or harmed by the government in the past? How well do federal rules that today govern human experimentation work? What lessons can be learned for application to the future? . . .

THE PRESIDENT'S CHARGE

The President directed the Advisory Committee to uncover the history of human radiation experiments during the period 1944 through 1974. It was in 1944 that the first known human radiation experiment of interest was planned, and in 1974 that the Department of

Health, Education and Welfare adopted regulations governing the conduct of human research, a watershed event in the history of federal protections for human subjects.

In addition to asking us to investigate human radiation experiments, the President directed us to examine cases in which the government had intentionally released radiation into the environment for research purposes. He further charged us with identifying the ethical and scientific standards for evaluating these events, and with making recommendations to ensure that whatever wrongdoing may have occurred in the past cannot be repeated.

We were asked to address human experiments and intentional releases that involved radiation. The ethical issues we addressed and the moral framework we developed are, however, applicable to all research involving human subjects. . . .

THE COMMITTEE'S APPROACH

. . . As we began our search into the past, we quickly discovered that it was going to be extremely difficult to piece together a coherent picture. Many critical documents had long since been forgotten and were stored in obscure locations throughout the country. Often they were buried in collections that bore no obvious connection to human radiation experiments. There was no easy way to identify how many experiments had been conducted, where they took place, and which government agencies had sponsored them. Nor was there a quick way to learn what rules applied to these experiments for the period prior to the mid-1960s. With the assistance of hundreds of federal officials and agency staff, the Committee retrieved and reviewed hundreds of thousands of government documents. Some of the most important documents were secret and were declassified at our request. Even after this extraordinary effort, the historical record remains incomplete. Some potentially important collections could not be located and were evidently lost or destroyed years ago.

Nevertheless, the documents that were recovered enabled us to identify nearly 4,000 human radiation experiments sponsored by the federal government between 1944 and 1974. In the great majority of cases, only fragmentary data was locatable; the identity of subjects and the specific radiation exposures involved were typically unavailable. Given the constraints of information, even more so than time, it was impossible for the Committee to review all these experiments, nor could we evaluate the experiences of countless individual subjects. We thus decided to focus our investigation on representative case studies reflecting eight different categories of experiments that together addressed our charge and priorities. These case studies included:

- experiments with plutonium and other atomic bomb materials
- the Atomic Energy Commission's program of radioisotope distribution
- nontherapeutic research on children
- total body irradiation
- research on prisoners
- human experimentation in connection with nuclear weapons testing
- intentional environmental releases of radiation
- observational research involving uranium miners and residents of the Marshall Islands

In addition to assessing the ethics of human radiation experiments conducted decades ago, it was also important to explore the current conduct of human radiation research. Insofar as wrongdoing may have occurred in the past, we needed to examine the likelihood that such things could happen today. We therefore undertook three projects:

- A review of how each agency of the federal government that currently conducts or funds research involving human subjects regulates this activity and oversees it.
- An examination of the documents and consent forms of research projects that are today sponsored by the federal government in order to develop insight into the current status of protections for the rights and interests of human subjects.
- Interviews of nearly 1,900 patients receiving outpatient medical care in private hospitals and federal facilities throughout the country. We asked them whether they were currently, or had been, subjects of research, and why they had agreed to participate in research or had refused.

THE HISTORICAL CONTEXT

Since its discovery 100 years ago, radioactivity has been a basic tool of medical research and diagnosis. In addition to the many uses of the x-ray, it was soon discovered that radiation could be used to treat cancer and that the introduction of "tracer" amounts of radioisotopes into the human body could help to diagnose disease and understand bodily processes. At the same time, the perils of overexposure to radiation were becoming apparent.

During World War II the new field of radiation science was at the center of one of the most ambitious and secret research efforts the world has known—the Manhattan Project. Human radiation experiments were undertaken in secret to help understand radiation risks to workers engaged in the development of the atomic bomb.

Following the war, the new Atomic Energy Commission used facilities built to make the atomic bomb to produce radioisotopes for medical research and other peacetime uses. This highly publicized program provided the radioisotopes that were used in thousands of human experiments conducted in research facilities throughout the country and the world. This research, in turn, was part of a larger postwar transformation of biomedical research through the infusion of substantial government monies and technical support.

The intersection of government and biomedical research brought with it new roles and new ethical questions for medical researchers. Many of these researchers were also physicians who operated within a tradition of medical ethics that enjoined them to put the interests of their patients first. When the doctor also was a researcher, however, the potential for conflict emerged between the advancement of science and the advancement of the patient's well-being.

Other ethical issues were posed as medical researchers were called on by government officials to play new roles in the development and testing of nuclear weapons. For example, as advisers they were asked to provide human research data that could reassure officials about the effects of radiation, but as scientists they were not always convinced that human research could provide scientifically useful data. Similarly, as scientists, they came from a tradition in which research results were freely debated. In their capacity as advisers to and officials of the government, however, these researchers found that the openness of science now needed to be constrained.

None of these tensions were unique to radiation research. Radiation represents just one of several examples of the exploration of the weapons potential of new scientific discoveries during and after World War II. Similarly, the tensions between clinical research and the treatment of patients were emerging throughout medical science, and were not found only in research involving radiation. Not only were these issues not unique to radiation, but they were not unique to the 1940s and 1950s. Today society still struggles with conflicts between the openness of science and the preservation of national security, as well as with conflicts between the advancement of medical science and the rights and interests of patients.

KEY FINDINGS

HUMAN RADIATION EXPERIMENTS

- Between 1944 and 1974 the federal government sponsored several thousand human radiation experiments. In the great majority of cases, the experiments were conducted to advance biomedical science; some experiments were conducted to advance national interests in defense or space exploration; and some experiments served both biomedical and defense or space exploration purposes. As noted, in the great majority of cases only fragmentary data are available.

- The majority of human radiation experiments identified by the Advisory Committee involved radioactive tracers administered in amounts that are likely to be similar to those used in research today. Most of these tracer studies involved adult subjects and are unlikely to have caused physical harm. However, in some nontherapeutic tracer studies involving children, radioisotope exposures were associated with increases in the potential lifetime risk for developing thyroid cancer that would be considered unacceptable today. The Advisory Committee also identified several studies in which patients died soon after receiving external radiation or radioisotope doses in the therapeutic range that were associated with acute radiation effects.

- Although the AEC, the Defense Department and the National Institutes of Health recognized at an early date that research should proceed only with the consent of the human subject, there is little evidence of rules or practices of consent except in research with healthy subjects. It was commonplace during the 1940s and 1950s for physicians to use patients as subjects of research without their awareness or consent. By contrast, the government and its researchers focused with substantial success on the minimization of risk in the conduct of experiments, particularly with respect to research involving radioisotopes. But little attention was paid during this period to issues of fairness in the selection of subjects.

- Government officials and investigators are blameworthy for not having had policies and practices in place to protect the rights and interests of human subjects who were used in research from which the subjects could not possibly derive direct medical benefit. To the extent that there was reason to believe that research might provide a direct medical benefit to subjects, government officials and biomedical professionals are less blameworthy for not having had such protections and practices in place.

INTENTIONAL RELEASES

- During the 1944–1974 period, the government conducted several hundred intentional releases of radiation into the environment for research purposes. Generally, these releases were not conducted for the purpose of studying the effects of radiation on humans. Instead they were usually conducted to test the operation of weapons, the safety of equipment, or the dispersal of radiation into the environment.
- For those intentional releases where dose reconstructions have been undertaken, it is unlikely that members of the public were directly harmed solely as a consequence of these tests. However, these releases were conducted in secret and despite continued requests from the public that stretch back well over a decade, some information about them was made public only during the life of the Advisory Committee.

URANIUM MINERS

- As a consequence of exposure to radon and its daughter products in underground uranium mines, at least several hundred miners died of lung cancer and surviving miners remain at elevated risk. These men, who were the subject of government study as they mined uranium for use in weapons manufacturing, were subject to radon exposures well in excess of levels known to be hazardous. The government failed to act to require the reduction of the hazard by ventilating the mines, and it failed to adequately warn the miners of the hazard to which they were being exposed.

SECRECY AND THE PUBLIC TRUST

- The greatest harm from past experiments and intentional releases may be the legacy of distrust they created. Hundreds of intentional releases took place in secret, and remained secret for decades. Important discussion of the policies to govern human experimentation also took place in secret. Information about human experiments was kept secret out of concern for embarrassment to the government, potential legal liability, and worry that public misunderstanding would jeopardize government programs.
- In a few instances, people used as experimental subjects and their families were denied the opportunity to pursue redress for possible wrongdoing because of actions taken by the government to keep the truth from them. Where programs were legitimately kept secret for national security reasons, the government often did not create or maintain adequate records, thereby preventing the public, and those most at risk, from learning the facts in a timely and complete fashion.

CONTEMPORARY HUMAN SUBJECTS RESEARCH

- Human research involving radioisotopes is currently subjected to more safeguards and levels of review than most other areas of research involving human subjects. There are no apparent differences between the treatment of human subjects of radiation research and human subjects of other biomedical research.
- Based on the Advisory Committee's review, it appears that much of human subjects research poses only minimal risk of harm to subjects. In our review of research documents that bear on human subjects issues, we found no problems or only minor problems in most of the minimal-risk studies we examined.
- Our review of documents identified examples of complicated, higher-risk studies in which human subjects issues were carefully and adequately addressed and that included excellent consent forms. In our interview project, there was little evidence that patient-subjects felt coerced or pressured by investigators to participate in research. We interviewed patients who had declined offers to become research subjects, reinforcing the impression that there are often contexts in which potential research subjects have a genuine choice.
- At the same time, however, we also found evidence suggesting serious deficiencies in aspects of the current system for the protection of the rights and interests of human subjects. For example, consent forms do not always provide adequate information and may be misleading about the impact of research participation on people's

lives. Some patients with serious illnesses appear to have unrealistic expectations about the benefits of being subjects in research.

CURRENT REGULATIONS ON SECRECY IN HUMAN RESEARCH AND ENVIRONMENTAL RELEASES

- Human research can still be conducted in secret today, and under some conditions informed consent in secret research can be waived.
- Events that raise the same concerns as the intentional releases mentioned in the Committee's charter could take place in secret today under current environmental laws. . . .

KEY RECOMMENDATIONS

APOLOGIES AND COMPENSATION

The government should deliver a personal, individualized apology and provide financial compensation to those subjects of human radiation experiments, or their next of kin, in cases where:

- efforts were made by the government to keep information secret from these individuals or their families, or the public, for the purpose of avoiding embarrassment or potential legal liability, and where this secrecy had the effect of denying individuals the opportunity to pursue potential grievances.
- there was no prospect of direct medical benefit to the subjects, or interventions considered controversial at the time were presented as standard practice, and physical injury attributable to the experiment resulted.

URANIUM MINERS

- The Interagency Working Group, together with Congress, should give serious consideration to amending the provisions of the Radiation Exposure Compensation Act of 1990 relating to uranium miners in order to provide compensation to *all* miners who develop lung cancer after some minimal duration of employment underground (such as one year), without requiring a specific level of exposure. The act should also be reviewed to determine whether the documentation standards for compensation should be liberalized.

IMPROVED PROTECTION FOR HUMAN SUBJECTS

- The Committee found no differences between human radiation research and other areas of research with respect to human subjects issues, either in the past or the present. In comparison to the practices and policies of the 1940s and 1950s, there have been significant advances in the federal government's system for the protection of the rights and interests of human subjects. But deficiencies remain. Efforts should be undertaken on a national scale to ensure the centrality of ethics in the conduct of scientists whose research involves human subjects.

- One problem in need of immediate attention by the government and the biomedical research community is unrealistic expectations among some patients with serious illnesses about the prospect of direct medical benefit from participating in research. Also, among the consent forms we reviewed, some appear to be overly optimistic in portraying the likely benefits of research, to inadequately explain the impact of research procedures on quality of life and personal finances, and to be incomprehensible to lay people.

- A mechanism should be established to provide for continuing interpretation and application in an open and public forum of ethics rules and principles for the conduct of human subjects research. Three examples of policy issues in need of public resolution that the Advisory Committee confronted in our work are: (1) clarification of the meaning of minimal risk in research with healthy children; (2) regulations to cover the conduct of research with institutionalized children; and (3) guidelines for research with adults of questionable competence, particularly for research in which subjects are placed at more than minimal risk but are offered no prospect of direct medical benefit.

SECRECY: BALANCING NATIONAL SECURITY AND THE PUBLIC TRUST

Current policies do not adequately safeguard against the recurrence of the kinds of events we studied that fostered distrust. The Advisory Committee concludes that there may be special circumstances in which it may be necessary to conduct human research or intentional releases in secret. However, to the extent that the government conducts such activities with elements of secrecy, special protections of the rights and interests of individuals and the public are needed.

Research Involving Human Subjects. The Advisory Committee recommends the adoption of federal policies requiring:

- the informed consent of all human subjects of classified research. This requirement should not be subject to exemption or waiver.
- that classified research involving human subjects be permitted only after the review and approval of an independent panel of appropriate non-governmental experts and citizen representatives, with all the necessary security clearances.

Environmental Releases. There must be independent review to assure that the action is needed, that risk is minimized, and that records will be kept to assure a proper accounting to the public at the earliest date consistent with legitimate national security concerns. Specifically, the Committee recommends that:

- Secret environmental releases of hazardous substances should be permitted only after the review and approval of an independent panel. This panel should consist of appropriate, nongovernmental experts and citizen representatives, all with the necessary security clearances.
- An appropriate government agency, such as the Environmental Protection Agency, should maintain a program directed at the oversight of classified programs, with suitably cleared personnel. . . .

Codes and Guidelines for Human Research

THE NUREMBERG MEDICAL TRIAL

The Nuremberg Code (1947)

The great weight of the evidence before us is to the effect that certain types of medical experiments on human beings, when kept within reasonably well-defined bounds, conform to the ethics of the medical profession generally. The protagonists of the practice of human experimentation justify their views on the basis that such experiments yield results for the good of society that are unprocurable by other methods or means of study. All agree, however, that certain basic principles must be observed in order to satisfy moral, ethical and legal concepts.

From *Trials of War Criminals before the Nuernberg Military Tribunals under Control Council Law No. 10.* (Nuernberg, October 1946–April 1949) (Washington, DC: U.S. Government Printing Office, 1949), II., 181–182.

1. The voluntary consent of the human subject is absolutely essential.

This means that the person involved should have legal capacity to give consent; should be so situated as to be able to exercise free power of choice, without the intervention of any element of force, fraud, deceit, duress, overreaching, or other ulterior form of constraint or coercion; and should have sufficient knowledge and comprehension of the elements of the subject matter involved as to enable him to make an understanding and enlightened decision. This latter element requires that before the acceptance of an affirmative decision by the experimental subject there should be made known to him the nature, duration, and purpose of the experiment; the method and means by which it is to be conducted; all inconveniences and hazards reasonably to be expected; and the effects upon his health or person which may possibly come from his participation in the experiment.

The duty and responsibility for ascertaining the quality of the consent rests upon each individual who initiates, directs or engages in the experiment. It is a personal duty and responsibility which may not be delegated to another with impunity.

2. The experiment should be such as to yield fruitful results for the good of society, unprocurable by other methods or means of study, and not random and unnecessary in nature.

3. The experiment should be so designed and based on the results of animal experimentation and a knowledge of the natural history of the disease or other problems under study that the anticipated results will justify the performance of the experiment.

4. The experiment should be so conducted as to avoid all unnecessary physical and mental suffering and injury.

5. No experiment should be conducted where there is an *a priori* reason to believe that death or disabling injury will occur; except perhaps, in those experiments where the experimental physicians also serve as subjects.

6. The degree of risk to be taken should never exceed that determined by the humanitarian importance of the problem to be solved by the experiment.

7. Proper preparations should be made and adequate facilities provided to protect the experimental subject against even remote possibilities of injury, disability, or death.

8. The experiment should be conducted only by scientifically qualified persons. The highest degree of skill and care should be required through all stages of the experiment of those who conduct or engage in the experiment.

9. During the course of the experiment the human subject should be at liberty to bring the experiment to an end if he has reached the physical or mental state where continuation of the experiment seems to him to be impossible.

10. During the course of the experiment the scientist in charge must be prepared to terminate the experiment at any stage, if he has probable cause to believe, in the exercise of the good faith, superior skill and careful judgment required of him that a continuation of the experiment is likely to result in injury, disability, or death to the experimental subject.

WORLD MEDICAL ASSOCIATION

Declaration of Helsinki: Ethical Principles for Medical Research Involving Human Subjects

A. INTRODUCTION

1. The World Medical Association has developed the Declaration of Helsinki as a statement of ethical principles to provide guidance to physicians and other participants in medical research involving human subjects. Medical research involving human subjects includes research on identifiable human material or identifiable data.

2. It is the duty of the physician to promote and safeguard the health of the people. The physician's knowledge and conscience are dedicated to the fulfillment of this duty.

3. The Declaration of Geneva of the World Medical Association binds the physician with the words, "The health of my patient will be my first consideration," and the International Code of Medical Ethics declares that, "A physician shall act only in the patient's interest when providing medical care which might have the effect of weakening the physical and mental condition of the patient."

The complete text of the following principles and notes of clarification is available online at the following URL: http://www.wma.net/e/policy/b3.htm/ Reprinted by permission of the World Medical Association.

Adopted by the 18th WMA General Assembly, Helsinki, Finland, June 1964, and amended by the 29th WMA General Assembly, Tokyo, Japan, October 1975; 35th WMA General Assembly, Venice, Italy, October 1983; 41st WMA General Assembly, Hong Kong, September 1989; 48th WMA General Assembly, Somerset West, Republic of South Africa, October 1996 and the 52nd WMA General Assembly, Edinburgh, Scotland, October 2000; Note of Clarification on Paragraph 29 added by the WMA General Assembly, Washington 2002; Note of Clarification on Paragraph 30 added by the WMA General Assembly, Tokyo 2004.

4. Medical progress is based on research which ultimately must rest in part on experimentation involving human subjects.

5. In medical research on human subjects, considerations related to the well-being of the human subject should take precedence over the interests of science and society.

6. The primary purpose of medical research involving human subjects is to improve prophylactic, diagnostic and therapeutic procedures and the understanding of the aetiology and pathogenesis of disease. Even the best proven prophylactic, diagnostic, and therapeutic methods must continuously be challenged through research for their effectiveness, efficiency, accessibility and quality.

7. In current medical practice and in medical research, most prophylactic, diagnostic and therapeutic procedures involve risks and burdens.

8. Medical research is subject to ethical standards that promote respect for all human beings and protect their health and rights. Some research populations are vulnerable and need special protection. The particular needs of the economically and medically disadvantaged must be recognized. Special attention is also required for those who cannot give or refuse consent for themselves, for those who may be subject to giving consent under duress, for those who will not benefit personally from the research and for those for whom the research is combined with care.

9. Research investigators should be aware of the ethical, legal and regulatory requirements for research on human subjects in their own countries as well as applicable international requirements. No national ethical, legal or regulatory

requirement should be allowed to reduce or eliminate any of the protections for human subjects set forth in this Declaration.

WORLD MEDICAL ASSOCIATION   73

B. BASIC PRINCIPLES FOR ALL MEDICAL RESEARCH

10. It is the duty of the physician in medical research to protect the life, health, privacy, and dignity of the human subject.

11. Medical research involving human subjects must conform to generally accepted scientific principles, be based on a thorough knowledge of the scientific literature, other relevant sources of information, and on adequate laboratory and, where appropriate, animal experimentation.

12. Appropriate caution must be exercised in the conduct of research which may affect the environment, and the welfare of animals used for research must be respected.

13. The design and performance of each experimental procedure involving human subjects should be clearly formulated in an experimental protocol. This protocol should be submitted for consideration, comment, guidance, and where appropriate, approval to a specially appointed ethical review committee, which must be independent of the investigator, the sponsor or any other kind of undue influence. This independent committee should be in conformity with the laws and regulations of the country in which the research experiment is performed. The committee has the right to monitor ongoing trials. The researcher has the obligation to provide monitoring information to the committee, especially any serious adverse events. The researcher should also submit to the committee, for review, information regarding funding, sponsors, institutional affiliations, other potential conflicts of interest and incentives for subjects.

14. The research protocol should always contain a statement of the ethical considerations involved and should indicate that there is compliance with the principles enunciated in this Declaration.

15. Medical research involving human subjects should be conducted only by scientifically qualified persons and under the supervision of a clinically competent medical person. The responsibility for the human subject must always rest with a medically qualified person and never rest on the subject of the research, even though the subject has given consent.

16. Every medical research project involving human subjects should be preceded by careful assessment of predictable risks and burdens in comparison with foreseeable benefits to the subject or to others. This does not preclude the participation of healthy volunteers in medical research. The design of all studies should be publicly available.

17. Physicians should abstain from engaging in research projects involving human subjects unless they are confident that the risks involved have been adequately assessed and can be satisfactorily managed. Physicians should cease any investigation if the risks are found to outweigh the potential benefits or if there is conclusive proof of positive and beneficial results.

18. Medical research involving human subjects should only be conducted if the importance of the objective outweighs the inherent risks and burdens to the subject. This is especially important when the human subjects are healthy volunteers.

19. Medical research is only justified if there is a reasonable likelihood that the populations in which the research is carried out stand to benefit from the results of the research.

20. The subjects must be volunteers and informed participants in the research project.

21. The right of research subjects to safeguard their integrity must always be respected. Every precaution should be taken to respect the privacy of the subject, the confidentiality of the patient's information and to minimize the impact of the study on the subject's physical and mental integrity and on the personality of the subject.

22. In any research on human beings, each potential subject must be adequately informed of the aims, methods, sources of funding, any possible conflicts of interest, institutional affiliations of the researcher, the anticipated benefits and potential risks of the study and the discomfort it may entail. The subject should be informed of the right to abstain from participation in the study or to withdraw consent to participate at any time without reprisal. After ensuring that the subject has understood the information, the physician should then obtain the subject's freely-given informed consent, preferably in writing. If the consent cannot be

obtained in writing, the non-written consent must be formally documented and witnessed.

23. When obtaining informed consent for the research project the physician should be particularly cautious if the subject is in a dependent relationship with the physician or may consent under duress. In that case the informed consent should be obtained by a well-informed physician who is not engaged in the investigation and who is completely independent of this relationship.

24. For a research subject who is legally incompetent, physically or mentally incapable of giving consent or is a legally incompetent minor, the investigator must obtain informed consent from the legally authorized representative in accordance with applicable law. These groups should not be included in research unless the research is necessary to promote the health of the population represented and this research cannot instead be performed on legally competent persons.

25. When a subject deemed legally incompetent, such as a minor child, is able to give assent to decisions about participation in research, the investigator must obtain that assent in addition to the consent of the legally authorized representative.

26. Research on individuals from whom it is not possible to obtain consent, including proxy or advance consent, should be done only if the physical/mental condition that prevents obtaining informed consent is a necessary characteristic of the research population. The specific reasons for involving research subjects with a condition that renders them unable to give informed consent should be stated in the experimental protocol for consideration and approval of the review committee. The protocol should state that consent to remain in the research should be obtained as soon as possible from the individual or a legally authorized surrogate.

27. Both authors and publishers have ethical obligations. In publication of the results of research, the investigators are obliged to preserve the accuracy of the results. Negative as well as positive results should be published or otherwise publicly available. Sources of funding, institutional affiliations and any possible conflicts of interest should be declared in the publication. Reports of experimentation not in accordance with the principles laid down in this Declaration should not be accepted for publication.

C. ADDITIONAL PRINCIPLES FOR MEDICAL RESEARCH COMBINED WITH MEDICAL CARE

28. The physician may combine medical research with medical care, only to the extent that the research is justified by its potential prophylactic, diagnostic or therapeutic value. When medical research is combined with medical care, additional standards apply to protect the patients who are research subjects.

29. The benefits, risks, burdens and effectiveness of a new method should be tested against those of the best current prophylactic, diagnostic, and therapeutic methods. This does not exclude the use of placebo, or no treatment, in studies where no proven prophylactic, diagnostic or therapeutic method exists.[1]

30. At the conclusion of the study, every patient entered into the study should be assured of access to the best proven prophylactic, diagnostic and therapeutic methods identified by the study.[2]

[1]**Note of clarification on paragraph 29 of the WMA Declaration of Helsinki**

The WMA hereby reaffirms its position that extreme care must be taken in making use of a placebo-controlled trial and that in general this methodology should only be used in the absence of existing proven therapy. However, a placebo-controlled trial may be ethically acceptable, even if proven therapy is available, under the following circumstances:

–Where for compelling and scientifically sound methodological reasons its use is necessary to determine the efficacy or safety of a prophylactic, diagnostic or therapeutic method; or

–Where a prophylactic, diagnostic or therapeutic method is being investigated for a minor condition and the patients who receive placebo will not be subject to any additional risk of serious or irreversible harm.

All other provisions of the Declaration of Helsinki must be adhered to, especially the need for appropriate ethical and scientific review.

[2]**Note of clarification on paragraph 30 of the WMA Declaration of Helsinki**

The WMA hereby reaffirms its position that it is necessary during the study planning process to identify post-trial access by study participants to prophylactic, diagnostic and therapeutic procedures identified as beneficial in the study or access to other appropriate care. Post-trial access arrangements or other care must be described in the study protocol so the ethical review committee may consider such arrangements during its review.

31. The physician should fully inform the patient which aspects of the care are related to the research. The refusal of a patient to participate in a study must never interfere with the patient-physician relationship.

32. In the treatment of a patient, where proven prophylactic, diagnostic and therapeutic methods do not exist or have been ineffective, the physician, with informed consent from the patient, must be free to use unproven or new prophylactic, diagnostic and therapeutic measures, if in the physician's judgement it offers hope of saving life, re-establishing health or alleviating suffering. Where possible, these measures should be made the object of research, designed to evaluate their safety and efficacy. In all cases, new information should be recorded and, where appropriate, published. The other relevant guidelines of this Declaration should be followed.

COUNCIL FOR INTERNATIONAL ORGANIZATIONS OF MEDICAL SCIENCES (CIOMS), IN COLLABORATION WITH THE WORLD HEALTH ORGANIZATION (WHO)

International Ethical Guidelines for Biomedical Research Involving Human Subjects (2002)

• • •

GENERAL ETHICAL PRINCIPLES

All research involving human subjects should be conducted in accordance with three basic ethical principles, namely respect for persons, beneficence and justice. It is generally agreed that these principles, which in the abstract have equal moral force, guide the conscientious preparation of proposals for scientific studies. In varying circumstances they may be expressed differently and given different moral weight, and their application may lead to different decisions or courses of action. The present guidelines are directed at the application of these principles to research involving human subjects.

Respect for persons incorporates at least two fundamental ethical considerations, namely:

From *International Ethical Guidelines for Biomedical Research Involving Human Subjects*, prepared by the Council for International Organizations of Medical Sciences (CIOMS) in collaboration with the World Health Organization (WHO) (Geneva: CIOMS, 2002), pp. 17–81. Reproduced by permission of CIOMS: The full text of the guidelines is available online at the following URL: http://www.cioms.ch/frame_guidelines_nov_2002.htm

a) respect for autonomy, which requires that those who are capable of deliberation about their personal choices should be treated with respect for their capacity for self-determination; and

b) protection of persons with impaired or diminished autonomy, which requires that those who are dependent or vulnerable be afforded security against harm or abuse.

Beneficence refers to the ethical obligation to maximize benefits and to minimize harms. This principle gives rise to norms requiring that the risks of research be reasonable in the light of the expected benefits, that the research design be sound, and that the investigators be competent both to conduct the research and to safeguard the welfare of the research subjects. Beneficence further proscribes the deliberate infliction of harm on persons; this aspect of beneficence is sometimes expressed as a separate principle, **non-maleficence** (do no harm).

Justice refers to the ethical obligation to treat each person in accordance with what is morally right and proper, to give each person what is due to him or her. In the ethics of research involving human subjects the principle refers primarily to **distributive justice,** which requires the equitable distribution of both the burdens and the benefits of participation in research. Differences in distribution of burdens and benefits are justifiable only if they are based on morally relevant distinctions between persons; one such distinction is vulnerability. "Vulnerability" refers to a substantial incapacity to protect one's own interests owing to such impediments as lack of capability to give informed consent, lack of alternative means of obtaining medical care or other expensive necessities, or being a junior or subordinate member of a hierarchical group. Accordingly, special provision must be made for the protection of the rights and welfare of vulnerable persons.

Sponsors of research or investigators cannot, in general, be held accountable for unjust conditions where the research is conducted, but they must refrain from practices that are likely to worsen unjust conditions or contribute to new inequities. Neither should they take advantage of the relative inability of low-resource countries or vulnerable populations to protect their own interests, by conducting research inexpensively and avoiding complex regulatory systems of industrialized countries in order to develop products for the lucrative markets of those countries.

In general, the research project should leave low-resource countries or communities better off than previously or, at least, no worse off. It should be responsive to their health needs and priorities in that any product developed is made reasonably available to them, and as far as possible leave the population in a better position to obtain effective health care and protect its own health.

Justice requires also that the research be responsive to the health conditions or needs of vulnerable subjects. The subjects selected should be the least vulnerable necessary to accomplish the purposes of the research. Risk to vulnerable subjects is most easily justified when it arises from interventions or procedures that hold out for them the prospect of direct health-related benefit. Risk that does not hold out such prospect must be justified by the anticipated benefit to the population of which the individual research subject is representative.

PREAMBLE

The term "research" refers to a class of activity designed to develop or contribute to generalizable knowledge. Generalizable knowledge consists of theories, principles or relationships, or the accumulation of information on which they are based, that can be corroborated by accepted scientific methods of observation and inference. In the present context "research" includes both medical and behavioural studies pertaining to human health. Usually "research" is modified by the adjective "biomedical" to indicate its relation to health.

Progress in medical care and disease prevention depends upon an understanding of physiological and pathological processes or epidemiological findings, and requires at some time research involving human subjects. The collection, analysis and interpretation of information obtained from research involving human beings contribute significantly to the improvement of human health.

Research involving human subjects includes:

- Studies of a physiological, biochemical or pathological process, or of the response to a specific intervention—whether physical, chemical or psychological—in healthy subjects or patients;
- controlled trials of diagnostic, preventive or therapeutic measures in larger groups of persons, designed to demonstrate a specific generalizable response to these measures against a background of individual biological variation;
- studies designed to determine the consequences for individuals and communities of specific preventive or therapeutic measures; and
- studies concerning human health-related behaviour in a variety of circumstances and environments.

Research involving human subjects may employ either observation or physical, chemical or psychological intervention; it may also either generate records or make use of existing records containing biomedical or other information about individuals who may or may not be identifiable from the records or information. The use of such records and the protection of the confidentiality of data obtained from those records are discussed in International Guidelines for Ethical Review of Epidemiological Studies (CIOMS, 1991).

The research may be concerned with the social environment, manipulating environmental factors in a way that could affect incidentally-exposed individuals. It is defined in broad terms in order to embrace field studies of pathogenic organisms and toxic chemicals under investigation for health-related purposes.

Biomedical research with human subjects is to be distinguished from the practice of medicine, public health and other forms of health care, which [are] designed to contribute directly to the health of individuals or communities. Prospective subjects may find it confusing when research and practice are to be conducted simultaneously, as when research is designed to obtain new information about the efficacy of a drug or other therapeutic, diagnostic or preventive modality.

As stated in Paragraph 32 of the Declaration of Helsinki, "In the treatment of a patient, where proven prophylactic, diagnostic and therapeutic methods do not exist or have been ineffective, the physician, with informed consent from the patient, must be free to use unproven or new prophylactic, diagnostic and therapeutic measures, if in the physician's judgement it offers hope of saving life, re-establishing health or alleviating suffering. Where possible, these measures should be made the object of research, designed to evaluate their safety and efficacy. In all cases, new information should be recorded and, where appropriate, published. The other relevant guidelines of this Declaration should be followed."

Professionals whose roles combine investigation and treatment have a special obligation to protect the rights and welfare of the patient-subjects. An investigator who agrees to act as physician-investigator undertakes some or all of the legal and ethical responsibilities of the subject's primary-care physician. In such a case, if the subject withdraws from the research owing to complications related to the research or in the exercise of the right to withdraw without loss of benefit, the physician has an obligation to continue to provide medical care, or to see that the subject receives the necessary care in the health-care system, or to offer assistance in finding another physician.

Research with human subjects should be carried out only by, or strictly supervised by, suitably qualified and experienced investigators and in accordance with a protocol that clearly states: the aim of the research; the reasons for proposing that it involve human subjects; the nature and degree of any known risks to the subjects; the sources from which it is proposed to recruit subjects; and the means proposed for ensuring that subjects' consent will be adequately informed and voluntary. The protocol should be scientifically and ethically appraised by one or more suitably constituted review bodies, independent of the investigators.

New vaccines and medicinal drugs, before being approved for general use, must be tested on human subjects in clinical trials; such trials constitute a substantial part of all research involving human subjects.

THE GUIDELINES

Guideline 1: Ethical justification and scientific validity of biomedical research involving human beings. The ethical justification of biomedical research involving human subjects is the prospect of discovering new ways of benefiting people's health. Such research can be ethically justifiable only if it is carried out in ways that respect and protect, and are fair to, the subjects of that research and are morally acceptable within the communities in which the research is carried out. Moreover, because scientifically invalid research is unethical in that it exposes research subjects to risks without possible benefit, investigators and sponsors must ensure that proposed studies involving human subjects conform to generally accepted scientific principles and are based on adequate knowledge of the pertinent scientific literature. . . .

Guideline 2: Ethical review committees. All proposals to conduct research involving human subjects must be submitted for review of their scientific merit and ethical acceptability to one or more scientific review and ethical review committees. The review committees must be independent of the research team, and any direct financial or other material benefit they may derive from the research should not be contingent on the outcome of their review. The investigator must obtain their approval or clearance before undertaking the research. The ethical review committee should conduct further reviews as necessary in the course of the research, including monitoring of the progress of the study. . . .

Guideline 3: Ethical review of externally sponsored research. An external sponsoring organization and individual investigators should submit the research protocol for ethical and scientific review in the country of the sponsoring organization, and the ethical standards applied should be no less stringent than they would be for research carried out in that country. The health authorities of the host country, as well as a national or local ethical review committee, should ensure that the proposed research is responsive to the health needs and priorities of the host country and meets the requisite ethical standards. . . .

Guideline 4: Individual informed consent. For all biomedical research involving humans the investigator must obtain the voluntary informed consent of the prospective subject or, in the case of an individual who is not capable of giving informed consent, the permission of a legally authorized representative in accordance with applicable law. Waiver of informed consent is to be regarded as uncommon and exceptional, and must in all cases be approved by an ethical review committee. . . .

Guideline 5: Obtaining informed consent: Essential information for prospective research subjects. Before requesting an individual's consent to participate in research, the investigator must provide the following information, in language or another form of communication that the individual can understand:

1. that the individual is invited to participate in research, the reasons for considering the individual suitable for the research, and that participation is voluntary;
2. that the individual is free to refuse to participate and will be free to withdraw from the research at any time without penalty or loss of benefits to which he or she would otherwise be entitled;
3. the purpose of the research, the procedures to be carried out by the investigator and the subject, and an explanation of how the research differs from routine medical care;
4. for controlled trials, an explanation of features of the research design (e.g., randomization, double-blinding), and that the subject will not be told of the assigned treatment until the study has been completed and the blind has been broken;
5. the expected duration of the individual's participation (including number and duration of visits to the research centre and the total time involved) and the possibility of early termination of the trial or of the individual's participation in it;
6. whether money or other forms of material goods will be provided in return for the individual's participation and, if so, the kind and amount;
7. that, after the completion of the study, subjects will be informed of the findings of the research in general, and individual subjects will be informed of any finding that relates to their particular health status;
8. that subjects have the right of access to their data on demand, even if these data lack imme-

diate clinical utility (unless the ethical review committee has approved temporary or permanent non-disclosure of data, in which case the subject should be informed of, and given, the reasons for such non-disclosure);
9. any foreseeable risks, pain or discomfort, or inconvenience to the individual (or others) associated with participation in the research, including risks to the health or well-being of a subject's spouse or partner;
10. the direct benefits, if any, expected to result to subjects from participating in the research;
11. the expected benefits of the research to the community or to society at large, or contributions to scientific knowledge;
12. whether, when and how any products or interventions proven by the research to be safe and effective will be made available to subjects after they have completed their participation in the research, and whether they will be expected to pay for them;
13. any currently available alternative interventions or courses of treatment;
14. the provisions that will be made to ensure respect for the privacy of subjects and for the confidentiality of records in which subjects are identified;
15. the limits, legal or other, to the investigators' ability to safeguard confidentiality, and the possible consequences of breaches of confidentiality;
16. policy with regard to the use of results of genetic tests and familial genetic information, and the precautions in place to prevent disclosure of the results of a subject's genetic tests to immediate family relatives or to others (e.g., insurance companies or employers) without the consent of the subject;
17. the sponsors of the research, the institutional affiliation of the investigators, and the nature and sources of funding for the research;
18. the possible research uses, direct or secondary, of the subject's medical records and of biological specimens taken in the course of clinical care . . . ;
19. whether it is planned that biological specimens collected in the research will be destroyed at its conclusion, and, if not, details about their storage (where, how, for how long, and final disposition) and possible future use, and that subjects have the right to decide about such

future use, to refuse storage, and to have the material destroyed . . . .

20. whether commercial products may be developed from biological specimens, and whether the participant will receive monetary or other benefits from the development of such products;

21. whether the investigator is serving only as an investigator or as both investigator and the subject's physician;

22. the extent of the investigator's responsibility to provide medical services to the participant;

23. that treatment will be provided free of charge for specified types of research-related injury or for complications associated with the research, the nature and duration of such care, the name of the organization or individual that will provide the treatment, and whether there is any uncertainty regarding funding of such treatment.

24. in what way, and by what organization, the subject or the subject's family or dependents will be compensated for disability or death resulting from such injury (or, when indicated, that there are no plans to provide such compensation);

25. whether or not, in the country in which the prospective subject is invited to participate in research, the right to compensation is legally guaranteed;

26. that an ethical review committee has approved or cleared the research protocol.

Guideline 6: Obtaining informed consent: Obligations of sponsors and investigators. Sponsors and investigators have a duty to:

• refrain from unjustified deception, undue influence, or intimidation;

• seek consent only after ascertaining that the prospective subject has adequate understanding of the relevant facts and of the consequences of participation and has had sufficient opportunity to consider whether to participate;

• as a general rule, obtain from each prospective subject a signed form as evidence of informed consent—investigators should justify any exceptions to this general rule and obtain the approval of the ethical review committee . . . ;

• renew the informed consent of each subject if there are significant changes in the conditions or procedures of the research or if new information

becomes available that could affect the willingness of subjects to continue to participate; and,

• renew the informed consent of each subject in long-term studies at pre-determined intervals, even if there are no changes in the design or objectives of the research. . . .

Guideline 7: Inducement to participate. Subjects may be reimbursed for lost earnings, travel costs and other expenses incurred in taking part in a study; they may also receive free medical services. Subjects, particularly those who receive no direct benefit from research, may also be paid or otherwise compensated for inconvenience and time spent. The payments should not be so large, however, or the medical services so extensive as to induce prospective subjects to consent to participate in the research against their better judgment ("undue inducement"). All payments, reimbursements and medical services provided to research subjects must have been approved by an ethical review committee. . . .

Guideline 8: Benefits and risks of study participation. For all biomedical research involving human subjects, the investigator must ensure that potential benefits and risks are reasonably balanced and risks are minimized.

• Interventions or procedures that hold out the prospect of direct diagnostic, therapeutic or preventive benefit for the individual subject must be justified by the expectation that they will be at least as advantageous to the individual subject, in the light of foreseeable risks and benefits, as any available alternative. Risks of such 'beneficial' interventions or procedures must be justified in relation to expected benefits to the individual subject.

• Risks of interventions that do not hold out the prospect of direct diagnostic, therapeutic or preventive benefit for the individual must be justified in relation to the expected benefits to society (generalizable knowledge). The risks presented by such interventions must be reasonable in relation to the importance of the knowledge to be gained. . . .

Guideline 9: Special limitations on risk when research involves individuals who are not capable of giving informed consent. When there is ethical and scientific justification to conduct research with individuals incapable of giving informed consent, the risk from research interventions that do not hold out the prospect of direct benefit for the individual subject should be no more likely and not greater than the risk attached to routine medical or psychological examination of such persons. Slight or minor increase above such risk may be permitted when there is an overriding scientific or medical rationale for such increases and when an ethical review committee has approved them. . . .

Guideline 10: Research in populations and communities with limited resources. Before undertaking research in a population or community with limited resources, the sponsor and the investigator must make every effort to ensure that:

- the research is responsive to the health needs and the priorities of the population or community in which it is to be carried out; and
- any intervention or product developed, or knowledge generated, will be made reasonably available for the benefit of that population or community. . . .

Guideline 11: Choice of control in clinical trials. As a general rule, research subjects in the control group of a trial of a diagnostic, therapeutic, or preventive intervention should receive an established effective intervention. In some circumstances it may be ethically acceptable to use an alternative comparator, such as placebo or "no treatment".

Placebo may be used:

- when there is no established effective intervention;
- when withholding an established effective intervention would expose subjects to, at most, temporary discomfort or delay in relief of symptoms;
- when use of an established effective intervention as comparator would not yield scientifically reliable results and use of placebo would not add any risk of serious or irreversible harm to the subjects. . . .

Guideline 12: Equitable distribution of burdens and benefits in the selection of groups of subjects in research. Groups or communities to be invited to be subjects of research should be selected in such a way that the burdens and benefits of the research will be equitably distributed. The exclusion of groups or communities that might benefit from study participation must be justified. . . .

Guideline 13: Research involving vulnerable persons. Special justification is required for inviting vulnerable individuals to serve as research subjects and, if they are selected, the means of protecting their rights and welfare must be strictly applied. . . .

Guideline 14: Research involving children. Before undertaking research involving children, the investigator must ensure that:

- the research might not equally well be carried out with adults;
- the purpose of the research is to obtain knowledge relevant to the health needs of children;
- a parent or legal representative of each child has given permission;
- the agreement (assent) of each child has been obtained to the extent of the child's capabilities; and,
- a child's refusal to participate or continue in the research will be respected. . . .

Guideline 15: Research involving individuals who by reason of mental or behavioural disorders are not capable of giving adequately informed consent. Before undertaking research involving individuals who by reason of mental or behavioural disorders are not capable of giving adequately informed consent, the investigator must ensure that:

- such persons will not be subjects of research that might equally well be carried out on persons whose capacity to give adequately informed consent is not impaired;
- the purpose of the research is to obtain knowledge relevant to the particular health needs of persons with mental or behavioural disorders;
- the consent of each subject has been obtained to the extent of that person's capabilities, and a prospective subject's refusal to participate in research is always respected, unless, in exceptional circumstances, there is no reasonable medical alternative and local law permits overriding the objection; and,
- in cases where prospective subjects lack capacity to consent, permission is obtained from a responsible family member or a legally authorized representative in accordance with applicable law. . . .

Guideline 16: Women as research subjects. Investigators, sponsors or ethical review committees should not exclude women of reproductive age from biomedical research. The potential for becoming pregnant during a study should not, in itself, be used as a reason for precluding or limiting participation. However, a thorough discussion of risks to the pregnant woman and to her fetus is a prerequisite for the woman's ability to make a rational decision to enroll in a clinical study. In this discussion, if participation in the research might be hazardous to a fetus or a woman if she becomes pregnant, the sponsors/investigators should guarantee the prospective subject a pregnancy test and access to effective contraceptive methods before the research commences. Where such access is not possible, for legal or religious reasons, investigators should not recruit for such possibly hazardous research women who might become pregnant. . . .

Guideline 17: Pregnant women as research participants. Pregnant women should be presumed to be eligible for participation in biomedical research. Investigators and ethical review committees should ensure that prospective subjects who are pregnant are adequately informed about the risks and benefits to themselves, their pregnancies, the fetus and their subsequent offspring, and to their fertility.

Research in this population should be performed only if it is relevant to the particular health needs of a pregnant woman or her fetus, or to the health needs of pregnant women in general, and, when appropriate, if it is supported by reliable evidence from animal experiments, particularly as to risks of teratogenicity and mutagenicity. . . .

Guideline 18: Safeguarding confidentiality. The investigator must establish secure safeguards of the confidentiality of subjects' research data. Subjects should be told the limits, legal or other, to the investigators' ability to safeguard confidentiality and the possible consequences of breaches of confidentiality. . . .

Guideline 19: Right of injured subjects to treatment and compensation. Investigators should ensure that research subjects who suffer injury as a result of their participation are entitled to free medical treatment for such injury and to such financial or other assistance as would compensate them equitably for any resultant impairment, disability or handicap. In the case of death as a result of their participation, their dependents are entitled to compensation. Subjects must not be asked to waive the right to compensation. . . .

Guideline 20: Strengthening capacity for ethical and scientific review and biomedical research. Many countries lack the capacity to assess or ensure the scientific quality or ethical acceptability of biomedical research proposed or carried out in their jurisdictions. In externally sponsored collaborative research, sponsors and investigators have an ethical obligation to ensure that biomedical research projects for which they are responsible in such countries contribute effectively to national or local capacity to design and conduct biomedical research, and to provide scientific and ethical review and monitoring of such research.

Capacity-building may include, but is not limited to, the following activities:

- establishing and strengthening independent and competent ethical review processes/committees
- strengthening research capacity
- developing technologies appropriate to health-care and biomedical research
- training of research and health-care staff
- educating the community from which research subjects will be drawn. . . .

Guideline 21: Ethical obligation of external sponsors to provide health-care services. External sponsors are ethically obliged to ensure the availability of:

- health-care services that are essential to the safe conduct of the research;
- treatment for subjects who suffer injury as a consequence of research interventions; and,
- services that are a necessary part of the commitment of a sponsor to make a beneficial intervention or product developed as a result of the research reasonably available to the population or community concerned. . . .

REFERENCE

[CIOMS (1991): Zbigniew Bankowski, John H. Bryant, and John M. Last, eds., *Ethics and Epidemiology: International Guidelines* (Geneva: CIOMS, 1991)].

PATRICIA A. KING

The Dangers of Difference

Patricia A. King is Cormack Waterhouse Professor of Law, Medicine, Ethics, and Public Policy at the Georgetown University Law School. She has served as a member of the National Commission for the Protection of Human Subjects, the President's Commission for the Study of Ethical Problems in Medicine and Biomedical and Behavioral Research, and the NIH Recombinant DNA Advisory Committee. She was also a member of the Institute of Medicine's Committee on the Ethical and Legal Issues Relating to the Inclusion of Women in Clinical Studies. Professor King is coeditor of a textbook entitled *Law, Medicine, and Ethics.* Before entering academia she was active in the enforcement of civil rights within the federal Equal Employment Opportunity Commission and the U.S. Department of Justice.

It has been sixty years since the beginning of the Tuskegee syphilis experiment and twenty years since its existence was disclosed to the American public. The social and ethical issues that the experiment poses for medicine, particularly for medicine's relationship with African Americans, are still not broadly understood, appreciated, or even remembered.[1] Yet a significant aspect of the Tuskegee experiment's legacy is that in a racist society that incorporates beliefs about the inherent inferiority of African Americans in contrast with the superior status of whites, any attention to the question of differences that may exist is likely to be pursued in a manner that burdens rather than benefits African Americans.

The Tuskegee experiment, which involved approximately 400 males with late-stage, untreated syphilis and approximately 200 controls free of the disease, is by any measure one of the dark pages in the history of American medicine. In this study of the natural course of untreated syphilis, the participants did not give informed consent. Stunningly, when penicillin was subsequently developed as a treatment for syphilis, measures were taken to keep the diseased participants from receiving it.

Patricia A. King, "The Dangers of Difference," *Haslings Center Report* 22, no. 6 (1992): 35–38. Reprinted by permission of the author and the Hastings Center.

Obviously, the experiment provides a basis for the exploration of many ethical and social issues in medicine, including professional ethics,[2] the limitations of informed consent as a means of protecting research subjects, and the motives and methods used to justify the exploitation of persons who live in conditions of severe economic and social disadvantage. At bottom, however, the Tuskegee experiment is different from other incidents of abuse in clinical research because all the participants were black males. The racism that played a central role in this tragedy continues to infect even our current well-intentioned efforts to reverse the decline in health status of African Americans.[3]

Others have written on the scientific attitudes about race and heredity that flourished at the time that the Tuskegee experiment was conceived.[4] There has always been widespread interest in racial differences between blacks and whites, especially differences that related to sexual matters. These perceived differences have often reinforced and justified differential treatment of blacks and whites, and have done so to the detriment of blacks. Not surprisingly, such assumptions about racial differences provided critical justification for the Tuskegee experiment itself.

Before the experiment began a Norwegian investigator had already undertaken a study of untreated syphilis in whites between 1890 and 1910. Although there had also been a follow-up study of these untreated patients from 1925 to 1927, the original study was abandoned when arsenic therapy became available. In light of the availability of therapy a substantial justification for replicating a study of untreated syphilis was required. The argument that provided critical support for the experiment was that the natural course of untreated syphilis in blacks and whites was not the same.[5] Moreover, it was thought that the differences between blacks and whites were not merely biological but that they extended to psychological and social responses to the disease as well. Syphilis, a sexually transmitted disease, was perceived to be rampant among blacks in part because blacks—unlike whites—were not inclined to seek or continue treatment for syphilis.

THE DILEMMA OF DIFFERENCE

In the context of widespread belief in the racial inferiority of blacks that surrounded the Tuskegee experiment, it should not come as a surprise that the experiment exploited its subjects. Recognizing and taking account of racial differences that have historically been utilized to burden and exploit African Americans poses a dilemma.[6] Even in circumstances where the goal of a scientific study is to benefit a stigmatized group or person, such well-intentioned efforts may nevertheless cause harm. If the racial difference is ignored and all groups or persons are treated similarly, unintended harm may result from the failure to recognize racially correlated factors. Conversely, if differences among groups or persons are recognized and attempts are made to respond to past injustices or special burdens, the effort is likely to reinforce existing negative stereotypes that contributed to the emphasis on racial differences in the first place.

This dilemma about difference is particularly worrisome in medicine. Because medicine is pragmatic, it will recognize racial differences if doing so will promote health goals. As a consequence, potential harms that might result from attention to racial differences tend to be overlooked, minimized, or viewed as problems beyond the purview of medicine.

The question of whether (and how) to take account of racial differences has recently been raised in the context of the current AIDS epidemic. The participation of African Americans in clinical AIDS trials has been disproportionately small in comparison to the numbers of African Americans who have been infected with the Human Immunodeficiency Virus. Because of the possibility that African Americans may respond differently to drugs being developed and tested to combat AIDS,[7] those concerned about the care and treatment of AIDS in the African American community have called for greater participation by African Americans in these trials. Ironically, efforts to address the problem of underrepresentation must cope with the enduring legacy of the Tuskegee experiment—the legacy of suspicion and skepticism toward medicine and its practitioners among African Americans.[8]

In view of the suspicion Tuskegee so justifiably engenders, calls for increased participation by African Americans in clinical trials are worrisome. The question of whether to tolerate racially differentiated AIDS research testing of new or innovative therapies, as well as the question of what norms should govern participation by African Americans in clinical research, needs careful and thoughtful attention. A generic examination of the treatment of racial differences in medicine is beyond the scope of this article. However, I will describe briefly what has occurred since disclosure of the Tuskegee experiment to point out the dangers I find lurking in our current policies.

INCLUSION AND EXCLUSION

In part because of public outrage concerning the Tuskegee experiment,[9] comprehensive regulations governing federal research using human subjects were revised and subsequently adopted by most federal agencies.[10] An institutional review board (IRB) must approve clinical research involving human subjects, and IRB approval is made contingent on review of protocols for adequate protection of human subjects in accordance with federal criteria. These criteria require among other things that an IRB ensure that subject selection is "equitable." The regulations further provide that:

[i]n making this assessment the IRB should take into account the purposes of the research and the setting in which the research will be conducted and should be particularly cognizant of the special problems of research involving vulnerable populations, such as women, mentally disabled persons, or economically or educationally disadvantaged persons.[11]

The language of the regulation makes clear that the concern prompting its adoption was the protection of vulnerable groups from exploitation. The obverse problem—that too much protection might promote the exclusion or underrepresentation of vulnerable groups, including African Americans—was not at issue. However, underinclusion can raise as much of a problem of equity as exploitation.[12]

A 1990 General Accounting Office study first documented the extent to which minorities and women were underrepresented in federally funded research. In response, in December 1990 the National Institutes of Health, together with the Alcohol, Drug Abuse and Mental Health Administration, directed that minorities and women be included in study populations,

so that research findings can be of benefit to all persons at risk of the disease, disorder or condition under study; special emphasis should be placed on the need for inclusion of minorities and women in studies of diseases, disorders and conditions that disproportionately affect them.[13]

If minorities are not included, a clear and compelling rationale must be submitted.

The new policy clearly attempts to avoid the perils of overprotection, but it raises new concerns. The policy must be clarified and refined if it is to meet the intended goal of ensuring that research findings are of benefit to all. There are at least three reasons for favoring increased representation of African Americans in clinical trials. The first is that there may be biological differences between blacks and whites that might affect the applicability of experimental findings to blacks, but these differences will not be noticed if blacks are not included in sufficient numbers to allow the detection of statistically significant racial differences. The second reason is that race is a reliable index for social conditions such as poor health and nutrition, lack of adequate access to health care, and economic and social disadvantage that might adversely affect potential benefits of new interventions and procedures. If there is indeed a correlation between minority status and these factors, then African Americans and all others with these characteristics will benefit from new information generated by the research. The third reason is that the burdens and benefits of research should be spread across the population regardless of racial or ethnic status.[14] Each of these reasons for urging that representation of minorities be increased has merit. Each of these justifications also raises concern, however, about whether potential benefits will indeed be achieved.

The third justification carries with it the obvious danger that the special needs or problems generated as a result of economic or social conditions associated with minority status may be overlooked and that, as a result, African Americans and other minorities will be further disadvantaged. The other two justifications are problematic and deserve closer examination. They each assume that there are either biological, social, economic, or cultural differences between blacks and whites.

THE WAY OUT OF THE DILEMMA

Understanding how, or indeed whether, race correlates with disease is a very complicated problem. Race itself is a confusing concept with both biological and social connotations. Some doubt whether race has biological significance at all.[15] Even if race is a biological fiction, however, its social significance remains.[16] As Bob Blauner points out, "Race is an essentially political construct, one that translates our tendency to see people in terms of their color or other physical attributes into structures that make it likely that people will act for or against them on such a basis."[17]

In the wake of Tuskegee and, in more recent times, the stigma and discrimination that resulted from screening for sickle cell trait (a genetic condition that occurs with greater frequency among African Americans), researchers have been reluctant to explore associations between race and disease. There is increasing recognition, however, of evidence of heightened resistance or vulnerability to disease along racial lines.[18] Indeed, sickle cell anemia itself substantiates the view that biological differences may exist. Nonetheless, separating myth from reality in determining the cause of disease and poor health status is not easy. Great caution should be exercised in attempting to validate biological differences in susceptibility to disease in light of this society's past experience with biological differences. Moreover, using race as an index for other conditions that might influence health and well-being is also dangerous. Such practices could emphasize social and economic differences that might also lead to stigma and discrimination.

If all the reasons for increasing minority participation in clinical research are flawed, how then can we promote improvement in the health status of African Americans and other minorities through participation in clinical research while simultaneously minimizing the harms that might flow from such participation? Is it possible to work our way out of this dilemma?

An appropriate strategy should have as its starting point the defeasible presumption that blacks and whites are biologically the same with respect to disease and treatment. Presumptions can be overturned of course, and the strategy should recognize the possibility that biological differences in some contexts are possible. But the presumption of equality acknowledges that historically the greatest harm has come from the willingness to impute biological differences rather than the willingness to overlook them. For some, allowing the presumption to be in any way defeasible is troubling. Yet I do not believe that fear should lead us to ignore the possibility of biologically differentiated responses to disease and treatment, especially when the goal is to achieve medical benefit.

It is well to note at this point the caution sounded by Hans Jonas. He wrote, "Of the new experimentation with man, medical is surely the most legitimate; psychological, the most dubious; biological (still to come), the most dangerous."[19] Clearly, priority should be given to exploring the possible social, cultural, and environmental determinants of disease before targeting the study of hypotheses that involve biological differences between blacks and whites. For example, rather than trying to determine whether blacks and whites respond differently to AZT, attention should first be directed to learning whether response to AZT is influenced by social, cultural, or environmental conditions. Only at the point where possible biological differences emerge should hypotheses that explore racial differences be considered.

A finding that blacks and whites are different in some critical aspect need not inevitably lead to increased discrimination or stigma for blacks. If there indeed had been a difference in the effects of untreated syphilis between blacks and whites such information might have been used to promote the health status of blacks. But the Tuskegee experiment stands as a reminder that such favorable outcomes rarely if ever occur. More often, either racist assumptions and stereotypes creep into the study's design, or findings broken down by race become convenient tools to support policies and behavior that further disadvantage those already vulnerable.

NOTES

1. For earlier examples of the use of African Americans as experimental subjects see Todd L. Savitt, "The Use of Blacks for Medical Experimentation and Demonstration in the Old South," *Journal of Southern History* 48, no. 3 (1982): 331–48.

2. David J. Rothman, "Were Tuskegee and Willowbrook 'Studies in Nature'?" *Hastings Center Report* 12, no. 2 (1982): 5–7.

3. For an in-depth examination of the health status of African Americans see Woodrow Jones, Jr., and Mitchell F. Rice, eds. *Health Care Issues in Black America: Policies, Problems, and Prospects* (New York: Greenwood Press, 1987).

4. See for example Allan M. Brandt, "Racism and Research: The Case of the Tuskegee Syphilis Study," *Hastings Center Report* 8, no. 6 (1978): 21–29; and James H. Jones, *Bad Blood: The Tuskegee Syphilis Experiment* (New York: Free Press, 1981).

5. Jones, *Bad Blood*, p. 106.

6. Martha Minow, *Making All the Difference: Inclusion, Exclusion, and American Law* (Ithaca, N.Y.: Cornell University Press, 1990).

7. Wafaa El-Sadr and Linnea Capps, "The Challenge of Minority Recruitment in Clinical Trials for AIDS," *JAMA* 267, no. 7 (1992): 954–57.

8. See for example Stephen B. Thomas and Sandra Crouse Quinn, "Public Health Then and Now," *American Journal of Public Health* 81, no. 11 (1991): 1498–1505; Henry C. Chinn, Jr., "Remember Tuskegee," *New York Times*, 29 May 1992.

9. Tuskegee Syphilis Study Ad Hoc Advisory Panel, *Final Report of the Tuskegee Syphilis Study Ad Hoc Advisory Panel* (Washington, D.C.: U.S. Department of Health, Education and Welfare, Public Health Service, 1973).

10. Federal Policy for the Protection of Human Subjects; Notices and Rules, *Federal Register* 56, no. 117 (1991): 28002.

11. 45 *Code of Federal Regulations* §46.111 (a) (3).

12. This problem is discussed in the context of research in prisons in Stephen E. Toulmin, "The National Commission on Human Experimentation: Procedures and Outcomes," in *Scientific Controversies: Case Studies in the Resolution and Closure of Disputes in Science and Technology*, ed. H. Tristram Engelhardt, Jr. and Arthur L. Caplan (New York: Cambridge University Press, 1987), pp. 602–6.

13. National Institutes of Health and Alcohol, Drug Abuse and Mental Health Administration, "Special Instructions to Applicants Using Form PHS 398 Regarding Implementation of the NIH/ ADAMHA Policy concerning Inclusion of Women and Minorities in Clinical Research Study Populations," December 1990.

14. Arthur L. Caplan, "Is There a Duty to Serve as a Subject in Biomedical Research?" *IRB: A Review of Human Subjects Research* 6, no. 5 (1984): 1–5.

15. See J. W. Green, *Cultural Awareness in the Human Services* (Englewood Cliffs, N.J.: Prentice-Hall, 1982), p. 59; Bob Blauner, "Talking Past Each Other: Black and White Languages of Race," *American Prospect* 61, no. 10 (1992): 55–64.

16. Patricia A. King, "The Past as Prologue: Race, Class, and Gene Discrimination," in *Using Ethics and Law as Guides*, ed. George J. Annas and Sherman Elias (New York: Oxford University Press, 1992), pp. 94–111.

17. Blauner, "Talking Past Each Other," p. 16.

18. See for example James E. Bowman and Robert F. Murray, Jr., *Genetic Variation and Disorders in People of African Origin* (Baltimore, Md.: Johns Hopkins University Press, 1981); Warren W. Leary. "Uneasy Doctors Add Race-Consciousness to Diagnostic Tools," *New York Times*, 15 September 1990.

19. Hans Jonas, "Philosophical Reflections on Experimenting with Human Subjects," in *Experimentation with Human Subjects*, ed. Paul A. Freund (New York: George Braziller, 1970), p. 1. Recent controversy in genetic research makes Jonas's warning particularly timely. See Daniel Goleman, "New Storm Brews on Whether Crime Has Roots in Genes," *New York Times*, 15 September 1992.

ANNA MASTROIANNI AND JEFFREY KAHN

Swinging on the Pendulum: Shifting Views of Justice in Human Subjects Research

Anna Mastroianni is Associate Professor at the University of Washington School of Law and the Institute for Public Health Genetics. She has coedited books entitled *Ethics and Public Health: Model Curriculum; Beyond Consent: Seeking Justice in Research; Ethics of Research with Human Subjects: Selected Policies and Resources*; and *Women and Health Research: Ethical and Legal Issues of Including Women in Clinical Studies*. She has published articles on human subjects research, surgical innovation, and reproduction. She is a coeditor of this textbook.

Jeffrey P. Kahn is Professor and Director, Center for Bioethics, University of Minnesota. With Anna Mastroianni and Jeremy Sugarman he has coedited *Beyond Consent: Seeking Justice in Research* and *Ethics of Research with Human Subjects: Selected Policies and Resources*. From 1994 to 1995 he served as Deputy Director for the White House Advisory Committee on Human Radiation Experiments. He has published articles on the ethical issues in clinical research, human embryonic stem cell research, genetic technologies, and organ donation and transplantation. He is a coeditor of this textbook.

Justice has long been one of the central principles in the ethical conduct of research on human subjects. But its application, as reflected in federal policies pertaining to human subjects research, has undergone a remarkable shift over a relatively short span of time. Understanding this shift is important not only for interpreting claims about justice in human subjects research, but also for assessing the status and adequacy of policies for protecting subjects.

In the 1970s, these policies emphasized the protection of human subjects from the risks of harm in research, and justice was seen as part of this protection. Since the early 1990s, however, justice as applied in research ethics has empasized the need to ensure access to the potential benefits that research has to offer. That such a dramatic shift could occur

so quickly is extraordinary, especially in light of the understanding, coalescing over the same period, that subjects have an inadequate understanding of the research in which they are participating and are inadequately protected by existing practices and policies. The tension between these developments offers an important lesson for research protection as the context of human subject research becomes more complex. Our goal here is to attempt to understand how the pendulum has swung from protection to access, where in its arc we are, and where we should be.

JUSTICE IN THE BELMONT ERA: PROTECTION FROM EXPLOITATION

The development of human subject protection policy in the United States was driven by a history of exploitation of subjects, most notably by research on "vulnerable" subject populations that came to light between the mid-1960s and the early 1970s. The landmark examples were the Willowbrook State School

Anna Mastroianni and Jeffrey Kahn, "Swinging on the Pendulum: Shifting Views of Justice in Human Subjects Research," *Hastings Center Report* 31, no. 3 (2001): 21–28. Reprinted by permission of the authors and the Hastings Center.

hepatitis vaccine research on institutionalized children; the Jewish Chronic Disease Hospital cancer research, involving the injection of cancer cells into elderly nursing home residents; and the so-called Tuskegee Syphilis Study, which had been under way for decades but was exposed to an appalled nation in 1972.[1] Those examples contributed to a sense that human subjects research in the United States permitted scandalous practices—inadequate attempts to inform subjects about research and obtain their consent, exploitive recruitment strategies, the use of vulnerable subject populations, and a willingness to expose subjects to significant risk without any potential for direct medical benefit. Further, there was a sense that the risks and benefits of research were split apart—the risks were borne by subjects, the benefits accrued to others.

Thus the early history of U.S. research ethics policy focused on the risks rather than the benefits of research, and on preventing subjects from being exposed to unacceptable or exploitive levels of risk, particularly without the prospect of offsetting direct medical benefits. *The Belmont Report*, issued by the National Commission for the Protection of Human Subjects of Biomedical and Behavioral Research in 1978, identified justice as requiring the fair distribution of the burdens and benefits of research in subject selection and recruitment; in practice, however, justice was interpreted as requiring the prevention of any further exploitation of vulnerable groups.[2] The emphasis was realized through the promulgation of research policies that staked much on protection and that singled out particular groups—namely, prisoners, children, and pregnant women and fetuses—for additional protections.

Prisoners were deemed vulnerable because of the nature of their living environment. Adequate informed consent, it was believed, was not possible when subjects lived in a setting that constrained the autonomy on which the concept of informed consent is based. This view actually ran counter to information collected by the National Commission, which found in interviews with prisoners who participated in research that the prisoners wanted to be enrolled in studies and were highly motivated research subjects, for a variety of reasons—the opportunity to earn a few extra dollars, the perks that might come with research participation, access to more frequent and potentially improved health care, and a belief that participating in research offered a way for them to make a contribution to society. Most interesting was the finding that

it was not the least powerful and arguably most vulnerable prisoners who participated in research, but the most powerful.[3] Prisoners often viewed research as an opportunity to be seized rather than a hazard to be avoided; they apparently did not worry that anyone was taking advantage of them. Even so, policies were promulgated, and remain in place today, that made it impossible to perform research on prison populations unless the research either offers a prospect of direct medical benefit to the individual subjects themselves, as in clinical trials for HIV infection, or aims at understanding or improving the prison environment, such that it would potentially benefit prison populations generally.

Children were deemed vulnerable because of similar concerns about informed consent and the potential for taking advantage of their reliance on others. Such concerns were vividly illustrated in the infamous Willowbrook case, where hepatitis vaccine research was performed on institutionalized, mentally retarded children whose parents seemed to have little choice but to agree to their children's participation—thereby picking out the most vulnerable from among the potential pool of children. The rules developed to prevent this sort of exploitation limited research in which children could participate to studies involving either minimal risk or direct medical benefit.

Pregnant women and fetuses were deemed especially vulnerable and deserving of protection. Influenced by the abortion debate and memories of thalidomide, policymakers protected pregnant women from research that carried risk of harm to protect them and their fetus. The implementation of this policy was expanded in practice to include not only pregnant women but also women of childbearing capacity, both to prevent unwitting risk to fetuses and to protect the future health of the women. This practice represented the logical conclusion of a regulatory culture and process that emphasized the protection of subjects from risk as paramount.

FROM PROTECTION TO ACCESS

The research regulatory culture that emphasized protection from risk in the 1970s began to shift during the late 1980s and early 1990s. Due to a growing belief that research increasingly offered real benefits, the application of justice in research began to emphasize the fair distribution of the benefits of research instead of its risks. Advocacy groups, particularly those representing the interests of people with AIDS and women's health groups, argued this view to great effect before Congress and elsewhere. The thrust of their position was that fairness demands not only protection from the risks of research, but increasingly demands the opportunity for inclusion in research. The shift was taking place: from justice as protection to justice as access.

The HIV/AIDS advocacy community was at the forefront of making the case for justice as access. As the first clinical trials for AZT were being undertaken, groups like ACTUP organized rallies protesting the limited enrollments in them. At a time when subjects were sharing their research medication with friends to spread around whatever potential benefit could be had from these drug trials, protestors were marching in large cities across the country carrying placards proclaiming "Clinical trials are health care too!"[4] Such a sentiment, conflating research participation with medical care, represented not just a shift in emphasis but a total reversal of the ethics of research from protection to access.

Through the late 1970s and 1980s, there was a growing sense that cutting edge therapy could be found in research participation, particularly for cancer, where the best therapeutic outcomes were thought to be in research protocols, and where standard treatment modalities were largely viewed as less effective. It was certainly true that the benefits from the major investments in biomedical research were being realized and applied. The problem was that those benefits were limited to the populations represented in the subject populations—largely although not exclusively adult males. Whatever the complex of reasons for excluding women, racial and ethnic minorities, and children from research participation, the policy was largely predicated on protection from harm and exploitation. But as advocates began to point out, such policies had the effect not only of preventing harm and exploitation, but also of preventing benefit—resulting, claimed one commentator, in a climate that protected some groups to death.[5] Exclusion denies access to the benefits of research at two levels—first to the individuals who may themselves receive the direct medical benefit of research participation, and more notably to the groups from which the subjects come.

There are numerous examples of the research system's failure to provide equitable benefits to women. Among the most notable is the United States Physicians Study, a longitudinal study that assessed the effectiveness of low dose aspirin for preventing heart attacks.[6] It yielded strong evidence of success, but it couldn't be applied outside the research population, comprised exclusively of men, because women are not merely smaller versions of men. Similarly, children are not merely smaller versions of adults, and racial and ethnic groups may differ from each other in disease pathology, drug response, and the like.

The realization that policy and practice had emphasized protection and a denial of the real and perceived benefits of research pushed the pendulum of research policy toward recognizing the importance of access to the benefits of biomedical research, by means of policies requiring inclusion in research set against a background of protection. In 1994, less than twenty years after the first federal policies on research protections were promulgated, the NIH issued the first policy requiring *inclusion* of particular groups in research—the Guideline on Inclusion of Women and Minorities in Research.[7] The guideline represents an unprecedented sea change in thinking about the ethics of research on human subjects.

IMPLEMENTING JUSTICE IN POLICY

The implementation of the 1994 NIH guideline flipped the presumption about research participation from exclusion to inclusion. Researchers were and are now required to include representative populations of women and minorities in their protocols unless there are special reasons for excluding them. It would make no sense, for example, to include women in a clinical trial testing a new drug for prostate cancer, nor would it be reasonable to conduct research on conditions in racial or ethnic groups in which those conditions are not found.

Policy on the participation of children in research is following a similar path, driven by similar arguments. In an effort to protect children, children have been excluded from research that carried greater than minimal risk unless the research also had the potential to provide direct medical benefit to the subjects. Thus federal regulations (subpart D of 45 CFR 46) bar the participation of children in phase I drug trials, which are used to assess the safety of new drugs before their approval. But excluding children from such research has meant there is limited information about the safety of drugs in pediatric populations. This information has instead been pieced together after the drugs are approved and marketed for adults: children have received drug doses based only on the most general calculations of their size relative to the adults for whom drugs are approved, and on the clinical experience (read "trial and error") of pediatricians who have begun to try the drugs on children.

Recent directions from both the NIH and the Food and Drug Administration are changing the presumption from exclusion to inclusion, and requiring a special justification to exclude children.[8] The change in approach has not been completely achieved, however. Reversing the presumption about participation has resulted in a policy that reflects the tension between ensuring access to the benefits of research and protecting subjects from research harms. The dictates of subpart D, as currently written, do not easily coexist with a policy of inclusion. It appears that the long-standing commitments to protection will be weakened as part of the trend toward assuring access to the benefits of research.

Changes in the rhetoric of health policy are further evidence of the emphasis on access to the benefits of research, reaching to the highest levels of our government. Richard Klausner, director of the National Cancer Institute, testifying before Congress in 1998 about the need for large increases in the overall NIH budget (which were eventually granted), argued that substantial additional resources were required "to ensure that all people who wish to participate in a clinical trial are able to do so."[9] The comment both presupposes that there is a real benefit to be had by the subjects of clinical research and reflects a remarkable commitment to universal access to research participation, particularly in a country where there is no similar commitment concerning basic health care.

Klausner's commitment has now been realized in policy, at least for those who have health insurance or are eligible for Medicare. In 1999, United Healthcare, one of the largest managed care organizations in the country, became the first third-party payer to agree to pay the costs associated with their subscribers' participation in clinical trials.[10] The decision was hailed as a major step in removing one of the substantial barriers to participation in clinical trials, since the policy of most health insurers has been to deny payment for the costs of clinical trial participation on the grounds that the treatment rendered is experimental. Whether the change in policy is a function of a changed view of the benefits of research participation, a response to the demands of its customers, or a commitment to supporting the research that yields the clinical advances on which health care depends, it certainly delivers a message to patients. If your insurance

company thinks research is worth paying for, it must be worth participating in. Not long after the decision was announced, then-President Bill Clinton directed the Health Care Financing Administration to ensure that all Medicare recipients would enjoy similar access to clinical trial participation, leaving it to policymakers to determine the conditions under which patients would be eligible for such a benefit.[11] This theme even became part of the rhetoric of the presidential campaign when Al Gore incorporated a reference to access to research participation in his standard stump speech on health care issues.[12]

The final piece of evidence that the pendulum has swung fully from protection to access is the waiver of informed consent in research in emergency settings, written into federal regulations in 1996.[13] The waiver is the ultimate endorsement of an emphasis on the benefits of research since it suggests that research participation is so beneficial, to individuals and society, that we must guarantee access even for those unable to consent. With this step we have now backed away from the cornerstone concept of informed consent, dating back to the Nuremberg era, in the protection of research subjects.

A NEW ERA IN THE PROTECTION OF HUMAN SUBJECTS?

What are the implications for research oversight of the swing from protection to access? The protection of the rights and interests of research subjects is rightly the preeminent concern in research oversight, but how do we ensure that protection is adequately balanced against access? There is ample evidence that even in an environment stressing protection there are serious shortcomings in the process of informed consent,[14] and subjects are persistently confused about the distinction between research and clinical care[15] and the benefits they stand to realize by participating in research.[16] Thus an overemphasis on the benefits of research participation can undermine the reality that research inherently carries risk and very often holds no benefits to the subject.

It is a confusing time to be a subject—or to be thinking about becoming one. The media presents stories about the need for more research and research funding alongside reports of serious harms to subjects in research trials. The death of Jesse Gelsinger in a gene transfer study at the University of Pennsylvania resulted in a swirl of reportage, congressional hearings, university investigations, and new restrictions and reporting policies for gene transfer research.[17] The *Seattle Times* recently reported on alleged conflicts of interest and failures to obtain informed consent in two clinical trials in which some subjects died unexpectedly, both at Seattle's Fred Hutchinson Cancer Research Center.[18] The *Los Angeles Times* ran a story on "seven deadly drugs" that were fast-tracked to approval by the Food and Drug Administration and were subsequently withdrawn from the market after they were discovered to have serious side effects, sometimes leading to death.[19] And it was recently reported that the FDA has asked for an additional $36 million in the next fiscal year to increase its "emphasis on high-risk trials, such as those enrolling vulnerable populations (mentally impaired and pediatric populations, for example) and sponsor-investigators who have a proprietary interest in the product under study."[20] How do we reconcile these divergent messages to subjects, investigators, IRBs, and institutions, and properly balance the requirements of justice in research? If we fail to answer this question adequately we risk a serious erosion of trust in the research enterprise.

LOOKING AHEAD

Accountability for balancing protection and access falls to those at every level in the conduct of research: the physicians who refer their patients to investigators, the investigators themselves, the IRBs that oversee research, and the institutions where research is performed. Policy-making does not occur in a vacuum; regulatory and spending decisions respond to the perceived needs and expressed desires of the public. Without trust from the public, there can be no research, as there will be no research subjects willing to participate and no willingness on the part of the public to support research with tax dollars. Research is a privilege not to be presumed or exploited, but earned through building and maintaining the public trust. This requires a careful balancing of access and protection.

Recent announcements by the Department of Health and Human Service's Office of Human Research Protections focus on conflicts of interest in research—at base an effort to secure public trust by ensuring that investigators are not motivated to overlook subjects' protection.[21] The Institute of Medicine recently completed a study recommending, among other things, the accreditation of IRBs.[22] But both of these steps seem to be aimed at assuring that paperwork requirements are met, which is at best a weak proxy for assuring adequate protection of subjects. Thus both efforts seem to miss the point—certification and oversight provide a way of inspecting the implementation of policies aimed at protection rather than a way of exercising them. And thus these approaches encourage us to overlook the nagging, recurring, and fundamental shortcomings in research protections that continue to undermine the trust central to any effort to protect the rights and interests of research subjects, including ensuring their access to the benefits of research.[23]

In the current research climate, the pendulum may have swung as far as it can toward an emphasis on benefits. When a pendulum has finished swinging in one direction, it inevitably starts back in the other, and it eventually comes to a rest in the middle. But the direction in which research ethics policy is swinging at any given time will be a function of how well we manage the balance between policies and practices at either of its two ends. Increasing policy attention to conflicts of interest, reporting, and regulatory oversight of the research environment seems to imply that the pendulum has begun its swing back toward an emphasis on protection. But paperwork requirements are not enough, and may distract us from efforts that will modulate the swing. What remains to be seen is how far the pendulum will go, and whether we have the tools to control it.

NOTES

1. J. Jones, *Bad Blood* (New York: Free Press, 1993).

2. National Commission for the Protection of Human Subjects of Biomedical and Behavioral Research, *The Belmont Report: Ethical Principles and Guidelines for the Protection of Human Subjects of Research* (Bethesda, Md.: Department of Health, Education, and Welfare, 1978).

3. National Commission for the Protection of Human Subjects of Biomedical and Behavioral Research, *Report and Recommendations: Research Involving Prisoners* (Bethesda, Md.: Department of Health, Education, and Welfare, 1976); V. Cohn, "Prisoner Test Ban Opposed," *Washington Post*, 14 March 1976.

4. R. Shilts, *And the Band Played On: Politics, People, and the AIDS Epidemic* (New York: St. Martin's Press, 1987).

5. R.A. Charo, "Protecting Us to Death: Women, Pregnancy, and Clinical Research Trials," *Saint Louis University Law Journal* 38, no. 1 (1993): 135–87.

6. J.E. Manson et al., "Aspirin in the Primary Prevention of Angina Pectoris in a Randomized Trial of United States Physicians." *American Journal of Medicine* 89 (1990): 772–76.

7. "NIH Guidelines on the Inclusion of Women and Minorities as Subjects in Clinical Research," *Federal Register* 59 (28 March 1994): 14508.

8. "NIH Policy and Guidelines on the Inclusion of Children as Participants in Research Involving Human Subjects," NIH Guide, 6 March 1998 <www.nih.gov/grants/guide/1998/98.03.06>.

9. R. Pear, "Medical Research to Get More Money from Government," *New York Times*, 3 January 1998.

10. G. Kolata and K. Eichenwald, "Insurers Come in from the Cold on Cancer," *New York Times*, 19 December 1999.

11. R. Pear, "Clinton to Order Medicare to Pay New Costs," *New York Times*, 7 June 2000.

12. J. Dao, "Gore Urges Doubling of Funds in War against Cancer," *New York Times*, 2 June 2000.

13. "Waiver of Informed Consent Requirements in Certain Emergency Research," *Federal Register* 61 (2 October 1996): 51531; "Protection of Human Subjects; Informed Consent," *Federal register* 61 (2 October 1996): 51498.

14. Advisory Committee on Human Radiation Experiments, "Research Proposal Review Project," in *The Human Radiation Experiments* (New York: Oxford University Press, 1996), 439–58; C.H. Braddock, "Advancing the Cause of Informed Consent: Moving from Disclosure to Understanding," *American Journal of Medicine* 105 (1998): 354–55; E.D. Kodish et al., "Informed Consent in the Children's Cancer Group: Results of Preliminary Research," *Cancer* 82 (1998): 2467–81.

15. Advisory Committee on Human Radiation Experiments, "Subject Interview Study," in *The Human Radiation Experiments* (New York: Oxford University Press. 1996): 459–81; N.E. Kass et al., "Trust: The Fragile Foundation of Contemporary Biomedical Research," *Hastings Center Report* 19, no. 5 (1996): 25–29.

16. P.S. Appelbaum, L.H. Roth, and C.W. Lidz, "The Therapeutic Misconception: Informed Consent in Psychiatric Research," *International Journal of Law and Psychiatry* 5 (1982): 319–29; C. Daugherty et al., "Perceptions of Cancer Patients and Their Physicians Involved in Phase I Trials," *Journal of Clinical Oncology* 13 (1995): 1062–72.

17. D.S. Greenberg, "Stricter Regulation Proposed for U.S. Gene Therapy Trials," *Lancet* 355 (1977): 2000.

18. D. Wilson and D. Heath, "Uninformed Consent," *Seattle Times*, 11–15 March 2001.

19. D. Willman, "How a New Policy Led to Seven Deadly Drugs," *Los Angeles Times*, 20 December 2000.

20. *Health News Daily*, 11 April 2001.

21. J. Brainard, "U.S. Agency Seeks Power to Fine Universities That Violate Rules on Human Research Subjects," *Chronicle of Higher Education*, 24 May 2000.

22. S.G. Stolberg, "Experts Call for New Rules on Research," *New York Times*, 18 April 2001.

23. J.P. Kahn and A.C. Mastroianni, "Moving From Compliance to Conscience: Why We Can and Should Improve on the Ethics of Clinical Research," *Archives of Internal Medicine* 161 (2001): 925–28.

SOLOMON R. BENATAR

Justice and Medical Research: A Global Perspective[1]

Solomon R. Benatar is a Professor of Medicine at the University of Cape Town in South Africa. He was the founding director of the university's Bioethics Centre. From 1980 to 1999 he also served as the Chief Physician at the Groote Schuur Hospital in Cape Town. Professor Benatar is a past president of the International Association of Bioethics. He has published articles on respiratory medicine, human rights, and global health.

INTRODUCTION

When Harold Macmillan (then Prime Minister of Britain) visited Africa in 1960, he referred to the "wind of change" that he perceived blowing through Africa— in the wake of decades of colonialism and oppression.[2] The history of sub-Saharan Africa since then has been stormy. Initial encouraging advances made by many countries in the early years of their independence have been followed by subsequent retrogression due to both external and internal influences. External factors include the adverse effects of neo-liberal economics on trade and the incurring of debts, the subsequent structural adjustment programs imposed by the IMF and World Bank, and the impact of arms trading and 'Cold War' interference in Africa. Internal factors include corruption, political patronage, power struggles and poor governance. Adverse environmental conditions and the HIV/AIDS pandemic have posed additional

From *Bioethics* 15, no. 4 (2001), 333–340. Copyright © 2001 Blackwell Publishers Ltd.

massive burdens to progress.[3] The "wind of change" associated with emancipation from oppression in apartheid South Africa has culminated in a much admired peaceful transition in that country.[4] How this transition will play out in the face of the HIV/AIDS pandemic and in the context of a globalising world is of great importance.[5]

THE WORLD AT THE BEGINNING OF THE 21ST CENTURY

It is necessary to appreciate that the "wind of change" is now being felt throughout the world, as globalising forces create ever widening disparities in wealth, with important implications for health and well being.[6] Despite great progress in science, technology and communication during the 20th century, the world at the beginning of the new millennium is characterized by chaos and despair at many levels.[7] Escalating economic disparities, especially during the past 30 years, illustrate the impact of the "visible hand" of the market place and the "squeezed up" effect, that is, the funneling of resources upwards resulting in wider disparities in wealth and health between rich and poor than ever before—rather than the so much spoken about and praised "invisible hand" and "trickle down effect." Indeed more than half the world's population lives in poverty—25% in abject poverty.

The shift in the accumulation of capital from the nation state to multinational corporations, and the creation of unpayable third world debt, have impoverished third world countries and reduced annual per capita health care expenditures to less than $10 in most poor countries—where less than 50% of the population have access to even essential drugs. Health care services are rudimentary for many in a world in which 87% of annual global expenditure on health is directed to 16% of the world's population, who only bear 7% of the global burden of disease, and in which increasingly unethical, market driven research neglects many diseases.[8] Of all US $56 billion spent annually on medical research 90% is spent on those diseases causing only 10% of the global burden of disease.[9]

Meanwhile vast expenditure continues on the military. Many small wars, fuelled by trade in weapons, have resulted in unprecedented numbers of civilian deaths and displacement of millions of people from their social roots, with profound disruption of their lives. In addition there is a world-wide movement of people, within and across national borders through urbanization, migration, tourism and illicit trading in drugs and people[10]—all favoring the rapid spread of infectious diseases. Growth of the world's population and massive increases in energy consumption (five and 30 fold increases respectively over the past 150 years) further threaten our ecology.[11]

New ecological niches created by these destructive social and environmental changes favor the emergence of many new infectious diseases, the worst being HIV/AIDS, and the recrudescence of old diseases such as tuberculosis and malaria that cause immense suffering and millions of premature deaths.[12] These and other infectious diseases that may emerge in the future challenge thinkers to better understand the world and how it could be improved.

HOW CAN THE WORLD BE EXPLAINED?

On the one hand the world can be considered as an unfortunate place in which most suffer disproportionately and unavoidably. On this account it is presumed that the manner and direction in which money flows, power is expressed, and social values develop are shaped by forces beyond the control of individuals or nations.

On the other hand an unjust world can be considered as one created by human activities, and one which can, and should be, changed. On this account the flow of money can be explained on the basis of national/international political forces and economic trends, and on such other aspects of globalization as advances in science and technology that have profoundly altered the nature of the global economy, as well as by exploitation at many levels (both overt–trade practices protecting the rich, and covert–debt trade and the arms trade as forms of enslavement). Some have used the term "global apartheid" for the processes that have promoted (and continue to aggravate) vast disparities between rich and poor across the world.[13] Others have described third world debt, an integral component of globalization, as analogous to slavery in its impact,[14] and have called for reflection on the magnificent achievements of the 20th century, and on how the human condition and health could be improved globally.[15]

CHALLENGES FOR INTERNATIONAL RESEARCH ETHICS

This brief review of the adverse effects of progress serves to locate the context in which the controversy about research ethics has arisen and the backdrop against which the goals of change need to be considered: how to construct universally valid guidelines for collaborative international medical research with the view to enhancing sensitivity to issues of justice and our common humanity. In brief, the rationale for embarking on this endeavor now more than ever before includes:

- The scale of injustice at a global level.
- Knowledge of the history of abuse of humans in medical research and the need to protect (vulnerable) research subjects.
- The need for research on diseases that know no boundaries and potentially threaten all—e.g., HIV/AIDS, and the diseases to which antimicrobial drug resistance is developing.
- Significant growth of research to promote the use of therapeutic drugs in a lucrative market.
- The attractiveness of doing research in developing countries: easy access to patients, reduced costs, and less stringent regulations—the "research sweat shop" equivalent.
- Understanding that researchers do not go to developing countries mainly for altruistic reasons.
- A perception by the vulnerable that they are being exploited.
- The need to balance the notion that solutions to disease and illness lie entirely in the realm of biomedicine with recognition that global forces promote emergence and resurgence of infectious diseases, and have many adverse effects on health.
- The goal of fostering empowerment through co-operation that may enhance human flourishing by making subjects essential partners in the research process.

The challenge to be faced in international research ethics is the development of universal rules for research world wide, at a time when health care is being delivered within very different health care systems (even within any single country) and in a multicultural world in which people live under radically different conditions—ranging from immense luxury to abject poverty. Variable trajectories of emancipation of individuals from communities have also given rise to a wide spectrum of how people view themselves, what it means to be ill and how health care systems should be structured.[16] With recognition of the role of social conditions in shaping the world, and how privileged people view the world and themselves, comes the realization that research cannot be considered in isolation.

Medical research, health care, conditions of life around the world and how humans flourish may seem separate, but they are all interdependent. Taking such a comprehensive global perspective adds complexity to the task of crafting universal research ethics guidelines.

SOME SOLUTIONS TO THE CONTROVERSY ON RESEARCH ETHICS

Against this background of the context in which the controversy regarding alterations to the Helsinki Declaration and other guidelines for research ethics has arisen[17] a choice which can be made from several options. First, the status quo could be upheld in the hope that the progress of science and of economic growth will continue uninterrupted with beneficial effects for all even if disparities persist or grow. This would be the easiest choice as it presupposes no responsibility for global injustice. However, it would also be immoral as current injustices will be perpetuated and aggravated.

The second choice would be to make piecemeal changes at the margins—for example in international research by tinkering with the Helsinki Declaration and making some minor modifications. This course is also appealing to those who wish to make research easier and less accountable, but there is powerful and justified resistance to diluting protection for vulnerable research subjects and any progress made would in all probability be insufficient and temporary.[18]

Third, there could be acknowledgment of the need for a paradigm shift in thinking and action—towards reciprocal relationships between individuals, society, and the notion of rational self-interest and long term interdependence.[19] This is a more difficult decision and one that may have higher costs in the short term. It would, however, reflect recognition of the adverse impact of globalization and allow use of such desirable universal values as human rights to build a more widely achievable universalism. Such a decision could advance human relationships to the high moral ground, with the consequent best hope for long-term results. South Africa's peaceful transition through a negotiated revolution is an example. It is suggested that privileged people need to hold up a mirror to their lives, and try to see themselves from the perspective of the marginalised and weak in the world today and as historians in the future may see them in retrospect—as decadent and selfish.

Given the responsibility to use power and knowledge wisely, it is suggested that the deliberations at this meeting should include the possibility of introducing several new components into the Declaration of Helsinki and other international research guidelines—to extend and honor the concepts of justice and of integrity in the research endeavor:

- Vulnerable groups should be provided with increasing accessibility to research, and this should apply to the vulnerable within all countries.
- Exploitation of subjects, or their use as mere means to the ends of others, should be explicitly excluded by ensuring that the research is of relevance to the individuals participating in the research as well as their communities.
- The potential benefits of research should considerably outweigh potential risks or harms to vulnerable individuals and communities.
- Research subjects should be encouraged to participate in planning and conducting studies.
- Research in developing countries should be linked with capacity building in health care, and with economic and educational empowerment that has beneficial effects on the delivery of health care and on progress generally in the host country.

The first Global Forum on International Research, which opened discussion of all the topics listed on this agenda, was an enlightened first step forward. The second step would be to promote the addition of the newly proposed clauses to the Helsinki and other declarations. Third, there should be consideration of an expanded role for Institutional Review Boards (Research Ethics Committees)—taking them beyond mere review bodies to include duties of audit and education. Fourth, there is the need to influence mind sets—for example through societal marketing processes, rewards for compliance, wider publicity for and marginalisation of those doing unethical research, and by bringing bioethics and human rights programs closer to each other. Such actions could act as bridges, levers, and moral examples for the process of narrowing disparities. Education, the acquisition of self-knowledge coupled to activism, and moral example are all necessary for the promotion of a "global new deal."[20]

In summary support is provided here for the suggestion that to help the world's poorest, and indeed to foster the interests of all, the dialogue between rich and poor should be enhanced, the power of science and technology should be mobilized to address the problems of poor countries, new institutional alliances should be constructed, the concept of intellectual property rights should be re-evaluated to avoid "ripping off the poor," and long term financing should be planned for the international good necessary for human flourishing.[21] Herein lie the challenges to which the international research ethics endeavor could contribute.[22]

NOTES

1. Based on the opening address given by the author at the Fogarty International Global Research Ethics Forum, Bethesda, Maryland, USA, November 1999.

2. H. Macmillan. "The wind of change is blowing through the continent. Whether we like it or not, this growth of national consciousness is a fact." Speech in the South African Parliament, Cape Town, February 3, 1960.

3. D. E. Logie, S. R. Benatar. Africa in the 21st century: can despair be turned to hope? *BMJ* 1997; 315: 1444–46. R. Sandbrook. 2000. *Closing the circle: democratization and development in Africa.* London. Zed Books.

4. H. Adam, K. Moodley, 1993. *The negotiated revolution: society and politics in post-apartheid South Africa.* Johannesburg. Jonathan Ball Publ.

5. K. Lee, A. B. Zwi. A global political economy approach to AIDS: ideology, interests and implications. *New Political Economy* 1996; 1: 355–73. S. R. Benatar. South Africa's transition in a globalising world: HIV/AIDS as a window and a mirror. *International Affairs* 2001; 77: 347–375.

6. S. R. Benatar. Global disparities in health and human rights. *American Journal of Public Health* 1998; 88: 295–300. J. Frenk et al., The new world order and international health. *BMJ,* 1997; 314: 1404–7.

7. E. Hobsbawm. 1994. *The age of extremes: a history of the world 1914–1991.* New York. Pantheon Books.

8. J. Iglehart. American health services: expenditure. *NEJM.* 1999; 340: 70–76.

9. Commission on Health Research for Development. 1990. *Health research: essential link to equity in development.* Oxford. Oxford University Press.

10. H. R. Friman, P. Andreas, (Eds). 1999. *Illicit global economy and state power.* New York. Rowan & Littlefield.

11. A. J. McMichael, *Planetary overload: global environmental change and the health of the human species.* Cambridge. Cambridge University Press.

12. WHO. *World health report 1996.* Geneva. K. Lee, A. B. Zwi. A global political economy approach to AIDS.

13. A. Richmond. 1994. *Global apartheid: refugees, racism and the new world order.* Oxford. Oxford University Press. T. Alexander. 1996. *Unraveling global apartheid.* Cambridge. Polity Press.

14. A. Pettifor. 1996. Debt, the most potent form of slavery. London. Jubilee 2000 Coalition. 2000. *Kicking the habit: finding a lasting solution to addictive lending and borrowing—and its corrupting side effects.* London.

15. The Jubilee 2000 campaign. www.jubilee2000.org

16. N. Smart. 1995. *World views: cross-cultural explorations of human beliefs.* New Jersey. Prentice Hall. R. Wilkinson. 1996. *Unhealthy societies: afflictions of inequality.* London. Routledge.

17. Revising the Declaration of Helsinki: a fresh start. *Bulletin of Medical Ethics.* 1999; 150: 3–44. Nuffield Council on Bioethics, 1999. *The ethics of clinical research in developing countries: a discussion paper.* London. D. Hellman. Trials on trial. *Report from the Institute for Philosophy and Public Policy.* 1998; 128: 142–147.

18. The Helsinki Declaration was modified at the 52nd World Medical Association (WMA) General Assembly in October 2000, Edinburgh, Scotland.

19. S. R. Benatar. 1997. Streams of global change. In: *Ethics, equity and health for all.* Z. Bankowski, J. H. Bryant, J. Gallagher (Eds). Geneva. CIOMS: 75–85. S. R. Benatar, P. A. Singer. A new look at international research ethics. *BMJ* 2000; 321: 824–26. A. Costello, A. Zumla. Moving to research partnerships in developing countries. *BMJ* 2000; 321: 827–29.

20. R. J. Barnett, J. Cavanagh. 1994. A global new deal. In: *Beyond Bretton Woods: alternatives to the new world order.*

J. Cavanagh, D. Wysham, M. Arruda (Eds). London. Pluto Press. R. Falk. 1999. *Predatory globalization: a critique.* Cambridge. Polity Press. A. J. McMichael. 1993. *Planetary overload.* Cambridge, Cambridge University Press. J. Rotblat (Ed).1997. *World citizenship: allegiance to humanity.* Basingstoke. Macmillan. G. Teeple. 2000. *Globalization and the decline of social reform.* 2nd ed. Aurora, Ontario. Garamond Press.

21. J. Sachs. Helping the world's poorest. *The Economist* 14 August, 1999: 17–20.

22. J. Stephens et al. The body hunters. A series of six articles in the *Washington Post* 17–21 December 2000, describing some of the horrors associated with the growing commercialization of drug research in developing countries.

NATIONAL BIOETHICS ADVISORY COMMISSION

Protecting Research Participants—A Time for Change

INTRODUCTION

Protecting the rights and welfare of those who volunteer to participate in research is a fundamental tenet of ethical research. A great deal of progress has been made in recent decades in changing the culture of research to incorporate more fully this ethical responsibility into protocol design and implementation. In the 1960s and 1970s, a series of scandals concerning social science research and medical research conducted with the sick and the illiterate underlined the need to systematically and rigorously protect individuals in research (Beecher 1966; Faden and Beauchamp 1986; Jones 1981; Katz 1972; Tuskegee Syphilis Study Ad Hoc Advisory Panel 1973). However, the resulting system of protections that evolved out of these rising concerns—although an improvement over past practices—is no longer sufficient. It is a patchwork arrangement associated with the receipt of federal research funding or the regulatory review and approval of new drugs and devices. In addition, it depends on the voluntary

cooperation of investigators, research institutions, and professional societies across a wide array of research disciplines. Increasingly, the current system is being viewed as uneven in its ability to simultaneously protect the rights and welfare of research participants and promote ethically responsible research.

Research involving human participants has become a vast academic and commercial activity, but this country's system for the protection of human participants has not kept pace with that growth. On the one hand, the system is too narrow in scope to protect all participants, while on the other hand, it is often so unnecessarily bureaucratic that it stifles responsible research. Although some reforms by particular federal agencies and professional societies are under way,[1] it will take the efforts of both the executive and legislative branches of government to put in place a streamlined, effective, responsive, and comprehensive system that achieves the protection of all human participants and encourages ethically responsible research.

Clearly, scientific investigation has extended and enhanced the quality of life and increased our understanding of ourselves, our relationships with others, and the natural world. It is one of the foundations of our

Reprinted from National Bioethics Advisory Commission, *Ethical and Policy Issues in Research Involving Human Participants: Summary* (Bethesda, MD: NBAC, August 2001), pp. i–ix.

society's material, intellectual, and social progress. For many citizens, scientific discoveries have alleviated the suffering caused by disease or disability. Nonetheless, the prospect of gaining such valuable scientific knowledge need not and should not be pursued at the expense of human rights or human dignity. In the words of philosopher Hans Jonas, "progress is an optional goal, not an unconditional commitment, and . . . its tempo . . . compulsive as it may become, has nothing sacred about it" (Jonas 1969, 245).

Since the 1974 formation of the National Commission for the Protection of Human Subjects of Biomedical and Behavioral Research and the activities in the early 1980s of the President's Commission for the Study of Ethical Problems in Medicine and Biomedical and Behavioral Research, American leaders have consistently tried to enhance the protections for human research participants. The research community has, in large part, supported the two essential protections for human participants: independent review of research to assess risks and potential benefits and an opportunity for people to voluntarily and knowledgeably decide whether to participate in a particular research protocol.

The charter of the National Bioethics Advisory Commission (NBAC), a presidential commission created in 1995, makes clear the Commission's focus: "As a first priority, NBAC shall direct its attention to consideration of protection of the rights and welfare of human research subjects." In our first five years, we focused on several issues concerning research involving human participants, issuing five reports and numerous recommendations that, when viewed as a whole, reflect our evolving appreciation of the numerous and complex challenges facing the implementation and oversight of any system of protections.[2] The concerns and recommendations addressed in these reports reflect our dual commitment to ensuring the protection of those who volunteer for research while supporting the continued advance of science and understanding of the human condition. This report views the oversight system as a whole, provides a rationale for change, and offers an interrelated set of recommendations to improve the protection of human participants and enable the oversight system to operate more efficiently.

RESPECTING RESEARCH PARTICIPANTS

Whether testing a new medical treatment, interviewing people about their personal habits, studying how people think and feel, or observing how they live within groups, research seeks to learn something new about the human condition. Unfortunately, history has also demonstrated that researchers sometimes treat participants not as persons but as mere objects of study. As Jonas observed: "Experimentation was originally sanctioned by natural science. There it is performed on inanimate objects, and this raises no moral questions. But as soon as animate, feeling beings become the subject of experiment . . . this innocence of the search for knowledge is lost and questions of conscience arise" (Jonas 1969, 219).

How, then, should people be studied? For over half a century, since the revelations of medical torture under the guise of medical experimentation were described at the Nuremberg Trials,[3] it has been agreed that people should participate in research only when the study addresses important questions, its risks are justifiable, and an individual's participation is voluntary and informed.

The principles underlying the *Belmont Report: Ethical Principles and Guidelines for the Protections of Human Subjects of Research* (*Belmont Report*) (National Commission 1979) have served for over 20 years as a leading source of guidance regarding the ethical standards that should govern research with human participants in the United States. The *Belmont Report* emphasized that research must respect the autonomy of participants, must be fair in both conception and implementation, and must maximize potential benefits while minimizing potential harms. The report's recommendations provided a coherent rationale for the federal policies and rules that created the current U.S. system of decentralized, independent research review coupled with some degree of federal oversight. But although the *Belmont Report* is rightly hailed as a key source of guidance on informed consent, assessment of risk, and the injustice of placing individuals (and groups) in situations of vulnerability, the principles the report espouses and the regulations adopted as federal policy 20 years ago have often fallen short in achieving their overarching goal of protecting human research participants. Moreover, since the *Belmont Report* was published, additional concerns have arisen that require much-needed attention today.

ENSURING INDEPENDENT REVIEW OF RISKS AND POTENTIAL BENEFITS

A central protection for research participants is the guarantee that someone other than the investigator will assess the risks of the proposed research. *No one should participate in research unless independent review concludes that the risks are reasonable in relation to the potential benefits.* In the United States, the Institutional Review Board, or IRB, has been the principal structure responsible for conducting such reviews.

Independent review of research is essential because it improves the likelihood that decisions are made free from inappropriate influences that could distort the central task of evaluating risks and potential benefits. Certainly, reviewers should not have a financial interest in the work, but social factors may be just as crucial. Reviewers may feel constrained because they are examining the work of their colleagues or their supervisors, and they should not participate in protocol review unless they are able to separate these concerns from their task. All reviewers who themselves are members of the research community should recognize that their familiarity with research and (perhaps) their predilection to support research are factors that could distort their judgment. Truly independent and sensitive review requires more involvement of individuals drawn from the ranks of potential research participants or those who can adequately represent the interests of potential research participants.

A critical purpose of independent review is to ensure that risks are reasonable in relation to potential personal and societal benefits. This is a precondition to offering people the opportunity to volunteer, since informed consent alone cannot justify enrollment. When reviewed for risks and potential benefits, research studies must be evaluated in their entirety. Studies often include different components, however, and the risks and potential benefits of each should also be examined separately, lest the possibility of great benefit or monetary enticement in one component cause potential participants or IRBs to minimize or overlook risk in another. No matter what potential benefit is offered to individual participants or society at large, the possibility of benefit from one element of a study should not be used to justify otherwise unacceptable elements.

In our view, IRBs should appreciate that for some components of a study, participants might incur risks with no personal potential benefit—for example, when a nondiagnostic survey is included among the components of a psychotherapy protocol or when placebos are given to some participants in a drug trial. For these elements, there should be some limitation on the amount of social and physical risk that can be imposed, regardless of the participants' willingness to participate

or the monetary (or other) enticement being offered. Further, the possibility of some benefit from one element of a study should not be used to justify otherwise unacceptable elements of research whose potential benefits, if any, accrue, solely to society at large. If aspects of a study present unacceptable risks, protocols should not be approved until these elements are eliminated. If removing the risky component would impair the study as a whole, then the entire study should be redesigned so that each of its elements presents risks that are reasonable in relation to potential benefits.

Other parts of studies can obscure risks, such as when standard medical interventions are compared in a patient population, leading some participants and researchers to discount the risks because they are associated with known therapies. It is essential that participants and investigators not be led to believe that participating in research is tantamount to being in a traditional therapeutic relationship. Regardless of whether there is the possibility or even the likelihood of direct benefit from participation in research, such participation still alters the relationship between a professional and the participant by introducing another loyalty beyond that to the participant, to wit, loyalty to doing good science. It is too often forgotten that even though the researchers may consider participants' interests to be important, they also have a serious, and perhaps conflicting, obligation to science.

Years of experience with the current system of independent review have demonstrated that there are enduring questions about how to arrive at such impartial judgments and how to go about deciding when potential benefits justify risks that are incurred solely by participants or the community from which they come. In recent years, increasing strains on the system have undermined the practice of independent review. IRBs are overburdened by the volume of research coming before them, a strain that is compounded by concerns about training of IRB members and possible conflicts of interest. In addition, the constantly changing nature of research challenges existing notions about what constitutes risks and potential benefits.

Because IRBs are so central to the current oversight system, they need better guidance on how to review and monitor research, how to assess potential benefits to research participants and their communities, and how to distinguish among levels of risk. This report provides such guidance in the following areas: determining the type of review necessary for minimal risk research; ensuring that research participants are able to make voluntary decisions and are appropriately informed prior to giving consent; providing adequate protections for privacy and confidentiality; identifying appropriate measures needed when participants are susceptible to coercion or are otherwise placed in vulnerable situations; and monitoring ongoing research. In addition, the report recommends that IRB members and staff complete educational and certification programs on research ethics before being permitted to review research studies.

OBTAINING VOLUNTARY INFORMED CONSENT

Even when risks are reasonable, however, *no one should participate in research without giving voluntary informed consent (except in the case of an appropriate authorized representative or a waiver). Investigators must make appropriate disclosures and ensure that participants have a good understanding of the information and their choices, not only at the time of enrollment, but throughout the research.* Engaging in this process is one of the best ways researchers can demonstrate their concern and respect for those they aim to enroll in a study. It also serves as the best means for those who do not wish to participate to protect themselves.[4]

Recommendations from our previous reports are reinforced in this report, which emphasizes the *process* of providing information and ensuring comprehension rather than the form of documentation of the decision to give consent. Both the information and the way it is conveyed—while meeting full disclosure requirements—must be tailored to meet the needs of the participants in the particular research context. In addition, documentation requirements must be adapted for varying research settings, and the criteria for deciding when informed consent is not necessary must be clarified so that participants' rights and welfare are not endangered.

The decision to participate in research must not only be informed; it must be voluntary. Even when risks are reasonable and informed consent is obtained, it may nonetheless be wrong to solicit certain people as participants. Those who are not fully capable of resisting the request to become participants—such as prisoners and other institutionalized or otherwise

vulnerable persons—should not be enrolled in studies merely because they are easily accessible or convenient. This historic emphasis on protecting people from being exploited as research participants, however, has failed to anticipate a time when, at least for some areas of medical research, people would be demanding to be included in certain studies because they might provide the only opportunity for receiving medical care for life-threatening diseases.

MAKING RESEARCH INCLUSIVE WHILE PROTECTING INDIVIDUALS AND CATEGORIZED AS VULNERABLE

Vulnerable individuals need additional protection in research. Although certain individuals and populations are more vulnerable as human participants than others, people whose circumstances render them vulnerable should not be arbitrarily excluded from research for this reason alone. This includes those viewed as more open to harm (e.g., children), more subject to coercion (e.g., institutionalized persons), more "complicated" (e.g., women, who are considered more biologically complicated than men), or more inconvenient (e.g., women with small children, who are viewed as less reliable research participants due to conflicting demands on time). Calling competent people intrinsically "vulnerable" can be both insulting and misleading. It is not their gender or other group designation that exposes them to injury or coercion, but rather their situation that can be exploited by ethically unacceptable research. That is, it is their circumstances, which are situational, that create the vulnerability. At other times it is the intrinsic characteristics of the person—for example, children or those with certain mental or developmental disorders—that make them generally vulnerable in the research setting.

The response, whenever possible, should not be to exclude people from research, but instead to change the research design so that it does not create situations in which people are unnecessarily harmed. To do otherwise is to risk developing knowledge that helps only a subset of the population. To the extent that the results are not generalizable, the potential societal benefits that justify doing the research are attenuated. *Research participants must be treated equally and with respect. Whenever possible, research should be designed to encourage the participation of all groups while protecting their rights and welfare.*

To accomplish this, we recommend that rather than focusing primarily on categorizing groups as vulnerable, investigators and IRBs should also recognize and avoid situations that create susceptibility to harm or coercion. Such situations may be as varied as patients being recruited by their own physicians; sick and desperate patients seeking enrollment in clinical trials; participants being recruited by those who teach or employ them; or studies involving participants with any characteristic that may make them less likely to receive care and respect from others (e.g., convicted criminals or intravenous drug users). In these circumstances, rather than excluding whole groups of people, researchers should design studies that reduce the risk of exploitation, whether by using a different method of recruitment, by using a recruiter who shares the participants' characteristics, or by some other technique. This is not always easy. It requires researchers to consider carefully their research design and the potential pool of participants. At times, it will mean anticipating that otherwise seemingly benign situations may become more complex because a particular participant or group of participants will be unusually susceptible to harm or manipulation. At other times, the nature of the vulnerability may require using a different research design. Ethical research does not avoid complexity. Rather, it acknowledges the full range and realities of the human condition.

COMPENSATING FOR HARMS

Despite all these precautions, however, some research participants might be harmed. *Participants who are harmed as a direct result of research should be cared for and compensated.* This is simple justice. The fact that they offered to participate in no way alters the view that mere decency calls for us to take care of these volunteers. Unfortunately, this is a greater challenge than it might appear. For those who endure harm while participating in research, it is often very difficult to separate injuries traceable to the research from those that stem from the underlying disease or social condition being studied. For others, appropriate care and compensation would be far beyond the means of the researchers, their sponsors, and their institutions. Two decades ago, the President's Commission for the Study of Ethical Problems in Medicine and Biomedical and Behavioral Research called for pilot studies of compensation programs—a recommendation that was not pursued. It is time to reconsider the need for some type of compensation program and to explore the possible mechanisms that could be used were one to be adopted. Regardless of individual motives, research participants are providing a service for society, and justice requires that they be treated with great respect and receive appropriate care for any related injuries. It should always be remembered that it is a privilege for any researcher to involve human participants in his or her research.

ESTABLISHING A COMPREHENSIVE, EFFECTIVE, AND STREAMLINED SYSTEM

In the United States, government regulations, professional guidelines, and the general principles highlighted in the *Belmont Report* (1979) form the basis of the current system of protections. In the earliest stages of adoption, the federal regulations were fragmented and confusing. Even today, they apply to most—but not all—research funded or conducted by the federal government, but have inconsistent and sometimes no direct application to research funded or conducted by state governments, foundations, or industry. They apply to medical drugs and devices and vaccines approved for interstate sale, but not to some medical innovations that would remain wholly within state borders. And they apply to other research only when the investigators and their institutions volunteer to abide by the rules.

A comprehensive and effective oversight system is essential to uniformly protect the rights and welfare of participants while permitting ethically and scientifically responsible research to proceed without undue delay. A fundamental flaw in the current oversight system is the ethically indefensible difference in the protection afforded participants in federally sponsored research and those in privately sponsored research that falls outside the jurisdiction of the Food and Drug Administration. As a result, people have been subjected to experimentation without their knowledge or informed consent in fields as diverse as plastic surgery, psychology, and infertility treatment. This is wrong. *Participants should be protected from avoidable harm, whether the research is publicly or privately financed.* We have repeated this assertion throughout our deliberations, and recommendations in this regard appear in four previous reports (NBAC 1997; NBAC 1999a; NBAC 1999b; NBAC 2001).

In this report, we recommend that the protections of an oversight system extend to the entire private sector for both domestic and international research. A credible, effective oversight system must apply to all research, and all people are entitled to the dignity that comes with freely and knowingly choosing whether to participate in research, as well as to protection from undue research risks. This is consistent with our 1997 resolution that no one should be enrolled in research absent the twin protections of independent review and voluntary informed consent.

Even when current protections apply, the interpretation of the federal regulations can vary unpredictably, depending on which federal agency oversees the research. Even the most basic, common elements of the federal rules took a decade to develop into regulations, because there was no single authority within the government to facilitate and demand cooperation and consistency. There still is no such single authority.[5] This has slowed the diffusion of basic protections and made it almost impossible to develop consistent interpretations of the basic protections or those relevant to especially problematic research, such as studies involving children or the decisionally impaired. Nor has there been a unified response to emerging areas of research, such as large-scale work on medical records and social science databases or on stored human biological materials.

Today's research protection system cannot react quickly to new developments. Efforts to develop rules for special situations, such as research on those who can no longer make decisions for themselves, have languished for decades in the face of bureaucratic hurdles, and there is no reason to believe that efforts to oversee other emerging research areas will be any more efficient. In addition, the current system leaves people vulnerable to new, virtually uncontrolled experimentation in emerging fields, such as some aspects of reproductive medicine and genetic research.

Indeed, some areas of research are not only uncontrolled, they are almost invisible. In an information age, poor management of research using medical records, human tissue, or personal interview data could lead to employment and insurance discrimination, social stigmatization, or even criminal prosecution.[6] The privacy and confidentiality concerns raised by this research are real, but the federal response has often been illusory. There is almost no guidance and certainly no coordination on these topics. The time has come to have a single source of guidance for these emerging areas, one that would be better positioned to effect change across all divisions of the government and private sector, as well as to facilitate development of specialized review bodies, as needed.

In this report *we propose a new independent oversight office that would have clear authority over all other segments of the federal government and extend protections to the entire private sector for both domestic and international research.* A single office would decide how to introduce consistency or reforms, and only that office would develop mechanisms to provide specialized review when needed. We recognize the challenges to such a proposal. For example, an independent office might lack the political support accorded an existing cabinet-level department. Although assigning one department, such as the Department of Health and Human Services, the role of "first among equals" would allow it to advocate forcefully for uniform rules across the government, without special provisions it would not have the authority to require other departments to comply, nor is it certain to escape the temptation to develop rules premised on a traditional, biomedical model rather than the wider range of research to be covered.

Federal research protections should be uniform across all government agencies, academe, and the private sector, but they should be flexible enough to be applied in widely different research settings or to emerging areas of research. Furthermore, any central coordinating body should be open to public input, have significant political or legal authority over research involving human participants—whether in the public or private sector—and have the support of the executive and legislative branches of government.

EDUCATION AS THE KEY TO PROMOTING LOCAL RESPONSIBILITY

Currently, federal protections depend on a decentralized oversight system involving IRBs, institutions, investigators, sponsors, and participants. We endorse the spirit and intent of this approach, specifically its contention that *the ethical obligation to protect participants lies first with researchers, their sponsors, and the IRBs that review their research.* Protecting research participants is a duty that researchers, research institutions, and sponsors cannot delegate completely to others or to the government. In addition, merely adhering to a set of rules and regulations does not fulfill this duty. Rather, it is accomplished by acting within a culture of concern and respect for research participants.

It is unrealistic to think that ethical obligations can be fully met without guidance and resources. *To help researchers and IRBs fulfill their responsibilities, the federal government should promote the development of education, certification, and accreditation systems that apply to all researchers, all IRB members and staff, and all institutions.* These tools should help researchers craft and IRBs review studies that pose few problems and to know when their work requires special oversight. Today, investigators and IRBs are rightly confused over issues as basic as which areas of inquiry should be reviewed and who constitutes a human participant.

Education is the foundation of the oversight system and is essential to protecting research participants. In all of our reports, we have highlighted the need to educate all those involved in research with human participants, including the public, investigators, IRB members, institutions, and federal agencies. In *Cloning Human Beings* (1997), we recommended federal support of public education in biomedical sciences that increasingly affect our cultural values. In *Research Involving Persons with Mental Disorders That May Affect Decisionmaking Capacity* (1998), we called for practice guidelines and ethics education on special concerns regarding this population. In *Ethical and Policy Issues in International Research: Clinical Trials in Developing Countries* (2001), we recommended measures to help developing countries build their capacity for designing and conducting clinical trials, for reviewing the ethics and science of proposed research, and for using research results after a trial is completed.

In this report, we again acknowledge the inadequacy of educational programs on research ethics in the United States. This deficiency begins at the highest level within the federal oversight system and extends to the local level at individual institutions. We recommend that investigators and IRB members and staff successfully complete educational programs on research ethics and become certified before they perform or review research, that research ethics be taught to the next generation of scientists, and that research ethics be included in continuing education programs.

CLARIFYING THE SCOPE OF OVERSIGHT

Many areas of scientific inquiry are "research," and many of these involve human participants, but only some need federal oversight, while others might be better regulated through professional ethics, social custom, or other state and federal law. For example, certain types of surveys and interviews are considered research, but they can be well managed to avoid harms without federal oversight, as the risks are few and participants are well situated to decide for themselves whether to participate. On the other hand, certain studies of medical records, databases, and discarded surgical tissue are often perceived as something other than human research, even when the information

retrieved is traceable to an identifiable person. Such research does need oversight to avoid putting people at risk of identity disclosure or discrimination without their knowledge. *Federal policies should clearly identify the kinds of research that are subject to review and the types of research participants to whom protections should apply.* When research poses significant risks or when its risks are imposed on participants without their knowledge, it clearly requires oversight. However, meaningless or overly rigid oversight engenders disdain on the part of researchers, creates an impossible and pointless workload for IRBs, and deters ethically sound research from going forward.

ENSURING THAT THE LEVEL OF REVIEW CORRESPONDS TO THE LEVEL OF RISK

Even within areas of research that need oversight, many individual studies will involve little or no risk to participants. Although current federal policies allow for some distinction between research involving minimal risk and research involving more than minimal risk, the distinction operates mostly in terms of how the research will be reviewed—that is, how procedures are to be followed. But the distinction should be based on how the research is pursued, how the participants are treated, and how the work is monitored over time. Overall, the emphasis should be on knowing how to protect participants rather than on knowing how to navigate research regulations. Instead of focusing so much on the period during which a research design is reviewed, oversight should also include an ongoing system of education and certification that helps researchers to anticipate and minimize research risks. Oversight should also make it easier for researchers to collaborate with their colleagues here and abroad without the burden of redundant reviews. *Research review and monitoring should be intensified as the risk and complexity of the research increase and at all times should emphasize protecting participants rather than following rigid rules. In addition, the review process should facilitate rather than hinder collaborative research among institutions and across national boundaries, provided that participants are protected.*

PROVIDING RESOURCES FOR THE OVERSIGHT SYSTEM

Creating a system that protects the rights and welfare of participants and facilitates responsible research demands political and financial support from the federal government as well as the presence of a central coordinating body to provide guidance and oversee education and accreditation efforts. *The oversight system should be adequately funded at all levels to ensure that research continues in a manner that demonstrates respect and concern for the interests of research participants.*

CONCLUSIONS

The current system for protecting human participants in research is in need of reform. It does not protect all research participants, and where protection is offered, it is often burdened by excessive bureaucracy, confusing or conflicting interpretations of rules, and an inability to respond to emerging areas of research. We recommend that a new oversight system be adopted that is led by a responsive and authoritative federal office, that emphasizes researcher education and research design as the primary means to protect participants, and that encourages responsible research while protecting all research participants.

NOTES

1. For example, the Office for Human Research Protections is implementing a new process by which institutions assure future compliance with human participant protections. The Institute of Medicine has recently issued a report on accreditation standards for IRBs (IOM 2001). Public Responsibility in Medicine and Research has established training programs and has co-founded a new organization, the Association for the Accreditation of Human Research Protection Programs.

2. To date, NBAC has issued five reports: *Cloning Human Beings* (NBAC 1997), *Research Involving Persons with Mental Disorders That May Affect Decisionmaking Capacity* (NBAC 1998), *Ethical Issues in Human Stem Cell Research* (NBAC 1999a), *Research Involving Human Biological Materials: Ethical Issues and Policy Guidance* (NBAC 1999b), and *Ethical and Policy Issues in International Research: Clinical Trials in Developing Countries* (NBAC 2001).

3. *United States* v. *Karl Brandt* et al., Trials of War Criminals Before the Nuremberg Military Tribunals Under Control Council Law 10. Nuremberg, October 1946–April 1949. Volumes I–II. Washington, D.C.: U.S. Government Printing Office.

4. There are, of course, some circumstances in which consent cannot be obtained and in which an overly rigid adherence to this principle would preclude research that is either benign or potentially needed by the participant him- or herself. Thus, NBAC endorses the current exceptions for research that is of minimal risk to participants and for potentially beneficial research in emergency

settings where no better alternative for the participants exists. NBAC also urges attention to emerging areas of record, database, and tissue bank research in which consent serves only as a sign of respect and in which alternative ways to respect participants do exist (NBAC 1999b; 21 CFR 50.24). In a previous report, the Commission made recommendations regarding persons who lack decisionmaking capacity and from whom informed consent cannot be obtained (NBAC 1998).

5. Porter, J., Testimony before NBAC. November 23, 1997. Bethesda, Maryland. See McCarthy, C.R., "Reflections on the Organizational Locus of the Office for Protection from Research Risks." This background paper was prepared for NBAC and is available in Volume II of this report.

6. See Goldman, J., and A. Choy, "Privacy and Confidentiality in Health Research" and Sieber, J., "Privacy and Confidentiality: As Related to Human Research in Social and Behavioral Science." These background papers were prepared for NBAC and are available in Volume II of this report. See also *Ferguson* v. *City of Charleston* 121 S. Ct. 1281. (2001).

REFERENCES

Beecher, H. K. 1966. "Ethics and Clinical Research." *New England Journal of Medicine* 274(24):1354–1360.

Faden, R. R., and T. L. Beauchamp. 1986. *A History and Theory of Informed Consent.* New York: Oxford University Press.

Institute of Medicine (IOM). 2001. *Preserving Public Trust: Accreditation and Human Research Participant Protection Programs.* Washington, D.C.: National Academy Press.

Jonas, H. 1969. "Philosophical Reflections on Experimenting with Human Subjects." *Daedalus* 98:219–247.

Jones, J. H. 1981. *Bad Blood: The Tuskegee Syphilis Experiment.* New York: The Free Press.

Katz, J. 1972. *Experimentation with Human Beings.* New York: Russell Sage Foundation.

National Bioethics Advisory Commission (NBAC). 1997. *Cloning Human Beings.* 2 vols. Rockville, MD: U.S. Government Printing Office.

———. 1998. *Research Involving Persons with Mental Disorders That May Affect Decisionmaking Capacity.* 2 vols. Rockville, MD: U.S. Government Printing Office.

———. 1999a. *Ethical Issues in Human Stem Cell Research.* 3 vols. Rockville, MD: U.S. Government Printing Office.

———. 1999b. *Research Involving Human Biological Materials: Ethical Issues and Policy Guidance.* 2 vols. Rockville, MD: U.S. Government Printing Office.

———. 2001. *Ethical and Policy Issues in International Research: Clinical Trials in Developing Countries.* 2 vols. Bethesda, MD: U.S. Government Printing Office.

National Commission for the Protection of Human Subjects of Biomedical and Behavioral Research (National Commission). 1979. *Belmont Report: Ethical Principles and Guidelines for the Protection of Human Subjects of Research.* Washington, D.C.: U.S. Government Printing Office.

Tuskegee Syphilis Study Ad Hoc Advisory Panel. 1973. *Final Report.* Washington, D.C.: U.S. Department of Health, Education, and Welfare.

Animal Research

DAVID DEGRAZIA

The Ethics of Animal Research: What Are the Prospects for Agreement?

David DeGrazia is Professor of Philosophy at George Washington University in Washington, DC. He is the author of *Human Identity and Bioethics; Animal Rights: A Very Short Introduction*; and *Taking Animals Seriously: Mental Life and Moral Status*. He is also coeditor of an anthology entitled *Biomedical Ethics* (6th ed., 2005). Professor DeGrazia's recent articles have focused on human embryo research, the common morality, personhood, and advance directives for health care.

Few human uses of nonhuman animals (hereafter simply "animals") have incited as much controversy as the use of animals in biomedical research. The political exchanges over this issue tend to produce much more heat than light, as representatives of both biomedicine and the animal protection community accuse opponents of being "Nazis," "terrorists," and the like. However, a healthy number of individuals within these two communities offer the possibility of a more illuminating discussion of the ethics of animal research.

One such individual is Henry Spira. Spira almost single-handedly convinced Avon, Revlon, and other major cosmetics companies to invest in the search for alternatives to animal testing. Largely due to his tactful but persistent engagement with these companies—and to their willingness to change—many consumers today look for such labels as "not tested on animals" and "cruelty free" on cosmetics they would like to buy.

Inspired by Spira, this paper seeks common ground between the positions of biomedicine and animal advocates. (The term "biomedicine" here refers to everyone who works in medicine or the life sciences, not just those conducting animal research. "Animal advocates" and "animal protection community" refer to those individuals who take a major interest in protecting the

interests of animals and who believe that much current usage of animals is morally unjustified. The terms are not restricted to animal activists, because some individuals meet this definition without being politically active in seeking changes.) The paper begins with some background on the political and ethical debate over animal research. It then identifies important points of potential agreement between biomedicine and animal advocates; much of this common ground can be missed due to distraction by the fireworks of the current political exchange. Next, the paper enumerates issues on which continuing disagreement is likely. Finally, it concludes with concrete suggestions for building positively on the common ground.

BACKGROUND ON THE DEBATE OVER ANIMAL RESEARCH

What is the current state of the debate over the ethics of animal research? Let us begin with the viewpoint of biomedicine. It seems fair to say that biomedicine has a "party line" on the ethics of animal research, conformity to which may feel like a political litmus test for full acceptability within the professional community. According to this party line, animal research is clearly justified because it is necessary for medical progress and therefore human health—and those who disagree are irrational, antiscience, misanthropic "extremists" whose views do not deserve serious attention. (Needless

From *Cambridge Quarterly of Healthcare Ethics* 8 (1999), 23–34. Copyright © 1999 Cambridge University Press. Reprinted with permission.

to say, despite considerable conformity, not everyone in biomedicine accepts this position.)

In at least some countries, biomedicine's leadership apparently values conformity to this party line more than freedom of thought and expression on the animal research issue. (In this paragraph, I will refer to the American situation to illustrate the point.) Hence the unwillingness of major medical journals, such as *JAMA* and *The New England Journal of Medicine*, to publish articles that are highly critical of animal research. Hence also the extraordinary similarity I have noticed in pro-research lectures by representatives of biomedicine. I used to be puzzled about why these lectures sounded so similar and why, for example, they consistently made some of the same philosophical and conceptual errors (such as dichotomizing animal welfare and animal rights, and taking the latter concept to imply identical rights for humans and animals). But that was before I learned of the "AMA [American Medical Association] Animal Research Action Plan" and the AMA's "White Paper." Promoting an aggressive pro-research campaign, these documents encourage AMA members to say and do certain things for public relations purposes, including the following: "Identify animal rights activists as anti-science and against medical progress"; "Combat emotion with emotion (eg [sic], 'fuzzy' animals contrasted with 'healing' children)"; and "Position the biomedical community as moderate—centrist—in the controversy, not as a polar opposite."[1]

It is a reasonable conjecture that biomedicine's party line was developed largely in reaction to fear—both of the most intimidating actions of some especially zealous animal advocates, such as telephoned threats and destruction of property, and of growing societal concern about animals. Unfortunately, biomedicine's reaction has created a political culture in which many or most animal researchers and their supporters do not engage in sustained, critical thinking about the moral status of animals and the basic justification (or lack thereof) for animal research. Few seem to recognize that there is significant merit to the opposing position, fewer have had any rigorous training in ethical reasoning, and hardly any have read much of the leading literature on animal ethics. The stultifying effect of this cultural phenomenon hit home with me at a small meeting of representatives of biomedicine, in which I had been invited to explain "the animal rights philosophy" (the invitation itself being exceptional and encour-

aging). After the talk, in which I presented ideas familiar to all who really know the literature and issues of animal ethics, several attendees pumped my hand and said something to this effect: "This is the first time I have heard such rational and lucid arguments for the other side. I didn't know there were any."

As for the animal protection community, there does not seem to be a shared viewpoint except at a very general level: significant interest in animal welfare and the belief that much current animal usage is unjustified. Beyond that, differences abound. For example, the Humane Society of the United States opposes factory farming but not humane forms of animal husbandry, rejects current levels of animal use in research but not animal research itself, and condemns most zoo exhibits but not those that adequately meet animals' needs and approximate their natural habitats.[2] Meanwhile, the Animal Liberation Front, a clandestine British organization, apparently opposes all animal husbandry, animal research, and the keeping of zoo animals.[3] Although there are extensive differences within the animal protection community, as far as our paper topic goes, it seems fair to say that almost everyone in this group opposes current levels of animal research.

That's a brief sketch of the perspectives of biomedicine and animal advocates on the issue of animal research. What about the state of animal ethics itself? The leading book-length works in this field exhibit a near consensus that the status quo of animal usage is ethically indefensible and that at least significant reductions in animal research are justified. Let me elaborate.

Defending strong animal rights positions in different ways, Tom Regan and Evelyn Pluhar advocate abolition of all research that involves harming animals.[4] Ray Frey and Peter Singer, by contrast, hold the use of animals to the very stringent utilitarian standard—accepting only those experiments whose benefits (factoring in the likelihood of achieving them) are expected to outweigh the harms and costs involved—where the interests of animal subjects (e.g., to avoid suffering) are given the same moral weight that we give comparable human interests.[5]

Without commiting either to a strong animal rights view or to utilitarianism, my own view shares with these theories the framework of equal consideration for animals: the principle that we must give equal moral weight to comparable interests, no matter who has those interests.[6] But unlike the aforementioned philosophers, I believe that the arguments for and against equal consideration are nearly equal in strength. I therefore have respect for progressive views that attribute moral standing to animals without giving them fully equal consideration. The unequal consideration view that I find most plausible gives moral weight to animals' comparable interests in accordance with the animals' cognitive, affective, and social complexity—a progressive, "sliding scale" view. Since I acknowledge that I might be mistaken about equal consideration, my approach tracks the practical implications both of equal consideration and of the alternative just described.

Arguing from pluralistic frameworks, which are developed in different ways, Steve Sapontzis, Rosemary Rodd, and Bernard Rollin support relatively little animal research in comparison with current levels.[7] Drawing significantly from feminist insights, Mary Midgley presents a view whose implications seem somewhat more accepting of the status quo of animal research but still fairly progressive.[8] Of the leading contributors to animal ethics, the only one who embraces the status quo of animal research and does not attribute significant moral status to animals is Peter Carruthers.[9] (It is ironic that while biomedicine characterizes those who are critical of animal research as irrational "extremists," nearly all of the most in-depth, scholarly, and respected work in animal ethics supports such a critical standpoint at a general level.)

In discussing the prospects for agreement between biomedicine and animal advocates, I will ignore political posturing and consider only serious ethical reflection. In considering the two sides of this debate, I will assume that the discussants are morally serious, intellectually honest, reflective, and well informed both about the facts of animal research and about the range of arguments that come into play in animal ethics. I will not have in mind, then, the researcher who urges audiences to dismiss "the animal rights view" or the animal activist who tolerates no dissent from an abolitionist position. The two representative interlocutors I will imagine differ on the issue of animal research, but their views result from honest, disciplined, well-informed ethical reflection. Clearly, their voices are worth hearing.

POINTS ON WHICH THE BIOMEDICAL AND ANIMAL PROTECTION COMMUNITIES CAN AGREE

The optimistic thesis of this paper is that the biomedical and animal protection communities can agree on a fair number of important points, and that much can be done to build upon this common ground. I will number and highlight (in italics) each potential point of agreement and then justify its inclusion by explaining how both sides can agree to it, without abandoning their basic positions, and why they should.

1. The use of animals in biomedical research raises ethical issues. Today very few people would disagree with this modest claim, and any who would are clearly in the wrong.[10] Most animal research involves harming animal subjects, provoking ethical concerns, and the leading goal of animal research, promotion of human health, is itself ethically important; even the expenditure of taxpayers' money on government-funded animal research raises ethical issues about the best use of such money. Although a very modest assertion, this point of agreement is important because it legitimates a process that is sometimes resisted: *discussing* the ethics of animal research.

It is worth noting a less obvious claim that probably enjoys strong majority support but not consensus: that animals (at least sentient ones, as defined below) have moral status. To say animals have moral status is to say that their interests have moral importance independently of effects on human interests. ('Interests' may be thought of as components of well-being. For example, sentient animals have an interest in avoiding pain, distress, and suffering.) If animals have moral status, then to brutalize a horse is wrong because of the harm inflicted on the horse, not simply because the horse is someone's property (if that is so) or because animal lovers' feelings may be hurt (if any animal lovers find out about the abuse). The idea is that gratuitously harming the horse *wrongs the horse.* Although nearly every leader in animal ethics holds that animals have moral status—and though most people, on reflection, are likely to find this idea commonsensical—Carruthers argues that it is mistaken.[11]

2. Sentient animals, a class that probably includes at least the vertebrates, deserve moral protection. Whether because they have moral status or because needlessly harming them strongly offends many people's sensibilities, sentient animals deserve some measure of moral protection. By way of definition, sentient animals are animals endowed with any sorts of feelings: (conscious) sensations such as pain or emotional states such as fear or suffering. But which animals are sentient? Addressing this complex issue implicates both the natural sciences and the philosophy of mind. Lately, strong support has emerged for the proposition that at least vertebrate animals are very likely sentient.[12] This proposition is implicitly endorsed by major statements of principles regarding the humane use of research animals, which often mention that they apply to vertebrates.[13] (Hereafter, the unqualified term "animals" will refer to sentient animals in particular.)

3. Many animals (at the very least, mammals) are capable of having a wide variety of aversive mental states, including pain, distress (whose forms include discomfort, boredom, and fear), and suffering. In biomedical circles, there has been some resistance to attributing suffering to animals, so government documents concerned with humane use of animals have often mentioned only pain, distress, and discomfort.[14] Because "suffering" refers to a *highly* unpleasant mental state (whereas pain, distress, and discomfort can be mild and transient), the attribution of suffering to animals is morally significant. An indication that resistance may be weakening is the attribution of suffering to sentient animals in the National Aeronautics and Space Administration's "Principles for the Ethical Care and Use of Animals."[15] Whatever government documents may say, the combined empirical and philosophical case for attributing suffering to a wide range of animals is very strong.[16]

4. Animals' experiential well-being (quality of life) deserves protection. If the use of animals raises ethical issues, meaning that their interests matter morally, we confront the question of what interests animals have. This question raises controversial issues. For example, do animals have an interest in remaining alive (life interests)? That is, does death itself—as opposed to any unpleasantness experienced in dying—harm an animal? A test case would be a scenario in which a contented dog in good health is painlessly and unwittingly killed in her sleep: Is she harmed?

Another difficult issue is whether animal well-being can be understood *entirely* in terms of experiential well-being—quality of life in the familiar sense in which (other things equal) pleasure is better than pain, enjoyment better than suffering, satisfaction better than frustration. Or does the exercise of an animal's natural capacities count positively toward well-being, even if quality of life is not enhanced? A test case would be a scenario in which conditioning, a drug, or brain surgery removes a bird's instinct and desire to fly without lowering quality of life: Does the bird's transformation to a new, nonflying existence represent a harm?

Whatever the answers to these and other issues connected with animal well-being, what is not controversial is that animals have an interest in experiential well-being, a good quality of life. That is why animal researchers are normally expected to use anesthesia or analgesia where these agents can reduce or eliminate animal subjects' pain, distress, or suffering.

5. Humane care of highly social animals requires extensive access to conspecifics. It is increasingly appreciated that animals have different needs based on what sorts of creatures they are. Highly social animals, such as apes, monkeys, and wolves, need social interactions with conspecifics (members of their own species). Under normal circumstances, they will develop social structures, such as hierarchies and alliances, and maintain long-term relationships with conspecifics. Because they have a strong instinct to seek such interactions and relationships, depriving them of the opportunity to gratify this instinct harms these animals. For example, in some species, lack of appropriate social interactions impedes normal development. Moreover, social companions can buffer the effects of stressful situations, reduce behavioral abnormalities, provide opportunities for exercise, and increase cognitive stimulation.[17] Thus in the case of any highly social animals used in research, providing them extensive access to conspecifics is an extremely high moral priority.

6. Some animals deserve very strong protections (as, for example, chimpanzees deserve not to be killed for the purpose of population control). Biomedicine and animal advocates are likely to disagree on many details of ethically justified uses of animals in research, as we will see in the next section. Still, discussants can agree that there is an obligation to protect not just the experiential well-being, but also the lives, of at least some animals. This claim might be supported by the (controversial) thesis that such animals have life interests. On the other hand, it might be supported by the goal of species preservation (in the case of an endangered species), or by the recognition that routine killing of such animals when they are no longer useful for research would seriously disturb many people.[18]

Without agreeing on all the specific justifications, members of the National Research Council's Committee on Long-Term Care of Chimpanzees were able to agree (with one dissent) that chimps should not be killed for the purpose of population control, although they could be killed if suffering greatly with no alternative means of relief.[19] This recommended protection of chimps' lives is exceptional, because animal research policies generally state no presumption against killing animal subjects, requiring only that killings be as painless as possible.[20] Since this committee represents expert opinion in biomedicine, it seems correct to infer that biomedicine and the animal protection community can agree that at least chimpanzees should receive some very strong protections—of their lives and of certain other components of their well-being, such as their needs for social interaction, reasonable freedom of movement, and stimulating environments.[21]

7. *Alternatives should now be used whenever possible and research on alternatives should expand.* Those who are most strongly opposed to animal research hold that alternatives such as mathematical models, computer simulations, and in vitro biological systems should replace nearly all use of animals in research. (I say "nearly all" because, as discussed below, few would condemn animal research that does not harm its subjects.) Even for those who see the animal research enterprise more favorably, there are good reasons to take an active interest in alternatives. Sometimes an alternative method is the most valid way to approach a particular scientific question; often alternatives are cheaper.[22] Their potential for reducing animal pain, distress, and suffering is, of course, another good reason. Finally, biomedicine may enjoy stronger public support if it responds to growing social concern about animal welfare with a very serious investment in nonanimal methods. This means not just using alternatives wherever they are currently feasible, but also aggressively researching the possibilities for expanding the use of such methods.

8. *Promoting human health is an extremely important biomedical goal.* No morally serious person would deny the great importance of human health, so its status as a worthy goal seems beyond question. What is sometimes forgotten, however, is that a worthy goal does not automatically justify all the means thereto. Surely it would be unethical to force large numbers of humans to serve as subjects in highly painful, eventually lethal research, even if its goal were to promote human health. The controversy over animal research focuses not on the worthiness of its principal goal—promoting human health—but rather on the means, involving animal subjects, taken in pursuit of that goal.

9. *There are some morally significant differences between humans and other animals.* Many people in biomedicine are not aware that the views of animal advocates are consistent with this judgment. Indeed, some animal advocates might not realize that their views are consistent with this judgment! So let me identify a couple of ideas, to which all should agree, that support it.

First, the principle of respect for autonomy applies to competent adult human beings, but to very few if any animals. This principle respects the self-regarding decisions of individuals who are capable of autonomous decisionmaking and action. Conversely, it opposes paternalism toward such individuals, who have the capacity to decide for themselves what is in their interests. Now, many sentient beings, including human children and at least most nonhuman animals, are not autonomous in the relevant sense and so are not covered by this principle.[23] Thus it is often appropriate to limit their liberty in ways that promote their best interests, say, preventing the human child from drinking alcohol, or forcing a pet dog to undergo a vaccination. We might say that where there is no autonomy to respect, the principles of beneficence (promoting best interests) and respect for autonomy cannot conflict; where there is autonomy to respect, paternalism becomes morally problematic.

Second, even if sentient animals have an interest, others things equal, in staying alive (as I believe), the moral presumption against taking human life is stronger than the presumption against killing at least some animals. Consider fish, who are apparently sentient yet cognitively extremely primitive in comparison with humans. I have a hard time imagining even very committed animal advocates maintaining that killing a fish is as serious a matter as killing a human being. Leaders in animal ethics consistently support—though in interestingly different ways—the idea that, ordinarily, killing humans is worse than killing at least some animals who have moral status. (It is almost too obvious to mention that it's worse to kill humans than to kill animals, such as amoebas, that *lack* moral status.[24])

The only notable exception seems to be Sapontzis, who tries to undermine the major arguments proffered to support such comparative claims. But the comparisons he opposes always involve humans and other mammals or birds.[25] The farther one goes down the phylogenetic scale, the more incredible it becomes to hold that it is equally prima facie wrong to kill humans and to kill other animals. At the very least, someone like Sapontzis will have to admit that killing humans tends to be worse than killing fish in that (1) humans tend to live much longer, so that untimely death generally robs them of more good years, and (2) untimely human death causes deep social sorrow and anguish to others in a way that is not paralleled in the fish world. So I believe that the comparative judgment I have made is well justified and embraceable by all parties to the present debate. There may be other morally interesting differences to which all should agree,[26] but these examples will suffice for present purposes.

10. Some animal research is justified. Many animal advocates would say that they disagree with this statement. But I'm not sure they do. Or, if they really do, they shouldn't. Let me explain by responding to the three likeliest reasons some animal advocates might take exception to the claim.

First, one might oppose all uses of animals that involve *harming them for the benefit of others* (even other animals)—as a matter of absolute principle—and overlook the fact that some animal research does not harm animal subjects at all. Although such nonharmful research represents a tiny sliver of the animal research enterprise, it exists. Examples are certain observational studies of animals in their natural habitats, some ape language studies, and possibly certain behavioral studies of other species that take place in laboratories but do not cause pain, distress, or suffering to the subjects. And if nonsentient animals cannot be harmed (in any morally relevant sense), as I would argue, then any research involving such animals falls under the penumbra of nonharming research.

Moreover, there is arguably no good reason to oppose research that imposes only *minimal* risk or harm on its animal subjects. After all, minimal risk research on certain human subjects who, like animals, cannot consent (namely, children) is permitted in many countries; in my view, this policy is justified. Such research might involve a minuscule likelihood of significant harm or the certainty of a slight, transient harm, such as the discomfort of having a blood sample taken.

Second, one might oppose all animal research because one believes that none of it actually benefits human beings. Due to physical differences between species, the argument goes, what happens to animal subjects when they undergo some biomedical intervention does not justify inferences about what will happen to humans who undergo that intervention. Furthermore, new drugs, therapies, and techniques must always be tried on human subjects before they

can be accepted for clinical practice. Rather than tormenting animals in research, the argument continues, we should drop the useless animal models and proceed straight to human trials (with appropriate protections for human subjects, including requirements for informed or proxy consent).

Although I believe a considerable amount of current animal research has almost no chance of benefiting humans,[27] I find it very hard to believe that no animal research does. While it is true that human subjects must eventually be experimented on, evidence suggests that animal models sometimes furnish data relevant to human health.[28] If so, then the use of animal subjects can often decrease the risk to human subjects who are eventually involved in experiments that advance biomedicine, by helping to weed out harmful interventions. This by itself does not justify animal research, only the claim that it sometimes benefits humans (at the very least human subjects themselves and arguably the beneficiaries of biomedical advances as well).

Note that even if animal research never benefited humans, it would presumably sometimes benefit conspecifics of the animals tested, in sound veterinary research.[29] It can't be seriously argued that animal models provide no useful information about animals! Moreover, in successful *therapeutic* research (which aims to benefit the subjects themselves), certain animals benefit directly from research and are not simply used to benefit other animals. For that reason, blanket opposition to animal research, including the most promising therapeutic research in veterinary medicine, strikes me as almost unintelligible.

Almost unintelligible, but not quite, bringing us to the third possible reason for opposing all animal research. It might be argued that, whether or not it harms its subjects, all animal research involves *using animals (without their consent) for other's benefit*, since—qua research—it seeks *generalizable knowledge.* But to use animals in this way reduces them to *tools* (objects to be used), thereby *disrespecting* the animals.

Now the idea that we may never use nonconsenting individuals, even in benign ways, solely for the benefit of others strikes me as an implausibly strict ethical principle. But never mind. The fact that some veterinary research is intended to benefit the subjects themselves (as well as other animals or humans down the road) where no other way to help them is known shows that such research, on any reasonable view, is *not* disrespectful toward its subjects. Indeed, in such cases, the animals *would* consent to taking part, if they could, because taking part is in their interests. I fully grant that therapeutic veterinary research represents a minuscule portion of the animal research conducted today. But my arguments are put forward in the service of a goal that I think I have now achieved: demonstrating, beyond a shadow of a doubt, that some animal research is justified.

If animal advocates and representatives of biomedicine were aware of these ten points of potential agreement, they might perceive their opponents' views as less alien than they had previously taken them to be. This change in perception might, in turn, convince all parties that honest, open discussion of outstanding issues has a decent chance of repaying the effort.

POINTS ON WHICH AGREEMENT BETWEEN THE TWO SIDES IS UNLIKELY

Even if biomedicine and the animal protection community approach the animal research issue in good faith, become properly informed about animal ethics and the facts of research, and so forth, they are still likely to disagree on certain important issues. After all, their basic views differ. It may be worthwhile to enumerate several likely points of difference.

First, disagreement is likely on the issue of *the moral status of animals in comparison with humans.* While representatives of biomedicine may attribute moral status to animals, they hold that animals may justifiably be used in many experiments (most of which are nontherapeutic and harm the subjects) whose primary goal is to promote human health. But for animal advocates, it is not at all obvious that much animal research is justified. This suggests that animal advocates ascribe higher moral status to animals than biomedicine does.[30]

Second, disagreement is likely to continue on the issue of *the specific circumstances in which the worthy goal of promoting human health justifies harming animals.* Biomedicine generally tries to protect the status quo of animal research. Animal advocates generally treat not using animals in research as a presumption, any departures from which would require careful justification. Clearly, animal advocates will have many disagreements with biomedicine over when it is appropriate to conduct animal research.

Third, in a similar vein, continuing disagreement is likely on the issue of *whether current protections for research animals are more or less adequate.* Biomedicine would probably answer affirmatively, with relatively minor internal disagreements over specific issues (e.g., whether apes should ever be exposed to dis-

eases in order to test vaccines). Animal advocates will tend to be much more critical of current protections for research animals. They will argue, for example, that animals are far too often made to suffer in pursuit of less than compelling objectives, such as learning about behavioral responses to stress or trauma.

In the United States, critics will argue that the basic principles that are supposed to guide the care and use of animals in federally funded research ultimately provide very weak protection for research animals. That is because the tenth and final principle begins with implicit permission to make exceptions to the previous nine: "Where exceptions are required in relation to the provisions of these Principles. . . ."[31] Since no limits are placed on permissible exceptions, this final principle precludes any absolute restraints on the harm that may be inflicted on research animals—an indefensible lack of safeguards from the perspective of animal advocates. (Although similar in several ways to these American principles, including some ways animal advocates would criticize, the International Guiding Principles for Biomedical Research Involving Animals avoids this pitfall of a global loophole. One of its relatively strong protections is Principle V: "Investigators and other personnel should never fail to treat animals as sentient, and should regard their proper care and use and the avoidance or minimization of discomfort, distress, or pain as ethical imperatives."[32])

Although protections of research animals are commonly thought of in terms of preventing unnecessary pain, distress, and suffering, they may also be thought of in terms of protecting animal life. A fourth likely area of disagreement concerns *whether animal life is morally protectable.* Return to a question raised earlier: whether a contented animal in good health is harmed by being painlessly killed in her sleep. Since government documents for the care and use of research animals generally require justification for causing pain or distress to animal subjects, but no justification for painless killing, it seems fair to infer that biomedicine generally does not attribute life interests to animals. Although I lack concrete evidence, I would guess that most animal advocates would see the matter quite differently, and would regard the killing of animals as a serious moral matter even if it is justified in some circumstances.

The four issues identified here as probable continuing points of difference are not intended to comprise an exhaustive list. But they show that despite the fact that the biomedical and animal protection communities can agree on an impressive range of major points, given their basic orientations they cannot be expected to agree on every fundamental question. Few will find this assertion surprising. But I also suggest, less obviously, that even if both sides cannot be entirely right in their positions, differences that remain after positions are refined through honest, open-minded, fully educated inquiry can be reasonable differences.

WHAT CAN BE DONE NOW TO BUILD UPON THE POINTS OF AGREEMENT

Let me close with a series of suggestions offered in the constructive yet critical-minded spirit of Henry Spira's work for how to build on the points of agreement identified above. For reasons of space, these suggestions will be stated somewhat tersely and without elaboration.

First, biomedical organizations and leaders in the profession can do the following: openly acknowledge that ethical issues involving animals are complex and important; educate themselves or acquire education about the ethical issues; tolerate views departing from the current party line; open up journals to more than one basic viewpoint; and stop disseminating one-sided propaganda.

Second, the more "militant" animal advocates can acknowledge that there can be reasonable disagreement on some of the relevant issues and stop intimidating people with whom they disagree.

Third, biomedicine can openly acknowledge, as NASA recently did in its principles, that animals can suffer and invite more serious consideration of animal suffering.

Fourth, the animal protection community can give credit to biomedicine where credit is due—for example, for efforts to minimize pain and distress, to improve housing conditions, and to refrain from killing old chimpanzees who are no longer useful for research but are expensive to maintain.

Fifth, animal researchers and members of animal protection organizations can be required by their organizations to take courses in ethical theory or animal ethics to promote knowledgeable, skilled, broad-minded discussion and reflection.

Sixth, the animal protection community can openly acknowledge that some animal research is justified (perhaps giving examples to reduce the potential for misunderstanding).

Seventh, more animal research ethics committees can bring aboard at least one dedicated animal advocate who (unlike mainstream American veterinarians) seriously questions the value of most animal research.

Eighth, conditions of housing for research animals can be improved—for example, with greater enrichment and, for social animals, more access to conspecifics.

Ninth, all parties can endorse and support the goal of finding ways to *eliminate* animal subjects' pain, distress, and suffering.[33]

Tenth, and finally, governments can invest much more than they have to date in the development and use of alternatives to animal research, and all parties can give strong public support to the pursuit of alternatives.

NOTES

1. American Medical Association. Animal Research Action Plan. (June 1989), p.6. See also American Medical Association. White Paper (1988).

2. See the Humane Society of the United States (HSUS). *Farm Animals and Intensive Confinement.* Washington, D.C.: HSUS, 1994; *Animals in Biomedical Research.* Washington, D.C.: HSUS, revised 1989; and *Zoos: Information Packet.* Washington, D.C.: HSUS, 1995.

3. Animal Liberation Front. Animal Liberation Frontline Information Service: the A.L.F. Primer. (website)

4. Regan T. *The Case for Animal Rights.* Berkeley: University of California Press, 1983; Pluhar E. *Beyond Prejudice.* Durham, North Carolina: Duke University Press, 1995.

5. Frey R. G. *Interests and Rights.* Oxford: Clarendon, 1980; Singer P. *Animal Liberation*, 2d ed. New York: New York Review of Books, 1990.

6. DeGrazia D. *Taking Animals Seriously.* Cambridge: Cambridge University Press, 1996.

7. Sapontzis S. F. *Morals, Reason, and Animals.* Philadelphia: Temple University Press, 1987; Rodd R. *Biology, Ethics, and Animals.* Oxford: Clarendon, 1990; and Rollin B. E. *Animal Rights and Human Morality*, 2d ed. Buffalo, New York: Prometheus, 1992.

8. Midgley M. *Animals and Why They Matter.* Athens, Georgia: University of Georgia Press, 1983.

9. Carruthers P. *The Animals Issue.* Cambridge: Cambridge University Press, 1992.

10. In a letter to the editor, Robert White, a neurosurgeon well known for transplanting monkeys' heads, asserted that "[a]nimal usage is not a moral or ethical issue . . ." (White R. Animal ethics? [letter]. *Hastings Center Report* 1990;20(6):43). For a rebuttal to White, see my letter, *Hastings Center Report* 1991;21(5):45.

11. See note 9, Carruthers 1992. For an attempt to undermine Carruthers' arguments, see note 6, DeGrazia 1996:53–6.

12. See Rose M., Adams D. Evidence for pain and suffering in other animals. In: Langley G., ed. *Animal Experimentation.* New York: Chapman and Hall, 1989:42–71; Smith J. A., Boyd K. M. *Lives in the Balance.* Oxford: Oxford University Press, 1991: ch. 4. See also note 7 Rodd 1990: ch. 3; and DeGrazia D., Rowan A. Pain, suffering, and anxiety in animals and humans. *Theoretical Medicine* 1991;12:193–211.

13. See, e.g., U.S. Government Principles for the Utilization and Care of Vertebrate Animals Used in Testing, Research, and Training. In: National Research Council. *Guide for the Care and*

Use of Laboratory Animals. Washington, D.C.: National Academy Press, 1996:117–8; National Aeronautics and Space Administration. *Principles for the Ethical Care and Use of Animals.* NASA Policy Directive 8910.1, effective 23 March 1998; and Council for International Organizations of Medical Sciences. *International Guiding Principles for Biomedical Research Involving Animals.* Geneva: CIOMS, 1985:18.

14. See note 13, National Research Council 1996; CIOMS 1985.

15. See note 13, NASA 1998.

16. See note 12, Rose, Adams 1989; DeGrazia, Rowan 1991. And see note 7, Rodd 1990: ch. 3. There is also much evidence that at least mammals can experience anxiety. (See note 12, DeGrazia, Rowan 1991; note 12, Smith, Boyd 1991: ch. 4.)

17. See note 13, National Research Council 1996:37.

18. Note that the term "euthanasia," which means a death that is good for the one who dies, is inappropriate when animals are killed because they are costly to maintain or for similarly human-regarding reasons.

19. National Research Council Committee on Long-Term Care of Chimpanzees. *Chimpanzees in Research.* Washington, D.C.: National Academy Press, 1997:38.

20. Such policies typically state that animals who would otherwise experience severe or chronic pain or distress should be painlessly killed. See, e.g., note 13, National Research Council 1996:117; CIOMS 1985:19; and [British] Home Office. *Home Office Guidance on the Operation of the Animals [Scientific Procedures] Act 1986.* London: Home Office, 1986. Although this directive addresses what to do with animals who could survive only in agony, it does not state any presumption against killing animals who could live well following research.

21. The committee addresses these chimpanzee interests in note 19, National Research Council 1997:ch. 3.

22. See note 12, Smith, Boyd 1991:334.

23. See note 6, DeGrazia 1996:204–10.

24. Admittedly, some unusual individuals would claim that amoebas have moral status, either because they think amoebas are sentient or because they think that sentience is unnecessary for moral status. I know of no one, however, who would claim that killing amoebas is as serious a matter as killing humans.

25. See note 7, Sapontzis 1987:216–22.

26. For example, if I am right, just as the moral presumption against taking life can differ in strength across species, so can the presumption against confining members of different species (the interest at stake being freedom). See note 6, DeGrazia 1996:254–6.

27. That is, except those humans who benefit directly from the conduct of research, such as researchers and people who sell animals and laboratory equipment.

28. See, e.g., note 12, Smith, Boyd 1991: ch. 3.

29. Peter Singer reminded me of this important point.

30. The idea of differences of moral status can be left intuitive here. Any effort to make it more precise will invite controversy. (See note 6, DeGrazia 1996:256–7.)

31. See note 13, National Research Council 1996:118.

32. See note 13, CIOMS 1985:18.

33. This is the stated goal of a new initiative of the Humane Society of the United States, which expects the initiative to expand to Humane Society International.

R . G . F R E Y

Animals

Raymond G. Frey is Professor of Philosophy at Bowling Green State University in Bowling Green, Ohio. In 1983 he published *Rights, Killing, and Suffering: Moral Vegetarianism and Applied Ethics.* Professor Frey has coedited *A Companion to Applied Ethics; Euthanasia and Physician-Assisted Suicide; The Works of Joseph Butler; Violence, Terrorism, and Justice;* and *Utility and Rights.* He has also published numerous articles on applied ethics and social and political theory.

• • •

[1.] THREE POSITIONS ON EXPERIMENTATION

We can distinguish (at least) three positions on animal experimentation, though there are permutations on each.

From *The Oxford Handbook of Practical Ethics* edited by Hugh La Follette (New York: Oxford University Press, 2003), pp. 166–87. Reprinted by permission of the author and publisher. Section numbers modified.

[1.1] ABOLITIONISM

There are two different types of view to be distinguished here. First, there is immediate abolitionism, to the effect that any and all animal experimentation should cease at once, no matter what the experiment or how promising it may be so far as human benefit is concerned or how far it has progressed. If something is wrong, it should be stopped. Tom Regan (1983) takes this position. Secondly, there is progressive abolitionism, of the sort advocated by FRAME (see Balls et al. 1983), in which animal experiments are eliminated as replacements become available by which to do the research in question. Sometimes, Regan (1997) has been ambivalent between these positions, but I see no reason why he should be. If he thinks it is wrong to experiment upon animals, then what permits us to continue to experiment upon them until we find replacements? In fact, an abolitionist who holds the progressive form can be accused by immediate abolitionists of having truck with evil. After all, it might be urged, who would accept the progressive closure of a concentration camp? Yet, in most public discussion, it is the progressive variety of abolitionism that is presented: as we develop alternative methods of obtaining the results or benefits of medical research, we can progressively shift away from the use of animals. But that is something that even defenders of experimentation can—and should—hold. As alternative methods become available, it becomes immoral to continue to use animals to obtain results that could be obtained by non-animal means.

The progressive form is preferred, of course, because the immediate form of abolitionism is too extreme: the removal of illnesses, the dramatic enhancement of human quality of life, and the extension of human life are clear benefits for most of us and so held to be worth having, even at the cost of animal lives. . . .

[1.2] ANYTHING GOES

If immediate abolitionism is too extreme for most people, so, too, is the "anything-goes" position. Here, the claim would be that we can do anything we please to research animals. If this position were ever in vogue, it clearly is no longer. Thus, very few people today would claim that animals do not feel pain, and those who might be so tempted, as Peter Carruthers (1992) is thought to be, usually go on at once to qualify the sense in which they might be understood to intend such a claim. Certainly medical people give every evidence of believing exactly the opposite. Hospital and research facilities have ethics review committees that oversee the institutional use and care of animals, and they have in place guidelines governing the infliction of pain and suffering upon animals. Medical periodicals have peer review policies that ask about what was done to animals in the course of research and about what in the

experiment justifies the infliction of pain and suffering. Guidelines demand that animal suffering be controlled, limited mitigated where feasible, and justified in the course of research, and where these guidelines are ignored or violated, government and institutional oversight committees can deny further funding for the research and so effectively terminate it. Of course, none of this denies that animals can be used and, at times, painfully, but the "anything-goes" position, in which the infliction of pain is viewed as uncontrolled and in which the value of animal life is held to be negligible or non-existent, can again seem too extreme.

Today, of course, the three-R approach, associated with the names of W. M. S. Russell and R. L. Burch (Russell and Burch 1959), is very much to the fore in animal welfare circles. The idea is to try to achieve *reduction* in the number of animals used and the pain and suffering inflicted, *refinement* in the experiment in order to eliminate, for example, repetitive uses of animals, continual duplication of results, and ultimately, the number of animals used, and *replacement* of animals with non-animal models (such as tissue cultures, computer adaptations, and so on). The three-R approach is widely endorsed today as the embodiment of a humane research ethic, so far as animals are concerned. But it must be understood clearly that, far from being an abolitionist position, it is in fact a pro-research position. It aims at forming a "humane" research ethic, one that animal welfarists can endorse but that working scientists can also attempt to achieve in their working lives.

[1.3] MIDDLE POSITION

To many people, of course, there has to be middle ground between the abolitionist and anything-goes positions. This middle ground needs to be described and defended, a task to which I now turn. It is characterized by several claims: animals possess moral standing and so are part of the moral community; therefore, their pains are to be taken seriously and their lives accorded value; progressive abolition occurs as replacement of animal models occurs; and trade-offs between benefit and loss with regard to humans and animals are accepted. This middle ground, adequately defended, constitutes, I think, a moral justification of animal experimentation.

[2.] HUMAN BENEFIT

Human benefit drives animal research (though benefit to animals is, of course, also a consideration), and virtually all attempts to justify animal research inevitably go through this appeal to benefit. This appeal, however, requires supplementation, and for an obvious reason: the benefits that animal research confer on us could be obtained from doing the research in humans. Indeed, using humans could confer those benefits as well, if not better, than doing the research in animals, since extrapolations from animals to humans are bound in some sense to be more problematic than extrapolations from humans to humans. Yet, everyone would agree, I presume, that it is wrong to do to humans what we presently do to research animals. Therefore, the claim of benefit needs to be supplemented with an argument that shows why, given some particular benefit, it would be wrong to do the research that obtains that benefit in humans but not in animals.

[3.] REJECTION OF THE TRADITIONAL JUSTIFICATION

This line of argument is sufficiently powerful, I think, that those in the pro-research camp are liable to be tempted to an extreme position here—namely, to suggest that humans are morally considerable or possess moral standing and that animals do not. Accordingly, what is done to animals will not matter morally, or, if it matters, it does so only derivatively, in terms, as Kant implied, of what it may lead us to do to humans. If, then, animals do not matter morally, then there is nothing wrong with using them to our research ends by, for example, giving them certain illnesses and then studying the progress and pathology of those illnesses in their lives. This extreme position does indeed differentiate humans from animals: humans are morally considerable in their own right and not derivatively; therefore, what is done to them counts morally in a way that what is done to animals does not.

What we might think of as the traditional justification of animal experimentation incorporates this extreme position. That justification rests upon three claims: first, animals are not members of the moral community and lack all moral standing; secondly, their lives have no or only very little value; and, thirdly, since humans are members of the moral community, we cannot use them in the way we presently use animals.

Behind these claims lay the Judaic/Christian ethic that posited a sharp break between humans and animals. The first two claims would indeed mark out a sharp moral difference. If animals are not members of the moral community, then what we do to them, including using them in painful ways, is not of moral concern (except in so far as it might lead us to use humans in painful ways), and if their lives had no or only very little value, then the destruction of those lives, lives that in any event lay outside the moral community, is also of little concern. The third claim simply applied the first two: no human who is a member of the moral community and whose life is of (considerable) value can be treated as we presently treat research animals.

This traditional justification must, I think, be given up. In very general terms, as we learn more about animals, it becomes more difficult to maintain a sharp break between animals and ourselves. From one side, as we learn more about animals and the feats they can perform, especially primates, it becomes difficult in the light of those feats to maintain a sharp break; from the other, as we learn more about the conditions in which humans can find themselves through illness, disease, and degeneration, conditions in which some humans can do little of what primates customarily do, it becomes equally difficult to maintain a sharp break. Besides, there is the sheer convenience of it all, of how our religious ethic advantages ourselves at the expense of the animate (and, indeed, inanimate) environment.

The main problem with the traditional justification of animal experimentation, of course, is that we cannot take for granted any longer the religious underpinning of the first two claims. In a pluralistic society, unanimity in religious opinion is no longer the case; not only do different religions, especially Eastern ones, take different views about animals, but the number of non-religious people also appears to have risen as well. In fact, those who offer a religious ethic sometimes do so in terms, for example, of distinctly human goods and conceptions of human flourishing, notions that are more amenable to non-religious people. In short, I do not think we can simply take for granted that the traditional justification of animal experimentation will any longer carry the day, and I think that any new attempt at justification, including one that involves appeal to human benefit, will almost certainly start by denying the first two claims of the traditional justification. That is, I think any justification must accept that animals have moral standing and so are members of the moral community and that their lives have value. In this regard, I think Singer [1975], Regan [1983], Clark (1982), and others are right to criticize past efforts to read animals out of the moral community.

They were read out of the moral community because their pain and suffering and their lives were postulated as being of no moral significance. But pain and suffering are moral-bearing characteristics for us, and throughout the USA and Europe there are guidelines that mandate that animal suffering be controlled, limited, mitigated, and justified in the research protocol and/or experiment. Moreover, the great care researchers extend to their experimental animals and their concern that such animals be euthanized before recovering from anaesthetic indicate that they take animal suffering seriously.

Besides, there is something odd about maintaining that pain and suffering are morally significant when felt by a human but not when felt by an animal. If a child burns a hamster alive, it seems quite incredible to maintain that what is wrong with this act has nothing essentially to do with the pain and suffering the hamster feels. To maintain that the act was wrong because it might encourage the child to burn other children or encourage anti-social behaviour, because the act failed to exhibit this or that virtue or violated some duty to be kind to animals—to hold these views seems almost perverse, if they are taken to imply that the hamster's pain and suffering are not central data bearing upon the morality of what was done to it. For us, pain and suffering are moral-bearing characteristics, so that, whether one burns the child or the child burns the hamster, the morality of what is done is determined at least in part by the pain and suffering the creature in question undergoes. Singer's utilitarianism picks this feature up quite nicely, and it seems to me exactly right. Of course, there may be other moral-bearing characteristics that apply in the case, but that fact in no way enables us to ignore, morally, the hamster's pains.

If the hamster's pain and suffering count morally, however, then it seems implausible to suggest that its life does not. The very reason that suffering so concerns us, in the case of any creature who can undergo it, is how it can blight and ruin a life (Rollin 1989). If the lives of experimental animals had no value, then why do researchers go to such lengths to justify the sacrifice of those lives? Why would we even bother to point to the benefits that such sacrifice can bring, if the lives sacrificed had no value whatever? If, however, those lives do have some value, then we certainly need to justify their destruction and the deliberate lowering through experimentation of their quality of life.

Though it perhaps sounds slightly offensive, I do not think the first two claims of the traditional justification of animal experimentation are even plausible beginnings of a defence of animal experimentation. As we shall see, I think what confers moral standing upon animal lives and gives them value is precisely what does these things in our lives—namely, their experiential content.

[4.] THE CENTRAL PROBLEM: HUMANS, NOT ANIMALS

There is an obvious way of making plain, so far as moral standing is concerned, the difficulty of separating the human and animal case. For example, it is widely agreed today that there are features of human lives, such as intelligence, sentiency, and self-direction, that bar using such beings in research without their consent (or, indeed, in certain cases, even with their consent), and a number of writers on "animal rights" have tried, not surprisingly, to find such features in animal lives, including some of the main types of research animals. In the face of this attempt, one might, I suppose, simply insist that animals do not share in the relevant characteristics picked out "to the same degree" or "enough" to warrant a similar bar to research in their cases. But the central problem with this kind of move has little to do with the success of those writers on "animal rights"; it has rather to do with the fact that not all human beings share in the characteristics picked out to the same degree. What do we do about these humans? If animals do not gain protection from research because they lack the relevant degree of the relevant characteristics, then what about those humans who lack that degree of those characteristics?

One suggestion here, of course, is that, side effects apart, we may use the humans in question as we use animals in research. But most people would be outraged by this suggestion. Yet, these same people are not outraged by the thought of using animals in medical research. So what can be the difference? What can make it wrong to use humans but right to use animals? An answer to this question simply must be forthcoming. The appeal to human benefit cannot stand alone as a justification of animal experimentation, since it would also justify human experimentation. It must be supplemented, therefore, with some account of why it would be wrong to use humans, any humans whatever, in order to obtain the benefits in question but not wrong to use animals.

What is driving the argument here is what I take to be a justified assumption—namely, that, for any characteristic selected as that around which to formulate a claim of protection, humans will be found who lack the characteristic altogether, or lack it to a degree sufficient to protect them from being used in medical experiments, or lack it to a degree that in fact means that some animals have it to a greater degree. Thus, any number of primates give evidence of being more intelligent than many severely mentally enfeebled humans, of being sentient to a degree beyond anything we associate with anencephalic infants, and of being better able to direct their lives than humans fully in the grip of senile dementia. Indeed, depending upon the characteristic selected, all kinds of animals, and of different species, will exceed the human case.

Certainly, the characteristic of having had two human parents may favour humans, but it does not appear to be the kind of characteristic required. For the nature of one's parentage says nothing about one's present quality of life, intelligence, capacity for pain and distress, the ability to direct one's life, and so on, and these sorts of characteristics appear much more like the kinds of things that would justify not treating a human life as we presently treat animal lives. For these sorts of characteristics say something about the life being lived, not what produced that life, something, that is, about the quality of the life being lived and so the welfare of the creature whose life it is. Thus, while anencephalic infants have had human parents, the nature and quality of their lives, by all the usual standards, appear to be far worse than the lives of many animals. Much the same appears to be true in the cases of all those who suffer from radically debilitating, degenerative illnesses, such as Huntington's disease, amyotrophic lateral sclerosis, and so on.

The central problem, then, in this discussion of animals turns out to be certain humans. Whatever characteristic we select around which to formulate some claim of protection from research, we seem inevitably to come across humans who lack that characteristic and animals who to a greater or lesser degree have it. Do we use these humans as we presently use animals in research? Or do we use neither humans nor animals, since the latter possess the characteristic selected around which to formulate the claim of protection? The first option will be repugnant to most; the second will virtually bar animal research. The problem, then, is that, if we cannot separate fully, in a morally significant way, the human and animal cases (Rachels 1990), then we must either endorse some version of animal research on humans or cease,

whether in an immediate or progressive fashion, research on all those animals who share in the characteristic selected. In this sense, the sense in which the argument from marginal cases (or unfortunate humans) looms large, the case for anti-vivisectionism, as I have always maintained, is stronger than most people allow.

It is obvious why the usual tactic at this juncture—namely, to select some strongly cognitive characteristic in order to bar all animals from the protected class—fails completely (Beauchamp 1992, 1997). The number of humans who fall outside the protected class will significantly increase, as the complexity of the cognitive task required for protection from research mounts; whereas to go in the other direction and to select a very much less complex task to acquire the relevant protection runs the obvious risk of including a good many animals in the protected group, even as some humans are excluded from it. Thus, the difficulty here is not that protection would be extended to some animals by this argument; it is that protection would not be extended to all humans. And those outside the protected class would then fall subject, side effects apart, to the benefit argument for experimentation.

In short, the search for some characteristic or set of characteristics, including cognitive ones, by which to separate us from animals runs headlong into the problem of marginal humans (or, in my less harsh expression, unfortunate humans). Do we use humans who fall outside the protected class, side effects apart, to achieve the benefits that animal research confers? Or do we protect these humans on some other ground, a ground that includes all humans, whatever their quality and condition of life, but no animals, whatever their quality and condition of life, a ground, moreover, that is reasonable for us to suppose can anchor a moral difference in how these different creatures are to be treated? But then what on earth is this other ground?

What in part bedevils the case of animals, then, is the case of humans. I shall return to this argument about marginal or unfortunate humans below, but first it is necessary to go back to the issue of moral standing, of who or what is morally considerable or a member of the moral community, in order now to indicate why I think animals have moral standing and lives of value and in what the value of their lives consists.

[5.] MORAL STANDING

In recent years, the search for a characteristic (or set) that transforms a creature from one that does not count morally into one that does so count has been protracted and heated. In some respects, this search has resembled that earlier in the abortion controversy, as claims about whether the fetus is a person, can feel pain, has rights, and so on all became ways of trying to give the fetus moral standing. In the case of animals, however, where many did not feel inclined to grant the fetus independent moral standing, no such reluctance was felt here. Numerous options have surfaced. Singer (1986) and a good many others have followed Bentham and urged sentiency or the ability to feel pain as the characteristic in question; Regan (2001) has talked about things that have inherent worth and a biography, with moral rights then used to protect such worth; Mary Anne Warren (1997) has urged a multiplicity of criteria, in addition to sentiency, as the required feature. A host of people, including Sapontzis (1987), DeGrazia (1996), and to some extent Rollin (1981), have urged the possession of interests as the crucial feature required for moral standing, with or without rights then deployed as the device by which interests are protected. Clark (1997), Linzey (1987), and others have urged a more theocratic view be taken of our relationship with both animate and inanimate nature and that moral standing be seen in the light of this relationship to God. Carruthers (1992) has put forward contractualist concerns and the ability to enter into voluntary agreements as a condition of standing, with the result that animals turn out to have moral standing only derivatively. Others treat this implication as a kind of *reductio* of the contractualist position. Scruton (1996) has talked of moral community in a more traditional sense, in which the interplay of reciprocity among persons, duty, responsibility, and virtuous action is characteristic, with some allowance then made for children and certain adults. John Harris (1988) takes being a person to be the central datum, where that notion is not identical with that of being human, and others have followed his lead. And Rosalind Hursthouse (2000) has even given, though in more indistinct form, some account of how a virtue theorist might try to address the issue of moral standing (given that the virtuous agent is the prime datum in the theory and animals are not virtuous agents) and the virtuous agent's treatment of animals. In short, all kinds of suggestions have been put forward over moral standing. I have not space to go into all these. It seems to me, however, that there is a central notion that many of these different accounts strive to capture in some form or other, one that enables us as well to keep the focus upon the interplay between our treatment of research animals and the claim that the benefits that research confers can be obtained through the use of (certain) humans.

Moral standing, I think, has nothing to do with agency on the part of the subject, nothing to do with the capacity to display virtues in the course of one's behaviour or with the capacity to make contracts, nothing to do with the possession of moral rights. Humans fully in the grip of Alzheimer's disease may cease to be agents, making choices and directing their own lives, but we do not think thereby that they cease being members of the moral community. In certain cases, the severely subnormal may never have risen to the station of agent in the first place, but they do not thereby cease being morally considerable and so part of the moral community.

In my view, moral standing or moral considerability turns upon whether a creature is an experiential subject, with an unfolding series of experiences that, depending upon their quality, can make that creature's life go well or badly. Such a creature has a welfare that can be positively or negatively affected, depending upon what is done to it. With a welfare that can be enhanced or diminished, a creature has a quality of life. People in the grip of senile dementia or who are severely subnormal nevertheless are beings with a quality of life that can be positively or negatively affected by what we do to them. At the same time, however, most people today would concede that hamsters, rabbits, and rodents, let alone chimps and other primates, are such creatures. They are experiential subjects with a welfare and quality of life that our actions can affect, and this is true whether they have rights, whether they are thought of as agents, and whatever their capacities for displaying virtues in their behaviour or making contracts. Of course, there are likely to be cases where we are doubtful about whether a creature is an experiential one (say, earthworms), but I cannot see that the usual experimental animals, such as rodents, rabbits, pigs, and primates, are doubtful cases at all. Accordingly, in this view, creatures who are experiential subjects have moral standing and are members of the moral community in exactly the same way that we are.

As I noted earlier, pain is a moral-bearing characteristic for us, and I cannot see what difference it makes as to which species feels pain. Pain is pain: to experiential creatures, it represents an evil in life, if not intrinsically, then certainly instrumentally, with respect to their quality of life. But, if the pains of animals count morally, then it is rather odd to conclude that their lives do not. As I indicated above, part of what matters about pain so much is how it can ruin a life and seriously reduce its quality, and this possibility of reduced quality exists in the cases of all those who can experience pain. After all, it would be absurd, whether in ourselves or in animals, to take excruciating agony to be an indication, other things being equal, of a high or desirable quality of life. Animals, then, are living creatures with experiential lives, creatures with a welfare and quality of life, and they are, therefore, creatures whose lives can be blighted and radically diminished in quality. For these reasons, I think that animal lives have value.

Given that animals and humans are experiential creatures, I see no reason to offer an account of the value of their respective lives that is different (Frey 1988), and quality-of-life views will typically treat them the same. What matters is the quality of life lived. Such a view makes the value of a life turn upon its content or experiences, whether that life be human or animal, and this in turn raises the interesting issue of the nature of, and the nature of our access to, the subjective lives and inner experiences of animals. Today, most informed people accept that animals— certainly, primates—have such experiences. It is these unfolding experiences that constitute their inner lives and make them, so to speak, psychological beings, in the way that we are psychological beings, and the difficulty of determining the exact nature of these experiences in their cases does not, in and of itself, undermine this fact.

In sum, animals and humans are living creatures with experiential lives and so things with a welfare and a quality of life. For these reasons, I take animal lives to have value, where the value of a life is a function of its quality. It is not just true of human lives that they can go well or badly: this is true of the lives of all experiential creatures. So, I think quality of life determines the value not only of human but also of animal lives, and I think that quality of life is a function of the scope and capacities of a creature for different kinds of experiences.

If the value of a life is a function of its quality, the quality of its richness, and the richness of its scope and capacities for enrichment, then the lives of normal adult humans are almost certainly going to turn out to be of a higher value than the lives of most animals. The capacities of enrichment of life in the normal adult case exceed anything we find in the animal case, or so the evidence suggests; thus, though we live lives with basic human needs, many, if not most, of which we share with animals, we also live lives at a level at which our mental, cultural, academic, and artistic talents, to name only a few things, deeply affect the texture of our lives. I do not have space here for more detail, but the general idea may be captured by a thought about death. When we say of a man after death that he lived a rich, full life or that he lived life to the full, we refer to things far beyond what evidence suggests that rodents, our main research animal, can enjoy. We cannot on a quality-of-life view, however, be dogmatic in the matter: if evidence turns up to suggest otherwise of rodent lives, then we shall have to change our view of their richness, quality, and value.

[6.] QUESTIONING TRADITION AND AVOIDING SPECIESISM

I cannot here go into all the qualifications that must attend any discussion of quality of life, including the obvious fact that, if this is often difficult to determine in the human case, how much more difficult it is likely to be in the animal case. Still, we use the notion constantly with regard to humans and in all kinds of contexts, from discussions about treatment and the allocation of medical goods to the evaluation of social policies as they affect the well-being of those they are intended to help. Granted that the concept is not an easy one to unravel, it is not, however, completely beyond us to do so. Yet, I do not need to go into these various qualifications here in order to show, if the notion of quality of life can be defended, how it can supply what is needed with the appeal to benefit in order to justify animal experimentation.

Why can we not do to humans what we presently do to experimental animals? The answer the traditional justification gave was that humans are members of the moral community and have lives of some value. On the view just sketched, however, animals are members of the moral community, because they, too, are experiential creatures, and they have lives of some value, because they, too, have a quality of life and welfare that our actions can augment or diminish. The fact is that these things are true of both humans and animals, and it is only speciesism that makes us think otherwise. By "speciesism," I mean discrimination on the basis of species alone.

So, whether we use animals to achieve the benefits of experimentation or we use humans, we shall be using creatures who are members of the moral community and who have lives of value. How, then, do we choose between them, in a non-speciesist way?

Any number of things may be said at this point, but virtually all of them strike me as attempts to hang on to past practices, when we have discarded the rationale and ethic that underlay those practices. For example, can we not just prefer humans to animals, say, because of the tradition (moral, social, cultural, religious) out of which we come? But how can this sort of thing make something, such as regarding black people as inferior to white, right? No one really believes today that citing tradition justifies the continuance of racism. So why should we think that it justifies a perpetual preference of animals over humans, in the case of experimentation?

How, then, are we to choose which creatures to use in order to achieve the benefits of the enhancement and extension of human life? The thought that underlies the quality-of-life position is that we use quality of life to decide. Other things being equal, in a hospital, if we can save one of two lives, we save the life of higher quality (actual and/or prospective); in taking life, other things being equal, we sacrifice the life of lower quality. Accordingly, we achieve the benefits of experimentation by using creatures of lower rather than higher quality of life. Plainly, then, a good deal of work needs to be done on the notion of quality of life, on how to determine it in humans and animals, and on gaining access to the inner lives of animals. This way of proceeding is non-speciesist, since we are preferring (most) human lives to (most) animal lives not in virtue of species but in virtue of quality of life.

I accept, then, that animals, and certainly the "higher" animals, have subjective experiences, that those experiences determine their quality of life, and that the quality of lives determines the value of those lives. This is exactly what I accept in the human case. We use behaviour and behavioural studies to gain access to the interior lives of animals, and we move slowly forward as these empirical studies of animal behaviour yield more information about them. If I can never know exactly what it is like to be a hamster, I can nevertheless come to know more and more in this regard, as we learn more about them and their responses to their environment.

Most of us do not think, however, that animal life is as valuable as human life, and a quality-of-life view of the value of a life can explain why. The richness of normal adult human life greatly exceeds that of animal life, in that the capacities for enrichment, in all their variety, extent, and depth, exceed anything that we associate with mice or even chimps. That an animal has a more acute sense of hearing than we do does not make up for this difference in variety, extent, and depth of capacities; for that to happen we should have to think that the animal's more acute hearing confers on its life a quality that approximates the quality that all of our capacities for enrichment along multidimensions that appear unavailable to the animal, on present scientific evidence, confer on our lives. Once again, however, we cannot be dogmatic on this score and must be prepared to revise our view of animal lives as more and better information on them becomes available to us.

Most importantly, the claim that the animal's capacities provide it with a perfectly full life for a creature of its kind is not to the point, for what quality-of-life concerns are being used to do here is to make comparative judgements about the value of different lives. The concession that animals lead full lives for creatures of their kind does not, in and of itself, answer the question about the comparative value of the animal's life versus the value of a normal adult human's life. Moreover, while one can object to making such comparative judgements, at least with any very great degree of refinement, we certainly make such judgements daily, whether in our hospitals, as we evaluate the comparative conditions of two patients, or in our veterinary schools, as we evaluate the comparative conditions of two animals. But the degree of refinement I am talking about does not need to be very great, in order for me to suggest that it is the comparative value of lives, not species, that supplements the argument from benefit.

Thus, in addition to the fact that pain is a moral-bearing characteristic for us, animals are members of the moral community because they are experiential creatures with a quality of life and welfare that can be affected by what we do to them. But they do not have the same moral standing as normal adult humans, since the value of these human lives far exceeds that of animals. The truth is that not all creatures who have moral standing have the same moral standing, and this truth, as we shall see, has as dramatic implications for human lives as it does for the comparative-value question for animal lives. Even so, animals are members of the moral community and have lives of some value; they are morally considerable. The "anything-goes" position on animal research, then, a position that might seem desirable from the point of view of research scientists, will not do: it simply fails to take account of the moral considerability of animals and the fact that their lives have value.

[7.] COMPARING LIVES

If one can kill a mouse or a man and obtain the relevant benefits, then, other things being equal, it is worse to kill the man. What makes it worse is not species membership, but the fact that human life is more valuable than animal life. While the mouse's life has value, it does not have the same value as the man's life, and it is worse to destroy lives of greater rather than lesser value. This comparative view of the value of a life will be speciesist, however, unless something other than species membership confers greater value on the man's life. Richness, capacity for enrichment, and quality of life are such things.

What matters, then, is how pronounced the capacities of an experiential creature are for a rich life, and science and observation teach us different things about mice and men. Neither the behavioural sciences nor observation give us reason to believe that the mouse, given the variety and extent of its capacities and the life appropriate to its species, approaches our own in richness, quality, and value, given the variety, extent, and depth of our capacities. So far as we know, the capacities for enrichment of the mouse are just too limited in number, scope, and variety to lead us to think differently, though we must retain an open mind on the matter and pay attention to opposing evidence. Where this evidence comes in the form of detailed observation of primates, we might have to be prepared, I think, to envisage something radically different from the case of the mouse, based on the accruing evidence of primate studies both in the wild and in captivity.

Certainly, much here is difficult because it is difficult to gain access to the inner lives of animals. It is quite wrong to suggest, however, that we can know nothing of the richness of animal lives, so that I am barred from using the notion. Animal behaviourists sympathetic to the "animal rights" cause, such as Donald Griffin (1981, 1992), Rosemary Rodd (1990), Marian Dawkins (1993), and Marc Bekoff (1998), all think that we can know something of the richness and quality of life of the "higher" animals. Certainly, all laymen think this, when they point out that pain and suffering, boredom, inability to scratch or peck, and so on, affect a creature's quality of life, something to which veterinarians, such as David Morton (1995), also attest. The fact that we cannot know everything about an animal's inner life does not mean that we cannot know a good deal. Yet, what we know leads us to think that the capacities associated with normal adult human life exceed anything we associate with the lives of mice, pigs, or baboons. This difference in capacities for enrichment affects the content of a life and so its quality and value. This, then, is why it is morally worse to kill the man rather than the mouse: it amounts to the destruction of something of greater value.

[8.] INTRA- AND INTER-SPECIES COMPARISONS

Difficulties arise, of course, with quality-of-life judgements even within our own species, as when we try, for example, to compare the quality of lives of two patients in a hospital. Such comparisons are not, however, entirely beyond us, and medical people make such judgements daily, often as a basis for treatment and decisions about allocation of scarce goods. Nor do I deny that different factors can be taken into account, especially as between subjective impressions as to how well one's life is going versus objective criteria about that life. One area where interesting work is being done on this kind of problem is in the quality-adjusted-life-year (QALY) literature, where the scales of measurement of quality of life, in order to assign a QALY ranking and so to be able to compare and contrast different lives, weave together subjective and objective criteria of richness of content (Mooney 1986). The point is that such weaving together is not entirely beyond us.

If intra-species comparisons are difficult, inter-species comparisons are likely to be more so, though, again, not impossible. Once we depart very far from the "higher" animals, we lose behavioural correlates that give us access to the interior lives of animals. Behavioural science and observation, both in captivity and the wild, have added enormously to our knowledge of the subjective lives of animals, and there is no doubt that this work has suggested that the interior lives of at least some animals are far richer than the traditional justification of animal experimentation ever envisaged. Yet, even so, ethologists and others are very hesitant to posit anything like similarity of richness of content with normal adult human life.

On two important points, we must be careful not to mistake what is at issue. First, to claim that I cannot be certain that the hamster's life is not as rich as the normal adult human's is not to meet the thrust of the capacities argument. If one wants to maintain that the two lives are equally valuable, then one must cite something that, however limited the capacities of the hamster in number and variety, confers on its life a richness comparable to what the differing capacities of the normal adult human confer on his life. The fact that the hamster has a keener sense of smell, the dog a keener sense of hearing, the eagle a keener sense of sight does not readily make us think otherwise. And to assume that the keener sense of smell confers on the hamster's life a vast dimension of joy that exceeds the various dimensions of richness conferred on human life by all its differing and extended capacities is again not something that science or observation will lead us readily to think. Secondly, we must be careful not to take the claim that both the hamster and we ourselves have but one life to live and that its value should be judged by the capacities appropriate to it as if it answered the comparative point. It does not. Based on what we know, we have no reason to believe that the hamster possesses anything like the extent, variety, and depth of ways of enrichment typical of normal adult humans, and we need some reason to believe that its keener sense of smell can confer on its life a richness similar to our own. There is nothing incommensurable here, nothing that as a matter of principle denies me access to the richness and quality of the hamster's life, even if it is difficult to gain that access. This fact supports the view that the difficulties in comprehending the richness and quality of life of (at least the "higher") animals is one of degree and not of kind.

Nor must we overlook several features of normal adult human life that enable us to add enormously to the value of our lives. First, no account of all the activities we share with animals, such as eating, sleeping, and reproducing, comes anywhere near exhausting the richness of a life in which art, music, literature, family, friendship, love, intellectual endeavours, and so on inform it. Indeed, the fact that we can mould our lives in particular ways, to live out certain conceptions of the good life, such as a painter, is an important fact about us. Even if ultimately all this is cashed out in terms of experiences, it shows that we can shape our lives in ways of our own choosing, that we are not condemned to a life appropriate to our own species, even if it is true that there are limits on the sorts of life we can make for ourselves. Secondly, this feature of our lives lies beyond any mere concern with our capacities. In fact, we can integrate our lives into wholes whose value is enhanced as a result. This integrative task is partly an intellectual one, governed by some conception of the good life, and by a psychological awareness of how we are as people, in terms both of our similarities to other people and creatures and of our differences from them. This integration of our lives is part of what makes them worth living, a part that we do not share with other animals, as far as we know. Yet, no account of the richness of our lives could ignore it, since we should fail to understand how people have moulded their lives into lives they take appropriate to being teachers, athletes, and artists. Thirdly, we cannot ignore the role of agency in our lives. Not every being who is an experiential one and a member of the moral community is also an agent; some are, and always remain, patients. Among agents, however, there is a further sense of moral community that informs their lives. In this further sense of community, members have duties to each other, reciprocity of action occurs, standards for the assessment of conduct occur, and reasons for action are proffered and received. The absence of agency in this sense means that the creature in question is not regarded as a moral being in the full sense of being held accountable for its actions. To be accountable for what one does, in a community of others who are accountable for what they do, is not the same thing as having moral standing, nor is agency construed as acting and weighing reasons for action in the light of standards required in order to be morally considerable.

Nevertheless, agency in this sense matters to the value of a life. The moral relations in which normal adult humans stand to each other are part of whom they take themselves to be. They are husbands and wives, sons and daughters, family and friends. These are important roles we play in life, and they are composed in part by a view of the moral burdens and duties they impose on us, as well as the opportunities for action they allow us. In these relations, we come to count on others, to see ourselves as interlocked with the fate of at least some others, to be moved by what happens to these others, and to be motivated to affect the fate of these others to the extent that we can. While there is nothing fixed about all this, being a functioning member of a community in this sense can be one of the great goods of life, enriching the very texture of the life one lives.

Our participation in a community of such agents enriches our lives. At a minimal level, it achieves this by allowing us to cooperate to achieve our cooperative ends. But the very way we live our lives—for example, as husbands and fathers—in order to fulfil what we see as our obligations within these moral relations in which we take ourselves to stand to others forms part of the texture and richness of our lives and so part of what we look at in order to determine whether our lives are going well or badly. In fact, these relations partly inform many of our prized ends in life, and we often find it difficult to explain why we did something at such obvious cost to ourselves except through citing how we see ourselves linked to certain others.

The above barely scratches the surface of the sorts of things that come to constitute the richness of our lives. Yet, they show clearly that, when we speak of someone as having led a "rich, full" life, we refer to something that we understand to be beyond the animal case. The relations in which we stand to each other aid us in pursuit of our ends and projects, many of which require the help of others to achieve, and the pursuit of these ends and projects, sometimes referred to collectively as one's "conception of the good life," adds enormously to how well we take our lives to be going. Since our welfare is bound up with these kinds of pursuits, to ignore this fact is to give an impoverished account of a characteristically human life. Since all these ends and projects can vary between persons, there is no life "appropriate" to our species, no single way of living to which every human being is condemned to conform. Agency enables us to make different lives for ourselves and so reflects, in this sense, how we want to live. Accomplishment of ends so moulded and shaped by ourselves is one of the important factors that can enrich individual human lives.

Agency, then, enables normal adult humans to enhance the quality and value of their lives in ways that no account of the activities we share with animals captures, and in seeking to give some account of the comparative value of human and animal life this kind of difference—to mention only one thing—is obviously important. It is just such a difference as this that evolutionary accounts of morality today can all too easily overlook, in their urge to show the common holdings of humans and animals.

Of course, on the comparative value of lives, we must be careful not to use in some unreflective manner criteria for assessing the richness of human lives as if they applied automatically to the animal case. This would be to make oneself into a speciesist in a second-order sense. We must use all we know about animals, especially primates, to try to gauge the quality of their lives in terms appropriate to their species. We must then try to assess the differences we allude to when we say, first of a rodent, then of a human, that each has led a rich, full life. What I am suggesting here is not merely that such assessments are within our capabilities, as we learn more about the subjective lives of animals, but also that they need to be informed by what we know in our own case about dimensions of our lives that neither science nor observation leads us to believe are characteristic of animal lives. For these differences will bear upon the issue of the comparative value of human and animal life.

We have, then, a non-speciesist reason for thinking that normal adult human life is more valuable than animal life. Its richness and quality exceed that of animal life. I said earlier that killing—between two lives, we take the life of lower quality and value—and saving—between two lives, we save the life of higher quality and value—are two sides of the same coin. Quality-of-life judgements dictate this. Accordingly, we have a non-speciesist reason for using the animal in preference to the human in medical experimentation, if we have to use some creature or other.

[9.] THE ARGUMENT FROM MARGINAL CASES

Yet, it should be apparent, as I remarked earlier, that there is a problem involving humans. Take the issue of moral standing: if those in the final stages of senile dementia or the very severely mentally enfeebled remain experiential creatures, it is unclear that those in permanently vegetative states or anencephalic infants do. Where the value of life is concerned, matters are even worse. It seems reasonably clear that many human lives, devastated by illness and disease, have diminished radically in richness and quality, quite apart from PVS [persistent vegetative state] patients and anencephalic infants, and it seems reasonably clear that numerous people undone by their medical conditions cannot adduce standards for the evaluation of conduct or conform their behaviour to such standards or receive and weigh reasons for action. (Indeed, even perfectly normal children and many of the very severely mentally enfeebled cannot do these things.) Today, of course, when the issue of physician-assisted suicide is much debated, virtually everyone is familiar with cases in which people living out certain lives seek relief from them, as they worsen, and where the quality and value of their lives are in inexorable decline. Such lives, even as they remain morally considerable, have plummeted in quality and value, and the fact is that they can plummet to such an extent that the quality and value of a perfectly healthy animal's life can exceed these things in their lives.

In truth, not all human lives have the same richness or scope for enrichment; they do not, therefore, have the same value. What the prominence of medical cases has taught us today is that the quality of human life can plummet to such a degree that neither we nor the people forced to live those lives wish to see them condemned to do so. Tragic cases abound, from infants with AIDS to adults dying from amyotrophic lateral sclerosis, cardiomyopathy, or pancreatic cancer. It seems absurd to pretend that lives of these sorts, lives that no one, not even the people living them, would wish to live, are as valuable as normal adult human life. Whereas, with ordinary children, we might appeal to some potentiality argument, in order to address the issue of the value of their lives, no such appeal is possible in the cases of some children or with adults stricken with severe, devastating illnesses. The truth seems to be that human lives vary in richness, quality, and value, and, when their value plummets drastically in severe cases, while these lives remain members of the moral community, their value can reach a point such that the value of quite ordinary animal lives appears to exceed that of the human. If, therefore, research involving the use of lives is required, a terrible problem confronts us. . . .

The argument from benefit, then, does not tell us which life to use; it needs to be supplemented with an argument that enables us to choose between lives, which I have attempted to provide. It turns out that lives of higher quality have greater value than lives of lower quality and that taking a life of higher quality in preference to a life of lower quality is worse. Assuming we have to use some lives in research in the first place, this tells us which lives to use. We should use lives of lower rather than higher quality. Typically, this will mean that we use animal lives. We simply cannot guarantee that this will always be so, however, unless we can find something that always ensures, whatever the richness and quality of human

life, that it exceeds in value the lives of any and all animals. Unfortunately, I know of no such thing.

I do not advocate that we conduct experiments upon humans. Mine is not a recipe for action, but an attempt to understand what underlies one major effort at or argument for justifying the use of animals in medical experimentation. After all, the adverse side effects of experiments on certain humans—admittedly, the weakest amongst us—would be immense, and public outrage would be vociferous. Yet, if the benefits of animal research are all that researchers would have us believe, how do we avoid envisaging this terrible outcome? The claim would be not that we replace animals with humans, but that we follow the logic of the argument and use creatures with lower qualities of life. If one cannot bring oneself to do this, then I think one is forced to re-examine the case for animal experimentation, at least if that case is held, either directly or indirectly, to run through the appeal to benefit. . . .

REFERENCES

Balls, M. et al. (1983) (ed.), *Animals and Alternatives in Toxicity Testing*. London: Academic Press.

Beauchamp, T. L. (1992), "The Moral Standing of Animals in Medical Research." *Journal of Law, Medicine, and Ethics*, 20: 7–16.

Beauchamp, T. L. (1997). "Opposing Views on Animal Experimentation: Do Animals Have Rights?" *Ethics and Behavior*, 7: 113–21.

Bekoff, M. (1998). "Cognitive Ethology: The Comparative Study of Animal Minds," in W. Bechtel and G. Graham (eds.), *Blackwell Companion to Cognitive Science*. Oxford: Blackwell, 371–9.

Carruthers, P. (1992). *The Animals Issue*. Cambridge: Cambridge University Press.

Clark, S. R. L. (1982). *The Nature of the Beast*. Oxford: Oxford University Press.

——— (1997). *Animals and their Moral Standing*. London: Routledge.

Dawkins, M. S. (1993). *Through our Eyes Only: The Search for Animal Consciousness*. New York: W. H. Freeman.

DeGrazia, D. (1996). *Taking Animals Seriously*. Cambridge: Cambridge University Press.

Frey, R. G. (1988). "Moral Standing, the Value of Lives, and Speciesism." *Between the Species*, 4: 191–201.

Griffin, D. 1981. *The Question of Animal Awareness*. New York: Rockefeller University Press.

——— (1992). *Animal Minds*. Chicago: University of Chicago Press.

Harris, J. (1988). *The Value of Life*. London: Methuen.

Hursthouse, R. (2000). *Ethics, Humans, and Other Animals*. London: Routledge.

Linzey, A. (1987). *Christianity and the Rights of Animals*. London: Herder & Herder.

Mooney, G. (1986). *Economics, Medicine, and Health Care*. Atlantic Heights, NJ: Humanities Press International.

Morton, D. (1995). "Recognition and Assessment of Adverse Effects in Animals," in N. E. Johnston (ed.), *Proceedings of Animals in Science Conference Perspectives on their Use, Care, and Welfare*. Melbourne: Monash University, 131–48.

Rachels, J. (1990). *Created from Animals: The Moral Implications of Darwinism*. Oxford: Oxford University Press.

Regan, T. (1983). *The Case for Animal Rights*. Berkeley and Los Angeles: University of California Press.

—— (1997). "Animals and Morality." *Ethics and Behavior*, 7: 95–110.

—— (2001). *Defending Animal Rights*. Urbana, IL: University of Illinois Press.

Rodd, R. (1990). *Biology, Ethics, and Animals*. Oxford: Oxford University Press.

Rollin, B. (1981). *Animal Rights and Human Morality*. Buffalo, NY: Prometheus.

—— (1989). *The Unheeded Cry: Animal Consciousness, Animal Pain, and Science*. Oxford: Oxford University Press.

Russell, W. M. S., and Burch, R. L. (1959). *The Principles of Humane Experimental Technique*. London: Methuen.

Sapontzis, S. F. (1987). *Morals, Reason, and Animals*. Philadelphia: Temple University Press.

Scruton, R. (1996). *Animal Rights and Wrongs*. London: Demos.

Singer, P. (1975). *Animal Liberation*. New York: New York Review, distributed by Random House.

—— (1986). *In Defense of Animals*. New York: Perennial Library.

Warren, M. A. (1997). *Moral Status: Obligations to Persons and Other Living Things*. Oxford: Oxford University Press.

GILLES DEMERS,[1] GILLY GRIFFIN,[2] GUY DE VROEY,[3] JOSEPH R. HAYWOOD,[4] JOANNE ZURLO,[5] AND MARIE BÉDARD[2]

Harmonization of Animal Care and Use Guidance

All of the authors are members of the Working Group on Harmonization of Guidelines for ICLAS [the International Council for Laboratory Animal Science]. G. Demers is the President of ICLAS, and G. De Vroey and J. R. Haywood are members of the ICLAS Governing Board; J. R. Haywood represents the International Union of Basic and Clinical Pharmacology. In addition, G. De Vroey was the chair of the subcommittee (of the ICLAS Working Group on Harmonization) on euthanasia and J. R. Haywood the chair of the subcommittee on endpoints. [1]ICLAS, St-Hilaire, Quebec, QC, Canada J3H 4W1. [2]Canadian Council on Animal Care, Ottawa, ON, Canada K1P 5G4. [3]Johnson & Johnson, B-2340 Beerse, Belgium. [4]Department of Pharmacology and Toxicology, Michigan State University, East Lansing, MI 48824, USA. [5]Institute for Laboratory Animal Research, National Academy of Sciences, Washington, DC 20001, USA.

Societal expectations for improvements in the health of humans and animals require scientific studies involving the use of animals. At the same time, the public is concerned about the welfare of animals used in science. Animal welfare is also of importance because of the link between healthy, well-cared-for animals and sound science.

Most national oversight mechanisms emphasize basic principles of humane science, in particular the "three R's" tenet of replacement, reduction, and refinement of animal use.[1] However, the oversight of animal care and use occurs through a wide variety of local, national, and international mechanisms, some based on legislation [the European Union (EU);[2]], others on peer review or other forms of nonlegislated oversight (Canada) and yet others on a combination of legislated and nonlegislated oversight (United States). This patchwork of mechanisms can cause problems, given the global nature of science.

Different standards for animal care and use can complicate the comparison of results from animal-based

From *Science* 312 (5774): May 5, 2006; 700–701. Reprinted by permission of the authors and the American Association for the Advancement of Science.

studies and the reproducibility of such results and can also slow international scientific collaboration. For example, CO_2 euthanasia is more commonly used for rodents in the United States than in the EU, and T-61 (a combination of three drugs—a local anesthetic, a general anesthetic, and a curariform drug) is available to animal users in Europe but not the United States. There are also international trade implications: multinational companies face the challenge of having to work with research and testing sites operating within very different regulatory structures. Specific standards of animal care and use required by scientific journals can also present a barrier to publication. The patchwork of mechanisms can be especially daunting for developing countries, in elaborating their own mechanisms and in international collaboration. Finally, there is concern that differences in animal care and use requirements may lead to the transfer of animal-based studies to countries with weaker requirements. As far back as 1985, the Committee of International Organizations of Medical Science (CIOMS), which works closely with the World Health Organization, said "The varying approaches in different countries to the use of animals for biomedical purposes, and the lack of relevant legislation or of formal self regulatory mechanisms in some, point to the need for international guiding principles elaborated as a result of international and interdisciplinary consultations."[3]

There are international efforts to use guidance that is based on performance standards [i.e., standards that define an outcome and provide criteria for assessing that outcome, but do not limit the methods by which that outcome may be achieved[4]], and to work on filling gaps in the science needed for sound animal welfare guidance. Examples of international collaboration include the CIOMS Principles, the Mutual Acceptance of Data Program of the Organisation for Economic Cooperation and Development (OECD), and the International Conference on Harmonization of Technical Requirements for Registration of Pharmaceuticals for Human Use (ICH). These instances of collaboration have reduced unnecessary duplication of studies involving animals by developing internationally accepted common methods for chemical testing and drug development.

Guidance on the recognition of clinical signs as humane end points is now being implemented by

---

1. There is strong evidence that animals experience pain and distress in situations comparable to those that cause pain and distress for humans.

2. Death or severe pain and distress should be avoided as end points.

3. The earliest possible end point should be used that is consistent with the scientific objectives.

4. Studies should be designed to minimize any pain or distress likely to be experienced by the animals, while meeting the scientific objectives.

5. The duration of studies involving pain and distress should be kept to a minimum.

6. Pilot studies should be encouraged as a means of determining morbidity, time course of effects, and frequency of observations required to set an earlier end point.

7. Before commencing the experiment, agreement should be reached on (i) appropriate end points for the study and (ii) the person or persons to be responsible for making the judgment that the end point has been reached.

8. A team approach should be used employing the professional judgment of the scientist, veterinarian, animal care staff, and ethics committee to agree on the appropriate end point for the study.

9. Research and animal care staff must be adequately trained and competent in recognition of species-specific behavior and, in particular, species-specific signs of pain, distress, and moribundity.

10. Animals should be monitored by means of behavioral, physiological, and/or clinical signs at an appropriate frequency to permit timely termination of the experiment once the end point has been reached.

---

member nations of the OECD, in conjunction with the OECD test guidelines for safety evaluation, which means that regulatory agencies in these countries should no longer require death in extremis as an end point for safety tests.[5] In countries that are not OECD members, death may still be commonly accepted as an end point.

The International Council for Laboratory Animal Science [ICLAS[6]], has brought members of the international community together to identify and to recommend acceptance of guidance documents. ICLAS believes in the harmonization of animal care and use guidance as a reflection of the globalization of research. However, harmonization must be distinguished from standardization (one world-wide set of regulations); ICLAS believes that each country should be able to maintain an oversight mechanism for animals used in science that reflects its cultures, traditions, religions, laws, and regulations.

ICLAS first worked with the Canadian Council on Animal Care (CCAC) on best practices to minimize pain and distress for animals used in regulatory testing; these were agreed upon and published.[7] Two guidance documents on humane end points were recognized as effective refinement tools.[5,8]

In November 2003, the Institute for Laboratory Animal Research (ILAR) organized an international workshop[9] to discuss harmonization. During this workshop, many experts from around the world independently reported about a desire for and worldwide pressures to have international benchmarks for animal welfare. However, many participants pointed out that there are strong attachments to existing national guidance and gaps in the science needed as a basis for some of the regulations, standards, and guidelines.

ICLAS held its First International Meeting for the Harmonization of Guidelines on the Use of Animals in Science in Nantes, France, on 13 and 14 June 2004.[10] An ICLAS Working Group on Harmonization of Guidelines, composed of representatives from major organizations producing and/or using guidelines for the use of animals in science, was created at the meeting.[11] The working group agreed on general principles for the establishment of humane end points that are based on the earlier documents from the OECD and CCAC.[5,8,12] The working group encourages consultation of the extensive literature available on end points and recognizes the need for research to support performance-based standards. The current general principles for humane end points defined by the working group are described in the table [on the preceding page].

The working group also agreed on general principles for euthanasia and recommended two documents[13,14] as international references.[15] Both documents provide general principles and guidance on ways to ensure that euthanasia methods meet the goal of assuring the humane death of animals. There are some areas of inconsistency between the two references. This is partly because the American Veterinary Medical Association document is designed for a more general audience (i.e., not only for animal use in science) and because of differing practices and traditions in the United States and Europe, but mostly it is due to insufficient knowledge about the best methods of euthanasia for various

Principles for Animal Euthanasia

1. Whenever an animal's life is to be taken, it should be treated with the highest respect.

2. Euthanasia should place emphasis on making the animal's death painless and distress-free. The method likely to cause the least pain and distress to the animals should be used whenever possible.

3. Euthanasia techniques should result in rapid loss of consciousness, followed by cardiac or respiratory arrest and ultimate loss of brain function.

4. Techniques should require minimum restraint of the animal and should minimize distress and anxiety experienced by the animal, before loss of consciousness.

5. Techniques used should be appropriate for the species, age, and health of the animal.

6. Death must be verified following euthanasia and before disposal of the animal.

7. Personnel responsible for carrying out the euthanasia techniques should be trained: (i) to carry out euthanasia in the most effective and humane manner; (ii) to recognize signs of pain, fear, and distress in relevant species; and (iii) to recognize and confirm death in relevant species.

8. Human psychological responses to euthanasia should be taken into account when selecting the method of euthanasia, but should not take precedence over animal welfare considerations.

9. Ethics committees should be responsible for approval of the method of euthanasia (in line with any relevant legislation). This should include euthanasia as part of the experimental protocol, as well as euthanasia for animals experiencing unanticipated pain and distress.

10. A veterinarian experienced with the species in question should be consulted when selecting the method of euthanasia, particularly when little species-specific euthanasia research has been done.

species at different life stages. The areas in which further research will be needed were identified as mass animal euthanasia, euthanasia of fetuses and neonates, euthanasia of cold-blooded animals, proper use of CO_2 for various species, decapitation with or without prior anesthesia, cervical dislocation, and the use of N_2 and/or argon gas. With more research in these areas, the working group felt that the discrepancies between the documents could be addressed and better guidance incorporated into future versions of the guidelines. The general principles for euthanasia defined by the working group are shown in the table above.

ICLAS will continue to work with its many partners around the world to identify solid, practical guidance that can easily be used by the international community to promote good animal welfare while conducting sound animal-based science.[16]

NOTES

1. W. M. S. Russell, R. L. Burch, *The Principles of Humane Experimental Technique* (Methuen, London, 1959; reprinted, Universities Federation for Animal Welfare, Wheathampstead, UK, 1992).

2. European Science Foundation (ESF) Policy Briefing, "Use of Animals in Research" (ESF, Strasbourg, France, August 2001); (www.esf.org/publication/115/ESPB15.pdf).

3. Z. Bankowski, N. Howard-Jones, Eds., *International Guiding Principles for Biomedical Research Involving Animals* [Committee of International Organizations of Medical Science (CIOMS), Geneva, 1986].

4. National Research Council, *Guide for the Care and Use of Laboratory Animals* (National Academies Press, Washington, DC, ed.7, 1996).

5. Organisation for Economic Cooperation and Development (OECD), "Guidance document on the recognition, assessment, and use of clinical signs as humane endpoints for experimental animals used in safety evaluation" (OECD, Paris, 2000); [www.olis.oecd.org/olis/2000doc.nsf/LinkTo/env-jm-mono (2000)7].

6. International Council for Laboratory Animal Science (ICLAS) (www.iclas.org/).

7. G. Griffin, W. Stokes, Eds., *Regulatory Testing and Animal Welfare: Proceedings of the ICLAS/CCAC International Symposium, Quebec City, Canada, 21 to 23 June 2001. ILAR J.* 43 (suppl.), 140 pp. (2002).

8. Canadian Council on Animal Care (CCAC), "[CCAC] guidelines on: choosing an appropriate endpoint in experiments using animals for research, teaching, and testing" (CCAC, Ottawa, 1998);(www.ccac.ca/en/CCAC_Programs/Guidelines_Policies/GDLINES/ENDPTS/APPOPEN.HTM).

9. National Research Council, *The Development of Science-based Guidelines for Laboratory Animal Care, Proceedings of the November 2003 International Workshop*, Washington, DC, 18 and 19 November 2003 (National Academies Press, Washington, DC, 2004).

10. Federation of European Laboratory Animal Science Associations (FELASA), "First ICLAS meeting for the harmonization of guidelines on the use of animals in science" in *Proceedings of the Ninth FELASA Symposium, Section 2, International Harmonisation of Care and Use Issues*, Nantes, France, 13 and 14 June 2004 (FELASA, London, 2005); (www.lal.org.uk/pdffiles/FELASA/Seciton2.pdf), p. 40.

11. List of participants available on *Science* Online.

12. ICLAS, "International harmonization of guidelines on humane endpoints" (ICLAS, Nantes, France, 2004), approved in Athens, Greece, May 2005, available on *Science* Online.

13. "2000 Report of the American Veterinary Medical Association (AVMA) Panel on Euthanasia" (www.avma.org/issues/animal_welfare/euthanasia.pdf).

14. "1996/1997 EC [European Commission] recommendations for euthanasia of experimental animals," parts 1 and 2 (www.lal.org.uk/workp. html).

15. ICLAS, "International harmonization of guidelines on euthanasia" (ICLAS, Nantes, France, 2004), approved in Buenos Aires, Argentina, November 2004, available on *Science* Online.

16. ICLAS thanks all those who have volunteered their time and expertise for its work, in particular those working on international harmonization.

Suggested Readings for Chapter 2

PAST ABUSES OF HUMAN RESEARCH SUBJECTS

Advisory Committee on Human Radiation Experiments. *Final Report*. Washington, DC: U.S. Government Printing Office, October 1995.

Annas, George J., and Grodin, Michael A., eds. *The Nazi Doctors and the Nuremberg Code: Human Rights in Human Experiments*. New York: Oxford University Press, 1992.

Dörner, Klaus, et al., eds. *The Nuremberg Medical Trial, 1946/47: Transcripts, Materials of the Prosecution and Defense, Related Documents*. Munich: K. G. Saur, 2001.

Faden, Ruth R., ed. *The Human Radiation Experiments: Final Report of the Advisory Committee*. New York: Oxford University Press, 1996.

Freedman, Benjamin. "Research, Unethical." In Stephen G. Post, ed. *Encyclopedia of Bioethics*. 3rd edition. New York: Macmillan Reference USA: Thomson/Gale; 2004: 2376–2379.

Gray, Fred D. *The Tuskegee Syphilis Study: The Real Story and Beyond*. Montgomery, AL: Black Belt Press, 1998.

Harris, Sheldon H. *Factories of Death: Japanese Biological Warfare 1932–45 and the American Cover Up*. Revised edition. New York: Routledge, 1994.

Hornblum. Allen M. *Acres of Skin: Human Experiments at Holmesburg Prison: A True Story of Abuse and Exploitation in the Name of Medical Science*. Baltimore, MD: Johns Hopkins University Press, 1998.

Lederer, Susan E. *Subjected to Science: Human Experimentation in America before the Second World War*. Baltimore, MD: Johns Hopkins University Press, 1995.

Jones, James H. *Bad Blood: The Tuskegee Syphilis Experiment*. New and expanded edition. New York: Free Press, 1993.

Katz, Jay, with the assistance of Alexander Morgan Capron and Eleanor Swift Glass. *Experimentation with Human Beings*. New York: Russell Sage Foundation, 1972.

Mitscherlich, Alexander, and Fred Mielke. *Doctors of Infamy: The Story of the Nazi Medical Crimes*. New York: Henry Schuman, 1949.

Moreno, Jonathan D. *Undue Risk: Secret State Experiments on Humans*. New York: Routledge, 2001.

Proctor, Robert N. *Racial Hygiene: Medicine under the Nazis.* Cambridge, MA: Harvard University Press, 1988.

Reverby, Susan M. *Tuskegee's Truths: Rethinking the Tuskegee Syphilis Study.* Chapel Hill, NC: University of North Carolina Press, 2000.

Schmidt, Ulf. *Justice at Nuremberg: Leo Alexander and the Nazi Doctors' Trial.* New York: Palgrave Macmillan, 2004.

———. "Cold War at Porton Down: Informed Consent in Britain's Biological and Chemical Warfare Experiments." *Cambridge Quarterly of Healthcare Ethics* 15 (2006), 366–80.

———. *Karl Brandt: the Nazi Doctor: Medicine and Power in the Third Reich.* London: Continuum, 2007.

Washington, Harriet A. *Medical Apartheid: The Dark History of Medical Experimentation on Black Americans from Colonial Times to the Present.* New York: Doubleday, 2006.

Weindling, Paul Julian. *Nazi Medicine and the Nuremberg Trials: From Medical War Crimes to Informed Consent.* Basingstoke, Hampshire/New York: Palgrave Macmillan, 2004.

Welsome, Eileen. *The Plutonium Files: America's Secret Medical Experiments in the Cold War.* New York: Dial Press, 1999.

CODES AND GUIDELINES FOR HUMAN RESEARCH

Annas, George J., and Grodin, Michael A., eds. *The Nazi Doctors and the Nuremberg Code: Human Rights in Human Experimentation.* Oxford: Oxford University Press, 1992.

Bankowski, Zbigniew, and Levine, Robert J., eds. *Ethics and Research on Human Subjects: International Guidelines.* Geneva: Council for International Organizations of Medical Sciences, 1993.

Brody, Baruch A. *The Ethics of Biomedical Research: An International Perspective.* New York: Oxford University Press, 1998, Appendixes 1–4.

Byk, Christian. "La déclaration d'Helsinki revisée: un nouveau contexte, de nouveaux défis pour la recherche biomedicale/The Declaration of Helsinki revised: a new context, new challenges for biomedical research." *Journal International de Bioéthique/International Journal of Bioethics* 2004 March; 15(1): 17–30, 130–131.

Canadian Institutes of Health Research, Natural Sciences and Engineering Research Council of Canada, Social Sciences and Humanities Research Council of Canada. *Tri-Council Policy Statement: Ethical Conduct for Research Involving Humans.* Ottawa: The Three Councils 1998 (with 2000, 2002 and 2005 amendments). [Online at http://pre.ethics.gc.ca/english/policystatement/policystatement.cfm]

Katz, Jay. "The Nuremberg Code and the Nuremberg Trial: A Reappraisal." *Journal of the American Medical Association* 276 (1996), 1662–66.

Knoppers, Bartha Maria, and Sprumont, Dominique. "Human Subjects Research, Ethics, and International Codes on Genetic Research." In Thomas H. Murray and Maxwell J. Mehlman, eds. *Ethical, Legal, and Policy Issues in Biotechnology.* 2 vols. New York: John Wiley & Sons, 2000, II, 566–76.

Levine, Robert J. "International Codes and Guidelines for Research Ethics: A Critical Appraisal." In Harold Y. Vanderpool, ed. *The Ethics of Research Involving Human Subjects: Facing the 21st Century.* Frederick, MD: University Publishing Group, 1996, 235–39.

Levine, Robert J., and Gorovitz, Samuel, with James Gallagher, eds. *Biomedical Research Ethics: Updating International Guidelines—A Consultation.* Geneva: Council for International Organizations of Medical Sciences, 2000.

Macklin, Ruth. "After Helsinki: Unresolved Issues in International Research." *Kennedy Institute of Ethics Journal* 11 (2001), 17–36.

Moreno, Jonathan D. "'The Only Feasible Means': The Pentagon's Ambivalent Relationship with the Nuremberg Code." *Hastings Center Report* 26 (September–October 1996), 11–19.

———. "Reassessing the Influence of the Nuremberg Code on American Medical Ethics." *Journal of Contemporary Health Law and Policy* 13 (1997), 347–60.

Parsi, Kayhan, and Spicer, Carol Mason. "Appendix I: Codes, Oaths, and Directives Related to Bioethics." In Stephen G. Post, ed. *Encyclopedia of Bioethics.* 3rd edition. New York: Macmillan Reference USA: Thomson/Gale; 2004: 2615–2909.

Shuster, Evelyne. "Fifty Years Later: The Significance of the Nuremberg Code." *New England Journal of Medicine* 337 (1997), 1436–40.

U.S., National Bioethics Advisory Commission. *Ethical and Policy Issues in International Research: Clinical Trials in Developing Countries.* 2 vols. Washington, DC: U.S. Government Printing Office, 2001.

U.S., National Commission for the Protection of Research Subjects. *The Belmont Report: Ethical Principles and Guidelines for the Protection of Human Subjects of Research and Appendix.* 3 vols. Washington, DC: U.S. Government Printing Office, 1978. [Excerpts published in *Federal Register* 44 (1979), 23192–97.]

Williams, John R. "The Promise and Limits of International Bioethics: Lessons from the Recent Revision of the Declaration of Helsinki." *Journal International de Bioethique / International Journal of Bioethics* 15 (2004), 31–42, 131.

CURRENT ETHICAL ISSUES IN HUMAN RESEARCH

Annas, George J.; Glantz, Leonard H.; and Katz, Barbara F. *Informed Consent to Human Experimentation: The Subject's Dilemma.* Cambridge, MA: Ballinger, 1977.

Baker, Robert. "Bioethics and Human Rights: A Historical Perspective." *Cambridge Quarterly of Healthcare Ethics* 10 (2001), 241–52.

———. "A Theory of International Bioethics: Multiculturalism, Postmodernism, and the Bankruptcy of Fundamentalism." *Kennedy Institute of Ethics Journal* 8 (1998), 201–31.

———. "A Theory of International Bioethics: The Negotiable and the Non-Negotiable." *Kennedy Institute of Ethics Journal* 8 (1998), 233–73.

Brainerd, Jeffrey. "Report Calls for Easing Rules on Research Involving Prisoners." *Chronicle of Higher Education* 52 (28 July 2006), A16.

Brody, Baruch A. *The Ethics of Biomedical Research: An International Perspective.* New York: Oxford University Press, 1998.

Capron, Alexander M. "Experimentation with Human Beings: Light or Only Shadows?" *Yale Journal of Health Policy, Law and Ethics* 6 (2006), 431–449.

Dresser, Rebecca. *When Science Offers Salvation: Patient Advocacy and Research Ethics.* New York: Oxford University Press, 2001.

Ellenberg, Susan; Fleming, Thomas; and DeMets, David. *Data Monitoring Committees in Clinical Trials: A Practical Perspective.* New York: John Wiley & Sons, 2002.

Emanuel, Ezekiel J.; Wendler, David; and Grady, Christine. "What Makes Clinical Research Ethical?" *Journal of the American Medical Association* 283 (2000), 2701–11.

Faden, Ruth R., Beauchamp, Tom L. with King, Nancy M. P. *A History and Theory of Informed Consent.* New York: Oxford University Press, 1986: Chapters 5–9.

Federman, Daniel D.; Hanna, Kathi E.; and Rodriguez, Laura Lyman, eds. Institute of Medicine [IOM] (United States). Committee on Assessing the System for Protecting Human Research Participants. *Responsible Research: A Systems Approach to Protecting Research Participants.* Washington, DC: National Academies Press, 2003.

Freund, Paul, ed. *Experimentation with Human Subjects.* New York: George Braziller, 1970.

Frewer, Andreas. "Debates on Human Experimentation in Weimar and Early Nazi Germany as Reflected in the Journal "Ethik" (1922–1938) and Its Context." In Volker Roelcke and Giovanni Maio, eds. *Twentieth Century Ethics of Human Subjects Research: Historical Perspectives on Values, Practices, and Regulations.* Stuttgart: Franz Steiner Verlag; 2004: 137–150.

Fried, Charles. *Medical Experimentation: Personal Integrity and Social Policy.* New York: American Elsevier, 1974.

Fry, Sara T., and Veatch, Robert M. "Experimentation on Human Beings." In their *Case Studies in Nursing Ethics.* Third edition. Sudbury, Mass.: Jones and Bartlett Publishers; 2006: 330–63.

Gostin, Lawrence O. "Biomedical Research Involving Prisoners: Ethical Values and Legal Regulation." *Journal of the American Medical Association* 297 (2007), 737–40.

Gray, Bradford H. *Human Subjects in Medical Experimentation.* New York: Wiley, 1975.

Grodin, Michael A., and Glantz, Leonard H., eds. *Children as Research Subjects: Science, Ethics, and Law.* New York: Oxford University Press, 1994.

Institute of Medicine (United States). Board on Health Sciences Policy. Committee on Assessing the System for Protecting Human Research Subjects. *Preserving Public Trust: Accreditation and Human Research Participant Protection Programs.* Washington, DC: National Academy Press, 2001.

Jonas, Hans. "Philosophical Reflections on Experimenting with Human Subjects." In his *Philosophical Essays: From Current Creed to Technological Man.* Chicago: University of Chicago Press, 1980, 105–31.

Kahn, Jeffrey P.; Mastroianni, Anna C.; and Sugarman, Jeremy, eds. *Beyond Consent: Seeking Justice in Research.* New York: Oxford University Press, 1998.

Kopelman, Loretta M. "Human Subjects Research, Ethics, Research on Children." In Thomas H. Murray and Maxwell J. Mehlman, eds. *Ethical, Legal, and Policy Issues in Biotechnology.* 2 vols. New York: John Wiley & Sons, 2000, 576–85.

Levine, Robert J. *Ethics and Regulation of Human Research.* 2nd ed. Baltimore, MD: Urban and Schwarzenberg, 1986.

Mastroianni, Anna C.; Faden, Ruth R.; and Federman, Daniel, eds. *Women and Health Research: Ethical and Legal Issues of Including Women in Clinical Studies.* 2 vols. Washington, DC: National Academy Press, 1994.

Nuffield Council on Bioethics. *The Ethics of Research Related to Healthcare in Developing Countries.* London: Nuffield Council on Bioethics, 2002.

Pence, Gregory. *Classic Cases in Medical Ethics.* 4th edition. New York: McGraw-Hill, 2004: Chapters 11, 12, and 14.

Rothman, David J. *Strangers at the Bedside: A History of How Law and Bioethics Transformed Medical Decision Making.* New York: Basic Books, 1991.

Temple, Robert, and Ellenberg, Susan S. "Placebo-Controlled Trials and Active-Control Trials in the Evaluation of New Treatments.

Part 1: Ethical and Scientific Issues." *Annals of Internal Medicine* 133 (2000), 455–63.

———. "Placebo-Controlled Trials and Active-Control Trials in the Evaluation of New Treatments. Part 2: Practical Issues and Specific Cases." *Annals of Internal Medicine* 133 (2000), 464–70.

Veatch, Robert M. *The Patient as Partner: A Theory of Human Experimentation Ethics.* Bloomington, IN: Indiana University Press, 1987.

ETHICAL ISSUES IN, AND GUIDELINES

FOR, ANIMAL RESEARCH

Bishop, Laura Jane, and Nolen, Anita Lonnes. "Animals in Research and Education: Ethical Issues." *Kennedy Institute of Ethics Journal* 11 (2001), 91–112.

Canadian Council on Animal Care. *Guide to the Care and Use of Experimental Animals.* Ottawa, Canada: The Council, Vol. 1, 2nd ed., 1993, Vol. 2, 1984. [Online at http://www.ccac.ca]

DeGrazia, David. *Taking Animals Seriously: Mental Life and Moral Status.* New York: Cambridge University Press, 1996.

European Union. Council Directive 86/609/EEC of 24 November 1986 on the approximation of laws, regulations and administrative provisions of the Member States regarding the protection of animals used for experimental and other scientific purposes [Online at http://eur-lex.europa.eu]

Haugen, David M., ed. *Animal Experimentation.* Detroit: Greenhaven Press, 2007.

Kahn, Jeffrey; Dell, Ralph; and Parry, Susan. "Animal Research: III: Law and Policy." In Stephen G. Post, ed. *Encyclopedia of Bioethics.* 3rd edition. New York: Macmillan Reference USA: Thomson/Gale; 2004: 178–183.

Kleinig, John. "Research on Animals, Ethics, Principles Governing Research on Animals." In Thomas H. Murray and Maxwell J. Mehlman, eds. *Ethical, Legal, and Policy Issues in Biotechnology.* 2 vols. New York: John Wiley & Sons, 2000, 1014–20.

Nuffield Council on Bioethics. *The Ethics of Research Involving Animals.* London: Nuffield Council on Bioethics, 2005.

Orlans, F. Barbara; Beauchamp, Tom L.; Dresser, Rebecca; Morton, David B.; and Gluck, John P., eds. *The Human Use of Animals: Case Studies in Ethical Choice.* New York: Oxford University Press, 1998.

Paul, Ellen Frankel, and Paul, Jeffrey. *Why Animal Experimentation Matters: The Use of Animals in Medical Research.* New Brunswick, NJ: Transaction Publishers, 2001.

Pluhar, Evelyn B. "Experimentation on Humans and Nonhumans." *Theoretical Medicine and Bioethics* 27 (2006), 333–355.

Regan, Tom. *The Case for Animal Rights.* Berkeley, CA: University of California Press, 1983.

———. *Defending Animal Rights.* Urbana, IL: University of Illinois Press, 2001.

Singer, Peter. *Animal Liberation,* 2nd ed. New York: New York Review of Books, 1990.

———. "Animal Research: II. Philosophical Issues." In Stephen G. Post, ed. *Encyclopedia of Bioethics.* 3rd edition. New York: Macmillan Reference USA: Thomson/Gale; 2004: 170–178.

United Kingdom, Home Office. *Guidance on the Operation of the Animals (Scientific Procedures) Act 1986.* 2000. Online at http://www.archive.official-documents.co.uk/document/hoc/321/321.htm.]

Whorton, James C. "Animal Research: I. Historical Aspects." In Stephen G. Post, ed. *Encyclopedia of Bioethics.* 3rd ed. New York: Macmillan Reference USA: Thomson/Gale; 2004: 166–170.

Chapter 3
The Patient–Professional Relationship

Introduction

This chapter explores a number of ethical issues that arise in the context of the relationship between the patient and the health care professional. These include (1) responsibilities of health care professionals in the management and protection of patients' health care information, (2) respective roles, rights, and obligations in medical decision making, and (3) challenges to communication in the health care setting.

MEDICAL CONFIDENTIALITY

The section on medical confidentiality in this chapter provides a strong link to traditional medical ethics, where rules of confidentiality have played a significant role since the Hippocratic Oath. There the physician vows: "What I may see or hear in the course of treatment or even outside of the treatment in regard to the life of men . . . I will keep to myself."

In the first selection in this chapter, Mark Siegler questions whether the tradition of confidentiality has been reduced to a "decrepit" concept of more symbolic than real value. Siegler maintains that traditional medical confidentiality has been systematically compromised in the course of modern bureaucratic health care and data storage systems that allow informational access to a large number of persons. He argues that infringements of confidentiality have become routine events in medical practice—the rule rather than the exception.

Siegler's article raises the question of whether medical confidentiality is an especially strict duty, a relic of the past, or a requirement in need of reconstruction. In addressing this question, we can begin by asking what would justify a practice of maintaining medical confidentiality in a profession in which access to vital information may mean the difference between life and death. Two general types of justification have been proposed for the confidentiality principle. The first type of justification appeals to the principle of respect for autonomy. The argument is that the health professional does not show proper respect for the patient's autonomy and privacy if he or she does not uphold the confidentiality of the professional–patient relationship. A variant of this approach asserts that there is an implied promise of confidentiality inherent in the professional–patient relationship, whether the professional explicitly recognizes the promise or not. In the absence of an explicit acknowledgment that confidentiality does *not* hold, the patient would always be entitled to assume that it does hold.

A second justification is that confidentiality should be maintained because it is a necessary condition of properly doing the work of a physician (or nurse or hospital). If confidentiality were ignored in medical practice, patients would be unwilling to reveal sensitive information to health professionals. This unwillingness would render diagnosis and cure more difficult and, in the long run, would be detrimental to the health of patients. The assumption is that the physician–patient relationship rests on a basis of trust that would be imperiled if physicians were not under an obligation to maintain confidence.

The second justification appeals to the positive *consequences* of confidentiality, whereas the first looks to a moral violation that would be wrong irrespective of the kinds of consequences envisaged in the second. That is, the first justification maintains that breaches of trust, broken promises, and failures to keep contractual obligations are themselves wrong, whereas the second looks not at what is intrinsically wrong but instead at whether the balance of the consequences supports maintaining confidentiality.

The second justification has been at the center of recent controversy about confidentiality. Its consequentialist commitments require that we compare the benefits of keeping confidences with the benefits of revealing confidential information in circumstances in which the information is desperately needed by another party. If through this comparison it turns out that there is an overriding duty to warn persons who might be seriously harmed if confidentiality were maintained, then confidentiality is not an absolute duty. Yet many have long held that confidentiality is an absolute duty.

A now classic case of conflict between the obligation of confidentiality and the obligation to protect others from harm occurred in *Tarasoff v. Regents of the University of California* (the second selection in this chapter). In this case a patient confided to his psychologist that he intended to kill a third party. The psychologist then faced the choice of preserving the confidentiality of the patient or of infringing his right of confidentiality to warn a young woman that her life might be in danger. The court finds that health care professionals have a duty to weigh a peril to the public that a patient discloses in confidence against the duty of maintaining confidentiality. But how is the one duty to be weighed against the other? How can we be confident that warning potential victims of a dangerous patient's disclosures will not undermine the benefits of a medical system that motivates disturbed individuals to seek help? As the *Tarasoff* opinion itself indicates, it is difficult to verify which alternative produces a better outcome for society.

One way out of this problem is to take the first justification very seriously and allow rights of patient autonomy to override the utilitarian social benefits of disclosing confidential information. There is a loss, however, by giving such stringent weight to rights of autonomy: The benefits of disclosure under desperate circumstances are lost if we allow no violations of confidentiality whatever. For example, physicians would not be able to report contagious diseases, child abuse, gunshot wounds, epilepsy (to a motor vehicle department), and the like.

To meet this challenge, perhaps one could support a *firm* rule of confidentiality without supporting an *absolute* rule. Using this approach, one could recognize a range of exceptions under which disclosure of clearly confidential information is permitted. One example of this problem is found in the contemporary discussion of the conditions under which confidential information about AIDS patients may be disclosed, especially when the disclosure constitutes a warning to persons such as health professionals of imminent danger.

Morton Winston considers a range of problems about AIDS and the limits of medical confidentiality in the final article in this section. He notes that rights of autonomy can often be limited by the *harm principle*, which requires persons to refrain from causing preventable wrongful harm to innocent others. This principle has special force when persons are vulnerable and dependent on others. Winston uses these premises to argue that breaches of confidentiality can be justified in a range of cases in which each of the following conditions is satisfied: (1) persons would be placed at risk of contracting AIDS, (2) carriers will not freely disclose their status, and (3) the identity and status of the carrier is known to a health professional.

Not all examples of the problem of confidentiality are so dramatic or socially significant as those discussed in the Tarasoff case and the Winston article. More troublesome and pervasive problems concern how much of a patient's medical record can be fed into a widely accessed "public" data bank, how much information about a patient's genetic makeup may be revealed to a sexual partner if there is a substantial likelihood of the couple's producing genetically handicapped children, what information employers and insurance companies should and should not receive, and to whom in a family the full range of test results in genetic screening should be disclosed. These are some of the many issues about confidentiality currently under discussion.

In addition, issues of confidentiality in the United States now arise in a highly regulated context. Indeed, the day-to-day process of ensuring confidentiality of health care records has become more routinized and bureaucratized in the past ten years with the passage of the federal Health Insurance Portability and Accountability Act of 1996, Public Law 104-191 (HIPAA). HIPAA was designed to encourage standardized communication among health care entities, but did not directly address confidentiality protections for the treatment and exchange of health care information. The 2000 HIPAA Privacy Rule, from the U.S. Department of Health and Human Services, instituted confidentiality protections, including formal notifications to patients about rights and uses of their identifiable health information and the formalization of institutional confidentiality practices and policies. Relevant laws at the state level also exist. While this legal context has forced attention to confidentiality of health care information, the ethical challenges discussed in this chapter persist, requiring ongoing attention and resolution.

TRUTH TELLING, NONDISCLOSURE, AND DISCLOSING MEDICAL ERROR

In modern medicine the nature and quality of the physician–patient relationship varies with prior contact, the mental or physical state of the patient, the manner in which the physician relates to the family, and problems in patient–family interactions. The patient's right to know the truth and the physician's obligation to tell it are contingent on these and other factors in the relationship.

Most writers in the history of medical ethics have held that departures from the general principle of truth telling are justified when information disclosure itself carries serious risks for patients. They view truth telling as limited by the Hippocratic principle that they should do no harm to patients in difficult circumstances by revealing upsetting conditions. If disclosure of a diagnosis of cancer, for example, would cause the patient anxiety or lead to an act of self-destruction, they believe that medical ethics requires that the physician carefully monitor and, at times, withhold the information that could cause additional harm. A common thesis is that in cases in which risks of harm from nondisclosure are low and benefits of nondisclosure to the patient are substantial, a physician may legitimately deceive or underdisclose the truth, and sometimes lie.

Deception is sometimes said to be easier to justify than blatant lying, because deception does not necessarily threaten the relationship of trust. Underdisclosure and nondisclosure are also thought to be more easily justified than lying. Those who share this perspective argue that it is important not to conflate the duties not to lie, not to deceive, and to disclose as if they were a single duty of veracity.

These justifications of nondisclosure seem especially plausible in cases in which bad news must be delivered to fragile patients or to strangers. Nevertheless, almost all authorities now agree that there is a strong duty of veracity in medicine because of respect for autonomous patients. Can these views about justified disclosure and justified nondisclosure be rendered consistent?

In the first essay in this section, David Thomasma explains both why truth telling is important and when truth telling rules might plausibly be overridden in the clinical setting. Thomasma defends the controversial thesis that "truth is a secondary good . . . [and] other primary values take precedence over the truth." Moreover, he says, "the only values that can trump the truth are recipient survival, community survival, and the ability to absorb the full impact of the truth at a particular time."

The recent patient safety movement has highlighted a somewhat different tension in the professional–patient relationship. The 2000 Institute of Medicine report, *To Err is Human*, estimated that up to 98,000 deaths per year were caused by preventable medical errors.[1] From a policy perspective, without error disclosure there is no opportunity to prevent repeated errors and harm to future patients. At an individual level, however, the interests of the patient and health care professional may diverge when the professional is involved in the commission of medical error during a patient's treatment. Even in cases where ethical consensus would urge disclosure, the realities of medical practice may discourage disclosure. The potential for negative professional consequences, including legal liability, institutional sanctions, or personal embarrassment, may persuade a health care provider to act in his or her own best interest rather than the best interest of a patient. At the same time, providers may also believe that nondisclosure is in the best interest of the patient, especially where the error is not significant or is remediable.

In the second selection, Wu and colleagues analyze the ethical responsibility of health care professionals to discuss medical mistakes with their patients. Except under limited conditions, they advocate for disclosure when medical errors occur. They also draw attention to the cultural and contextual challenges in integrating disclosure into medical practice.

The context in which disclosures are made has shifted somewhat in the last few years. The federal government, many state legislatures, and health care accrediting bodies have taken a keen interest in disclosure of medical mistakes. A few states now legally mandate disclosure of significant errors by providers or health care institutions. Other states have attempted to create a legal climate that is supportive of disclosure. For example, a number of states protect an apology from a provider to the patient from being used as an admission of the provider's liability in a medical malpractice lawsuit. Nonetheless, the tensions and ethical issues in disclosure of medical error remain.

Despite the mitigating conditions mentioned by Thomasma and Wu and colleagues, many writers in contemporary bioethics believe that all intentional suppression of pertinent information violates a patient's autonomy rights and violates the fundamental duties of the health professional. Here the duty of veracity is derived from obligations of respect for the autonomy of persons. This thesis has been especially prominent in the recent literature on informed consent.

INFORMED CONSENT

It is now widely believed that the physician has a moral obligation not only to tell patients the truth, but also to help them decide important matters that affect their health. This ability to make an educated decision is dependent on the availability of truthful information and the patient's capacity to handle the information. For this reason it is often said that before a physician performs a medical procedure on a competent patient, he or she has an obligation to obtain the patient's informed consent and to engage in mutual decision making with the patient.

The history of informed consent is not ancient. Prior to the 1950s, there was no firm ground in which a commitment to informed consent could take root. This is not to say that there is no relevant history of the physician's management of medical information in the encounter with patients. However, with few exceptions, no serious consideration was given to issues of either consent or self-determination by patients and research subjects. Proper principles, practices, and virtues of "truthfulness" in disclosure were occasionally discussed, but the perspective was largely one of how to make disclosures without harming patients by revealing their condition too abruptly and starkly.

Because of the vagueness that surrounds the term *informed consent*, some writers have been interested in analyzing the concept so that its meaning is as clear as possible. If overdemanding criteria such as "full disclosure and complete understanding" are adopted, an informed consent becomes impossible to obtain. Conversely, if underdemanding criteria such as "the patient signed the form" are used, an informed consent becomes too easy to obtain and the term loses all moral significance. Many interactions between a physician and a patient or an investigator and a subject that have been called informed consents have been so labeled only because they rest on underdemanding criteria; they are inappropriately referred to as informed consents. For example, a physician's truthful disclosure to a patient has often been declared the essence of informed consent, as if a patient's silence following disclosure could add up to an informed consent.

Jay Katz has been at the forefront of this effort to analyze the concept of informed consent. He argues that *informed consent* and *shared decision making* should be treated as virtually synonymous terms. His basic moral conviction is that the primary goal of informed consent in medical care and in research is to enable potential subjects and patients to make autonomous decisions about whether to grant or refuse authorization for medical and research interventions.

Ruth Faden and Tom Beauchamp agree that there is a historical relationship between shared decision making and informed consent, but believe it is confusing to treat them as *synonymous*. They argue that decision making should be distinguished from a subject's or patient's act of knowledgeably *authorizing* the intervention, that is, giving an informed consent. The essence of an informed consent, on this analysis, is an autonomous authorization. Such an authorization requires more than merely acquiescing in, yielding to, or complying with an arrangement or a proposal made by a physician or investigator.

One crucial question addressed in the articles on informed consent in this chapter is whether a valid informed consent can be given if a patient or subject does *not* autonomously authorize an intervention. The authors in this chapter all appear to answer "No" to this question. Yet most of the "consents" obtained in health care institutions at the present time probably do not constitute autonomous authorizations, in the sense of autonomy discussed in Chapter 1. That is, it is doubtful that a patient substantially understands the circumstances, makes a decision absent coercion, and intentionally authorizes a professional to proceed with a medical or research intervention. This situation opens up a range of questions about the validity of the practices of consent currently at work in contemporary medicine and research.

Another problem addressed in these articles concerns adequate standards of disclosure in informed consent contexts. Legal history reveals an evolving doctrine of informed consent from a 1767 case to the 1972 *Canterbury v. Spence* case (and its aftermath). *Canterbury* was the first and most influential of the recent landmark informed consent cases. In *Canterbury*, surgery on the patient's back and a subsequent accident in the hospital led to further injuries and unexpected paralysis, the possibility of which had not yet been disclosed. Judge Spottswood Robinson's opinion focuses on the needs of the reasonable person and the right to self-determination. As for sufficiency of information, the court holds: "The patient's right of self-decision shapes the boundaries of the duty to reveal. That right can be effectively exercised only if the patient possesses enough information to enable an intelligent choice." Katz delivers a blistering attack on the development of these standards in the precedent legal cases, especially *Canterbury*.

Many have challenged whether any legal standard could be adequate for clinical ethics (as distinct from a standard in law), because the law is almost uniformly directed at adequate *disclosures*. In recent bioethics the focus on informed consent has turned somewhat away from disclosure duties and more toward the quality of understanding and consent in the patient. Much has been made of Katz's claim that the key to effective communication is to invite participation by patients or subjects in an exchange of information and dialogue. Asking questions, eliciting the concerns and interests of the patient or subject, and establishing a climate that encourages the patient or subject to ask questions seems to be more important for medical ethics than the full body of requirements of disclosed information in law.

In the final selection in this section, Robert Levine discusses why the Western model of informed consent is unsuitable in much of the remainder of the world, where he thinks the concept of "person" differs substantially from that in Western societies. Levine concludes that we would be better off if we used a procedural solution to these problems when they are encountered rather than insisting on rules of obtaining consent. Levine's treatment also suggests how we might handle the growing problem of cultural diversity in Western nations when patients from non-Western countries present to health professionals.

REFUSAL OF TREATMENT

The subject of the fourth section of this chapter is refusal of treatment by a patient or a duly authorized representative of the patient (when a patient is incompetent or seriously ill). The major question is, "Under what conditions, if any, is it permissible for patients, health professionals, and surrogate decision makers to forgo treatment with the foreknowledge that there may be serious health consequences for the patient (such as death or disability)?"

It is now generally agreed, in both law and ethics, that a competent patient has an autonomy right to forgo treatment at any time, including the right to refuse medical nutrition and hydration. Indeed, refusals in medical settings have a moral power lacking in mere requests for assistance: A physician is morally and legally required to comply with a refusal. However, competent persons sometimes exercise their rights in a way inconsistent with the beliefs of other members of their family or inconsistent with the commitments of a health care institution—a problem that arises in this chapter in the case of Elizabeth Bouvia. She suffered from cerebral palsy that left her with virtually no motor function in her limbs or skeletal muscles, but she was unaffected cognitively. The court asserts that patients like Bouvia have a moral and constitutional right to refuse treatment even if its exercise creates a "life-threatening condition" of which physicians disapprove and consider against standards of practice.

Several celebrated legal cases have centered on whether formerly competent patients have some kind of right to refuse treatment despite their present incompetence. Among the best-known cases, and the only one to reach the U.S. Supreme Court, is that of Nancy Cruzan. The 25-year-old Ms. Cruzan was in a persistent vegetative state for over three years. Her parents then petitioned for permission to remove the feeding tube, knowing that, by doing so, their daughter would die. A lower court's authorization of termination of treatment was reversed by the Missouri Supreme Court, which ruled that no one may order an end to life-sustaining treatment for an incompetent person in the absence of a valid living will or clear and convincing evidence of the patient's wishes.

This decision was appealed to the U.S. Supreme Court, which handed down its decision in 1990. The majority opinion—the second selection in this section—holds that a state may constitutionally require "clear and convincing evidence" whenever surrogates claim to represent a patient's autonomous wishes about continuing or refusing life-sustaining treatment. The majority insists that its findings rest on a judgment by society that it is better to err in preserving life in a vegetative state than to err through a decision that leads directly to death. The dissenting justices express a particularly vigorous disagreement with this majority opinion. Justices Brennan, Marshall, and Blackmun find that "Nancy Cruzan has a fundamental right to be free of unwanted artificial nutrition and hydration"—a direct challenge to the line of argument in the majority opinion.

Whether the Court's opinion is adequate to protect the autonomy interests of patients is still under discussion. One of the major issues raised by *Cruzan* is whether a protected autonomy interest in refusing medical treatment can be meaningfully exercised only by competent patients or also by incompetent patients, either through their surrogates or through some forms of advance directive to health care authorities. These questions have fostered an active discussion of the role of advance directives in health care—our final topic in this chapter.

ADVANCE DIRECTIVES

In an advance directive—a device intended to implement patients' rights of autonomy— a person, while competent, either writes a directive for health care professionals or selects a surrogate to make decisions about treatments during periods of incompetence. Two types of advance directive have been recognized: *living wills*, which are substantive directives regarding medical procedures that should be provided or forgone in specific circumstances, and *durable powers of attorney* (DPA) for health care. A durable power of attorney is a legal document in which one person assigns another person as authority to perform specified actions on behalf of the signer.

Both kinds of advance directive can reduce stress for individuals, families, and health professionals who fear wrong outcomes or decisions, but they also generate practical and moral problems. First, relatively few persons compose them or leave explicit instructions. Second, a designated decision maker might be unavailable when needed, might be incompetent to make good decisions for the patient, or might have a conflict of interest. Third, laws often severely restrict the use of advance directives. For example, advance directives have legal effect in some states if and only if the patient is terminally ill and death is imminent. But decisions must be made in some cases when death is not imminent or the medical condition cannot appropriately be described as a terminal illness. Fourth, in the case of living wills, individuals have difficulty in specifying decisions or guidelines that adequately anticipate the full range of medical situations that might occur. The directive given may provide no basis for health professionals to overturn instructions that turn out not to be in the patient's best medical interest, although the patient could not have reasonably anticipated this circumstance while competent. Surrogate decision makers also make decisions with which physicians sharply disagree.

Despite these problems, the advance directive is widely recognized as a promising and valid way for competent persons to exercise their autonomy. On December 1, 1991, the Patient Self-Determination Act—a federal law known as PSDA—went into effect in the United States. This law requires health care facilities certified by Medicare or Medicaid to notify competent adult patients of their right to accept or refuse medical treatment and their right to execute an advance directive. This law gave powerful legal effect to advance directives in the United States.

The intent of this law—and of almost all rules and regulations pertaining to advance directives—is to allow patients to take control of their medical fate, on the grounds that their interests will ultimately be best served by making their own decisions, rather than having the decisions made for them. In their article in this chapter, Linda Emanuel and colleagues attempt to provide a practically oriented set of basic steps and skills for advance care planning. Their model of advance care planning *as a process* should be viewed as augmenting and updating (rather than replacing) executed advance directive forms. They identify several steps of providing information, facilitating discussion, recording statements, reviewing directives, and implementing decisions. They argue that their model will minimize risks and maximize benefits for patients and health professionals alike.

In the final article in this chapter, Ben A. Rich assesses advance directives as a form of anticipatory decision making that moves "beyond informed consent and refusal." Rich distinguishes between and assesses oral directives, living wills, and the durable power of attorney. He points to several flaws and limitations in these forms of advance planning, especially living wills and durable powers of attorney. He also discusses why there has been so much physician inattention to advance directives. Rich concludes that it is not the concept of advance directives that is flawed, but rather "our fledgling efforts at crafting them." He provides some reasons for optimism that "the next generation of advance directives will succeed where the others have failed."

T.L.B.
A.C.M.

NOTE

1. Institute of Medicine, *To Err is Human: Building a Safer Health System*, Linda T. Kohn, Janet M. Corrigan, and Molla S. Donaldson, eds., Committee on Quality of Health Care in America (Washington DC: National Academies Press, 2000).

The Confidentiality of Medical Information

MARK SIEGLER

Confidentiality in Medicine—A Decrepit Concept

Mark Siegler is director of the MacLean Center for Clinical Medical Ethics and Lindy Bergman Professor of Medicine and Surgery in the Department of Medicine at the University of Chicago. With Albert Jonsen and William Winslade, he published *Clinical Ethics*, which is widely consulted by health professionals. Among his many articles in bioethics are "The External Control of Private Medical Decisions: A Major Change in the Doctor-Patient Relationship," *Journal of American Geriatrics Society* and a collaboration entitled "A Procedure for Balancing the Rights of Patients and the Responsibilities of Physicians," *The Law-Medicine Relation: A Philosophical Exploration*.

Medical confidentiality, as it has traditionally been understood by patients and doctors, no longer exists. This ancient medical principle, which has been included in every physician's oath and code of ethics since Hippocratic times, has become old, worn-out, and useless; it is a decrepit concept. Efforts to preserve it appear doomed to failure and often give rise to more problems than solutions. Psychiatrists have tacitly acknowledged the impossibility of ensuring the confidentiality of medical records by choosing to establish a separate, more secret record. The following case illustrates how the confidentiality principle is compromised systematically in the course of routine medical care.

A patient of mine with mild chronic obstructive pulmonary disease was transferred from the surgical intensive-care unit to a surgical nursing floor two days after an elective cholecystectomy. On the day of transfer, the patient saw a respiratory therapist writing in his medical chart (the therapist was recording the results of an arterial blood gas analysis) and became concerned about the confidentiality of his hospital records. The patient threatened to leave the hospital prematurely unless I could guarantee that the confidentiality of his hospital record would be respected.

This patient's complaint prompted me to enumerate the number of persons who had both access to his hospital record and a reason to examine it. I was amazed to learn that at least 25 and possibly as many as 100 health professionals and administrative personnel at our university hospital had access to the patient's record and that all of them had a legitimate need, indeed a professional responsibility, to open and use that chart. These persons included 6 attending physicians (the primary physician, the surgeon, the pulmonary consultant, and others); 12 house officers (medical, surgical, intensive-care unit, and "covering" house staff); 20 nursing personnel (on three shifts); 6 respiratory therapists; 3 nutritionists; 2 clinical pharmacists; 15 students (from medicine, nursing, respiratory therapy, and clinical pharmacy); 4 unit secretaries; 4 hospital financial officers; and 4 chart reviewers (utilization review, quality assurance review, tissue review, and insurance auditor). It is of interest that this patient's problem was straightforward, and he therefore did not require many other technical and support services that the modern hospital provides. For example, he did not need multiple consultants and fellows, such specialized procedures as dialysis, or social workers, chaplains, physical therapists, occupational therapists, and the like.

Upon completing my survey I reported to the patient that I estimated that at least 75 health professionals and hospital personnel had access to his medical record. I suggested to the patient that these people were all involved in providing or supporting his health care services. They were, I assured him, working for him. Despite my reassurances the patient was obviously distressed and retorted, "I always believed that medical confidentiality was part of a doctor's code of ethics. Perhaps you should tell me just what you people mean by 'confidentiality'!"

TWO ASPECTS OF MEDICAL CONFIDENTIALITY

CONFIDENTIALITY AND THIRD-PARTY INTERESTS

Previous discussions of medical confidentiality usually have focused on the tension between a physician's responsibility to keep information divulged by patients secret and a physician's legal and moral duty, on occasion, to reveal such confidences to third parties, such as families, employers, public-health authorities, or police authorities. In all these instances, the central question relates to the stringency of the physician's obligation to maintain patient confidentiality when the health, well-being, and safety of identifiable others or of society in general would be threatened by a failure to reveal information about the patient. The tension in such cases is between the good of the patient and the good of others.

CONFIDENTIALITY AND THE PATIENT'S INTEREST

As the example above illustrates, further challenges to confidentiality arise because the patient's personal interest in maintaining confidentiality comes into conflict with his personal interest in receiving the best possible health care. Modern high-technology health care is available principally in hospitals (often, teaching hospitals), requires many trained and specialized workers (a "health-care team"), and is very costly. The existence of such teams means that information that previously had been held in confidence by an individual physician will now necessarily be disseminated to many members of the team. Furthermore, since health-care teams are expensive and few patients can afford to pay such costs directly, it becomes essential to grant access to the patient's medical record to persons who are responsible for obtaining third-party payment. These persons include chart reviewers, financial officers, insurance auditors, and quality-of-care assessors. Finally, as medicine expands from a narrow, disease-based model to a model that encompasses psychological, social, and economic problems,

not only will the size of the health-care team and medical costs increase, but more sensitive information (such as one's personal habits and financial condition) will now be included in the medical record and will no longer be confidential.

The point I wish to establish is that hospital medicine, the rise of health-care teams, the existence of third-party insurance programs, and the expanding limits of medicine will appear to be responses to the wishes of people for better and more comprehensive medical care. But each of these developments necessarily modifies our traditional understanding of medical confidentiality.

THE ROLE OF CONFIDENTIALITY IN MEDICINE

Confidentiality serves a dual purpose in medicine. In the first place, it acknowledges respect for the patient's sense of individuality and privacy. The patient's most personal physical and psychological secrets are kept confidential in order to decrease a sense of shame and vulnerability. Secondly, confidentiality is important in improving the patient's health care—a basic goal of medicine. The promise of confidentiality permits people to trust (i.e., have confidence) that information revealed to a physician in the course of a medical encounter will not be disseminated further. In this way patients are encouraged to communicate honestly and forthrightly with their doctors. This bond of trust between patient and doctor is vitally important both in the diagnostic process (which relies on an accurate history) and subsequently in the treatment phase, which often depends as much on the patient's trust in the physician as it does on medications and surgery. These two important functions of confidentiality are as important now as they were in the past. They will not be supplanted entirely either by improvements in medical technology or by recent changes in relations between some patients and doctors toward a rights-based, consumerist model.

POSSIBLE SOLUTIONS TO THE CONFIDENTIALITY PROBLEM

First of all, in all nonbureaucratic, noninstitutional medical encounters—that is, in the millions of doctor–patient encounters that take place in physician's offices, where more privacy can be preserved—meticulous care should be taken to guarantee that patients' medical and personal information will be kept confidential.

Secondly, in such settings as hospitals or large-scale group practices, where many persons have opportunities to examine the medical record, we should aim to provide access only to those who have "a need to know." This could be accomplished through such administrative changes as dividing the entire record into several sections—for example, a medical and financial section—and permitting only health professionals access to the medical information.

The approach favored by many psychiatrists—that of keeping a psychiatric record separate from the general medical record—is an understandable strategy but one that is not entirely satisfactory and that should not be generalized. The keeping of separate psychiatric records implies that psychiatry and medicine are different undertakings and thus drives deeper the wedge between them and between physical and psychological illness. Furthermore, it is often vitally important for internists or surgeons to know that a patient is being seen by a psychiatrist or is taking a particular medication. When separate records are kept, this information may not be available. Finally, if generalized, the practice of keeping a separate psychiatric record could lead to the unacceptable consequence of having a separate record for each type of medical problem.

Patients should be informed about what is meant by "medical confidentiality." We should establish the distinction between information about the patient that generally will be kept confidential regardless of the interest of third parties and information that will be exchanged among members of the health-care team in order to provide care for the patient. Patients should be made aware of the large number of persons in the modern hospital who require access to the medical record in order to serve the patient's medical and financial interests.

Finally, at some point most patients should have an opportunity to review their medical record and to make informed choices about whether their entire record is to be available to everyone or whether certain portions of the record are privileged and should be accessible only to their principal physician or to others designated explicitly by the patient. This approach would rely on traditional informed-consent procedural standards and might permit the patient to balance the personal value of medical confidentiality against the personal value of high-technology, team health care. There is no reason that the same procedure should not be used with psychiatric records instead of the arbitrary system now employed, in which everything related to psychiatry is kept secret.

AFTERTHOUGHT: CONFIDENTIALITY AND INDISCRETION

There is one additional aspect of confidentiality that is rarely included in discussions of the subject. I am referring here to the wanton, often inadvertent, but avoidable exchanges of confidential information that occur frequently in hospital rooms, elevators, cafeterias, doctors' offices, and at cocktail parties. Of course, as more people have access to medical information about the patient the potential for this irresponsible abuse of confidentiality increases geometrically.

Such mundane breaches of confidentiality are probably of greater concern to most patients than the broader issues of whether their medical records may be entered into a computerized data bank or whether a respiratory therapist is reviewing the results of an arterial blood gas determination. Somehow, privacy is violated and a sense of shame is heightened when intimate secrets are revealed to people one knows or is close to—friends, neighbors, acquaintances, or hospital roommates—rather than when they are disclosed to an anonymous bureaucrat sitting at a computer terminal in a distant city or to a health professional who is acting in an official capacity.

I suspect that the principles of medical confidentiality, particularly those reflected in most medical codes of ethics, were designed principally to prevent just this sort of embarrassing personal indiscretion rather than to maintain (for social, political, or economic reasons) the absolute secrecy of doctor–patient communications. In this regard, it is worth noting that Percival's Code of Medical Ethics (1803) includes the following admonition: "Patients should be interrogated concerning their complaint in a tone of voice which cannot be overheard."* We in the medical profession frequently neglect these simple courtesies.

CONCLUSION

The principle of medical confidentiality described in medical codes of ethics and still believed in by patients no longer exists. In this respect, it is a decrepit concept. Rather than perpetuate the myth of confidentiality and invest energy vainly to preserve it, the public and the profession would be better served if they devoted their attention to determining which aspects of the original principle of confidentiality are worth retaining. Efforts could then be directed to salvaging those.

*Leake C. D., ed. *Percival's Medical Ethics.* Baltimore: Williams & Wilkins, 1927.

TARASOFF v. REGENTS OF THE UNIVERSITY OF CALIFORNIA

California Supreme Court, 1976

TOBRINER, JUSTICE

On October 27, 1969, Prosenjit Poddar killed Tatiana Tarasoff. Plaintiffs, Tatiana's parents, allege that two months earlier Poddar confided his intention to kill Tatiana to Dr. Lawrence Moore, a psychologist employed by the Cowell Memorial Hospital at the University of California at Berkeley. They allege that on Moore's request, the campus police briefly detained Poddar, but released him when he appeared rational. They further claim that Dr. Harvey Powelson, Moore's superior, then directed that no further action be taken to detain Poddar. No one warned plaintiffs of Tatiana's peril. . . .

We shall explain that defendant therapists cannot escape liability merely because Tatiana herself was not their patient. When a therapist determines, or pursuant to the standards of his profession should determine, that his patient presents a serious danger of violence to another, he incurs an obligation to use reasonable care to protect the intended victim against such danger. The discharge of this duty may require the therapist to take one or more of various steps, depending upon the nature of the case. Thus it may call for him to warn the intended victim or others likely to apprise the victim of the danger, to notify the police, or to take whatever other steps are reasonably necessary under the circumstances. . . .

1. PLAINTIFFS' COMPLAINTS

Plaintiffs, Tatiana's mother and father, filed separate but virtually identical second amended complaints. The issue before us on this appeal is whether those complaints now state, or can be amended to state,

From 131 *California Reporter* 14, 551 P.2d 334, decided July 1, 1976. All footnotes and numerous references in the text of the decision and a dissent have been omitted.

causes of action against defendants. We therefore begin by setting forth the pertinent allegations of the complaints.

Plaintiffs' first cause of action, entitled "Failure to Detain a Dangerous Patient," alleges that on August 20, 1969, Poddar was a voluntary outpatient receiving therapy at Cowell Memorial Hospital. Poddar informed Moore, his therapist, that he was going to kill an unnamed girl, readily identifiable as Tatiana, when she returned home from spending the summer in Brazil. Moore, with the concurrence of Dr. Gold, who had initially examined Poddar, and Dr. Yandell, assistant to the director of the department of psychiatry, decided that Poddar should be committed for observation in a mental hospital. Moore orally notified Officers Atkinson and Teel of the campus police that he would request commitment. He then sent a letter to Police Chief William Beall requesting the assistance of the police department in securing Poddar's confinement.

Officers Atkinson, Brownrigg, and Halleran took Poddar into custody, but, satisfied that Poddar was rational, released him on his promise to stay away from Tatiana. Powelson, director of the department of psychiatry at Cowell Memorial Hospital, then asked the police to return Moore's letter, directed that all copies of the letter and notes that Moore had taken as therapist be destroyed, and "ordered no action to place Prosenjit Poddar in 72-hour treatment and evaluation facility."

Plaintiffs' second cause of action, entitled "Failure to Warn On a Dangerous Patient," incorporates the allegations of the first cause of action, but adds the assertion that defendants negligently permitted Poddar to be released from police custody without "notifying the parents of Tatiana Tarasoff that their daughter was in grave danger from Prosenjit Poddar." Poddar persuaded Tatiana's brother to share an apartment with him near

2. PLAINTIFFS CAN STATE A CAUSE OF ACTION AGAINST DEFENDANT THERAPISTS FOR NEGLIGENT FAILURE TO PROTECT TATIANA

The second cause of action can be amended to allege that Tatiana's death proximately resulted from defendants' negligent failure to warn Tatiana or others likely to apprise her of her danger. Plaintiffs contend that as amended, such allegations of negligence and proximate causation, with resulting damages, establish a cause of action. Defendants, however, contend that in the circumstances of the present case they owed no duty of care to Tatiana or her parents and that, in the absence of such duty, they were free to act in careless disregard of Tatiana's life and safety. . . .

In the landmark case of *Rowland v. Christian* (1968), Justice Peters recognized that liability should be imposed "for an injury occasioned to another by his want of ordinary care or skill" as expressed in section 1714 of the Civil Code. Thus, Justice Peters, quoting from *Heaven v. Pender* (1883) stated: "'whenever one person is by circumstances placed in such a position with regard to another . . . that if he did not use ordinary care and skill in his own conduct . . . he would cause danger of injury to the person or property of the other, a duty arises to use ordinary care and skill to avoid such danger.'"

We depart from "this fundamental principle" only upon the "balancing of a number of considerations"; major ones "are the foreseeability of harm to the plaintiff, the degree of certainty that the plaintiff suffered injury, the closeness of the connection between the defendant's conduct and the injury suffered, the moral blame attached to the defendant's conduct, the policy of preventing future harm, the extent of the burden to the defendant and consequences to the community of imposing a duty to exercise care with resulting liability for breach, and the availability, cost and prevalence of insurance for the risk involved."

The most important of these considerations in establishing duty is foreseeability. As a general principle, a "defendant owes a duty of care to all persons who are foreseeably endangered by his conduct, with respect to all risks which make the conduct unreasonably dangerous."

As we shall explain, however, when the avoidance of foreseeable harm requires a defendant to control the conduct of another person, or to warn of such conduct, the common law has traditionally imposed liability only if the defendant bears some special relationship to the dangerous person or to the potential victim. Since the relationship between a therapist and his patient satisfies this requirement, we need not here decide whether foreseeability alone is sufficient to create a duty to exercise reasonable care to protect a potential victim of another's conduct. . . .

A relationship of defendant therapists to either Tatiana or Poddar will suffice to establish a duty of care; as explained in section 315 of the Restatement Second of Torts, a duty of care may arise from either "(a) a special relation . . . between the actor and the third person which imposes a duty upon the actor to control the third person's conduct, or (b) a special relation . . . between the actor and the other which gives to the other a right of protection." . . .

The courts hold that a doctor is liable to persons infected by his patient if he negligently fails to diagnose a contagious disease, or, having diagnosed the illness, fails to warn members of the patient's family.

Since it involved a dangerous mental patient, the decision in *Merchants Nat. Bank & Trust Co. of Fargo v. United States* (1967) comes closer to the issue. The Veterans Administration arranged for the patient to work on a local farm, but did not inform the farmer of the man's background. The farmer consequently permitted the patient to come and go freely during non-working hours; the patient borrowed a car, drove to his wife's residence and killed her. Notwithstanding the lack of any "special relationship" between the Veterans Administration and the wife, the court found the Veterans Administration liable for the wrongful death of the wife.

In their summary of the relevant rulings Fleming and Maximov conclude that the "case law should dispel any notion that to impose on the therapists a duty to take precautions for the safety of persons threatened by a patient, where due care so requires, is in any way opposed to contemporary ground rules on the duty relationship. On the contrary, there now seems to be sufficient authority to support the conclusion that by entering into a doctor-patient relationship the therapist becomes sufficiently involved to assume some responsibility for the safety, not only of the patient himself, but also of any third person whom the doctor knows to be threatened by the patient." (Fleming & Maximov, *The Patient or His Victim: The Therapist's Dilemma* [1974] 62 Cal.L.Rev. 1025, 1030.)

Defendants contend, however, that imposition of a duty to exercise reasonable care to protect third persons is unworkable because therapists cannot accurately predict whether or not a patient will resort to violence. In support of this argument amicus representing the American Psychiatric Association and other professional societies cites numerous articles which indicate that therapists, in the present state of the art, are unable reliably to predict violent acts; their forecasts, amicus claims, tend consistently to overpredict violence, and indeed are more often wrong than right. Since predictions of violence are often erroneous, amicus concludes, the courts should not render rulings that predicate the liability of therapists upon the validity of such predictions. . . .

We recognize the difficulty that a therapist encounters in attempting to forecast whether a patient presents a serious danger of violence. Obviously we do not require that the therapist, in making that determination, render a perfect performance; the therapist need only exercise "that reasonable degree of skill, knowledge, and care ordinarily possessed and exercised by members of [that professional specialty] under similar circumstances." Within the broad range of reasonable practice and treatment in which professional opinion and judgment may differ, the therapist is free to exercise his or her own best judgment without liability; proof, aided by hindsight, that he or she judged wrongly is insufficient to establish negligence.

In the instant case, however, the pleadings do not raise any question as to failure of defendant therapists to predict that Poddar presented a serious danger of violence. On the contrary, the present complaints allege that defendant therapists did in fact predict that Poddar would kill, but were negligent in failing to warn.

Amicus contends, however, that even when a therapist does in fact predict that a patient poses a serious danger of violence to others, the therapist should be absolved of any responsibility for failing to act to protect the potential victim. In our view, however, once a therapist does in fact determine, or under applicable professional standards reasonably should have determined, that a patient poses a serious danger of violence to others, he bears a duty to exercise reasonable care to protect the foreseeable victim of that danger.

While the discharge of this duty of due care will necessarily vary with the facts of each case, in each instance the adequacy of the therapist's conduct must be measured against the traditional negligence standard of the rendition of reasonable care under the circumstances. As explained in Fleming and Maximov, *The Patient or His Victim: The Therapist's Dilemma* (1974) 62 Cal.L.Rev. 1025, 1967: ". . . the ultimate question of resolving the tension between the conflicting interests of patient and potential victim is one of social policy, not professional expertise. . . . In sum, the therapist owes a legal duty not only to his patient, but also to his patient's would-be victim and is subject in both respects to scrutiny by judge and jury." . . .

The risk that unnecessary warning may be given is a reasonable price to pay for the lives of possible victims that may be saved. We could hesitate to hold that the therapist who is aware that his patient expects to attempt to assassinate the President of the United States would not be obligated to warn the authorities because the therapist cannot predict with accuracy that his patient will commit the crime.

Defendants further argue that free and open communication is essential to psychotherapy, that "Unless a patient . . . is assured that . . . information [revealed by him] can and will be held in utmost confidence, he will be reluctant to make the full disclosure upon which diagnosis and treatment . . . depends." The giving of a warning, defendants contend, constitutes a breach of trust which entails the revelation of confidential communications.

We recognize the public interest in supporting effective treatment of mental illness and in protecting the rights of patients to privacy, and the consequent public importance of safeguarding the confidential character of psychotherapeutic communication. Against this interest, however, we must weigh the public interest in safety from violent assault. . . .

We realize that the open and confidential character of psychotherapeutic dialogue encourages patients to express threats of violence, few of which are ever executed. Certainly a therapist should not be encouraged routinely to reveal such threats; such disclosures could seriously disrupt the patient's relationship with his therapist and with the persons threatened. To the contrary, the therapist's obligations to his patient require that he not disclose a confidence unless such disclosure is necessary to avert danger to others, and even then that he do so discreetly, and in a fashion that would preserve the privacy of his patient to the fullest extent compatible with the prevention of the threatened danger.

The revelation of a communication under the above circumstances is not a breach of trust or a violation of professional ethics; as stated in the Principles of Medical Ethics of the American Medical Association

(1957), section 9: "A physician may not reveal the confidence entrusted to him in the course of medical attendance . . . *unless he is required to do so by law or unless it becomes necessary in order to protect the welfare of the individual or of the community.*" (Emphasis added.) We conclude that the public policy favoring protection of the confidential character of patient–psychotherapist communications must yield to the extent to which disclosure is essential to avert danger to others. The protective privilege ends where the public peril begins. . . .

For the foregoing reasons, we find that plaintiffs' complaints can be amended to state a cause of action against defendants Moore, Powelson, Gold, and Yandell and against the Regents as their employer, for breach of a duty to exercise reasonable care to protect Tatiana.

• • •

CLARK, JUSTICE (dissenting).

Until today's majority opinion, both legal and medical authorities have agreed that confidentiality is essential to effectively treat the mentally ill, and that imposing a duty on doctors to disclose patient threats to potential victims would greatly impair treatment. Further, recognizing that effective treatment and society's safety are necessarily intertwined, the Legislature has already decided effective and confidential treatment is preferred over imposition of a duty to warn.

The issue of whether effective treatment for the mentally ill should be sacrificed to a system of warnings is, in my opinion, properly one for the Legislature, and we are bound by its judgment. Moreover, even in the absence of clear legislative direction, we must reach the same conclusion because imposing the majority's new duty is certain to result in a net increase in violence. . . .

Overwhelming policy considerations weigh against imposing a duty on psychotherapists to warn a potential victim against harm. While offering virtually no benefit to society, such a duty will frustrate psychiatric treatment, invade fundamental patient rights and increase violence.

The importance of psychiatric treatment and its need for confidentiality have been recognized by this court. "It is clearly recognized that the very practice of psychiatry vitally depends upon the reputation in the community that the psychiatrist will not tell." (Slovenko, *Psychiatry and a Second Look at the Medical Privilege* (1960) 6 Wayne L.Rev. 175, 188.)

Assurance of confidentiality is important for three reasons.

DETERRENCE FROM TREATMENT

First, without substantial assurance of confidentiality, those requiring treatment will be deterred from seeking assistance. It remains an unfortunate fact in our society that people seeking psychiatric guidance tend to become stigmatized. Apprehension of such stigma— apparently increased by the propensity of people considering treatment to see themselves in the worst possible light—creates a well-recognized reluctance to seek aid. This reluctance is alleviated by the psychiatrist's assurance of confidentiality.

FULL DISCLOSURE

Second, the guarantee of confidentiality is essential in eliciting the full disclosure necessary for effective treatment. The psychiatric patient approaches treatment with conscious and unconscious inhibitions against revealing his innermost thoughts. "Every person, however well-motivated, has to overcome resistances to therapeutic exploration. These resistances seek support from every possible source and the possibility of disclosure would easily be employed in the service of resistance." (Goldstein & Katz, 36 Conn. Bar J. 175, 179.) Until a patient can trust his psychiatrist not to violate their confidential relationship, "the unconscious psychological control mechanism of repression will prevent the recall of past experiences." (Butler, *Psychotherapy and Griswold: Is Confidentiality a Privilege or a Right?* (1971) 3 Conn.L.Rev. 599, 604.)

SUCCESSFUL TREATMENT

Third, even if the patient fully discloses his thoughts, assurance that the confidential relationship will not be breached is necessary to maintain his trust in his psychiatrist—the very means by which treatment is effected. "[T]he essence of much psychotherapy is the contribution of trust in the external world and ultimately in the self, modelled upon the trusting relationship established during therapy." (Dawidoff, *The Malpractice of Psychiatrists*, 1966 Duke L.J. 696, 704.) Patients will be helped only if they can form a trusting relationship with the psychiatrist. All authorities appear to agree that if the trust relationship cannot be developed because of collusive communication between the psychiatrist and others, treatment will be frustrated.

Given the importance of confidentiality to the practice of psychiatry, it becomes clear the duty to warn imposed by the majority will cripple the use and effectiveness of psychiatry. Many people, potentially violent—yet susceptible to treatment—will be deterred from seeking it; those seeking it will be inhibited from making revelations necessary to effective treatment; and, forcing the psychiatrist to violate the patient's trust will destroy the interpersonal relationship by which treatment is effected.

VIOLENCE AND CIVIL COMMITMENT

By imposing a duty to warn, the majority contributes to the danger to society of violence by the mentally ill and greatly increases the risk of civil commitment—the total deprivation of liberty—of those who should not be confined. The impairment of treatment and risk of improper commitment resulting from the new duty to warn will not be limited to a few patients but will extend to a large number of the mentally ill. Although under existing psychiatric procedures only a relatively few receiving treatment will ever present a risk of violence, the number making threats is huge, and it is the latter group—not just the former—whose treatment will be impaired and whose risk of commitment will be increased.

Both the legal and psychiatric communities recognize that the process of determining potential violence in a patient is far from exact, being fraught with complexity and uncertainty. In fact precision has not even been attained in predicting who of those having already committed violent acts will again become violent, a task recognized to be of much simpler proportions.

This predictive uncertainty means that the number of disclosures will necessarily be large. As noted above, psychiatric patients are encouraged to discuss all thoughts of violence, and they often express such thoughts. However, unlike this court, the psychiatrist does not enjoy the benefit of overwhelming hindsight in seeing which few, if any, of his patients will ultimately become violent. Now, confronted by the majority's new duty, the psychiatrist must instantaneously calculate potential violence from each patient on each visit. The difficulties researchers have encountered in accurately predicting violence will be heightened for the practicing psychiatrist dealing for brief periods in his office with heretofore nonviolent patients. And, given the decision not to warn or commit must always be made at the psychiatrist's civil peril, one can expect most doubts will be resolved in favor of the psychiatrist protecting himself.

MORTON E. WINSTON

AIDS, Confidentiality, and The Right to Know

Morton Winston is professor of philosophy at the College of New Jersey. His work has focused on applied ethics, human rights, cognitive science, and philosophy of the mind. He is also a former chair of the board of directors of Amnesty International. He coauthored *Society, Ethics, and Technology* (Wadsworth) as well as *Global Ethics: Human Rights and Responsibilities* (University of Pennsylvania).

In June of 1987, a young woman who was nine months pregnant was shot with an arrow fired from a hunting bow on a Baltimore street by a man who was engaged in an argument with another person. Emergency workers from the city fire fighting unit were called to the scene, administered resuscitation to the profusely bleeding woman and took her to a local hospital where she died shortly afterwards. Her child, delivered by emergency Caesarian section, died the next day.

From *Public Affairs Quarterly* 2, no. 2 (April 1988), 91–104. Footnotes renumbered. Reprinted with permission.

This tragedy would have been quickly forgotten as yet another incident of random urban violence if it had not been later learned that the woman was infected with the AIDS virus. A nurse at the hospital decided on her own initiative that the rescue workers who had brought the woman to the emergency room should be informed that they had been exposed to HIV-infected blood and contacted them directly. Several days after this story hit the newspapers two state legislators introduced a bill adding AIDS to the list of diseases that hospitals would be required to inform workers about. A hospital spokeswoman was quoted in the newspaper as opposing the proposed legislation on the grounds that it would violate patient confidentiality and that, "People taking care of patients should assume that everyone is a potential AIDS patient and take precautions. The burden is on you to take care of yourself."[1]

This case, and others like it, raises difficult and weighty ethical and public policy issues. What are the limits of medical confidentiality? Who, if anyone, has a right to know that they may have been exposed to AIDS or other dangerous infectious diseases? Whose responsibility is it to inform the sexual contacts of AIDS patients or others who may have been exposed to the infection? Can public health policies be framed which will effectively prevent the spread of the epidemic while also protecting the civil and human rights of its victims?

I. THE LIMITS OF CONFIDENTIALITY

The rule of medical confidentiality enjoins physicians, nurses, and health care workers from revealing to third parties information about a patient obtained in the course of medical treatment. The rule protecting a patient's secrets is firmly entrenched in medical practice, in medical education, and receives explicit mention in all major medical oaths and codes of medical ethics. Sissela Bok has argued that the ethical justification for confidentiality rests on four arguments.[2]

The first and most powerful justification for the rule of confidentiality derives from the individual's right, flowing from autonomy, to control personal information and to protect privacy. The right of individuals to control access to sensitive information about themselves is particularly important in cases where revelation of such information would subject the individual to invidious discrimination, deprivation of rights, or physical or emotional harm. Since persons who are HIV-infected or who have AIDS or ARC (AIDS-Related Complex), are often subjected to discrimination, loss of employment, refusal of housing and insurance, many physicians believe that the confidentiality of HIV antibody test results and diagnoses of AIDS should be safeguarded under all circumstances. Since many infected persons and AIDS patients are members of groups which have traditionally been subject to discrimination or social disapproval—homosexuals, drug users, or prostitutes—the protection of confidentiality of patients who belong to these groups is especially indicated.

The second and third arguments for confidentiality concern the special moral relationship which exists between physicians and their patients. Medical practice requires that patients reveal intimate personal secrets to their physicians, and that physicians live up to the trust that is required on the part of patients to reveal such information; to fail to do so would violate the physician's duty of fidelity. Additionally, since medical practice is normally conducted under a tacit promise of confidentiality, physicians would violate this expectation by revealing their patients' secrets.

The fourth argument for confidentiality is based on utilitarian or broadly pragmatic considerations. Without a guarantee of confidentiality, potential patients in need of medical care would be deterred from seeking medical assistance from fear that sensitive personal information will be revealed to third parties thereby exposing the individual to the risk of unjust discrimination or other harm. Many physicians who work with AIDS patients find such pragmatic arguments particularly compelling, believing, perhaps correctly, that breaches of medical confidentiality concerning antibody status or a diagnosis of AIDS, would have a "chilling effect" preventing people in high-risk groups from seeking voluntary antibody testing and counselling. . . .

Bok believes that confidentiality is at best a prima facie obligation, one that while generally justified, can be overridden in certain situations by more compelling moral obligations. Among the situations which license breaches of confidentiality Bok cites are: cases involving a minor child or incompetent patient who would be harmed if sensitive information were not disclosed to a parent or guardian, cases involving threats of violence against identifiable third parties, cases involving contagious sexually transmitted diseases, and other cases where identifiable third parties would be harmed or placed at risk unknowingly by failure to disclose information known to a physician obtained through therapeutic communication.

In general, personal autonomy, and the derivative right of individuals to control personal information, is limited by the "Harm Principle" [HP], which requires moral agents to refrain from acts and omissions which would foreseeably result in preventable wrongful harm to innocent others. Bok argues that when HP (or a related ethical principle which I will discuss shortly) comes into play, "the prima facie premises supporting confidentiality are overridden" . . .[3] If this argument is correct, then the strict observance of confidentiality cannot be ethically justified in all cases, and physicians and nurses who invoke the rule of confidentiality in order to justify their not disclosing information concerning threats or risks to innocent third parties, may be guilty of negligence.

Before accepting this conclusion, however, it is necessary that we clarify the force of HP in the context of the ethics of AIDS, and refine the analysis of the conditions under which breaches of confidentiality pertaining to a patient's antibody status or a diagnosis of AIDS may be ethically justifiable.

II. VULNERABILITY, DISEASE CONTROL, AND DISCRIMINATION

Defenders of HP typically hold that all moral agents have a general moral obligation with respect to all moral patients to (a) avoid harm, (b) prevent or protect against harm, and (c) remove harm. One problem with HP is that not all acts and omissions which result in harm to others appear to be wrong. For instance, if I buy the last pint of Haagen-Daz coffee ice cream in the store, then I have, in some sense, harmed the next customer who wants to buy this good. Similarly, if one baseball team defeats another, then they have harmed the other team. But neither of these cases represent *wrongful* harms. Why then are some harms wrongful and others not?

Robert Goodin has recently developed a theory which provides at least a partial answer to this question. According to Goodin, the duty to protect against harm tends to arise most strongly in contexts in which someone is specially dependent on others or in some way specially vulnerable to their choices and actions.[4] He dubs this the Vulnerability Principle [VP]. Vulnerability, implying risk or susceptibility to harm, should be understood in a relational sense: being vulnerable to another is a condition which involves both a relative inability of the vulnerable party to protect themselves from harm or risk, and a correlative ability of another individual to act (or refrain from actions) which would foreseeably place the vulnerable party in a position of harm or risk or remove them from such a position. . . .

The Vulnerability Principle is related to the Harm Principle in giving a more precise analysis of the circumstances in which a strict duty to protect others arises. For example, under HP it might be thought that individuals, qua moral agents, have a duty to insure that persons be inoculated against contagious, preventable diseases, such as polio. However, while we have no strong obligations under HP to ensure that other adults have been inoculated, we *do* have a strong general obligation under VP to see to it that all young children are inoculated, and I have a special duty as a parent to see that my own children are inoculated. Children, as a class, are especially vulnerable and lack the ability to protect themselves. Being a parent *intensifies* the duty to prevent harm to children, by focusing the duty to protect the vulnerable on individuals who are specially responsible for the care of children. For other adults, on the other hand, I have no strong duty to protect, since I may generally assume that mature moral agents have both the ability and the responsibility to protect themselves.

Viewed in this light, the remarks quoted earlier by the hospital spokeswoman take on new meaning and relevance. She argued that it is the responsibility of health care workers to protect themselves by taking appropriate infection control measures in situations in which they may be exposed to blood infected with HIV. This argument might be a good one if people who occupy these professional roles are trained in such measures and are equipped to use them when appropriate. If they were so equipped, then in the Baltimore case, the nurse who later informed the rescue workers of the patient's antibody status was *not* specially responsible to prevent harm; the paramedics were responsible for their own safety.

The main problem with this argument is that it is not always possible to assume that emergency workers and others who provide direct care to AIDS patients or HIV-infected individuals are properly trained and equipped in infection control, nor, even if they are, that it is always feasible for them to employ these procedures in emergency situations. The scene of an emergency is not a controlled environment, and while emergency and public safety workers may take precautions such as wearing gloves and masks, these measures can be rendered ineffective, say, if a glove is torn and the worker cut while wrestling someone from a mass of twisted metal that was a car. While *post hoc* notification of the antibody status of people whom public safety workers have handled may not prevent them from contracting infection, it can alert them to the need to be tested, and thus can prevent them from spreading the infection (if they are in fact infected) to others, e.g. their spouses.

Health care workers, public safety workers, paramedics, and others who come into direct contact with blood which may be infected with the AIDS virus represent a class of persons for whom the Vulnerability Principle suggests a special "duty to protect" is appropriate. It is appropriate in these cases because such workers are routinely exposed to blood in the course of their professional activities, and exposure to infected blood is one way in which people can become infected with the AIDS virus. Such workers could protect themselves by simply refusing to handle anyone whom they suspected of harboring the infection. Doing this, however, would mean violating their professional responsibility to provide care. Hence, morally, they can only protect themselves by reducing their risk of exposure, in this case, by employing infection control measures and being careful. In this respect, health care workers, whether they work inside or outside of the hospital, are in a relevantly different moral situation than ordinary people who are not routinely exposed to blood and who have no special duty to provide care, and this makes them specially vulnerable. It thus appears that the nurse who informed the emergency workers of their risk of exposure did the right thing in informing them, since in doing so she was discharging a duty to protect the vulnerable.

But do similar conclusions follow with respect to "ordinary" persons who need not expose themselves to infection in the course of their professional activities? Consider the case in which a patient who is known to have a positive antibody status informs his physician that he does not intend to break off having sexual relations and that he will not tell his fiancée that he is infected with the AIDS virus.

In this case, we have a known, unsuspecting party, the fiancée, who will be placed at risk by failure to discharge a duty to protect. The fiancée is vulnerable in this case to the infected patient, since it is primarily *his* actions or omissions which place her at risk. According to HP + VP, the patient has a strong special responsibility to protect those with whom he has or will have sexual relations against infection. There are a number of ways in which he can discharge this duty. For instance, he can break off the relationship, abstain from sexual intercourse, practice "safe sex," or he can inform his fiancée of his antibody status. This last option protects the fiancée by alerting her to the need to protect herself. But does the physician in

this case also have a special responsibility to protect the fiancée?

She does, in this case, if she has good reason to believe that her patient will not discharge his responsibility to protect his fiancée or inform her of his positive antibody status. Since the physician possesses the information which would alert her patient's fiancée to a special need to protect herself, and the only other person who has this information will not reveal it, the fiancée is specially dependent upon the physician's choices and actions. Were she to fail to attempt to persuade her patient to reveal the information, or if he still refused to do so, to see to it that the patient's fiancée was informed, she would be acting in complicity with a patient who was violating his duty to prevent harm, and so would also be acting unethically under the Vulnerability Principle.

It thus appears that the rule of confidentiality protecting a patient's HIV antibody status cannot be regarded as absolute. There are several sorts of cases where HP + VP override the rule of confidentiality. However, finding there are justified exceptions to a generally justified rule of practice does not allow for unrestricted disclosure of antibody status to all and sundry. The basic question which must be answered in considering revealing confidential information concerning a patient's HIV antibody status is: *Is the individual to be notified someone who is specially vulnerable? That is, are they someone who faces a significant risk of exposure to the infection, and, will revealing confidential information to them assist them in reducing this risk to themselves or others?*

Answering this question is not always going to be easy, and applying HP + VP and balancing its claims against those of confidentiality will require an extraordinary degree of moral sensitivity and discretion. Because the rule of confidentiality describes a valid prima facie moral responsibility of physicians, the burden of proof must always fall on those who would violate it in order to accommodate the claims of an opposing ethical principle. Perhaps this is why physicians tend to assume that if the rule of confidentiality is not absolute, it might as well be treated as such. Physicians, nurses, and others who are privy to information about patients' antibody status, by and large, are likely to lack the relevant degree of ethical sensitivity to discriminate the cases in which confidentiality can be justifiably violated from those where it cannot. So if we must err, the argument goes, it is better to err on the side of confidentiality.

Aside from underestimating the moral sensitivity of members of these professional groups, this argument fails to take into account that there are two ways of erring—one can err by wrongfully disclosing confidential information to those who have no right to know it, and one can err by failing to disclose confidential information to those who do have a right to know it. The harm that can result from errors of the first kind [is] often significant, and sometimes irreparable. But so are the harms that result from errors of the second kind. While the burden of proof should be placed on those who would breach the prima facie rule of confidentiality, it should sometimes be possible for persons to satisfy this burden and act in accordance with HP + VP without moral fault.

The strength of conviction with which many physicians in the forefront of AIDS research and treatment argue for the protection of confidentiality can be explained partly by recognizing that they view themselves as having a special responsibility to prevent harm to AIDS patients. The harm which they seek to prevent, however, is not only harm to their patient's health. It is also social harm caused by discrimination that these physicians are trying to prevent. This is yet a different application of HP + VP in the context of AIDS which merits close attention. . . .

Medical personnel and public health authorities who take the position that confidentiality is absolute in order to shield their patients from discrimination, will increasingly find themselves in the uncomfortable position of being accomplices to the irresponsible behavior of known noncompliant positives. What is needed, then, is a finely drawn public policy that includes strong and effective anti-discrimination standards, a public education program which encourages individual and professional responsibility, and a set of clear effective guidelines for public health authorities concerning when and to whom confidential information necessary for disease control and the protection of those at risk may be revealed.

III. WHO HAS A RIGHT TO KNOW?

The Vulnerability Principle suggests that breaches of confidentiality may be justified in cases where the following conditions obtain: (1) there is an identifiable person or an identifiable group of people who are "at risk" of contracting AIDS from a known carrier, (2) the carrier has not or will not disclose his/her antibody status to those persons whom he/she has placed or will place at risk, and (3) the identity of the carrier and his/her antibody status is known to a physician, nurse, health care worker, public health authority, or another person privileged to this information. It is justifiable, under these circumstances, to reveal information which might enable others to identify an AIDS patient or HIV-infected person. Revelation of confidential information is justified under this rule by the fact that others are vulnerable to infection, or may be unknowingly infecting others, and the information to be revealed may serve as an effective means of protecting those at risk.

NOTES

1. *The Baltimore Sun*, June 11, 1987, p. D1.

2. Sissela Bok, *Secrets: On the Ethics of Concealment and Revelation* (New York: Vintage Books, 1983); Chapter IX.

3. Bok, Op. Cit., pp. 129–130.

4. Robert E. Goodin, *Protecting the Vulnerable: A Reanalysis of Our Social Responsibilities* (Chicago: The University of Chicago Press, 1985).

Truth Telling, Nondisclosure, and Disclosing Medical Error

DAVID C. THOMASMA

Telling the Truth to Patients: A Clinical Ethics Exploration

David Thomasma was professor of medical ethics in the Neiswanger Institute for Bioethics and Health Policy at Loyola University Chicago Medical Center, where he directed the Medical Humanities Program. His many publications focused heavily on the Doctor-Patient Relationship. His collaborations with Dr. Edmund Pellegrino produced several books, including *For the Patient's Good: The Restoration of Beneficence in Health Care* (Oxford).

REASONS FOR TELLING THE TRUTH

. . . In all human relationships, the truth is told for a myriad of reasons. A summary of the prominent reasons are that it is a right, a utility, and a kindness.

It is a right to be told the truth because respect for the person demands it. As Kant argued, human society would soon collapse without truth telling, because it is the basis of interpersonal trust, covenants, contracts, and promises.

The truth is a utility as well, because persons need to make informed judgments about their actions. It is a mark of maturity that individuals advance and grow morally by becoming more and more self-aware of their needs, their motives, and their limitations. All these steps toward maturity require honest and forthright communication, first from parents and later also from siblings, friends, lovers, spouses, children, colleagues, co-workers, and caregivers.[1]

Finally, it is a kindness to be told the truth, a kindness rooted in virtue precisely because persons to whom lies are told will of necessity withdraw from important, sometimes life-sustaining and life-saving relationships. Similarly, those who tell lies poison not only their relationships but themselves, rendering themselves incapable of virtue and moral growth.[2] . . .

OVERRIDING THE TRUTH

. . . Not all of us act rationally and autonomously at all times. Sometimes we are under sufficient stress

that others must act to protect us from harm. This is called necessary paternalism. Should we become seriously ill, others must step in and rescue us if we are incapable of doing it ourselves. . . .

IN GENERAL RELATIONSHIPS

In each of the three main reasons why the truth must be told, as a right, a utility, and a kindness, lurk values that may from time to time become more important than the truth. When this occurs, the rule of truth telling is trumped, that is, overridden by a temporarily more important principle. The ultimate value in all instances is the survival of the community and/or the well-being of the individual. Does this mean for paternalistic reasons, without the person's consent, the right to the truth, the utility, and the kindness, can be shunted aside? The answer is "yes." The truth in a relationship responds to a multivariate complexity of values, the context for which helps determine which values in that relationship should predominate.

Nothing I have said thus far suggests that the truth may be treated in a cavalier fashion or that it can be withheld from those who deserve it for frivolous reasons. The only values that can trump the truth are recipient survival, community survival, and the ability to absorb the full impact of the truth at a particular time. All these are only temporary trump cards in any event. They only can be played under certain limited conditions because respect for persons is a foundational value in all relationships.

From *Cambridge Quarterly of Healthcare Ethics* 3 (1994), 375–82. Copyright © 1994 Cambridge University Press. Reprinted with permission.

It is time to look more carefully at one particular form of human relationship, the relationship between the doctor and the patient or sometimes between other healthcare providers and the patient.

Early in the 1960s, studies were done that revealed the majority of physicians would not disclose a diagnosis of cancer to a patient. Reasons cited were mostly those that derived from nonmaleficence. Physicians were concerned that such a diagnosis might disturb the equanimity of a patient and might lead to desperate acts. Primarily physicians did not want to destroy their patients' hope. By the middle 1970s, however, repeat studies brought to light a radical shift in physician attitudes. Unlike earlier views, physicians now emphasized patient autonomy and informed consent over paternalism. In the doctor–patient relation, this meant the majority of physicians stressed the patient's right to full disclosure of diagnosis and prognosis.

One might be tempted to ascribe this shift of attitudes to the growing patients' rights and autonomy movements in the philosophy of medicine and in public affairs. No doubt some of the change can be attributed to this movement. But also treatment interventions for cancer led to greater optimism about modalities that could offer some hope to patients. Thus, to offer them full disclosure of their diagnosis no longer was equivalent to a death sentence. Former powerlessness of the healer was supplanted with technological and pharmaceutical potentialities.

A more philosophical analysis of the reasons for a shift comes from a consideration of the goal of medicine. The goal of all healthcare relations is to receive/provide help for an illness such that no further harm is done to the patient, especially in that patient's vulnerable state.[3] The vulnerability arises because of increased dependency. Presumably, the doctor will not take advantage of this vulnerable condition by adding to it through inappropriate use of power or the lack of compassion. Instead, the vulnerable person should be assisted back to a state of human equality, if possible, free from the prior dependency.[4]

First, the goal of the healthcare giver–patient relation is essentially to restore the patient's autonomy. Thus, respect for the right of the patient to the truth is measured against this goal. If nothing toward that goal can be gained by telling the truth at a particular time, still it must be told for other reasons. Yet, if the truth would impair the restoration of autonomy, then it may be withheld on grounds of potential harm. Thus the goal of the healing relationship enters into the calculus of values that are to be protected.

Second, most healthcare relationships of an interventionist character are temporary, whereas relationships involving primary care, prevention, and chronic or dying care are more permanent. These differences also have a bearing on truth telling. During a short encounter with healthcare strangers, patients and healthcare providers will of necessity require the truth more readily than during a long-term relation among near friends. In the short term, decisions, often dramatically important ones, need to be made in a compressed period. There is less opportunity to maneuver or delay for other reasons, even if there are concerns about the truth's impact on the person.

Over a longer period, the truth may be withheld for compassionate reasons more readily. Here, the patient and physician or nurse know one another. They are more likely to have shared some of their values. In this context, it is more justifiable to withhold the truth temporarily in favor of more important long-term values, which are known in the relationship.

Finally, the goal of healthcare relations is treatment of an illness. An illness is far broader than its subset, disease. Illness can be viewed as a disturbance in the life of an individual, perhaps due to many nonmedical factors. A disease, by contrast, is a medically caused event that may respond to more interventionist strategies.[5]

Helping one through an illness is a far greater personal task than doing so for a disease. A greater, more enduring bond is formed. The strength of this bond may justify withholding the truth as well, although in the end "the truth will always out."

CLINICAL CASE CATEGORIES

The general principles about truth telling have been reviewed, as well as possible modifications formed from the particularities of the healthcare professional–patient relationship. Now I turn to some contemporary examples of how clinical ethics might analyze the hierarchy of values surrounding truth telling.

There are at least five clinical case categories in which truth telling becomes problematic: intervention cases, long-term care cases, cases of dying patients, prevention cases, and nonintervention cases.

INTERVENTION CASES

Of all clinically difficult times to tell the truth, two typical cases stand out. The first usually involves a mother of advanced age with cancer. The family might beg the surgeon not to tell her what has been discovered for fear that "Mom might just go off the deep end." The movie *Dad*, starring Jack Lemmon, had as its centerpiece the notion that Dad could not tolerate the idea of cancer. Once told, he went into a psychotic shock that ruptured standard relationships with the doctors, the hospital, and the family. However, because this diagnosis requires patient participation for chemotherapeutic interventions and the time is short, the truth must be faced directly. Only if there is not to be intervention might one withhold the truth from the patient for a while, at the family's request, until the patient is able to cope with the reality. A contract about the time allowed before telling the truth might be a good idea.

The second case is that of ambiguous genitalia. A woman, 19 years old, comes for a checkup because she plans to get married and has not yet had a period. She is very mildly retarded. It turns out that she has no vagina, uterus, or ovaries but does have an undescended testicle in her abdomen. She is actually a he. Should she be told this fundamental truth about herself? Those who argue for the truth do so on grounds that she will eventually find out, and more of her subsequent life will have been ruined by the lies and disingenuousness of others. Those who argue against the truth usually prevail. National standards exist in this regard. The young woman is told that she has something like a "gonadal mass" in her abdomen that might turn into cancer if not removed, and an operation is performed. She is assisted to remain a female.

More complicated still is a case of a young Hispanic woman, a trauma accident victim, who is gradually coming out of a coma. She responds only to commands such as "move your toes." Because she is now incompetent, her mother and father are making all care decisions in her case. Her boyfriend is a welcome addition to the large, extended family. However, the physicians discover that she is pregnant. The fetus is about 5 weeks old. Eventually, if she does not recover, her surrogate decision makers will have to be told about the pregnancy, because they will be involved in the terrible decisions about continuing the life of the fetus even if it is a risk to the mother's recovery from the coma. This revelation will almost certainly disrupt current family relationships and the role of the boyfriend. Further, if the mother is incompetent to decide, should not the boyfriend, as presumed father, have a say in the decision about his own child?

In this case, revelation of the truth must be carefully managed. The pregnancy should be revealed only on a "need to know" basis, that is, only when the survival of the young woman becomes critical. She is still progressing moderately towards a stable state.

LONG-TERM CASES

Rehabilitation medicine provides one problem of truth telling in this category. If a young man has been paralyzed by a football accident, his recovery to some level of function will depend upon holding out hope. As he struggles to strengthen himself, the motivation might be a hope that caregivers know to be false, that he may someday be able to walk again. Yet this falsehood is not corrected, lest he slip into despair. Hence, because this is a long-term relationship, the truth will be gradually discovered by the patient under the aegis of encouragement by his physical therapists, nurses, and physicians, who enter his life as near friends.

CASES OF DYING PATIENTS

Sometimes, during the dying process, the patient asks directly, "Doctor, am I dying?" Physicians are frequently reluctant to "play God" and tell the patient how many days or months or years they have left. This reluctance sometimes bleeds over into a less-than-forthright answer to the question just asked. A surgeon with whom I make rounds once answered this question posed by a terminally ill cancer patient by telling her that she did not have to worry about her insurance running out!

Yet in every case of dying patients, the truth can be gradually revealed such that the patient learns about dying even before the family or others who are resisting telling the truth. Sometimes, without directly saying "you are dying," we are able to use interpretative truth and comfort the patient. If a car driver who has been in an accident and is dying asks about other family members in the car who are already dead, there is no necessity to tell him the truth. Instead, he can be told that "they are being cared for" and that the important thing right now is that he be comfortable and not in pain. One avoids the awful truth because he may feel responsible and guilt ridden during his own dying hours if he knew that the rest of his family were already dead.

PREVENTION CASES

A good example of problems associated with truth telling in preventive medicine might come from screening. The high prevalence of prostate cancer among men over 50 years old may suggest the utility of cancer screening. An annual checkup for men over

40 years old is recommended. Latent and asymptomatic prostate cancer is often clinically unsuspected and is present in approximately 30% of men over 50 years of age. If screening were to take place, about 16.5 million men in the United States alone would be diagnosed with prostate cancer, or about 2.4 million men each year. As of now, only 120,000 cases are newly diagnosed each year. Thus, as Timothy Moon noted in a recent sketch of the disease, "a majority of patients with prostate cancer that is not clinically diagnosed will experience a benign course throughout their lifetime."[6]

The high incidence of prostate cancer coupled with a very low malignant potential would entail a whole host of problems if subjected to screening. Detection would force patients and physicians to make very difficult and life-altering treatment decisions. Among them are removal of the gland (with impotence a possible outcome), radiation treatment, and most effective of all, surgical removal of the gonads (orchiectomy). But why consider these rather violent interventions if the probable outcome of neglect will overwhelmingly be benign? For this reason the U.S. Preventive Services Task Force does not recommend either for or against screening for prostate cancer.[7] Quality-of-life issues would take precedence over the need to know.

NONINTERVENTION CASES

This last example more closely approximates the kind of information one might receive as a result of gene mapping. This information could tell you of the likelihood or probability of encountering a number of diseases through genetic heritage, for example, adult onset or type II diabetes, but could not offer major interventions for most of them (unlike a probability for diabetes).

Some evidence exists from recent studies that the principle of truth telling now predominates in the doctor–patient relationship. Doctors were asked about revealing diagnosis for Huntington's disease and multiple sclerosis, neither of which is subject to a cure at present. An overwhelming majority would consider full disclosure. This means that, even in the face of diseases for which we have no cure, truth telling seems to take precedence over protecting the patient from imagined harms.

The question of full disclosure acquires greater poignancy in today's medicine, especially with respect to Alzheimer's disease and genetic disorders that may be diagnosed in utero. There are times when our own

scientific endeavors lack a sufficient conceptual and cultural framework around which to assemble facts. The facts can overwhelm us without such conceptual frameworks. The future of genetics poses just such a problem. In consideration of the new genetics, this might be the time to stress values over the truth.

CONCLUSION

Truth in the clinical relationship is factored in with knowledge and values.

First, truth is contextual. Its revelation depends upon the nature of the relationship between the doctor and patient and the duration of that relationship.

Second, truth is a secondary good. Although important, other primary values take precedence over the truth. The most important of these values is survival of the individual and the community. A close second would be preservation of the relationship itself.

Third, truth is essential for healing an illness. It may not be as important for curing a disease. That is why, for example, we might withhold the truth from the woman with ambiguous genitalia, curing her disease (having a gonad) in favor of maintaining her health (being a woman).

Fourth, withholding the truth is only a temporary measure. *In vino, veritas* it is said. The truth will eventually come out, even if in a slip of the tongue. Its revelation, if it is to be controlled, must always aim at the good of the patient for the moment.

At all times, the default mode should be that the truth is told. If, for some important reason, it is not to be immediately revealed in a particular case, a truth-management protocol should be instituted so that all caregivers on the team understand how the truth will eventually be revealed.

NOTES

1. Bok, S. *Lying: Moral Choice in Public and Personal Life.* New York: Vintage Books, 1989.

2. Pellegrino, E. D., Thomasma, D. C. *The Virtues in Medical Practice.* New York: Oxford University Press, 1993.

3. Pellegrino, E. D., Thomasma, D. C. *For the Patient's Good: The Restoration of Beneficence in Health Care.* New York: Oxford University Press, 1998.

4. Cassell, E. The nature of suffering and the goals of medicine. *New England Journal of Medicine* 1982; 306(11): 639–45.

5. See Nordenfelt, L., issue editor. Concepts of health and their consequences for health care. *Theoretical Medicine* 1993; 14(4).

6. Moon, T. D. Prostate cancer. *Journal of the American Geriatrics Society* 1992; 40: 622–7 (quote from 626).

7. See note 6. Moon. 1992; 40: 622–7.

ALBERT W. WU, THOMAS A. CAVANAUGH, STEPHEN J. MCPHEE, BERNARD LO, AND GUY P. MICCO

To Tell the Truth: Ethical and Practical Issues in Disclosing Medical Mistakes to Patients

Albert W. Wu is Professor of Health Policy and Management at the Johns Hopkins Bloomberg School of Public Health. His research and publications focus on measuring health and patient outcomes to assess treatments and quality of care. He currently serves on the Institute of Medicine's Identifying and Preventing Medical Errors Committee.

Thomas A. Cavanaugh is Professor and Chair of the Department of Philosophy at the University of San Francisco. He has published numerous books and articles on medical ethics and moral psychology, including *Double-Effect Reasoning: Doing Good and Avoiding Evil* (Oxford).

Stephen J. McPhee is Professor in the Department of Medicine and a faculty member in the Institute for Health Policy Studies, at the University of California, San Francisco. His publications focus on the practice of medicine in ethnically diverse communities.

Bernard Lo is Professor of Medicine and Director of the Program in Medical Ethics at the University of California, San Francisco. He served as a member of President Clinton's National Bioethics Advisory Commission. He has published extensively in many areas of bioethics, including medical decision making, HIV infection, human subjects research, and stem cell research. His publications include *Resolving Ethical Dilemmas: A Guide for Clinicians* (Lippincott Williams & Wilkins).

Guy P. Micco is Clinical Professor in the Division of Health and Medical Sciences at the University of California, Berkeley. He is a practicing physician in internal medicine, is the chair of the ethics committee at Alta Bates Medical Center, and is the director of the University of California Berkeley Center on Aging. A number of his publications examine ethical issues in disclosure of mistakes to patients and dealing with the errors of colleagues.

While moonlighting in an emergency room, a resident physician evaluated a 35-year-old woman who was 6 months pregnant and complaining of a headache. The physician diagnosed a "mixed tension/sinus headache." The patient returned to the ER 3 days later with an intracerebral bleed, presumably related to eclampsia, and died.

From *Journal of Internal Medicine* 12 (1997), 770–775.
Copyright © 1997 Blackwell Publishing Ltd.

Errare humanum est: "to err is human." In medical practice, mistakes are common, expected, and understandable. Virtually all practicing physicians have made mistakes, but physicians often do not tell patients or families about them. Even when a definite mistake results in a serious injury, the patient often is not told. In one study, house officers reported telling their attending physicians about serious medical mistakes only half the time, and telling the patients or families in less than a quarter of cases. Highly publicized cases of fatal mistakes have heightened public and professional concerns about how physicians and hospitals respond to serious mistakes. When mistakes are not acknowledged in a timely manner, there may be a perception of a cover-up, and public confidence in physicians may be undermined.

The American Medical Association's (AMA's) *Principles of Medical Ethics* (1957) states that a physician must report an accident, injury, or bad result stemming from his or her treatment.[1] However, many physicians interpret these requirements to mean that they should report to their superiors or to the hospital quality assurance or risk management committee, rather than to the patient. More recently, the *American College of Physicians Ethics Manual* states, "physicians should disclose to patients information about procedural and judgment errors made in the course of care, if such information significantly affects the care of the patient.[2] The AMA's Council on Ethical and Judicial Affairs states, "Situations occasionally occur in which a patient suffers significant medical complications that may have resulted from the physician's mistake or judgment. In these situations, the physician is ethically required to inform the patient of all facts necessary to ensure understanding of what has occurred.[3]

In this article, we analyze the various ethical arguments for and against disclosing serious mistakes to patients. We also provide practical suggestions for how to discuss the sensitive topic of mistakes with patients.

WHAT IS A MISTAKE?

We define a medical mistake as a commission or an omission with potentially negative consequences for the patient that would have been judged wrong by skilled and knowledgeable peers at the time it occurred, independent of whether there were any negative consequences. This definition excludes the natural history of disease that does not respond to treatment and the foreseeable complications of a correctly performed procedure, as well as cases in which there is reasonable disagreement over whether a mistake occurred.

We categorize errors according to their genesis. System errors, also referred to as latent errors, derive primarily from flaws inherent in the system of medical practice. In such errors, the system "sets up" individuals to make mistakes, i.e., through the unavailability of medical records, by confusing labeling of medications, and the like. When a system error occurs, the physician shares responsibility with other elements of the health care delivery system.

Conversely, individual errors are those deriving primarily from deficiencies in the physician's own knowledge, skill, or attentiveness. For instance, a physician mistakenly prescribed a nonsteroidal anti-inflammatory agent to a patient with renal insufficiency, resulting in permanently worsened renal failure. In such a case of individual error, the physician has primary responsibility.

The considerations in the disclosure of latent errors differ from those in the disclosure of individual errors. For example, in a latent error, the physician is often one link in a chain of causes generating the error. Accordingly, the disclosure of such an error may not be the sole responsibility of the physician. In what follows, we consider only the arguments for a physician to disclose his or her individual error to a patient. We also restrict ourselves to mistakes that cause significant harm, without regard to their detectability.

Errors causing harm can be subdivided into cases that are not medically remediable and those that are medically remediable. We argue that the physician has an obligation to disclose mistakes that cause significant harm, which in the judgment of a risk manager or malpractice insurer is likely to be remediable, mitigable, or compensable. Only in rare cases would a physician be permitted not to disclose a mistake causing harm to the patient. Specifically, physicians might be permitted not to tell if they have good reason to believe that disclosure would undermine the patient's autonomy in some way (e.g., incapacitate the already severely depressed patient). Or the patient might have told the doctor explicitly, "Doctor, if anything goes wrong, I don't want to know about it."

Two ethical theories assist in thinking about the disclosing of a mistake: consequentialism and deontology. A consequentialist ethical theory holds that one ought to do that act which will realize the best overall consequences. A deontological theory maintains that one ought to do that act by which one fulfills one's duties or obligations. Both consequentialist and deontological theories ground arguments for disclosure. In what follows, we first consider arguments based on consequences; then, we attend to arguments based on a physician's duties.

POTENTIAL BENEFITS AND HARMS OF DISCLOSURE

POTENTIAL BENEFITS OF DISCLOSURE TO THE PATIENT

The patient could benefit in many ways from knowing that a mistake had occurred. Such knowledge would allow the patient to obtain timely and appropriate treatment to correct problems resulting from the mistake. Disclosure therefore can prevent further harm to the patient. In some situations, close monitoring or a medical procedure may be necessary to mitigate the consequences of a mistake. Patients may be unwilling to permit or cooperate with necessary measures if they are unaware of the reason for doing so. When further treatment is indicated, disclosure is essential for informed consent. Otherwise, the uninformed patient is placed at risk of subsequent misdiagnosis and improper or inadequate treatment.

Disclosure of a mistake may also prevent the patient from worrying needlessly about the etiology of a medical problem. For example, a patient who was prescribed too much warfarin resulting in excessive anticoagulation suffered a gastrointestinal bleed. Telling patients about such mistakes may resolve their uncertainty about the cause of their condition, possibly allowing them to feel better by explaining that recurrence would be unlikely.

Disclosure of a mistake also provides patients with information needed to make informed decisions. Patients may develop more realistic expectations about their doctors' interventions. Acknowledgment of fallibility brings uncertainties into the open, reduces the possibility of misunderstandings, and encourages the patient to take greater responsibility for his or her own care.

In the case of an injury, knowing about a mistake may allow the patient to obtain compensation for lost earnings or to pay for care necessitated by the injury or to at least get a bill written off. Such compensation might be obtained through settlement rather than lawsuit; under the current system, obtaining such compensation would be difficult or impossible without disclosure of the mistake.

Finally, disclosure of a mistake can promote trust in physicians. Patients have a presumption of truthtelling. Thus, a patient who is not informed of a mistake may feel angry and betrayed; the patient may think that a privileged relationship has been violated.

POTENTIAL HARMS OF DISCLOSURE TO THE PATIENT

Patients may be harmed by learning that a mistake was made in their care. The knowledge may cause alarm, anxiety, and discouragement. It may destroy patients' faith and confidence in the physician's ability to help them. Patients may become disillusioned with the medical profession in general. This may cause them to decline beneficial treatments, or decrease their adherence to beneficial treatment regimens or habits.

Not all patients want to know everything about their medical care. Some would rather not be burdened with the complexities of their illness. The well-meaning disclosure of potentially serious, but inconsequential mistakes may cause unwelcome confusion. In such cases, patients may feel they would be better off not knowing that a mistake had been made in their care. As the *American College of Physicians Ethics Manual* states, "society recognizes the 'therapeutic privilege,' which is an exemption from detailed disclosure when such disclosure has a high likelihood of causing serious and irreversible harm to the patient." However, the American College of Physicians offers the following caution: "On balance, this privilege should be interpreted narrowly; invoking it too broadly can undermine the entire concept of informed consent."[2]

POTENTIAL BENEFITS OF DISCLOSURE TO THE PHYSICIAN

The physician might also benefit from disclosing a mistake to the patient or family. The knowledge of making a mistake that harmed a patient can cause the physician to experience great emotional distress. The physician may be relieved to admit the mistake. In the case of a serious mistake, the patient or family member may be the only person able to forgive the physician for making the mistake. This may be the only way for the physician to gain absolution for the mistake. Many patients appreciate the physician's honesty, and disclosure of a mistake actually may strengthen the doctor-patient relationship. For example, when one of the authors failed to obtain a serum ferritin test during the evaluation of a patient referred for an enlarged liver, the diagnosis of hemochromatosis was delayed significantly. When the patient was told about the omission, he responded, "That's O.K. After all, doctor, you can't think of everything."

Candid disclosure of a mistake may decrease the likelihood of legal liability. Some have suggested that a strong doctor-patient relationship makes patients less likely to bring suit. Furthermore, if the patient learns about a mistake and brings a lawsuit, failure to disclose may place the physician in greater jeopardy.

Disclosing mistakes may help physicians to learn and improve their practice. In a survey by Quill and Williamson, responding physicians reported that sharing errors with colleagues, students, friends, and sometimes patients prevented isolation, and marked the beginning of grieving about and learning from the mistake. Admitting a mistake may also help the physician accept responsibility for it, and may help the physician make constructive changes in practice. Physicians may also learn vicariously from mistakes made by others, and be able to avoid making similar mistakes themselves.

POTENTIAL HARMS OF DISCLOSURE TO THE PHYSICIAN

Revealing a medical mistake to a patient is often difficult and painful for the physician. The patient may become angry and upset, and such reactions can be highly stressful to doctors.

Many physicians fear that disclosing a serious medical mistake will expose them to the risk of a malpractice suit. If a lawsuit ensues, the physician may be subjected to increased malpractice premiums as well as psychological stress.

Disclosure of a mistake may harm the physician through loss of referrals, hospital admitting privileges, preferred provider status, credentials, and even licensure. Selective contracting and physician profiling by managed care organizations create more tangible threats to the physician's livelihood. The development of the National Practitioner Data Bank adds the possibility that an incident will leave a permanent mark on the physician's record. Disclosure of mistakes may also damage the physician's reputation through the loss of respect or status among colleagues. In small communities, the physician's public reputation may also suffer.

Following disclosure of a serious error, the career of a physician-in-training may be harmed by poor evaluations or letters of recommendation, or even dismissal. Even without the expectation of overt punishment, it is difficult to admit wrongdoing.

A consequentialist argument for the disclosure of mistakes to patients would be framed in terms of the above-noted benefits and harms to individual patients and physicians. In the doctor-patient relationship, a physician is to act for the sake of the patient; therefore, in weighing the benefits and harms of disclosure, the benefits and harms to the patient should have greater weight than those to the physician. There are also duty-based grounds for holding that, in certain cases, a physician should disclose medical error to a patient. We now turn to such arguments.

THE PHYSICIAN'S DUTIES

In what follows, we argue that a physician's responsibility to disclose a mistake to a patient can be derived from the fiduciary character of the doctor-patient relationship (that is, the fact that this relationship is based on trust). The fiduciary character of this relationship can be further articulated in accordance with the principles of nonmaleficence, beneficence, respect for patient autonomy, and justice.

Primum non nocere, "first, do no harm," states the principle of nonmaleficence: a caregiver has a grave responsibility to avoid harming the patient. The principle of beneficence enjoins physicians to act for the best interests of their patients' health even if the physician's own financial or professional well-being is not benefited by so acting. In cases in which harm resulting from a mistake can be reversed or ameliorated, the physician is obligated to do so. For example, if a sponge has been left in a patient after surgery, the sponge can be removed and infection can be prevented. In such cases, remedying or mitigating the harms caused by a mistake often requires the physician to disclose the mistake to the patient.

Respect for patient autonomy enjoins physicians to disclose a mistake that seriously harmed a patient. This is the case when full disclosure frees patients of mistaken beliefs concerning their past, present, or future medical conditions, thus enabling them to make informed decisions about future medical care. It may also be the case even if the patient does not need to know of the error in order to make future decisions about medical care. This is because patients have a claim to know their own history and to be free of mistaken beliefs concerning their past, present, or future medical condition. In short, a physician's obligation to respect patient autonomy indicates that a doctor has an ethical obligation to disclose mistakes to patients.

When a nonremediable mistake has been made, the doctor may have an ethical duty to disclose it to the patient so that the patient can be compensated. Justice requires that people be given what is due to them. It would be unfair not to compensate a patient who was seriously harmed by mistake, e.g., for further medical care necessitated by the mistake, for income lost due to the mistake, for pain and suffering, or for loss of function. The more serious the harm and the greater the need of the patient for compensation, the greater the physician's responsibility to make amends.

Physicians may be less obligated or not obligated at all to disclose a mistake that had little marginal impact, such as a serious medication error involving a moribund patient or the failure to recognize a pneumothorax caused during a failed attempt at cardiopulmonary resuscitation. Although it can be argued that disclosure is discretionary in these cases, the counterargument can be advanced that even these mistakes should generally be disclosed. The physician has little to lose by so doing. These cases may provide a good opportunity for open and honest discussion and may strengthen the relationship with the patient or family.

In summary, the fiduciary character of the doctor-patient relationship indicates that a physician has the ethical duty to disclose error to a patient when disclosure furthers the patient's health, respects the patient's autonomy, or enables the patient to be compensated for serious, irreparable harm.

PRACTICAL ISSUES IN DISCLOSURE OF MISTAKES

Accepting the physician's obligation to disclose mistakes, there are practical issues concerning whether, when, who, and how to tell about the mistake. For uncertain cases, who should decide whether or not to tell? Is there an ideal time to tell the patient? What should be done in the case of the incompetent patient? When more than one physician was involved, who should tell the patient? What should be the role of hospital quality assurance and risk management personnel?

Deciding Whether to Disclose a Mistake. In cases in which disclosing a mistake seems controversial, who should decide whether or not to tell? The individual physician is biased against disclosure, and can easily rationalize the decision not to tell. The burden of proof should be on the physician to justify not disclosing a mistake. However, the decision should not be left to the individual physician's judgment. It would be important to obtain a second opinion to represent what a reasonable physician would do and be willing to defend in public. This second opinion would be particularly important in cases in which there was an adverse out-

come, and the physician is inclined *not* to tell. A formal body such as an institution's ethics committee or quality review board seems preferable to informal consultation with peers, who might be similarly reticent.

Timing of Disclosure. The timing of disclosure should be considered. Although the patient might benefit from learning about a mistake as soon as possible after it occurred, disclosure should be made at a time when the patient is physically and emotionally stable. For example, disclosure of a surgical error should be delayed, if possible, until the patient has recovered sufficiently to be able to understand and deal with the information.

Who Should Disclose the Mistake? When a mistake is made by a physician-in-training, responsibility is shared with the attending physician of record. It may be most appropriate for the attending physician and house officer to disclose the mistake to the patient together. Sometimes it may be appropriate to involve an institutional representative, such as a hospital administrator, risk manager, or quality assurance representative, in the disclosure.

The Incompetent Patient. Many patients with impaired decision-making capacity can still appreciate an apology. However, some patients lack the mental capacity to understand and appreciate what the physician tells them about medical errors, even if the discussion is simplified. There is no need to inform an incompetent patient. However, if there is a family member or other effective decision maker, this surrogate should be informed. The physician who will be taking care of the patient in the ambulatory setting should also be informed.

What to Say? Disclosure is often difficult, for several reasons. The facts of the case may be too complicated to be explained easily, and may not be known precisely. The physician may be tempted to frame the disclosure in a way that obscures that a mistake was made.

Disclosure of a mistake is an instance of "breaking bad news" to patients. There is need for medical education about conducting these discussions. The upsetting news that a mistake has occurred and information regarding the consequences should be presented to the patient in a way that minimizes distress. The *American*

College of Physicians Ethics Manual offers the following guidance, which could be applied to the disclosure of a mistake: "Information should be given in terms the patient can understand. The physician should be sensitive to the patient's responses in setting the pace of disclosure. . . Disclosure should never be a mechanical or perfunctory process."[2] The physician should recognize that patients or families may become upset or angry, and accept this as a natural response, taking care not to react defensively.

In telling the patient about an error, the physician should begin by stating simply that he or she has made a mistake. It may be helpful to describe the decisions that were made, including those in which the patient participated. The course of events should then be described in detail, using nontechnical language. The nature of the mistake, consequences, and corrective action taken or to be undertaken should be stated. The physician should then express personal regret and apologize for the mistake. Finally, the physician should elicit questions or concerns from the patient and address them.

The harm of disclosing a mistake may be minimized if disclosure is made promptly and openly, if apologies are offered, and if charges for associated care are forgone. When the mistake had a major adverse impact on the patient, an offer should be made to cancel charges for subsequent care needed to remedy the mistake and to provide the necessary supportive services.

Financial amends should include all extra expenses incurred, such as physician services, error-generated laboratory fees, hospital expenses, and drug costs. Hospital risk management teams sometimes adopt and malpractice insurers sometimes encourage such an approach, which may reduce the number and size of malpractice suits. The physician rarely if ever pays for any of these services out of pocket. Under capitated payment, the hospital or group absorbs the costs (if individual physicians are capitated for pharmacy services they may also share the costs). If health insurance is available to pay for medical care, a decision should be made whether or not to bill the insurer for the services. It can be argued that the insurance company bears some co-equal responsibility because it insures the patient for all outcomes. However, companies may want recourse to reclaim some of the money. In all cases, it is important that hospital administration and risk management be involved in decisions and negotiations about billing.

A physician who had prescribed a sulfonamide to a patient known to be allergic to sulfa, causing an anaphylactoid reaction, might say, "Mrs. Smith, I have discovered what has caused you to become so ill. I regret to say that I made a mistake. Before prescribing the medication for your infection, I failed to check whether you were allergic to it. You are. The itchy rash, joint pains, and fever you now have are due to the allergy. I am giving you ibuprofen and diphenhydramine to help you feel better, and I expect you will gradually improve over the next several days. I feel very badly that my not checking has caused you to have this reaction. I am sorry. Of course, there will be no charges for the antibiotic or the medications I am now prescribing to remedy my mistake. Do you have any questions for me?"

OVERCOMING BARRIERS TO DISCLOSURE

From a pragmatic point of view, physicians are often most concerned about the potentially harmful personal consequences of disclosing a mistake. In blunt terms, physicians may question whether any possible benefits to the patient are worth the possible risks of a lawsuit to their career or livelihood. This clash between ethical ideals and pragmatic reality is a difficult one. It may sound unconvincing to exhort physicians to do what is best for the patient. However, the AMA's Council on Ethical and Judicial Affairs states, "Concern regarding legal liability which might result following truthful disclosure should not affect the physician's honesty with a patient."[3]

We would make several responses to physicians who hesitate to disclose mistakes that cause significant harm to patients because of fears of litigation. First, disclosing mistakes may reduce the risk of litigation, if patients appreciate physicians' honesty and fallibility. Second, serious mistakes may come to light, even if physicians do not disclose them. Patients may wonder about the cause of their changed condition, ask other caregivers, or even ask their physicians directly. Any perception that the physician tried to cover up a mistake might make a patient more angry and more litigious. Third, in disclosing mistakes physicians can take steps to mitigate any harms that may occur to them. Physicians can learn how to disclose mistakes in a manner that diffuses patient anger. Furthermore, when mistakes have caused serious harm to patients, physicians can take the initiative in recommending to institutional risk management personnel or malpractice insurers that a prompt and fair settlement is made out of court.

For an injured patient to obtain compensation through the tort system requires proof of negligence, defined as violation of professional standards. This creates an untenable conflict for physicians, for whom compensation to the patient demands the demonstration of malpractice. Acts of negligence constituted only a small proportion of the errors in the Harvard Medical Practice Study and only a small proportion of injuries resulted in compensation for the patient. Thus, the current system obstructs detection and just compensation for errors and inhibits disclosure. The need to report and reduce errors constitutes a major ethical impetus for reform to a system of no-fault, nonadversarial patient compensation. Such a system would facilitate a move to a systems approach incorporating human factors research to reduce errors.

The fear of damage to reputation and loss of respect from peers may also inhibit physicians from disclosing mistakes. To overcome this barrier will require increased recognition and acceptance of mistakes as part of clinical practice. Guidelines should be created to describe what physicians should do when they make a mistake. Such guidelines should also describe what to do when a colleague tells you about a mistake you have made or a mistake he or she has made. The importance of providing emotional support needs to be emphasized. It is particularly important to help physicians-in-training cope with their mistakes in such a way as to help them maintain their confidence and develop professionally.

DISCLOSURE OF MISTAKES MADE BY OTHER PHYSICIANS

A physician who, in the care of one of his or her own patients, learns of or witnesses a major error (e.g., a surgical mishap) made by another physician, has several options. These include waiting for the other physician to disclose the mistake, advising the other physician to disclose the mistake, arranging a joint meeting to discuss the mistake, or telling the patient directly. Insofar as the doctor-patient relationship obtains in such a case, physicians have an obligation to facilitate disclosure. However, they may be reluctant to say anything because of lack of definitive information, because of the thought that "there but for the grace of God go I," or because of fear of hurting the feelings of colleagues, or of straining professional relationships. Social norms militate against disclosing when a colleague makes a mistake. From an early age, we are socialized against "tattling" on our peers. In addition, physicians may fear that disclosure would lead to libel suits. Unfortunately, there are no guidelines describing the obligations of a physician who learns of a mistake made by another physician on his or her own patient.

The simplest solution is to leave the discussion up to the physician who made the mistake. However, there is no assurance that the patient actually will be informed. By advising the physician who erred to tell the patient, the observing physician may fulfill his or her responsibility for disclosure, but the patient also may not be informed. Simultaneously advising quality assurance or risk management personnel would increase the likelihood that the patient would be told. Arranging a joint conference with the patient and original physician would assure the observing physician that appropriate disclosure was made, while preserving the primacy of the relationship between the other physician and patient. These other options failing, one might tell the patient directly of the error. Although this conversation may be awkward and may interfere with the other physician's relationship with the patient, it does guarantee disclosure. Policy statements from medical staff offices and medical societies, as well as potential involvement by these bodies, are needed to guide and facilitate these difficult interactions.

CONCLUSIONS

Consideration of the doctor-patient relationship indicates that a physician has ethical obligations to disclose significant errors when disclosure benefits the health of the patient, respects the patient's autonomy, or is called for by justice. This is so even if such disclosure does not benefit the physician. Only in rare cases, when disclosure would threaten to undermine the patient's autonomy, or when the patient explicitly states a preference not to be told about such untoward events, should the physician not disclose the mistake. These same considerations suggest that a physician also has a considerable duty to ensure that disclosure occurs when, in the care of his or her own patient, another physician makes a serious mistake.

NOTES

1. American Medical Association. *Principles of Medical Ethics*; 1957: section 4.

2. American College of Physicians. *American College of Physicians Ethics Manual.* 3rd ed. Ann Intern Med. 1992; 117: 947–60.

3. AMA Council on Ethical and Judicial Affairs and Southern Illinois University School of Law. *Code of Medical Ethics, Annotated Current Opinions.* Chicago, Ill: American Medical Association; 1994.

CANTERBURY v. SPENCE

United States Court of Appeals, 1972

SPOTTSWOOD W. ROBINSON, III, CIRCUIT JUDGE

Suits charging failure by a physician adequately to disclose the risks and alternatives of proposed treatment are not innovations in American law. They date back a good half-century, and in the last decade they have multiplied rapidly. There is, nonetheless, disagreement among the courts and the commentators on many major questions, and there is no precedent of our own directly in point. For the tools enabling resolution of the issues on this appeal, we are forced to begin at first principles.

The root premise is the concept, fundamental in American jurisprudence, that "[e]very human being of adult years and sound mind has a right to determine what shall be done with his own body. . . ." True consent to what happens to one's self is the informed exercise of a choice, and that entails an opportunity to evaluate knowledgeably the options available and the risks attendant upon each. The average patient has little or no understanding of the medical arts, and ordinarily has only his physician to whom he can look for enlightenment with which to reach an intelligent decision. From these almost axiomatic considerations springs the need, and in turn the requirement, of a reasonable divulgence by physician to patient to make such a decision possible.

• • •

Once the circumstances give rise to a duty on the physician's part to inform his patient, the next inquiry is the scope of the disclosure the physician is legally obliged to make. The courts have frequently confronted this problem, but no uniform standard defin-

No. 22099, U.S. Court of Appeals, District of Columbia Circuit, May 19, 1972. 464 *Federal Reporter,* 2nd Series, 772.

ing the adequacy of the divulgence emerges from the decisions. Some have said "full" disclosure,[1] a norm we are unwilling to adopt literally. It seems obviously prohibitive and unrealistic to expect physicians to discuss with their patients every risk of proposed treatment—no matter how small or remote—and generally unnecessary from the patient's viewpoint as well. Indeed, the cases speaking in terms of "full" disclosure appear to envision something less than total disclosure,[2] leaving unanswered the question of just how much.

The larger number of courts, as might be expected, have applied tests framed with reference to prevailing fashion within the medical profession. Some have measured the disclosure by "good medical practice," others by what a reasonable practitioner would have bared under the circumstances, and still others by what medical custom in the community would demand. We have explored this rather considerable body of law but are unprepared to follow it. The duty to disclose, we have reasoned, arises from phenomena apart from medical custom and practice. The latter, we think, should no more establish the scope of the duty than its existence. Any definition of scope in terms purely of a professional standard is at odds with the patient's prerogative to decide on projected therapy himself. That prerogative, we have said, is at the very foundation of the duty to disclose, and both the patient's right to know and the physician's correlative obligation to tell him are diluted to the extent that its compass is dictated by the medical profession.

In our view, the patient's right of self-decision shapes the boundaries of the duty to reveal. That right can be effectively exercised only if the patient possesses enough information to enable an intelligent choice. The scope of the physician's communications to the patient, then, must be measured by the patient's need, and that need is the information material to the decision. Thus the test for determining whether a particular peril must be divulged is its materiality to the patient's decision: all risks potentially affecting the decision must be unmasked. And to safeguard the patient's interest in achieving his own determination on treatment, the law must itself set the standard for adequate disclosure.

Optimally for the patient, exposure of a risk would be mandatory whenever the patient would deem it significant to his decision, either singly or in combination with other risks. Such a requirement, however, would summon the physician to second-guess the patient, whose ideas on materiality could hardly be known to the physician. That would make an undue demand upon medical practitioners, whose conduct, like that of others, is to be measured in terms of reasonableness. Consonantly with orthodox negligence doctrine, the physician's liability for nondisclosure is to be determined on the basis of foresight, not hindsight; no less than any other aspect of negligence, the issue of nondisclosure must be approached from the viewpoint of the reasonableness of the physician's divulgence in terms of what he knows or should know to be the patient's informational needs. If, but only if, the fact-finder can say that the physician's communication was unreasonably inadequate is an imposition of liability legally or morally justified.

Of necessity, the content of the disclosure rests in the first instance with the physician. Ordinarily it is only he who is in a position to identify particular dangers; always he must make a judgment, in terms of materiality, as to whether and to what extent revelation to the patient is called for. He cannot know with complete exactitude what the patient would consider important to his decision, but on the basis of his medical training and experience he can sense how the average, reasonable patient expectably would react. Indeed, with knowledge of, or ability to learn, his patient's background and current condition, he is in a position superior to that of most others—attorneys, for example—who are called upon to make judgments on pain of liability in damages for unreasonable miscalculation.

From these considerations we derive the breadth of the disclosure of risks legally to be required. The scope of the standard is not subjective as to either the physician or the patient; it remains objective with due regard for the patient's informational needs and with suitable leeway for the physician's situation. In broad outline, we agreed that "[a] risk is thus material when a reasonable person, in what the physician knows or should know to be the patient's position, would be likely to attach significance to the risk or cluster of risks in deciding whether or not to forgo the proposed therapy."[3]

The topics importantly demanding a communication of information are the inherent and potential hazards of the proposed treatment, the alternatives to that treatment, if any, and the results likely if the patient remains untreated. The factors contributing significance to the dangerousness of a medical technique are, of course, the incidence of injury and the degree of the harm threatened. A very small chance of death or serious disablement may well be significant; a potential disability which dramatically outweighs the potential benefit of the therapy or the detriments of the existing malady may summon discussion with the patient.

There is no bright line separating the significant from the insignificant; the answer in any case must abide a rule of reason. Some dangers—infection, for example—are inherent in any operation; there is no obligation to communicate those of which persons of average sophistication are aware. Even more clearly, the physician bears no responsibility for discussion of hazards the patient has already discovered, or those having no apparent materiality to patients' decision on therapy. The disclosure doctrine, like others marking lines between permissible and impermissible behavior in medical practice, is in essence a requirement of conduct prudent under the circumstances. Whenever nondisclosure of particular risk information is open to debate by reasonable-minded men, the issue is for the finder of the facts.

Two exceptions to the general rule of disclosure have been noted by the courts. Each is in the nature of a physician's privilege not to disclose, and the reasoning underlying them is appealing. Each, indeed, is but a recognition that, as important as is the patient's right to know, it is greatly outweighed by the magnitudinous circumstances giving rise to the privilege. The first comes into play when the patient is unconscious or otherwise incapable of consenting, and harm from a failure to treat is imminent and outweighs any harm threatened by the proposed treatment. When a genuine emergency of that sort arises, it is settled that the impracticality of conferring with the patient dispenses with need for it. Even in situations of that character the physician should, as current law requires, attempt to secure a relative's consent if possible. But if time is too short to accommodate discussion obviously the physician should proceed with the treatment.

The second exception obtains when risk-disclosure poses such a threat of detriment to the patient as to become unfeasible or contraindicated from a medical point of view. It is recognized that patients occasionally become so ill or emotionally distraught on disclosure as to foreclose a rational decision, or complicate or hinder the treatment, or perhaps even pose psychological damage to the patient. Where that is so, the cases have generally held that the physician is armed with a privilege to keep the information from the patient, and we think it clear that portents of that type may justify the physician in action he deems medically warranted. The critical inquiry is whether the physician responded to a sound medical judgment that communication of the risk information would present a threat to the patient's well-being.

The physician's privilege to withhold information for therapeutic reasons must be carefully circumscribed, however, for otherwise it might devour the disclosure rule itself. The privilege does not accept the paternalistic notion that the physician may remain silent simply because divulgence might prompt the patient to forgo therapy the physician feels the patient really needs. That attitude presumes instability or perversity for even the normal patient, and runs counter to the foundation principle that the patient should and ordinarily can make the choice for himself. Nor does the privilege contemplate operation save where the patient's reaction to risk information, as reasonably foreseen by the physician, is menacing. And even in a situation of that kind, disclosure to a close relative with a view to securing consent to the proposed treatment may be the only alternative open to the physician.

NOTES

1. *E.g., Salgo v. Leland Stanford Jr. Univ. Bd. of Trustees*, 154 Cal. App. 2d 560, 317 P.2d 170, 181 (1975); *Woods v. Brumlop, supra* note 13 [in original text], 377 P.2d at 524–525.

2. See, Comment, Informed Consent in Medical Malpractice, 55 Calif. L. Rv. 1396, 1402–03 (1967).

3. Waltz and Scheuneman, Informed Consent to Therapy, 64, Nw. U.L. Rev. 628, 640 (1970).

JAY KATZ

Physicians and Patients: A History of Silence

Jay Katz, MD, is Elizabeth K. Dollard Professor Emeritus of Law, Medicine, and Psychiatry, as well as Harvey L. Karp Professorial Lecturer in Law and Psychoanalysis at Yale Law School. In the field of bioethics, he published two foundational works in the field: the edited work *Experimentation with Human Beings* (Russell Sage Foundation) and the authored work *The Silent World of Doctor and Patient* (Johns Hopkins University Press).

Disclosure and consent, except in the most rudimentary fashion, are obligations alien to medical thinking and practice. Disclosure in medicine has served the function of getting patients to "consent" to what physicians wanted them to agree to in the first place. "Good" patients follow doctor's orders without question. Therefore, disclosure becomes relevant only with recalcitrant patients. Since they are "bad" and "ungrateful," one does not need to bother much with them. Hippocrates once said, "Life is short, the Art

Reprinted by permission of the author.

long, Opportunity fleeting, Experiment treacherous, Judgment difficult. The physician must be ready, not only to do his duty himself, but also to secure the cooperation of the patient, of the attendants and of externals." These were, and still are, the lonely obligations of physicians: to wrestle as best they can with life, art, opportunity, experiment and judgment. Sharing with patients the vagaries of available opportunities, however perilous or safe, or the rationale underlying judgments, however difficult or easy, is not part of the Hippocratic task. For doing that, the Art is too long and Life too short.

Physicians have always maintained that patients are only in need of caring custody. Doctors felt that in order to accomplish that objective they were obligated to attend to their patients' physical and emotional needs and to do so on their own authority, without consulting with their patients about the decisions that needed to be made. Indeed, doctors intuitively believed that such consultations were inimical to good patient care. The idea that patients may also be entitled to liberty, to sharing the burdens of decision with their doctors, was never part of the ethos of medicine. Being unaware of the idea of patient liberty, physicians did not address the possible conflict between notions of custody and liberty. When, however, in recent decades courts were confronted with allegations that professionals had deprived citizen-patients of freedom of choice, the conflict did emerge. Anglo-American law has, at least in theory, a long-standing tradition of preferring liberty over custody; and however much judges tried to sidestep law's preferences and to side with physicians' traditional beliefs, the conflict remained and has ever since begged for a resolution. . . .

The legal doctrine remained limited in scope, in part, because judges believed or wished to believe that their pronouncements on informed consent gave legal force to what good physicians customarily did; therefore they felt that they could defer to the disclosure practices of "reasonable medical practitioners." Judges did not appreciate how deeply rooted the tradition of silence was and thus did not recognize the revolutionary, alien implications of their appeal for patient "self-determination." In fact, precisely because of the appeal's strange and bewildering novelty, physicians misinterpreted it as being more far-reaching than courts intended it to be.

Physicians did not realize how much their opposition to informed consent was influenced by suddenly encountering obligations divorced from their history, their clinical experience, or medical education. Had they appreciated that even the doctrine's modest appeal to patient self-determination represented a radical break with medical practices, as transmitted from teacher to student during more than two thousand years of recorded medical history, they might have been less embarrassed by standing so unpreparedly, so nakedly before this new obligation. They might then perhaps have realized that their silence had been until most recently a historical necessity, dictated not only by the inadequacy of medical knowledge but also by physicians' incapacity to discriminate between therapeutic effectiveness based on their actual physical interventions and benefits that must be ascribed to

other causes. They might also have argued that the practice of silence was part of a long and venerable tradition that deserved not to be dismissed lightly. . . .

When I speak of silence I do not mean to suggest that physicians have not talked to their patients at all. Of course, they have conversed with patients about all kinds of matters, but they have not, except inadvertently, employed words to invite patients' participation in sharing the burden of making joint decisions. . . .

Judges have made impassioned pleas for patient self-determination, and then have undercut them by giving physicians considerable latitude to practice according to their own lights, exhorting them only to treat each patient with the utmost care. Judges could readily advance this more limited plea because generally doctors do treat their patients with solicitude. The affirmation of physicians' commitment to patients' physical needs, however, has failed to address physicians' lack of commitment to patients' decision making needs. These tensions have led judges to fashion a doctrine of informed consent that has secured for patients the right to better custody but not to liberty—the right to choose how to be treated. . . .

CANTERBURY v. SPENCE (1972)

Judge Robinson, of the D.C. Court of Appeals, who authored the . . . last landmark informed consent decision, also had good intentions. . . . The lesson to be learned from a study of *Canterbury* [is that]: The strong commitment to self-determination at the beginning of the opinion gets weaker as the opinion moves from jurisprudential theory to the realities of hospital and courtroom life. By the end, the opinion has only obscured the issue it intended to address: the nature of the relationship between the court's doctrine of informed consent, as ultimately construed, and its root premise of self-determination. . . .

Respect for the patient's right of self-determination on particular therapy demands a standard set by law for physicians rather than one which physicians may or may not impose upon themselves.

For this apparently bold move, *Canterbury* has been widely celebrated, as well as followed in many jurisdictions.

The new rule of law laid down in *Canterbury*, however, is far from clear. Judge Robinson, returning to basic principles of expert testimony, simply said that there is "no basis for operation of the special medical standard where the physician's activity does not bring his medical knowledge and skills peculiarly into play," and that ordinarily disclosure is not such a situation. But he left room for such situations by adding: "When medical judgment enters the picture and for that reason the special standard controls, prevailing medical practice must be given its *just due*." He did not spell out the meaning of *"just due."*

Both standards tend to confuse the need for *medical knowledge* to elucidate the risks of and alternatives to a proposed procedure in the light of professional experience with the need for *medical judgment* to establish the limits of appropriate disclosure to patients. The difference is crucial to the clarification of the law of informed consent. In *Natanson* and many subsequent cases, judges lumped the two together uncritically, relying solely on current medical practice to resolve the question of reasonableness of disclosure. In *Canterbury*, the distinction was formally recognized. The plaintiff was required to present expert evidence of the applicable medical knowledge, while the defendant had to raise the issue of medical judgment to limit disclosure in defense. But even *Canterbury* did not undertake a detailed judicial analysis of the nature of medical judgment required, precisely because judges were hesitant to make rules in an area that doctors strongly believed was solely the province of medicine.

In *Canterbury*, Dr. Spence claimed that "communication of that risk (paralysis) to the patient is not good medical practice because it might deter patients from undergoing needed surgery and might produce adverse psychological reactions which could preclude the success of the operation." Such claims will almost invariably be raised by physicians since they are derived from deeply held tenets of medical practice. Judge Robinson's enigmatic phrase of "just due" certainly suggests that the medical professional standard would be applicable in such a case, raising profound questions about the extent to which the novel legal standard has been swallowed up by the traditional and venerable medical standard.

In fact, medical judgment was given its "just due" twice. It could also be invoked under the "therapeutic privilege" not to disclose, which Judge Robinson retained as a defense to disclosure:

It is recognized that patients occasionally become so ill or emotionally distraught on disclosure as to foreclose a rational decision, or complicate or hinder the treatment, or perhaps even pose psychological damage to the patient. . . . The critical inquiry is whether the physician responded to a sound medical judgment that communication of the risk information would present a threat to the patient's well-being.

The therapeutic privilege not to disclose is merely a procedurally different way of invoking the professional standard of care. . . .

Since the court wished to depart from medical custom as the standard, it had to give some indication as to the information it expected physicians to disclose. The court said that "the test for determining whether a particular peril must be divulged is its materiality to the patient's decision: all risks potentially affecting the decision must be unmasked." It added that physicians must similarly disclose alternatives to the proposed treatment and the "results likely if the patient remains untreated."

But then the court chose to adopt an "objective" test for disclosure of risks and alternatives—what a [reasonable] *prudent* person in the patient's position would have decided if suitably informed—and rejected a "subjective" test of materiality—"what an *individual* patient would have considered a significant risk." In opting for an "objective" standard, self-determination was given unnecessarily short shrift. The whole point of the inquiry was to safeguard the right of *individual* choice, even where it may appear idiosyncratic. Although law generally does not protect a person's right to be unreasonable and requires reasonably prudent conduct where injury to another may occur, it remains ambiguous about the extent to which prudence can be legally enforced where the potential injury is largely confined to the individual decision maker. For example, courts have split on the question of whether society may require the wearing of motorcycle helmets and whether an adult patient may be compelled to undergo unwanted blood transfusions.

The "objective" standard for disclosure contradicts the right of each individual to decide what will be done with his or her body. The belief that there is one "reasonable" or "prudent" response to every situation inviting medical intervention is nonsense, from the point of view of both the physician and the patient. The most cursory examination of medical practices demonstrates that what is reasonable to the internist may appear unreasonable to the surgeon or even to other internists and, more significantly, that the value preferences of physicians may not coincide with those of their patients. For example, doctors generally place a higher value on physical longevity than their patients do. But physical longevity is not the only touchstone of prudence. Why should not informed consent law countenance a wide range of potentially reasonable responses by patients to their medical condition based on other value preferences? . . .

Ascertaining patients' informational needs is difficult. Answers do not lie in guessing or "sensing" patients' particular concerns or in obliterating the "subjective" person in an "objective" mass of persons. The "objective" test of materiality only tempts doctors to introduce their own unwarranted subjectivity into the disclosure process. It would have been far better if the court had not committed itself prematurely to the labels "objective" and "subjective." Instead it should have considered more the patients' plight and required physicians to learn new skills: how to inquire openly about their patients' *individual* informational needs and patients' concerns, doubts, and misconceptions about treatment—its risks, benefits, and alternatives. Safeguarding self-determination requires assessing whether patients' informational needs have been satisfied by asking them whether they understand what has been explained to them. Physicians should not try to "second-guess" patients or "sense" how they will react. Instead, they need to explore what questions require further explanation. Taking such unaccustomed obligations seriously is not easy. . . .

SUMMING UP

The legal life of "informed consent," if quality of human life is measured not merely by improvements in physical custody but also by advancement of liberty, was over almost as soon as it was born. Except for the . . . law promulgated in a handful of jurisdictions and the more generally espoused dicta about "self-determination" and "freedom of choice," this is substantially true. Judges toyed briefly with the idea of patients' right to self-determination and largely cast it aside. . . .

Treatment decisions are extremely complex and require a more sustained dialogue, one in which patients are viewed as participants in medical decisions affecting their lives. This is not the view of most physicians, who believe instead that patients are too ignorant to make decisions on their own behalf, that disclosure increases patients' fears and reinforces "foolish" decisions, and that informing them about the uncertainties of medical interventions in many instances seriously undermines faith so essential to the success of therapy. Therefore, physicians asserted that they must be the ultimate decision makers. Judges did not probe these contentions in depth but were persuaded to refrain from interfering significantly with traditional medical practices.

I have not modified my earlier assessment of law's informed consent vision:

[T]he law of informed consent is substantially mythic and fairy tale-like as far as advancing patients' rights to self-decisionmaking is concerned. It conveys in its dicta about such rights a fairy tale-like optimism about human capacities for "intelligent" choice and for being respectful of other persons' choices; yet in its implementation of dicta, it conveys a mythic pessimism of human capacities to be choice-makers. The resulting tensions have had a significant impact on the law of informed consent which only has made a bow toward a commitment to patients' self-determination, perhaps in an attempt to resolve these tensions by a belief that it is "less important that this commitment be total than that we believe it to be there."

Whether fairy tale and myth can and should be reconciled more satisfactorily with reality remains to be seen. If judges contemplate such a reconciliation, they must acquire first a more profound understanding and appreciation of medicine's vision of patients and professional practice, of the capacities of physicians and patients for autonomous choice, and of the limits of professional knowledge. Such understanding cannot readily be acquired in courts of law, during disputes in which inquiry is generally constrained by claims and counter-claims that seek to assure victory for one side.

The call to liberty, embedded in the doctrine of informed consent, has only created an atmosphere in which freedom has the potential to survive and grow. The doctrine has not as yet provided a meaningful blueprint for implementing patient self-determination. The message . . . is this: Those committed to greater patient self-determination can, if they look hard enough, find inspiration in the common law of informed consent, and so can those, and more easily, who seek to perpetuate medical paternalism. Those who look for evidence of committed implementation will be sadly disappointed. The legal vision of informed consent, based on *self-determination*, is still largely a mirage. Yet a mirage, since it not only deceives but also can sustain hope, is better than no vision at all. . . .

RUTH R. FADEN AND TOM L. BEAUCHAMP

The Concept of Informed Consent

Ruth R. Faden is Philip Franklin Wagley Professor of Biomedical Ethics and executive director of the Berman Institute of Bioethics at the Johns Hopkins University. She is also a senior research scholar at the Kennedy Institute, Georgetown University and former chair of the President's Advisory Committee on Human Radiation Experiments. Among her books are *Social Justice: The Moral Foundations of Public Health and Health Policy* (Oxford), written with Madison Powers, *A History and Theory of Informed Consent* (Oxford), written with Tom Beauchamp, and *HIV, AIDS, and Childbearing* (Oxford), edited with Nancy Kass.

Tom L. Beauchamp is professor of philosophy and senior research scholar at the Kennedy Institute, Georgetown University. He has written widely in applied ethics, concentrating in research ethics and medical ethics, and also specializes in the philosophy of David Hume. Among his books are *Principles of Biomedical Ethics* (Oxford), written with James Childress, and *A History and Theory of Informed Consent* (Oxford), written with Ruth Faden. He has published three volumes in the Clarendon Hume (a critical edition of Hume's *Works*) and is currently working on one more volume.

What is an informed consent? Answering this question is complicated because there are two common, entrenched, and starkly different meanings of "informed consent." That is, the term is analyzable in two profoundly different ways—not because of mere subtle differences of connotation that appear in different contexts, but because two different *conceptions* of informed consent have emerged from its history and are still at work, however unnoticed, in literature on the subject.

In one sense, which we label *sense₁*, "informed consent" is analyzable as a particular kind of action by individual patients and subjects: an autonomous authorization. In the second sense, *sense₂*, informed consent is analyzable in terms of the web of cultural and policy rules and requirements of consent that collectively form the social practice of informed consent in institutional contexts where *groups* of patients and subjects must be treated in accordance with rules,

From *A History and Theory of Informed Consent* by Ruth R. Faden and Tom L. Beauchamp, 276–86 (1986). Copyright © 1986 by Oxford University Press, Inc. www.oup.com. Used by permission.

policies, and standard practices. Here, informed consents are not always *autonomous* acts, nor are they always in any meaningful respect *authorizations*.

SENSE₁: INFORMED CONSENT AS AUTONOMOUS AUTHORIZATION

The idea of an informed consent suggests that a patient or subject does more than express agreement with, acquiesce in, yield to, or comply with an arrangement or a proposal. He or she actively *authorizes* the proposal in the act of consent. John may *assent* to a treatment plan without authorizing it. The assent may be a mere submission to the doctor's authoritative order, in which case John does not call on his own authority in order to give permission, and thus does not authorize the plan. Instead, he acts like a child who submits, yields, or assents to the school principal's spanking and in no way gives permission for or authorizes the spanking. Just as the child merely submits to an authority in a system where the lines of authority are quite clear, so often do patients.

Accordingly, an informed consent in sense₁ should be defined as follows: An informed consent is an autonomous action by a subject or a patient that authorizes a professional either to involve the subject in research or to initiate a medical plan for the patient (or both). We can whittle down this definition by saying that an informed consent in sense₁ is given if a patient or subject with (1) substantial understanding and (2) in substantial absence of control by others (3) intentionally (4) authorizes a professional (to do intervention I).

All substantially autonomous acts satisfy conditions 1–3; but it does not follow from that analysis alone that all such acts satisfy 4. The fourth condition is what distinguishes informed consent as one *kind* of autonomous action. (Note also that the definition restricts the kinds of authorization to medical and research contexts.) A person whose act satisfies conditions 1–3 but who refuses an intervention gives an *informed refusal.*

The Problem of Shared Decisionmaking. This analysis of informed consent in sense₁ is deliberately silent on the question of how the authorizer and agent(s) being authorized *arrive at an agreement* about the performance of "I." Recent commentators on informed consent in clinical medicine, notably Jay Katz and the President's Commission, have tended to equate the idea of informed consent with a model of "shared decisionmaking" between doctor and patient. The President's Commission titles the first chapter of its report on informed consent in the patient-practitioner relationship "Informed Consent as Active, Shared Decision Making," while in Katz's work "the idea of informed consent" and "mutual decisionmaking" are treated as virtually synonymous terms.[1]

There is of course an historical relationship in clinical medicine between medical decisionmaking and informed consent. The emergence of the legal doctrine of informed consent was instrumental in drawing attention to issues of decisionmaking as well as authority in the doctor-patient relationship. Nevertheless, it is a confusion to treat informed consent and shared decisionmaking as anything like *synonymous.* For one thing, informed consent is not restricted to clinical medicine. It is a term that applies equally to biomedical and behavioral research contexts where a model of shared decisionmaking is frequently inappropriate. Even in clinical contexts, the social and psychological dynamics involved in selecting medical interventions should be distinguished from the patient's *authorization.*

We endorse Katz's view that effective communication between professional and patient or subject is often instrumental in obtaining informed consents (sense₁), but we resist his conviction that the idea of informed consent entails that the patient and physician "share decisionmaking," or "reason together," or reach a consensus about what is in the patient's best interest. This is a manipulation of the concept from a too singular and defined moral perspective on the practice of medicine that is in effect a moral program for changing the practice. Although the patient and physician *may* reach a decision together, they need not. It is the essence of informed consent in sense₁ only that the patient or subject *authorizes autonomously*; it is a matter of indifference where or how the proposal being authorized originates.

For example, one might advocate a model of shared decisionmaking for the doctor-patient relationship without simultaneously advocating that every medical procedure requires the consent of patients. Even relationships characterized by an ample slice of shared decisionmaking, mutual trust, and respect would and should permit many decisions about routine and low-risk aspects of the patient's medical treatment to remain the exclusive province of the physician, and thus some decisions are likely always to remain subject exclusively to the physician's authorization. Moreover, in the uncommon situation, a patient could autonomously authorize the physician to make *all* decisions about medical treatment, thus giving his or her informed consent to an arrangement that scarcely resembles the sharing of decisionmaking between doctor and patient.

Authorization. In authorizing, one both assumes responsibility for what one has authorized and transfers to another one's authority to implement it. There is no informed consent unless one *understands* these features of the act and *intends* to perform that act. That is, one must understand that one is assuming responsibility and warranting another to proceed.

To say that one assumes responsibility does not quite locate the essence of the matter, however, because a *transfer* of responsibility as well as of authority also occurs. The crucial element in an authorization is that the person who authorizes uses whatever right, power, or control he or she possesses in the situation to endow another with the right to act. In so doing, the authorizer assumes some responsibility for the actions taken by the other person. Here one could either authorize *broadly* so that a person can act in accordance with general guidelines, or *narrowly* so as to authorize only a particular, carefully circumscribed procedure.

SENSE₂: INFORMED CONSENT AS EFFECTIVE CONSENT

By contrast to sense$_1$, sense$_2$, or *effective* consent, is a policy-oriented sense whose conditions are not derivable solely from analyses of autonomy and authorization, or even from broad notions of respect for autonomy. "Informed consent" in this second sense does not refer to *autonomous* authorization, but to a legally or institutionally *effective* (sometimes misleadingly called *valid*) authorization from a patient or a subject. Such an authorization is "effective" because it has been obtained through procedures that satisfy the rules and requirements defining a specific institutional practice in health care or in research.

The social and legal practice of requiring professionals to obtain informed consent emerged in institutional contexts, where conformity to operative rules was and still is the sole necessary and sufficient condition of informed consent. Any consent is an informed consent in sense$_2$ if it satisfies whatever operative rules apply to the practice of informed consent. Sense$_2$ requirements for informed consent typically do not focus on the autonomy of the act of giving consent (as sense$_1$ does), but rather on regulating the behavior of the *consent-seeker* and on establishing *procedures and rules* for the context of consent. Such requirements of professional behavior and procedure are obviously more readily monitored and enforced by institutions.

However, because formal institutional rules such as federal regulations and hospital policies govern whether an act of authorizing is effective, a patient or subject can autonomously authorize an intervention, and so give an informed consent in sense$_1$, and yet *not effectively authorize* that intervention in sense$_2$.

Consider the following example. Carol and Martie are nineteen-year-old, identical twins attending the same university. Martie was born with multiple birth defects, and has only one kidney. When both sisters are involved in an automobile accident, Carol is not badly hurt, but her sister is seriously injured. It is quickly determined that Martie desperately needs a kidney transplant. After detailed discussions with the transplant team and with friends, Carol consents to be

the donor. There is no question that Carol's authorization of the transplant surgery is substantially autonomous. She is well informed and has long anticipated being in just such a circumstance. She has had ample opportunity over the years to consider what she would do were she faced with such a decision. Unfortunately, Carol's parents, who were in Nepal at the time of the accident, do not approve of her decision. Furious that they were not consulted, they decide to sue the transplant team and the hospital for having performed an unauthorized surgery on their minor daughter. (In this state the legal age to consent to surgical procedures is twenty-one.)

According to our analysis, Carol gave her informed consent in sense$_1$ to the surgery, but she did not give her informed consent in sense$_2$. That is, she autonomously authorized the transplant and thereby gave an informed consent in sense$_1$ but did not give a consent that was effective under the operative legal and institutional policy, which in this case required that the person consenting be a legally authorized agent. Examples of other policies that can define sense$_2$ informed consent (but not sense$_1$) include rules that consent be witnessed by an auditor or that there be a one-day waiting period between solicitation of consent and implementation of the intervention in order for the person's authorization to be effective. Such rules can and do vary, both within the United States by jurisdiction and institution, and across the countries of the world.

Medical and research codes, as well as case law and federal regulations, have developed models of informed consent that are delineated entirely in a sense$_2$ format, although they have sometimes attempted to justify the rules by appeal to something like sense$_1$. For example, disclosure conditions for informed consent are central to the history of "informed consent" in sense$_2$, because disclosure has traditionally been a *necessary* condition of effective informed consent (and sometimes a *sufficient* condition!). The legal doctrine of informed consent is primarily a law of disclosure; satisfaction of disclosure rules virtually consumes "informed consent" in law. This should come as no surprise, because the legal system needs a generally applicable informed consent mechanism by which injury and responsibility can be readily and fairly assessed in court. These disclosure requirements in the legal and regulatory contexts are not conditions of "informed consent" in sense$_1$; indeed disclosure may be entirely irrelevant to giving an informed consent in sense$_1$. If a person has an adequate *understanding* of relevant information without benefit of a disclosure, then it makes no difference whether someone *discloses* that information.

Other sense$_2$ rules besides those of disclosure have been enforced. These include rules requiring evidence of adequate comprehension of information and the aforementioned rules requiring the presence of auditor witnesses and mandatory waiting periods. Sense$_2$ informed consent requirements generally take the form of rules focusing on disclosure, comprehension, the minimization of potentially controlling influences, and competence. These requirements express the present-day mainstream conception in the federal government of the United States. They are also typical of international documents and state regulations, which all reflect a sense$_2$ orientation.

THE RELATIONSHIP BETWEEN SENSE$_1$ AND SENSE$_2$

A sense$_1$ "informed consent" can fail to be an informed consent in sense$_2$ by a lack of conformity to applicable rules and requirements. Similarly, an informed consent in sense$_2$ may not be an informed consent in sense$_1$. The rules and requirements that determine sense$_2$ consents need not result in autonomous authorizations at all in order to qualify as informed consents.

Such peculiarities in informed consent law have led Jay Katz to argue that the legal doctrine of "informed consent" bears a "name" that "promises much more than its construction in case law has delivered." He has argued insightfully that the courts have, in effect, imposed a mere duty to warn on physicians, an obligation confined to risk disclosures and statements of proposed interventions. He maintains that "This judicially imposed obligation must be distinguished from the *idea* of informed consent, namely, that patients have a decisive role to play in the medical decision-making process. The idea of informed consent, though alluded to also in case law, cannot be implemented, as courts have attempted, by only expanding the disclosure requirements." By their actions and declarations, Katz believes, the courts have made informed consent a "cruel hoax" and have allowed "the idea of informed consent . . . to wither on the vine."[2]

The most plausible interpretation of Katz's contentions is through the sense$_1$/sense$_2$ distinction. If a physician obtains a consent under the courts' criteria, then an informed consent (sense$_2$) has been obtained. But it does not follow that the courts are using the *right* standards, or *sufficiently rigorous* standards in light of a stricter autonomy-based model—or "idea" as Katz puts it—of informed consent (sense$_1$).[3] If Katz

is correct that the courts have made a mockery of informed consent and of its moral justification in respect for autonomy, then of course his criticisms are thoroughly justified. At the same time, it should be recognized that people can proffer legally or institutionally effective authorizations under prevailing rules even if they fall far short of the standards implicit in sense$_1$.

Despite the differences between sense$_1$ and sense$_2$, a definition of informed consent need not fall into one or the other class of definitions. It may conform to both. Many definitions of informed consent in policy contexts reflect at least a strong and definite reliance on informed consent in sense$_1$. Although the conditions of sense$_1$ are not logically necessary conditions for sense$_2$, we take it as morally axiomatic that they *ought* to serve—and in fact have served—as the benchmark or model against which the moral adequacy of a definition framed for sense$_2$ purposes is to be evaluated. This position is, roughly speaking, Katz's position.

A defense of the moral viewpoint that policies governing informed consent in sense$_2$ *should* be formulated to conform to the standards of informed consent in sense$_1$ is not hard to express. The goal of informed consent in medical care and in research—that is, the purpose behind the obligation to obtain informed consent—is to enable potential subjects and patients to make autonomous decisions about whether to grant or refuse authorization for medical and research interventions. Accordingly, embedded in the reason for having the social institution of informed consent is the idea that institutional requirements for informed consent in sense$_2$ *should* be intended to maximize the likelihood that the conditions of informed consent in sense$_1$ will be satisfied.

A major problem at the policy level, where rules and requirements must be developed and applied in the aggregate, is the following: The obligations imposed to enable patients and subjects to make authorization decisions must be evaluated not only in terms of the demands of a set of abstract conditions of "true" or sense$_1$ informed consent, but also in terms of the impact of imposing such obligations or requirements on various institutions with their concrete concerns and priorities. One must take account of what is fair and reasonable to require of health care professionals and researchers, the effect of alternative consent requirements on efficiency and effectiveness in the delivery of health care and the advancement of science, and—particularly in medical care—the effect of requirements on the welfare of patients. Also relevant are considerations peculiar to the particular social context, such as proof, precedent, or liability theory in case law, or regulatory authority and due process in the development of federal regulations and IRB consent policies.

Moreover, at the sense$_2$ level, one must resolve not only which requirements will define effective consent; one must also settle on the rules stipulating the conditions under which effective consents must be obtained. In some cases, hard decisions must be made about whether requirements of informed consent (in sense$_2$) should be imposed at all, even though informed consent (in sense$_1$) *could* realistically and meaningfully be obtained in the circumstances and could serve as a model for institutional rules. For example, should there be any consent requirements in the cases of minimal risk medical procedures and research activities?

This need to balance is not a problem for informed consent in sense$_1$, which is not policy oriented. Thus,

it is possible to have a *morally acceptable* set of requirements for informed consent in sense$_2$ that deviates considerably from the conditions of informed consent in sense$_1$. However, the burden of moral proof rests with those who defend such deviations since the primary moral justification of the obligation to obtain informed consent is respect for autonomous action.

NOTES

1. President's Commission, *Making Health Care Decisions*, Vol. 1, 15 and Jay Katz, *The Silent World of Doctor and Patient* (New York: The Free Press, 1984), 87 and "The Regulation of Human Research—Reflections and Proposals," *Clinical Research* 21 (1973): 758–91. Katz does not provide a sustained analysis of joint or shared decisionmaking, and it is unclear precisely how he would relate this notion to informed consent.

2. Jay Katz, "Disclosure and Consent," in A. Milunsky and G. Annas, eds., *Genetics and the Law II* (New York: Plenum Press, 1980), 122, 128.

3. We have already noted that Katz's "idea" of informed consent—as the active involvement of patients in the medical decisionmaking process—is different from our sense$_1$.

ROBERT J. LEVINE

Informed Consent: Some Challenges to the Universal Validity of the Western Model

Robert J. Levine is professor of medicine and lecturer in pharmacology at the Yale University School of Medicine. He has served as president of the American Society of Law, Medicine, and Ethics and as a fellow at both the Hastings Center and the American College of Physicians. Dr. Levine's focus in bioethics is research ethics. His works include "The Need to Revise the Declaration of Helsinki" (*New England Journal of Medicine*), "Ethics of Clinical Trials: Do They Help the Patient?" (*Cancer*), and the influential textbook *Ethics and Regulation of Clinical Research* (Yale University Press).

INFORMED CONSENT

Informed consent holds a central place in the ethical justification of research involving human subjects. This position is signaled by the fact that it is the first stated and, by far, the longest principle of the Nuremberg Code.[1]

From *Law, Medicine, and Health Care* 19 (1991), 207–13. Reprinted by permission of the American Society of Law, Medicine & Ethics. © 1991. All rights reserved.

I. The voluntary consent of the human subject is absolutely essential. This means that the person involved should have the legal capacity to give consent; should be so situated as to be able to exercise free power of choice, without the intervention of any element of force, fraud, deceit, duress, overreaching, or other ulterior form of constraint or coercion; and should have sufficient knowledge and comprehension of the elements of the subject matter involved as to enable him to make an understanding and enlightened decision. This latter element requires that before the acceptance of an affirmative decision by the experimental subject there should be made known to him the nature, duration, and purpose of the experiment; the method and means by which it is to be conducted; all inconveniences and hazards reasonably to be expected; and the effects upon his health or person which may possibly come from his participation in the experiment. . . .

The Nuremberg Code identifies four attributes of consent without which consent cannot be considered valid: consent must be "voluntary," "legally competent," "informed," and "comprehending." These four attributes stand essentially unchanged to this day. Although there has been extensive commentary on the meaning of each of these attributes and how they are to be interpreted in specific contexts, there has been no authoritative agreement reached that any of them may be omitted or that there should be any additional attribute elevated to the status of the original four. . . .

The National Commission grounded the requirement for informed consent in the ethical principle of respect for persons which it defined as follows:

Respect for persons incorporates at least two basic ethical convictions: First, that individuals should be treated as autonomous agents, and second, that persons with diminished autonomy and thus in need of protection are entitled to such protections.

The National Commission defined an "autonomous person" as ". . . an individual capable of deliberation about personal goals and of acting under the direction of such deliberation." To show respect for autonomous persons requires that we leave them alone, even to the point of allowing them to choose activities that might be harmful, unless they agree or consent that we may do otherwise. We are not to touch them or to encroach upon their private spaces unless such touching or encroachment is in accord with their wishes. Our actions should be designed to affirm their authority and enhance their capacity to be self-determining; we are not to obstruct their actions unless they are clearly detrimental to others. We show disrespect for autonomous persons when we either repudiate their considered judgments or deny them the freedom to act on those judgments in the absence of compelling reasons to do so.

The National Commission's discussion of an autonomous person is consistent with the prevailing perception of the nature of the "moral agent" in Western civilization. A moral agent is an individual who is capable of forming a rational plan of life, capable of rational deliberation about alternative plans of action with the aim of making choices that are compatible with his or her life plan and who assumes responsibility for the consequences of his or her choices.

Although the National Commission did not cite either of the following sources as authoritative in developing its definition of respect for persons, it is clear to this observer that they found them influential: The first is the statement of the principle of respect for persons as articulated by the German philosopher, Immanuel Kant: "So act as to treat humanity, whether in thine own person or in that of any other, in every case as an end withal, never as a means only." A second influential statement is that of the American judge, Benjamin Cardozo: "Every human being of adult years and sound mind has the right to determine what will be done with his own body . . ."

. . . In the actual process of negotiating informed consent and in the reviews of plans for informed consent conducted by Institutional Review Boards (IRBs), there is a tendency to concentrate on the information to be presented to the prospective subject. Among the IRB's principal concerns are the following questions: Is there a full statement of each of the elements of informed consent? Is the information presented in a style of language that one could expect the prospective subject to understand? Implicit in this is a vision of informed consent as a two step process. First, information is presented to the subject by the investigator. Secondly, the subject satisfies himself or herself that he or she understands, and based upon this understanding either agrees or refuses to participate in the research project. . . .

In the paper I presented at an earlier CIOMS [Council for International Organizations of Medical Sciences] conference[2] I concluded:

This brief survey of descriptions of relationships between health professionals and patients in three disparate cultures leads me to conclude that the informed consent standards of the Declaration of Helsinki are not universally valid. Imposition of these standards as they are now written will not accomplish their purposes; i.e., they will not guide physicians in their efforts to show respect for persons because they do not reflect adequately the views held in these cultures of the nature of the person in his or her relationship to society.

This conclusion was based on a review of observations of the doctor–patient relationship, subject–investigator relationship and perspectives on the nature of disease in three cultures: Western Africa, China, and a Central American Mayan Indian culture.

The concept of personhood as it exists in various cultures has been addressed in an excellent paper by Willy De Craemer.[3] De Craemer is a cross-cultural sociologist with extensive experience in the field in, among other places, Central Africa and Japan.

In this paper he makes it clear that the Western vision of the person is a minority viewpoint in the world. The majority viewpoint manifest in most other societies, both technologically developing (e.g., Central Africa) and technologically developed (e.g., Japan), does not reflect the American perspective of radical individualism. . . .

Although I commend to the readers' attention De Craemer's entire essay, I shall here excerpt some passages from his description of the Japanese vision of the person. I do this because Japan is unquestionably a highly developed society technologically as well as in other respects. Thus, it is less easy to dismiss its vision of the person as exotic, as could be done with some of the examples examined in my earlier paper: . . .

The special status that the Japanese accord to human relationships, with its emphasis on the empathic and solidary interdependence of many individuals, rather than on the autonomous independence of the individual person, includes within it several other core attributes. To begin with, the kind of reciprocity (*on*) that underlies human relationships means that both concretely and symbolically what anthropologist Marcel Mauss . . . termed "the theme of the gift" is one of its dominant motifs. A continuous, gift-exchange-structured flow of material and nonmaterial "goods" and "services" takes place between the members of the enclosed human nexus to which each individual belongs. Through a never-ending process of mutual giving, receiving, and repaying . . . a web of relations develops that binds donors and recipients together in diffuse, deeply personal, and overlapping creditor-debtor ways. Generalized benevolence is involved, but so is generalized obligation, both of which take into account another crucial parameter of Japanese culture: the importance attached to status, rank, and hierarchical order in interpersonal relationships, and to . . . "proper-place occupancy" within them. The triple obligation to give, receive, and repay are tightly regulated by this status-formalism and sense of propriety. . . .

It is not difficult to imagine how a research ethics committee in the Western world—particularly in the United States—would evaluate the custom of exchange of gifts—both material and immaterial—in a system that recognized the legitimacy of "status, rank, and hierarchical order." Attention would soon be focused on the problems of "conflicts of interest." Questions would be raised as to whether consent would be invalidated by "undue inducement," or what the Nuremberg Code calls "other ulterior form(s) of constraint or coercion." In my views, it is impossible to evaluate the meaning of cash payments, provision of free services, and other "inducements" without a full appreciation of the cultural significance of such matters.

It is against this backdrop that I have been asked by the CIOMS Conference Programme Committee to "provide a definition [of informed consent] which is widely applicable to different countries and cultures." Given that the purpose of informed consent is to show respect for persons, in recognition of the vastly different perspectives of the nature of "person," I cannot do this. Since I cannot provide a substantive definition of informed consent, I shall suggest a procedural approach to dealing with the problem.

As an American I am firmly committed to the Western vision of the person and deeply influenced by my experience with the American variant of this vision. . . .

Thus, it would not be prudent to trust an American to provide a universally applicable definition of informed consent. I suggest further, that it would not be prudent to rely on any person situated in any culture to provide a universally applicable definition of informed consent.

Before proceeding, I wish to comment on the continuing controversy on the topic of ethical justification of research that crosses national boundaries. There are those who contend that all research, wherever it is conducted, should be justified according to universally applicable standards; I refer to them as "universalists." Those opposed to the universalist position, whom I call "pluralists," accept some standards as universal, but argue that other standards must be adapted to accommodate the mores of particular cultures. Pluralists commonly refer to the universalist position as "ethical imperialism," while universalists often call that of their opponents, "ethical relativism."

Universalists correctly point out that most therapeutic innovations are developed in industrialized nations. Investigators from these countries may go to technologically developing countries to test their innovations for various reasons; some of these reasons are good and some of them are not (e.g., to save money and to take advantage of the less complex and sophisticated regulatory systems typical to technologically developing countries). Moreover, universalists observe that, once the innovations have been proved safe and effective, economic factors often limit their availability to citizens of the country in which they were tested. Requiring investigators to conform to the ethical standards of their own country when conducting research abroad is one way to restrain exploitation of this type. Universalists also point to the Declaration of Helsinki as a widely accepted universal standard for biomedical research that has been endorsed by most countries, including those labeled "technologically developing." This gives weight to their claim that research must be conducted according to universal principles. Furthermore, the complex regulations characteristic of technologically developed countries are, in general, patterned after the Declaration of Helsinki.

Marcia Angell, in a particularly incisive exposition of the universalists' position, suggests this analogy.[4]

Does apartheid offend universal standards of justice, or does it instead simply represent the South African custom that should be seen as morally neutral? If the latter view is accepted, then ethical principles are not much more than a description of the mores of a society. I believe they must have more meaning than that. There must be a core of human rights that we would wish to see honored universally, despite local variations in their superficial aspects . . . The force of local custom or law cannot justify abuses of certain fundamental rights, and the right of self-determination, on which the doctrine of informed consent is based, is one of them.

Pluralists join with universalists in condemning economic exploitation of technologically developing countries and their citizens.[5] Unlike the universalists, however, they see the imposition of ethical standards for the conduct of research by a powerful country on a developing country as another form of exploitation. In their view, it is tantamount to saying, "No, you may not participate in this development of technology, no matter how much you desire it, unless you permit us to replace your ethical standards with our own." Pluralists call attention to the fact that the Declaration of Helsinki, although widely endorsed by the nations of the world, reflects a uniquely Western view of the nature of the person; as such it does not adequately guide investigators in ways to show respect for all persons in the world.

An example of pluralism may be found in the diversity of national policies regarding blind HIV-seroprevalence studies. The United States Centers for Disease Control are now conducting anonymous tests of leftover blood drawn for other purposes without notification in studies designed to "determine the level of HIV-seroprevalence in a nationwide sample of hospital patients and clients at family planning, sexually transmitted disease, tuberculosis, and drug treatment clinics. . . ." No personal identifiers are kept.[6] Although there seems to be widespread agreement among US commentators that such anonymous testing without notification is ethically justified, different judgments have been reached in other countries, most notably in the United Kingdom and in the Netherlands.[7] Who is to say which of these nations has the correct ethical perspective that should be made part of the "universal standard?"

The legitimacy of the pluralists' position is recognized implicitly in U.S. policy on whether research subjects are required to be informed of the results of HIV antibody testing.[8] In general, this policy requires that all individuals "whose test results are associated with personal identifiers must be informed of their own test results . . . individuals may not be given the option 'not to know' the result. . . ." This policy permits several narrowly defined exceptions. One of these provides that research "conducted at foreign sites should be carefully evaluated to account for cultural norms, the health resource capability and official health policies of the host country." Then "the reviewing IRB must consider if any modification to the policy is significantly justified by the risk/benefit evaluation of the research."

WHO/CIOMS Proposed International Guidelines provide specific guidance for the conduct of research in which an investigator or an institution in a technologically developed country serves as the "external sponsor" of research conducted in a technologically developing "host country."[9] In my judgment these guidelines strike a sensitive balance between the universalist and pluralist perspectives. They require that "the research protocol should be submitted to ethical review by the initiating agency. The ethical standards applied should be no less exacting than they would be for research carried out within the initiating country" (Article 28). They also provide for accommodation to the mores of the culture within the "host country." For example:

Where individual members of a community do not have the necessary awareness of the implications of participation in an experiment to give adequately informed consent directly to the investigators, it is desirable that the decision whether or not to participate should be elicited through the intermediary of a trusted community leader. (Article 15).

The conduct of research involving human subjects must not violate any universally applicable ethical standards. Although I endorse certain forms of cultural relativism, there are limits to how much cultural relativism ought to be tolerated. Certain behaviors ought to be condemned by the world community even though they are sponsored by a nation's leaders and seem to have wide support of its citizens. For example, the Nuremberg tribunal appealed to universally valid principles in order to determine the guilt of the physicians (war criminals) who had conducted research according to standards approved by their nation's leaders.

I suggest that the principle of respect for persons is one of the universally applicable ethical standards. It is universally applicable when stated at the level of formality employed by Immanuel Kant: "So act as to treat humanity, whether in thine own person or in that of any other, in every case as an end withal, never as a means only." The key concept is that persons are never to be treated only or merely as means to another's ends. When one goes beyond this level of formality or abstraction, the principle begins to lose its universality. When one restates the principle of respect for persons in a form that reflects a peculiarly Western view of the person, it begins to lose its relevance to some people in Central Africa, Japan, Central America, and so on.

The Conference Programme Committee asked me to address the problem "of obtaining consent in cultures where non-dominant persons traditionally do not give consent, such as a wife." Having subscribed to the Western vision of the meaning of person, I believe that all persons should be treated as autonomous agents, wives included. Thus, I believe that we should show respect for wives in the context of research by soliciting their informed consent. But, if this is not permitted within a particular culture, would I exclude wives from participation in research?

Not necessarily. If there is a strong possibility either that the wife could benefit from participation in the research or that the class of women of which she is a representative could benefit (and there is a reasonable balance of risks and potential benefits), I would offer her an opportunity to participate. To do otherwise would not accomplish anything of value (e.g., her entitlement to self-determination); it would merely deprive her of a chance to secure the benefits of participation in the research. I would, of course, offer her an opportunity to decline participation,

understanding that in some cultures she would consider such refusal "unthinkable."

. . . Finally, the Conference Programme Committee has asked me to consider "the special problems of obtaining consent when populations are uneducated or illiterate." Lack of education in and of itself presents no problems that are unfamiliar to those experienced with negotiating informed consent with prospective subjects. These are barriers to comprehension which are not generally insurmountable. Greater problems are presented by those who hold beliefs about health and illness that are inconsistent with the concepts of Western medicine. It may, for example, be difficult to explain the purpose of vaccination to a person who believes that disease is caused by forces that Western civilization dismisses as supernatural or magical.[10] The meaning of such familiar (in the Western world) procedures as blood-letting may be vastly different and very disturbing in some societies.[11] Problems with such explanations can, I believe, be dealt with best by local ethical review committees.

Illiteracy, in and of itself, presents no problems to the process of informed consent which, when conducted properly, entails talking rather than reading. Rather, it presents problems with the documentation of informed consent, designed to show respect for persons, fosters their interests by empowering them to pursue and protect their own interests. The consent form, by contrast, is an instrument designed to protect the interests of investigators and their institutions and to defend them against civil or criminal liability. If it is necessary to have such protection of investigators, subjects may be asked to make their mark on a consent document and a witness may be required to countersign and attest to the fact that the subject received the information.

A PROCEDURAL RESOLUTION

In "Proposal Guidelines for International Testing of Vaccines and Drugs Against HIV Infection and AIDS" (hereafter referred to as "Proposed HIV Guidelines"), reference is made to an ethical review system.[12] This system is based on that set forth in the WHO/CIOMS Proposed International Guidelines for Biomedical Research Involving Human Subjects. In the Proposed HIV Guidelines, there are suggestions for divisions of responsibility for ethical review. Here I shall elaborate how responsibilities should be divided for determining the adequacy of informed consent procedures.

This proposal presupposes the existence of an international standard for informed consent. I suggest that the standards for informed consent as set forth in the WHO/CIOMS Proposed International Guidelines and as elaborated in the Proposed HIV Guidelines, be recognized as the international standard for informed consent.

1. All plans to conduct research involving human subjects should be reviewed and approved by a research ethics committee (REC). Ideally the REC should be based in the community in which the research is to be conducted. However, as noted in CIOMS/WHO Proposed International Guidelines, under some circumstances regional or national committees may be adequate for these purposes. In such cases it is essential that regional or national committees have as members or consultants individuals who are highly familiar with the customs of the community in which the research is to be done.

    The authority of the REC to approve research should be limited to proposals in which the plans for informed consent conform either to the international standard or to a modification of the international standard that has been authorized by a national ethical review body.

2. Proposals to employ consent procedures that do not conform to the international standard should be justified by the researcher and submitted for review and approval by a national ethical review body. Earlier in this paper I identified some conditions or circumstances that could justify such omissions or modifications.

    The role of the national ethical review body is to authorize consent procedures that deviate from the international standard. The responsibility for review and approval of the entire protocol (with the modified consent procedure) remains with the REC. Specific details of consent procedures that conform to the international standard or to a modified version of the international standard approved by the national ethical review body should be reviewed and approved by the local ethical review committee.

3. There should be established an international ethical review body to provide advice, consultation and guidance to national ethical review bodies when such is requested by the latter.

4. In the case of externally sponsored research: Ethical review should be conducted in the initiating country. Although it may and should provide advice to the host country, its approval should be based on its finding that plans for informed consent are consistent with the international standard. If there has been a modification of consent procedures approved by the national ethical review body in the host country, the initiating country may either endorse the modification or seek consultation with the international review body.

NOTES

1. Reprinted in R. J. Levine: *Ethics and Regulation of Clinical Research.* Urban & Schwarzenberg, Baltimore & Munich, Second Edition, 1986.

2. R. J. Levine, "Validity of Consent Procedures in Technologically Developing Countries. In: *Human Experimentation and Medical Ethics*. Ed. by Z. Bankowski and N. Howard-Jones, Council for International Organizations of Medical Sciences, Geneva, 1982, pp. 16–30.

3. W. De Craemer, "A Cross-Cultural Perspective on Personhood," *Milbank Memorial Fund Quarterly* 61: 19–34, Winter 1983.

4. M. Angell, "Ethical Imperialism? Ethics in International Collaborative Clinical Research." *New England Journal of Medicine* 319: 1081–1083, 1988.

5. M. Barry, "Ethical Considerations of Human Investigation in Developing Countries: The AIDS Dilemma." *New England Journal of Medicine* 319: 1083–1086, 1988; N. A. Christakis, "Responding to a Pandemic: International Interests in AIDS Control." *Daedalus* 118 (No. 2): 113–114, 1989; and N. A. Christakis, "Ethical Design of an AIDS Vaccine Trial in Africa." *Hastings Center Report* 18 (No. 3): 31–37, June/July, 1988.

6. M. Pappaioanou, et al., "The Family of HIV Seroprevalence Studies: Objectives, Methods and Uses of Sentinel Surveillance in the United States." *Public Health Reports* 105(2): 113–119, 1990.

7. R. Bayer, L. H. Lumey, and L. Wan, "The American, British and Dutch Responses to Unlinked Anonymous HIV Seroprevalence Studies: An International Comparison." *AIDS* 4: 283–290, 1990, reprinted in this issue of *Law, Medicine and Health Care*, 19: 3–4.

8. R. E. Windom, Assistant Secretary for Health, policy on informing those tested about HIV serostatus, letter to PHS agency heads, Washington, DC, May 9, 1988.

9. Proposed International Guidelines for Biomedical Research Involving Human Subjects, A Joint Project of the World Health Organization and the Council for International Organizations of Medical Sciences, CIOMS, Geneva, 1982.

10. See De Craemer, supra note 6 and Levine, supra note 5.

11. A. J. Hall, "Public Health Trials in West Africa: Logistics and Ethics," *IRB: A Review of Human Subjects Research* 11 (No. 5): 8–10, Sept/Oct 1989. See also Christakis, supra note 8.

12. R. J. Levine, and W. K. Mariner, "Proposed Guidelines for International Testing of Vaccines and Drugs Against HIV Infection and AIDS," prepared at the request of WHO, Global Programme on AIDS and submitted January 5, 1990.

BOUVIA v. SUPERIOR COURT

California Court of Appeals, 1986

BEACH, ASSOCIATE JUSTICE

Petitioner, Elizabeth Bouvia, a patient in a public hospital seeks the removal from her body of a nasogastric tube inserted and maintained against her will and without her consent by physicians who so placed it for the purpose of keeping her alive through involuntary forced feeding. . . .

The trial court denied petitioner's request for the immediate relief she sought. It concluded that leaving the tube in place was necessary to prolong petitioner's life, and that it would, in fact, do so. With the tube in place petitioner probably will survive the time required to prepare for trial, a trial itself and an appeal, if one proved necessary. The real party physicians also assert, and the trial court agreed, that physically petitioner tolerates the tube reasonably well and thus is not in great physical discomfort. . . .

FACTUAL BACKGROUND

Petitioner is a 28-year-old woman. Since birth she has been afflicted with and suffered from severe cerebral palsy. She is quadriplegic. She is now a patient at a public hospital maintained by one of the real parties in interest, the County of Los Angeles. . . . Petitioner's physical handicaps of palsy and quadriplegia have progressed to the point where she is completely bedridden. Except for a few fingers of one hand and some slight head and facial movements, she is immobile. She is physically helpless and wholly unable to care for herself. She is totally dependent upon others for all of her needs. These include feeding, washing, cleaning, toileting, turning, and helping her with elimination and other bodily functions. She cannot stand

Reprinted from the *California Reporter*, 225. Cal. Rptr. 297 (Cal, App. 2 Dist.)

or sit upright in bed or in a wheelchair. She lies flat in bed and must do so the rest of her life. She suffers also from degenerative and severely crippling arthritis. She is in continual pain. Another tube permanently attached to her chest automatically injects her with periodic doses of morphine which relieves some, but not all of her physical pain and discomfort.

She is intelligent, very mentally competent. She earned a college degree. She was married but her husband has left her. She suffered a miscarriage. She lived with her parents until her father told her that they could no longer care for her. She has stayed intermittently with friends and at public facilities. A search for a permanent place to live where she might receive the constant care which she needs has been unsuccessful. She is without financial means to support herself and, therefore, must accept public assistance for medical and other care.

She has on several occasions expressed the desire to die. In 1983 she sought the right to be cared for in a public hospital in Riverside County while she intentionally "starved herself to death." A court in that county denied her judicial assistance to accomplish that goal. She later abandoned an appeal from that ruling. Thereafter, friends took her to several different facilities, both public and private, arriving finally at her present location. . . .

Petitioner must be spoon fed in order to eat. Her present medical and dietary staff have determined that she is not consuming a sufficient amount of nutrients. Petitioner stops eating when she feels she cannot orally swallow more, without nausea and vomiting. As she cannot now retain solids, she is fed soft liquid-like food. Because of her previously announced resolve to starve herself, the medical staff feared her weight loss might reach a life-threatening level. Her weight since admission to real parties' facility seems to hover between 65 and 70 pounds. Accordingly, they inserted the subject tube against her will and contrary to her express written instruction. . . .

THE RIGHT TO REFUSE MEDICAL TREATMENT

"[A] person of adult years and in sound mind has the right, in the exercise of control over his own body, to determine whether or not to submit to lawful medical treatment." (*Cobbs v. Grant* (1972) 104 Cal.Rptr, 505.) It follows that such a patient has the right to refuse any medical treatment, even that which may save or prolong her life. (*Barber v. Superior Court* (1983) 195 Cal.Rptr. 484; *Bartling v. Superior Court* (1984) 209 Cal.Rptr. 220.) In our view the foregoing authorities are dispositive of the case at bench. Nonetheless, the County and its medical staff contend that for reasons unique to this case, Elizabeth Bouvia may not exercise the right available to others. Accordingly, we again briefly discuss the rule in the light of real parties' contentions.

The right to refuse medical treatment is basic and fundamental. It is recognized as a part of the right of privacy protected by both the state and federal constitutions. . . . Its exercise requires no one's approval. It is not merely one vote subject to being overridden by medical opinion.

In *Barber v. Superior Court* we considered this same issue although in a different context. Writing on behalf of this division, Justice Compton thoroughly analyzed and reviewed the issue of withdrawal of life-support systems beginning with the seminal case of the *Matter of Quinlan* (N.J. 1976), and continuing on to the then recent enactment of the California Natural Death Act (Health & Saf. Code. §§ 7185–7195). His opinion clearly and repeatedly stresses the fundamental underpinning of its conclusion, i.e., the patient's right to decide: "In this state a clearly recognized legal right to control one's own medical treatment predated the Natural Death Act. A long line of cases, approved by the Supreme Court in *Cobbs v. Grant* (1972) have held that where a doctor performs treatment in the absence of an informed consent, there is an actionable battery. The obvious corollary to this principle is that *a competent adult patient has the legal right to refuse medical treatment.*". . .

Bartling v. Superior Court, was factually much like the case at bench. Although not totally identical in all respects, the issue there centered on the same question here present: i.e., "May the patient refuse even life continuing treatment?" Justice Hastings, writing for another division of this court, explained:

"In this case we are called upon to decide whether a competent adult patient, with serious illness which are probably incurable but have not been diagnosed as terminal, has the right, over the objection of his physicians and the hospital, to have life-support equipment disconnected despite the fact that withdrawal of such devices will surely hasten his death." (209 Cal.Rptr. 220) . . .

The description of Mr. Bartling's condition fits that of Elizabeth Bouvia. The holding of that case applies here and compels real parties to respect her decision even though she is not "terminally" ill. . . .

THE CLAIMED EXCEPTIONS TO THE PATIENT'S RIGHT TO CHOOSE ARE INAPPLICABLE

. . . At bench the trial court concluded that with sufficient feeding petitioner could live an additional 15 to 20 years; therefore, the preservation of petitioner's life for that period outweighed her right to decide. In so holding the trial court mistakenly attached undue importance to the *amount of time* possibly available to petitioner, and failed to give equal weight and consideration for the *quality* of that life; an equal, if not more significant, consideration.

All decisions permitting cessation of medical treatment or life-support procedures to some degree hastened the arrival of death. In part, at least, this was permitted because the quality of life during the time remaining in those cases had been terribly diminished. In Elizabeth Bouvia's view, the quality of her life has been diminished to the point of hopelessness, uselessness, unenjoyability and frustration. She, as the patient, lying helplessly in bed, unable to care for herself, may consider her existence meaningless. . . .

Here Elizabeth Bouvia's decision to forego medical treatment or life-support through a mechanical means belongs to her. It is not a medical decision for her physicians to make. Neither is it a legal question whose soundness is to be resolved by lawyers or judges. It is not a conditional right subject to approval by ethics committees or courts of law. It is a moral and philosophical decision that, being a competent adult, is hers alone. . . .

Here, if force fed, petitioner faces 15 to 20 years of a painful existence, endurable only by the constant administrations of morphine. Her condition is irreversible. There is no cure for her palsy or arthritis. Petitioner would have to be fed, cleaned, turned, bedded, toileted by others for 15 to 20 years! Although alert, bright, sensitive, perhaps even brave and feisty, she must lie immobile, unable to exist except through physical acts of others. Her mind and spirit may be free to take great flights but she herself is imprisoned and must lie physically helpless subject to the ignominy, embarrassment, humiliation, and dehumanizing aspects created by her helplessness. We do not believe it is the policy of this State that all and every life must be preserved against the will of the sufferer. It is incongruous, if not monstrous, for medical practitioners to assert their right to preserve a life that someone else must live, or, more accurately, endure, for "15 to 20 years." We cannot conceive it to be the policy of this State to inflict such an ordeal upon anyone.

It is, therefore, immaterial that the removal of the nasogastric tube will hasten or cause Bouvia's eventual death. Being competent she has the right to live out the remainder of her natural life in dignity and peace. It is precisely the aim and purpose of the many decisions upholding the withdrawal of life-support systems to accord and provide a large measure of dignity, respect and comfort as possible to every patient for the remainder of his days, whatever be their number. This goal is not to hasten death, though its earlier arrival may be an expected and understood likelihood. . . .

It is not necessary to here define or dwell at length upon what constitutes suicide. Our Supreme Court dealt with the matter in the case of *In re Joseph G.* (1983) 194 Cal.Rptr. 163, wherein declaring that the State has an interest in preserving and recognizing the sanctity of life, it observed that it is a crime to aid in suicide. But it is significant that the instances and the means there discussed all involved affirmative, assertive, proximate, direct conduct such as furnishing a gun, poison, knife, or other instrumentality or usable means by which another could physically and immediately inflict some death-producing injury upon himself. Such situations are far different than the mere presence of a doctor during the exercise of his patient's constitutional rights.

This is the teaching of *Bartling* and *Barber*. No criminal or civil liability attaches to honoring a competent, informed patient's refusal of medical service.

We do not purport to establish what will constitute proper medical practice in all other cases or even other aspects of the care to be provided petitioner. We hold only that her right to refuse medical treatment even of the life-sustaining variety, entitles her to the immediate removal of the nasogastric tube that has been involuntarily inserted into her body. The hospital and medical staff are still free to perform a substantial, if not the greater part of their duty, i.e., that of trying to alleviate Bouvia's pain and suffering.

Petitioner is without means to go to a private hospital and, apparently, real parties' hospital as a public facility was required to accept her. Having done so it may not deny her relief from pain and suffering merely because she has chosen to exercise her fundamental right to protect what little privacy remains to her. . . .

IT IS ORDERED

Let a peremptory writ of mandate issue commanding the Los Angeles Superior Court immediately upon receipt thereof, to make and enter a new and different order granting Elizabeth Bouvia's request for a preliminary injunction, and the relief prayed for therein; in particular to make an order (1) directing real parties in interest forthwith to remove the nasogastric tube from petitioner, Elizabeth Bouvia's, body, and (2) prohibiting any and all of the real parties in interest from replacing or aiding in replacing said tube or any other or similar device in or on petitioner without her consent. . . .

COMPTON, ASSOCIATE JUSTICE, CONCURRING OPINION

. . . I have no doubt that Elizabeth Bouvia wants to die; and if she had the full use of even one hand, could probably find a way to end her life—in a word—commit suicide. In order to seek the assistance which she needs in ending her life by the only means she sees available—starvation—she has had to stultify her position before this court by disavowing her desire to end her life in such a fashion and proclaiming that she will eat all that she can physically tolerate. Even the majority opinion here must necessarily "dance" around the issue.

Elizabeth apparently has made a conscious and informed choice that she prefers death to continued existence in her helpless and, to her, intolerable condition. I believe she has an absolute right to effectuate that decision. This state and the medical profession instead of frustrating her desire, should be attempting to relieve her suffering by permitting and in fact assisting her to die with ease and dignity. The fact that she is forced to suffer the ordeal of self-starvation to achieve her objective is in itself inhumane.

The right to die is an integral part of our right to control our own destinies so long as the rights of others are not affected. That right should, in my opinion, include the ability to enlist assistance from others, including the medical profession, in making death as painless and quick as possible. . . .

CRUZAN v. DIRECTOR, MISSOURI DEPARTMENT OF HEALTH

United States Supreme Court, 1990

CHIEF JUSTICE REHNQUIST delivered the opinion of the Court.

Petitioner Nancy Beth Cruzan was rendered incompetent as a result of severe injuries sustained during an automobile accident. Co-petitioners Lester and Joyce Cruzan, Nancy's parents and co-guardians, sought a court order directing the withdrawal of their daughter's artificial feeding and hydration equipment after it became apparent that she had virtually no chance of recovering her cognitive faculties. The Supreme Court of Missouri held that because there was no clear and convincing evidence of Nancy's desire to have life-sustaining treatment withdrawn under such circumstances, her parents lacked authority to effectuate such a request. . . .

She now lies in a Missouri state hospital in what is commonly referred to as a persistent vegetative state: generally, a condition in which a person exhibits motor reflexes but evinces no indications of significant cognitive function.[1] The State of Missouri is bearing the cost of her care.

After it had become apparent that Nancy Cruzan had virtually no chance of regaining her mental facilities her parents asked hospital employees to terminate the artificial nutrition and hydration procedures. All agree that such a removal would cause her death. The employees refused to honor the request without court approval. The parents then sought and received authorization from the state trial court for termination. The court found that a person in Nancy's condition had a fundamental right under the State and Federal Constitutions to refuse or direct the withdrawal of "death prolonging procedures." App to Pet for Cert A99. The court also found that Nancy's

"expressed thoughts at age twenty-five in somewhat serious conversation with a housemate friend that if sick or injured she would not wish to continue her life unless she could live at least halfway normally suggest that given her present condition she would not wish to continue with her nutrition and hydration." Id., at A97–A98.

The Supreme Court of Missouri reversed by a divided vote. The court recognized a right to refuse treatment embodied in the common-law doctrine of informed consent, but expressed skepticism about the application of that doctrine in the circumstances of this case. *Cruzan v. Harmon*, 760 SW2d 408, 416–417 (Mo 1988) (en banc). The court also declined to read a broad right of privacy into the State Constitution which would "support the right of a person to refuse medical treatment in every circumstance," and expressed doubt as to whether such a right existed under the United States Constitution. Id., at 417–418. It then decided that the Missouri Living Will statue, Mo Rev Stat § 459.010 et seq. (1986), embodied a state policy strongly favoring the preservation of life. The court found that Cruzan's statements to her roommate regarding her desire to live or die under certain conditions were "unreliable for the purpose of determining her intent," id., at 424, "and thus insufficient to support the co-guardians claim to exercise substituted judgment on Nancy's behalf." Id., at 426. It rejected the argument that Cruzan's parents were entitled to order the termination of her medical treatment, concluding that "no person can assume that choice for an incompetent in the absence of the formalities required under Missouri's Living Will statutes or the clear and convincing, inherently reliable evidence absent here." Id., at 425. The court also expressed its view that "[b]road policy questions bearing on life and death are more properly addressed

From *United States [Supreme Court] Reports* 497 (1990), 261–357 (excerpts). Footnotes and some references omitted.

by representative assemblies" than judicial bodies. Id., at 426. . . .

[The] notion of bodily integrity has been embodied in the requirement that informed consent is generally required for medical treatment. Justice Cardozo, while on the Court of Appeals of New York, aptly described this doctrine: "Every human being of adult years and sound mind has a right to determine what shall be done with his own body; and a surgeon who performs an operation without his patient's consent commits an assault, for which he is liable in damages." *Schloendorff v. Society of New York Hospital*, 105 NE 92, 93 (1914). The informed consent doctrine has become firmly entrenched in American tort law. . . .

The common-law doctrine of informed consent is viewed as generally encompassing the right of a competent individual to refuse medical treatment. Beyond that, [court] decisions demonstrate both similarity and diversity in their approach to decision of what all agree is a perplexing question with unusual strong moral and ethical overtones. State courts have available to them for decision a number of sources— state constitutions, statutes, and common law—which are not available to us. In this Court, the question is simply and starkly whether the United States Constitution prohibits Missouri from choosing the rule of decision which it did. This is the first case in which we have been squarely presented with the issue of whether the United States Constitution grants what is in common parlance referred to as a "right to die." . . .

The Fourteenth Amendment provides that no State shall "deprive any person of life, liberty, or property, without due process of law." The principle that a competent person has a constitutionally protected liberty interest in refusing unwanted medical treatment may be inferred from our prior decisions. . . .

But determining that a person has a "liberty interest" under the Due Process Clause does not end the inquiry; "whether respondent's constitutional rights have been violated must be determined by balancing his liberty interests against the relevant state interests." *Youngberg v. Romeo*, 457 US 307, 321 (1982). See also *Mills v. Rogers*, 457 US 291, 299 (1982).

Petitioners insist that under the general holdings of our cases, the forced administration of life-sustaining medical treatment, and even of artificially delivered food and water essential to life, would implicate a competent person's liberty interest. . . . The dramatic consequences involved in refusal of treatment would inform the inquiry as to whether the deprivation of the interest is constitutionally permissible. But for purposes of this case, we assume that the United States Constitution would grant a competent person a constitutionally protected right to refuse lifesaving hydration and nutrition.

Petitioners go on to assert that an incompetent person should possess the same right in this respect as is possessed by a competent person. . . .

The difficulty with petitioners' claim is that in a sense it begs the question: an incompetent person is not able to make an informed and voluntary choice to exercise a hypothetical right to refuse treatment or any other right. Such a "right" must be exercised for her, if at all, by some sort of surrogate. Here, Missouri has in effect recognized that under certain circumstances a surrogate may act for the patient in electing to have hydration and nutrition withdrawn in such a way as to cause death, but it has established a procedural safeguard to assure that the action of the surrogate conforms as best it may to the wishes expressed by the patient while competent. Missouri requires that evidence of the incompetent's wishes as to the withdrawal of treatment be proved by clear and convincing evidence. The question, then, is whether the United States Constitution forbids the establishment of this procedural requirement by the State. We hold that it does not.

Whether or not Missouri's clear and convincing evidence requirement comports with the United States Constitution depends in part on what interests the State may properly seek to protect in this situation. Missouri relies on its interest in the protection and preservation of human life, and there can be no gainsaying this interest. . . .

But in the context present here, a State has more particular interests at stake. The choice between life and death is a deeply personal decision of obvious and overwhelming finality. We believe Missouri may legitimately seek to safeguard the personal element of this choice through the imposition of heightened evidentiary requirements. It cannot be disputed that the Due Process Clause protects an interest in life as well as an interest in refusing life-sustaining medical treatment. Not all incompetent patients will have loved ones available to serve as surrogate decision makers. And even where family members are present "[t]here will, of course, be some unfortunate situations in which family members will not act to protect a patient.". . . Finally, we think a State may properly decline to make judgments about the "quality" of life that a particular individual may enjoy, and simply assert an unqualified interest in the preservation of human life to be weighed against the constitutionally protected interests of the individual.

In our view, Missouri has permissibly sought to advance these interests through the adoption of a "clear and convincing" standard of proof to govern such proceedings. "The function of a standard of proof, as that concept is embodied in the Due Process Clause and in the realm of factfinding, is to 'instruct the factfinder concerning the degree of confidence our society thinks he should have in the correctness of factual conclusions for a particular type of adjudication.'" . . .

There is no doubt that statutes requiring wills to be in writing, and statutes of frauds which require that a contract to make a will be in writing, on occasion frustrate the effectuation of the intent of a particular decedent, just as Missouri's requirement of proof in this case may have frustrated the effectuation of the not-fully-expressed desires of Nancy Cruzan. But the Constitution does not require general rules to work faultlessly; no general rule can. . . .

The Supreme Court of Missouri held that in this case the testimony adduced at trial did not amount to clear and convincing proof of the patient's desire to have hydration and nutrition withdrawn. In so doing, it reversed a decision of the Missouri trial court which had found that the evidence "suggest[ed]" Nancy Cruzan would not have desired to continue such measures, but which had not adopted the standard of "clear and convincing evidence" enunciated by the Supreme Court. The testimony adduced at trial consisted primarily of Nancy Cruzan's statements made to a housemate about a year before her accident that she would not want to live should she face life as a "vegetable," and other observations to the same effect. The observations did not deal in terms with withdrawal of medical treatment or of hydration and nutrition. We cannot say that the Supreme Court of Missouri committed constitutional error in reaching the conclusion that it did. . . .

No doubt is engendered by anything in this record but that Nancy Cruzan's mother and father are loving and caring parents. If the States were required by the United States Constitution to repose a right of "substituted judgment" with anyone, the Cruzans would surely qualify. But we do not think the Due Process Clause requires the State to repose judgment on these matters with anyone but the patient herself. Close

family members may have a strong feeling—a feeling not at all ignoble or unworthy, but not entirely disinterested, either—that they do not wish to witness the continuation of the life of a loved one which they regard as hopeless, meaningless, and even degrading. But there is no automatic assurance that the view of close family members will necessarily be the same as the patient's would have been had she been confronted with the prospect of her situation while competent. All of the reasons previously discussed for allowing Missouri to require clear and convincing evidence of the patient's wishes lead us to conclude that the State may choose to defer only to those wishes, rather than confide the decision to close family members.

The judgment of the Supreme Court of Missouri if affirmed.

SEPARATE OPINIONS

JUSTICE O'CONNOR, concurring.

[T]he Court does not today decide the issue whether a State must also give effect to the decisions of a surrogate decisionmaker. . . . In my view, such a duty may well be constitutionally required to protect the patient's liberty interest in refusing medical treatment. Few individuals provide explicit oral or written instructions regarding their intent to refuse medical treatment should they become incompetent. States which decline to consider any evidence other than such instructions may frequently fail to honor a patient's intent. Such failures might be avoided if the State considered an equally probative source of evidence: the patient's appointment of a proxy to make health care decisions on her behalf. Delegating the authority to make medical decisions to a family member or friend is becoming a common method of planning for the future. . . .

Today's decision, holding only that the Constitution permits a State to require clear and convincing evidence of Nancy Cruzan's desire to have artificial hydration and nutrition withdrawn, does not preclude a future determination that the Constitution requires the States to implement the decisions of a patient's duly appointed surrogate. Nor does it prevent States from developing other approaches for protecting an incompetent individual's liberty interest in refusing medical treatment. As is evident from the Court's survey of state court decisions, . . . no national consensus has yet emerged on the best solution for this difficult and sensitive problem. Today we decide only that one State's practice does not violate the Constitution; the more challenging task of crafting appropriate procedures for safeguarding incompetents' liberty interests is entrusted to the "laboratory" of the States, *New State Ice Co. v. Liebmann*, 285 US 262, 311 (1932) (Brandeis, J., dissenting), in the first instance.

JUSTICE BRENNAN, with whom JUSTICE MARSHALL and JUSTICE BLACKMUN join, DISSENTING

. . . .A grown woman at the time of the accident, Nancy had previously expressed her wish to forgo continuing medical care under circumstances such as these. Her family and her friends are convinced that this is what she would want. A guardian ad litem appointed by the trial court is also convinced that this is what Nancy would want. See 760 SW2d at 444 (Higgins, J., dissenting from denial of rehearing). Yet the Missouri Supreme Court, alone among state courts deciding such a question, has determined that an irreversibly vegetative patient will remain a passive prisoner of medical technology—for Nancy, perhaps for the next 30 years. . . . Because I believe that Nancy Cruzan has a fundamental right to be free of unwanted artificial nutrition and hydration, which right is not outweighed by any interests of the State, and because I find that the improperly biased procedural obstacles imposed by the Missouri Supreme Court impermissibly burden that right, I respectfully dissent. Nancy Cruzan is entitled to choose to die with dignity. . . .

I

. . . .The right to be free from medical attention without consent, to determine what shall be done with one's own body, is deeply rooted in this Nation's traditions, as the majority acknowledges. . . . This right has long been "firmly entrenched in American tort law" and is securely grounded in the earliest common law. . . . "'Anglo-American law starts with the premise of thoroughgoing self determination. It follows that each man is considered to be master of his own body, and he may, if he be of sound mind, expressly prohibit the performance of lifesaving surgery, or other

medical treatment.'" *Natanson v. Kline*, 350 P2d 1093, 1104 (1960) . . . .

No material distinction can be drawn between the treatment to which Nancy Cruzan continues to be subject—artificial nutrition and hydration—and any other medical treatment. . . .

Artificial delivery of food and water is regarded as medical treatment by the medical profession and the Federal Government. According to the American Academy of Neurology, "[t]he artificial provision of nutrition and hydration is a form of medical treatment . . . analogous to other forms of life-sustaining treatment, such as the use of the respirator. When a patient is unconscious, both a respirator and an artificial feeding device serve to support or replace normal bodily functions that are compromised as a result of the patient's illness." . . .

II

A

The right to be free from unwanted medical attention is a right to evaluate the potential benefit of treatment and its possible consequences according to one's own values and to make a personal decision whether to subject oneself to the intrusion. For a patient like Nancy Cruzan, the sole benefit of medical treatment is being kept metabolically alive. . . .

There are also affirmative reasons why someone like Nancy might choose to forgo artificial nutrition and hydration under these circumstances. Dying is personal. And it is profound. For many, the thought of an ignoble end, steeped in decay, is abhorrent. A quiet, proud death, bodily integrity intact, is a matter of extreme consequence. "In certain, thankfully rare, circumstances the burden of maintaining the corporeal existence degrades the very humanity it was meant to serve." *Brophy v. New England Sinai Hospital, Inc.*, 497 NE2d 626, 635–636 (1986). . . .

Such conditions are, for many, humiliating to contemplate, as is visiting a prolonged and anguished vigil on one's parents, spouse, and children. A long, drawn-out death can have a debilitating effect on family members. . . .

B

Although the right to be free of unwanted medical intervention, like other constitutionally protected interests, may not be absolute, no State interest could outweigh the rights of an individual in Nancy Cruzan's position. Whatever a State's possible interests in mandating life-support treatment under other circumstances, there is no good to be obtained here by Missouri's insistence that Nancy Cruzan remain on life-support systems if it is indeed her wish not to do so. Missouri does not claim, nor could it, that society as a whole will be benefited by Nancy's receiving medical treatment. No third party's situation will be improved and no harm to others will be averted.

The only state interest asserted here is a general interest in the preservation of life. But the State has no legitimate general interest in someone's life, completely abstracted from the interest of the person living that life, that could outweigh the person's choice to avoid medical treatment. . . . Thus, the State's general interest in life must accede to Nancy Cruzan's particularized and intense interest in self-determination in her choice of medical treatment. There is simply nothing legitimately within the State's purview to be gained by superseding her decision.

Moreover, there may be considerable danger that Missouri's rule of decision would impair rather than serve any interest the State does have in sustaining life. Current medical practice recommends use of heroic measures if there is a scintilla of a chance that the patient will recover, on the assumption that the measures will be discontinued should the patient improve. When the President's Commission in 1982 approved the withdrawal of life support equipment from irreversibly vegetative patients, it explained that "[a]n even more troubling wrong occurs when a treatment that might save life or improve health is not started because the health care personnel are afraid that they will find it very difficult to stop the treatment if, as is fairly likely, it proves to be of little benefit and greatly burdens the patient." President's Commission 75. . . .

III

. . . Missouri may constitutionally impose only those procedural requirements that serve to enhance the accuracy of a determination of Nancy Cruzan's wishes or are at least consistent with an accurate determination. The Missouri "safeguard" that the Court upholds today does not meet that standard. The determination needed in this context is whether the incompetent person would choose to live in a persistent vegetative state on life-support or to avoid this medical treatment. Missouri's rule of decision imposes a markedly asymmetrical evidentiary burden. Only evidence of specific statements of treatment choice made by the patient when competent is admissible to support a finding that the patient, now in a persistent vegetative state, would wish to avoid further medical treatment. Moreover, this evidence must be clear and convincing. No proof is required to support a finding that the incompetent person would wish to continue treatment. . . .

Even more than its heightened evidentiary standard, the Missouri court's categorical exclusion of relevant evidence dispenses with any semblance of accurate factfinding. The court adverted to no evidence supporting its decision, but held that no clear and convincing, inherently reliable evidence had been presented to show that Nancy would want to avoid further treatment. In doing so, the court failed to consider statements Nancy had made to family members and a close friend. The court also failed to consider testimony from Nancy's mother and sister that they were certain that Nancy would want to discontinue artificial nutrition and hydration, even after the court found that Nancy's family was loving and without malignant motive. The court also failed to consider the conclusions of the guardian ad litem, appointed by the trial court, that there was clear and convincing evidence that Nancy would want to discontinue medical treatment and that this was in her best interests. The court did not specifically define what kind of evidence it would consider clear and convincing, but its general discussion suggests that only a living will or equivalently formal directive from the patient when competent would meet this standard. . . .

The Missouri Court's disdain for Nancy's statements in serious conversations not long before her accident, for the opinions of Nancy's family and friends as to her values, beliefs and certain choice, and even for the opinion of an outside objective factfinder appointed by the State evinces a disdain for Nancy Cruzan's own right to choose. The rules by which an incompetent person's wishes are determined must represent every effort to determine those wishes. The rule that the Missouri court adopted and that this Court upholds, however, skews the result away from a determination that as accurately as possible reflects the individual's own preferences and beliefs. It is a rule that transforms human beings into passive sub-jects of medical technology. . . .

That Missouri and this Court may truly be moti-vated only by concern for incompetent patients makes no matter. As one of our most prominent jurists warned us decades ago: "Experience should teach us to be most on our guard to protect liberty when the gov-ernment's purposes are beneficent. . . . The greatest dangers to liberty lurk in insidious encroachment by men of zeal, well meaning but without understanding." *Olmstead v. United States,* 277 US 438, 479 (1928) (Brandeis, J., dissenting).

I respectfully dissent.

Editor's Note: The concurring opinion of JUSTICE SCALIA and the dissenting opinion of JUSTICE STEVENS are omitted.

NOTE

1. See 2 President's Commission for the Study of Ethical Problems in Medicine and Biomedical and Behavioral Research, Making Health Care Decision 241–242 (1982) (36% of those surveyed gave instructions regarding how they would like to be treated if they ever became too sick to make decisions: 23% put those instructions in writing) (Lou Harris Poll, September 1982); American Medical Association Surveys of Physicians and Public Opinion on Health Care Issues 29–30 (1988) (56% of those surveyed had told family members their wishes con-cerning the use of life-sustaining treatment if they entered an irreversible coma; 15% had filled out a living will specifying those wishes).

Advance Directives

LINDA A. EMANUEL, MARION DANIS, ROBERT A. PEARLMAN, AND PETER A. SINGER

Advance Care Planning as a Process: Structuring the Discussions in Practice

Linda A. Emanuel is Professor of Medicine at Northwestern University Medical School and Director of the Buehler Center on Aging and Professor of Health Industry Management at the Kellogg School of Management. She is also founder and principal of the Education for Physicians in End-of-Life Care (EPEC) Project. Former Vice President of Ethics Standards and head of the Institute for Ethics at the American Medical Association, she has published extensively in the field of bioethics, with particular attention to end-of-life care, the doctor-patient relationship, academic integrity, and organizational ethics.

Marion Danis is the Chief of the Bioethics Consultation Service and Head of the Section on Ethics and Health Policy in the Department of Clinical Bioethics in the Clinical Center of the National Institutes of Health. In this position, she has focused on the connection between ethical values and health policy. Some of her other articles on advanced directives include "Following Advanced Directives" (*Hastings Center Report*) and "A Prospective Study of Advance Directives for Life-Sustaining Care" (*New England Journal of Medicine*).

Robert A. Pearlman is Chief of the Ethics Evaluation Service at the National Center for Ethics in Health Care of the Veterans Health Administration and Director of the Ethics Program at the Veterans Administration Puget Sound Health Care System. He is also a professor of medicine, specializing in geriatric medicine and gerontology, at the University of Washington School of Medicine. He has published extensively on issues of consent, advance-care planning, the quality of life, and empirical research in clinical ethics.

Peter A. Singer holds the Sun Life Financial Chair in Bioethics at the University of Toronto, as well as being director of the University of Toronto Joint Centre for Bioethics. He is a professor in the Department of Medicine and is extensively involved in bioethics in Canada. In addition to his longstanding interests in advance directives, he has worked on problems of euthanasia and physician-assisted suicide, global health ethics, and research ethics.

From *Journal of the American Geriatrics Society* 43 (1995), 440–446. Reprinted by permission.

A PROCESS OF ADVANCE PLANNING

FACILITATING A STRUCTURED DISCUSSION

The structured discussion should be aimed at framing the issues, and tentatively identifying wishes. It need not aim to resolve all issues or come to final determination of all prior wishes. Neither should it aim to be a deep personal revelation seeking perfect knowledge of the patient's core self; this is unrealistic and unnecessary. Nevertheless, this step is the core of all advanced planning processes.

The skills required of the professional for this stage are those of communicating pertinent medical understanding and of supportive elicitation of the patient's wishes, as in most ideal informed consent discussions. Specific training sessions may be needed to acquire the information, skills, and judgment involved in this critical part of the process of advance planning because, unlike most medical decisions, in this case patients' preferences are cast forward into future scenarios.

Initial Decisions About the Mode of Advance Planning. An early part of the discussion may focus on whether proxy designation, instructional directives, or both are most suitable for the particular patient. Most patients should be advised to combine the two forms of planning so that the proxy may be guided by the patient's stated prior wishes. Thus, the conversation might continue as follows:

"Ms/r. X, I suggest we start by considering a few examples as a way of getting to know your thinking. I will use examples that I use for everyone."

If, in the physician's judgment, a particular patient proves not competent to make prior directives, he or she might nevertheless be competent to designate a proxy decision-maker. In such a case the conversation might go rather differently. For example, the physician might proceed as follows:

"These decisions may be hard to think about when they are not even relevant right now. You have had a long and trusting relationship with Ms/r. Y. You might even have had discussions like this before with her/him. Would you want to give Ms/r. Y, or someone else you trust, the authority to make decisions for you in case of need?"

Understanding the Patient's Goals for Treatment in a Range of Scenarios. When instructional directives are suitable, we believe that the physician should help the patient articulate abstract values, goals of treatment, and concrete examples of treatment preferences in order to provide all the major components of decision-making. Discussions can be well structured by going through an illustrative predrafted document together; this approach can prevent long confusing and overwhelming encounters. With such structuring, this portion of advance planning can be informative, accessible to patients with a wide range of educational levels, and still quite brief. Many documents that can be used for structuring discussions are available; however, a property validated document should be chosen to maximize the chance that patients are accurately representing their wishes.

Scenarios representative of the range of prognosis and of the range of disability usually encountered in circumstances of incompetence should be presented to the patient. The physician might start like this:

"So, let's try to imagine several circumstances. We will go through four and then perhaps another one or two. First imagine you were in a coma with no awareness. Assume there was a chance that you might wake up and be yourself again, but it wasn't likely. Some people would want us to withdraw treatment and let them die, others would want us to attempt everything possible, and yet others would want us to try to restore health but stop treatment and allow death if it was not working. What do you think you would want?"

After a standard set of scenarios, tailored scenarios can be considered. When a patient has a serious diagnosis with a predictable outcome involving incompetence that is not covered in the standard document, the physician might continue:

"We should also consider the situations that your particular illness can cause; that way you can be sure we will do what you want. For sure, all people are different and you may never face these circumstances. Nevertheless, let's imagine . . ."

While illness scenarios may be difficult for people to imagine, we suggest that preferences arrived at without illness scenarios are unlikely to be accurate or realistic wishes; a treatment preference without a specified illness circumstance is meaningless.

A patient considering illness scenarios also may be able to articulate which states, if any, are greatly feared and/or are felt to be worse than death for them. So, for example, the physician may go on:

"People often think about circumstances they have seen someone in or heard about in the news. Some may seem worse than death. Do you have such concerns?"

When a range of scenarios have been considered it is often possible to go back and identify the scenario(s) in which the patient's goals changed from "treat" to "don't treat." This can provide a useful personal threshold to guide the physician and proxy later. The physician may also use it to check back at the time with the patient that his or her wishes are properly reflected, saying, for example:

"Well, we've gone through several scenarios now. It seems to me that you feel particularly strongly about . . . Indeed, you move from wanting intervention to wanting to be allowed to die in peace at the point when . . . Do I speak for you correctly if I say that your personal threshold for deciding to let go is . . . ?"

Raising Specific Examples and Asking About General Values. In any scenario after the patient's response about goals, specific examples may be used:

"So, let us take an example to be sure I understand you, not only in general but also in specific. Say you were in a coma with a very small chance of recovery, and you had pneumonia; to cure the pneumonia we would have to put you on a breathing machine. Would you want us to use the breathing machine and try to cure; allow the pneumonia to cause death; or perhaps try the treatment, withdrawing the breathing machine if you did not get better?"

Checking and specifying a patient's views by providing concrete examples may be a useful way to reduce the incidence of clinically unrealistic choices by patients. So, for example, a patient who declines intubation but wants resuscitation may need more information on resuscitation and a suggestion as to how his or her wishes may be translated into a clinically reasonable decision.

The preceding discussion about goals for treatment and specific choices may be usefully combined with an open ended question about the patient's reasons for particular decisions and the values that pertain to such decisions.

"I think you have given a good picture of particular decisions you would want. Can you also say something about the values or beliefs that you hold? Understanding your more general views can be an important part of getting specific decisions right."

Patients' statements might refer to their wish to act in accord with the positions of their religious denomination, or to their views on the sanctity of life or dignity of death, or they might articulate their disposition to take a chance or to favor a secure choice.

Including the Proxy. The proxy, if already known at this point, should be encouraged to attend this discussion. Much understanding of the patient's wishes can be gained from hearing this part of the process. The clinician can guide the proxy to adopt a listening role; the proxy may ask clarifying questions but should avoid biasing the patient's expressions. Sometimes the proxy can be following the conversation with a predrafted document in hand, noting down the patient's statements. The ground can be set for future discussions between any of the patient, physician, and proxy. The proxy becomes part of the working team, and future interactions between proxy and physician, if the patient does become incompetent, are likely to go more smoothly than they might without such prior discussions.

At this stage, the advance directive should be, at most, pencilled in. The tentative draft can be taken home by the patient for further reflection and review with other involved parties, such as the proxy, family, friends, or pastor. This step can be a useful mechanism for dealing with difference among the parties ahead of time. The structured discussion should be brief and followed by a subsequent meeting when a directive may be finalized. Physicians will initially take longer in these interviews, but with training in the requisite skills and with experience, time will be reduced.

COMPLETING AN ADVISORY DIRECTIVE AND RECORDING IT

. . . The professional's main required skill here is to ascertain whether the patient has reached resolution and is ready to articulate well considered preferences. Any facet of the first two steps not yet complete should be completed at this step. Even if a patient has reached resolution, there should be a reminder that advance directives can be revised if his/her wishes are changed. If the proxy has not been present at previous stages, the physician should particularly encourage the proxy to enter the process at this point. The proxy should again be encouraged to adopt a listening and clarifying role, avoiding undue influence on the patient. It can be helpful for the physician to co-sign the document at this stage to endorse physician involvement and to document the primary physician for ease of future follow up.

REVIEWING AND UPDATING DIRECTIVES

Along with other regular check-ups and screening tests, patients should be told to expect periodic review of their directives. The clinician may re-introduce the topic.

"Ms/r. X, a year has gone by since we completed your advance care plans, and in that time a lot has happened. People do sometimes change their wishes so let's review the wishes you wrote down a year ago."

Competent people are often known to change their minds about all matters, whether they are of great import or not. Reasonable but imperfect consistency has also been found in advance planning decisions by competent individuals. Physicians should be aware of this and should review directives with the patient periodically. Physicians should check which decisions a patient maintains and which are changed. Changed positions should prompt the physician to pay particular attention to the source of change; some changes will be well reasoned, and others will be markers for misunderstandings that need to be clarified. Some people will be generally changeable; the physician should address this observation to the patient, inquiring after the reason. If supportive guidance and education do not permit the patient to reach reasonable stability in his or her advance directives, more emphasis must be placed on proxy decision-making for the patient. The physician will often be able to come to this decision jointly with the patient and proxy:

"Your choices changed on several decisions both times when we reviewed your statement, even though we have discussed the issues a lot. You have already said that you want Ms/r. Y to be your proxy. Would you prefer to give these decisions over to Ms/r. Y to decide according to what she/he thinks would be in your best interests?"

Some changed decisions may occur after the onset of incompetence. There is continuing debate on how to deal with such circumstances. The physician should be careful to evaluate the exact nature of the patient's incompetence; some patients will be globally incompetent while others will be competent to make some decisions and incompetent for other decisions. The role of the proxy and possibly a further adjudicating party may be crucial in such circumstances.

The skills that physicians require for this portion of advance planning are not as yet matched by detailed understanding of how patients might make or can be encouraged to make valid and enduring decisions, or the type of circumstances that tend to prompt changes. It is reasonable to expect that researchers will continue to study how best to elicit patient's enduring and valid wishes.

Clinicians will require both interpersonal and interpretive skills in this difficult final step. Patients will often end up in need of decisions that are not accurately specified in their advance directive. The physicians and proxy, then, must work from the information they have to make a good guess as to what the patient would have wanted. Knowledge of the patient's values, goals, choices in a range of scenarios, and thresholds for withholding or withdrawing specific interventions can all be helpful. Choices in scenarios can often provide very accurate predictors.

The spirit as much as the letter of the directive should be the focus of the physician and the proxy. Documents that are given as an advisory statement rather than a legal imperative are less likely to lead to blind application of irrelevant decisions. So, for example, if a patient has a poorly drafted document stating only that he or she does not want to be on a respirator, the physicians should try to clarify what circumstances this preference applies to; the patient may have intended the statement to apply to circumstances of hopeless prognosis, but may actually be facing a reversible life threatening illness. The physicians and proxy would need to "override" the simple statement in order to honor the true wishes of the patient in such a case; they would be interpreting simple statements to match presumed true wishes, not trumping the patient's wishes. The full responsibility of this interpretive process and the risks of misusing it in parentalistic judgments should be clear to the physician and proxy.

When the physician writes orders for the incompetent patient's care they should be as detailed as the advance directive permits. Thus a "Do Not Resuscitate" order can usually be supplemented with orders such as "evaluate and treat infection," "do not intubate," "provide full comfort care," and so forth. They can be gathered together in a series of orders altogether intended to translate the directive into doctors orders. Life threatening illness often prompts a change in health care facility or attending physician and will, therefore, entail transfer of advance directives from the physician who has guided the process to a new physician. At a minimum, physicians, patients, proxies, and institutions should all be aware of the need to transfer advance care documents with the patient to the new facility and physician. However, transmittal of accurate portrayals of a patient's wishes will rarely be adequately completed by simply passing on a document; whenever possible, the earlier physician should remain available as a key resource as the patient's prior wishes are brought to bear on specific decisions. It is likely that the physician and proxy who have undertaken the entire process of advance planning with the patient will have a more accurate sense of the patient's actual wishes than those who were simply presented with a document after patient incompetence has already occurred. Those who attempt substituted judgments in the absence of specific patient guidance are known to have discrepancies in their decisions compared with the wishes of the patient, and it is reasonable to assume that explicit communication on the matter should reduce the gap.

Decision-making, especially when there is a proxy involved, is a collaborative matter. The physician and the proxy have distinct roles that should be understood. The physician's role is to diagnose the condition and convey information, opinions, and judgment, and then to discuss them with the proxy, as would ordinarily occur with the patient. The proxy's role is to attempt substituted judgments and speak for the patient wherever possible, or to make best interest judgments as a second best approach if there is no way of surmising what the patient would have wanted. Unless the patient or the local state statutes say otherwise, the proxy should take on the "voice" of the patient and assume equal levels of authority—nor more or less—that would have been the patient's.

FURTHER CONCERNS

ARE ADVANCED DIRECTIVES FOR EVERYONE?

Time constraints and other practical considerations may lead physicians to target their sicker and older patients. However, younger and healthier patients are often quite interested in the approach. Furthermore, advance planning for those who suffer an accident or sudden illness may be most helpful. Advance planning may be considered as a branch of preventive medicine.

There will be a proportion of patients who should not be advised to undertake advance care planning. For example, there are people with no one they wish to choose as a proxy who also have limited ability to imagine future hypothetical situations. Others might find the notion so dissonant with the type of care relationship they want that they do not wish to consider the process. This latter group of patients should still have sufficient discussion to permit understanding of how decisions get made in the absence of directives. For example, the different powers of proxy and next

of kin should be clear, as should the occasional role of a guardian ad lidum, and the limited ability of substituted decisions to match the patient's prior wishes in the absence of guidance from the patient. Neither physician nor patient should allow themselves the assumption that this is a topic they need not even raise. If the patient and physician are explicitly content with the hitherto more traditional approaches to decision-making at the end of life, this is acceptable.

A considerable proportion of people have no primary care physician or health professional, and the only educational materials that reach them will be through the public media. Some of these people are able to have a physician; they should seek out a physician for the purposes of advance planning if they wish to undertake it. They should be aware that many directives are highly dependent on medical knowledge and understanding of the individual patient's medical circumstances; decisions made in the absence of medical expertise may be inaccurate reflections of the person's true preferences.

People who face limited access to the health care system should not be discouraged from advance care planning if they are inclined toward it. However, people who complete directives without talking to a physician should be encouraged to discuss their views in as much depth as possible with their next-of-kin or proxy so that ultimately someone will be able to discuss with a physician how the patient's known prior wishes relate to actual circumstances and treatment decisions. Publicly provided information or work sheets to guide persons and their proxy in such discussions can be helpful.

WHEN AND WHERE SHOULD ADVANCE DIRECTIVES BE DISCUSSED?

Advanced care planning should ideally be initiated in the outpatient setting, where such discussions are known to be well received. Then, when the topic is raised on admission to the hospital, as required by the Patient Self Determination Act, it is likely to be less threatening. Inquiry can be continued to an indepth inpatient discussion in selected cases. For example, it is appropriate with patients who are at risk of needing life-sustaining intervention soon, and discussions in this setting can be well conducted, providing guidance and welcome coordination of goals and expectations for all concerned. Although judgment of need for such intervention is known to be difficult, physicians may be guided in part by published criteria. For those with a completed directive, review during an admission may also be advisable. Other patients with a good prognosis who want to complete directives should first be advised of the merits of deferring the process to an outpatient setting. While there is little data on the question, we fear that those patients who complete directives for the first time in the hospital setting risk making more unstable decisions because of the emotional turbulence of the moment. For those who do complete a directive for the first time during hospital admission, review of the directives after health has stabilized may be particularly important.

TIME CONSTRAINTS

No step in the process of advance care planning needs to take longer than standard doctor-patient encounters. Furthermore, advance care planning probably reduces difficult and time-consuming decisions made in the absence of such planning and should, therefore, be understood as a wise investment of time. Like any other clinical process, skill and experience will make the planning process more time-efficient.

WHAT IS THE ROLE FOR NONPHYSICIAN HEALTHCARE PROFESSIONALS?

Decision-making for incompetent patients has always been among the central tasks of the physician. We regard the facilitation of a structured discussion as the central step in the process of advance planning and, therefore, as particularly dependent on physician involvement. Nevertheless, time constraints and the different communication styles of physicians will make it inevitable that some, and perhaps many, physicians will not include all the steps of advance planning in the routine activities that are the core of good doctoring. Thus, there is likely to be a need for other healthcare professionals to engage in the process of advance planning. Some facilities may form interdisciplinary source groups or consult services that will be available to physicians or patients who seek extra help. Other facilities may train nursing staff in advance planning. Social workers may have a role in facilitating communication around these difficult concepts. However, we view it as essential that the physician, who must ultimately take responsibility for life-sustaining treatment decisions, communicate with the patient at some point and at least check with the patient for possible misunderstandings, unrealistic

expectations, or wishes for treatment that the physician would find contrary to standards of medical practice or contrary to his or her conscience. Omission of this step risks discovery of advance directives which have internal inconsistencies or other major problems when it is too late to correct the problem. If the physician cannot participate in this step of advance planning, then another appropriate point may be at the next step of completing a signed advisory statement.

HELPING PROXIES UNDERSTAND THEIR ROLE

The proxy will need to distinguish his or her emotional and personal motives from concerns appropriate to their role as a proxy. Some will have emotional connections with the patient or personal views of their own that will drive them toward more aggressive intervention; others may have monetary or other concerns which may cause a conflict of interest and motivate them toward less aggressive intervention than the patient would have wanted. The physician should be sensitive to these and related possibilities and be able to help the proxy disentangle and understand the relevant motivations, both during the planning process and when making actual decisions. Complex or destructive cases may require further professional counseling and support. Together, the physician and proxy should deliberate the various therapeutic options available. The goal is to avoid any need for one party to assert authority over the other and to achieve consensus instead.

RISKS OF PLACING THE ADVANCE DIRECTIVE IN THE PATIENT'S CHART

Concerns have arisen about how to record the statement in such a fashion that it is least likely to result in inappropriate care and most likely to be available when it becomes relevant. Advance directives placed in hospital records may run the same risk as "Do Not Resuscitate" orders, which are known to sometimes result in inappropriate cessation of other therapies. Education of health professionals on the matter is clearly necessary. Detailed doctors orders can help too. In addition, sections in the medical records for advance directives may be prominently stamped with a statement to the effect that prior directives are (1) intended as an extension of patient autonomy beyond *wishlessness*, (2) may be for the purposes of requesting as well as declining treatment, and (3) have no relevance to care before incompetence.

Copies of the advisory statement and statutory document are best kept not only by the physician but also the proxy and any other person likely to be in early contact in the event of changed medical circumstances. The physician's copy should be recorded as part of the patient's medical records.

DEALING WITH LEGAL CONCERNS

Advance planning statements with physicians should be considered as advisory statements rather than adversarial challenges. (We use the term "advisory statement" in order to distinguish planning devices from narrower statutory documents, which have different legal purposes.) Physicians should make it clear to patients that the advisory statement is the area where medical counsel is most relevant and that the advisory statement is one of the best means of expressing their wishes. An advisory statement can be considered a portrait of a patient's wishes, a profile that should be interpreted to fit with whatever circumstances ultimately pertain. Such a statement can be interpreted with the flexibility needed to meet the complexities of medical decision-making and uncertainties of human decision-making.

Clinicians should be reassured that it has been well argued that such advisory statements will be honored under Common, Statutory, or Constitutional Law, even if they are not part of a statutory document. We nevertheless urge health care professionals to be less concerned with legal issues and more concerned with the medical task of translating a patient's deepest wishes into sound medical decisions. Usually, an advisory statement does not need to raise legal issues because its primary purpose is to provide a valid description of the patient's wishes. However, points of legal concern such as whether living will and proxy statutes in other states are significantly different, may require legal expertise; in such a case the physician should avoid offering unauthorized legal advice and refer to a lawyer.

Physicians may encourage simultaneous use of statutory documents, i.e., predrafted statements designed for specific state statutes, because this is what gives physicians most legal immunity from prosecution when the physician carries out the patient's or proxy's directions. Some statutory documents may contain an advisory section. If not, the advisory and statutory documents may be combined or filed together.

BEN A. RICH

Advance Directives: The Next Generation

Ben A. Rich is Associate Professor of Bioethics at the University of California–Davis School of Medicine. He is also visiting professor at the U.C. Davis School of Law. As a lawyer, he specialized in litigation and health law. Later in his career he focused his interests on bioethics. He has published numerous works on pain management and advance directives, including *Strange Bedfellows: How Medical Jurisprudence has Influenced Medical Ethics and Medical Practice* (Kluwer Academic/ Plenum Publishers).

PROSPECTIVE AUTONOMY AND THE RECOGNITION OF ADVANCE DIRECTIVES

• • •

BEYOND INFORMED CONSENT AND REFUSAL

The doctrine of informed consent, in respecting the individual autonomy of the patient, presupposes that the person has present decisional capacity. Thus, the circumstances of diagnosis, prognosis, and proposed treatment are directly and immediately confronting the patient and are ripe for decisionmaking. When the patient gives or refuses consent to a recommended procedure or a course of treatment, it is one that is deemed by the physician to be appropriate given the patient's present and/or immediately anticipated circumstances. While there is always a certain amount of speculation or uncertainty involved, it is probably as low as it ever will be.

When, on the other hand, a healthy person states preferences for treatment or nontreatment of a hypothetical condition that might arise during some possible future period of decisional incapacity, the level of potential uncertainty is greatly increased. The question then arises whether the uncertainty is so great that, as a matter of ethics, law, and public policy, it is reason-

able to honor such declarations. Perhaps we can best consider this question in the context of a few judicial decisions involving oral directives. In doing so, we also can begin to appreciate why a movement in support of statutorily recognized written directives developed.

ORAL DIRECTIVES

It is not uncommon for people, when reflecting upon serious illness or disabling injury, to share with relatives and close friends their views on how they would wish to be cared for under such circumstances. If, at some future time, the individual does become a victim of such an illness or disability, and is also decisionally incapacitated, then the concern is whether the person, when making those statements, actually intended such expressions to dictate subsequent treatment or nontreatment.

The case of *In re Eichner*[1] presented such a scenario. Brother Fox, the member of a Catholic religious order, had discussed the highly publicized case of Karen Ann Quinlan with other members of the order. He indicated that he did not wish to have his life sustained if he were to become, as she was, permanently unconscious. Some years later, during a surgical procedure, Brother Fox suffered cardiac arrest. Although he was resuscitated, he remained in a persistent vegetative state with no reasonable prospect of regaining consciousness. Father Eichner, acting on behalf of Brother Fox, petitioned the court for an order directing the hospital to remove all life support.

The testimony was uncontroverted that Brother Fox, in his prior statements, had fortuitously addressed precisely the medical contingency that had now befallen him—permanent unconsciousness, which might be prolonged indefinitely through medical interventions. The decision of the court turned upon the seriousness with which Brother Fox had made the statement. The continuum along which such statements run appears to be that of "casual remarks" at one end and "solemn pronouncements" at the other. The court concluded that Brother Fox's statements constituted solemn pronouncements, and therefore met the clear and convincing evidence standard applied in such cases.[2] . . .

[In *In re Martin*,][3] Michael Martin had a tremendous fear of becoming and remaining severely debilitated and disabled, regardless of whether it was mental, physical, or both. He discussed this profound concern on several occasions with his wife, indicating that he would not wish to have his life sustained by medical interventions if he were incapable of performing various functions such as walking, conversing with others, dressing and bathing himself, or tending to his basic needs. For example, after a conversation about frail and demented patients in long-term care facilities who were completely dependent upon others, Michael Martin's wife quoted him as saying: "I would never want to live like that. Please don't ever let me exist that way because those people don't even have their dignity."[4] On another occasion, after viewing the motion picture "Brian's Song," the story of an athlete with a terminal illness, Michael Martin said to his wife: "If I ever get sick don't put me on any machines to keep me going if there is no hope of getting better." He then said to her, in an obvious effort to emphasize the point, that if she ever did that to him: "I'll always haunt you, Mary."[5] On still another occasion, Michael Martin, who was an avid hunter, indicated to his wife that, if he were to become the victim of a hunting accident in which he was seriously and permanently injured, so that he would never again be the same person, then he would not want to go on living. To further reinforce his point, he said to his wife: "Mary, promise me you wouldn't let me live like that if I can't be the person I am right now, because if you do, believe me I'll haunt you every day of your life."[6]

Within months after the last in a series of conversations of this nature with his wife, Michael Martin sustained grave injuries in an automobile accident. As a result of these injuries, he was rendered decisionally incapacitated, unable to walk or talk, and dependent upon a colostomy tube for elimination and a gastrostomy tube for nutrition and hydration. His wife was appointed his guardian, and respecting his repeatedly expressed views, she sought to have his life-sustaining interventions withdrawn. The ethics committee of the institution where he was being treated reviewed the case and concluded that withdrawing his nutritional support was both medically and ethically appropriate, but suggested that prior judicial authorization should be obtained.[7] When Mary Martin filed a petition in the probate court requesting such authorization, Michael Martin's mother and sister opposed the petition and sought to have Mary removed as Michael's guardian. Remarkably, the probate court ruled that, although clear and convincing evidence had been presented that Michael's present condition was one in which he had indicated he would not wish to have his life maintained, his wishes could not be considered because they were never expressed in writing. The court also declined to remove Mary as Michael's guardian.[8]

Following the remand by the appellate court for additional evidentiary proceedings, the trial court found that nutritional support could be withdrawn by the guardian based upon the clear and convincing evidence that Michael's present, irreversible condition was one in which he had indicated he would not wish to be maintained. The appellate court affirmed, based upon the determination that Michael Martin's present condition fell within the parameters that he had described when competent.

The Michigan Supreme Court, in a fashion reminiscent of the Missouri Supreme Court in the case of Nancy Cruzan,[9] disagreed on the weight and sufficiency of the evidence as determined by the trial court, and reversed on the grounds that the majority was not satisfied that the evidence in the record is "so clear, direct, weighty and convincing as to enable [the fact finder] to come to a clear conviction, without hesitancy, of the truth of the precise facts in issue."[10] The majority cites with favor the following language from the brief filed by the respondents regarding the various remarks made by Michael Martin:

[The remarks] were remote in time and place from his present circumstances. At the time the remarks were supposedly made, Michael was young and healthy. The remarks were general, vague and casual, because Mr. Martin was not presently experiencing and likely had never experienced the form of "helplessness" he supposedly disliked, and thus he could not bring to bear his specific views about specific circumstances of which he was intimately knowledgeable. Not being informed by his actual experience, Michael's purported remarks thus were "no different than those that many of us might make after witnessing an agonizing death of another."[11]

The implications of this proposition for the exercise of prospective autonomy are immense and profoundly negative. A few of them are discussed here. First, young and healthy persons would be precluded from issuing directives (that such courts will honor) refusing treatment in the event of grave and permanent injury because (1) they have never experienced life under such circumstances, and (2) the occurrence of such catastrophic illness or injury may come years later. Second, and more significant, no competent person may ever prospectively decline treatment for a future period of incompetence because the person will have no first-hand experience of what life is like as an incompetent individual. Their refusal, from this point of view, is fatally uninformed and therefore need not be respected. Followed to its natural conclusion, 20 years of public policy in support of advance care planning would be completely annihilated.

Because Michigan, like New York, is one of the few jurisdictions that refuses to apply a best interests approach in the absence (real or purported) of clear and convincing evidence, there was no basis upon which the petitioner could argue for withdrawal of nutritional support. Again echoing the Missouri Supreme Court in *Cruzan*, the Michigan Supreme Court asserted: "Our determination is consistent with the furtherance of this state's interest in preserving the sanctity of life and does not abridge Mr. Martin's right to refuse life-sustaining medical treatment."[12] This facile and self-serving observation by the court to the contrary notwithstanding, the conclusion for the citizens of Michigan is inescapable: if you wish your views on withholding or withdrawing life-sustaining treatment to overcome the almost insurmountable burdens imposed by the clear and convincing evidence standard (as interpreted by the state's highest court) and the state's strong interest in preserving the sanctity of life (regardless of its quality or the disproportion between the burdens and benefits of continued existence to the individual), then you must express those views in a formal written directive. Furthermore,

do not just state your views so that anyone can understand them, state them so that no one can misunderstand them.

Cases such as those considered in this section help to explain why citizens concerned about their ability to exercise a purported right to prospective autonomy turned to the state legislatures for redress.

THE LIVING WILL

The first type of written advance directive to be recognized by law was the living will. It is the most well known, to the extent that it has (problematically) become in common parlance a generic term for any type of directive. A living will is usually a declaration that, under certain medical conditions, the declarant would not wish to have his or her life sustained through major medical interventions such as artificial respiration, nutrition or hydration, or cardiopulmonary resuscitation. Living wills were designed to prevent the use of medical technology that could not cure disease or reverse an ultimately terminal condition, and thus might reasonably be viewed as merely prolonging the dying process rather than saving life.

What is both interesting and ironic about living wills is that the most significant impetus for their development came from highly publicized cases such as that of Karen Ann Quinlan, a woman in her early twenties whose life was sustained for years while she remained in a persistent vegetative state (PVS) with no hope of recovery to a competent, sapient state.[13] Many of the people who executed living wills believed that, in so doing, they were ensuring they would avoid Karen Quinlan's fate. However, many state living will statutes require, before the will can take effect, that an attending and one other physician certify in writing not only that the patient is unconscious, comatose, or otherwise decisionally incapacitated, but also that the patient's condition is terminal (that is, will result in the patient's death within six months). Many physicians do not consider a PVS to be terminal, because with proper care, such patients may live for many years. Thus, the fate worse than death, which those executing living wills sought to avoid (being kept alive biologically with no hope of regaining consciousness), was something from which those directives could not protect them.

The other ironic aspect of the *Quinlan* case as an impetus for the use of living wills is that, as previously noted, Quinlan was a very young and otherwise healthy woman when she entered a PVS. Yet it is rarely the case that people in their twenties or even thirties execute living wills. Similarly, even those physicians who have become proponents of living wills acknowledge that they do not make a practice of discussing these instruments with their young, healthy patients, even though they are perhaps most at risk of severe brain injury through trauma.

Another difficulty with the terminal illness requirement is that it means different things to different physicians. If the statute recognizing living wills defines terminal condition, then it may characterize it as an irreversible condition from which the patient will die in six months. Medicine is not good at making such predictions except for patients who are only a few hours or at most a few days away from death, regardless of the medical interventions they receive. This is another fact confirmed by SUPPORT. If the statute does not define terminal illness in terms of a maximum life expectancy, then there is likely to be wide variation among physicians as to when they would be willing to certify in writing that a condition is terminal. A conservative view may reject the terminal label until death is imminent (a matter of hours), thereby essentially nullifying the living will. A liberal view may take the position that any irreversible condition that ultimately will result in the patient's death should be deemed a terminal condition, including a PVS.

The other common limitation of living will statutes is that certain types of interventions are specifically excluded. The Missouri living will statute, which was discussed by the Missouri Supreme Court (with highly questionable relevance) in the *Cruzan* case, provides a dramatic example. One of the dissenting judges in that case described the Missouri Living Will Act as "a fraud on Missourians who believe we have been given a right to execute a living will, and to die naturally, respectably, and in peace."[14] The Missouri Living Will Act excludes from the phrase "death-prolonging procedure" comfort care, artificial nutrition and hydration, or the administration of any medication (presumably even antibiotics in the case of pneumonia). Even statutes that do not completely exclude certain procedures from the ambit of living will declarations may, as is the case in Colorado, require that declarants specifically state that they do not wish to receive artificial nutrition and hydration if they are decisionally incapacitated and suffering from a terminal condition.

THE DURABLE POWER OF ATTORNEY FOR HEALTH CARE

The primary purpose of this type of advance directive is the designation of a particular individual as the attorney-in-fact for the making of surrogate health care decisions. To be valid, a health care power of attorney need not contain any indication of the person's views about life, death, life-sustaining medical interventions, or other information that might be informative and helpful to the designated surrogate or treating physicians. There seems to be an assumption, which may not necessarily be accurate, that the person executing the health care power of attorney has made his or her wishes with regard to various forms of treatment, and the medical interventions they might entail, known to the attorney-in-fact and perhaps the individual's primary care physician as well. Such an assumption may be nothing more than wishful thinking, however.

In many states, the health care power of attorney constitutes a means by which to avoid the serious limitations that characterize the living will. Typically, the statutes recognizing this form of directive require only the decisional incapacity of the patient in order for the power of attorney to take effect. Similarly, most statutes do not single out any particular intervention (such as artificial nutrition and hydration), which the attorney-in-fact may not reject or reject only when certain conditions have been met. Consequently, the attorney-in-fact has the same, virtually unlimited, authority to reject any or all medical procedures, including those necessary to sustain the life of the patient, as the patient has when competent.

Although the durable power of attorney for health care can be viewed as a significant improvement on the living will in terms of the exercise of prospective autonomy, use of this form of directive carries potential risks for the declarant. An often-repeated critique of advance directives generally, which was noted in *Martin*, is that no one who is competent and reasonably healthy can anticipate accurately how he or she might feel about major medical interventions, especially potentially life-saving ones, during a later period of incompetence and grave illness. To the extent that this critique is valid, it can be asserted even more strongly with regard to a surrogate decisionmaker. Particularly in those situations in which the document contains no personal statement, and the declarant and the attorney-in-fact have not had extensive discussions on this subject, there exists a considerable risk that the surrogate, in making health care decisions for the incompetent patient, will project his or her own views onto the patient. Indeed, health care professionals often (wittingly or unwittingly) encourage such behaviors on the part of surrogates by posing the critical question to them in terms such as: "What do you want us to do for the patient?" rather than using the more appropriate phraseology: "Knowing the patient as you do, what do you believe that he/she would want us to do under the circumstances as we have described them?"

When the person executing the durable power of attorney provides explicit indications of the kinds of interventions he or she would wish to receive in particular situations, as well as those the person would not wish, an objective standard can be said to have been applied by the attorney-in-fact acting as the duly appointed surrogate decisionmaker. However, when explicit indications are not provided in the durable power, and the author simply trusts that the designated attorney-in-fact will know the right thing to do, then a subjective standard will have to be applied. The practice of referring to the standard of decisionmaking under these circumstances as one of "substituted judgment" can be misleading. Courts using such terminology state that the surrogate substitutes his or her judgment for that of the incompetent patient. Typically, however, when a person designates another to be a health care proxy, it is not because that person has demonstrated a capacity to make good decisions in general. Rather, the proxy is selected because he or she knows the patient well, and based upon that familiarity will be in the best position to know, or at least intuit, what the now incompetent patient would decide if he or she were still competent and had been apprised fully of the circumstances.

A person who wishes to create a durable power of attorney for health care that provides the designated proxy (attorney-in-fact), and the health care professionals with whom the proxy will interact on behalf of the incompetent patient, with reasonably explicit guidance on the values and preferences that should inform the decisionmaking process, must expend some significant amount of time and effort. Personal views and wishes on these matters must be assessed accurately and clearly expressed in the directive as well as in discussions with the individual's primary care physician, designated attorney-in-fact, and one or more alternate surrogates in the event that the primary surrogate is no longer available at the critical time. The more out of the mainstream the patient's views are with regard to desired treatment or nontreatment during grave or terminal illness, the greater

will be the need to document those views. Otherwise, physicians responsible for the incompetent patient's care reasonably may believe that the proxy is not acting in good faith and in pursuit of the patient's best interests.

A health care proxy document that is neither too general nor too specific presents a genuine challenge in draftsmanship. If too general, then the document will not provide the attorney-in-fact with sufficient guidance or documentation of views that may have been previously expressed in conversation. If too specific, then the document may be viewed as addressing only the situations actually mentioned, thereby suggesting that any other circumstance, no matter how similar, was not intended to be governed by it. One solution for the version that errs on the side of specificity is to include the phrase "by way of example and not limitation" in conjunction with the discussion of particular medical conditions or interventions. Another solution is to utilize one of the next generation of advance care planning documents. . . .

CONCLUSION

A common explanation for physician inattention to advance directives is the lack of time and reimbursement for such discussions. However, in the era of cost containment, such an attitude is counterproductive. Most patients who engage in advance care planning choose to limit care at the end of life rather than demand care that would be described as "futile." Thus, the time spent in assisting patients in carefully and clearly constraining the use of heroic measures in their care ultimately will produce significant reductions in the cost of care, not to mention stress and anxiety on the part of caregivers. A health care system that seeks to contain costs and minimize inappropriate care (which certainly should include within its ambit care the patient would not want) has every reason to embrace wholeheartedly all forms of advance care planning.

Patients, physicians, hospitals, and health plans all can benefit immensely from the utilization of some combination of health care proxies, medical directives, and a values history. The emphasis should be upon the creation of a clear, cogent, yet concise record of patient wishes and preferences, including the identity of surrogate decisionmakers. In addition to the tangible benefits discussed, engaging in the process of creating and reviewing the next generation of directives offers the intangible benefit of countering the increasingly common patient perception that physicians are cold, impersonal, and more interested in moving on to the next case than in relating to them as a unique individual.

As we move into our new millennium, we would do well to learn from the past, lest we repeat it. It is not the concept of advance directives that is flawed and unworkable, but merely our fledgling efforts at crafting them. The next generation of advance directives will succeed where the others have failed. They will do so, in significant part, because they remedy the fatal flaw of the earlier versions—removal of the physician from a fundamental aspect of the professional relationship, which is to provide guidance, counsel, and moral support in planning for care at the end of life.

NOTES

1. 420 N.E.2d 64 (N.Y. 1981).
2. *Id.* at 72.
3. *In re Martin*, 538 N.W.2d 399 (Mich. 1995).
4. *Id.* at 412.
5. *Id.*
6. *Id.*
7. *Id.* at 402.
8. *Id.* at 403.
9. *Cruzan v. Harmon*, 760 S.W.2d 408 (Mo. 1988) (en banc).
10. *Martin*, 538 N.W.2d at 413.
11. *Id.* at 411.
12. *Id.* at 413.
13. *In re Quinlan*, 355 A.2d 647 (N.J. 1976).
14. *Cruzan*, 760 S.W.2d at 442 (Welliver, J., dissenting).

Suggested Readings for Chapter 3

MEDICAL CONFIDENTIALITY

American Society of Human Genetics. "Professional Disclosure of Familial Genetic Information." *American Journal of Human Genetics* 62 (1998), 474–83.

Beauchamp, Tom L., and Childress, James F. *Principles of Biomedical Ethics,* 6th ed. New York: Oxford University Press, 2008, chaps. 3 and 7.

Black, Sir Douglas. "Absolute Confidentiality?" In Raanan Gillon, ed. *Principles of Health Care Ethics.* London: John Wiley & Sons, 1994.

Bok, Sissela. *Secrets: On the Ethics of Concealment and Revelation.* New York: Pantheon Books, 1983.

Gostin, Lawrence O., and Hodge, James G. "Piercing the Veil of Secrecy in HIV/AIDS and Other Sexually Transmitted Diseases: Theories of Privacy and Disclosure in Partner Notification." *Duke Journal of Gender Law & Policy* 5 (1998), 9–88.

Kipnis, K. "A Defense of Unqualified Medical Confidentiality." *American Journal of Bioethics* 6 (2006), 7–18 [with following commentary].

Offit, Kenneth; Groeger, Elizabeth; Turner, Sam; Wadsworth, Eve A.; and Weisner, Mary A. "The 'Duty to Warn' a Patient's Family Members about Hereditary Disease Risks." *The Journal of the American Medical Association* 292 (2004), 1469–73.

Sankar, P., Moran, S., Merz, J. F., and Jones, N. L. "Patient Perspectives of Medical Confidentiality: A Review of the Literature." *Journal of General Internal Medicine* 18 (2003), 659–69.

TRUTH TELLING, NONDISCLOSURE, AND DISCLOSING MEDICAL ERROR

Baylis, Francoise. "Errors in Medicine: Nurturing Truthfulness." *Journal of Clinical Ethics* 8 (Winter 1997), 336–40.

Bok, Sissela. *Lying: Moral Choice in Public and Private Life.* New York: Pantheon Books, 1978.

Bostick, Nathan A., Sade, Robert, McMahon, John W., and Benjamin, Regina. "Report of the American Medical Association Council on Ethical and Judicial Affairs: Withholding Information from Patients: Rethinking the Propriety of 'Therapeutic Privilege.'" *Journal of Clinical Ethics* 17 (Winter 2006), 302–06.

Buckman, R. F. *How to Break Bad News.* Baltimore: Johns Hopkins University Press, 1992.

Cabot, Richard C. "The Use of Truth and Falsehood in Medicine," as edited by Jay Katz from the 1909 version. *Connecticut Medicine* 42 (1978), 189–94.

Gallagher, Thomas H., Waterman, Amy D., Ebers, Alison G., Fraser, Victoria J., and Levinson, Wendy. "Patients' and Physicians' Attitudes Regarding the Disclosure of Medical Errors." *Journal of the American Medical Association* 289 (February 26, 2003), 1001–07.

Gillon, Raanan. "Is There an Important Moral Distinction for Medical Ethics between Lying and Other Forms of Deception?" *Journal of Medical Ethics* 19 (1993), 131–32.

Gold, M. "Is Honesty Always the Best Policy? Ethical Aspects of Truth Telling." *Internal Medicine Journal* 34 (2004), 578–80.

Jones, James W., McCullough, Laurence B., and Richman, Bruce W. "Truth-telling About Terminal Diseases." *Surgery* 137 (March 2005), 380–82.

Klitzman, Robert, and Bayer, Ronald. *Mortal Secrets: Truth and Lies in the Age of AIDS*. Baltimore: Johns Hopkins University Press, 2003.

Orona, Celia J., Koenig, Barbara A., and Davis, Anne J. "Cultural Aspects of Nondisclosure." *Cambridge Quarterly of Healthcare Ethics* 3 (1994), 338–46.

Sirotin, Nicole, and Lo, Bernard. "The End of Therapeutic Privilege?" *Journal of Clinical Ethics* 17 (Winter 2006), 312–16.

Surbone, Antonella. "Telling the Truth to Patients with Cancer: What Is the Truth?" *Lancet Oncology* 7 (November 2006), 944–50.

Wu, Albert W. "Is There an Obligation to Disclose Near-Misses in Medical Care?" In Virginia A. Sharpe, ed. *Accountability: Patient Safety and Policy Reform.* Washington, D.C.: Georgetown University Press, 2004, ch. 8.

INFORMED CONSENT

Beauchamp, Tom L., and Childress, James F. *Principles of Biomedical Ethics,* 6th ed. New York: Oxford University Press, 2008, chap. 3.

Berg, Jessica W., Appelbaum, Paul S., Lidz, Charles W., and Parker, Lisa S. *Informed Consent: Legal Theory and Clinical Practice,* 2nd ed. New York: Oxford University Press, 2001.

Bok, Sissela. "Shading the Truth in Seeking Informed Consent." *Kennedy Institute of Ethics Journal* 5 (1995), 1–17.

Buchanan, Allen E., and Brock, Dan W. *Deciding for Others: The Ethics of Surrogate Decision Making.* Cambridge: Cambridge University Press, 1989.

Dworkin, Roger B. "Getting What We Should from Doctors: Rethinking Patient Autonomy and the Doctor-Patient Relationship." *Health Matrix* 13 (2003), 235–96.

Faden, Ruth R., and Beauchamp, Tom L. *A History and Theory of Informed Consent.* New York: Oxford University Press, 1986.

Geller, Gail, Strauss, Misha, Bernhardt, Barbara A., and Holtzman, Neil A. "'Decoding' Informed Consent: Insights from Women Regarding Breast Cancer Susceptibility Testing." *Hastings Center Report* 27 (March-April 1997), 28–33.

Gostin, Lawrence O. "Informed Consent, Cultural Sensitivity, and Respect for Persons." *Journal of American Medical Association* 274 (September 13, 1995), 844–45.

Karlawish, Jason H. T., Fox, Ellen, and Pearlman, Robert. "How Changes in Health Care Practices, Systems, and Research Challenge the Practice of Informed Consent." *Medical Care* 40 (Supplement 2002), V12–V19.

Katz, Jay. *The Silent World of Doctor and Patient.* New York: Free Press, 1984.

King, Jaime Staples, and Moulton, Benjamin W. "Rethinking Informed Consent: The Case for Shared Medical Decision-making." *American Journal of Law and Medicine* 32 (2006), 429–93.

Meisel, Alan, and Kuczewski, Mark. "Legal and Ethical Myths About Informed Consent." *Archives of Internal Medicine* 156 (December 1996), 2521–26.

Rich, Ben A. "Medical Paternalism v. Respect for Patient Autonomy: The More Things Change the More They Remain the Same." *Michigan State University Journal of Medicine & Law* 10 (2006), 87–124.

Veatch, Robert M. "Abandoning Informed Consent." *Hastings Center Report* 25 (March-April 1995), 5–12.

White, Becky Cox, and Zimbelman, Joe. "Abandoning Informed Consent: An Idea Whose Time Has Not Yet Come." *Journal of Medicine and Philosophy* 23 (1998), 477–99.

Wolf, Susan M. "Doctor and Patient: An Unfinished Revolution." *Yale Journal of Health Policy, Law & Ethics* 6 (Summer, 2006), 485–500.

Beauchamp, Tom L., and Veatch, Robert, eds. *Ethical Issues in Death and Dying,* 2nd ed. Upper Saddle River, NJ: Prentice-Hall, 1996.

Kelley, Maureen. "Limits on Patient Responsibility." *Journal of Medicine and Philosophy* 30 (2005) 189–206.

Kliever, Lonnie D., ed. *Dax's Case: Essays in Medical Ethics and Human Meaning.* Dallas, TX: Southern Methodist University Press, 1989.

Kon, Alexander A. "When Parents Refuse Treatment for Their Child." *JONA'S Healthcare Law, Ethics and Regulation* 8 (January-March 2006), 5–9.

Lynn, Joanne. *By No Extraordinary Means: The Choice to Forego Life-Sustaining Food and Water.* Reprint ed. Bloomington, IN: Indiana University Press, 1989.

Murphy, Peter. "Are Patients' Decisions to Refuse Treatment Binding on Health Care Professionals?" *Bioethics* 19 (June 2005), 189–201.

President's Commission for the Study of Ethical Problems in Medicine and Biomedical and Behavioral Research. *Deciding to Forego Life-Sustaining Treatment.* Washington, DC: U.S. Government Printing Office, 1983.

Ravitsky, Vardit, and Wendler, David, "Dissolving the Dilemma over Forced Treatment." *Lancet* 365 (April 30, 2005), 1525–26.

Sullivan, Mark D., and Youngner, Stuart J. "Depression, Competence, and The Right to Refuse Lifesaving Medical Treatment." *American Journal of Psychiatry* 151 (July 1994), 971–78.

Youngner, Stuart J. "Competence To Refuse Life-Sustaining Treatment." In Maurice D. Steinberg and Stuart J. Youngner, eds. *End-of-Life Decisions: A Psychosocial Perspective.* Washington, DC: American Psychiatric Press, 1998, 19–54.

ADVANCE DIRECTIVES

Ackerman, Terrence F. "Forsaking the Spirit for the Letter of the Law: Advance Directives in Nursing Homes." *Journal of the American Geriatrics Society* 45 (1997), 114–16.

Bradley, Elizabeth H., and Rizzo, John A. "Public Information and Private Search: Evaluating the Patient Self-Determination Act." *Journal of Health Politics, Policy and Law* 24 (April 1999), 239–73.

Hickman, Susan E., Hammes, Bernard J., Moss, Alvin H., and Tolle, Susan W. "Hope for the Future: Achieving the Original Intent of Advance Directives." *Improving End of Life Care: Why Has It Been So Difficult? Hastings Center Report Special Report* 35 (2005), S26–30.

King, Nancy. *Making Sense of Advance Directives.* Dordrecht: Kluwer Academic Publishers, 1991.

Mappes, Thomas A. "Persistent Vegetative State, Prospective Thinking, and Advance Directives." *Kennedy Institute of Ethics Journal* 13 (June 2003), 119–39.

Olick, Robert S. *Taking Advance Directives Seriously: Prospective Autonomy and Decisions Near the End of Life.* Washington, D.C.: Georgetown University Press, 2001.

Teno, Joan M., Lynn, Joanne, Wenger, Neil S., Phillips, Russell S., Murphy, Donald, Youngner, Stuart J., and Bellamy, Paul. "Do Formal Advance Directives Affect Resuscitation Decisions and the Use of Resources for Seriously Ill Patients?" *Journal of Clinical Ethics* 5 (1994), 23–30 [with following commentary].

Chapter 4
Eugenics and Human Genetics

Introduction

The last decade of the twentieth century and the first decade of this new century have been exciting times for human genetics. The detailed sequencing of the human genome was completed in 2004, fifty-one years after the discovery of the double helix by James Watson and Francis Crick. Parallel genome projects have already provided the genetic sequences for the fruit fly, a roundworm called *C. elegans,* a mustard-like plant named *Arabidopsis,* at least sixty types of bacteria, the mouse, the rat, the dog, the chimpanzee, and the rhesus macaque monkey.[1] These impressive achievements of multiple genome projects will provide new understandings of health and disease, information about evolution and migration, and, more controversially, insight into genetic influences on behavior.

The readings in this chapter explore two medical applications of new genetic knowledge: genetic testing and screening on one hand and human gene transfer aimed at treating disease (sometimes called *human gene therapy*) on the other. In a more research-oriented mode, the final readings in the chapter consider what is known, and what is not known, about the interrelationships between human genes and human behavior.

EUGENICS IN THE TWENTIETH CENTURY

While new scientific findings offer grounds for optimism about the future, some past attempts to apply genetic knowledge suggest that caution and vigilance may also be warranted. The initial readings in this chapter recount government-sponsored attempts to improve society by intervening in the reproductive decisions, or modifying the reproductive capacities, of human beings. The first of these eugenic programs emerged in the United States during the first half of the twentieth century. A second program, modeled in part on the U.S. experience and the writings of American eugenicists, was enacted in Germany when that country was governed by Adolf Hitler and the National Socialists.

The definition of *eugenics* is controversial. One simple definition is that eugenics means "the study of human improvement by genetic means."[2] If this definition is accepted, one can discover eugenic proposals in writings as old as Plato's *Republic*, where selective breeding was proposed as a means of improving society.[3] The word *eugenics* was coined in 1883 by an English scientist, Francis Galton, who was a cousin of Charles Darwin. In his first major book, *Hereditary Genius*, published in 1869, and in later works Galton advocated a system of arranged marriages between men and women of distinction, with the aim of producing a group of gifted children and ultimately an improved British population.

In twentieth-century eugenics programs, the element of coercion by the state was added to the social goal of promoting human betterment. The first systematic attempts to develop mandatory eugenic programs occurred in several states of the United States. Within these state-based programs the central aim was to prevent reproduction by people who were judged to have intellectual disabilities—people who, it was thought, were likely to transmit their disabilities to their offspring. (In the language of the time, people who had such disabilities were said to be "feeble-minded.") The method by which this potential harm was to be prevented was surgical sterilization—the tying off or cutting of the fallopian tubes in females and the severing of the *vasa deferentia* in males.

Daniel Kevles's essay chronicles the history of eugenic sterilization in the United States. While several state courts struck down mandatory sterilization statutes as unconstitutional, the U.S. Supreme Court found Virginia's involuntary sterilization law to be compatible with the guarantees of the U.S. Constitution. Oliver Wendell Holmes wrote for the Supreme Court's majority and argued that if Carrie Buck's mother, Carrie herself, and Carrie's daughter were all feeble-minded, the state of Virginia was justified in attempting to prevent any further reproduction by Carrie Buck through involuntary sterilization. In Holmes's chilling words, "Three generations of imbeciles are enough." The full text of the court's 1927 *Buck v. Bell* decision is reprinted in this chapter. In his essay "Carrie Buck's Daughter" paleontologist Stephen Jay Gould critically examines both the factual premises accepted and the moral arguments advanced by the Supreme Court majority.

The eugenic programs undertaken in several states of the United States were closely monitored by academics and policy makers in other parts of the world, and especially in Germany. There the method of mandatory sterilization was found to be compatible both with the academic field called "racial hygiene" and with the political agenda of the National Socialists. Jonathan Glover discusses the theory and practice of the Nazi sterilization program during the 1930s, when approximately 350,000 persons deemed unfit to reproduce were sterilized. As is well known, this sterilization effort was later followed by more radical measures that sought to exterminate "unworthy" individuals and groups in Nazi killing centers and concentration camps.[4]

GENETICS AND SOCIETY

There can be no doubt that we live in the golden age of genetics, especially human genetics. Even before the 1950s, Gregor Mendel's classic work on various modes of inheritance was available as a framework for understanding how certain traits, like the colors of flowers, are transmitted from one generation to the next. However, Watson and Crick's discovery of the molecular structure of DNA in 1953 and the rapid advances made feasible by recombinant DNA techniques from the 1970s to the present have opened up entirely new possibilities for genetic diagnosis and therapy.

The genetic structure of human cells is incredibly intricate and complex. Within the nuclei of each human cell there are forty-six chromosomes. These chromosomes, in turn, are comprised of approximately 20,000–25,000 genes plus intervening sequences.[5] The function of the intervening sequences is not yet well understood. The simplest units into which the genes and intervening sequences can be analyzed are individual nucleotides or bases, designated by the familiar letters A, C, G, and T; two corresponding nucleotides form a base pair. It is estimated that each human cell contains approximately 3 billion base pairs. Only about 1.5 percent of the human genome seems to be involved in the encoding of proteins.[6]

In an essay that combines history with ethical and political analysis, James Watson describes the sequence of events that led a reluctant community of U.S. biomedical scientists to accept the importance of mapping and sequencing the human genome. As Watson notes with satisfaction, he insisted that a fixed percentage of the human genome project budget—initially 3 percent, later 5 percent—be set aside to study the ethical, legal, and social implications of the project. The ELSI program, as it came to be known, has allowed philosophers, theologians, lawyers, social scientists, and clinicians to perform normative research on issues like those discussed in the current chapter. At the conclusion of his essay Watson predicts that behavioral genetics and genetic enhancement will become important topics as genetic knowledge continues to accrue. He argues that the main lesson to be drawn from the eugenic excesses of the past is that governments must be prevented from telling citizens what to do, and what not to do, in the genetic sphere.

Philosophers Allen Buchanan, Dan Brock, Norman Daniels, and Daniel Wikler have written an important book entitled *From Chance to Choice*: *Genetics and Justice*.[7] In the excerpt from this book reprinted here the authors explore multiple options for allocating new genetic technologies. Rejecting both the public health model and the personal services model, Buchanan and his colleagues seek to develop a third approach to the public policy issues raised by genetic research and its applications. The authors' constructive proposal draws heavily on John Rawls's theory of justice and on a robust notion of equal opportunity that is indebted both to Rawls and to the writings of Norman Daniels on just health care.

European scholar Svante Pääbo considers possible nonmedical implications of the human genome project. The findings of this research will help us as humans to reconstruct our ancient history—that is, our sites of origin and the patterns of migration and conquest that have led to the current configuration of human ethnic groups and nations. At the same time, however, the genome project will reveal to what extent the human genome contains genes that are closely related to corresponding genes in "simple" organisms like the fruit fly and roundworms. Further research will also delineate more clearly the similarities and differences between humans and our closest nonhuman relatives, the great apes. In Pääbo's view, the fact that humans and chimpanzees show 99 percent similarity in their DNA sequences may raise intriguing questions about traditional notions of human uniqueness.

GENETIC TESTING AND SCREENING

Advances in human genome mapping and sequencing will facilitate more precise genetic *testing*. This type of testing will be applicable to the diagnosis of disease, or even a higher-than-average predisposition to develop a certain kind of disease later in life. However, as the science develops, more sophisticated types of genetic testing may also make possible the discovery of at least approximate correlations between genes (or small constellations of genes) and complex behavioral traits—for example, exceptional memory or specific personality characteristics. (Please see the section on Genetics and Behavior.) The various techniques of genetic testing can be employed at any of several stages in the human life cycle: with most methods of assisted reproduction, between in vitro fertilization and embryo transfer (preimplantation diagnosis); after implantation but before birth (prenatal diagnosis); immediately after birth (newborn genetic testing); during childhood or adolescence; and in adulthood (for example, when reproductive decisions are being made). It is not yet clear whether the genetic testing of sperm and egg cells can be performed in ways that are both highly accurate and nondestructive to the cells being tested. Genetic *screening* involves the use of genetic testing in large populations—for example, with most or virtually all newborn infants.

The essays in this section consider multiple dimensions of genetic testing and screening. Canadian philosopher Michael Burgess questions the exclusive focus on disclosure and consent that often characterizes discussions of genetic testing and screening. Burgess argues that a wide-ranging and culturally sensitive consideration of genetic testing's potential benefits and harms is an essential complement to respect for individual autonomy. The moral and practical dimensions of predictive genetic testing are considered by genetic counselor Kimberly Quaid. People who are healthy but who are thought to be at higher-than-average risk for either developing or transmitting a genetic condition often face agonizing decisions about being tested and about disclosing test results to the members of their extended families. In the final essay of this section pediatrician and lawyer Ellen Wright Clayton considers the moral justifications for the genetic testing of children. Without denying the obvious benefits of screening newborns for treatable disorders such as phenylketonuria (PKU), Clayton argues that parents of children should be consulted about proposed neonatal tests and that their decisions about such testing should be treated with respect. In most cases that involve a clear-cut risk of harm to a child, she notes, parents can be convinced to accept neonatal testing. Like Burgess and Quaid, Clayton advocates a thoughtful, nuanced evaluation of both medical and psychosocial benefits and harms.

HUMAN GENE TRANSFER RESEARCH

In the history of medicine, diagnosis is often the necessary prelude to a cure. It thus seems likely that the capacity to identify genetic diseases and susceptibilities will provide new impetus for already existing efforts to develop ways to correct, or at least to compensate for, genetic defects. The general name usually given to these therapeutic initiatives is *gene therapy*, or, more broadly, *genetic intervention.*

A central distinction in any discussion of genetic intervention is the distinction between reproductive and nonreproductive cells, which are often called germ-line and somatic cells, respectively. Somatic cells, like skin or muscle cells, contain the full complement of forty-six chromosomes and cannot transmit genetic information to succeeding generations. In other words, the genetic information contained in somatic cells stops with us and is not passed on to our descendants. In contrast, germ-line cells, the egg and sperm cells, contain only twenty-three chromosomes and are capable of transmitting genetic information to our progeny in the next generation, as well as to their children and grandchildren.

A second important distinction in discussions of human genetic intervention is that between the cure or prevention of disease on one hand and the enhancement of human capabilities on the other. A genetic approach to the treatment of cystic fibrosis clearly would be regarded as gene therapy. In contrast, the attempt to increase stature or to improve the efficiency of long-term memory—in a child whose height or memory fall within the normal range—would probably be regarded by most observers as an effort to enhance capabilities rather than to cure disease. The two distinctions discussed in this and the preceding paragraph can be arrayed in the following two-by-two matrix:

	Somatic	Germ-line
Cure or prevention of disease	1	2
Enhancement of capabilities	3	4

In the late 1980s and early 1990s, the name generally applied to somatic-cell gene transfer to treat disease was gene therapy. This phrase had originally been suggested by scientists in 1970 as a less frightening alternative to the then-prevalent phrase *genetic engineering.*[8] However, the term *therapy* was potentially misleading because it tended to obscure the experimental character of human gene transfer. By 1995 at the latest, it had also become clear that human gene transfer would not immediately produce the dramatic therapeutic results that both scientists and the public had anticipated. Thus, in the late 1990s, several commentators recommended that the word *therapy* be replaced by the more neutral term *transfer* and that the entire phrase describing this technique include the word *research*.[9] The phrase *human gene transfer research* is therefore employed in this introduction as a more neutral and more accurate descriptor than *human gene therapy*.

By February 2007 approximately 816 formal gene transfer protocols had been submitted to the National Institutes of Health for formal public review. Of these, approximately 766 studies were oriented toward the alleviation of disease. More than 70 percent of the disease-oriented studies were conducted in human subjects who were afflicted with various kinds of cancers. Another 8.6 percent of the studies involved subjects with genetic disorders—for example, cystic fibrosis, a progressive disease of the lungs. Still other studies enlisted people with HIV infection or AIDS.[10]

During the year 2000 the first clear-cut success occurred in human gene transfer research. Alain Fischer and his colleagues at the Necker Hospital in Paris, France, demonstrated decisive improvement in several children born with a genetically caused condition called "severe combined immunodeficiency."[11] David, the so-called boy in the bubble, had suffered from the same disease in the 1970s and early 1980s.[12] Fischer and his colleagues succeeded in transferring the gene that produces a missing enzyme into enough of the children's bone marrow cells to produce a clinical benefit in nine patients.[13] However, two of the nine patients in whom immune reconstitution had occurred later developed leukemias because the vector for the gene transfer had activated an oncogene.[14]

The four essays on human gene transfer research discuss several facets of this promising, but still very young, field. In his essay pediatrician Theodore Friedmann describes the requirements for ethically acceptable, publicly accountable human gene transfer research. He tacitly acknowledges that the public oversight system for this field of research was weakened in 1997 and urges that the monitoring of serious adverse events in gene-transfer studies be enhanced. In Friedmann's view, researchers, universities, and companies should scrupulously avoid even the appearance of financial conflicts of interest in conducting such studies. Oxford scholar Julian Savulescu and LeRoy Walters, a coeditor of this textbook, review the tragic death of an 18-year-old young man, Jesse Gelsinger, in a gene-transfer study conducted at the University of Pennsylvania. After documenting numerous deficiencies in the way the Penn study was conducted, Savulescu goes on to argue that gene-transfer research in infants afflicted with life-threatening disorders can be morally justifiable if certain conditions are fulfilled. Walters describes multiple ways in which the public-oversight system for human transfer research faltered in the years preceding the Gelsinger tragedy. He advocates disinterested, robust, and transparent prior review of all human gene transfer research protocols, without regard to the source of their funding.

In the final essay included in this section, philosopher and lawyer David Resnik devotes particular attention to human genetic changes that are likely to be, and in many cases are intended to be, passed on to future generations. These changes were recently termed "inheritable genetic modifications" by a U.S. working group. In a calm, non-alarmist mode, Resnik arrays the arguments for and against such proposed modifications. If the techniques for effecting such modifications become more precise or targeted in the future, the benefit–harm ratio for inheritable modifications may shift dramatically in favor of employing this novel technique.

GENETICS AND BEHAVIOR

The final two essays of this chapter venture into highly controversial territory. The late Glayde Whitney, a well-known psychologist, and Kenneth Schaffner, a philosopher of science and a physician, review the sometimes heated public debates that have sometimes accompanied efforts to trace connections between human genetics and human behavior. Whitney and Schaffner also seek to map the terrain of behavioral genetics, displaying the various methods employed by the interdisciplinary group of contributors to this field. The authors carefully employ the phrase "genetic influences" to avoid conveying the impression that genes affect behavior in any mechanistic or deterministic way. In a recent and influential survey of genes and behavior, British psychiatrist Michael Rutter distinguishes between (1) human disorders and traits in which genetic factors predominate and (2) disorders and traits where conceptual or diagnostic questions continue to be debated and/or the current evidence about the respective contributions of nature and nurture remains unclear. Rutter is optimistic that further research will bring greater clarity to this important discussion and that additional relationships between genes and human behavior will be discovered and validated.

L.W.

NOTES

1. Rhesus Macaque Genome Sequencing and Analysis Consortium. "Evolutionary and Biomedical Insights from the Rhesus Macaque Genome." *Science* 316: 5822 (13 April 2007), 222–34.

2. International Human Genome Sequencing Consortium. "Finishing the Euchromatic Sequence of the Human Genome." *Nature* 431: 7011 (21 October 2004), 931–45.

3. International Human Genome Sequencing Consortium. "Initial Sequencing and Analysis of the Human Genome." *Nature* 409: 6822 (14 February 2001), 860–921.

4. *Encyclopedia Britannica*, Micropaedia. "Eugenics." (1989), 593.

5. Plato, *Republic*, III (410), IV, 456–61.

6. For the history of Nazi policies on the "unfit" and the "unworthy," see the following works: Robert N. Proctor. *Racial Hygiene: Medicine under the Nazis*. Cambridge, MA: Harvard University Press, 1988; Michael Burleigh and Wolfgang Wipperman. *The Racial State: Germany 1933–1945*. Cambridge: Cambridge University Press, 1991; and Michael Burleigh. *Death and Deliverance: "Euthanasia" in Germany c. 1900–1945*. Cambridge: Cambridge University Press, 1994.

7. Allen Buchanan, Dan W. Brock, Norman Daniels, and Daniel Wikler. *From Chance to Choice: Genetics and Justice*. New York: Cambridge University Press, 2000.

8. LeRoy Walters. "Gene Therapy: Overview." In Thomas H. Murray and Maxwell J. Mehlman, eds., *Encyclopedia of Ethical, Legal, and Policy Issues in Biotechnology*, 2 vols. New York: John Wiley and Sons, 2000, 336–42.

9. See, for example, Larry R. Churchill, Myra L. Collins, Nancy M. P. King, Stephen G. Pemberton, and Keith A. Wailoo. "Genetic Research as Therapy: Implications of 'Gene Therapy' for Informed Consent." *Journal of Law, Medicine, and Ethics* 26: 1 (Spring 1998), 38–47.

10. Source: Web site of the Office of Biotechnology Activities at the U.S. National Institutes of Health (URL: http://www4.od.nih.gov/oba/rac/PROTOCOL.pdf; accessed April 12, 2007).

11. Marina Cavazzana-Calvo et al. "Gene Therapy of Severe Combined Immunodeficiency (SCID)-XI Disease." *Science* 288: 5466 (28 April 2000), 627–29.

12. See LeRoy Walters and Julie Gage Palmer. *The Ethics of Human Gene Therapy*. New York: Oxford University Press, 1997, xiii–xvi.

13. Salima Hacein-Bey-Abina et al. "Sustained Correction of X-Linked Severe Combined Immunodeficiency by *ex vivo* Gene Therapy." *New England Journal of Medicine* 346: 16 (18 April 2002), 1241–43.

14. Salima Hacein-Bey-Abina, et al. "LMO2-Associated Clonal T Cell Proliferation in Two Patients after Gene Therapy for SCID-X1." *Science* 302: 5644 (17 October 2003), 415–19.

Eugenics in the Twentieth Century

DANIEL J. KEVLES

Eugenics and Human Rights

Daniel Kevles is the Stanley Woodward Professor of History at Yale University. He has published extensively about the history of science in America; the interplay of science and society past and present; and scientific fraud and misconduct. His publications include *In the Name of Eugenics: Genetics and the Uses of Human Heredity* (Harvard University Press) and *The Baltimore Case: A Trial of Politics, Science, and Character* (Norton).

During the Nazi era in Germany, eugenics prompted the sterilisation of several hundred thousand people, then helped lead to antisemitic programmes of euthanasia and ultimately, of course, to the death camps. The association of eugenics with the Nazis is so strong that many people were surprised at the news several years ago that Sweden had sterilised around 60,000 people (mostly women) between the 1930s and 1970s. The intention was to reduce the number of children born with genetic diseases and disorders. After the turn of the century, eugenics movements—including demands for sterilisation of people considered unfit—had, in fact, blossomed in the United States, Canada, Britain, and Scandinavia, not to mention elsewhere in Europe and in parts of Latin America and Asia. Eugenics was not therefore unique to the Nazis. It could, and did, happen everywhere.

ORIGINS OF EUGENICS

Modern eugenics was rooted in the social darwinism of the late 19th century, with all its metaphors of fitness, competition, and rationalisations of inequality. Indeed, Francis Galton, a cousin of Charles Darwin and an accomplished scientist in his own right, coined the word eugenics. Galton promoted the ideal of improving the human race by getting rid of the "undesirables" and multiplying the "desirables." Eugenics began to flourish after the rediscovery, in 1900, of Mendel's theory that the biological make up of organisms is determined by certain factors, later identified with genes. The application of mendelism to human beings reinforced the idea that we are determined almost entirely by our "germ plasm."

Eugenic doctrines were articulated by physicians, mental health professionals, and scientists—notably biologists who were pursuing the new discipline of genetics—and were widely popularised in books, lectures, and articles for the educated public of the day. Publications were bolstered by the research pouring out of institutes for the study of eugenics or "race biology." These had been established in several countries, including Denmark, Sweden, Britain, and the United States. The experts raised the spectre of social degeneration, insisting that "feebleminded" people (the term then commonly applied to people believed to be mentally retarded) were responsible for a wide range of social problems and were proliferating at a rate that threatened social resources and stability. Feebleminded women were held to be driven by a heedless sexuality, the product of biologically grounded flaws in their moral character that led them to prostitution and producing illegitimate children. "Hereditarian" biology attributed poverty and criminality to bad genes rather than to flaws in the social corpus.

A DRIVE FOR SOCIAL IMPROVEMENT

Much of eugenics belonged to the wave of progressive social reform that swept through western Europe and North America during the early decades of the century. For progressives, eugenics was a branch of

Reprinted from the *British Medical Journal* 319 (1999):435–438, with permission from BMJ Publishing Group. Copyright © 1999, the British Medical Association.

the drive for social improvement or perfection that many reformers of the day thought might be achieved through the deployment of science to good social ends. Eugenics, of course, also drew appreciable support from social conservatives, concerned to prevent the proliferation of lower income groups and save on the cost of caring for them. The progressives and the conservatives found common ground in attributing phenomena such as crime, slums, prostitution, and alcoholism primarily to biology and in believing that biology might be used to eliminate these discordances of modern, urban, industrial society.

Race was a minor subtext in Scandinavian and British eugenics, but it played a major part in the American and Canadian versions of the creed. North American eugenicists were particularly disturbed by the immigrants from eastern and southern Europe who had been flooding into their countries since the late 19th century. They considered these people not only racially different from but inferior to the Anglo-Saxon majority, partly because their representation among the criminals, prostitutes, slum dwellers, and feeble-minded in many cities was disproportionately high. Anglo-American eugenicists fastened on British data indicating that half of each generation was produced by no more than a quarter of married people in the preceding generation, and that the prolific quarter was disproportionately located among the "dregs" of society. Eugenic reasoning in the United States had it that if deficiencies in immigrants were hereditary and eastern European immigrants outreproduced natives of Anglo-Saxon stock, then inevitably the quality of the American population would decline.

POSITIVE AND NEGATIVE EUGENICS

Eugenicists on both sides of the Atlantic argued for a two pronged programme that would increase the frequency of "socially good" genes in the population and decrease that of "bad genes." One prong was positive eugenics, which meant manipulating human heredity or breeding, or both, to produce superior people; the other was negative eugenics, which meant improving the quality of the human race by eliminating or excluding biologically inferior people from the population.

In Britain between the wars, positive eugenic thinking led to proposals (unsuccessful ones) for family allowances that would be proportional to income. In the United States, it fostered "fitter family" competitions. These became a standard feature at a number of state fairs and were held in the "human stock" sections. At the 1924 Kansas Free Fair, winning families in the three categories—small, average, and large—were awarded a governor's fitter family trophy. "Grade A" individuals received a medal that portrayed two diaphanously garbed parents, their arms outstretched toward their (presumably) eugenically meritorious infant. It is hard to know exactly what made these families and individuals stand out as fit, but the fact that all entrants had to take an IQ test and the Wasserman test for syphilis says something about the organisers' views of necessary qualities.

Much more was urged for negative eugenics, notably the passage of eugenic sterilisation laws. By the late 1920s, sterilisation laws had been enacted in two dozen American states, largely in the middle Atlantic region, the Midwest, and California. By 1933, California had subjected more people to eugenic sterilisation than had all other states of the union combined. Similar measures were passed in Canada, in the provinces of British Columbia and Alberta. Almost everywhere they were passed, however, the laws reached only as far as the inmates of state institutions for the mentally handicapped or mentally ill. People in private care or in the care of their families escaped them. Thus, the laws tended to discriminate against poorer people and minority groups. In California, for example, the sterilisation rates of blacks and foreign immigrants were twice as high as would be expected from their representation in the general population.

SOCIETY BEFORE INDIVIDUAL RIGHTS

The sterilisation laws rode roughshod over private human rights, holding them subordinate to an allegedly greater public good. This reasoning figured explicitly in the US Supreme Court's eight to one decision, in 1927, in the case of Buck versus Bell, which upheld Virginia's eugenic sterilisation law. Justice Oliver Wendell Holmes, writing for the majority, averred: "We have seen more than once that the public welfare may call upon the best citizens for their lives. It would be strange if it could not call upon those who already sap the strength of the State for these lesser sacrifices, often not felt to be such by those concerned, in order to prevent our being swamped with incompetence. It is better for all the world, if instead of waiting to execute degenerate offspring for crime, or to let them starve for their imbecility, society can prevent those who are manifestly unfit from continuing their kind. The principle that sustains compulsory vaccination is

Three generations of imbeciles are enough."[1]

In Alberta, the premier called sterilisation far more effective than segregation and, perhaps taking a leaf from Holmes's book, insisted that "the argument of freedom or right of the individual can no longer hold good where the welfare of the state and society is concerned."[2,3]

Sterilisation rates climbed with the onset of the worldwide economic depression in 1929. In parts of Canada, in the deep south of the United States, and throughout Scandinavia, sterilisation acquired broad support. This was not primarily on eugenic grounds (though some hereditarian-minded mental health professionals continued to urge it for that purpose) but on economic ones. Sterilisation raised the prospect of reducing the cost of institutional care and of poor relief. Even geneticists who disparaged sterilisation as the remedy for degeneration held that sterilising mentally disabled people would yield a social benefit because it would prevent children being born to parents who could not care for them.

In Scandinavia, sterilisation was broadly endorsed by Social Democrats as part of the scientifically oriented planning of the new welfare state. Alva Myrdal spoke for her husband, Gunnar, and for numerous liberals like themselves when in 1941 she wrote, "In our day of highly accelerated social reforms the need for sterilization on social grounds gains new momentum. Generous social reforms may facilitate homemaking and childbearing more than before among the groups of less desirable as well as more desirable parents. [Such a trend] demands some corresponding corrective."[4] On such foundations among others, sterilisation programmes continued in several American states, in Alberta, and in Scandinavia well into the 1970s.

EUGENICS UNDER FIRE

During the interwar years, however, eugenic doctrines were increasingly criticised on scientific grounds and for their class and racial bias. It was shown that many mental disabilities have nothing to do with genes; that those which do are not simple products of genetic make up; and that most human behaviours (including deviant ones) are shaped by environment at least as much as by biological heredity, if they are fashioned by genes at all. Science aside, eugenics became malodorous precisely because of its connection with Hitler's regime, especially after the second world war, when its complicity in the Nazi death camps was revealed.

All along, many people on both sides of the Atlantic had ethical reservations about sterilisation and were squeamish about forcibly subjecting people to the knife. Attempts to authorise eugenic sterilisation in Britain had reached their high water mark in the debates over the Mental Deficiency Act in 1913. They failed not least because of powerful objections from civil libertarians insistent on defending individual human rights. More than a third of the American states declined to pass sterilisation laws, and so did the eastern provinces of Canada. Most of the American states which passed the laws declined to enforce them, and British Columbia's law was enforced very little.

The opposition comprised coalitions that varied in composition. It came from mental health professionals who doubted the scientific underpinnings of eugenics and from civil libertarians, some of whom warned that compulsory sterilisation constituted "Hitlerisation." Sterilisation was also vigorously resisted by Roman Catholics—partly because it was contrary to church doctrine and partly because many recent immigrants to the United States were Catholics and thus disproportionately placed in jeopardy of the knife. For many people before the second world war, individual human rights mattered far more than those sanctioned by the science, law, and perceived social needs of the era.

The revelations of the holocaust strengthened the moral objections to eugenics and sterilisation, and so did the increasing worldwide discussion of human rights, a foundation for which was the Universal Declaration of Human Rights that the General Assembly of the United Nations adopted and proclaimed in 1948. Since then, the movement for women's rights and reproductive freedom has further transformed moral sensibilities about eugenics, so that we recoil at the majority's ruling in Buck versus Bell. History at the least has taught us that concern for individual rights belongs at the heart of whatever stratagems we may devise for deploying our rapidly growing knowledge of human and medical genetics.

NOTES

1. Buck v Bell [1927] 274 US 201–7.

2. Christian T. The mentally ill and human rights in Alberta: a study of the Alberta Sexual Sterilisation Act. Edmonton: Faculty of Law, University of Alberta, nd: 27.

3. McLaren A. Our own master race: eugenics in Canada, 1885–1945. Toronto: McClelland and Stewart, 1990.

4. Broberg G., Roll-Hansen N., eds. Eugenics and the welfare state: sterilization policy in Denmark, Sweden, Norway, and Finland. East Lansing: Michigan State University Press, 1996.

BUCK v. BELL

United States Supreme Court, 1927

Argued April 22, 1927. Decided May 2, 1927.

On Writ of Error to the Supreme Court of Appeals of the State of Virginia to review a judgment affirming a judgment of the Circuit Court for Amherst County directing the sterilization of an inmate of a Colony for Epileptics and Feeble Minded. Affirmed. . . .*

The facts are stated in the opinion.

Mr. I. P. Whitehead argued the cause and filed a brief for plaintiff in error:

The act of assembly of Virginia does not provide due process of law guaranteed by the 14th Amendment to the Constitution of the United States. . . .

The act of assembly of Virginia denies to the plaintiff and other inmates of the State Colony for Epileptics and Feebleminded the equal protection of the law guaranteed by the 14th Amendment to the Constitution of the United States. . . .

Mr. Aubrey E. Strode argued the cause and filed a brief for defendant in error:

The act affords due process of law. . . .

The act is a valid exercise of the police power.

The statute may be sustained as based upon a reasonable classification. . . .

MR. JUSTICE HOLMES delivered the opinion of the court:

This is a writ of error to review a judgment of the supreme court of appeals of the state of Virginia, affirming a judgment of the circuit court of Amherst county, by which the defendant in error, the superintendent of the State Colony for Epileptics and Feeble Minded, was ordered to perform the operation of salpingectomy upon Carrie Buck, the plaintiff in error,

for the purpose of making her sterile. 143 Va. 310, 51 A.L.R. 855, 130 S. E. 516. The case comes here upon the contention that the statute authorizing the judgment is void under the 14th Amendment as denying to the plaintiff in error due process of law and the equal protection of the laws.

Carrie Buck is a feeble minded white woman who was committed to the State Colony above mentioned in due form. She is the daughter of a feeble minded mother in the same institution, and the mother of an illegitimate feeble minded child. She was eighteen years old at the time of the trial of her case in the circuit court, in the latter part of 1924. An Act of Virginia approved March 20, 1924, recites that the health of the patient and the welfare of society may be promoted in certain cases by the sterilization of mental defectives, under careful safeguard, etc.; that the sterilization may be effected in males by vasectomy and in females by salpingectomy, without serious pain or substantial danger to life; that the Commonwealth is supporting in various institutions many defective persons who if now discharged would become a menace but if incapable of procreating might be discharged with safety and become self-supporting with benefit to themselves and to society; and that experience has shown that heredity plays an important part in the transmission of insanity, imbecility, etc. The statute then enacts that whenever the superintendent of certain institutions including the above named State Colony shall be of opinion that it is for the best interests of the patients and of society that an inmate under his care should be sexually sterilized, he may have the operation performed upon any patient afflicted with hereditary forms of insanity, imbecility, etc., on complying with the very careful provisions by which the act protects the patients from possible abuse.

The superintendent first presents a petition to the special board of directors of his hospital or colony,

---

*Editor's note: Some references to other court decisions are omitted or abbreviated.

From *United States [Supreme Court] Reports* 274 (1927), 200–208.

stating the facts and the grounds for his opinion, verified by affidavit. Notice of the petition and of the time and place of the hearing in the institution is to be served upon the inmate, and also upon his guardian, and if there is no guardian the superintendent is to apply to the circuit court of the county to appoint one. If the inmate is a minor notice also is to be given to his parents if any with a copy of the petition. The board is to see to it that the inmate may attend the hearings if desired by him or his guardian. The evidence is all to be reduced to writing, and after the board has made its order for or against the operation, the superintendent, or the inmate, or his guardian, may appeal to the circuit court of the county. The circuit court may consider the record of the board and the evidence before it and such other admissible evidence as may be offered, and may affirm, revise, or reverse the order of the board and enter such order as it deems just. Finally any party may apply to the supreme court of appeals, which, if it grants the appeal, is to hear the case upon the record of the trial in the circuit court and may enter such order as it thinks the circuit court should have entered. There can be no doubt that so far as procedure is concerned the rights of the patient are most carefully considered, and as every step in this case was taken in scrupulous compliance with the statute and after months of observation, there is no doubt that in that respect the plaintiff in error has had due process of law.

The attack is not upon the procedure but upon the substantive law. It seems to be contended that in no circumstances could such an order be justified. It certainly is contended that the order cannot be justified upon the existing grounds. The judgment finds the facts that have been recited and that Carrie Buck "is the probable potential parent of socially inadequate offspring, likewise afflicted, that she may be sexually sterilized without detriment to her general health and that her welfare and that of society will be promoted by her sterilization," and thereupon makes the order. In view of the general declarations of the legislature and the specific findings of the court obviously we cannot say as matter of law that the grounds do not exist, and if they exist they justify the result. We have seen more than once that the public welfare may call upon the best citizens for their lives. It would be strange if it could not call upon those who already sap the strength of the state for these lesser sacrifices, often not felt to be such by those concerned, in order to prevent our being swamped with incompetence. It is better for all the world, if instead of waiting to execute degenerate offspring for crime, or to let them starve for their imbecility, society can prevent those who are manifestly unfit from continuing their kind. The principle that sustains compulsory vaccination is broad enough to cover cutting the Fallopian tubes. Jacobson v. Massachusetts, 197 U.S. 11. Three generations of imbeciles are enough.

But, it is said, however it might be if this reasoning were applied generally, it fails when it is confined to the small number who are in the institutions named and is not applied to the multitudes outside. It is the usual last resort of constitutional arguments to point out shortcomings of this sort. But the answer is that the law does all that is needed when it does all that it can, indicates a policy, applies it to all within the lines, and seeks to bring within the lines all similarly situated so far and so fast as its means allow. Of course so far as the operations enable those who otherwise must be kept confined to be returned to the world, and thus open the asylum to others, the equality aimed at will be more nearly reached.

Judgment affirmed.

MR. JUSTICE BUTLER dissents.

STEPHEN JAY GOULD

Carrie Buck's Daughter

Stephen Jay Gould (d. 2002) was Professor of Geology and Zoology at Harvard University. His main interests lay in palaeontology and evolutionary biology. He was a frequent and popular speaker on the sciences. His published work included *The Mismeasure of Man* (Norton), *The Panda's Thumb: More Reflections in Natural History* (Norton), and *The Flamingo's Smile* (Norton).

The Lord really put it on the line in his preface to that prototype of all prescriptions, the Ten Commandments:

> . . . for I, the Lord thy God, am a jealous God, visiting the iniquity of the fathers upon the children unto the third and fourth generation of them that hate me (Exod. 20:5).

The terror of this statement lies in its patent unfairness—its promise to punish guiltless offspring for the misdeeds of their distant forebears.

A different form of guilt by genealogical association attempts to remove this stigma of injustice by denying a cherished premise of Western thought—human free will. If offspring are tainted not simply by the deeds of their parents but by a material form of evil transferred directly by biological inheritance, then "the iniquity of the fathers" becomes a signal or warning for probable misbehavior of their sons. Thus Plato, while denying that children should suffer directly for the crimes of their parents, nonetheless defended the banishment of a personally guiltless man whose father, grandfather and great-grandfather had all been condemned to death.

It is, perhaps, merely coincidental that both Jehovah and Plato chose three generations as their criterion for establishing different forms of guilt by association. Yet we maintain a strong folk, or vernacular, tradition for viewing triple occurrences as minimal evidence of regularity. Bad things, we are told, come in threes. Two may represent an accidental association; three is a pattern. Perhaps, then, we should not wonder that our own century's most famous pronouncement of blood guilt employed the same criterion—Oliver Wendell Holmes's defense of compulsory sterilization in Virginia (Supreme Court decision of 1927 in *Buck v. Bell*): "three generations of imbeciles are enough."

Restrictions upon immigration, with national quotas set to discriminate against those deemed mentally unfit by early versions of IQ testing, marked the greatest triumph of the American eugenics movement—the flawed hereditarian doctrine, so popular earlier in our century and by no means extinct today . . . that attempted to "improve" our human stock by preventing the propagation of those deemed biologically unfit and encouraging procreation among the supposedly worthy. But the movement to enact and enforce laws for compulsory "eugenic" sterilization had an impact and success scarcely less pronounced. If we could debar the shiftless and the stupid from our shores, we might also prevent the propagation of those similarly afflicted but already here.

The movement for compulsory sterilization began in earnest during the 1890s, abetted by two major factors—the rise of eugenics as an influential political movement and the perfection of safe and simple operations (vasectomy for men and salpingectomy, the cutting and tying of Fallopian tubes, for women) to replace castration and other socially unacceptable forms of mutilation. Indiana passed the first sterilization act based on eugenic principles in 1907 (a few states had previously mandated castration as a punitive measure for certain sexual crimes, although such laws were rarely enforced and usually overturned by judicial review). Like so many others to follow, it provided for sterilization of afflicted people residing in the state's "care," either as inmates of mental hospitals and homes for the feeble-minded or as inhabitants of prisons. Sterilization could be imposed upon those judged insane, idiotic, imbecilic, or moronic, and upon convicted rapists or criminals when recommended by a board of experts.

By the 1930s, more than thirty states had passed similar laws, often with an expanded list of so-called hereditary defects, including alcoholism and drug addiction in some states, and even blindness and deafness in others. These laws were continually challenged and rarely enforced in most states; only California and Virginia applied them zealously. By January 1935, some 20,000 forced "eugenic" sterilizations had been performed in the United States, nearly half in California.

No organization crusaded more vociferously and successfully for these laws than the Eugenics Record Office, the semiofficial arm and repository of data for the eugenics movement in America. Harry Laughlin, superintendent of the Eugenics Record Office, dedicated most of his career to a tireless campaign of writing and lobbying for eugenic sterilization. He hoped, thereby, to eliminate in two generations the genes of what he called the "submerged tenth"—"the most worthless one-tenth of our present population." He proposed a "model sterilization law" in 1922, designed

to prevent the procreation of persons socially inadequate from defective inheritance, by authorizing and providing for eugenical sterilization of certain potential parents carrying degenerate hereditary qualities.

This model bill became the prototype for most laws passed in America, although few states cast their net as widely as Laughlin advised. (Laughlin's categories encompassed "blind, including those with seriously impaired vision; deaf, including those with seriously impaired hearing; and dependent, including orphans, ne'er-do-wells, the homeless, tramps, and paupers.") Laughlin's suggestions were better heeded in Nazi Germany, where his model act inspired the infamous and stringently enforced *Erbgesundheitsrecht*, leading by the eve of World War II to the sterilization of some 375,000 people, most for "congenital feeble-mindedness," but including nearly 4,000 for blindness and deafness.

The campaign for forced eugenic sterilization in America reached its climax and height of respectability in 1927, when the Supreme Court, by an 8–1 vote, upheld the Virginia sterilization bill in *Buck v. Bell*. Oliver Wendell Holmes, then in his mid-eighties and the most celebrated jurist in America, wrote the majority opinion with his customary verve and power of style. It included the notorious paragraph, with its chilling tag line, cited ever since as the quintessential statement of eugenic principles. Remembering with pride his own distant experiences as an infantryman in the Civil War, Holmes wrote:

We have seen more than once that the public welfare may call upon the best citizens for their lives. It would be strange if it could not call upon those who already sap the strength of the state for these lesser sacrifices. . . . It is better for all the world, if instead of waiting to execute degenerate offspring for crime, or to let them starve for their imbecility, society can prevent those who are manifestly unfit from continuing their kind. The principle that sustains compulsory vaccination is broad enough to cover cutting the Fallopian tubes. Three generations of imbeciles are enough.

Who, then, were the famous "three generations of imbeciles," and why should they still compel our interest?

When the state of Virginia passed its compulsory sterilization law in 1924, Carrie Buck, an eighteen-year-old white woman, lived as an involuntary resident at the State Colony for Epileptics and Feeble-Minded. As the first person selected for sterilization under the new act, Carrie Buck became the focus for a constitutional challenge launched, in part, by conservative Virginia Christians who held, according to eugenical "modernists," antiquated views about individual preferences and "benevolent" state power. (Simplistic political labels do not apply in this case, and rarely in general for that matter. We usually regard eugenics as a conservative movement and its most vocal critics as members of the left. This alignment has generally held in our own decade. But eugenics, touted in its day as the latest in scientific modernism, attracted many liberals and numbered among its most vociferous critics groups often labeled as reactionary and antiscientific. If any political lesson emerges from these shifting allegiances, we might consider the true inalienability of certain human rights.)

But why was Carrie Buck in the State Colony and why was she selected? Oliver Wendell Holmes upheld her choice as judicious in the opening lines of his 1927 opinion:

Carrie Buck is a feeble-minded white woman who was committed to the State Colony. . . . She is the daughter of a feeble-minded mother in the same institution, and the mother of an illegitimate feeble-minded child.

In short, inheritance stood as the crucial issue (indeed as the driving force behind all eugenics). For if measured mental deficiency arose from malnourishment, either of body or mind, and not from tainted genes, then how could sterilization be justified? If decent food, upbringing, medical care, and education might make a worthy citizen of Carrie Buck's daughter, how could the State of Virginia justify the severing of Carrie's Fallopian tubes against her will? (Some forms of mental deficiency are passed by inheritance in family lines, but most are not—a scarcely surprising conclusion when we consider the thousand shocks that beset us all during our lives, from abnormalities in embryonic growth to traumas of birth, malnourishment, rejection, and poverty. In any case, no fair-minded person today would credit Laughlin's social criteria for the identification of hereditary deficiency—ne'er-do-wells, the homeless, tramps, and paupers—although we shall soon see that Carrie Buck was committed on these grounds.)

When Carrie Buck's case emerged as the crucial test of Virginia's law, the chief honchos of eugenics understood that the time had come to put up or shut up on the crucial issue of inheritance. Thus, the Eugenics Record Office sent Arthur H. Estabrook, their crack fieldworker, to Virginia for a "scientific" study of the case. Harry Laughlin himself provided a deposition, and his brief for inheritance was presented at the local trial that affirmed Virginia's law and later worked its way to the Supreme Court as *Buck v. Bell*.

Laughlin made two major points to the court. First, that Carrie Buck and her mother, Emma Buck, were feebleminded by the Stanford-Binet test of IQ then in its own infancy. Carrie scored a mental age of nine years, Emma of seven years and eleven months. (These figures ranked them technically as "imbeciles" by definitions of the day, hence Holmes's later choice of words—though his infamous line is often misquoted as "three generations of idiots." Imbeciles displayed a mental age of six to nine years; idiots performed worse,

morons better, to round out the old nomenclature of mental deficiency.) Second, that most feeblemindedness resides ineluctably in the genes, and that Carrie Buck surely belonged with this majority. Laughlin reported:

Generally feeble-mindedness is caused by the inheritance of degenerate qualities; but sometimes it might be caused by environmental factors which are not hereditary. In the case given, the evidence points strongly toward the feeble-mindedness and moral delinquency of Carrie Buck being due, primarily, to inheritance and not to environment.

Carrie Buck's daughter was then, and has always been, the pivotal figure of this painful case. I noted in beginning this essay that we tend (often at our peril) to regard two as potential accident and three as an established pattern. The supposed imbecility of Emma and Carrie might have been an unfortunate coincidence, but the diagnosis of similar deficiency for Vivian Buck (made by a social worker, as we shall see, when Vivian was but six months old) tipped the balance in Laughlin's favor and led Holmes to declare the Buck lineage inherently corrupt by deficient heredity. Vivian sealed the pattern—*three* generations of imbeciles are enough. Besides, had Carrie not given illegitimate birth to Vivian, the issue (in both senses) would never have emerged.

Oliver Wendell Holmes viewed his work with pride. The man so renowned for his principle of judicial restraint, who had proclaimed that freedom must not be curtailed without "clear and present danger"—without the equivalent of falsely yelling "fire" in a crowded theater—wrote of his judgment in *Buck v. Bell:* "I felt that I was getting near the first principle of real reform."

And so *Buck v. Bell* remained for fifty years, a footnote to a moment of American history perhaps best forgotten. Then, in 1980, it reemerged to prick our collective conscience, when Dr. K. Ray Nelson, then director of the Lynchburg Hospital where Carrie Buck had been sterilized, researched the records of his institution and discovered that more than 4,000 sterilizations had been performed, the last as late as 1972. He also found Carrie Buck, alive and well near Charlottesville, and her sister Doris, covertly sterilized under the same law (she was told that her operation was for appendicitis), and now, with fierce dignity, dejected and bitter because she had wanted a child more than anything else in her life and had finally, in her old age, learned why she had never conceived.

As scholars and reporters visited Carrie Buck and her sister, what a few experts had known all along became abundantly clear to everyone. Carrie Buck was a woman of obviously normal intelligence. For example, Paul A. Lombardo of the School of Law at the University of Virginia, and a leading scholar of *Buck v. Bell,* wrote in a letter to me:

As for Carrie, when I met her she was reading newspapers daily and joining a more literate friend to assist at regular bouts with the crossword puzzles. She was not a sophisticated woman, and lacked social graces, but mental health professionals who examined her in later life confirmed my impressions that she was neither mentally ill nor retarded.

On what evidence, then, was Carrie Buck consigned to the State Colony for Epileptics and Feeble-Minded on January 23, 1924? I have seen the text of her commitment hearing; it is, to say the least, cursory and contradictory. Beyond the bald and undocumented say-so of her foster parents, and her own brief appearance before a commission of two doctors and a justice of the peace, no evidence was presented. Even the crude and early Stanford-Binet test, so fatally flawed as a measure of innate worth . . . but at least clothed with the aura of quantitative respectability, had not yet been applied.

When we understand why Carrie Buck was committed in January 1924, we can finally comprehend the hidden meaning of her case and its message for us today. The silent key, again as from the first, is her daughter Vivian, born on March 28, 1924, and then but an evident bump on her belly. Carrie Buck was one of several illegitimate children borne by her mother, Emma. She grew up with foster parents, J. T. and Alice Dobbs, and continued to live with them as an adult, helping out with chores around the house. She was raped by a relative of her foster parents, then blamed for the resulting pregnancy. Almost surely, she was (as they used to say) committed to hide her shame (and her rapist's identity), not because enlightened science had just discovered her true mental status. In short, she was sent away to have her baby. Her case never was about mental deficiency; Carrie Buck was persecuted for supposed sexual immorality and social deviance. The annals of her trial and hearing reek with the contempt of the well-off and well-bred for poor people of "loose morals." Who really cared whether Vivian was a baby of normal intelligence; she was the illegitimate child of an illegitimate woman. Two generations of bastards are enough. Harry Laughlin began his "family history" of the Bucks by writing: "These people belong to the shiftless, ignorant and worthless class of anti-social whites of the South."

We know little of Emma Buck and her life, but we have no more reason to suspect her than her daughter Carrie of true mental deficiency. Their supposed deviance was social and sexual; the charge of imbecility was a cover-up, Mr. Justice Holmes notwithstanding.

We come then to the crux of the case, Carrie's daughter, Vivian. What evidence was ever adduced for her mental deficiency? This and only this: At the original trial in late 1924, when Vivian Buck was seven months old, a Miss Wilhelm, social worker for the Red Cross, appeared before the court. She began by stating honestly the true reason for Carrie Buck's commitment:

Mr. Dobbs, who had charge of the girl, had taken her when a small child, had reported to Miss Duke [the temporary secretary of Public Welfare for Albemarle County] that the girl was pregnant and that he wanted to have her committed somewhere—to have her sent to some institution.

Miss Wilhelm then rendered her judgment of Vivian Buck by comparing her with the normal granddaughter of Mrs. Dobbs, born just three days earlier:

It is difficult to judge probabilities of a child as young as that, but it seems to me not quite a normal baby. In its appearance—I should say that perhaps my knowledge of the mother may prejudice me in that regard, but I saw the child at the same time as Mrs. Dobbs' daughter's baby, which is only three days older than this one, and there is a very decided difference in the development of the babies. That was about two weeks ago. There is a look about it that is not quite normal, but just what it is, I can't tell.

This short testimony, and nothing else, formed all the evidence for the crucial third generation of imbeciles. Cross-examination revealed that neither Vivian nor the Dobbs grandchild could walk or talk, and that "Mrs. Dobbs' daughter's baby is a very responsive baby. When you play with it or try to attract its attention—it is a baby that you can play with. The other baby is not. It seems very apathetic and not responsive." Miss Wilhelm then urged Carrie Buck's sterilization: "I think," she said, "it would at least prevent the propagation of her kind." Several years later, Miss Wilhelm denied that she had ever examined Vivian or deemed the child feebleminded.

Unfortunately, Vivian died at age eight of "enteric colitis" (as recorded on her death certificate), an ambiguous diagnosis that could mean many things but may well indicate that she fell victim to one of the preventable childhood diseases of poverty (a grim reminder of the real subject in *Buck v. Bell*). She is therefore mute as a witness in our reassessment of her famous case.

When *Buck v. Bell* resurfaced in 1980, it immediately struck me that Vivian's case was crucial and that evidence for the mental status of a child who died at age eight might best be found in report cards. I have therefore been trying to track down Vivian Buck's school records for the past four years and have finally succeeded. (They were supplied to me by Dr. Paul A. Lombardo, who also sent other documents, including Miss Wilhelm's testimony, and spent several hours answering my questions by mail and Lord knows how much time playing successful detective in re Vivian's school records. I have never met Dr. Lombardo; he did all this work for kindness, collegiality, and love of the game of knowledge, not for expected reward or even requested acknowledgment. In a profession— academics—so often marred by pettiness and silly squabbling over meaningless priorities, this generosity must be recorded and celebrated as a sign of how things can and should be.)

Vivian Buck was adopted by the Dobbs family, who had raised (but later sent away) her mother, Carrie. As Vivian Alice Elaine Dobbs, she attended the Venable Public Elementary School of Charlottesville for four terms, from September 1930 until May 1932, a month before her death. She was a perfectly normal, quite average student, neither particularly outstanding nor much troubled. In those days before grade inflation, when C meant "good, 81–87" (as defined on her report card) rather than barely scraping by, Vivian Dobbs received A's and B's for deportment and C's for all academic subjects but mathematics (which was always

difficult for her, and where she scored D) during her first term in Grade 1A, from September 1930 to January 1931. She improved during her second term in 1B, meriting an A in deportment, C in mathematics, and B in all other academic subjects; she was placed on the honor roll in April 1931. Promoted to 2A, she had trouble during the fall term of 1931, failing mathematics and spelling but receiving A in deportment, B in reading, and C in writing and English. She was "retained in 2A" for the next term—or "left back" as we used to say, and scarcely a sign of imbecility as I remember all my buddies who suffered a similar fate. In any case, she again did well in her final term, with B in deportment, reading, and spelling, and C in writing, English, and mathematics during her last month in school. This daughter of "lewd and immoral" women excelled in deportment and performed adequately, although not brilliantly, in her academic subjects.

In short, we can only agree with the conclusion that Dr. Lombardo has reached in his research on *Buck v. Bell*—there were no imbeciles, not a one, among the three generations of Bucks. I don't know that such correction of cruel but forgotten errors of history counts for much, but I find it both symbolic and satisfying to learn that forced eugenic sterilization, a procedure of such dubious morality, earned its official justification (and won its most quoted line of rhetoric) on a patent falsehood.

Carrie Buck died last year. By a quirk of fate, and not by memory or design, she was buried just a few steps from her only daughter's grave. In the umpteenth and ultimate verse of a favorite old ballad, a rose and a brier—the sweet and the bitter—emerge from the tombs of Barbara Allen and her lover, twining about each other in the union of death. May Carrie and Vivian, victims in different ways and in the flower of youth, rest together in peace.

JONATHAN GLOVER

Eugenics: Some Lessons from the Nazi Experience

Jonathan Glover is Professor of Ethics at King's College, University of London, and Director of the college's Centre of Medical Law and Ethics. He has published several books on ethics, including *Choosing Children: The Ethical Dilemmas of Genetic Intervention* (2006), *Humanity: A Moral History of the Twentieth Century* (1999), *What Sort of People Should There Be?* (1984), and *Causing Death and Saving Lives* (1977). He chaired a European Commission Working Party on Assisted Reproduction, which issued *The Glover Report* in 1989. His current research interests include global ethics and ethical issues in psychiatry.

In one way, the existence of bioethics is very cheering. It is a fine thing that in our time there is so much ethical discussion about what we should do with the remarkable new developments in biology and medicine. But it is also hard not to be struck by the feeling that much work in bioethics is un-philosophical, in the sense of being unreflective on its own methods.

In particular, much of bioethics seems uncritically Cartesian in approach, in a way which makes the whole subject too easy. People writing about certain practical issues, for instance in medical ethics, often start off with principles which are taken to be self-evident. Or else there is a perfunctory attempt to explain why these are the appropriate principles and then practical conclusions are simply derived from them. Often the result is the mechanical application of some form of utilitarianism to various bioethical problems. Or, alternatively, there is a list of several principles about autonomy, beneficence, and so on, which is again mechanically applied.

What worries me about this approach is that it does not reflect real ethical thinking, which is a two-way process. We do not just start off with a set of axioms and apply them to particular cases. We also try to learn from experience. There is something to be said

From John Harris and Søren Holm, eds., *The Future of Human Reproduction: Ethics, Choice, and Regulation,* pp. 55–65. (Oxford: Clarendon Press, 1998). Reprinted with the permission of Oxford University Press.

for a more empirical approach to bioethics. This involves not only looking at principles and thinking about what they imply. It involves also looking at particular experiences which, collectively, we have had, and seeing what can be learnt from them. Perhaps from these experiences we can learn something about the sorts of approach it would be a good idea to adopt. Sometimes these historical experiences can teach us a different, but still useful, lesson about the kinds of approach it would be a good idea not to adopt. That is one of the reasons for looking at the Nazi experiment in eugenics.

Before talking about the Nazi episode, it is worth mentioning a quite different case which might also be described as, in one sense, a kind of eugenics. In thinking about the Nazis, it is important to bear in mind how very different their concerns were from the motives which sometimes make people these days want to be able to choose to have one kind of child rather than another.

A letter was published in an English newspaper, the *Guardian,* a few years ago. It was at a time when there was a move to try to lower the time limit for legal abortion. Part of the aim of this proposal was to restrict the possibility of so-called "therapeutic abortion," since many of the tests for medical disorders would not give results by the proposed new time limit. Behind the proposal was an opposition to abortion on the "eugenic" grounds of wanting a child without disability, as opposed to one who had a disability.

Two parents wrote to the *Guardian* in these terms:

In December 1986 our newly born daughter was diagnosed to be suffering from a genetically caused disease called Dystrophic epidermolysis Bullosa (EB). This is a disease in which the skin of the sufferer is lacking in certain essential fibres. As a result, any contact with her skin caused large blisters to form, which subsequently burst leaving raw open skin that only healed slowly and left terrible scarring. As EB is a genetically caused disease it is incurable and the form that our daughter suffered from usually causes death within the first six months of life. In our daughter's case the condition extended to her digestive and respiratory tracts and as a result of such internal blistering and scarring, she died after a painful and short life at the age of only 12 weeks.

Following our daughter's death we were told that if we wanted any more children, there was a one-in-four probability that any child we conceived would be affected by the disease but that it was possible to detect the disease antenatally. In May 1987 we decided to restart our family only because we knew that such a test was available and that should we conceive an affected child the pregnancy could be terminated; such a decision is not taken lightly or easily . . .

We have had to watch our first child die slowly and painfully and we could not contemplate having another child if there was a risk that it too would have to die in the same way.

My reaction to this letter is one of complete sympathy with the parents' predicament and complete support for the decision that they took. Of course, this kind of decision raises very real questions. If you choose not to have a disabled child, there is a question about the impact on disabled people already alive, about what it does to the idea of equality of respect for the disabled. There is also an alarming slippery slope. How far should we go in choosing what kinds of people should be born? As soon as we start choosing at all, we enter a zone of great moral difficulty where there are important boundaries to be drawn.

But many people, when they think about this sort of issue, also have a feeling of horror and revulsion, linked in a vague way to the Nazi episode. Of course any morally serious person at our end of the twentieth century is bound to have reactions which are coloured by what the Nazis did. All the same, the Nazi episode is greatly misused in bioethics. People too readily reach for the argument that "the Nazis did this" and that therefore we should not. It is a poor

case for eating meat that Hitler was a vegetarian. It is necessary to look and see precisely what the Nazis did, and to look a bit harder than people usually do at exactly what was wrong with what they did.

In the case of the decision not to have another child with EB, there are two issues. First, is choosing not to have a child with EB in itself a "eugenic" decision, in the objectionable way the Nazi policies were? Second, are we on a slippery slope, which may lead to objectionable Nazi-like policies?

It is worth making a brief mention of the parallel appeal to the Nazi example that is often made in the euthanasia debate. Here it is fairly obvious that the argument is used too crudely. The Nazi "euthanasia" programme (as the quotation marks indicate) was extraordinarily different from anything that other advocates of euthanasia support. The Nazi euthanasia programme was itself bound up with their ideas about eugenics. It was driven by a highly distinctive ideology. For them, it was not at all important to consider the interests of the individual person whose life was in question. Their project was one of tidying up the world, in the interest of what they called "racial hygiene."

The Nazi theorists were concerned with Darwinian natural selection. They were afraid that the "natural" selective pressures, which had functioned to ensure the survival of healthy and strong human beings, no longer functioned in modern society. Because of such things as medical care, and support for the disabled, people who in tougher times would have died were surviving to pass on their genes.

In the Nazi "euthanasia" programme, 70,723 mental patients were killed by carbon monoxide gas. The thinking behind this is not a matter of acting on the patients' wishes. Nor is it a matter of asking whether someone's life is such a nightmare for them that it is in their own interests that they should die. The thinking does not try to see things from the perspective of the individual person at all.

The bible of the Nazi "euthanasia" programme was a book by a lawyer, Karl Binding, and a psychiatrist, Alfred Hoche, called *Permission for the Destruction of Life Unworthy of Life*. In it, Karl Binding wrote: "The relatives would of course feel the loss badly, but mankind loses so many of its members through mistakes that one more or less hardly matters." That is very different from the agonized thought that goes into the decisions taken by doctors nowadays, when they wonder whether someone's life should be terminated. "One more or less hardly matters" is not the thinking behind the moral case for euthanasia.

The impersonal approach characteristic of the Nazi programme was expressed in 1939 in Berlin. Victor Brack chaired a meeting about who should be killed. The minutes report his remarks: "The number is arrived at through a calculation on the basis of a ratio of 1000 to 10 to 5 to 1. That means, out of 1000 people 10 require psychiatric treatment, of these 5 in residential form, and of these 1 patient will come out of the programme. If one applies this to the population of the Greater German Reich, then one must reckon with 65 to 75,000 cases. With this statement the question of who can be regarded as settled."[1]

This impersonal approach went all the way through the Nazi programme. A nurse described one of the first transports from the asylum of Jestetten in Württemberg: "The senior sister introduced the patients by name. But the transport leader replied that they did not operate on the basis of names but numbers. And in fact the patients who were to be transported then had numbers written in ink on their wrists, which had been previously dampened with a sponge. In other words the people were transported not as human beings but as cattle."[2]

We all know how the later murder of the Jews was preceded by transport in cattle trucks. Many of the people who ran the Nazis' so-called euthanasia programme moved to Poland to work in the extermination camps there. The ideology behind the murder of the Jews was a mixture of race hatred and the same racial hygiene outlook found in the euthanasia programme.

The ideology was one of racial purity. There was the idea that genetic mixing with other races lowered the quality of people. One of the great fathers of the Nazi eugenics movement was Dr. Eugen Fischer. Many years before, he had been to South Africa and in 1913 had published a study of people who he called "Rehoboth bastards." They were children of mixed unions between Boers and Hottentots. He reached the conclusion, on a supposedly scientific basis, that these children were, as he put it, "of lesser racial quality." He wrote that "We should provide them with the minimum amount of protection which they require, for survival as a race inferior to ourselves, and we should do this only as long as they are useful to us. After this, free competition should prevail and, in my opinion, this will lead to their decline and destruction."[3]

In 1933 Dr Fischer was made the new Rector of Berlin University. In his Rectoral Address he said: "The new leadership, having only just taken over the reins of power, is deliberately and forcefully intervening in the course of history and in the life of the nation, precisely when this intervention is most urgently, most decisively, and most immediately needed . . . This intervention can be characterized as a biological population policy, biological in this context signifying the safeguarding by the state of our hereditary endowment and our race." Fischer in 1939 extended this line of thinking specifically to the Jews. He said: "When a people wants to preserve its own nature it must reject alien racial elements. And when these have already insinuated themselves it must suppress them and eliminate them. This is self-defence."[4]

As well as belief in racial purity, there was the idea that in a given race only the "best people" should be encouraged to procreate. And the view was that those who are not "the best people" should be discouraged from having children, or even prevented from doing so. In 1934, one of the other fathers of the Nazi eugenics movement, Professor Fritz Lenz, said: "As things are now, it is only a minority of our fellow citizens who are so endowed that their unrestricted procreation is good for the race."[5] Fisher and Lenz, together with their colleagues, had perhaps more impact on the world than any other academics in the twentieth century. In 1923, Adolf Hitler, while confined in Landsberg prison, read their recently published textbook *Outline of Human Genetics and Racial Hygiene*. He incorporated some of its ideas in *Mein Kampf*.[6] These ideas influenced the Sterilization Law brought in when Hitler came to power in 1933. This made sterilization compulsory for people with conditions including schizophrenia, manic depression, and alcoholism.

This ideology is not one of the importance of the individual. There is a conception of the pure race and the biologically desirable human being. Reproductive freedom and individual lives are to be sacrificed to these abstractions. One medical model had great influence on the Nazis. It is an appalling medical model: the idea that in treating people who are "racially inferior," you are like the doctor who is dealing with a diseased organ in an otherwise healthy body. This analogy was put forward in a paper in 1940 by Konrad Lorenz, the very distinguished ethologist, now remembered for his work on aggression, and whose books on animals had an enormous charm. Lorenz wrote this:

> There is a certain similarity between the measures which need to be taken when we draw a broad biological analogy between bodies and malignant tumours, on the one hand, and a nation and individuals within it who have become asocial because of their defective constitution, on the other hand . . . Fortunately, the elimination of such elements is easier for the public health position and less dangerous for the supra-individual organism, than such an operation by a surgeon would be for the individual organism.[7]

The influence in practice of this thinking can be seen very clearly in Robert Jay Lifton's book on the Nazi doctors. He quotes a doctor called Fritz Klein. Dr. Klein was asked how he would reconcile the appalling medical experiments he carried out in Auschwitz with his oath as a doctor. He replied: "Of course I am a doctor and I want to preserve life. And out of respect for human life, I would remove a gangrenous appendix from a diseased body. The Jew is the gangrenous appendix in the body of mankind."[8] This brings out the importance, not just of things people literally believe, but also of the imagery which colours their thinking. Dr Klein cannot literally have believed that Jews were a gangrenous appendix. It would be easier to think that the Nazis were all mad if they literally thought that.

The role of such imagery can be seen again in the way in which racism was given a biological justification. Appalling images likened Jews to vermin, or to dirt and disease. When all Jews were removed from an area, it was called "Judenrein"—clean of Jews. Hans Frank, talking about the decline of a typhus epidemic, said that the removal of what he called "the Jewish element" had contributed to better health in Europe. The Foreign Office Press Chief Schmidt said that the Jewish question was, as he put it, "a question of political hygiene."[9]

This kind of medical analogy was important in Nazi thinking. Hitler said, "The discovery of the Jewish virus is one of the greatest revolutions that have taken place in the world. The battle in which we are engaged today is of the same sort as the battle waged during the last century by Pasteur and Koch. How many diseases have their origin in the Jewish virus! . . . We shall regain our health only by eliminating the Jew."[10]

The medical analogies and the idea of racial hygiene were supplemented by the ideology of Social Darwinism. To study either Nazism or, further back, the origins of the First World War is to see how enormously more influential Social Darwinist ideas have been in our century than one would guess. Social Darwinist ideas were not confined to Germany. They originated in England. It would be unfair to blame Darwin, who was a very humane person, for these ideas. They were developed by people like Francis Galton and Karl Pearson. Before the First World War, Karl Pearson said that the nation should be kept up to a high pitch of external efficiency by contest, chiefly by way of war with inferior races. The influence of Social Darwinism in Germany was partly the result of the Englishman Houston Stewart Chamberlain, who became an adopted German nationalist, holding that the Germans were a superior race.

Social Darwinism fuelled the naval arms race between Germany and Britain, a contest which helped to cause the First World War. Admiral Tirpitz thought naval expansion was necessary because, if Germany did not join the biological struggle between races, it would go under. When the danger of the arms race was obvious, the British Foreign Secretary, Sir Edward Grey, proposed a naval moratorium on both sides. The German Chancellor, Bethmann-Hollweg, rejected Grey's proposal: "The old saying still holds good that the weak will be the prey of the strong. When a people will not or cannot continue to spend enough on its armaments to be able to make its way in the world, then it falls back into the second rank . . . There will always be another and a stronger there who is ready to take the place in the world which it has vacated."[11]

Nazism emerged against this background of belief in life as a ruthless struggle for survival. According to Social Darwinism, victory goes to the strong, the tough, and the hard rather than to those who are gentle and co-operative. The Nazis took this up. They extolled struggle and the survival of the fittest. This led them to abandon traditional moral restraints. One Nazi physician, Dr Arthur Guett, said: "The ill-conceived 'love of thy neighbour' has to disappear . . . It is the supreme duty of the . . . state to grant life and livelihood only to the healthy and hereditarily sound portion of the population in order to secure . . . a hereditarily sound and racially pure people for all eternity."[12]

The Nazis also extolled hardness, which they thought led to victory in the struggle for survival. Hitler was proud of his own hardness. He said, "I am perhaps the hardest man this nation has had for 200 years."[13]

The belief in hardness came partly from Nietzsche. He was contemptuous of English biologists, and so was predictably cool about Darwin. Despite this, Nietzsche was in certain respects a Social Darwinist. He too thought compassion for the weak was sentimental nonsense, and advocated struggle and hardness.

Hitler, an admirer of the darker side of Nietzsche, was also a Social Darwinist. One day at lunch he said, "As in everything, nature is the best instructor, even as regards selection. One couldn't imagine a better activity on nature's part than that which consists in deciding the supremacy of one creature over another by means of a constant struggle." He went on to express disapproval of the way "our upper classes give way to a feeling of compassion regarding the fate of the Jews who we claim the right to expel."[14]

This outlook influenced the people who worked in the Nazi eugenic and "euthanasia" programmes. They felt guilty about feelings of compassion, which they were taught were a weakness to overcome. One Nazi doctor involved in killing psychiatric patients as part of the "euthanasia" programme expressed this in a letter to the director of the asylum where he worked, explaining his reluctance to take part in murdering the children there. He wrote,

I am very grateful for you willingly insisting that I should take time to think things over. The new measures are so convincing that I had hoped to be able to discard all personal considerations. But it is one thing to approve state measures with conviction and another to carry them out yourself down to their last consequences. I am thinking of the difference between a judge and an executioner. For this reason, despite my intellectual understanding and good will, I cannot help stating that I am temperamentally not fitted for this. As eager as I often am to correct the natural course of events, it is just as repugnant to me to do so systematically, after cold blooded consideration, according to the objective principles of science, without being affected by a doctor's feeling for his patient . . . I feel emotionally tied to the children as their medical guardian, and I think this emotional contact is not necessarily a weakness from the point of view of a National Socialist doctor . . . I prefer to see clearly and to recognise that I am too gentle for this work than to disappoint you later.[15]

This apology for his concern for his patients, his emotional tie to these children, as "not necessarily a weakness in a National Socialist doctor," shows how deeply ingrained this ideology was.

What lessons can be drawn from this grim episode? Any conclusions from this more empirical approach to ethics have to be tentative. There is always the danger of the mistake attributed to generals and strategists, of preparing for the previous war. There will not be an exact rerun of the Nazi episode, so we have to be flexible in learning from it.

The Nazi episode is evil on such a grand scale that any conclusions drawn from it are likely to seem puny by comparison with the events themselves. But it is worth not being deterred by this, and, at the risk of banality, trying to focus on some of the things we should guard against.

One conclusion may be that it is a mistake to let any system of belief, including a system of ethics, become too abstract. There are dangers in getting too far away from ordinary human emotional responses to people. The worry behind "racial hygiene," the worry about the consequences of removing "natural" evolutionary selective pressures, was a thought you did not have to be a very evil person to have. We see it as a misguided thought, but it is still one a morally good person might have had. The danger is to get hooked on an idea, such as this one, and then to follow it ruthlessly, trampling on all the normal human feelings and responses to individual people in front of you. This is a general danger in ethics. Even a humane outlook such as utilitarianism can do great harm when applied with ruthless abstraction.

Another lesson, in our time fortunately a platitude, is that we should not be thinking in terms of racial purity and of lesser racial quality. It is not at all clear what these phrases mean. They are woolly and muddled ideas, which are manifestly incredibly dangerous. (I mention this platitude because sometimes what was once a platitude stops being one. Who, a few years ago, would have thought it worth stating that "ethnic cleansing" should be utterly rejected?)

There is need for more thought about the answer to the claim about the necessity of replacing evolutionary selective pressures. All of us shudder when we see where this kind of thought led, but few do the thinking to find out exactly what is wrong with the arguments.

It is worth mentioning one thought about this. The fact that we can deal with some disorders, so that people with them are able to survive and have children who then may inherit the disorder, is supposed to be the problem. But, in the case of a disorder where people find their lives worth living, it is not a disaster if they pass on their genes. In the Stone Age, people with poor sight may have lost out in the evolutionary competition. Glasses and contact lenses are among the reasons why they now survive to have children. Their lives are not a disaster, and there is no reason why it is a disaster if their children inherit short-sightedness. To the extent that modern medicine makes possible, not just survival, but a decent quality of life, the supposed problem to which eugenics seemed to be the answer is not a real one.

Another lesson is the dangers of the group approach. The Nazis thought mainly in terms of nations and races. In decisions about who is to be born, decisions for instance about access to fertility treatment or about genetic screening, it is important to look first and foremost at those immediately involved: at the person who may be born and at the family. In the case of the kind of reproductive intervention where we are choosing the creation of one person rather than another, our central thought ought to be about what one kind of life or another would be like from the point of view of the person living it.

The case is like that of euthanasia. If we are to justify euthanasia at all, it has to be justified by saying either that a particular person wants not to go on living, or, where the person is past expressing any view, that their life must seem to them so terrible that it would be a kindness to kill them. We have to look at things from inside in taking these decisions. (Of course this is very difficult, which is a reason for extreme caution.)

It is utterly repugnant that "euthanasia" should be defended for instance on grounds of general social utility, such as the cost of keeping certain people alive. Killing on those grounds is not euthanasia, despite the Nazi attempt to hijack the term for such policies. People now sometimes ignorantly misuse the Nazi policy as though it were a knock-down argument against genuine euthanasia. Those of us who study what the Nazis really did tend to dislike this propagandist move. As with the casual use of "fascist" to describe political opponents, it makes light of something truly terrible, and leaves us without a vocabulary for the real thing. But the one place where the argument from Nazism really does apply is where killing the old or the sick or the insane to benefit other people is advocated.

In the same sort of way, I find repugnant the idea that decisions about the kind of children to be born should be made on grounds of general social utility.

Finally, there are issues about Social Darwinism. Rather few people these days hold Hitler's maniac racist views. But Social Darwinism may be a continuing danger. A crude interpretation of some claims in sociobiology could lend support to a renewed Social Darwinism. In mentioning this, I am not lending support to one crude reaction against sociobiology, a reaction which takes the form of denying any genetic contribution to the explanation of human behaviour. That sort of absolute denial is going to lose out in the intellectual debate. No doubt sometimes the evidence will suggest the existence of a genetic component. But, if people propose social policies supposed to follow from this, we need to look very hard at the supporting arguments. Claims about simple links between biology and social policy are often backed by very dubious arguments. And it is not just that the thinking is poor. The Nazi experience suggests that the conclusions may also be dangerous. The victims of the Nazis were not killed just by gas but also by beliefs, which can be poisonous too.

NOTES

1. Quoted in J. Noakes and G. Pridham, *Nazism, 1919–1945,* iii: *Foreign Policy, War and Racial Extermination: A Documentary Reader* (Exeter, 1988), 1010.

2. Quoted ibid. 1023–4.

3. Quoted in Benno Muller-Hill, *Murderous Science: Elimination by Scientific Selection of Jews, Gypsies, and Others, Germany 1933–1945*, trans. George R. Fraser (Oxford, 1988), 7–8.

4. Quoted ibid. 10, 12.

5. Quoted ibid. 10.

6. Cf. Robert N. Proctor, *Racial Hygiene: Medicine under the Nazis* (Cambridge, Mass.: Harvard University Press, 1988).

7. Quoted in Muller-Hill, *Murderous Science*, 14.

8. Quoted in Robert Jay Lifton, *The Nazi Doctors: A Study in the Psychology of Evil* (London, 1986), 16.

9. Quoted in Raul Hilberg, *The Destruction of the European Jews*, student edn. (New York, 1985), 287.

10. *Hitler's Table Talk, 1941–44,* introd. Hugh Trevor-Roper (Oxford, 1988), 332.

11. Quoted in Michael Howard, 'The Edwardian Arms Race', in Michael Howard, *The Lessons of History* (Oxford, 1993).

12. Quoted in Lifton, *The Nazi Doctors*.

13. Hitler, 8 Nov. 1940, quoted in J. P. Stern, *Hitler: The Führer and the People*, 62.

14. *Hitler's Table Talk*, 396–7.

15. Noakes and Pridham, *Nazism, 1919–1945,* iii. 1014–15.

Genetics and Society

JAMES D. WATSON

Genes and Politics

James D. Watson is the Chancellor of the Cold Spring Harbor Laboratory and shared the Nobel Prize for the discovery of the structure of DNA. He has been a member of the Harvard faculty and was the first Director of the National Center for Human Genome Research at the National Institutes of Health, where he helped to launch the Human Genome Project. Dr. Watson has coedited three widely-used textbooks, *Molecular Biology of the Gene*, *Molecular Biology of the Cell*, and *Recombinant DNA*.

• • •

GENUINE HUMAN GENETICS EMERGES FROM RECOMBINANT DNA METHODOLOGIES

Long holding back the development of human genetics as a major science was the lack of a genetic map allowing human genes to be located along the chromosomes on which they reside. As long as conventional breeding procedures remained the only route to gene mapping, the precise molecular changes underpinning most human genetic diseases seemed foreordained to remain long mysterious. The key breakthrough opening a path around this seemingly insuperable obstacle came in the late 1970s when it was discovered that the exact sequence (order of the genetic letters A, G, T, and C) of a given gene varies from one person to another. Between any two individuals, roughly 1 in 1000 bases are different, with such variations most frequently occurring within the noncoding DNA regions not involved in specifying specific amino acids. Initially most useful were base differences (polymorphisms) which affected DNA cutting by one of the many just discovered "restriction enzymes" that cut DNA molecules within very specific base sequences.

Reprinted with the permission of the author and the publisher from the *Journal of Molecular Medicine* 75 (September 1997), 632–36. Copyright © 1997 Springer and Kluwer Academic Publishers. Reprinted with kind permission from Springer Science and Business Media.

Soon after the existence of DNA polymorphisms became known, proposals were made that they could provide the genetic markers needed to put together human genetic maps. In a 1980 paper, David Botstein, Ron Davis, Mark Scolnick, and Ray White argued that human maps could be obtained through studying the pattern through which polymorphisms were inherited in the members of large multigenerational families. Those polymorphisms that stay together were likely to be located close to each other on a given chromosome. During the next 5 years, two groups, one led by Helen Donis-Keller in Massachusetts, the other led by Ray White in Utah, rose to this challenge, both using DNA from family blood samples stored at CEPH (Centre d'Étude de Polymorphisme Humain), the mapping center established in Paris by Jean Dausset. By 1985, the mutant genes responsible for Huntington's disease and cystic fibrosis (CF) had been located on chromosomes 4 and 7, respectively.

By using a large number of additional polymorphic markers in the original chromosome 7 region implicated in CF, Francis Collins' group in Ann Arbor and L. C. Tsui's group in Toronto located the DNA segment containing the responsible gene. Its DNA sequence revealed that the CF gene coded for a large membrane protein involved in the transport of chloride ions. The first CF mutant they found contained three fewer bases than its normal equivalent and led to a protein product that was nonfunctional because of its lack of a phenylalanine residue.

THE HUMAN GENOME PROJECT: RESPONDING TO THE NEED FOR EFFICIENT DISEASE GENE MAPPING AND ISOLATION

Although the genes responsible for cystic fibrosis and Huntington's disease were soon accurately mapped using only a small number of DNA polymorphic markers, the genes behind many other important genetic diseases quickly proved to be much harder to map to a specific chromosome, much less assign to a DNA chromosomal segment short enough to generate hopes for its eventual cloning. All too obviously, the genes behind the large set of still very badly understood diseases like Alzheimer's disease, late-onset diabetes, or breast cancer would be mapped much, much sooner if several thousands more newly mapped DNA polymorphisms somehow became available. Likewise, the task of locating the chromosomal DNA segment(s) in which the desired disease genes reside would be greatly shortened if all human DNA were publicly available as sets of overlapping cloned DNA segments (contigs). And the scanning of such DNA segments to look for mutationally altered base sequences would go much faster if the complete sequence of all the human DNA were already known. However, to generate these importantly new resources for human genetics, major new sources of money would be needed. So, by early 1986, serious discussions began as to how to start, soon, the complete sequencing of the 3×10^9 [3 billion] base pairs that collectively make up the human genome (the Human Genome Project or HGP).

Initially, there were more scientific opponents than proponents for what necessarily would be biology's first megaproject. It would require thousands of scientists and the consumption of some $3 billion-like sums. Those disliking its prospects feared that, inevitably, it would be run by governmental bureaucrats not up to the job and would employ scientists too dull for assignment to this intellectually challenging research. Out of many protracted meetings held late in 1986 and through 1987, the argument prevailed that the potential rewards for medicine as well as for biological research itself would more than compensate for the monies the Human Genome Project would consume during the 15 years then thought needed to complete it. Moreover, completion of each of the two stages— the collection of many more mapped DNA markers and the subsequent ordering of cloned DNA segments into long overlapping sets (contigs)—would by themselves greatly speed up disease gene isolation.

Always equally important to point out, the 15 years projected to complete the Human Genome Project meant that its annual cost of $200 million at most would represent only 1–2% of the money spent yearly for fundamental biomedical research over the world. There was also the realization that some 100,000 human genes believed sited along their chromosomes would be much easier to find and functionally understand if genome sequences were first established for the much smaller, well-studied model organisms such as *Escherichia coli* [a bacterium], *Saccharomyces cerevisiae* [yeast], *Caenorhabditis elegans* [a roundworm], and *Drosophila melanogaster* [the fruitfly]. Thus, the biologists who worked with these organisms realized that their own research would be speeded up if the Human Genome Project went ahead.

The American public, as represented by their congressional members, proved initially to be much more enthusiastic about the objectives of the Human Genome Project than most supposedly knowledgeable biologists, with their parochial concerns for how federal monies for biology would be divided up. The first congressionally mandated monies for the Human Genome Project became available late in 1987, when many intelligent molecular geneticists still were sitting on the fence as to whether it made sense. In contrast, Congress, being told that big medical advances would virtually automatically flow out of genome knowledge, saw no reason not to move fast. In doing so, they temporarily set aside the question of what human life would be like when the bad genes behind so many of our major diseases were found. Correctly, to my mind, their overwhelming concern was the current horror of diseases like Alzheimer's, not seeing the need then to, perhaps prematurely, worry about the dilemmas arising when individuals are genetically shown at risk for specific diseases years before they show any symptoms.

GENOME ETHICS: PROGRAMS TO FIND WAYS TO AMELIORATE GENETIC INJUSTICE

The moment I began in October 1988 my almost 4-year period of helping lead the Human Genome Project, I stated that 3% of the NIH-funded component should support research and discussion on the Ethical, Legal, and Social Implications (ELSI) of the new resulting genetic knowledge. A lower percentage might be seen as tokenism, while I then could not see wise use of a larger sum. Under my 3% proposal, some $6 million (3% of $200 million) would eventually be so available, a much larger sum than ever before provided by our government for the ethical implications of biological research.

In putting ethics so soon into the Genome agenda, I was responding to my own personal fear that all too soon critics of the Genome Project would point out that I was a representative of the Cold Spring Harbor Laboratory that once housed the controversial Eugenics Record Office. My not forming a genome ethics program quickly might be falsely used as evidence that I was a closet eugenicist, having as my real long-term purpose the unambiguous identification of genes that lead to social and occupational stratification as well as to genes justifying racial discrimination. So I saw the need to be proactive in making ELSI's major purpose clear from its start—to devise better ways to combat the social injustice that has at its roots bad draws of the genetic dice. Its programs should not be turned into public forums for debating whether genetic inequalities exist. With imperfect gene copying always the evolutionary imperative, there necessarily will always be a constant generation of the new gene disease variants and consequential genetic injustice.

The issues soon considered for ELSI monies were far-ranging. For example, how can we ensure that the results of genetic diagnosis are not misused by prospective employers or insurers? How should we try to see that individuals know what they are committing themselves to when they allow their DNA to be used for genetic analyzing? What concrete steps should be taken to ensure the accuracy of genetic testing? And when a fetus is found to possess genes that will not allow it to develop into a functional human being, who, if anyone, should have the right to terminate the pregnancy?

From their beginnings, our ELSI programs had to reflect primarily the needs of individuals at risk of the oft tragic consequences of genetic disabilities. Only long-term harm would result in the perception of genetics as an honest science if ELSI-type decisions were perceived to be dominated either by the scientists who provided the genetic knowledge or by the government bodies that funded such research. And since women are even in the distant future likely to disproportionately share the burden of caring for the genetically disabled, they should lead the discussion of how more genetic knowledge is to come into our lives.

HUMAN HESITATIONS IN LEARNING THEIR OWN GENETIC FATE

With the initial distribution of American genome monies and the building and equipping the resulting genome centers taking 2 years, the Human Genome Project in its megaphase did not effectively start until the fall of 1990. Decisions to go ahead by funding bodies in the United States helped lead to the subsequent inspired creation of Genethon outside Paris by the French genetic disease charity, Association Française contre les Myopathies (AFM), as well as the building of the now immense Sanger Centre, just south of Cambridge, England, by the British medically oriented charity, the Wellcome Trust. Now effectively 7 years into its projected 15-year life, the Human Genome Project has more than lived up to its role in speeding up genetic disease mapping and subsequent gene cloning. It quickly made successful the search for the gene behind the fragile X syndrome that leads to severe mental retardation in boys preferentially affected by this sex-linked genetic affliction. The molecular defect found was an expansion of preexisting three-base repetitive sequences that most excitingly increase in length from one generation to the next. The long mysterious phenomenon of anticipation, in which the severity of a disease grows through subsequent generations, was thus given a molecular explanation. Then at long last, in 1994, the gene for Huntington's disease was found. Its cause was likewise soon found to be the expansion of a repetitive gene sequence.

While the mapping to a chromosome per se of any disease gene remains an important achievement, the cloning of the disease gene itself is a bigger milestone. Thus, the 1990 finding by Mary Claire King that much hereditary breast cancer is due to a gene on chromosome 17 set off a big gene-cloning race. With that gene in hand, there was a chance that its DNA sequence would reveal the normal function of the protein it codes for. In any case, it gives its possessors the opportunity to examine directly the DNA from individuals known to be at risk for a disease to see whether they had the unwanted gene. Thus, when in 1993 the chromosome 17 breast cancer gene (BRCA1) was isolated by Myriad, the Utah disease gene-finding company, it could inform women so tested for BRCA1 whether or not they had the feared gene.

Initially, concerns were voiced that unbridled commercialization of this capability would all too easily give women knowledge they would not be psychologically prepared to handle. If so, the ethical way to prevent such emotional setbacks might be to regulate both how the tests were given and who should be allowed to be tested. I fear, however, that a major reason behind many such calls for regulation of genetic testing is the hidden agenda of wanting to effectively stop widespread genetic testing by making it so difficult to obtain.

Now, however, calls for governmental regulation may fall on increasingly deaf ears. To Myriad's great disappointment, it appears that the great majority of women at 50% risk of being breast cancer gene carriers don't want to be tested. Rather than receive the wrong verdict, they seem to prefer living with uncertainty. Likewise, a very large majority of the individuals at risk for Huntington's disease are also psychologically predisposed against putting themselves at risk of possibly knowing of their genetic damnation.

Although we are certain to learn in the future of many individuals regretting that they subjected themselves to genetic tests and wishing they had been more forewarned of the potential perils of such knowledge, I do not see how the state can effectively enter into such decisions. Committees of well-intentioned outsiders will never have the intimate knowledge to assess a given individual's psychological need, or not, for a particular piece of scientific or medical knowledge. In the last analysis, we should accept the fact that if scientific knowledge exists, individual persons or families should have the right to decide whether it will lead to their betterment.

INARGUABLE EXISTENCE OF GENES PREDISPOSING HUMANS TO BEHAVIORAL DISORDERS

The extraordinarily negative connotation that the term eugenics now conveys is indelibly identified with its past practitioners' unjustified statements that behavioral differences, whether between individuals, families, or the so-called races, largely had their origins in gene differences. Given the primitive power of human genetics, there was no way for such broad-ranging assertions to have been legitimatized by the then methods of science. Even the eugenically minded psychiatrists' claims that defective genes were invariably at the root of their mental patients' symptoms were no more than hunches. Yet, it was by their imputed genetic imperfection that the mentally ill were first sterilized and then, being of no value to the wartime Third Reich, released from their lives by subsequent "mercy killings."

But past eugenic horrors in no way justify the "Not in Our Genes" politically correct outlook of many left-wing academics. They still spread the unwarranted message that only our bodies, not our minds, have genetic origins. Essentially protecting the ideology that all our troubles have capitalistic exploitative origins, they are particularly uncomfortable with the thought that genes have any influence on intellectual abilities or that unsocial criminal behavior might owe its origins to other than class or racially motivated oppression. Whether these scientists on the left actually believe, say, that the incidence of schizophrenia would seriously lessen if class struggles ended, however, is not worth finding out.

Instead, we should employ, as fast as we can, the powerful new techniques of human genetics to find soon the actual schizophrenia predisposing genes. The much higher concordance of schizophrenia in identical versus nonidentical twins unambiguously tells us that they are there to find. Such twin analysis, however, reveals that genetics cannot be the whole picture. Since the concordance rates for schizophrenia, as well as for manic-depressive disease, are more like 60%, not 100%, environmental predisposing factors must exist and, conceivably, viral infections that affect the brain are sometimes involved.

Unfortunately, still today, the newer statistical tricks for analyzing polymorphic inheritance patterns have not yet led to the unambiguous mapping of even one major schizophrenic gene to a defined chromosomal site. The only convincing data involve only the 1% of schizophrenics whose psychoses seemingly are caused by the small chromosome 22 deletions responsible also for the so-called St. George facial syndrome. Manic-depressive disease also has been more than hard to understand genetically. Only last year did solid evidence emerge for a major predisposing gene on the long arm of chromosome 18. This evidence looks convincing enough for real hopes that the actual gene involved will be isolated over the next several years.

Given that over half the human genes are thought to be involved in human brain development and functioning, we must expect that many other behavioral differences between individuals will also have genetic origins. Recently, there have been claims that both "reckless personalities" and "unipolar depressions" associate with specific polymorphic forms of genes coding for the membrane receptors involved in the transmission of signals between nerve cells. Neither claim now appears to be reproducible, but we should not be surprised to find some subsequent associations to hold water. Now anathematic to left-wing ideologues is the highly convincing report of a Dutch family, many of whose male members display particularly violent behavior. Most excitingly, all of the affected males possess a mutant gene coding for an inactive form of the enzyme monoamine oxidase.

Conceivably having too little of this enzyme, which breaks down neurotransmitters, leads to the persistence of destructive thoughts and the consequential aggressive patterns. Subsequent attempts to detect in other violent individuals this same mutant gene have so far failed. We must expect someday, however, to find that other mutant genes that lead to altered brain chemistry also lead to asocial activities. Their existence, however, in no way should be taken to mean that gene variants are the major cause of violence. Nonetheless, continued denials by the scientific left that genes have no role in how people interact with each other will inevitably further diminish their already tainted credibility.

KEEPING GOVERNMENTS OUT OF GENETIC DECISIONS

No rational person should have doubts whether genetic knowledge properly used has the capacity to improve the human condition. Through discovering those genes whose bad variants make us unhealthy or in some other way unable to function effectively, we can fight back in several different ways. For example, knowing what is wrong at the molecular level should let us sometimes develop drugs that will effectively neutralize the harm generated by certain bad genes. Other genetic disabilities should effectively be neutralized by so-called gene therapy procedures restoring normal cell functioning by adding good copies of the missing normal genes. Although gene therapy enthusiasts have promised too much for the near future, it is difficult to imagine that they will not with time cure some genetic conditions.

For the time being, however, we should place most of our hopes for genetics on the use of antenatal diagnostic procedures, which increasingly will let us know whether a fetus is carrying a mutant gene that will seriously proscribe its eventual development into a functional human being. By terminating such pregnancies, the threat of horrific disease genes continuing to blight many families' prospects for future success can be erased. But even among individuals who firmly place themselves on the pro-choice side and do not want to limit women's rights for abortion, opinions frequently are voiced that decisions obviously good for individual persons or families may not be appropriate for the societies in which we live. For example, by not wanting to have a physically or mentally handicapped child or one who would have to fight all its life against possible death from cystic fibrosis, are we not reinforcing the second-rate status

of such handicapped individuals? And what would be the consequences of isolating genes that give rise to the various forms of dyslexia, opening up the possibility that women will take antenatal tests to see if their prospective child is likely to have a bad reading disorder? Is it not conceivable that such tests would lead to our devoting less resources to the currently reading-handicapped children whom now we accept as an inevitable feature of human life?

That such conundrums may never be truly answerable, however, should not concern us too much. The truly relevant question for most families is whether an obvious good to them will come from having a child with a major handicap. Is it more likely for such children to fall behind in society or will they through such affliction develop the strengths of character and fortitude that lead, like Jeffrey Tate, the noted British conductor, to the head of their packs? Here I'm afraid that the word handicap cannot escape its true definition—being placed at a disadvantage. From this perspective, seeing the bright side of being handicapped is like praising the virtues of extreme poverty. To be sure, there are many individuals who rise out of its inherently degrading states. But we perhaps most realistically should see it as the major origin of asocial behavior that has among its many bad consequences the breeding of criminal violence.

Only harm, thus, I fear will come from any form of society-based restriction on individual genetic decisions. Decisions from committees of well-intentioned individuals will too often emerge as vehicles for seeming to do good as opposed to doing good. Moreover, we should necessarily worry that once we let governments tell their citizens what they cannot do genetically, we must fear they also have power to tell us what we must do. But for us as individuals to feel comfortable making decisions that affect the genetic makeups of our children, we correspondingly have to become genetically literate. In the future, we must necessarily question any government which does not see this as its responsibility. Will it so not act because it wants to keep such powers for itself?

THE MISUSE OF GENETICS BY HITLER SHOULD NOT DENY ITS USE TODAY

Those of us who venture forth into the public arena to explain what Genetics can or cannot do for society seemingly inevitably come up against individuals who feel that we are somehow the modern equivalents of

Hitler. Here we must not fall into the absurd trap of being against everything Hitler was for. It was in no way evil for Hitler to regard mental disease as a scourge on society. Almost everyone then, as still true today, was made uncomfortable by psychotic individuals. It is how Hitler treated German mental patients that still outrages civilized societies and lets us call him immoral. Genetics per se can never be evil. It is only when we use or misuse it that morality comes in. That we want to find ways to lessen the impact of mental illness is inherently good. The killing by the Nazis of the German mental patients for reasons of supposed genetic inferiority, however, was barbarianism at its worst.

Because of Hitler's use of the term Master Race, we should not feel the need to say that we never want to use genetics to make humans more capable than they are today. The idea that genetics could or should be used to give humans power that they do not now possess, however, strongly upsets many individuals first exposed to the notion. I suspect such fears in some ways are similar to concerns now expressed about the genetically handicapped of today. If more intelligent human beings might someday be created, would we not think less well about ourselves as we exist today? Yet anyone who proclaims that we are now perfect as humans has to be a silly crank. If we could honestly promise young couples that we knew how to give them offspring with superior character, why should we assume they would decline? Those at the top of today's societies might not see the need. But if your life is going nowhere, shouldn't you seize the chance of jump-starting your children's future?

Common sense tells us that if scientists find ways to greatly improve human capabilities, there will be no stopping the public from happily seizing them.

ALLEN BUCHANAN, DAN W. BROCK, NORMAN DANIELS, AND DANIEL WIKLER

From Chance to Choice: Genetics and Justice

Allen Buchanan is the James B. Duke Professor of Philosophy and the James B. Duke Professor of Public Policy Studies at Duke University. In the early 1980s he served as Staff Philosopher for the President's Council on Ethical Issues in Medicine and Biomedical and Behavioral Research, where he was the principal author of the Commission's two reports on genetics. His books include *Ethics, Efficiency, and the Market* (1982) and *Justice, Legitimacy, and Self-Determination: Moral Foundations for International Law* (2003).

Dan Brock is the Frances Glessner Lee Professor of Medical Ethics in the Department of Social Medicine, the Director of the Division of Medical Ethics at the Harvard Medical School, and the Director of the Harvard University Program in Ethics and Health. He also served as Staff Philosopher for the President's Council on Bioethics. He is the author (with Allen Buchanan) of *Deciding For Others: The Ethics of Surrogate Decision Making* (1989) and of *Life and Death: Philosophical Essays in Biomedical Ethics* (1993), as well as of numerous articles. His current research interests include ethical issues in health resource prioritization and genetic selection for enhancement and to prevent disability.

Norman Daniels is Mary B. Saltonstall Professor of Population Ethics in the Department of Population and International Health at the Harvard School of Public Health. His research encompasses issues of distributive justice and health policy, philosophy of science, ethics, political and social philosophy, and medical ethics. Professor Daniels's publications include *Justice and Justification: Reflective Equilibrium in Theory and Practice* (1996) and *Seeking Fair Treatment: From the AIDS Epidemic to National Health Care Reform* (2002).

Daniel Wikler is the second Mary B. Saltonstall Professor of Population Ethics in the Department of Population and International Health at the Harvard School of Public Health. He served as the first Staff Ethicist for the World Health Organization. He was also the co-founder and second president of the International Association of Bioethics. Professor Wikler's recent essays have focused on ethical issues in resource allocation and new product development, personal and social responsibility for health, and ethical issues in global public health.

• • •

TWO MODELS FOR GENETIC INTERVENTION

THE PUBLIC HEALTH MODEL

[We have identified] two quite different perspectives from which genetic intervention may be viewed. The first is what we call the public health model; the second is the personal choice model.

The public health model stresses the production of benefits and the avoidance of harms for groups. It uncritically assumes that the appropriate mode of evaluating options is some form of cost-benefit (or cost-effectiveness) calculation. To the extent that the public health model even recognizes an ethical dimension to decisions about the application of scientific knowledge or technology, it tends to assume that sound ethical reasoning is exclusively consequentialist (or utilitarian) in nature. In other words, it assumes that whether a policy or an action is deemed to be right is thought to depend solely on whether it produces the greatest balance of good over bad outcomes.

More important, consequentialist ethical reasoning—like cost-benefit and cost-effectiveness calculations—assumes that it is not only possible but permissible and even mandatory to aggregate goods and bads (costs and benefits) across individuals. Harms to some can be offset by gains to others; what matters is the sum. Critics of such simple and unqualified consequentialist reasoning, including ourselves, are quick to point out its fundamental flaws: Such reasoning is distributionally insensitive because it fails to take seriously the separateness and inviolability of persons.

In other words, as simple and unqualified consequentialist reasoning looks only to the aggregate balance of good over bad, it does not recognize fairness in the distribution of burdens and benefits to be a fundamental value. As a result, it not only allows but in some circumstances requires that the most fundamental interests of individuals be sacrificed in order to produce the best overall outcome.

Consequentialist ethical theory is not unique in allowing or even requiring that the interests of individuals sometimes yield to the good of all. Any reasonable ethical theory must acknowledge this. But it is unique in maintaining that in principle such sacrifice is justified whenever it would produce any aggregate gain, no matter how small. Because simple and unqualified consequentialism has this implication, some conclude that it fails to appreciate sufficiently that each individual is an irreducibly distinct subject of moral concern.

The public health model, with its affinity for consequentialist ethical reasoning, took a particularly troubling form among some prominent eugenicists. Individuals who were thought to harbor "defective germ plasm" (what would now be called "bad genes") were likened to carriers of infectious disease. While persons infected with cholera were a menace to those with whom they came into contact, individuals with defective germ plasm were an even greater threat to society: They transmitted harm to an unlimited line of persons across many generations.

The only difference between the "horizontally transmitted" infectious diseases and "vertically transmitted" genetic diseases, according to this view, was that the potential harm caused by the latter was even greater. So if measures such as quarantine and restrictions on travel into disease areas that infringed individual freedom were appropriate responses to the former, then they were even more readily justified to avert the greater potential harm of the latter. This variant of the public health model may be called the *vertical epidemic model*. Once this point of view is adopted and combined with a simple and unqualified consequentialism, the risks of infringing liberty and of exclusion and discrimination increase dramatically.

THE PERSONAL SERVICE MODEL

Today eugenics is almost universally condemned. Partly in reaction to the tendency of the most extreme eugenicists to discount individual freedom and welfare for the supposed good of society, medical geneticists and genetic counselors since World War II have adopted an almost absolute commitment to "nondirectiveness" in their relations with those seeking genetic services. Recoiling from the public health model that dominated the eugenics movement, and especially from the vertical disease metaphor, they publicly endorse the view that genetic tests and interventions are simply services offered to individuals—goods for private consumption—to be accepted or refused as individuals see fit.

This way of conceiving of genetic interventions takes them out of the public domain, relegating them to the sphere of private choice. Advocates of the personal service model proclaim that the fundamental value on which it rests is individual autonomy. Whether a couple at risk for conceiving a child with a genetic disease takes a genetic test and how they use the knowledge thus obtained is their business, not society's, even if the decision to vaccinate a child for common childhood infectious diseases is a matter of public health and as such justifies restricting parental choice.

The personal service model serves as a formidable bulwark against the excesses of the crude consequentialist ethical reasoning that tainted the application of the public health model in the era of eugenics. But it does so at a prohibitive price: It ignores the obligation to prevent harm as well as some of the most basic requirements of justice. By elevating autonomy to the exclusion of all other values, the personal service model offers a myopic view of the moral landscape.

In fact, it is misleading to say that the personal service model expresses a commitment to autonomy. Instead, it honors only the autonomy of those who are in a position to exercise choice concerning genetic interventions, not all of those who may be affected by such choices. . . . [T]his approach wrongly subordinates the autonomy of children to that of their parents.

In addition, if genetic services are treated as goods for private consumption, the cumulative effects of many individual choices in the "genetic marketplace" may limit the autonomy of many people, and perhaps of all people. Economic pressures, including requirements for insurability and employment, as well as social stigma directed toward those who produce children with "defects" that could have been avoided, may narrow rather than expand meaningful choice. Finally, treating genetic interventions as personal services may exacerbate inequalities in opportunities if the prevention of genetic diseases or genetic enhancements are available only to the rich. It would be more accurate to say, then, that the personal service model gives free reign to some dimensions of the autonomy of some people, often at the expense of others.

A THIRD APPROACH

Much current thinking about the ethics of genetic intervention assumes that the personal service model is not an adequate moral guide. However, the common response to its deficiencies is not to resurrect the public health model associated with eugenics. Instead, there is a tendency to assume the appropriateness of the personal service model in general and then to erect ad hoc—and less than convincing—"moral firebreaks" to constrain the free choices of individuals in certain areas. For example, some ethicists have urged that the cloning of human beings be strictly prohibited, that there be a moratorium or permanent ban on human germline interventions, or that genetic enhancements (as opposed to treatments of diseases) be outlawed. In each case the proposed moral firebreak shows a distrust of the unalloyed personal service model but at the same time betrays the lack of a systematic, principled account of why and how the choices of individuals should be limited.

[We] aim to avoid both the lack of attention to the moral equality, separateness, and inviolability of persons that afflicted the eugenics movement's public health model of genetic intervention and the narrow concern with autonomous individual choice that characterizes the personal service model. We argue that although respect for individual autonomy requires an extensive sphere of protected reproductive freedoms and hence a broad range of personal discretion in decisions to use genetic interventions, both the need to prevent harm to offspring and the demands of justice, especially those regarding equal opportunity, place systematic limits on individuals' freedom to use or not use genetic interventions.

We try to develop a systematic, defensible moral framework for choices about the use of genetic intervention technologies. Our view steers a course between a public health model in which individuals count only so far as what they do or what is done to them affects the genetic health of "society" and a personal service model in which the choice to use genetic interventions is morally equivalent to the decision to buy goods for private consumption in an ordinary market. Because our account locates the ethics of genetic intervention within the larger enterprise of ethical theorizing, it avoids the arbitrariness and lack of system of the moral firebreaks approach.

ETHICAL ANALYSIS AND ETHICAL THEORY

Although we discuss ethical principles for individuals, our focus more often than not is primarily on ethical principles for institutions. In most cases we try to refine, and sometimes reinterpret or modify, institutional ethical principles that are quite familiar. Prominent examples include the principle that the basic institutions in a society should ensure equal opportunity and the principle of individual self-determination (or autonomy). We also evaluate certain distinctions, such as that between positive and negative genetic interventions or between treatments and enhancements, that some have tried to elevate to the status of institutional ethical principles.

One of the main results of our analysis is that a proper respect for individual self-determination in the realm of reproductive choices must recognize an asymmetry between institutional ethical principles and those for private individuals who are prospective parents: In general, parents should have considerably more latitude to use genetic interventions to shape their children than governments should have to shape their citizens. So even though our emphasis is on institutional ethical principles, determining their proper scope and limits requires an exploration of principles for individuals.

A comprehensive ethical theory—which we do not pretend to provide here—would include an account of virtues as well as principles. Our concern is not to attempt to provide a theory of the connection between ethical virtues and choices concerning the uses of genetic interventions. Nevertheless, some of what we say has direct and important implications for the sorts of virtues persons will need to have, both in their capacities as private individuals and as citizens concerned with public policy, in a society of heightened genetic powers. In particular, we have a good deal to say about the attitudes toward genetically based disabilities and the commitments to "the morality of inclusion" that members of such a society must exhibit if our new powers are to be used justly and humanely.

By way of partial preview, this much can be said about the institutional ethical principles we believe are most essential for a just and humane society equipped with robust capabilities for genetic intervention. As a first approximation, we can say that among the most important principles are those of justice and the prevention of harm. This is hardly surprising or controversial. Things become more complex and interesting as we explore different concepts of what justice requires and different understandings of what constitutes harm, and as we attempt to ascertain the scope and limits of the obligation to prevent harm.

JUSTICE

Following Rawls (1971, p. 3), we focus on the justice of basic social institutions and only by implication on the justice of particular policies or actions. We identify two main headings under which considerations of justice arise in a society of developed powers of genetic intervention: equal opportunity and the morality of inclusion (the latter concept is introduced at the end of this section).

One important conception of equal opportunity requires protection against limitations on individuals' opportunities imposed by racial, ethnic, religious, or gender discrimination. This principle, we argue, is important but incomplete. We opt for a somewhat more inclusive concept of equal opportunity—a version of what John Roemer has called a level playing field conception, of which Rawls's notion of fair equality of opportunity is the most prominent exemplar. Level playing field conceptions require efforts to eliminate or ameliorate the influence of some or all other social factors that limit opportunity over and above discrimination.

The most direct and compelling implication of this conception of the principle of equal opportunity lies in the domain of just health care. Here we adopt the main lines of Norman Daniels's theory of just health care, as developed in several books and a number of articles over the past 15 years. The core idea is that a just health care system should strive to remove barriers to opportunity that are due to disease. ("Disease" here is understood as any "adverse departures from normal species functioning.")

Regardless of how the term "genetic disease" is defined, the etiologies of many diseases include a genetic component. If just health care puts a premium on eliminating barriers to opportunity posed by disease, the question is not whether or in what sense a disease is genetic, but whether there is an intervention (genetic or otherwise) that can cure or prevent it. Thus the level playing field conception has direct implications for genetic intervention: In general, genetic intervention will be an important means of achieving equal opportunity, at least through its use to cure or prevent disease.

We also argue that equal opportunity, as an important principle of justice, has another bearing on genetic intervention. This principle can impose conditions on access to genetic interventions that go beyond the prevention or cure of disease. If, for example, it should ever become possible to enhance some normal desirable characteristics, a consistent commitment to equal opportunity might rule out an unrestricted market for the dissemination of the relevant technology, for if valuable enhancements were available only to the better-off, existing inequalities in opportunity might be exacerbated. Under such conditions, equal opportunity might require either making the enhancements available to all, even those who cannot pay for them or preventing anyone from having them. . . .

A deeper and more perplexing question is whether equal opportunity may require or permit genetic interventions for the sake of preventing natural inequalities that do not constitute diseases. On the account we endorse, health care does not include everything of benefit that biomedical science can deliver. Health care, so far as it is a concern of justice, has to do only with the treatment and prevention of disease. However, we argue that some versions of the level playing field conception extend the requirements of equal opportunity, at least in principle, to interventions to counteract natural inequalities that do not constitute diseases.

The rationale for such an extension is straightforward: If one of the key intuitions underpinning a level playing field conception of equal opportunity is the conviction that people's opportunities should not be significantly limited due to factors that are wholly beyond their control, then it appears that equal opportunity may require the interventions to counteract the more serious opportunity-limiting effects of bad luck in the "natural lottery," regardless of whether the disadvantage conferred by a person's genes is a disease, strictly speaking. . . .

Examples such as that of the person with the "mild depression gene" may pull one toward the conclusion that equal opportunity requires genetic interventions in such cases, even if the intervention is not treatment for a disease, for the same reason that equal opportunity requires efforts to counteract the effects of being born into a family of lower educational attainment. In both cases, it seems wrong that a person's opportunities should be limited by wholly undeserved and unchosen factors.

We will also see, however, that there are other interpretations of the level playing field conception that stop short of the conclusion that equal opportunity generally requires interventions to prevent natural disadvantages beyond the realm of disease. One such interpretation, which we believe to be Rawls's, does not hold that all undeserved disadvantages as such, including less desirable genetic endowments, require redress as a matter of justice. Instead, this understanding of equal opportunity only asserts that it is unjust to structure social institutions so as to base persons' entitlements to goods on their possession of natural advantages. According to this view, equal opportunity would not require intervention to prevent any and all instances in which an individual would have less desirable genetic endowments. Natural inequalities as such would not be problematic from the standpoint of justice. These alternative understandings of the level playing field conception of equal opportunity appear to have radically different implications for action: One seems to require

what might be called genetic equality, the other does not. . . .

This divergence between different versions of the level playing field conception of equal opportunity provides the first illustration of one of the major aims of this [essay]: to explore how the prospects of genetic interventions with human beings challenge existing ethical theory. The challenge takes two distinct forms. First, the prospect of vastly increased powers of genetic intervention brings with it the inevitability of new choices, the contemplation of which stimulates us to articulate existing ethical theories in greater detail (in this case distinguishing different variants of level playing field theories of equal opportunity, which appear to have different practical implications). Second, by placing within human control features of our condition that we have heretofore regarded as given and unalterable (the fate assigned to us by the natural lottery), the prospect of genetic interventions forces us to rethink the boundary we have traditionally drawn between misfortune and injustice, and indeed between the natural and the social.

PREVENTING HARM

[W]e argue that the most straightforward and compelling case for developing and using genetic interventions is to fulfill one of the most basic moral obligations human beings have: the obligation to prevent harm. People have especially demanding obligations to prevent harm to their offspring, but through the agency of their political institutions, they also have obligations to prevent harm to others.

Taking seriously the potential of genetic interventions to prevent harm pushes the limits of ethical theory in two ways: first, by forcing us to ascertain more precisely the scope and limits of the obligation to prevent harm; and second, by putting pressure on our very understanding of how harm is to be understood in ethical theory. Meeting the first challenge requires us to determine how the sometimes conflicting values of reproductive freedom and the obligation to prevent harm limit each other. Meeting the second requires us to take a stand on a fundamental question of ethical theory: whether behavior is subject to ethical evaluation only if it worsens or betters the condition of particular, individual persons. Some genetic interventions—those that prevent a genetic impairment by preventing an individual who would have the impairment from coming into existence—cannot be described as preventing harm, if a harm is a worsening of the condition of a particular individual. If the individual does not exist, then the intervention cannot worsen his condition.

In addition, our exploration of the obligation to prevent harm through genetic interventions calls into question common dogmas concerning "nondirective" genetic counseling and the right to refuse medical treatment in cases of "maternal/fetal" conflict—where a woman who intends to carry a fetus to term refuses treatment that would prevent a disability in the future child. Thus, whether it is morally permissible to require or at least encourage individuals to avoid a high risk of transmitting a genetic disease . . . will depend in part on how the obligation to prevent harm is understood.

LIMITS ON THE PURSUIT OF "GENETIC PERFECTION"

Parents, of course, are typically not just concerned with preventing harm to their children; they want what is best for them. As the capability for genetic intervention increases, however, ethical issues arise concerning the proper expression of this benevolent parental impulse. [W]e distinguish between permissible and obligatory genetic enhancements, examine the social implications of some of the enhancements that parents might consider undertaking for their children, and argue that what Joel Feinberg has called the child's right to an open future places significant limitations on what it is permissible for parents to do in this regard.

We also distinguish between the ethical implications of the pursuit of improvements by individual parents and those that might be pursued by collectivities in the name of some communitarian vision of human perfection. . . .

THE MORALITY OF INCLUSION

The dawning of the age of genetic intervention also pushes the limits of theories of justice in another way—by calling into question the manner in which the fundamental problem of justice is characteristically framed.

Theories of justice generally begin with the assumption that the most fundamental problem is how to distribute fairly the burdens and benefits of a society—understood as a single, cooperative framework in which all members are active and effective participants. This way of formulating the issue of justice overlooks two vital points: first, that increasingly human

beings can exert some control over the character of the basic cooperative framework within which the most fundamental questions of fair distribution arise; and second, that the character of the most basic cooperative framework in a society will determine who is and who is not "disabled." In other words, what the most basic institutions for production and exchange are like will determine the capacities an individual must have in order to be an effective participant in social cooperation (Wikler 1983; Buchanan 1993, 1996).

But if the choice of a framework of cooperation has profound implications for whether some people will be able to participate effectively, there is a prior question of justice: What is required for fairness in the choice of a society's most basic and comprehensive cooperative scheme? Attempting to answer this question stimulates us to gain a deeper understanding of the very nature of disability.

[W]e distinguish genetic impairments from disabilities that have a genetic component, noting that whether or to what extent a genetic impairment results in disability depends on the character of the dominant cooperative framework and the kinds of abilities required for effective participation in it. We then argue that there is an important but often ignored obligation to choose a dominant cooperative framework that is inclusive—that minimizes exclusion from participation on account of genetic impairments. If obligations of inclusion are to be taken seriously, they too impose significant restrictions on the personal choice model for the ethics of genetic intervention.

Justice in the choice of cooperative schemes turns out to be complex, however. The obligation of inclusion is not the sole morally relevant factor, so it cannot be a moral absolute. There is also the morally legitimate interest that persons have in having access to the most productive, enriching, and challenging cooperative scheme in which they are capable of being effective participants. Where there are significant differences in persons' natural assets, the obligation of inclusion and this legitimate interest can come into conflict.

However this conflict is resolved, we argue, a just society of considerable powers of genetic intervention may require changes in both directions: genetic interventions to enable individuals to be effective participants in social cooperation who would not otherwise be able to, and efforts to design the structure of cooperation in ways that make it possible for more people to be effective participants. Appreciation of the problem of justice in the choice of cooperative schemes leads us to the conclusion that regardless of whether we choose to use genetic interventions to promote inclusiveness or refuse to do so, we are in a very real sense choosing who will and who will not be disabled.

REFERENCES

Buchanan, Allen. "Genetic Manipulation and the Morality of Inclusion." *Social Philosophy and Policy* 13 (1996), 18–46.

Buchanan, Allen. "The Morality of Inclusion." *Social Philosophy and Policy* 10 (1993), 233–57.

Rawls, John. *A Theory of Justice.* Cambridge, MA: Harvard University Press, 1971.

Wikler, Daniel I. "Paternalism and the Mildly Retarded," in Rolf Sartorius, ed., *Paternalism.* Minneapolis: University of Minnesota Press, 1983, 83–94.

SVANTE PÄÄBO

The Human Genome and Our View of Ourselves

Svante Pääbo is one of the founding directors of the Max-Planck-Institute for Evolutionary Anthropology in Leipzig and Honorary Professor of Genetics and Evolutionary Biology at the University of Leipzig. He studies molecular evolution, with an emphasis on human history and origins. In particular, he works on the retrieval of DNA from archaeological and paleontological remains and comparative studies of genomes and gene expression in humans and the great apes.

Perhaps for the pragmatic biologist, the determination of the human genome sequence is a prosaic event—the delivery of a wonderfully powerful tool, but a tool nonetheless. For the general public, however, the human genome sequence is of enormous symbolic significance, and its publication [in] this issue[1] [of *Science*] and in this week's *Nature*[2] is likely to be greeted with the same awestruck feeling that accompanied the landing of the first human on the moon and the detonation of the first atomic bomb.

Why are certain achievements—the first lunar landing, atomic fission, the determination of the human genome sequence—imbued with such emblematic significance? The reason is, I believe, that they change how we think about ourselves. Landing a person on the moon gave us an extraterrestrial perspective on human life; atomic fission gave us the power to create enormous energy reserves and to extinguish all human life on Earth; and now the human genome sequence gives us a view of the internal genetic scaffold around which every human life is molded. This scaffold has been handed down to us from our ancestors, and through it we are connected to all other life on Earth.

How does the complete human genome sequence affect the way that we think about ourselves? Clearly, the availability of a reference human DNA sequence is a milestone toward understanding how humans have evolved, because it opens the door to large-scale comparative studies. The major impact of such studies will be to reveal just how similar humans are to each other and to other species.

The first comparisons will be between the human genome and distantly related genomes such as those of yeast, flies, worms, and mice. A glimpse of what this will show us comes from considering the fact that about 26,000 to 38,000 genes are found in the draft version of our own genome, a number that is only two to three times larger than the 13,600 genes in the fruit fly genome. Furthermore, some 10% of human genes are clearly related to particular genes in the fly and the worm. So, obviously, we share much of our genetic scaffold even with very distant relatives. The similarity between humans and other animals will become even more evident when genome sequences from organism such as the mouse, with whom we share a more recent common ancestor, become available. For these species,

Reprinted with permission from *Science* 291 (16 February 2001), 1219–20. Copyright © 2001, American Association for the Advancement of Science. Reprinted by permission from Macmillan Publishers Ltd: Kaessmann, et al., DNA Sequence Variation, *Nature Genetics* 22 78 (1999), © 1999, Nature Publishing Group.

both the number of genes and the general structure of the genome are likely to be very similar to ours. Although this has long been realized by insiders in the genetics community, the close similarity of our genome to those of other organisms will make the unity of life more obvious to everyone. No doubt the genomic view of our place in nature will be both a source of humility and a blow to the idea of human uniqueness.

However, the most obvious challenge to the notion of human uniqueness is likely to come from comparisons of genomes of closely related species. We already know that the overall DNA sequence similarity between humans and chimpanzees is about 99%.[3] When the chimpanzee genome sequence becomes available, we are sure to find that its gene content and organization are very similar (if not identical) to our own. Perhaps it is our subconscious discomfort with this expectation that explains the slowness with which the genomics community has embraced the idea of a chimpanzee genome project. Be that as it may, with most of the human genome sequence now complete, it will be easy to determine the chimpanzee sequence using the human sequence as a guide to assembly. The result is sure to be an even more powerful challenge to the notion of human uniqueness than the comparison of the human genome to those of other mammals.

Yet the few differences between our genome and those of the great apes will be profoundly interesting because among them lie the genetic prerequisites that make us different from all other animals. In particular, these differences may reveal the genetic foundation for our rapid cultural evolution and geographic expansion, which started between 150,000 and 50,000 years ago[4] and led to our current overbearing domination of Earth. The realization that one or a few genetic accidents made human history possible will provide us with a whole new set of philosophical challenges to think about.

Large-scale comparisons of human genomes from many individuals are now possible with the emergence of high-throughput techniques for DNA sequence determination. The general picture already apparent from such studies is that the gene pool in Africa contains more variation than elsewhere, and that the genetic variation found outside of Africa represents only a subset of that found within the African continent.[5] From a genetic perspective, all humans are therefore Africans, either residing in Africa or in recent exile.

In view of the sad part that race and ethnicity still play in most societies, concerns that genetic analyses of different human populations could be abused are appropriate. Fortunately, from the few studies of nuclear DNA sequences, it is clear that what is called "race," although culturally important, reflects just a few continuous traits determined by a tiny fraction of our genes. This tiny fraction gives no indication of variations at other parts of our genome. Thus, from the perspective of nuclear genes, it is often the case that two persons from the same part of the world who look superficially alike are less related to each other than they are to persons from other parts of the world who may look very different (see the figure p. 235).[6] Although small segments of the genome—such as mitochondrial DNA and Y chromosomal DNA (which are inherited in an unusual way) or the few genes that encode visible traits (which may have been selected for)—show a pattern where the genes in a particular human population can be traced back to a single common ancestor, this is not the case for the vast majority of our genes. Indeed, one way in which we humans seem to differ from apes is that we have evolved with very little subdivision. This is surely because we are a young species (in evolutionary terms) and have a greater tendency for migration than many other mammals. I suspect, therefore, that genome-wide studies of genetic variation among human populations may not be so easy to abuse—in terms of using data as "scientific support" for racism or other forms of bigotry—as is currently feared. If anything, such studies will have the opposite effect because prejudice, oppression, and racism feed on ignorance. Knowledge of the genome should foster compassion, not only because our gene pool is extremely mixed, but also because a more comprehensive understanding of how our genotype relates to our phenotype will demonstrate that everyone carries at least some deleterious alleles. Consequently, stigmatizing any particular group of individuals on the basis of ethnicity or carrier status for certain alleles will be revealed as absurd.

From a medical standpoint, improved predictive capabilities provided by the identification of disease-associated alleles harbor great potential benefits but also problems. The benefits will come from using individualized risk assessment to modify the environmental and behavioral components of common diseases. Relatively minor measures implemented early in life may prove to be extremely effective in postponing or even preventing the onset of disease. But individualized risk assessment may come at the price of "genetic hypochondria," causing many to spend their lives waiting for a disease that may never

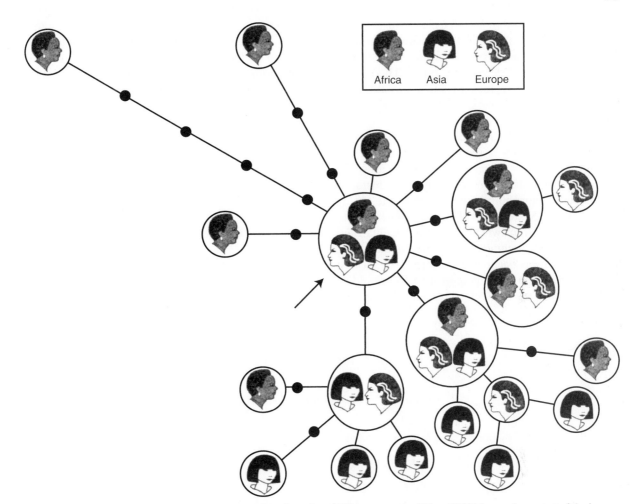

The global family. A network illustrating the relatedness of a series of DNA sequences within a 10,000-base pair segment of the human X chromosome sampled from 70 individuals worldwide. Identical DNA sequences found in people living on three different continents are illustrated by circles containing three faces; identical DNA sequences found in individuals from two continents are depicted as circles containing two faces; sequences that are found only among individuals inhabiting one continent are depicted as circles containing one face. A DNA sequence that is ancestral to all of the other sequences (arrow) is found in individuals from all continents. Black dots on the lines connecting the circles denote nucleotide substitutions in the DNA sequences. The network demonstrates that people from different continents often carry identical DNA sequences. Consequently, how a person looks gives little or no clue to what alleles he or she may carry at any particular locus. [Modified from (6)]

arrive. Finally, increased medical predictive power obviously represents a societal challenge in terms of medical insurance, especially in countries that, unlike most Western European countries, are not blessed with health insurance systems that share risks in an equitable fashion among the whole population. Legislators in such countries would be wise to act now to counteract future temptations to "personalize" insurance risks. Later on, once powerful genetic diagnostic tests are in place, it will be hard to withstand

pressure from the insurance lobby to prevent such legislation.

As we enter a genomic era in medicine and biology, perhaps the greatest danger I see stems from the enormous emphasis placed on the human genome by the media. The successes of medical genetics and genomics during the last decade have resulted in a sharp shift toward an almost completely genetic view of ourselves. I find it striking that 10 years ago, a geneticist had to defend the idea that not only the environment but also genes shape human development. Today, one feels compelled to stress that there is a large environmental component to common diseases, behavior, and personality traits! There is an insidious tendency to look to our genes for most aspects of our "humanness," and to forget that the genome is but an internal scaffold for our existence.

We need to leave behind the view that the genetic history of our species is *the* history par excellence. We must realize that our genes are but one aspect of our history, and that there are many other histories that are even more important. For example, many people in the Western world feel a connection to ancient Greece, from which arose fundamental features of Western architecture, science, technology, and political ideals (such as democracy). Yet, at best a tiny fraction of the gene pool of the Western industrialized world came from the ancient Greeks.

Obviously, this fact in no way diminishes the importance of ancient Greece. So it is a delusion to think that genomics in isolation will ever tell us what it means to be human. To work toward that lofty goal, we need an approach that includes the cognitive sciences, primatology, the social sciences, and the humanities. But with the availability of the complete human genome sequence now at hand, genetics is in a prime position to play a prominent part in this endeavor.

NOTES

1. J. C. Venter *et al., Science* 291, 1304 (2001).

2. International Human Genome Sequencing Consortium, *Nature* **409,** 860 (2001).

3. M.-C. King, A. C. Wilson, *Science* **188,** 107 (1975).

4. R. G. Klein, *The Human Career* (Univ. of Chicago Press, Chicago, IL, 1999).

5. L. B. Jorde, M. Bamshad, A. R. Rogers, *Bioessays* **20,** 126 (1998).

6. H. Kaessmann, F. Heissig, A. von Haeseler, S. Pääbo, *Nature Genet.* **22,** 78 (1999).

Genetic Testing and Screening

MICHAEL M. BURGESS

Beyond Consent: Ethical and Social Issues in Genetic Testing

Michael Burgess holds the Chair in Biomedical Ethics at the W. Maurice Young Centre for Applied Ethics and in the Department of Medical Genetics at the University of British Columbia in Vancouver. His current research activities concern ethical issues raised by genetic knowledge and technology. He has served as a member of the Management Committee for the Canadian Genetic Assessment and Technology Program and the Social Issues Committee of the American Society of Human Genetics. He currently leads a project on "Democracy, Ethics and Genomics: Consultation, Deliberation and Modeling."

INFORMED CONSENT promotes patient participation and AUTONOMY in health-care decisions by requiring the provision of information and recognizing that patients must voluntarily authorize interventions. In the case

Reprinted with permission from Macmillan Publishers Ltd., *Nature Reviews: Genetics* 2 (February 2001), 147–151. Copyright © 2001, Nature Publishing Group.

of genetic testing, genetic counselling provides the means to achieve informed consent. Genetic counselling explains the nature, usefulness and risks associated with genetic tests, and assures that participation in genetic testing is autonomous, or based on participants' understanding of the relevant information. Because informed consent is highly dependent on comprehension of information and good communication, genetic counselling provides excellent support, although evaluation of counselling is not well established and some researchers express concern about the ability of counsellors to be non-directive.[1-3]

However, genetic testing raises issues that cannot be managed through informed consent. To begin with, there might be few, if any, clinical benefits from genetic testing. As far as genetic counselling is concerned, the STANDARD OF PRACTICE is primarily directed at imparting understanding of possible test results, because the net benefit of a genetic test is often highly dependent on how much the participant values the information and what they want to do with it (Box 1). Genetic counselling also involves careful consideration of the social and psychological risks of genetic testing, but evolving social contexts, such as the workplace, the insurance industry and the family, shape whether and how these risks materialize. Genetic information produced by testing individuals also affects other family members, and those who share, or are perceived to share, a common genetic heritage.

Genetic testing therefore raises ethical issues that concern standard of practice, indeterminacy of risks and collective acceptability of risks and benefits. This article discusses each of these issues, indicating the extent to which informed consent addresses the ethical

issues, and suggests fruitful avenues of research into the ethics of the social context of genetic practice.

GENETIC TESTING: A STANDARD OF PRACTICE

Because of the complexity of genetic information and its interpretation, genetic counselling has become a cornerstone of genetic research and clinical practice. Counsellors must explain the highly variable, and often changing, views about the relation between genetic test results and the associated conditions, as well as information about the conditions themselves and possible treatments or preventions.

One of the first and most influential studies of genetic testing for an adult onset disease was the predictive testing for Huntington disease. The concerns associated with predictive genetic testing[4,5] were managed in the Canadian multi-centre research protocol by requiring four pre-test and several post-test counselling sessions.[6] Although there were no definitive medical benefits in this instance, testing was felt to promote individual patient autonomy and emotional welfare. The conclusion of the Canadian study was that, with the provision of pre- and post-test counselling that included psychological assessments, genetic testing for Huntington disease did not pose unacceptable risks for consenting participants.[7] Clinical recommendations supporting genetic counselling of adults have been based on this research experience,[8] although in clinical practice and with other genetic tests, pre- and post-test counselling have become streamlined with little study of the effects of counselling itself or of modifications to clinical protocols.[9] The clinical availability of predictive testing for Huntington disease is based on the ethical assessment that the promotion of autonomy and the psychological and social benefits for people can justify the risks for those who want the test and undergo genetic counselling.

The case of Huntington disease illustrates the general trend for genetic testing to become the *de facto* standard of practice—available for those who wish to have the information once it is established that a genetic test can identify a genetic contribution to a disease. This is probably due to the low cost of the test, and the difficulty of justifying withholding the test on a clinical basis once it is established as accurate in the research context.[10,11] This emphasis on individual participant autonomy in the research setting might explain what some have referred to as "premature implementation"

Box 1 Possible benefits from tests

Clinical
- Avoidance of onset of disease
- Curative treatment due to timely and accurate diagnosis
- Avoidance of harms from inappropriate treatment or monitoring
- Symptomatic treatment

Psychological or social
- Relief from uncertainty
- Personal planning
- Improved well-being
- Fulfilment of patient wishes to be tested

Public health
- Decrease population morbidity and/or mortality from genetic disease
- Decrease population frequency of treatment-related morbidity or mortality

before establishing clinical benefit, particularly in the case of tests that are not predictive but that indicate an increase in disease susceptibility.[12]

There are, of course, genetic tests that direct clinical care. In the case of prenatal testing, the possibility of abortion as a clinical intervention does provide a clinical option with a clear outcome. A family history of colon cancer initiates invasive monitoring, and testing that eliminates a genetic contributor might reduce or eliminate the need for monitoring and the accompanying risks and discomforts. But, in many cases, the genetic information together with the choices that it provides to people are the primary benefits.

Providing access to a genetic test because it is accurate is different from evidence-based standards that are applied to other clinical interventions. These standards require that there is a measurable difference in clinical outcomes or population health measures for a test, screen or intervention to become the standard of practice. However, most genetic tests develop well in advance of effective interventions because of their usefulness in research. Many genetic tests are therefore available simply because they provide accurate information. This standard of practice does not protect patients from risks, but makes them responsible for evaluating whether the social and psychological risks are justified by the benefits. The historical association of genetics with eugenics has probably contributed to the vehemence with which patient autonomy and non-directive counselling have been asserted as the ethical standard for such assessments.[13]

Potential test participants cannot assume that there is benefit simply because genetic testing is offered as a clinical service. They have to evaluate for themselves whether the knowledge likely to result from the genetic test is beneficial. This poses an additional challenge to informed consent. It is not enough to provide information—patients must also be supported in evaluating their own responses and views of benefit. Policy decisions related to health-care insurance must also evaluate whether accurate genetic tests provide sufficient health benefits to justify coverage (and whether private and therefore unequal access constitutes a problem for justice in national health-care systems).[14] So it is not ethically sufficient to establish test accuracy and assure counselling and consent for test participants.

Participant evaluation of the benefits of testing engages a larger context than just the genetic counselling sessions. Media, marketing and some public enthusiasm for genetic testing and biotechnology in general will tend to raise participants' expectations of genetic testing.[15,16] Although the advent of preventive or ameliorating interventions will strengthen the benefits, the psychological and social risks will always be an important factor and make it difficult to consider genetic tests as being innocuous.

THE INDETERMINATE NATURE OF RISKS

Establishing the risks that are associated with genetic testing is also critical for both the standard of practice and for informed consent. In the absence of clear and dependable clinical benefits, the social and psychological risks might overwhelm the benefits. Even in cases for which there is clinical benefit from a particular test, the psychological and social risks should be disclosed in counselling, and there is a need for policies or regulation to minimize these risks. But evaluating the social and psychological risks (or benefits) that come from genetic testing and information is difficult. The same genetic information can pose harm or benefit owing to the highly variable nature of familial and social circumstances.

For example, a person told that they have not inherited the Huntington disease mutation might experience relief or increased responsibility for family members who are less fortunate. The experience of relief from being told that one is not at risk for a familial disease hardly needs explanation. But clinical reports, interviews and focus group discussions also describe the experiences of people receiving the same news whose relief is qualified by the misfortune of other family members, or who assume or are assigned caregiving responsibilities.[17] Whereas some people might experience caregiving roles as fulfilling and desirable, others find that their personal resources and social supports are inadequate, and describe their lives as still dominated by Huntington disease. Women receiving news that they have not inherited the mutation associated with breast cancer in their family certainly will experience relief, although they might also feel an obligation to educate family members and to encourage others at risk to seek genetic testing. For some, this responsibility might be grasped with enthusiasm, but for others, familial responses will be marginalizing. Although genetic counselling might include discussion of familial responses to genetic information as well as sharing of test results within the family, it is unrealistic to expect genetic counsellors or individual test participants to be able to anticipate the actual familial responses and personal experiences.

The unpredictability of familial and personal responses makes it difficult to assess the net benefit of genetic testing for any individual.

Another context that will shape the social and psychological effects of genetic testing is the work place. On the positive side, the identification of a genetic contributor to an environmental sensitivity can motivate an intervention to reduce exposure to the specific environmental agent (if it is readily alterable).[18] But increased susceptibility identified by a genetic test might also lead employers to discriminate against some people to minimize employees' sick time. Liability, disability and life insurance create incentives for employers to increase scrutiny of those with genetic-based susceptibilities to minimize overhead costs or legal risks. It is not the genetic information itself that poses the risk, but individual and social system responses.[19,20]

Although confidentiality of health-care records could reduce some discriminatory uses of genetic testing information, it is controversial whether mere disclosure of the risks and the current privacy regulations for genetic information are adequate.[21,22] The privacy issue is particularly problematic for insurance policies, because insurance contracts are based on the sharing of medical information to assess risk and to establish proportionate or market-related premiums.[23–26] It is controversial whether broad social policy to restrict the insurance industry's access to genetic information is necessary to protect fair access to insurance,[27] despite strong international pressures either to restrict access or to require the provision of basic levels of insurance without scrutiny of medical records.[28–31] The various uses of genetic information in these social contexts emphasize the need to identify, evaluate and regulate for possible discrimination.

The occurrence of social and psychological effects, and whether they are experienced as harms or benefits, is sensitive to many factors such as individual resources, family support, supportive social services, insurance company policies and social attitudes. Although informed consent must explain that these broader social contexts are relevant to assessing the effects of genetic testing, the actual effects remain unpredictable owing to the complexity and variability of social systems. Whenever genetic testing provides a definitive response to a pressing clinical problem, these more abstract concerns appropriately recede into the background. But when genetic tests provide primarily social or psychological benefits, these social contexts are critical for assessing whether the anticipated benefits will materialize, and whether the harms will be justified. Such an assessment is inevitably part of informed consent. But the genetic counselling must clearly articulate uncertainty about the harms and benefits of genetic testing.

Ethical evaluations of genetic tests must assess the social and psychological effects of testing and consider the actual and possible responses of social systems. Although informed consent and genetic counselling might disclose or discuss these ethical dimensions for the test candidate, they must not be construed as adequate to manage these risks. The social context is beyond the control of geneticists and participants; neither can be held responsible for deciding whether to expose the participant to effects that are essentially unstable and not universally experienced as good or bad. Ultimately, the acceptance of genetic testing in society must be accompanied by investment in social research that will identify social system responses, provide ethical and social analyses and alternatives for reform.

EFFECTS ON NON-CONSENTING PERSONS

Genetic testing produces information that is familial and not only individual. A participant's genetic test for an inherited mutation reveals whether they received the mutation from their parents, whether their siblings might have inherited the mutation, and whether their children could inherit it. The previous discussion of the subjectivity of non-clinical benefit established that the same test result could be beneficial or harmful, or some mix of the two, and that consent depended on the evaluation of the individual. But the model of consent presumes that harms and benefits can be isolated to consenting persons. Therefore, the combination of the familial effects of genetic testing and individual authorization of the acceptance of risks and benefits seems to entail the impractical requirement that every family member, for whom the test participant's information might have relevance, should provide consent before the participant is tested. The usual compromise is to suggest to a test candidate that he or she discuss the testing possibilities with family members, and, whenever possible, to first counsel and test potential carriers, such as parents. If the persons most likely to be affected by one family member's test are already tested, then the effects on the rest of the family will be minimized. But even if family members insist on their "right not to know," the presumption of the ethical sufficiency of informed consent for clinical services makes it difficult to justify refusing genetic testing to the consenting person.

The effects of genetic testing on groups larger than families are probably most familiar with inherited disease related to minorities or religious communities. Tay-Sachs disease, sickle cell anaemia and specific mutations associated with breast and ovarian cancers are the best-known examples. In these instances, historical reproductive and immigration patterns have preserved a degree of genetic homogeneity in ethnocultural communities, which makes the genetic contributions to some diseases easier to identify in these groups. Such communities are therefore attractive as research populations. It is important to recognize that the frequency of a condition in a specific population might not be higher than in the general population, but that the reduced heterogeneity makes it easier to search for meaningful genetic variations.[32] And it is this same association of heritage, race or social group with the identification of genetic risk that can lead to stigmatization of ethnic populations as genetically 'defective.'[33]

Informed consent of individual ethno-cultural COMMUNITY members is wholly inadequate for authorizing the acceptability of the risks of stigmatization for the entire group.[34,35] Even if there are collective benefits likely to accrue from the clinical testing of individuals or from research, consent from individual community members cannot authorize the acceptability of the effects to the community. Although researchers might sometimes seek authoritative acceptance by leaders, even this approach begs important ethical questions about the representativeness of leadership and heterogeneity of moral beliefs and judgments within communities.[36] The authority of leadership might, in some cases, require consent processes that encourage independence and strong confidentiality to leave room for people to refuse to participate.[37] Despite some views that if ethics gets in the way of science and benefits then the ethics should be examined,[38] there is considerable recognition that some kind of collective acceptability of research must be negotiated with identified populations.[39]

Untested and non-consenting members of disease-related charitable organizations and patient support groups can also experience the effects of genetic testing of persons within their group. For instance, a complex genetic disease might have several genetic components that interact with each other and with the environment in which the disease is manifested.

Understanding these genetic components might differentiate between those who would benefit from one form of intervention rather than another, or show that environmental contributors can be controlled to avoid disease in some subset of the affected population. But characterization of the disease as genetic could lead to insurance discrimination for the entire population. Some persons with the disease who lack the social and financial resources so relevant to a sense of empowerment might assume fatalism with respect to the disease, avoiding possibly ameliorating measures. Affected persons might be stigmatized for not avoiding the environmental contributors. These are the effects on the population that result from a genetic understanding of disease and, as such, are the result of individuals' consent to genetic research on their own disease. Contrary to some attempts to extend informed consent to groups, the collective acceptability of research,[40] or its justifiability in the case of diverse opinion, requires detailed negotiation and specific ethical assessments.[41]

BEYOND CONSENT

Individualized ideas about autonomy and informed consent are a part of the CULTURE of bioethics in Western health-care practice and politics. Cultural studies indicate that the concept of culture should not be understood as a set of beliefs that explain the behaviour of others,[42] but instead as the nest of practices and assumptions that underlie everyday practice for all people, however diverse. Cultural dimensions shape what is considered desirable research for researchers, granting agencies, health-care systems and commercial enterprises, as well as for families, "ethnic groups" and groups organized around fund raising and research for particular diseases. In other words, the development of genetic testing as well as the trend towards genomic science are themselves cultural phenomena that can be understood as being made possible and supported by particular cultural views.[43]

The orientation towards accurate knowledge as a benefit independent of clinical relevance is a part of the culture of science and is promoted by a tradition that emphasizes individual autonomy. Resorting to the individual to assess net benefit in the face of ambiguity is a feature of liberal political philosophy. Contemporary bioethics tends to support the insulation of scientists, institutions and commercial producers from responsibility for social contexts in which scientific knowledge is used, without suggesting alternative responsible parties. Social research and explicit discussion of the culture of research, commercialization, and risk-orientated health education allow the wider public to participate in meaningful discussions about technology and health policy,[44–46] a critical but often neglected feature of democracy in this area.

Clinical research and health policy analysis must return to an evaluation of the clinical and non-clinical benefits related to the standard of practice. The current *ad hoc* addition of genetic tests to the standard of practice merely because they provide accurate genetic information is not justifiable. This is particularly true as social and psychological effects cannot be adequately described or predicted. Some of the most important research related to genetic testing has to do with the use of genetic information and ideas of inheritance in social institutions, ranging from the family to whole communities. Finally, as the social effects of genetic and inheritance information are better described, it will be vital to establish collaborative research with communities and other groups who have collective interests in the effects of research on themselves.

GLOSSARY

Autonomy The capacity to be rational and self-directing. Autonomy creates the possibility of moral responsibility, and is therefore accorded strong ethical protection in bioethics.
Community Communities usually share some element of value or practice that provides cohesiveness despite considerable heterogeneity. Aggregates might be identified as having a common feature, such as a disease, but lack any social cohesiveness. Disease-related groups might move from being an aggregate to a community as they organize activities around their common features.
Culture Culture is constituted by the practices and assumptions that underlie a group's everyday activities, and is typically heterogeneous and constantly evolving.
Informed consent A doctrine intended to assure patient participation in health-care decisions. It requires that the recommended and alternative interventions be explained, together with their harms and benefits. Authorization of treatment is based on comprehension of this information and voluntary agreement.
Standard of practice Historically rooted in clinical practice, the standard of practice is the service or intervention that is recognized by the relevant group of health professionals as appropriate care. The move to evidence-based standards of practice evaluates whether the benefits of a new intervention outweigh the possible harms.

NOTES

1. Rapp, R. Chromosomes and communication: the discourse of genetic counseling. *Med. Anthrop. Quart.* **2,** 143–157 (1988).

2. Lippman, A. in *The Future of Human Reproduction* (ed. Overall, C.) 182–194 (The Women's Press, Toronto, 1989).

3. Clarke, A. Is non-directive genetic counseling possible? *Lancet* **338,** 998–1001 (1991).

4. Farrer, L. A. Suicide and attempted suicide in Huntington disease: implications for preclinical testing of persons at risk. *Am. J. Med. Genet.* **24,** 305–3111 (1986).

5. Kessler, S. & Bloch, M. Social system responses to Huntington disease. *Family Processes* **28,** 59–68 (1989).

6. Fox, S., Bloch, M., Fahy, M. & Hayden, M. R. Predictive testing for Huntington disease: description of a pilot study in British Columbia. *Am. J. Med. Genet.* **32,** 211–216 (1988).

7. Benjamin, C. M. *et al.* and the Canadian collaborative groups for predictive testing for Huntington disease. Proceed with care: direct predictive testing for Huntington disease. *Am. J. Hum. Genet.* **55,** 606–617 (1994).

8. Quaid, K. A. Presymptomatic testing for Huntington disease: recommendations for counseling. *Am. J. Med. Genet.* **39,** 347–354 (1992).

9. Biesecker, B. B. & Marteau, T. M. The future of genetic counseling: an international perspective. *Nature Genet.* **22,** 133–137 (1999).

10. DeGrazia, D. The ethical justification for minimal paternalism in the use of the predictive test for Huntington's disease. *J. Clin. Ethics* **2,** 219–228 (1991).

11. Burgess, M. M. & Hayden, M. R. Patients' rights to laboratory data: trinucleotide repeat length in Huntington disease. *Am. J. Med. Genet.* **162,** 6–9 (1996).

12. Koenig, B. *et al.* Genetic testing for BRCA1 and BRCA2; recommendations of the Stanford program in genomics, ethics and society. *J. Women's Health* **7,** 531–545 (1998).

13. Kerr, A. & Cunningham-Burley, S. On ambivalence and risk: reflexive modernity and the new human genetics. *Sociology* **34,** 283–304 (2000).

14. Burgess, M. M. in *The Commercialization of Genetics Research: Ethical, Legal, and Policy Issues* (eds Caulfield, T. A. & Williams-Jones, B.) 181–194 (Kluwer Academic/Plenum Publishers, New York, 1999).

15. Nelkin, D. & Lindee, M. S., *The DNA Mystique: The Gene as a Cultural Icon* (New York: Freeman, 1995).

16. Harper, P. S. Direct marketing of cystic fibrosis carrier screening: commercial push or population need? *J. Med. Genet.* **32,** 249–250 (1995).

17. Huggins, M. *et al.* Predictive testing for Huntington disease in Canada: adverse effects and unexpected results in those receiving a decreased risk. *Am. J. Med. Genet.* **42,** 508 (1992).

18. Vineis, P. & Schulte, P. A. Scientific and ethical aspects of genetic screening of workers for cancer risk: the case of *N*-acetyltransferase phenotype. *J. Clin. Epidemiol.* **48,** 189–197 (1995).

19. MacDonald, C. & Williams-Jones, B. Ethics and genetics: susceptibility testing in the workplace. *J. Business Ethics* [**35** (2002), 235–41.]

20. Lemmens, T. What about your genes? Ethical, legal and policy dimensions of genetics in the workplace. *Politics and the Life Sciences* **16,** 57–75 (1997).

21. Working Group on Ethical, Legal and Social Implications of Human Genome Research. *Genetic Information and Health Insurance. Report of the Task Force*: (National Institutes of Health, Bethesda, Maryland, 1993).

22. Abbott, A. Israel split on rights to genetic privacy. *Nature* **394,** 214 (1998).

23. McGleenan, T., Weising, U. & Ewald, F. (eds) *Genetics and Insurance* (Springer, New York, 1999).

24. NIH-DOE Working Group on Ethical, Legal, and Social Implications of Human Genome Research. *Genetic Information and Health Insurance* (Human Genome Project, Washington DC, 1993).

25. Lemmens, T. & Bahamin, P. in *Socio-Ethical Issues in Human Genetics* (ed. Knoppers, B. M.) 115–275 (Les Editions Yvons-Blais Inc., Cowansville, Quebec, 1998).

26. Greely, H. T. in *The Code of Codes: Scientific and Social Issues in the Human Genome Project* (eds Kelves, D. J. & Hood, L.) 274–280 (Harvard Univ. Press, Cambridge, Massachusetts, 1992).

27. McGleenan, T. & Wiesing, U. in *Genetics and Insurance* (eds McGleenan, T. *et al.*) 116–117 (Springer, New York, 1999).

28. Murray, T. Genetics and the moral mission of health insurance. *Hastings Center Report* **22,** no. 6, 12–15 (1992).

29. Wilkie, T. Genetics and insurance in Britain: why more than just the Atlantic divides the English-speaking nations. *Nature Genet.* **20,** 119–121 (1998).

30. Dutch Health Council. *Genetics, Science & Society* (Dutch Health Council, The Hague, 1989).

31. Sandberg, P. Genetic information and life insurance: a proposal for an ethical European policy. *Social Sci. Med.* **40,** 1549–1559 (1995).

32. Collins, F. cited in Wadman, M. News: Jewish leaders meet NIH chiefs on genetic stigmatisation fears. *Nature* **392,** 851 (1998).

33. Editorial. Privacy matters. *Nature Genet.* **19,** 207–208 (1998).

34. Weijer, C., Goldsand, G. & Emanuel, E. J. Protecting communities in research: current guidelines and limits of extrapolation. *Nature Genet.* **23,** 275–280 (1999).

35. Weijer, C. Protecting communities in research: Philosophical and pragmatic challenges. *Cam. Q. Health Ethics* **8,** 501–513 (1999).

36. Burgess, M. M. & Brunger, F. in *The Governance of Health Research involving Human Subjects* (ed. McDonald, M.) 141–175 (Law Commission of Canada, Ottawa, 2000). Also see http://www.lcc.gc.ca/en/themes/gr/hrish/macdonald/macdonald.pdf

37. Foster, M. W., Berensten, D. & Carter, T. H., A model agreement for genetic research in socially identifiable populations. *Am. J. Hum. Genet.* **63,** 696–702 (1998).

38. Scheuermann, R. H. & Picker, L. J. Letter to the editor. *Nature* **392,** 14 (1998).

39. Council for International Organizations of Medical Sciences (CIOMS) *International Ethical Guidelines for Biomedical Research Involving Human Subjects* (CIOMS, Geneva, 1993).

40. Weijer, C., Goldsand, G. & Emanuel, E. J. Protecting communities in research: current guidelines and limits of extrapolation. *Nature Genet.* **23,** 275–280 (1999).

41. Burgess, M. M. & Brunger, F. in *The Governance of Health Research involving Human Subjects* (ed. McDonald, M.) 117–151 (Law Commission of Canada, 2000).

42. Stephenson, P. in *A Cross-Cultural Dialogue on Health Care Ethics* (eds Coward, H. & Ratanakul, P.) 68–91. (Wilfrid Laurier Univ. Press, 1999).

43. Brunger, F. & Bassett, K. *Culture and Genetics in Socioethical Issues in Human Genetics* (ed. Knoppers, B. M.) 30–34 (Les Editions Yvon Blais Inc., Cowansville, Quebec, 1998).

44. Sclove, R. E. *Democracy and Technology* (The Guilford Press, New York, 1995).

45. Kerr, A, Cunningham-Burley, S. & Amos, A. The new genetics and health: Mobilizing lay expertise. *Public Understanding of Science* **7,** 41–60 (1998).

46. Kerr, A., Cunningham-Burley, S. & Amos, A. Drawing the line: an analysis of lay people's discussions about the new genetics. *Public Understanding of Science* **7,** 113–133 (1998).

KIMBERLY A. QUAID

Predictive Genetic Testing

Kimberly A. Quaid is Professor of Clinical Medical and Molecular Genetics, Clinical Psychiatry and Clinical Medicine, as well as a Core Faculty Member of the Center for Bioethics, in the Indiana University School of Medicine. She is also the Co-Director of the Master's Program in Genetic Counseling in the Department of Medical and Molecular Genetics and the Director of the Predictive Testing Program. Her recent publications have focused on risk assessment in people with a family history of Alzheimer's disease, the disclosure of information obtained through genetic testing, and the collection, storage, and research use of human biological materials.

. . . The ability to provide currently healthy individuals with DNA-based risk assessments for diseases that will manifest in the future, especially in the absence of effective treatment for those diseases, presents challenges for those at risk, health professionals, and society. This [essay] explores some of those challenges, concentrating on tests that can detect mutations associated with adult-onset disorders.

AVAILABLE TESTS

The beginning of the era of genetic prediction can be dated to 1983, when Huntington's disease (HD) became the first disease to be mapped to a previously unknown genetic location through the use of restriction enzymes that cleave deoxyribonucleic acid (DNA) at sequence-specific sites (Gusella et al.). Huntington's disease is a late-onset autosomal dominant neuropsychiatric disorder. The child of an affected parent has a 50 percent chance of inheriting the genetic mutation that causes HD. Disease onset usually occurs in the fourth decade of life and is marked by a movement disorder, alterations in mood, and cognitive decline. There is no treatment or cure.

Inherited variations of these DNA sequences, which also are known as restriction fragment length polymorphisms (RFLPs), can be used as genetic markers to map diseases on chromosomes and to trace the inheritance of diseases in families. The discovery of these markers represented a significant advance in HD research. Not only did the markers provide a possible clue for finding the HD gene and understanding the mechanism by which the gene causes brain cells to die, this discovery meant that predictive testing for some individuals at risk for HD was possible through the use of a technique called linkage. Linkage testing requires the collection and analysis of blood samples from affected and elderly unaffected relatives of the at-risk individual who asks for testing to trace the pattern of inheritance of the HD gene in a specific family. Linkage testing is labor-intensive and expensive and can result in erroneous conclusions caused by incorrectly attributed paternity, misdiagnosis, and the distance between the gene and the markers used for testing. The discovery of the HD gene in 1993 (Huntington's Disease Collaborative Research Group) made testing more accurate, less expensive, faster, and possible for every person at risk for HD.

Since that time new discoveries in molecular genetics have shifted the focus from relatively rare single-gene disorders such as HD to common adult-onset disorders that cause substantial morbidity and mortality. Examples include the identification of mutations in the BRCA1 and BRCA2 genes as causes of susceptibility to breast and ovarian cancers (Miki et al.; Wooster et al.), the discovery of multiple genetic mutations associated with the risk of colorectal cancer (Laken et al.; Lynch and Lynch), the reported association between the APOE e4 allele and late-onset Alzheimer disease (Strittmatter et al.), associations between factor V Leiden and thromboembolic disease (Hille et al.; Ridker et al.; Simioni et al.), and the identification of the HFE gene for hereditary hemochromatosis (Beutler et al.; Edwards et al.). In the second decade of the twenty-first century it has been predicted that genetic tests will be available for diabetes, asthma, dyslexia, attention deficit hyperactivity disorder, obesity, and schizophrenia. These discoveries point to the potential use of genetic tests for population screening in adult populations and an increasing role in public health for genetic testing.

EVALUATING NEW TESTS

The National Institutes of Health–Department of Education–Department of Energy (NIH–DOE) Task Force on Genetic Testing stated in 1998 that any proposed initiation of population-based genetic screening requires careful attention to the parameters of both analytical and clinical validity. For DNA-based tests analytical validity requires establishing that a test will be positive when a particular sequence is present (analytical sensitivity) and establishing the probability that that test will be negative when the sequence is absent (analytical specificity). Clinical validity involves establishing measures of clinical performance, including the probability that the test will be positive in people with the disease (clinical sensitivity), the probability that the test will be negative in people without the disease (clinical specificity), and the positive and negative predictive value (PV) of the test. The positive PV is the probability that people with a positive test eventually will get the disease. The negative PV is the probability that people with negative test results will not get the disease.

Two features of most of the genetic diseases discussed as candidates for population-wide screening also affect the clinical validity of any test designed to screen for those diseases. The first is heterogeneity, or the fact that the same genetic disease may result from the presence of any of several different variants of the same gene (an example would be cystic fibrosis, with over 900 mutations found in the CF gene) or of different genes (such as the genes for breast cancer BRCA1 and BRCA2). The second is penetrance, the probability that disease will appear when the disease-related genotype is present. Both heterogeneity and penetrance may differ in different populations, causing difficulties in the interpretation of test results. The final Report of the Task Force on Genetic Testing stated that "clinical use of a genetic test must be based on evidence that the gene being examined is associated with the disease in question, that the test itself has analytical and clinical validity, and that the test results will be useful to the people being tested" (Task Force on Genetic Testing).

From a public health perspective the value of implementing these tests on a population-wide basis will depend to a large extent on whether early treatment of diseases discovered through screening improves the prognosis (Burke et al.). That can be determined only through randomized clinical trials, an expensive process for the array of tests likely to be developed in the near future. However, experience with hormone replacement therapy (HRT) for healthy postmenopausal women in which HRT was found to cause more health problems than a placebo (Writing Group for the Women's Health Initiative Investigators) and a widely used knee surgery technique for osteoarthritis that was found to be ineffective (Moseley et al.) suggests that such trials may be a necessary component of any proposed large-scale screening effort.

Critics of this approach say that the prospective studies necessary to gather this type of information can take years. If widespread use of a test is withheld until the positive predictive value is determined fully and the risks and benefits of testing are known clearly, manufacturers and laboratories could be inhibited from developing tests, and consequently, people will be denied the benefits of being tested. Even without an effective treatment these benefits might include a reduction in uncertainty, the ability to avoid the conception or birth of a child carrying the disease-causing mutation, escape from frequent monitoring for signs of disease or prophylactic surgery, and freedom from concerns about employment or insurance discrimination.

In the absence of a consensus on the public health benefits of widespread screening, tests continue to be developed and in some cases marketed directly to physicians and consumers. For example, in June 2002 Myriad Genetics, based in Salt Lake City, Utah, announced that it would market genetic tests for familial cancers to the general public despite the fact that those tests were appropriate only for a very small percentage of the population. This practice has been the subject of some controversy (Holtzman and Watson), especially in cases in which predictive tests have become available without adequate assessment of their positive predictive value or benefits and risks. Without this information it is difficult for providers or consumers to make thoughtful and fully informed decisions about whether to offer or to use the tests. In another case a test based on the association of the APOE e4 allele with late-onset Alzheimer's disease was marketed directly to physicians just months after the first paper about that association was published. The genetics community decried this development, asserting that the actual interpretation of those associational data for any single individual could not be determined and that any test result based on it would be misleading if not worthless. The public outcry was so great that the test was withdrawn from the market in a matter of months.

THE TESTING PROCESS

Requests for testing can arise from a variety of circumstances and for a number of reasons. For example, although genetic test results can be used to guide individual healthcare and reproductive decisions, genetic testing often is sought to fulfill familial, domestic, or vocational responsibilities (Burgess and d'Agincourt-Canning). For this reason healthcare professionals must be adept at presenting and discussing the potential ramifications of testing in light of the at-risk individual's reason for requesting testing. Genetics practice also calls for pretest and posttest counseling and formal informed consent procedures to ensure that people deciding whether to undergo genetic testing are informed about the risks and potential harms, benefits, and limitations of the test, as well as alternatives and treatment options (National Advisory Council for Human Genome Research; Holtzman and Watson).

At the beginning of the twenty-first century, the volume of genetic testing was not great and the vast majority of testing occurred in genetic centers or in consultation with highly trained geneticists and genetics counselors. As the number of tests increases, the demand for testing may outstrip the capacity of genetics-trained individuals to respond. This scenario suggests that it is likely that more and more testing decisions will be made by physicians with little formal training or experience in genetics. Some question the ability of physicians to perform this function and continue to

recommend referrals to health professionals with specific training in genetics to ensure proper counseling, informed consent, and correct interpretation of test results (Giardello et al.).

A related issue is the fear that physicians will be more likely to take a directive approach to decisions about testing. This approach is antithetical to the concept of the value-neutral nondirective counseling that is a main tenet of all genetic counseling. Historically, this commitment to nondirective counseling can be understood as a moral stance designed to disassociate modern genetics from the eugenics movements of the first half of the twentieth century, which often advocated forced sterilization for individuals deemed to be genetically abnormal (Paul).

Philosophically, nondirective counseling also reflects the centrality of respect for autonomy (the right to self-determination or self-governance) in modern bioethics. Because decisions about genetic testing often involve reproduction and/or an individual's most personal desires and fears, the genetics community has adopted the view that the role of the genetics professional is to help an individual make a decision about testing that is consistent with that person's most strongly held values. Genetic counselors in training are taught specifically not to let their own opinions and attitudes influence the information that is given to people or recommendations for a course of action.

THE DECISION TO BE TESTED

The process of genetic testing can challenge traditional concepts of autonomy and privacy. The desire to be tested on the part of one individual can place pressure on other family members if their cooperation is required for the test to be done. In testing for familial cancers, for example, it is often necessary for a family member who is already affected to be tested first to identify the specific disease-associated mutation in the family. If the affected family member refuses to cooperate, that refusal can frustrate the desire of other family members to learn about their risk. This need to identify an index case also makes it difficult for an individual who wishes to be tested to keep that decision private.

Some authors have advanced the concept of *relational responsibility* as playing a key role in decisions regarding testing (Burgess and d'Agincourt-Canning). This ethical concept emphasizes that decisions about genetic testing occur within complex social relationships that are embedded in and shaped by notions of responsibility to specific others. Thus, although testing guidelines often emphasize that the decision whether to undergo genetic testing should be solely that of the individual for his or her own purposes and free from coercion by a spouse or another family member, research suggests that in reality people often make decisions about testing on the basis of the wishes and desires of others, primarily close family members, about whom they care deeply. Rosamund Rhodes has taken the notion of relational responsibility further, arguing that individuals have a moral duty to pursue genetic information about themselves, especially in cases in which that information has ramifications for others, such as spouses or children (Rhodes).

ORDERING TESTS

Once the decision has been made to pursue testing, tests for relatively common disorders usually are obtained from commercial laboratories (GeneTests). Blood is drawn and mailed to the laboratory, and the test results are conveyed back to the healthcare professional who ordered the test. That person then has the responsibility of conveying the results, usually in person, to the individual who has been tested. Genetic tests for rare disorders sometimes are available only from laboratories in academic medical centers that have a particular interest in the disease in question. Those laboratories may not have satisfied the ongoing quality and proficiency assessments required of commercial laboratories, thus raising questions about the reliability of testing obtained from this source.

SHARING GENETIC INFORMATION

When a test has been performed and a result has been obtained, other considerations come into play. Perhaps the most vexing is whether and when a person has a moral duty to share genetic information. Genetic test results for a specific individual also reveal information about that person's relatives. Parents and children share half their genes, as do siblings. If a woman learns that she carries a gene associated with breast cancer, does she have a responsibility to share that information with her sister? Many writers agree that that responsibility exists, with Dorothy Wertz and colleagues suggesting that at the level of the person genetic information, although individual, should "be shared among family members" as a form of shared familial property (Wertz et al.). Indeed, most people, once they are aware of the implications of genetic information for other family members, willingly share the information with those for whom it is especially relevant.

However, what if a woman with a breast cancer mutation does not wish to share that information? May her physician breach her confidentiality and warn her sister? Several groups have addressed this issue in depth (President's Commission for the Study of Ethical Problems in Medicine and Biomedical and Behavioral Research; Andrews et al.). Guidelines published by the American Society of Human Genetics Social Issues Subcommittee on Familial Disclosure in 1998 state that the legal and ethical norm of patient confidentiality should be respected, with breaches of confidentiality permitted only in exceptional cases. Those exceptions are (1) when attempts to encourage disclosure by the patient have failed, when the harm is highly likely to occur and is serious and foreseeable, when the at-risk relative or relatives are identifiable, and when the disease is preventable/treatable or medically accepted standards indicate that early monitoring will reduce the genetic risk and (2) when the harm that may result from failure to disclose outweighs the harm that may result from disclosure (Knoppers et al.). At least one author has argued that knowledge about the risk for conceiving a child with a deleterious gene does not pose the type of serious, imminent harm that generally would require disclosure (Andrews).

In regard to the issue of disclosure Ruth Macklin suggests the institution of a patient "Miranda" warning so that before genetic testing occurs, a patient would be warned about the circumstances that would result in the disclosure of genetic information to other family members regardless of the patient's intentions to disclose (Macklin).

Two court decisions appear to indicate an increasing trend toward disclosure. In *Pate v. Threkel*, Florida, 1995, a physician was held to a duty to warn patients of the familial implications of a genetic disease. In *Safer v. Estate of Pack*, New Jersey, 1996, the court held that a physician has a duty to warn relatives known to be at risk for a genetic disorder regardless of potential conflicts between the duty to warn and the obligations of confidentiality. The courts have not yet addressed a physician's obligation to disclose information concerning individuals whose occupations may place the lives of others in danger, such as pilots and air traffic controllers.

The completion of the Human Genome Project will result in a proliferation of genetic tests for a wide variety of disorders. Some public health advocates argue for a broader role for population-based testing, whereas critics believe that further work needs to be done to understand the value of testing on a widespread basis. Concerns exist about the ability of consumers and physicians to make informed decisions about whether to use genetic tests and are exacerbated by a growing trend on the part of commercial laboratories to market the tests directly to consumers. Once a test has been ordered and the results have been obtained, questions remain about the duties of both individuals and healthcare professionals regarding disclosure of test results.

BIBLIOGRAPHY

Andrews, Lori. 1997. "The Genetic Information Superhighway: Rules of the Road for Contacting Relatives and Recontacting Former Patients." In *Human DNA: Law and Policy: International and Comparative Perspectives*, ed. Bartha M. Knoppers and Claude Laberge. The Hague: Kluwer Law International.

Andrews, Lori; Fullerton, Jane; Holtman, Neil, et al. 1994. *Assessing Genetic Risks: Implications for Health and Social Policy*. Washington, D.C.: Institute of Medicine.

Beutler, Ernest; Felitti, Vincent; Gelbart, Terri, et al. 2000. "The Effect of HFE Genotypes on Measurements of Iron Overload in Patients Attending a Health Appraisal Clinic." *Annals of Internal Medicine* 133: 328–337.

Burgess, Michael M., and d'Agincourt-Canning, Lori. 2001. "Genetic Testing for Hereditary Disease: Attending to Relational Responsibility." *Journal of Clinical Ethics* 12: 361–372.

Burke, Wylie; Coughlin, Steven; Lee, Nancy, et al. 2001. "Application of Population Screening Principles to Genetic Screening for Adult-Onset Conditions." *Genetic Testing* 5: 201–211.

Edwards, Corwin Q.; Griffen, Linda M.; Ajioka, Richard S., et al. 1998. "Screening for Hemochromatosis: Phenotypes versus Genotypes." *Hematology* 35: 72–76.

Giardello, Francis M.; Brensinger, Jill D.; Petersen, Gloria M., et al. 1997. "The Use and Interpretation of Commercial APC Gene Testing for Familial Adenomatous Polyposis." *New England Journal of Medicine* 336(12): 823–827.

Gusella, James F.; Wexler, Nancy S.; Conneally, P. Michael, et al. 1983. "A Polymorphic DNA Marker Genetically Linked to Huntington Disease." *Nature* 306: 234–238.

Hille, Elysee T.; Westendorp, Rudi G.; Vandenbroucke, Jan P., et al. 1997. "Mortality and the Causes of Death in a Family with Factor V Leiden Mutation (Resistance to Activated Protein C)." *Blood* 89: 1963–1967.

Holtzman, Neil A., and Watson, Michael S., eds. 1998. *Promoting Safe and Effective Genetic Testing in the United States: Final Report of the Task Force on Genetic Testing, National Human Genome Research Institute.* Baltimore: Johns Hopkins University Press.

Huntington's Disease Collaborative Research Group. 1993. "A Novel Gene Containing a Trinucleotide Repeat That Is Expanded and Unstable on Huntington's Disease Chromosomes." *Cell* 72: 971–983.

Knoppers, Bartha M.; Strom, Charles; Clayton, Ellen Wright, et al., for the American Society of Human Genetics Social Issues Subcommittee on Familial Disclosure. 1998. "Professional Disclosure of Familial Genetic Information." *American Journal of Human Genetics* 62(2): 474–483.

Laken, Steven J.; Petersen, Gloria M.; Gruber, Stephen B., et al. 1997. "Familial Colorectal Cancer in Ashkenazim Due to a Hypermutable Tract in APC." *Nature Genetics* 17(1): 79–83.

Lynch, Henry T., and Lynch, Jane F. 1998. "Genetics of Colonic Cancer." *Digestion* 59: 481–492.

Macklin, Ruth. 1992. "Privacy Control of Genetic Information." In *Gene Mapping: Using Law and Ethics as Guides*, ed. George Annas and Sherman Elias. New York: Oxford University Press.

Miki, Yoshio; Swensen, Jeff; Shattuck-Eidens, Donna, et al. 1994. "A Strong Candidate for the Breast and Ovarian Cancer Susceptibility Gene BRCA1." *Science* 266: 66–71.

Moseley, J. Bruce; O'Malley, Kimberly; Petersen, Nancy J., et al. 2002. "A Controlled Trial of Arthroscopic Surgery for Osteoarthritis of the Knee." *New England Journal of Medicine* 27(2): 81–88.

National Advisory Council for Human Genome Research. 1994. "Statement on the Use of DNA Testing for Presymptomatic Identification of Cancer Risk." *Journal of the American Medical Association* 271: 785.

Paul, Diane. 1995. *Controlling Human Heredity, 1865—Present.* Atlantic Highlands, NJ: Humanities Press.

President's Commission for the Study of Ethical Problems in Medicine and Biomedical and Behavioral Research. 1983. *Screening and Counseling for Genetic Conditions: A Report on the Ethical, Social and Legal Implications of Genetic Screening, Counseling and Education Program.* Washington, D.C.: U.S. Government Printing Office.

Rhodes, Rosamond. 1998. "Genetic Links, Family Ties, and Social Bonds: Rights and Responsibilities in the Face of Genetic Knowledge." *Journal of Medicine and Philosophy* 23(1): 10–30.

Ridker, Paul M.; Glynn, Robert J.; Miletich, Joseph P., et al. 1997. "Age-Specific Incidence Rates of Venous Thromboembolism among Heterozygous Carriers of Factor V Leiden Mutation." *Annals of Internal Medicine* 126: 528–531.

Simioni, Paolo; Prandoni, Paolo; Lensing, Anthonie W., et al. 1997. "The Risk of Recurrent Venous Thromboembolism in Patients with an ARG^{506} →Gln Mutation in the Gene for Factor V (Factor V Leiden)." *New England Journal of Medicine* 336: 399–403.

Strittmatter, Warren J.; Saunders, Ann M.; Schmechel, Donald E., et al. 1993. "Apolipoprotein E: High-Avidity Binding to B-Amyloid and Increased Frequency of Type 4 Allele in Late-Onset Familial Alzheimer's Disease." *Proceedings of the National Academy of Science of the United States of America* 90: 1977–1981.

Wertz, Dorothy; Fletcher, John; and Berg, Kare. 1995. *Guidelines on Ethical Issues in Medical Genetics and the Provision of Genetic Services.* Geneva: World Health Organization.

Wooster, Richard; Neuhausen, Susan L.; Mangion, Jonathan, et al. 1994. "Localization of a Breast Cancer Susceptibility Gene, BRCA2, to Chromosome 13q12–13." *Science* 265: 2088–2090.

Writing Group for the Women's Health Initiative Investigators. 2002. "Risks and Benefits of Estrogen Plus Progestin in Healthy Postmenopausal Women: Principal Results from the Women's Health Initiative Randomized Controlled Trial." *Journal of the American Medical Association* 288(3): 321–333.

INTERNET RESOURCES

GeneTests. 2003. Available from <http://www.genetests.org>.

Task Force on Genetic Testing. 1998. Available from <http://www.hopkinsmedicine.org/tfgtelsi/>.

ELLEN WRIGHT CLAYTON

Newborn Genetic Screening

Ellen Wright Clayton is Professor of Pediatrics and Law; Professor of Law; Rosalind E. Franklin Professor of Genetics and Health Policy; and Director of the Genetics Health Policy Center at Vanderbilt University in Nashville. She holds degrees in both medicine and law. Her current research interests include newborn screening, genetic testing for children and adults, and guidelines to promote inclusion of children in clinical trials. Professor Clayton's publications have focused on genetics and public health, possible mass screening programs for hereditary hemochromatosis, and arguments for and against the disclosure of genetic information to the relatives of a person who has a positive genetic test.

Throughout the United States, and in many other countries around the world, newborns are tested within the first few days to weeks of life for a varying array of metabolic disorders. Until recently, newborns were typically screened for only a handful of disorders, but recent technological advances and new knowledge about genetics have led to pressure for greatly expanded screening. At first glance, newborn screening might seem unremarkable. Much of medical practice is devoted to the early detection of disease to allow the delivery of effective interventions, and new developments are often received enthusiastically. But newborn screening programs have several features that individually and collectively pose particular ethical challenges.

All U.S. states require that newborns be screened, either prior to discharge or, if delivered outside a healthcare facility, within the first two to three days of life (AAP). Maryland, Wyoming, and, for some but not all tests, Georgia and Massachusetts require that parents give their permission for screening, though many states do permit parents to refuse screening (generally for religious reasons). This option may be difficult to exercise in practice, however, since few states require that parents even be told that screening is occurring, much less

that they have a right to refuse. Thus, one of the more remarkable aspects of newborn screening is that parents are not even nominally part of the decision-making process for their new infants (AAP; Paul; Clayton).

Those who argue against either notifying parents or seeking their permission reason that all children should be screened, and it would thus be a waste of money and effort to talk with parents (Cunningham). Proponents of mandatory screening argue that most parents would agree to screening, but that they might be unduly worried if they knew about the test (Cunningham). They assert further that parents who refuse would be harming their own children. These arguments raise two separate issues: (1) the justifiability of excluding parents, and (2) the characteristics of newborn screening programs (and the disorders they seek).

THE ROLE OF PARENTS

. . . In general, parents are presumed to have a role to play in [healthcare decisions for their infants; such decisions] can be overridden only to avert serious harm. But clinicians cannot decide not to talk with parents simply because they think it would take too much time, would make parents worry, or that it would be a waste of effort because parents usually agree to the clinician's recommendations anyway.

These principles suggest to the advocates of seeking parental permission that parents cannot justifiably be denied the opportunity to be informed about and participate in decisions about newborn screening. Most parents agree to screening, and informed parents are more likely to ensure that screening is performed, as well as to obtain any follow-up that may be required (Andrews). Even if parents refuse screening, it is unlikely that their children will come to harm, for the disorders sought in these programs are very rare.

NEWBORN SCREENING PROGRAMS

Universal newborn screening was first adopted for phenylketonuria (PKU), an inherited metabolic disorder that causes severe mental retardation unless treatment is started in the first few weeks of life (NAS). Children with this disease have few symptoms early on, but the metabolic abnormality can be detected in the first few days of life by testing either the urine or the blood. Thus, several factors converged to support the idea of early detection:

- The disease has a devastating outcome
- Treatment is highly effective in averting this outcome, but only if it is started early
- Affected children cannot be detected on the basis of symptoms in time to start effective treatment
- Screening reliably detects most affected children (NAS)

When clinicians were slow to adopt these tests in their clinical practice, in part because they were uncertain about the efficacy of treatment, advocates went to their legislators to get them to enact laws requiring PKU screening (AAP; Clayton; NAS).

In the two decades that followed the enactment of these initial laws, the diseases that were added to the testing panels generally had similar characteristics. Congenital hypothyroidism requires early treatment to prevent severe retardation, and it frequently is not detected clinically during the newborn period. The risk of overwhelming bacterial infection faced by young children with sickle-cell disease can be greatly reduced by giving prophylactic penicillin. Children with galactosemia are often critically ill by the time the condition is detected on the basis of their symptoms, an outcome that can be averted by using a formula that does not contain lactose (milk sugar). Typically, programs were expanded to these and other disorders in response to a combination of mounting medical evidence and political pressure by families and clinicians.

Pressure to expand the number of disorders being screened for expanded dramatically during the 1990s,

largely as a result of the development of tandem mass spectrometry ("MS/MS") (AAP). This technology permits the detection of a large number of metabolic abnormalities on a single specimen of blood. Unfortunately, no treatment exists for many of the disorders detectable by MS/MS, which raises issues of whether to test for these abnormalities, and of what to tell families whose children may have one of the untreatable diseases.

Until recently, most state statutes focused on identifying affected children. Most state programs tried to ensure that these children were directed to appropriate sources of care, but few actually ensured the availability of needed medications and diets. Since children do not have universal access to healthcare, some children received no treatment, and some parents suffered job lock. Increasingly, states, practitioners, and clinicians have begun to work together to develop systems to ensure the delivery of care for these children (AAP), a laudable goal which is threatened by the increasing pressure to privatize newborn screening.

THE PROBLEM OF FALSE POSITIVES

Screening tests are assessed according to their sensitivity (the percentage of affected individuals detected) and their specificity (the percentage of unaffected individuals who are correctly excluded from further testing). The actual number of people who receive inaccurate initial screening results depends in large part on the frequency of the disease in the population. The more common the disease, the more likely it is that a person who receives a positive (abnormal) test result will actually be affected. (The rhetoric of screening and testing is confusing in that "positive" test results almost always mean that something is wrong.) As the disease becomes less frequent, the proportion of initial results that turn out to be "false positives" increases. Suppose a disease has an incidence of 1 in 10,000 and a population of 100,000 people is tested with a screening test that has a sensitivity of 90 percent (so that 9 out of 10 affected people will test positive) and a specificity of 99 percent (so that 99 out of 100 unaffected people will test negative). The results overall would be as follows:

	Test positive	Test negative
Affected	9 "true positive"	1 "false negative"
Unaffected	999 "false positive"	98,991 "true negative"

Put another way, for every person who was truly affected (and tested positive), 100 people who did not have the disease would also (falsely) test positive. In addition, nine people who did have the disease would test negative, While most people who get false positive test results are ultimately reassured by further testing, some may continue to be worried. Affected children who are missed in these programs may face substantial delays in diagnosis if clinicians reason that the child could not have the disorder because it would have been identified in the newborn period.

The disorders sought in newborn screening programs typically are quite rare, usually having frequencies in the 1-in-5,000 to 1-in-15,000 range. Some of the diseases that are being added to newborn screening panels are as rare as 1 in 100,000. Without denying the benefits that can come to affected children who are detected in these programs, it is important to acknowledge the possible harms that may befall the many children who inevitably receive falsely abnormal results. The newborn period is a particularly vulnerable time. Parents are just beginning to know and bond with their infants. Bad news, even if incorrect, can interfere with the formation of this central relationship and lead parents to view their new infants as medically fragile. One study revealed that almost 10 percent of parents whose infants received initial false-positive screening results for cystic fibrosis were still worried a year later that their children were affected or otherwise sickly.

Thus, the trend has been to increase the disorders for which newborns are screened, including some for which the benefits of early invention are unclear or may be absent, all the while causing a growing number of infants to receive false-positive test results, which will cause some of them harm.

THE IMPLICATIONS OF THESE DISORDERS

Most of the disorders sought by newborn screening are inherited, usually as autosomal recessive disorders. If parents have a child with one of these diseases, they have a one in four chance in each subsequent pregnancy of having another affected child. Children with such a disease can have affected children themselves if they have children with partners who have one or two copies of the same mutated gene. Some screening protocols, such as those for sickle-cell disease and cystic fibrosis, also detect carriers (children who have a single copy of a mutated gene).

While these children do not have the disease, the presence of a mutated gene signals an increased risk of having a truly affected child, both for them and for their parents. From an ethical perspective, it seems obvious that parents should be told about all of these implications, but this sort of communication often does not occur.

One of the more difficult ethical questions is whether parents should be encouraged to alter their future reproductive plans in order to decrease the costs of disease to society. The general consensus is that decisions about having children are to be made by the prospective parents according to their own values, and that genetic counseling is to be nondirective (Andrews, Fullerton, Holtzman, et al.).

Another complex issue is whether decreasing the number of affected children born, whether as a result of state intervention or even of independent decisions by prospective parents, should be seen as an additional goal or benefit of newborn screening. Some governmental officials have made this argument, even calculating the decreased healthcare expenditures that follow from the birth of fewer affected children in their efforts to calculate the cost efficacy of newborn screening (Cunningham). Others, including advocates of disability rights and opponents of prenatal diagnosis, find these arguments distasteful and potentially coercive (Asch).

UNINTENDED CONSEQUENCES

Untreated women with PKU are profoundly retarded and rarely have children. As a result of the successful implementation of newborn screening and treatment for PKU, however, many affected females are now in their reproductive years, have intelligence in the normal range, and can and do become pregnant. Unless these women adhere to the highly restrictive and burdensome PKU diet prior to conception and throughout their pregnancy, their children will be born with severe brain injury.

These children typically do not have PKU themselves because their fathers are not likely to be carriers since those mutations are not common. The injuries they suffer during pregnancy result instead from the high levels of phenylalanine that exist in their mothers' blood when they eat a normal diet, levels which are particularly toxic to the developing brain. The irony then is that improving the lives of women with PKU creates a high level of risk to the children they may bear. Clearly, these women need to be educated about the importance of adhering to the proper diet prior to and during pregnancy. The ethical dilemma is whether it is ever appropriate, and if so, how, to bring pressure to bear to lead these women to either follow this onerous diet or avoid childbearing altogether (Robertson and Schulman).

NEWBORN SCREENING SAMPLES AS DNA DATABANKS

Birth is the only time of life when the government collects blood from virtually everyone. Some states discard these samples within a few months after birth, while others retain them indefinitely. In the past it was not possible to extract much information from these samples because most metabolites deteriorate quickly, but recent advances, particularly in DNA testing, have created new possibilities. Newborn samples can be used for DNA identification, for further investigation when a child subsequently becomes sick, or for research, for which they may be particularly attractive as a true population sample. However, all these uses are secondary to the purpose for which they were initially collected—to detect children with diseases that urgently require treatment.

The appropriateness of using these samples for these other purposes raises many of the questions that attend any use of stored tissue samples for research, including: (1) whether it is necessary to ask the donor (or in this case the parent) for permission; (2) when, if ever, it is appropriate to inform individuals of their personal results; and (3) what sort of review needs to occur before these samples can be used. The fact that these samples are typically obtained without parental knowledge or permission makes these issues that much more urgent, particularly in a society that is so deeply concerned about issues of genetic privacy. It would be rather ironic if a system of universal DNA identification were developed as a by-product of newborn screening rather than as a result of an explicit policy decision.

CONCLUSION

The particular ethical issues posed by newborn screening arise because these programs are required and run by the government, typically do not involve parents in decision making, often implicate reproductive decision making, and can provide samples for a growing number of secondary uses. These unique factors suggest that parents should have a greater role to play in these programs, and that these programs should remain narrowly focused on detecting diseases for which treatment is urgently needed to avert serious sequelae.

BIBLIOGRAPHY

American Academy of Pediatrics (AAP); Newborn Screening Task Force. 2000. "Serving the Family From Birth to the Medical Home, Newborn Screening: A Blueprint for the Future, A Call for a National Agenda on State Newborn Screening Programs." *Pediatrics* 106 (suppl.): 383–427.

Andrews, Lori B. 1985. "New Legal Approaches to Newborn Screening and the Rationale behind the Recommendations for Quality Assurance in Newborn Screening." In *Legal Liability and Quality Assurance in Newborn Screening*, ed. Lori B. Andrews. Chicago: American Bar Foundation.

Andrews Lori B.; Fullerton, Jane E.; Holtzman, Neil A., et al., eds. 1994. *Assessing Genetic Risks: Implications for Health and Science Policy*. Washington, D.C.: National Academy Press.

Asch, A. 1989. "Reproductive Technology and Disability." In *Reproductive Laws for the 1990s*, ed. S. Cohen and N. Taub. Clifton, NJ: Humana Press.

Clayton, Ellen W. 1992. "Screening and Treatment of Newborns." *Houston Law Review* 29(1): 85–148.

Cunningham, George. 1990. "Balancing the Individual's Rights to Privacy against the Need for Information to Protect and Advance Public Health," In *Genetic Screening: From Newborns to DNA Typing*, ed. Bartha M. Knoppers and Claude M. Laberge. Amsterdam: Excerpta Medica.

Faden, Ruth; Chwalow, A. J.; Holtzman, Neil A.; et al. 1982. "A Survey to Evaluate Parental Consent as Public Policy for Neonatal Screening." *American Journal of Public Health* 72: 1347–52.

Hannon, W. Harry, and Grosse, Scott D. 2001. "Using Tandem Mass Spectrometry for Metabolic Disease Screening Among Newborns," *Morbidity and Mortality Weekly Report* 50(RR03): 1–22.

National Research Council, Committee for the Study of Inborn Errors of Metabolism. 1975. *Genetic Screening: Programs, Principles, and Research*. (NAS) Washington, D.C.: National Academy Press.

"Newborn Screening for Sickle Cell Disease and Other Hemoglobinopathies." 1989. *Pediatrics* 83(5/2): 813–914.

Paul, D. 1999. "Contesting Consent: The Challenge to Compulsory Neonatal Screening for PKU." *Perspectives in Biology and Medicine* 42: 207–219.

Robertson, J. A., and Schulman, J. D. 1987. "Pregnancy and Prenatal Harm to Offspring: The Case of Mothers with PKU." *Hastings Center Report* 17(4): 23–33.

Tluczek A.; Mischler, E. H.; Farrell, P. M.; et al. (1992). "Parents' Knowledge of Neonatal Screening and Response to False-Positive Cystic Fibrosis Testing." *Journal of Developmental Behavioral Pediatrics*. 13(3): 181–186.

Waisbren S. E., Hanley, W; and Levy, H. L.; et al. 2000. "Outcome at Age 4 Years in Offspring of Women with Maternal Phenylketonuria: the Maternal PKU Collaborative Study." *Journal of the American Medical Association* 283(6): 756–762.

THEODORE FRIEDMANN

Principles for Human Gene Therapy Studies

Theodore Friedmann is Professor of Pediatrics and Whitehill Professor of Biomedical Ethics at the University of California, San Diego (UCSD) and Director of the UCSD Program in Human Gene Therapy. He was one of the first to publish on the need for gene therapy for human disease. He formerly served as Chair of the NIH Recombinant DNA Advisory Committee. In June 2006 he was elected President of the American Society of Gene Therapy.

The human gene therapy community finds itself struggling with technical and policy problems arising from several recently publicized adverse events in human gene therapy studies. The current discussion was catalyzed by the tragic death of Jesse Gelsinger, an 18-year-old patient with ornithine transcarbamylase (OTC) deficiency who died, apparently as a direct result of the experimental gene therapy studies being carried out by investigators at the University of Pennsylvania in Philadelphia and the National Children's Medical Center in Washington, DC.

Preliminary public review of the events leading to the tragedy in the Philadelphia OTC study was presented at a recent public meeting of the Recombinant DNA Advisory Committee (RAC) of the Office of Biotechnology Activities (OBA) of the National Institutes of Health. An ongoing Food and Drug Administration (FDA) investigation has already resulted in a compulsory hold of indefinite duration being placed on gene therapy studies at the Institute for Human Gene Therapy at the University of Pennsylvania and a voluntary hold on at least one other academic institution until possible deficiencies can be corrected. One commercially sponsored study was placed on temporary hold but now has been resumed. Additional inquiries by the involved universities, the Advisory Committee to the Director of the NIH, the United States Senate, and the executive branch are under way.

These events suggest that the gene therapy community has not fully succeeded in developing mechanisms to ensure the highest possible quality of clinical research. The intention of this discussion is to derive lessons from the preliminary information available and to reexamine the principles that constitute the foundation of clinical research in gene therapy.

HUMAN EXPERIMENTATION REQUIRES CAREFUL PATIENT SELECTION AND PROTECTION

Human disease and therapy are, eventually, best studied in human subjects. Codes of medical ethics recognize the importance of appropriate human studies, as long as they rest on strong basic and preclinical science and voluntary informed consent by patients. To be truly "informed," a patient's consent must be based on current and complete information of the procedures and their potential risks and benefits.

The patient population with potentially the most to gain in the Philadelphia OTC study, patients with the neonatal lethal form of the disease, were justifiably included in the initial study design. However, investigators were advised by their institutional review board (IRB) and medical ethics consultants that phase I experiments (in which dose and safety are being tested) would be ethically unacceptable in these infants because of the danger of implying a potential benefit to desperate parents. The next-best study population was used instead—less severely affected older patients from whom informed consent and meaningful data might be more readily obtained. There is debate in the medical ethics community whether this decision to exclude desperately ill newborns was appropriate. The quandary of patient selection in this case underscores this general dilemma in medical ethics and the unrealistic degree to which we have come to expect therapeutic results in phase I studies.

HUMAN EXPERIMENTATION INVOLVES RISKS

Human experimental studies, genetic or otherwise, are "experimental" precisely because the results are not known beforehand. Preclinical studies sometimes indicate adverse outcomes that can be readily avoided. In other instances, adverse results are found, only in retrospect, to have been foreshadowed by clues during early testing that investigators were neither alert nor wise enough to appreciate. In still other studies, adverse outcomes could not have been predicted in animals and limited human trials. Preclinical studies did not predict the discovery that the diet medication fen-phen is associated with potentially life-threatening cardiac valvular damage. Likewise, the recent withdrawal from the market by the FDA of a rotavirus vaccine came only after large-scale human experience with the vaccine.

ADVERSE RESULTS DO NOT INVALIDATE THE RATIONALE OF GENE THERAPY

Apparent "failures" in early phaseI/II or even phase III studies do not necessarily indicate a therapeutic wild-goose chase. Because gene therapy is highly experimental and many patients are desperately ill, serious adverse events and even deaths will occur. It is vital to understand the reasons for unexpected results or clinical failures to allow the development of corrected procedures and improved experimental methods. For example, problems with polio vaccines due to persistence of live disease-causing poliovirus in incompletely inactivated preparations and the presence of SV40 in the vaccine were identified early, corrected, and used to develop improved programs.

The development of gene therapy is similar to vaccine and drug development. Drug development is difficult and expensive, and gene therapy will not be simpler. The pharmaceutical industry, more mature and experienced than the gene therapy community, devotes enormous research and financial resources to studies of the biodistribution, pharmacological properties, stability, and metabolic properties of a potential new drug, as well as the physiological, immunological, and teratogenic effects on the host. Despite such care, because of the enormous complexity of human physiology and disease, and because even the most extensive animal data do not always faithfully predict responses in humans, adverse clinical responses have occurred and will again. The same understanding of pharmacokinetics and mechanisms has not been available for gene therapy trials. Some clinical applications have simply outstripped scientific understanding of the disease model or the properties of the vectors, resembling an army too far ahead of its supply lines. Despite clinical urgency, there is a need to develop a similar degree of rigor for gene transfer agents as for small molecule therapeutics or viral vaccines.

Despite the caveats regarding the need for better knowledge, the search for optimum methods should not paralyze attempts to use available tools to conduct clinical research studies. To make progress, one must accept the limitations of knowledge and simultaneously use available information to ease suffering and to continue research into improvements in technology.

INFORMED CONSENT IS CRUCIAL TO PATIENT PROTECTION

The single most important mechanism for ensuring patient protection from inherent risks of clinical experiments, unrealistic expectations, and potential conflicts of interest of the investigator is accurate and full disclosure of potential risks and benefits and a well-executed informed consent process. For gene therapy studies, the FDA and RAC review the adequacy of locally approved informed consent procedures during the protocol approval process. The FDA concluded that there were deficiencies in the informed consent process in the OTC study that resulted in incomplete disclosure of all potential risks to the subjects or their families. Additional troublesome public revelations of potential lapses in quality control and in patient protection have been made for other gene therapy studies.

Exaggerated expectations and potential conflicts of interest of investigators pose additional problems to the informed consent process. In 1995, an NIH advisory committee chaired by Stuart Orkin and Arno Motulsky criticized the gene therapy community for its overly optimistic public portrayal of gene therapy experiments and for unsubstantiated claims for efficacy.[1] There is still too ready a tendency by some in the gene therapy community to exaggerate potential benefits at the expense of full disclosure of potential risks. If that tendency is the result of optimism, it is at least unfortunate and should be guarded against. If it was determined that risks were intentionally omitted or misstated, appropriate sanctions by the gene therapy community and oversight bodies should be applied.

DEALING WITH FINANCIAL CONFLICT OF INTEREST

The issue of conflicts of interest is magnified by the very large role that biotechnology and pharmaceutical industries have come to play in gene therapy. In many cases, academic investigators have had to forge commercial collaborations to implement clinical studies because of the high costs (production and testing of a gene vector usually exceeds several hundred thousand dollars). Although commercial interactions have facilitated clinical studies, they have also introduced corporate financial interests and investigator economic conflicts. Therefore, at minimum, involved investigators should disclose direct commercial ties in the informed consent process. Those investigators with direct financial interest in the study outcome should recuse themselves from patient selection, the informed consent process, and study direction.

IMPROVEMENTS ARE NEEDED IN REVIEW AND REGULATION

During the early phase of clinical studies of human gene transfer, the RAC played a major role by providing an avenue for public evaluation of the scientific basis and patient protection aspects of a proposed study. The FDA shared responsibility for oversight of gene therapy studies through its traditional regulatory function of ensuring safety and efficacy. In 1997, in response to an advisory committee report to the NIH director, the FDA assumed the principal regulatory and oversight responsibility for gene therapy proposals, and the RAC was given the function of catalyzing public awareness and understanding of the issues of gene therapy. It also retained a secondary responsibility to determine whether studies submitted to the FDA utilized technological concepts and tools so novel that they required further public review.

An important difference between the RAC and FDA processes is that the RAC reviews of proposals and adverse-event reporting are public and open, whereas FDA is required by statute to carry out these functions privately and without provision for public disclosure. In a field as immature and filled with public interest and concern as gene therapy, more, rather than less, public review seems desirable. A cohesive mechanism must be developed in which primary regulatory control stays with the appropriate regulatory agency—the FDA—but which more effectively takes advantage of the advisory role of the RAC or a RAC-like body and also uses the RAC as a conduit for public discussion and disclosure before protocol approval. It is encouraging that discussions are under way between the RAC, FDA, and NIH through the Advisory Committee to the NIH director on potential mechanisms to provide this kind of process.

GENE THERAPY TRIALS REQUIRE IMPROVED MONITORING

For the field to progress, investigators must have more ready access to the clinical experience in other studies, and it is therefore particularly encouraging that the OBA has reaffirmed its intention to develop a gene therapy database that will make the occurrence and nature of adverse events available online to other gene therapy investigators.[2] Such a database can only succeed if investigators report their adverse events, and disclosure is useful only if mechanisms exist to collate, evaluate, and promulgate such information.

The existence of widely different reporting requirements has contributed to uncertainty and, quite probably, to deficiencies in reporting. The FDA requires that serious, unexpected, or related events be reported to the agency within 7 days if there is a patient death, or within 15 days for other serious adverse events. All other events are to be included in annual reports.[3] The words "serious," "unexpected," and "related" allow room for interpretation by investigators and study sponsors; the NIH requirements are less flexible. It is therefore possible, as the oversight agencies and several investigators have recently discovered, to be in compliance with the FDA requirements but not with the NIH guidelines. The NIH has recently proposed strengthening its reporting requirements through amendments of the NIH guidelines in which the definition of adverse events is clarified, and there is notification that such reports may not contain any confidential trade secrets or commercial and financial information.[4] The NIH has also notified all federally supported institutions to review their policies and procedures to ensure that they are in compliance with reporting requirements.[5] The FDA has stated that it will notify the RAC of the receipt of all adverse events in a gene therapy study.[6]

CONCLUSIONS

Scientific and policy problems in gene therapy studies, together with the explosive growth of clinical studies, challenge the academic gene therapy community, commercial biotechnology and pharmaceutical firms, regulatory agencies, and professional societies such as the American Society of Human Gene Therapy to work together to improve current practices and infrastructures. Announcements of new initiatives for FDA and NIH that would require earlier review of researcher's plans for monitoring safety and quarterly meetings to promote communication are encouraging developments. Further critical steps toward that goal would include RAC determination of the need for full public evaluation of protocols before investigational new drug (IND) assignment by FDA and IRB approval; the development of a single, uniform mechanism for reporting adverse events to the RAC, FDA, and other relevant agencies; establishment by OBA of its proposed public database of all adverse events; and nonparticipation of investigators with financial interests in study outcomes in patient selection, the informed consent process, and direct management of clinical studies. While there is need for improvements,

there is also much to celebrate—major technical advances that promise imminent proof that the lives of patients can eventually be made better by gene therapy.

NOTES

1. S. Orkin and A. Motulsky, www.nih.gov/news/panelrep.html, 7 December 1995.

2. Testimony of A. Patterson, www4.od.nih.gov/oba/patterson 2-00.pdf, 2 February 2000.

3. FDA Manual of Regulatory Standard Operating Procedures and Policies, www.fda.gov/cber/regsopp/91101.htm; www.fda.gov/cber/regsopp/91102.htm; and www.fda.gov/cber/ind/21cfr312.pdf.

4. Minutes of RAC meeting, 5 September 1999, www4.od.nih.gov/oba/9%2D99pro.htm.

5. Letter from A. Patterson to federally funded institutions, 22 November 1999.

6. Letter from K. Zoon to Investigational New Drug Sponsors and Principal Investigators, www.fda.gov/cber/ltr/gt110599.htm, 5 November 1999.

JULIAN SAVULESCU

Harm, Ethics Committees and the Gene Therapy Death

Julian Savulescu is Uehiro Professor of Practical Ethics at the University of Oxford, Fellow of St. Cross College, Oxford, and Director of the Oxford Uehiro Centre for Practical Ethics. He is also Head of the Melbourne-Oxford Stem Cell Collaboration, which is devoted to examining the ethical implications of cloning and embryonic stem cell research. Professor Savulescu edits the *Journal of Medical Ethics*. His research interests include the ethics of genetics, especially predictive genetic testing, preimplantation genetic diagnosis, prenatal testing, behavioral genetics, genetic enhancement, and gene therapy.

The recent tragic and widely publicised death of Jesse Gelsinger in a gene therapy trial has many important lessons for those engaged in the ethical review of research. One of the most important lessons is that ethics committees can give too much weight to ensur-

ing informed consent and not enough attention to minimising the harm associated with participation in research. The first responsibility of ethics committees should be to ensure that the expected harm associated with participation is reasonable.

Jesse was an 18-year-old man with a mild form of ornithine transcarbamylase (OTC) deficiency, a disorder of nitrogen metabolism. His form of the disease could be controlled by diet and drug treatment. On September 13 1999 a team of researchers led by James

From the *Journal of Medical Ethics* 27 (2001), 148–50. Copyright © 2001. Reprinted with permission from the BMJ Publishing Group.

Wilson at the University of Pennsylvania's Institute for Human Gene Therapy (IHGT) injected 3.8×10^{13} adenovirus vector particles containing a gene to correct the genetic defect. He was the eighteenth and final patient in the trial. The virus particles were injected directly into the liver. He received the largest number of virus particles in a gene therapy trial.[1] Four days later he was dead from what was probably an immune reaction to the virus vector. This was the first death directly attributed to gene therapy. It resulted in worldwide publicity, an independent investigation, the Federal Drug Administration (FDA) suspending all trials at the IHGT, an FDA, and a senate subcommittee investigation.

At a special public meeting at the National Institutes of Health (NIH) in December 1999, James Wilson, also the director of the IHGT, said they still did not understand fully what had gone wrong.[2] Even though a massive dose had been used, only 1% of transferred genes reached the target cells. (None of the patients in the trial showed significant gene expression. Art Caplan, the University of Pennsylvania's outspoken bioethicist, is reported to have said: "if you cured anyone from a Phase 1 trial, it would be a miracle" and "there was never a chance that anyone would benefit from these experiments."[3]) Wilson claimed the death was the result of an anomalous response. Jesse's bone marrow had very low levels of red blood cell precursors, which probably predated the experiment. This may have reflected another genetic defect or a parvovirus infection. While most gene therapists at the meeting agreed that Jesse's response was unusual, some claimed it was foreseeable, given the ability of adenovirus to elicit an immune response and the high dose employed.[2]

The death also resulted in a wrongful death lawsuit which alleged[3]:

- that members of the IHGT team and others were careless, negligent and reckless in failing to adequately evaluate Jesse's condition and eligibility. Jesse had an ammonia level 30%–60% higher than the eligibility criterion stated in the protocol approved by the FDA;
- that the adenovirus vector was unreasonably dangerous;
- that storage of the vector for 25 months led researchers to underestimate its potency;
- that a conflict of interest existed. Researchers and members of the University of Pennsylvania held patents covering several aspects of the technology employed. Wilson and colleagues also hold equity holdings in Genovo, the private sector biotechnology collaborator in the project. These conflicts of interest were alleged to have not been disclosed to the participant;
- that researchers failed to notify the FDA of adverse events in prior patients and animals.

The lawsuit also named Art Caplan, director of the University of Pennsylvania's Bioethics Center. It was also suggested but not explicitly alleged that Caplan had a conflict of interest because his centre was funded by Wilson's department. The complaint also drew attention to Caplan's intervention to persuade Wilson and others to use older participants who could consent (but who had a mild form of the disease) rather than newborns who could not consent (but had an otherwise lethal form of the disease).[3]

Other concerns related to this trial have included[4]:

- Researchers continued to increase the dose despite signs of toxicity in other patients;
- Volunteers were recruited by direct appeal on a patient advocacy website which described "very low doses" and "promising results." Such appeals had been rejected by federal officials as being coercive.
- The original consent reviewed publicly by the NIH mentioned that monkeys had died from the treatment but the final version did not mention that.
- The NIH's Recombinant DNA Advisory Committee (RAC) discussed the potential for lethal liver inflammation related to this experiment in December 1995, after reviewing toxicity results in rhesus monkeys and the death of one monkey from an extremely high dose of a first-generation vector. They recommended administration through a peripheral vein rather than directly into the liver. Food and Drug Administration regulators were concerned about infection of reproductive cells (germ line modification) and made researchers go back to direct liver injection.[1]

In February 2000, at a separate hearing, Paul Geisinger, Jesse's father, asserted:

1. that his son had not been told important preclinical evidence of toxicity (including the deaths of monkeys);
2. that his son was led to believe that his participation would be clinically beneficial, despite this being a Phase 1 trial where no benefit was envisaged.[5]

James Wilson while acting as director of the IHGT, was also involved in several clinical trials and basic research. Judith Rodin, the University of Pennsylvania's president and William Danceforth, the lead author of an independent report into Jesse's death, said that Wilson was "overloaded."[6] The IHGT has been downsized and no longer conducts clinical trials. The Department of Health and Human Services has said it intends to introduce laws which will fine researchers up to $250,000 and instructions up to one million dollars for failing to meet new stricter standards.[6]

INTERESTING INSIGHTS

This experiment yields many interesting insights into the problems related to ethics review of research in general. But there is perhaps one lesson which is more important than all the others. Research ethics review is concerned primarily with two goals: ensuring that the expected harm involved in participation is reasonable and that participants give valid consent. The requirement to give valid consent has led many in the research ethics community to suggest that non-therapeutic research on incompetent patients is unethical. This trial illustrates *par excellence* the increasing and mistaken tendency of ethics committees to give too much weight to consent and to fail to give sufficient attention to protecting participants from harm.

One simple justification for conducting this trial in adults with the mild form of the disease rather than severely affected newborns goes like this. "There are serious risks including a risk of death associated with participation in this trial. Since the risks are significant, it is better that the trial be conducted on humans who consent to those risks rather than on those who cannot consent."

However, it is important to distinguish between the *chance* of a bad outcome occurring and *expected harm*. Expected harm is the probability of a harm occurring multiplied by the magnitude of that harm. Being harmed by an intervention is being made worse off than one would otherwise have been if that intervention had not been performed.

Consider an illustration using a quality adjusted life year (QALY) approach. Let's assume for simplicity's sake that the only harm in this experiment was death from the virus vector. Let's assign a value of 1 to perfect health and 0 to death. Jesse's existing quality of life was less than perfect, but still acceptable. Let's say it was 0.8. Assume that he would have lived another 50 years. Assume that the risk of the gene therapy killing him was small—1/10,000 (this is a conservative estimate: Jesse's death was the first death in nearly 400 gene therapy trials involving over 4000 patients).[7] That means that the expected harm of Jesse participating was $0.8 \times 50/10,000 = 40/10,000 = 0.004$ quality adjusted life year. This is a very small expected harm.

Now compare this to the expected harm that severely affected newborns would experience. Imagine that a newborn boy, who is already very likely to die of his disease, dies as a result of a similar gene therapy trial. Has he been harmed? He is not worse off than he would otherwise have been, since he would have died if the trial had not been conducted. He would have died of the severe form of the underlying disease. The magnitude of the expected harm to adult participants with milder forms of this disease was significantly greater than to newborns with the severe form of the disease.

Put simply, Jesse had something to lose while the seriously affected newborn did not. Even though the expected harm to Jesse prior to commencing the trial may have been small, why prefer a small expected harm to no harm? There is no good reason, regardless of whether someone is prepared to consent. It is irrational to prefer more harm to less harm.

The ethics committee which persuaded Wilson and colleagues to invite adults to participate either:

1. misunderstood the nature of expected harm and/or ethics committees' responsibilities in evaluating it, or
2. (more likely) gave greater weight to consent than to expected harm.

Attempting to draw lessons from Jesse's death, Friedmann, director of the Program in Human Gene Therapy at the University of California, stated: "The single most important mechanism for ensuring patient protection from inherent risks of clinical experiments, unrealistic expectations, and potential conflicts of interest of the investigator is accurate and full disclosure of potential risks and benefits and a well-executed informed consent process."[8]

Fine rhetoric but probably false. In Jesse's case, there were allegedly significant omissions in the consent process, allegedly involving failure to disclose relevant risks and conflicts of financial interest. But would these have made a difference? Jesse understood the trial would not cure him and there was a small chance it could hurt him. But, as his father said:

"He wanted to help the babies. . . . My son had the purest intent." Indeed, strong intentions. He attempted to enrol when he was 17 but had to return when he turned 18 and was eligible.[7] Even if Jesse Gelsinger would not have participated if disclosure had been more frank, someone would have. (After all, one healthy person offered his own heart when Barney Clark received the first artificial heart!) The key to research review is not only consent, but a responsible objective evaluation of the reasonableness of harm in research.[9]

There are complex issues about whether this trial should have been conducted on human beings at all. But if it was justified, it would have been better to conduct it on newborns with the severe form of the disease. Sometimes it is better that an incompetent person participate in research than a competent person who can consent. Consent is important. But the fact that a human being is not able to consent should not paralyse ethics committees. It is a mistake to give more weight to consent than to expected harm. Ethics committees must make an evaluation of the expected harm and whether less harmful avenues should be pursued.

NOTES

1. Lehrman S. Virus treatment questioned after gene therapy death. *Lancet* 1999;**401:** 517–8.

2. Marshall E. Gene therapy death prompts review of adenovirus vector. *Science* 1999; **286:** 2244–5.

3. Fox J. L. Gene-therapy death prompts broad civil lawsuit. *Nature Biotechnology* 2000;**18:** 1136.

4. Nelson D., Weiss R. Is Jesse's death a stain on the new science? *The Age* 1999 Dec 5: news section: 1.

5. Walters L. "Gene therapy: overview." In: Murray T., Mehlman M. J., eds. *Encyclopedia of ethical, legal and policy issues in biotechnology.* New York: Wiley, 2000: 341.

6. Smaglik P. Clinical trials end at gene therapy institute. *Nature* 2000; **405:** 497.

7. Verma I. M. A tumultuous year for gene therapy. *Molecular Therapy* 2000; **2:** 415–6.

8. Friedmann T. Principles for human gene therapy studies. *Science* 2000; **287:** 2163–5.

9. Savulescu J. Safety of participants of non-therapeutic research must be ensured. *British Medical Journal* 1998; **16:** 891–2.

L E R O Y   W A L T E R S

Public Oversight for Human Gene Transfer Research

LeRoy Walters is a coeditor of this anthology. He is a Professor of Philosophy at Georgetown University and the Joseph P. Kennedy, Sr. Professor of Christian Ethics at Georgetown's Kennedy Institute of Ethics. He is coeditor of the annual *Bibliography of Bioethics* (1975–present; 33 volumes to date), co-author with Julie Gage Palmer of *The Ethics of Human Gene Therapy* (1997), and coeditor of the *Source Book in Bioethics* (1998). From 1992 to 1996 he served as Chair of the NIH Recombinant DNA Advisory Committee.

I will begin with a proposal about terminology. The phrase "human gene therapy" was always in danger of seeming to overpromise benefits to the participants in the early clinical trials of human gene transfer. Especially in light of the meager results of human gene transfer studies from 1990 to the present, it seems more accurate and honest to use a neutral phrase that simply describes the procedure that is undertaken. In English, this more neutral phrase is "human gene transfer." The phrase parallels a term like *transplantation*, which also describes the movement of cells or tissues from one individual to another but does not run the risk of unduly raising the expectations of recipients. In this [essay], then, I will employ the [word "transfer" instead of "therapy"] except in cases where the alternative language appears in the original document. . . .

From Harold W. Baillie and Timothy K. Casey, eds., *Is Human Nature Obsolete? Genetics, Bioengineering, and the Future of the Human Condition*, pp. 367, 369–384. © 2004 Massachusetts Institute of Technology. Reprinted by permission of MIT Press.

. . . [T]he clearest example so far of success in a human gene transfer clinical protocol occurred in France, where Doctor Alain Fischer and his colleagues at the Necker Hospital in Paris treated several young male children who had inherited X-linked severe combined immunodeficiency. In this disorder, neither of the two major components of the immune system functions properly. In Fischer's study, the children received their own genetically modified bone marrow cells, presumably including bone marrow stem cells. The modified cells seemed to have a competitive advantage over the native, malfunctioning cells, and produced positive results in all but one child. Fischer and his colleagues reported their positive results in *Science* in April 2000, and the *New England Journal of Medicine* in April 2002.[1] Much to everyone's regret, news reports from early October 2002 and additional information published in January 2003 indicated that two of the first nine children given gene transfer in this protocol had developed T cell leukemias. The retroviral vector used in Fischer's study activated an oncogene (LMO2) in some of the cells that were transferred into the children after genetic modification.[2]

PUBLIC OVERSIGHT: A BRIEF HISTORY

Three stages can be distinguished in the history of public oversight for this field in the United States. The first stage began in the 1980s and continued through the first half of the 1990s. From 1983 through 1995, the public oversight system for human gene transfer research was established. The second stage began in 1996 and continued through 1999; during this time, the existing public oversight system was substantially weakened. A third stage was triggered by the death of a research subject in a gene transfer trial in September 1999. From the time of Jesse Gelsinger's death forward, and especially from the years 2000 to 2002, an effective oversight system for gene transfer research was restored.

In the United States, there was an effective, though somewhat unstable, national oversight system in place for human gene transfer research between 1990 and 1995. During the early 1990s, every interested citizen and policy maker in this country and the world as a whole knew exactly what was happening in the field of human gene transfer research in the United States. In fact, several other countries established advisory committees that paralleled the NIH's Recombinant DNA Advisory Committee (RAC) in its public review of human gene transfer clinical research protocols.

The public oversight system established in the United States was an important precedent. Although it followed by several years the premature attempts by Martin Cline of the University of California at Los Angeles to perform human gene transfer, it was nonetheless an anticipatory system.[3] In fact, those of us who helped to develop the guidelines for research in this field in late 1984 and early 1985 were concerned that we might not conclude our work before the first research protocol was submitted. The first gene-marking study was proposed to RAC in 1988, however, and the first gene transfer study aimed at the treatment of subjects came forward only in early 1990.

There were weaknesses and ambiguities in the public oversight system, to be sure. The most critical weakness, in retrospect, was the failure of the NIH and the Food and Drug Administration (FDA) to establish precise, complementary roles in the review of gene transfer protocols. With the benefit of hindsight, one can also ask why the NIH, a funding agency, was involved in the regulation of research that it funded? Even more problematically, why was the NIH attempting to regulate clinical research being conducted by private-sector biotechnology and pharmaceutical companies? The short answer to these latter two concerns is that the NIH had developed a model in the mid-1970s by taking the initiative in reviewing recombinant DNA research proposals for the entire nation.[4] The NIH and the researchers that the agency funded preferred this mode of self-regulation to the possibly less flexible regulatory proposals that members of Congress were suggesting in 1976 and 1977.

Other questions also confronted RAC and the NIH during these years. Among them were the following:

- How high a standard should be set for the scientific merit of human gene transfer protocols?
- How much time and effort should be devoted to reviewing the consent forms for such trials?
- How could RAC and the NIH avoid having their approval of human gene transfer studies construed as a Good Housekeeping Seal that companies could then use to attract investors?
- How could RAC and the NIH counteract the hyperbole that researchers and companies sometimes employed in publicizing what seemed to be modest research successes?

- Could an advisory committee that was comprised primarily of academics and that met only once each quarter keep pace with a rapidly evolving field like human gene transfer research?

Despite the ambiguities in its role, RAC performed a creditable job in keeping pace with an accelerating number of research protocols from 1990 to 1995. Thanks to the insight and creativity of the late Brigid Leventhal, a pediatric oncologist from Johns Hopkins University, RAC devised a system that asked researchers to report annually on serious adverse events that had occurred to subjects in their gene transfer studies. In June 1995, RAC conducted a comprehensive audit of all U.S. human gene transfer research to date, noting the numbers of protocols reviewed, the various applications of gene transfer, and the target diseases in the studies that aimed to treat patients for a variety of genetic and nongenetic diseases. This comprehensive review constituted one of the finest moments in the history of RAC.[5]

In 1996 and 1997, this oversight system was substantially weakened by policy makers at the NIH and the FDA. Between 1994 and early 1996, opposition to RAC's role in reviewing human gene transfer research began to be expressed by some members of the biotechnology and pharmaceutical industries, AIDS activists, and academic researchers. The opposition ostensibly was based on the notion that RAC, meeting only quarterly, could not respond in a timely manner to new developments in a fast-moving arena of research. Suddenly, draft legislation appeared that, in the course of reforming the FDA's regulatory practices, would have abolished RAC oversight of the field. This provision was never adopted, but a warning about RAC's unpopularity in some quarters had clearly been sent by an antiregulatory Congress. For its part, Congress was responding to advocates for the biotechnology and pharmaceutical industries.

The grounds for this opposition to RAC's role were based in part on the ambiguities cited above. In other respects, however, the amount of hostility engendered by RAC during this time remains puzzling even now. One can only speculate about the motives of the opponents. They surely wanted to avoid unnecessary duplication and delay in the oversight system for this important field. Other critics may have concluded that RAC's quasi-regulatory review function should be located at a regulatory agency, the FDA. And one factor in the opposition of at least some private companies may have been the desire for the more confidential, and therefore less transparent, mode of regulation that occurs in the interactions between companies and FDA regulators.

Whatever the background for his decision, NIH director Harold Varmus announced his plans for the future of RAC in a May 1996 speech given at Hilton Head, South Carolina. No text of the speech is available, but on the basis of reports on the speech and an interview with Varmus, Eliot Marshall of *Science* published an article on the director's plans to "scrap the RAC."[6]

Varmus's speech was followed in June 1996 by attempts by NIH officials to explain the rationale for his new plan to members of Congress and their staff members. In July 1996, the *Federal Register* published the formal NIH proposal to abolish RAC and turn over virtually all public oversight responsibility for human gene transfer research to the FDA.

Between June and August 1996, substantial opposition to the NIH plans for RAC was expressed by four members of Congress and a majority of letters written in response to the *Federal Register* notice, including several authored by prominent figures in the field of bioethics.[7] Meanwhile, RAC skipped its March, June, and September 1996 meetings—in part, it was said, because there was an insufficient number of novel protocols requiring review. The director of the Office of Recombinant DNA Activities, which supported RAC's activities, departed the NIH for an academic position at the end of June 1996, thus further complicating RAC's situation.

In November 1996, February 1997, and October 1997, three further proposals for the new public oversight system were published in the *Federal Register*. The upshot of this long process was the following compromise:

- RAC would continue to discuss, at its quarterly meetings, gene transfer protocols that raised novel issues, used new vectors, or aimed to treat new diseases.
- There would, however, no longer be RAC approval or disapproval of human gene transfer protocols; approval or disapproval (more technically, permission to proceed) belonged solely to the FDA.
- The size of RAC was reduced from twenty-five to fifteen members.

- A new type of forum, the Gene Therapy Policy Conferences, would be associated with RAC's work and would discuss a theme—for example, in utero gene transfer—rather than a particular protocol. This innovation was, in my view, an excellent addition to RAC's role.

The most immediate and obvious effects of the 1996–97 changes were the loss of transparency in the oversight system, and the weakening of RAC's role in reviewing research protocols and monitoring the state of the art in the field. A University of Pennsylvania proposal to study gene transfer in subjects who had ornithine transcarbamylase (OTC) deficiency can perhaps serve as a paradigm case for the new situation that emerged in early 1996. RAC had discussed this protocol in detail at its December 1995 meeting and had provided the researchers with several suggestions for changes that might, in the committee's view, improve the study. Yet with RAC's missed meetings in March, June, and September 1996, and the ongoing debate about both the continuation and the proper role of RAC, the OTC deficiency protocol simply disappeared from public view. Here are several questions about the Penn protocol for which there were no clear answers in the years 1996 through 1999:

- Had the FDA given Penn approval to proceed with the OTC deficiency protocol in response to Penn's Investigational New Drug Application?
- Had the design of the study been changed after public RAC review?
- Had the consent form been changed after RAC review?
- Had the clinical trial been initiated?
- If so, had any serious adverse events occurred?

In fairness to the NIH, I should note that the new guidelines published in the *Federal Register* on October 31, 1997 did require researchers to report to the NIH and RAC all post-RAC-review changes and serious adverse events.

There was also more general evidence that RAC's role had been weakened and the national oversight system was less effective from 1996 on. There was no annual audit of the human gene transfer field conducted in 1996, 1997, 1998, or 1999. Thus, policy makers, the public, and researchers around the world lost the kind of comprehensive overview that RAC had provided in June 1995. Such an audit would have been difficult to conduct during these years for at least three reasons. No senior person (PhD or MD) was

appointed to direct the staff that served RAC for more than two years after the former director's departure at the end of June 1996. Second, in 1995, the FDA had withdrawn its agreement to cooperate with the NIH and RAC in developing a public, online database to track serious adverse events in human gene transfer trials; NIH efforts to create such a database alone proceeded slowly and had not borne fruit four years later. Third, as noted above, the size of RAC was reduced from twenty-five to fifteen members early in 1997; thus, the shared workload that allowed the 1995 audit to be performed was more difficult to achieve.

In 1998 and 1999, the refusal by one researcher and one company to provide public disclosure of serious adverse events in their gene transfer trials was symptomatic of additional problems in the public oversight system. In preparation for their September 1999 meeting, RAC members were asked to sign a confidentiality agreement stating that they would be able to review serious adverse event reports from two protocols, but that they would not be permitted to discuss the adverse event reports in the public meeting. Some members of RAC were clearly not comfortable with this lack of transparency and drafted language, approved by a majority of RAC members, that sought to clarify the existing RAC policy—namely, that no adverse event reports were to be considered confidential. Press stories about these refusals to disclose serious adverse events also began to appear.

During 1997 and 1998, there was also a parallel development that has not been as widely reported; a few academic researchers and companies began recruiting subjects into novel gene transfer research protocols before RAC review had occurred, but after the FDA had given the researchers permission to proceed with their Investigational New Drug Applications. To their credit, the RAC chair, RAC's staff, and the NIH general counsel stood firm, ultimately threatening the academic institutions collaborating with the private companies in these protocols with the termination of all NIH grant and contract funding to those academic institutions if they did not wait until after RAC review before beginning the actual conduct of their trials.

The most dramatic event in the history of human gene transfer research occurred in September 1999. As mentioned above, Gelsinger died while participating in a gene transfer study. The death of this eighteen-year-old, relatively healthy research subject and the subsequent investigation revealed fundamental flaws in the oversight system and led to an agonizing reappraisal of clinical research involving human gene transfer.

As noted earlier, researchers at the University of Pennsylvania submitted an OTC deficiency protocol to the NIH and RAC in fall 1995. The director of the university's Institute for Human Gene Therapy (IHGT), James Wilson, took the lead in presenting the protocol to RAC. Yet the principal investigator for the protocol was Wilson's associate, Mark Batshaw, a pediatrician. In brief, OTC deficiency is a single-gene disorder that causes the buildup of excessive levels of ammonia in the liver. According to the protocol design, six cohorts, each comprised of three subjects, were to receive increasing doses of an adenoviral vector and an inserted gene. The protocol was designated a phase 1 study; that is, the goal of the study was to investigate the potential toxicity of the vector and the transgene rather than to provide a treatment for the subjects' underlying disease.

The OTC deficiency protocol disappeared from public view after the December 1995 RAC review, during which RAC voted to recommend several changes in the study design. The protocol did not become visible again until the June 1999 meeting of the American Society for Gene Therapy, for which Wilson and his colleagues prepared an abstract reporting results from their first four cohorts of subjects. Most members of the public and most RAC members did not attend this meeting, however, and were thus unaware of the study's progress. From the public record of the study compiled in late 1999 and 2000, we now know that this clinical trial proceeded through several stages between early 1996 and September 1999, the month during which a study participant died.

From February through December 1996, the FDA reviewed the OTC deficiency protocol. In December, the agency permitted the study to proceed. Recruitment of subjects began early in 1997, and in April the first subject in the first cohort completed her participation in the protocol. During the remainder of 1997, 1998, and the first nine months of 1999 the trial continued; three subjects were recruited into each of the first three cohorts, four were recruited into the fourth cohort, three into the fifth, and two into the sixth. The second subject in the sixth cohort, Gelsinger, died as a result of his participation in the trial.

There are contextual factors related to this trial that deserve more detailed review. The first set of factors concerns the local level—that is, actions taken and policies adopted by the researchers and the University of Pennsylvania. In June or July 1995, a funding arrangement was entered into by the IHGT, the University of Pennsylvania, and Genovo, a company that had been founded by IHGT's Wilson in 1992. According to the terms of the five-year agreement, Genovo would provide funding for IHGT's research in exchange for the exclusive right to license patents resulting from Wilson's human gene therapy research. This financial arrangement supplied approximately $4.7 million per year to IHGT, or approximately 20 percent of the institute's budget. The arrangement was approved by the University of Pennsylvania's Conflict of Interest Standing Committee.[8]

During late 1996 and the following year, there were two instances of miscommunication between the Penn researchers and the FDA. As both the IHGT and the FDA agree, in November 1996 the Penn research group failed to submit Protocol Version 1.0 to the FDA after the protocol was reviewed by Penn's Institutional Review Board. According to the FDA, nine months later, in August 1997, the Penn research group raised the permissible ammonia level for subjects entering the trial from fifty to seventy micromolar in Protocol Version 2.0 without listing this alteration in the summary of changes for the revision that was sent to the FDA.[9]

It would be possible to dismiss these omissions as failures to file routine paperwork with a regulatory agency. In retrospect, though, the next instance of miscommunication was potentially more important. According to the FDA, in October and November 1998, Grade 3 (moderately serious) laboratory toxicities in two subjects at the fourth dose level were not reported immediately to Penn's Institutional Review Board or the FDA, and the study was not placed on clinical hold. In response, the Penn research group agreed with the FDA's assertions, but replied that it [had reported] these Grade 3 toxicities to the FDA in a January 1999 letter and a March 1999 annual report. The research group also summarized the toxicities in a table prepared for an annual review by the Penn Institutional Review Board on August 9, 1999.

There was also a breakdown in communication about parallel animal studies that were being conducted in 1998 by the Penn research group. From October through December 1998, the group conducted a preclinical study with three monkeys using adenoviral vectors. According to the FDA, two monkeys had serious reactions to early versions of the vector and were therefore euthanized; a third had milder symptoms in response to the third-generation vector that was simultaneously being used in the OTC deficiency trial. In reviewing the tragic events of September 1999, the FDA contended that the results of this preclinical study should have been reported to the agency because they were directly relevant to the OTC deficiency study. The Penn researchers agreed that the results of this study should have been communicated to the FDA in the annual report of March 2000, but argued that the doses of vector in the preclinical study were seventeen times higher than those used in the clinical trial. The researchers also noted that the response of the monkey that received the third-generation vector was less severe than that of the monkeys receiving the earlier-generation vectors.

In September 1999, patient 019, Gelsinger, was infused with the vector and the inserted gene even though his ammonia level was ninety-one micromolar on the day before he received the infusion. (The permissible level was either fifty or seventy micromolar, depending on the version of the protocol.) The Penn researchers [asserted] that Gelsinger's ammonia levels were within the stated range when he was screened for possible participation in the trial in June 1999, that he was given a drug to reduce his ammonia levels, and that they had made a clinical judgment that an ammonia level of ninety-one would not be harmful to the subject.

In addition to the foregoing questions at the local level, the tragic history of the Penn OTC deficiency protocol revealed serious problems in the national oversight system for human gene transfer research. As noted above, there was a long period of uncertainty that stretched from May 1996 to October 1997, at least. During this time, there were multiple proposals about the role and the very existence of RAC. There were also multiple versions of the NIH guidelines. Researchers received quite clear signals from the NIH: "You in the research community will be dealing primarily with the FDA from now on." The net effect of these developments was confusion and an undermining of RAC's authority.

Perhaps the most important system problem was the failure of most gene transfer researchers to report serious adverse events to the NIH and RAC in a timely fashion. A December 21, 1999, letter from NIH director Varmus to Congressman Henry Waxman contains this sobering concession: "Of the 691 serious adverse events reported [in trials using adenoviral vectors], 39 had been previously reported as required by the *NIH Guidelines*."[10] Thirty-nine out of 691 is 5.6 percent.

The great unknown at the national level is how the FDA was exercising its oversight responsibilities for the Penn OTC deficiency protocol and other human gene transfer protocols between 1996 and 1999. One would like to know the answers to honest questions such as the following:

- How many FDA medical officers and reviewers were involved in overseeing the OTC deficiency protocol?
- How carefully did they read correspondence and annual reports on this and other Investigational New Drug applications?
- What types of database capabilities did they have?
- Did they see patterns of serious adverse events in trials involving adenoviral vectors?

The follow-up to the death of Gelsinger was arduous for his family, the federal government, and the research community. In December 1999, the RAC meeting was devoted to reviewing what had caused Gelsinger's death and how the oversight system could be modified to prevent similar tragedies in the future. In January 2000, the FDA sent the Penn research group a series of inspectional observations and placed a clinical hold on the OTC deficiency trial. One month later, Senator Bill Frist convened a hearing on the oversight of human gene transfer research at which Gelsinger's father, Paul, and I testified. The FDA sent a formal warning letter in March to Wilson and the IHGT at Penn. Two months later, an external review committee chaired by former senator John Danforth reported its findings to University of Pennsylvania president Judith Rodin, who in response, decided to discontinue all clinical research at the institute.[11]

During the summer of 2000, the University of Pennsylvania decided not to renew its agreement with Genovo. According to published reports in the *Wall Street Journal* and the *Philadelphia Inquirer*, Genovo was sold to Targeted Genetics for newly issued shares of stock valued at $89.9 million. The newspapers also disclosed that Penn had owned a 3.2 percent equity stake in Genovo, for which it received Targeted Genetics stock valued at $1.4 million, and that Wilson had owned a 30 percent nonvoting equity stake, for which he received Targeted Genetics stock valued at

$13.5 million. Biogen was to receive $50 million worth of Targeted Genetics stock in exchange for its stake in Genovo.[12]

In September 2000, the Gelsinger family sued the University of Pennsylvania for the wrongful death of Jesse Gelsinger. After six weeks of negotiation between the parties, the case was settled without going to trial. The terms of the settlement were not disclosed.[13]

The tragic death of Gelsinger in 1999 has had a decisive impact on the public oversight of human gene transfer research in the United States. Since October 2000, there have been several promising developments at the NIH and the FDA. One of the most encouraging developments of late 2000, 2001, and early 2002 has been the step-by-step restoration of RAC's traditional role. An October 2000 *Federal Register* notice stipulated that RAC review and subsequent local institutional approval must be completed before a clinical trial of human gene transfer can begin.[14] In December 2000 and again in November 2001, the NIH proposed the establishment of a Human Gene Transfer Safety Assessment Board to evaluate adverse events in gene transfer trials in an organized, systematic manner and to report regularly to RAC.[15] This board received final approval from the Office of Management and Budget in January 2002, and the revision of the guidelines that authorizes its establishment was published in the *Federal Register* in May 2002.[16] Moreover, in September and December 2001, RAC engaged in an extended discussion about the serious adverse events that had occurred in two clinical trials designed to study gene transfer in subjects with hemophilia. In response to the adverse events in the French trial of gene transfer for severe combined immunodeficiency, RAC provided detailed public analyses in December 2002 and February 2003. Finally, the number of RAC members has been expanded beyond fifteen so that more areas of scientific and clinical expertise can be represented on the committee.

For its part, the FDA announced in January 2001, during the waning days of the second Clinton administration, its intention to make public "certain data and information related to human gene therapy and xenotransplantation."[17] Public comments on this proposal will be considered before the new policy is enacted. The death of a healthy volunteer in an asthma study being conducted at Johns Hopkins University in June 2001 reminded researchers and the public alike that research subjects can be at serious risk even in seemingly innocuous trials.[18] Several months after this volunteer's death, the FDA established a new Office for Good Clinical Practice within the Commissioner's Office "to improve the conduct and oversight of clinical research and to ensure the protection of participants in FDA-regulated research."[19] Like RAC, the FDA has also analyzed the leukemias that occurred in the French gene transfer trial—at public advisory committee meetings held in October 2002 and February 2003.

ISSUES FOR THE FUTURE

When we look to the future, it is quite clear that the most critical issues involving human gene transfer research will involve the brain (especially behavioral traits), enhancement by genetic means, and the human germ line. I should add a caveat: in my view, it is probably too early to know what the relative contributions to human health will be of gene transfer, cell transplantation (including human embryonic stem cell transplantation), and drugs. A recent article suggests that a combination of factors may be involved.[20]

THE BRAIN

In this arena, one can imagine that the brain, which has until now been off-limits except in efforts to treat diseases like glioma, will become a legitimate target for gene transfer research. A foretaste of things to come could be a recent gene transfer study that attempted to introduce the dopamine D2 receptor into rats, in a effort to decrease alcohol consumption.[21]

ENHANCEMENT

An obvious physical enhancement that also would be disease related would be a fine-tuning of the human immune system, so that it is much less likely to go awry either in attacking an individual's own body in the event of autoimmune diseases or in overreacting to environmental allergens. A candidate for intellectual enhancement would be the preservation of memory during the process of aging, in contrast to the dementia that afflicts so many elderly people. Important theoretical questions with regard to enhancement will be, What is enhancement? What is remediation of an undesirable condition? And can we draw a clear line between these two categories?[22]

GERM LINE INTERVENTION

To many people, the final and most forbidding frontier in genetics may seem to be deliberately attempting to transmit particular genes to our children and grandchildren. This may be a case in which incremental steps will lead to a point where each major industrial society will need to pause and consider what it wants its future policy on human germ line intervention to be. Here are several foreseeable steps that could be leading us toward this decision point:

- Germ line changes as unintended side effects of somatic cell gene transfer.
- Nuclear transfer in human eggs, to prevent mitochondrial disease.
- The genetic "repair" of sperm or egg cells to prevent disease.
- The genetic "repair" of preimplantation embryos to prevent disease.[23]

CONCLUSION

There are no easy answers to these breathtaking technological possibilities. . . . Perhaps what we will need to do is commit ourselves to *procedures* and *modes of deliberation* that allow us to be prepared for such possibilities when they become actual. The first step will be both academic and political. . . . It involves calm, rational, anticipatory, and interdisciplinary discussion—discussion that also involves members of the public. The second step will be primarily political, but one hopes that it will not lose touch either with academia or the will of the general public. In order to be ready for and to cope with the genetic technologies of the future, we will need transparent, flexible, and vigorous oversight systems.

NOTES

An earlier version of this chapter was presented in March 2001 in Berlin, Germany, at the international conference on "The Impact of Genetic Knowledge on Human Life," cosponsored by the Deutsches Referenzzentrum für Ethik in den Biowissenschaften. See LeRoy Walters, "Genforschung und Gesellschaft: Erwartungen, Ziele und Grenzen," in Ludger Honnefelder, et al., eds., *Das genetische Wissen und die Zukunft des Menschen* (Berlin: Walter de Gruyter, 2003), 152–166.

1. Marina Cavazana-Calvo, Salima Hacein-Bey, Genevieve de Saint Basile, et al., "Gene Therapy of Severe Combined Immunodeficiency (SCID)-X1 Disease," *Science* 288, no. 5466 (April 28, 2000): 627–629; and Salima Hacein-Bey-Abina, Francoise Le Deist, Fredoriove Carlier, "Sustained Correction of X-Linked Severe Combined Immunodeficiency by *ex vivo* Gene Therapy," *New England Journal of Medicine* 346, no. 16 (April 18, 2002): 1185–1193.

2. See, for example, Sheryl Gay Stolberg, "Trials Are Halted on a Gene Therapy Experiment," *New York Times*, October 9, 2002, A1, A20; Salima Hacein-Bey-Abina, Christol von Kalle, Manfred Schmidt, "A Serious Adverse Event after Successful Gene Therapy for X-Linked Severe Combined Immunodeficiency," letter to the editor, *New England Journal of Medicine* 348, no. 3 (January 16, 2003): 255–256; and Rick Weiss, "Second Boy Receiving Gene

Therapy Develops Cancer," *Washington Post,* January 15, 2003, A9.

3. See Larry Thompson, *Correcting the Code: Inventing the Genetic Cure for the Human Body* (New York: Simon and Schuster, 1994), 230–267.

4. For a fascinating study of this process, see Donald S. Fredrickson, *The Recombinant DNA Controversy: A Memoir* (Washington, DC: American Society for Microbiology, 2001).

5. The audit was published as "Gene Therapy in the United States: A Five-Year Status Report," *Human Gene Therapy* 7, no. 14 (September 10, 1996): 1781–1790.

6. Eliot Marshall, "Varmus Proposes to Scrap the RAC," *Science* 272, no. 5264 (May 17, 1996): 945.

7. On the opposition by members of Congress, see David Pryor, Mark Hatfield, Ron Wyden, and Henry A. Waxman, "A Word to Varmus," letter to the editor, *Hastings Center Report* 26, no. 4 (July–August 1996): 46–47.

8. See Scott Hensley, "Targeted Genetics Agrees to Buy Genovo," *Wall Street Journal,* August 9, 2000, B2; Scott Hensley, "Targeted Genetics' Genovo Deal Leads to Windfall for Researcher," *Wall Street Journal,* August 10, 2000, B12; and Andrea Knox and Huntley Collins, "Rival to Buy Local Biotech Pioneer Genovo," *Philadelphia Inquirer,* August 10, 2000, A1.

9. The communications are warning letters to James M. Wilson, March 3, 2000, http://www.fda.gov/foi/warning letters/m3435n.pdf (January 26, 2004) and July 3, 2000 http://www.fda.gov/foi/warning letters/m3897n. pdf (January 26, 2004), one warning letter each to Mark L. Batshaw and Steven E. Raper, November 30, 2000, http://www.fda.gov/foi/warning letters/m4911n.pdf (January 26, 2004) and http://www.fda.gov/foi/warning letters/m4912n.pdf (January 26, 2004) and a notice of initiation of disqualification proceeding and opportunity to explain letter to James M. Wilson, November 30, 2002 http://www.fda.gov/foi/nidpoe/n121.pdf (January 26, 2004). Unfortunately the replies of the University of Pennsylvania researchers are not part of the public record.

10. Letter from Harold Varmus to Henry Waxman, December 21, 1999 http://www.house.gov/waxman/issues/health/issues health gene therapy.htm/ (January 26, 2004).

11. For the information in this paragraph, see Deborah Nelson and Rick Weiss, "Penn Ends Gene Trials on Humans," *Washington Post,* May 25, 2000, A1.

12. Hensley, "Targeted Genetics"; Hensley, "Genovo Deal"; and Knox and Collins, "Rival."

13. See Deborah Nelson and Rick Weiss, "Penn Researchers Sued in Gene Therapy Death," *Washington Post,* September 19, 2000, A3; and Rick Weiss and Deborah Nelson, "Penn Settles Gene Therapy Suit," *Washington Post,* November 4, 2000, A4.

14. Office of Biotechnology Activities, "Recombinant DNA Research: Action under the NIH Guidelines; Notice," *Federal Register* 10, no. 65 (October 10, 2000): 60327–60332.

15. Office of Biotechnology Activities, "Recombinant DNA Research: Action under the NIH Guidelines," *Federal Register* 65, no. 239 (December 12, 2000): 77655–77659; and Office of Biotechnology Activities, "Recombinant DNA Research: Proposed Actions under the NIH Guidelines," *Federal Register* 66, no. 223 (November 19, 2001): 57970–57977.

16. Office of Biotechnology Activities, "Recombinant DNA Research: Notice under the NIH Guidelines," *Federal Register* 67, no. 101 (May 24, 2002): 36619–36620.

17. Food and Drug Administration, "Availability for Public Disclosure and Submission to FDA for Public Disclosure of Certain Data and Information Related to Human Gene Therapy or

Xenotransplantation," *Federal Register* 66, no. 12 (January 18, 2001): 4688–4706.

18. See Jonathan Bor and Gary Cohn, "Research Volunteer Dies in Hopkins Asthma Study," *Baltimore Sun*, 14 July 2001, A1.

19. Food and Drug Administration, press release, October 26, 2001 (no longer available).

20. See William M. Rideout III, Konrao Hochedlinger, Michael Kyba "Correction of a Genetic Defect by Nuclear Transplantation and Combined Cell and Gene Therapy," *Cell* 109, no. 1 (April 5, 2002): 17–27.

21. See Panayotis K. Thanos, Nora D. Volkow, Paul Freimuth, "Overexpression of Dopamine D2 Receptors Reduces Alcohol Self-Administration," *Journal of Neurochemistry* 78, no. 5 (September 2001): 1094–1103.

22. On this topic, see LeRoy Walters and Julie Gage Palmer, *The Ethics of Human Gene Therapy* (New York: Oxford University Press 1997), 99–142.

23. On the topic of germ line intervention, see Walters and Palmer, *The Ethics of Human Gene Therapy*, 143–153.

DAVID B. RESNIK

Human Genetic Engineering

Through 2004, David B. Resnik was Professor of Medical Humanities at the Brody School of Medicine at East Carolina University and Director of New Programs for the Bioethics Center at University Health Systems of Eastern North Carolina. He now serves as the bioethicist at the National Institute of Environmental Health Sciences, NIH, in Research Triangle Park, North Carolina. Dr. Resnik is author of *The Ethics of Science: An Introduction* (1998), *Human Germ-Line Gene Therapy: Scientific, Moral, and Political Issues* (1999), and *Owning the Genome: A Moral Analysis of DNA Patenting* (2004).

The development of recombinant DNA techniques in the 1970s enabled scientists to create genetically engineered organisms. In 1975 molecular biologists and geneticists held a conference in Asilomar, California, to discuss the biosafety issues relating to the new technology as well as policies for regulation and oversight. In 1978 fertility specialists used in vitro fertilization (IVF) techniques to assist a British couple in conceiving Louise Brown, the world's first "test tube" baby. In the early 1980s researchers began using embryo-splitting technologies to produce desirable livestock clones for agriculture. By the end of the decade universities and biotechnology companies were manufacturing and patenting transgenic mice for use in drug testing and medical research.

During the course of those events many people expressed concern that these discoveries and innovations eventually would lead to human genetic engineering (HGE). In early discussions of HGE (circa 1965–1980) scientists, journalists, and scholars conjured up the familiar allegories of Mary Shelly's *Frankenstein* and Aldous Huxley's *Brave New World* to question the wisdom of pursuing the new technologies (Gaylin; Boone). Science fiction novels such as *Mutant 59* and *The Boys from Brazil* depicted the disastrous effects of genetic engineering experiments gone awry. The biotechnology critic Jeremy Rifkin (1983) warned of the Faustian bargain of genetic engineering and the dangers of meddling with nature. Theologians such as Paul Ramsey (1970) and bioethicists such as Leon Kass (1972) spoke about the dangers of "playing God" and disrupting family relationships. However, scientists, such as Joshua Lederberg (1966) and James Watson (1971) and philosophers such as Jonathan Glover (1984) and Joseph Fletcher (1965) embraced the possibilities of using HGE to advance scientific and social goals.

From *Encyclopedia of Bioethics* 3rd edition by Stephen G. Post, ed., 2003. Reprinted with permission from Gale, a division of Thomson Learning: www.thomsonrights.com Fax 800-730-2215.

While the public debate continued, scientists, clinicians, and scholars began to envision potential medical uses of HGE as they developed a framework for justifying the application of gene transfer technologies to human beings. Two key distinctions defined this framework: the somatic versus germline distinction and the therapy versus enhancement distinction (Walters; Anderson, 1985, 1989). Those distinctions implied four types of HGE:

Somatic gene therapy (SGT)

Somatic genetic enhancement (SGE)

Germline gene therapy (GLGT)

Germline genetic enhancement (GLGE)

Anderson (1989) and others argued that SGT could be justified on the grounds that it was morally similar to other types of medical treatments, such as pharmaceutical therapy and surgery. The goal of SGT is to transfer genes into human somatic cells to enable those cells to produce functional proteins in the appropriate quantities at the appropriate time. In 1990 the first SGT clinical trial involved an attempt to transfer normal adenosine deaminase (ADA) genes into patients with ADA deficiency, a disease of the immune system caused by mutations that prevent the patient from producing sufficient quantities of ADA (Walters and Palmer). Because SGT targets somatic cells, it probably will not transmit genetic changes to future generations as a result of the fact the genetic inheritance in human beings occurs through germ cells. However, there is a slight chance that an SGT protocol will result in an accidental gene transfer to germ cells, and that chance increases as one performs the experiment earlier in human development. For example, SGT administered to a developing fetus entails a significant risk of accidental gene transfer to germ cells (Zanjani and Anderson).

The goal of GLGT, in contrast, is to transfer genes into human germ cells to prevent the development of a genetic disease in a child who has not yet been born. A GLGT protocol for ADA deficiency would attempt to transfer normal genes into the parents' gametes or a zygote so that the progeny would have the correct gene and therefore would not develop the disease. Because GLGT targets germ cells, it is likely to transmit genetic changes to future generations; therefore, it poses far greater risks than does SGT. According to many authors and organizations, SGT can be morally justified but GLGT cannot because it is too risky. Thus, many clinician-scientists who saw the promise of SGT attempted to draw a firm moral boundary between SGT and GLGT.

After the first SGT experiments began, many writers made the case for crossing the line between somatic therapy and germline therapy (Zimmerman; Berger and Gert; Munson and Davis). Those writers argued that some germline interventions are morally justifiable because they promote medical goals such as disease prevention and the relief of suffering. Most of the approximately 5,000 known genetic diseases cause disabilities, premature death, and suffering. Although couples often can use nongenetic methods such as prenatal genetic testing and preimplantation genetic testing to give birth to children without genetic diseases, for some diseases germline therapy offers the only hope of producing a healthy child who is genetically related to the couple. For example, if a male and a female are both homozygous for a recessive genetic disease such as cystic fibrosis (CF), the only way they can produce a healthy child is to use gene transfer techniques to create embryos with normal genes (Resnik and Langer).

THERAPY VERSUS ENHANCEMENT

Many of the writers, clinicians, and scientists who defended genetic therapy also had moral qualms about genetic enhancement. In genetic enhancement the goal of the intervention is not to treat or prevent a disease but to achieve another result, such as increased height, intelligence, disease resistance, or musical ability. Thus, according to many authors, there is a moral distinction between genetic therapy, which is morally acceptable, and genetic enhancement, which is morally unacceptable or questionable (Suzuki and Knudtson; Anderson, 1989; Berger and Gert). Until society achieves a moral consensus on genetic enhancement, HGE protocols should not attempt to enhance human beings genetically.

By making these two fundamental distinctions, SGT proponents were able to obtain public approval of and funding for SGT experiments and dispel some of the fears associated with HGE. Under this twofold classification, SGT experiments were ethical and should be conducted but other types of HGE experiments were unethical or at least ethically questionable and should not be conducted.

Whereas the somatic versus germline distinction has stood the test of time, the therapy versus enhancement distinction has been criticized (Juengst, 1997; Stock and Campbell; Parens; Resnik, 2000a). Some critics of the second distinction argue that many genetic *enhancements* would be morally acceptable. For example, some day it may be possible to transfer disease-resistance genes to human beings. If childhood immunizations, which enhance the human immune system in order to prevent disease, are morally acceptable, what is wrong with *genetic immunizations*? It also may be possible some day to manipulate genes that affect the aging process. If nongenetic means of prolonging life such as organ transplants are morally acceptable, what is wrong with genetic means of prolonging life?

Other critics question the cogency of the distinction because it is founded on the concepts of health and disease (Parens). Therapy is an intervention designed to treat or prevent disease; enhancement is an intervention that serves another purpose. However, how should one define health and disease? Several decades of reflection on these concepts have not solved the problem (Caplan). According to an influential approach, disease is an objective concept that is defined as a deviation from normal human functioning that causes suffering and places limitations on a person's range of opportunities (Boorse; Buchanan et al.).

For example, CF is a disease because patients with CF do not breath normally. As a result, they have a variety of symptoms, such as shortness of breath and a persistent cough, which cause suffering and interfere with physical activity. CF patients also usually die many years before the normal human life span of seventy-plus years. Thus, a genetic intervention designed to treat or prevent CF is therapeutic.

However, this approach has some well-known problems and limitations. First, social and cultural factors play an important role in delineating the normal range of values that define disease. For example, dyslexia is recognized as a disease in developed nations because it interferes with reading, but it does not cause that problem in a nonliterate society. An adult in the United States who is shorter than four feet tall is regarded as having a disease—dwarfism—but the same adult living in an African pygmy tribe would be regarded as normal. Modern psychiatrists recognize depression as a mental illness, but it was regarded as a lifestyle or bad mood a hundred years ago.

Second, social and political values affect the range of opportunities in society and therefore have an impact on diseases; societies choose who will be disabled (Buchanan et al.). For example, if a person has an allergy to cigarette smoke, he or she would have a difficult time breathing in a society in which smoking is permitted in public places. That person may become disabled, and his or her condition therefore would be a disease. However, that person would not have those difficulties [in] a society that bans smoking in public. The allergy would not prevent that person from working or participating in public activities. He or she therefore would not be disabled and would not have a disease.

Third, health usually is not defined as merely the opposite of disease. According to an influential definition of health, "Health is a state of complete physical, mental, and social well-being and not merely the absence of disease or infirmity" (World Health Organization [WHO]). This definition implies that some enhancements of human functioning are necessary to promote health because health is understood not only as the absence of disease but as an ideal state of functioning and flourishing. Thus, immunizations that enhance the immune system promote health, as do exercise regimens that enhance human musculature and endurance.

As a result of these and other problems with the therapy versus enhancement distinction, several authors have argued that it does not mark any absolute moral or metaphysical boundaries. One cannot equate *therapy* with *morally acceptable* or *morally required*, and one cannot equate *enhancement* with *morally unacceptable* or *morally forbidden*. To determine the moral justifiability of a genetic intervention in a particular case, one must assess that intervention in light of the relevant facts as well as moral values and principles such as autonomy, beneficence, and justice (Resnik and Langer). Some writers who criticize the distinction nevertheless maintain that it may be useful in setting an agenda for policy discussions or for raising moral warning flags (Buchanan et al.).

INHERITABLE GENETIC MODIFICATIONS

In the early debates about germline interventions most writers viewed GLGT and GLGE as methods for transferring genes to human germs cells such as sperm, ova, and zygotes or to human germ tissues such as the testes and ovaries. A human germline intervention would be similar to a genetic engineering experiment in a mammal in that it would attempt to transfer a gene into the DNA in the chromosomes in the cell nucleus. Writers on both sides of the GLGT debate agreed that random gene insertion would be an extremely risky procedure and that targeted gene replacement (TGR) would pose the fewest risks to progeny (Resnik, Steinkraus, and Langer).

Several important scientific and technical developments in the 1990s challenged this way of thinking about genetic interventions in the germline. In 1997 the experiment that produced Dolly, the world's first cloned sheep, demonstrated that nuclear transfer (NT) techniques could be applied to human beings (Pence). In this procedure one removes the nucleus from a zygote and transfers a nucleus from another egg or a somatic cell to the enucleated egg. The resulting embryo has a donor nucleus combined with the cytoplasm of the recipient. An NT procedure, like a GLGT procedure, produces inheritable genetic changes. However, an NT procedure does not attempt to modify human chromosomes. Since the early 1990s scientists and scholars around the world have had a vigorous debate about the ethical and social issues of human cloning (Kristol and Cohen). Several European countries, including Germany and France, have outlawed all human cloning. At the time of this writing the United States was considering a ban on human cloning, although no bill has been signed into law.

While the world was debating the ethics of NT, researchers conducted a more modest form of genetic manipulation in human beings: ooplasm transfer (OT). OT already has resulted in over thirty live births (Barritt et al.). In OT one infuses ooplasm (the cytoplasm from an egg) into a zygote. The resulting embryo has its original nucleus and a modified ooplasm containing ooplasm from the donor egg. OT also produces inheritable genetic changes because it modifies DNA that resides in the mitochondria: mitochondrial DNA (mtDNA). Because the mitochondria facilitate many important metabolic processes in cells, mtDNA plays an important role in cellular metabolism. Some metabolic disorders are caused by mutations in mtDNA. Less than 1 percent of human DNA consists of mtDNA; the majority of human DNA, nuclear DNA (nDNA), resides in the nucleus.

Although OT experiments and NT experiments do not appear to be as risky as experiments that manipulate human chromosomes, they are not risk-free because they can result in a mismatch between nDNA and mtDNA known as hetereoplasmy, which can affect the expression of both nDNA and mtDNA (Resnik and Langer; Templeton).

Artificial chromosomes pose an additional challenge to the earlier paradigm because they would not modify the chromosomes but would carry genes on a separate structure that would be segregated from the chromosomes (Stock and Campbell). One reason for developing artificial chromosomes is to avoid tampering with existing chromosomes. However, because an artificial chromosome could carry dozens of genes, it would transmit genetic changes to future generations.

As these developments unfolded, scholars discussed ethical and policy issues related to NT, OT, and artificial chromosomes (McGee; Bonnickson; Pence; Robertson, 1998; Stock and Campbell; Parens and Juengst; Davis). Some writers suggested that it would be useful to develop a typology for different interventions in the human germline to allow a distinction between various techniques, procedures, and methods (Richter and Baccheta; Resnik and Langer). For example, some techniques, such as TGR, attempt to modify the nDNA in human chromosomes. Other procedures, such as OT, attempt to change the composition of mtDNA. One could classify these procedures according to the degree of risk they entail, with OT being *low-risk* and TGR being *high-risk* (Resnik and Langer).

In light of the scientific, technical, and philosophical developments that occurred after the early discussions of germline interventions, in 2001 a working group convened by the American Association for the Advancement of Science proposed that people use the term *inheritable genetic modification* (IGM) instead of GLGT or GLGE because it provides a more accurate description of the techniques and methods that have been the subject of so much debate. According to the working group, IGM refers to "the technologies, techniques, and interventions that are capable of modifying the set of genes that a subject has available to transmit to his or her offspring" (Frankel and Chapman, p. 12). Under that definition, TGR, OT, NT, and the use of artificial chromosomes all would be classified as types of IGM. IGM could include methods that are used to treat or prevent diseases as well as methods intended to enhance human traits.

ARGUMENTS FOR AND AGAINST IGM

There is not sufficient space in this [essay] for an in-depth discussion of the arguments for and against applying IGM procedures to human beings, and so the entry will provide only a quick summary of those arguments (for further discussion, see Resnik, Steinkraus, and Langer; Walters and Palmer; President's Commission; Holtug).

Arguments for IGM. The following arguments have been made in favor of IGM.

1. IGM can benefit patients by preventing genetic disease as well as the disability, pain, and suffering associated with those diseases (Zimmerman; Berger and Gert; Munson and Davis). IGM also can benefit patients who will enjoy the effects of enhancements of health, longevity, intelligence, and so on (Stock and Campbell; Glover; Silver).

2. IGM can benefit parents by enabling them to have healthy children who are genetically related to the parents (Zimmerman; Robertson, 1994).

3. IGM can benefit society by reducing the social and economic burdens of genetic disease. Society also can benefit from IGM if enhancements of human traits increase human knowledge; productivity, performance, aesthetic experience, and other social goals (Harris; Silver).

4. IGM can benefit the human gene pool by enabling society to promote "good" genes and weed out "bad" genes. For a critique of this argument, see Suzuki and Knudtson (1989).

5. Parents have a right to use IGM to prevent genetic diseases and promote the overall health and well-being of their children (Robertson, 1994).

Arguments Against IGM. The following arguments have been made against IGM.

1. IGM can cause biological harms to patients that result from genetic defects caused by IGM procedures, such as underproduction or overproduction of important proteins, the production of a protein at the wrong time, and the production of nonfunctional proteins. Although some procedures, such as OT, are safer than other procedures, such as TGR, IGM entails many risks that scientists do not understand fully (Resnik and Langer). IGM also could cause psychological harms to patients, who may view themselves as products of their parents' desires or as mere commodities (Kass, 1985; Andrews).

2. IGM could cause harm to a mother who carries a genetically modified child. For example, IGM might carry an increased risk of preeclampsia or complications during labor and delivery.

3. IGM could harm future generations. Because some genetic defects may not manifest themselves until the second or third generation, it may be difficult to estimate the potential harm to future generations (Suzuki and Knudtson).

4. IGM could harm the gene pool by reducing genetic diversity, which is important for the survival of the human species (Suzuki and Knudtson). For a critique, see Resnik (2000b).

5. IGM could cause harms to society, such as the increased social and economic burden of caring for patients with genetic defects caused by IGM, increased discrimination and bias against racial and ethnic groups and people with disabilities, the breakdown of the traditional family and traditional methods of reproduction, the loss of respect for the value of human life as a result of treating children as commodities, and the loss of human diversity (Kass, 1985; Kitcher; Kimbrell; Parens and Asch; Andrews).

6. IGM could waste health-care resources that could be better spent elsewhere (Juengst, 1991).

7. IGM could violate the rights of children, including the right not to be harmed, the right to an open future, and the right not be the subject of an experiment (Kimbrell; Andrews; Davis; McGee, Kass, 1985; Resnik, Steinkraus, and Langer).

8. IGM subverts natural reproduction and the natural human form (Rifkin; Kass, 1985). See Resnik, Steinkraus, and Langer (1999) for a discussion of this argument.

9. IGM is a form of "playing God" because people do not have the wisdom or the authority to design themselves (Rifkin; Kimbrell; Ramsey). See Peters (1997) for a critique of this view.

10. IGM is the vain pursuit of human perfection (Kass, 1985). See McGee (1997) for a critique of this view.

11. IGM is nothing more than a modern version of the eugenics movement (Kevles). It will repeat all the errors of the Social Darwinists and the Nazis (Kass, 1985). See Buchanan et al. and Kitcher (1997) for a discussion of this view.

12. IGM will cause social injustice by increasing the gap between the genetic "haves" and the genetic "have-nots." See Buchanan et al. and Mehlman and Botkin (1998) for further discussion of this argument. . . .

CONCLUSION

It is likely that societies will debate the ethical and legal aspects of IGM for many years. The field of biotechnology is advancing so rapidly that interventions that were merely conceivable at the end of the twentieth century are fast becoming a practical reality. It is to be hoped that people will develop effective and well-balanced laws and policies pertaining to IGM before the first genetically engineered baby is born.

BIBLIOGRAPHY

American Medical Association, Council on Ethical and Judicial Affairs. 1998. *Code of Medical Ethics. Current Opinions with Annotations.* Chicago: American Medical Association.

American Society for Reproduction Medicine. 2000. "Human Somatic Nuclear Transfer." *Fertility and Sterility* 74: 873–876.

Anderson, French. 1985. "Human Gene Therapy: Scientific and Ethical Considerations." *Journal of Medicine and Philosophy* 10: 275–291.

Anderson, French. 1989. "Why Draw a Line?" *Journal of Medicine and Philosophy* 14: 681–693.

Andrews, Lori. 2000. *The Clone Age: Adventures in the New World of Reproductive Technology.* New York: Henry Holt.

Annas, George. 1998. "The Shadowlands—Secrets, Lies, and Assisted Reproduction." *New England Journal of Medicine* 339: 935–937.

Barritt, John; Willadsen, Stephen; Brenner, Carl; and Cohen, Jonathan. 2001. "Cytoplasmic Transfers in Assisted Reproduction." *Human Reproduction Update* 7: 428–435.

Berger, Edward, and Gert, Bernie. 1991. "Genetic Disorders and the Ethical Status of Germline Therapy." *Journal of Medicine and Philosophy* 16: 667–683.

Bonnickson, Andrea. 1998. "Transplanting Nuclei between Human Eggs: Implications for Germ-Line Genetics." *Politics and the Life Sciences* 17: 3–10.

Boone, Charles. 1988. "Bad Axioms in Genetic Engineering." *Hastings Center Report* 18(4): 9–13.

Boorse, Christopher. 1977. "Health as a Theoretical Concept." *Philosophy of Science* 44: 542–577.

Buchanan, Alen; Brock, Dan; Daniels, Normal; and Wikler, Dan. 2000. *From Chance to Choice: Genetics and Justice.* Cambridge, MA: Cambridge University Press.

Caplan, Arthur. 1997. "The Concepts of Health, Disease, and Illness." In *Medical Ethics,* 2nd edition, ed. Robert Veatch. Sudbury, MA: Jones and Bartlett.

Council for Responsible Genetics. 1993. "Position Paper on Human Germ Line Manipulation." *Human Gene Therapy* 4: 35–37.

Council for the Organization of Medical Sciences, World Health Organization, and United Nations Educational, Scientific, and Cultural Organization. 1990. "Declaration of Inuyama and Reports of the Working Groups." *Human Gene Therapy* 2: 123–129.

Davis, Dena. 2001. *Genetic Dilemmas.* New York: Routledge.

Fletcher, Joseph. 1965. *Morals and Medicine.* New York: Beacon Press.

Frankel, Mark, and Chapman, Audrey, eds. 2000. *Human Inheritable Genetic Modifications: Assessing Scientific, Religious, and Policy Issues.* Washington, D.C.: American Association for the Advancement of Science.

Gaylin, Willard. 1977. "The Frankenstein Factor." *New England Journal of Medicine* 297: 665–666.

Glover, Jonathan. 1984. *What Sort of People Should There Be?* New York: Penguin Books.

Group of Advisors on the Ethical Implications of Biotechnology of the European Commission. 1993. *The Ethical Implications of Gene Therapy.* Brussels: European Commission.

Harris, John. 1992. *Wonderwoman and Superman: The Ethics of Human Biotechnology.* New York: Oxford University Press.

Holtug, Nils. 1997. "Altering Humans—The Case for and against Human Gene Therapy." *Cambridge Quarterly of Healthcare Ethics* 6: 157–174.

Juengst, Eric. 1991. "Germ-Line Gene Therapy: Back to Basics." *Journal of Medicine and Philosophy* 16: 587–592.

Juengst, Eric. 1997. "Can Enhancement be Distinguished from Therapy in Genetic Medicine?" *Journal of Medicine and Philosophy* 22: 125–142.

Kass, Leon. 1972. "Making Babies—The New Biology and the 'Old' Morality." *The Public Interest* 26: 18–56.

Kass, Leon. 1985. *Toward a More Natural Science.* New York: Free Press.

Kevles, Daniel, 1985. *In the Name of Eugenics.* Cambridge, MA: Harvard University Press.

Kimbrell, Andrew. 1997. *The Human Body Shop.* Washington, D.C.: Regnery.

Kitcher, Philip. 1997. *The Lives to Come.* New York: Simon & Schuster.

Kristol, William, and Cohen, Eric. 2001. *The Future Is Now: America Confronts the New Genetics.* New York: Routledge.

Lederberg, Joshua. 1966. "Experimental Genetics and Human Evolution." *The American Naturalist* 100(915): 519–531.

McGee, Glenn. 1997. *The Perfect Baby.* Lanham, MD: Rowman and Littlefield.

Mehlman, Maxwell, and Botkin, Jeffrey. 1998. *Access to the Genome.* Washington, D.C.: Georgetown University Press.

Munson, Ron, and Davis, Larry. 1992. "Germline Gene Therapy and the Medical Imperative." *Kennedy Institute of Ethics Journal* 2: 137–158.

National Bioethics Advisory Commission. 1997. *Report on Cloning Human Beings.* Washington, D.C.: Author.

Parens, Erik, and Asch, Adrienne, eds. 2000. *Prenatal Testing and Disability Rights.* Washington, D.C.: Georgetown University Press.

Parens, Erik, and Juengst, Eric. 2001. "Inadvertently Crossing the Germline." *Science* 292: 397.

Parens, Erik, ed. 1999. *Enhancing Human Traits.* Washington, D.C.: Georgetown University Press.

Pence, Gregory E. 1998. *Who's Afraid of Human Cloning?* New York: Routledge.

Peters, Ted. 1997. *Playing God?: Genetic Determinism and Human Freedom.* New York: Routledge.

President's Commission for the Study of Ethical Problems in Medicine and Biomedical and Behavioral Research. 1982.

Splicing Life: The Social and Ethical Issues of Genetic Engineering with Human Beings. Washington, D.C.: President's Commission.

Ramsey, Paul. 1970. *Fabricated Man: The Ethics of Genetic Control.* New Haven, CT: Yale University Press.

Recombinant DNA Advisory Committee. 1995. "Recombinant DNA Research: Actions under the Guidelines." *Federal Register* 60 (810: 20731–20737, April 27).

Resnik, David. 2000a. "The Moral Significance of the Therapy/Enhancement Distinction in Human Genetics." *Cambridge Quarterly of Healthcare Ethics* 9: 365–377.

Resnik, David. 2000b. "Of Maize and Men: Reproductive Control and the Threat to Genetic Diversity." *Journal of Medicine and Philosophy* 25: 451–467.

Resnik, David, and Langer, Pamela. 2001. "Human Germline Therapy Reconsidered." *Human Gene Therapy* 12: 1449–1458.

Resnik, David; Steinkraus, Holly; and Langer, Pamela. 1999. *Human Germline Gene Therapy: Scientific, Moral and Political Issues.* Austin, TX: R.G. Landes.

Richter, Gerd, and Baccheta, Matthew. 1998. "Interventions in the Human Genome: Some Moral and Ethical Considerations." *Journal of Medicine and Philosophy* 23: 303–317.

Rifkin, Jeremy. 1983. *Algeny.* New York: Viking Press.

Robertson, John. 1994. *Children of Choice.* Princeton, NJ: Princeton University Press.

Robertson, John. 1998. "Oocyte Cytoplasm Transfers and the Ethics of Germ-Line Intervention." *Journal of Law, Medicine, and Ethics* 26(3): 211–220.

Silver, Lee. 1998. *Remaking Eden: How Genetic Engineering and Cloning Will Transform the American Family.* New York: Avon.

Stock, Gregory, and Campbell, John. 2000. *Engineering the Human Germline.* New York: Oxford University Press.

Suzuki, David, and Knudtson, Peter. 1989. *Genethics.* Cambridge, MA: Harvard University Press.

Templeton, Allan. 2002. "Ooplasmic Transfer—Proceed with Care." *New England Journal of Medicine* 346: 773–775.

Walters, Le Roy. 1986. "The Ethics of Human Gene Therapy." *Nature* 320: 225–227.

Walters, Le Roy, and Palmer, Julie. 1997. *The Ethics of Human Gene Therapy.* New York: Oxford University Press.

Watson. James. 1971. "Moving Toward Clonal Man." *Atlantic Monthly* 227(5): 50–53.

Zanjani, Esmail, and Anderson, French. 1999. "Prospects for in Utero Human Gene Therapy." *Science* 285: 2084–2088.

Zimmerman, Burke. 1991. "Human Germline Therapy: The Case for Its Development and Use." *Journal of Medicine and Philosophy* 16: 593–612.

INTERNET RESOURCES

Human Genetic Advisory Commission/Human Fertilization and Embryology Authority. 1998. "Cloning Issues in Reproduction, Science and Medicine." Available from <http://www.dgwsoft.co.uk/homepages/cloning/>.

International Bioethics Committee. 1994. "Report on Human Gene Therapy." Available from <http://www.unesco.org/ibc/en/>.

U.S. Food and Drug Administration. 2002a. *Human Gene Therapy and the Role of the Food and Drug Administration.* Available from <http://www.fda.gov/cber/>.

U.S. Food and Drug Adminstration. 2002b. *Use of Cloning Technology to Clone a Human Being.* Available from <http://www.fda.gov/cber/genetherapy/clone.htm>.

World Health Organization. "Definition of Health." Available from <http://www.who.int/aboutwho/en/>.

GLAYDE WHITNEY AND KENNETH F. SCHAFFNER

Genetics and Human Behavior: Scientific and Research Issues

Glayde Whitney (d. 2002) was a behavioral geneticist and professor of psychology at Florida State University. His laboratory research focused on the genetics of sensory system function in mice. He served as president of the Behavior Genetics Association during the mid-1990s. Professor Whitney was a frequent contributor to the journal *Mankind Quarterly*. In his later years his views on genetics and race and genetics and intelligence led to considerable public controversy.

Kenneth F. Schaffner is University Professor of History and Philosophy of Science, and of Philosophy, as well as Professor of Psychiatry at the University of Pittsburgh. He is also Emeritus University Professor of Medical Humanities and Professor of Philosophy at George Washington University in Washington, DC. He holds graduate degrees in both medicine and philosophy. Professor Schaffner has published *Discovery and Explanation in Biology and Medicine* (1993) and contributed to a 2006 volume entitled *Wrestling with Behavioral Genetics: Science, Ethics, and Public Conversation*, edited by Erik Parens, Audrey R. Chapman, and Nancy Press. His primary research interests are in the conceptual, historical, and social issues raised by behavioral genetics and, more generally, the philosophy of biology, medicine, and psychiatry.

Interest in the possible effects of genetic inheritance on human behavior is a perennial one, with its modern roots dating back the writings of Sir Francis Galton in the late nineteenth century. The issue is often framed as a debate over "nature versus nurture." After the "rediscovery" of the work of Gregor Mendel (1822–1884) in the twentieth century, the issue came to be couched in terms of genes versus environments and their respective influences on the organism, while more recently the talk has been of DNA and its role in relation to other causal factors. Themes revolving around genetics and environment are especially contentious when behavioral and mental traits (and disorders) are brought into the picture. This has been the case for views about the self and responsibility, as well as in society in general, where the specter of eugenics is quickly raised. According to the Nobel Laureate Thorsten Wiesel, "Perhaps most disturbing to our sense of being free individuals, capable to a large degree of shaping our character and our minds, is the idea that our behavior, mental abilities, and mental health can be determined or destroyed by a segment of DNA." The inflammatory appearance in 1994 of *The Bell Curve* by social scientists Richard Herrnstein and Charles Murray, which argued IQ is substantially inherited and may differ among races for genetic reasons, represents a major example of this social contentiousness. Another highly fractious example revolved around the University of Maryland's project on genetics and criminal behavior, and especially the September 1995 conference. The conference was strongly criticized by groups opposed to any inquiries into genetics and crime, and some of these groups' representatives invaded the conference and had to be escorted away by the authorities (Wasserman and Wachbroit).

The academic discipline that studies the effect of genetics on human behavior is termed *behavior genetics* or *behavioral genetics*. In addition to studying humans, this discipline has a long history of examining the behaviors of simpler organisms, including the round worm (*C. elegans*), the fruit fly (*Drosophila*), and the common mouse (*Mus*), as well as dogs, primates, and many other organisms. The organized discipline began to coalesce from a wide variety of disciplines in the 1960s with the appearance of the first textbook in the subject, *Genetics* by John Fuller and Robert Thompson. The disciplines contributing to behavioral (and psychiatric) genetics included biology (including genetics), psychology, statistics, zoology, medicine, and psychiatry. Especially significant was the psychology of *individual differences*, which perhaps provided the main themes of the new subject (see psychiatric geneticist Irving Gottesman's 2003 article for a brief but excellent historical introduction and references).

In the realm of behavioral disorders and genetics, the years since 1970 have seen a shift from the view of psychiatric disorders being primarily environmental (due to poor parenting, for example) to the contemporary view that amalgamates both genetic and what are called *nonshared* environmental influences as major causal determinants of mental disorders. This has not been a shift without controversy, and it reflects broader shifts in psychosocial studies of the contributions of nature and nurture (Reiss and Neiderhiser). Further, though psychology has paid increasing attention to behavioral genetics, cultural anthropology and sociology have been strongly resistant to any genetic approaches (Rowe and Jacobson).

MAJOR METHODS OF STUDYING GENETIC INFLUENCES

Traditional genetics, of the type investigated by Mendel and his followers, was able to identify genes that had large effects and often displayed typical patterns, such as those involving dominant, recessive, or sex-linked traits. Genes that affect human behaviors and exhibit such patterns are well-known, including Huntington's disease (caused by an autosomal dominant mutation) and phenylketonuria, or PKU (a recessive mutation). Symptoms of Huntington's disease include degeneration of the nervous system, usually beginning in middle age and resulting in death. In this devastating disease, there is usually a gradual loss of intellectual ability and emotional control. The genetic pattern is that of a condition caused by a rare, single, dominant gene. Since affected people have one copy of the dominant disease gene and one copy of a recessive gene (for a "normal" nervous system), half of their offspring develop the disease. Huntington's never skips a generation. Since the gene is dominant, the person who inherits it will manifest the disease (if he or she lives long enough). If one full sibling has the condition, there is a fifty-fifty chance that any other sibling will also get the disease.

In contrast to dominant conditions, recessive conditions show a very different pattern of occurrence. *Recessive* means that both copies of the gene must be of the same form (the same allele) in order to show the condition. Two parents, neither of whom shows a trait, can have a child affected by a recessive trait (this happens if both parents are carriers of one copy of the recessive allele—the child thus has two copies, one from each parent, and manifests the condition). Recessive traits can skip generations because parents and their offspring can carry one copy of the recessive gene and not display the associated trait. In the population there are many recessive genes that cause various abnormal conditions. Each particular recessive allele may be rare, but since there are many of them, their combined impact on a population can be substantial.

Among humans, a classic example of recessive inheritance is the condition of phenylketonuria (PKU). Individuals with PKU usually are severely mentally impaired. Most never learn to talk; many have seizures and display temper tantrums. PKU is a form of severe mental retardation that is both genetic and treatable. It is genetic in that it is caused by a recessive genetic allele. Without two copies of that particular allele, a person will not develop the set of symptoms, including mental impairment, that is characteristic of PKU. However, scientific knowledge has led to a treatment. It was discovered that the recessive PKU gene prevents the normal metabolism of a substance that is common in food, making many normal foods toxic to the individual with two PKU alleles. A special diet that is low in the offending substance can prevent or minimize the nervous system damage that leads to the profound intellectual disabilities of untreated PKU individuals.

The example of PKU demonstrates that inherited (genetic) conditions can be treated—that knowledge of specific causation can result in effective treatment. This is an extremely important point both ethically and philosophically, because it is often misunderstood and misinterpreted.

Well over one hundred different genes are known for which relatively rare recessive alleles cause conditions that include severe mental impairment among their symptoms. The rapidly developing knowledge of basic genetic chemistry, from molecular genetics to biotechnology and the Human Genome Project, which produced a mapping of some 30,000 human genes early in the twenty-first century on April 15, 2003, holds out the hope that many more of these devastating genetic conditions may soon be treatable. As part of the Human Genome Project, genes for Huntington's disease and PKU have been identified and sequenced, though as yet no new therapies have been developed for these disorders.

In spite of these clear scientific successes related to Mendelian genetic-pattern disorders, many human traits—including normal traits, as well as somatic, behavioral, and psychiatric disorders—have *not* exhibited clear Mendelian patterns of inheritance. For those traits, an extension of Mendel's work to quantitative traits that was first developed by Sir Ronald Fisher, has been used extensively. Beginning in the 1990s, an additional, more molecular, set of techniques was developed to examine possible influences of genetics on human behavior. These two broad approaches to studying the influences of nature and nurture in psychiatry are termed *quantitative* (or *epidemiological*) and *molecular*. A brief summary of the two approaches is presented here, including some examples of their results and their problems (an overview of them can be found in Neiderhiser and in Schaffner [2001], and a systematic analysis is presented in *Behavioral Genetics* by Plomin et al.).

Quantitative Methods. Quantitative, or epidemiological, methods are utilized to distinguish genetic and environmental contributions to quantitative traits or features of an organism, as well as to assess correlations and interactions between genetic and environmental factors that account for differences between individuals. These methods do not examine individual genes, but report on proportions of differences in traits due to heredity or environment, or to their interactions, broadly conceived. The methods include family, twin, and adoption studies. Adoption studies examine genetically related individuals in different familial environments, and thus can *prima facie* disentangle contributions of nature and nurture. Twin studies compare identical and fraternal twins, both within the same familial environment and (in adoption studies) in different familial circumstances.

Twin studies have been used extensively in psychiatry to indicate whether a disorder is genetic or environmentally influenced, and to what extent. Twin studies make several assumptions to analyze gathered data, including that the familial environment is the same for twins raised together but different for twins raised apart, an assumption called the *equal environments assumption*. Though critics of genetic influence often question this assumption empirical studies have confirmed it (Kendler et al.). The example of schizophrenia may help make some twin results clearer. Employing what are termed *concordance studies* of twins, Gottesman and his associates have reported over many years that the risk of developing schizophrenia if a twin or sibling has been diagnosed with the condition is about 45 percent for monozygotic (MZ) twins, 17 percent for dizygotic (DZ) twins, and 9 percent for siblings (Gottesman and Erlenmeyer-Kimling). This concordance pattern supports what is called a non-Mendelian polygenic (many genes) quantitative trait etiology for schizophrenia with a major environmental effect (> 50%), i.e., more than half of the differences in liability to schizophrenia among individuals is due to environmental factors. Twin studies can also be used to estimate the heritability of a trait or a disorder, which for schizophrenia is about 80 percent. *Heritability* is a technical term, one that is often confusing even to experts, and one which only loosely points toward the existence of underlying genetic factors influencing a trait. Investigators note that "it does *not* describe the quantitative contribution of genes to . . . any . . . phenotype of interest; it describes the quantitative contribution of genes to *interindividual differences* in a phenotype studied in a particular population" (Benjamin et al., p. 334). If there are no interindividual differences in a trait, then the heritability of that trait is zero—leading to the paradoxical result that the heritability of a human having a brain is virtually zero. Heritability is also conditional on the environment in which the population is studied, and the heritability value can significantly change if the environment changes.

Keeping these caveats in mind, heritability estimates for many major psychiatric disorders appear to be in the 70 to 80 percent range, and personality studies indicate heritabilities of about 30 to 60 percent for traits such as emotional stability and extraversion, suggesting that these differences among humans are importantly genetically influenced. But even with a heritability of schizophrenia of about 80 percent, it is also wise to keep in mind that approximately 63 percent of all persons suffering from schizophrenia will have *neither first- nor second-degree* relatives diagnosed with schizophrenia, reinforcing the complex genetic-environmental patterns found in this disorder.

Twin studies were also the basis of a distinction between *shared* and *nonshared* environments. The meaning of environment in quantitative genetics is extremely broad, denoting everything that is not genetic (thus environment would include *in utero* effects). The shared environment comprises all the nongenetic factors that cause family members to be similar, and the nonshared environment is what makes family members different. Remarkably, quantitative genetics studies of normal personality factors, as well as of mental disorders, indicate that of all environmental factors, it is the *nonshared* ones that have the major effect. A meta-analysis of forty-three studies undertaken by psychologists Eric Turkheimer and Mary Waldron in 2000 indicated that though the non-shared environment is responsible for 50 percent of the total variation of behavioral outcomes, *identified and measured nonshared environmental factors* accounted for only 2 percent of the total variance. Turkheimer infers that these nonshared differences are nonsystematic and largely accidental, and thus have been, and will continue to be, very difficult to study (Turkheimer, 2000). This possibility had been considered in 1987 by Robert Plomin and Denise Daniels but dismissed as a "gloomy prospect"—though it looks more plausible.

Epidemiological investigations have also identified two important features of how genetic and environmental contributions work together. The first, genotype-environment *correlation* (GsE), represents possible effects of an individual's genetics on the environment (e.g., via that individual's evoking different responses or selecting environments). Such effects were found for both normal and pathological traits in the large Nonshared Environmental Adolescent Development (NEAD) study, described in detail in the 2000 book *The Relationship Code*, written by David Reiss and colleagues. Secondly, different genotypes have different sensitivities to environments, collectively called genotype×environmental *interaction* (G×E). Differential sensitivity is important in many genetic

disorders, including the neurodevelopmental models of schizophrenia genetics and in a recent study on the cycle of violence in maltreated children (discussed later).

Molecular Methods. Classical quantitative or epidemiological studies can indicate the genetic contributions to psychiatric disorders at the population level, but they do not identify any specific genes or how genes might contribute (patho)physiologically to behavioral outcomes. According to psychiatric geneticist Peter McGuffin and his colleagues, "quantitative approaches can no longer be seen as ends in themselves," and the field must move to the study of specific genes, assisted by the completed draft versions of the human genome sequence (McGuffin et al., p. 1232). In point of fact, a review of the recent literature indicates that most research in behavioral genetics, and especially in psychiatric genetics, has taken a "molecular turn."

It is widely acknowledged that most genes playing etiological and/or pathophysiological roles in human behaviors, as well as in psychiatric disorders, will *not* be single locus genes of large effect following Mendelian patterns of the Huntington's and PKU type discussed earlier. The neurogeneticist Steven Hyman notes that mental disorders will typically be heterogeneous and have multiple contributing genes, and likely have different sets of overlapping genes affecting them. Mental disorders will thus be what are called *complex traits*, technically defined as conforming to *non*-Mendelian inheritance patterns.

There are two general methods that are widely used by molecular behavioral and molecular psychiatric geneticists in their search for genes related to mental disorders: (1) linkage analysis, and (2) alleleic association. Linkage analysis is the traditional approach to gene identification, but it only works well when genes have reasonably large effects, which does not appear to be the case in normal human behavior or in psychiatry. Allelic association studies are more sensitive, but they require "candidate genes" to examine familial data. An influential 1996 paper by statisticians Neil Risch and Kathleen Merikangas urged this strategy.

Studies in schizophrenia are again illustrative of these approaches, as are the Alzheimer's disease genetic studies reviewed later. Though there was an erroneous 1988 report of an autosomal dominant gene for schizophrenia on chromosome 5 that is seen as a false positive, evidence has been accumulating for genes or gene regions of small effect related to schizophrenia on many chromosomes, including 1q, 2, 3p, 5q, 6p, 8p, 11q, 13q, 20p, and 22q (Harrison and Owen). Replication difficulties with these results in different populations of schizophrenics and their families have been a recurring problem, however.

ENVIRONMENTAL RESEARCH AND THE ENVIROME

It is clear from epidemiological studies that more than half the variance of typical behavioral traits, as well as half of the liability for psychiatric disorders (including schizophrenia), is environmental. This has fueled major searches for various environmental causes. In schizophrenia, this work has been reviewed by Ming Tsuang and his colleagues, who note that the major environmental risk factors in schizophrenia are due to the nonshared environment. These include problems in pregnancy (e.g., preeclampsia) and obstetric complications, urban birth, winter birth, and maternal communicational deviance. Thus far, *identified* predisposing environmental factors have small values in comparison with genetic risk factors. Using a term coined in 1995 by James C. Anthony, Tsuang et al. have proposed that the entire *envirome* needs to be searched for extragenetic causes of disorders, including schizophrenia. These factors are believed to affect susceptible genotypes, involving G×E interactions.

Though evidence for susceptibility genes for major mental disorders continues to accumulate, there has been no strongly replicated result that might be used in diagnosis or in early detection and prevention interventions. Of all the *psychiatric* disorders that have been investigated to date by genetic strategies, only Alzheimer's disease (AD) provides both a classical Mendelian etiological picture and complex trait patterns, and thus can function as a concrete prototype for psychiatric genetics and for research on genetic influences on human behavior in general. There are three Mendelian forms of early-onset AD, due to dominant mutations in genes APP, PS1, and PS2. The strongly replicated APOE4 locus associated with late-onset Alzheimer's disease (LOAD), in contrast, is a *susceptibility gene*, neither necessary nor sufficient for the disease. The APOE4 and APOE2/3 alleleic forms also interact with other genes and with the environment. APOE alleles 2 and 3 appear to protect individuals with the APP mutation (Roses). Other susceptibility genes for LOAD continue to be investigated. A possible locus on chromosome 12 has been identified, and one was reported in 2000 on chromosome 9 (Pericak-Vance et al.; Roses).

COGNITIVE ABILITIES AND INTELLIGENCE

Though there are more data about the inheritance of intelligence than about any other complex behavioral characteristic of humans, the word *intelligence* is viewed even by the proponents of IQ testing as misleading because it has too many different meanings. IQ researchers seem to prefer to use the expression "general cognitive ability," represented by the letter *g* (Jensen; Plomin, DeFries, et al., 2001). The notion of substantial genetic influences on individual variation in *g* or "intelligence" remains controversial even after almost a century of investigation.

Most investigators in behavioral genetics view the level of intellectual functioning (abstract reasoning, ability to perform complex cognitive tasks, score on tests of general intelligence, IQ) as a strongly heritable trait. In 1963, psychologists Nikki Erlenmeyer-Kimling and Lissy Jarvik summarized the literature dealing with correlations between the measured intelligence of various relatives. After eliminating studies based on specialized samples or employing unusual tests or statistics, they reviewed eighty-one investigations. Included were data from eight countries on four continents spanning more than two generations and containing over 30,000 correlational pairings. The overview that emerged from that mass of data was unequivocal. Intelligence appeared to be a quantitative polygenic trait; that is, a trait influenced by many genes, as are such physical characteristics as height and weight.

The results did not suggest that environmental factors were unimportant, but that genetic variation was quite important. The less sensitive trait of height (or weight) can be used to illustrate this distinction. It is well known that an individual's height can be influenced by nutrition, and inadequate diets during development can result in reduced height. The average height of whole populations has changed along with changes in public health and nutrition. Yet at the same time, individual differences in height (or weight) among the members of a population are strongly influenced by heredity. In general, taller people tend to have taller children across the population as a whole, and the relative height of different people is strongly influenced by their genes. This also appears to be the case with intelligence. The Erlenmeyer-Kimling and Jarvik survey data suggest that about

70 percent of the variation among individuals in measured intelligence is due to genetic differences. The remaining 30 percent of the variation is due to unspecified (and still unknown) environmental effects.

Two decades later, in 1981, Thomas Bouchard and Matt McGue at the University of Minnesota also compiled a summary of the world literature on intelligence correlations between relatives. They summarized 111 studies, 59 of which had been reported during the seventeen years since the Erlenmeyer-Kimling and Jarvik review. Bouchard and McGue summarized 526 familial correlations from 113,942 pairings. The general picture remained the same, with roughly 70 percent of normal-range variation attributable to genetic differences and about 30 percent due to environmental effects.

However, researchers examining the behavioral genetics of cognitive ability estimate the heritability of g (or IQ) as substantially lower, about 30 to 35 percent. Statisticians Bernie Devlin, Michael Daniels, and Kathryn Roeder argue that much of the difference between the high and low heritabilities can be accounted for by a substantial maternal environmental component. As in the height and weight example above, there is also a substantial general environmental component that increased IQ scores by about 30 points between 1950 and 2000. This is known as the Flynn effect (see Flynn).

Robert Plomin and colleagues have attempted to identify specific genes or gene regions, also known as quantitative trait loci (QTLs), that influence IQ. Though there has been one publication reporting an IQ-related gene (see Plomin, Hill, et al.), replication has not yet been forthcoming.

Much is known about the genetics of mental retardation and learning disabilities. The most common single causes of severe general learning disabilities are chromosomal anomalies (having too many or too few copies of one of the many genes that occur together on a chromosome). These genes may reside on additional chromosomes, for example trisomy 21 (an extra chromosome 21, or three instead of the normal two) is the cause of Down's syndrome, and the "fragile X" condition may by itself account for most, if not all, of the excess of males among people with severe learning disabilities (Plomin, DeFries, et al., 2001). A large number of rare single-gene mutations, many of them recessive, induce metabolic abnormalities that severely affect nervous system function and thus lead to mental retardation. Because the specific alleles involved are individually rare and recessive, such metabolic abnormalities can cause learning-disabled individuals to appear sporadically in otherwise unaffected families. The new field of molecular genetic technology holds a promise of future therapeutic regimens for many learning disabilities.

PERSONALITY STUDIES

Dimensions of personality tend to be familial (Benjamin et al.). Modern studies of twins and adoptees suggest that for adults, some major dimensions are influenced by differences in family environments, while some are not. For the dimension of extroversion, which encompasses such tendencies as sociability and impulsivity, genetic factors account for about 30 to 60 percent of the variation among adults, with about 50 percent of the variation being environmental in origin. But, surprisingly, none of the variation among adults appears to be related to environmental differences within families.

For neuroticism, which taps such traits as anxiousness (a characteristic state of anxiety), emotional instability, and anxious arousability (a tendency to react with anxiety to events), about 40 percent of the adult variation appears to be caused by genetic differences, and again none of the variation is from environmental differences that are shared by members of the same family. In contrast, social desirability, which measures a tendency to answer questions in socially approved ways and to want to appear accepted by and acceptable to society, does not show evidence of genetic causation. Essentially all of the measurable variation in social desirability appears to be environmental, with about 20 percent due to family environment.

Some authors, including Robert Plomin and colleagues, the authors of *Behavioral Genetics* (2001), suggest that because extroversion and neuroticism are general factors involved in many other personality scales or dimensions, most of the others also show moderate genetic variation. For example, a twin study involving eleven personality scales found genetic influence of various degrees for them all (Tellegen et al.). On average, across the eleven personality scales, 54 percent of the variation was attributable to genetic differences among the people, and 46 percent to environmental differences.

Tendencies toward affective (mood) disorders, including psychotic depression and bipolar disorder type I (manic depression), also are clearly influenced by genetics. A lack of familial co-occurrence has established the separateness of schizophrenia from the affective psychoses. Unipolar depression and bipolar affective disorder do co-occur, and there may be a genetically influenced major depressive syndrome distinct from manic depression. The affective disorders probably include a diversity of genetic conditions.

OTHER TRAITS

Although data are sparse for many traits, modern studies are revealing genetic involvement in many conditions of importance to society. Plomin and colleagues point out that, for males, the best single predictor of alcoholism is alcoholism in a first-degree biological relative. Alcoholism clearly runs in biological families. Severe alcoholism affects about 5 percent of males in the general population, but among male relatives of alcoholics the incidence is about 25 percent. The incidence remains about the same for adopted-away sons of male alcoholics. However, biological children of nonalcoholics are not at increased risk for alcoholism when raised by alcoholic adoptive parents.

Behavioral and psychiatric geneticists have studied genetic influence on antisocial behavior and adult criminality. Studies tend to report that shared environment is more important as a cause in juveniles and that genetics plays more of a role in adults (Lyons et al.). These studies have been extremely contentious, however (Wasserman and Wachbroit). Since the early 1990s several molecular studies of genetics and violence have also emerged, two of which are cited here. In 1993 Hans Brunner and his group reported on a Dutch family with a missing gene on the X chromosome which governed the monoamine oxidase A (MAOA) enzyme, an enzyme that metabolizes some key neurotransmitters (Brünner et al.). The Dutch families' males exhibited an unusual number of antisocial behaviors of varied sorts (assaults, rape, arson, etc.). Males, lacking a second X chromosome, were more vulnerable to the effects of this mutation. The mutation was subsequently determined to be extremely rare, and behavioral geneticists largely lost interest in the MAOA gene. In August 2002, however, a major study involving about 1000 New Zealand families found that a less severe MAOA gene mutation had a significant effect on males' display of antisocial behaviors, including their being convicted for violent offenses (Caspi et al.). But the antisocial behaviors only appeared in those subjects (in as much as 85% of them) who had experienced abuse during childhood, indicating an important G×E interaction effect of gene with environment. This carefully designed study is yet to be replicated, but it has received widespread attention.

Both twin and adoption studies indicate that obesity is highly heritable, probably about 70 percent (Grilo and Pogue-Geile). In addition, a large adoption study of obesity among adults found that family environment by itself had no apparent effect—in adulthood, the body mass index of the adoptees showed a strong relationship to that of their biological parents, but there was no relationship between weight classification of adoptive parents and the adoptees. The relation between biological parent and adoptee weight extended across the spectrum, from very thin to very obese. Once again, cumulative effects of the rearing home environment were not important determinants of individual differences among adults (Stunkard et al.).

PHILOSOPHICAL AND THEORETICAL PERSPECTIVES

Biologists, psychologists, and philosophers have engaged in high-level theorizing about the effects of genes on traits in general and on human behavior in particular. Perhaps the most vigorous and ongoing discussion has been generated by a variety of papers and books that can be loosely characterized as a "developmentalist challenge" to the separability of genetic and environmental contributions to an organism's features (Schaffner, 1998). Over the years, the biologist Richard Lewontin's views have been particularly influential in this regard. Similar views critical of an overemphasis of genetic influence on traits have been articulated by several other scholars (see *Cycles of Contingency* [2001], by Susan Oyama, Paul Griffiths, and Russell Gray, which presents a number of contributions to "developmental systems theory" [DST]). Thus far, DST has largely been directed at critiquing DNA priority in molecular developmental and evolutionary claims, and at recommending more epigenetic-driven research. It is conceivable that as DST develops further, it will be applied more specifically to the relation of nature and nurture in a number of psychiatric disorders.

INTEGRATED APPROACHES

Some recent articles suggest that research integrating quantitative and molecular approaches with neuroscientific strategies will be the most fruitful way to provide a framework for genetic and environmental effects on organisms. Reiss and Neiderhiser recommend an "integrated" approach. In their 1991 book *Schizophrenia Genesis,* Irving Gottesman and Dorothea Wolfgram envision the future promise of neuroscience programs to assist progress in schizophrenia. The increasingly important neurodevelopmental perspective approach to schizophrenia has been championed by Tsuang and colleagues and implemented in recent papers from the Pittsburgh group (Mirnics et al.). In addition, a series of ethical issues have arisen in neuroscience that mirror many of those first generated by behavioral genetics, including issues of reduction, determinism, and responsibility. A new term, *neuroethics,* has been coined to describe these issues (Marcus).

The completion of the draft mapping of the human genome has led to a realization that the next stage of inquiry into examining human behavioral traits, and both somatic and mental disorders, will need to be very complex, involving functional genomics, proteomics (the study of proteins and their effects) (Pandey and Mann), and enviromics (Anthony). These will be difficult and complex projects that will also need to attend carefully to developmental issues, since most human diseases, including psychiatric disorders, probably represent the culmination of "lifelong interactions between our genome and the environment" (Peltonen and McKusick, p. 1228). Animal models will be helpful here, as will new technologies using DNA genetic chips, also known as *microarrays.*

CONCLUSION

There are diverse methodological approaches to studying the effects of genetics on human behavior and in relation to psychiatric disorders. The working out of the partitioning of genetic and environmental causes and their interactions at multiple levels of aggregation in complex systems, as humans are, will require many research programs extending over many years, hopefully producing a number of useful interim results such as those discussed above. These results, however, will not silence the continuing debates over the roles that genes and environments play in the complex choreography of organism development and behaviors.

BIBLIOGRAPHY

Anthony, James C. 2001. "The Promise of Psychiatric Enviromics." *British Journal of Psychiatry* 40 (suppl.): 8–11.

Benjamin, Jonathan; Ebstein, Richard P.; and Belmaker, Robert H. 2002. *Molecular Genetics and the Human Personality.* Washington, D.C.: American Psychiatric Publications.

Bouchard, Thomas J., Jr., and McGue, Matt. 1981. "Familial Studies of Intelligence: A Review." *Science* 212(4498):1055–1059.

Brunner, H. G.; Nelen, M.; Breakefield, X. O.; et al. 1993. "Abnormal Behavior Associated with a Point Mutation in the Structural Gene for Monoamine Oxidase A." *Science* 262(5133): 578–580.

Caspi, Avshalom; McClay, Joseph; Moffitt, Terrie E.; et al. 2002. "Role of Genotype in the Cycle of Violence in Maltreated Children." *Science* 297(5582): 851–854.

Devlin, Bernie; Daniels, Michael; and Roeder, Kathryn. 1997. "The Heritability of IQ." *Nature* 388(6641): 468–471.

Erlenmeyer-Kimling, L., and Jarvik, Lissy F. "Genetics and Intelligence: A Review." *Science* 142(3598): 1477–1479.

Flynn, J. R. 1999. "Searching for Justice: The Discovery of IQ Gains over Time." *American Psychologist* 54: 5–20.

Fuller, John L., and Thompson, William Robert. 1960. *Behavioral Genetics.* New York: Wiley.

Gottesman, Irving I. 2003. "A Behavioral Genetics Perspective." In *Behavioral Genetics in the Postgenomic Era,* ed. R. Plomin, J. DeFries, I. Craig, P. McGuffin, et al. Washington, D.C.: American Psychological Association.

Gottesman, Irving I., and Erlenmeyer-Kimling, L. 2001. "Family and Twin Strategies As a Head Start in Defining Prodromes and Endophenotypes for Hypothetical Early-Interventions in Schizophrenia." *Schizophrenia Research* 51(1): 93–102.

Gottesman, Irving I., and Wolfgram, Dorothea L. 1991. *Schizophrenia Genesis: The Origins of Madness.* New York: Freeman.

Grilo, C. M., and Pogue-Geile, M. F. 1991. "The Nature of Environmental Influences on Weight and Obesity: A Behavior Genetic Analysis." *Psychology Bulletin* 110(3): 520–537.

Harrison, P. J., and Owen, M. J. 2003. "Genes for Schizophrenia? Recent Findings and Their Pathophysiological Implications." *Lancet* 361(9355): 417–419.

Herrnstein, Richard J., and Murray, Charles A. 1994. *The Bell Curve: Intelligence and Class Structure in American Life.* New York: Free Press.

Hyman, Steven E. 2000. "The Genetics of Mental Illness: Implications for Practice." *Bulletin of the World Health Organization* 78(4): 455–463.

Jensen, Arthur R. 1998. *The g Factor: The Science of Mental Ability.* Westport, CT: Praeger.

Kendler, K. S.; Neale, M. C.; Kessler, R. C.; et al. 1993. "A Test of the Equal-Environment Assumption in Twin Studies of Psychiatric Illness." *Behavioral Genetics* 23(1): 21–27.

Lewontin, Richard C.; Rose, Steven P. R.; and Kamin, Leon J. 1984. *Not in Our Genes: Biology, Ideology, and Human Nature.* New York: Pantheon.

Lyons, M. J.; True, W. R.; Eisen, S. A.; et al. 1995. "Differential Heritability of Adult and Juvenile Antisocial Traits." *Archives of General Psychiatry* 52(11): 906–915.

Marcus, Steven, ed. 2002. *Neuroethics: Mapping the Field: Conference Proceedings.* New York: Dana Foundation.

McGuffin, Peter; Riley, Brien; and Plomin, Robert. 2001. "Genomics and Behavior. Toward Behavioral Genomics." *Science* 291(5507): 1232–1249.

Mirnics, K.; Middleton, F.; Marquez, A. A.; et al. 2000. "Molecular Characterization of Schizophrenia Viewed by Microarray Analysis of Gene Expression in Prefrontal Cortex." *Neuron* 28(1): 53–67.

Neiderhiser, Jenae M. 2001. "Understanding the Roles of Genome and Envirome: Methods in Genetic Epidemiology." *British Journal of Psychiatry* 40 (suppl.): 12–17.

Oyama, Susan; Griffiths, Paul E.; and Gray, Russell D. 2001. *Cycles of Contingency: Developmental systems and Evolution.* Cambridge, MA: MIT Press.

Pandey, A., and Mann, M. 2000. "Proteomics to Study Genes and Genomes." *Nature* 405(6788): 837–846.

Peltonen, Leena, and McKusick, Victor A. 2001. "Genomics and Medicine. Dissecting Human Disease in the Postgenomic Era." *Science* 291(5507): 1224–1229.

Pericak-Vance, M. A.; Grubber, J.; Bailey, L. R.; et al. 2000. "Identification of Novel Genes in Late-Onset Alzheimer's Disease." *Experimental Gerontology* 35(9–10): 1343–1352.

Plomin, Robert, and Daniels, D. 1987. "Why Are Children in the Same Family So Different from One Another?" *Behavioral and Brain Sciences* 10: 1–60.

Plomin, Robert; DeFries, John C.; McClearn; Gerald E.; et al. 2001. *Behavioral Genetics.* New York: Worth.

Plomin, Robert; Hill, L.; Craig, I. W.; et al. 2001. "A Genome-Wide Scan of 1842 DNA Markers for Allelic Associations with General Cognitive Ability: A Five-Stage Design Using DNA Pooling and Extreme Selected Groups." *Behavioral Genetics* 31(6): 497–509.

Reiss, David, and Neiderhiser, Jenae M. 2000. "The Interplay of Genetic Influences and Social Processes in Developmental Theory: Specific Mechanisms Are Coming into View." *Developmental Psychopathology* 12(3): 357–374.

Reiss, David; Neiderhiser, Jenae M.; Hetherington, E. Mavis; et al. 2000. *The Relationship Code: Deciphering Genetic and Social Influences on Adolescent Development.* Cambridge, MA: Harvard University Press.

Risch, Neil, and Merikangas, Kathleen. 1996. "The Future of Genetic Studies of Complex Human Diseases." *Science* 273(5281): 1516–1517.

Roses, Allen D. 2000. "Pharmacogenetics and the Practice of Medicine." *Nature* 405(6788): 857–865.

Rowe, David C., and Jacobson, Kristin C. 1999. "In the Mainstream: Research in Behavioral Genetics." In *Behavioral Genetics: The Clash of Culture and Biology,* ed. Ronald A. Carson and Mark A. Rothstein. Baltimore: Johns Hopkins University Press.

Schaffner, Kenneth F. 1998. "Genes, Behavior, and Developmental Emergentism: One Process, Indivisible?" *Philosophy of Science* 65(June): 209–252.

Schaffner, Kenneth F. 2001. "Nature and Nurture." *Current Opinion in Psychiatry* 14(Sept): 486–490.

Stunkard, A. J.; Foch, T. T.; and Hrubec, Z. 1986. "A Twin Study of Human Obesity." *Journal of the American Medical Association* 256(1): 51–54.

Tellegen, A.; Lykken, D. T.; Bouchard, T. J., Jr.; et al. 1988. "Personality Similarity in Twins Reared Apart and Together." *Journal of Personality and Social Psychology* 54(6): 1031–1039.

Tsuang, Ming. 2000. "Schizophrenia: Genes and Environment." *Biological Psychiatry* 47(3): 210–220.

Turkheimer, Eric. 2000. "Three Laws of Behavior Genetics and What They Mean." *Current Directions in Psychological Science* 9: 160–161.

Turkheimer, Eric, and Waldron, Mary. 2000. "Nonshared Environment: A Theoretical, Methodological, and Quantitative Review." *Psychology Bulletin* 126(1): 78–108.

Wasserman, David T., and Wachbroit, Robert S. 2001. *Genetics and Criminal Behavior.* Cambridge, Eng.: Cambridge University Press.

Wiesel, T. 1994. "Genetics and Behavior." *Science* 264:1647.

MICHAEL RUTTER

The Heritability of Different Mental Disorders and Traits

Sir Michael Rutter was appointed to the first United Kingdom Chair in Child Psychiatry in 1973. Since his retirement in 1998 he has held a research chair as Professor of Developmental Psychopathology at the Institute of Psychiatry, Kings College, London. He has written or edited approximately 40 books. His ongoing research interests are autism, child psychiatry, psychiatric epidemiology, and psychological development.

Before summarizing the findings on the heritability of a selective sample of different mental disorders and traits, it is necessary to consider how best to decide on the confidence that can be placed in the estimates derived from research findings. Basically, four main

From Michael Rutter, *Genes and Behavior: Nature-Nurture Interplay Explained* (Oxford: Blackwell Publishing, 2006), pp. 64–80, 89–91. Reprinted by permission of Blackwell Publishing.

approaches may be followed. First, attention needs to be paid to the results of putting together all the findings from the twin studies of acceptable quality. Sometimes, this has been done through a statistical technique called meta-analysis that provides a quantitative estimate based on the findings of all the studies but taking into account the relative size of the samples in the individual investigations. However, it is also sometimes done by considering both the average figure and the confidence interval around that figure—meaning the range covered by 95 percent of the findings. The second approach is to focus on the best quality studies in terms of sampling and measurement, in order to see whether they provide findings that are substantially different from the overall average. The third approach is to determine the extent to which the findings from the twin studies are in line with other evidence—meaning, for the most part, family studies and adoption studies. Finally, attention needs to be paid to whether or not cautions or reservations need to be added because of conceptual or methodological concerns raised by critics. These four approaches are illustrated with respect to some uncommon severely handicapping disorders, some more common disorders and traits for which there are rather more in the way of queries over diagnosis and definition, and, thirdly, findings on life experiences.

UNCOMMON DISORDERS FOR WHICH GENETIC INFLUENCES PREDOMINATE

SCHIZOPHRENIA

Schizophrenia is a serious mental disorder (occurring in males and females at roughly the same rate) that most often begins in early adult life and which is characterized by a combination of both positive and negative phenomena.[1] Positive symptoms (meaning those involving qualitative abnormalities) include thought disorder, auditory hallucinations, and delusions. Negative symptoms (meaning those that involve impairment in normal functions) include social withdrawal and a loss of motivation. Although about a fifth of people with schizophrenia do recover or markedly improve, in the majority of instances, the disorder runs a chronic or a current course. There is a much increased risk of suicide and also an increased rate of death from a variety of causes. There is major social impairment and considerable personal suffering. About one in a hundred people develop schizophrenia. Although the onset is characteristically in early adult life, in many cases there have been manifest precursors in childhood that involve neurodevelopmental impairment, social deficits, and solitary antisocial behavior.

Cardno and Gottesman[2] have brought together the findings from the five systematically ascertained twin studies reported in the late 1990s. The proband-wise **concordance** rate for schizophrenia in monozygotic (MZ) twin pairs was 41–65 percent, as compared with 0–28 percent for dizygotic (DZ) twin pairs, giving rise to a heritability estimate of approximately 80 to 85 percent. Considering the five studies separately, the heritability estimates range from 82 percent (with a confidence interval of 71–90) to 84 percent (with a confidence interval of 19–92). These figures are closely similar to the findings from the much earlier, methodologically less satisfactory, studies summarized by Gottesman.[3]

In many respects the best twin studies are the Scandinavian investigations—such as the Finnish Twin Study—because they are based on systematic coverage of the whole population as well as systematic diagnosis.[4] However, the Maudsley Twin Register has the special merit of a systematic recording of all twins attending the hospital since 1948 (albeit not on a population sample), and it has the advantages of a substantial sample size, zygosity determination undertaken on all available information and blind to diagnosis, and the use of systematic standardized diagnostic methods.[5] Both these studies produced heritability estimates closely in line with other twin studies.

Adoption studies, similarly, have indicated a strong genetic effect on the individual variations to the liability to schizophrenia. Thus, when data from the Danish adoption study were reanalyzed using modern diagnostic criteria, nearly 8 percent of the first-degree biological relatives of adoptees with schizophrenia had schizophrenia themselves, compared with just less than 1 percent of the first-degree relatives of control adoptees.[6] The comparable figures for schizophrenia spectrum disorders were 24 percent vs. 5 percent. Most of Joseph's[7] criticisms of this study were met by this more rigorous approach to both the data used and the diagnostic methods, as well as the separation of full and half siblings. The Finnish Adoption Study findings by Tienari et al.[8] provided broadly comparable figures for the offspring: an 8 percent rate of schizophrenia in the adopted-away offspring of mothers with schizophrenia, compared with 2 percent in the offspring of a comparison group of parents without schizophrenia.

Family studies, similarly, have shown consistently that the risk of schizophrenia in the relatives of individuals with schizophrenia is a function of the extent to which they share their genes. Thus, in the general population the rate of schizophrenia is approximately 1 percent, in second-degree relatives it is about 2–6 percent, whereas in first-degree relatives it is about 6–13 percent.[9]

Various objections have been raised in relation to the genetic findings on schizophrenia.[7] Some of the concerns refer to the reporting of the earlier adoptee study findings, some to the problems that derive from the uncertainties over diagnostic boundaries,[10] and some focus on the variations within groups of similar genetic relatedness (for example, the fact that the rate in non-identical co-twins is nearly twice as high as that in siblings, although they have the same genetic relatedness[3]). Also, the rate in parents (about 6 percent) is half that in children (about 13 percent), despite the fact that they are similar in their genetic relatedness. However, this last difference is almost certainly due to the fact that, as compared with the general population, individuals with schizophrenia are less likely to marry and have children.[11] Some of the detailed methodological criticisms are valid but the overall consistency of findings, and in particular the fact that the findings of the best studies are so consistent, makes the overall estimate of heritability sound. It can be inferred that, in the populations studied, the heritability is something of the order of 80 percent.

However, there are two further points that need emphasis. The early genetic studies all indicated that schizophrenia seemed to be genetically rather distinct from bipolar affective disorder. Recent evidence[12] has indicated that if the diagnostic criteria are somewhat broadened and if rather arbitrary traditional diagnostic hierarchies are set aside, the evidence indicates that, to some extent at least, genetic liability for schizophrenia and for bipolar disorder may overlap. A recent brain imaging study[13] showed that the genetic risks for schizophrenia and for bipolar disorder were associated with similar findings regarding the white matter of the brain, but with differences regarding the gray matter. As the author concluded, the evidence points to overlap between these two psychoses in some respects, but separateness in others. The other consideration is that the genetic risk for schizophrenia may interact with environmental risk factors.[14]

BIPOLAR AFFECTIVE DISORDER

Bipolar affective disorder (previously called manic-depressive disorder) is a serious recurrent condition involving one or more episodes of mania, usually (but not always) with episodes of depression at other times. The mania is characterized by euphoria, an exaggerated sense of self-esteem, racing thoughts and undue talkativeness, sleeplessness, distractibility, and reckless impulsive behavior. Typically each episode begins and ends rather suddenly, after a period of disability that lasts several months, but may be as brief as a week. It has an incidence of about 1 percent in the general population and occurs at much the same frequency in males and females.

The evidence on bipolar affective disorder is substantially less than that available for schizophrenia. Jones, Kent, and Craddock[15] pooled the findings from six twin studies using a modern concept of bipolar disorder. None was methodologically strong, and only three had a sample size that warranted statistical analysis. The monozygotic concordance rates ranged from 36 to 75 percent and those for dizygotic from 0 to 7 percent. This is consistent with high heritability but the data are too sparse for any quantitative estimate to be made with confidence. However, there are rather more data from family studies, there being eight with appropriate control findings. The risk of bipolar disorder in first-degree relatives is about 5–10 percent, which is much higher than the general population rate of about 0.5–1.5 percent. It has generally been concluded that the heritability is in excess of 70 percent, but inevitably this is a very approximate figure given the limitations of the evidence. The main area of uncertainty stems from the difficulty in knowing quite where to place the diagnostic boundary. Recently, long-term follow-up studies have suggested that the concept should be substantially broadened.[16] It is not at all clear how this would affect the estimates of the strength of genetic contribution to the population variance for this disorder.

AUTISM SPECTRUM DISORDERS

Autism spectrum disorders are serious conditions that involve deficits in social communication, deficits in social reciprocity, and the presence of stereotyped repetitive patterns of behavior, and which are much more common in males.[17] Although many findings indicate the likelihood that the basis of the disorder is first evident in brain development before birth and in the infancy period,[18] in most instances the manifestations of the disorder are not readily apparent until about the age of 18 months. It is now generally accepted that it is a neurodevelopmental disorder with characteristic cognitive deficits, of which the most prominent are a difficulty in telling from social situations what another person is likely to be thinking (a so-called "theory of mind" or mentalizing deficit) and a difficulty in appreciating the overall gestalt of pictures (in other words, a tendency to focus on details rather than the meaning of the whole[19]). There are also characteristic findings from functional brain imaging.[20]

There have been three epidemiologically based twin studies of autism.[21] The concordance rate in monozygotic pairs ranged from 36 to 91 percent; in dizygotic pairs the rate was just 0 percent (but probably 5 percent is a more realistic figure, this reflecting the rate in siblings as well as DZ twins on the grounds that the two are genetically comparable). The two combined British twin studies[22] had the considerable advantage of using well-tested standardized methods of diagnosis with DNA testing for zygosity in the great majority of cases, and checks that the findings were not an artifact of obstetric complications. The finding in the second study that very few new cases were found that would have been eligible for the first study (but were unused) means that the general population coverage was successfully thorough.

Family studies have provided further evidence of a strong genetic influence on the liability to autism. The rate of about 3 to 6 percent in the siblings of individuals with autism is many times higher than that in the general population. At the time the twin and family studies were undertaken, the evidence suggested a general population rate of approximately 1 per 1,000, meaning that the increase in rate among siblings was of the order of 30 to 60-fold. More recent epidemiological studies[23] have suggested that the true figure in the general population might be as high as 3 to 6 per 1,000. That would still mean an increase of 10-fold. However, for a proper comparison, the broad definition of autism used in the modern epidemiological studies would have to be applied to the twin and family studies, and this would mean that the increase in risk would be somewhat higher. Putting the findings together, the estimate of heritability is something of the order of about 90 percent. Because the twin and family studies provide the same conclusions, there can be considerable confidence that the heritability is very high, with genetic factors accounting for the majority of the population variance in liability to develop the disorder.

The main caution about the findings stems from the evidence that the genetic liability to autism extends much more broadly than the traditional diagnostic category of a seriously handicapping condition.[24]

ATTENTION DEFICIT DISORDER WITH HYPERACTIVITY (ADHD)

The fourth disorder for which the evidence suggests that genetic factors account for the majority of the population variance in liability is attention deficit disorder with hyperactivity (ADHD). It is a disorder that is more common in males and that is characterized by severe hyperactivity, impulsiveness, and inattention, that is pervasive across situations (although the intensity of its manifestations may vary according to circumstances), that is evident by the time the children start school, that shows substantial persistence into adult life, and which is associated with a range of other problems including antisocial behavior and poor scholastic achievement.[25] The majority of children with this disorder show a beneficial response to stimulant medication provided that it is part of a well thought out therapeutic plan tailored to the needs of the individual child.[26] Not surprisingly, because the diagnostic features overlap with "ordinary" forms of disruptive behavior seen in many normal children, there has been controversy over the validity of the diagnostic concept. Both the genetic evidence and the findings of longitudinal studies suggest that the liability is dimensionally distributed, without a clear watershed between variations within the normal range and a clinical condition requiring treatment.[27] On the other hand, there is much evidence showing important differences between ADHD and other forms of disruptive behavior, brain imaging findings show distinctive features, and the disorder is associated with substantial social impairment. Accordingly, although there is legitimate concern over the excessive use of stimulants in the United States for the treatment of very young children (an age group for which there is a lack of good evidence that stimulants are effective), there is every reason to regard ADHD as a clinically meaningful disorder that, when severe, warrants treatment by methods that include the use of stimulant medication.

There have been at least a dozen twin studies of ADHD symptoms.[28] The heritability estimates range from 60 to 88 percent when based on information from parents and 39 to 72 percent when based on ratings by teachers. Consistency of the heritability estimates across studies using a diverse range of questionnaire and interview measures is certainly impressive; the inference of a strong heritability seems justified. Nevertheless, there are reasons for being somewhat cautious about the strength of genetic influences. The data from family studies are supportive in showing an increased risk in biological first-degree relatives, as compared with controls, but the estimated increase of 4 to 5-fold[29] would seem to suggest a moderate rather than a very high heritability. There have been a number of adoption studies but, because of their weak methodology, they are essentially non-contributory.

There are also concerns with respect to some uncertainties on the diagnostic boundaries of ADHD, the fact that the findings are based on symptom scores rather than clinical diagnoses (although the evidence suggests that the heritability findings are similar for the two), and that there is some evidence that there may be contrast effects. What this means is that parents, when rating hyperactivity or inattention in their twins, under-rate these behaviors in the one twin because the contrast with the more seriously affected twin is so great. There are ways of dealing with this problem and, when this has been done, the heritability rate is still well above 60 percent.[30] Despite these concerns, the consistency of the evidence is sufficient to conclude that genetic influences on ADHD are substantial. Moreover, there is evidence that the well-documented association between ADHD and cognitive impairment arises to a predominant extent from a shared genetic liability.[31]

DISORDERS AND TRAITS WITH QUERIES OVER DIAGNOSIS OR DEFINITION

ANTISOCIAL BEHAVIOR

Antisocial behavior is a general term used to cover acts that involve breaking the law irrespective of whether the individual is caught or prosecuted.[32] However, children below the age of criminal responsibility (which varies widely among different countries) engage in similar behavior for which they cannot be prosecuted and these are similarly incorporated in the same overall term. The origins of antisocial behavior frequently lie in early-onset physical aggression, which tends to be accompanied by oppositional/defiant behavior. Accordingly, both of these may be included in a broader concept of antisocial behavior. Overall, it is more common in males, but the sex difference varies according to the type of antisocial behavior.

In many respects, claims on the strength of genetic influences on antisocial behavior have proved particularly controversial because of the fact that it involves socially defined behavior occurring in social contexts, rather than something that can be unambiguously measured in an objective fashion. However, that concern, although relevant for interpretation of the meaning of the findings, is not relevant with respect to the heritability findings. There have been a huge number of twin studies on large samples using sound measures

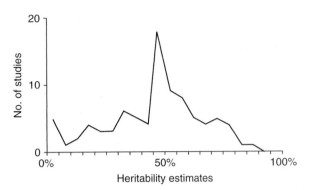

Figure 4.1   Percentage of genetic influence reported in behavioral genetic studies of antisocial behaviour.

Source: Moffitt, personal communication, derived from Moffitt, 2005.

of antisocial behavior. Rhee and Waldman[33] undertook a meta-analysis of the findings, which produced an overall heritability estimate of 41 percent. Moffitt[34] adopted a slightly different approach by examining the distribution of heritability estimates across studies, as shown in Figure 4.1. The findings show that the peak is around the 50 percent mark, with small tails to the bell-shaped distribution at both extremes. On the whole, the findings at the extremes derive from somewhat unusual samples or measures. This variation across studies is precisely what one would expect in putting a heterogeneous group of studies together.

Because of the need to be concerned about possible rater biases, the greatest confidence can be placed on the studies that have used multiple informants and multiple measures. These have tended to give heritability estimates that are rather higher than most. There are a few adoptee studies but the evidence they provide is too limited to offer much help in conclusions. Family studies are consistent in showing a 3 to 4-fold increase in the rate of antisocial behavior in the first degree of biological relatives of individuals showing antisocial behavior themselves.[32]

Putting the evidence together,[34] it is clear that there is a moderately strong genetic influence on the liability to exhibit antisocial behavior but the effects of genetic factors are far from determinative. The heritability of 40–50 percent means that there are strong non-genetic influences, and more detailed findings indicate that these account for both similarities among siblings in the same family and also differences. That is to say, some of the environmental influences tend to impinge similarly on all children in the family whereas others are particularly focused on just one child.

It is necessary to come back, however, to just what this moderate, but not overwhelmingly strong, heritability means. To begin with, it certainly does not mean that it is at all likely that antisocial behavior as such is inherited. That is really rather unlikely. What is much more probable is that the genetic factors influence temperamental or personality features that play a contributory role in making it more or less likely that individuals will engage in antisocial behavior. In other words, the effects are indirect. Also, . . . the genetic factors may be important in rendering people more vulnerable to adverse environmental features. It also should not be assumed that the genetic influence operates equally across all varieties of antisocial behavior. For example, there is some preliminary evidence that genetic influences may be more important in relation to early-onset antisocial behavior associated with hyperactivity and which tends to persist into adult life. There is a strong tendency for hyperactivity/inattention to be associated with oppositional/defiant behavior and with conduct problems and the evidence indicates that genetic factors play the major role in the associations among these different forms of disruptive behavior. The public tends to assume that genetic factors are likely to be maximal with violent crime, rather than with petty theft, but, although the evidence is far from conclusive, it does suggest that the reverse may be the case.

In summary, antisocial behavior constitutes a good example of behavior that is certainly heterogeneous in type and which is much influenced by social factors of both a societal and personal kind, but which, nevertheless, involves moderate genetic influences on individual differences in the liability to behave in antisocial ways.

UNIPOLAR DEPRESSION

Common varieties of depressive disorder constitute another example of the same kind. The adjective unipolar means depression that is not associated with episodes of mania or hypomania (meaning a lesser degree of mania) in which there is an abnormal elevation in mood that is accompanied by widespread disturbances in behavior. These ordinary varieties of depression are very common and indeed it is part of the normal human condition to feel depressed in some circumstances. What is called depressive disorder differs from this normal variation in mood in that it is accompanied by marked suffering and impairments in social functioning. Thus, the depressed mood tends to be accompanied by a loss of energy and of interest in life, changes in sleep and appetite, psychomotor agitation or retardation, feelings of worthlessness or unwarranted guilt, diminished concentration, and recurrent thoughts of death or suicidal ideation. In short, it is not at all like ordinary sadness, although there is unhappiness. Over the course of a lifetime, probably about one in four females and one in ten males suffer from a major depressive disorder. For some people, there is just one such episode but for others there are many recurrences and it has been shown from many studies that not only is there a substantial increase in the rate of suicide but there is also a substantial increase in mortality from other disorders. Numerous twin studies, based on both general population and hospital clinic samples, have been undertaken. Sullivan et al.[35] undertook a meta-analysis from the five twin studies meeting the most stringent criteria, and produced a heritability estimate of 37 percent (with a confidence interval extending from 31 to 42 percent). However, the McGuffin et al.[36] study based on the Maudsley Hospital Twin Register found a heritability of between 48 and 75 percent, depending on what assumption was made about the rate in the general population. Kendler et al.[37] also showed that the heritability tended to be substantially greater when account was taken of both the reliability of measurement and multiple times of measurement.

Several concerns have been expressed with respect to the genetic findings on depression.[38] Thus, in relation to the general population studies, it has been objected that, because most of the sample will not have been depressed, the findings mainly show a genetic effect on not being depressed, rather than on having a depressive disorder. Of course, in a sense, that is correct because most of the variance will be within the normal range, but the objection does not really have validity because . . . the liability to depression is based on a continuously distributed dimension that extends throughout the population. The findings do not suggest that the disorder of depression is inherited as such; rather, the evidence suggests that the liability to have such an episode is influenced by genetic and environmental factors to an approximately equal degree. Surprise has also been expressed that relatively small differences between monozygotic and dizygotic pairs result in an estimated heritability as high as 40 percent. However, that, too, represents a misunderstanding of the situation. Heritability of 40 percent means that, overall in the population, environmental influences are having more effect than genes and, therefore, you would not expect a very big difference between monozygotic and dizygotic pairs. The situation is quite different from that seen with, say, schizophrenia or autism. Attention has also been drawn to the difficulties of defining the boundaries of depression, a problem that pervades the whole field of mental disorders. None of these concerns seriously challenges the conclusion that genetic factors are of moderate strength in relation to the ordinary varieties of depression, but that environmental influences are of roughly comparable importance. It is scarcely a very startling or surprising finding.

TEMPERAMENT, PERSONALITY
AND PERSONALITY DISORDER

The notion that people differ in their temperamental qualities goes back at least to the time of Galen in the second century, who postulated a subdivision into four qualities—melancholic, sanguine, choleric and phlegmatic.[39] With various modifications, the concept of biologically based differences in psychological style persisted until the twentieth century when, following the emergence of both psychoanalysis and behaviorism (led respectively by Freud and Pavlov), a belief in the overwhelming importance of the rearing environment took over. A key turning point was provided by the research and ideas of Alexander Thomas, Stella Chess, and Herbert Birch, working in New York. Based on an inductive analysis of detailed parental accounts of their children's behavior from infancy onwards, they emphasized the importance of distinctive styles of behavior, rather than motives, goals and competence.[40] Initially, they used the term "primary reaction patterns" in order to focus on both the constitutional origin and the role of the behavioral style in shaping children's responses to their environment. Later, they adopted the more straightforward term of "**temperament**."

During the years that followed, in keeping with the concepts of Buss and Plomin, it came to be accepted that temperamental features constituted a subclass of traits that showed marked individual variability and that were distinctive in emerging early in life, in exhibiting high stability over time and over situations, and in showing high heritability.[41] This view has not

stood the test of time[42] because temperamental features are not noticeably more heritable than other behaviors, because there is low stability in early infancy (although much higher stability from age 3 years onwards[43]), and because traits that index reactivity to the environment will be most evident in high stress or challenge situations, rather than in ordinary everyday life.[44] Accordingly, although there is no clear consensus on how temperament should be conceptualized, many researchers follow Kagan's preference for low-level traits that are concerned with some aspect of reactivity and which show good conceptual and empirical links with biology (and hence are best measured through a combination of behavior and physiology). He has argued that such temperamental features create an envelope of potential outcomes, creating a behavioral tendency that is not easily limited by life events but yet does not determine a particular personality type.

A quite different approach has been adopted by researchers who have focused on the coherence of reported behavioral features as observed in adult life. The preference here is for higher-order abstractions as exemplified by the so-called Big Five traits of extraversion/positive emotionality, neuroticism/negative emotionality, conscientiousness/constraint, agreeableness, and openness to experience.[45] This approach differs from Kagan's notion of temperamental reactivity in its inclusion of coherences that stem from attitudinal features, patterns of thought, and from motivational considerations, as well as simple dispositional attributes.[42] Although derived initially from adult research, the approach works reasonably well in childhood[46] and the measures provide important predictors of later mental functioning. Nevertheless, longitudinal evidence indicates that personality is far from fixed in early childhood; changes continue well into adult life.[45]

Personality disorder involves yet another concept that needs to be differentiated from temperament and personality. Traditionally, [personality disorders] have been conceptualized as malfunctioning extremes of personality traits, but this concept has little empirical justification.[42] Probably, the personality disorder concept of the greatest contemporary interest is "psychopathy," a category first put forward by Cleckley to describe a lack of normal socio-emotional responsiveness characterized by lack of remorse for wrong-doing, an absence of close relationships, egocentricity, and a general poverty of affect.[47] Some researchers have sought to relate "psychopathy" to the Big Five dimensions of personality but, in my view, it is more fruitful to define it in terms of an abnormal lack of responsiveness to emotionally laden cues, as examined by both Blair and Patrick using experimental paradigms with adult criminals.[48] The interest lies in the possibility that the emotional detachment constitutes an unusual risk factor for antisocial behavior that is not particularly associated with social disadvantage or family adversity.

These three aspects of psychological individuality (temperament, personality, and personality disorder) have been discussed at some length because of their centrality in dimensional approaches to risk . . . and in considerations of gene–environment interplay. . . . However, that being noted, it has to be added that twin and adoptee studies have not been particularly informative in casting light on causal mechanisms. There is consistency in the finding of a substantial genetic influence on personality dimensions with heritabilities of about 50 percent from twin studies and about 30 percent from adoptee studies,[49] but with not much variation across different dimensions. There is rather less evidence on temperament studies[50] but the findings are broadly comparable. There is some suggestion that genetic influences on psychopathy are possibly somewhat stronger than other dimensions studies.[51] It is reasonable to infer that temperament, personality, and personality disorder all show a moderate heritability (as is the case with most behaviors), but caution is needed in going any further than that in view of the fact that most research is based on single informant measures (parent reports in childhood and self-reports in adult life). The very limited evidence from the few multi-informant studies provides much the same picture, but the hope that behavioral genetics would show how temperament leads on to personality functioning and mental disorder has yet to be realized.

SUBSTANCE USE, AND SUBSTANCE USE DISORDER

A key feature of substance use and abuse is the very high frequency of occasional recreational use of illicit drugs (and of alcohol and tobacco products), but the relative infrequency of abuse and dependency.[52] The terminology applied to the various patterns of misuse and their consequences is both complex and varied.

However, the patterns include "dependence" (meaning a state involving various admixtures of increasing tolerance, physical withdrawal effects, difficulties in controlling the use of the substance, and a strong desire to take the substance despite harmful consequences), and "harmful use" (meaning that it leads to psychological, social, or somatic complications). It is also typical that the use of illicit substances includes a range of chemically disparate drugs, and that it is usual for the substance misuse to be associated with a mixture of mental health problems. A particularly common pattern is for early conduct disturbance to lead on to drug use and misuse and for such misuse to increase the later development of depression.[52]

In undertaking twin and adoptee studies, it is obvious that a developmental approach is essential. Thus, it cannot be assumed that the genetic and environmental influences on occasional recreational use of substances will be identical to those predisposing to later regular heavy use or to those involved in dependence. Because of these complications, it is perhaps not surprising that the estimates of heritability vary considerably,[53] although overall most estimates are in the 25 to 50 percent range. The more interesting aspects of the findings concern the evidence that genetic influences tend to be much weaker for initial experimental use of drugs than for abuse or dependency, which has quite a strong heritability, and that there is substantial overlap in the genetic liability for the use and abuse of different drugs. On the other hand, there is some drug-specificity. Also, adoption study findings suggest that there are two genetic pathways leading to drug abuse/dependency.[54] The first involves a main effect on drug problems, and the second involves a more indirect causal route that operates through antisocial behavior. Moreover, the genetic effects on antisocial behavior include a gene–environment interaction whereby the genetic risk involves an effect on susceptibility to environmental hazards.

DYSLEXIA

Dyslexia, a specific reading disability, is characterized by a persistent failure to acquire skills in reading despite adequate intelligence, adequate opportunity, and satisfactory teaching.[55] Although there is evidence from twin studies of a substantial genetic influence, dyslexia is a multifactorial disorder that is influenced by environmental as well as genetic factors. Thus, for example, specific reading disability was found to be much more common in inner London children than in those living in a less disadvantaged area of small towns.[56] This geographical difference held up after taking account of the children's measured intelligence and also patterns of in- and out-migration from the area.[57] Also, there are differences among schools in rates of reading difficulties that cannot be accounted for by differences in intake to the schools.[58] As well, there is evidence that children's opportunities to read at home affect their reading.[59] It is also notable that there are important differences in the rate of difficulties according to the language of upbringing.[60] The genetic findings cannot be used to infer that the reading difficulties have been caused by changes in the brain but they can be used to infer important connections between the workings of the brain and the acquisition, or failure to acquire, reading skills, as well as the fact that reading difficulties have a strong tendency to persist from childhood into adult life.

Dyslexia has also been found to be about twice as common in males as females.[61] Because of the influence of environmental factors, and because of difficulties of providing a satisfactory unambiguous definition of the disorder, the concept has given rise to some controversy. However, there is now substantial evidence that the reading difficulties are associated with measurable changes in brain functioning as studied through functional imaging. Moreover, brain changes are associated with both learning to read[62] and persistence of reading difficulties.[63]

Much of the uncertainty over genetic influences on dyslexia (specific reading disability) stems from the difficulties in knowing how best to conceptualize and measure it. It is generally regarded as a specific disorder that is not accounted for by limitations in general intelligence. However, IQ and reading skills are associated and therefore there is a need to separate the two when examining dyslexia. Also, although conceptualized as a specific disorder, from a genetic perspective it may function as a dimensionally distributed liability.

It has been known for many years that specific reading disability tends to run in families and both the Colorado Twin Study[64] and the London Twin Study[65] have shown that there is a substantial genetic influence.[66] Interestingly, heritability may be higher for reading disability in children of above average IQ (72 percent) than for those of below average IQ (43 percent)[64]; this finding still needs confirmation.

The sampling and measurement in the Colorado Twin Study were good and provide sound evidence of a substantial genetic influence but, in the absence of sound data from multiple studies of equal quality, uncertainty remains on the aspects of reading disability that are most influenced by genetics.

SPECIFIC DEVELOPMENTAL DISORDERS OF LANGUAGE (SPECIFIC LANGUAGE IMPAIRMENT – SLI)

Specific developmental disorders of language, now more commonly termed **specific language impairment**—SLI—concern marked delays in language development in children whose psychological development is proceeding relatively normally otherwise and who do not have an obvious disorder that might be causal (such as hearing loss, an acquired neurological condition, or mental retardation).[67] Such delay may involve only expressive language (i.e., use of language), or may include receptive abnormalities (i.e., the understanding of language), or may largely concern pragmatics (i.e., the social communicative aspects of language). Although essentially normal children may be remarkably late in gaining spoken language, the research findings are clear-cut in showing that the deficits associated with SLI that includes receptive problems often persist into adult life, with accompanying social deficits.[68] It is unlikely that this form of SLI constitutes just a variant of normal.

There are only a small number of twin studies but both those based on clinic samples and those based on general population epidemiological samples are in agreement in showing that SLI has substantial heritability.[69] In Viding et al.'s 2004 general population study, it was notable that the heritability was significantly greater for severe SLI than milder degrees of SLI.[70] It is notable that the genetic liability in high-risk groups, however, extends to include milder, as well as severe, SLI and that it does not fit at all neatly into the traditional diagnostic categories of SLI.

ALZHEIMER'S DISEASE

Alzheimer's disease is a progressive neurodegenerative disorder involving memory loss and then a more global decline in intellectual function, which typically comes on in old age. In the later stages, there is a loss of self-help skills (feeding, dressing, etc.), there may be wandering, and also episodes of delusions and hallucinations. It has a distinctive pattern of brain changes that can be seen microscopically after death. Thus, there is extensive loss of **neurones** and the deposition of extracellular plaques (made up of beta amyloid protein) and intracellular neurofibrillary tangles (made up from a particular kind of tau). There are two varieties of Alzheimer's disease: a rare early-onset variety (beginning before the age of 65 years), that is inherited in autosomal dominant fashion; and a much commoner late-onset variety that occurs in some 40 percent of individuals (both male and female) over the age of 90 years.

It is generally considered that Alzheimer's disease is quite distinct from normal ageing and from the deterioration in short-term memory and new learning that is so common in extreme old age. Certainly Alzheimer's disease involves a serious and general dementia that extends far beyond decrements in memory and new learning. Nevertheless, it may be that the genetic liability spans both the disease and normal memory decline.

Although Alzheimer's disease is a common condition, there are three main problems in assessing heritability.[71] First, clinical diagnosis is not completely accurate because of possible confusion with dementia due to cerebrovascular disease; second, because of the late onset of the condition, many individuals with a genetic liability die before reaching the age of risk; and third, family members may be assessed as free of the disease but nevertheless develop it some years later. Nevertheless, it is apparent that some 6 to 14 percent of the first-degree relatives of people with Alzheimer's disease also have the disease—approximately a doubling or trebling of risk. The twin data are based on very small samples but suggest a heritability of 40 to 80 percent. The family data suggest that most of the genetically influenced familial increase in risk has already come into play by age 90, with a lesser effect on Alzheimer's disease with an onset in extreme old age.

LIFE EXPERIENCES

There are now quite a number of studies that have examined genetic effects on a diverse range of experiences including threatening life events, differential parenting, parental negativity, and divorce.[72] Because the life experiences examined have been rather diverse and have involved a disparate range of measures, it is not possible to combine the studies in quite the same way that was done with the various mental disorders. Nevertheless, the findings are consistent in showing a significant genetic effect on people's likelihood of experiencing negative events or happenings of the kind that could be influenced by their own behavior. That is to say, the genetic influence is not on the events as such, but rather on the way people behave, and it is through their behavior that they shape and select their environments. The genetic effect is a far from overwhelming one, with most heritabilities in the region of 20 percent or so, although sometimes they have been higher than that. The evidence is certainly quite sufficient by now to conclude that there are genetic effects on the likelihood that people will have negative experiences that put them at risk of mental disorders, that the genetic effects are modest rather than strong, but they are pervasive. . . .

CONCLUSIONS

In conclusion, it is evident that quantitative genetic findings have been most useful in causing people to think somewhat differently about the nature of mental disorders. In particular, the findings are clear-cut in indicating that genetic influences apply to some degree to all forms of behavior, both normal and abnormal. However, in both cases the relevant genes are likely often to involve common, normal allelic variations rather than rare pathological mutations with major effects. It is not that, on its own, it matters very much whether the heritability is 20 percent or 80 percent, but the more hypothesis-driven multivariate analyses using twin and adoptee data have been helpful both in elucidating some matters and in raising fundamental questions about others. None of the findings are in the least bit compatible with a genetically deterministic view. The evidence does indicate that genetic influences are all-pervasive but the same evidence also indicates that they operate through a variety of mechanisms both direct and indirect. . . .

NOTES

See Reference list for full details.

1. Jablensky, 2000; Liddle, 2000

2. Cardno & Gottesman, 2000

3. See Gottesman, 1991. The **proband**-wise concordance rate is that based on probands, rather than pairs. In other words, a concordant pair is counted twice, once for each proband. This is appropriate provided that each proband has been independently ascertained; that is, the schizophrenia (or whatever disorder is being studied) has not been diagnosed only as a result of special assessment as a consequence of being a co-twin. For a variety of technical reasons, the proband-wise concordance rate is usually regarded as preferable to the pair-wise concordance rate.

4. Cannon et al., 1998

5. Cardno et al., 1999

6. Kendler et al., 1994

7. Joseph, 2003

8. Tienari et al., 2000

9. Gottesman, 1991; Jablensky, 2000

10. See, e.g., Kendler et al., 1995

11. McGuffin et al., 1994

12. Cardno et al., 2002

13. McDonald et al., 2004

14. Carter et al., 2002; van Os & Sham, 2003; Wahlberg et al., 1997

15. Jones, Kent, & Craddock, 2002

16. Angst et al., 2003

17. Lord & Bailey, 2002

18. Bock & Goode, 2003; Courchesne et al., 2003

19. Frith, U., 2003

20. Frith, C., 2003; Volkmar et al., 2004

21. Rutter, 2000 a and in press b; Steffenburg et al., 1989

22. Bailey et al., 1995

23. Rutter, 2005 a

24. Bailey et al., "A clinicopathological study"; Bailey et al., "Autism"; Pickles et al., 2000; Rutter, 2000 a, 2005 a

25. Schachar & Tannock, 2002

26. MTA, 1999 a & b, 2004 a & b

27. Levy & Hay, 2001

28. Levy & Hay, 2001; Thapar et al., 1995; Waldman & Rhee, 2002

29. Faraone et al., 1998

30. Eaves et al., 1997; Simonoff et al., 1998 a

31. Kuntsi et al., 2004

32. Moffitt et al., 2001; Rutter et al., 1998

33. Rhee & Waldman, 2002

34. Moffitt, 2005

35. Sullivan et al., 2000

36. McGuffin et al., 1996

37. Kendler et al., 1993 a

38. Brown, 1996

39. Kagan, 1994; Kagan & Snidman, 2004

40. Thomas et al., 1963; Thomas et al., 1968

41. Buss & Plomin 1984; Kohnstamm et al., 1989

42. Rutter, 1987

43. Caspi et al., 2005 a; Shiner & Caspi, 2003

44. Higley & Suomi, 1989; Kagan, 1994; Kagan & Snidman, 2004

45. Caspi et al., 2005 a

46. Shiner & Caspi, 2003

47. See Cleckley, 1941; Rutter, 2005 f

48. Blair et al., 1997 & 2002; Patrick et al., 1997

49. Bouchard & Loehlin, 2001

50. Nigg & Goldsmith, 1998

51. Viding et al., 2005

52. Rutter, 2002 c

53. Ball & Collier, 2002; Rutter, 2002 c

54. Cadoret et al., 1995 a & b

55. Démonet et al., 2004; Fisher & DeFries, 2002; Knopik et al., 2002

56. Berger et al., 1975; Rutter et al., 1975 a, b

57. Rutter & Quinton, 1977

58. Rutter et al., 1979

59. Hewison & Tizard, 1980

60. Wimmer & Goswami, 1994; Aro & Wimmer, 2003; Paulesu et al., 2001

61. Rutter et al., 2004

62. Turkeltaub et al., 2003

63. Shaywitz et al., 2003

64. Wadsworth et al., 2000

65. Stevenson et al., 1987

66. Williams, 2002

67. Bishop, 2002 b

68. Clegg et al., 2005

69. Bishop, 2001

70. Viding et al., 2004

71. Liddell et al., 2002

72. Plomin, 1994; Rutter, 2000 b; Rutter, Moffitt, & Caspi, in press

REFERENCE LIST

Angst, J., Gamma, A., Benazzi, F., Ajdacic, V., Eich, S., & Rössler, W. (2003). Toward a re-definition of subthreshold bipolarity: Epidemiology and proposed criteria for bipolar-II, minor bipolar disorders and hypomania. *Journal of Affective Disorders* 73, 133–146.

Aro, M., & Wimmer, H. (2003). Learning to read: English in comparison to six more regular orthographies. *Applied Psycholinguistics* 24, 621–635.

Bailey, A., Le Couteur, A., Gottesman, I., Bolton, P., Simonoff, E., Yuzda, E., & Rutter, M. (1995). Autism as a strongly genetic disorder: Evidence from a British twin study. *Psychological Medicine* 25, 63–77.

Bailey, A., Luthert, P., Dean, A., Harding, B., Janota, I., Montgomery, M., Rutter, M., & Lantos, P. (1998). A clinicopathological study of autism. *Brain* 121, 889–905.

Bailey, A., Palferman, S., Heavey, L., & Le Couteur, A. (1998). Autism: The phenotype in relatives. *Journal of Autism and Developmental Disorders* 28, 381–404.

Ball, D., & Collier, D. (2002). Substance misuse. In P. McGuffin, M.J. Owen, & I.I. Gottesman (Eds.), *Psychiatric genetics and genomics.* Oxford: Oxford University Press. pp. 267–302.

Berger, M., Yule, W., & Rutter, M. (1975). Attainment and adjustment in two geographical areas: II. The prevalence of specific reading retardation. *British Journal of Psychiatry* 126, 510–519.

Bishop, D.V.M. (2001). Genetic and environmental risks for specific language impairment in children. *Philosophical Transactions of the Royal Society, Series B* 356, 369–380.

Bishop, D.V.M. (2002 b). Speech and language difficulties. In M. Rutter & E. Taylor (Eds.), *Child and adolescent psychiatry, 4th ed.* Oxford: Blackwell Science. pp. 664–681.

Blair, R.J.R., Jones, L., Clark, F., & Smith, M. (1997). The psychopathic individual: A lack of responsiveness to distress cues? *Psychophysiology* 34, 192–198.

Blair, R.J.R., Mitchell, D.G., Richell, R.A., Kelly, S., Leonard, A., Newman, C., & Scott, S.K. (2002). Turning a deaf ear to fear: Impaired recognition of vocal affect in psychopathic individuals. *Journal of Abnormal Psychology* 11, 682–686.

Bock, G., & Goode, J.A. (2003). *Autism: Neural basis and treatment possibilities.* Novartis Foundation Symposium 251. Chichester, West Sussex: John Wiley & Sons Ltd.

Bouchard, T.J. Jr., & Loehlin, R.C. (2001). Genes, evolution, and personality. *Behavior Genetics* 31, 243–73.

Brown, G.W. (1996). Genetics of depression: A social science perspective. *International Review of Psychiatry* 8, 387–401.

Buss, A.H., & Plomin, R. (1984). *Temperament: Early developing personality traits.* Hillsdale, NJ: Erlbaum.

Cadoret, R.J., Yates, W.R., Troughton, E., Woodworth, G., & Stewart, M.A. (1995 a). Adoption study demonstrating two genetic pathways to drug abuse. *Archives of General Psychiatry* 52, 42–52.

Cadoret, R.J., Yates, W.R., Troughton, E., Woodworth, G., & Stewart, M.A.S. (1995 b). Genetic–environmental interaction in the genesis of aggressivity and conduct disorders. *Archives of General Psychiatry* 52, 916–924.

Cannon, T.D., Kaprio, J., Lonnqvist, J., Huttunen, M., & Koskenvuo, M. (1998). The genetic epidemiology of schizophrenia in a Finnish twin cohort: A population-based modeling study. *Archives of General Psychiatry* 55, 67–74.

Cardno, A.G., & Gottesman, I.I. (2000). Twin studies of schizophrenia: From bow-and-arrow concordances to star wars Mx and functional genomics. *American Journal of Medical Genetics* 97, 12–17.

Cardno, A.G., Marshall, E.J., Coid, B., Macdonald, A.M., Ribchester, T.R., Davies, N.J., Venturi, P., Jones, L.A., Lewis, S.W., Sham, P.C., Gottesman, I.I., Farmer A.E., McGuffin, P., Reveley, A.M., & Murray, R.M. (1999). Heritability estimates for psychotic disorders: The Maudsley twin psychosis series. *Archives of General Psychiatry* 56, 162–168.

Cardno, A.G., Rijsdijk, F.V., Sham, P.C., Murray, R.M., & McGuffin, P. (2002). A twin study of genetic relationships between psychotic symptoms. *American Journal of Psychiatry* 159, 539–545.

Carter, J.W., Schulsinger, F., Parnas, J., Cannon, T., & Mednick, S.A. (2002). A multivariate prediction model of schizophrenia. *Schizophrenia Bulletin* 28, 649–682.

Caspi, A., Roberts, B.W., & Shiner, R.L. (2005 a). Personality development: Stability and change. *Annual Review of Psychology* 56, 17.1–17.32.

Cleckley, H.C. (1941). *The mask of sanity: An attempt to reinterpret the so-called psychopathic personality.* St Louis, MO: Mosby.

Clegg, J., Hollis, C., Mawhood, L., & Rutter, M. (2005). Developmental language disorder—a follow-up in later adult life. Cognitive, language, and psychosocial outcomes. *Journal of Child Psychology and Psychiatry* 46, 128–149.

Courchesne, E., Carper, R., & Akshoomoff, N. (2003). Evidence of brain overgrowth in the first year of life in autism. *Journal of the American Medical Association* 290, 337–344.

Démonet, J.F., Taylor, M.J., & Chaix, Y. (2004). Developmental dyslexia. *Lancet* 363, 1451–1460.

Eaves, L.J., Silberg, J.L., Meyer, J.M., Maes, H.H., Simonoff, E., Pickles, A., Rutter, M., Neale, M.C., Reynolds, C.A., Erikson, M.T., Heath, A.C., Loeber, R., Truett, T.R., & Hewitt. J.K. (1997). Genetics and developmental psychopathology: 2. The main effects of genes and environment on behavioral problems in the Virginia Twin Study of Adolescent Behavioral Development. *Journal of Child Psychology and Psychiatry* 38, 965–980.

Faraone, S.V., Biederman, J., Mennin, D., Russell, R., & Tsuang, M.T. (1998). Familial subtypes of attention deficit hyperactivity disorder: A 4-year follow-up study of children from antisocial-ADHD families. *Journal of Child Psychology and Psychiatry* 39, 1045–1053.

Fisher, S.E., & DeFries, J.C. (2002). Developmental dyslexia: Genetic dissection of a complex cognitive trait. *Nature Reviews Neuroscience* 3, 767–780.

Frith, C. (2003). What do imaging studies tell us about the neural basis of autism? In G. Bock and J. Goode (Eds.). *Autism: Neural basis and treatment possibilities.* Chichester: John Wiley & Sons Ltd. pp. 149–176.

Frith, U. (2003). *Autism: Explaining the enigma, 2nd ed.* Oxford: Blackwell.

Gottesman, I.I. (1991). *Schizophrenia genesis: The origins of madness.* New York: W.H. Freeman & Company.

Hewison. J., & Tizard. J. (1980). Parental involvement and reading attainment. *British Journal of Educational Psychology* 50, 209–215.

Higley, J.D., & Suomi, S.J. (1989). Temperamental reactivity in non-human primates. In G.A. Kohnstamm, J.E. Bates, & M.K. Rothbart (Eds.), *Temperament in childhood.* Chichester: John Wiley & Sons. pp. 153–167.

Jablensky, A. (2000). Epidemiology of schizophrenia. In M.G. Gelder, J.L. López-Ibor, & N. Andreasen (Eds.), *New Oxford textbook of psychiatry, vol. 1.* Oxford: Oxford University Press. pp. 585–599.

Jones, I., Kent, L., & Craddock, N. (2002). Genetics of affective disorders. In P. McGuffin, M.J. Owen, & I.I. Gottesman (Eds.), *Psychiatric genetics and genomics.* Oxford: Oxford University Press. pp. 211–245.

Joseph, J. (2003). *The gene illusion: Genetic research in psychiatry and psychology under the microscope.* Ross on Wye: PCCS Books.

Kagan, J. (1994). *Galen's prophecy.* London: Free Association Books Ltd.

Kagan, J., & Snidman, N. (2004). *The long shadow of temperament.* Cambridge, MA: The Belknap Press.

Kendler, K.S., Neale, M.C., Kessler, R.C., Heath, A.C., & Eaves, L.J. (1993 a). The lifetime history of major depression in women: Reliability of diagnosis and heritability. *Archives of General Psychiatry*, 50, 863–870.

Kendler, K.S., Neale, M.C., Kessler, R.C., Heath, A.C., & Eaves, L.J. (1994). Parental treatment and the equal environment assumption in twin studies of psychiatric illness. *Psychological Medicine* 24, 579–590.

Kendler, K.S., Neale, M.C., & Walsh, D. (1995). Evaluating the spectrum concept of schizophrenia in the Roscommon Family Study. *American Journal of Psychiatry* 152, 749–754.

Knopik, V.S., Smith, S.D., Cardon, L., Pennington, B., Gayan, J., Olson, R.K., & DeFries, J.C. (2002). Differential genetic etiology of reading component processes as a function of IQ. *Behavior Genetics* 32, 181–198.

Kohnstamm, G.A., Bates, J.E., & Rothbart, M.K. (Eds.) (1989). *Temperament in childhood.* Chichester: John Wiley, & Sons.

Kuntsi, J., Eley, T.C., Taylor, A., Hughes, C., Asherson, P., Caspi, A., & Moffitt, T.E. (2004). Co-occurrence of ADHD and low IQ has genetic origins. *American Journal of Medical Genetics B (Neuropsychiatric Genetics)* 124B, 41–47.

Levy, F., & Hay, D. (Eds.) (2001). *Attention, genes and ADHD.* Hove, Sussex: Brunner-Routledge.

Liddell, M.B., Williams, J., & Owen, M.J. (2002). The dementias. In P. McGuffin, M.J. Owen, & I.I. Gottesman (Eds.), *Psychiatric genetics and genomics.* Oxford: Oxford University Press. pp. 341–393.

Liddle, P.F. (2000). Descriptive clinical features of schizophrenia. In M.G. Gelder, J.L. López-Ibor, & N. Andreasen (Eds.), *New Oxford textbook of psychiatry, vol. 1.* Oxford: Oxford University Press. pp. 571–576.

Lord, C., & Bailey, A. (2002). Autism spectrum disorders. In M. Rutter & E. Taylor (Eds.), *Child and adolescent psychiatry, 4th ed.* Oxford: Blackwell Scientific. pp. 636–663.

McDonald, C., Bullmore, E.T., Sham, P.C., Chitnis, X., Wickham, H., Bramon, E., & Murray. R.M. (2004). Association of genetic risks for schizophrenia and bipolar disorder with specific and generic brain structural endophenotypes. *Archives of General Psychiatry* 61, 974–984.

McGuffin, P., Asherson, P., Owen. M., & Farmer, A. (1994). The strength of the genetic effect. Is there room for an environmental influence in the aetiology of schizophrenia? *British Journal of Psychiatry* 164, 593–599.

McGuffin. P., Katz, R., Watkins, S., & Rutherford, J. (1996). A hospital-based twin register of the heritability of DSM-IV unipolar depression. *Archives of General Psychiatry* 53, 129–136.

Moffitt, T.E. (2005). The new look of behavioral genetics in developmental psychopathology: Gene-environment interplay in antisocial behaviors. *Psychological Bulletin* 131, 533–554.

Moffitt, T.E., Caspi, A., Rutter, M., & Silva, P.A. (2001). *Sex differences in antisocial behaviour: Conduct disorder, delinquency, and violence in the Dunedin Longitudinal Study.* Cambridge: Cambridge University Press.

MTA Cooperative Group. (1999 a). A 14-month randomized clinical trial of treatment strategies for attention-deficit/hyperactivity disorder, *Archives of General Psychiatry* 56, 1073–1086.

MTA Cooperative Group. (1999 b). Moderators and mediators of treatment response for children with attention-deficit/hyperactivity disorder. *Archives of General Psychiatry* 56, 1088–1096.

MTA Cooperative Group. (2004 a). National Institute of Mental Health Multimodal Treatment Study of ADHD follow-up: 24-month outcomes of treatment strategies for attention-deficit/hyperactivity disorder. *Pediatrics* 113, 754–761.

MTA Cooperative Group. (2004 b). National Institute of Mental Health Multimodal Treatment Study of ADHD follow-up: Changes in effectiveness and growth after the end of treatment. *Pediatrics* 113, 762–769.

Nigg, J.T., & Goldsmith, H.H. (1998). Developmental psychopathology, personality, and temperament: Reflections on recent behavioral genetics research. *Human Biology* 70, 387–412.

Patrick, C.J., Zempolich, K.A., & Levenston, G.K. (1997). Emotionality and violent behavior in psychopaths: A biosocial analysis. In A. Raine, P. Brennan, D.P. Farrington, & S.A. Mednick (Eds.), *Biosocial bases of violence.* New York: Plenum. pp. 145–163.

Paulesu, E., Démonet, J., Fazio, F., McCrory, E., Chanoine, V., Brunswick, N., Cappa, S., Cossu, G., Habib, M., Frith, C., & Frith, U. (2001). Dyslexia: Cultural diversity and biological unity. *Science* 291, 2165–2167.

Pickles, A., Starr, E., Kazak, S., Bolton, P., Papanikolau, K., Bailey, A.J., Goodman, R., & Rutter, M. (2000). Variable expression of the autism broader phenotype: Findings from extended pedigrees. *Journal of Child Psychology and Psychiatry* 41, 491–502.

Plomin, R. (1994). *Genetics and experience: The interplay between nature and nurture.* Thousand Oaks, CA: Sage Publications.

Rhee, S.H., & Waldman, I.D. (2002). Genetic and environmental influences on antisocial behavior: A meta-analysis of twin and adoption studies. *Psychological Bulletin* 128, 490–529.

Rutter, M. (1987). Continuities and discontinuities from infancy. In J. Osofsky (Ed.), *Handbook of infant development, 2nd ed.* New York: Wiley. pp. 1256–1296.

Rutter, M. (2000 a). Genetic studies of autism: From the 1970s into the millennium. *Journal of Abnormal Child Psychology* 28, 3–14.

Rutter, M. (2000 b). Negative life events and family negativity: Accomplishments and challenges. In T. Harris (Ed.), *Where inner and outer worlds meet: Psychosocial research in the tradition of George W. Brown.* London: Routledge/Taylor & Francis. pp. 123–149.

Rutter, M. (2002 c). Substance use and abuse: Causal pathways considerations. In M. Rutter & E. Taylor (Eds.), *Child and adolescent psychiatry, 4th ed.* Oxford: Blackwell Scientific. pp. 455–462.

Rutter, M. (2005 a). Incidence of autism spectrum disorders: Changes over time and their meaning. *Acta Paediatrica* 94, 2–15.

Rutter, M. (2005 f). What is the meaning and utility of the psychopathy concept? *Journal of Abnormal Child Psychology* 33, 499–503.

Rutter, M. (in press b). The psychological effects of institutional rearing. In P. Marshall & N. Fox (Eds.). *The development of social engagement.* New York: Oxford University Press.

Rutter, M., Caspi, A., Fergusson, D., Horwood, L.J., Goodman, R., Maughan, B., Moffitt, T.E., Meltzer, H., & Carroll, J. (2004). Sex differences in developmental reading disability: New findings from 4 epidemiological studies. *Journal of American Medical Association* 291, 2007–2012.

Rutter, M., Cox, A., Tupling, C., Berger, M., & Yule, W. (1975 a). Attainment and adjustment in two geographical areas: I. The prevalence of psychiatric disorder. *British Journal of Psychiatry* 126, 493–509.

Rutter, M., Giller, H., & Hagell, A. (1998). *Antisocial behavior by young people.* New York: Cambridge University Press.

Rutter, M., Maughan, B., Mortimore, P., Ouston, J., & Smith, A. (1979). *Fifteen thousand hours: Secondary schools and their effects on children.* London: Open Books.

Rutter, M., Moffitt, T.E., & Caspi, A. (in press). Gene–environment interplay and psychopathology: Multiple varieties but real effects. *Journal of Child Psychology and Psychiatry.*

Rutter, M., & Quinton, D. (1977). Psychiatric disorder – ecological factors and concepts of causation. In H. McGurk (Ed.), *Ecological factors in human development.* Amsterdam: North-Holland. pp. 173–187.

Rutter, M., Yule, B., Quinton, D., Rowlands, O., Yule, W., & Berger, M. (1975 b). Attainment and adjustment in two geographical areas: III Some factors accounting for area differences. *British Journal of Psychiatry* 126, 520–533.

Schachar, R., & Tannock, R. (2002). Syndromes of hyperactivity and attention deficit. In M. Rutter & E. Taylor (Eds.), *Child and adolescent psychiatry, 4th ed.* Oxford: Blackwell Scientific. pp. 399–418.

Shaywitz, S.E., Shaywitz, B.A., Fulbright, R.K. Skudlarski, P., Mencl, W.E., Constable, R.T., Pugh, K.R., Holahan, J.M., Marchione, K.E., Fletcher, J.M., Lyon, G.R., & Gore, J.C. (2003). Neural systems for compensation and persistence: Young adult outcome of childhood reading disability. *Biological Psychiatry* 54, 25–33.

Shiner, R., & Caspi, A. (2003). Personality differences in childhood and adolescence: Measurement, development, and consequences. *Journal of Child Psychology and Psychiatry* 44, 2–32.

Simonoff, E., Pickles, A., Hervas, A., Silberg, J.L., Rutter, M., & Eaves, L. (1998 a). Genetic influences on childhood hyperactivity: Contrast effects imply parental rating bias, not sibling interaction. *Psychological Medicine* 28, 825–837.

Steffenburg, S., Gillberg, C., Hellgren, L., Andersson, L., Gillberg, I., Jakobsson, G., & Bohman, M. (1989). A twin study of autism in Denmark, Finland, Iceland, Norway and Sweden. *Journal of Child Psychology and Psychiatry* 30, 405–416.

Stevenson, L., Graham, P., Fredman, G., & McLoughlin, V. (1987). A twin study of genetic influences on reading and spelling ability and disability. *Journal of Child Psychology and Psychiatry* 28, 229–247.

Sullivan, P.F., Neale, M.C., & Kendler, K.S. (2000). Genetic epidemiology of major depression: Review and meta-analysis. *American Journal of Psychiatry* 157, 1552–1562.

Thapar, A., Hervas, A., & McGuffin, P. (1995). Childhood hyperactivity scores are highly heritable and show sibling competition effects: Twin study evidence. *Behavior Genetics* 25, 537–544.

Thomas, A., Chess, S., & Birch, H. (1968). *Temperament and behavior disorders in childhood.* New York: New York University Press.

Thomas, A., Chess, S., Birch, H., Hertzig, M., & Korn, S. (1963). *Behavioral individuality in early childhood.* New York: New York University Press.

Tienari, P., Wynne, L.C., Moring, J., Läsky, K., Nieminen, P., Sorri, A., Lahti, I., Wahlberg, K-E., Naarala, M., Kurki-Suonio, K., Saarento, O., Koistinen, P., Tarvainen, T., Hakko, H., & Miettunen, J. (2000). Finnish adoptive family study: Sample selection and adoptee DSM-III-R diagnoses. *Acta Psychiatrica Scandinavica* 101, 433–443.

Turkeltaub, P.E., Gareau, L., Flowers, D.L., Zeffiro, T.A., & Eden, G.F. (2003). Development of neural mechanisms for reading. *Nature Neuroscience* 6, 767–773.

Van Os, J., & Sham, P. (2003). Gene–environment correlation and interaction in schizophrenia. In R.M. Murray, P.B. Jones, E. Susser, J. van Os, & M. Cannon (Eds.), *The epidemiology of schizophrenia.* Cambridge: Cambridge University Press. pp. 235–253.

Viding, E., Blair, R.J., Moffitt, T.E., & Plomin, R. (2005). Evidence for substantial genetic risk for psychopathy in 7-year-olds. *Journal of Child Psychology and Psychiatry* 46, 592–597.

Viding, E., Spinath, F., Price, T.S., Bishop, D.V.M., Dale, P.S., & Plomin, R. (2004). Genetic and environmental influence on language impairment in 4-year old same-sex and opposite-sex twins. *Journal of Child Psychology and Psychiatry* 45 315–325.

Volkmar, F.R., Lord, C., Bailey, A., Schultz, R.T., Klin, A., & Wadsworth, S.J. (2004). Autism and pervasive developmental disorders. *Journal of Child Psychology and Psychiatry* 41, 135–170.

Wadsworth, S.J., Knopik, V.S., & DeFries, J.C. (2000). Reading disability in boys and girls: No evidence for a differential genetic etiology. *Reading and Writing: An Interdisciplinary Journal* 13, 133–145.

Wahlberg, K-E., Wynne, L.C., Oja, H., Keskitalo, P., Pykalainen, L., Lahti, I., Moring, J., Naarala, M., Sorri, A., Seitarnaa, M., Laksy, K., Kolassa, J., & Tienari, P. (1997). Gene–environment interaction in vulnerability to schizophrenia: Findings from the Finnish Adoptive Family Study of Schizophrenia. *American Journal of Psychiatry* 154, 355–362.

Waldman, I.D., & Rhee, S.H. (2002). Behavioural and molecular genetic studies. In S. Sandberg (Ed.), *Hyperactivity and attention disorders of childhood, 2nd ed.* Cambridge; Cambridge University Press. pp. 290–335.

Williams, J. (2002). Reading and language disorders. In P. McGuffin, M.J. Owen, & I.I. Gottesman (Eds.), *Psychiatric genetics and genomics.* Oxford: Oxford University Press. pp. 129–145.

Wimmer, H., & Goswami, U. (1994). The influence of orthographic consistency on reading development: Word recognition in English and German children. *Cognition* 51, 91–103.

Suggested Readings for Chapter 4

EUGENICS IN THE TWENTIETH CENTURY

Adams, Mark B., ed. *The Wellborn Science: Eugenics in Germany, France, Brazil, and Russia.* New York: Oxford University Press, 1990.

Biesold, Horst. *Crying Hands: Eugenics and Deaf People in Nazi Germany.* Washington DC: Gallaudet University Press, 1999.

Bruinius, Harry. *Better for All the World: The Secret History of Forced Sterilization and America's Quest for Racial Purity.* New York: Knopf, 2006.

Burleigh, Michael, and Wippermann, Wolfgang. *The Racial State: Germany 1933–1945.* Cambridge: Cambridge University Press, 1991.

Carlson, Elof Axel. *The Unfit: A History of a Bad Idea.* Woodbury, NY: Cold Spring Harbor Laboratory Press, 2000.

China, People's Republic of. "Presidential Decree No. 33 of 27 October 1994 Promulgating the Law of the People's Republic of China on the Protection of Maternal and Child Health." *International Digest of Health Legislation* 46, no. 1 (1995), 39–42.

Dikötter, Frank. *Imperfect Conceptions: Medical Knowledge, Birth Defects, and Eugenics in China.* New York: Columbia University Press, 1998.

———. "Race Culture: Recent Perspectives on the History of Eugenics." *American Historical Review* 103 (1998), 467–78.

Dowbiggin, Ian Robert. *Keeping America Sane: Psychiatry and Eugenics in the United States and Canada, 1880–1940.* Ithaca, NY: Cornell University Press, 1997.

Dubow, Saul. *Scientific Racism in Modern South Africa.* New York: Cambridge University Press, 1995.

Duster, Troy. *Backdoor to Eugenics.* 2nd edition. New York: Routledge, 2003.

Engs, Ruth C., ed. *The Eugenics Movement: An Encyclopedia.* Westport, CT: Greenwood Press, 2005.

Field, Martha A., and Sanchez, Valerie A. *Equal Treatment for People with Mental Retardation: Having and Raising Children.* Cambridge, MA: Harvard University Press, 2001.

Gallagher, Nancy L. *Breeding Better Vermonters: The Eugenics Project in the Green Mountain State.* Hanover, NH: University Press of New England, 1999.

Gillham, Nicholas Wright. *A Life of Sir Frances Galton: From African Exploration to the Birth of Eugenics.* New York: Oxford University Press, 2001.

Haller, Mark H. *Eugenics: Hereditarian Attitudes in American Thought.* New Brunswick, NJ: Rutgers University Press, 1963.

Hesketh, Therese, and Zhu,Wei Xiang. "Maternal and Child Health in China." *British Medical Journal* 314 (1997), 1898–1900.

Kevles, Daniel J. *In the Name of Eugenics: Genetics and the Uses of Human Heredity.* Cambridge, MA: Harvard University Press, 1995.

Kline, Wendy. *Building of a Better Race: Gender, Sexuality, and Eugenics From the Turn of the Century to the Baby Boom.* Berkeley, CA: University of California Press, 2001.

Kühl, Stefan. *The Nazi Connection: Eugenics, American Racism, and German National Socialism.* New York: Oxford University Press, 2002.

Larson, Edward J. *Sex, Race, and Science: Eugenics and the Deep South.* Baltimore, MD: Johns Hopkins University Press, 1996.

Ludmerer, Kenneth M. *Genetics and American Society: A Historical Appraisal*. Baltimore: Johns Hopkins University Press, 1972.

McGee, Glenn, and Magus, David. "Eugenics, Ethics." In Thomas H. Murray and Maxwell J. Mehlman, eds., *Encyclopedia of Ethical, Legal, and Policy Issues in Biotechnology*. 2 vols. New York: John Wiley & Sons, 2000, 199–204.

Mazumdar, Pauline M. H. *The Eugenics Movement: An International Perspective*. 6 vols. New York: Routledge, 2007.

———. *Eugenics, Human Genetics, and Human Failings: The Eugenics Society, Its Sources and Its Critics in Britain*. New York: Routledge, 2005.

Paul, Diane B. *Controlling Human Heredity, 1865 to the Present*. Atlantic Highlands, NJ: Humanities Press International, 1995.

Pearson, Veronica. "Population Policy and Eugenics in China." *British Journal of Psychiatry* 167 (1995), 1–4.

Pernick, Martin S. *The Black Stork: Eugenics and the Death of "Defective" Babies in American Medicine and Motion Pictures Since 1915*. New York: Oxford University Press, 1999.

———. "Eugenics and Public Health in American History." *American Journal of Public Health* 87 (1997), 1767–72.

Proctor, Robert N. "Genomics and Eugenics: How Fair Is the Comparison?" In George J. Annas and Sherman Elias, eds., *Gene Mapping: Using Law and Ethics as Guides*. New York: Oxford University Press, 1992, 75–93.

———. *Racial Hygiene: Medicine under the Nazis*. Cambridge, MA: Harvard University Press, 1988.

Rafter, Nicole Hahn. *Creating Born Criminals*. Urbana, IL: University of Illinois Press, 1998.

Reilly, Phillip R. *The Surgical Solution: A History of Involuntary Sterilization in the United States*. Baltimore: Johns Hopkins University Press, 1991.

Roll-Hansen, Nils, and Broberg, Gunnar, eds. *Eugenics and the Welfare State: Sterilization Policy in Denmark, Sweden, Norway, and Finland*. East Lansing, MI: Michigan State University Press, 1996.

Schafft, Gretchen Engle. *From Racism to Genocide: Anthropology in the Third Reich*. Urbana: University of Illinois Press, 2004.

Smith, J. David, and Nelson, K. Ray. *The Sterilization of Carrie Buck*. Far Hills, NJ: New Horizon Press, 1989.

Stepan, Nancy Leys. *The Hour of Eugenics: Race, Gender, and Nation in Latin America*. Ithaca, NY: Cornell University Press, 1996.

Thomson, Mathew. *Problem of Mental Deficiency: Eugenics and Social Policy in Britain*. New York, Oxford University Press, 1998.

Turda, Marius, and Weindling, Paul, eds. *"Blood and Homeland": Eugenics and Racial Nationalism in Central and Southeastern Europe, 1900–1940*. Budapest, New York: Central European University Press, 2007.

Watson, James D., Witkowski, Jan Anthony, and Inglis, John R., eds. *Davenport's Heredity in Relation to Eugenics: A View from the 21st Century*. New York: Cold Spring Harbor Press, 2005.

Weikart, Richard. *From Darwin to Hitler: Evolutionary Ethics, Eugenics, and Racism in Germany*. New York: Palgrave Macmillan, 2004.

Weindling, Paul. *Health, Race, and German Politics between National Unification and Nazism, 1870–1945*. Cambridge: Cambridge University Press, 1989.

Winfield, Ann Gibson. *Eugenics and Education in America: Institutionalized Racism and the Implications of History, Ideology, and Memory*. New York: Peter Lang, 2007.

Zenderland, Leila. *Measuring Minds: Henry Herbert Goddard and the Origins of American Intelligence Testing*. New York: Cambridge University Press, 1997.

GENETICS AND SOCIETY

Asch, Adrienne, and Geller, Gail. "Feminism, Bioethics, and Genetics." In Susan M. Wolf, ed., *Feminism and Bioethics: Beyond Reproduction*. New York: Oxford University Press, 1996, 318–50.

Buchanan, Allen; Brock, Dan W.; Daniels, Norman; and Wikler. *From Chance to Choice: Genetics and Justice*. Cambridge: Cambridge University Press, 2000.

Collins, Francis S.; Guttmacher, Alan E.; and Drazen, Jeffrey M. *Genomic Medicine: Articles from the New England Journal of Medicine*. Baltimore: Johns Hopkins University Press, 2004.

Deane-Drummond, Celia. *Genetics and Christian Ethics*. Cambridge: Cambridge University Press, 2006.

Evans, John H. *Playing God?: Human Genetic Engineering and the Rationalization of Public Bioethical Debate*. Chicago: University of Chicago Press, 2002.

Fukuyama, Francis. *Our Posthuman Future: Consequences of the Biotechnology Revolution*. New York: Farrar, Straus and Giroux, 2002.

Harris, John. *Clones, Genes, and Immortality: Ethics and the Genetic Revolution*. New York: Oxford University Press, 1998.

Kristol, William, and Cohen, Eric, eds. *The Future Is Now: America Confronts the New Genetics*. New York: Rowman & Littlefield, 2002.

Murray, Thomas H., Rothstein, Mark A., and Murray, Robert F., eds. *The Human Genome Project and the Future of Health Care*. Bloomington: Indiana University Press, 1996.

Nelkin, Dorothy, and Lindee, M. Susan. *The DNA Mystique: The Gene as a Cultural Icon*. New York: Freeman, 1995.

Ramsey, Paul. *Fabricated Man: The Ethics of Genetic Control*. New Haven: Yale University Press, 1970.

Rifkin, Jeremy. *The Biotech Century: Harnessing the Gene and Remaking the World*. New York: Penguin Putnam, 1998.

U.S. Congress, Office of Technology Assessment. *New Developments in Biotechnology—Background Paper: Public Perceptions of Biotechnology*. Washington, DC: U.S. Government Printing Office, May 1987.

GENETIC TESTING AND SCREENING

Anderlik, Mary R., and Pentz, Rebecca D. "Genetic Information, Legal, Genetic Privacy Laws." In Thomas H. Murray and Maxwell J. Mehlman, eds., *Encyclopedia of Ethical, Legal, and Policy Issues in Biotechnology*. 2 vols. New York: John Wiley & Sons, 2000, 456–68.

Anderlik, Mary R. "Genetic Information, Legal, Genetics and the Americans with Disabilities Act." In Thomas H. Murray and Maxwell J. Mehlman, eds., *Encyclopedia of Ethical, Legal, and Policy Issues in Biotechnology*. 2 vols. New York: John Wiley & Sons, 2000, 468–78.

Andre, Judith, et al. "On Being Genetically 'Irresponsible.'" *Kennedy Institute of Ethics Journal* 10 (2000), 129–46.

Andrews, Lori B. *Future Perfect: Confronting Decisions about Genetics*. New York: Columbia University Press, 2001.

———, et al. Institute of Medicine, Committee on Assessing Genetic Risks. *Assessing Genetic Risks: Implications for Health and Social Policy*. Washington, DC: National Academy Press, 1994.

Annas, George J. "The Limits of State Laws to Protect Genetic Information." *New England Journal of Medicine* 345 (2001), 385–88.

Betta, Michaela. *The Moral, Social, and Commercial Imperatives of Genetic Testing and Screening: The Australian Case.* Dordrecht: Springer, 2006.

Bobinski, Mary Anne. "Genetic Information, Legal, ERISA Preemption, and HIPAA Protection." In Thomas H. Murray and Maxwell J. Mehlman, eds., *Encyclopedia of Ethical, Legal, and Policy Issues in Biotechnology.* 2 vols. New York: John Wiley & Sons, 2000, 427–40.

Botkin, Jeffrey R. "Reproduction, Law, Wrongful Birth, and Wrongful Life Actions." In Thomas H. Murray and Maxwell J. Mehlman, eds., *Encyclopedia of Ethical, Legal, and Policy Issues in Biotechnology.* 2 vols. New York: John Wiley & Sons, 2000, 996–1003.

Chadwick, Ruth, et al., eds. *The Ethics of Genetic Screening.* Boston: Kluwer Academic Publishers, 1999.

———, et al. "Euroscreen 2: Towards Community Policy on Insurance, Commercialization and Public Awareness." *Journal of Medicine and Philosophy* 26 (2001), 263–272.

Clayton, Ellen Wright. "Genetic Testing Is Different." *Journal of Health Politics, Policy and Law* 26 (2001), 457–64.

Cunningham, George S. "Genetic Information, Legal, Regulating Genetic Services." In Thomas H. Murray and Maxwell J. Mehlman, eds., *Encyclopedia of Ethical, Legal, and Policy Issues in Biotechnology.* 2 vols. New York: John Wiley & Sons, 2000, 478–83.

European Commission, European Group on Ethics in Science and New Technologies. *Opinion on the Ethical Aspects of Genetic Testing in the Workplace.* Luxembourg: Office for Official Publications of the European Communities, 2003.

Great Britain, Human Genetics Advisory Committee. *Our Genes, Ourselves: Towards Appopriate Genetic Testing: Third Annual Report of the Human Genetics Commission.* London: The Commission, 2003.

Great Britain, Human Genetics Commission. *Profiling the Newborn: A Prospective Gene Technology?* London: the Commission, 2005.

Grodin, Michael A., et al. "Susceptibility Genes and Neurological Disorders." *Archives of Neurology* 57 (2000), 1569–74.

Holtzman, Neil A. *Proceed with Caution: Predicting Genetic Risks in the Recombinant DNA Era.* Baltimore: Johns Hopkins University Press, 1989.

———, and Watson, Michael S., eds. *Promoting Safe and Effective Genetic Testing in the United States: Final Report of the Task Force on Genetic Testing.* Baltimore, MD: Johns Hopkins University Press, 1998.

Hudson, Kathy L., et al. "Genetic Discrimination and Health Insurance: An Urgent Need for Reform." *Science* 270 (1995), 391–393.

Juengst, Eric T. "Genetic Information, Ethics, Family Issues." In Thomas H. Murray and Maxwell J. Mehlman, eds., *Encyclopedia of Ethical, Legal, and Policy Issues in Biotechnology.* 2 vols. New York: Johns Wiley & Sons, 2000, 390–396.

Kass, Nancy F. "The Implications of Genetic Testing for Health and Life Insurance." In Mark A. Rothstein, ed. *Genetic Secrets.* New Haven: Yale University Press, 1997, 299–316.

Knoppers, Bartha M. "Cancer Genetics: A Model for Multifactorial Conditions?" *Medicine and Law* 20 (2001), 177–82.

Laurie, Graeme. *Genetic Privacy: A Challenge to Medico-Legal Norms.* New York: Cambridge University Press, 2002.

Long, Clarisa, ed. *Genetic Testing and Use of Information.* Washington, DC: The American Enterprise Institute for Public Policy Research, 1999.

McNally, Eryl, and Cambon-Thomsen, Anne, eds. Commission of the European Communities, Directorate-General for Research. *Ethical, Legal and Social Aspects of Genetic Testing: Research, Development and Clinical Applications.* Luxembourg: Office for Official Publications of the European Communities, 2004.

Naff, Clay Farris. *Gene Therapy.* Detroit: Thomson/Gale, 2005.

National Academy of Sciences, Committee on DNA Technology in Forensic Science. *DNA Technology in Forensic Science.* Washington, DC: National Academy Press, 1992.

National Research Council, Committee for the Study of Inborn Errors of Metabolism. *Genetic Screening: Programs, Principles and Research.* Washington, DC: National Academy of Science, 1975.

Nelkin, Dorothy, and Tancredi, Laurence. *Dangerous Diagnostics: The Social Power of Biological Information.* Chicago, IL: University of Chicago Press, 1994.

New York State Task Force on Life and the Law. *Genetic Testing and Screening in the Age of Genomic Medicine.* New York: The Task Force, November 2000.

Nikas, Juth. *Genetic Information Values and Rights: The Morality of Presymptomatic Genetic Testing.* Göteberg: Acta Universitatis Gothoburgensis, 2005.

Nuffield Council on Bioethics. *Genetic Screening: Ethical Issues.* London: The Council, 1993.

Organization for Economic Cooperation and Development (OECD) Staff. *Genetic Testing: Policy Issues for the New Millenium.* Organization for Economic Cooperation and Development, 2001.

Parens, Erik, Asch, Adrienne, and Powell, Cynthia. "Reproduction, Ethics, Prenatal Testing and the Disability Rights Critique." In Thomas H. Murray and Maxwell J. Mehlman, eds., *Encyclopedia of Ethical, Legal, and Policy Issues in Biotechnology.* 2 vols. New York: John Wiley & Sons, 2000, 957–69.

Powers, Madison. "Genetic Information, Ethics, Privacy and Confidentiality: Overview." In Thomas H. Murray and Maxwell J. Mehlman, eds., *Encyclopedia of Ethical, Legal, and Policy Issues in Biotechnology.* 2 vols. New York: John Wiley & Sons, 2000, 405–13.

———. "Privacy and the Control of Genetic Information." In Mark S. Frankel, and Albert Teich, eds., *The Genetic Frontier: Ethics, Law, and Policy.* Washington, DC: American Association for the Advancement of Science, 1994, 77–100.

Quaid, Kimberly A. "Genetic Information, Ethics, Informed Consent to Testing and Screening." In Thomas H. Murray and Maxwell J. Mehlman, eds., *Encyclopedia of Ethical, Legal, and Policy Issues in Biotechnology.* 2 vols. New York: John Wiley & Sons, 2000, 397–405.

Roche, Patricia A., and Annas, George J. "Protecting Genetic Privacy." *Nature Reviews: Genetics* 2 (2001), 392–396.

Ross, Lainie Friedman. "Heterozygote Carrier Testing in High Schools Abroad: What Are the Lessons for the U.S.? " *Journal of Law, Medicine and Ethics* 34 (2006), 753–764.

———, and Moon, Margaret R. "Ethical Issues in the Genetic Testing of Children," *Archives of Pediatrics and Adolescent Medicine* 154 (2000), 873–879.

Rothstein, Mark A. *Genetic Ties and the Family: The Impact of Paternity Testing on Parents and Children.* Baltimore: Johns Hopkins University Press, 2005.

———, ed. *Genetic Secrets: Protecting Privacy and Confidentiality in the Genetic Era.* New Haven: Yale University Press, 1997.

Smith, David H., et al. *Early Warning: Cases and Ethical Guidance for Presymptomatic Testing in Genetic Diseases.* Bloomington, IN: Indiana University Press, 1998.

Thomson, Elizabeth J., et al., eds. *Genetics and Public Health in the Twenty-First Century: Using Genetic Information to Improve Health and Prevent Disease.* New York: Oxford University Press, 2000.

Tong, Rosemarie. "Feminist and Nonfeminist Perspectives on Genetic Screening, Diagnosis, Counseling, and Therapy." In Rosemarie Tong, ed., *Feminist Approaches to Bioethics: Theoretical Reflections and Practical Applications.* Boulder, CO: Westview Press: 213–42, 268–71.

U.S. Congress, Office of Technology Assessment. *Cystic Fibrosis and DNA Tests: Implications of Carrier Screening.* Washington, DC: U.S. Government Printing Office, August 1992.

———. *Genetic Monitoring and Screening in the Workplace.* Washington, DC: U.S. Government Printing Office, October 1990.

———. *Genetic Witness: Forensic Uses of DNA Tests.* Washington, DC: U.S. Government Printing Office, July 1990.

U.S. President's Commission for the Study of Ethical Problems in Medicine and Biomedical and Behavioral Research. *Screening and Counseling for Genetic Conditions.* Washington, DC: U.S. Government Printing Office, February 1983.

Wasserstrom, David T. Wachbroit, Robert S., and Bickenbach, Jerome E., eds. *Quality of Life and Human Difference: Genetic Testing, Health Care, and Disability.* New York: Cambridge University Press, 2005.

Wolf, Susan M. "Beyond 'Genetic Discrimination': Toward the Broader Harm of Geneticism." *Journal of Law, Medicine and Ethics* 23 (1995), 345–353.

Zallen, Doris Teichler. *Does It Run in the Family? A Consumer's Guide to DNA Testing for Genetic Disorders.* Piscataway, NJ: Rutgers University Press, 1997.

HUMAN GENE TRANSFER RESEARCH

Ackerman, Terrence F., and Nienhuis, Arthur W., eds. *Ethics of Cancer Genetics and Gene Therapy.* Totowa, NJ: Humana Press, 2001.

Agius, Emmanuel, et al., eds. *Germ-Line Intervention and Our Responsibilities to Future Generations.* New York: Kluwer Academic Publishers, 1998.

Bonnicksen, Andrea A. "Gene Therapy, Ethics, and International Perspectives." In Thomas H. Murray and Maxwell J. Mehlman, eds., *Encyclopedia of Ethical, Legal, and Policy Issues in Biotechnology.* 2 vols. New York: John Wiley & Sons, 2000, 275–85.

Fletcher, John C., and Anderson, W. French. "Germ-Line Gene Therapy: A New Stage of Debate." *Law, Medicine and Health Care* 20 (1992), 26–39.

Fletcher, John C., and Richter, Gerd. "Human Fetal Gene Therapy: Moral and Ethical Questions." *Human Gene Therapy* 7 (1996), 1605–14.

Fowler, Gregory; Juengst, Eric T.; and Zimmerman, Burke K. "Germ-Line Gene Therapy and the Clinical Ethos of Medical Genetics." *Theoretical Medicine* 10 (1989), 151–65.

Frankel, Mark S., and Chapman, Audrey R., eds. *Human Inheritable Genetic Modifications: Assessing Scientific, Ethical, Religious, and Policy Issues.* Washington, DC: American Association for the Advancement of Science, 2000.

Friedmann, Theodore, ed. *The Development of Human Gene Therapy.* New York: Cold Spring Harbor Laboratory Press, 1999.

Grady, Denise, and Pollack, Andrew. "Patient in Experimental Gene Therapy Study Dies, F.D.A. Says," *New York Times,* 27 July 2007, 20.

Henderson, Gail E., Easter, Michele M., Zimmer, Catherine, King, Nancy M. P., et al. "Therapeutic Misconception in Early Phase Gene Transfer Trials." *Social Science and Medicine* 62 (2006), 239–253.

Jaffé, A., Prasad, S.A., Larcher, V., and Hart, S. "Gene Therapy for Children with Cystic Fibrosis – Who Has the Right to Choose?" *Journal of Medical Ethics* 32 (2006), 361–364.

Juengst, Eric T., ed. "Human Germ-Line Engineering." *Journal of Medicine and Philosophy* 16 (1991), 587–694. Thematic issue.

Kaiser, Jocelyn. "Death Prompts a Review of Gene Therapy Vector." *Science* 317 (2007), 580.

McKenny, Gerald P. "Gene Therapy, Ethics, Religious Perspectives." In Thomas H. Murray and Maxwell J. Mehlman, eds. *Encyclopedia of Ethical, Legal, and Policy Issues in Biotechnology.* 2 vols. New York: John Wiley & Sons, 2000: 300–311.

McLean, Sheila, ed. *Genetics and Gene Therapy.* Burlington, VT: Ashgate, 2005.

Nelson, Robert. "Gene Therapy, Ethics, Germ Cell Gene Transfer." In Thomas H. Murray and Maxwell J. Mehlman, eds., *Encyclopedia of Ethical, Legal, and Policy Issues in Biotechnology.* 2 vols. New York: John Wiley & Sons, 2000, 292–300.

Panno, Joseph. *Gene Therapy: Treating Diseases by Repairing Genes.* New York: Facts on File, 2005.

Proctor, Robert N. "Genomics and Eugenics: How Fair Is the Comparison?" In George J. Annas and Sherman Elias, eds., *Gene Mapping: Using Law and Ethics as Guides.* New York: Oxford University Press, 1992, 75–93.

Resnik, David B. *Human Germ-Line Therapy: Scientific, Moral and Political Issues.* Georgetown, TX: Landes Bioscience, 1999.

Ross, Gail, et al. "Gene Therapy in the United States: A Five-Year Status Report." *Human Gene Therapy* 7 (1996), 1781–90.

Scharschmidt, Tiffany, and Lo, Bernard. "Clinical Design Issues Raised During Recombinant DNA Advisory Committee Review of Gene Transfer Protocols." *Human Gene Therapy* 17 (2006), 448–454.

Stock, Gregory, and Campbell, John, eds. *Engineering the Human Germline: An Exploration of the Science and Ethics of Altering the Genes We Pass to Our Children.* New York: Oxford University Press, 2000.

Swazo, Norman K. "Calculating Risk/Benefit in X-linked Severe Combined Immune Deficiency Disorder (X-SCID) Gene Therapy Trials: The Task of Ethical Evaluation." *Journal of Medicine and Philosophy* 31 (2006), 533–564

Tauer, Carol A. "Gene Therapy, Ethics, Gene Therapy for Fetuses and Embryos." In Thomas H. Murray and Maxwell J. Mehlman, eds., *Encyclopedia of Ethical, Legal, and Policy Issues in Biotechnology.* 2 vols. New York: John Wiley & Sons, 2000, 285–292.

U.K. Department of Health, Gene Therapy Advisory Committee. "Guidance on Making Proposals to Conduct Gene Therapy Research on Human Subjects." *Human Gene Therapy* 12 (2001), 711–20.

U.S. Congress. Office of Technology Assessment. *Human Gene Therapy: Background Paper.* Washington, DC: U.S. Government Printing Office, 1984.

U.S. President's Commission for the Study of Ethical Problems in Medicine and Biomedical and Behavioral Research. *Splicing*

Life: A Report on the Social and Ethical Issues of Genetic Engineering with Human Beings. Washington, DC: U.S. Government Printing Office, November 1982.

Walters, LeRoy. "Ethical Issues in Human Gene Therapy." *Journal of Clinical Ethics* 2 (1991), 267–74.

———. "Human Gene Therapy: Ethics and Public Policy." *Human Gene Therapy* 2 (1991), 115–22.

———. "Gene Therapy: Overview." In Thomas H. Murray and Maxwell J. Mehlman, eds., *Encyclopedia of Ethical, Legal, and Policy Issues in Biotechnology.* 2 vols. New York: John Wiley & Sons, 2000, 336–42.

———, and Palmer, Julie G. "Germ-Line Gene Therapy." *The Ethics of Human Gene Therapy.* New York: Oxford University Press, 1997, 60–98.

———, and Palmer, Julie Gage. *The Ethics of Human Gene Therapy.* New York: Oxford University Press, 1997.

Weiss, Rick. "Death Points to Risks in Research: One Woman's Experience in Gene Therapy Trial Highlights Weaknesses in the Patient Safety Net." *Washington Post,* 6 August 2007, A1, A7.

———. "Patient in Gene Therapy Study Dies." *Washington Post,* 27 July 2007, A12.

Wivel, Nelson A. "Gene Therapy, Ethics, Somatic Cell Gene Therapy." In Thomas H. Murray and Maxwell J. Mehlman, eds., *Encyclopedia of Ethical, Legal, and Policy Issues in Biotechnology.* 2 vols. New York: John Wiley & Sons, 2000, 310–21.

Wivel, Nelson A., and Walters, LeRoy. "Germ-Line Gene Modification and Disease Prevention: Some Medical and Ethical Perspectives." *Science* 262 (1993), 533–38.

GENETICS AND BEHAVIOR

Carson, Ronald A., and Rothstein, Mark A., eds. *Behavioral Genetics: The Clash of Culture and Biology.* Baltimore: Johns Hopkins University Press, 1999.

Clarke, William R., and Grunstein, Michael. *Are We Hardwired? The Role of Genes in Human Behavior.* New York: Oxford University Press, 2000.

Dawkins, Richard. *The Selfish Gene.* 30th anniversary edition. New York: Oxford University Press, 2006.

Institute of Medicine. Hernandez, Lyla M., and Blazer, Dan G., eds. *Genes, Behavior, and the Social Environment: Moving Beyond the Nature/Nurture Debate.* Washington, DC: National Academies Press, 2006

Lewontin, Richard C., Rose, Steven P. R., and Kamin, Leon J. *Not in Our Genes: Biology, Ideology, and Human Nature.* New York: Pantheon Books, 1984.

McGuffin, Peter, Owen, Michael J., and Gottesmann, Irving L., eds. *Psychiatric Genetics and Genomics.* New York: Oxford University Press, 2002.

Nuffield Council on Bioethics. *Genetics and Human Behaviour: The Ethical Context.* London: Nuffield Council on Bioethics, 2002.

Parens, Erik; Chapman, Audrey R.; and Press, Nancy, eds. *Wrestling with Behavioral Genetics: Science, Ethics and Public Conversation.* Baltimore: Johns Hopkins University Press, 2006.

Plomin, Robert; DeFries, John C.; McClearn, Gerald E.; and McGuffin, Peter. *Behavioral Genetics.* 4th edition. New York: Worth, 2001.

Plomin, Robert, ed. *Behavioral Genetics in the Postgenomic Era.* Washington, DC: American Psychological Association, 2003.

Richerson, Peter J., and Boyd, Robert. *Not by Genes Alone: How Culture Transformed Human Evolution.* Chicago: University of Chicago Press, 2005.

Rutter, Michael. *Genes and Behavior: Nature-Nurture Interplay Explained.* Malden, MA: Blackwell, 2006.

Wachbroit, Robert. "Genetic Determinism, Genetic Reductionism, and Genetic Essentialism." In Thomas H. Murray and Maxwell J. Mehlman, eds., *Encyclopedia of Ethical, Legal, and Policy Issues in Biotechnology.* 2 vols. New York: John Wiley & Sons, 2002, 352–56.

Wasserman, David T. "Behavioral Genetics, Human." In Thomas H. Murray and Maxwell J. Mehlman, eds., *Encyclopedia of Ethical, Legal, and Policy Issues in Biotechnology.* 2 vols. New York: John Wiley & Sons, 2000, 117–27.

Wasserman, David, and Wachbroit, Robert, eds. *Genetics and Criminal Behavior.* Cambridge: Cambridge University Press, 2001.

REFERENCE WORKS

Burley, Justine, and Harris, John, eds. *A Companion to Genethics.* Malden, MA: Blackwell, 2004.

Chadwick, Ruth F., ed. *The Concise Encyclopedia of the Ethics of New Technologies.* San Diego, CA: Academic Press, 2001.

Chapter 5
Reproduction

Introduction

This chapter explores two different aspects of human reproduction. The first section focuses on moral quandaries that arise in decisions by individuals and couples who actively seek to have children and propose to use some form of medical intervention toward that end. The second section of this chapter focuses on decisions about whether to terminate a pregnancy. Despite the fact that abortion is legal in many western nations, questions of its ethical acceptability continue to be widely debated. In the United States, the legality of abortion continues to be controversial.

ASSISTED REPRODUCTION AND REPROGENETICS

The first section of this chapter presents ethical issues that arise in the use of assisted reproduction and reprogenetics. Those who cannot achieve pregnancy without medical assistance may choose to use assisted reproductive technologies (ART) in their attempts to become pregnant. Individuals or couples with a family history of genetically transmissible disease or conditions, or other interest in the genetic makeup of a future child, may choose to use genetic technologies during or prior to pregnancy. The use of genetic technologies during reproduction, with or without the intervention of reproductive technologies, is sometimes referred to as reprogenetics.

ASSISTED REPRODUCTION

In the traditional model of reproduction, a heterosexual couple makes a rational decision to have a child. They proceed through sexual intercourse. A related process of rational decision making also may occur after the unintended initiation of a pregnancy.

The traditional model is not the only possible practice. In the latter decades of the twentieth century and the early years of the twenty-first century, health professionals and couples alike have made the general public increasingly aware of the problem of involuntary infertility. Infertility is defined as the failure to become pregnant after twelve months of unprotected (no contraceptive use) sexual intercourse. In response to this problem, both old and new technologies designed to enable women to achieve pregnancy, known collectively as ART, have been developed and increasingly employed. Artificial insemination, for example, is an older and relatively simple and inexpensive technique where sperm are collected from a man and inserted directly into the woman using a syringe. No drugs or surgical interventions are typically required. Newer approaches are costlier and require increased scientific and medical involvement for pregnancy success. These technologies can be used to extract and combine eggs and sperm to create embryos outside a woman's body and subsequently place the embryos in her to achieve pregnancy.

Although ART was developed to address infertility, the technologies have also permitted individuals and nontraditional couples to conceive biologically related children.

Understanding Infertility. The primary motivation for developing new reproductive technologies is involuntary infertility. Over 7 percent of U.S. married couples experience infertility.[1] The causes of infertility vary from couple to couple, but include lower fertility rates among couples who delay having children until their thirties or older and the deleterious effects on fertility of sexually transmitted diseases such as chlamydia.

Various ways of handling infertility have been viewed as ethically questionable. Some critics of the new reproductive technologies have argued that infertility is not a disease and that physicians are responding inappropriately with interventions that are socially desired by patients rather than medically necessitated.[2] However, other commentators see it differently. For example, a distinguished committee in the United Kingdom, the Warnock Committee, issued an influential 1984 report arguing that even if infertility is not a disease in the strict sense, it is a bodily "malfunction" that health professionals can and should help to remedy.[3] Others have employed a different metaphor, suggesting that involuntary infertility should be regarded as a disability. As a disability, infertility can sometimes be prevented, sometimes cured, or must otherwise be compensated for. Using this metaphor, whatever path is chosen, it is the person herself and not a successful reproductive outcome that should remain the central focus of attention.[4]

A decision by the U.S. Supreme Court supports the disability view. The case turned on whether a woman's HIV infection placed a substantial limitation on her ability "to reproduce and to bear children" and, if so, whether reproduction is one of the "major life activities" covered by the Americans with Disabilities Act (ADA). By a 5–4 margin, the Supreme Court agreed that limitations on a person's ability to reproduce *do* constitute a disability under the terms of the ADA.[5]

In Vitro Fertilization and Other Reproductive Technologies. The birth of Louise Brown in Lancashire, England, in 1978 inaugurated a new era in reproductive technologies. Brown had not been conceived inside her mother's body but in a Petri dish, where eggs removed from her mother had been mixed with sperm from her father, and fertilization had taken place.

In vitro fertilization (literally, "fertilization in glass") is most often proposed as a technique for overcoming infertility in married couples. The simplest case involves the use of semen from the husband and eggs from the wife. No reproductive cells (sperm or eggs) are donated to the couple, so all embryos that result from IVF contain the parents' genes. Technology currently permits the freezing of sperm and human embryos. In this simplest case, all created embryos are transferred to the uterus of the wife. No surplus embryos are created, and thus there is no freezing and storage of the early human embryos.

There are, however, variations on this simplest case. The created embryos may be frozen and stored for future use, donated to other infertile couples, donated to research, or disposed of as medical waste. Either the sperm or the eggs—or even the embryo—may be derived from sources other than the husband and the wife (viz., from donors or vendors).

In addition to IVF, other forms of ART have recently been developed to enhance the likelihood of conceiving. Gamete intrafallopian transfer (GIFT), for example, is similar to IVF. In GIFT, the egg and sperm are transferred surgically to the woman's fallopian tubes rather than her uterus. Unlike IVF, the eggs are not fertilized outside the body and no extra embryos are created, making it an attractive option for those who have religious objections to IVF. Some technological approaches are being used in conjunction with IVF to increase the likelihood of success. For example, intracytoplasmic sperm injection (ICSI), where only one single sperm is injected into an egg, was developed to address certain types of male infertility.

Assisted reproduction is no longer considered radically new. Since the birth of Louise Brown, more than three million infants have been born worldwide with the assistance of ART.[6] In the United States today more than one out of every hundred children born is conceived using some form of ART.[7]

In separating the intimacy of sexual intercourse from family creation, ART has raised unique issues about the nature of parenthood and families; the commodification of children, women's bodies and gametes; the health and safety of the participating individuals (including harm to future children); and, the rights of individuals to use and access the technology. For example, the use of ART in the practice of surrogacy permits an egg donor (surrogate) or another woman (gestational carrier) to carry a pregnancy on behalf of married or unmarried couples and individuals. The surrogate is genetically related to the child, whereas the gestational carrier is not. The intended parents who will raise the child may or may not be biologically related to the child. A surrogacy arrangement could technically result in five individuals who could claim a right to parentage in some form: the egg donor, the sperm donor, the gestational surrogate, the intended father, and the intended mother. Difficult issues arise when the child is born and a party to the arrangement asserts parental rights contrary to the original agreement. State courts have been the arbiter of last resort in such conflicts, forced to resolve whether the biological relationship or the social relationship should prevail and decide whether agreements for these types of services should even be recognized as legally binding and enforceable. Some states have completely banned the commercial practice of surrogacy, finding the contractual and commercial nature of surrogacy morally offensive and reflecting concerns about commodification of children and about the health, safety, and exploitation of women who donate eggs or are paid to carry a pregnancy.

ART has played a significant role in the emergence of nontraditional families and has also highlighted the role of health care providers in controlling access to technologies. Single women can choose a sperm donor from the donor profiles listed on sperm bank websites. They can then utilize the relatively inexpensive low-tech ART procedure of artificial insemination, purchasing semen to be inserted into the woman's uterus. Gay and lesbian couples can use ART to conceive children who are genetically related to at least one of the individuals in the couple. Women who are past the age of menopause may be able to use reproductive technologies to successfully conceive a biologically related child. Children can even be conceived after a man's death by using stored frozen sperm or sperm retrieved immediately after death. These techniques require application of some form of technology that an individual or couple cannot access without a third party, raising the possibility of discrimination in access against those who do not fit a health care provider or sperm bank's traditional concept of a heterosexual, married, young couple.[8]

The use of ART in the creation of human life has been ethically contentious. Some commentators have asked whether it is appropriate to place limitations or controls on ART. In the first article of this chapter, John Robertson advocates for recognition of an unrestricted procreative liberty right for individuals and couples to make reproductive choices involving assisted reproduction. He argues that procreative liberty in the context of coital reproduction has a strong moral, legal, and social foundation that should similarly be reflected in public policymaking concerning noncoital reproduction. His critics question the primacy of procreative liberty in the context of ART, and claim in contrast that reproductive technologies have the potential to cause harms that should outweigh an individual's or couple's procreative liberty right. His detractors advocate restrictions or prohibitions on various uses of reproductive technologies.

Among Robertson's critics is Bonnie Steinbock. In the second selection in this chapter, she argues for continued respect for individual choice regarding reproduction, but also for the recognition and support of a right to reproduce only where there is an intention or ability to raise a child. That is, she maintains that a right to reproduce would not apply when there is no such intention or ability. The implication is that there should be no recognized right to be a sperm donor, egg donor, or surrogate mother. She counters Robertson's unrestricted liberty right by introducing the concept of procreative *responsibility,* reflecting concern for potential harms to children. Steinbock also examines the religious, health, safety, and feminist objections to IVF. She believes that these objections do not justify a ban on ART. She asserts that fertile and infertile individuals have a right to reproduce, but limitations on such a right may be justifiable in light of the interests of society in preventing harm to children and exploitation of individuals who use the technologies.

Ethical and legal concerns about the oversight of business practices associated with ART are also being raised. More than one million people in the United States are estimated to have used some form of fertility treatment.[9] ART has also become a $4 billion a year business enterprise in the United States alone.[10] Various countries have adopted divergent approaches to the public oversight of assisted reproductive technologies. In the United Kingdom, for example, the Human Fertilisation and Embryology Authority (HFEA) is a statutory body that regulates donor insemination, IVF, storage of gametes, and research involving early human embryos.[11] This British agency publishes annual reports that detail the success rates of individual clinics with donor insemination and IVF. The HFEA also sets practice standards on matters as specific as the number of early embryos that can be transferred to the body of a woman in a given ovulatory cycle.

In the United States, reproductive technologies have developed within an environment that can be described as laissez-faire. There is no comprehensive mechanism beyond professional regulation to oversee this area. In addition to Steinbock's suggestions that appropriate controls may be needed, there have been several calls in the United States for oversight of reproductive medicine practices. In 2004, George W. Bush's President's Council on Bioethics focused attention on the lack of data, regulation, and oversight in the converging fields of assisted reproduction, genetics, and embryo research. In this chapter's excerpt from their report, *Reproduction and Responsibility*, the Council investigates and expresses concerns about the growing markets for gametes and the commercialization of ART services.

On one hand, it can be argued that the exchange of money for eggs and sperm creates an environment that may ultimately diminish human meaning. On the other hand, some would argue that such commerce is not ethically and practically distinguishable from other areas of commerce and that the physical and emotional contribution of gamete donors deserves recognition through financial compensation. They place significance on the outcome—the availability of gametes enables infertile couples to participate in procreation and child rearing.

The Council also explored issues raised by the competitive market for ART services. Irresponsible practitioners may persuade and exploit gamete donors and users of ART by offering financial incentives, including discounted fees for services. Some contend, though, that competition among clinics is essential to keep ART's high costs under control, that it offers choices to patients, and that informed consent can help protect against exploitation.

Ultimately, the Council suggests that commerce in this area may be ripe for possible government intervention and oversight.

REPROGENETICS

Like ART, technological advances in reprogenetics have been rapid, spurred by the brisk development of new genetic tests. The primary use of genetic technology in combination with reproduction is through prenatal genetic testing (PNT). PNT allows for the detection of genetic abnormalities in the fetus while the fetus is still inside the mother. Methods include testing of fluid or tissue obtained through (1) amniocentisis, where a small amount of the fluid surrounding the fetus is extracted, (2) chorionic villi sampling, where tissue that will become the placenta is aspirated, and (3) maternal serum alpha-fetoprotein (MSAFP) screening for certain limited conditions, such as Down's syndrome or neural tube impairments, where the mother's blood is tested for certain biochemical markers and positive results are followed up with other PNT methods. Ultrasound may also be used to diagnose structural defects in the fetus. With PNT, the fetus may have been conceived naturally or through assisted reproduction. Once the woman is informed of the test results, her options are limited. She can choose to continue the pregnancy, prepared with the knowledge that the child will be born with a particular genetic condition. Alternatively, she can choose to abort the fetus. Very infrequently, surgical options may be available to address an identified abnormality while the fetus is in utero.

Preimplantation genetic diagnosis (PGD) is another reprogenetic technology. In contrast to PNT, it tests early-stage embryos outside of the mother and *prior* to implantation. ART techniques are used to create embryos *in vitro* that undergo genetic testing. Based on the test results, a particular embryo can either be used to establish a pregnancy through assisted reproduction or be discarded. Frequently, multiple embryos are tested using PGD, and those with the desired traits (or lack of undesired traits) will be selected for use. Unlike PNT, abortion is not an issue because no pregnancy is established at the preimplantation stage.

Combining reproduction and genetics provides society with an impressive array of diagnostic possibilities, an array that is likely to become more impressive and confounding with greater knowledge of the human genome, genetic diseases and conditions. Close to one thousand conditions can currently be diagnosed through reprogenetic applications.[12] The primary ethical issue arising in reprogenetics concerns the avoidance of the birth of a child affected by a genetic disorder. The end result—never being born—starkly contrasts with traditional medical interventions, which ameliorate or cure affected children.

In the United States, autonomous decision making in areas of reproduction is highly valued. But should parents be permitted to choose freely from the ever-growing testing menu of diseases, conditions, and traits available through reprogenetics? Should testing for benign conditions, or even testing for sex selection, be permitted? Are concerns about eugenic implications (discussed in Chapter 4) valid? What is the appropriate role of health care professionals in supporting or counseling patients about reprogenetic options?

In this chapter, Adrienne Asch raises issues about the impact of PNT and selective abortion on people with disabilities. She argues that individuals and society are generally misinformed about disability. Abortion in this context threatens the full acceptance and inclusion of people with disabilities in society, and further threatens parent–child relationships. The societal and medical acceptability of PNT disvalues human variation and individuals with disabilities. At the core of her argument is the contention that disability should be understood as a social issue, rather than a medical issue. The medical paradigm understands disability in terms of biological limitations and treatments and a diminished quality of life. A social paradigm understands disability in terms of societal barriers that are capable of remedy. Unaccommodating building access, communication, and transit options prevent people with disabilities from participating in work and society. In the social paradigm, people with disabilities do not question their quality of life until they are confronted by socially constructed obstacles.

In the next selection, Allen Buchanan and colleagues critically examine the assertion that the use of medical genetics, in PNT and otherwise, will bring an improvement in lives, distinguishing today's genetic interventions from eugenics. These authors methodically address and challenge a number of the disability-rights critiques of genetic interventions. In their opinion, these critiques ultimately do not justify hindering the progress and use of genetic technologies and therapies.

THE PROBLEM OF JUSTIFYING ABORTION

The four excerpts in the second section explore the moral justification for abortion.

THE PROBLEM OF MORAL JUSTIFICATION

Abortions are sought for many reasons: psychological trauma, pregnancy caused by rape, the inadvertent use of fetus-deforming drugs, genetic predisposition to disease, prenatally diagnosed birth defects, and many personal and family reasons such as the financial burden of a child. These circumstances explain why abortions are obtained. But an *explanation* of this sort does not address the problem of *justification:* What reasons, if any, are sufficient to justify the act of aborting a human fetus?

Some contend that abortion is never acceptable or, at most, is permissible only if it is necessary to bring about a moral good such as saving a pregnant woman's life. This view is commonly called the *conservative theory of abortion* because it emphasizes conserving life. Roman Catholics are well-known proponents of this approach, but they are by no means its only advocates. A philosophical case for this point of view is presented in this chapter by Don Marquis, who does not rely on any form of religious claim to defend his views.

The opposed view is that abortion is always permissible, whatever the state of fetal development. This outlook is commonly termed the *liberal theory of abortion* because it emphasizes freedom of choice and the right of a woman to make decisions that affect her body. Mary Anne Warren defends this approach in this chapter.

Many writers defend theories that are intermediate between liberal and conservative approaches. They hold that abortion is ethically permissible up to a specified stage of fetal development or for moral reasons that warrant abortions under limited circumstances (such as pregnancy from rape and pregnancy that presents a risk of death to the woman). Baruch Brody presents an intermediate theory that leans toward conservatism, whereas Judith Thomson's essay suggests an intermediate theory that leans toward liberalism.

THE ONTOLOGICAL STATUS OF THE FETUS

Recent controversies about abortion focus on ethical problems of our obligations to fetuses and on what rights, if any, fetuses possess. One basic issue concerns the *kind of entities* fetuses are. This is the problem of the *ontological status* of the fetus.

Several layers of questions can be distinguished about ontological status: (1) Is the fetus an individual organism? (2) Is the fetus biologically a human being? (3) Is the fetus psychologically a human being? and (4) Is the fetus a person? It is widely agreed that one attributes a more significant status to the fetus by granting that it is fully a human being (biologically and psychologically), rather than merely saying that it is an individual organism, and that one enhances its status still further by attributing personhood to the fetus.

Many are willing to concede that an individual life begins at fertilization but not willing to concede that a psychological human being or a person exists at fertilization. Others claim that the fetus is human biologically and psychologically at fertilization but not a person. Still others grant full personhood at fertilization. Those who espouse these views sometimes differ because they define one or more central terms differently. Other critical differences derive from theories of humanity or personhood.

THE CONCEPT OF HUMANITY

The concept of human life has long been at the center of the abortion discussion. It is a complicated notion, because "human life" carries two very different meanings. On one hand, it can mean *biological human life*, that group of biological characteristics that set the human species apart from nonhuman species. On the other hand, "human life" can be used to mean *life that is distinctively human*—that is, a life characterized by psychological rather than biological properties. For example, the ability to use symbols, to imagine, to love, and to perform higher intellectual skills are among the most distinctive human properties.

A simple example illustrates the differences between these two senses of "human life": Some infants with extreme disabilities die shortly after birth. They are born of human parents, and they are biologically human; but they never exhibit the distinctively human psychological traits just mentioned and (in many cases) have no potential to do so. For these individuals it is not possible to make human life in the biological sense match human life in the psychological sense. It is noteworthy that we do not differentiate these two aspects of life in discourse about any other animal species. We do not, for example, speak of making feline life more distinctively feline. But we do meaningfully speak of making human life more human, and this usage makes sense because of the dual meaning just mentioned.

In discussions of abortion, it is important to be clear about which meaning is being employed when using the expression "the taking of human life."

THE CONCEPT OF PERSONHOOD

The concept of personhood may or may not be different from either the biological sense or the psychological sense of human life. That is, it could be argued that what it means to be a person is simply to have some properties that make an organism human in one or both of these senses. However, many writers have suggested a list of more demanding criteria for being a person. They have suggested that an entity is a person if and only if it possesses certain *cognitive* properties, not merely *human* properties. Cognitive conditions of personhood similar to the following have been promoted by several writers, among them Warren:

1. Self-consciousness (of oneself as existing over time)
2. Capacity to act on reason
3. Capacity to communicate with others using a language
4. Capacity to act freely
5. Rationality

Sometimes it is said by those who propose such a list that in order to be a person an individual need only satisfy one of the aforementioned criteria—for example, bona fide linguistic behavior (condition 3)—but need not also satisfy the other conditions (nos. 1–2, 4–5). Others say that all of these conditions must be satisfied. In theories in which more than one of these criteria is necessary to qualify as a person, it is not uncommon to say that fetuses, profoundly brain-damaged persons, and most if not all animals fail one of the criteria, and so do not have the moral standing conferred by the category of person. Here the critical question is whether any list approximating criteria 1–5 is acceptable. Marquis, Brody, and Thomson (unlike Warren) seem not to view the core problems of abortion as turning on the acceptance or rejection of any such list.

The problem of ontological status is further complicated by a factor related to the biological development of the fetus. It is important, in some theories, to be able to specify the point during development at which an entity achieves the status of a human or a person. Locating this point of development is a central task in Brody's essay and also in the U.S. Supreme Court opinions in *Roe v. Wade* and *Planned Parenthood v. Casey*. Many positions have been advanced on how to establish this point of development. Moderate theories draw the line somewhere between the extremes of conception and birth. For example, the line may be drawn at quickening, at viability, or when brain waves are first present, as Brody argues.

A very different position is that the fetus fails to satisfy any of the specified criteria and therefore has *no ontological status* (of any moral importance). Warren defends this view. The opposite position is that the fetus always has *full ontological status* in regard to all of the significant measures of status. Marquis supports a version of this view, but one closely tied to what will now be discussed as "the moral status of the fetus."

THE MORAL STATUS OF THE FETUS

Philosophers have explicated the notion of *moral status* in several ways. In a weak sense, this term refers to a standing, grade, or rank of moral importance or of moral value. In a stronger and more common sense, *status* means to have rights, or the functional equivalent of rights, in the form of having protected interests and being positioned to make valid claims (or to have them asserted on one's behalf). Thus, having moral status is to qualify under some range of moral protections. If fetuses have *full moral status* then they possess the same rights as those who have been born. Brody holds this thesis for at least some periods of fetal development, and Marquis's analysis suggests it for all periods.

By contrast, many writers hold that fetuses have only a *partial moral status* and therefore only a partial set of rights, and some maintain that fetuses possess no moral status and therefore no rights, as Warren maintains. If Warren's account is accepted, then the fetus has no more right to life than a body cell or a tumor, and an abortion is no more morally objectionable than surgery to remove the tumor. But if the full-status view is accepted, fetuses possess the rights possessed by all human beings, and an abortion is as objectionable as any common killing of an innocent person.

Theories of moral status have direct links to theories of ontological status. Many writers in philosophy, religion, science, and popular culture have suggested that some special properties of persons, such as self-consciousness and rationality, confer a unique moral standing on those individuals who possess it (though many others have been skeptical that such a property or set of properties does or even could confer moral status).

A typical conservative thesis is that because the line between the human and the nonhuman is properly drawn at conception, the fetus has full ontological status and, therefore, full moral status. A typical liberal claim is that the line between the human and the nonhuman must be drawn at birth; the fetus has no significant ontological status and, therefore, no significant moral status. Some liberals argue that even though the fetus is biologically human, it is nonetheless not human in an ontologically significant sense and, therefore, has no significant moral status. This claim is usually accompanied by the thesis that *only* persons have a significant ontological status, and because fetuses are not persons they have no moral status (see Warren).

Moderates use a diverse mixture of arguments, which sometimes do and sometimes do not combine an ontological account with a moral one. Typical of moderate views is the claim that the line between the human and the nonhuman or the line between persons and nonpersons should be drawn at some point between conception and birth. Therefore, the fetus has no significant moral status during some stages of growth but does have significant moral status beginning at some later stage. For example, the line may be drawn at viability, with the result that the fetus is given either full moral status or partial moral status at viability. Some arguments in U.S. Supreme Court cases involve a similar (although not identical) premise about the role of viability.

PROBLEMS OF CONFLICTING RIGHTS

If either the liberal or the conservative view of the moral status of the fetus is adopted, the problem of morally justifying abortion may seem straightforward. If one holds that a fetus does not have human rights, abortions do not seem morally reprehensible and are prudentially justified just as surgical procedures are. In contrast, if one accepts that a fetus at any stage of development is a human life with full moral status, then the equation "abortion is murder" (at the designated stage of development) seems to follow.

However, establishing a position on abortion is not this straightforward. Even on a conservative theory there may be cases of justified abortion. For example, it has been argued by many writers that a pregnant woman may legitimately abort the fetus in "self-defense" if both will die unless the life of the fetus is terminated. In order to claim that abortion is always wrong, one must justify the claim that the fetus's "right to life" always overrides the pregnant woman's rights to life and liberty. Even if a theory held that human fetuses are owed equal consideration or have equal rights, these rights might not always override all other moral rights. Here rights are *conflicting:* The unborn possess some rights (including a right to life) and pregnant women also possess rights (including a right to life). Those who possess the rights have a (prima facie) moral claim to be treated in accordance with their rights. But what happens when the rights conflict?

This problem is also present for many moderate theories of the moral status of the fetus. These theories provide moral grounds against arbitrary termination of fetal life (the fetus has some claim to protection against the actions of others) yet do not grant to the fetus (at least in some stages of development) the same rights to life possessed by persons. Advocates of these theories are also faced with the problem of specifying which rights should take precedence in situations of conflict. Does the woman's right to decide what happens to her body justify abortion? Does pregnancy resulting from rape justify abortion? Does self-defense justify abortion? Does psychological damage justify abortion? Does knowledge of a grossly deformed fetus justify abortion? And further, does the fetus have a right to a "minimum quality of life," that is, to protection against wrongful life? Some of these issues about conflicting rights are raised by Thomson, who is criticized by both Brody and Warren.

LEGAL ISSUES SURROUNDING ABORTION

The remaining excerpts in this chapter explore the legal status of abortion in the United States. The 1973 U.S. Supreme Court case of *Roe v. Wade* set a precedent for how abortion legislation may and may not be formulated in the United States. In the opinion of the Court, the majority held that the right to privacy implicit in the Fourteenth Amendment is broad enough to encompass a woman's decision to have an abortion. This right overrides all other concerns until the fetus reaches the point of viability. After that point, the Court finds that states have a legitimate interest in protecting the life of the fetus, even if the protection afforded directly competes with the woman's interest in liberty.

The Court's arguments in *Roe v. Wade* have often come under attack. Even some Supreme Court justices have expressed significant disagreement with this opinion. Justice Sandra Day O'Connor presented an influential criticism in the case of *City of Akron v. Center for Reproductive Health.* She attacked the framework of *Roe,* maintaining that the Court's reasoning was not sufficient to justify its fundamental analytical framework of "stages" of pregnancy. She also argued that the notion of compelling interests in maternal and fetal health will change as medical technology changes. O'Connor envisioned the following possibility: As the point of viability is pushed back to earlier stages of development by technological advancement, the point at which abortion is legally allowed must also be pushed back; as medical practices improve, the need to protect maternal health will also be reduced. She concluded that the *Roe* framework is unworkable and "on a collision course with itself."[13]

In *Planned Parenthood v. Casey,* which appears as the second reading in the legal section of this chapter, O'Connor and two other justices join forces in reaffirming the essential holding in *Roe* that a woman has a legal right to seek an abortion prior to fetal viability, but they strip *Roe* of what they consider its untenable parts, especially the "trimester" conception of three stages of pregnancy. They argue that an undue burden test should replace the trimester framework in evaluating legal restrictions placed on access to abortion prior to viability. They also maintain that certain restrictions do not constitute undue burdens, including requirements of informed consent, parental notification and consent, and a 24-hour waiting period. However, they argue that a spousal notification provision would place an undue burden on a woman, and they therefore declare it legally invalid.

The third legal opinion in this section, *Gonzales v. Carhart,* involved a statute passed by the United States Congress, the Partial Birth Abortion Act of 2003. This Act prohibits doctors from performing a second trimester procedure that has become known as "partial birth abortion." As described in graphic detail by the United States Supreme Court, the procedure involves a physician extracting part of the fetus from the uterus prior to ending its life. Under the federal statute, a physician could be criminally prosecuted for performing the procedure except when it would save the pregnant woman's life. The statute prohibits the procedure in any other circumstance, including when the pregnant woman's health is at risk. In a 5–4 decision, the Supreme Court applied the "undue burden" test from the *Casey* opinion, finding that the ban on this abortion procedure did not unduly burden a woman's right to abortion. With reference to "ethical and moral" considerations, the Court's majority opinion emphasized the government's substantial interest in preserving fetal life without making a distinction between pre-viability and post-viability abortions. This decision was issued seven years after the Court's decision *Stenberg v. Carhart* (2000) where, in a 5–4 vote, it overturned a Nebraska's statute banning partial birth abortion because it did not contain an exception permitting a physician to perform the procedure where necessary to preserve the health of the mother. There is no doubt that future challenges to the legality of abortion will continue.

T.L.B.

L.W.

A.C.M.

NOTES

1. Elizabeth Hervey Stephen and Anjani Chandra, "Declining Estimates of Infertility in the United States: 1982–2002," *Fertility and Sterility* 86 (2006), 516–23.

2. See, for example, Leon R. Kass, "Making Babies: The New Biology and the 'Old' Morality," *Public Interest* 26 (1972), 18–56.

3. U.K., Department of Health and Social Security, *Report of the Committee of Inquiry into Human Fertilisation and Embryology* (The Warnock Committee Report). London: Her Majesty's Stationery Office, July 1984, 8–10.

4. See, for example, Barbara Katz Rothman, "Infertility as Disability." In *Recreating Motherhood: Ideology and Technology in a Patriarchal Society.* New York: W. W. Norton & Company, 1989, 143–51.

5. *Bragdon v. Abbott*, 524 U.S. 624 (1998).

6. European Society of Human Reproduction & Embryology, "Three Million Babies Born Using Assisted Reproductive Technologies," *Press Releases ESHRE* (2006) available at http://www.eshre.com/emc.asp? pageId=806.

7. U.S. Dept. of Health and Human Services, Centers for Disease Control and Prevention. *2004 Assisted Reproductive Technology Success Rates: National Summary and Fertility Clinic Reports* (December 2006). Available at http://ftp.cdc.gov/pub/Publications/art/2004ART508.pdf.

8. See, for example, The Ethics Committee of the American Society for Reproductive Medicine, "Access To Fertility Treatment By Gays, Lesbians, and Unmarried Persons," *Fertility and Sterility* 86 (2006), 1333–35, available at http://www.asrm.org/Media/Ethics/fertility_gaylesunmarried.pdf.

9. President's Council on Bioethics, *Reproduction and Responsibility: The Regulation of New Biotechnologies.* Washington, DC: March 2004 (available at www.bioethics.gov).

10. President's Council on Bioethics, *Reproduction and Responsibility: The Regulation of New Biotechnologies.* Washington, DC: March 2004 (available at www.bioethics.gov).

11. Human Fertilisation and Embryology Authority (HFEA), www.hfea.gov.uk.

12. Cynthia M. Powell, "The Current State of Prenatal Genetic Testing in the United States." In Erik Parens and Adrienne Asch eds., *Prenatal Testing and Disability Rights.* Washington, DC: Georgetown University Press, 2000, 44–53.

13. *City of Akron v. Akron Center for Reproductive Health*, 462 U.S. 416, 458 (1983).

Assisted Reproduction and Reprogenetics

JOHN A. ROBERTSON

The Presumptive Primacy of Procreative Liberty

John A. Robertson holds the Vinson and Elkins Chair at the University of Texas School of Law at Austin. He has written and lectured widely on law and bioethical issues. He is the author of two books in bioethics—*The Rights of the Critically Ill* (Bantam Books) and *Children of Choice: Freedom and the New Reproductive Technologies* (Princeton) and numerous articles on reproductive rights, genetics, organ transplantation, and human experimentation. He has served on or been a consultant to many national bioethics advisory bodies, and is currently Chair of the Ethics Committee of the American Society for Reproductive Medicine.

Procreative liberty has wide appeal but its scope has never been fully elaborated and often is contested. The concept has several meanings that must be clarified if it is to serve as a reliable guide for moral debate and public policy regarding new reproductive technologies.

WHAT IS PROCREATIVE LIBERTY?

At the most general level, procreative liberty is the freedom either to have children or to avoid having them. Although often expressed or realized in the context of a couple, it is first and foremost an individual interest. It is to be distinguished from freedom in the ancillary aspects of reproduction, such as liberty in the conduct of pregnancy or choice of place or mode of childbirth.

The concept of reproduction, however, has a certain ambiguity contained within it. In a strict sense, reproduction is always genetic. It occurs by provision of one's gametes to a new person, and thus includes having or producing offspring. While female reproduction has traditionally included gestation, in vitro fertilization (IVF) now allows female genetic and gestational reproduction to be separated. Thus a woman who has provided the egg that is carried by another has reproduced, even if she has not gestated and does not rear resulting offspring. Because of the close link between gestation and female reproduction, a woman who gestates the embryo of another may also reasonably be viewed as having a reproductive experience, even though she does not reproduce genetically.

In any case, reproduction in the genetic or gestational sense is to be distinguished from child rearing. Although reproduction is highly valued in part because it usually leads to child rearing, one can produce offspring without rearing them and rear children without reproduction. One who rears an adopted child has not reproduced, while one who has genetic progeny but does not rear them has.

In this [excerpt] the terms "procreative liberty" and "reproductive freedom" will mean the freedom to reproduce or not to reproduce in the genetic sense, which may also include rearing or not, as intended by the parties. Those terms will also include female gestation whether or not there is a genetic connection to the resulting child. . . .

Two further qualifications on the meaning of procreative liberty should be noted. One is that "liberty" as used in procreative liberty is a negative right. It means that a person violates no moral duty in making a procreative choice, and that other persons have a duty not to interfere with that choice. However, the negative right to procreate or not does not imply the duty of others to provide the resources or services necessary to exercise one's procreative liberty despite plausible moral arguments for governmental assistance.

As a matter of constitutional law, procreative liberty is a negative right against state interference with choices to procreate or to avoid procreation. It is not a right against private interference, though other laws might provide that protection. Nor is it a positive right to have the state or particular persons provide the means or resources necessary to have or avoid having children. The exercise of procreative liberty may be severely constrained by social and economic circumstances. Access to medical care, child care, employment, housing, and other services may significantly affect whether one is able to exercise procreative liberty. However, the state presently has no constitutional obligation to provide those services. Whether the state should alleviate those conditions is a separate issue of social justice.

The second qualification is that not everything that occurs in and around procreation falls within liberty interests that are distinctively procreative. Thus whether the father may be present during childbirth, whether midwives may assist birth, or whether childbirth may occur at home rather than in a hospital may be important for the parties involved, but they do not implicate the freedom to reproduce (unless one could show that the place or mode of birth would determine whether birth occurs at all). Similarly, questions about a pregnant woman's drug use or other conduct during pregnancy, . . . implicates liberty in the course of reproduction but not procreative liberty in the basic sense. . . .

Procreative liberty should enjoy presumptive primacy when conflicts about its exercise arise because control over whether one reproduces or not is central to personal identity, to dignity, and to the meaning of one's life. For example, deprivation of the ability to avoid reproduction determines one's self-definition in the most basic sense. It affects women's bodies in a direct and substantial way. It also centrally affects one's psychological and social identity and one's social and moral responsibilities. The resulting burdens are especially onerous for women, but they affect men in significant ways as well.

On the other hand, being deprived of the ability to reproduce prevents one from an experience that is central to individual identity and meaning in life. Although the desire to reproduce is in part socially constructed, at the most basic level transmission of one's genes through reproduction is an animal or species urge closely linked to the sex drive. In connecting us with nature and future generations, reproduc-tion gives solace in the face of death. As Shakespeare noted, "nothing 'gainst Time's scythe can make defense/ save breed." For many people "breed"—reproduction and the parenting that usually accompanies it—is a central part of their life plan, and the most satisfying and meaningful experience they have. It also has primary importance as an expression of a couple's love or unity. For many persons, reproduction also has religious significance and is experienced as a "gift from God." Its denial—through infertility or governmental restriction—is experienced as a great loss, even if one has already had children or will have little or no rearing role with them.

Decisions to have or to avoid having children are thus personal decisions of great import that determine the shape and meaning of one's life. The person directly involved is best situated to determine whether that meaning should or should not occur. An ethic of personal autonomy as well as ethics of community or family should then recognize a presumption in favor of most personal reproductive choices. Such a presumption does not mean that reproductive choices are without consequence to others, nor that they should never be limited. Rather, it means that those who would limit procreative choice have the burden of showing that the reproductive actions at issue would create such substantial harm that they could justifiably be limited. Of course, what counts as the "substantial harm" that justifies interference with procreative choice may often be contested, as the discussion of reproductive technologies in this [excerpt] will show. . . .

• • •

TWO TYPES OF PROCREATIVE LIBERTY

• • •

An essential distinction is between the freedom to avoid reproduction and the freedom to reproduce. When people talk of reproductive rights, they usually have one or the other aspect in mind. Because different interests and justifications underlie each and countervailing interests for limiting each aspect vary, recognition of one aspect does not necessarily mean that the other will also be respected; nor does limitation of one mean that the other can also be denied.

However, there is a mirroring or reciprocal relationship here. Denial of one type of reproductive liberty necessarily implicates the other. If a woman is not able to avoid reproduction through contraception or abortion, she may end up reproducing, with all the burdens that unwanted reproduction entails. Similarly, if one is denied the liberty to reproduce through forcible sterilization, one is forced to avoid reproduction, thus experiencing the loss that absence of progeny brings. By extending reproductive options, new reproductive technologies present challenges to both aspects of procreative choice.

AVOIDING REPRODUCTION: THE LIBERTY NOT TO REPRODUCE

One sense in which people commonly understand procreative liberty is as the freedom to avoid reproduction—to avoid begetting or bearing offspring and the rearing demands they make. Procreative liberty in this sense could involve several different choices, because decisions to avoid procreation arise at several different stages. A decision not to procreate could occur prior to conception through sexual abstinence, contraceptive use, or refusal to seek treatment for infertility. At this stage, the main issues concern freedom to refrain from sexual intercourse, the freedom to use contraceptives, and the freedom to withhold gametes for use in noncoital conception. Countervailing interests concern societal interests in increasing population, a partner's interest in sexual intimacy and progeny, and moral views about the unity of sex and reproduction.

Once pregnancy has occurred, reproduction can be avoided only by termination of pregnancy. Procreative freedom here would involve the freedom to abort the pregnancy. Competing interests are protection of embryos and fetuses and respect for human life generally, the most heated issue of reproductive rights. They may also include moral or social beliefs about the connectedness of sex and reproduction, or views about a woman's reproductive and work roles.

Once a child is born, procreation has occurred, and the procreators ordinarily have parenting obligations. Freeing oneself from rearing obligations is not strictly speaking a matter of procreative liberty, though it is an important personal interest. Even if parents relinquish the child for adoption, the psychological reality that one has reproduced remains. Opposing interests at this stage involve the need to provide parenting, nurturing, and financial support to offspring. The right to be free of those obligations, as well as the right to assume them after birth occurs, is not directly addressed in this [excerpt] except to the extent that those rights affect reproductive decisions. . . .

THE FREEDOM TO PROCREATE

In addition to freedom to avoid procreation, procreative liberty also includes the freedom to procreate—the freedom to beget and bear children if one chooses. As with avoiding reproduction, the right to reproduce is a negative right against public or private interference, not a positive right to the services or the resources needed to reproduce. It is an important freedom that is widely accepted as a basic, human right. But its various components and dimensions have never been fully analyzed, as technologies of conception and selection now force us to do.

As with avoiding reproduction, the freedom to procreate involves the freedom to engage in a series of actions that eventuate in reproduction and usually in child rearing. One must be free to marry or find a willing partner, engage in sexual intercourse, achieve conception and pregnancy, carry a pregnancy to term, and rear offspring. Social and natural barriers to reproduction would involve the unavailability of willing or suitable partners, impotence or infertility, and lack of medical and child-care resources. State barriers to marriage, to sexual intercourse, to conception, to infertility treatment, to carrying pregnancies to term, and to certain child-rearing arrangements would also limit the freedom to procreate. The most commonly asserted reasons for limiting coital reproduction are overpopulation, unfitness of parents, harm to offspring, and costs to the state or others. Technologies that treat infertility raise additional concerns that are discussed below.

The moral right to reproduce is respected because of the centrality of reproduction to personal identity, meaning, and dignity. This importance makes the liberty to procreate an important moral right, both for an ethic of individual autonomy and for ethics of community or family that view the purpose of marriage and sexual union as the reproduction and rearing of offspring. Because of this importance, the right to reproduce is widely recognized as a prima facie moral right that cannot be limited except for very good reason.

Recognition of the primacy of procreation does not mean that all reproduction is morally blameless, much less that reproduction is always responsible and praiseworthy and can never be limited. However, the presumptive primacy of procreative liberty sets a very high standard for limiting those rights, tilting the balance in favor of reproducing but not totally determining its acceptability. A two-step process of analysis is envisaged here. The first question is whether a distinctively procreative interest is involved. If so, the question then is whether the harm threatened by reproduction satisfies the strict standard for overriding this liberty interest. . . .

• • •

Charges that noncoital reproduction is unethical or irresponsible arise because of its expense, its highly technological character, its decomposition of parenthood into genetic, gestational, and social components, and its potential effects on embryos, women, and offspring. To assess whether these effects justify moral condemnation or public limitation, we must first determine whether noncoital reproduction implicates important aspects of procreative liberty.

THE RIGHT TO REPRODUCE AND NONCOITAL TECHNOLOGY

If the moral right to reproduce presumptively protects coital reproduction, then it should protect noncoital reproduction as well. The moral right of the coitally infertile to reproduce is based on the same desire for offspring that the coitally fertile have. They too wish to replicate themselves, transmit genes, gestate, and rear children biologically related to them. Their infertility should no more disqualify them from reproductive experiences than physical disability should disqualify persons from moving about with mechanical assistance. The unique risks posed by noncoital reproduction may provide independent justifications for limiting its use, but neither the noncoital nature of the means used nor the infertility of their beneficiaries mean that the presumptively protected moral interest in reproduction is not present.

A major question about this position, however, is whether the noncoital or collaborative nature of the means used truly implicates reproductive interests. For example, what if only one aspect of reproduction—genetic transfer, gestation, or rearing—occurs, as happens with gamete donors or surrogates who play no rearing role? Is a person's procreative liberty substantially implicated in such partial reproductive roles? The answer will depend on the value attributed to the particular collaborative contribution and on whether the collaborative enterprise is viewed from the donor's or recipient's perspective.

Gamete donors and surrogates are clearly reproducing even though they have no intention to rear. Because reproduction *tout court* may seem less important than reproduction with intent to rear, the donor's reproductive interest may appear less important. However, more experience with these practices is needed to determine the inherent value of "partial" reproductive experiences to donors and surrogates. Experience may show that it is independently meaningful, regardless of their contact with offspring. If not, then countervailing interests would more easily override their right to enter these roles.

Viewed from the recipient's perspective, however, the donor or surrogate's reproduction *tout court* does not lessen the reproductive importance of her contribution. A woman who receives an egg or embryo donation has no genetic connection with offspring but has a gestational relation of great personal significance. In addition, gamete donors and surrogates enable one or both rearing partners to have a biological relation with offspring. If one of them has no biological connection at all, they will still have a strong interest in rearing their partner's biologic offspring. Whether viewed singly through the eyes of the partner who is reproducing, or jointly as an endeavor of a couple seeking to rear children who are biologically related to at least one of the two, a significant reproductive interest is at stake. If so, noncoital, collaborative treatments for infertility should be respected to the same extent as coital reproduction is.

Questions about the core meaning of reproduction will also arise in the temporal dislocations that cryopreservation of sperm and embryos make possible. For example, embryo freezing allows siblings to be conceived at the same time, but born years apart and to different gestational mothers. Twins could be created by splitting one embryo into two. If one half is frozen for later use, identical twins could be born at widely different times. Sperm, egg, and embryo freezing also make posthumous reproduction possible.

Such temporally dislocative practices clearly implicate core reproductive interests when the ultimate recipient has no alternative means of reproduction. However, if the procreative interests of the recipient couple are not directly implicated, we must ask whether those whose gametes are used have an independent procreative interest, as might occur if they directed that gametes or embryos be thawed after their death for purposes of posthumous reproduction. In that case the question is whether the expectancy of posthumous reproduction is so central to an individual's procreative identity or life-plan that it should receive the same respect that one's reproduction when alive receives. The answer to such a question will be important in devising policy for storing and posthumously disposing of gametes and embryos. The answer will also affect inheritance questions and have implications for management of pregnant women who are irreversibly comatose or brain dead.

The problem of determining whether technology implicates a major reproductive interest also arises with technologies that select offspring characteristics. . . . Some degree of quality control would seem logically to fall within the realm of procreative liberty. For many couples the decision whether to procreate depends on the ability to have healthy children. Without some guarantee or protection against the risk of handicapped children, they might not reproduce at all.

Thus viewed, quality control devices become part of the liberty interest in procreating or in avoiding procreation, and arguably should receive the same degree of protection. If so, genetic screening and selective abortion, as well as the right to select a mate or a source for donated eggs, sperm, or embryos should be protected as part of procreative liberty. The same arguments would apply to positive interventions to cure disease at the fetal or embryo stage. However, futuristic practices such as nontherapeutic enhancement, cloning, or intentional diminishment of offspring characteristics may so deviate from the core interests that make reproduction meaningful as to fall outside the protective canopy of procreative liberty.

Finally, technology will present questions of whether one may use one's reproductive capacity to produce gametes, embryos, and fetuses for nonreproductive uses in research or therapy. Here the purpose is not to have children to rear, but to get material for research or transplant. Are such uses of reproductive capacity tied closely enough to the values and interests that underlie procreative freedom to warrant similar respect? Even if procreative choice is not directly involved, other liberties may protect the activity.

ARE NONCOITAL TECHNOLOGIES UNETHICAL?

If this analysis is accepted, then procreative liberty would include the right to use noncoital and other technologies to form a family and shape the characteristics of offspring. Neither infertility nor the fact that one will only partially reproduce eliminates the existence of a prima facie reproductive experience for someone. However, judgments about the proximity of these partial reproductive experiences to the core meanings of reproduction will be required in balancing those claims against competing moral concerns.

Judgment about the reproductive importance of noncoital technologies is crucial because many people have serious ethical reservations about them, and are more than willing to restrict their use. The concerns here are not the fears of overpopulation, parental unfitness, and societal costs that arise with allegedly irresponsible coital reproduction. Instead, they include reduction of demand for hard-to-adopt children, the coercive or exploitive bargains that will be offered to poor women, the commodification of both children and reproductive collaborators, the objectification of women as reproductive vessels, and the undermining of the nuclear family.

However, often the harms feared are deontological in character. In some cases they stem from a religious or moral conception of the unity of sex and reproduction or the definition of family. Such a view characterizes the Vatican's strong opposition to IVF, donor sperm, and other noncoital and collaborative techniques. Other deontological concerns derive from a particular conception of the proper reproductive role of women. Many persons, for example, oppose paid surrogate motherhood because of a judgment about the wrongness of a woman's willingness to sever the mother-child bond for the sake of money. They also insist that the gestational mother is always morally entitled to rear, despite her preconception promise to the contrary. Closely related are dignitary objections to allowing any reproductive factors to be purchased, or to having offspring selected on the basis of their genes.

Finally, there is a broader concern that noncoital reproduction will undermine the deeper community interest in having a clear social framework to define boundaries of families, sexuality, and reproduction. The traditional family provides a container for the narcissism and irrationality that often drives human reproduction. This container assures commitments to the identifications and taboos that protect children from various types of abuse. The technical ability to disaggregate and recombine genetic, gestational, and rearing connections and to control the genes of offspring may thus undermine essential protections for offspring, couples, families, and society.

These criticisms are powerful ones that explain much of the ambivalence that surrounds the use of certain reproductive technologies. They call into question the wisdom of individual decisions to use them, and the willingness of society to promote or facilitate their use. Unless one is operating out of a specific religious or deontological ethic, however, they do not show that all individual uses of these techniques are immoral, much less that public policy should restrict or discourage their use.

. . . [T]hese criticisms seldom meet the high standard necessary to limit procreative choice. Many of them are mere hypothetical or speculative possibilities. Others reflect moralisms concerning a "right" view of reproduction, which individuals in a pluralistic society hold or reject to varying degrees. In any event, without a clear showing of substantial harm to the tangible interests of others, speculation or mere moral objections alone should not override the moral right of infertile couples to use those techniques to form families. Given the primacy of procreative liberty, the use of these techniques should be accorded the same high protection granted to coital reproduction. . . .

RESOLVING DISPUTES OVER PROCREATIVE LIBERTY

. . . If procreative liberty is taken seriously, a strong presumption in favor of using technologies that centrally implicate reproductive interests should be recognized. Although procreative rights are not absolute, those who would limit procreative choice should have the burden of establishing substantial harm. This is the standard used in ethical and legal analyses of restrictions on traditional reproductive decisions. Because the same procreative goals are involved, the same standard of scrutiny should be used for assessing moral or governmental restrictions on novel reproductive techniques.

In arbitrating these disputes, one has to come to terms with the importance of procreative interests relative to other concerns. The precise procreative interest at stake must be identified and weighed against the core values of reproduction. As noted, this will raise novel and unique questions when the technology deviates from the model of two-person coital reproduction, or otherwise disaggregates or alters ordinary reproductive practices. However, if an important reproductive interest exists, then use of the technology should be presumptively permitted. Only substantial harm to tangible interests of others should then justify restriction.

In determining whether such harm exists, it will be necessary to distinguish between harms to individuals and harms to personal conceptions of morality, right order, or offense, discounted by their probability of occurrence. . . . [M]any objections to reproductive technology rest on differing views of what "proper" or "right" reproduction is aside from tangible effects on others. For example, concerns about the decomposition of parenthood through the use of donors and surrogates, about the temporal alteration of conception, gestation and birth, about the alienation or commercialization of gestational capacity, and about selection and control of offspring characteristics do not directly affect persons so much as they affect notions of right behavior. . . .

At issue . . . is the symbolic or constitutive meaning of actions regarding prenatal life, family, maternal gestation, and respect for persons over which people in a secular, pluralistic society often differ. A majoritarian view of "right" reproduction or "right" valuation of prenatal life, family, or the role of women should not suffice to restrict actions based on differing individual views of such preeminently personal issues. At a certain point, however, a practice such as cloning, enhancement, or intentional diminishment of offspring may be so far removed from even pluralistic notions of reproductive meaning that they leave the realm of protected reproductive choice. People may differ over where that point is, but it will not easily exclude most reproductive technologies of current interest.

To take procreative liberty seriously, then, is to allow it to have presumptive priority in an individual's life. This will give persons directly involved the final say about use of a particular technology, unless tangible harm to the interests of others can be shown. Of course, people may differ over whether an important procreative interest is at stake or over how serious the harm posed from use of the reproductive technology is. Such a focused debate, however, is legitimate and ultimately essential in developing ethical standards and public policy for use of new reproductive technologies.

THE LIMITS OF PROCREATIVE LIBERTY

The emphasis on procreative liberty that informs this [excerpt] provides a useful but by no means complete or final perspective on the technologies in question. Theological, social, psychological, economic, and feminist perspectives would emphasize different aspects of reproductive technology, and might be much less sanguine about potential benefits and risks. Such perspectives might also offer better guidance in how to use these technologies to protect offspring, respect women, and maintain other important values.

A strong rights perspective has other limitations as well. Recognition of procreative liberty, whether in traditional or in new technological settings, does not guarantee that people will achieve their reproductive goals, much less that they will be happy with what they do achieve. Nature may be recalcitrant to the latest technology. Individuals may lack the will, the perseverance, or the resources to use effective technologies. Even if they do succeed, the results may be less satisfying than envisaged. In addition, many individual instances of procreative choice may cumulate into larger social changes that from our current vantage point seem highly undesirable. But these are the hazards and limitations of any scheme of individual rights.

Recognition of procreative liberty will protect the right of persons to use technology in pursuing their reproductive goals, but it will not eliminate the ambivalence that such technologies engender. Societal ambivalence about reproductive technology is recapitulated at the individual level, as individuals and couples struggle with whether to use the technologies in question. Thus recognition of procreative liberty will not eliminate the dilemmas of personal choice and responsibility that reproductive choice entails. The freedom to act does not mean that we will act wisely, yet denying that freedom may be even more unwise, for it denies individuals' respect in the most fundamental choices of their lives.

BONNIE STEINBOCK

A Philosopher Looks at Assisted Reproduction

Bonnie Steinbock is Professor in the Department of Philosophy, State University of New York at Albany. A Fellow of the Hastings Center, and a member of the Ethics Committee of the American Society for Reproductive Medicine (ASRM), her specialization is biomedical ethics, particularly reproduction and genetics. She has served on a number of working groups in the United States and Europe, including a Hastings Center working group on reprogenetics. Recent articles focus on defining parenthood, moral status, embryonic stem cell research, payment to egg donors, and sex selection. She is the author of numerous books and articles, including *Life Before Birth: The Moral and Legal Status of Embryos and Fetuses* (Oxford), and the editor of *Legal and Ethical Issues in Human Reproduction* (Ashgate).

INTRODUCTION

To assess anything morally—whether an action, character trait, institution, policy, or technological advance—we must consider its impact on the interests of people (and perhaps other affected individuals). Will the item under assessment do good? cause harm? treat people fairly? respect them as autonomous agents? What will be the impact on the community as a whole? These are the fundamental questions of ethical assessment. . . .

IVF allows some infertile couples who could not otherwise have biological children to become parents. Since having children is fervently desired by many people, and the inability to have children is often a source of grief and pain, IVF would seem to be a very good thing.

Nevertheless, IVF and other forms of assisted reproduction have been strongly criticized on a number of grounds. In the first section of this paper, I examine the various objections to IVF, starting with religious objections, coming primarily from the Roman Catholic Church, moving to health and safety objections, and turning finally to social, especially feminist, objections. I argue that none of these objections provides good

From *Journal of Assisted Reproduction and Genetics* 12 (1995): 543–51, Springer and Kluwer Academic Publishers. Reprinted with kind permission of Springer Science and Business Media.

reasons for banning IVF, though certain controls and procedures to protect individuals from harm and exploitation may be appropriate. In the second section, I present and critique John Robertson's strong conception of procreative liberty, arguing that it misconceives the nature and value of the right to reproduce. I argue that the right to reproduce is best interpreted as a right to have one's own children to rear. Where there is no intent or ability to rear, there is no fundamental moral right to reproduce. However, since assisted reproduction is used to enable individuals to have their own children to rear, it should be available to infertile individuals who cannot otherwise reproduce.

OBJECTIONS TO THE NEW REPRODUCTIVE TECHNOLOGIES

RELIGIOUS OBJECTIONS

The Roman Catholic Church opposes any procreative technique which severs reproduction from sexual intercourse. Thus, the Church opposes even the "simple case" of IVF where the husband and wife provide the gametes, and the resulting embryos are implanted in the wife's uterus. The Church's objection is based partly on the means by which the husband's sperm is obtained (masturbation), but more importantly on the fact that reproduction is achieved without an act of sexual intercourse. The Church teaches that the unitive and generative functions of sexual intercourse must not be separated. Thus, the Church opposes both artificial birth control and virtually all forms of assisted reproduction.[1]

It is sometimes speculated that the Church's univocal stance against IVF is premised on the fear that if it were to accept reproduction without sex, that would weaken the Church's absolute rejection of the prohibition on sex without (openness to the possibility of) reproduction. Whatever the merits of this concern, it can have force only for those who think that birth control is morally problematic. The fact that sexual intercourse and reproduction *are* connected is no reason why they *should* be connected, and no reason why it is wrong to try to achieve one without the other.

Some commentators have emphasized the importance of the link between the pleasure of sex, the communication of love, and the desire for children. Reproduction occurs through lovemaking; couples can express their love for each other as they create offspring together. By contrast, reproduction which takes place in a laboratory is cold and sterile. However, this is not a moral objection to assisted reproduction. Undoubtedly, lovemaking is a more enjoyable, not to mention cheaper, way of having a child than IVF, but it is simply not effective for infertile couples. This is unfortunate, but it is no reason why they should be prevented from receiving medical assistance to enable them to have children together.

Another religious objection to IVF comes from the probable destruction of surplus embryos. The Catholic Church considers embryos to be human persons, and their destruction to be impermissible homicide. The only way to avoid destroying surplus embryos is not to create them in the first place. This creates a dilemma. If more than three or four embryos are transplanted to the woman's uterus, there is an increased risk of multiple births, which is risky both for mother and offspring. However, there is no guarantee that the three or four embryos transferred will implant. If implantation fails to occur, another treatment cycle to extract eggs is necessary—at added expense, discomfort, and risk to the patient.

A way out of this dilemma is to extract more eggs than can be implanted—perhaps as many as 20 or 30—and to fertilize all of them. The resulting embryos with the best chance of implanting can be transferred, while the remainder can be frozen for future use. If they are not needed, the surplus embryos can be discarded, used in research and ultimately discarded, or donated to another couple. However, if preimplantation embryos are considered to be human subjects, then discard is not a permissible option.

A complete discussion of the moral status of the embryo is impossible within the confines of this paper. Very briefly, there are two main reasons given for regarding embryos as human persons: their genetic humanity and their potential to develop into persons. Neither is persuasive. Genetic humanity (or species membership) has been attacked by numerous philosophers, on both sides of the abortion issue, as arbitrary or irrelevant. As a merely biological characteristic, the moral relevance of genetic humanity remains dubious. As Don Marquis expresses the objection, "Why . . . is it any more reasonable to base a moral conclusion on the number of chromosomes in one's cells than on the color of one's skin?"[2] Potentially [sic] has been criticized as leading to a *reductio ad absurdum* in which contraception is immoral, since gametes as well as embryos may be said to have the potential, under the right conditions, to become persons. Potentiality theorists protest that there is a great difference between gametes and embryos in terms of their potentiality. Once implanted, an embryo has quite a good chance of developing into a baby, all by itself, without further intervention. By contrast, all by themselves, gametes do not develop into anything. However, whatever the plausibility of this argument in the context of an established pregnancy, it seems to have less force in the context of assisted reproduction, where both gametes and pre-embryos require intervention if they are to develop into persons. The difference in potentiality between gametes and embryos *in vitro* appears to be one of degree, not kind.

While the status of the embryo and fetus remains controversial, it is worth pointing out that some opponents of abortion distinguish between embryos and pre-embryos, regarding only the former to have the moral status and rights of human persons. These prolifers do not oppose forms of "contraception" that prevent implantation, such as the IUD, or very early abortifacients, such as the "morning-after" pill. By the same token, they would not regard the discarding [of] surplus embryos to be a moral objection to assisted reproduction, especially since the intention is to achieve the birth of a child.

Another religious (though not specifically Catholic) objection to assisted reproduction is that it is "playing God." It is sometimes suggested that infertility is

God's will, and that the appropriate response is resignation. Such an argument can obviously have force only with those who believe in God, but it is scarcely persuasive even for them. For the same argument could be applied to all medical intervention. Why treat infections with antibiotics? Why vaccinate children? Why remove a ruptured spleen? Unless we are to adopt the Christian Scientist approach and reject all medical treatment, there seems to be no reason to single out infertility treatment as "playing God."

To this it is sometimes responded that many so-called infertility treatments do not treat the patient's infertility at all. Rather, they enable an infertile couple to have a biologically related child by using the gametes or womb of others. The objection to "collaborative reproduction" is not so much that it is "playing God," as that it muddies lineage and genetic connection. Leon Kass voices this line of criticism. In contrast to the position taken by the Catholic Church, Kass does not object to the "simplest case" of IVF, in which both gametes come from the intended rearing parents, and the wife gestates the resulting embryo. However, he objects to IVF on the ground that it is likely to lead to practices that deprive people of clarity about their origins. He writes:[3]

[C]larity about who your parents are, clarity in the lines of generation, clarity about whose is whose, are the indispensable foundations of a sound family life, itself the sound foundation of civilized community. Clarity about your origins is crucial for self-identity, itself important for self-respect. It would be, in my view, deplorable further to erode such fundamental beliefs, values, institutions, and practices. This means, concretely, no encouragement of embryo adoption or, especially, of surrogate pregnancy.

The dangers of surrogate parenting have been covered at length in the literature.[4] Interestingly, Kass does not object to surrogacy on the usual grounds, such as the commercialization of reproduction or the exploitation of women. Instead, his objection is to the existence of multiple parents and thus a complicated lineage. But is having different genetic, gestational, and rearing parents in itself harmful? There is little empirical data to consult, aside from some limited studies of sperm donation. Robertson comments:[5]

The data available on offspring of sperm donation, however, do not show that those families or children are at especially high risk for psychological or social problems. They have fewer problems than adopted children and their families. Healthy adjustment usually occurs, though problems can arise if the parents have not accepted their infertility or worked through the emotional conflicts that donor sperm raises for them. Children who learn of their missing donor father are sometimes angry at their parents for having kept it secret, and may be frustrated at not being able to obtain more information about him. But they typically do not feel rejected or abandoned as adopted children often do, and many express gratitude for the "gift" that made their existence possible.

Robertson goes on to say, "There is no reason to suppose that egg and embryo donation or gestational surrogacy will pose any greater problems." It seems somewhat disingenuous to lump together gamete donation and gestational surrogacy. A child who is not bothered by the knowledge that he is the product of donated sperm or egg may be considerably more upset at learning that his biological mother agreed to conceive, gestate, and give him up at birth for money.

It is this aspect of surrogacy—that it amounts to babyselling—that is most disturbing to many people. Surrogacy is widely regarded as one of the worst potential harms on a very slippery slope. To avoid making the slide, it is held that "certain aspects of the human experience must never be commercialized," a view expressed by Canada's Royal Commission on New Reproductive Technologies in its Final Report, *Proceed with Care.*[6] One of the Royal Commission's broadest conclusions was that "[h]uman beings, their reproductive capacities or tissues should not be treated as commodities to be traded for money or other goods."[7] Using this conclusion as a guiding principle, the Royal Commission opposed the buying or selling of eggs, sperm, zygotes, embryos, or fetuses, and the use of financial incentives in preconception or adoption arrangements. . . . Canadians testifying at hearings before the Commission expressed the fear that commercial motives may be driving the development and provision of reproductive technologies inappropriately, and that the private sector's pursuit of profit may promote high-tech approaches to the treatment of infertility to the detriment of other alternatives.

These are legitimate concerns about assisted reproduction which deserve serious consideration in determining social policy regarding assisted reproduction. By contrast, the claim that collaborative reproduction, even when noncommercial, is inherently harmful seems unsupported and, on the face of it, implausible.

Secrecy about origins or the withholding of important medical information can be harmful to individuals, but this can be prevented by disclosing to children information about their biological origins.

HEALTH AND SAFETY OBJECTIONS

What are the health risks of assisted reproduction for women and their children? In the early days of IVF, the fear was expressed that the resulting offspring might be abnormal. However, the fears of abnormal offspring have not proved to be well founded. IVF has shown no higher rate of congenital deformity than coital reproduction. There was some research in Australia in the early 1990s that indicated that IVF children were two to three times more likely to suffer from spina bifida and heart defects. However, the number of IVF births in Australia was too small to know if the differences were statistically significant. In any event, recent surveys no longer confirm this suggestion. Thus, there is no evidence that IVF poses greater risks to offspring than ordinary reproduction.

The health risks for women from IVF are significant. Each treatment cycle requires exposing the woman to drugs to stimulate her ovaries. The common side effects from drugs such as Pergonal include bloating, weight gain, fatigue, hot flashes, depression, and mood swings. Ovarian overstimulation, in which the ovaries become enlarged and produce too many follicles, is a severe side effect which happens to about one in five women being treated with Pergonal. Even more dangerous is ovarian hyperstimulation, which happens in 1% to 2% of women, in which the ovaries become enlarged, blood hormone levels skyrocket, and excess fluid may collect in the abdominal cavity or the lungs. Cysts that have formed within the ovaries may rupture, causing internal bleeding. Rarely, blood clots will develop, which can be fatal. [One] study found that women treated with infertility drugs have a risk of ovarian cancer that is 2.5 times higher than that of women in the general population. The invasive procedures used to retrieve the eggs also pose risks, including bleeding, adverse reaction to anesthesia, and infection. The replacement of the fertilized ovum in the uterus may cause infection, physical damage, or ectopic pregnancy. An abnormally high percentage of IVF births end in spontaneous abortion or stillbirth.

In addition to the physical risks of IVF, there are the financial and emotional costs. IVF [is costly*] and may require two or three cycles to achieve pregnancy, if it is successful at all. Insurance may pay none or only some of the costs. The psychological burdens to women "include the emotional ups and down inherent in the cycle of hope and disappointment; the disruption of work and, often, personal relationships; and the humiliation and depersonalization that may result from the submission to painful and embarrassing invasions of their bodies."[8]

Finally, the chances of giving birth to a viable baby after participating in IVF are relatively slim:[9]

In the very best programs, pregnancy and take-home baby rates are around 20 percent of IVF egg retrieval ccles, which means that fewer than one in ten IVF-created embryos implant and come to term. Only ten to twenty programs achieve this level of success. Many other programs have much weaker records, and many have very few pregnancies at all. One survey in 1987 found that over half of the then existing American IVF programs had never produced a live birth. Other programs have misstated their success rates to consumers and been the subject of Federal Trade Commission charges of misleading advertising.

Obviously, consumers must have complete and accurate information about the success rate of IVF clinics. Without complete knowledge of the health risks, emotional pitfalls, and chance of success, potential patients cannot make an informed decision about whether the benefits are worth the risks.

FEMINIST OBJECTIONS

Some feminists support access to assisted reproduction because of its potential for enhancing women's reproductive choices. They believe that women should be free to decide for themselves whether the benefits of IVF outweigh the risks, insisting only on legal regulation and ethical supervision necessary to ensure that women's consent to IVF is adequately informed and voluntary, and that precautions are taken to make the procedure as safe as possible.[10] But other feminists reject this argument as superficial. They maintain that women cannot give truly voluntary consent to IVF treatments, regardless of how well-informed they may be about the risks, costs, and odds of success, because their choices are conditioned by the patriarchal power structure and the pronatalist ideology with which it is

---

*Editor's note: In 2007, the average cost in the United States was $12,400 per cycle. American Society for Reproductive Medicine, www.asrm.org/patients/faqs.html.

associated. If women were not conditioned to think that motherhood is their supreme fulfillment, or anxious to provide male partners with biological children, they would not be willing to submit to the dangers and expense of infertility treatments.

A variation on this theme is the claim that there is something suspect about wanting children "of one's own." Susan Sherwin writes:[11]

Why is it so important to so many people to produce their "own" child? . . . We must look at the sort of social arrangements and cultural values that underlie the drive to assume such risks for the sake of biological parenthood. We find that the capitalism, racism, sexism, and elitism of our culture have combined to create a set of attitudes which views children as commodities whose value is derived from their possession of parental chromosomes.

If it were not for pernicious cultural values, so this line of thinking goes, infertile people who wanted to have children would simply adopt existing children who need homes. However, adoption is not a solution for all couples wishing to adopt, because of the shortage of healthy newborns available for adoption. To this, it is sometimes responded that there are plenty of children available for adoption if one is willing to take an older child, especially one with physical or emotional problems. However, adopting a child with special needs involves taking on special burdens above and beyond those ordinarily associated with parenting. It is not clear why this burden should be placed solely or primarily on individuals who are unable to reproduce coitally. If adoption is morally preferable to procreation as a means of having children, there is no reason why this moral requirement should be placed on those who happen to be infertile. As Peter Singer says, "We cannot demand more of infertile couples than we are ready to demand of ourselves. If fertile couples are free to have large families of their own, rather than adopt destitute children from overseas, infertile couples must also be free to do what they can to have their own families."[12]

In any case, adoption does not fulfill all of the interests individuals may have in procreation. First, adoption does not allow a women to experience pregnancy, childbirth, and lactation, which many women view as joyous and special parts of motherhood. Nor does it allow the father to participate in labor and delivery, an experience which many couples find enriching and meaningful. Second, although adoption allows a couple to raise a child together, it is not the creation of a child together. This is valued as an expression of the couple's love for each other. The child is the living embodiment of the physical union of the couple. Third, people may value having "their own child" over adopting, because they would like a genetic connection with their child. Such a connection makes it more likely that the child will resemble them or other relatives physically or in personality traits, something which is a source of pleasure for parents. For all of these reasons, most people prefer to have children of their own, rather than adopt. Of course, this does not mean that adopting cannot be a wonderful experience. At the same time, there is no reason to "guilt-trip" people who prefer to have biologically related children. There is nothing racist, sexist, elitist, or unreasonable about this preference.

Sherwin thinks that many infertile women are desperate to have children because our culture provides few other outlets for women to have real intimacy and the sense of accomplishment which comes from doing work one judges to be valuable. She says, "[T]here is something very wrong with a culture where childrearing is the only outlet available to most women in which to pursue fulfillment."[13] This argument against reproduction, assisted or otherwise, seems very dated. Today, there are many avenues of fulfillment open to women. The fact that women with satisfying careers still choose to become mothers indicates that they find the experience valuable and important. To insist that the desire for children must be a mere social construction—false consciousness—is as untrue and offensive as insisting that women never freely choose abortion. Ultimately, individuals must decide for themselves whether the benefits of IVF treatment outweigh its costs and risks. As Mary Anne Warren eloquently expresses it:[14]

If women's right to reproductive autonomy means anything, it must mean that we are entitled to take some risks with our physical and psychological health, in the attempt to either have or not have children. Neither abortion nor many forms of contraception are entirely safe, but women sometimes reasonably judge that the alternatives are even less desirable. Having a wanted child can be as important a goal as avoiding an unwanted birth.

However, IVF is not available to every women who wants it and is medically suitable. This raises another feminist concern, namely, the problem of access. Most programs accept only married women in a stable marriage. It is not generally available to single women or lesbian women. Susan Sherwin comments, "The supposed freedom of choice, then, is provided only to selected women who have been screened by the personal values of those administering the technology.[15]

There is an irony in Sherwin's concern that IVF is not available to all women, given her skepticism of its benefits for any women. This is reminiscent of the old joke that the food in a certain restaurant was terrible—"and the portions are so small!" However, feminists may respond that what they object to is not the lack of access to IVF per se, but rather the bases on which it is allocated. In particular, they oppose withholding technologies on the basis of race, class, sexual orientation, or ability to pay. Ironically, the poor and minorities have higher rates of infertility than middle and upper classes, yet only well-off people can afford the high costs of IVF and other assisted reproductive treatments. John Robertson agrees that there is a fairness issue here, but adds:[16]

Yet it does not follow that society's failure to assure access to reproductive technologies for all who would benefit justifies denying access to those who have the means to pay. Such a principle has not been followed with other medical procedures, even life-saving procedures such as heart transplants. As troubled as we might be by differential access, the demands of equality should not bar access for those fortunate enough to have the means.

THE STRONG PROCREATIVE LIBERTY VIEW

John Robertson's . . . book, *Children of Choice,* espouses a very strong interpretation of procreative liberty. According to Robertson, procreative liberty is an important value because "whether one reproduces or not is central to personal identity, to dignity, and to the meaning of one's life." A corollary to this principle is that procreative decisions should be left to the individuals whose procreative desires are most directly involved. Reproductive rights can be limited only for "compelling" reasons, i.e., when reproduction would "clearly harm the tangible interests of others."

Robertson maintains that both fertile and infertile people have the right to reproduce. "Because the values and interests that undergird the right of coital reproduction clearly exist with the coitally infertile, their actions to form a family also deserve respect." Robertson argues that noncoital reproduction should be given the same protection as coital reproduction. However, Robertson goes beyond advocating a right

of access to the new reproductive technologies. His strong interpretation of procreative liberty includes a right to engage in collaborative reproduction, such as commercial surrogacy, because these arrangements may be necessary for some individuals to reproduce. Indeed, Robertson holds that enforcement of surrogate contracts by the state is required by procreative liberty. "A failure to enforce preconception agreements to rear could block the only avenue open to infertile couples to have offspring genetically related to one or both rearing partners." In fact, not only do infertile couples have a right to use surrogates to reproduce, but women who want to act as surrogates have a fundamental moral and legal right to do so. This means that, whatever qualms people may have about commercial surrogacy, "it may have to be tolerated because the procreative liberty of all the parties is so intimately involved."

Whether commercial surrogacy should be permitted is a complex legal and ethical question, which requires a careful balancing of the interests of infertile couples against the potential harm to surrogates and offspring. However that issue is resolved, it seems very unlikely that there is a fundamental moral or legal right to be a donor or surrogate. The view that there is such a right stems, in my view, from a misconception of the nature and value of the right to reproduce.

THE NATURE AND VALUE OF THE RIGHT TO REPRODUCE

The right to reproduce can be separated into two components: genetic replication and rearing. Ideally, the two go together, but it is possible to rear without genetic connection, and to pass on one's genes without rearing. Robertson thinks that both aspects of reproduction are protected by procreative liberty. This leads, as I will show, to implausible conclusions. A better interpretation of the right to reproduce emphasizes the connection with rearing, and maintains that where there is no intention or ability to rear, there is no right to reproduce.

The question we need to ask is, why is procreation important? Why does it deserve the protection of a fundamental right? The answer to this question is likely to be complex. Part of the answer has to do with the connection between procreation and sexual activity. The decision to have or refrain from having children is among the most intimate decisions a person can make. For this reason, it should remain an individual and personal decision. Another reason for regarding procreative choice as a personal decision is that any attempt to intervene into procreative decisions infringes bodily integrity. What people do with their own bodies should be a private and individual decision, unless there are compelling reasons for interference.

In addition to reasons having to do with the personal and intimate nature of reproductive decisions, and the issue of bodily integrity, a third reason for respecting individual choice regarding procreation stems from the profound impact such decisions are likely to have on people's lives. Having a child one does not want imposes serious physical, financial, and emotional burdens, as noted by the Supreme Court in *Roe v. Wade*.[17] Equally, being unable to have a child can be a source of lasting grief and disappointment. However, this grief and disappointment does not ordinarily stem from the frustration of genetic replication per se. Being childless is usually a source of grief because people want to raise children, to have a family. Admittedly, there may be some individuals for whom reproduction *tout court* (as Robertson calls it) has enormous personal meaning. However, not every idiosyncratic desire deserves the protection of a right. Procreation is valuable because of its connection with the raising of children. As Elizabeth Scott says, "It is the objective of rearing the child—of establishing a family—that elevates the right to procreate to a lofty status."[18] Where there is no intention or ability to rear, procreation is of significantly less importance. In other words, I am suggesting that the right to reproduce is not primarily a right to pass on one's genes. The right to reproduce is rather a right to have one's own children to rear.

If rearing is an essential component of the right to reproduce, then the claim of people who lack the intention to rear to reproduce is considerably weakened. This means, first, that there is no right to be a sperm or egg donor, or a surrogate mother. Whether commercial surrogacy should be tolerated or banned is, as I have indicated, a complicated question, but it does not have to be tolerated because there is a fundamental right to use one's reproductive capacity for hire.

This interpretation of the right to reproduce also has implications for those who lack the ability to rear. Consider the example of retarded individuals. A severely retarded person will never be able to care for a child, not even with monitoring and help. If the right

to procreate entails the ability to rear, then severely retarded people do not have a right to reproduce. Involuntary sterilization is not wrong because it violates their procreative autonomy—they do not have procreative autonomy—although it might be wrong for other reasons, such as subjecting them to risky, painful, or unnecessary surgery. . . .

The conception of procreative liberty I am proposing balances the right to reproduce with responsibility in procreating. The notion of procreative responsibility plays almost no role on Robertson's account of procreative liberty, because of his conviction that it is virtually impossible to harm or wrong a person by bringing him into existence. Consider the example of a woman who is HIV-positive. Would it be wrong of her, knowing her diagnosis, deliberately to conceive a child? We may assume that the woman wants very much to have a baby, that this is central to her identity and sense of the meaning of life. But is that all she should consider? I take it that most of us think that responsible reproduction requires that she think about the kind of life her baby will have. AIDS is a terrible and, so far as we know, invariably fatal, disease. Many afflicted children do not survive infancy. Those who do face years of illness before they die. Many are orphaned; some are left languishing in hospitals. Anyone contemplating parenthood should weigh her own desire to love and care for a baby, or to leave something of herself behind, against the possibility of a miserable life for her child. Whether reproduction is responsible depends, therefore, on such things as the degree of the risk of transmission, the possibility of therapies to cure or ameliorate the child's condition after birth, and whether she is likely to live long enough to care for her child.

However, although Robertson pays lip service to balancing the costs to offspring against the value of the reproductive experience, in fact, he does not think that there *are* any costs to offspring. It does not matter how high the rate of transmission, or how sick the kid will be, or how likely it is that he or she will end up as an orphan or "border baby" in some hospital. The reason why none of this matters is that, even under the worst circumstances, the child will probably value its own life, and prefer to go on living. Thus, its life is not "wrongful." If life is not wrongful, then the child has not been harmed or injured by being brought into existence. Robertson concludes, "If there is no injury to offspring from their birth alone, then reproduction is not irresponsible solely because children are born in undesirable circumstances."[19]

This view has startling consequences for clinics and doctors who provide fertility treatment. Nearly all IVF programs test couples for HIV and may refuse the procedure if one or both test positive. Robertson writes, "The exclusion is usually justified on the 'ethical' ground of protecting offspring who would be born in disadvantageous circumstances. However, providing IVF services to these groups would not harm children who have no other way to be born, and thus may ethically be provided if a program is so inclined."[20] However, on Robertson's view, clinics are not merely *free* to provide IVF services to HIV-positive couples, if they are so inclined. If an HIV-positive couple were to apply to an infertility clinic for treatment, the clinic would be morally, and perhaps legally, *required* to treat them. To deny them treatment would be to discriminate against them and to violate their right to reproduce. I regard this as a bizarre interpretation of the right to reproduce, and one that would be rejected by most fertility specialists.

CONCLUSIONS

The right to reproduce belongs to both fertile and infertile people. This does not mean that restrictions on assisted reproduction are never justified, but rather that restrictions need to be justified, balancing the interests of patients, offspring, and society as a whole. Opposition to assisted reproduction stemming from religious arguments based on faith, mere speculation about the importance of genetic lineage, or patronizing assumptions about what women ought to want, is not justified and should not be used to prevent individuals who are so inclined to have the chance to have their own children to rear.

NOTES

1. Congregation for the Doctrine of the Faith: Instruction on respect for human life in its origin and on the dignity of procreation: replies to certain questions of the day, February 22, 1987. Reprinted in Intervention and Reflection: Basic Issues in Medical Ethics, 4th ed, R Munson (ed). Belmont, CA, Wadsworth, 1992, pp 479–487.

2. Marquis D: Why abortion is immoral. J Philos 1989; 86: 183–202, at 186.

3. Kass L: 'Making babies' revisited, Public Interest 1979, no. 54. Reprinted in Arras JD, Steinbock B: Ethical Issues in Modern Medicine, 4th ed. Mountain View, CA, Mayfield, 1995, 431–432.

4. For an excellent summary, see The New York State Task Force on Life and the Law, Surrogate Parenting: Analysis and Recommendations for Public Policy, May 1988.

5. Robertson J: Children of Choice: Freedom and the New Reproductive Technologies. Princeton, NJ, Princeton University Press, 1994, p 122.

6. Proceed with Care: Final Report of the Royal Commission on New Reproductive Technologies, Vol. 2, Nov 30, 1993, at 718.

7. Royal Commission on New Reproductive Technologies: Update, December 1993, at 8.

8. Warren, MA: IVF and womens' interests: an analysis of feminist concerns, *Bioethics* 1988; 2, 37–57 at 38.

9. Robertson, *supra* note 5, at 114.

10. Warren, *supra* note 8, at 39–40.

11. Sherwin S: Feminist ethics and in vitro fertilization. *In* Science, Morality, and Feminist Theory, M Haene, K Nielsen (eds). Calgary, Alberta, University of Calgary Press, 1987, pp 265–284.

12. Singer P: Creating embryos. *In* Ethical Issues at the Outset of Life, WB Weil, M Benjamin (eds). Cambridge, MA, Blackwell, 1987, pp 43–62. Reprinted in Arras JD, Steinbock B (eds). Ethical Issues in Modern Medicine, 4th ed. Mountain View, CA, Mayfield, 1995, at 438.

13. Sherwin, *supra* note 11, at 229.

14. Warren, *supra* note 8, at 39.

15. Sherwin, *supra* note 11, at 228.

16. Robertson, *supra* note 5, at 226.

17. *Roe v. Wade,* 410 U.S. 113, 153 (1973).

18. Scott ES: Sterilization of mentally retarded persons: reproductive rights and family privacy. Duke Law J 1986; 806, at 828–829.

19. Robertson, *supra* note 5, at 73.

20. Robertson, *supra* note 5, at 117.

THE PRESIDENT'S COUNCIL ON BIOETHICS

The Regulation of New Biotechnologies: Commerce

The President's Council on Bioethics is a seventeen-member committee appointed by President George W. Bush in November 2001 to advise the President on ethical issues related to advances in biomedical science and technology. The Council has issued seven reports under the chairmanship of Leon R. Kass. Edmund D. Pellegrino is the current Council chair.

With advances and innovations in assisted reproduction, embryo research, and genetic screening and selection, there have arisen new markets for elements of these technologies and practices, including markets for gametes and embryos. These developments have significant implications for society's approach to reproductive biotechnologies, and for the formation of public and private attitudes about the ethical and social significance of these technologies and practices. They also have significant implications for the way we understand property in the human body more broadly.

This [excerpt] discusses commerce involving (1) gametes and embryos [and] (2) assisted reproductive technologies (ART) services. . . .

I. GAMETES AND EMBRYOS

A. CURRENT PRACTICES

There has long been a market for donated sperm in the United States. According to one commentator, there are at present "thousands of sperm banks . . . in this country offering modest, yet significant remuneration."[1] In 2000, the average payment to sperm donors was between $60 and $70 per donation.[2] At the margins, there are individuals who aggressively market their sperm for thousands of dollars per vial, and Internet sperm brokers such as ManNotIncluded.com,

From *Reproduction and Responsibility: The Regulation of New Biotechnologies*, (Washington, DC: March 2004), 147–165, 178, 200 (available at www.bioethics.gov). Notes renumbered.

which offers baby-making kits to its customers. In the early 1980s, multimillionaire Robert Graham established the "Repository for Germinal Choice," which offered infertile couples the opportunity to buy sperm donated by Nobel laureates.

Donated ova are generally procured by one of the following means: informally, from a close relative; indirectly, through a brokerage; or directly, from an individual or an ART clinic.

In vitro fertilization (IVF) clinics, brokers, and infertile couples advertise for gamete donors. The structures of the ensuing transactions vary. Typically donors are compensated for their time, efforts, and reasonable expenses, rather than for the gametes themselves. While there do not seem to be any definitive studies on the subject, it appears that the vast majority of donors provide gametes anonymously and without regard to specifically desired traits. There is, however, evidence of some noteworthy exceptions to this approach.

For example, some brokerages ("pooled brokerages") solicit a pool of potential donors, create individual profiles (including photographs, biographical data, information on physical characteristics, medical histories, etc.), and establish a database. One such brokerage, Egg Donation, Inc., seeks in a donor someone who is "bright and attractive, between the ages of 21 years to 30 years, of any ethnic background, preferably who has completed a college degree or is presently pursuing a college degree and is in excellent health."[3] Another brokerage, Tiny Treasures, specializes in Ivy League ovum donors. Its database includes photographs, SAT scores, grade-point averages, and compensation requests. Compensation for ovum donors from pooled brokerages varies. Egg Donation, Inc., advises potential donors that the donor fee "will range from $3,500 to $12,000." As to which variables drive cost, the website explains: "Asian and Jewish ovum donors are always in demand. A tall, attractive donor with a masters [sic] or doctorate degree will always receive higher compensation than most other donors." Ivy League donors from Tiny Treasures seek anywhere from $8,000 to $20,000 compensation for a cycle of ova retrieval.

Pooled brokerages charge potential recipients a fee to browse their database of donors. Once a donor is selected, the brokerage begins the "matching process," which includes psychological screening, medical screening, and legal consultation. Thereafter, a contract is executed between the parties, and the process of stimulation and retrieval is initiated.

Some couples advertise directly for ovum donors. Many advertise in campus newspapers at prestigious colleges and universities. One such advertisement at Vassar College offered $25,000 in exchange for the ova of a "healthy, intelligent college student or college graduate, age 21–33 with blue eyes and blonde or light brown hair." Another advertisement in the *Stanford Daily* offered $50,000.

An alternative means of acquiring ova is through so-called "oocyte sharing," an arrangement by which women undergoing infertility treatment are given a price discount in exchange for agreeing to share their ova with other patients. According to the American Society for Reproductive Medicine (ASRM), few details are published on how these transactions are structured, but "[i]t seems that IVF patients in these sharing programs generally donate up to half the oocytes retrieved in a single cycle to another patient, in return for a 50%–60% reduction in the total costs of the IVF cycle."[4]

There does not seem to be a market in human embryos. There is no evidence that early extracorporeal embryos are bought or sold in the United States. . . . [I]ndividuals and couples may donate to researchers and to other infertile couples any "excess" embryos that remain after the completion of infertility treatment.

B. ETHICAL CONSIDERATIONS

Payments for human gametes raise several ethical concerns. Some argue that the commercialization of reproductive tissues might diminish respect for the human body and human procreation. By putting human reproductive tissue—the seeds of the next generation—up for sale in the marketplace, it is argued that we stand to introduce a commercial character into human reproduction, and to introduce commercial concerns into the coming-to-be of the next generation. If the essential materials of human procreation are regularly bought, sold, and esteemed in accordance with market valuations (and indeed valued differently based on the desirability of certain traits, as in ads in college newspapers that offer premium prices for donors with particular characteristics), the human meaning of bringing forward the next generation may be obscured or undermined.

Others see such concerns as misleading and unjustified. They argue that commerce in human gametes is no different from commerce in other meaningful activities of life (like paying one's doctor) or commerce in other articles of special significance (like a religious text or a wedding ring). They point out that the clinics and laboratories are making money from assisting reproduction, and they suggest that it is unfair that only the donor is excluded from financial benefit. They further argue that the ability to buy and sell gametes helps otherwise infertile couples to participate in the activities of human procreation and child-rearing.

Ovum sales raise additional ethical concerns. The process of retrieving ova is onerous and risky for donors. The high fees paid to ovum donors—who are often from financially vulnerable populations, such as full-time students—might create pressure to undergo these invasive procedures. For those undergoing infertility treatment themselves, incentive programs like oocyte sharing may reduce the probability of successful pregnancy, because such a program reduces the number of ova a donor has available for transfer during a given ART cycle. An additional concern is that a free market in ova could lead to discrimination and greater inequality. The 1994 National Institutes of Health (NIH) Human Embryo Research Panel speculated that an open market for ova would lead to a two-tiered system in which wealthy white ovum donors would receive high payments primarily from IVF patients, whereas poor minority women would receive substantially lower payments primarily from researchers.[5]

Finally, financial incentives for donation encourage individuals to become the biological parents—sometimes many times over—of children they will never know. Alternatively, with the advent of laws providing children with the right to know their biological parentage, such donors may become involved in the lives of these children despite their wish to remain anonymous.

However, *not* compensating individuals for donating gametes raises still other ethical concerns. Financial incentives increase supply in other markets and are likely to do the same in the market for gametes for IVF. If there are no payments for gametes, some couples might remain childless because of an inadequate supply of eggs and sperm. Furthermore, given the sacrifice that is made by many gamete donors—especially ova donors—many argue that it would be unjust not to compensate them. Finally, some argue that a free market in gametes ultimately benefits all parties: those willing to provide their gametes get the compensation they desire, and those willing to pay for such gametes get the reproductive tissues they need to undergo assisted reproduction.

C. REGULATION

There are now no federal laws directly regulating the sale of gametes. The National Organ Transplantation Act "makes it unlawful for any person to knowingly acquire, receive, or otherwise transfer any human organ for valuable consideration for use in human transplantation if the transfer affects interstate commerce."[6] While the term "organ" in this statute has been construed to include fetal organs, it has never been extended to include sperm, ova, or embryos. A number of states ban or otherwise restrict the sale of embryos.[7] Only Louisiana explicitly bans the sale of ova. Virginia, on the other hand, explicitly exempts ova from its prohibition on the sale of body parts. California bans the sale of ova for use in attempts at cloning-to-produce-children. Some states broadly prohibit or limit the sale of organs or nonrenewable tissues, but it is an open question whether ova fall within the ambit of such prohibitions.

ASRM has issued ethical guidelines for its members on financial incentives for oocyte donation. Following a discussion of the ethical considerations implicated in payment or oocyte-sharing programs, it concludes that these transactions are acceptable, subject to certain limitations. First, ASRM calculates a "reasonable" payment for oocyte donation by taking the average fee for sperm donation ($60 to $75 for one hour) and multiplying it by the number of hours

spent in a medical setting during oocyte donation (fifty-six hours). Thus, ASRM concludes that the reasonable fee for an oocyte donor is $3,360 to $4,200. But because this calculus might not account for the more onerous nature of oocyte donation, ASRM concludes that "at this time sums of $5,000 or more require justification and sums above $10,000 go beyond what is appropriate."[8]

ASRM concludes that oocyte sharing is permissible provided that programs "formulate and disclose clear policies on how oocytes are allocated, especially if a low number of oocytes or oocytes of varying quality are produced." The Society advises that the reduction in fees resulting from oocyte donation should not be contingent on the number or quality of ova retrieved. Additionally, ASRM advises its members to adhere to certain guidelines: to ensure that there is a physician assigned to the oocyte donor (preferably not the fertility specialist for the ova recipient), to disclose policies regarding medical coverage for any complications experienced by the oocyte donor, to ensure that advertising is accurate and responsible, to avoid donors from recruiting agencies who have been paid exorbitant fees, and to limit the number of times a woman undergoes retrieval procedures "purely to provide oocytes to others."[9]

In a separate Practice Committee Report, ASRM advises its members to limit the number of stimulated cycles per oocyte donor to six, in light of health risks associated with the procedure. In the same document, ASRM advises its members to "strive to limit successful donations from a single donor to no more than 25 families per population of 800,000, given concerns regarding inadvertent consanguinity in offspring."[10]

II. SALE OF ART SERVICES

A. CURRENT PRACTICES

Assisted reproduction is a growing economic enterprise, with gross revenues of $4 billion per year, serving one in six infertile couples in the United States. The costs of assisted reproduction services are variable, depending largely on the particular procedures undertaken. For example, at one prominent clinic, the cost of an initial consultation is $370, one IVF cycle using never-frozen embryos is $9,345 (while transfer of cryopreserved embryos is only $4,000 per transfer), preimplantation genetic diagnosis (PGD) (for sex selection or disease screening) is $4,000, and intracytoplasmic sperm injection (ICSI) (generally a prerequisite for PGD) is $2,000. Preconception sex selection (by sperm sorting) adds another $2,000. Most couples must undergo more than one cycle to achieve a successful result—the most recently reported percentage of live births per cycle (using never-frozen, nondonor embryos) was 27 percent.

ART clinics advertise for business, emphasizing the range of procedures they offer to infertile couples.

Most infertility patients pay for ART services out-of-pocket, for reasons discussed below. To reduce their financial burdens, some clinics offer alternatives. One alternative, discussed above, is oocyte sharing. Another offered by some clinics is a "shared-risk" or "refund" program, in which infertile patients pay a higher fee, with the understanding that if they achieve an "ongoing pregnancy or delivery, the provider keeps the entire fee."[11] However, if the treatment fails, "90%–100% of the fee is returned."[12]

B. ETHICAL CONSIDERATIONS

The commercialization of ART services raises ethical concerns. Some of these are similar to those already raised in other contexts. Irresponsible clinicians may exploit the vulnerability and despair of the infertile with misleading advertisements and solicitations. . . . [C]ommercial competition may induce IVF clinics to try to boost their success rates by adopting risky procedures (such as the transfer of an excessive number of embryos per cycle) or by selectively excluding certain types of patients (such as older patients or those whose chances of becoming pregnant are for other reasons low). Finally, given that infertility treatment is expensive and that in the United States insurance coverage for such services is rare, inequality becomes a real concern, with ART available only to those who can afford it. Many advocates for the infertile argue that the absence of insurance coverage for assisted reproduction is the single greatest problem facing such patients. They argue, for example, that the high costs to patients create incentives to transfer many embryos per cycle, leading to a greater incidence of multiple gestations.

Ethical questions may also be raised regarding ova sharing and shared-risk programs. Ova sharing might induce women who are providing the sharable supply of eggs to undergo risks in greater superovulation, in order to harvest as many ova as possible, or it may reduce a woman's ultimate chances for success, given that fewer ova are available for her own use. Ova sharing also causes individuals to become biological parents to children they will never meet. Shared-risk programs may promote unrealistic expectations for

success. Such programs may induce clinicians to undertake unnecessary risks, or they may create a conflict of interest between doctor and patient.

Many see this range of concerns as unjustified or excessive. They argue that competition among clinics improves the quality of ART services, by making each clinic accountable in the marketplace. Some argue that the variety of treatment options—such as ova sharing and shared-risk programs—allow patients to choose which form of treatment and payment plan is best for them, and that normal informed consent procedures ensure against coercion and exploitation. To criticize irresponsible clinicians, they argue, is not to criticize the commercialization of assisted reproduction as such, but simply those who behave as irresponsible practitioners of medicine, who should be held accountable not through restrictions of commerce but enforceable standards for all ART practitioners. Some argue that the high cost of assisted reproduction is not a case against commerce as such, but rather a case for states to require insurance coverage of ART or for public subsidies for ART treatment. Finally, some argue that competition among ART clinics is the only way to control or reduce the cost of fertility treatment.

C. CURRENT REGULATION

Fourteen states now regulate insurance coverage of infertility treatment.[13] Some of these states mandate coverage of IVF, subject to certain conditions: for example, by requiring that the treatment be provided in conformity with guidelines of the American College of Obstetricians and Gynecologists and ASRM. Certain states require coverage only of fertilization of a donor's own ova with her spouse's sperm.[14]

Although most states do not specifically mandate coverage of assisted reproduction services, an insurance company's failure to cover such services may in some cases be challenged by patients as a violation of the terms of their particular contract. For example, if the contract provides coverage for "illness" or "medically necessary procedures"—as most do—and does not specifically exclude infertility services, patients may argue that infertility falls into these categories and must be covered. Courts are divided on such questions. For example, in *Kinzie v. Physician's Liability Insurance Co.*, an Oklahoma appellate court held (as a matter of law) that IVF is not medically necessary but rather elective. In *Egert v. Connecticut General Life Insurance Co.*, the court rejected the defendant insurance company's claim that infertility is not an illness but rather the result of an illness, holding such a claim to be an improper construction of the insurance contract's provisions and the insurance company's internal guidelines. Some insurance companies have refused to cover IVF on the grounds that it is experimental, citing its less than 50 percent rate of success.

The Federal Trade Commission (FTC) has the authority to investigate deceptive claims in advertising by health care providers, including ART clinics, engaged in interstate commerce. It has jurisdiction, for example, to investigate claims of pregnancy success rates. FTC has the specific authority to investigate claims made in promotional materials, advertisements, contracts, consent forms, and other point-of-sale materials. To prove deception, FTC must show that there has been a "representation, omission, or practice that is likely to mislead the consumer" and that such deception is likely to affect the consumer's choice regarding the purchase of a service or product. For those clinics or individuals found to be engaged in deceptive advertising or unfair competition, FTC can impose civil penalties and cease-and-desist orders.

ASRM has issued guidelines on the subjects of advertising and shared-risk or refund programs. ASRM enumerates eight principles for advertising that should be followed by members: (1) advertising must comply with FTC guidelines; (2) claims must be supported by reliable data; (3) clinics should not rank or compare success rates; (4) advertisements should not unreasonably inflate expectations about success; (5) advertisements including references to outcomes may not selectively omit unfavorable data; (6) the method used to calculate success must be clear; (7) the Practice Director is ultimately responsible for all advertising content; and (8) when quoting statistics, the following statement must be included: "A comparison of clinic success rates may not be meaningful because patient medical characteristics and treatment approaches may vary from clinic to clinic."[15]

In a separate ethics opinion, ASRM sets forth the ethical concerns raised by "shared-risk" or "refund" programs, whereby patients pay a higher initial fee that is refunded if the treatment fails. Such concerns include the risks of exploitation, unreasonable expectations, overly aggressive and unsafe efforts to maximize chances for success, and conflict of interest. Following this discussion, ASRM concludes that shared-risk transactions may be ethically offered to patients lacking health insurance coverage for treatment, provided certain conditions are satisfied, namely, "that the criterion for success is clearly specified, that patients are fully informed of the financial costs and advantages and disadvantages of such programs, that informed consent materials clearly inform patients of their chances of success if found eligible for the shared risk program, and that the program is not guaranteeing pregnancy and delivery." Additionally, ASRM advises its members to clearly inform patients that "they will be paying a higher cost for IVF if they in fact succeed on the first or second cycle than if they had not chosen the shared risk program, and that, in any event, the costs of screening and drugs are not included." To prevent the danger that shared-risk programs may create incentives for clinicians to take actions that might harm patients in pursuit of success (and to avoid a refund), ASRM advises that patients be informed of the potential conflicts of interest. Moreover, such patients should not be given unusually high doses of hormones, and should be advised of the risks of multifetal gestation.[16] As with all other ASRM guidelines, these are suggestions rather than directives.

• • •

[To summarize,] [t]here is no comprehensive mechanism for regulation of commerce in gametes, embryos, and ART services. Professional guidelines exist that attempt to place limits on commerce in human reproductive tissue and human embryos, primarily in order to safeguard the health of women and the dignity of gamete donors, but these guidelines are unenforced. Regarding the sale of ART services generally, there are overall federal guidelines relating to truth in advertising, and professional societies have propounded guidelines on this matter as well.

• • •

The commercialization of various elements of human reproduction is, for some, a . . . cause for concern and . . . potential target for regulation. At present, the buying and selling of gametes is essentially unrestricted in most states, as is, in principle, the buying and selling of embryos, though there is no evidence to suggest the existence of any market in embryos. . . .

Possible policies in this arena include:

1. Limits or Restrictions on the Buying and Selling of Gametes. If the buying and selling of human

gametes is deemed troubling, Congress, or state governments, could set certain limits, potentially including a ceiling on the price of eggs or sperm, limits on
advertising for or by gamete donors, or perhaps even
a restriction on the selling of gametes altogether.

*2. Limits or Restrictions on the Buying and Selling
of Human Embryos.* Similarly, Congress, or state
governments, might set limits on the buying and selling of human embryos, whether for research or for
implantation.

• • •

NOTES

1. Baum, K., "Golden Eggs: Towards the Rational Regulation of
Oocyte Donation," *Brigham Young University Law Review* 107–166
(2001).

2. Ethics Committee, American Society for Reproductive
Medicine, "Financial Incentives in Recruitment of Oocyte Donors,"
Fertility and Sterility 74: 216–220 (2000).

3. *See* http://www.eggdonor.com (February 26, 2004).

4. Ethics Committee, ASRM, "Financial Incentives," *op. cit.*

5. *Ibid.*

6. 42 U.S.C. § 274e.

7. See, for example, Florida, Illinois, Louisiana, Michigan,
South Dakota, and Utah.

8. Ethics Committee, ASRM, "Financial Incentives," *op. cit.*

9. *Ibid.*

10. American Society for Reproductive Medicine, Practice
Committee Report, "Repetitive Oocyte Donation," November 2000,
http://www.asrm.org/Media/Practice/oocyte_donation.pdf
(accessed June 4, 2003).

11. Ethics Committee, American Society for Reproductive
Medicine, "Shared-Risk or Refund Programs in Assisted Repro-
duction," http://www.asrm.org/Media/Ethics/shared.html (accessed
May 16, 2003).

12. *Ibid.*

13. Arkansas, California, Connecticut, Hawaii, Illinois, Maryland, Massachusetts, Montana, New Jersey, New York, Ohio, Rhode
Island, Texas, and West Virginia. (Source: ASRM website.)

14. See, for example, Arkansas.

15. American Society for Reproductive Medicine, Practice
Committee Report, "Guidelines for Advertising by ART Programs,"
October 1999, http://www.asrm.org/Media/Practice/ArtAdvertising
.pdf (accessed June 4, 2003).

16. Ethics Committee, ASRM, "Shared-Risk," *op. cit.*

ADRIENNE ASCH

Prenatal Diagnosis and Selective Abortion:
A Challenge to Practice and Policy

Adrienne Asch is the Edward and Robin Milstein Professor of Bioethics at the
Wurzweiler School of Social Work and Professor of Epidemiology and Population
Health at the Albert Einstein College of Medicine at Yeshiva University. She has
authored numerous articles and book chapters on ethical, political, psychological,
and social implications of human reproduction and the family and is editor with
Erik Parens of *Prenatal Testing and Disability Rights* (Georgetown) and co-editor of *The
Double-Edged Helix: Social Implications of Genetics in a Diverse Society* (Johns Hopkins).

. . . Prenatal tests designed to detect the condition of
the fetus include ultrasound, maternal serum [alpha]-
fetoprotein screening, chorionic villus sampling, and
amniocentesis. Some (ultrasound screenings) are routinely performed regardless of the mother's age and
provide information that she may use to guide her
care throughout pregnancy; others, such as chorionic
villus sampling or amniocentesis, do not influence the
woman's care during pregnancy but provide information intended to help her decide whether to continue
the pregnancy if fetal impairment is detected. Amniocentesis, the test that detects the greatest variety of
fetal impairments, is typically offered to women who

From *American Journal of Public Health* 89, no. 11 (November
1999), 1649–57. Notes renumbered. Reprinted with permission
from the American Public Health Association.

will be 35 years or older at the time they are due to deliver, but recently commentators have urged that the age threshold be removed and that the test be available to women regardless of age. Such testing is increasingly considered a standard component of prenatal care for women whose insurance covers these procedures, including women using publicly financed clinics in some jurisdictions.

These tests, which are widely accepted in the field of bioethics and by clinicians, public health professionals, and the general public, have nonetheless occasioned some apprehension and concern among students of women's reproductive experiences, who find that women do not uniformly welcome the expectation that they will undergo prenatal testing or the prospect of making decisions depending on the test results. Less often discussed by clinicians is the view, expressed by a growing number of individuals, that the technology is itself based on erroneous assumptions about the adverse impact of disability on life. Argument from this perspective focuses on what is communicated about societal and familial acceptance of diversity in general and disability in particular. Like other women-centered critiques of prenatal testing, this article assumes a pro-choice perspective but suggests that unreflective uses of testing could diminish, rather than expand, women's choices. Like critiques stemming from concerns about the continued acceptance of human differences within the society and the family, this critique challenges the view of disability that lies behind social endorsement of such testing and the conviction that women will, or should, end their pregnancies if they discover that the fetus has a disabling trait.

If public health frowns on efforts to select for or against girls or boys and would oppose future efforts to select for or against those who would have a particular sexual orientation, but promotes people's efforts to avoid having children who would have disabilities, it is because medicine and public health view disability as extremely different from and worse than these other forms of human variation. At first blush this view may strike one as self-evident. To challenge it might even appear to be questioning our professional mission. Characteristics such as chronic illnesses and disabilities (discussed together throughout this article) do not resemble traits such as sex, sexual orientation, or race, because the latter are not in themselves perceived as inimical to a rewarding life. Disability is thought to be just that—to be incompatible with life satisfaction. When public health considers matters of sex, sexual orientation, or race, it examines how factors in social and economic life pose obstacles to health and to health care, and it champions actions to improve the well-being of those disadvantaged by the discrimination that attends minority status. By contrast, public health fights to eradicate disease and disability or to treat, ameliorate, or cure these when they occur. For medicine and public health, disease and disability is the problem to solve, and so it appears natural to use prenatal testing and abortion as one more means of minimizing the incidence of disability.

In the remainder of this article I argue, first, that most of the problems associated with having a disability stem from discriminatory social arrangements that are changeable, just as much of what has in the past made the lives of women or gays difficult has been the set of social arrangements they have faced (and which they have begun to dismantle). After discussing ways in which the characteristic of disability resembles and differs from other characteristics, I discuss why I believe the technology of prenatal testing followed by selective abortion is unique among means of preventing or ameliorating disability, and why it offends many people who are untroubled by other disease prevention and health promotion activities. I conclude by recommending ways in which health practitioners and policymakers could offer this technology so that it promotes genuine reproductive choice and helps families and society to flourish.

CONTRASTING MEDICAL AND SOCIAL PARADIGMS OF DISABILITY

The definitions of terms such as "health," "normality," and "disability" are not clear, objective, and universal across time and place. Individual physical characteristics are evaluated with reference to a standard of normality, health, and what some commentators term "species-typical functioning."[1,2] These commentators point out that within a society at a particular time, there is a shared perception of what is typical physical functioning and role performance for a girl or boy, woman or man. . . .

Chronic illness, traumatic injury, and congenital disability may indeed occasion departures from "species-typical functioning," and thus these conditions do constitute differences from both a statistical average and a desired norm of well-being. Certainly society prizes some characteristics, such as intelligence, athleticism, and musical or artistic skill, and rewards people with more than the statistical norm of these attributes; I will return to this point later. Norms on many health-related attributes change over time; as the life span for people in the United States and Canada increases, conditions that often lead to death before 40 years of age (e.g., cystic fibrosis) may become even more dreaded than they are today. The expectation that males will be taller than females and that adults will stand more than 5 feet in height leads to a perception that departures from these norms are not only unusual but undesirable and unhealthy. Not surprisingly, professionals who have committed themselves to preventing illness and injury, or to ameliorating and curing people of illnesses and injuries, are especially attuned to the problems and hardships that affect the lives of their patients. Such professionals, aware of the physical pain or weakness and the psychological and social disruption caused by acute illness or sudden injury, devote their lives to easing the problems that these events impose.

What many scholars, policymakers, and activists in the area of disability contend is that medically oriented understandings of the impact of disability on life contain 2 erroneous assumptions with serious adverse consequences: first, that the life of a person with a chronic illness or disability is forever disrupted, as one's life might be temporarily disrupted as a result of a back spasm, an episode of pneumonia, or a broken leg; second, that if a disabled person experiences isolation, powerlessness, unemployment poverty, or low social status, these are inevitable consequences of biological limitation. Body, psyche, and social life do change immediately following an occurrence of disease, accident, or injury, and medicine, public health, and bioethics all correctly appreciate the psychological and physical vulnerability of patients and their families and friends during immediate medical crises. These professions fail people with disabilities, however, by concluding that because there may never be full physical recovery, there is never a regrouping of physical, cognitive, and psychological resources with which to participate in a rewarding life. Chronic illness and disability are not equivalent to acute illness or sudden injury, in which an active disease process or unexpected change in physical function disrupts life's routines. Most people with conditions such as spina bifida, achondroplasia, Down syndrome, and many other mobility and sensory impairments perceive themselves as healthy, not sick, and describe their conditions as givens of their lives—the equipment with which they

meet the world. The same is true for people with chronic conditions such as cystic fibrosis, diabetes, hemophilia, and muscular dystrophy. These conditions include intermittent flare-ups requiring medical care and adjustments in daily living, but they do not render the person as unhealthy as most of the public—and members of the health profession—imagine.

People with disabilities are thinking about a traffic jam, a disagreement with a friend, which movie to attend, or which team will win the World Series—not just about their diagnosis. Having a disability can intrude into a person's consciousness if events bring it to the fore: if 2 lift-equipped buses in a row fail to stop for a man using a wheelchair; if the theater ticket agent insults a patron with Down syndrome by refusing to take money for her ticket; if a hearing-impaired person misses a train connection because he did not know that a track change had been announced.

The second way in which medicine, bioethics, and public health typically err is in viewing all problems that occur to people with disabilities as attributable to the condition itself, rather than to external factors. When ethicists, public health professionals, and policymakers discuss the importance of health care, urge accident prevention, or promote healthy lifestyles, they do so because they perceive a certain level of health not only as intrinsically desirable but as a prerequisite for an acceptable life. One commentator describes such a consensual view of types of life in terms of a "normal opportunity range": "The normal opportunity range for a given society is the array of life plans reasonable persons in it are likely to construct for themselves."[2] Health care includes that which is intended to "maintain, restore, or provide functional equivalents where possible, to normal species functioning."[2]

The paradigm of medicine concludes that the gaps in education, employment, and income that persist between adults with disabilities and those without disabilities are inevitable because the impairment precludes study or limits work. The alternative paradigm, which views people with disabilities in social, minority-group terms, examines how societal arrangements—rules, laws, means of communication, characteristics of buildings and transit systems, the typical 8-hour workday—exclude some people from participating in school, work, civic, or social life. This newer paradigm is expressed by enactment of the Individuals with Disabilities Education Act and the Americans with Disabilities Act and is behind the drive to ensure that employed disabled people will keep their access to health care through Medicaid or Medicare. This paradigm—still more accepted by people outside medicine, public health, and bioethics than by those within these fields—questions whether there is an inevitable, unmodifiable gap between people with disabilities and people without disabilities. Learning that in 1999, nine years after the passage of laws to end employment discrimination, millions of people with disabilities are still out of the work force, despite their readiness to work, the social paradigm asks what remaining institutional factors bar people from the goal of productive work. . . .

It is estimated that 54 million people in the United States have disabilities, of which impairments of mobility, hearing, vision, and learning; arthritis; cystic fibrosis; diabetes; heart conditions; and back problems are some of the most well-known. Thus, in discussing discrimination, stigma, and unequal treatment for people with disabilities, we are considering a population that is larger than the known gay and lesbian population or the African American population. These numbers take on new significance when we assess the rationale behind prenatal diagnosis and selective abortion as a desirable strategy to deal with disability.

PRENATAL DIAGNOSIS FOR DISABILITY PREVENTION

If some forms of disability prevention are legitimate medical and public health activities, and if people with disabilities use the health system to improve and maintain their own health, there is an acknowledgment that the characteristic of disability may not be desirable. Although many within the disability rights movement challenge prenatal diagnosis as a means of disability prevention, no one objects to public health efforts to clean up the environment, encourage seat-belt use, reduce tobacco and alcohol consumption, and provide prenatal care to all pregnant women. All these activities deal with the health of existing human beings (or fetuses expected to come to term) and seek to ensure their well-being. What differentiates prenatal testing followed by abortion from other forms of disability prevention and medical treatment is that prenatal testing followed by abortion is intended not to prevent the disability or illness of a born or future human being but to pre-

vent the birth of a human being who will have one of these undesired characteristics. . . .

Professionals fail to recognize that along with whatever impairment may be diagnosed come all the characteristics of any other future child. The health professions suggest that once a prospective parent knows of the likely disability of a future child, there is nothing else to know or imagine about who the child might become: disability subverts parental dreams. . . .

I focus on the view of life with disability that is communicated by society's efforts to develop prenatal testing and urge it on every pregnant woman. If public health espouses goals of social justice and equality for people with disabilities, as it has worked to improve the status of women, gays and lesbians, and members of racial and ethnic minorities, it should reconsider whether it wishes to continue endorsing the technology of prenatal diagnosis. . . .

RATIONALES FOR PRENATAL TESTING

The medical professions justify prenatal diagnosis and selective abortion on the grounds of the costs of childhood disability—the costs to the child, to the family, and to the society. Some proponents of the Human Genome Project from the fields of science and bioethics argue that in a world of limited resources, we can reduce disability-related expenditures if all diagnoses of fetal impairment are followed by abortion.[3]

On both empirical and moral grounds, endorsing prenatal diagnosis for societal reasons is dangerous. Only a small fraction of total disability can now be detected prenatally, and even if future technology enables the detection of predisposition to diabetes, forms of depression, Alzheimer disease, heart disease, arthritis, or back problems—all more prevalent in the population than many of the currently detectable conditions—we will never manage to detect and prevent most disability. Rates of disability increase markedly with age, and the gains in life span guarantee that most people will deal with disability in themselves or someone close to them. Laws and services to support people with disabilities will still be necessary, unless society chooses a campaign of eliminating disabled people in addition to preventing the births of those who would be disabled. Thus, there is small cost-saving in money or in human resources to be achieved by even the vigorous determination to test every pregnant woman and abort every fetus found to exhibit disabling traits.

My moral opposition to prenatal testing and selective abortion flows from the conviction that life with disability is worthwhile and the belief that a just society must appreciate and nurture the lives of all people, whatever the endowments they receive in the natural lottery. I hold these beliefs because . . . there is abundant evidence that people with disabilities can thrive even in this less than welcoming society. Moreover, people with disabilities do not merely take from others, they contribute as well—to families, to friends, to the economy. They contribute neither in spite of nor because of their disabilities, but because along with their disabilities come other characteristics of personality, talent, and humanity that render people with disabilities full members of the human and moral community.

IMPLICATIONS FOR PEOPLE WITH DISABILITIES

Implications for children and adults with disabilities, and for their families, warrant more consideration. Several prominent bioethicists claim that to knowingly bring into the world a child who will live with an impairment (whether it be a "withered arm," cystic fibrosis, deafness, or Down syndrome) is unfair to the child because it deprives the child of the "right to an open future" by limiting some options.[4] Green's words represent a significant strand of professional thinking: "In the absence of adequate justifying reasons, a child is morally wronged when he/she is knowingly, deliberately, or negligently brought into being with a health status likely to result in significantly greater disability or suffering, or significantly reduced life options relative to the other children with whom he/she will grow up."[5] Green is not alone in his view that it is irresponsible to bring a child into the world with a disability.[6,7]

The biology of disability can affect people's lives, and not every feature of life with a disability is socially determined or mediated. . . . People who use a wheelchair for mobility will not climb mountains; people with the intellectual disabilities of Down syndrome or fragile X chromosome are not likely to read this article and engage in debate about its merits and shortcomings. Yet, as disability scholars point out, such limitations do not preclude a whole class of experiences, but only certain instances in which these experiences might occur. People who move through the world in wheelchairs may not be able to climb mountains, but they can and do participate in other athletic activities that are challenging and exhilarating and call for stamina, alertness, and teamwork. . . .

The child who will have a disability may have fewer options for the so-called open future that philosophers and parents dream of for children. Yet I suspect that disability precludes far fewer life possibilities than members of the bioethics community claim. That many people with disabilities find their lives satisfying has been documented. For example, more than half of people with spinal cord injury (paraplegia) reported feeling more positively about themselves since becoming disabled.[8] Similarly, Canadian teenagers who had been extremely-low-birthweight infants were compared with nondisabled teens and found to resemble them in terms of their own subjective ratings of quality of life.[9]

Interestingly, professionals faced with such information often dismiss it and insist that happy disabled people are the exceptions.[10] Here . . . , James Watson expresses a common view when he says,

> Is it more likely for such children to fall behind in society or will they through such afflictions develop the strengths of character and fortitude that lead . . . to the head of their packs? Here I'm afraid that the word handicap cannot escape its true definition—being placed at a disadvantage. From this perspective seeing the bright side of being handicapped is like praising the virtues of extreme poverty. To be sure, there are many individuals who rise out of its inherently degrading states. But we perhaps most realistically should see it as the major origin of asocial behavior.[11]

I return to the points made earlier regarding how many of the supposed limits and problems associated with disability are socially, rather than biologically, imposed. . . . Nonetheless, I do not deny that disability can entail physical pain, psychic anguish, and social isolation—even if much of the psychological and social pain can be attributed to human cruelty rather than to biological givens. In order to imagine bringing a child with a disability into the world when abortion is possible, prospective parents must be able to imagine saying to a child, "I wanted you enough and believed enough in who you could be that I felt you could have a life you would appreciate even with the difficulties your disability causes." If parents and siblings, family members and friends can genuinely love and enjoy the child for who he or she is and not lament what he or she is not; if child care centers, schools, and youth groups routinely include disabled children; if television programs, children's books, and toys take children with disabilities into account by including them naturally in programs and products, the child may not live with the anguish and isolation that have marred life for generations of disabled children.

IMPLICATIONS FOR FAMILY LIFE

Many who are willing to concede that people with disabilities could have lives they themselves would enjoy nonetheless argue that the cost to families of raising them justifies abortion. Women are seen to carry the greatest load for the least return in caring for such a child. Proponents of using the technology to avoid the births of children with disabilities insist that the disabled child epitomizes what women have fought to change about their lives as mothers: unending labor, the sacrifice of their work and other adult interests, loss of time and attention for the other children in the family as they juggle resources to give this disabled child the best available support, and uncertain recompense in terms of the mother's relationship with the child.[12]

Writing in 1995 on justifications for prenatal testing, Botkin proposed that only conditions that impose "burdens" on parents equivalent to those of an unwanted child warrant society-supported testing.

> The parent's harms are different in many respects from the child's, but include emotional pain and suffering, loss of a child, loss of opportunities, loss of freedom, isolation, loneliness, fear, guilt, stigmatization, and financial expenses. . . . Some conditions that are often considered severe may not be associated with any experience of harm for the child. Down syndrome is a prime example. Parents in this circumstance are not harmed by the suffering of a child . . . but rather by their time, efforts, and expenses to support the special needs of an individual with Down syndrome. . . . It might also be added that parents are harmed by their unfulfilled expectations with the birth of an impaired child. In general terms, the claim is that parents suffer a sufficient harm to justify prenatal testing or screening when the severity of a child's condition raises problems for the parents of a similar magnitude to the birth of an unwanted child. . . . [P]arents of a child with unwanted disability have their interests impinged upon by the efforts, time, emotional burdens, and expenses added by the disability that they would not have otherwise experienced with the birth of a healthy child.[13]

I believe the characterizations found in the writings of Wertz and Fletcher[12] and Botkin[13] are at the heart of professionals' support for prenatal testing and deserve careful scrutiny. Neither Wertz and Fletcher nor Botkin offer citations to literature to support their claims of family burden, changed lifestyle, disappointed expectations, or additional expenses, perhaps because they believe these are indisputable. Evaluating the claims, however, requires recognizing an assumption implied in them: that there is no benefit to offset the "burden," in the way that parents can expect rewards of many kinds in their relationship with children who do not have disabilities. This assumption, which permeates much of the medical, social science, and bioethics literature on disability and family life and disability in general, rests on a mistaken notion. As rehabilitation psychologist Beatrice Wright has long maintained,[14,15] people imagine that incapacity in one arena spreads to incapacity in all—the child with cystic fibrosis is always sick and can never play; the child who cannot walk cannot join classmates in word games, parties, or sleepovers; someone who is blind is also unable to hear or speak. Someone who needs assistance with one activity is perceived to need assistance in all areas and to contribute nothing to the social, emotional, or instrumental aspects of family life. . . .

Parents, professionals working with the family, and the larger society all value the gift of the violin prodigy, the talent of the future Olympic figure skater, the aptitude of a child who excels in science and who might one day discover the cure for cancer. They perceive that all the extra work and rearrangement associated with raising such children will provide what people seek in parenthood: the opportunity to give ourselves to a new being who starts out with the best we can give, who will enrich us, gladden others, contribute to the world, and make us proud.

If professionals and parents believed that children with disabilities could indeed provide their parents many of the same satisfactions as any other child in terms of stimulation, love, companionship, pride, and pleasure in influencing the growth and development of another, they might reexamine their belief that in psychological, material, and social terms, the burdens of raising disabled children outweigh the benefits. A vast array of literature, both parental narrative and social science quantitative and qualitative research, powerfully testifies to the rewards—typical and atypical—of raising children with many of the conditions for which prenatal testing is considered de rigueur and abortion is expected (Down syndrome, hemophilia, cystic fibrosis, to name only some). Yet bioethics, public health, and genetics remain woefully—scandalously—oblivious, ignorant, or dismissive of any information that challenges the conviction that disability dooms families.

Two years before the gene mutation responsible for much cystic fibrosis was identified, Walker et al. published their findings about the effects of cystic fibrosis on family life. They found that mothers of children with cystic fibrosis did not differ from mothers of children without the condition on measures of

> . . . Child Dependency and Management Difficulty, Limits on Family Opportunity, Family Disharmony, and Financial Stress. The difference between the two groups of mothers almost reached statistical significance on a fifth subscale, Personal Burden, which measured the mother's feeling of burden in her caretaking role. . . . The similarities between mothers of children with cystic fibrosis and those with healthy children were more apparent than the differences. Mothers of children with cystic fibrosis did not report significantly higher levels of stress than did the control group mothers of healthy children. Contrary to suggestions that mothers of children with cystic fibrosis feel guilty and inadequate as parents, the mothers in this study reported levels of parenting competence equal to those reported by the mothers of healthy children.[16]

The literature on how disability affects family life is, to be sure, replete with discussions of stress; anger at unsupportive members of the helping professions; distress caused by hostility from extended family, neighbors, and strangers; and frustration that many disability-related expenses are not covered by health insurance. And it is a literature that increasingly tries to distinguish why—under what conditions some families of disabled children founder and others thrive. Contrary to the beliefs still much abroad in medicine, bioethics, and public health, recent literature does not suggest that, on balance, families raising children who have disabilities experience more stress and disruption than any other family.

IMPLICATIONS FOR PROFESSIONAL PRACTICE

. . . I call for change to ensure that everyone obtaining testing or seeking information about genetic or prenatally diagnosable disability receives sufficient information about predictable difficulties, supports, and life events associated with a disabling condition to enable them to consider how a child's disability would fit into their own hopes for parenthood. . . . For some people, any mobility, sensory, cognitive, or health impairment may indeed lead to disappointment of parental hopes; for others, it may be far easier to imagine incorporating disability into family life without believing that the rest of their lives will be blighted. . . . Testing and abortion guarantee little about the child and the life parents create and nurture, and all parents and children will be harmed by inflated notions of what parenting in an age of genetic knowledge can bring in terms of fulfilled expectations. . . .

Given that more than 50 million people in the U.S. population have disabling traits and that prenatal tests may become increasingly available to detect more of them, we are confronting the fact that tests may soon be available for characteristics that we have until now considered inevitable facts of human life, such as heart disease.

In order to make testing and selecting for or against disability consonant with improving life for those who will inevitably be born with or acquire disabilities, our clinical and policy establishments must communicate that it is as acceptable to live with a disability as it is to live without one and that society will support and appreciate everyone with the inevitable variety of traits. We can assure prospective parents that they and their future child will be welcomed whether or not the child has a disability. If that professional message is conveyed, more prospective parents may envision that their lives can be rewarding, whatever the characteristics of the child they are raising. When our professions can envision such communication and the reality of incorporation and appreciation of people with disabilities, prenatal technology can help people to make decisions without implying that only one decision is right. If the child with a disability is not a problem for the world, and the world is not a problem for the child, perhaps we can diminish our desire for prenatal testing and selective abortion and can comfortably welcome and support children of all characteristics.

NOTES

1. Boorse C. Concepts of health. In: Van de Veer D, Regan T, eds. *Health Care Ethics.* Philadelphia, Pa: Temple University Press; 1987: 359–393.

2. Daniels NL. *Just Health Care: Studies in Philosophy and Health Policy.* Cambridge, England: Cambridge University Press; 1985.

3. Shaw MW. Presidential address: to be or not to be, that is the question. *Am J Human Genetics* 1984; 36: 1–9.

4. Feinberg J. The child's right to an open future. In: Aiken W, LaFollette H, eds. *Whose Child? Children's Rights, Parental Authority, and State Power.* Totowa, NJ: Rowman & Littlefield 1980: 124–153.

5. Green R. Prenatal autonomy and the obligation not to harm one's child genetically. *J Law Med Ethics.* 1996; 25(1): 5–16.

6. Davis DS. Genetic dilemmas and the child's right to an open future. *Hastings Cent Rep* 1997; 27(2): 7–15.

7. Purdy L. Loving future people. In: Callahan J, ed. *Reproduction, Ethics and the Law.* Bloomington: Indiana University Press; 1995: 300–327.

8. Ray C, West J. Social, sexual and personal implications of paraplegia. *Paraplegia.* 1984; 22: 75–86.

9. Saigal S, Feeny D, Rosenbaum P, Furlong W, Burrows E, Stoskopf B. Self-perceived health status and health-related quality of life of extremely low-birth-weight infants at adolescence. *JAMA.* 1996; 276: 453–459.

10. Tyson JE, Broyles RS. Progress in assessing the long-term outcome of extremely low-birth-weight infants. *JAMA.* 1996; 276: 492–493.

11. Watson JD. President's essay: genes and politics. *Annual Report Cold Springs Harbor.* 1996: 1–20.

12. Wertz DC, Fletcher JC. A critique of some feminist challenges to prenatal diagnosis. *J Womens Health.* 1993; 2: 173–188.

13. Botkin J. Fetal privacy and confidentiality. *Hastings Cent Rep.* 1995; 25(3): 32–39.

14. Wright BA. Attitudes and the fundamental negative bias: conditions and correlates. In: Yuker HE, ed. *Attitudes Toward Persons With Disabilities.* New York, NY. Springer; 1988: 3–21.

15. Wright BA. *Physical Disability: A PyschoSocial Approach.* New York, NY: Harper & Row; 1983.

16. Walker LS, Ford MB, Donald WD. Cystic fibrosis and family stress: effects of age and severity of illness. *Pediatrics.* 1987; 79: 239–246.

ALLEN BUCHANAN, DAN W. BROCK, NORMAN DANIELS, AND DANIEL WIKLER

Genetic Intervention and the Morality of Inclusion

Allen Buchanan is the James B. Duke Professor of Philosophy and James B. Duke Professor of Public Policy Studies in the Terry Sanford Institute of Public Policy at Duke University. He is a former staff philosopher on the President's Commission for the Study of Ethical Problems in Medicine. His books include *Marx and Justice: The Radical Critique of Liberalism* (Rowman & Littlefield), *Ethics, Efficiency, and the Market* (Oxford), *Justice, Legitimacy, and Self-Determination: Moral Foundations for International Law* (Oxford), and (with Dan W. Brock) *Deciding for Others: The Ethics of Surrogate Decision Making* (Cambridge).

Dan W. Brock is the Frances Glessner Lee Professor of Medical Ethics and Director of the Division of Medical Ethics at the Harvard Medical School. He was formerly the Charles C. Tillinghast, Jr. University Professor, Professor of Philosophy and Biomedical Ethics, and Director of the Center for Biomedical Ethics at Brown University. He is a former staff philosopher on the President's Commission for the Study of Ethical Problems in Medicine. His books include *Life and Death: Philosophical Essays in Biomedical Ethics* (Cambridge), and (with Allen Buchanan) *Deciding for Others: The Ethics of Surrogate Decision Making* (Cambridge).

Norman Daniels is the Mary B. Saltonstall Professor of Population Ethics at the Harvard School of Public Health. He publishes in ethics, political and social philosophy, and medical ethics. Among his authored and co-authored books are *Seeking Fair Treatment: From the AIDS Epidemic to National Health Care Reform* (Oxford), *Just Health Care* (Cambridge), and *Benchmarks of Fairness for Health Care Reform* (Oxford).

Daniel Wikler is the Mary B. Saltonstall Professor of Population Ethics at the Harvard School of Public Health. He served as the first Staff Ethicist for the World Health Organization. He publishes on ethical issues in reproduction, transplantation, end-of-life decision making, and population and international health. His authored and co-authored publications include the book series *Studies in Philosophy and Health Policy* (Cambridge) and *Population-level Bioethics: Mapping a New Agenda* (Oxford).

. . . Enthusiasts for the new genetics react defensively to any suggestion that current scientific endeavors harbor the taint of eugenics. After all, what could be

From *From Chance to Choice: Genetics and Justice* (New York and Cambridge, MA: Cambridge University Press, 2000), pp. 264–281. Notes omitted. Reprinted with permission.

controversial about the goal of improving human life through the application of a scientific knowledge of genes? Surely the difference between the old eugenics and the new genetics is unmistakable: The former was particularistic and exclusionary, condemning as defective all those who failed to meet supposed criteria of racial purity or human perfection; the latter is universalistic and inclusive, seeking to prevent suffering for all of humanity through the eradication of genetic disease. In addition, the exclusionary vision of the old eugenics was aided and abetted by faulty science, whereas the new genetics is truly scientific.

CHALLENGING THE RHETORIC: THE RADICAL DISABILITIES RIGHTS ADVOCATES' COMPLAINTS

Where enthusiasts for the new genetics see inclusion and progress, some in the disabilities rights movement see exclusion and moral retrogression. The charge is that the very conception of progress that lies at the core of the ideology of the new genetics radically devalues individuals with disabilities, inflicting on them what may be the gravest injury of all—a denial of their equal moral worth and even their very right to exist.

The source of injury is said to be a fundamentally flawed conception of the value of human lives. . . . Lives that include impairments are assumed to be without value if not a positive evil to be eradicated. Thus the disabilities rights advocates' view stands the new geneticists' claim to universalistic progress on its head. Not only is the alleged universalism indicated as exclusion, but also the very notion of progress is said to rest on a distorted view of the basic value that is supposed to guide the quests for progress. Scientific control over natural endowments will not mean improvements for all of humanity. Instead, it will result in harm to the fundamental interest of some human beings—those with disabilities.

The disabilities rights advocates' critique of the new genetics appears to be nothing short of a rejection of the basic idea of striving "to make human lives better by selection based on genetic knowledge." . . . "Selection" here includes not only choosing who will be born and who will not (through genetic testing and abortion to avoid the birth of individuals with certain conditions) but also choosing the characteristics of those who will be born by genetic interventions on gametes (sperm and egg cells) or embryos (fertilized eggs) to eliminate or counteract genetic influences that would cause disease.

Furthermore, the charge is not simply that the effort at improvement through selection in either of these ways is unwise or in some way morally questionable. The claim is that it is unjust—that it violates the most fundamental rights of people with disabilities and is nothing less than a degradation of the core of morality, the proper appreciation of the value of human lives. What is striking about the radical disabilities advocates' critique, then, is that it is directed squarely against medical genetics—which proponents of the new genetics have taken to be the most laudable and uncontroversial application of genetic knowledge. Taken at face value, this critique condemns any effort to eliminate disabilities through medical interventions, genetic or otherwise (although it is true that the radical disabilities rights critique has focused primarily on genetic intervention). For if taken literally the slogan "change society, not individuals" does not merely insist that we try to make the social world more accessible to those whose impairments cannot be corrected; it would require accommodating those with impairments *rather than* using medical science to prevent or correct impairments.

Given the universalistic and progressive self-image of those who engage in or support the new genetics, this critique evokes incredulity and indignation. Indeed, it is tempting to dismiss the radical disabilities advocates' objections as hysterical, paranoid, or extremist. This, however, would be a mistake. . . . For there is some truth in this critique. Humanity's emerging powers of genetic intervention do raise important and in some ways novel issues of justice and exclusion—issues the rhetoric of universal progress obscures. On closer examination, however, it will turn out that neither the disabilities rights advocates nor the enthusiasts for the new genetics have grasped the fundamental implications of genetic intervention for our understanding of justice, of the moral significance of disabilities, or of the morality of inclusion.

SORTING OUT THE CONCERNS OF DISABILITIES RIGHTS ADVOCATES

Several distinct objections can be discerned in the disabilities rights advocates' critique. Here we will concentrate on what we take to be the objections that strike at the heart of the legitimating rhetoric of the new genetics, those that challenge the claim that, at least so far as the application of genetic science is restricted to the prevention of disease, the new genetics is nonexclusionary and benign.

THE LOSS OF SUPPORT ARGUMENT

Before proceeding to the most fundamental objections to the new genetics, however, we should note a different criticism of "improvement through selection" that is often voiced by those from the disabilities rights movement. This is the charge that as the application of genetic science reduces the number of persons suffering from disabilities, public support for those who have disabilities will dwindle. Although we discuss this "loss of support argument" mainly to distinguish it from what we take to be more fundamental objections, three points merit consideration.

First, the objection rests on a sweeping empirical generalization: that as the number of persons with a certain disability decreases, support for those who have that disability will decrease, and that this is true for disabilities generally. Without attempting to settle the empirical issue, we would only point out that it is not enough to state the generalization. Data to support it must be marshaled. To our knowledge, those who advance the "loss of support argument" have not borne this burden of evidence. Moreover, we do know of at least one instance in which a reduction in the incidence of a genetic disease (achieved through voluntary carrier testing) resulted in more resources being used to support the decreasing number of those who had the disease. This was the case of the Thalassemia testing program in Greece. . . .

Second, whether or not support will diminish in a particular case will depend on a number of factors, not the least significant of which is whether the public is alerted in advance to the danger of reduced support. In fact, the prediction that support will decrease as science reduces the incidence of genetic diseases is much less plausible today than it would have been twenty years ago, precisely because the disabilities rights movement has succeeded in awakening the public and policy makers to the need for support.

Third, even if there should turn out to be some loss of support for certain genetically based diseases as their incidence declines, it would not follow that seeking to reduce their incidence is wrong, all things considered. The most fundamental problem with the loss of support argument is that it only considers the interests of those who will have disabilities in a world in which disabilities are less common. It entirely neglects the legitimate interests that people have in not having disabilities. (In addition, . . . this argument also fails to recognize that those who are not disabled and who are not at significant risk of being disabled can have legitimate interests in reducing the incidence of disabilities.)

Consider first the interest a person has in not having disabilities. Surely this is a morally legitimate interest. It is true that in some cases this interest is not rel-

evant, because the disability is avoided only by preventing the existence of the person who would have been born with it. Obviously, in this case, one cannot justify the intervention by citing the interest some person has in not having the disability.

But there are other interventions that do serve the interest that individuals have in not having disabilities. For example, it will very likely become possible to correct some genetic anomalies by intervening on the embryo. In this case, it will be correct to speak of preventing an identified individual from having a disability and to justify the intervention by appealing to that individual's interest in not having a disability. Similarly, genetic science will be able to prevent disabling genetic conditions in other, perhaps less dramatic, ways, not by manipulating the genes of embryos but by administering drugs that mimic the products of normal genes or that counteract the deleterious effects of abnormal genes. In these cases, too, we may correctly say that the application of genetic science makes identifiable individuals' lives better by preventing genetically based diseases, and that such individuals have a legitimate interest in avoiding the damage to them that would occur without the intervention.

Once it is recognized that the incidence of genetically based diseases may be reduced without preventing the birth of individuals who would have disabilities, it should be evident that the loss of support argument must be rejected. It fails to give any weight to the legitimate interests that individuals have in avoiding disabilities. This can be seen more clearly once we recognize that the general form of this argument has nothing peculiarly to do with genetic interventions. If the risk of loss of support is a reason for not undertaking genetic interventions, then it is also a reason for not undertaking conventional medical interventions as well. By this logic, it would be wrong to treat babies' eyes at birth to prevent blindness due to contact with gonococcus bacteria during vaginal delivery. But surely it is not only permissible but morally obligatory to prevent babies from being blinded, if this can be done safely and effectively, even if it could be shown that there is some significant risk of loss of support for the blind. . . .

Suppose that Jill is a young adult who faces life with paraplegia unless she undergoes a surgical procedure. If she has the surgery, she can look forward to a life with all the opportunities that go with normal mobility.

She chooses to have the surgery. As a result of her choice, the ranks of the disabled will diminish by one. Does her action harm people with disabilities? Presumably not—her cure is very unlikely to make much of a difference. Suppose that many people in her situation make the same choice, with the result that there is a significant reduction in the number of people with paraplegia. Have those who had the surgery harmed the people with paraplegia who cannot be cured or who for some reason chose not to be cured? If by harming someone is meant worsening their condition, then it may well be true that large numbers of surgical cures for paraplegia might harm those who remain paraplegic. It does not follow, however, that widespread use of the curative surgical intervention should be prohibited or that it would be morally wrong.

It is necessary here to distinguish between being harmed and being wrongly harmed. Even if the minority who remain uncured are harmed by widespread use of the surgical intervention it would not follow that they have been *wrongly* harmed, unless one is willing to make the implausible claim that those who elected to be cured had no right to make this choice. But whether they have a right to make such a choice will depend primarily upon whether they have a legitimate interest in avoiding being disabled and whether that legitimate interest is of such moral weight that it warrants the special protection implied in the notion of a right. Having a right to do something means having a sphere of discretion to do what might otherwise be wrong, including what may contribute to a worsening of the condition of others. For example, if you have a right to compete with me for a certain prize, then the fact that your entering the competition worsens my condition does not show that you wrong me by competing.

. . . [O]ur critique of the loss of support argument reveals quite general features of other arguments advanced on behalf of persons with disabilities. First, whether their proponents recognize it or not, these arguments are not limited to interventions to prevent genetic diseases. They apply to all disabilities regardless of their etiology, and their general implications are highly implausible. Second, like the loss of support argument, the other arguments considered here are flawed because they consider only some of the legitimate interests at stake. They give no weight to the legitimate interests that persons have in not having

disabilities. Thus, ironically, their arguments are exclusionary.

THE JUSTICE TRUMPS BENEFICENCE ARGUMENT

We have just seen that the "loss of support argument" overlooks the legitimate interests that people have in avoiding disabilities. This interest is not merely legitimate—that is, not subject to any moral criticism as such. . . . [It] is the basis of a claim of justice. We argued [elsewhere] that there are cases in which justice requires interventions to correct or prevent genetic defects. The chief basis for this conclusion is that an adequate account of justice includes a commitment to equal opportunity, and that genetically based disabilities, like other disabilities, impair opportunity.

The conclusion that genetic interventions can be required by justice has a direct and devastating implication for another argument advanced on behalf of persons with disabilities and against genetic intervention. This is the "justice trumps beneficence" argument. This argument asserts that while only beneficence, not justice, speaks in favor of genetic intervention to prevent disabilities, the widespread use of genetic interventions to prevent disabilities puts disabled persons at risk of suffering grave injustices. . . . More explicitly, the argument is:

1. Genetic intervention to prevent disabilities is not required by justice but only by the value or principle of beneficence.
2. The widespread use of genetic intervention to prevent disabilities would create a serious risk of injustices to disabled people.
3. Justice trumps beneficence (when the pursuit of beneficence creates a risk of serious injustice, the avoidance of injustice should take precedence).
4. Therefore, widespread genetic intervention to prevent disabilities ought not to be undertaken.

In a nutshell, the "justice trumps beneficence" argument contends that it is wrong to act on the principle of beneficence to the detriment of the principle of justice.

Consider premise 2. Our critique of the loss of support argument has already shown that even if a reduction in the incidence of disabilities does put disabled persons at risk for loss of support, it does not follow that we should forgo the effort to prevent disabilities by genetic or other means. [Elsewhere] we examine another interpretation of premise 2 of the "justice trumps beneficence" argument, one that focuses on a different risk to those with disabilities.

There we evaluate the allegation that genetic intervention to prevent disabilities expresses a radical devaluation of persons with disabilities, which violates their right to be recognized as persons of equal moral worth. But here we wish to attack the third premise, which is false for two reasons.

First, some benefits are not "mere benefits." Achieving a great good or avoiding a great harm can in some cases be obligatory, not merely commendable or desirable. Indeed, there can be instances in which the obligation to achieve a great good or to prevent a great harm trumps obligations of justice, because those particular obligations of justice are less weighty.

To fail to consider this possibility is to make the mistake of assuming that obligations of justice are the weightiest obligations in all circumstances. What distinguishes these obligations from others, including obligations to provide benefits and to avoid harms, is not their relative strength, but their grounds—the kinds of considerations that are appealed to in justifying the assertion that there is an obligation. . . . So even if it were true that beneficence but not justice speaks in favor of genetic intervention to prevent disabilities, it would not follow that we ought never to intervene when intervention creates a risk of injustice.

Second, . . . justice—and more specifically, equal opportunity as one component of justice—sometimes requires genetic intervention to prevent disabilities. And . . . our obligations to prevent harm can also require genetic interventions, whether these obligations are understood to be obligations of justice or not. So it is a mistake to say that the prospect of genetic intervention to prevent disabilities pits mere beneficence against justice, even if it can be shown that such intervention would put people with disabilities at risk of being treated unjustly.

The justice trumps beneficence argument portrays an unequal contest between the need to protect people with disabilities against the most fundamental injustice, on the one hand, and the merely desirable goal of conferring benefits, on the other. But this is inaccurate. Instead, we have either a conflict between obligations of justice (or to prevent serious harms) and obligations to minimize the risk of injustice. Whether we should underake genetic interventions to protect equal opportunity (or for the sake of preventing serious harm) or refrain from intervening in order to avoid the risk of injustice to people with disabilities will depend on the nature of the injustice for

which people with disabilities are put at risk and the likelihood that this injustice will occur.

But if this is so, then we can proceed to examine the claim that the widespread use of genetic intervention to prevent disabilities puts people with disabilities at risk for being treated unjustly and we can dispense with the justice trumps beneficence argument, which we have seen is unsound anyway because of its oversimplified conception of strength of obligations of justice relative to those of beneficence.

THE EXPRESSIVIST OBJECTION

This objection, or rather this family of objections, focuses on what may be called the expressive character of decisions to use genetic interventions to prevent disabilities. The claim is that decisions to intervene—and indeed the whole enterprise of developing the knowledge and technology to make such interventions possible—express negative judgments about people with disabilities, and that these judgments themselves constitute a profound injustice to those people.

The negative judgments allegedly expressed in the enterprise of genetic intervention are said to betray a profound miscomprehension of the core concept of morality: the value of human life. The mistake is to assume that only "perfect" human lives are of sufficient value to be allowed to exist or to come into existence.

According to the expressivist objection, this error is not merely a mistake in ethical theory. To express these negative judgments about people with disabilities is itself an injury to them, a violation of their most fundamental right—the right to be regarded as persons of equal worth.

In addition, the social acceptance of the enterprise that expresses these negative judgments, the project of using genetic knowledge for improvement through selection, puts persons with disabilities at risk in more concrete ways. Those who are not regarded as members of the community of persons with equal worth, those whose fundamental value is denied, are likely to be neglected and abused, if not exterminated. The negative judgments allegedly expressed in the new genetics, then, are these:

1. The lives of individuals with disabilities are not worth living.
2. Only perfect individuals should be brought into the world. (Imperfect individuals have no right to exist.)

Disabilities rights advocates rightly reject both judgments. Those who advance the expressivist argument are quick to emphasize that the first judgment reveals an ignorance of the joys and fulfillments that even severely disabled individuals can experience. The second judgment is rejected on the grounds that it rests on a false assumption about what makes individuals worthy of equal respect and concern, and hence of life. It is not whether or not someone measures up to some supposed standard of perfection that matters so far as equal worth is concerned, but rather an individual's humanity (or, on some accounts, personhood).

It is no doubt true that people who have not experienced serious disabilities themselves, or been close to people who are seriously disabled, sometimes—perhaps often—fail to appreciate the quality of life of people with disabilities. They may focus only on the suffering and limitations the disability entails, underestimating both the positive experiences people with disabilities can have and the remarkable capacity that human beings have to adapt their expectations and goals to changes in their abilities. . . .

Even if this is true, however, it does not follow that all or even most of those who are not disabled believe that disabilities as such, or even serious disabilities, make life not worth living. It may well be true that many people believe that there are some disabilities so severe that they make life not worth living. And it may be that some interventions to prevent disabilities are undertaken out of this belief. But from this it does not follow that whenever we intervene to prevent a disability our action betrays a belief that the lives of disabled persons are not worth living.

What, then, would lead some disabilities rights advocates to conclude that the enthusiasm for using genetic science to reduce the incidence of disabilities expresses the judgment that the lives of disabled people are not worth living or that such people ought not to exist? The answer, apparently, is that they believe that central to the new genetics is the decision to prevent disabilities by avoiding the birth of individuals with disabilities—and that this decision must rest on the judgment that life with disabilities is not worth living or that less-than-perfect individuals ought not to exist or have no right to exist. . . .

As a general form of argument, the expressivist objection is invalid. An example that has nothing to do with genetic intervention will show why this is so.

Suppose that a woman can either conceive a child when she has German measles (rubella), knowing that if she does there is a significant risk that the child she bears will suffer a serious impairment, or she can delay conception until her illness passes. Surely the woman's decision to postpone conceiving a child need not be an expression of the belief either that if the child were born with an impairment its life would not be worth living or that were it born with an impairment it would have no right to live or be unworthy of equal respect and concern.

To reveal more conclusively the weakness of the expressivist argument, we must clarify what it means to say that a decision expresses (or presupposes) a particular judgment. This happens if and only if either, as a matter of psychological fact, one could only be motivated to make this judgment if the person ascribed to the judgment (i.e., that one could not psychologically make the decision if he or she did not believe to be true what the judgment affirms), or one cannot rationally make the decision without believing what the judgment affirms. So the expressivist objection is that decisions to use genetic intervention to prevent disabilities rationally or motivationally presuppose either the judgment that the lives of disabled individuals are not worth living, or the judgment that less-than-perfect individuals ought not to exist, or both.

Preventing Disabilities without Terminating the Lives of Individuals with Disabilities It should be clear that the expressivist objection only applies to those genetic interventions that prevent disabilities by preventing the existence of individuals who would have the disabilities in question. If the disability is prevented in other ways, there is no reason whatsoever to believe that the decision expresses a judgment that life with those disabilities would not be worth living or that the individual who had those disabilities ought not to exist.

This is a significant point because some modes of genetic intervention do not prevent disability by preventing the existence of individuals who would have the disability. To see that this is so, it is useful to distinguish the following four types of intervention:

- Preventing a genetic condition that would be disabling by "switching off" the gene that produces the disabling condition or by inserting normal genes either into embryos or gametes or into individuals after they are born.
- Avoiding conceiving a fetus with a genetic condition that would produce a disability by using

contraceptives when genetic testing reveals a significant risk of the condition.

- Avoiding conceiving a fetus with a genetic condition that would produce a disability by using artificial insemination or embryo transplant.
- Preventing the birth of an individual determined to have a genetic condition that would produce a disability or to be at high risk of having that condition by aborting the fetus.

Opting for the first form of intervention in no way presupposes—either motivationally or rationally—a judgment that only perfect individuals should exist or that people with disabilities ought not to exist, any more than performing conventional surgery to restore a blind person's sight does. In either case the motive may be, and often is, simply the desire to remove serious limitations on the individual's opportunities and to avoid needless suffering. One can be motivated by this desire and can rationally decide to act on it without believing either that the individual's life with the limitation is not worth living or that only perfect individuals should exist. If Jill decides to undergo the surgical procedure to cure her paraplegia, she need not believe that her life or anyone else's life as a paraplegic is not worth living, nor need she consciously or unconsciously believe that only perfect individuals should exist.

Similarly, the second and third modes of intervening to prevent disabilities need not express either of the negative judgments the expressivist argument attributes to those who advocate genetic interventions. To be willing to undertake either of these options, all that is necessary is the desire not to bring into the world an individual whose opportunities will be severely limited and who may also experience considerable suffering.

A number of beliefs may account for this desire, any of which would make the decision fully rational. First, someone may simply wish to be spared avoidable and serious strains on his or her marriage or family. Or he or she may wish to avoid putting additional pressure on limited social resources needed for the achievement of distributive justice in health care and in other areas, including the support of existing individuals who have disabilities.

In the second and third interventions, using contraception, artificial insemination, or embryo transplant, acting on these desires does not violate anyone's rights because there is no existing individual who has rights that might be violated. It is the coming to be of an individual that is avoided. No existing individual's life is terminated. So even if one believes that fetuses are

persons with all the rights that persons have, including the right not to be killed, avoiding disabilities by avoiding conception of individuals who would be disabled neither violates anyone's rights nor necessarily expresses any negative judgments about the lives of people with disabilities. Furthermore, to judge that it is morally permissible to avoid bringing a disabled person into the world, a person need not judge that disabled persons ought not to be born any more than judging that it is not wrong to refrain from getting a Ph.D. commits someone to the judgment that no one ought to get a Ph.D.

Only the fourth mode of intervention has any prospect of being vulnerable to the expressivist objection, because it is only in that case that there is a decision to terminate a life that will involve a disability. This point is extremely important because it shows that even in principle the expressivist objection cannot provide a reason for abandoning or restricting genetic interventions per se, but at most only one mode of intervention.

Genetic Intervention and the Status of Fetuses
Notice, however, that even in the fourth type of intervention the decision to intervene—to abort a fetus with a disabling genetic condition—need not express either of the two negative judgments about people with disabilities. Someone who decides to terminate a pregnancy after learning that the fetus she is carrying has Down syndrome may simply be motivated by the very same desire that motivates the decision to undertake any of the other three modes of intervention: the desire not to bring into the world an individual with seriously limited opportunities. Nor is there anything illogical or irrational about acting on this desire while firmly rejecting the judgment that the lives of disabled people are not worth living or that people with disabilities have no right to exist.

In the case of the fourth mode of intervention, as with the other three modes, the desire to avoid the birth of an individual with disabilities may be based on any of several quite morally unexceptionable considerations. A person may wish to avoid serious strains on a marriage or the ability to fulfill responsibilities to existing children, or to avoid diverting scarce resources needed for the achievement of distributive justice—and yet the individual may consistently believe that the lives of many or even of all individuals with Down syndrome are worth living and that every child and adult with this genetic condition has the same right to life and to recognition of equal worth as any other person.

Nor need the person believe that only perfect individuals ought to exist. An individual can rationally decide to abort a fetus with a genetic defect while nevertheless believing that persons with disabilities are of equal worth if he believes that fetuses (or at least fetuses up to and including the stage at which the abortion is performed) are not persons and hence do not have the rights and equal moral status of persons.

To believe that it is permissible to avoid a serious disability by selective abortion one need not believe that individuals with that disability ought not to be born. All that is necessary is the belief that the fetus has no right to be born. Furthermore, one can—and many people apparently do—consistently believe both that fetuses, whether they will have disabilities or not, have no right to be born (because they are not persons) while believing that all persons, including those with disabilities, have a right to exist, and hence a right not to be killed, because they are persons.

Similarly, there is nothing inconsistent or motivationally incoherent about believing that one ought not bring a disabled child into the world and believing that it is not the case that individuals with disabilities ought not to be born. (Someone can believe that she ought not to marry without believing that marriages ought not to occur.)

Perhaps those who advance the expressivist argument will still not be convinced of our rebuttal. The appeal of the argument is its simplicity. Thus a person who herself has a disability, impatient with the subtleties and hair-splitting of the preceding arguments, might reply:

No analysis of the possible motives or of the coherence of the possible reasons for preventing disabilities can erase one simple fact: When you endorse the use of genetic science to prevent disabilities, you are saying that people like me ought not to exist. And when you say that people like me ought not to exist, you devalue me in the most fundamental and threatening way imaginable. Your conception of the value of human life denies that my life, imperfect as it is in your eyes, has value.

Recall, however, that to say that it is permissible to avoid disabilities by genetic interventions is not to say that we ought to reduce the incidence of disabilities, much less that disabled persons ought not to exist. . . . [We] have argued [elsewhere] that there can be obligations of justice, as well as obligations to prevent harm, that require genetic interventions. From this perspective, we are committed to the judgment that in the future the world should not include so many disabilities and hence so many individuals with disabilities. But it is not the people with the disabilities that we devalue; it is the disabilities themselves. We do not wish to reduce the number of people with disabilities by taking the life of any individual who has a disability.

Devaluing Disabilities, Not People with Disabilities
We devalue disabilities because we value the opportunities and welfare of the people who have them. And it is because we value people, all people, that we care about limitations on their welfare and opportunities. We also know that disabilities as such diminish opportunities and welfare, even when they are not so severe that the lives of those who have them are not worth living, and even if those individuals do not literally suffer as a result of their disabilities. Thus there is nothing irrational, motivationally incoherent, or disingenuous in saying that we devalue the disabilities and wish to reduce their incidence while valuing existing persons with disabilities, and that we value them the same as those who do not have disabilities. . . .

Summary of Response to Expressivist Objection It may be useful at this point to summarize the main points of our complex discussion of the expressivist argument against genetic intervention. To be sound, the argument either must show that it is motivationally impossible or irrational both to devalue and seek to avoid disabilities while at the same time valuing equally individuals who have disabilities or it must defend the view that fetuses are persons, with all the rights that persons have, and that avoiding disabilities by aborting fetuses with disabilities is the moral equivalent of reducing the incidence of disabilities by exterminating disabled children and adults.

The first alternative is unconvincing. There are many instances in which we devalue (and seek to avoid) certain characteristics that some individuals have without devaluing individuals who have them. The second alternative comes at a steep price: Not only must the disabilities rights advocate articulate and defend an account of personhood that shows that fetuses are persons, he must also acknowledge that the fundamental error of those who advocate selective abortion to avoid disabilities is not that they devalue individuals with disabilities but that they fail to recognize that fetuses, whether disabled or not, are persons. The argument, then, would have nothing to do with disabilities as such.

Moreover, even if it were assumed that fetuses are persons and that hence killing them to reduce the incidence of disabilities is morally indistinguishable from exterminating disabled children and adults, this would have no negative implications for the other three modes of genetic intervention to avoid disabilities. None of these involves killing a fetus, so none can be described as killing a person, even if we assume that fetuses are persons. Therefore endorsing these modes of reducing disabilities need not express and does not presuppose the judgment that existing individuals with disabilities have no right to live.

To repeat: Advocating the fourth mode of intervention (selective abortion) is tantamount to saying that people like you (who have disabilities) have no right to exist only on the highly controversial assumption that fetuses are persons. Opting for the first, second, and third modes of intervention has no implications at all for the worthiness or unworthiness of "disabled lives," regardless of which view of the moral status of fetuses is correct. What appeared to be a distinctive objection to a new technology turns out to be a familiar objection to the age-old practice of abortion.

None of this is to deny that some members of the disabilities community are genuinely offended by what they take to be the misplaced zeal to harness the powers of science to prevent disabilities. Granted the shameful history of discrimination against and insensitivity toward persons with disabilities, their taking offense is perfectly understandable. However, it is one thing to say that certain behavior is offensive to a particular group, and quite another to say that the fact that the group is offended constitutes a violation of anyone's rights.

In general, a liberal society cannot count the occurrence of offense, as distinct from rights violations, as a sufficient ground for curtailing liberty, whether it is the liberty of a person to choose a surgical procedure that will cure her own paraplegia or that of her child, or the liberty of a researcher to try to develop a technique for preventing a genetically based impairment. . . .

The Problem of Justifying Abortion

DON MARQUIS

Why Abortion Is Immoral

Donald Marquis, professor of philosophy at the University of Kansas, has maintained active interests in the history of ethics as well as problems of abortion, social ethics, and research ethics. Representative publications include "Leaving Therapy to Chance: An Impasse in the Ethics of Randomized Clinical Trials," *The Hastings Center Report*; "An Ethical Problem Concerning Recent Therapeutic Research on Breast Cancer," *Hypatia*; and "Four Versions of Double Effect," *The Journal of Medicine and Philosophy*.

The view that abortion is, with rare exceptions, seriously immoral has received little support in the recent philosophical literature. No doubt most philosophers affiliated with secular institutions of higher education believe that the anti-abortion position is either a symptom of irrational religious dogma or a conclusion generated by seriously confused philosophical argument. The purpose of this essay is to undermine this general belief. This essay sets out an argument that purports

From *Journal of Philosophy* 86, no. 4 (April 1989), 183–202. Footnotes renumbered.

to show, as well as any argument in ethics can show, that abortion is, except possibly in rare cases, seriously immoral, that it is in the same moral category as killing an innocent adult human being.

The argument is based on a major assumption. Many of the most insightful and careful writers on the ethics of abortion . . . believe that whether or not abortion is morally permissible stands or falls on whether or not a fetus is the sort of being whose life it is seriously wrong to end. The argument of this essay will assume, but not argue, that they are correct.

Also, this essay will neglect issues of great importance to a complete ethics of abortion. Some antiabortionists will allow that certain abortions, such as abortion before implantation or abortion when the life of a woman is threatened by a pregnancy or abortion after rape, may be morally permissible. This essay will not explore the casuistry of these hard cases. The purpose of this essay is to develop a general argument for the claim that the overwhelming majority of deliberate abortions are seriously immoral. . . .

I

Passions in the abortion debate run high. There are both plausibilities and difficulties with the standard positions. Accordingly, it is hardly surprising that partisans of either side embrace with fervor the moral generalizations that support the conclusions they preanalytically favor, and reject with disdain the moral generalizations of their opponents as being subject to inescapable difficulties. It is easy to believe that the counterexamples to one's own moral principles are merely temporary difficulties that will dissolve in the wake of further philosophical research, and that the counterexamples to the principles of one's opponents are as straightforward as the contradiction between *A* and *O* propositions in traditional logic. This might suggest to an impartial observer (if there are any) that the abortion issue is unresolvable.

There is a way out of this apparent dialectical quandary. The moral generalizations of both sides are not quite correct. The generalizations hold for the most part, for the usual cases. This suggests that they are all *accidental* generalizations, that the moral claims made by those on both sides of the dispute do not touch on the *essence* of the matter.

This use of the distinction between essence and accident is not meant to invoke obscure metaphysical categories. Rather, it is intended to reflect the rather atheoretical nature of the abortion discussion. If the generalization a partisan in the abortion dispute adopts were derived from the reason why ending the life of a human being is wrong, then there could not be exceptions to that generalization unless some special case obtains in which there are even more powerful countervailing reasons. Such generalizations would not be merely accidental generalizations; they would point to, or be based upon, the essence of the wrongness of killing, what it is that makes killing wrong. All this suggests that a necessary condition of resolving the abortion controversy is a more theoretical account of the wrongness of killing. After all, if we merely believe, but do not understand, why killing adult human beings such as ourselves is wrong, how could we conceivably show that abortion is either immoral or permissible?

II

In order to develop such an account, we can start from the following unproblematic assumption concerning our own case: It is wrong to kill *us*. Why is it wrong? Some answers can be easily eliminated. It might be said that what makes killing us wrong is that a killing brutalizes the one who kills. But the brutalization consists of being inured to the performance of an act that is hideously immoral; hence, the brutalization does not explain the immorality. It might be said that what makes killing us wrong is the great loss others would experience due to our absence. Although such hubris is understandable, such an explanation does not account for the wrongness of killing hermits, or those whose lives are relatively independent and whose friends find it easy to make new friends.

A more obvious answer is better. What primarily makes killing wrong is neither its effect on the murderer nor its effect on the victim's friends and relatives, but its effect on the victim. The loss of one's life is one of the greatest losses one can suffer. The loss of one's life deprives one of all the experiences, activities, projects, and enjoyments that would otherwise have constituted one's future. Therefore, killing someone is wrong, primarily because the killing inflicts (one of) the greatest possible losses on the victim. To describe this as the loss of life can be misleading, however. The change in my biological state does not by itself make killing me wrong. The effect of the loss of my biological life is the loss to me of all those activities, projects, experiences, and enjoyments which would otherwise have constituted my future personal life. These activities, projects, experiences, and enjoyments are either valuable for their own sakes or are means to something else that is valuable for its own sake. Some parts of my future are not valued by me now, but will come to be valued by me as I grow older and as my values and capacities change. When I am killed, I am deprived both of what I now value which would have been part of my future personal life, but also what I would come to value. Therefore, when I die, I am deprived of all of the value of my future. Inflicting this loss on me is ultimately what makes killing me wrong. This being the case, it would seem that what makes killing *any* adult human being prima facie seriously wrong is the loss of his or her future.

How should this rudimentary theory of the wrongness of killing be evaluated? It cannot be faulted for deriving an "ought" from an "is," for it does not. The analysis assumes that killing me (or you, reader) is prima facie seriously wrong. The point of the analysis is to establish which natural property ultimately explains the wrongness of the killing, given that it is wrong. A natural property will ultimately explain the wrongness of killing, only if (1) the explanation fits with our intuitions about the matter and (2) there is no other natural property that provides the basis for a better explanation of the wrongness of killing. This analysis rests on the intuition that what makes killing a particular human or animal wrong is what it does to that particular human or animal. What makes killing wrong is some natural effect or other of the killing. Some would deny this. For instance, a divine-command theorist in ethics would deny it. Surely this denial is, however, one of those features of divine-command theory which renders it so implausible.

The claim that what makes killing wrong is the loss of the victim's future is directly supported by two considerations. In the first place, this theory explains why we regard killing as one of the worst of crimes. Killing is especially wrong, because it deprives the victim of more than perhaps any other crime. In the second place, people with AIDS or cancer who know they are dying believe, of course, that dying is a very bad thing for them. They believe that the loss of a future to them that they would otherwise have experienced is what makes their premature death a very bad thing for them. A better theory of the wrongness of killing would require a different natural property associated with killing which better fits with the attitudes of the dying. What could it be?

The view that what makes killing wrong is the loss to the victim of the value of the victim's future gains additional support when some of its implications are examined. In the first place, it is incompatible with the view that it is wrong to kill only beings who are biologically human. It is possible that there exists a different species from another planet whose members have a future like ours. Since having a future like that is what makes killing someone wrong, this theory entails that it would be wrong to kill members of such a species. Hence, this theory is opposed to the claim that only life that is biologically human has great moral worth, a claim which many anti-abortionists have seemed to adopt. This opposition, which this theory has in common with personhood theories, seems to be a merit of the theory.

In the second place, the claim that the loss of one's future is the wrong-making feature of one's being killed entails the possibility that the futures of some actual nonhuman mammals on our own planet are sufficiently like ours that it is seriously wrong to kill them also. Whether some animals do have the same right to life as human beings depends on adding to the account of the wrongness of killing some additional account of just what it is about my future or the futures of other adult human beings which makes it wrong to kill us. No such additional account will be offered in this essay. Undoubtedly, the provision of such an account would be a very difficult matter. Undoubtedly, any such account would be quite controversial. Hence, it surely should not reflect badly on this sketch of an elementary theory of the wrongness of killing that it is indeterminate with respect to some very difficult issues regarding animal rights.

In the third place, the claim that the loss of one's future is the wrong-making feature of one's being killed does not entail, as sanctity of human life theories do, that active euthanasia is wrong. Persons who are severely and incurably ill, who face a future of pain and despair, and who wish to die will not have suffered a loss if they are killed. It is, strictly speaking, the value of a human's future which makes killing wrong in this theory. This being so, killing does not necessarily wrong some persons who are sick and dying. Of course, there may be other reasons for a prohibition of active euthanasia, but that is another matter. Sanctity-of-human-life theories seem to hold that active euthanasia is seriously wrong even in an individual case where there seems to be good reason for it independently of public policy considerations. This consequence is most implausible, and it is a plus for the claim that the loss of a future of value is what makes killing wrong that it does not share this consequence.

In the fourth place, the account of the wrongness of killing defended in this essay does straightforwardly entail that it is prima facie seriously wrong to kill children and infants, for we do presume that they have futures of value. Since we do believe that it is wrong to kill defenseless little babies, it is important that a theory of the wrongness of killing easily account for this. Personhood theories of the wrongness of killing, on the other hand, cannot straightforwardly account for the wrongness of killing infants and young children. Hence, such theories must add special ad hoc accounts of the wrongness of killing the young. The plausibility of such ad hoc theories seems to be a function of how desperately one wants such theories to work. The claim that the primary wrong-making feature of a killing is the loss to the victim of the value of its future accounts for the wrongness of killing young children and infants directly; it makes the wrongness of such acts as obvious as we actually think it is. This is a further merit of this theory. Accordingly, it seems that this value of a future-like-ours theory of the wrongness of killing shares strengths of both sanctity-of-life and personhood accounts while avoiding weaknesses of both. In addition, it meshes with a central intuition concerning what makes killing wrong.

The claim that the primary wrong-making feature of a killing is the loss to the victim of the value of its future has obvious consequences for the ethics of abortion. The future of a standard fetus includes a set of experiences, projects, activities, and such which are identical with the futures of adult human beings and are identical with the futures of young children. Since the reason that is sufficient to explain why it is wrong to kill human beings after the time of birth is a reason that also applies to fetuses, it follows that abortion is prima facie seriously morally wrong.

This argument does not rely on the invalid inference that, since it is wrong to kill persons, it is wrong to kill potential persons also. The category that is morally central to this analysis is the category of having a valuable future like ours; it is not the category of personhood. The argument to the conclusion that abortion is prima facie seriously morally wrong proceeded independently of the notion of person or potential person or any equivalent. Someone may wish to start with this analysis in terms of the value of a human future, conclude that abortion is, except perhaps in rare circumstances, seriously morally wrong, infer that fetuses have the right to life, and then call fetuses "persons" as a result of their having the right to life. Clearly, in this case, the category of person is being used to state the *conclusion* of the analysis rather than to generate the *argument* of the analysis.

The structure of this anti-abortion argument can be both illuminated and defended by comparing it to what appears to be the best argument for the wrongness of the wanton infliction of pain on animals. This latter argument is based on the assumption that it is prima facie wrong to inflict pain on me (or you, reader). What is the natural property associated with the infliction of pain which makes such infliction wrong? The obvious answer seems to be that the infliction of pain causes suffering and that suffering is a misfortune. The suffering caused by the infliction of pain is what makes the wanton infliction of pain on me wrong. The wanton infliction of pain on other adult humans causes suffering. The wanton infliction of pain on animals causes suffering. Since causing suffering is what makes the wanton infliction of pain wrong and since the wanton infliction of pain on animals causes suffering, it follows that the wanton infliction of pain on animals is wrong.

This argument for the wrongness of the wanton infliction of pain on animals shares a number of structural features with the argument for the serious prima facie wrongness of abortion. Both arguments start with an obvious assumption concerning what it is wrong to do to me (or you, reader). Both then look for the characteristic or the consequence of the wrong action which makes the action wrong. Both recognize that the wrong-making feature of these immoral actions is a property of actions sometimes directed at individuals other than postnatal human beings. If the structure of the argument for the wrongness of the wanton infliction of pain on animals is sound, then the structure of the argument for the prima facie serious wrongness of abortion is also sound, for the structure of the two arguments is the same. The structure common to both is the key to the explanation of how the wrongness of abortion can be demonstrated without recourse to the category of person. In neither argument is that category crucial.

This defense of an argument for the wrongness of abortion in terms of a structurally similar argument for the wrongness of the wanton infliction of pain on animals succeeds only if the account regarding animals is the correct account. Is it? In the first place, it seems plausible. In the second place, its major competition is Kant's account. Kant believed that we do not have direct duties to animals at all, because they are not persons. Hence, Kant had to explain and justify the wrongness of inflicting pain on animals on the grounds that "he who is hard in his dealings with animals becomes hard also in his dealing with men."[1] The problem with Kant's account is that there seems to be no reason for accepting this latter claim unless Kant's account is rejected. If the alternative to Kant's account is accepted, then it is easy to understand why someone who is indifferent to inflicting pain on animals is also indifferent to inflicting pain on humans, for one is indifferent to what makes inflicting pain wrong in both cases. But, if Kant's account is accepted, there is no intelligible reason why one who is hard in his dealings with animals (or crabgrass or stones) should also be hard in his dealings with men. After all, men are persons: animals are no more persons than crabgrass or stones. Persons are Kant's crucial moral category. Why, in short, should a Kantian accept the basic claim in Kant's argument?

Hence, Kant's argument for the wrongness of inflicting pain on animals rests on a claim that, in a world of Kantian moral agents, is demonstrably false. Therefore, the alternative analysis, being more plausible anyway, should be accepted. Since this alternative analysis has the same structure of the anti-abortion argument being defended here, we have further support for the argument for the immorality of abortion being defended in this essay.

Of course, this value of a future-like-ours argument, if sound, shows only that abortion is prima facie wrong, not that it is wrong in any and all circumstances. Since the loss of the future to a standard fetus, if killed, is, however, at least as great a loss as the loss of the future to a standard adult human being who is killed, abortion, like ordinary killing, could be justified only by the most compelling reasons. The loss of one's life is almost the greatest misfortune that can happen to one. Presumably abortion could be justified in some circumstances, only if the loss consequent on failing to abort would be at least as great. Accordingly, morally permissible abortions will be rare indeed unless, perhaps, they occur so early in pregnancy that a fetus is not yet definitely an individual. Hence, this argument should be taken as showing that abortion is presumptively very seriously wrong, where the presumption is very strong—as strong as the presumption that killing another adult human being is wrong.

III

How complete an account of the wrongness of killing does the value of a future-like-ours account have to be in order that the wrongness of abortion is a consequence? This account does not have to be an account of the necessary conditions for the wrongness of killing. Some persons in nursing homes may lack valuable human futures, yet it may be wrong to kill them for other reasons. Furthermore, this account does not obviously have to be the sole reason killing is wrong where the victim did have a valuable future. This analysis claims only that, for any killing where the victim did have a valuable future like ours, having that future by itself is sufficient to create the strong presumption that the killing is seriously wrong.

One way to overturn the value of a future-like-ours argument would be to find some account of the wrongness of killing which is at least as intelligible and which has different implications for the ethics of abortion. Two rival accounts possess at least some degree of plausibility. One account is based on the obvious fact that people value the experience of living and wish for that valuable experience to continue. Therefore, it might be said, what makes killing wrong is the discontinuation of that experience for the victim. Let us call this the *discontinuation account*. Another rival account is based upon the obvious fact that people strongly desire to continue to live. This suggests that what makes killing us so wrong is that it interferes with the fulfillment of a strong and fundamental desire, the fulfillment of which is necessary for the fulfillment of any other desires we might have. Let us call this the *desire account*.[2]

Consider first the desire account as a rival account of the ethics of killing which would provide the basis for rejecting the anti-abortion position. Such an account will have to be stronger than the value of a future-like-ours account of the wrongness of abortion if it is to do the job expected of it. To entail the wrongness of abortion, the value of a future-like-ours account has only to provide a sufficient, but not a necessary, condition for the wrongness of killing. The desire account, on the other hand, must provide us also with a necessary condition for the wrongness of killing in order to generate a pro-choice conclusion on abortion.

The reason for this is that presumably the argument from the desire account moves from the claim that what makes killing wrong is interference with a very strong desire to the claim that abortion is not wrong because the fetus lacks a strong desire to live. Obviously, this inference fails if someone's having the desire to live is not a necessary condition of its being wrong to kill that individual.

One problem with the desire account is that we do regard it as seriously wrong to kill persons who have little desire to live or who have no desire to live or, indeed, have a desire not to live. We believe it is seriously wrong to kill the unconscious, the sleeping, those who are tired of life, and those who are suicidal. The value-of-a-human-future account renders standard morality intelligible in these cases; these cases appear to be incompatible with the desire account.

The desire account is subject to a deeper difficulty. We desire life, because we value the goods of this life. The goodness of life is not secondary to our desire for it. If this were not so, the pain of one's own premature death could be done away with merely by an appropriate alteration in the configuration of one's desires. This is absurd. Hence, it would seem that it is the loss of the goods of one's future, not the interference with the fulfillment of a strong desire to live, which accounts ultimately for the wrongness of killing.

It is worth noting that, if the desire account is modified so that it does not provide a necessary, but only a sufficient, condition for the wrongness of killing, the desire account is compatible with the value of a future-like-ours account. The combined accounts will yield an anti-abortion ethic. This suggests that one can retain what is intuitively plausible about the desire account without a challenge to the basic argument of this paper.

It is also worth noting that, if future desires have moral force in a modified desire account of the wrongness of killing, one can find support for an anti-abortion ethic even in the absence of a value of a future-like-ours account. If one decides that a morally relevant property, the possession of which is sufficient to make it wrong to kill some individual, is the desire at some future time to live—one might decide to justify one's refusal to kill suicidal teenagers on these grounds, for example—then, since typical fetuses will have the desire in the future to live, it is wrong to kill typical fetuses. Accordingly, it does not seem that a desire account of the wrongness of killing can provide a justification of a pro-choice ethic of abortion which is nearly as adequate as the value of a human-future justification of an anti-abortion ethic.

The discontinuation account looks more promising as an account of the wrongness of killing. It seems just as intelligible as the value of a future-like-ours account, but it does not justify an anti-abortion position. Obviously, if it is the continuation of one's activities, experiences, and projects, the loss of which makes killing wrong, then it is not wrong to kill fetuses for that reason, for fetuses do not have experiences, activities, and projects to be continued or discontinued. Accordingly, the discontinuation account does not have the anti-abortion consequences that the value of a future-like-ours account has. Yet it seems as intelligible as the value of a future-like-ours account, for when we think of what would be wrong with our being killed, it does seem as if it is the discontinuation of what makes our lives worthwhile which makes killing us wrong.

Is the discontinuation account just as good an account as the value of a future-like-ours account? The discontinuation account will not be adequate at all, if it does not refer to the *value* of the experience that may be discontinued. One does not want the discontinuation account to make it wrong to kill a patient who begs for death and who is in severe pain that cannot be relieved short of killing. (I leave open the question of whether it is wrong for other reasons.) Accordingly, the discontinuation account must be more than a bare discontinuation account. It must make some reference to the positive value of the patient's experiences. But, by the same token, the value of a future-like-ours account cannot be a bare future account either. Just having a future surely does not itself rule out killing the above patient. This account must make some reference to the value of the patient's future experiences and projects also. Hence, both accounts involve the value of experiences, projects, and activities. So far we still have symmetry between the accounts.

The symmetry fades, however, when we focus on the time period of the value of the experiences, etc., which has moral consequences. Although both accounts leave open the possibility that the patient in our example may be killed, this possibility is left open only in virtue of the utterly bleak future for the patient. It makes no difference whether the patient's immediate past contains intolerable pain, or consists in being in a coma (which we can imagine is a situation of indifference), or consists in a life of value. If the patient's future is a future of value, we want our account to make it wrong to kill the patient. If the patient's future is intolerable, whatever his or her immediate past, we want our account to allow killing the patient. Obviously, then, it is the value of that patient's future which is doing the work in rendering the morality of killing the patient intelligible.

This being the case, it seems clear that whether one has immediate past experiences or not does not work in the explanation of what makes killing wrong. The addition the discontinuation account makes to the value of a human future account is otiose. Its addition to the value-of-a-future account plays no role at all in rendering intelligible the wrongness of killing. Therefore, it can be discarded with the discontinuation account of which it is a part.

IV

The analysis of the previous section suggests that alternative general accounts of the wrongness of killing are either inadequate or unsuccessful in getting around the anti-abortion consequences of the value of a future-like-ours argument. A different strategy for avoiding these anti-abortion consequences involves limiting the scope of the value of a future argument. More precisely, the strategy involves arguing that fetuses lack a property that is essential for the value-of-a-future argument (or for any anti-abortion argument) to apply to them.

One move of this sort is based upon the claim that a necessary condition of one's future being valuable is that one values it. Value implies a valuer. Given this, one might argue that, since fetuses cannot value their futures, their futures are not valuable to them. Hence, it does not seriously wrong them deliberately to end their lives.

This move fails, however, because of some ambiguities. Let us assume that something cannot be of value unless it is valued by someone. This does not entail that my life is of no value unless it is valued by me. I may think, in a period of despair, that my future is of no worth whatsoever, but I may be wrong because others rightly see value—even great value—in it. Furthermore, my future can be valuable to me even if I do not value it. This is the case when a young person attempts suicide, but is rescued and goes on to significant human achievements. Such young people's futures are ultimately valuable to them, even though such futures do not seem to be valuable to them at the

moment of attempted suicide. A fetus's future can be valuable to it in the same way. Accordingly, this attempt to limit the anti-abortion argument fails.

Another similar attempt to reject the anti-abortion position is based on Tooley's claim that an entity cannot possess the right to life unless it has the capacity to desire its continued existence. It follows that, since fetuses lack the conceptual capacity to desire to continue to live, they lack the right to life. Accordingly, Tooley concludes that abortion cannot be seriously prima facie wrong (*op. cit.,* pp. 46/7). . . .

One might attempt to defend Tooley's basic claim on the grounds that, because a fetus cannot apprehend continued life as a benefit, its continued life cannot be a benefit or cannot be something it has a right to or cannot be something that is in its interest. This might be defended in terms of the general proposition that, if an individual is literally incapable of caring about or taking an interest in some X, then one does not have a right to X or X is not a benefit or X is not something that is in one's interest.[3]

Each member of this family of claims seems to be open to objections. . . . As Tooley himself has pointed out, persons who have been indoctrinated, or drugged, or rendered temporarily unconscious may be literally incapable of caring about or taking an interest in something that is in their interest or is something to which they have a right, or is something that benefits them. Hence, the Tooley claim that would restrict the scope of the value of a future-like-ours argument is undermined by counterexamples.[4]

Finally, Paul Bassen[5] has argued that, even though the prospects of an embryo might seem to be a basis for the wrongness of abortion, an embryo cannot be a victim and therefore cannot be wronged. An embryo cannot be a victim, he says, because it lacks sentience. His central argument for this seems to be that, even though plants and the permanently unconscious are alive, they clearly cannot be victims. What is the explanation of this? Bassen claims that the explanation is that their lives consist of mere metabolism and mere metabolism is not enough to ground victimizability. Mentation is required.

The problem with this attempt to establish the absence of victimizability is that both plants and the permanently unconscious clearly lack what Bassen calls "prospects" or what I have called "a future life like ours." Hence, it is surely open to one to argue that the real reason we believe plants and the permanently unconscious cannot be victims is that killing them cannot deprive them of a future life like ours; the real reason is not their absence of present mentation. . . .

V

In this essay, it has been argued that the correct ethic of the wrongness of killing can be extended to fetal life and used to show that there is a strong presumption that any abortion is morally impermissible. If the ethic of killing adopted here entails, however, that contraception is also seriously immoral, then there would appear to be a difficulty with the analysis of this essay.

But this analysis does not entail that contraception is wrong. Of course, contraception prevents the actualization of a possible future of value. Hence, it follows from the claim that futures of value should be maximized that contraception is prima facie immoral. This obligation to maximize does not exist, however; furthermore, nothing in the ethics of killing in this paper entails that it does. The ethics of killing in this essay would entail that contraception is wrong only if something were denied a human future of value by contraception. Nothing at all is denied such a future by contraception, however.

Candidates for a subject of harm by contraception fall into four categories: (1) some sperm or other, (2) some ovum or other, (3) a sperm and an ovum separately, and (4) a sperm and an ovum together. Assigning the harm to some sperm is utterly arbitrary, for no reason can be given for making a sperm the subject of harm rather than an ovum. Assigning the harm to some ovum is utterly arbitrary, for no reason can be given for making an ovum the subject of harm rather than a sperm. One might attempt to avoid these problems by insisting that contraception deprives both the sperm and the ovum separately of a valuable future like ours. On this alternative, too many futures are lost. Contraception was supposed to be wrong, because it deprived us of one future of value, not two. One might attempt to avoid this problem by holding that contraception deprives the combination of sperm and ovum of a valuable future like ours. But here the definite article misleads. At the time of contraception, there are hundreds of millions of sperm, one (released) ovum and millions of possible combinations of all of these. There is no actual combination at all. Is the subject of the loss to be a merely possible combination? Which

one? This alternative does not yield an actual subject of harm either. Accordingly, the immorality of contraception is not entailed by the loss of a future-like-ours argument simply because there is no nonarbitrarily identifiable subject of the loss in the case of contraception.

VI

The purpose of this essay has been to set out an argument for the serious presumptive wrongness of abortion subject to the assumption that the moral permissibility of abortion stands or falls on the moral status of the fetus. Since a fetus possesses a property, the possession of which in adult human beings is sufficient to make killing an adult human being wrong, abortion is wrong. This way of dealing with the problem of abortion seems superior to other approaches to the ethics of abortion, because it rests on an ethics of killing which is close to self-evident, because the crucial morally relevant property clearly applies to fetuses, and because the argument avoids the usual equivocations on "human life," "human being," or "person." The argument rests neither on religious claims nor on Papal dogma. It is not subject to the objection of "speciesism." Its soundness is compatible with the moral permissibility of euthanasia and contraception. It deals with our intuitions concerning young children.

Finally, this analysis can be viewed as resolving a standard problem—indeed, *the* standard problem—concerning the ethics of abortion. Clearly, it is wrong to kill adult human beings. Clearly, it is not wrong to end the life of some arbitrarily chosen single human cell. Fetuses seem to be like arbitrarily chosen human cells in some respects and like adult humans in other respects. The problem of the ethics of abortion is the problem of determining the fetal property that settles this moral controversy. The thesis of this essay is that the problem of the ethics of abortion, so understood, is solvable.

NOTES

1. "Duties to Animals and Spirits," in *Lectures on Ethics*, Louis Infeld, trans. (New York: Harper, 1963), p. 239.

2. Presumably a preference utilitarian would press such an objection. Tooley once suggested that his account has such a theoretical underpinning. See his "Abortion and Infanticide," *Philosophy and Public Affairs* 2 (1972), pp. 44–5.

3. Donald VanDeVeer seems to think this self-evident. See his "Whither Baby Doe?" in *Matters of Life and Death*, p. 233.

4. See Tooley again in "Abortion and Infanticide," pp. 47–49.

5. "Present Sakes and Future Prospects: The Status of Early Abortion," *Philosophy and Public Affairs*, XI, 4 (1982): 322–326.

JUDITH JARVIS THOMSON

A Defense of Abortion[1]

Judith Jarvis Thomson, Professor of Philosophy at the Massachusetts Institute of Technology, works in both ethics and metaphysics. Her book *Realm of Rights* (Harvard) is a comprehensive theory of the subject. Representative publications include "Self-Defense," *Philosophy and Public Affairs*, "On Some Ways in which a Thing Can Be Good," *Social Philosophy and Policy*, and "Physician-Assisted Suicide: Two Moral Arguments," *Ethics*.

Most opposition to abortion relies on the premise that the fetus is a human being, a person, from the moment of conception. The premise is argued for, but, as I think, not well. Take, for example, the most common argument. We are asked to notice that the development of a human being from conception through birth into childhood is continuous; then it is said that to draw a line, to choose a point in this development and say "before this point the thing is not a person, after this point it is a person" is to make an arbitrary choice, a choice for which in the nature of things no good reason can be given. It is concluded that the fetus is, or anyway that we had better say it is, a person from the moment of conception. But this conclusion does not follow. Similar things might be said about the development of an acorn into an oak tree, and it does not follow that acorns are oak trees, or that we had better say they are. Arguments of this form are sometimes called "slippery slope arguments"—the phrase is perhaps self-explanatory—and it is dismaying that opponents of abortion rely on them so heavily and uncritically.

I am inclined to agree, however, that the prospects for "drawing a line" in the development of the fetus look dim. I am inclined to think also that we shall probably have to agree that the fetus has already become a human person well before birth. Indeed, it comes as a surprise when one first learns how early in its life it begins to acquire human characteristics. By

the tenth week, for example, it already has a face, arms and legs, fingers and toes; it has internal organs, and brain activity is detectable.[2] On the other hand, I think that the premise is false, that the fetus is not a person from the moment of conception. A newly fertilized ovum, a newly implanted clump of cells, is no more a person than an acorn is an oak tree. But I shall not discuss any of this. For it seems to me to be of great interest to ask what happens if, for the sake of argument, we allow the premise. How, precisely, are we supposed to get from there to the conclusion that abortion is morally impermissible? Opponents of abortion commonly spend most of their time establishing that the fetus is a person, and hardly any time explaining the step from there to the impermissibility of abortion. Perhaps they think the step too simple and obvious to require much comment. Or perhaps instead they are simply being economical in argument. Many of those who defend abortion rely on the premise that the fetus is not a person, but only a bit of tissue that will become a person at birth; and why pay out more arguments than you have to? Whatever the explanation, I suggest that the step they take is neither easy nor obvious, that it calls for closer examination than it is commonly given, and that when we do give it this closer examination we shall feel inclined to reject it.

I propose, then, that we grant that the fetus is a person from the moment of conception. How does the argument go from here? Something like this, I take it. Every person has a right to life. So the fetus has a right to life. No doubt the mother has a right to decide

From *Philosophy and Public Affairs* 1, no. 1 (1971), 47–66. Copyright © 1971 by Blackwell Publishing. Reprinted with permission.

what shall happen in and to her body; everyone would grant that. But surely a person's right to life is stronger and more stringent than the mother's right to decide what happens in and to her body, and so outweighs it. So the fetus may not be killed; an abortion may not be performed.

It sounds plausible. But now let me ask you to imagine this. You wake up in the morning and find yourself back to back in bed with an unconscious violinist. A famous unconscious violinist. He has been found to have a fatal kidney ailment, and the Society of Music Lovers has canvassed all the available medical records and found that you alone have the right blood type to help. They have therefore kidnapped you, and last night the violinist's circulatory system was plugged into yours, so that your kidneys can be used to extract poisons from his blood as well as your own. The director of the hospital now tells you, "Look, we're sorry the Society of Music Lovers did this to you—we would never have permitted it if we had known. But still, they did it, and the violinist now is plugged into you. To unplug you would be to kill him. But never mind, it's only for nine months. By then he will have recovered from his ailment, and can safely be unplugged from you." Is it morally incumbent on you to accede to this situation? No doubt it would be very nice of you if you did, a great kindness. But do you *have* to accede to it? What if it were not nine months, but nine years? Or longer still? What if the director of the hospital says, "Tough luck, I agree, but you've now got to stay in bed, with the violinist plugged into you, for the rest of your life. Because remember this. All persons have a right to life, and violinists are persons. Granted you have a right to decide what happens in and to your body, but a person's right to life outweighs your right to decide what happens in and to your body. So you cannot ever be unplugged from him." I imagine you would regard this as outrageous, which suggests that something really is wrong with that plausible-sounding argument I mentioned a moment ago.

In this case, of course, you were kidnapped; you didn't volunteer for the operation that plugged the violinist into your kidneys. Can those who oppose abortion on the ground I mentioned make an exception for a pregnancy due to rape? Certainly. They can say that persons have a right to life only if they didn't come into existence because of rape; or they can say

that all persons have a right to life, but that some have less of a right to life than others, in particular, that those who came into existence because of rape have less. But these statements have a rather unpleasant sound. Surely the question of whether you have a right to life at all, or how much of it you have, shouldn't turn on the question of whether or not you are the product of a rape. And in fact the people who oppose abortion on the ground I mentioned do not make this distinction, and hence do not make an exception in case of rape.

Nor do they make an exception for a case in which the mother has to spend the nine months of her pregnancy in bed. They would agree that would be a great pity, and hard on the mother; but all the same, all persons have a right to life, the fetus is a person, and so on. I suspect, in fact, that they would not make an exception for a case in which, miraculously enough, the pregnancy went on for nine years, or even the rest of the mother's life.

Some won't even make an exception for a case in which continuation of the pregnancy is likely to shorten the mother's life; they regard abortion as impermissible even to save the mother's life. Such cases are nowadays very rare, and many opponents of abortion do not accept this extreme view. All the same, it is a good place to begin: a number of points of interest come out in respect to it.

1. Let us call the view that abortion is impermissible even to save the mother's life "the extreme view." I want to suggest first that it does not issue from the argument I mentioned earlier without the addition of some fairly powerful premises. Suppose a woman has become pregnant, and now learns that she has a cardiac condition such that she will die if she carries the baby to term. What may be done for her? The fetus, being a person, has a right to life, but as the mother is a person too, so has she a right to life. Presumably they have an equal right to life. How is it supposed to come out that an abortion may not be performed? If mother and child have an equal right to life, shouldn't we perhaps flip a coin? Or should we add to the mother's right to life her right to decide what happens in and to her body, which everybody seems to be ready to grant—the sum of her rights now outweighing the fetus's right to life?

The most familiar argument here is the following. We are told that performing the abortion would be directly killing[3] the child, whereas doing nothing would not be killing the mother, but only letting her die. Moreover, in killing the child, one would be killing an innocent person, for the child has committed no crime, and is not aiming at his mother's death. And then there are a variety of ways in which this might be continued. (a) But as directly killing an innocent person is always and absolutely impermissible, an abortion may not be performed. Or, (b) as directly killing an innocent person is murder, and murder is always and absolutely impermissible, an abortion may not be performed.[4] Or, (c) as one's duty to refrain from directly killing an innocent person is more stringent than one's duty to keep a person from dying, an abortion may not be performed. Or, (d) if one's only options are directly killing an innocent person or letting a person die, one must prefer letting the person die, and thus an abortion may not be performed.[5]

Some people seem to have thought that these are not further premises which must be added if the conclusion is to be reached, but that they follow from the very fact that an innocent person has a right to life.[6] But this seems to me to be a mistake, and perhaps the simplest way to show this is to bring out that while we must certainly grant that innocent persons have a right to life, the theses in (a) through (d) are all false. Take (b), for example. If directly killing an innocent person is murder, and thus is impermissible, then the mother's directly killing the innocent person inside her is murder, and thus is impermissible. But it cannot seriously be thought to be murder if the mother performs an abortion on herself to save her life. It cannot seriously be said that she *must* refrain, that she *must* sit passively by and wait for her death. Let us look again at the case of you and the violinist. There you are, in bed with the violinist, and the director of the hospital says to you, "It's all most distressing, and I deeply sympathize, but you see this is putting an additional strain on your kidneys, and you'll be dead within the month. But you *have* to stay where you are all the same. Because unplugging you would be directly killing an innocent violinist, and that's murder, and that's impermissible." If anything in the world is true, it is that you do not commit murder, you do not do what is impermissible, if you reach around to your back and unplug yourself from that violinist to save your life.

The main focus of attention in writings on abortion has been on what a third party may or may not do in answer to a request from a woman for an abortion. This is in a way understandable. Things being as they are, there isn't much a woman can safely do to abort herself. So the question asked is what a third party may do, and what the mother may do, if it is mentioned at all, is deduced, almost as an afterthought, from what it is concluded that third parties may do. But it seems to me that to treat the matter in this way is to refuse to grant to the mother that very status of person which is so firmly insisted on for the fetus. For we cannot simply read off what a person may do from what a third party may do. Suppose you find yourself trapped in a tiny house with a growing child. I mean a very tiny house, and a rapidly growing child—you are already up against the wall of the house and in a few minutes you'll be crushed to death. The child on the other hand won't be crushed to death; if nothing is done to stop him from growing he'll be hurt, but in the end he'll simply burst open the house and walk out a free man. Now I could well understand it if a bystander were to say, "There's nothing we can do for you. We cannot choose between your life and his, we cannot be the ones to decide who is to live, we cannot intervene." But it cannot be concluded that you too can do nothing, that you cannot attack it to save your life. However innocent the child may be, you do not have to wait passively while it crushes you to death. Perhaps a pregnant woman is vaguely felt to have the status of house, to which we don't allow the right of self-defense. But if the woman houses the child, it should be remembered that she is a person who houses it.

I should perhaps stop to say explicitly that I am not claiming that people have a right to do anything whatever to save their lives. I think, rather, that there are drastic limits to the right of self-defense. If someone threatens you with death unless you torture someone else to death, I think you have not the right, even to save your life, to do so. But the case under consideration here is very different. In our case there are only two people involved, one whose life is threatened, and one who threatens it. Both are innocent: the one who is threatened is not threatened because of any fault, the one who threatens does not threaten because of any fault. For this reason we may feel that we bystanders cannot intervene. But the person threatened can.

In sum, a woman surely can defend her life against the threat to it posed by the unborn child, even if doing so involves its death. And this shows not merely that the theses in (a) through (d) are false; it shows also that the extreme view of abortion is false, and so we need not canvass any other possible ways of arriving at it from the argument I mentioned at the outset.

2. The extreme view could of course be weakened to say that while abortion is permissible to save the mother's life, it may not be performed by a third party, but only by the mother herself. But this cannot be right either. For what we have to keep in mind is that the mother and the unborn child are not like two tenants in a small house which has, by an unfortunate mistake, been rented to both: the mother *owns* the house. The fact that she does adds to the offensiveness of deducing that the mother can do nothing from the supposition that third parties can do nothing. But it does more than this: it casts a bright light on the supposition that third parties can do nothing. Certainly it lets us see that a third party who says "I cannot choose between you" is fooling himself if he thinks this is impartiality. If Jones has found and fastened on a certain coat, which he needs to keep him from freezing, but which Smith also needs to keep him from freezing, then it is not impartiality that says "I cannot choose between you" when Smith owns the coat. Women have said again and again "This body is *my* body!" and they have reason to feel angry, reason to feel that it has been like shouting into the wind. Smith, after all, is hardly likely to bless us if we say to him, "Of course it's your coat, anybody would grant that it is. But no one may choose between you and Jones who is to have it."

We should really ask what it is that says "no one may choose" in the face of the fact that the body that houses the child is the mother's body. It may be simply a failure to appreciate this fact. But it may be something more interesting, namely, the sense that one has a right to refuse to lay hands on people, even where it would be just and fair to do so, even where justice seems to require that somebody do so. Thus justice might call for somebody to get Smith's coat back from Jones, and yet you have a right to refuse to be the one to lay hands on Jones, a right to refuse to do physical violence to him. This, I think, must be granted. But then what should be said is not "no one may choose," but only "I cannot choose," and indeed not even this, but "*I* will not *act*," leaving it open that somebody else can or should, and in particular that anyone in a position of authority, with the job of securing people's rights, both can and should. So this is no difficulty. I have not been arguing that any given third party must accede to the mother's request that he perform an abortion to save her life, but only that he may.

I suppose that in some views of human life the mother's body is only on loan to her, the loan not being one which gives her any prior claim to it. One who held this view might well think it impartiality to say "I cannot choose." But I shall simply ignore this possibility. My own view is that if a human being has any just, prior claim to anything at all, he has a just, prior claim to his own body. And perhaps this needn't be argued for here anyway, since, as I mentioned, the arguments against abortion we are looking at do grant that the woman has a right to decide what happens in and to her body.

But although they do grant it, I have tried to show that they do not take seriously what is done in granting it. I suggest the same thing will reappear even more clearly when we turn away from cases in which the mother's life is at stake, and attend, as I propose we now do, to the vastly more common cases in which a woman wants an abortion for some less weighty reason than preserving her own life.

3. Where the mother's life is not at stake, the argument I mentioned at the outset seems to have a much stronger pull. "Everyone has a right to life, so the unborn person has a right to life." And isn't the child's right to life weightier than anything other than the mother's own right to life, which she might put forward as ground for an abortion?

This argument treats the right to life as if it were unproblematic. It is not, and this seems to me to be precisely the source of the mistake.

For we should now, at long last, ask what it comes to, to have a right to life. In some views having a right to life includes having a right to be given at least the bare minimum one needs for continued life. But suppose that what in fact *is* the bare minimum a man needs for continued life is something he has no right at all to be given. If I am sick unto death, and the only thing that will save my life is the touch of Henry Fonda's cool hand on my fevered brow, then all the same, I have no right to be given the touch of Henry Fonda's cool hand on my fevered brow. It would be frightfully nice of him to fly in from the West Coast to provide it. It would be less nice, though no doubt well meant, if my friends flew out to the West Coast and carried Henry Fonda back with them. But I have no right at all against anybody that he should do this for me. Or again, to return to the story I told earlier, the fact that for continued life that violinist needs the continued use of your kidneys does not establish that he has a right to be given the continued use of your kidneys. He certainly has no right against you that *you* should give him continued use of your kidneys. For nobody has any right to use your kidneys unless you give him such a right; and nobody has the right against you that you shall give him this right—if you do allow him to go on using your kidneys, this is a kindness on your part, and not something he can claim from you as his due. Nor has he any right against anybody else that they should give him continued use of your kidneys. Certainly he had no right against the Society of Music Lovers that *they* should plug him into you in the first place. And if you now start to unplug yourself, having learned that you will otherwise have to spend nine years in bed with him, there is nobody in the world who must try to prevent you, in order to see to it that he is given something he has a right to be given.

Some people are rather stricter about the right to life. In their view, it does not include the right to be given anything, but amounts to, and only to, the right not to be killed by anybody. But here a related difficulty arises. If everybody is to refrain from killing that violinist, then everybody must refrain from doing a great many different sorts of things. Everybody must refrain from slitting his throat, everybody must refrain from shooting him—and everybody must refrain from unplugging you from him. But does he have a right against everybody that they shall refrain from unplugging you from him? To refrain from doing this is to allow him to continue to use your kidneys. It could be argued that he has a right against us that we should allow him to continue to use your kidneys. That is, while he had no right against us that we should give him the use of your kidneys, it might be argued that he anyway has a right against us that we shall not now intervene and deprive him of the use of your kidneys. I shall come back to third-party interventions later. But certainly the violinist has no right against you that *you* shall allow him to continue to use your kidneys. As I said, if you do allow him to use them, it is a kindness on your part, and not something you owe him.

The difficulty I point to here is not peculiar to the right to life. It reappears in connection with all the other natural rights; and it is something which an adequate account of rights must deal with. For present purposes it is enough just to draw attention to it. But I would stress that I am not arguing that people do not have a right to life—quite to the contrary, it seems to me that the primary control we must place on the acceptability of an account of rights is that it should turn out in that account to be a truth that all persons have a right to life. I am arguing only that having a right to life does not guarantee having either a right to be given the use of or a right to be allowed continued use of another person's body—even if one needs it for life itself. So the right to life will not serve the opponents of abortion in the very simple and clear way in which they seem to have thought it would.

4. There is another way to bring out the difficulty. In the most ordinary sort of case, to deprive someone of what he has a right to is to treat him unjustly. Suppose a boy and his small brother are jointly given a box of chocolates for Christmas. If the older boy takes the box and refuses to give his brother any of the chocolates, he is unjust to him, for the brother has been given a right to half of them. But suppose that, having learned that otherwise it means nine years in bed with that violinist, you unplug yourself from him. You surely are not being unjust to him for you gave him no right to use your kidneys, and no one else can have given him any such right. But we have to notice that in unplugging yourself, you are killing him; and violinists, like everybody else, have a right to life, and thus in the view we were considering just now, the right not to be killed. So here you do what he supposedly has a right you shall not do, but you do not act unjustly to him in doing it.

The emendation which may be made at this point is this: the right to life consists not in the right not to be killed, but rather in the right not to be killed unjustly. This runs a risk of circularity, but never mind: it would enable us to square the fact that the violinist has a right to life with the fact that you do not act unjustly toward him in unplugging yourself, thereby killing him. For if you do not kill him unjustly, you do not violate his right to life, and so it is no wonder you do him no injustice.

But if this emendation is accepted, the gap in the argument against abortion stares us plainly in the face: It is by no means enough to show that the fetus is a person, and to remind us that all persons have a right to life—we need to be shown also that killing the fetus violates its right to life, i.e., that abortion is unjust killing. And is it?

I suppose we may take it as a datum that in a case of pregnancy due to rape the mother has not given the unborn person a right to the use of her body for food and shelter. Indeed, in what pregnancy could it be supposed that the mother has given the unborn person such a right? It is not as if there were unborn persons drifting about the world, to whom a woman who wants a child says "I invite you in."

But it might be argued that there are other ways one can have acquired a right to the use of another person's body than by having been invited to use it by that person. Suppose a woman voluntarily indulges in intercourse, knowing of the chance it will issue in pregnancy, and then she does become pregnant; is she not in part responsible for the presence, in fact the very existence, of the unborn person inside her? No doubt she did not invite it in. But doesn't her partial responsibility for its being there itself give it a right to the use of her body?[7] If so, then her aborting it would be more like the boy's taking away the chocolates, and less like your unplugging yourself from the violinist—doing so would be depriving it of what it does have a right to, and thus would be doing it an injustice.

And then, too, it might be asked whether or not she can kill it even to save her own life: If she voluntarily called it into existence, how can she now kill it, even in self-defense?

The first thing to be said about this is that it is something new. Opponents of abortion have been so concerned to make out the independence of the fetus, in order to establish that it has a right to life, just as its mother does, that they have tended to overlook the possible support they might gain from making out that the fetus is *dependent* on the mother, in order to establish that she has a special kind of responsibility for it, a responsibility that gives it rights against her which are not possessed by any independent person—such as an ailing violinist who is a stranger to her.

On the other hand, this argument would give the unborn person a right to its mother's body only if her pregnancy resulted from a voluntary act, undertaken in full knowledge of the chance a pregnancy might result from it. It would leave out entirely the unborn person whose existence is due to rape. Pending the availability of some further argument, then, we would be left with the conclusion that unborn persons whose existence is due to rape have no right to the use of their mothers' bodies, and thus that aborting them is not depriving them of anything they have a right to and hence is not unjust killing.

And we should also notice that it is not at all plain that this argument really does go even as far as it purports to. For there are cases and cases, and the details make a difference. If the room is stuffy, and I therefore open a window to air it, and a burglar climbs in,

it would be absurd to say, "Ah, now he can stay, she's given him a right to the use of her house—for she is partially responsible for his presence there, having voluntarily done what enabled him to get in, in full knowledge that there are such things as burglars, and that burglars burgle." It would be still more absurd to say this if I had had bars installed outside my windows, precisely to prevent burglars from getting in, and a burglar got in only because of a defect in the bars. It remains equally absurd if we imagine it is not a burglar who climbs in, but an innocent person who blunders or falls in. Again, suppose it were like this: people-seeds drift about in the air like pollen, and if you open your windows, one may drift in and take root in your carpets or upholstery. You don't want children, so you fix up your windows with fine mesh screens, the very best you can buy. As can happen, however, and on very, very rare occasions does happen, one of the screens is defective; and a seed drifts in and takes root. Does the person-plant who now develops have a right to the use of your house? Surely not—despite the fact that you voluntarily opened your windows, you knowingly kept carpets and upholstered furniture, and you knew that screens were sometimes defective. Someone may argue that you are responsible for its rooting, that it does have a right to your house, because after all you *could* have lived out your life with bare floors and furniture, or with sealed windows and doors. But this won't do—for by the same token anyone can avoid a pregnancy due to rape by having a hysterectomy, or anyway by never leaving home without a (reliable!) army.

It seems to me that the argument we were looking at can establish at most that there are *some* cases in which the unborn person has a right to the use of its mother's body, and therefore *some* cases in which abortion is unjust killing. There is room for much discussion and argument as to precisely which, if any. But I think we should sidestep this issue and leave it open, for at any rate the argument certainly does not establish that all abortion is unjust killing.

5. There is room for yet another argument here, however. We surely must all grant that there may be cases in which it would be morally indecent to detach a person from your body at the cost of his life. Suppose you learn that what the violinist needs is not nine years of your life, but only one hour. All you need do to save his life is to spend one hour in that bed with him. Suppose also that letting him use your kidneys for that one hour would not affect your health in the slightest. Admittedly you were kidnapped. Admittedly

you did not give anyone permission to plug him into you. Nevertheless it seems to me plain you *ought* to allow him to use your kidneys for that hour—it would be indecent to refuse.

Again, suppose pregnancy lasted only an hour, and constituted no threat to life or health. And suppose that a woman becomes pregnant as a result of rape. Admittedly she did not voluntarily do anything to bring about the existence of a child. Admittedly she did nothing at all which would give the unborn person a right to the use of her body. All the same it might well be said, as in the newly emended violinist story, that she *ought* to allow it to remain for that hour—that it would be indecent in her to refuse.

Now some people are inclined to use the term "right" in such a way that it follows from the fact that you ought to allow a person to use your body for the hour he needs, that he has a right to use your body for the hour he needs, even though he has not been given that right by any person or act. They may say that it follows also that if you refuse, you act unjustly toward him. This use of the term is perhaps so common that it cannot be called wrong; nevertheless it seems to me to be an unfortunate loosening of what we would do better to keep a tight rein on. Suppose that box of chocolates I mentioned earlier had not been given to both boys jointly, but was given only to the older boy. There he sits, stolidly eating his way through the box, his small brother watching enviously. Here we are likely to say "You ought not to be so mean. You ought to give your brother some of those chocolates." My own view is that it just does not follow from the truth of this that the brother has any right to any of the chocolates. If the boy refuses to give his brother any, he is greedy, stingy, callous—but not unjust. I suppose that the people I have in mind will say it does follow that the brother has a right to some of the chocolates, and thus that the boy does act unjustly if he refuses to give his brother any. But the effect of saying this is to obscure what we should keep distinct, namely the difference between the boy's refusal in this case and the boy's refusal in the earlier case, in which the box was given to both boys jointly, and in which the small brother thus had what was from any point of view clear title to half.

A further objection to so using the term "right" that from the fact that A ought to do a thing for B, it follows that B has a right against A that A do it for him, is that it is going to make the question of whether or not a man has a right to a thing turn on how easy it is to provide him with it; and this seems not merely unfortunate, but morally unacceptable. Take the case

of Henry Fonda again. I said earlier that I had no right to the touch of his cool hand on my fevered brow, even though I needed it to save my life. I said it would be frightfully nice of him to fly in from the West Coast to provide me with it, but that I had no right against him that he should do so. But suppose he isn't on the West Coast. Suppose he has only to walk across the room, place a hand briefly on my brow—and lo, my life is saved. Then surely he ought to do it, it would be indecent to refuse. Is it to be said "Ah well, it follows that in this case she has a right to the touch of his hand on her brow, and so it would be an injustice in him to refuse"? So that I have a right to it when it is easy for him to provide it, though no right when it's hard? It's rather a shocking idea that anyone's right should fade away and disappear as it gets harder and harder to accord them to him.

So my own view is that even though you ought to let the violinist use your kidneys for the one hour he needs, we should not conclude that he has a right to do so—we would say that if you refuse, you are, like the boy who owns all the chocolates and will give none away, self-centered and callous, indecent in fact, but not unjust. And similarly, that even supposing a case in which a woman pregnant due to rape ought to allow the unborn person to use her body for the hour he needs, we should not conclude that he has a right to do so; we should conclude that she is self-centered, callous, indecent, but not unjust, if she refuses. The complaints are no less grave; they are just different. However, there is no need to insist on this point. If anyone does wish to deduce "he has a right" from "you ought," then all the same he must surely grant that there are cases in which it is not morally required of you that you allow that violinist to use your kidneys, and in which he does not have a right to use them, and in which you do not do him an injustice if you refuse. And so also for mother and unborn child. Except in such cases as the unborn person has a right to demand it—and we were leaving open the possibility that there may be such cases—nobody is morally *required* to make large sacrifices, of health, of all other interests and concerns, of all other duties and commitments, for nine years, or even for nine months, in order to keep another person alive.

6. We have in fact to distinguish between two kinds of Samaritan: the Good Samaritan and what we might call the Minimally Decent Samaritan. The story of the Good Samaritan, you will remember, goes like this:

A certain man went down from Jerusalem to Jericho, and fell among thieves, which stripped him of his raiment, and wounded him, and departed, leaving him half dead.

And by chance there came down a certain priest that way; and when he saw him, he passed by on the other side.

And likewise a Levite, when he was at the place, came and looked on him, and passed by on the other side.

But a certain Samaritan, as he journeyed, came where he was; and when he saw him he had compassion on him.

And went to him, and bound up his wounds, pouring in oil and wine, and set him on his own beast, and brought him to an inn, and took care of him.

And on the morrow, when he departed, he took out two pence, and gave them to the host, and said unto him, "Take care of him; and whatsoever thou spendest more, when I come again, I will repay thee."

(Luke 10:30–35)

The Good Samaritan went out of his way, at some cost to himself, to help one in need of it. We are not told what the options were, that is, whether or not the priest and the Levite could have helped by doing less than the Good Samaritan did, but assuming they could have, then the fact they did nothing at all shows they were not even Minimally Decent Samaritans, not because they were not Samaritans, but because they were not even minimally decent.

These things are a matter of degree, of course, but there is a difference, and it comes out perhaps most clearly in the story of Kitty Genovese, who, as you will remember, was murdered while thirty-eight people watched or listened, and did nothing at all to help her. A Good Samaritan would have rushed out to give direct assistance against the murderer. Or perhaps we had better allow that it would have been a Splendid Samaritan who did this, on the ground that it would have involved a risk of death for himself. But the thirty-eight not only did not do this, they did not even trouble to pick up a phone to call the police. Minimally Decent Samaritanism would call for doing at least that, and their not having done it was monstrous.

After telling the story of the Good Samaritan, Jesus said, "Go, and do thou likewise." Perhaps he meant that we are morally required to act as the Good Samaritan did. Perhaps he was urging people to do more than is morally required of them. At all events it seems plain that it was not morally required of any of the thirty-eight that he rush out to give direct assistance at the risk of his own life, and that it is not morally required of anyone that he give long stretches of his life—nine years or nine months—to sustaining the life of a person who has no special right (we were leaving open the possibility of this) to demand it.

Indeed, with one rather striking class of exceptions, no one in any country in the world is *legally* required to do anywhere near as much as this for anyone else. The class of exceptions is obvious. My main concern here is not the state of the law in respect to abortion, but it is worth drawing attention to the fact that in no state in this country is any man compelled by law to be even a Minimally Decent Samaritan to any person; there is no law under which charges could be brought against the thirty-eight who stood by while Kitty Genovese died. By contrast, in most states in this country women are compelled by law to be not merely Minimally Decent Samaritans, but Good Samaritans to unborn persons inside them. This doesn't by itself settle anything one way or the other, because it may well be argued that there should be laws in this country—as there are in many European countries—compelling at least Minimally Decent Samaritanism.[8] But it does show that there is a gross injustice in the existing state of the law. And it shows also that the groups currently working against liberalization of abortion laws, in fact working toward having it declared unconstitutional for a state to permit abortion, had better start working for the adoption of Good Samaritan laws generally, or earn the charge that they are acting in bad faith.

I should think, myself, that Minimally Decent Samaritan laws would be one thing, Good Samaritan laws quite another, and in fact highly improper. But we are not here concerned with the law. What we should ask is not whether anybody should be compelled by law to be a Good Samaritan, but whether we must accede to a situation in which somebody is being compelled—by nature, perhaps—to be a Good Samaritan. We have, in other words, to look now at third-party interventions. I have been arguing that no person is morally required to make large sacrifices to sustain the life of another who has no right to demand them, and this even where the sacrifices do not include life itself; we are not morally required to be Good Samaritans or anyway Very Good Samaritans to one another. But what if a man cannot extricate himself from such a situation? What if he appeals to us to extricate him? It seems to me plain that there are cases in which we can, cases in which a Good Samaritan would extricate him. There you are, you were kidnapped, and nine years in bed with that violinist lie ahead of you. You have your own life to lead. You are sorry, but you simply cannot see giving up so much of your life to the sustaining of his. You cannot extricate yourself, and ask us to do so.

I should have thought that—in light of his having no right to the use of your body—it was obvious that we do not have to accede to your being forced to give up so much. We can do what you ask. There is no injustice to the violinist in our doing so.

7. Following the lead of the opponents of abortion, I have throughout been speaking of the fetus merely as a person, and what I have been asking is whether or not the argument we began with, which proceeds only from the fetus's being a person, really does establish its conclusion. I have argued that it does not.

But of course there are arguments and arguments, and it may be said that I have simply fastened on the wrong one. It may be said that what is important is not merely the fact that the fetus is a person, but that it is a person for whom the woman has a special kind of responsibility issuing from the fact that she is its mother. And it might be argued that all my analogies are therefore irrelevant—for you do not have that special kind of responsibility for that violinist, Henry Fonda does not have that special kind of responsibility for me. And our attention might be drawn to the fact that men and women both *are* compelled by law to provide support for their children.

I have in effect dealt (briefly) with this argument in section 4 above; but a (still briefer) recapitulation now may be in order. Surely we do not have any such "special responsibility" for a person unless we have assumed it, explicitly or implicitly. If a set of parents do not try to prevent pregnancy, do not obtain an abortion, and then at the time of birth of the child do not put it out for adoption, but rather take it home with them, then they have assumed responsibility for it, they have given it rights, and they cannot *now* withdraw support from it at the cost of its life because they now find it difficult to go on providing for it. But if they have taken all reasonable precautions against having a child, they do not simply by virtue of their biological relationship to the child who comes into existence have a special responsibility for it. They may wish to assume responsibility for it, or they may not wish to. And I am suggesting that if assuming responsibility for it would require large sacrifices, then they may refuse. A good Samaritan would not refuse—or anyway, a Splendid Samaritan, if the sacrifices that had to be made were enormous. But then so would a Good Samaritan assume responsibility for that violinist; so would Henry Fonda, if he is a Good Samaritan, fly in from the West Coast and assume responsibility for me.

8. My argument will be found unsatisfactory on two counts by many of those who want to regard abortion as morally permissible. First, while I do argue that abortion is not impermissible, I do not argue that it is always permissible. There may well be cases in which carrying the child to term requires only Minimally Decent Samaritanism of the mother, and this is a standard we must not fall below. I am inclined to think it a merit of my account precisely that it does *not* give a general yes or a general no. It allows for and supports our sense that, for example, a sick and desperately frightened fourteen-year-old schoolgirl, pregnant due to rape, may *of course* choose abortion, and that any law which rules this out is an insane law. And it also allows for and supports our sense that in other cases resort to abortion is even positively indecent. It would be indecent in the woman to request an abortion, and indecent in a doctor to perform it, if she is in her seventh month and wants the abortion just to avoid the nuisance of postponing a trip abroad. The very fact that the arguments I have been drawing attention to treat all cases of abortion, or even all cases of abortion in which the mother's life is not at stake, as morally on a par ought to have made them suspect at the outset.

Secondly, while I am arguing for the permissibility of abortion in some cases, I am not arguing for the right to secure the death of the unborn child. It is easy to confuse these two things in that up to a certain point in the life of the fetus it is not able to survive outside the mother's body; hence removing it from her body guarantees its death. But they are importantly different. I have argued that you are not morally required to spend nine months in bed, sustaining the life of that violinist; but to say this is by no means to say that if, when you unplug yourself, there is a miracle and he survives, you then have a right to turn around and slit his throat. You may detach yourself even if this costs him his life; you have no right to be guaranteed his death, by some other means, if unplugging yourself does not kill him. There are some people who will feel dissatisfied by this feature of my argument. A woman may be utterly devastated by the thought of a child, a bit of herself, put out for adoption and never seen or heard of again. She may therefore want not merely that the child be detached from her, but more, that it die. Some opponents of abortion are inclined to regard this as beneath contempt—thereby showing insensitivity to what is surely a powerful source of despair. All the same, I agree that the desire for the child's death is not one which anybody may gratify, should it turn out to be possible to detach the child alive.

At this place, however, it should be remembered that we have only been pretending throughout that the fetus is a human being from the moment of conception. A very early abortion is surely not the killing of a person, and so is not dealt with by anything I have said here.

NOTES

1. I am very much indebted to James Thomson for discussion, criticism, and many helpful suggestions.

2. Daniel Callahan, *Abortion: Law, Choice and Morality* (New York, 1970), p. 373. This book gives a fascinating survey of the available information on abortion. The Jewish tradition is surveyed in David M. Feldman, *Birth Control in Jewish Law* (New York, 1968), Part 5; the Catholic tradition in John T. Noonan, Jr., "An Almost Absolute Value in History," in *The Morality of Abortion*, ed. John T. Noonan, Jr. (Cambridge, Mass., 1970).

3. The term "direct" in the arguments I refer to is a technical one. Roughly, what is meant by "direct killing" is either killing as an end in itself, or killing as a means to some end, for example, the end of saving someone else's life. See note 6, below, for an example of its use.

4. Cf. *Encyclical Letter of Pope Pius XI on Christian Marriage*, St. Paul Editions (Boston, n.d.), p. 32: "however much we may pity the mother whose health and even life is gravely imperiled in the performance of the duty allotted to her by nature, nevertheless what could ever be a sufficient reason for excusing in any way the direct murder of the innocent? This is precisely what we are dealing with here." Noonan (*The Morality of Abortion*, p. 43) reads this as follows: "What cause can ever avail to excuse in any way the direct killing of the innocent? For it is a question of that."

5. The thesis in (d) is in an interesting way weaker than those in (a), (b), and they rule out abortion even in cases in which both mother and child will die if the abortion is not performed. By contrast, one who held the view expressed in (d) could consistently say that one needn't prefer letting two persons die to killing one.

6. Cf. the following passage from Pius XII, *Address to the Italian Catholic Society of Midwives*: "The baby in the maternal breast has the right to life immediately from God.—Hence there is no man, no human authority, no science, no medical eugenic, social, economic or moral 'indication' which can establish or grant a valid juridical ground for a direct deliberate disposition of an innocent human life, that is a disposition which looks to its destruction either as an end or as a means to another end perhaps in itself not illicit.—The baby, still not born, is a man in the same degree and for the same reason as the mother" (quoted in Noonan, *The Morality of Abortion*, p. 45).

7. The need for a discussion of this argument was brought home to me by members of the Society for Ethical and Legal Philosophy, to whom this paper was originally presented.

8. For a discussion of the difficulties involved, and a survey of the European experience with such laws, see *The Good Samaritan and the Law*, ed. James M. Ratcliffe (New York, 1966).

BARUCH BRODY

The Morality of Abortion

Baruch Brody is Leon Jaworski Professor of Biomedical Ethics, director of the Center for Medical Ethics and Health Policy at the Baylor College of Medicine, Andrew Mellow Professor of Humanities in the Department of Philosophy at Rice University, and director of the Ethics Program at Methodist Hospital. Brody is a prolific writer in many areas of bioethics. Representative works include *Abortion and the Sanctity of Human Life* (MIT), *Life and Death Decision-Making* (Oxford), and *Taking Issue: Pluralism and Casuistry in Bioethics* (Georgetown).

THE WOMAN'S RIGHT TO HER BODY

It is a common claim that a woman ought to be in control of what happens to her body to the greatest extent possible, that she ought to be able to use her

From *Abortion and the Sanctity of Human Life: A Philosophical View* (Cambridge, MA: MIT Press, 1975), pp. 26–30, 37–39, and "Fetal Humanity and the Theory of Essentialism," in *Philosophy and Sex*, Robert Baker and Frederick Elliston, eds. (Buffalo, NY: Prometheus Books, 1975), pp. 348–352. (Some parts of these essays were later revised by Professor Brody.)

body in ways that she wants to and refrain from using it in ways that she does not want to. This right is particularly pressed where certain uses of her body have deep and lasting effects upon the character of her life, personal, social, and economic. Therefore, it is argued, a woman should be free either to carry her fetus to term, thereby using her body to support it, or to abort the fetus, thereby not using her body for that purpose.

In some contexts in which this argument is advanced, it is clear that it is not addressed to the issue of the morality of abortion at all. Rather, it is made in opposition to laws against abortion on the ground that the choice to abort or not is a moral decision that should belong only to the mother. But that specific direction of the argument is irrelevant to our present purposes; I will consider it [later] when I deal with the issues raised by laws prohibiting abortions. For the moment, I am concerned solely with the use of this principle as a putative ground tending to show the permissibility of abortion, with the claim that because it is the woman's body that carries the fetus and upon which the fetus depends, she has certain rights to abort the fetus that no one else may have.

We may begin by remarking that it is obviously correct that, as carrier of the fetus, the mother has it within her power to choose whether or not to abort the fetus. And, as an autonomous and responsible agent, she must make this choice. But let us notice that this in no way entails either that whatever choice she makes is morally right or that no one else has the right to evaluate the decision that she makes.

• • •

At first glance, it would seem that this argument cannot be used by anyone who supposes, as we do for the moment, that there is a point in fetal development from which time on the fetus is a human being. After all, people do not have the right to do anything whatsoever that may be necessary for them to retain control over the uses of their bodies. In particular, it would seem wrong for them to kill another human being in order to do so.

In a recent article,[1] Professor Judith Thomson has, in effect, argued that this simple view is mistaken. How does Professor Thomson defend her claim that the mother has a right to abort the fetus, even if it is a human being, whether or not her life is threatened and whether or not she has consented to the act of intercourse in which the fetus is conceived? At one point,[2] discussing just the case in which the mother's life is threatened, she makes the following suggestion:

In [abortion], there are only two people involved, one whose life is threatened and one who threatens it. Both are innocent: the one who is threatened is not threatened because of any fault, the one who threatens does not threaten because of any fault. For this reason, we may feel that we bystanders cannot intervene. But the person threatened can.

But surely this description is equally applicable to the following case: A and B are adrift on a lifeboat, B has

a disease that he can survive, but A, if he contracts it, will die, and the only way that A can avoid that is by killing B and pushing him overboard. Surely, A has no right to do this. So there must be some special reason why the mother has, if she does, the right to abort the fetus.

There is, to be sure, an important difference between our lifeboat case and abortion, one that leads us to the heart of Professor Thomson's argument. In the case that we envisaged, both A and B have equal rights to be in the lifeboat, but the mother's body is hers and not the fetus's and she has first rights to its use. The primacy of these rights allows an abortion whether or not her life is threatened. Professor Thomson summarizes this argument in the following way:[3]

I am arguing only that having a right to life does not guarantee having either a right to be given the use of, or a right to be allowed continued use of, another person's body—even if one needs it for life itself.

One part of this claim is clearly correct. I have no duty to X to save X's life by giving him the use of my body (or my life savings, or the only home I have, and so on), and X has no right, even to save his life, to any of those things. Thus, the fetus conceived in the laboratory that will perish unless it is implanted into a woman's body has in fact no right to any woman's body. But this portion of the claim is irrelevant to the abortion issue, for in abortion of the fetus that is a human being the mother must kill X to get back the sole use of her body, and that is an entirely different matter.

This point can also be put as follows: . . . we must distinguish the taking of X's life from the saving of X's life, even if we assume that one has a duty not to do the former and to do the latter. Now that latter duty, if it exists at all, is much weaker than the first duty; many circumstances may relieve us from the latter duty that will not relieve us from the former one. Thus, I am certainly relieved from my duty to save X's life by the fact that fulfilling it means the loss of my life savings. It may be noble for me to save X's life at the cost of everything I have, but I certainly have no duty to do that. And the same observation may be made about cases in which I can save X's life by giving him the use of my body for an extended period of time. However, I am not relieved of my duty not to take X's life by the fact that fulfilling it means the loss of everything I have and not even by the fact that fulfilling it means the loss of my life. . . .

At one point in her paper, Professor Thomson does consider this objection. She has previously imagined the following case: a famous violinist, who is dying from a kidney ailment, has been, without your consent, plugged into you for a period of time so that his body can use your kidneys:

Some people are rather stricter about the right to life. In their view, it does not include the right to be given anything, but amounts to, and only to, the right not to be killed by anybody. But here a related difficulty arises. If everybody is to refrain from killing that violinist, then everybody must refrain from doing a great many different sorts of things . . . everybody must refrain from unplugging you from him. But does he have a right against everybody that they shall refrain from unplugging you from him? To refrain from doing this is to allow him to continue to use your kidneys . . . certainly the violinist has no right against you that you shall allow him to continue to use your kidneys.

Applying this argument to the case of abortion, we can see that Professor Thomson's argument would run as follows:

a. Assume that the fetus's right to life includes the right not to be killed by the woman carrying him.
b. But to refrain from killing the fetus is to allow him the continued use of the woman's body.
c. So our first assumption entails that the fetus's right to life includes the right to the continued use of the woman's body.
d. But we all grant that the fetus does not have the right to the continued use of the woman's body.
e. Therefore, the fetus's right to life cannot include the right not to be killed by the woman in question.

And it is also now clear what is wrong with this argument. When we granted that the fetus has no right to the continued use of the woman's body, all that we meant was that he does not have this right merely because the continued use saves his life. But, of course, there may be other reasons why he has this right. One would be that the only way to take the use of the woman's body away from the fetus is by killing him, and that is something that neither she nor we have the right to do. So, I submit, the way in which Assumption d is true is irrelevant, and cannot be used by Professor Thomson, for Assumption d is true only in cases where the saving of the life of the fetus is at stake and not in cases where the taking of his life is at stake.

I conclude therefore that Professor Thomson has not established the truth of her claims about abortion, primarily because she has not sufficiently attended to the distinction between our duty to save X's life and our duty not to take it. Once one attends to that distinction, it would seem that the mother, in order to regain control over her body, has no right to abort the fetus from the point at which it becomes a human being.

It may also be useful to say a few words about the larger and less rigorous context of the argument that the woman has a right to her own body. It is surely true that one way in which women have been oppressed is by their being denied authority over their own bodies. But it seems to me that, as the struggle is carried on for meaningful amelioration of such oppression, it ought not to be carried so far that it violates the steady responsibilities all people have to one another. Parents may not desert their children, one class may not oppress another, one race or nation may not exploit another. For parents, powerful groups in society, races or nations in ascendancy, there are penalties for refraining from these wrong actions, but those penalties can in no way be taken as the justification for such wrong actions. Similarly, if the fetus is a human being, the penalty of carrying it cannot, I believe, be used as the justification for destroying it.

•   •   •

THE MODEL PENAL CODE CASES

All of the arguments that we have looked at so far are attempts to show that there is something special about abortion that justifies its being treated differently from other cases of the taking of human life. We shall now consider claims that are confined to certain special cases of abortion: the case in which the mother has been raped, the case in which bearing the child would be harmful to her health, and the case in which having the child may cause a problem for the rest of her family (the latter case is a particular case of the societal argument). In addressing these issues, we shall see whether there is any point to the permissibility of abortions in some of the cases covered by the Model Penal Code[4] proposals.

When the expectant mother has conceived after being raped, there are two different sorts of considerations that might support the claim that she has the right to take the life of the fetus. They are the following: (A) the woman in question has already suffered immensely from the act of rape and the physical and/or psychological aftereffects of that act. It would be particularly unjust, the argument runs, for her to have to live through an unwanted pregnancy owing to that act of rape. Therefore, even if we are at a stage at which the fetus is a human being, the mother has the right to abort it; (B) the fetus in question has no right to be in that woman. It was put there as a result of an act of aggression upon her by the rapist, and its continued presence is an act of aggression against the mother. She has a right to repel that aggression by aborting the fetus.

The first argument is very compelling. We can all agree that a terrible injustice has been committed on the woman who is raped. The question that we have to consider, however, is whether it follows that it is morally permissible for her to abort the fetus. We must make that consideration reflecting that, however unjust the act of rape, it was not the fetus who committed or commissioned it. The injustice of the act, then, should in no way impinge upon the rights of the fetus, for it is innocent. What remains is the initial misfortune of the mother (and the injustice of her having to pass through the pregnancy, and, further, to assume responsibility of at least giving the child over for adoption or assuming the burden of its care). However unfortunate that circumstance, however unjust, the misfortune and the injustice are not sufficient cause to justify the taking of the life of an innocent human being as a means of mitigation.

It is at this point that Argument B comes in, for its whole point is that the fetus, by its mere presence in the mother, is committing an act of aggression against her, one over and above the one committed by the rapist, and one that the mother has a right to repel by abortion. But . . . (1) the fetus is certainly innocent (in the sense of not responsible) for any act of aggression against the mother and . . . (2) the mere presence of the fetus in the mother, no matter how unfortunate for her, does not constitute an act of aggression by the fetus against the mother. Argument B fails then at just that point at which Argument A needs its support, and we can therefore conclude that the fact that pregnancy is the result of rape does not give the mother the right to abort the fetus.

We turn next to the case in which the continued existence of the fetus would threaten the mental and/or physical health but not necessarily the life of the mother. Again, . . . the fact that the fetus's continued existence poses a threat to the life of the mother does not justify her aborting it.[*] It would seem to be true, a fortiori, that the fact that the fetus's continued existence poses a threat to the mental and/or physical health of the mother does not justify her aborting it either.

We come finally to those cases in which the continuation of the pregnancy would cause serious problems for the rest of the family. There are a variety of cases that we have to consider here together. Perhaps the health of the mother will be affected in such a way that she cannot function effectively as a wife and mother during, or even after, the pregnancy. Or perhaps the expenses incurred as a result of the pregnancy would be utterly beyond the financial resources of the family. The important point is that the continuation of the pregnancy raises a serious problem for other innocent people involved besides the mother and the fetus, and it may be argued that the mother has the right to abort the fetus to avoid that problem.

By now, the difficulties with this argument should be apparent. We have seen earlier that the mere fact that the continued existence of the fetus threatens to harm the mother does not, by itself, justify the aborting of the fetus. Why should anything be changed by the fact that the threatened harm will accrue to the other members of the family and not to the mother? Of course, it would be different if the fetus were committing an act of aggression against the other members of the family. But, once more, this is certainly not the case.

Editor's note: Professor Brody provided a lengthy argument to this effect in a chapter not here excerpted. His summary of that argument is as follows: "Is it permissible, as an act of killing a pursuer, to abort the fetus in order to save the mother? The first thing that we should note is that Pope Pius's objection to aborting the fetus as a permissible act of killing a pursuer is mistaken. His objection is that the fetus shows no knowledge or intention in his attempt to take the life of the mother, that the fetus is, in a word, innocent. But that only means that the condition of guilt is not satisfied, and we have seen that its satisfaction is not necessary."

"Is, then, the aborting of the fetus, when necessary to save the life of the mother, a permissible act of killing a pursuer? It is true that in such cases the fetus is a danger to the mother. But it is also clear that the condition of attempt is not satisfied. The fetus has neither the beliefs nor the intention to which we have referred. Furthermore, there is on the part of the fetus no action that threatens the life of the mother. So not even the condition of action is satisfied. It seems to follow, therefore, that aborting the fetus could not be a permissible act of killing a pursuer."

We conclude, therefore, that none of these special circumstances justifies an abortion from that point at which the fetus is a human being.

• • •

FETAL HUMANITY AND BRAIN FUNCTION

The question which we must now consider is the question of fetal humanity. Some have argued that the fetus is a human being with a right to life (or, for convenience, just a human being) from the moment of conception. Others have argued that the fetus only becomes a human being at the moment of birth. Many positions in between these two extremes have also been suggested. How are we to decide which is correct?

The analysis which we will propose here rests upon certain metaphysical assumptions which I have defended elsewhere. These assumptions are: (a) the question is when has the fetus acquired all the properties essential (necessary) for being a human being, for when it has, it is a human being; (b) these properties are such that the loss of any one of them means that the human being in question has gone out of existence and not merely stopped being a human being; (c) human beings go out of existence when they die. It follows from these assumptions that the fetus becomes a human being when it acquires all those characteristics which are such that the loss of any one of them would result in the fetus's being dead. We must, therefore, turn to the analysis of death.

• • •

We will first consider the question of what properties are essential to being human if we suppose that death and the passing out of existence occur only if there has been an irreparable cessation of brain function (keeping in mind that that condition itself, as we have noted, is a matter of medical judgment). We shall then consider the same question on the supposition that [Paul] Ramsey's more complicated theory of death (the modified traditional view) is correct.

According to what is called the brain-death theory, as long as there has not been an irreparable cessation of brain function the person in question continues to exist, no matter what else has happened to him. If so, it seems to follow that there is only one property—leaving aside those entailed by this one property—that is essential to humanity, namely, the possession of a brain that has not suffered an irreparable cessation of function.

Several consequences follow immediately from this conclusion. We can see that a variety of often advanced claims about the essence of humanity are false. For example, the claim that movement, or perhaps just the ability to move, is essential for being human is false. A human being who has stopped moving, and even one who has lost the ability to move, has not therefore stopped existing. Being able to move, and a fortiori moving, are not essential properties of human beings and therefore are not essential to being human. Similarly, the claim that being perceivable by other human beings is essential for being human is also false. A human being who has stopped being perceivable by other humans (for example, someone isolated on the other side of the moon, out of reach even of radio communication) has not stopped existing. Being perceivable by other human beings is not an essential property of human beings and is not essential to being human. And the same point can be made about the claims that viability is essential for being human, that independent existence is essential for being human, and that actual interaction with other human beings is essential for being human. The loss of any of these properties would not mean that the human being in question had gone out of existence, so none of them can be essential to that human being and none of them can be essential for being human.

Let us now look at the following argument: (1) A functioning brain (or at least, a brain that, if not functioning, is susceptible of function) is a property that every human being must have because it is essential for being human. (2) By the time an entity acquires that property, it has all the other properties that are essential for being human. Therefore, when the fetus acquires that property it becomes a human being. It is clear that the property in question is, according to the brain-death theory, one that is had essentially by all human beings. The question that we have to consider is whether the second premise is true. It might appear that its truth does follow from the brain-death theory. After all, we did see that the theory entails that only one property (together with those entailed by it) is essential for being human. Nevertheless, rather than relying solely on my earlier argument, I shall adopt an alternative approach to strengthen the conviction that this second premise is true: I shall note the important ways in which the fetus resembles and differs from an ordinary human being by the time it definitely has a functioning brain (about the end of the sixth week of development). It shall then be evident, in light of our theory of essentialism, that none of these differences involves the lack of some property in the fetus that is essential for its being human.

Structurally, there are few features of the human being that are not fully present by the end of the sixth week. Not only are the familiar external features and all the internal organs present, but the contours of the body are nicely rounded. More important, the body is functioning. Not only is the brain functioning, but the heart is beating sturdily (the fetus by this time has its own completely developed vascular system), the stomach is producing digestive juices, the liver is manufacturing blood cells, the kidney is extracting uric acid from the blood, and the nerves and muscles are operating in concert, so that reflex reactions can begin.

What are the properties that a fetus acquires after the sixth week of its development? Certain structures do appear later. These include the fingernails (which appear in the third month), the completed vocal chords (which also appear then), taste buds and salivary glands (again, in the third month), and hair and eyelashes (in the fifth month). In addition, certain functions begin later than the sixth week. The fetus begins to urinate (in the third month), to move spontaneously (in the third month), to respond to external stimuli (at least in the fifth month), and to breathe (in the sixth month). Moreover, there is a constant growth in size. And finally, at the time of birth the fetus ceases to receive its oxygen and food through the placenta and starts receiving them through the mouth and nose.

I will not examine each of these properties (structures and functions) to show that they are not essential for being human. The procedure would be essentially the one used previously to show that various essentialist claims are in error. We might, therefore, conclude, on the supposition that the brain-death theory is correct, that the fetus becomes a human being about the end of the sixth week after its development.

There is, however, one complication that should be noted here. There are, after all, progressive stages in the physical development and in the functioning of the brain. For example, the fetal brain (and nervous system) does not develop sufficiently to support spontaneous motion until some time in the third month after conception. There is, of course, no doubt that that stage of development is sufficient for the fetus to be human. No one would be likely to maintain that a spontaneously moving human being has died; and similarly, a spontaneously moving fetus would seem to have become human. One might, however, want to claim that the fetus does not become a human being until the point of spontaneous movement. So then, on the supposition that the brain-death theory of death is correct, one ought to conclude that the fetus becomes a human being at some time between the sixth and twelfth week after its conception.

But what if we reject the brain-death theory, and replace it with its equally plausible contender, Ramsey's theory of death? According to that theory—which we can call the brain, heart, and lung theory of death—the human being does not die, does not go out of existence, until such time as the brain, heart, and lungs have irreparably ceased functioning naturally. What are the essential features of being human according to this theory?

Actually, the adoption of Ramsey's theory requires no major modifications. According to that theory, what is essential to being human, what each human being must retain if he is to continue to exist, is the possession of a functioning (actually or potentially) heart, lung, or brain. It is only when a human being possesses none of these that he dies and goes out of existence; and the fetus comes into humanity, so to speak, when he acquires one of these.

On Ramsey's theory, the argument would now run as follows: (1) The property of having a functioning brain, heart, or lungs (or at least organs of the kind that, if not functioning, are susceptible of function) is one that every human being must have because it is essential for being human. (2) By the time that an entity acquires that property it has all the other properties that are essential for being human. Therefore, when the fetus acquires that property it becomes a human being. There remains, once more, the problem of the second premise. Since the fetal heart starts operating rather early, it is not clear that the second premise is correct. Many systems are not yet operating, and many structures are not yet present. Still, following our theory of essentialism, we should conclude that the fetus becomes a human being when it acquires a functioning heart (the first of the organs to function in the fetus).

There is, however, a further complication here, and it is analogous to the one encountered if we adopt the brain-death theory: When may we properly say that the fetal heart begins to function? At two weeks, when occasional contractions of the primitive fetal heart are present? In the fourth to fifth week, when the heart, although incomplete, is beating regularly and pumping blood cells through a closed vascular system, and when the tracings obtained by an ECG exhibit the classical elements of an adult tracing? Or after the end of the seventh week, when the fetal heart is functionally complete and "normal"?

We have not reached a precise conclusion in our study of the question of when the fetus becomes a human being. We do know that it does so some time between the end of the second week and the end of the third month. But it surely is not a human being at the moment of conception and it surely is one by the end of the third month. Though we have not come to a final answer to our question, we have narrowed the range of acceptable answers considerably.

[In summary] we have argued that the fetus becomes a human being with a right to life some time between the second and twelfth week after conception. We have also argued that abortions are morally impermissible after that point except in rather unusual circumstances. What is crucial to note is that neither of these arguments appeal to any theological considerations. We conclude, therefore, that there is a human-rights basis for moral opposition to abortions.

NOTES

1. J. Thomson, "A Defense of Abortion," *Philosophy and Public Affairs*, Vol. 1 (1971), pp. 47–66.

2. Ibid., p. 53.

3. Ibid., p. 56.

4. On the Model Penal Code provisions, see American Law Institute, *Model Penal Code:* Tentative Draft No. 9 (1959).

MARY ANNE WARREN

On the Moral and Legal Status of Abortion

Mary Anne Warren was professor of philosophy at San Francisco State University. She has written on many topics concerning abortion and feminism. Representative publications include "The Abortion Struggle in America," *Bioethics, Moral Status: Obligations to Persons and Other Living Things* (Oxford), *Gendercide: The Implications of Sex Selection* (Rowman & Littlefield), and *The Nature of Woman: An Encyclopedia & Guide to the Literature* (Edgepress).

I will argue that, while it is not possible to produce a satisfactory defense of a woman's right to obtain an abortion without showing that a fetus is not a human being, in the morally relevant sense of that term, we ought not to conclude that the difficulties involved in determining whether or not a fetus is human make it impossible to produce any satisfactory solution to the problem of the moral status of abortion. For it is possible to show that, on the basis of intuitions which we may expect even the opponents of abortion to share, a fetus is not a person, and hence not the sort of entity to which it is proper to ascribe full moral rights.

From *The Monist* 57, no. 1 (January 1973), pp 43–61. Copyright © 1973, *The Monist: An International Quarterly Journal of General Philosophical Inquiry,* Peru, Illinois, USA 61354. Reprinted by permission.

In Section I, we will consider whether or not it is possible to establish that abortion is morally permissible even on the assumption that a fetus is an entity with a full-fledged right to life. I will argue that in fact this cannot be established, at least not with the conclusiveness which is essential to our hopes of convincing those who are skeptical about the morality of abortion, and that we therefore cannot avoid dealing with the question of whether or not a fetus really does have the same right to life as a (more fully developed) human being.

In Section II, I will propose an answer to this question, namely, that a fetus cannot be considered a member of the moral community, the set of beings with full and equal moral rights, for the simple reason that it is not a person, and that it is personhood, and not genetic humanity, i.e., humanity as defined by Noonan, which is the basis for membership in this community. I will argue that a fetus, whatever its stage of development, satisfies none of the basic criteria of personhood, and is not even enough *like* a person to be accorded even some of the same rights on the basis of this resemblance. Nor, as we will see, is a fetus's *potential* personhood a threat to the morality of abortion, since, whatever the rights of potential people may be, they are invariably overridden in any conflict with the moral rights of actual people.

I

We turn now to Professor [Judith] Thomson's case for the claim that even if a fetus has full moral rights, abortion is still morally permissible, at least sometimes, and for some reasons other than to save the woman's life.[1] Her argument is based upon a clever, but I think faulty, analogy. She asks us to picture ourselves waking up one day, in bed with a famous violinist. Imagine that you have been kidnapped, and your bloodstream hooked up to that of the violinist, who happens to have an ailment which will certainly kill him unless he is permitted to share your kidneys for a period of nine months. No one else can save him, since you alone have the right type of blood. He will be unconscious all that time, and you will have to stay in bed with him, but after the nine months are over he may be unplugged, completely cured, that is, provided that you have cooperated.

Now then, she continues, what are your obligations in this situation? The antiabortionist, if he is consistent, will have to say that you are obligated to stay in bed with the violinist: for all people have a right to life, and violinists are people, and therefore it would be murder for you to disconnect yourself from him and let him die (p. 49). But this is outrageous, and so there must be something wrong with the same argument when it is applied to abortion. It would certainly be commendable of you to agree to save the violinist, but it is absurd to suggest that your refusal to do so would be murder. His right to life does not obligate you to do whatever is required to keep him alive; nor does it justify anyone else in forcing you to do so. A law which required you to stay in bed with the violinist would clearly be an unjust law, since it is no proper function of the law to force unwilling people to make huge sacrifices for the sake of other people toward whom they have no such prior obligation.

Thomson concludes that, if this analogy is an apt one, then we can grant the antiabortionist his claim that a fetus is a human being, and still hold that it is at least sometimes the case that a pregnant woman has the right to refuse to be a Good Samaritan towards the fetus, i.e., to obtain an abortion. For there is a great gap between the claim that *x* has a right to life, and the claim that *y* is obligated to do whatever is necessary to keep *x* alive, let alone that he ought to be forced to do so. It is *y*'s duty to keep *x* alive only if he has somehow contracted a *special* obligation to do so; and a woman who is unwillingly pregnant, e.g., who was raped, has done nothing which obligates her to make the enormous sacrifice which is necessary to preserve the conceptus.

This argument is initially quite plausible, and in the extreme case of pregnancy due to rape it is probably conclusive. Difficulties arise, however, when we try to specify more exactly the range of cases in which abortion is clearly justifiable even on the assumption that the fetus is human. Professor Thomson considers it a virtue of her argument that it does not enable us to conclude that abortion is *always* permissible. It would, she says, be "indecent" for a woman in her seventh month to obtain an abortion just to avoid having to postpone a trip to Europe. On the other hand, her argument enables us to see that "a sick and desperately frightened schoolgirl pregnant due to rape may *of course* choose abortion, and that any law which rules this out is an insane law" (p. 65). So far, so good; but what are we to say about the woman who becomes pregnant not through rape but as a result of her own carelessness, or because of contraceptive failure, or who gets pregnant intentionally and then changes her mind about wanting a child? With respect to such cases, the violinist analogy is of much less use to the defender of the woman's right to obtain an abortion.

Indeed, the choice of a pregnancy due to rape, as an example of a case in which abortion is permissible even if a fetus is considered a human being, is extremely significant; for it is only in the case of pregnancy due to rape that the woman's situation is adequately analogous to the violinist case for our intuitions about the latter to transfer convincingly. The crucial difference between a pregnancy due to rape and the *normal* case of an unwanted pregnancy is that in the normal case we cannot claim that the woman is in no way responsible for her predicament; she could have remained chaste, or taken her pills more faithfully, or abstained on dangerous days, and so on. If, on the other hand, you are kidnapped by strangers, and hooked up to a strange violinist, then you are free of any shred of responsibility for the situation, on the basis of which it would be argued that you are obligated to keep the violinist alive. Only when her pregnancy is due to rape is a woman clearly just as non-responsible.[2]

Consequently, there is room for the antiabortionist to argue that in the normal case of unwanted pregnancy a woman has, by her own actions, assumed responsibility for the fetus. For if x behaves in a way which he could have avoided, and which he knows involves, let us say, a 1 percent chance of bringing into existence a human being, with a right to life, and does so knowing that if this should happen then that human being will perish unless x does certain things to keep him alive, then it is by no means clear that when it does happen x is free of any obligation to what he knew in advance would be required to keep that human being alive.

The plausibility of such an argument is enough to show that the Thomson analogy can provide a clear and persuasive defense of a woman's right to obtain an abortion only with respect to those cases in which the woman is in no way responsible for her pregnancy, e.g., where it is due to rape. In all other cases, we would almost certainly conclude that it was necessary to look carefully at the particular circumstances in order to determine the extent of the woman's responsibility, and hence the extent of her obligation. This is an extremely unsatisfactory outcome, from the viewpoint of the opponents of restrictive abortion laws, most of whom are convinced that a woman has a right to obtain an abortion regardless of how and why she got pregnant.

Of course a supporter of the violinist analogy might point out that it is absurd to suggest that forgetting her pill one day might be sufficient to obligate a woman to complete an unwanted pregnancy. And indeed it *is* absurd to suggest this. As we shall see, the moral right to obtain an abortion is not in the least dependent upon the extent to which the woman is responsible for her pregnancy. But unfortunately, once we allow the assumption that a fetus has full moral rights, we cannot avoid taking this absurd suggestion seriously. Perhaps we can make this point more clear by altering the violinist story just enough to make it more analogous to a normal unwanted pregnancy and less to a pregnancy due to rape, and then seeing whether it is still obvi-

ous that you are not obligated to stay in bed with the fellow.

Suppose, then, that violinists are peculiarly prone to the sort of illness the only cure for which is the use of someone else's bloodstream for nine months, and that because of this there has been formed a society of music lovers who agree that whenever a violinist is stricken they will draw lots and the loser will, by some means, be made the one and only person capable of saving him. Now then, would you be obligated to cooperate in curing the violinist if you had voluntarily joined this society, knowing the possible consequences, and then your name had been drawn and you had been kidnapped? Admittedly, you did not promise ahead of time that you would, but you did deliberately place yourself in a position in which it might happen that a human life would be lost if you did not. Surely this is at least a prima facie reason for supposing that you have an obligation to stay in bed with the violinist. Suppose that you had gotten your name drawn deliberately; surely *that* would be quite a strong reason for thinking that you had such an obligation.

It might be suggested that there is one important disanalogy between the modified violinist case and the case of an unwanted pregnancy, which makes the woman's responsibility significantly less, namely, the fact that the fetus *comes into existence* as the result of the woman's actions. This fact might give her a right to refuse to keep it alive, whereas she would not have had this right had it existed previously, independently, and then as a result of her actions become dependent upon her for its survival.

My own intuition, however, is that x has no more right to bring into existence, either deliberately or as a foreseeable result of actions he could have avoided, a being with full moral rights (y), and then refuse to do what he knew beforehand would be required to keep that being alive, than he has to enter into an agreement with an existing person, whereby he may be called upon to save that person's life, and then refuse to do so when so called upon. Thus, x's responsibility for y's existence does not seem to lessen his obligation to keep y alive, if he is also responsible for y's being in a situation in which only he can save him.

Whether or not this intuition is entirely correct, it brings us back once again to the conclusion that once we allow the assumption that a fetus has full moral rights it becomes an extremely complex and difficult question whether and when abortion is justifiable. Thus the Thomson analogy cannot help us produce a clear and persuasive proof of the moral permissibility of abortion. Nor will the opponents of the restrictive laws thank us for anything less; for their conviction (for the most part) is that abortion is obviously *not* a morally serious and extremely unfortunate, even though sometimes justified act, comparable to killing in self-defense or to letting the violinist die, but rather is closer to being a morally neutral act, like cutting one's hair.

The basis of this conviction, I believe, is the realization that a fetus is not a person, and thus does not have a full-fledged right to life. Perhaps the reason why this claim has been so inadequately defended is that it seems self-evident to those who accept it. And so it is, insofar as it follows from what I take to be perfectly obvious claims about the nature of personhood, and about the proper grounds for ascribing moral rights, claims which ought, indeed, to be obvious to both the friends and foes of abortion. Nevertheless, it is worth examining these claims, and showing how they demonstrate the moral innocuousness of abortion, since this apparently has not been adequately done before.

II

The question which we must answer in order to produce a satisfactory solution to the problem of the moral status of abortion is this: How are we to define the moral community, the set of beings with full and equal moral rights, such that we can decide whether a human fetus is a member of this community or not? What sort of entity, exactly, has the inalienable rights to life, liberty, and the pursuit of happiness? Jefferson attributed these rights to all *men*, and it may or may not be fair to suggest that he intended to attribute them *only* to men. Perhaps he ought to have attributed them to all human beings. If so, then we arrive, first, at Noonan's problem of defining what makes a being human, and second, at the equally vital question which Noonan does not consider, namely, What reason is there for identifying the moral community with the set of all human beings, in whatever way we have chosen to define that term?

ON THE DEFINITION OF "HUMAN"

One reason why this vital second question is so frequently overlooked in the debate over the moral status of abortion is that the term "human" has two distinct, but not often distinguished, senses. This fact results in a slide of meaning, which serves to conceal the fallaciousness of the traditional argument that since (1) it is wrong to kill innocent human beings, and (2) fetuses are innocent human beings, then (3) it is wrong to kill fetuses. For if "human" is used in the same sense in both (1) and (2) then, whichever of the two senses is meant, one of these premises is question-begging. And if it is used in two different senses, then of course the conclusion doesn't follow.

Thus, (1) is a self-evident moral truth,[3] and avoids begging the question about abortion, only if "human being" is used to mean something like "a full-fledged member of the moral community." (It may or may not also be meant to refer exclusively to members of the species *Homo sapiens*.) We may call this the *moral* sense of "human." It is not to be confused with what we will call the *genetic* sense, i.e., the sense in which any member of the species is a human being, and no member of any other species could be. If (1) is acceptable only if the moral sense is intended, (2) is non-question-begging only if what is intended is the genetic sense.

In "Deciding Who Is Human," Noonan argues for the classification of fetuses with human beings by pointing to the presence of the full genetic code, and the potential capacity for rational thought (p. 135). It is clear that what he needs to show, for his version of the traditional argument to be valid, is that fetuses are human in the moral sense, the sense in which it is analytically true that all human beings have full moral rights. But, in the absence of any argument showing that whatever is genetically human is also morally human, and he gives none, nothing more than genetic humanity can be demonstrated by the presence of the human genetic code. And, as we will see, the *potential* capacity for rational thought can at most show that an entity has the potential for *becoming* human in the moral sense.

DEFINING THE MORAL COMMUNITY

Can it be established that genetic humanity is sufficient for moral humanity? I think that there are very good reasons for not defining the moral community in this way. I would like to suggest an alternative way of defining the moral community, which I will argue for only to the extent of explaining why it is, or should be, self-evident. The suggestion is simply that the moral community consists of all and only *people*, rather than all and only human beings;[4] and probably the best way of demonstrating its self-evidence is by considering the concept of personhood, to see what sorts of entity are and are not persons, and what the decision that a being is or is not a person implies about its moral rights.

What moral characteristics entitle an entity to be considered a person? This is obviously not the place to attempt a complete analysis of the concept of personhood, but we do not need such a fully adequate analysis just to determine whether and why a fetus is or isn't a person. All we need is a rough and approximate list of the most basic criteria of personhood, and some idea of which, or how many, of these an entity must satisfy in order to properly be considered a person.

In searching for such criteria, it is useful to look beyond the set of people with whom we are acquainted, and ask how we would decide whether a totally alien being was a person or not. (For we have no right to assume that genetic humanity is necessary for personhood.) Imagine a space traveler who lands on an unknown planet and encounters a race of beings utterly unlike any he has ever seen or heard of. If he wants to be sure of behaving morally toward these beings, he has to somehow decide whether they are people, and hence have full moral rights, or whether they are the sort of thing which he need not feel guilty about treating as, for example, a source of food.

How should he go about making this decision? If he has some anthropological background he might look for such things as religion, art, and the manufacturing of tools, weapons, or shelters, since these factors have been used to distinguish our human from our prehuman ancestors, in what seems to be closer to the moral than the genetic sense of "human." And no doubt he would be right to consider the presence of such factors as good evidence that the alien beings were people, and morally human. It would, however, be overly anthropocentric of him to take the absence of these things as adequate evidence that they were not, since we can imagine people who have progressed beyond, or evolved without ever developing, these cultural characteristics.

I suggest that the traits which are most central to the concept of personhood, or humanity in the moral sense, are, very roughly, the following:

1. Consciousness (of objects and events external and/or internal to the being), and in particular the capacity to feel pain;
2. Reasoning (the *developed* capacity to solve new and relatively complex problems);
3. Self-motivated activity (activity which is relatively independent of either genetic or direct external control);
4. The capacity to communicate, by whatever means, messages of an indefinite variety of types, that is, not just with an indefinite number of possible contents, but on indefinitely many possible topics;
5. The presence of self-concepts, and self-awareness, either individual or racial, or both.

Admittedly, there are apt to be a great many problems involved in formulating precise definitions of these criteria, let alone in developing universally valid behavioral criteria for deciding when they apply. But I will assume that both we and our explorer know approximately what (1)–(5) mean, and that he is also able to determine whether or not they apply. How, then, should he use his findings to decide whether or not the alien beings are people? We needn't suppose that an entity must have *all* of these attributes to be properly considered a person; (1) and (2) alone may well be sufficient for personhood, and quite probably (1)–(3) are sufficient. Neither do we need to insist that any one of these criteria is *necessary* for personhood, although once again (1) and (2) look like fairly good candidates for necessary conditions, as does (3), if "activity" is construed so as to include the activity of reasoning.

All we need to claim, to demonstrate that a fetus is not a person, is that any being which satisfies *none* of (1)–(5) is certainly not a person. I consider this claim to be so obvious that I think anyone who denied it, and claimed that a being which satisfied none of (1)–(5) was a person all the same, would thereby demonstrate that he had no notion at all of what a person is—perhaps because he had confused the concept of a person with that of genetic humanity. If the opponents of abortion were to deny the appropriateness of these five criteria, I do not know what further arguments would convince them. We would probably have to admit that our conceptual schemes were indeed irreconcilably different, and that our dispute could not be settled objectively.

I do not expect this to happen, however, since I think that the concept of a person is one which is very nearly universal (to people), and that it is common to both proabortionists and antiabortionists, even though neither group has fully realized the relevance of this concept to the resolution of their dispute. Furthermore, I think that on reflection even the antiabortionists ought to agree not only that (1)–(5) are central to the concept of personhood, but also that it is a part of this concept that all and only people have full moral rights. The concept of a person is in part a moral concept; once we have admitted that *x* is a person we have recognized, even if we have not agreed to respect, *x*'s right to be treated as a member of the moral community. It is true that the claim that *x* is a *human being* is more commonly voiced as part of an appeal to treat *x* decently than is the claim that *x* is a person, but this is either because "human being" is here used in the sense which implies personhood, or because the genetic and moral senses of "human" have been confused.

Now if (1)–(5) are indeed the primary criteria of personhood, then it is clear that genetic humanity is neither necessary nor sufficient for establishing that an entity is a person. Some human beings are not people, and there may well be people who are not human beings. A man or woman whose consciousness has been permanently obliterated but who remains alive is a human being which is no longer a person; defective human beings, with no appreciable mental capacity, are not and presumably never will be people; and a fetus is a human being which is not yet a person, and which therefore cannot coherently be said to have full moral rights. Citizens of the next century should be prepared to recognize highly advanced, self-aware robots or computers, should such be developed, and intelligent inhabitants of other worlds, should such be found, as people in the fullest sense, and to respect their moral rights. But to ascribe full moral rights to an entity which is not a person is as absurd as to ascribe moral obligations and responsibilities to such an entity.

FETAL DEVELOPMENT AND THE RIGHT TO LIFE

Two problems arise in the application of these suggestions for the definition of the moral community to the determination of the precise moral status of a human fetus. Given that the paradigm example of a person is a normal adult being, then (1) How like this paradigm, in particular how far advanced since conception, does a human being need to be before it begins to have a right to life by virtue, not of being fully a person as of yet, but of being *like* a person? and (2) To what extent, if any, does the fact that a fetus has the *potential* for becoming a person endow it with some of the same rights? Each of these questions requires some comment.

In answering the first question, we need not attempt a detailed consideration of the moral rights of organ-isms which are not developed enough, aware enough, intelligent enough, etc., to be considered people, but which resemble people in some respects. It does seem reasonable to suggest that the more like a person, in the relevant aspects, a being is, the stronger is the case for regarding it as having a right to life, and indeed the stronger its right to life is. Thus we ought to take seriously the suggestion that, insofar as "the human individual develops biologically in a continuous fashion . . . the rights of a human person might develop in the same way."[5] But we must keep in mind that the attributes which are relevant in determining whether or not an entity is enough like a person to be regarded as having some of the same moral rights are no different from those which are relevant to determining whether or not it is fully a person—i.e., are not different from (1)–(5)—and that being genetically human, or having recognizably human facial and other physical features, or detectable brain activity, or the capacity to survive outside the uterus, are simply not among these relevant attributes.

Thus it is clear that even though a seven- or eight-month fetus has features which make it apt to arouse in us almost the same powerful protective instinct as is commonly aroused by a small infant, nevertheless it is not significantly more personlike than is a very small embryo. It is *somewhat* more personlike; it can apparently feel and respond to pain, and it may even have a rudimentary form of consciousness, insofar as its brain is quite active. Nevertheless, it seems safe to say that it is not fully conscious, in the way that an infant of a few months is, and that it cannot reason, or communicate messages of indefinitely many sorts, does not engage in self-motivated activity, and has no self-awareness. Thus, in the *relevant* respects, a fetus, even a fully developed one, is considerably less personlike than is the average mature mammal, indeed the average fish. And I think that a rational person must conclude that if the right to life of a fetus is to be based upon its resemblance to a person, then it cannot be said to have any more right to life than, let us say, a newborn guppy (which also seems to be capable of feeling pain), and that a right of that magnitude could never override a woman's right to obtain an abortion, at any stage of her pregnancy.

There may, of course, be other arguments in favor of placing legal limits upon the stage of pregnancy in which an abortion may be performed. Given the relative safety of the new techniques of artificially inducing labor during the third trimester, the danger to the woman's life or health is no longer such an argument. Neither is the fact that people tend to respond to the thought of abortion in the later stages of pregnancy with emotional repulsion, since mere emotional responses cannot take the place of moral reasoning in determining what ought to be permitted. Nor, finally, is the frequently heard argument that legalizing abortion, especially late in the pregnancy, may erode the level of respect for human life, leading, perhaps to an increase in unjustified euthanasia and other crimes. For this threat, if it is a threat, can be better met by educating people to the kinds of moral distinctions which we are making here than by limiting access to abortion (which limitation may, in its disregard for the rights of women, be just as damaging to the level of respect for human rights).

Thus, since the fact that even a fully developed fetus is not personlike enough to have any significant right to life on the basis of its person-likeness shows that no legal restrictions upon the stage of pregnancy in which an abortion may be performed can be justified on the grounds that we should protect the rights of the older fetus; and since there is no other apparent justification for such restrictions, we may conclude that they are entirely unjustified. Whether or not it would be *indecent* (whatever that means) for a woman in her seventh month to obtain an abortion just to avoid having to postpone a trip to Europe, it would not, in itself, be *immoral*, and therefore it ought to be permitted.

POTENTIAL PERSONHOOD AND THE RIGHT TO LIFE

We have seen that a fetus does not resemble a person in any way which can support the claim that it has even some of the same rights. But what about its *potential*, the fact that if nurtured and allowed to develop naturally it will very probably become a person? Doesn't that alone give it at least some right to life? It is hard to deny that the fact that an entity is a potential person is a strong prima facie reason for not destroying it; but we need not conclude from this that a potential person has a right to life, by virtue of that potential. It may be that our feeling that it is better, other things being equal, not to destroy a potential person is better explained by the fact that potential people are still (felt to be) an invaluable resource, not to be lightly squandered. Surely, if every speck of

dust were a potential person, we would be much less apt to conclude that every potential person has a right to become actual.

Still, we do not need to insist that a potential person has no right to life whatever. There may well be something immoral, and not just imprudent, about wantonly destroying potential people, when doing so isn't necessary to protect anyone's rights. But even if a potential person does have some prima facie right to life, such a right could not possibly outweigh the right of a woman to obtain an abortion, since the rights of any actual person invariably outweigh those of any potential person, whenever the two conflict. Since this may not be immediately obvious in the case of a human fetus, let us look at another case.

Suppose that our space explorer falls into the hands of an alien culture, whose scientists decide to create a few hundred thousand or more human beings, by breaking his body into its component cells, and using these to create fully developed human beings, with, of course, his genetic code. We may imagine that each of these newly created men will have all of the original man's abilities, skills, knowledge, and so on, and also have an individual self-concept, in short that each of them will be a bona fide (though hardly unique) person. Imagine that the whole project will take only seconds, and that its chances of success are extremely high, and that our explorer knows all of this, and also knows that these people will be treated fairly. I maintain that in such a situation he would have every right to escape if he could, and thus to deprive all of these potential people of their potential lives; for his right to life outweighs all of theirs together, in spite of the fact that they are all genetically human, all innocent, and all have a very high probability of becoming people very soon, if only he refrains from action.

Indeed, I think he would have a right to escape even if it were not his life which the alien scientists planned to take, but only a year of his freedom, or, indeed, only a day. Nor would he be obligated to stay if he had gotten captured (thus bringing all these people-potentials into existence) because of his own carelessness, or even if he had done so deliberately, knowing the consequences. Regardless of how he got captured, he is not morally obligated to remain in captivity for *any* period of time for the sake of permitting any number of potential people to come into actuality, so great is the margin by which one actual person's right to liberty outweighs whatever rights to life even a hundred thousand potential people have. And it seems reasonable to conclude that the rights of a woman will outweigh by a similar margin whatever right to life a fetus may have by virtue of its potential personhood.

Thus, neither a fetus's resemblance to a person, nor its potential for becoming a person provides any basis whatever for the claim that it has any significant right to life. Consequently, a woman's right to protect her health, happiness, freedom, and even her life,[6] by terminating an unwanted pregnancy will always override whatever right to life it may be appropriate to ascribe to a fetus, even a fully developed one. And thus, in the absence of any overwhelming social need for every possible child, the laws which restrict the right to an abortion, or limit the period of pregnancy during which an abortion may be performed, are a wholly unjustified violation of a woman's most basic moral and constitutional rights.[7]

POSTSCRIPT ON INFANTICIDE

Since the publication of this [essay], many people have written to point out that my argument appears to justify not only abortion, but infanticide as well. For a new-born infant is not significantly more personlike than an advanced fetus, and consequently it would seem that if the destruction of the latter is permissible so too must be that of the former. Inasmuch as most people, regardless of how they feel about the morality of abortion, consider infanticide a form of murder, this might appear to represent a serious flaw in my argument.

Now, if I am right in holding that it is only people who have a full-fledged right to life, and who can be murdered, and if the criteria of personhood are as I have described them, then it obviously follows that killing a new-born infant isn't murder. It does *not* follow, however, that infanticide is permissible, for two reasons. In the first place, it would be wrong, at least in this country and in this period of history, and other things being equal, to kill a new-born infant, because even if its parents do not want it and would not suffer from its destruction, there are other people who would like to have it, and would, in all probability, be deprived of a great deal of pleasure by its destruction. Thus, infanticide is wrong for reasons analogous to those which make it wrong to wantonly destroy natural resources, or great works of art.

Secondly, most people, at least in this country, value infants and would much prefer that they be preserved, even if foster parents are not immediately available. Most of us would rather be taxed to support orphanages than allow unwanted infants to be destroyed. So long as there are people who want an infant preserved, and who are willing and able to provide the means of caring for it, under reasonably humane conditions, it is, *certeris paribus*, wrong to destroy it.

But, it might be replied, if this argument shows that infanticide is wrong, at least at this time and in this country, doesn't it also show that abortion is wrong? After all, many people value fetuses, are disturbed by their destruction, and would much prefer that they be preserved, even at some cost to themselves. Furthermore, as a potential source of pleasure to some foster family, a fetus is just as valuable as an infant. There is, however, a crucial difference between the two cases: so long as the fetus is unborn, its preservation, contrary to the wishes of the pregnant woman, violates her rights to freedom, happiness, and selfdetermination. Her rights override the rights of those who would like the fetus preserved, just as if someone's life or limb is threatened by a wild animal, his right to protect himself by destroying the animal overrides the rights of those who would prefer that the animal not be harmed.

The minute the infant is born, however, its preservation no longer violates any of its mother's rights, even if she wants it destroyed, because she is free to put it up for adoption. Consequently, while the moment of birth does not mark any sharp discontinuity in the degree to which an infant possesses the right to life, it does mark the end of its mother's right to determine its fate. Indeed, if abortion could be performed without killing the fetus, she would never possess the right to have the fetus destroyed, for the same reasons that she has no right to have an infant destroyed.

On the other hand, it follows from my argument that when an unwanted or defective infant is born into a society which cannot afford and/or is not willing to care for it, then its destruction is permissible. This conclusion will, no doubt, strike many people as heartless and immoral; but remember that the very existence of people who feel this way, and who are willing and able to provide care for unwanted infants, is reason enough to conclude that they should be preserved.

NOTES

1. Judith Thomson, "A Defense of Abortion," *Philosophy and Public Affairs*, 1, No. 1 (Fall, 1971), 47–66.

2. We may safely ignore the fact that she might have avoided getting raped, e.g., by carrying a gun, since by similar means you might likewise have avoided getting kidnapped, and in neither case does the victim's failure to take all possible precautions against a highly unlikely event (as opposed to reasonable precautions against a rather likely event) mean that he is morally responsible for what happens.

3. Of course, the principle that it is (always) wrong to kill innocent human beings is in need of many other modifications, e.g., that it may be permissible to do so to save a greater number of other innocent human beings, but we may safely ignore these complications here.

4. From here on, we will use "human" to mean genetically human, since the moral sense seems closely connected to, and perhaps derived from, the assumption that genetic humanity is sufficient for membership in the moral community.

5. Thomas L. Hayes, "A Biological View," *Commonweal*, 85 (March 17, 1967), 677–78; quoted by Daniel Callahan, in *Abortion, Law, Choice, and Morality* (London: Macmillan & Co., 1970).

6. That is, insofar as the death rate, for the woman, is higher for childbirth than for early abortion.

7. My thanks to the following people, who were kind enough to read and criticize an earlier version of this paper: Herbert Gold, Gene Glass, Anne Lauterbach, Judith Thomson, Mary Mothersill, and Timothy Binkley.

Legal Issues Surrounding Abortion

R O E v . W A D E

United States Supreme Court, 1973

JUSTICE BLACKMUN delivered the opinion of the Court.

It is . . . apparent that at common law, at the time of the adoption of our Constitution, and throughout the major portion of the nineteenth century, abortion was viewed with less disfavor than under most American statutes currently in effect. Phrasing it another way, a woman enjoyed a substantially broader right to terminate a pregnancy than she does in most states today. At least with respect to the early stage of pregnancy, and very possibly without such a limitation, the opportunity to make this choice was present in this country well into the nineteenth century. Even later, the law continued for some time to treat less punitively an abortion procured in early pregnancy. . . .

Three reasons have been advanced to explain historically the enactment of criminal abortion laws in the nineteenth century and to justify their continued existence.

It has been argued occasionally that these laws were the product of a Victorian social concern to

discourage illicit sexual conduct. Texas, however, does not advance this justification in the present case, and it appears that no court or commentator has taken the argument seriously. . . .

A second reason is concerned with abortion as a medical procedure. When most criminal abortion laws were first enacted, the procedure was a hazardous one for the woman. This was particularly true prior to the development of antisepsis. Antiseptic techniques, of course, were based on discoveries by Lister, Pasteur, and others first announced in 1867, but were not generally accepted and employed until about the turn of the century. Abortion mortality was high. Even after 1900, and perhaps until as late as the development of antibiotics in the 1940s, standard modern techniques such as dilation and curettage were not nearly so safe as they are today. Thus it has been argued that a state's real concern in enacting a criminal abortion law was to protect the pregnant woman, that is, to restrain her from submitting to a procedure that placed her life in serious jeopardy.

Modern medical techniques have altered this situation. Appellants and various *amici* refer to medical data indicating that abortion in early pregnancy, that

Reprinted from 410 *United States Reports* 113: decided January 22, 1973.

is, prior to the end of first trimester, although not without its risk, is now relatively safe. Mortality rates for women undergoing early abortions, where the procedure is legal, appear to be as low as or lower than the rates for normal childbirth. Consequently, any interest of the state in protecting the woman from an inherently hazardous procedure, except when it would be equally dangerous for her to forgo it, has largely disappeared. Of course, important state interests in the area of health and medical standards do remain. The state has a legitimate interest in seeing to it that abortion, like any other medical procedure, is performed under circumstances that insure maximum safety for the patient. This interest obviously extends at least to the performing physician and his staff, to the facilities involved, to the availability of after-care, and to adequate provision for any complication or emergency that might arise. The prevalence of high mortality rates at illegal "abortion mills" strengthens, rather than weakens, the state's interest in regulating the conditions under which abortions are performed. Moreover, the risk to the woman increases as her pregnancy continues. Thus the state retains a definite interest in protecting the woman's own health and safety when an abortion is performed at a late stage of pregnancy.

The third reason is the state's interest—some phrase it in terms of duty—in protecting prenatal life. Some of the argument for this justification rests on the theory that a new human life is present from the moment of conception. The state's interest and general obligation to protect life then extends, it is argued, to prenatal life. Only when the life of the pregnant mother herself is at stake, balanced against the life she carries within her, should the interest of the embryo or fetus not prevail. Logically, of course, a legitimate state interest in this area need not stand or fall on acceptance of the belief that life begins at conception or at some other point prior to live birth. In assessing the state's interest, recognition may be given to the less rigid claim that as long as at least *potential* life is involved, the state may assert interests beyond the protection of the pregnant woman alone.

Parties challenging state abortion laws have sharply disputed in some courts the contention that a purpose of these laws, when enacted, was to protect prenatal life. Pointing to the absence of legislative history to support the contention, they claim that most state laws were designed solely to protect the woman. Because medical advances have lessened this concern, at least with respect to abortion in early pregnancy, they argue that with

respect to such abortions the laws can no longer be justified by any state interest. There is some scholarly support for this view of original purpose. The few states courts called upon to interpret their laws in the late nineteenth and early twentieth centuries did focus on the state's interest in protecting the woman's health rather than in preserving the embryo and fetus. . . .

The Constitution does not explicitly mention any right of privacy. In a line of decisions, however, going back perhaps as far as *Union Pacific R. Co. v. Botsford* (1891), the Court has recognized that a right of personal privacy, or a guarantee of certain areas or zones of privacy, does exist under the Constitution. In varying contexts the Court or individual Justices have indeed found at least the roots of that right in the First Amendment, . . . in the Fourth and Fifth Amendments, . . . in the penumbras of the Bill of Rights, . . . in the Ninth Amendment, . . . or in the concept of liberty guaranteed by the first section of the Fourteenth Amendment. . . . These decisions make it clear that only personal rights that can be deemed "fundamental" or "implicit in the concept of ordered liberty" . . . are included in this guarantee of personal privacy. They also make it clear that the right has some extension to activities relating to marriage, . . . procreation, . . . contraception, . . . family relationships, . . .and child rearing and education. . . .

This right of privacy, whether it be founded in the Fourteenth Amendment's concept of personal liberty and restrictions upon state action, as we feel it is, or, as the District Court determined, in the Ninth Amendment's reservation of rights to the people, is broad enough to encompass a woman's decision whether or not to terminate her pregnancy. . . .

Appellants and some *amici* argue that the woman's right is absolute and that she is entitled to terminate her pregnancy at whatever time, in whatever way, and for whatever reason she alone chooses. With this we do not agree. Appellants' arguments that Texas either has no valid interest at all in regulating the abortion decision, or no interest strong enough to support any limitation upon the woman's sole determination, is unpersuasive. The Court's decisions recognizing a right of privacy also acknowledge that some state regulation in areas protected by that right is appropriate. As noted above, a state may properly assert important interests in safeguarding health, in maintaining medical standards, and in protecting potential life. At some point in pregnancy, these respective interests become sufficiently compelling to sustain regulation of the factors that govern the abortion decision. The privacy rights involved, therefore, cannot be said to be absolute. . . .

We therefore conclude that the right of personal privacy includes the abortion decision, but that this right is not unqualified and must be considered against important state interests in regulation.

We note that those federal and state courts that have recently considered abortion law challenges have reached the same conclusion. . . .

Although the results are divided, most of these courts have agreed that the right of privacy, however based, is broad enough to cover the abortion decision; that the right, nonetheless, is not absolute and is subject to some limitations; and that at some point the state interests as to protection of health, medical standards, and prenatal life, become dominant. We agree with this approach. . . .

The appellee and certain *amici* argue that the fetus is a "person" within the language and meaning of the Fourteenth Amendment. In support of this they outline at length and in detail the well-known facts of fetal development. If this suggestion of personhood is established, the appellant's case, of course, collapses, for the fetus's right to life is then guaranteed specifically by the Amendment. The appellant conceded as much on reargument. On the other hand, the appellee conceded on reargument that no case could be cited that holds that a fetus is a person within the meaning of the Fourteenth Amendment. . . .

All this, together with our observation, *supra*, that throughout the major portion of the nineteenth century prevailing legal abortion practices were far freer than they are today, persuades us that the word "person," as used in the Fourteenth Amendment, does not include the unborn. . . . Indeed, our decision in *United States v. Vuitch* (1971), inferentially is to the same effect, for we there would not have indulged in statutory interpretation favorable to abortion in specified circumstances if the necessary consequence was the termination of life entitled to Fourteenth Amendment protection.

. . . As we have intimated above, it is reasonable and appropriate for a state to decide that at some point in time another interest, that of health of the mother or that of potential human life, becomes significantly involved. The woman's privacy is no longer sole and any right of privacy she possesses must be measured accordingly.

Texas urges that, apart from the Fourteenth Amendment, life begins at conception and is present throughout pregnancy, and that, therefore, the state has a compelling interest in protecting that life from and after conception. We need not resolve the difficult question of when life begins. When those trained in the respective disciplines of medicine, philosophy, and theology are unable to arrive at any consensus, the judiciary, at this point in the development of man's knowledge, is not in a position to speculate as to the answer.

It should be sufficient to note briefly the wide divergence of thinking on this most sensitive and difficult question. There has always been strong support for the view that life does not begin until live birth. This was the belief of the Stoics. It appears to be the predominant, though not the unanimous, attitude of the Jewish faith. It may be taken to represent also the position of a large segment of the Protestant community, insofar as that can be ascertained; organized groups that have taken a formal position on the abortion issue have generally regarded abortion as a matter for the conscience of the individual and her family. As we have noted, the common law found greater significance in quickening. Physicians and their scientific colleagues have regarded that event with less interest and have tended to focus either upon conception or upon live birth or upon the interim point at which the fetus becomes "viable," that is, potentially able to live outside the mother's womb, albeit with artificial aid. Viability is usually placed at about seven months (28 weeks) but may occur earlier, even at 24 weeks. . . .

In areas other than criminal abortion the law has been reluctant to endorse any theory that life, as we recognize it, begins before live birth or to accord legal rights to the unborn except in narrowly defined situations and except when the rights are contingent upon live birth. . . . In short, the unborn have never been recognized in the law as persons in the whole sense.

In view of all this, we do not agree that, by adopting one theory of life, Texas may override the rights of the pregnant woman that are at stake. We repeat, however, that the state does have an important and legitimate interest in preserving and protecting the health of the pregnant woman, whether she be a resident of the state or a nonresident who seeks medical consultation and treatment there, and that it has still *another* important and legitimate interest in protecting the potentiality of human life. These interests are separate and distinct. Each grows in substantiality as the woman approaches term and, at a point during pregnancy, each becomes "compelling."

With respect to the state's important and legitimate interest in the health of the mother, the "compelling" point, in the light of present medical knowledge, is at approximately the end of the first trimester. This is so because of the now established medical fact . . . that until the end of the first trimester mortality in abortion is less than mortality in normal childbirth. It follows that, from and after this point, a state may regulate the abortion procedure to the extent that the regulation reasonably relates to the preservation and protection of maternal health. Examples of permissible state regulation in this area are requirements as to the qualifications of the person who is to perform the abortion; as to the licensure of that person; as to the facility in which the procedure is to be performed, that is, whether it must be a hospital or may be a clinic or some other place of less-than-hospital status; as to the licensing of the facility; and the like.

This means, on the other hand, that, for the period of pregnancy prior to this "compelling" point, the attending physician, in consultation with his patient, is free to determine, without regulation by the state, that in his medical judgment the patient's pregnancy should be terminated. If that decision is reached, the judgment may be effectuated by an abortion free of interference by the state.

With respect to the state's important and legitimate interest in potential life, the "compelling" point is at viability. This is so because the fetus then presumably has the capability of meaningful life outside the mother's womb. State regulation protective of fetal life after viability thus has both logical and biological justifications. If the state is interested in protecting fetal life after viability, it may go so far as to proscribe abortion during that period except when it is necessary to preserve the life or health of the mother. . . .

To summarize and repeat:

1. A state criminal abortion statute of the current Texas type, that excepts from criminality only a *life-saving* procedure on behalf of the mother, without regard to pregnancy stage and without recognition of the other interests involved, is violative of the Due Process Clause of the Fourteenth Amendment.

(a) For the stage prior to approximately the end of the first trimester, the abortion decision and its effectuation must be left to the medical judgment of the pregnant woman's attending physician.

(b) For the stage subsequent to approximately the end of the first trimester, the state, in promoting its interest in the health of the mother, may, if it chooses, regulate the abortion procedure in ways that are reasonably related to maternal health.

(c) For the stage subsequent to viability the state, in promoting its interest in the potentiality of human life, may, if it chooses, regulate, and even proscribe, abortion except where it is necessary, in appropriate medical judgment, for the preservation of the life or health of the mother.

2. The state may define the term "physician" . . . to mean only a physician currently licensed by the state, and may proscribe any abortion by a person who is not a physician as so defined.

. . . The decision leaves the state free to place increasing restrictions on abortion as the period of pregnancy lengthens, so long as those restrictions are tailored to the recognized state interests. The decision vindicates the right of the physician to administer medical treatment according to his professional judgment up to the points where important state interests provide compelling justifications for intervention. Up to those points the abortion decision in all its aspects is inherently, and primarily, a medical decision, and basic responsibility for it must rest with the physician. If an individual practitioner abuses the privilege of exercising proper medical judgment, the usual remedies, judicial and intraprofessional, are available. . . .

JUSTICE WHITE, with whom JUSTICE REHNQUIST joins, dissenting.

At the heart of the controversy in these cases are those recurring pregnancies that pose no danger whatsoever to the life or health of the mother but are, nevertheless, unwanted for any one or more of a variety of reasons—convenience, family planning, economics, dislike of children, the embarrassment of illegitimacy, etc. The common claim before us is that for any one of such reasons, or for no reason at all, and without asserting or claiming any threat to life or health, any woman is entitled to an abortion at her request if she is able to find a medical advisor willing to undertake the procedure.

The Court for the most part sustains this position: During the period prior to the time the fetus becomes viable, the Constitution of the United States values the convenience, whim, or caprice of the putative mother more than the life or potential life of the fetus; the Constitution, therefore, guarantees the right to an abortion as against any state law or policy seeking to protect the fetus from an abortion not prompted by more compelling reasons of the mother.

With all due respect, I dissent. I find nothing in the language or history of the Constitution to support the Court's judgment. The Court simply fashions and announces a new constitutional right for pregnant mothers and, with scarcely any reason or authority for its action, invests that right with sufficient substance to override most existing state abortion statutes. The upshot is that the people and the legislatures of the 50 states are constitutionally disentitled to weigh the relative importance of the continued existence and development of the fetus, on the one hand, against a spectrum of possible impacts on the mother, on the other hand. As an exercise of raw judicial power, the Court perhaps has authority to do what it does today; but in my view its judgment is an improvident and extravagant exercise of the power of judicial review that the Constitution extends to this Court.

The Court apparently values the convenience of the pregnant mother more than the continued existence and development of the life or potential life that she carries. Whether or not I might agree with that marshaling of values, I can in no event join the Court's judgment because I find no constitutional warrant for imposing such an order of priorities on the people and legislatures of the states. In a sensitive area such as this, involving as it does issues over which reasonable men may easily and heatedly differ, I cannot accept the Court's exercise of its clear power of choice by interposing a constitutional barrier to state efforts to protect human life and by investing mothers and doctors with the constitutionally protected right to exterminate it. This issue, for the most part, should be left with the people and to the political processes the people have devised to govern their affairs.

It is my view, therefore, that the Texas statute is not constitutionally infirm because it denies abortions to those who seek to serve only their convenience rather than to protect their life or health. Nor is this plaintiff, who claims no threat to her mental or physical health, entitled to assert the possible rights of those women whose pregnancy assertedly implicated their health. This, together with *United States v. Vuitch*, 402 U.S. 62 (1971), dictates reversal of the judgment of the District Court.

Editor's note: The vote in *Roe* was 7–2, with Justices Rehnquist and White dissenting.

PLANNED PARENTHOOD v. CASEY

United States Supreme Court, 1992

JUSTICE O'CONNOR, JUSTICE KENNEDY, and JUSTICE SOUTER announced the judgment of the Court and delivered the opinion of the Court.

I

Liberty finds no refuge in a jurisprudence of doubt. Yet 19 years after our holding that the Constitution protects a woman's right to terminate her pregnancy in its early stages, *Roe v. Wade*, 410 U.S. 113 (1973), that definition of liberty is still questioned. Joining the respondents as *amicus curiae*, the United States, as it has done in five other cases in the last decade, again asks us to overrule *Roe*. . . .

At issue in these cases are five provisions of the Pennsylvania Abortion Control Act of 1982 as amended in 1988 and 1989. . . . The Act requires that a woman seeking an abortion give her informed consent prior to the abortion procedure, and specifies that she be provided with certain information at least 24 hours before the abortion is performed. For a minor to obtain an abortion, the Act requires the informed consent of one of her parents, but provides for a judicial bypass option if the minor does not wish to or cannot obtain a parent's consent. Another provision of the Act requires that, unless certain exceptions apply, a married woman seeking an abortion must sign a statement indicating that she has notified her husband of her intended abortion. The Act exempts compliance with these three requirements in the event of a "medical emergency," which is defined in § 3203 of the Act. In addition to the above provisions regulating the performance of abortions, the Act imposes certain reporting requirements on facilities that provide abortion services. . . .

We find it imperative to review once more the principles that define the rights of the woman and the legitimate authority of the State respecting the termination of pregnancies by abortion procedures.

After considering the fundamental constitutional questions resolved by *Roe*, principles of institutional integrity, and the rule of *stare decisis*, we are led to conclude this: the essential holding of *Roe v. Wade* should be retained and once again reaffirmed.

It must be stated at the outset and with clarity that *Roe*'s essential holding, the holding we reaffirm, has three parts. First is a recognition of the right of the woman to choose to have an abortion before viability and to obtain it without undue interference from the State. Before viability, the State's interests are not strong enough to support a prohibition of abortion or the imposition of a substantial obstacle to the woman's effective right to elect the procedure. Second is a confirmation of the State's power to restrict abortions after fetal viability, if the law contains exceptions for pregnancies which endanger a woman's life or health. And third is the principle that the State has legitimate interests from the outset of the pregnancy in protecting the health of the woman and the life of the fetus that may become a child. These principles do not contradict one another; and we adhere to each.

II

Constitutional protection of the woman's decision to terminate her pregnancy derives from the Due Process Clause of the Fourteenth Amendment. It declares that no State shall "deprive any person of life, liberty, or property, without due process of law." The controlling word in the case before us is "liberty." . . .

It is a promise of the Constitution that there is a realm of personal liberty which the government may not enter. We have vindicated this principle before. Marriage is mentioned nowhere in the Bill of Rights

and interracial marriage was illegal in most States in the 19th century, but the Court was no doubt correct in finding it to be an aspect of liberty protected against state interference by the substantive component of the Due Process Clause. . . .

In *Griswold*, we held that the Constitution does not permit a State to forbid a married couple to use contraceptives. That same freedom was later guaranteed, under the Equal Protection Clause, for unmarried couples. See *Eisenstadt v. Baird*, 405 U.S. 438 (1972). Constitutional protection was extended to the sale and distribution of contraceptives in *Carey v. Population Services International*. It is settled now, as it was when the Court heard arguments in *Roe v. Wade*, that the Constitution places limits on a State's right to interfere with a person's most basic decisions about family and parenthood. . . .

The inescapable fact is that adjudication of substantive due process claims may call upon the Court in interpreting the Constitution to exercise that same capacity which by tradition courts always have exercised: reasoned judgment. Its boundaries are not susceptible of expression as a simple rule. That does not mean we are free to invalidate state policy choices with which we disagree; yet neither does it permit us to shrink from the duties of our office. . . .

It should be recognized, moreover, that in some critical respects the abortion decision is of the same character as the decision to use contraception, to which *Griswold v. Connecticut, Eisenstadt v. Baird*, and *Carey v. Population Services International*, afford constitutional protection. We have no doubt as to the correctness of those decisions. They support the reasoning in *Roe* relating to the woman's liberty because they involve personal decisions concerning not only the meaning of procreation but also human responsibility and respect for it. As with abortion, reasonable people will have differences of opinion about these matters. One view is based on such reverence for the wonder of creation that any pregnancy ought to be welcomed and carried to full term no matter how difficult it will be to provide for the child and ensure its well-being. Another is that the inability to provide for the nurture and care of the infant is a cruelty to the child and an anguish to the parent. These are intimate views with infinite variations, and their deep, personal character underlay our decisions in *Griswold, Eisenstadt*, and *Carey*. The same concerns are present where the woman confronts the reality that, perhaps despite her attempts to avoid it, she has become pregnant. . . .

III

. . . No evolution of legal principle has left *Roe*'s doctrinal footings weaker than they were in 1973. No development of constitutional law since the case was decided has implicitly or explicitly left *Roe* behind as a mere survivor of obsolete constitutional thinking. . . .

The *Roe* Court itself placed its holding in the succession of cases most prominently exemplified by *Griswold v. Connecticut*, see *Roe*, 410 U.S., at 152–153. When it is so seen, *Roe* is clearly in no jeopardy, since subsequent constitutional developments have neither disturbed, nor do they threaten to diminish, the scope of recognized protection accorded to the liberty relating to intimate relationships, the family, and decisions about whether or not to beget or bear a child. . . .

[However], time has overtaken some of *Roe*'s factual assumptions: advances in maternal health care allow for abortions safe to the mother later in pregnancy than was true in 1973, and advances in neonatal care have advanced viability to a point somewhat earlier. . . . But these facts go only to the scheme of time limits on the realization of competing interests, and the divergences from the factual premises of 1973 have no bearing on the validity of *Roe*'s central holding, that viability marks the earliest point at which the State's interest in fetal life is constitutionally adequate to justify a legislative ban on nontherapeutic abortions. The soundness or unsoundness of that constitutional judgment in no sense turns on whether viability occurs at approximately 28 weeks, as was usual at the time of *Roe*, at 23 to 24 weeks, as it sometimes does today, or at some moment even slightly earlier in pregnancy, as it may if fetal respiratory capacity can somehow be enhanced in the future. Whenever it may occur, the attainment of viability may continue to serve as the critical fact, just as it has done since *Roe* was decided; which is to say that no change in *Roe*'s factual underpinning has left its central holding obsolete, and none supports an argument for overruling it. . . .

. . . Liberty must not be extinguished for want of a line that is clear. And it falls to us to give some real substance to the woman's liberty to determine whether to carry her pregnancy to full term.

We conclude the line should be drawn at viability, so that before that time the woman has a right to choose to terminate her pregnancy. We adhere to this principle for two reasons. First . . . is the doctrine of *stare decisis*. Any judicial act of line-drawing may seem somewhat arbitrary, but *Roe* was a reasoned statement, elaborated with great care. We have twice reaffirmed it in the face of great opposition. . . .

The second reason is that the concept of viability, as we noted in *Roe*, is the time at which there is a realistic possibility of maintaining and nourishing a life outside the womb, so that the independent existence of a second life can in reason and all fairness be the object of state protection that now overrides the rights of the woman. See *Roe*, at 163. Consistent with other constitutional norms, legislatures may draw lines which appear arbitrary without the necessity of offering a justification. But courts may not. We must justify the lines we draw. And there is no line other than viability which is more workable. To be sure, as we have said, there may be some medical developments that affect the precise point of viability, but this is an imprecision within tolerable limits given that the medical community and all those who must apply its discoveries will continue to explore the matter. The viability line also has, as a practical matter, an element of fairness. In some broad sense it might be said that a woman who fails to act before viability has consented to the State's intervention on behalf of the developing child.

The woman's right to terminate her pregnancy before viability is the most central principle of *Roe v. Wade*. It is a rule of law and a component of liberty we cannot renounce.

On the other side of the equation is the interest of the State in the protection of potential life. The *Roe* Court recognized the State's "important and legitimate interest in protecting the potentiality of human life." *Roe*, at 162. The weight to be given this state interest, not the strength of the woman's interest, was the difficult question faced in *Roe*. We do not need to say whether each of us, had we been Members of the Court when the valuation of the State interest came before it as an original matter, would have concluded, as the *Roe* Court did, that its weight is insufficient to justify a ban on abortions prior to viability even when it is subject to certain exceptions. The matter is not before us in the first instance, and coming as it does after nearly 20 years of litigation in *Roe*'s wake we are satisfied that the immediate question is not the soundness of *Roe*'s resolution of the issue, but the precedential force that must be accorded to its holding. And we have concluded that the essential holding of *Roe* should be reaffirmed.

Yet it must be remembered that *Roe v. Wade* speaks with clarity in establishing not only the woman's liberty but also the State's "important and legitimate interest in potential life." *Roe, supra*, at 163. That portion of the decision in *Roe* has been given too little acknowledgement and implementation by the Court in its subsequent cases. . . .

Roe established a trimester framework to govern abortion regulations. Under this elaborate but rigid construct, almost no regulation at all is permitted during the first trimester of pregnancy; regulations designed to protect the woman's health, but not to further the State's interest in potential life, are permitted during the second trimester; and during the third trimester, when the fetus is viable, prohibitions are permitted provided the life or health of the mother is not at stake. *Roe v. Wade*, at 163–166. Most of our cases since *Roe* have involved the application of rules derived from the trimester framework. . . .

The trimester framework no doubt was erected to ensure that the woman's right to choose not become so subordinate to the State's interest in promoting fetal life that her choice exists in theory but not in fact. We do not agree, however, that the trimester approach is necessary to accomplish this objective. A framework of this rigidity was unnecessary and in its later interpretation sometimes contradicted the State's permissible exercise of its powers.

Though the woman has a right to choose to terminate or continue her pregnancy before viability, it does not at all follow that the State is prohibited from taking steps to ensure that this choice is thoughtful and informed. Even in the earliest stages of pregnancy, the State may enact rules and regulations designed to encourage her to know that there are philosophic and social arguments of great weight that can be brought to bear in favor of continuing the pregnancy to full term and that there are procedures and institutions to allow adoption of unwanted children as well as a certain degree of state assistance if the mother chooses to raise the child herself. . . .

Numerous forms of state regulation might have the incidental effect of increasing the cost or decreasing the availability of medical care, whether for abortion or any other medical procedure. The fact that a law which serves a valid purpose, one not designed to strike at the right itself, has the incidental effect of making it more difficult or more expensive to procure an abortion cannot be enough to invalidate it. Only where state regulation imposes an undue burden on a woman's ability to make this decision does the power of the State reach into the heart of the liberty protected by the Due Process Clause. . . .

These considerations of the nature of the abortion right illustrate that it is an overstatement to describe it as a right to decide whether to have an abortion "without interference from the State," *Planned Parenthood of Central Mo. v. Danforth*, 428 U.S. 52, 61 (1976). All abortion regulations interfere to some degree with a woman's ability to decide whether to terminate her pregnancy. . . .

Roe v. Wade was express in its recognition of the State's "important and legitimate interest[s] in preserving and protecting the health of the pregnant woman [and] in protecting the potentiality of human life." 410 U.S., at 162. The trimester framework, however, does not fulfill *Roe*'s own promise that the State has an interest in protecting fetal life or potential life. *Roe* began the contradiction by using the trimester framework to forbid any regulation of abortion designed to advance that interest before viability. *Id.*, at 163. Before viability, *Roe* and subsequent cases treat all governmental attempts to influence a woman's decision on behalf of the potential life within her as unwarranted. This treatment is, in our judgment, incompatible with the recognition that there is a substantial state interest in potential life throughout pregnancy.

The very notion that the State has a substantial interest in potential life leads to the conclusion that not all regulations must be deemed unwarranted. Not all burdens on the right to decide whether to terminate a pregnancy will be undue. In our view, the undue burden standard is the appropriate means of reconciling the State's interest with the woman's constitutionally protected liberty. . . .

A finding of an undue burden is a shorthand for the conclusion that a state regulation has the purpose or effect of placing a substantial obstacle in the path of a woman seeking an abortion of a nonviable fetus. A statute with this purpose is invalid because the means chosen by the State to further the interest in potential life must be calculated to inform the woman's free choice, not hinder it. . . . That is to be expected in the application of any legal standard which must accommodate life's complexity. We do not expect it to be otherwise with respect to the undue burden standard. We give this summary:

(a) To protect the central right recognized by *Roe v. Wade* while at the same time accommodating the State's profound interest in potential life, we will employ the undue burden analysis as explained in this opinion. An undue burden exists, and therefore a provision of law is invalid, if its purpose or effect is to place a substantial obstacle in the path of a woman seeking an abortion before the fetus attains viability.

(b) We reject the rigid trimester framework of *Roe v. Wade.* To promote the State's profound interest in potential life, throughout pregnancy the State may take measures to ensure that the woman's choice is informed, and measures designed to advance this interest will not be invalidated as long as their purpose is to persuade the woman to choose childbirth over abortion. These measures must not be an undue burden on the right.

(c) As with any medical procedure, the State may enact regulations to further the health or safety of a woman seeking an abortion. Unnecessary health regulations that have the purpose or effect of presenting a substantial obstacle to a woman seeking an abortion impose an undue burden on the right.

(d) Our adoption of the undue burden analysis does not disturb the central holding of *Roe v. Wade*, and we reaffirm that holding. Regardless of whether exceptions are made for particular circumstances, a State may not prohibit any woman from making the ultimate decision to terminate her pregnancy before viability.

(e) We also reaffirm *Roe*'s holding that "subsequent to viability, the State in promoting its interest in the potentiality of human life may, if it chooses, regulate, and even proscribe, abortion except where it is necessary, in appropriate medical judgment, for the preservation of the life or health of the mother." *Roe v. Wade*, 410 U.S., at 164–165.

These principles control our assessment of the Pennsylvania statute, and we now turn to the issue of the validity of its challenged provisions.

V

The Court of Appeals applied what it believed to be the undue burden standard and upheld each of the provisions except for the husband notification requirement. We agree generally with this conclusion, but refine the undue burden analysis in accordance with the principles articulated above. . . .

B

We next consider the informed consent requirement. 18 Pa. Cons. Stat. Ann. § 3205. Except in a medical emergency, the statute requires that at least 24 hours before performing an abortion a physician inform the woman of the nature of the procedure, the health risks of the abortion and of childbirth, and the "probable gestational age of the unborn child." The physician or a qualified nonphysician must inform the woman of the availability of printed materials published by the State describing the fetus and providing information about medical assistance for childbirth, information about child support from the father, and a list of agencies which provide adoption and other services as alternatives to abortion. An abortion may not be performed unless the woman certifies in writing that she has been informed of the availability of these printed materials and has been provided them if she chooses to view them.

Our prior decisions establish that as with any medical procedure, the State may require a woman to give her written informed consent to an abortion. . . .

In *Akron I*, 462 U.S. 416 (1983), we invalidated an ordinance which required that a woman seeking an abortion be provided by her physician with specific information "designed to influence the woman's informed choice between abortion or childbirth." *Id.*, at 444. As we later described the *Akron I* holding in *Thornburgh v. American College of Obstetricians and Gynecologists*, 476 U.S., at 762, there were two purported flaws in the Akron ordinance: the information was designed to dissuade the woman from having an abortion and the ordinance imposed "a rigid requirement that a specific body of information be given in all cases, irrespective of the particular needs of the patient. . . ." *Ibid.* . . .

In attempting to ensure that a woman apprehend the full consequences of her decision, the State furthers the legitimate purpose of reducing the risk that a woman may elect an abortion, only to discover later, with devastating psychological consequences, that her decision was not fully informed. If the information the State requires to be made available to the woman is truthful and not misleading, the requirement may be permissible.

We also see no reason why the State may not require doctors to inform a woman seeking an abortion of the availability of materials relating to the consequences to the fetus, even when those consequences have no direct relation to her health. An example illustrates the point. We would think it constitutional for the State to require that in order for there to be informed consent to a kidney transplant operation the recipient must be supplied with information about risks to the donor as well as risks to himself or herself. . . .

Whether the mandatory 24-hour waiting period is nonetheless invalid because in practice it is a substantial obstacle to a woman's choice to terminate her pregnancy is a closer question. The findings of fact by the District Court indicate that because of the distances many women must travel to reach an abortion provider, the practical effect will often be a delay of much more than a day because the waiting period requires that a woman seeking an abortion make at least two visits to the doctor. The District Court also found that in many instances this will increase the exposure of women seeking abortions to "the harassment and hostility of anti-abortion protestors demonstrating outside a clinic." 744 F. Supp., at 1351. As a result, the District Court found that for those women who have the fewest financial resources, those who must travel long distances, and those who have difficulty explaining their whereabouts to husbands, employers, or others, the 24-hour waiting period will be "particularly burdensome." . . .

We are left with the argument that the various aspects of the informed consent requirement are unconstitutional because they place barriers in the way of abortion on demand. Even the broadest reading of *Roe*, however, has not suggested that there is a constitutional right to abortion on demand. See, *e.g., Doe v. Bolton*, 410 U.S., at 189. Rather, the right protected by *Roe* is a right to decide to terminate a pregnancy free of undue interference by the State. Because the informed consent requirement facilitates the wise exercise of that right it cannot be classified as an interference with the right *Roe* protects. The informed consent requirement is not an undue burden on that right.

C

Section 3209 of Pennsylvania's abortion law provides, except in cases of medical emergency, that no physician shall perform an abortion on a married woman without receiving a signed statement from the woman that she has notified her spouse that she is about to undergo an abortion. The woman has the option of providing an alternative signed statement certifying that her husband is not the man who impregnated her; that her husband could not be located; that the pregnancy is the result of spousal sexual assault which she has reported; or that the woman believes that notifying her husband will cause him or someone else to inflict bodily injury upon her. A physician who performs an abortion on a married woman without receiving the appropriate signed statement will have his or her license revoked, and is liable to the husband for damages. . . .

The American Medical Association (AMA) has published a summary of the recent research in this field, which indicates that in an average 12-month period in this country, approximately two million women are the victims of severe assaults by their male partners. In a 1985 survey, women reported that nearly one of every eight husbands had assaulted their wives during the past year. The AMA views these figures as "marked underestimates," because the nature of these incidents discourages women from reporting them, and because surveys typically exclude the very poor, those who do not speak English well, and women who are homeless or in institutions or hospitals when the survey is conducted. According to the AMA, "[r]esearchers on family violence agree that the true incidence of partner violence is probably *double* the above estimates; or four million severely assaulted women per year. Studies suggest that from one-fifth to one-third of all women will be physically assaulted by a partner or ex-partner during their lifetime." AMA Council on Scientific Affairs, Violence Against Women 7 (1991) (emphasis in original). Thus on an average day in the United States, nearly 11,000 women are severely assaulted by their male partners. Many of these incidents involve sexual assault. . . . In families where wife-beating takes place, moreover, child abuse is often present as well. . . .

In well-functioning marriages, spouses discuss important intimate decisions such as whether to bear a child. But there are millions of women in this country who are the victims of regular physical and psychological abuse at the hands of their husbands. Should these women become pregnant, they may have very good reasons for not wishing to inform their husbands of their decision to obtain an abortion. Many may have justifiable fears of physical abuse, but may be no less fearful of the consequences of reporting prior abuse to the Commonwealth of Pennsylvania. Many may have a reasonable fear that notifying their husbands will provoke further instances of child abuse; these women are not exempt from § 3209's notification requirement. . . . If anything in this field is certain, it is that victims of spousal sexual assault are extremely reluctant to report the abuse to the government; hence, a great many spousal rape victims will not be exempt from the notification requirement imposed by § 3209.

The spousal notification requirement is thus likely to prevent a significant number of women from obtaining an abortion. It does not merely make abortions a little more difficult or expensive to obtain; for many women, it will impose a substantial obstacle. We must not blind ourselves to the fact that the significant number of women who fear for their safety and the safety of their children are likely to be deterred from procuring an abortion as surely as if the Commonwealth had outlawed abortion in all cases. . . .

This conclusion is in no way inconsistent with our decisions upholding parental notification or consent requirements. Those enactments, and our judgment that they are constitutional, are based on the quite reasonable assumption that minors will benefit from consultation with their parents and that children will often not realize that their parents have their best interests at heart. We cannot adopt a parallel assumption about adult women. . . .

Our cases establish, and we reaffirm today, that a State may require a minor seeking an abortion to obtain the consent of a parent or guardian, provided that there is an adequate judicial bypass procedure. Under these precedents, in our view, the one-parent consent requirement and judicial bypass procedure are constitutional. . . .

VI

Our Constitution is a covenant running from the first generation of Americans to us and then to future generations. It is a coherent succession. Each generation must learn anew that the Constitution's written terms embody ideas and aspirations that must survive more ages than one. We accept our responsibility not to retreat from interpreting the full meaning of the covenant in light of all of our precedents. We invoke it once again to define the freedom guaranteed by the Constitution's own promise, the promise of liberty. . . .

Editor's note: Casey is a plurality decision, which means that the opinion issued by Justices O'Connor, Kennedy, and Souter was not supported in its totality by a majority of the nine Supreme Court justices. Parts of the opinion, however, were each joined by at least two other justices, creating a majority on those parts.

GONZALES v. CARHART

United States Supreme Court, 2007

JUSTICE KENNEDY delivered the opinion of the Court.

These cases require us to consider the validity of the Partial-Birth Abortion Ban Act of 2003(Act), a federal statute regulating abortion procedures.

. . .

I

A

The Act proscribes a particular manner of ending fetal life, so it is necessary here, as it was in *Stenberg* [*v. Carhart*, 530 U.S. 914 (2000)] to discuss abortion procedures in some detail. . . .

Abortion methods vary depending to some extent on the preferences of the physician and, of course, on the term of the pregnancy and the resulting stage of the unborn child's development. Between 85 and 90 percent of the approximately 1.3 million abortions performed each year in the United States take place in the first three months of pregnancy, which is to say in the first trimester. . . . . The Act does not regulate these procedures.

Of the remaining abortions that take place each year, most occur in the second trimester. The surgical procedure referred to as "dilation and evacuation" or "D & E" is the usual abortion method in this trimester. Although individual techniques for performing D & E differ, the general steps are the same. . . .

. . . .

After sufficient dilation the surgical operation can commence. The woman is placed under general anesthesia or conscious sedation. The doctor, often guided by ultrasound, inserts grasping forceps through the woman's cervix and into the uterus to grab the fetus. The doctor grips a fetal part with the forceps and pulls it back through the cervix and vagina, continuing to pull even after meeting resistance from the cervix. The friction causes the fetus to tear apart. For example, a leg might be ripped off the fetus as it is pulled through the cervix and out of the woman. The process of evacuating the fetus piece by piece continues until it has been completely removed. A doctor may make 10 to 15 passes with the forceps to evacuate the fetus in its entirety, though sometimes removal is completed with fewer passes. Once the fetus has been evacuated, the placenta and any remaining fetal material are suctioned or scraped out of the uterus. The doctor examines the different parts to ensure the entire fetal body has been removed. . . .

Some doctors, especially later in the second trimester, may kill the fetus a day or two before performing the surgical evacuation. They inject digoxin or potassium chloride into the fetus, the umbilical cord, or the amniotic fluid. Fetal demise may cause contractions and make greater dilation possible. Once dead, moreover, the fetus' body will soften, and its removal will be easier. Other doctors refrain from injecting chemical agents, believing it adds risk with little or no medical benefit. . . .

The abortion procedure that was the impetus for the numerous bans on "partial-birth abortion," including the Act, is a variation of [the] standard D & E. . . . For discussion purposes this D & E variation will be referred to as intact D & E. The main difference between the two procedures is that in intact D & E a doctor extracts the fetus intact or largely intact. . . . There are no comprehensive statistics indicating what percentage of all D & Es are performed in this manner. . . .

In an intact D & E procedure the doctor extracts the fetus in a way conducive to pulling out its entire body, instead of ripping it apart. . . .

From 2007 WL 1135596 (U.S.)

Intact D & E gained public notoriety when, in 1992, Dr. Martin Haskell gave a presentation describing his method of performing the operation. In the usual intact D & E the fetus' head lodges in the cervix, and dilation is insufficient to allow it to pass. Haskell explained the next step as follows:

"'At this point, the right-handed surgeon slides the fingers of the left [hand] along the back of the fetus and "hooks" the shoulders of the fetus with the index and ring fingers (palm down).

"'While maintaining this tension, lifting the cervix and applying traction to the shoulders with the fingers of the left hand, the surgeon takes a pair of blunt curved Metzenbaum scissors in the right hand. He carefully advances the tip, curved down, along the spine and under his middle finger until he feels it contact the base of the skull under the tip of his middle finger.

"'[T]he surgeon then forces the scissors into the base of the skull or into the foramen magnum. Having safely entered the skull, he spreads the scissors to enlarge the opening.

"'The surgeon removes the scissors and introduces a suction catheter into this hole and evacuates the skull contents. With the catheter still in place, he applies traction to the fetus, removing it completely from the patient.'" H.R. Rep. No. 108–58, p. 3 (2003).

This is an abortion doctor's clinical description. Here is another description from a nurse who witnessed the same method performed on a $26^1/_2$-week fetus and who testified before the Senate Judiciary Committee:

"'Dr. Haskell went in with forceps and grabbed the baby's legs and pulled them down into the birth canal. Then he delivered the baby's body and the arms—everything but the head. The doctor kept the head right inside the uterus . . . .

"'The baby's little fingers were clasping and unclasping, and his little feet were kicking. Then the doctor stuck the scissors in the back of his head, and the baby's arms jerked out, like a startle reaction, like a flinch, like a baby does when he thinks he is going to fall.

"'The doctor opened up the scissors, stuck a high-powered suction tube into the opening, and sucked the baby's brains out. Now the baby went completely limp. . . .

"'He cut the umbilical cord and delivered the placenta. He threw the baby in a pan, along with the placenta and the instruments he had just used.'" *Ibid.*

Dr. Haskell's approach is not the only method of killing the fetus once its head lodges in the cervix, and "the process has evolved" since his presentation. Another doctor, for example, squeezes the skull after

it has been pierced "so that enough brain tissue exudes to allow the head to pass through." Still other physicians reach into the cervix with their forceps and crush the fetus' skull. Others continue to pull the fetus out of the woman until it disarticulates at the neck, in effect decapitating it. These doctors then grasp the head with forceps, crush it, and remove it . . . .

D & E and intact D & E are not the only second-trimester abortion methods. Doctors also may abort a fetus through medical induction. The doctor medicates the woman to induce labor, and contractions occur to deliver the fetus. Induction, which unlike D & E should occur in a hospital, can last as little as 6 hours but can take longer than 48. It accounts for about five percent of second-trimester abortions before 20 weeks of gestation and 15 percent of those after 20 weeks. Doctors turn to two other methods of second-trimester abortion, hysterotomy and hysterectomy, only in emergency situations because they carry increased risk of complications. In a hysterotomy, as in a caesarean section, the doctor removes the fetus by making an incision through the abdomen and uterine wall to gain access to the uterine cavity. A hysterectomy requires the removal of the entire uterus. These two procedures represent about .07% of second-trimester abortions.

B

After Dr. Haskell's procedure received public attention, with ensuing and increasing public concern, bans on "'partial birth abortion'" proliferated. By the time of the *Stenberg* decision, about 30 States had enacted bans designed to prohibit the procedure. In 1996, Congress also acted to ban partial-birth abortion. President Clinton vetoed the congressional legislation, and the Senate failed to override the veto. Congress approved another bill banning the procedure in 1997, but President Clinton again vetoed it. In 2003, after this Court's decision in *Stenberg*, Congress passed the Act at issue here. On November 5, 2003, President Bush signed the Act into law. It was to take effect the following day.

The Act responded to *Stenberg* in two ways. First, Congress made factual findings. Congress determined that this Court in *Stenberg* "was required to accept the very questionable findings issued by the district court judge," but that Congress was "not bound to accept the same factual findings". Congress found, among other things, that "[a] moral, medical, and ethical consensus exists that the practice of performing a partial-birth abortion . . . is a gruesome and inhumane procedure that is never medically necessary and should be prohibited."

Second, and more relevant here, the Act's language differs from that of the Nebraska statute struck down in *Stenberg*. The operative provisions of the Act provide in relevant part:

"(a) Any physician who, in or affecting interstate or foreign commerce, knowingly performs a partial-birth abortion and thereby kills a human fetus shall be fined under this title or imprisoned not more than 2 years, or both. This subsection does not apply to a partial-birth abortion that is necessary to save the life of a mother whose life is endangered by a physical disorder, physical illness, or physical injury, including a life-endangering physical condition caused by or arising from the pregnancy itself. This subsection takes effect 1 day after the enactment.

"(b) As used in this section—

"(1) the term 'partial-birth abortion' means an abortion in which the person performing the abortion—

"(A) deliberately and intentionally vaginally delivers a living fetus until, in the case of a head-first presentation, the entire fetal head is outside the body of the mother, or, in the case of breech presentation, any part of the fetal trunk past the navel is outside the body of the mother, for the purpose of performing an overt act that the person knows will kill the partially delivered living fetus; and

"(B) performs the overt act, other than completion of delivery, that kills the partially delivered living fetus; and

"(2) the term 'physician' means a doctor of medicine or osteopathy legally authorized to practice medicine and surgery by the State in which the doctor performs such activity, or any other individual legally authorized by the State to perform abortions: *Provided, however*, That any individual who is not a physician or not otherwise legally authorized by the State to perform abortions, but who nevertheless directly performs a partial-birth abortion, shall be subject to the provisions of this section. . . . . .

"(d)(1) A defendant accused of an offense under this section may seek a hearing before the State Medical Board on whether the physician's conduct was necessary to save the life of the mother whose life was endangered by a physical disorder, physical illness, or physical injury, including a life-endangering physical condition caused by or arising from the pregnancy itself.

"(2) The findings on that issue are admissible on that issue at the trial of the defendant. Upon a motion of the defendant, the court shall delay the beginning of the trial for not more than 30 days to permit such a hearing to take place.

"(e) A woman upon whom a partial-birth abortion is performed may not be prosecuted under this section, for a conspiracy to violate this section, or for an offense under section 2, 3, or 4 of this title based on a violation of this section." 18 U.S.C. § 1531 (2000 ed., Supp. IV). . . . .

· · · ·

II

· · · ·

Casey involved a challenge to *Roe v. Wade*, 410 U.S. 113 (1973). . . .

We assume the following principles for the purposes of this opinion. Before viability, a State "may not prohibit any woman from making the ultimate decision to terminate her pregnancy." 505 U.S., at 879 (plurality opinion). It also may not impose upon this right an undue burden, which exists if a regulation's "purpose or effect is to place a substantial obstacle in the path of a woman seeking an abortion before the fetus attains viability." *Id.*, at 878. On the other hand, "[r]egulations which do no more than create a structural mechanism by which the State, or the parent or guardian of a minor, may express profound respect for the life of the unborn are permitted, if they are not a substantial obstacle to the woman's exercise of the right to choose." *Id.*, at 877. *Casey*, in short, struck a balance. The balance was central to its holding. We now apply its standard to the cases at bar.

· · · ·

[*Editor's note:* Portions of the opinion have been omitted here. The court concludes that the Act is not constitutionally void for vagueness and that the statutory text of the Act specifying restrictions on second trimester abortions does not impose an undue burden because it only applies to intact D & E, and does not prohibit a D & E procedure where the fetus is removed "in parts."]

IV

Under the principles accepted as controlling here, the Act, as we have interpreted it, would be unconstitutional "if its purpose or effect is to place a substantial obstacle in the path of a woman seeking an abortion before the fetus attains viability." *Casey*, 505 U.S., at 878 (plurality opinion). The abortions affected by the Act's regulations take place both previability and postviability; so the quoted language and the undue burden analysis it relies upon are applicable. The question is whether the Act, measured by its text in this facial attack, imposes a substantial obstacle to late-term, but previability, abortions. The Act does not on its face impose a substantial obstacle, and we reject this further facial challenge to its validity.

A

The Act's purposes are set forth in recitals preceding its operative provisions. A description of the prohibited abortion procedure demonstrates the rationale for the congressional enactment. The Act proscribes a method of abortion in which a fetus is killed just inches before completion of the birth process. Congress stated as follows: "Implicitly approving such a brutal and inhumane procedure by choosing not to prohibit it will further coarsen society to the humanity of not only newborns, but all vulnerable and innocent human life, making it increasingly difficult to protect such life." Congressional Findings (14)(N), in notes following 18 U.S.C. § 1531 (2000 ed., Supp. IV), p. 769. The Act expresses respect for the dignity of human life.

Congress was concerned, furthermore, with the effects on the medical community and on its reputation caused by the practice of partial-birth abortion. The findings in the Act explain:

"Partial-birth abortion . . . confuses the medical, legal, and ethical duties of physicians to preserve and promote life, as the physician acts directly against the physical life of a child, whom he or she had just delivered, all but the head, out of the womb, in order to end that life." Congressional Findings (14)(J), *ibid.*

There can be no doubt the government "has an interest in protecting the integrity and ethics of the medical profession." *Washington v. Glucksberg*, 521 U.S. 702, 7311997); see also. Under our precedents it is clear the State has a significant role to play in regulating the medical profession.

Casey reaffirmed these governmental objectives. The government may use its voice and its regulatory authority to show its profound respect for the life within the woman. A central premise of the opinion was that the Court's precedents after *Roe* had "undervalue[d] the State's interest in potential life." The plurality opinion indicated "[t]he fact that a law which serves a valid purpose, one not designed to strike at the right itself, has the incidental effect of making it more difficult or more expensive to procure an abortion cannot be enough to invalidate it." This was not an idle assertion. The three premises of *Casey* must coexist. The third premise, that the State, from the inception of the pregnancy, maintains its own regulatory interest in protecting the life of the fetus that may become a child, cannot be set at naught by interpreting *Casey's* requirement of a health exception so it becomes tantamount to allowing a doctor to choose the abortion method he or she might prefer. Where it has a rational basis to act, and it does not impose an undue burden, the State may use its regulatory power to bar certain procedures and substitute others, all in furtherance of its legitimate interests in regulating the medical profession in order to promote respect for life, including life of the unborn.

The Act's ban on abortions that involve partial delivery of a living fetus furthers the Government's objectives. No one would dispute that, for many, D & E is a procedure itself laden with the power to devalue human life. Congress could nonetheless conclude that the type of abortion proscribed by the Act requires specific regulation because it implicates additional ethical and moral concerns that justify a special prohibition. Congress determined that the abortion methods it proscribed had a "disturbing similarity to the killing of a newborn infant," Congressional Findings (14)(L), in notes following 18 U.S.C. § 1531 (2000 ed., Supp. IV), p. 769, and thus it was concerned with "draw[ing] a bright line that clearly distinguishes abortion and infanticide." Congressional Findings (14)(G), *ibid.* The Court has in the past confirmed the validity of drawing boundaries to prevent certain practices that extinguish life and are close to actions that are condemned. *Glucksberg* found reasonable the State's "fear that permitting assisted suicide will start it down the path to voluntary and perhaps even involuntary euthanasia." 521 U.S., at 732–735.

Respect for human life finds an ultimate expression in the bond of love the mother has for her child. The Act recognizes this reality as well. Whether to have an abortion requires a difficult and painful moral decision. While we find no reliable data to measure the phenomenon, it seems unexceptionable to conclude some women come to regret their choice to abort the infant life they once created and sustained. Severe depression and loss of esteem can follow.

In a decision so fraught with emotional consequence some doctors may prefer not to disclose precise details of the means that will be used, confining themselves to the required statement of risks the procedure entails. From one standpoint this ought not to be surprising. Any number of patients facing imminent surgical procedures would prefer not to hear all details, lest the usual anxiety preceding invasive medical procedures become the more intense. This is likely the case with the abortion procedures here in issue.

It is, however, precisely this lack of information concerning the way in which the fetus will be killed that is of legitimate concern to the State. The State has an interest in ensuring so grave a choice is well informed. It is self-evident that a mother who comes to regret her choice to abort must struggle with grief more anguished and sorrow more profound when she learns, only after the event, what she once did not know: that she allowed a doctor to pierce the skull and vacuum the fast-developing brain of her unborn child, a child assuming the human form.

It is a reasonable inference that a necessary effect of the regulation and the knowledge it conveys will be to encourage some women to carry the infant to full term, thus reducing the absolute number of late-term abortions. The medical profession, furthermore, may find different and less shocking methods to abort the fetus in the second trimester, thereby accommodating legislative demand. The State's interest in respect for life is advanced by the dialogue that better informs the political and legal systems, the medical profession, expectant mothers, and society as a whole of the consequences that follow from a decision to elect a late-term abortion.

It is objected that the standard D & E is in some respects as brutal, if not more, than the intact D & E, so that the legislation accomplishes little. What we have already said, however, shows ample justification for the regulation. Partial-birth abortion, as defined by the Act, differs from a standard D & E because the former occurs when the fetus is partially outside the mother to the point of one of the Act's anatomical landmarks. It was reasonable for Congress to think that partial-birth abortion, more than standard D & E, "undermines the public's perception of the appropriate role of a physician during the delivery process, and perverts a process during which life is brought into the world." Congressional Findings (14)(K), in notes following 18 U.S.C. § 1531 (2000 ed., Supp. IV), p. 769. There would be a flaw in this Court's logic, and an irony in its jurisprudence, were we first to conclude a ban on both D & E and intact D & E was overbroad and then to say it is irrational to ban only intact D & E because that does not proscribe both procedures. In sum, we reject the contention that the congressional purpose of the Act was "to place a substantial obstacle in the path of a woman seeking an abortion." 505 U.S., at 878, 112 S.Ct. 2791 (plurality opinion).

B

The Act's furtherance of legitimate government interests bears upon, but does not resolve, the next question: whether the Act has the effect of imposing an unconstitutional burden on the abortion right because it does not allow use of the barred procedure where "'necessary, in appropriate medical judgment, for [the] preservation of the . . . health of the mother.'" *Ayotte,* 546 U.S., at 327–328 (quoting *Casey*). The prohibition in the Act would be unconstitutional, under precedents we here assume to be controlling, if it "subject[ed] [women] to significant health risks." *Ayotte* at 328; see also *Casey* at 880 (opinion of the Court). In *Ayotte* the parties agreed a health exception to the challenged parental-involvement statute was necessary "to avert serious and often irreversible damage to [a pregnant minor's] health." 546 U.S., at 328. Here, by contrast, whether the Act creates significant health risks for women has been a contested factual question. The evidence presented in the trial courts and before Congress demonstrates both sides have medical support for their position.

• • • •

The question becomes whether the Act can stand when this medical uncertainty persists. . . .

Medical uncertainty does not foreclose the exercise of legislative power in the abortion context any more than it does in other contexts. The medical uncertainty over whether the Act's prohibition creates significant health risks provides a sufficient basis to conclude in this facial attack that the Act does not impose an undue burden.

The conclusion that the Act does not impose an undue burden is supported by other considerations. Alternatives are available to the prohibited procedure. As we have noted, the Act does not proscribe D & E. . . . In addition the Act's prohibition only applies to the delivery of "a living fetus." If the intact D & E procedure is truly necessary in some circumstances, it appears likely an injection that kills the fetus is an alternative under the Act that allows the doctor to perform the procedure. . . .

In reaching the conclusion the Act does not require a health exception we reject certain arguments made by the parties on both sides of these cases. On the one hand, the Attorney General urges us to uphold the Act on the basis of the congressional findings alone. Although we review congressional factfinding under a deferential standard, we do not in the circumstances here place dispositive weight on Congress' findings. The Court retains an independent constitutional duty to review factual findings where constitutional rights are at stake. . . . .

As respondents have noted, and the District Courts recognized, some recitations in the Act are factually incorrect. Whether or not accurate at the time, some of the important findings have been superseded. . . . Congress determined no medical schools provide instruction on the prohibited procedure. The testimony in the District Courts, however, demonstrated intact D & E is taught at medical schools. Congress also found there existed a medical consensus that the prohibited procedure is never medically necessary. The evidence presented in the District Courts contradicts that conclusion. Uncritical deference to Congress' factual findings in these cases is inappropriate.

On the other hand, relying on the Court's opinion in *Stenberg*, respondents contend that an abortion regulation must contain a health exception "if 'substantial medical authority supports the proposition that banning a particular procedure could endanger women's health.'" Brief for Respondents in No. 05-380, p. 19 (quoting 530 U.S., at 938, 120 S.Ct. 2597); see also Brief for Respondent Planned Parenthood et al. in No. 05-1382, at 12 (same). As illustrated by respondents' arguments and the decisions of the Courts of Appeals, *Stenberg* has been interpreted to leave no margin of error for legislatures to act in the face of medical uncertainty.

A zero tolerance policy would strike down legitimate abortion regulations, like the present one, if some part of the medical community were disinclined to follow the proscription. This is too exacting a standard to impose on the legislative power, exercised in this instance under the Commerce Clause, to regulate the medical profession. Considerations of marginal safety, including the balance of risks, are within the legislative competence when the regulation is rational and in pursuit of legitimate ends. When standard medical options are available, mere convenience does not suffice to displace them; and if some procedures have different risks than others, it does not follow that the State is altogether barred from imposing reasonable regulations. The Act is not invalid on its face where there is uncertainty over whether the barred procedure is ever necessary to preserve a woman's health, given the availability of other abortion procedures that are considered to be safe alternatives.

•   •   •

It is so ordered.

JUSTICE GINSBURG, WITH WHOM JUSTICE STEVENS, JUSTICE SOUTER, AND JUSTICE BREYER JOIN, DISSENTING.

•   •   •   •

Today's decision is alarming. It refuses to take *Casey* and *Stenberg* seriously. It tolerates, indeed applauds, federal intervention to ban nationwide a procedure found necessary and proper in certain cases by the American College of Obstetricians and Gynecologists (ACOG). It blurs the line, firmly drawn in *Casey*, between previability and postviability abortions. And, for the first time since *Roe*, the Court blesses a prohibition with no exception safeguarding a woman's health.

I dissent from the Court's disposition. Retreating from prior rulings that abortion restrictions cannot be imposed absent an exception safeguarding a woman's health, the Court upholds an Act that surely would not survive under the close scrutiny that previously attended state-decreed limitations on a woman's reproductive choices.

•   •   •   •

II

A

The Court offers flimsy and transparent justifications for upholding a nationwide ban on intact D & E *sans* any exception to safeguard a women's health. Today's ruling, the Court declares, advances "a premise central to [*Casey's*] conclusion"-*i.e.*, the Government's "legitimate and substantial interest in preserving and promoting fetal life." But the Act scarcely furthers that interest: The law saves not a single fetus from destruction, for it targets only a *method* of performing abortion. And surely the statute was not designed to protect the lives or health of pregnant women. In short, the Court upholds a law that, while doing nothing to "preserv[e] . . . fetal life," bars a woman from choosing intact D & E although her doctor "reasonably believes [that procedure] will best protect [her]." *Stenberg*, 530 U.S., at 946 (STEVENS, J., concurring).

As another reason for upholding the ban, the Court emphasizes that the Act does not proscribe the nonintact D & E procedure. But why not, one might ask. Nonintact D & E could equally be characterized as "brutal," involving as it does "tear[ing] [a fetus] apart" and "ripp[ing] off" its limbs. "[T]he notion that either of these two equally gruesome procedures . . . is more akin to infanticide than the other, or that the State furthers any legitimate interest by banning one but not the other, is simply irrational." *Stenberg*, 530 U.S., at 946–947 (STEVENS, J., concurring).

Delivery of an intact, albeit nonviable, fetus warrants special condemnation, the Court maintains, because a fetus that is not dismembered resembles an infant. But so, too, does a fetus delivered intact after it is terminated by injection a day or two before the surgical evacuation, or a fetus delivered through medical induction or caesarean. Yet, the availability of those procedures—along with D & E by dismemberment—the Court says, saves the ban on intact D & E from a declaration of unconstitutionality. Never mind that the procedures deemed acceptable might put a woman's health at greater risk.

Ultimately, the Court admits that "moral concerns" are at work, concerns that could yield prohibitions on any abortion. Notably, the concerns expressed are untethered to any ground genuinely serving the Government's interest in preserving life. By allowing such concerns to carry the day and case, overriding fundamental rights, the Court dishonors our precedent. . . .

Revealing in this regard, the Court invokes an antiabortion shibboleth for which it concededly has no reliable evidence: Women who have abortions come to regret their choices, and consequently suffer from "[s]evere depression and loss of esteem." Because of women's fragile emotional state and because of the "bond of love the mother has for her child," the Court worries, doctors may withhold information about the nature of the intact D & E procedure. The solution the Court approves, then, is *not* to require doctors to inform women, accurately and adequately, of the different procedures and their attendant risks. Instead, the Court deprives women of the right to make an autonomous choice, even at the expense of their safety.

This way of thinking reflects ancient notions about women's place in the family and under the Constitution—ideas that have long since been discredited. . . .

Though today's majority may regard women's feelings on the matter as "self-evident," this Court has repeatedly confirmed that "[t]he destiny of the woman must be shaped . . . on her own conception of her spiritual imperatives and her place in society." *Casey*, 505 U.S., at 852.

B

In cases on a "woman's liberty to determine whether to [continue] her pregnancy," this Court has identified viability as a critical consideration. See *Casey*, 505 U.S., at 869–870 (plurality opinion). "[T]here is no line [more workable] than viability," the Court explained in *Casey*, for viability is "the time at which there is a realistic possibility of maintaining and nourishing a life outside the womb, so that the independent existence of the second life can in reason and all fairness be the object of state protection that now overrides the rights of the woman. . . . In some broad sense it might be said that a woman who fails to act before viability has consented to the State's intervention on behalf of the developing child." *Id.*, at 870.

Today, the Court blurs that line, maintaining that "[t]he Act [legitimately] appl[ies] both previability and postviability because . . . a fetus is a living organism while within the womb, whether or not it is viable outside the womb." Instead of drawing the line at viability, the Court refers to Congress' purpose to differentiate "abortion and infanticide" based not on whether a fetus can survive outside the womb, but on where a fetus is anatomically located when a particular medical procedure is performed.

One wonders how long a line that saves no fetus from destruction will hold in face of the Court's "moral concerns." The Court's hostility to the right *Roe* and *Casey* secured is not concealed. Throughout, the opinion refers to obstetrician-gynecologists and surgeons who perform abortions not by the titles of their medical specialties, but by the pejorative label "abortion doctor." A fetus is described as an "unborn child," and as a "baby," second-trimester, previability abortions are referred to as "late-term,"; and the reasoned medical judgments of highly trained doctors are dismissed as "preferences" motivated by "mere convenience." Instead of the heightened scrutiny we have previously applied, the Court determines that a "rational" ground is enough to uphold the Act. And, most troubling, *Casey's* principles, confirming the continuing vitality of "the essential holding of *Roe*," are merely "assume[d]" for the moment, rather than "retained" or "reaffirmed."

III

A

Without attempting to distinguish *Stenberg* and earlier decisions, the majority asserts that the Act survives review because respondents have not shown that the ban on intact D & E would be unconstitutional "in a large fraction of relevant cases." But *Casey* makes clear that, in determining whether any restriction poses an undue burden on a "large fraction" of women, the relevant class is *not* "all women," nor "all pregnant women," nor even all women "seeking abortions." 505 U.S., at 895. Rather, a provision restricting access to abortion, "must be judged by reference to those [women] for whom it is an actual rather than an irrelevant restriction," *ibid.* Thus the absence of a health exception burdens *all* women for whom it is relevant—women who, in the judgment of their doctors, require an intact D & E because other procedures would place their health at risk. It makes no sense to conclude that this facial challenge fails because respondents have not shown that a health exception is necessary for a large fraction of second-trimester abortions, including those for which a health exception is unnecessary: The very purpose of a health *exception* is to protect women in *exceptional* cases.

IV

Though today's opinion does not go so far as to discard *Roe* or *Casey*, the Court, differently composed than it was when we last considered a restrictive abortion regulation, is hardly faithful to our earlier invocations of "the rule of law" and the "principles of *stare decisis*." Congress imposed a ban despite our clear prior holdings that the State cannot proscribe an abortion procedure when its use is necessary to protect a woman's health. Although Congress' findings could not withstand the crucible of trial, the Court defers to the legislative override of our Constitution-based rulings. A decision so at odds with our jurisprudence should not have staying power.

In sum, the notion that the Partial-Birth Abortion Ban Act furthers any legitimate governmental interest is, quite simply, irrational. The Court's defense of the statute provides no saving explanation. In candor, the Act, and the Court's defense of it, cannot be understood as anything other than an effort to chip away at a right declared again and again by this Court—and with increasing comprehension of its centrality to women's lives. When "a statute burdens constitutional rights and all that can be said on its behalf is that it is the vehicle that legislators have chosen for expressing their hostility to those rights, the burden is undue." *Stenberg*, 530 U.S., at 952 (GINSBURG, J., concurring).

* * *

For the reasons stated, I dissent from the Court's disposition and would affirm the judgments before us for review.

Suggested Readings for Chapter 5

ASSISTED REPRODUCTION AND REPROGENETICS

Andrews, Lori B., and Douglass, Lisa. "Alternative Reproduction." *Southern California Law Review* 65 (November 1991), 623–82.

Buchanan, Allen, Brock, Dan W., Daniels, Norman, and Wikler, Daniel. *From Chance to Choice: Genetics and Justice.* Cambridge: Cambridge University Press, 2000.

Charo, R. Alta. "Children by Choice: Reproductive Technologies and the Boundaries of Personal Autonomy." *Nature Cell Biology* S1 (2002), S23–29.

Cohen, Cynthia B. "'Give Me Children Or I Shall Die': New Reproductive Technologies and Harm to Children." *Hastings Center Report* 26 (1996), 19–27.

———. *New Ways of Making Babies: The Case of Egg Donation.* Bloomington and Indianapolis, IN: Indiana University Press, 1996.

The Council on Ethical and Judicial Affairs, American Medical Association. "Ethical Issues Related to Prenatal Genetic Testing." *Archives of Family Medicine* 3 (1994), 633–42.

Lebacqz, Karen. "Choosing Our Children: The Uneasy Alliance of Law and Ethics in John Robertson's Thought." In Arthur W. Galston and Christiana Z. Peppard, eds. *Expanding Horizons in Bioethics.* Dordrecht, The Netherlands: Springer, 2005, 123–39.

Macklin, Ruth. "Artificial Means of Reproduction and Our Understanding of the Family, *The Hastings Center Report* 21 (1991), 5–11.

———. "What Is Wrong with Commodification?" In Cynthia B. Cohen, ed. *New Ways of Making Babies: The Case of Egg Donation.* Bloomington and Indianapolis, IN: Indiana University Press, 1996.

Mahowald, Mary Briody. *Genes, Women, Equality.* New York: Oxford University Press, 2000, ch. 12.

McGee, G. *The Perfect Baby: Parenthood in the New World of Cloning and Genetics.* Lanham, MD: Rowman & Littlefield, 2000.

Murray, Thomas H. *The Worth of a Child.* Berkeley: University of California Press, 1996, ch. 6.

Nelson, Hilde Lindemann. "Dethroning Choice: Analogy, Personhood, and the New Reproductive Technologies." In Wanda Teays and Laura M. Purdy, eds. *Bioethics, Justice and Health Care.* Belmont, CA: Wadsworth, 2001, 555–64.

The New York State Task Force on Life and the Law. *Assisted Reproductive Technologies: Analysis and Recommendations for Public Policy.* New York: The New York State Task Force on Life and the Law, 1998.

Noah, Lars. "Assisted Reproductive Technologies and the Pitfalls of Unregulated Biomedical Innovation." *Florida Law Review* 55 (April 2003), 603–65

Parens, Erik, and Asch, Adrienne, eds. *Prenatal Testing and Disability Rights.* Washington, DC: Georgetown University Press, 2000.

Parens, Erik, and Knowles, Lori P. "Reprogenetics and Public Policy: Reflections and Recommendations." *The Hastings Center Report* 33 (July–August 2004), S1–24.

Peterson, M. M. "Assisted Reproductive Technologies and Equity of Access Issues." *Journal of Medical Ethics* 31 (2005), 280–85.

President's Council on Bioethics. *Reproduction and Responsibility: The Regulation of New Biotechnologies.* Washington, DC: President's Council on Bioethics, 2004.

Purdy, Laura. "Genetics and Reproductive Risk: Can Having Children be Immoral?" In Helga Kuhse and Peter Singer, eds. *Bioethics: An Anthology,* 2nd ed. Oxford: Blackwell Publishing, 2006, 115–21.

Rao, Radhika. "Assisted Reproductive Technology and the Threat to the Traditional Family." *Hastings Law Journal* 47 (April 1996), 951–65.

Roberts, Dorothy E. "Race and the New Reproduction." *Hastings Law Journal* 47 (April 1996), 935–49.

Robertson, John A. *Children of Choice: Freedom and the New Reproductive Technologies.* Princeton, NJ: Princeton University Press, 1994.

———. "Procreative Liberty and Harm to Offspring in Assisted Reproduction." *American Journal of Law & Medicine* 30 (2004), 7–40.

Rothenberg, Karen H., and Thomson, Elizabeth J., eds. *Women and Prenatal Testing: Facing the Challenges of Genetic Technology.* Columbus, OH: Ohio State University Press, 1994.

Rothman, Barbara Katz. *The Tentative Pregnancy: How Amniocentesis Changes the Experience of Motherhood.* New York: W.W. Norton & Company, 1993.

Ryan, Maura A. *Ethics and Economics of Assisted Reproduction: The Cost of Longing.* Washington, DC: Georgetown University Press, 2001.

———. "The Argument for Unlimited Procreative Liberty: A Feminist Critique." *Hastings Center Report* 20 (July–August 1990), 6–12.

Sherwin, Susan. "Feminist Ethics and In Vitro Fertilization." In Wanda Teays and Laura M. Purdy, eds. *Bioethics, Justice and Health Care.* Belmont, CA: Wadsworth, 2001, 537–42.

Silver, Lee M. *Remaking Eden: How Genetic Engineering and Cloning Will Transform the American Family.* New York: Avon Books, 1998.

Stanworth, Michelle. "Birth Pangs: Conceptive Technologies and the Threat to Motherhood." In Wanda Teays and Laura M. Purdy, eds. *Bioethics, Justice and Health Care.* Belmont, CA: Wadsworth, 2001, 549–54.

Steinbock, Bonnie. *Life before Birth.* New York: Oxford University Press, 1992.

———. "Sex Selection: Not Obviously Wrong." *The Hastings Center Report* 32 (January–February 2002), 23–28.

Wachbroit, Robert, and Wasserman, David. "Reproductive Technology." In Hugh LaFollette, ed. *The Oxford Handbook of Practical Ethics.* New York: Oxford, 2003, 136–60.

Warnock, Mary. *Making Babies: Is There a Right to Have Children?* New York: Oxford University Press, 2002, 55–63, 87–96.

Wasserman, David, Bickenbach, Jerome, Wachbroit, Robert, eds. *Quality of Life and Human Difference: Genetic Testing, Health Care, and Disability.* New York: Cambridge University Press, 2005.

ABORTION

Beckwith, Francis. "Thomson's Equal Reasonableness Argument for Abortion Rights: A Critique." *American Journal of Jurisprudence* 49 (2004), 185–98.

Browne, Alister. "Abortion in Canada." *Cambridge Quarterly of Healthcare Ethics* 14 (2005–07), 287–91.

Callahan, Daniel, and Callahan, Sidney, eds. *Abortion: Understanding Differences.* New York: Plenum Press, 1984.

Card, Robert F. "Two Puzzles For Marquis's Conservative View On Abortion." *Bioethics* 20 (2006), 264–277.

Davis, Michael. "Fetuses, Famous Violinists, and the Right to Continued Aid." *Philosophical Quarterly* 33 (1983), 259–78.

Davis, Nancy (Ann). "The Abortion Debate: The Search for Common Ground." Parts 1–2. *Ethics* 103 (1993), 516–39, 731–78.

Dworkin, Ronald. *Life's Dominion: An Argument about Abortion, Euthanasia and Individual Freedom.* New York: Knopf, 1993.

Dwyer, Susan, and Feinberg, Joel, eds. *The Problem of Abortion,* 3rd ed. Belmont, CA: Wadsworth, 1997.

Engelhardt, H. Tristram. *The Foundations of Bioethics,* 2nd ed. New York: Oxford University Press, 1996, chap. 6.

Gert, Bernard. "Moral Disagreement and Abortion." *Australian Journal of Professional and Applied Ethics* 6 (June 2004), 1–19.

Gevers, Sjef. "Third Trimester Abortion for Fetal Abnormality." *Bioethics* 13 (1999), 306–13.

Ginsburg, Ruth Bader. "Some Thoughts on Autonomy and Equality in Relation to *Roe v. Wade.*" *North Carolina Law Review* 63 (1985), 375–86.

Hall, Timothy. "Abortion, the Right to Life, and Dependence." *Social Theory and Practice: An International and Interdisciplinary Journal of Social Philosophy* 31 (2005–07), 405–29.

Harris, John. "The Concept of the Person and the Value of Life." *Kennedy Institute of Ethics Journal* 9 (December 1999), 293–308.

Harris, John, and Holm, Soren. "Abortion." In Hugh LaFollette, ed. *The Oxford Handbook of Practical Ethics.* New York: Oxford, 2003, 112–35.

Hursthouse, Rosalind. "Virtue Theory and Abortion." *Philosophy & Public Affairs* 20 (1991), 223–46.

Kamm, Frances M. *Creation and Abortion.* New York: Oxford University Press, 1992.

Little, Margaret Olivia. *Abortion, Intimacy, and Responsibilities to Gestate.* Oxford: Clarendon Press, 2003.

Marquis, D. "Abortion and the Beginning and End of Human Life." *Journal of Law, Medicine & Ethics* 34 (2006), 16–25.

Morgan, Lynn M. "Life Begins When They Steal Your Bicycle: Cross-Cultural Practices of Personhood at the Beginnings and Ends of Life." *Journal of Law, Medicine & Ethics* 34 (2006), 8–15.

Noonan, John T., Jr., ed. *The Morality of Abortion: Legal and Historical Perspectives.* Cambridge, MA: Harvard University Press, 1970.

Persson, Ingmar. "Harming the Non-Conscious." *Bioethics* 13 (1999), 294–305.

Pojman, Louis P., and Beckwith, Francis J., eds. *The Abortion Controversy.* Boston: Jones and Bartlett, 1994.

Quinn, Warren. "Abortion: Identity and Loss." *Philosophy & Public Affairs* 13 (1984), 24–54.

Regan, Tom, ed. *Matters of Life and Death.* 3rd ed. New York: Random House, 1992.

Rhoden, Nancy K. "A Compromise on Abortion." *Hastings Center Report* 19 (1989), 32–37.

Sumner, L. W. *Abortion and Moral Theory.* Princeton, NJ: Princeton University Press, 1981.

Thomson, Judith Jarvis. "Rights and Deaths." *Philosophy & Public Affairs* 2 (1973), 146–55.

Tribe, Laurence H. *Abortion: The Clash of Absolutes.* New York: Norton, 1990.

Warren, Mary Anne. "The Moral Significance of Birth." In Wanda Teays and Laura M. Purdy, eds. *Bioethics, Justice and Health Care.* Belmont, CA: Wadsworth, 2001, 477–80.

Chapter 6
Death and Dying

Introduction

In recent decades patients have demanded, and physicians have given, greater deference to patients' wishes regarding how they will die. Respect for a patient's autonomy has grown to encompass a patient's decisions about life-sustaining treatment and whether to hasten death. But what are the precise boundaries of the legitimate practice of medicine when patients request help in ending their lives? There is no consensus among health care professionals, the public, or in public policy about this matter. Many physicians feel strongly that, under appropriate circumstances, assistance in hastening death is a legitimate form of addressing a patient's needs, but other physicians are equally strongly opposed to this idea. The bioethics community is similarly divided. The moral problems underlying this profound disagreement are addressed in the present chapter.

KEY TERMS AND DISTINCTIONS

Physicians and nurses have long worried that if they withdraw treatment and a patient dies, they will be accused of killing the patient. A parallel concern exists that patients who refuse life-sustaining treatment or hasten death are killing themselves and that health professionals assist in the suicide if they comply with refusals or satisfy requests to refuse treatment. A related concern is that physicians who help patients "actively" hasten the time of their deaths are involved either in physician-assisted suicide or euthanasia. What do these key moral notions refer to and what is their moral import?

The Distinction between Killing and Letting Die. Those who reject physician assistance in hastening death often distinguish between overseeing a refusal of treatment and assisting in a suicide. They ground this distinction in the difference between "letting die" and "killing." This distinction is applied to distinguish between practices considered permissible from practices that are always impermissible. Withdrawals or withholdings of treatment have generally been classified in the "letting die" category—depending on the nature of the illness and the intent of the physician. In its ordinary language meaning, *killing* represents a family of ideas whose central condition is direct causation of another's death, whereas *letting die* represents another family of ideas whose central condition is intentional avoidance of intervention so that a death is caused by a disease, injury, or some other "natural" cause.

This distinction between killing and letting die is controversial. A person can be killed by intentionally letting him or her die of a "natural" condition of disease when the death should have been prevented by a physician. If a physician removes a respirator from a patient who needs it and wants to continue to use it, the action is wrong, even though the physician has only removed artificial life support and let nature take its course. Absent the patient's authorization, such "letting die" is morally unacceptable and looks like a case of killing. Is this circumstance properly characterized as a killing, a letting die, or both? Can an act be both? What are we to say about a circumstance in which a physician prescribes a lethal medication at a patient's request, which the patient then voluntarily ingests? Is this a killing, a letting die, or something else altogether?

Of course, physicians could use a so-called "active" means to bring about death, and many would argue that it is the use of an "active" means that accounts for the language of "killing." But there are also problems inherent in the idea that we can determine appropriate and inappropriate conduct by considering whether or not an active means to death was involved. This is notably true in the case of laws (such as the law of Oregon, as discussed later) that allow physicians to prescribe lethal medication to a patient, but do not allow physicians to administer what they prescribe. This does not look like a case of killing, but it also does not look like a case of letting die. What, then, is it; and is it morally permissible?

Euthanasia. Killing, especially by an active means, is often said to be "euthanasia," but this term needs careful definition. *Euthanasia* is the act or practice of ending a person's life in order to release the person from an incurable disease, intolerable suffering, or undignified death. The term is used to refer both to painlessly causing death—an "active" means to death—and to failing to prevent death from natural causes for merciful reasons—a "passive" means to death. Accordingly, two main types of euthanasia are commonly distinguished: *active* euthanasia and *passive* euthanasia. If a person requests the termination of his or her life, the action is called *voluntary euthanasia*. (See the introduction to Dan Brock's essay in this chapter.) If the person is not mentally competent to make an informed request, the action is called *nonvoluntary euthanasia*. Both forms should be distinguished from *involuntary euthanasia*, in which a person capable of making an informed request has not done so. Involuntary euthanasia has been universally condemned and is not under discussion in this chapter. Articles in this chapter that are concerned with euthanasia are exclusively concerned with voluntary active euthanasia (or VAE).

Physician-Assisted Suicide. The term "euthanasia" is today less central to discussions of the problems discussed in this chapter than is the term "physician-assisted suicide." Physician-assisted suicide is a patient's voluntary choice of death (hence the language of suicide) with the assistance of a physician. Unlike voluntary active euthanasia, physician-assisted suicide does not entail that the person who dies be acutely suffering or terminally ill, though these conditions are usually the reasons for electing suicide.

Physician-assisted suicide can be difficult to distinguish from both treatment withdrawals and aggressive physician assistance to control pain. Like many suicides, patients who refuse a treatment often *intend* to end their lives because of their grim prospects, not because they seek death as an end in itself. In some cases, physicians heavily sedate dying patients and the drugs have the *unintended* though *foreseen* effect of causing death. From this perspective, an act of controlling pain causes the death, under the foreknowledge that death might be the outcome. Is this circumstance one of either suicide or physician-hastened death?

It is critically important to be clear about the meanings of all of the central terms in this chapter in order to avoid biased discussion of the issues. As Alan Meisel points out in his article, terms like "active euthanasia," "physician-assisted suicide," and "mercy killing" have deeply negative connotations that may predispose a reader to a negative conclusion even prior to hearing the arguments on both sides of an issue.

LEGISLATION AND LANDMARK CASE LAW

Particular acts of assisting patients in hastening death may be humane, compassionate, and in a patient's best interest. But a social policy that authorizes such acts in medicine, it is often argued, would weaken existing moral restraints that we cannot replace, threatening practices that provide a basis of trust between patients and health care professionals. Should we, then, *legalize* physician involvement in hastening death? If so, what are the limits of the ways in which physicians may be involved? Moral and legal questions in this area are often difficult to separate.

Several issues about killing, letting die, and physician-assisted death have been discussed under the general heading of the "right to die." The notion of a right to die, in particular, points to a liberty right. It derives historically in the United States from a series of landmark "right-to-die" cases dating from *In re Quinlan* (1976). In *Quinlan*, the New Jersey Supreme Court held that it is permissible for a guardian to direct a physician and hospital to discontinue all extraordinary measures. The court asserted that the patient's rights and autonomous judgment are to prevail over the physician's judgment in decisions at the end of life.

The main ethical and legal issue became whether all medical treatments, depending on the circumstances, can be construed as optional. It soon became widely agreed that a passive letting die at a patient's or family's request is acceptable, but an active hastening of death or killing is not. The accepted rule became that there is a right to refuse treatment, but no right to request (or perform) an intentionally hastened death. However, withdrawal or withholding of treatment will hasten death only for persons whose lives are being sustained by such treatment. Many other individuals face a protracted period of dying even when respirators and other life-preserving technology are not being utilized.

Legal and related moral arguments about how these matters should be treated in law are discussed in two articles in this chapter, one by Yale Kamisar and the other by Alan Meisel. Both look carefully at early and late precedent right-to-die cases. Kamisar points out that more than one right is under discussion, so that a patient might have a right against intrusion and a right to privacy, but not a right to assisted suicide. Likewise, one might have a moral right, but not a constitutional right to something—for example, a (moral) right to pain relief, but not a (constitutional) right to lethal drugs, etc. After carefully assessing the status of rights in the precedent legal cases, Kamisar argues that the Supreme Court has not, should not, and likely will not reach a finding of a right to physician-assisted suicide. By contrast, Meisel argues that almost the entire superstructure of the law rests on a body of untenable moral distinctions, such as those between passively and actively hastening death, intending death and merely foreseeing that death will occur, causing death and merely intentionally allowing death, and so on. Meisel tries to show that all major legal arguments advanced by the courts are "fundamentally unsound," using "stock arguments" that are spurious. Most notably, he finds that the courts' persistent reliance on the distinction between a right to passively hasten death and a right to actively hasten death is untenable. At his hands, there truly is a right to die—passively and actively—and it is rooted in rights of self-determination.

The so-called right-to-die movement—a diverse collection of social groups and institutions—has exerted pressure to reform current laws so that physicians are allowed more leeway in facilitating the wishes of patients. A major right-to-die initiative was accepted by the majority of citizens in the state of Oregon. A ballot measure (Measure 16) was first approved by voters in that state in November 1994. It allowed physicians to prescribe lethal drugs for those terminally ill patients who wish to escape unbearable suffering. Under the provisions of the Oregon Death with Dignity Act, which is reprinted in this chapter, a physician is authorized to comply with the request of a terminally ill, mentally competent patient for a prescription for a lethal dose of medication, which the patient can ingest if the dying process becomes intolerable. Eligibility is limited to patients who have received a diagnosis from their attending physician that they have a terminal illness that will cause their death within six months. Patients must manifest a durable, verifiable desire for assistance, and there are various procedural safeguards to ensure that the patient's request is informed and truly voluntary. The patient must ingest the prescribed drug; the physician may not administer it.

This Oregon legislation was upheld as a result of two 1997 U.S. Supreme Court decisions: *Vacco v. Quill* and *Washington v. Glucksberg*, both reprinted in this chapter. The Supreme Court reviewed two decisions in circuit courts that had endorsed a constitutional right to limited physician-assisted suicide (or a right to die). The decisions of these lower courts were reversed by the Supreme Court, which found that there are no *constitutional* rights to physician-hastened dying, but that each state may set its own policy on patients' rights. By returning the issue to the states, the Supreme Court effectively recognized the legal validity of statutes that allow physician-hastened death as well as those that disallow it.

Chief Justice Rehnquist maintains in these opinions that a doctor may provide "aggressive palliative care" that "hastens a patient's death" if the doctor's intent is "only to ease his patient's pain." This doctor is presumably distinguished from the doctor who has the intention of assisting in a suicide because, according to Rehnquist, doctors involved in physician-assisted suicide "must, necessarily and indubitably, intend primarily that the patient be made dead." The Chief Justice appears to be using intention to distinguish between killing and letting die, while assuming that the former is unwarranted and the latter permissible.

This approach has generated controversy. The doctor who prescribes a fatal medication with the intention of giving the patient the choice of using or not using it need have no ill intention; the physician may even try to convince the patient not to use the medication. The doctor's intention may be a benevolent one of easing the patient's anxiety about a loss of control over the dying process, while giving the patient an option he or she has requested. This raises the question of whether the physician's intention is an important consideration at all in assessing the morality of the physician's action.

Despite Rehnquist's stated reservations about physician-assisted suicide, the U.S. Supreme Court decision had the effect of clearing the way for a right to physician-assisted death to be enacted by individual states, which then occurred in Oregon in 1997. The Oregon law appears to reflect the new frontier of issues about whether society should expand autonomy rights to control the moment of death. The cutting edge of the right-to-die movement seems, from this perspective, to have shifted from *refusal* of treatment to *request* for aid.

However, the Oregon law is itself morally controversial. In November 2001, then-U.S. Attorney General John Ashcroft attempted to trump the Oregon law by issuing a rule asserting that "assisting suicide is not a 'legitimate medical purpose'" under the U.S. Code of Federal Regulations. The cited regulation requires all prescriptions for controlled substances to "be issued for a legitimate medical purpose by an individual practitioner acting in the usual course of professional practice." The Attorney General sought to make the prescribing of lethal substances a violation of the Controlled Substances Act, allowing him to revoke the license of any physician who would prescribe the very drugs used in Oregon. The state of Oregon, in turn, sued the U.S. government. The state challenged Ashcroft's authority to limit the practice of medicine under Oregon law. The case—known as *Gonzales v. Oregon*—was eventually decided in 2006 by the U.S. Supreme Court and is included in this chapter. The Supreme Court determined that the Attorney General has no authority to prevent states from authorizing physicians to prescribe lethal medications in the practice of medicine. The Attorney General claimed that intentionally prescribing fatal drugs is not part of acceptable medical practice, which is fundamentally "a healing or curative art." The Court acknowledged that this is one proper understanding of "medicine's boundaries," but the Court also allowed a broader understanding and asserted that the Attorney General could not dictate to physicians the nature of medicine.

The implications of the Gonzales case for the near future in bioethics are discussed in the article by Ronald Lindsay, Tom Beauchamp, and Rebecca Dick. One result of the Supreme Court's series of decisions (the cases in this chapter) is that physician assistance in hastening death remains a legal option in Oregon. Oregon and all states are therefore legally allowed to determine what a physician may do in the way of helping to hasten death. Of course, a legal right does not entail a moral right, and the question of a moral right to physician-hastened death is clearly the central bioethical issue.

MORAL ISSUES ABOUT PHYSICIAN-ASSISTED DEATH

Many who are opposed to the legalization of killing or any form of intentional hastening of death appeal neither to the law nor to the intrinsic moral wrongness of helping someone hasten his or her death. Rather, they appeal to the social consequences that would result from a public policy that supports physician-assisted dying. They argue that assistance in hastening death could not be effectively regulated and would have serious adverse consequences for many, including for those who do not desire such assistance. They believe that the practice inevitably would be expanded to include euthanasia (including nonvoluntary euthanasia), that the quality of palliative care for all patients would deteriorate, that patients would be manipulated or coerced into requesting assistance in hastening death, that patients whose judgment was impaired would be allowed to request such assistance, and that members of allegedly vulnerable groups (the elderly, women, members of racial and ethnic minorities, etc.) would be adversely affected in disproportionate numbers.

A prominent argument in this discussion is the *slippery slope argument*. It proceeds as follows: Although particular acts of active killing are sometimes morally justified, the social consequences of sanctioning practices of killing would run serious risks of abuse and misuse and, on balance, would cause more harm than benefit. The argument is not that these negative consequences will occur immediately, but that they will grow incrementally over time. Although society might start by carefully restricting the number of patients who qualify for assistance in suicide or homicide, these restrictions would be revised and expanded over time, with an ever-increasing risk of unjustified killing. Unscrupulous persons would learn how to abuse the system, just as they learn how to be tax evaders. Slippery slope and other consequence-oriented arguments are discussed in this chapter by several authors, including Brock, Felicia Cohn and Joanne Lynn, Kamisar, and Meisel.

Supporters of a public policy that permits physician-hastened death argue that there is a certain range of cases in which respect for the rights of patients obligates society to respect their decisions. Brock supports this position. Clearly competent patients have a legal and moral right to refuse treatment that brings about their deaths. Why, then, should there not be a similar right to arrange for death by an active means? Proponents of assisted death, such as Brock, point to circumstances in which a condition has become overwhelmingly burdensome for a patient, pain management for the patient is inadequate, and only a physician seems capable of bringing relief. Brock argues that the "central ethical argument" for voluntary active euthanasia is that it promotes patient autonomy and well-being in circumstances in which persons have a strong need to be in control of their lives. Brock does not balk at the thesis that euthanasia involves intentionally killing the innocent, but he argues that such killing is justified under specifiable circumstances. Brock views the argument against euthanasia at the policy level as stronger than the argument against it at the level of individual cases, but he maintains that the objections are unpersuasive at both levels.

In the next selection in this section, Cohn and Lynn rebut the types of arguments (as they see it) that are relied upon by writers of Brock's persuasion. They consider a wide variety of arguments advanced in defense of physician-assisted means to death and try to show that every major argument fails. They argue that the legalization of physician-assisted suicide would pose serious and predictable social harms, especially to the elderly, the frail, the disabled, and the poor, who are already vulnerable to the effects of inadequate health care. Among their basic convictions is that supporters of allowing physician-hastened deaths underestimate how much medicine has to offer to persons who are dying. They believe that a correct approach to pain relief and end-of-life care would eliminate the need for physician-hastened death. Accordingly, they think that the main faults in the current system are in the area of poor palliative and end-of-life care, not in the area of a lack of patient choices about how to die. The best public policy, they suggest, is one that would improve end-of-life care—especially a policy that would promote excellence in palliative care—and not a policy that confers a right to physician-assisted suicide.

In the final article in this section of the chapter, H. Tristram Engelhardt denies that anyone holding any of the persuasions thus far discussed can or will prevail in controversies over physician-hastened death. He thinks that this controversy must be situated in the culture wars that run deeply across all societies that allow open discussion of these issues. Although figures in bioethics may present themselves as having the imprint of morality ("a canonical moral vision") in their views on physician-hastened death, in fact those views are contestable at every important level. Bioethicists therefore need to take moral diversity more seriously than they have in the past and allow "moral difference to have its place" in society and in the negotiation of public policies.

If dire consequences or systemic failures of care will flow from the legal legitimation of hastened death, then it would appear that such practices should be legally prohibited, as Kamisar and Cohn and Lynn recommend. However, Brock and Meisel insist that we need to establish what the evidence is that dire consequences will occur in a system with a strong right to die. In particular, is there a sufficient reason to think that we cannot provide safeguards and maintain control over a public policy of assisted death?

ALTERNATIVES TO PHYSICIAN-ASSISTED DEATH

The final two articles in this chapter discuss alternatives to physician-hastened death that either increase the range of patient autonomy or offer better end-of-life care. In the first, Bernard Gert, Charles M. Culver, and K. Danner Clouser argue that no patient should feel constrained by the health care or long-term care systems to stay alive, because every patient can refuse hydration and nutrition, which will ultimately cause death—a form of so-called *passive* euthanasia. All patients therefore already have the right to control their own destinies, and there is no need to rush to physician-assisted suicide or voluntary *active* euthanasia. These authors maintain that key questions turn on whether a competent patient has rationally refused treatment. What makes a circumstance one of letting a competent person die is the patient's refusal of treatment, not some omission by the physician. Therefore, the distinction between killing and letting die should be retained, but should be based on the difference between patients' *requests* and patients' *refusals*: Dying by self-determined refusal of nutrition (often said to be starvation) is, on this analysis, a case of letting die, not of killing, despite the fact that the physician cares for the patient during, and oversees, the dying process. In this theory, the administration of a lethal dose by the physician would be a case of killing.

In the final article in this chapter, Dan Brock discusses four options that might be presented to patients, so that they can choose how they will die. He argues that both terminal sedation and voluntarily stopping eating and drinking would allow physicians to be responsive to the suffering of certain types of patients, but he argues that these strategies are ethically and clinically closer to physician-assisted suicide and voluntary active euthanasia than has generally been appreciated. He proposes safeguards for a system in which patients can choose to die as they wish and maintains that explicit public policy allowing these alternatives (rather than leaving them hidden, as is now often the case) would reassure many patients who fear a bad death in their future. Unlike Gert and colleagues, he considers physician-assisted suicide as one among the four viable options for patients, the other three being improved palliative care, terminal sedation, and refusal of hydration and nutrition.

Virtually all parties to these controversies believe that improved pain management has made circumstances at least bearable for many patients, reducing the need for physician-hastened death and increasing the need for adequate medical facilities, training, and hospice programs. Nonetheless, as Brock points out, some patients cannot be satisfactorily relieved by medical means because they experience intolerable suffering. If physicians can benefit patients of this description by means of physician-hastened death, should they be restricted by law or morals from doing so? This question is at the center of the contemporary discussion and likely will be for many years into the future.

T.L.B.

THE OREGON DEATH WITH DIGNITY ACT

ALLOWS TERMINALLY ILL ADULTS TO OBTAIN PRESCRIPTION FOR LETHAL DRUGS

Question. Shall law allow terminally ill adult patients voluntary informed choice to obtain physician's prescription for drugs to end life?

Summary. Adopts law. Allows terminally ill adult Oregon residents voluntary informed choice to obtain physician's prescription for drugs to end life. Removes criminal penalties for qualifying physician-assisted suicide. Applies when physicians predict patient's death within 6 months. Requires:

15-day waiting period;
2 oral, 1 written request;
second physician's opinion;
counseling if either physician believes patient has mental disorder, impaired judgment from depression.

Person has choice whether to notify next of kin. Health care providers immune from civil, criminal liability for good faith compliance. . . .

SECTION 2: WRITTEN REQUEST FOR MEDICATION TO END ONE'S LIFE IN A HUMANE AND DIGNIFIED MANNER

§ 2.01 WHO MAY INITIATE A WRITTEN REQUEST FOR MEDICATION

An adult who is capable, is a resident of Oregon, and has been determined by the attending physician and consulting physician to be suffering from a terminal disease, and who has voluntarily expressed his or her wish to die, may make a written request for medication for the purpose of ending his or her life in a humane and dignified manner in accordance with this Act. . . .

SECTION 3: SAFEGUARDS

§ 3.01 ATTENDING PHYSICIAN RESPONSIBILITIES

The attending physician shall:

1. Make the initial determination of whether a patient has a terminal disease, is capable, and has made the request voluntarily;
2. Inform the patient of:
   (a) his or her medical diagnosis;
   (b) his or her prognosis;
   (c) the potential risks associated with taking the medication to be prescribed;
   (d) the probable result of taking the medication to be prescribed;
   (e) the feasible alternatives, including, but not limited to, comfort care, hospice care and pain control.
3. Refer the patient to a consulting physician for medical confirmation of the diagnosis, and for a determination that the patient is capable and acting voluntarily;
4. Refer the patient for counseling if appropriate pursuant to Section 3.03;
5. Request that the patient notify next of kin;
6. Inform the patient that he or she has an opportunity to rescind the request at any time and in any manner, and offer the patient an opportunity to rescind at the end of the 15-day waiting period pursuant to Section 3.06;
7. Verify, immediately prior to writing the prescription for medication under this Act, that the patient is making an informed decision;
8. Fulfill the medical record documentation requirements of Section 3.09;
9. Ensure that all appropriate steps are carried out in accordance with this Act prior to writing a prescription for medication to enable a qualified patient to end his or her life in a humane and dignified manner.

§ 3.02 CONSULTING PHYSICIAN CONFIRMATION

Before a patient is qualified under this Act, a consulting physician shall examine the patient and his or her relevant medical records and confirm, in writing, the attending physician's diagnosis that the patient is suffering from a terminal disease, and verify that the patient is capable, is acting voluntarily and has made an informed decision.

§ 3.03 COUNSELING REFERRAL

If in the opinion of the attending physician or the consulting physician a patient may be suffering from a psychiatric or psychological disorder, or depression causing impaired judgment, either physician shall refer the patient for counseling. No medication to end a patient's life in a humane and dignified manner shall be prescribed until the person performing the counseling determines that the patient is not suffering from a psychiatric or psychological disorder, or depression causing impaired judgment. . . .

§ 3.06 WRITTEN AND ORAL REQUESTS

In order to receive a prescription for medication to end his or her life in a humane and dignified manner, a qualified patient shall have made an oral request and a written request, and reiterate the oral request to his or her attending physician no less than fifteen (15) days after making the initial oral request. At the time the qualified patient makes his or her second oral request, the attending physician shall offer the patient an opportunity to rescind the request.

§ 3.07 RIGHT TO RESCIND REQUEST

A patient may rescind his or her request at any time and in any manner without regard to his or her mental state. No prescription for medication under this Act may be written without the attending physician offering the qualified patient an opportunity to rescind the request.

§ 3.08 WAITING PERIODS

No less than fifteen (15) days shall elapse between the patient's initial oral request and the writing of a prescription under this Act. No less than 48 hours shall elapse between the patient's written request and the writing of a prescription under the Act. . . .

§ 3.11 REPORTING REQUIREMENTS

1. The Health Division shall annually review a sample of records maintained pursuant to this Act.
2. The Health Division shall make rules to facilitate the collection of information regarding compliance with this Act. The information collected shall not be a public record and may not be made available for inspection by the public.

3. The Health Division shall generate and make available to the public an annual statistical report of information collected under Section 3.11(2) of this Act. . . .

§ 3.13 INSURANCE OR ANNUITY POLICIES

The sale, procurement, or issuance of any life, health, or accident insurance or annuity policy or the rate charged for any policy shall not be conditioned upon or affected by the making or rescinding of a request, by a person, for medication to end his or her life in a humane and dignified manner. Neither shall a qualified patient's act of ingesting medication to end his or her life in a humane and dignified manner have an effect upon a life, health, or accident insurance or annuity policy.

§ 3.14 CONSTRUCTION OF ACT

Nothing in this Act shall be construed to authorize a physician or any other person to end a patient's life by lethal injection, mercy killing or active euthanasia. Actions taken in accordance with this Act shall not, for any purpose, constitute suicide, assisted suicide, mercy killing or homicide, under the law.

SECTION 4: IMMUNITIES AND LIABILITIES

§ 4.01 IMMUNITIES

Except as provided in Section 4.02:

1. No person shall be subject to civil or criminal liability or professional disciplinary action for participating in good faith compliance with this Act. This includes being present when a qualified patient takes the prescribed medication to end his or her life in a humane and dignified manner.
2. No professional organization or association, or health care provider, may subject a person to censure, discipline, suspension, loss of license, loss of privileges, loss of membership or other penalty for participating or refusing to participate in good faith compliance with this Act.
3. No request by a patient for or provision by an attending physician of medication in good faith compliance with the provisions of this Act shall constitute neglect for any purpose of law or provide the sole basis for the appointment of a guardian or conservator. . . .

§ 4.02 LIABILITIES

1. A person who without authorization of the patient willfully alters or forges a request for medication or conceals or destroys a rescission of that request with the intent or effect of causing the patient's death shall be guilty of a Class A felony.
2. A person who coerces or exerts undue influence on a patient to request medication for the pur-pose of ending the patient's life, or to destroy a rescission of such a request, shall be guilty of a Class A felony. . . .

SECTION 6: FORM OF THE REQUEST

§ 6.01 FORM OF THE REQUEST

A request for medication as authorized by this act shall be in substantially the [boxed] form.

REQUEST FOR MEDICATION TO END MY LIFE IN A HUMANE AND DIGNIFIED MANNER

I, _____, am an adult of sound mind.

I am suffering from _____, which my attending physician has determined is a terminal dis-ease and which has been medically confirmed by a consulting physician.

I have been fully informed of my diagnosis, prognosis, the nature of medication to be prescribed and potential asso-ciated risks, the expected result, and the feasible alternatives, including comfort care, hospice care and pain control.

I request that my attending physician prescribe medication that will end my life in a humane and dignified manner.

INITIAL ONE:

_____ I have informed my family of my decision and taken their opinions into consideration.

_____ I have decided not to inform my family of my decision.

_____ I have no family to inform of my decision.

I understand that I have the right to rescind this request at any time.

I understand the full import of this request and I expect to die when I take the medication to be prescribed.

I make this request voluntarily and without reservation, and I accept full moral responsibility for my actions.

Signed:_____

Dated:_____

DECLARATION OF WITNESSES

We declare that the person signing this request:

    (a) Is personally known to us or has provided proof of identity;

    (b) Signed this request in our presence;

    (c) Appears to be of sound mind and not under duress, fraud or undue influence;

    (d) Is not a patient for whom either of us is attending physician.

_____Witness 1/Date

_____Witness 2/Date

NOTE: one witness shall not be a relative (by blood, marriage or adoption) of the person signing this request, shall not be entitled to any portion of the person's estate upon death and shall not own, operate or be employed at a health care facility where the person is a patient or resident. If the patient is an inpatient at a health care facility, one of the witnesses shall be an individual designated by the facility.

DENNIS C. VACCO, ATTORNEY GENERAL OF NEW YORK, ET AL., PETITIONERS V. TIMOTHY E. QUILL ET AL.

United States Supreme Court, 1997
ON WRIT OF CERTIORARI TO THE UNITED STATES COURT
OF APPEALS FOR THE SECOND CIRCUIT

CHIEF JUSTICE REHNQUIST delivered the opinion of the Court.

In New York, as in most States, it is a crime to aid another to commit or attempt suicide, but patients may refuse even lifesaving medical treatment. The question presented by this case is whether New York's prohibition on assisting suicide therefore violates the Equal Protection Clause of the Fourteenth Amendment. We hold that it does not. . . .

The Equal Protection Clause commands that no State shall "deny to any person within its jurisdiction the equal protection of the laws." This provision creates no substantive rights. . . . Instead, it embodies a general rule that States must treat like cases alike but may treat unlike cases accordingly. . . .

On their faces, neither New York's ban on assisting suicide nor its statutes permitting patients to refuse medical treatment treat anyone differently than anyone else or draw any distinction between persons. *Everyone,* regardless of physical condition, is entitled, if competent, to refuse unwanted lifesaving medical treatment; *no one* is permitted to assist a suicide. Generally speaking, laws that apply evenhandedly to all "unquestionably comply" with the Equal Protection Clause. . . .

The Court of Appeals, however, concluded that some terminally ill people—those who are on life-support systems—are treated differently than those who are not, in that the former may "hasten death" by ending treatment, but the latter may not "hasten death" through physician-assisted suicide. 80 F. 3d, at 729. This conclusion depends on the submission that ending or refusing lifesaving medical treatment "is nothing more nor less than assisted suicide." *Ibid.* Unlike the Court of Appeals, we think the distinction between assisting suicide and withdrawing life-sustaining treatment, a distinction widely recognized and endorsed in the medical profession and in our legal traditions, is both important and logical; it is certainly rational. . . .

The distinction comports with fundamental legal principles of causation and intent. First, when a patient refuses life-sustaining medical treatment, he dies from an underlying fatal disease of pathology; but if a patient ingests lethal medication prescribed by a physician, he is killed by that medication. . . .

Furthermore, a physician who withdraws, or honors a patient's refusal to begin, life-sustaining medical treatment purposefully intends, or may so intend, only to respect his patient's wishes and "to cease doing useless and futile or degrading things to the patient when [the patient] no longer stands to benefit from them." Assisted Suicide in the United States, Hearing before the Subcommittee on the Constitution of the House Committee on the Judiciary, 104th Cong., 2d Sess., 368 (1996) (testimony of Dr. Leon R. Kass). The same is true when a doctor provides aggressive palliative care; in some cases, painkilling drugs may hasten a patient's death, but the physician's purpose and intent is, or may be, only to ease his patient's pain.

521 U.S. 793; 117 S. Ct. 2293; 138 L. Ed. 2d 834; 1997 U.S. LEXIS 4038; 65 U.S.L.W. 4695; 97 Cal. Daily Op. Service 5027; 97 Daily Journal DAR 8122; 11 Fla. L. Weekly Fed. S 174

A doctor who assists a suicide, however, "must, necessarily and indubitably, intend primarily that the patient be made dead." *Id.*, at 367. Similarly, a patient who commits suicide with a doctor's aid necessarily has the specific intent to end his or her own life, while a patient who refuses or discontinues treatment might not. . . .

The law has long used actors' intent or purpose to distinguish between two acts that may have the same result. See, *e.g., United States v. Bailey*, 444 U.S. 394, 403–406 (1980). . . . Put differently, the law distinguishes actions taken "because of" a given end from actions taken "in spite of" their unintended but foreseen consequences. *Feeney*, 442 U.S., at 279; *Compassion in Dying v. Washington*, 79 F. 3d 790, 858. . . .

Given these general principles, it is not surprising that many courts, including New York courts, have carefully distinguished refusing life-sustaining treatment from suicide. See, *e.g., Fosmire v. Nicoleau*, 75 N.Y. 2d 218, 227, and n. 2, 551 N.E. 2d 77, 82, and n. 2 (1990) ("[M]erely declining medical . . . care is not considered a suicidal act").[1] In fact, the first state-court decision explicitly to authorize withdrawing lifesaving treatment noted the "real distinction between the self-infliction of deadly harm and a self-determination against artificial life support." *In re Quinlan*, 70 N.J. 10, 43, 52. . . .

Similarly, the overwhelming majority of state legislatures have drawn a clear line between assisting suicide and withdrawing or permitting the refusal of unwanted lifesaving medical treatment by prohibiting the former and permitting the latter. And "nearly all states expressly disapprove of suicide and assisted suicide either in statutes dealing with durable powers of attorney in health-care situations, or in 'living will' statutes." *Kevorkian*, 447 Mich., at 478–479, and nn. 53–54, 527 N.W 2d, at 731–732, and nn. 53–54. Thus, even as the States move to protect and promote pa-

tients' dignity at the end of life, they remain opposed to physician-assisted suicide. . . .

For all these reasons, we disagree with respondents' claim that the distinction between refusing life-saving medical treatment and assisted suicide is "arbitrary" and "irrational." Brief for Respondents 44. Granted, in some cases, the line between the two may not be clear, but certainty is not required, even were it possible. Logic and contemporary practice support New York's judgment that the two acts are different, and New York may therefore, consistent with the Constitution, treat them differently. By permitting everyone to refuse unwanted medical treatment while prohibiting anyone from assisting a suicide, New York law follows a longstanding and rational distinction.

New York's reasons for recognizing and acting on this distinction—including prohibiting intentional killing and preserving life; preventing suicide; maintaining physicians' role as their patients' healers; protecting vulnerable people from indifference, prejudice, and psychological and financial pressure to end their lives; and avoiding a possible slide towards euthanasia—are discussed in greater detail in our opinion in *Glucksberg, ante*. These valid and important public interests easily satisfy the constitutional requirement that a legislative classification bear a rational relation to some legitimate end.

The judgment of the Court of Appeals is reversed.

It is so ordered.

NOTE

1. Thus, the Second Circuit erred in reading New York law as creating a "right to hasten death"; instead, the authorities cited by the court recognize a right to refuse treatment, and nowhere equate the exercise of this right with suicide. *Schloendorff v. Society of New York Hospital*, 211 N.Y. 125, 129–130, 105 N.E. 92, 93 (1914), which contains Justice Cardozo's famous statement that "[e]very human being of adult years and sound mind has a right to determine what shall be done with his own body," was simply an informed-consent case. . . .

WASHINGTON, ET AL., PETITIONERS V. HAROLD GLUCKSBERG ET AL.

United States Supreme Court, 1997

ON WRIT OF CERTIORARI TO THE UNITED STATES COURT
OF APPEALS FOR THE NINTH CIRCUIT

CHIEF JUSTICE REHNQUIST delivered the opinion of the Court. . . .

[T]he States are currently engaged in serious, thoughtful examinations of physician-assisted suicide and other similar issues. . . .

Attitudes toward suicide itself have changed . . . but our laws have consistently condemned, and continue to prohibit, assisting suicide. Despite changes in medical technology and notwithstanding an increased emphasis on the importance of end-of-life decision-making, we have not retreated from this prohibition. Against this backdrop of history, tradition, and practice, we now turn to respondents' constitutional claim.

II

The Due Process Clause guarantees more than fair process, and the liberty it protects includes more than the absence of physical restraint. . . . The Clause also provides heightened protection against government interference with certain fundamental rights and liberty interests. . . . We have . . . assumed, and strongly suggested, that the Due Process Clause protects the traditional right to refuse unwanted lifesaving medical treatment. *Cruzan*, 497 U.S., at 278–279. . . .

By extending constitutional protection to an asserted right or liberty interest, we, to a great extent, place the matter outside the arena of public debate and legislative action. . . .

521 U.S. 702; 117 S. Ct. 2258; 117 S. Ct. 2302; 138 L. Ed. 2d 772; 1997 U.S. LEXIS 4039; 65 U.S.L.W. 4669; 97 Cal. Daily Op. Service 5008; 97 Daily Journal DAR 8150; 11 Fla. L. Weekly Fed. S 190

Our established method of substantive-due-process analysis has two primary features: First, we have regularly observed that the Due Process Clause specially protects those fundamental rights and liberties which are, objectively, "deeply rooted in this Nation's history and tradition," *id.*, at 503 (plurality opinion); . . . Second, we have required in substantive-due-process cases a "careful description" of the asserted fundamental liberty interest. . . .

The Washington statute at issue in this case prohibits "aid[ing] another person to attempt suicide," Wash. Rev. Code §9A.36.060(1) (1994), and, thus, the question before us is whether the "liberty" specially protected by the Due Process Clause includes a right to commit suicide which itself includes a right to assistance in doing so.

We now inquire whether this asserted right has any place in our Nation's traditions. Here, as discussed above . . . we are confronted with a consistent and almost universal tradition that has long rejected the asserted right . . .

Respondents contend, however, that the liberty interest they assert *is* consistent with this Court's substantive-due-process line of cases, if not with this Nation's history and practice. Pointing to *Casey* and *Cruzan*, respondents read our jurisprudence in this area as reflecting a general tradition of "self-sovereignty," Brief of Respondents 12, and as teaching that the "liberty" protected by the Due Process Clause includes "basic and intimate exercises of personal autonomy," *id.*, at 10; see *Casey*, 505 U.S., at 847 ("It is a promise of the Constitution that there is a realm of personal liberty which the government may not enter"). According to respondents, our liberty jurisprudence, and the broad, individualistic principles it reflects, protects the "liberty of competent, terminally ill adults to make end-of-life decisions free of undue government interference." Brief for Respondents 10. . . .

[O]ur decisions lead us to conclude that the asserted "right" to assistance in committing suicide is not a fundamental liberty interest protected by the Due Process Clause. The Constitution also requires, however, that Washington's assisted-suicide ban be rationally related to legitimate government interests. . . . This requirement is unquestionably met here. As the court below recognized, 79 F. 3d, at 816–817,[1] Washington's assisted-suicide ban implicates a number of state interests.[2] . . .

First, Washington has an "unqualified interest in the preservation of human life." *Cruzan*, 497 U.S., at 282. The State's prohibition on assisted suicide, like all homicide laws, both reflects and advances its commitment to this interest. . . .

Next, the State has an interest in protecting vulnerable groups—including the poor, the elderly, and disabled persons—from abuse, neglect, and mistakes. The Court of Appeals dismissed the State's concern that disadvantaged persons might be pressured into physician-assisted suicide as "ludicrous on its face." 79 F. 3d, at 825. We have recognized, however, the real risk of subtle coercion and undue influence in end-of-life situations. *Cruzan*, 497 U.S., at 281. Similarly, the New York Task Force warned that "[l]egalizing physician-assisted suicide would pose profound risks to many individuals who are ill and vulnerable. . . . The risk of harm is greatest for the many individuals in our society whose autonomy and well-being are already compromised by poverty, lack of access to good medical care, advanced age, or membership in a stigmatized social group." New York Task Force 120. . . .

We need not weigh exactly the relative strengths of these various interests. They are unquestionably important and legitimate, and Washington's ban on assisted suicide is at least reasonably related to their promotion and protection. We therefore hold that Wash. Rev. Code §9A.36.060(1) (1994) does not violate the Fourteenth Amendment, either on its face or "as applied to competent, terminally ill adults who wish to hasten their deaths by obtaining medication prescribed by their doctors." 79 F. 3d, at 838.

• • •

Throughout the Nation, Americans are engaged in an earnest and profound debate about the morality, legality, and practicality of physician-assisted suicide. Our holding permits this debate to continue, as it should in a democratic society. The decision of the en banc Court of Appeals is reversed, and the case is remanded for further proceedings consistent with this opinion.

It is so ordered.

JUSTICE STEVENS, concurring in the judgments. . . .

A State, like Washington, that has authorized the death penalty and thereby has concluded that the sanctity of human life does not require that it always be preserved, must acknowledge that there are situations in which an interest in hastening death is legitimate. Indeed, not only is that interest sometimes legitimate, I am also convinced that there are times when it is entitled to constitutional protection.

• • •

The state interests supporting a general rule banning the practice of physician-assisted suicide do not have the same force in all cases. . . . That interest not only justifies—it commands—maximum protection of every individual's interest in remaining alive, which in turn commands the same protection for decisions about whether to commence or to terminate life-support systems or to administer pain medication that may hasten death. Properly viewed, however, this interest is not a collective interest that should always outweigh the interests of a person who because of pain, incapacity, or sedation finds her life intolerable, but rather, an aspect of individual freedom. . . .

Although as a general matter the State's interest in the contributions each person may make to society outweighs the person's interest in ending her life, this interest does not have the same force for a terminally ill patient faced not with the choice of whether to live, only of how to die. Allowing the individual, rather than the State, to make judgments "'about the "quality" of life that a particular individual may enjoy'" *ante*, at 25 (quoting *Cruzan*, 497 U.S., at 282), does not mean that the lives of terminally-ill, disabled people have less value than the lives of those who are healthy, see *ante*, at 28. Rather, it gives proper recognition to the individual's interest in choosing a final chapter that accords with her life story, rather than one that demeans her values and poisons memories of her. . . .

Similarly, the State's legitimate interests in preventing suicide, protecting the vulnerable from coercion and abuse, and preventing euthanasia are less significant in this context. I agree that the State has a compelling interest in preventing persons from committing suicide because of depression, or coercion by third parties. But the State's legitimate interest in preventing abuse does not apply to an individual who is not victimized by abuse, who is not suffering from depression, and who makes a rational and voluntary decision to seek assistance in dying. . . .

Relatedly, the State and *amici* express the concern that patients whose physical pain is inadequately treated will be more likely to request assisted suicide. Encouraging the development and ensuring the availability of adequate pain treatment is of utmost importance; palliative care, however, cannot alleviate all pain and suffering. . . . An individual adequately informed of the care alternatives thus might make a rational choice for assisted suicide. For such an individual, the State's interest in preventing potential abuse and mistake is only minimally implicated.

The final major interest asserted by the State is its interest in preserving the traditional integrity of the medical profession. The fear is that a rule permitting physicians to assist in suicide is inconsistent with the perception that they serve their patients solely as healers. But for some patients, it would be a physician's refusal to dispense medication to ease their suffering and make their death tolerable and dignified that would be inconsistent with the healing role. . . . For doctors who have long-standing relationships with their patients, who have given their patients advice on alternative treatments, who are attentive to their patient's individualized needs, and who are knowledgeable about pain symptom management and palliative care options, see Quill, Death and Dignity, A Case of Individualized Decision Making, 324 New England J. of Med. 691–694 (1991), heeding a patient's desire to assist in her suicide would not serve to harm the physician–patient relationship. Furthermore, because physicians are already involved in making decisions that hasten the death of terminally ill patients—through termination of life support, withholding of medical treatment, and terminal sedation—there is in fact significant tension between the traditional view of the physician's role and the actual practice in a growing number of cases. . . .

I agree that the distinction between permitting death to ensue from an underlying fatal disease and causing it to occur by the administration of medication or other means provides a constitutionally suffi-

cient basis for the State's classification. Unlike the Court, however, . . . I am not persuaded that in all cases there will in fact be a significant difference between the intent of the physicians, the patients or the families in the two situations.

There may be little distinction between the intent of a terminally-ill patient who decides to remove her life-support and one who seeks the assistance of a doctor in ending her life; in both situations, the patient is seeking to hasten a certain, impending death. The doctor's intent might also be the same in prescribing lethal medication as it is in terminating life support. A doctor who fails to administer medical treatment to one who is dying from a disease could be doing so with an intent to harm or kill that patient. Conversely, a doctor who prescribes lethal medication does not necessarily intend the patient's death—rather that doctor may seek simply to ease the patient's suffering and to comply with her wishes. The illusory character of any differences in intent or causation is confirmed by the fact that the American Medical Association unequivocally endorses the practice of terminal sedation—the administration of sufficient dosages of pain-killing medication to terminally ill patients to protect them from excruciating pain even when it is clear that the time of death will be advanced. The purpose of terminal sedation is to ease the suffering of the patient and comply with her wishes, and the actual cause of death is the administration of heavy doses of lethal sedatives. This same intent and causation may exist when a doctor complies with a patient's request for lethal medication to hasten her death.

Thus, although the differences the majority notes in causation and intent between terminating life-support and assisting in suicide support the Court's rejection of the respondents' facial challenge, these distinctions may be inapplicable to particular terminally ill patients and their doctors. Our holding today in *Vacco v. Quill* that the Equal Protection Clause is not violated by New York's classification, just like our holding in *Washington v. Glucksberg* that the Washington statute is not invalid on its face, does not foreclose the possibility that some applications of the New York statute may impose an intolerable intrusion on the patient's freedom.

There remains room for vigorous debate about the outcome of particular cases that are not necessarily resolved by the opinions announced today. How such cases may be decided will depend on their specific facts. In my judgment, however, it is clear that the so-called "unqualified interest in the preservation of human life," *Cruzan*, 497 U.S., at 282, *Glucksberg, ante*, at 24, is not itself sufficient to outweigh the interest in liberty that may justify the only possible means of preserving a dying patient's dignity and alleviating her intolerable suffering. . . .

JUSTICE O'CONNOR, concurring.*

. . . I join the Court's opinions because I agree that there is no generalized right to "commit suicide." But respondents urge us to address the narrower question whether a mentally competent person who is experiencing great suffering has a constitutionally cognizable interest in controlling the circumstances of his or her imminent death. I see no need to reach that question in the context of the facial challenges to the New York and Washington laws at issue here. . . . The parties and *amici* agree that in these States a patient who is suffering from a terminal illness and who is experiencing great pain has no legal barriers to obtaining medication, from qualified physicians, to alleviate that suffering, even to the point of causing unconsciousness and hastening death. . . . In this light, even assuming that we would recognize such an interest, I agree that the State's interests in protecting those who are not truly competent or facing imminent death, or those whose decisions to hasten death would not truly be voluntary, are sufficiently weighty to justify a prohibition against physician-assisted suicide. . . .

Every one of us at some point may be affected by our own or a family member's terminal illness. There is no reason to think the democratic process will not strike the proper balance between the interests of terminally ill, mentally competent individuals who would seek to end their suffering and the State's interests in protecting those who might seek to end life mistakenly or under pressure. As the Court recognizes, States are presently undertaking extensive and serious evaluation of physician-assisted suicide and other related issues. . . . In such circumstances, "the . . . challenging task of crafting appropriate procedures for safeguarding . . . liberty interests is entrusted to the 'laboratory' of the States . . . in the first instance." *Cruzan v. Director, Mo. Dept. of Health*, 497 U.S. 261, 292 (1990) (O'CONNOR, J., concurring) (citing *New State Ice Co. v. Liebmann*, 285 U.S. 262, 311 (1932)).

In sum, there is no need to address the question whether suffering patients have a constitutionally cognizable interest in obtaining relief from the suffering that they may experience in the last days of their lives. There is no dispute that dying patients in Washington and New York can obtain palliative care, even when doing so would hasten their deaths. The difficulty in defining terminal illness and the risk that a dying patient's request for assistance in ending his or her life might not be truly voluntary justifies the prohibitions on assisted suicide we uphold here.

NOTES

1. The court identified and discussed six state interests: (1) preserving life; (2) preventing suicide; (3) avoiding the involvement of third parties and use of arbitrary, unfair, or undue influence; (4) protecting family members and loved ones; (5) protecting the integrity of the medical profession; and (6) avoiding future movement toward euthanasia and other abuses. 79 F. 3d, at 816–832.

2. Respondents also admit the existence of these interests, Brief for Respondents 28–39, but contend that Washington could better promote and protect them through regulation, rather than prohibition, of physician-assisted suicide. Our inquiry, however, is limited to the question whether the State's prohibition is rationally related to legitimate state interests.

---

*JUSTICE GINSBURG concurs in the Court's judgments substantially for the reasons stated in this opinion. JUSTICE BREYER joins this opinion except insofar as it joins the opinion of the Court.

ALBERTO R. GONZALES, ATTORNEY GENERAL, ET AL., PETITIONERS v. OREGON ET AL.,

United States Supreme Court, 2006
ON WRIT OF CERTIORARI TO THE UNITED STATES COURT
OF APPEALS FOR THE NINTH CIRCUIT

JUSTICE KENNEDY delivered the opinion of the Court.

The question before us is whether the Controlled Substances Act allows the United States Attorney General to prohibit doctors from prescribing regulated drugs for use in physician-assisted suicide, notwithstanding a state law permitting the procedure. As the Court has observed, "Americans are engaged in an earnest and profound debate about the morality, legality, and practicality of physician-assisted suicide." *Washington* v. *Glucksberg*, 521 U. S. 702, 735 (1997). The dispute before us is in part a product of this political and moral debate, but its resolution requires an inquiry familiar to the courts: interpreting a federal statute to determine whether Executive action is authorized by, or otherwise consistent with, the enactment.

In 1994, Oregon became the first State to legalize assisted suicide when voters approved a ballot measure enacting the Oregon Death With Dignity Act (ODWDA). Ore. Rev. Stat. §127.800 *et seq.* (2003). ODWDA, which survived a 1997 ballot measure seeking its repeal, exempts from civil or criminal liability state-licensed physicians who, in compliance with the specific safeguards in ODWDA, dispense or prescribe a lethal dose of drugs upon the request of a terminally ill patient.

The drugs Oregon physicians prescribe under ODWDA are regulated under a federal statute, the Controlled Substances Act (CSA or Act). 84 Stat. 1242, as amended, 21 U. S. C. §801 *et seq.* The CSA allows these particular drugs to be available only by a written prescription from a registered physician. In the ordinary course the same drugs are prescribed in smaller doses for pain alleviation.

A November 9, 2001 Interpretive Rule issued by the Attorney General addresses the implementation and enforcement of the CSA with respect to ODWDA. It determines that using controlled substances to assist suicide is not a legitimate medical practice and that dispensing or prescribing them for this purpose is unlawful under the CSA. The Interpretive Rule's validity under the CSA is the issue before us. . . .

The present dispute involves controlled substances listed in Schedule II, substances generally available only pursuant to a written, nonrefillable prescription by a physician. 21 U. S. C. §829(a). A 1971 regulation promulgated by the Attorney General requires that every prescription for a controlled substance "be issued for a legitimate medical purpose by an individual practitioner acting in the usual course of his professional practice." 21 CFR §1306.04(a) (2005).

To prevent diversion of controlled substances with medical uses, the CSA regulates the activity of physicians. To issue lawful prescriptions of Schedule II drugs, physicians must "obtain from the Attorney General a registration issued in accordance with the rules and regulations promulgated by him." 21 U. S. C. §822(a)(2). The Attorney General may deny, suspend, or revoke this registration if, as relevant here, the physician's registration would be "inconsistent with the public interest." §824(a)(4); §822(a)(2). When deciding whether a practitioner's registration is in the public interest, the Attorney General "shall" consider:

"1. The recommendation of the appropriate State licensing board or professional disciplinary authority.

"2. The applicant's experience in dispensing, or conducting research with respect to controlled substances.

"3. The applicant's conviction record under Federal or State laws relating to the manufacture, distribution, or dispensing of controlled substances.

"4. Compliance with applicable State, Federal, or local laws relating to controlled substances.

"5. Such other conduct which may threaten the public health and safety." §823(f).

The CSA explicitly contemplates a role for the States in regulating controlled substances, as evidenced by its preemption provision. . . .

The reviewing physicians must keep detailed medical records of the process leading to the final prescription, §127.855, records that Oregon's Department of Human Services reviews, §127.865. Physicians who dispense medication pursuant to ODWDA must also be registered with both the State's Board of Medical Examiners and the federal Drug Enforcement Administration (DEA). §127.815(1)(L). In 2004, 37 patients ended their lives by ingesting a lethal dose of medication prescribed under ODWDA. Oregon Dept. of Human Servs., Seventh Annual Report on Oregon's Death with Dignity Act 20 (Mar. 10, 2005). . . .

On November 9, 2001, without consulting Oregon or apparently anyone outside his Department, the Attorney General issued an Interpretive Rule announcing his intent to restrict the use of controlled substances for physician-assisted suicide. Incorporating the legal analysis of a memorandum he had solicited from his Office of Legal Counsel, the Attorney General ruled

"assisting suicide is not a 'legitimate medical purpose' within the meaning of 21 CFR 1306.04 (2001), and that prescribing, dispensing, or administering federally controlled substances to assist suicide violates the Controlled Substances Act. Such conduct by a physician registered to dispense controlled substances may 'render his registration . . . inconsistent with the public interest' and therefore subject to possible suspension or revocation under 21 U. S. C. 824(a)(4). The Attorney General's conclusion applies regardless of whether state law authorizes or permits such conduct by practitioners or others and regardless of the condition of the person whose suicide is assisted." 66 Fed. Reg. 56608 (2001).

There is little dispute that the Interpretive Rule would substantially disrupt the ODWDA regime. Respondents contend, and petitioners do not dispute, that every prescription filled under ODWDA has specified drugs classified under Schedule II. A physician cannot prescribe the substances without DEA registration, and revocation or suspension of the registration would be a severe restriction on medical practice. Dispensing controlled substances without a valid prescription, furthermore, is a federal crime. . . .

In response the State of Oregon, joined by a physician, a pharmacist, and some terminally ill patients, all from Oregon, challenged the Interpretive Rule in federal court. The United States District Court for the District of Oregon entered a permanent injunction against the Interpretive Rule's enforcement.

A divided panel of the Court of Appeals for the Ninth Circuit granted the petitions for review and held the Interpretive Rule invalid. . . . It reasoned that, by making a medical procedure authorized under Oregon law a federal offense, the Interpretive Rule altered the "'"usual constitutional balance between the States and the Federal Government"'" without the requisite clear statement that the CSA authorized such action. . . .

The Government first argues that the Interpretive Rule is an elaboration of one of the Attorney General's own regulations, 21 CFR §1306.04 (2005), which requires all prescriptions be issued "for a legitimate medical purpose by an individual practitioner acting in the usual course of his professional practice." . . .

The regulation uses the terms "legitimate medical purpose" and "the course of professional practice," ibid., but this just repeats two statutory phrases and attempts to summarize the others. It gives little or no instruction on a central issue in this case: Who decides whether a particular activity is in "the course of professional practice" or done for a "legitimate medical purpose"? Since the regulation gives no indication how to decide this issue, the Attorney General's effort to decide it now cannot be considered an interpretation of the regulation. . . .

Turning first to the Attorney General's authority to make regulations for the "control" of drugs, this delegation cannot sustain the Interpretive Rule's attempt to define standards of medical practice. . . .

It is not enough that the terms "public interest," "public health and safety," and "Federal law" are used in the part of the statute over which the Attorney General has authority. The statutory terms "public interest" and "public health" do not call on the Attorney General, or any other Executive official, to make an independent assessment of the meaning of federal law. The Attorney General did not base the Interpretive Rule on an application of the five-factor test generally, or the "public health and safety" factor specifically. Even if he had, it is doubtful the Attorney General could cite the "public interest" or "public health" to deregister a physician simply because he deemed a controversial practice permitted by state law to have an illegitimate medical purpose. . . .

The importance of the issue of physician-assisted suicide, which has been the subject of an "earnest and profound debate" across the country, *Glucksberg*, 521 U. S., at 735, makes the oblique form of the claimed delegation all the more suspect. Under the Government's theory, moreover, the medical judgments the Attorney General could make are not limited to physician-assisted suicide. Were this argument accepted, he could decide whether any particular drug may be used for any particular purpose, or indeed whether a physician who administers any controversial treatment could be deregistered. This would occur, under the Government's view, despite the statute's express limitation of the Attorney General's authority to registration and control, with attendant restrictions on each of those functions, and despite the statutory purposes to combat drug abuse and prevent illicit drug trafficking. . . .

In deciding whether the CSA can be read as prohibiting physician-assisted suicide, we look to the statute's text and design. The statute and our case law amply support the conclusion that Congress regulates medical practice insofar as it bars doctors from using their prescription-writing powers as a means to engage in illicit drug dealing and trafficking as conventionally understood. Beyond this, however, the statute manifests no intent to regulate the practice of medicine generally. . . .

Oregon's regime is an example of the state regulation of medical practice that the CSA presupposes. Rather than simply decriminalizing assisted suicide, ODWDA limits its exercise to the attending physcians of terminally ill patients, physicians who must be licensed by Oregon's Board of Medical Examiners. . . .

In the face of the CSA's silence on the practice of medicine generally and its recognition of state regulation of the medical profession it is difficult to defend the Attorney General's declaration that the statute impliedly criminalizes physician-assisted suicide. . . . A prescription, the Government argues, necessarily implies that the substance is being made available to a patient for a legitimate medical purpose. The statute, in this view, requires an anterior judgment about the term "medical" or "medicine." The Government contends ordinary usage of these words ineluctably refers to a healing or curative art, which by these terms cannot embrace the intentional hastening of a patient's death. It also points to the teachings of Hippocrates, the positions of prominent medical organizations, the Federal Government, and the judgment of the 49 States that have not legalized physician-assisted suicide as further support for the proposition that the practice is not legitimate medicine. . . .

On its own, this understanding of medicine's boundaries is at least reasonable. The primary problem with the Government's argument, however, is its assumption that the CSA impliedly authorizes an Executive officer to bar a use simply because it may be inconsistent with one reasonable understanding of medical practice. . . .

The Government, in the end, maintains that the prescription requirement delegates to a single Executive officer the power to effect a radical shift of authority from the States to the Federal Government to define general standards of medical practice in every locality. The text and structure of the CSA show that Congress did not have this far-reaching intent to alter the federal-state balance and the congressional role in maintaining it.

The judgment of the Court of Appeals is

Affirmed.

SCALIA, J., dissenting

JUSTICE SCALIA, with whom CHIEF JUSTICE ROBERTS and JUSTICE THOMAS join, dissenting.

The Court concludes that the Attorney General lacked authority to declare assisted suicide illicit under the Controlled Substances Act (CSA), because the CSA is concerned only with "*illicit* drug dealing and trafficking," *ante,* at 23 (emphasis added). This question-begging conclusion is obscured by a flurry of arguments that distort the statute and disregard settled principles of our interpretive jurisprudence. . . .

The [Attorney General's] Directive . . . purports to do three distinct things: (1) to interpret the phrase "legitimate medical purpose" in the Regulation to exclude physician-assisted suicide; (2) to determine that prescribing, dispensing, and administering federally controlled substances to assist suicide violates the CSA; and (3) to determine that participating in physician-assisted suicide may render a practitioner's registration "inconsistent with the public interest" within the meaning of 21 U. S. C. §§823(f) and 824(a)(4) (which incorporates §823(f) by reference). The Court's analysis suffers from an unremitting failure to distinguish among these distinct propositions in the Directive. . . .

It is beyond dispute . . . that a "prescription" under §829 must issue for a "legitimate medical purpose." . . .

The Directive is assuredly valid insofar as it interprets "prescription" to require a medical purpose that is "legitimate" as a matter of *federal* law—since that is an interpretation of "prescription" that we ourselves have adopted. *Webb* v. *United States*, 249 U. S. 96 (1919), was a prosecution under the Harrison Act of a doctor who wrote prescriptions of morphine "for the purpose of providing the user with morphine sufficient to keep him comfortable by maintaining his customary use," *id.*, at 99. The dispositive issue in the case was whether such authorizations were "prescriptions" within the meaning of §2(b) of the Harrison Act, predecessor to the CSA. *Ibid.* We held that "to call such an order for the use of morphine a physician's prescription would be so plain a perversion of meaning that no discussion of the subject is required." *Id.*, at 99–100. Like the Directive, this interprets "prescription" to require medical purpose that is legitimate as a matter of federal law. And the Directive is also assuredly valid insofar as it interprets "legitimate medical purpose" as a matter of federal law to exclude physician-assisted suicide, because that is not only a permissible but indeed the most natural interpretation of that phrase. . . .

In sum, the Directive's construction of "legitimate medical purpose" is a perfectly valid agency interpretation of its own regulation; and if not that, a perfectly valid agency interpretation of the statute. No one contends that the construction is "plainly erroneous or inconsistent with the regulation." . . . In fact, as explained below, the Directive provides *the most natural* interpretation of the Regulation and of the

statute. The Directive thus definitively establishes that a doctor's order authorizing the dispensation of a Schedule II substance for the purpose of assisting a suicide is not a "prescription" within the meaning of §829. . . .

Virtually every relevant source of authoritative meaning confirms that the phrase "legitimate medical purpose"* does not include intentionally assisting suicide. "Medicine" refers to "[t]he science and art dealing with the prevention, cure, or alleviation of disease." Webster's Second 1527. The use of the word "legitimate" connotes an *objective* standard of "medicine," and our presumption that the CSA creates a uniform federal law regulating the dispensation of controlled substances, see *Mississippi Band of Choctaw Indians* v. *Holyfield*, 490 U. S. 30, 43 (1989), means that this objective standard must be a federal one. As recounted in detail in the memorandum for the Attorney General that is attached as an appendix to the Directive (OLC Memo), virtually every medical authority from Hippocrates to the current American Medical Association (AMA) confirms that assisting suicide has seldom or never been viewed as a form of "prevention, cure, or alleviation of disease," and (even more so) that assisting suicide is not a "legitimate" branch of that "science and art." See OLC Memo, App. to Pet. for Cert. 113a–130a. Indeed, the AMA has determined that "[p]hysician-assisted suicide is fundamentally incompatible with the physician's role as a healer." . . . "[T]he overwhelming weight of authority in judicial decisions, the past and present policies of nearly all of the States and of the Federal Government, and the clear, firm and unequivocal views of the leading associations within the American medical and nursing professions, establish that assisting in suicide . . . is not a legitimate medical purpose." . . .

The only explanation for such a distortion is that the Court confuses the *normative* inquiry of what the boundaries of medicine *should be*—which it is laudably hesitant to undertake—with the *objective* inquiry of what the accepted definition of "medicine" *is*. The same confusion is reflected in the Court's remarkable statement that "[t]he primary problem with the Government's argument . . . is its assumption that the CSA impliedly authorizes an Executive officer to bar

---

*This phrase appears only in the Regulation and not in the relevant section of the statute. But as pointed out earlier, the Court does not contest that this is the most reasonable interpretation of the section—regarding it, indeed, as a mere "parroting" of the statute.

a use simply because it may be inconsistent with *one reasonable understanding* of medical practice." *Ibid.* (emphasis added). The fact that many in Oregon believe that the boundaries of "legitimate medicine" *should be* extended to include assisted suicide does not change the fact that the overwhelming weight of authority (including the 49 States that condemn physician-assisted suicide) confirms that they have not yet been so extended. Not even those of our Eighth Amendment cases most generous in discerning an "evolution" of national standards would have found, on this record, that the concept of "legitimate medicine" has evolved so far. See *Roper* v. *Simmons*, 543 U. S. 551, 564–567 (2005).

The Court contends that the phrase "legitimate medical purpose" *cannot* be read to establish a broad, uniform federal standard for the medically proper use of controlled substances. *Ante*, at 22. But it also rejects the most plausible alternative proposition, urged by the State, that any use authorized under state law constitutes a "legitimate medical purpose." . . .

Even assuming, however, that the *principal* concern of the CSA is the curtailment of "addiction and recreational abuse," there is no reason to think that this is its *exclusive* concern. We have repeatedly observed that Congress often passes statutes that sweep more broadly than the main problem they were designed to address. "[S]tatutory prohibitions often go beyond the principal evil to cover reasonably comparable evils, and it is ultimately the provisions of our laws rather than the principal concerns of our legislators by which we are governed." *Oncale* v. *Sundowner Offshore Services, Inc.*, 523 U. S. 75, 79 (1998). See also *H. J. Inc.* v. *Northwestern Bell Telephone Co.*, 492 U. S. 229, 248 (1989). . . .

Even if we could rewrite statutes to accord with sensible "design," it is far from a certainty that the Secretary, rather than the Attorney General, ought to control the registration of physicians. Though registration decisions sometimes require judgments about the legitimacy of medical practices, the Department of Justice has seemingly had no difficulty making them. See *In re Harline*, 65 Fed. Reg. 5665; *In re Tecca*, 62 Fed. Reg. 12842; *In re Roth*, 60 Fed. Reg. 62262. But unlike decisions about whether a substance should be scheduled or whether a narcotics addiction treatment is legitimate, registration decisions are not exclusively, or even primarily, concerned with "medical [and] scientific" factors. See 21 U. S. C. §823(f). Rather, the decision to register, or to bring an action to deregister, an individual *physician* implicates all

the policy goals and competing enforcement priorities that attend any exercise of prosecutorial discretion. It is entirely reasonable to think (as Congress evidently did) that it would be easier for the Attorney General occasionally to make judgments about the legitimacy of medical practices than it would be for the Secretary to get into the business of law enforcement. It is, in other words, perfectly consistent with an intelligent "design of the statute" to give the Nation's chief law enforcement official, not its chief health official, broad discretion over the substantive standards that govern registration and deregistration. That is *especially* true where the contested "scientific and medical" judgment at issue has to do with the legitimacy of physician-assisted suicide, which ultimately rests, not on "science" or "medicine," but on a naked value judgment. It no more depends upon a "quintessentially medical judgmen[t]," *ante*, at 20, than does the legitimacy of polygamy or eugenic infanticide. And it requires no particular *medical* training to undertake the objective inquiry into how the continuing traditions of Western medicine have consistently treated this subject. See OLC Memo, App. to Pet. for Cert. 113a–130a. The Secretary's supposedly superior "medical expertise" to make "medical judgments," *ante*, at 19–20, is strikingly irrelevant to the case at hand. . . .

In sum, the Directive's first conclusion—namely that physician-assisted suicide is not a "legitimate medical purpose"—is supported both by the deference we owe to the agency's interpretation of its own regulations and by the deference we owe to its interpretation of the statute. The other two conclusions—(2) that prescribing controlled drugs to assist suicide violates the CSA, and (3) that such conduct is also "inconsistent with the public interest"—are inevitable consequences of that first conclusion. Moreover, the third conclusion, standing alone, is one that the Attorney General is authorized to make.

The Court's decision today is perhaps driven by a feeling that the subject of assisted suicide is none of the Federal Government's business. It is easy to sympathize with that position. The prohibition or deterrence of assisted suicide is certainly not among the enumerated powers conferred on the United States by the Constitution, and it is within the realm of public morality (*bonos mores*) traditionally addressed by the so-called police power of the States. But then, neither is prohibiting the recreational use of drugs or discouraging drug addiction among the enumerated powers. From an early time in our national history, the Federal Government has used its enumerated powers, such as its power to regulate interstate commerce, for the purpose of protecting public morality—for example, by banning the interstate shipment of lottery tickets, or the interstate transport of women for immoral purposes. See *Hoke* v. *United States*, 227 U. S. 308, 321–323 (1913); *Lottery Case*, 188 U. S. 321, 356 (1903). Unless we are to repudiate a long and well-established principle of our jurisprudence, using the federal commerce power to prevent assisted suicide is unquestionably permissible. The question before us is not whether Congress *can* do this, or even whether Congress *should* do this; but simply whether Congress *has* done this in the CSA. I think there is no doubt that it has. If the term "*legitimate* medical purpose" has any meaning, it surely excludes the prescription of drugs to produce death.

For the above reasons, I respectfully dissent from the judgment of the Court.

Moral Arguments about the Law

YALE KAMISAR

The Rise and Fall of the "Right" to Assisted Suicide

Yale Kamisar is the Clarence Darrow Distinguished University Professor of Law Emeritus at the University of Michigan Law School. In his work in constitutional law and criminal procedure, he has published *The Supreme Court: Trends and Developments* (five annual volumes). He has written numerous articles on euthanasia and assisted suicide, dating from the earliest discussions of the issues in the United States and Great Britain.

When, more than forty years ago, I first wrote about the law and policy governing death and dying,[1] I never thought that someday it would be seriously argued that there is (or ought to be) a constitutional right to assisted suicide or active voluntary euthanasia, or both. Some would say I lacked the foresight or imagination to contemplate such a development. But I believe my attitude was understandable. As my colleague Carl Schneider recently observed, "Throughout most of American history no one would have supposed biomedical policy could or should be made through constitutional adjudication. No one would have thought that the Constitution spoke to biomedical issues, that those issues were questions of federal policy, or that judges were competent to handle them.[2] However, *Roe v. Wade*[3] and *Cruzan v. Director, Missouri Department of Health*[4] were to change all that. . . .

Proponents of physician-assisted suicide . . . relied heavily on *Cruzan*, the first Supreme Court case on death, dying, and the right of privacy ever decided and the only Supreme Court case on the subject until the 1997 physician-assisted suicide cases, *Washington v. Glucksberg* and *Vacco v. Quill*. The *Cruzan* Court did not need to, and did not, discuss the right or liberty interest in determining the time and manner of one's death, hastening one's death, or obtaining the active intervention of a physician to help bring about one's suicide. The only assumption that the *Cruzan* Court made for purposes of that case was that a competent person had a constitutionally protected interest in refusing unwanted

From *The Case against Assisted Suicide: For the Right to End-of-Life Care*, ed. Kathleen Foley, M.D. and Herbert Hendin, M.D., pp. 71–93. © 2002 The Johns Hopkins University Press.

life-sustaining medical treatment (even artificially delivered food and water).

Although the right to terminate artificial life-support systems and the right to enlist the assistance of another in committing suicide can be, and have been, lumped together under the rubric of "right to die," the two "rights" are different in important respects. As the New York State Task Force on Life and the Law noted, the so-called right to die should mean only, and until recently meant only, "a right against intrusion," a right to resist "a direct invasion of bodily integrity, and in some cases, the use of physical restraints, both of which are flatly inconsistent with society's basic conception of personal dignity."[5] To be sure, a total prohibition against assisted suicide does close an "avenue of escape," but, unlike a refusal to honor a competent patient's request to terminate life-sustaining treatment, it does not force one into "a particular, all-consuming, totally dependant, and indeed rigidly standardized life: the life of one confined to a hospital bed, attached to medical machinery, and tended to by medical professionals."[6]

Not only would a prohibition against rejecting life-sustaining treatment impose a more onerous burden on persons affected than does a ban against assisted suicide (indeed, in some cases a ban against forgoing or terminating life support could lead to the almost total "occupation" of a person's life by medical machinery and the "expropriation" of a person's body from his or her own will), it also would impair the autonomy of a great many more people. As Justice William Brennan pointed out in his dissenting opinion in *Cruzan*, more than three-fourths of the two million people who die in this country every year do so in hospitals and long-term care institutions, and most of these individuals die "after a decision to forgo life-sustaining treatment has been made."[7] If life-sustaining treatment could not be rejected, vast numbers of patients would be "at the mercy of every technological advance."[8] Moreover, if patients could refuse potentially lifesaving treatment at the outset but not discontinue the treatment once it went into effect, many patients probably would not seek such treatment in the first place. In short, allowing a patient to die at some point is a practical condition on the successful operation of medicine.

The same can hardly be said of physician-assisted suicide or physician-administered active voluntary euthanasia. . . .

However, the U.S. Court of Appeals for the Ninth and Second Circuits read *Roe* and *Cruzan* very differently from the way I and many other commentators have. As a result, in 1996, within the span of a single month, both the Ninth Circuit in *Compassion in Dying v. Washington* (renamed, when the case reached the U.S. Supreme Court, *Washington v. Glucksberg*) and the Second Circuit in *Quill v. Vacco* held that there was a constitutional right to physician-assisted suicide under certain circumstances. Until these decisions were handed down, no state or federal appellate court in this country had ever held that there was a constitutional right to assisted suicide no matter how narrow the circumstances or stringent the conditions.

The Ninth Circuit and Second Circuit decisions shattered a general consensus that withholding or withdrawing lifesaving treatment constitutes neither suicide nor assisted suicide nor homicide. Starting with the landmark *Quinlan* case, various state supreme courts had explicitly recognized the significance of the distinction between refusal of medical treatment and active intervention to end life. To be sure, "the moral significance of the distinction has been subjected to periodic philosophical challenge," but the distinction "has remained a basic tenet of health care law and mainstream medical ethics."[9] As Alexander Morgan Capron has pointed out,[10] the Ninth Circuit viewed the right to forgo unwanted medical treatment and the right to enlist the assistance of a physician in committing suicide as nothing more than *sub*categories of *the same* broad right or liberty interest: "controlling the time and manner of one's death" or "hastening one's death."[11] The Ninth Circuit did not merely smudge the distinction between "letting die" and actively intervening to promote or to bring about death—it disparaged the distinction: "We see no ethical or constitutionally cognizable difference between a doctor's pulling the plug on a respirator and his prescribing drugs which will permit a terminally ill patient to end his own life. In fact, some might argue that pulling the plug is a more culpable and aggressive act on the doctor's part and provides more reason for the criminal prosecution. To us, what matters most is that the death of the patient is the intended result as surely in one case as in the other."[12]

If the Ninth Circuit belittled the distinction between letting die and actively intervening to help bring about death, it did not treat more kindly another distinction long relied on by opponents of physician-assisted suicide: the distinction between giving a patient a drug for the purpose of killing the patient and administering drugs for the purpose of relieving pain, with the knowledge that it may have a "double effect"—hastening the patient's death as well as reducing the patient's pain. The Ninth Circuit could "see little, if any, difference for constitutional or ethical purposes between providing medication with a double effect and providing medication with a single effect, as long as one of the known effects in each case is to hasten the end of the patient's life."

Although the Second Circuit summarily rejected the Ninth Circuit's due process analysis, it was no more impressed than the other federal court of appeals with the distinction between "allowing nature to take its course" and "intentionally using an artificial death-producing device." Indeed, the *Quill* court went a step further. What it considered to be "the moral and legal identity of those two modes of hastening death [became] the crux of [its] argument for prohibiting laws banning assisted suicide." The Second Circuit maintained that New York had not treated terminally ill people facing similar circumstances alike: terminally ill persons on life support systems "are allowed to hasten their death by directing the removal of such systems," but persons off life support who are "similarly situated" except for being attached to life-sustaining equipment "are not allowed to hasten death by self-administering prescribed drugs." The Second Circuit would have us believe that much like a person who has been speaking prose throughout life without being aware of it, many physicians and other health professionals have been helping people commit suicide almost every day of their professional lives without realizing it: "Withdrawal of life support requires physicians or those acting on their direction physically to remove equipment and, often, to administer palliative drugs which may themselves contribute to death. The ending of life by these means is nothing more nor less than assisted suicide. It simply cannot be said that those mentally competent, terminally-ill persons who seek to hasten death but whose treatment does not include life support are treated equally."

The 1996 decisions by the two federal courts of appeals generated a good deal of momentum in favor of physician-assisted suicide. . . . But then the U.S. Supreme Court entered the fray—and brought the momentum to a screeching halt.

CHIEF JUSTICE REHNQUIST'S OPINIONS IN *GLUCKSBERG* AND *QUILL*

Chief Justice Rehnquist wrote the opinion of the Court in both *Washington v. Glucksberg* (the Ninth Circuit case) and *Vacco v. Quill* (the Second Circuit case). The chief justice disagreed with the two lower federal courts virtually point by point, and he in effect eradicated all the lower courts' stirring language in favor of a constitutional right to physician-assisted suicide. It may be useful to summarize briefly the main arguments the *Glucksberg* and *Quill* plaintiffs made in assailing a *total* prohibition against physician-assisted suicide and the reasons Chief Justice Rehnquist gave for rejecting each of these arguments (using the chief justice's own language wherever possible).

Argument: Withdrawal of life support is nothing more or less than assisted suicide; there is no significant moral or legal distinction between the two practices. The right to forgo unwanted life-sustaining medical treatment and the right to enlist a physician's assistance in dying by suicide are merely *sub*categories of *the same* broad right or liberty interest—controlling the time and manner of one's death or hastening one's death.

Response: The distinction between assisting suicide and terminating lifesaving treatment is "widely recognized and endorsed in the medical profession and in our legal traditions [and] is both important and logical." The decision to commit suicide with a physician's assistance "may be just as personal and profound as the decision to refuse unwanted medical treatment, but it has never enjoyed similar legal protection. Indeed, the two acts are widely and reasonably regarded as quite distinct."

Argument: There is no significant difference between administering palliative drugs with the knowledge that it is likely to hasten the patient's death and prescribing a lethal dose of drugs for the very purpose of killing the patient. As the Ninth Circuit put it, there is no real distinction between providing medication with a double effect and providing it with a single effect "as long as one of the known effects in each case is to hasten the end of the patient's life."

Response: In some cases, to be sure, "painkilling drugs may hasten a patient's death, but the physician's purpose and intent is, or may be, only to ease his patient's pain. . . . The law has long used actors' intent or purpose to distinguish between two acts that may have the same result. . . . The law distinguishes actions taken 'because of' a given end [dispensing drugs in order to bring about death] from actions taken 'in spite of' their unintended but foreseen consequences [providing aggressive palliative care that may hasten death, or increase its risk]."

Argument: The 1990 *Cruzan* case is not simply a case about the right to forgo unwanted medical treatment. Considering the facts, it is really a case about personal autonomy and the right to control the time and manner of one's death. *Cruzan*'s extension of the right to refuse medical treatment to include the right to forgo life-sustaining nutrition and hydration was "influenced by the profound indignity that would be wrought upon an unconscious patient by the slow atrophy and disintegration of her body [and] can only be understood as a recognition of the liberty, at least in some circumstances, to physician assistance in ending one's life."

Response: Cruzan is *not* a suicide or an assisted suicide case. The Court's assumption in that case was not based, as the Second Circuit supposed, "on the proposition that patients have a general and abstract 'right to hasten death,' but on well established, traditional rights to bodily integrity and freedom from unwanted touching." Indeed, "in *Cruzan* itself, we recognized that most States outlawed assisted suicide—and even more do today—and we certainly gave no intimation that the right to refuse unwanted medical treatment could be somehow transmuted into a right to assistance in committing suicide."

Argument: Fourteenth Amendment Due Process protects one's right to make intimate and personal choices, such as those relating to marriage, procreation, and child rearing—as well as the time and manner of one's death. As the Ninth Circuit observed, quoting language from *Planned Parenthood v. Casey*: "Like the decision of whether or not to have an abortion, the decision how and when to die is one of 'the most intimate and personal choices a person may make in a lifetime,' a choice 'central to personal dignity and autonomy.'"

Response: The capacious, one might even say majestic, language in *Casey* simply "described, in a general way and in light of our prior cases, those personal activities and decisions that this Court has iden-

tified as so deeply rooted in our history and traditions, or so fundamental to our concept of constitutionally ordered liberty, that they are protected by the Fourteenth Amendment." However, the fact that many of the rights and liberties protected by due process "sound in personal autonomy does not warrant the sweeping conclusion that any and all important, intimate, and personal decisions are so protected, and *Casey* did not suggest otherwise."

JUSTICE O'CONNOR'S CONCURRING OPINION

I am well aware that in both *Glucksberg* and *Quill* Justice O'Connor provided the fifth vote (along with Justices Scalia, Kennedy, and Thomas) to make the chief justice's opinions the opinions of the Court—by stating that she joined Chief Justice Rehnquist's opinion, yet writing separately. I am aware, too, that in large measure two other members of the Court, Justices Ginsburg and Breyer, joined O'Connor's opinion.

However, there is no indication in Justice O'Connor's brief concurring opinion that she found any of the principal arguments made by physician-assisted suicide proponents any more persuasive than the chief justice did. There is no suggestion, for example, that she reads the *Cruzan* opinion any more broadly than does the chief justice or that she interprets the stirring language in *Casey* any more expansively. Nor is there any suggestion that she has any more difficulty accepting the distinction between forgoing life-sustaining medical treatment and actively intervening to bring about death. Nor is there any reason to think that she has more trouble grasping the double effect principle.

Indeed, in one respect at least Justice O'Connor may have gone a step further than the chief justice. I think she may be saying—she is certainly implying—that the principle of double effect is not only plausible but *necessary*. Her position (and Justice Breyer's as well) seems to be that if, for example, a state were to prohibit the pain relief that a patient desperately needs when the increased dosage of medication is so likely to hasten death or cause unconsciousness that, according to the state, the procedure smacks of assisted suicide or euthanasia, she (presumably along with Justices Breyer and Ginsburg) would want to revisit the question.

Early in her concurring opinion, Justice O'Connor does say that there is no need to address "the narrower question whether a mentally competent person who is experiencing great suffering has a constitutionally cognizable interest in *controlling the circumstances* of his or her imminent death." As her opinion continues, the general question about a constitutionally protected interest in controlling the circumstances of one's death is put aside and the opinion turns into a narrower and more focused discussion about the liberty interest in obtaining needed pain relief or in preventing a state from erecting legal barriers preventing access to such relief.

This is why, I believe, Justice O'Connor deems it important that the parties and amici agree that the states of Washington and New York have imposed no legal barriers to pain relief. "*In this light,*" she continues, "even assuming" that there is a constitutionally protected interest in controlling the circumstances of one's death, "the State's interests . . . are sufficiently weighty to justify a prohibition against physician-assisted suicide." Moreover, at the end of her opinion, Justice O'Connor describes the "constitutionally cognizable interest" rather narrowly: "In sum, there is no need to address the question whether suffering patients have a constitutionally cognizable interest *in obtaining relief from the suffering that they may experience in the last days of their lives.* There is no dispute that dying patients in Washington and New York *can obtain* palliative care, *even when doing so would hasten their deaths.*"

In isolation, "obtaining relief from suffering" could mean assisted suicide or euthanasia. In context, however, I think it means only a liberty interest in obtaining pain relief. In light of her entire opinion, I believe Justice O'Connor's description of the constitutionally cognizable interest at the end of her opinion is more accurate than the one she refers to at the outset. Justice O'Connor's overall view appears to be that *so long as a state erects no legal barriers to obtaining pain relief* (even when the analgesics may hasten death or cause unconsciousness), the state's interests in protecting those who are not truly competent or whose wish to commit suicide is not truly voluntary (and the difficulties involved in defining "terminal illness" and ascertaining who fits that category) are sufficiently strong to uphold a total ban against physician-assisted suicide.

As best I can tell, Justice Breyer, who joined Justice O'Connor's opinion (except insofar as her opinion joined the majority) and also wrote separately, took essentially the same position as O'Connor. Even assuming that there is something like a "right to die with dignity," Justice Breyer saw no need to decide whether such a right is "fundamental." Why not? Because, as he saw it, "the avoidance of severe physical pain (connected with death) would have to comprise an essential part of any successful claim" and "as Justice O'Connor points out, the laws before us do not *force* a dying patient to undergo that kind of pain." "Rather," continued Breyer, the laws of New York and of Washington allow physicians to provide patients with pain-relieving drugs "despite the risk that those drugs themselves will kill." *So long as this is the case,* concluded Breyer, laws prohibiting physician-assisted suicide "would overcome any remaining significant interests" making up a "dying with dignity" claim and thus withstand constitutional challenge.

Justice Breyer emphasized that the crucial question is not whether a patient is receiving adequate palliative care but whether *state laws* prevent a patient from obtaining such care: "We [are] . . . told that there are many instances in which patients do not receive the palliative care that, in principle, is available, but that is so for institutional reasons or inadequacies or obstacles, which would seem possible to overcome, and which do not include a *prohibitive set of laws.*" I believe some passages in Solicitor General Dellinger's amicus brief and some of his remarks during the oral arguments significantly illuminate the views of both Justice O'Connor and Justice Breyer.

Although the solicitor general denied that "there is a broad liberty interest in deciding the timing and manner of one's death," he went on to say that the term *liberty* in the Due Process Clause "is broad enough to encompass an interest on the part of terminally ill, mentally competent adults in obtaining relief from the kind of suffering experienced by the plaintiffs in this case." Not only is a liberty interest implicated when a state inflicts severe pain or suffering on someone, continued the solicitor general, but also when a state "compels a person" to suffer severe pain caused by an illness by "prohibiting access to medication that would alleviate the condition." During the oral arguments General Dellinger maintained:

A person states a cognizable liberty interest when he or she alleges that the state is imposing severe pain and suffering *or has adopted a rule which prevents someone from the only means of relieving that pain and suffering.* . . .

If one alleges the kind of severe pain and agony that is being suffered here and that *the state is the cause of standing between you and the only method of relieving that,* you have stated a constitutionally cognizable liberty interest.[13]

Kathryn Tucker, the lead lawyer for the plaintiffs in the *Glucksberg* case, addressed the Court immediately after Solicitor General Dellinger. She was not pleased with the solicitor general's description of the liberty interest at stake: "The Solicitor General's comment that what we're dealing with here is simply a liberty interest in avoiding pain and suffering . . . absolutely trivializes the claim. We have a constellation of interests [including decisional autonomy and the interest in bodily integrity], each of great Constitutional dimension."[14] It may well be that a liberty interest in obtaining pain relief or not being denied access to such relief is only a "trivialized" version of the liberty interest really at stake. But Justices O'Connor and Breyer focused heavily, perhaps exclusively, on that trivialized or downsized version. . . .

In a sense, the Court's support for the principle of double effect is a victory for everybody. For whatever position they may take on assisted suicide or euthanasia, surely most people want those who are dying and severely ill to suffer as little physical pain as possible. And as Howard Brody observed, "Clinicians need to believe to some degree in some form of the principle of double effect in order to provide optimal symptom relief at the end of life. . . . A serious assault on the logic of the principle of double effect could do major violence to the (already reluctant and ill-informed) commitment of the mass of physicians to the goals of palliative care and hospice."[15]

In a way, however, the showing of support for the principle of double effect by the highest court in the land was a special victory for opponents of assisted suicide and euthanasia. For they have long defended the principle. And they did so again in the *Glucksberg* and *Quill* cases. . . .

A good number of those favoring the legalization (or constitutionalization) of physician-assisted suicide have sharply criticized the principle of double effect. They have condemned the supposed hypocrisy in both permitting the use of analgesics that hasten death and banning euthanasia. They have further maintained that killing to relieve suffering has already been sanctioned in the context of "risky pain relief." Moreover, it is worth recalling that it was the 8-3 majority of the U.S. Court of Appeals for the Ninth Circuit that disparaged the double effect principle—as Brody puts it, dismissing the principle as "moral hypocrisy." A robust version of the principle of double effect—the view that even when the level of medication is likely to cause death, the principle may be constitutionally required—helps *opponents* of physician-assisted suicide, *not* pro-

ponents of the practice. For one of the main arguments against the legalization of physician-assisted suicide is that "properly trained health care professionals can effectively meet their patients' needs for compassionate end-of-life care without acceding to requests for suicide."[16] . . . The principle of double effect eases the task of health care professionals—and eases the plight of their patients—and thus weakens the case for physician-assisted suicide.

SOME FINAL THOUGHTS ON JUSTICE O'CONNOR'S CONCURRING OPINION

. . . Since one of the principal arguments made by opponents of physician-assisted suicide is that once established for terminally ill patients assisted suicide would not remain so limited for very long, it was not surprising that several justices voiced doubts about whether the claimed right or liberty interest would or could or should be limited to those on the threshold of death.[17] But Tucker stood her ground.

She told the Court that "we do draw the line at a patient who is confronting death" because, unlike other individuals who wish to die by suicide, one on the threshold of death *no longer* has a choice between living and dying, but "only the choice of *how* to die."[18] She also recognized that a state may prevent a *non*–terminally ill person from choosing suicide because one day that person might "rejoice in that," but the same could not be said for the person who is terminally ill—for his or her life is about to end anyhow.

Moreover, when asked to define the liberty interest Timothy Quill and other plaintiffs in the New York case were claiming, Tucker's co-counsel, Professor Laurence Tribe, told the Court that it "is the liberty, *when facing imminent and inevitable death*, not to be forced by the government to endure . . . pain and suffering"; "the freedom, *at this threshold at the end of life*, not to be a creature of the state but to have some voice in the question of how much pain one is really going through" [emphasis added]. This caused Justice Scalia to respond, "Why does the voice just [arise] when death is imminent?" . . .

THE FUTURE OF THE "RIGHT" TO PHYSICIAN-ASSISTED SUICIDE IN THE SUPREME COURT

I have to agree with the many Court watchers (especially those who were unhappy with the result in the assisted suicide cases) who say that *Glucksberg* and

Quill will not be the Court's last word on the subject. But it hardly follows that the next time the Court confronts the issue it will establish a right to assisted suicide in some limited form. There were a number of factors at work when the Supreme Court decided the 1997 physician-assisted suicide cases, and most of them will still be operating when the Court addresses the issue [in the future]. . . .

Still another factor that must have had some impact on at least some members of the Court, and is bound to influence at least some of the justices in future cases, is the strong opposition of the AMA and other medical groups to the constitutionalization or legalization of physician-assisted suicide, regardless of how narrowly limited the constitutional right or the statutory authorization might be. . . .

Finally, another factor at work in the assisted suicide cases, and one that will operate as well the next time the Court confronts the issue, is the justices' realization that if they were to establish a right to assisted suicide, however limited, the need to enact legislation implementing and regulating any such right would generate many problems—which inevitably would find their way back to the Court.

Whether a regulatory mechanism would be seen as providing patients and physicians with much-needed protection or as unduly burdening the underlying right would be largely in the eye of the beholder. Thus it is not surprising that proponents of physician-assisted suicide even disagree among themselves as to how a particular procedural requirement should be regarded. . . .

THE FUTURE OF THE "RIGHT" TO PHYSICIAN-ASSISTED SUICIDE IN THE POLITICAL ARENA

. . . Anecdotes about individual cases and stirring rhetoric about personal autonomy and self-determination are one thing; concrete and detailed proposals designed to cover thousands of cases are something else. As the eminent ethicist Sissela Bok recently observed, "No society has yet worked out the hardest questions of how to help those patients who desire to die, without endangering others who do not."[19] This is not the only problem confronting proponents of physician-assisted suicide. The Supreme Court not only reversed the Ninth and Second Circuit physician-assisted suicide decisions, it disagreed with the lower federal courts virtually point by point. As noted earlier, the Supreme Court in effect wiped out all the lower courts' very strong and very quotable language in favor of physician-assisted suicide. . . .

There are only so many arguments one can make in favor of a "right" to physician-assisted suicide—and almost all of them were addressed by the Supreme Court in *Glucksberg* and *Quill*. I think it fair to say the Court did not find any of them convincing. Thus these arguments have lost a considerable amount of credibility and will be easier to rebuff when made again, albeit in a different setting.

NOTES

1. See Y. Kamisar, "Some Non-Religious Views against Proposed 'Mercy-Killing' Legislation," *Minnesota Law Review* 42 (1958):969–1042.

2. C. E. Schneider, "Making Biomedical Policy through Constitutional Adjudication: The Example of Physician-Assisted Suicide," in *Law at the End of Life: The Supreme Court and Assisted Suicide*, ed. C. E. Schneider (Ann Arbor, Mich.: University of Michigan Press, 2000), 164–217, 164.

3. 410 U.S. 113 (1973).

4. 497 U.S. 261 (1990).

5. New York State Task Force on Life and the Law, *When Death Is Sought: Assisted Suicide and Euthanasia in the Medical Context* (New York: New York State Task Force on Life and the Law, 1994), 71.

6. J. Rubenfeld, "The Right to Privacy," *Harvard Law Review* 102 (1989):737–94, 794.

7. *Cruzan*, 497 U.S. at 302–3.

8. See n. 5, New York State Task Force 1994, 75.

9. F. G. Miller, "Legalizing Physician-Assisted Suicide by Judicial Decision: A Critical Appraisal," *BioLaw* 2, Special Section (1996):S136–45, S141.

10. A. M. Capron, "Liberty, Equality, Death!" *Hastings Center Report* 26, no. 3 (1996):23–24.

11. See *Compassion in Dying*, 79 F.3d at 802.

12. *Compassion in Dying*, 79 F.3d at 824.

13. Transcript of Oral Argument, *Glucksberg* (No. 96-110), available in 1997 WL 13671, at *18, *20–21 (8 January 1997), emphasis added.

14. Transcript of Oral Argument, *Glucksberg* (No. 96-110), available in 1997 WL 13671, at *35–36.

15. See H. Brody, "Physician-Assisted Suicide in the Courts: Moral Equivalence, Double Effect, and Clinical Practice," *Minnesota Law Review* 82 (1998):939–63, 960.

16. Brief of the American Medical Association, the American Nurses Association, and the American Psychiatric Association et al. as Amicus Curiae in Support of Petitioners at 3, *Glucksberg* (No. 96-110), available in 1996 WL 656263.

17. See Transcript of Oral Argument, *Glucksberg* (No. 96-110), available in 1997 WL 13671, at *27, *29, *33–35, *50–51 (8 January 1997).

18. Transcript of Oral Argument, *Glucksberg* (No. 96-110), available in 1997 WL 13671, at *28, emphasis added.

19. S. Bok, "Physician-Assisted Suicide," in *Euthanasia and Physician-Assisted Suicide*, G. Dworkin et al. (Cambridge: Cambridge University Press, 1998), 83–139, 139.

ALAN MEISEL

Physician-Assisted Suicide: A Common Law Roadmap

Alan Meisel is Dickie, McCamey & Chilcote Professor of Bioethics, and Professor of Law and Psychiatry, University of Pittsburgh School of Law. He is co-author of *The Right to Die* (3d ed. 2004) and *Informed Consent: Legal Theory and Clinical Practice* (1987). He has published extensively on physician-assisted suicide and the right to die as well as on health law.

Although the Supreme Court has upheld the constitutionality of state prohibitions on physician-assisted suicide, efforts to legalize physician-assisted suicide on state-law grounds are likely to continue. One way to legalize such action would be the enactment of referenda like Oregon's in other states. This may occur in a few states, but will be unlikely in most because the process of placing a question on a statewide ballot is extremely cumbersome. State legislatures could also revise existing legislation prohibiting assisted suicide by creating an exception, hedged with safeguards like the Oregon statute's, for physician-assisted suicide for the terminally ill. This too seems unlikely to occur to any great extent. Physician-assisted suicide, like abortion, is just too controversial a subject for legislatures to vote to approve regardless of individual legislators' views on the subject. . . .

THE CONSENSUS ABOUT FORGOING LIFE-SUSTAINING TREATMENT AND THE BRIGHT LINE BETWEEN ACTIVELY AND PASSIVELY HASTENING DEATH

. . . Some forms of physician aid-in-dying have been accepted in American law for the past two decades. The celebrated *In re Quinlan* case, decided in 1976, marked the first step in the legalization of physician aid-in-dying. *Quinlan* has more than 100 progeny in half the states,[1] and has spawned a variety of legislative

This article was originally published in the *Fordham Urban Law Journal* as *Physician-Assisted Suicide: A Common Law Roadmap for State Courts*, 24 FORDHAM URB. L. J. 817 (1997).

enactments that recognize the legal right to "passively" hasten death. Passively hastening death includes refusal of treatment, termination of life support, forgoing treatment, or withholding and withdrawing treatment, and variants on these terms.

This agglomeration of case and statutory law comprises a well-accepted legal consensus from which it is reasonable to infer how the case law on passively hastening death will develop in the states that have not yet had an authoritative appellate case. This consensus rests on three fundamental points: (1) there is a legal right of autonomy or self-determination which vests in competent individuals the right to refuse medical treatment, even if death results; (2) persons who have lost decision-making capacity have a right to have their families decide to withhold or withdraw medical treatment, even if death results; and (3) there is a bright line between the refusal of treatment that results in death and more "active" means of hastening death.

Quinlan, and the consensus that has evolved from it, acknowledge a clear awareness of the distinction between passively and actively hastening death. Courts and legislatures are mindful of this distinction and have taken special pains to distinguish the two forms of hastening death. In fact, it is fair to say that this distinction has been the bedrock of the consensus. Without this distinction, it is doubtful that *Quinlan* would have been decided as it was or that the legal consensus about forgoing life-sustaining treatment would have evolved.

Opponents of the legalization of physician-assisted suicide object that *Quinlan* and its progeny are different because the current movement is for the legalization of *actively* hastening death. Regardless of terminology, the common feature is that life-sustaining medical treatment is either stopped or not started. In actuality, there never was a bright legal, logical or moral line between the two; the distinction was never more than semantic.

Only a few judges have been willing to acknowledge this, the best known of whom is Justice Scalia. In *Cruzan v. Director*,[2] he devoted a substantial part of his concurring opinion to arguing that there was no constitutional right to passively hasten death because it was the equivalent of killing and the states had the constitutional authority to prohibit such conduct if they so chose. Many illustrations could be plucked from his opinion, but one should suffice:

Starving oneself to death [his characterization of forgoing artificial nutrition and hydration procedures] is no different from putting a gun to one's temple as far as the common-law definition of suicide is concerned; the cause of death in both cases is the suicide's conscious decision to "pu[t] an end to his own existence."[3]

Yet, for two decades courts created and maintained the fiction, with little, if any, in-depth analysis, that there is a difference, a determinative difference, between passively and actively hastening death. . . .

Synonyms for actively hastening death, such as suicide, assisted suicide, active euthanasia, and mercy killing, have deeply negative connotations. They would have been like Typhoid Mary to the development of the law of end-of-life decision-making. No one wanted to associate with these terms for fear of becoming tainted. Thus, courts that wanted to recognize a right of both competent and incompetent individuals to be free of unwanted medical treatment realistically appraised the situation and determined that the best way to establish this right was to conceptualize, compartmentalize, and package the "right to die" to make it more acceptable. The most fundamental way in which courts did this was to proclaim not merely a significant difference, but a legally determinative difference between actively and passively hastening death, even if such a difference did not exist. This was accomplished by concluding that passively hastening death does not meet the requirements of the criminal offenses of homicide or assisted suicide, but actively hastening death does.

PURPORTED DISTINCTIONS BETWEEN PASSIVELY AND ACTIVELY HASTENING DEATH

The primary motivation for seeking judicial review in end-of-life decision-making cases is the fear of liability arising from forgoing life-sustaining treatment. Although the opinions of the appellate courts allude to the fear of both civil and criminal liability, the major concern has been with criminal liability. It has been asserted that forgoing life-sustaining treatment would constitute some form of criminal homicide in the case of patients lacking decision-making capacity, and aiding, assisting, or abetting suicide in the case of competent patients. The possibility of liability for conspiracy or accessory liability has also lurked in the background of the cases.

Beginning with *Quinlan*, the courts have steadfastly hewed to the position that forgoing life-sustaining treatment does *not* subject the participants—either those who make the decision or those who actually withhold or withdraw the treatment—to criminal liability. In so doing, judges have not merely legitimated the forgoing of life-sustaining treatment, they have also endeavored to distinguish passively hastening death from actively hastening death, and to condemn the latter.

The courts have achieved this dual effort by employing three stratagems, sometimes alone and sometimes in combination. The fundamental idea is that passively hastening death is not a crime because (1) death results from an omission rather than an act, (2) the intent necessary to support a crime is lacking, and/or (3) the omission is not the cause of the patient's death. Each of these stratagems, in effect, negates an essential element of a crime: act, intent, or causation. In addition, a small number of courts have taken a fourth tack and concluded that there is no criminal liability because the patient has a legal right to refuse treatment.

A.   ACT AND OMISSION

1.   THE TRADITIONAL EXPLANATION

The first method of avoiding criminal liability when life-sustaining medical treatment is forgone begins with the assertion that forgoing treatment is an omission, not an act. The locution sometimes used is that when treatment is forgone, the patient is allowed to die; no one is killing him. In the case of a competent patient, it is maintained that the patient is not committing suicide but merely omitting treatment. These arguments are founded on the assumption that acts are culpable but omissions are not. Thus, passively hastening death by forgoing life-sustaining treatment is not culpable, but actively hastening death is.

2. DIFFICULTIES WITH THE TRADITIONAL EXPLANATION

There are at least three problems with this approach, any one of which is fatal.

a. Liability for Omissions The most general flaw with the traditional explanation is that this assertion about the nature of criminal liability is flat-out wrong; liability may be imposed for an omission. Although it is well accepted black-letter law, both in criminal law and the civil law of torts, that an omission to act is not culpable, this is merely a general rule or presumption that can be overcome by showing that the party who omitted to act was under a duty to do so.

There are various ways to show an individual had a duty to act. In the context of life-sustaining medical treatment, one can look for a duty established by contract or by the actor's voluntarily undertaking to act on behalf of the victim. In the present context, the two are essentially indistinguishable: the doctor-patient relationship is generally agreed to be contractual in nature; and although as a general rule a physician has no obligation to treat a patient, once there is an agreement to do so, a duty arises to continue to provide treatment until the relationship is terminated in any one of a number of legally acceptable ways. . . .

b. Forgoing Treatment May Be Accomplished by an Act The second problem with the argument that forgoing life-sustaining treatment is not criminally culpable because it is an omission rather than an act is that sometimes "forgoing" treatment *is* accomplished by an act, not by an omission. There are two ways in which treatment may be forgone. "Withholding" treatment is readily and uncontroversially denominated an omission. The one almost universally involved in the reported cases, however, is "withdrawing" treatment.

Withdrawing treatment ordinarily requires the physician, or someone under the physician's authority and acting at the physician's direction, to *do* something to stop treatment, such as removing ventilatory support or a feeding tube. That being the case, someone performs an act which leads to the patient's death.

c. Difficulty in Distinguishing Between Act and Omission A third problem with the traditional expla-

nation is the difficulty in characterizing behavior as either an act or an omission. The New Jersey Supreme Court addressed this problem in *In re Conroy:*[4]

Characterizing conduct as active or passive is often an elusive notion, even outside the context of medical decision-making.

Saint Anselm of Canterbury was fond of citing the trickiness of the distinction between "to do" (facere) and "not to do" (non facere). In answer to the question "What's he doing?" we say "He's just sitting there" (positive), really meaning something negative: "He's not doing anything at all." . . .

The distinction is particularly nebulous, however, in the context of decisions whether to withhold or withdraw life-sustaining treatment.[5]

That the very same treatment can be forgone either by withholding (omitting to act) or by withdrawing (acting) strongly suggests that the legal consequences should not depend on such slim semantic differences having no practical difference between them.

Take the case of a patient who is being kept alive by a feeding tube, as has so often been the situation in litigated cases. When a decision is made to forgo tube-feeding, there are two general ways to accomplish it: one is to take the feeding tube out; the other is to leave it in place but not introduce any further fluids or nourishment through the tube. Is death achieved by an act or by an omission? More fundamentally, should legal culpability turn on such hair-splitting distinctions that have no practical differences? Thus, as the New Jersey Supreme Court concluded, "'merely determining whether what was done involved a fatal act or omission does not establish whether it was morally acceptable. . . . [In fact, a]ctive steps to terminate life-sustaining interventions may be permitted, indeed required, by the patient's authority to forgo therapy even when such steps lead to death.'"[6]

Similar scenarios can be sketched for other common forms of life support. A ventilator could be turned off and the tube removed from the patient. This seems to be an act, and, thus, would be legally culpable as long as the other elements of a crime could be proved. Instead, the patient could be left on the ventilator and the gases not properly adjusted or replenished when they run out. Death, by this latter course, would result from an omission, and it would not be culpable. . . .

B. INTENT

1. THE TRADITIONAL EXPLANATION

Some courts have distinguished actively from passively hastening death on the basis of their having a different intent, and they have justified nonliability for the latter on the absence of the kind of intent necessary to constitute a crime. According to conventional reasoning, in cases of genuine suicide, the individual's intent is to bring about his death. By contrast, forgoing life-sustaining treatment does not constitute suicide because the patient's wish is not to end life. Indeed, the patient is said to have no specific intent to die.

Rather, in forgoing life-sustaining treatment, the patient's intent is said to be the relief of suffering. Under this explanation, because death from forgoing life-sustaining treatment is not suicide, the physician has not aided suicide and is not subject to criminal liability. By contrast, actively hastening death is said to be quite different because the intent is unabashedly to cause the patient's death.

2. DIFFICULTIES WITH THE TRADITIONAL EXPLANATION: THE NATURE OF CRIMINAL INTENT

On closer analysis, the intent-based explanations of why there is no liability for a patient's death from forgoing treatment and the purported distinction between passively and actively hastening death are unsupportable. The courts in right-to-die cases have been content to substitute platitudes about intent for analysis. They have utterly failed to examine the conventional meanings of intent in criminal law. Had they done so, they might have concluded that when death is passively hastened, it is hard to avoid the conclusion that criminal intent exists.

For there to be criminal liability, there must be proof of a requisite mental element, traditionally referred to as mens rea, malice, or scienter. This requirement in modern American criminal law, as exemplified by the Model Penal Code, has been replaced by the concept of culpability. Under the Model Penal Code, the general requirement of culpability is established by proof that the actor acted "purposely, knowingly, recklessly or negligently, as the law may require, with respect to each material element of the offense." To convict a person of murder, there must be proof that the actor acted "purposely or knowingly."

The courts have taken the position that when life-sustaining medical treatment is forgone, the physician's purpose was to relieve suffering. Therefore, in passively hastening death there is no liability for assisted suicide, homicide, or related crimes because the actor's purpose was not to cause death. This explanation, however, suffers from two defects. First, it overlooks the fact that culpability (or mens rea) may be established in other ways. Second, it confuses intent with motive.

a. Establishing Culpability Culpability need not be proved exclusively by demonstrating that the actor's purpose was to cause death. An alternative is to prove that the actor acted "knowingly." That is, one may be criminally liable, even absent a purpose to cause death, if one knew that one's conduct would cause death.

The assertion that the intent was to relieve suffering is certainly credible in end-of-life decisions. That it is credible, however, does not negate the existence of another intent—the intent to cause death. No reason exists in law or in fact why an actor cannot possess and be driven to action simultaneously by two intents, especially when those intents are complementary. The existence of a nonblameworthy intent (the intent to relieve suffering) certainly does not eliminate the possibility of the actor's simultaneously possessing a blameworthy intent (the intent to cause death), nor in law does the existence of the former somehow cancel the effect of the latter.

b. Avoiding Culpability by the Use of Double Effect One possible way to avoid this trap is to claim that the actor's intent was to relieve suffering but acknowledge that this intent can only be accomplished by causing death; that is, death is the unintended consequence of another, intended consequence. This is the reasoning used to explain and validate the so-called doctrine of double effect in end-of-life decision-making. This doctrine is employed to legitimate the decades', if not centuries', old practice of using medication for the relief of pain and anxiety in terminally ill patients, even if the patient dies from the medication. Such medications, given in adequate doses to be effective, are capable of killing the patient because of their depressing effect on respiration. Thus, a physician who gives a patient an analgesic or sedative adequate to relieve the patient's symptoms might actively hasten the patient's death. By applying the doctrine of double effect, however, as long as the physician's primary purpose in prescribing the medication is to manage the patient's pain or suffering, the unintended result of the patient's death should not expose the physician to criminal liability.

Although the doctrine of double effect is well accepted by medical ethicists and physicians to justify giving a patient possibly lethal doses of medication to relieve serious pain and/or anxiety, this mode of justification has received scant attention from the courts. Perhaps this is because the logic of this doctrine skirts the edges of accepted principles of intent and causation in criminal (and tort) law. If courts were seriously to challenge the doctrine of double effect, the result might be quite the opposite of promoting the humane practice of medicine.

c. Confusion of Motive and Intent Another difficulty with the argument that forgoing life-sustaining treatment does not implicate criminal liability because the actor's intent is not blameworthy is that it confuses intent with motive. . . .

If a patient's suffering or own evaluation of his quality of life is such that he wishes to end his life, then it is correct to say that his motive, *i.e.*, what motivates him to end his life or to authorize another to do so, is to relieve suffering. His legally relevant intent, however, is to die because that is the consequence he seeks to achieve. A physician may also be motivated to end a patient's suffering, and the patient's surrogate may authorize the physician to forgo life-sustaining treatment motivated by the same concern, but the intent, as far as the law is concerned, is still to bring about the patient's death. Thus, although we might not wish to call a death resulting from forgoing life-sustaining treatment a suicide or homicide, it is hard to see how this result can be achieved simply by saying that the intent to bring about death is absent.

d. Equivalent Intent in Actively and Passively Hastening Death A final problem with the effort to distinguish passively and actively hastening death on the basis of differential intent is that whatever one can say about intent in the former is true about the latter as well. If we assume that all of the above arguments about intent are incorrect (*i.e.*, when treatment is forgone, there is no intent in law to cause death but rather the legally relevant intent is to relieve suffering, which is insufficient to support criminal liability) then precisely the same can be said of intent in actively hastening death. If we believe that forgoing life-sustaining treatment involves only an intent to relieve suffering

and not to cause death, then when a patient takes an overdose of medication (either provided by a physician or obtained by some other means), the patient is merely intending to relieve suffering. Death is the incidental by-product of this effort, as it is in forgoing treatment. Thus, the patient's death is not a suicide and the physician who provides the patient with the means of "relieving suffering," or who administers a lethal medication to the patient at the patient's request to relieve suffering, is not assisting suicide nor committing homicide.

Phrasing the analysis in this way helps illustrate the hollowness of this argument. In both actively and passively hastening death, the clear intent—or at least the intent with which law traditionally is concerned—is to bring about death. The motive for doing so in both cases may be the relief of suffering, but motive is not necessary to establish liability.

C.   CAUSATION

1. THE TRADITIONAL EXPLANATION

The third stratagem used by courts to avoid characterizing the passive hastening of death as unlawful killing is to claim that when life-sustaining medical treatment is withheld or withdrawn, death results from natural causes, not from the behavior of those caring for the patient. Death results from the fact that the patient's underlying illness or injury, for which treatment was being provided or was proposed, prevents the patient from breathing (when ventilatory support is forgone), taking nourishment (when tube-feeding is forgone), ridding the body of wastes (when renal dialysis is forgone), or fighting infections (when antibiotics are forgone). By saying that the patient dies a natural death or that nature is taking its course, Mother Nature, who is beyond prosecution, is made the causal agent of death rather than the health care professionals who withhold or withdraw treatment.

Essentially what the courts have done in right-to-die cases is revive the long-discredited "cause/condition" distinction. Although they have not used this terminology, the courts are concluding that forgoing life-sustaining treatment is not the *cause* of death, but merely a necessary *condition* for death to occur. As such, it is not blameworthy under the traditional rules of criminal liability. In so concluding, however, they are conveniently overlooking well-established rules of criminal liability routinely applied in other contexts.

By contrast, it is said that when a physician engages in conduct that *actively* hastens death, it is the physician's conduct which is the cause of death.[7] Certainly causation is clearer in instances of actively hastening death than in passively hastening death, but this does not end the inquiry. It merely means that there must be a deeper probing into the latter, which courts have been steadfastly disinclined to do.

2. DIFFICULTIES WITH THE TRADITIONAL EXPLANATION

Further inquiry demonstrates that causation-based efforts to find a difference between passively and actively hastening death do not wash.

a. Sine Qua Non Test If a sine qua non test of causation, the primary one accepted by the Model Penal Code,[8] is employed to escape liability, we must be able to say "but for" the act or omission of a human, the patient would not have died. When life-sustaining treatment is withheld or withdrawn, however, this is clearly not the case. If treatment had been initiated or continued, the patient would *not* have died—at least not then and there—and it is a well-established principle that the shortening of a life, even the life of one who is close to death, is criminally culpable.[9]

b. Natural and Probable Consequences Test Another test of causation used in the criminal law is the "natural and probable consequences" test. Under this test, an actor's conduct is said to be the legally responsible cause of a result if the result is the natural and probable consequence of the actor's conduct. For example, if a patient is being maintained by some form of life support, it is because there is reasonable medical certainty that the patient will die without treatment. Therefore, if treatment is withdrawn, death is the natural and probable consequence of the withdrawal. There would be no difficulty making a prima facie showing that this test of causation is met.

In situations in which life-sustaining medical treatment is withheld rather than withdrawn, it may be more difficult to establish that not initiating treatment caused the patient's death. If the treatment in question is truly "life-sustaining" treatment, *ex hypothesi*, the failure to administer it is the cause of the patient's death. These are, however, questions of fact. What is important for present purposes is that causation could be established in some situations of withholding treatment. Thus, one cannot make the blanket statement that withholding treatment could never be the legal cause of death. . . .

The concept of legal causation is ultimately a mix of factual and policy considerations of who should be responsible for what, and under what circumstances. Nonetheless, to deny that there is legal causation in passively hastening death, and yet to find it in actively hastening death, requires more than a mere assertion that causation in the two types of hastening death is different. Factually it is different. The question is whether this fact ought to make a difference with respect to the ultimate issue of culpability. If it does, one must be able to point to important, relevant differences between passively and actively hastening death. Perhaps some exist but they cannot be found in the realm of legal causation, as they are not in the nature of the act or intent. . . .

What is it, at core, that *does* legitimate passively hastening death? One might assert that it is the patient's legal right to refuse medical treatment, but there is a deeper explanation. The right to refuse medical treatment is itself based on the more fundamental legal value of self-determination, which in turn is implemented through the mechanism of consent to treatment—or more precisely, informed consent. . . .

Thus, consent functions as a defense in right-to-die cases, just as other justifications are recognized as defenses under appropriate circumstances. Consent, however, is not merely a defense. To speak of it as such degrades its status in all medical decision-making. Consent is the fundamental validating property of forgoing life-sustaining treatment whether by withholding or withdrawing, whether by a competent patient or a surrogate. . . .

PROTECTING AGAINST THE "ABUSE" OF ACTIVELY HASTENING DEATH

Even if there is no bright line between actively and passively hastening death—both are manifestations of the fundamental right of self-determination and both are legitimated by consent—there are still arguments which can be lodged against the prima facie claim for the validity of actively hastening death. These claims must be examined to determine whether the prima facie case can be overcome. This is what the Second[10] and Ninth Circuits[11] did, albeit within a constitutional framework, and found them to be unpersuasive support for statutes criminalizing physician-assisted suicide.[12]

In defending against claims of unconstitutionality, opponents of physician-assisted suicide have cited a number of reasons why the state has an important interest in maintaining the criminality of this conduct. A list of these reasons could be compiled from many sources, in a number of ways. I will rely on the reasons set forth by the majority opinion in *Compassion in Dying*,[13] the purpose here being illustrative, not comprehensive:

1. Disadvantaged individuals, the poor, the elderly, the disabled, and minorities, will be pressured to submit to physician-assisted suicide, becoming victims rather than beneficiaries.

2. The real problem is the "lack of universal access to medical care" resulting from misplaced national priorities. If high quality medical and other care were provided to the dying, they would not seek physician-assisted suicide.

3. Acceptance of physician-assisted suicide would make doctors insensitive "to the plight of terminally ill patients, and . . . they will treat requests to die in a routine and impersonal manner, rather than affording the careful, thorough, individualized attention that each request deserves."

4. Acceptance of physician-assisted suicide would have a substantial adverse effect on the patient's "children, other family members, and loved ones."

5. Acceptance of physician-assisted suicide would undermine "the integrity of the medical profession" and require doctors to act "contrary to their individual principles."

6. Acceptance of physician-assisted suicide will lead us down the slippery slope, converting a right to die into an obligation to die in which "courts will sanction putting people to death, not because they are desperately ill and want to die, but because they are deemed to pose an unjustifiable burden on society."

The purpose here is not to attempt to refute these arguments. There is no denying the truth to these claims and they must be taken seriously. There is, however, no evidence, nor is there any abstract reason, why these arguments should be considered more compelling in the context of actively hastening death than they are in the context of passively hastening death. Any argument that can be made against actively hastening death can be levelled with equal vigor against passively hastening death. There is no significant difference between the two that would warrant acceptance in the latter and rejection in the former.

It will come as no surprise that patients (whether belonging to some categorically vulnerable group, or merely vulnerable because they are patients) are susceptible to pressure by physicians. Physicians can subtly or heavy-handedly pressure patients into forgoing life-sustaining treatment by telling them that it is useless, painful, and expensive. Moreover, the lack of access to health care may cause patients to reluctantly request or accede to a suggestion that they forgo life-sustaining treatment because they cannot afford the treatment they need and want. Physicians can also become hardened to the plight of the terminally ill by the knowledge that forgoing life-sustaining treatment is an easy out for the physician. Family members suffer either way. They experience severe loss when a terminally ill patient dies from forgoing treatment, but they also suffer if the patient is forced to continue suffering by not being allowed to forgo treatment if that is his wish. Forgoing life-sustaining treatment was once at odds with the ethics of the medical profession. One of the important factors in its acceptance by the medical community has been its legalization. Finally, predictions that terminally ill patients should be prohibited from forgoing life-sustaining treatment because it would be subject to widespread abuse have similarly proved to be untrue.

Why has the experiment in passively hastening death, begun by *Quinlan*, turned out as well as it has? The key to the answer is consent. Consent is not only the validating principle underlying passively or actively hastening death, it is also the mechanism which protects against abuse in both situations. Just as procedural and substantive protections have been developed to assure that abuse does not occur when forgoing life-sustaining treatment occurs, similar protection must be created for actively hastening death. . . .

CONCLUSION

I have attempted to show several things. First, the arguments that courts have put forth for two decades to justify the criminal nonculpability of passively hastening death are fundamentally unsound. Nonetheless, passively hastening death should not invoke criminal sanctions against those whose conduct causes it if there is legally adequate consent to the conduct and its consequences. Second, once we see that the stock arguments used to justify passively hastening death are spurious and that the true justification for its legitimacy is self-determination implemented through consent, the purported legal distinctions between actively and passively hastening death fade. Finally, although there are sound, indeed strong, arguments against the legitimation of actively hastening death, these same arguments can be made with equal force against passively hastening death. Yet, they are not made, or when made they have been rejected. In light of the virtual indistinguishability of the two practices, there are no sound legal reasons for continuing the prohibition against actively hastening death. What is critical is not the means by which death occurs but that there be adequate protections against abuse, whatever the means of hastening death. . . .

While it may have been useful, or even necessary, for courts to employ a variety of fictions to establish the right to passively hasten death, they no longer serve any useful purpose in that realm. These fictions must now be discarded so that their perpetuation does not undermine the very ends they were originally devised to promote and protect: the humane care of the dying.

NOTES

1. *See* 1 Alan Meisel, The Right to Die § 1.7 (2d ed. 1995 & Supp. 1997) [hereinafter 1 Meisel].

2. Cruzan v. Director, 497 U.S. 261 (1990).

3. *Id.* at 296–97, *quoting* 4 Blackstone, Commentaries *189. *See also* Mack v. Mack, 618 A.2d 744, 774 (Md. 1993).

4. 486 A.2d 1209 (N.J. 1985).

5. *Id.* at 1234 (citations omitted).

6. *Conroy*, 486 A.2d at 1234.

7. *See, e.g., Vacco*, 117 S. Ct. at 2298 ("[I]f a patient ingests lethal medication prescribed by a physician, he is killed by that medication.").

8. Model Penal Code § 2.03(1)(a) ("Conduct is the cause of a result when . . . it is an antecedent but for which the result in question would not have occurred").

9. *See, e.g.*, Barber v. Superior Court, 195 Cal. Rptr. 484 (Ct. App. 1983).

10. *See* Quill v. Vacco, 80 F.3d 716 (2d Cir. 1996), *rev'd*, 117 S. Ct. 2293 (1997).

11. *See* Compassion in Dying v. Washington, 79 F.3d 790 (9th Cir. 1996), *rev'd sub nom.* Washington v. Glucksberg, 117 S. Ct. 2258 (1997).

12. In *Glucksberg*, the Supreme Court also evaluated these claims but found them to be persuasive. *But see Glucksberg*, 117 S. Ct. at 2271–2275.

13. 79 F.3d 790 (9th Cir. 1996) (en banc).

RONALD A. LINDSAY, TOM L. BEAUCHAMP, AND REBECCA P. DICK

Hastened Death and the Regulation of the Practice of Medicine

Ronald A. Lindsay is a professional philosopher and also a lawyer in private practice in Washington, DC. His scholarly publications have focused on issues in bioethics, especially physician-assisted dying. He co-authored an amicus brief that supported the position of the state of Oregon in *Gonzales v. Oregon.*

Tom L. Beauchamp is Professor of Philosophy in the Philosophy Department and Senior Research Scholar at the Kennedy Institute of Ethics, Georgetown University. His co-authored works include *Principles of Biomedical Ethics* (5th ed. 2001) and *A History and Theory of Informed Consent* (1986). He has published widely in the areas of death and dying since the early 1970s.

Rebecca P. Dick is counsel in the antitrust, trade practices, and litigation groups of her law firm, Dechert LLP, Washington, DC. She has extensive experience in litigation in the areas in which she specializes. She formerly served as Director of a division of the U.S. Department of Justice. Legal issues of physician-assisted suicide have been a special interest of hers in the last decade.

GONZALES V. OREGON

On November 9, 2001, then-Attorney General John Ashcroft issued an interpretive rule (hereinafter "November 2001 Interpretive Rule" or "Interpretive Rule") stating that "assisting suicide is not a 'legitimate medical purpose' within the meaning of 21 CFR § 1306.04." The Attorney General's directive purported to make the prescribing, dispensing, or administering of a controlled substance to assist in a suicide a violation of the Controlled Substances Act (CSA).[1]

On January 17, 2006, the Supreme Court, in a 6-3 ruling, with the majority opinion authored by Justice Kennedy, concluded that the Interpretive Rule was an invalid exercise of the Attorney General's authority.[2] Specifically, the Court held that the CSA does not grant the Attorney General authority to prohibit physicians

from prescribing controlled substances to assist in hastening death if such a practice is authorized by state law.

We will argue that, correctly understood, assistance in hastening death is properly regarded as a *medical* practice, or, more broadly stated, that a physician legitimately may assist in various ways in helping to bring about the death of a terminally ill patient who has explicitly and competently requested this assistance from the physician.

Withdrawal or withholding of treatment will hasten death only for those individuals who are being sustained by such treatment. Many other individuals, including cancer patients, may face a protracted period of dying even when respirators and other life-preserving technology are not being utilized. For some of these patients, palliative care and the ability to refuse treatment do not adequately address their concerns. During their prolonged period of dying, they may endure a loss of functional capacity, unremitting pain and suffering, an inability to experience the simplest

Reprinted with permission from Ronald A. Lindsay, Tom L. Beauchamp, and Rebecca P. Dick. *Washington University Journal of Law & Policy,* vol. 22 (2006).

of pleasures, and long hours aware of the hopelessness of their condition. Some patients find this prospect unbearable. They desire a means to hasten their deaths.

Efforts to enact legislation that would legalize assistance in hastening death have met determined resistance. Much of this resistance stems from religious objections to the practice. Other objections, however, reflect concerns that assistance in hastening death could not be effectively regulated and would have serious adverse consequences for many, including for those who do not desire such assistance. Moreover, opponents of legalization have maintained that the practice inevitably would be expanded to include euthanasia (including non-voluntary euthanasia), the quality of palliative care for all patients would deteriorate, patients would be manipulated or coerced into requesting assistance in hastening death, patients whose judgment was impaired would be allowed to request such assistance, and members of allegedly vulnerable groups (the elderly, women, members of racial and ethnic minorities, etc.) would be adversely affected in disproportionate numbers. Proponents of legal assistance in hastening death have tried to meet these objections by incorporating various procedural safeguards into their proposed legislation.

In 1994 the voters of Oregon, by referendum, adopted the ODWDA, the first and still the only statute in the United States expressly to permit assistance in hastening death.

In providing assistance in hastening death under the ODWDA, a physician is to exercise his or her professional judgment in prescribing the most effective drug. The drug prescribed in almost all instances in Oregon is a form of barbiturate, the use of which is regulated by the CSA.

The CSA classifies controlled substances in five categories or schedules based on their potential for abuse, their accepted medical use, and the risks associated with their use under medical supervision. Schedule I substances have a high potential for abuse and have no currently accepted use in medical treatment. Schedule II through Schedule V substances are approved for medical use but are subject to a descending hierarchy of restrictions on their use, reflecting the likelihood of abuse and the likely degree of harm if abuse occurs. Barbiturates are listed on Schedule II.

There is little dispute that the primary purposes of the CSA are to control drug abuse and to eliminate illicit trafficking in drugs.

Finally, the Court addressed the federal government's argument that the CSA's mandate that prescriptions be issued only for "a legitimate medical purpose" necessarily implies that prescriptions under the ODWDA are unlawful. The government contended that intentionally hastening death cannot be part of accepted medical practice, which is "a healing or curative art." In response, the Court acknowledged that limiting medical care to treatment designed to cure a patient was only one understanding of "medicine's boundaries." The Court also pointed out that there are alternative understandings of the scope of medicine. The CSA does not authorize the Attorney General to impose on physicians *his* particular understanding of the practice of medicine.

The Court both noted the absence of any statutory warrant for the government's position and emphasized that the implications of that position are dangerous. It stated that were this interpretation of the CSA accepted, the Attorney General's authority to make medical judgments would not be limited to the issue of physician assistance in hastening death. The Attorney General would have the authority to interfere with any medical practice he deemed inappropriate if it involved use of controlled substances.

ASSISTANCE IN HASTENING DEATH AS A LEGITIMATE FORM OF MEDICAL PRACTICE

We start with the premise that physician assistance in hastening death is best viewed as part of a continuum of medical care. A physician who encounters a sick patient should initially seek, if possible, to rid the patient's body of injuries, diseases, or related infirmities. Restoration of health is morally mandatory as a goal as long as there is a reasonable prospect of success and the patient supports the means necessary to this end. However, to direct the physician to stop at this point and confine the practice of medicine to those measures designed to cure diseases or heal injuries is an unduly narrow way of thinking about what the physician has to offer the patient. The value of physicians is broader.

When in the patient's eyes the burdens of continued attempts at a cure outweigh their probable benefits, the caring physician, in consultation with the patient, should redirect the course of treatment so that its primary focus is the relief of pain and suffering. For many patients, palliative care with aggressive use of analgesics will prove sufficient to accomplish this goal. For other patients, relief of intolerable distress or suffering will come only with death, which some patients will therefore seek to hasten.

To prevent a physician from using her skills to bring comfort and relief to a patient on the ground that the measures available are not curative is to prevent the physician from meeting what both the physician and the patient may consider the physician's commitment to and responsibility for her incurably ill patients.

There are prudential reasons for permitting physicians to provide such assistance legally and publicly. First, if physicians are barred from providing assistance lawfully, some patients will resort to self-help in causing their own deaths, with adverse consequences. A few, being concerned about waiting until it is "too late" (that is, until they lack the physical or mental ability to hasten their own deaths), will end their lives prematurely. If they had access to the security of a lethal drug, they might find their situation bearable and continue to live until a natural death arrives.

A regulatory scheme that minimizes the chance that patients will be manipulated or coerced into dying also diminishes the risk that they will make an ill-advised choice while cognitively impaired or experiencing depression, and it encourages them to live as long as they find their lives worthwhile. For this reason alone, a scheme that allows physicians to provide legal assistance in hastening death is preferable to a total ban on that assistance.

Some who contend that assistance in hastening death lies outside the boundaries of medical practice rely on a mechanical and telescoped concept of the physician's role. Under this view, assisting a patient to die does not make use of medical skills or judgment, but rather consists only of utilizing technical knowledge about how to cause a patient's death. These arguments treat assistance in hastening death as if it begins and ends with a doctor's prescription of a lethal dose of medication. This view of the physician's role is again too narrow.

A physician who assists a patient in hastening his or her death is not a mere technician, nor does this physician provide services that could be provided, just as easily and competently, by a layperson. Sensitive physicians use the full extent of their professional training and experience when they assess the patient's condition and determine whether the patient is terminally ill; they assess the prospects for effective palliative care for the patient through a meaningful dialogue with the patient; they evaluate what alternatives may be feasible and acceptable to the patient; they determine whether the patient is competent to make a decision regarding the course of treatment; they ensure that the patient's judgment is not impaired by depression or other factors; and they consult with other physicians to confirm the accuracy of the diagnosis, the exhaustion of other alternatives, and the competence of the patient. To be performed well, these activities all require the experience, knowledge, and skills of the physician.

Significantly, the activities a physician undertakes in providing assistance in hastening death are the same as those often carried out by a physician who oversees a withdrawal of treatment.[3] As a purely medical matter, there is little to distinguish a physician's activities in withdrawing treatment from activities in hastening death through other means.

THE INADEQUACY OF THE DISTINCTION BETWEEN "LETTING DIE" AND "KILLING"

The distinction between killing and letting die has long been the most critical one in attempts in law and moral philosophy to distinguish appropriate from inappropriate means to death.

However, the distinction between "killing" and "letting die" is not a reliable way to distinguish impermissible from permissible acts. It is unsatisfactory for a number of reasons, not least because it tends to mask, rather than promote, consideration of the relevant factors that ought to be considered in determining permissible conduct. For example, we believe that withdrawing treatment from a competent patient is not morally justifiable unless the patient has made an informed decision authorizing this withdrawal. If a physician removes a respirator from a patient who needs it and wants to continue to use it, the action is wrong, even though the physician has only removed artificial life support and let nature take its course. Absent the patient's authorization, such "letting die" is simply killing. The lack of authorization by the patient is the relevant consideration in assessing the act as unacceptable. Focusing on the distinction between letting die and killing obscures what should be the determinative factor in evaluating the physician's conduct: the patient's decision.

A physician's validly authorized nonintervention in circumstances in which the patient dies as a result is appropriate where the physician is following the patient's instruction. By contrast, comparable action or inaction is inappropriate in medicine if a physician has a duty to treat but the physician withholds or withdraws, without patient authorization, a life-sustaining technology, and the patient subsequently dies for lack of the technology. A physician is the relevant cause of death, and thereby acts wrongly, if he or she has no valid authorization from the patient to withhold or withdraw treatment. By contrast, the physician is not the relevant cause of death and does not act wrongly if he or she does have valid authorization for withholding or withdrawing treatment.

Of course, physicians also may kill by using a so-called "active" means to death, but there are several problems inherent in the idea that we can determine appropriate and inappropriate conduct by considering whether an active means to death was involved. This is especially true in the context of the ODWDA, where the distinction between "letting die" and "killing" is not helpful in determining appropriate and inappropriate physician conduct. Physicians who act under the ODWDA do not "kill" patients in any meaningful sense. A physician who prescribes a lethal medication at a patient's request is simply writing a prescription. That act no more "kills" a person than does the writing of a prescription for sedatives or analgesics for a patient who is undergoing withdrawal of treatment. Under the ODWDA, the patient must make a conscious decision to use the drug. About one-third of the patients who seek a prescription under the ODWDA never ingest the lethal drug; others ingest it months after it has been prescribed. For those who do take the drug, the physician's writing of the prescription is a necessary step in the process that leads to the patient's death, but it is not the determinative or even the final step. Under any reasonable interpretation of the term, the Oregon physician does not "kill" the patient. Nor, however, does this physician "let the patient die." Use of the terms "letting die" and "killing" is simply not an illuminating way to view what happens when a physician provides a patient who so requests with the means to escape the ravages of a fatal illness.

RESOLVING DISPUTES BETWEEN DIFFERENT MODELS OF MEDICAL PRACTICE

It is undeniable that the physician-as-healer model of medical practice derives from a resilient tradition that retains considerable support today, both in the medical community and among the public at large. The reasons it enjoys such support are understandable: it is in some ways a comfortable view and it avoids confrontation of some difficult issues. However, this model no longer appears to be the dominant view, either in the medical community or among the public. We have supported a very different model, the continuum-of-care model, that takes a broader view of the range of activities legitimate for physicians. It is likely that both models will continue to enjoy significant support in the years to come. How, then, should we resolve disputes between these inherently contestable models? Is there any way other than sheer political muscle? Can the models co-exist?

The key issue is how to determine the goals of regulation. Fortunately, the historical record may provide useful direction. Regulatory questions regarding whether a particular action serves a legitimate medical purpose are not new. Historically these disputes have focused on whether a proposed treatment is safe and effective. These disputes continue today, as the controversies over various forms of alternative medicine illustrate. In resolving such disputes regulatory bodies, be they federal or state, have not only looked at the implications for patients receiving the disputed drug, device, or treatment, but also at implications for society as a whole. A critical question is the effect the practice will have not only on patients receiving the care but on society as a whole. Will the welfare of many be adversely affected by tolerance of the benefits afforded others by the practice?

We urge that similar considerations of public health and safety be utilized for adjudicating normative disputes about appropriate restrictions on a physician's actions in caring for terminally ill patients. Protection of the health and safety of both patients and the public is a presumptively legitimate goal and well-established in the laws regulating medicine. The question we should ask is this: Is the proposed restriction necessary to protect the public from consequences that are regarded as serious and adverse by all or almost all? In the context of assistance in hastening death, the question becomes, is prohibition necessary to ensure that those who wish to die naturally are not tricked, maneuvered, or otherwise manipulated into ending their lives earlier? Might legalization reduce opportunities for effective palliative care, to the detriment of many?

Concerns that legalizing assistance in hastening death might result in serious harms, especially for those *not* seeking such assistance, have been raised by many opposed to assistance in hastening death. If legalization were to bring about unwarranted, involuntary deaths, reduce the quality of palliative care, result in deep-seated and widespread mistrust of physicians, and so on, then we agree that these consequences would support arguments against legalizing physician assistance in hastening death. However, none of these consequences has come to pass in the only state that has legalized physician assistance in dying.

Focusing on public health and safety is the only way that we see to define the limits of medical care without turning this issue into a political football.

We recommend the following general principle for regulation of medical practice: neither the states nor the federal government should limit the type of care physicians provide their patients in the absence of evidence that the practice at issue poses a significant threat to the health and safety of the public. Utilizing this standard avoids unresolvable disputes about the goals or ends of medicine while ensuring that legitimate public concerns are taken into account. Under this standard, there is no sound basis for state or federal legislation that would prevent physicians from assisting patients in hastening their deaths pursuant to the provisions like those of the ODWDA.

CONCLUSION

The touchstone for decisions over legalization should not be whether assistance in hastening death can be characterized as "healing" or "letting die," but whether legalization causes significant harm to the public health and safety. The Oregon experience demonstrates that the health and safety of the citizens of that state have been protected, and even promoted, by legalization of physician assistance in dying.

NOTES

1. The Controlled Substances Act (CSA), 21 U.S.C. §§ 801–904 (2000), is Title II of the Comprehensive Drug Abuse Prevention and Control Act.

2. Gonzales v. Oregon, 126 S. Ct. 904 (2006).

3. We say "significantly" because given the widespread acceptance of withdrawal of treatment, there is relatively little scrutiny of what most physicians actually do in such situations.

Moral Issues about Physician-Assisted Death

DAN W. BROCK

Voluntary Active Euthanasia

Dan W. Brock is the Frances Glessner Lee Professor of Medical Ethics and Director of the Division of Medical Ethics at the Harvard Medical School. He was formerly Charles C. Tillinghast, Jr. University Professor, Professor of Philosophy and Biomedical Ethics, and Director of the Center for Biomedical Ethics at Brown University. He is a former staff philosopher on the President's Commission for the Study of Ethical Problems in Medicine. His books include *Life and Death: Philosophical Essays in Biomedical Ethics*, and (with Allen Buchanan) *Deciding for Others: The Ethics of Surrogate Decision Making*.

In the recent bioethics literature some have endorsed physician-assisted suicide but not euthanasia. Are they sufficiently different that the moral arguments for one often do not apply to the other? A paradigm case of

From *Hastings Center Report* 22, no. 2 (March/April 1992), 10–22 (edited). © The Hastings Center. Reprinted by permission of the publisher.

physician-assisted suicide is a patient's ending his or her life with a lethal dose of a medication requested of and provided by a physician for that purpose. A paradigm case of voluntary active euthanasia is a physician's administering the lethal dose, often because the patient is unable to do so. The only difference that need exist between the two is the person who actually administers the lethal dose—the physician or the patient. In each, the physician plays an active and necessary causal role.

In physician-assisted suicide the patient acts last (for example, Janet Adkins herself pushed the button after Dr. Kevorkian hooked her up to his suicide machine), whereas in euthanasia the physician acts last by performing the physical equivalent of pushing the button. In both cases, however, the choice rests fully with the patient. In both the patient acts last in the sense of retaining the right to change his or her mind until the point at which the lethal process becomes irreversible. How could there be a substantial moral difference between the two based only on this small difference in the part played by the physician in the causal process resulting in death? Of course, it might be held that the moral difference is clear and important—in euthanasia the physician kills the patient whereas in physician-assisted suicide the patient kills him- or herself. But this is misleading at best. In assisted suicide the physician and patient together kill the patient. To see this, suppose a physician supplied a lethal dose to a patient with the knowledge and intent that the patient will wrongfully administer it to another. We would have no difficulty in morality or the law recognizing this as a case of joint action to kill for which both are responsible.

If there is no significant, intrinsic moral difference between the two, it is also difficult to see why public or legal policy should permit one but not the other; worries about abuse or about giving anyone dominion over the lives of others apply equally to either. As a result, I will take the arguments evaluated below to apply to both and will focus on euthanasia.

My concern here will be with *voluntary* euthanasia only—that is, with the case in which a clearly competent patient makes a fully voluntary and persistent request for aid in dying. Involuntary euthanasia, in which a competent patient explicitly refuses or opposes receiving euthanasia, and nonvoluntary euthanasia, in which a patient is incompetent and unable to express his or her wishes about euthanasia, will be considered here only as potential unwanted side-effects of permitting voluntary euthanasia. I emphasize as well that I am concerned with *active* euthanasia, not withholding or withdrawing life-sustaining treatment, which some commentators characterize as "passive euthanasia.". . .

THE CENTRAL ETHICAL ARGUMENT FOR VOLUNTARY ACTIVE EUTHANASIA

The central ethical argument for euthanasia is familiar. It is that the very same two fundamental ethical values supporting the consensus on patient's rights to decide about life-sustaining treatment also support the ethical permissibility of euthanasia. These values are individual self-determination or autonomy and individual well-being. By self-determination as it bears on euthanasia, I mean people's interest in making important decisions about their lives for themselves according to their own values or conceptions of a good life, and in being left free to act on those decisions. Self-determination is valuable because it permits people to form and live in accordance with their own conception of a good life, at least within the bounds of justice and consistent with others doing so as well. In exercising self-determination people take responsibility for their lives and for the kinds of persons they become. A central aspect of human dignity lies in people's capacity to direct their lives in this way. The value of exercising self-determination presupposes some minimum of decisionmaking capacities or competence, which thus limits the scope of euthanasia supported by self-determination; it cannot justifiably be administered, for example, in cases of serious dementia or treatable clinical depression. . . .

The other main value that supports euthanasia is individual well-being. It might seem that individual well-being conflicts with a person's self-determination when the person requests euthanasia. Life itself is commonly taken to be a central good for persons, often valued for its own sake, as well as necessary for pursuit of all other goods within a life. But when a competent patient decides to forgo all further life-sustaining treatment, then the patient, either explicitly or implicitly, commonly decides that the best life possible for him or her with treatment is of sufficiently poor quality that it is worse than no further life at all. Life is no longer considered a benefit by the patient, but has now become a burden. The same judgment underlies a request for euthanasia: continued life is seen by the patient as no longer a benefit, but now a burden. Especially in the often severely compromised and debilitated states of many critically ill or dying patients, there is no objective standard, but only the competent patient's judgment of whether continued life is no longer a benefit. . . .

The claim that any individual instance of euthanasia is a case of deliberate killing of an innocent person is, with only minor qualifications, correct. Unlike forgoing life-sustaining treatment, commonly understood as allowing to die, euthanasia is clearly killing, defined as depriving of life or causing the death of a living being. While providing morphine for pain relief at doses where the risk of respiratory depression and an earlier death may be a foreseen but unintended side effect of treating the patient's pain, in a case of euthanasia the patient's death is deliberate or intended even if in both the physician's ultimate end may be respecting the patient's wishes. If the deliberate killing of an innocent person is wrong, euthanasia would be nearly always impermissible.

In the context of medicine, the ethical prohibition against deliberately killing the innocent derives some of its plausibility from the belief that nothing in the currently accepted practice of medicine is deliberate killing. Thus, in commenting on the "It's Over, Debbie" case, four prominent physicians and bioethicists could entitle their paper "Doctors Must Not Kill."[1] The belief that doctors do not in fact kill requires the corollary belief that forgoing life-sustaining treatment, whether by not starting or by stopping treatment, is allowing to die, not killing. Common though this view is, I shall argue that it is confused and mistaken.

Why is the common view mistaken? Consider the case of a patient terminally ill with ALS disease. She is completely respirator dependent with no hope of ever being weaned. She is unquestionably competent but finds her condition intolerable and persistently requests to be removed from the respirator and allowed to die. Most people and physicians would agree that the patient's physician should respect the patient's wishes and remove her from the respirator, though this will certainly cause the patient's death. The common understanding is that the physician thereby allows the patient to die. But is that correct?

Suppose the patient has a greedy and hostile son who mistakenly believes that his mother will never decide to stop her life-sustaining treatment and that even if she did her physician would not remove her from the respirator. Afraid that his inheritance will be dissipated by a long and expensive hospitalization, he enters his mother's room while she is sedated, extubates her, and she dies. Shortly thereafter the medical staff discovers what he has done and confronts the son. He replies, "I didn't kill her, I merely allowed her to die. It was her ALS disease that caused her death." I think this would rightly be dismissed as transparent sophistry—the son went into his mother's room and deliberately killed her. But, of course, the son performed just the same physical actions, did just the same thing, that the physician would have done. If that is so, then doesn't the physician also kill the patient when he extubates her? . . .

I have argued elsewhere that this alternative account is deeply problematic, in part because it commits us to accepting that what the greedy son does is to allow to die, not kill. Here, I want to note two other reasons why the conclusion that stopping life support is killing is resisted.

The first reason is that killing is often understood, especially within medicine, as unjustified causing of death; in medicine it is thought to be done only accidentally or negligently. It is also increasingly widely accepted that a physician is ethically justified in stopping life support in a case like that of the ALS patient. But if these two beliefs are correct, then what the physician does cannot be killing, and so must be allowing to die. Killing patients is not, to put it flippantly, understood to be part of physicians' job description. What is mistaken in this line of reasoning is the assumption that all killings are *unjustified* causings of death. Instead, some killings are ethically justified, including many instances of stopping life support.

Another reason for resisting the conclusion that stopping life support is often killing is that it is psychologically uncomfortable. Suppose the physician had stopped the ALS patient's respirator and had made the son's claim, "I didn't kill her, I merely allowed her to die. It was her ALS disease that caused her death." The clue to the psychological role here is how naturally the "merely" modifies "allowed her to die." The characterization as allowing to die is meant to shift felt responsibility away from the agent—the physician—and to the lethal disease process. Other language common in death and dying contexts plays a similar role; "letting nature take its course" or "stopping prolonging the dying process" both seem to shift responsibility from the physician who stops life support to the fatal disease process. However psychologically helpful these conceptualizations may be in making the difficult responsibility of a physician's role in the patient's death bearable, they nevertheless are confusions. Both physicians and family members can instead be helped to understand that it is the patient's decision and consent to stopping treatment that limits their responsibility for the patient's death and that shifts that responsibility to the patient. . . .

Suppose both my arguments are mistaken. Suppose that killing is worse than allowing to die and that withdrawing life support is not killing, although euthanasia is. Euthanasia still need not for that reason be morally wrong. To see this, we need to determine the basic principle for the moral evaluation of killing persons. What is it that makes paradigm cases of wrongful killing wrongful? One very plausible answer is that killing denies the victim something that he or she values greatly—continued life or a future. Moreover, since continued life is necessary for pursuing any of a person's plans and purposes, killing brings the frustration of all of these plans and desires as well. In a nutshell, wrongful killing deprives a person of a valued future, and of all the person wanted and planned to do in that future.

A natural expression of this account of the wrongness of killing is that people have a moral right not to be killed. But in this account of the wrongness of killing, the right not to be killed, like other rights, should be waivable when the person makes a competent decision that continued life is no longer wanted or a good, but is instead worse than no further life at all. In this view, euthanasia is properly understood as a case of a person having waived his or her right not to be killed. . . .

WOULD THE BAD CONSEQUENCES OF EUTHANASIA OUTWEIGH THE GOOD?

The argument against euthanasia at the policy level is stronger than at the level of individual cases, though even here I believe the case is ultimately unpersuasive, or at best indecisive. The policy level is the place where the main issues lie, however, and where moral considerations that might override arguments in favor of euthanasia will be found, if they are found anywhere. It is important to note two kinds of disagreement about the consequences for public policy of permitting euthanasia. First, there is empirical or factual disagreement about what the consequences would be. This disagreement is greatly exacerbated by the lack of firm data on the issue. Second, since on any reasonable assessment there would be both good and bad consequences, there are moral disagreements about

the relative importance of different effects. In addition to these two sources of disagreement, there is also no single, well-specified policy proposal for legalizing euthanasia on which policy assessments can focus. But without such specification, and especially without explicit procedures for protecting against well-intentioned misuse and ill-intentioned abuse, the consequences for policy are largely speculative. Despite these difficulties, a preliminary account of the main likely good and bad consequences is possible. This should help clarify where better data or more moral analysis and argument are needed, as well as where policy safeguards must be developed.

POTENTIAL GOOD CONSEQUENCES
OF PERMITTING EUTHANASIA

What are the likely good consequences? First, if euthanasia were permitted it would be possible to respect the self-determination of competent patients who want it, but now cannot get it because of its illegality. . . .

One important factor substantially affecting the number of persons who would seek euthanasia is the extent to which an alternative is available. The widespread acceptance in the law, social policy, and medical practice of the right of a competent patient to forgo life-sustaining treatment suggests that the number of competent persons in the United States who would want euthanasia if it were permitted is probably relatively small.

A second good consequence of making euthanasia legally permissible benefits a much larger group. Polls have shown that a majority of the American public believes that people should have a right to obtain euthanasia if they want it.[2] No doubt the vast majority of those who support this right to euthanasia will never in fact come to want euthanasia for themselves. Nevertheless, making it legally permissible would reassure many people that if they ever do want euthanasia they would be able to obtain it. This reassurance would supplement the broader control over the process of dying given by the right to decide about life-sustaining treatment. . . .

A third good consequence of the legalization of euthanasia concerns patients whose dying is filled with severe and unrelievable pain or suffering. When there is a life-sustaining treatment that, if forgone, will lead relatively quickly to death, then doing so can bring an end to these patients' suffering without recourse to euthanasia. For patients receiving no such treatment, however, euthanasia may be the only release from their otherwise prolonged suffering and agony. This argument from mercy has always been the strongest argument for euthanasia in those cases to which it applies.[3]

The importance of relieving pain and suffering is less controversial than is the frequency with which patients are forced to undergo untreatable agony that only euthanasia could relieve. If we focus first on suffering caused by physical pain, it is crucial to distinguish pain that *could* be adequately relieved with modern methods of pain control, though it in fact is not, from pain that is relievable only by death.[4] . . .

Specialists in pain control, as for example the pain of terminally ill cancer patients, argue that there are very few patients whose pain could not be adequately controlled, though sometimes at the cost of so sedating them that they are effectively unable to interact with other people or their environment. Thus, the argument from mercy in cases of physical pain can probably be met in a large majority of cases by providing adequate measures of pain relief. This should be a high priority, whatever our legal policy on euthanasia—the relief of pain and suffering has long been, quite properly, one of the central goals of medicine. Those cases in which pain could be effectively relieved, but in fact is not, should only count significantly in favor of legalizing euthanasia if all reasonable efforts to change pain management techniques have been tried and have failed.

Dying patients often undergo substantial psychological suffering that is not fully or even principally the result of physical pain.[5] The knowledge about how to relieve this suffering is much more limited than in the case of relieving pain, and efforts to do so are probably more often unsuccessful. If the argument from mercy is extended to patients experiencing great and unrelievable psychological suffering, the numbers of patients to which it applies are much greater.

One last good consequence of legalizing euthanasia is that once death has been accepted, it is often more humane to end life quickly and peacefully, when that is what the patient wants. Such a death will often be seen as better than a more prolonged one. People who suffer a sudden and unexpected death, for example by dying quickly or in their sleep from a heart attack or stroke, are often considered lucky to have died in this way. We care about how we die in part because we care about how others remember us, and we hope they will remember us as we were in "good times" with them and not as we might be when disease has robbed us of our dignity as human beings. . . .

POTENTIAL BAD CONSEQUENCES OF PERMITTING EUTHANASIA

Some of the arguments against permitting euthanasia are aimed specifically against physicians, while others are aimed against anyone being permitted to perform it. I shall first consider one argument of the former sort. Permitting physicians to perform euthanasia, it is said, would be incompatible with their fundamental moral and professional commitment as healers to care for patients and to protect life. Moreover, if euthanasia by physicians became common, patients would come to fear that a medication was intended not to treat or care, but instead to kill, and would thus lose trust in their physicians. This position was forcefully stated in a paper by Willard Gaylin and his colleagues:

> The very soul of medicine is on trial. This issue touches medicine at its moral center; if this moral center collapses, if physicians become killers or are even licensed to kill, the profession—and, therewith, each physician—will never again be worthy of trust and respect as healer and comforter and protector of life in all its frailty.

These authors go on to make clear that, while they oppose permitting anyone to perform euthanasia, their special concern is with physicians doing so:

> We call on fellow physicians to say that they will not deliberately kill. We must also say to each of our fellow physicians that we will not tolerate killing of patients and that we shall take disciplinary action against doctors who kill. And we must say to the broader community that if it insists on tolerating or legalizing active euthanasia, it will have to find nonphysicians to do its killing.[6]

If permitting physicians to kill would undermine the very "moral center" of medicine, then almost certainly physicians should not be permitted to perform euthanasia. But how persuasive is this claim? Patients should not fear, as a consequence of permitting *voluntary* active euthanasia, that their physicians will substitute a lethal injection for what patients want and believe is part of their care. If active euthanasia is restricted to cases in which it is truly voluntary, then no patient should fear getting it unless she or he has voluntarily requested it. (The fear that we might in time also come to accept nonvoluntary, or even involuntary, active euthanasia is a slippery slope worry I address below.) Patients' trust of their physicians could be increased, not eroded, by knowledge that physicians will provide aid in dying when patients seek it. . . .

A second bad consequence that some foresee is that permitting euthanasia would weaken society's commitment to provide optimal care for dying patients. We live at a time in which the control of health care costs has become, and is likely to continue to be, the dominant focus of health care policy. If euthanasia is seen as a cheaper alternative to adequate care and treatment, then we might become less scrupulous about providing sometimes costly support and other services to dying patients. Particularly if our society comes to embrace deeper and more explicit rationing of health care, frail, elderly, and dying patients will need to be strong and effective advocates for their own health care and other needs, although they are hardly in a position to do this. We should do nothing to weaken their ability to obtain adequate care and services.

This second worry is difficult to assess because there is little firm evidence about the likelihood of the feared erosion in the care of dying patients. There are at least two reasons, however, for skepticism about this argument. The first is that the same worry could have been directed at recognizing patients' or surrogates' rights to forgo life-sustaining treatment, yet there is no persuasive evidence that recognizing the right to refuse treatment has caused a serious erosion in the quality of care of dying patients. The second reason for skepticism about this worry is that only a very small proportion of deaths would occur from euthanasia if it were permitted. In the Netherlands, where euthanasia under specified circumstances is permitted by the courts, though not authorized by statute, the best estimate of the proportion of overall deaths that result from it is about 2 percent.[7] Thus, the vast majority of critically ill and dying patients will not request it, and so will still have to be cared for by physicians, families, and others. Permitting euthanasia should not diminish people's commitment and concern to maintain and improve the care of these patients. . . .

[A third] potential bad consequence of permitting euthanasia has been developed by David Velleman and turns on the subtle point that making a new option or choice available to people can sometimes make them worse off, even if once they have the choice they go on to choose what is best for them.[8] Ordinarily, people's continued existence is viewed by them as given, a fixed condition with which they must cope.

Making euthanasia available to people as an option denies them the alternative of staying alive by default. If people are offered the option of euthanasia, their continued existence is now a choice for which they can be held responsible and which they can be asked by others to justify. We care, and are right to care, about being able to justify ourselves to others. To the extent that our society is unsympathetic to justifying a severely dependent or impaired existence, a heavy psychological burden of proof may be placed on patients who think their terminal illness or chronic infirmity is not a sufficient reason for dying. Even if they otherwise view their life as worth living, the opinion of others around them that it is not can threaten their reason for living and make euthanasia a rational choice. Thus the existence of the option becomes a subtle pressure to request it.

This argument correctly identifies the reason why offering some patients the option of euthanasia would not benefit them. Velleman takes it not as a reason for opposing all euthanasia, but for restricting it to circumstances where there are "unmistakable and overpowering reasons for persons to want the option of euthanasia," and for denying the option in all other cases. But there are at least three reasons why such restriction may not be warranted. First, polls and other evidence support that most Americans believe euthanasia should be permitted (though the recent defeat of the referendum to permit it in the state of Washington raises some doubt about this support). Thus, many more people seem to want the choice than would be made worse off by getting it. Second, if giving people the option of ending their life really makes them worse off, then we should not only prohibit euthanasia, but also take back from people the right they now have to decide about life-sustaining treatment. The feared harmful effect should already have occurred from securing people's right to refuse life-sustaining treatment, yet there is no evidence of any such widespread harm or any broad public desire to rescind that right. Third, since there is a wide range of conditions in which reasonable people can and do disagree about whether they would want continued life, it is not possible to restrict the permissibility of euthanasia as narrowly as Velleman suggests without thereby denying it to most persons who would want it; to permit it only in cases in which virtually everyone would want it would be to deny it to most who would want it.

A [fourth] potential bad consequence of making euthanasia legally permissible is that it might weaken the general legal prohibition of homicide. This prohibition is so fundamental to civilized society, it is argued, that we should do nothing that erodes it. If most cases of stopping life support are killing, as I have already argued, then the court cases permitting such killing have already in effect weakened this prohibition. However, neither the courts nor most people have seen these cases as killing and so as challenging the prohibition of homicide. The courts have usually grounded patients' or their surrogates' rights to refuse life-sustaining treatment in rights to privacy, liberty, self-determination, or bodily integrity, not in exceptions to homicide laws.

Legal permission for physicians or others to perform euthanasia could not be grounded in patients' rights to decide about medical treatment. Permitting euthanasia would require qualifying, at least in effect, the legal prohibition against homicide, a prohibition that in general does not allow the consent of the victim to justify or excuse the act. Nevertheless, the very same fundamental basis of the right to decide about life-sustaining treatment—respecting a person's self-determination—does support euthanasia as well. Individual self-determination has long been a well-entrenched and fundamental value in the law, and so extending it to euthanasia would not require appeal to novel legal values or principles. That suicide or attempted suicide is no longer a criminal offense in virtually all states indicates an acceptance of individual self-determination in the taking of one's own life analogous to that required for voluntary active euthanasia. The legal prohibition (in most states) of assisting in suicide and the refusal in the law to accept the consent of the victim as a possible justification of homicide are both arguably a result of difficulties in the legal process of establishing the consent of the victim after the fact. If procedures can be designed that clearly establish the voluntariness of the person's request for euthanasia, it would under those procedures represent a carefully circumscribed qualification on the legal prohibition of homicide. Nevertheless, some remaining worries about this weakening can be captured in the final potential bad consequence, to which I will now turn.

This final potential bad consequence is the central concern of many opponents of euthanasia and, I believe, is the most serious objection to a legal policy permitting it. According to this "slippery slope" worry, although active euthanasia may be morally permissible in cases in which it is unequivocally voluntary and the patient finds his or her condition unbearable, a legal policy permitting euthanasia would inevitably lead to active euthanasia being performed in many other cases in which it would be morally wrong. To prevent those other wrongful cases of euthanasia we should not permit even morally justified performance of it.

Slippery slope arguments of this form are problematic and difficult to evaluate.[9] From one perspective, they are the last refuge of conservative defenders of the status quo. When all the opponent's objections to the wrongness of euthanasia itself have been met, the opponent then shifts ground and acknowledges both that it is not in itself wrong and that a legal policy which resulted only in its being performed would not be bad. Nevertheless, the opponent maintains, it should still not be permitted because doing so would result in its being performed in other cases in which it is not voluntary and would be wrong. In this argument's most extreme form, permitting euthanasia is the first and fateful step down the slippery slope to Nazism. Once on the slope we will be unable to get off.

Now it cannot be denied that it is *possible* that permitting euthanasia could have these fateful consequences, but that cannot be enough to warrant prohibiting it if it is otherwise justified. A similar *possible* slippery slope worry could have been raised to securing competent patients' rights to decide about life support, but recent history shows such a worry would have been unfounded. It must be relevant how likely it is that we will end with horrendous consequences and an unjustified practice of euthanasia. How *likely* and *widespread* would the abuses and unwarranted extensions of permitting it be? By abuses, I mean the performance of euthanasia that fails to satisfy the conditions required for voluntary active euthanasia, for example, if the patient has been subtly pressured to accept it. By unwarranted extensions of policy, I mean later changes in legal policy to permit not just voluntary euthanasia, but also euthanasia in cases in which, for example, it need not be fully voluntary. Opponents of voluntary euthanasia on slippery slope grounds have not provided the data or evidence necessary to turn their speculative concerns into well-grounded likelihoods.

It is at least clear, however, that both the character and likelihood of abuses of a legal policy permitting euthanasia depend in significant part on the procedures put in place to protect against them. I will not try to detail fully what such procedures might be, but will just give some examples of what they might include:

1. The patient should be provided with all relevant information about his or her medical condition, current prognosis, available alternative treatments, and the prognosis of each.
2. Procedures should ensure that the patient's request for euthanasia is stable or enduring (a brief waiting period could be required) and fully voluntary (an advocate for the patient might be appointed to ensure this).
3. All reasonable alternatives must have been explored for improving the patient's quality of life and relieving any pain or suffering.
4. A psychiatric evaluation should ensure that the patient's request is not the result of a treatable psychological impairment such as depression.[10]

These examples of procedural safeguards are all designed to ensure that the patient's choice is fully informed, voluntary, and competent, and so a true exercise of self-determination. Other proposals for euthanasia would restrict its permissibility further—for example, to the terminally ill—a restriction that cannot be supported by self-determination. Such additional restrictions might, however, be justified by concern for limiting potential harms from abuse. At the same time, it is important not to impose procedural or substantive safeguards so restrictive as to make euthanasia impermissible or practically infeasible in a wide range of justified cases. . . .

THE SLIP INTO NONVOLUNTARY ACTIVE EUTHANASIA

While I believe slippery slope worries can largely be limited by making necessary distinctions both in principle and in practice, one slippery slope concern is legitimate. There is reason to expect that legalization of voluntary active euthanasia might soon be followed by strong pressure to legalize some nonvoluntary euthanasia of incompetent patients unable to express their own wishes. Respecting a person's self-determination and recognizing that continued life is not always of value to a person can support not only voluntary active euthanasia, but some nonvoluntary euthanasia as well. These are the same values that ground competent patients' right to refuse life-sustaining treatment. Recent history here is instructive. In the medical ethics literature, in the courts since Quinlan, and

in norms of medical practice, that right has been extended to incompetent patients and exercised by a surrogate who is to decide as the patient would have decided in the circumstances if competent.[11] It has been held unreasonable to continue life-sustaining treatment that the patient would not have wanted just because the patient now lacks the capacity to tell us that. Life-sustaining treatment for incompetent patients is today frequently forgone on the basis of a surrogate's decision, or less frequently on the basis of an advance directive executed by the patient while still competent. The very same logic that has extended the right to refuse life-sustaining treatment from a competent patient to the surrogate of an incompetent patient (acting with or without a formal advance directive from the patient) may well extend the scope of active euthanasia. The argument will be, Why continue to force unwanted life on patients just because they have now lost the capacity to request euthanasia from us? . . .

Even if voluntary active euthanasia should slip into nonvoluntary active euthanasia, with surrogates acting for incompetent patients, the ethical evaluation is more complex than many opponents of euthanasia allow. Just as in the case of surrogates' decisions to forgo life-sustaining treatment for incompetent patients, so also surrogates' decisions to request euthanasia for incompetent persons would often accurately reflect what the incompetent person would have wanted and would deny the person nothing that he or she would have considered worth having. Making nonvoluntary active euthanasia legally permissible, however, would greatly enlarge the number of patients on whom it might be performed and substantially enlarge the potential for misuse and abuse. As noted above, frail and debilitated elderly people, often demented or otherwise incompetent and thereby unable to defend and assert their own interests, may be especially vulnerable to unwanted euthanasia.

For some people, this risk is more than sufficient reason to oppose the legalization of voluntary euthanasia. But while we should in general be cautious about inferring much from the experience in the Netherlands to what our own experience in the United States might be, there may be one important lesson that we can learn from them. One commentator has noted that in the Netherlands families of incompetent patients have less authority than do families in the United States to act as surrogates for incompetent patients in making decisions to forgo life-sustaining treatment.[12] From the Dutch perspective, it may be we in the United

States who are *already* on the slippery slope in having given surrogates broad authority to forgo life-sustaining treatment for incompetent persons. In this view, the more important moral divide, and the more important with regard to potential for abuse, is not between forgoing life-sustaining treatment and euthanasia, but instead between voluntary and nonvoluntary performance of either. If this is correct, then the more important issue is ensuring the appropriate principles and procedural safeguards for the exercise of decisionmaking authority by surrogates for incompetent persons in *all* decisions at the end of life. This may be the correct response to slippery slope worries about euthanasia. . . .

NOTES

1. Willard Gaylin, Leon R. Kass, Edmund D. Pellegrino, and Mark Siegler, "Doctors Must Not Kill," *JAMA* 259 (1988): 2139–40.

2. P. Painton and E. Taylor, "Love or Let Die," *Time,* 19 March 1990, pp. 62–71; *Boston Globe*/Harvard University Poll, *Boston Globe,* 3 November 1991.

3. James Rachels, *The End of Life* (Oxford: Oxford University Press, 1986).

4. Marcia Angell, "The Quality of Mercy," *NEJM* 306 (1982): 98–99; M. Donovan, P. Dillon, and L. Mcguire, "Incidence and Characteristics of Pain in a Sample of Medical-Surgical Inpatients," *Pain* 30 (1987): 69–78.

5. Eric Cassell, *The Nature of Suffering and the Goals of Medicine* (New York: Oxford University Press, 1991).

6. Gaylin et al., "Doctors Must Not Kill."

7. Paul J. Van der Maas et al., "Euthanasia and Other Medical Decisions Concerning the End of Life," *Lancet* 338 (1991): 669–674.

8. My formulation of this argument derives from David Velleman's statement of it in his commentary on an earlier version of this paper delivered at the American Philosophical Association Central Division meetings; a similar point was made to me by Elijah Milgram in discussion on another occasion.

9. Frederick Schauer, "Slippery Slopes," *Harvard Law Review* 99 (1985): 361–83; Wibren van der Burg, "The Slippery Slope Argument," *Ethics* 102 (October 1991): 42–65.

10. There is evidence that physicians commonly fail to diagnose depression. See Robert I. Misbin, "Physicians Aid in Dying," *NEJM* 325 (1991): 1304–7.

11. Allen E. Buchanan and Dan W. Brock, *Deciding for Others: The Ethics of Surrogate Decision Making* (Cambridge: Cambridge University Press, 1989).

12. Margaret P. Battin, "Seven Caveats Concerning the Discussion of Euthanasia in Holland," *American Philosophical Association Newsletter on Philosophy and Medicine* 89, no. 2 (1990).

FELICIA COHN AND JOANNE LYNN

Vulnerable People: Practical Rejoinders to Claims in Favor of Assisted Suicide

Felicia G. Cohn is Director of Medical Ethics Education at the University of California, Irvine, College of Medicine. Her training was in religious ethics, with a concentration in bioethics. She has published on end-of-life issues in medical ethics as well as appropriate care for the terminally ill.

Joanne Lynn is a physician who specializes in end-of-life issues, geriatrics, and quality improvement. She has published widely on facing serious illness, improving care at the end of life, and reforming health care. She is the director of the Center to Improve Care of the Dying at the George Washington Medical School, Washington, DC.

Though everyone recognizes that death is a certainty, few know how to live with fatal illness. The realities of dying are difficult, for serious illness usually lasts many months, with substantial burdens and expenses. Death itself is not a choice, but its timing sometimes is, or could be. For those persons who conclude that they do not wish to endure the suffering and the costs associated with prolonged dying, physician-assisted suicide seems to offer an answer. It appears to provide individuals the chance to prevent suffering and maintain control over what once seemed uncontrollable.

For others, however, physician-assisted suicide conjures fear that someone else will determine what is to be considered excessive suffering or costs, and that others might seek to eliminate the suffering or the costs by eliminating those persons who are perceived to be suffering or costly. The elderly and the poor are particularly vulnerable to the effects of inadequate health care resources and the attendant constraints on medical decision making. . . .

Health care providers and institutions face increasing pressure to reduce the costs of care. Medicare benefits, for example, remain a regular political issue,

sparking controversy over the costs of preserving the program and the introduction of additional benefits deemed desirable or necessary. In an era when resources are increasingly being squeezed while the population ages and health care needs increase, the elderly and the dying compete against other portions of the population for health care services.[1] Given the high and seemingly disproportionate costs of health care for the elderly and those in the final phase of life, these "users of excessive medical resources" may be the targets of cost-saving efforts.[2] . . .

A number of voices have emerged that speak to the potential for abuse of physician-assisted suicide against members of various groups (e.g., people with disabilities, AIDS patients, members of minorities). Though these people do not speak with one voice, either within or across communities, their insights help us to demonstrate why . . . the most common and most compelling arguments for legalizing physician-assisted suicide are unpersuasive or misleading.

THE PUBLIC WANTS PHYSICIAN-ASSISTED SUICIDE

One opinion poll after another has indicated that a majority of the American public favors legalizing physician-assisted suicide.[3] However, a survey by the

From *The Case against Assisted Suicide: For the Right to End-of-Life Care,* ed. Kathleen Foley, M.D. and Herbert Hendin, M.D., 238–260. © 2002 The Johns Hopkins University Press.

American Medical Association demonstrated that support for physician-assisted suicide reverses when respondents are given information about abuses in the Netherlands and about other options for care at the end of life.[4] Applying the rate of physician-assisted suicide in the Netherlands to the American population indicates that physician-assisted suicide could account for over 61,000 deaths in the United States annually. The Dutch experience also reveals that there are a significant number of unreported cases and instances in which physician-assisted suicide was provided without patient request or consent, contrary to stated guidelines.[5] When presented with Dutch data, one-half of those who supported legalizing physician-assisted suicide reversed their positions. Once provided with descriptions of hospice and palliative care options, only 14 percent said they would still opt for legal access to physician-assisted suicide.[6]

Furthermore, reports of the polls hide the distribution of preferences among various subpopulations of our society. Those favoring legalization of physician-assisted suicide tend to be young, male, and white.[7] Those opposing legalization of physician-assisted suicide are often elderly, female, or from minority groups—some of the very people who face progressive disability and suffering before death and who therefore would seem most likely to support having the option of assisted suicide. . . .

The situation changes as people experience the progressive declines that often accompany aging. As people approach death, they commonly have very few financial resources and often are profoundly dependent on the arrangements others make for their care. Which services are available largely reflects federal financing, including the coverage gaps when Medicare and Medicaid do not pay for services. Many people's poorest years are those nearest death, when income is low, care needs are high, and lack of community support for personal care during disability takes its largest toll. The prospect of increasing disability and eventual death is disheartening enough, but the added anxiety over the adequacy of savings and the "safety net" of government services is often terrifying.

For many, no reasonably desirable choices may exist. Then, physician-assisted suicide may not merely be a choice, one option among others; rather, it may become a coercive offer.[8] If physician-assisted suicide becomes a more popular choice, ending one's own life could come to be perceived as an obligation, that is, a societally endorsed course of action that is the only way to avoid suffering, indignity, and impoverishment. Physician-assisted suicide may not be what dying people would reasonably prefer if given a choice of reliable, comprehensive care, an option that is not now usually available. Thus rather than increasing the choices one has as death approaches, legalizing physician-assisted suicide may actually have the effect of constraining choices. . . .

WHEN MEDICINE CAN DO "NOTHING MORE," PHYSICIAN-ASSISTED SUICIDE IS ONE APPROPRIATE RESPONSE

Medical care often works to the detriment of those reaching life's inevitable and natural end. However, only rarely can "nothing more" be done, though current patterns of medical care may miss the opportunities to provide appropriate assistance.

Medicine has much to offer those who are dying. That many do not get what they need is not justification for physician-assisted suicide but an indictment of the current approach to end-of-life care. Appropriate health care could relieve overwhelming pain in those near death, support family caregivers, and provide reliable, trustworthy care. However, most patients cannot count on any of this. Currently, the only program for end-of-life care covered by Medicare is hospice. Yet hospice serves a very small population. In 1998, hospice provided benefits to 540,000 dying patients in their last few weeks of life.[9] The hospice benefit is limited to people who have a "terminal illness with a life expectancy of six months or less." Cancer and AIDS are virtually the only diseases that follow predictable courses of decline near death; thus, about 60 percent of hospice patients have cancer and many of the rest have AIDS.[10] Cancer patients are usually referred to hospice when the individual's functioning declines, usually three to six weeks before death.[11] By electing hospice, Medicare patients agree to forgo "life-prolonging" interventions and instead receive comprehensive medical and supportive services not otherwise covered by Medicare. In addition to this prognostic requirement, hospice effectively requires that the beneficiary have a home and a family or nursing home caregiver. . . .

In addition to the constraints of uncertain prognosis, many elderly people live alone, often in inadequate homes and without social support. Such patients are not generally eligible for hospice, though they desperately need hospice-like services, including advance planning, prescription medication, support services, symptom management, and coordinated care services—none of which are readily available. Providing comprehensive end-of-life care services to these individuals could significantly improve the quality of their remaining days. . . .

Consideration of the legalization of physician-assisted suicide should be taken as a challenge to improve end-of-life care and make it available to everyone. If dying is miserable and expensive, it is because we have allowed it to become that way. . . .

WHEN A PATIENT IS SUFFERING DREADFULLY AND REQUESTS ASSISTANCE IN BRINGING ABOUT A DESIRED KIND OF DEATH, LEGALIZED PHYSICIAN-ASSISTED SUICIDE WOULD BE APPROPRIATE

The common vision is that of a suffering patient who visits his or her physician to request a lethal prescription. The patient expects to leave the office with prescription in hand, heading home to place those pills on the counter so they are ready for use whenever the "right time" arrives.

A number of misperceptions plague this image, particularly with regard to alternatives at the end of life and the rapid access to physician-assisted suicide. First, physical suffering need not be a part of dying, and physician-assisted suicide is not the only remedy for suffering. Rates of intractable pain, even among cancer patients, are low; and if the patient is willing to accept sedation, pain can practically be eliminated.[12] Providing pain medication is already legal, even if it is perceived to have the side effect of hastening death. Other symptoms, such as nausea, depression, and shortness of breath, can also be medically relieved. Virtually all patients with serious illness can be physically comfortable.

Second, patients may bring about their deaths without physician-assisted suicide (e.g., by committing suicide unassisted, refusing life-sustaining treatment, or forgoing nutrition and fluids). Dehydration, for example, requires no assistance and is a generally comfortable way to die, especially for a very ill person who may have little interest in food and water or may actually be harmed by the imposition of feedings.[13] Contrary to public perception, forgoing artificial nutrition and hydration does not leave patients hungry or thirsty.[14] Furthermore, physician-assisted suicide does not provide an immediate solution. According to understandable safeguards built into virtually every proposed physician-assisted suicide statute as well as

the law in effect in Oregon, a physician can act on a request for physician-assisted suicide only following a substantial waiting period, often at least two weeks. This is hardly the response envisioned by proponents' arguments and may even take longer than death by dehydration. . . .

THE RIGHT TO FORGO LIFE-SUSTAINING TREATMENT LOGICALLY INCLUDES PHYSICIAN-ASSISTED SUICIDE

Many claim that no reasonable line can be drawn between acts of forgoing (withdrawing and withholding) life-sustaining treatment and acts of physician-assisted suicide. This argument holds that if forgoing life-sustaining treatment is ethically and legally acceptable, physician-assisted suicide is also justifiable. Physician-assisted suicide occurs "when a physician provides either equipment or medication, or informs the patient of the most efficacious use of already available means, for the sole purpose of assisting the patient to end his or her own life." Forgoing life-sustaining treatment by definition occurs when "medical intervention is either not given or the ongoing use of the intervention is discontinued, allowing natural progression of the underlying disease state."[15] In each, death predictably results from the action taken. Therefore some claim that no cognizable difference exists between forgoing life-sustaining treatment and having physician-assisted suicide. In both, someone, usually a health care professional, acts to bring about death. The lower courts in the two physician-assisted suicide cases decided in 1997 found no justification for distinguishing physician-assisted suicide from withholding or withdrawing life-sustaining treatment.[16] Timothy Quill also argues that any purported difference is ethically irrelevant and that both methods ought to be available to physicians who desire to help their patients die comfortably.[17]

However, crucial distinctions do exist and have been serving medicine and patients well. Major American medical associations maintain distinctions between physician-assisted suicide and forgoing life-sustaining treatment.[18] Within the practice of medicine, physician-assisted suicide and withholding or withdrawing life-sustaining treatment may be distinguished according to practical and conceptual descriptions, legal ramifications for medical practice, and the procedural consequences of collapsing the distinction. Indeed, very few cases arise that would occasion any dispute as to which category was involved. . . .

When patients forgo life-sustaining treatment, the intent is not to bring about the patient's death but to respect the patient's wishes not to be subjected to undesired treatment. Medical treatment is withdrawn or withheld, and the underlying disease process then leads to the patient's death. Thus the patient is allowed to die following the natural course of his or her illness, but death is not artificially hastened. Although a physician may be active in removing life support, the physician's action is not a proximate cause of the death. If the particular life-sustaining technique had not been available, death would already have resulted. Additionally, the patient may continue to live, even when life support is removed. The physician would not proceed to suffocate a patient who resumes spontaneous respiration after a ventilator is withdrawn.

This scenario differs from physician-assisted suicide. In physician-assisted suicide, the intent is to bring about the patient's death. Certainly, a physician may be acting in accord with a patient's wishes and will eliminate the patient's suffering, but at the cost of explicitly and intentionally causing the patient's death in a manner distinct from the natural course to death. The physician is not preventing patient abuse nor alleviating pain, but actively abetting death. . . .

ALLOWING USE OF PAIN MEDICATIONS THAT MAY INADVERTENTLY HASTEN DEATH PROVIDES SUPPORT FOR LEGALIZING PHYSICIAN-ASSISTED SUICIDE

Proponents of physician-assisted suicide also rely on an analogy to the provision of potentially life-shortening palliative care. The intent of a person providing palliative care is not to bring about the patient's death but to decrease the patient's pain and suffering. A recognized, but perhaps unavoidable, side effect may be the hastening of the patient's death. However, pain management techniques do not necessarily hasten death for a particular patient, nor is it clear that they actually often have that effect. As commonly used, pain medications rarely accelerate the patient's death. Patients using opioids chronically do not experience respiratory depressant side effects at doses that are effective in suppressing pain. Once the patient is habitually taking opioids, only a quite extraordinary dose would be lethal. Only for patients who have received no opioids is the respiratory depressant effect present at analgesic doses, and few dying patients are in this situation.

Even if a physician's act may hasten death, the physician is not acting to ensure an earlier death. The provision of "comfort care" also does not involve the exercise of a right to die, but instead is a matter of sound medical practice, aiming to relieve symptoms. . . .

PHYSICIANS POSSESS THE UNIQUE EXPERTISE AND SINGULAR ABILITY TO BRING ABOUT AN EASY SUICIDE AND SO ARE NECESSARILY INVOLVED

Underlying claims about a right to physician-assisted suicide are fears of botched suicides and desires for ensured death. Physician involvement is thought to afford a guarantee of easy suicide. Only physicians are thought to have both the knowledge of pharmacology and the access to controlled substances believed necessary to facilitate successful suicides. To that end, proposals for legalized assisted suicide have required physician involvement.

Yet physician involvement guarantees neither an easy nor a successful suicide. Often physicians are not even taught effective symptom management; certainly, they are not schooled in how to take life. Indeed, expertise in how to ensure death is not commonly available in medical textbooks or journals. If advocates wish to ensure expertise, those who implement the death penalty may be more qualified than physicians generally.

Because of either patient condition or incorrect dosing, many patients will be unable to swallow or keep the pills down. This raises the probability that assistance beyond prescribing lethal medications will be essential and may even suggest that active euthanasia, or lethal injection, would be more effective and likely would seem more humane. Furthermore, the question of how to deal with a failed attempt remains, particularly if that act has rendered the patient worse off or unable to request or complete another attempt. . . .

CURRENTLY WIDESPREAD BUT CLANDESTINE PHYSICIAN-ASSISTED SUICIDE WOULD BE REGULATED APPROPRIATELY

Advocates frequently claim that physician-assisted suicide is practiced regularly. Their claims appear to be supported by studies in which physicians anonymously admit to having assisted in suicide or even to have euthanized a patient.[19] Most such studies have utilized quite inadequate methods. For example, these studies often do not provide an explicit definition of physician-assisted suicide.

For physician-assisted suicide to occur with regularity would require widespread complicity in illegal behaviors, since three-quarters or more of patients dying of serious illness are in hospitals and nursing homes. Widespread criminal activity could hardly go unnoticed by regulators and the general public.

According to one methodologically superior study of the rate of physician-assisted suicide,[20] about 3 percent of American physicians report that they have been party to physician-assisted suicide at least once. However, even with good definitions, many respondents confused physician-assisted suicide with euthanasia and with side effects of medications to relieve symptoms, so the actual rate is lower. While not an insignificant rate, it is hardly evidence of widespread violation of the law.

Furthermore, the fact that physician-assisted suicide may be occurring hardly provides a reason for making it legal. Although many in the United States now use illicit drugs and engage in underage drinking and agitate for the legalization of these activities, our society has decided that there are important reasons for maintaining their illegality. Foremost among these reasons is the protection of certain portions of society, both from their own bad decisions and from new societal expectations. The same may be true of physician-assisted suicide. Unless our society achieves a consensus on the value of life, works out the practical difficulties, and resolves the role conflict for physicians, any policy allowing physician-assisted suicide will continue to be problematic. . . .

THE LAW CAN PROTECT PEOPLE FROM ABUSES OF PHYSICIAN-ASSISTED SUICIDE

Most proposed legislation requires that physician-assisted suicide be confined to patients who are terminally ill, suffering, and competent and who voluntarily and repeatedly request assistance from their physicians. Those who propose legalization of physician-assisted suicide contend that each of these conditions in part justifies legalization and that the needed categories can be clearly delineated. The legal constraints are thought to be sufficient to limit physician-assisted suicide to those who have made informed decisions to escape intolerable suffering in the final phase of life and to avoid subjecting others to abusive impositions. However, each of these conditions is problematic. Some are undefinable or unsustainable, or both, and undoubtedly each would lead to a number of contested cases. Even regulation of physician-assisted suicide does not guarantee that its practice will be limited according to the legal and clinical boundaries we create, nor can it ensure protection of those who may be most in need of protection.

Terminal illness and *terminal condition* have been "defined repeatedly . . . in a model statute, the Uniform Rights of the Terminally Ill Act, and in over 40 state natural death statutes."[21] However, the terms are notoriously difficult to define, have uncertain criteria, and, as with any set of criteria, lead to myriad contentious cases. Despite the existence of what may be working definitions of *terminal illness*, a more rigorous definition seems necessary when its application may have such significant and irreversible consequences. Three general approaches might be used in attempting to define the category *terminally ill*: subjective judgment, statistical criteria, or disease severity threshold. However, none of these approaches yields the certainty and clarity necessary for implementing good public policy.

A subjective determination of who is "terminally ill" requires that some person or persons render a judgment that integrates an array of information about the patient's situation, prognosis, and appropriate care. Often patients, family, and professional caregivers negotiate the designation while discussing plans and making decisions that collectively mark a change from a strategy of correcting abnormalities with the expectation of long survival to a strategy focusing on function, comfort, and emotional and spiritual support with the expectation of death. In matters of routine patient care, various participants can arrive at the designation at somewhat different times, and the labeling can unfold differently with different participants in the conversation.

The obvious variation in this process would be troubling if physician-assisted suicide were available only for those categorized as "terminally ill." Availability of physician-assisted suicide contingent on this designation may result in pressure to accelerate the application of or resist the label. Thus this category would not describe an objectively determined status, independent of its effect. Rather, the possibility of physician-assisted suicide could alter the designation and the dynamics of its negotiation.

Regional and situational variation probably would be substantial and perceived as unfair, especially since no standards or assessment mechanisms exist. A rigorous or regularized process would sacrifice the personalization that commends this approach. Furthermore, no approach overcomes the problem that being labeled as terminally ill turns, in part, on the desirability of having physician-assisted suicide available. The variation, the inability to standardize, and the likelihood of significant litigation make this an unlikely determinant

In general, we use *terminal illness* to refer to those patients for whom there is no available curative treatment, who are losing weight and function, and who are, or ought to be, psychologically "ready" to die. Any statistical threshold will include many persons who do not now merit this social label, or will exclude many who do, or both. For example, half of all persons who die of lung cancer today will have had a prognosis of better than 30 percent to live two months just one week ago,[22] so any more restrictive threshold will miss most persons dying of lung cancer. Yet such a threshold will include many persons with acute respiratory, cardiac, or liver failure, who usually are vigorously treated and qualify for transplantation only when seriously ill. If the category were expanded to include everyone with up to a 50 percent chance to live six months, most nursing home residents would qualify. If the category were restricted to those with a 1 percent chance to live two months, not only would one exclude virtually all cancer patients but those in the category would be so sick that they would, on average, die within a day.[23] Every option yields a mismatch between perceptions and achievable goals that renders the designation of terminal illness almost meaningless with regard to physician-assisted suicide. . . .

A very different way to define terminal illness is based on the extent of illness. While this approach is loosely tied to prognosis, it allows substantial uncertainty about an individual's expected survival time. The threshold could be linked to clinically significant and morally important events, such as the recurrence of cancer in a different site or the onset of fecal incontinence in a demented person. These events and thresholds could be understandable to patients, practitioners, and the public in a way that the statistical modeling is not. This would allow for the possibility of public accord on the general nature and some of the specifics of the thresholds.

However, there are problems with this approach. An individual's status is not well characterized by the extent of one serious disease. Rather, a person's future is shaped by the particular illness; reserve capacity of various body systems; social situation; personal orientation; and availability, use of, and response to treatment. Thus there unquestionably will be much variation. Additionally, many of the patients included will actually have long life spans. If one purpose of defining *terminal illness* is to restrict physician-assisted suicide to persons who have only a short time to live, this method of categorization will not succeed. This method is also afflicted with some of the problems already described: lack of data for groups of persons generally and for specific patients individually, inability to arbitrate the effects of inducing "terminal illness" through treatment choices, and incompatibility with existing social construction of the category.

In addition to the requirement for terminal illness, physician-assisted suicide proposals and law limit access to persons who are competent to make such a decision at the time it is implemented. Thus there is a need to determine who is and is not competent for this purpose. As with categorizing the terminally ill, identifying competence is a difficult and perhaps impossible task, especially as there are difficulties with both legal and clinical considerations. . . .

As another option, measurement and performance requirements for physician-assisted suicide could be established. Competence is a multifactorial concept, which includes, for example, ability to learn and recall information, consider likely outcomes, assess desirability of outcomes, communicate about the situation and the choices, and reach a decision. An individual can lack capacity to make some decisions but not others. A person also can be generally confused but clear about a particular situation. Since the combinations and complications are legion, using a specific threshold in one or in just a few domains oversimplifies what actually is a complex task. That simplification could mean that a fixed threshold will find some persons to be competent despite obvious and relevant disabilities while others could actually handle this choice well despite a determination of incompetence.

A special problem with lengthy dying is fear of the indignity associated with incompetence. If policy is to allow physician assistance in suicide for only those with contemporaneous competence, then those who have conditions likely to lead to incompetence may feel pressure to undertake preemptive suicide. This is a special risk in early dementia, when patients retain the ability to understand but have failing memory. At this stage, a patient may have nonprogressive memory loss or a very slow rate of progression, and thus the chance for additional comfortable and capable years. However, a patient also may rapidly progress to cognitive disability. Persons in this situation might seek to avoid the dreaded outcomes by preemptive physician-assisted suicide. This pattern could create substantial pressures for allowing some forms of advance direction by which a person could specify the degree of disability that would trigger lethal actions. Once a person is no longer competent or capable of acting himself or herself, assisted suicide is no longer an option. Thus policy may be forced to move beyond assisted suicide to considerations of euthanasia.

Not only must an individual be terminally ill and competent to make decisions to have access to physician-assisted suicide, but also he or she must be acting voluntarily or without undue influence. Yet the experience of illness appears inherently coercive: dying persons are very sick and usually experience a welter of strong emotions, such as anger, fear, exhilaration, and self-disparagement. They are generally vulnerable to the suggestions, expectations, and guidance of others. In this context, pressure or encouragement from family, friends, and caregivers or even general societal expectations may become inappropriately coercive. . . .

While it is easy enough to bar decisions made under threat of violence, gentle coercion of the very sick is hard to discern or to prevent. Would we count it as undue influence if we found that most persons in certain nursing homes, or certain capitated managed care systems, were "freely choosing" to commit suicide? Would we count it as undue influence if heirs encouraged physician-assisted suicide? What if an elderly, terminally ill grandfather felt that he had become unreasonably burdensome for his aging adult child? . . .

[P]ersons approaching death are often severely pressured by financial concerns. Is financial concern to count as undue influence or not? This is a particular dilemma for those who serve frail, disabled, and poor patients. The availability of physician-assisted suicide may itself become coercive in a society where health care services are not a right but a privilege that is circumscribed by individual situation, location, and finances. . . .

Some proposals for physician-assisted suicide also require that the patient be "suffering," "in pain," or "acting rationally." The nature and measurement of these conditions have not been articulated and justified. The interaction with treatment is again important, since sedation can always eliminate physical symptoms. This course is available at present, without any change in the law. Then again, most patients can be made physically comfortable without sedation. Perhaps many would be eligible for physician-assisted

suicide only if they turned down these available treatments and therefore had severe symptoms. . . .

Given the possibilities of suffering, physician-assisted suicide may appear to be a "rational" option. Indeed, many advocates see rationality as a necessary and worthy attribute. Suicide may often be understandable, but weighing the outcome of nonexistence against other outcomes requires some distinctly nonrational considerations. Furthermore, any decision of this import should not be wholly rational but should include a nonrational emotional commitment. One would find it quite incomprehensible to advocate merely "rational" choices for most major life choices—having children, for example. . . .

Even the experience of physician-assisted suicide in Oregon and the Netherlands has not yielded clear, consistent, readily understandable guidelines. Without such guidelines, public policy is limited to guesswork and many patients will be subject to arbitrary, possibly discriminatory decisions. Possibilities abound for manipulation so that physician-assisted suicide is effectively easier for those who are elderly, poor, or frail, and for other vulnerable populations. Clearly, legislated guidelines will not be enough to protect everyone, no matter how well intentioned. . . .

CONCLUSION

The most powerful calls for physician-assisted suicide come from individuals experiencing suffering we would all prefer to avoid. But for every tragic case of individual suffering spotlighted in the media, whole categories of people suffer without similar attention. Certainly, in some particular situations, physician-assisted suicide may seem appropriate, even necessary. However, justifying an individual act does not mean that a widespread practice can or should be justified. What is good for one person may not be good for groups of people and may be harmful to several groups of people—as physician-assisted suicide appears likely to be. In developing policy, we must remember that physician-assisted suicide is about more than individual rights and distressing situations. Oliver Wendell Holmes reminded us, "Hard cases make bad law." Now we need a corollary about population well-being and policy: Hard individual situations make bad public policy.

The calls for legalizing physician-assisted suicide arise in a social system that is inattentive to the complex physical, emotional, and spiritual needs of people as they near the end of life. Additionally, abuse is a real risk, especially among those who are elderly, frail, disabled, and economically disadvantaged. Resolving a patient's suffering should not rely on assisting that patient's suicide. Rather, providing comfort care, especially when cure is no longer possible, is an important task for health care professionals. Making good palliative care a real option involves developing a new research agenda, enhancing medical education, and changing priorities in health care delivery and funding. With a priority on palliative care, physician assistance in dying could come to mean supportive and comfort care rather than a lethal prescription.

NOTES

1. D. Callahan, "Controlling the Costs of Health Care for the Elderly: Fair Means Foul," *New England Journal of Medicine* 10 (1996):744–46; H. M. Chochinov and K. Janson, "Dying to Pay: The Cost of End-of-Life Care," *Journal of Palliative Care* 14, no. 4 (1998):5–15.

2. N. G. Levinsky, "The Purpose of Advance Medical Planning: Autonomy for Patients or Limitation of Care?" *New England Journal of Medicine* 333 (1996):741–43.

3. R. A. Knox, "Poll: Americans Favor Mercy Killing," *Boston Globe*, 3 November 1991, A1; Hemlock Society, *1996 Gallup Poll on Doctor-Assisted Suicide* (Princeton, N.J.: Gallup Organization, 1997); Hemlock Society, *1997 Gallup/CNN/USA Today Poll on Doctor-Assisted Suicide* (Princeton, N.J.: Gallup Organization, 1997).

4. American Medical Association, *AMA End of Life Survey*, December 1996.

5. J. S. Shapiro, "Euthanasia's Home: What the Dutch Experience Can Teach Americans about Assisted Suicide," *U.S. News & World Report*, 13 January 1997, 24–27.

6. See American Medical Association 1996.

7. K. Stewart, "Physician Aid in Dying," *Polling Report* 13, no. 15 (1997): 1, 6–7.

8. See Hardwig 1997.

9. National Hospice Organization, at http://www.nho.org/facts.htm.

10. Ibid.

11. J. Lynn, F. E. Harrell, F. Cohn, et al., for the SUPPORT Investigators, "Defining the 'Terminally Ill': Insights from SUPPORT," *Duquesne Law Review* 25 (1996): 311–36; V. Mor and D. Kidder, "Cost Savings in Hospice: Final Results of the National Hospice Study," *Health Services Research* 20 (1985): 407–22.

12. See Knox 1991.

13. J. L. Bernat, B. Gert, and R. P. Mogielnicki, "Patient Refusal of Hydration and Nutrition: An Alternative to Physician-Assisted Suicide or Voluntary Euthanasia," *Archives of Internal Medicine* 153 (1993):2723–28.

14. J. Lynn and J. Harrold, *Handbook for Mortals* (New York: Oxford University Press, 1999), 113.

15. American Geriatrics Society Ethics Committee, "Physician-Assisted Suicide and Voluntary Active Euthanasia," *Journal of the American Geriatrics Society* 43 (1995):579–80.

16. *Dennis C. Vacco et al. v. Timothy E. Quill, M.D., et al.*, 80 F.3d 716 (2d Cir. 1996), and *State of Washington v. Harold Glucksberg, et al.* (formerly *Compassion in Dying v. Washington*) 79 F.3d 790 (9th Cir. 1996).

17. T. E. Quill, *A Midwife through the Dying Process: Stories of Healing and Hard Choices at the End of Life* (Baltimore: Johns Hopkins University Press, 1996).

18. E. J. Larson, "Seeking Compassion in Dying: The Washington State Law against Assisted Suicide," *Seattle University Law Review* 18 (1995):509–17; New York State Task Force on Life and the Law, *When Death Is Sought: Assisted Suicide and Euthanasia in the Medical Context* (New York: New York State Task Force on Life and the Law, 1994), 102.

19. A. Back, "Physician Assisted Death" [editorial], *Journal of the American Medical Association* 276 (1996):1688.

20. D. Meier, C. A. Emmons, S. Wallenstein, et al., "A National Survey of Physician Assisted Death in the United States," *New England Journal of Medicine* 338 (1998):1193–1201.

21. *Quill*, 80 F.3d at 731; *Compassion in Dying v. State of Washington*, 79 F.3d 790, 831 (9th Cir. 1996).

22. See Lynn et al. 1997.

23. See Teno et al. 1994.

H. TRISTRAM ENGELHARDT, JR.

Physician-Assisted Suicide and Euthanasia: Another Battle in the Culture Wars

H. Tristram Engelhardt, Jr. is a Professor of Bioethics, Medicine, and Community Medicine at the Baylor College of Medicine, as well as Professor of Philosophy at Rice University. His areas of scholarship are bioethics, philosophy of medicine, and continental philosophy. Among his books are *Foundations of Bioethics, Bioethics and Secular Humanism,* and *The Foundations of Christian Bioethics.*

1. THE CULTURE WARS

. . . Depending on the moral framework affirmed, physician-assisted suicide will be an element of patient empowerment or assisted self-murder. Physician-assisted suicide and voluntary active euthanasia evoke controversies that reflect foundationally contrasting moral visions with important implications for bioethics and health care policy. To place the disputes regarding physician-assisted suicide in a larger context, this essay explores the depth of the moral disagreements that exist in secular bioethics. . . .

The debates go very deep. They depend not just on different understandings of freedom, equality, justice, and ownership. The differences often turn on the meaning of the universe itself, the existence of God, as well as duties to God regarding one's own life and that of others. In the debates regarding physician-assisted suicide and euthanasia, one finds, as with abortion, that secular philosophical differences are more strident because they are joined with religious understandings that consider both as forms of murder and assisted murder. If anything, the conflict of moralities regarding physician-assisted suicide and euthanasia will be even more pervasive. Not all reproduce. Not all who reproduce find an occasion for abortion. However, everyone dies; there will likely be more

occasions under which issues of physician-assisted suicide and euthanasia will come to the fore than with regard to abortion. . . .

These foundational disagreements raise a number of important moral and policy issues, three of which deserve special attention. First, to what extent do such disagreements bring into question claims regarding the existence of a common morality? Second, how do these disagreements press us to take moral diversity seriously? Third, what implications do such moral disagreement and diversity have for a secular state and its health care policy?

2. CULTURAL WARS: WHY WE THOUGHT WE COULD AVOID THEM

First, in the shadow of the Second World War and in the light of new medical technologies, scientific advances, and with the challenge of new medical costs, many clamored for moral direction. Since nearly everyone recognized the horrors of National Socialist medical atrocities, the hope was that similar agreement could be secured regarding most substantive issues in bioethics. Few noticed that not only were the atrocities of National Socialism signally horrendous, they violated the core canons of secular morality as well as of most religious morality: the National Socialists were engaged in atrocities against individuals without their consent. . . . If the Enlightenment project of discovering by reason a content-full moral vision were successful, then:

From Loretta M. Kopelman and Kenneth A. De Ville (eds.), *Physician-Assisted Suicide,* 29–41. © 2001 Kluwer Academic Publishers.

1. all would be disclosed as really being members of one moral community, superficial differences to the contrary notwithstanding;
2. all would be bound by a content-full morality that could be rejected only at the risk of being found irrational;
3. those who imposed a public policy elaborated in conformity with that morality would act with the authority of reason;
4. those subjected to coercive force to conform to that policy should not find that force alien to their true moral selves, but rather restorative of their true, rational, autonomous behavior; and
5. there would be jobs aplenty for bioethicists to elaborate the policy that should direct those who govern society.
6. bioethicists would assume the role of secular priests: they would disclose the morality that should shape law and public policy as well as being able to serve as expert witnesses before court.

It is therefore in the interest of both those who govern and their bioethical collaborators to claim that:

1. philosophers and bioethicists can by reason discover the canonical content-full morality, or
2. philosophers and bioethicists can elaborate the common morality shared by all as humans, or
3. philosophers and bioethicists can produce a moral consensus that can authoritatively guide those who govern, or some variation on one of these claims.

Bioethicists have strong interests in advancing a recapitulation of the Enlightenment project. Like the *philosophes* of the 18th century, they can hope to be engaged in fashioning an enlightened future. . . .

3. PHYSICIAN-ASSISTED SUICIDE: ASSISTED SELF-MURDER VS. ASSISTED SELF-DELIVERANCE

In the absence of a canonical moral vision that establishes a priority to life itself over other goods, or in the absence of a metaphysical understanding that establishes a duty to God not to take one's own life, it will not be possible to justify in principle the moral proscription of suicide, physician-assisted suicide, and physician-assisted euthanasia. As already indicated, such a canonical ranking of values cannot be established in general secular terms without begging the crucial question or engaging an infinite regress in

the pursuit of a normative value perspective. Nor in general secular arguments will the invocation of duties to God be a clincher. As a consequence, disputes regarding a good death will be resolved among moral strangers by agreement and by not interfering with those who peaceably go their own ways. Since moral authority will be derived from permission, there will by default be moral zones of privacy, areas where one cannot enter save by permission (Engelhardt, 1996, pp. 68–74).

Insofar as one recognizes consent as core to the procedural morality binding moral strangers, the prime moral focus in physician-assisted suicide will be on the consent of those who participate, as well as on the costs and benefits of different policies. There will be an attention (1) to the authorization by moral agents of their own deaths, as well as (2) to the consequences of different policies for aiding and accomplishing voluntary killings. Under such circumstances, it will be impossible to establish secular moral barriers in principle to physician-assisted suicide and voluntary active euthanasia. Instead, the focus will fall on:

1. the adequacy of the consent of those seeking assisted suicide,
2. the absence of invalidating coercion,
3. the presence of defeating duties to third parties,
4. the possibility of untoward consequences, including the abuse of innocent parties as well as being prematurely dispatched, and
5. the special effects of different policies on particular, historically conditioned understandings of the health care professions.

None of these considerations offers a bar in principle to secular bioethics, but rather raises various considerations to be addressed in determining how to establish moral rules or practices regarding physician-assisted suicide and other forms of consented-to killings.

Indeed, the secular moral burden of proof will fall on anyone who would coercively forbid physician-assisted suicide or voluntary active euthanasia. The ethos of death with dignity and the affirmation of rational self-determination makes death marked by suffering and lack of control profoundly unacceptable, especially in a society whose dominant culture values individual dignity and self-control. One should note that the focus is not on pain in such pleadings on behalf of physician-assisted suicide and voluntary active euthanasia. It is a loss of mastery over one's own life and destiny, which can be experienced as suffering. The argument in favor of suicide will, in such circumstances, not be blunted by adequate pain control or the availability of better analgesics. A death is unacceptable for many if (1) (a) it involves the indignity of the loss of control of bodily functions, (b) dependency on others, and/or (c) an inability to engage in that which gives one's life meaning when (2) there is the possibility of an earlier dignified death. . . .

As the secular moral culture of the West becomes disconnected from traditional Western Christianity's proscription of directly intending the death of an innocent person, it will appear precious at best, if not perversely misguided, to draw distinctions between intention and foresight in the care of the dying. It will be a mystery to many, if not most, why one may engage in activities associated with an earlier death as long as one only foresees but does not intend the death of the person treated. It will be a puzzle as to why one may not also intend death. . . .

[T]raditional Christians, Orthodox Jews, and others will still appreciate the moral wrongness of physician-assisted suicide and voluntary active euthanasia (Engelhardt, 2000, esp. ch. 6). This wrongness will be acknowledged within understandings at variance with the metaphysical, epistemological, and axiological commitments of a general secular morality. In particular, such will acknowledge duties to God not to take life, which duties are not defeated by concerns with suffering, dignity, or interest in self-control. Because of God-regarding obligations, physician-assisted suicide will be recognized by them as a grave moral evil. . . .

4. TOLERANCE AND CONFRONTATION

Although traditional Christians and Orthodox Jews should tolerate the involvement of others in physician-assisted suicide and voluntary active euthanasia in the sense of eschewing coercive interventions, tolerance does not require acceptance. Just as many find the condemnatory language of abortion as murder to be morally disruptive, so, too, the recognition and condemnation of physician-assisted suicide and voluntary active euthanasia as assisted murder and murder will be perceived on the one hand as morally disturbing and on the other hand as morally obligatory. As with abortion, so too with physician-assisted suicide, the judgment of the moral actions of those involved is likely to be forceful, substantive, and conflicting.

As with abortion, many will find it impossible to be moral collaborators. As a result, many physicians and institutions will likely not only refuse to provide physician-assisted suicide services and voluntary active euthanasia, they will also not refer for such services. One may even find some geographical areas without easily accessible providers offering physician-assisted suicide and voluntary active euthanasia, as currently is the case with abortion services. As a result, there will not only be moral controversies, but disputes engendered by the refusal to provide services that many will consider essential to a dignified death. On the one hand, the availability of physician-assisted suicide is likely inevitable. On the other hand, deep and persistent disagreements concerning physician-assisted suicide will likely lead to strong mutual moral condemnations and the refusal to provide such services.

5. TAKING MORAL DIVERSITY SERIOUSLY

One way to come to terms with the depth of these disagreements is to recognize and respect the integrity of moral diversity: to take moral diversity seriously. . . .

Acceptance of moral diversity would require true tolerance on the part of those who preach tolerance: one would need to allow moral difference to have its place. Much today is said about the virtues of diversity. Societies, so it is held, are enriched by cultural and ethnic diversity. However, much of the praise for such diversity, though likely not disingenuous, is usually on behalf of a domesticated diversity without moral substance. . . . Secular bioethics and health care will need to take this moral diversity seriously. The emerging acceptance of physician-assisted suicide and voluntary active euthanasia may support claims in favor of recognizing and coming to terms with this diversity.

REFERENCES

Engelhardt, H.T., Jr.: 1996, *The Foundations of Bioethics*, 2nd ed., Oxford University Press, New York, New York.

Engelhardt, H.T., Jr.: 2000, *The Foundations of Christian Bioethics*, Swets & Zeitlinger, Lisse, The Netherlands.

Seneca: 1958, 'On the sadness of life', in *The Stoic Philosophy of Seneca*, trans. Moses Hadas, Norton, New York, New York.

Palliation and Other Alternatives to Physician-Assisted Death

BERNARD GERT, CHARLES M. CULVER, AND K. DANNER CLOUSER

An Alternative to Physician-Assisted Suicide

Bernard Gert is the Stone Professor of Intellectual and Moral Philosophy at Dartmouth College and Adjunct Professor of Psychiatry at Dartmouth Medical School. He is first author of *Morality and the New Genetics* (1996), and (with Charles M. Culver and K. Danner Clouser) *Bioethics: A Return to Fundamentals* (1997). He is also author of *Morality: Its Nature and Justification* (rev. ed. 2005) and *Common Morality: Deciding What to Do* (2004)—two works in general ethical theory.

Charles Culver is a physician and Professor of Medical Education at Barry University. He is a psychiatrist who has co-authored (with Bernard Gert and K. Danner Clouser) *Bioethics: A Return to Fundamentals*. Dr. Culver is also the co-author of *Philosophy in Medicine: Conceptual and Ethical Problems in Medicine and Psychiatry* and editor of *Ethics at the Bedside*.

The late K. Danner Clouser was a University Professor of Humanities at the Penn State College of Medicine from 1968 until his retirement in 1996. He was instrumental in building the first humanities department established at a medical school and was a pioneer in the newly emerging field of bioethics. His publications include (with Bernard Gert and Charles M. Culver) *Bioethics: A Return to Fundamentals* and *Teaching Bioethics: Strategies, Problems, and Resources*. His work was examined in a book entitled *Building Bioethics: Conversations with Clouser and Friends on Medical Ethics* (Kluwer).

Two tasks are necessary in order to determine whether physician-assisted suicide should be legalized. The first is to clarify the meaning of the phrase "physician-assisted suicide" (PAS) so that one can be precise about what procedures are correctly specified by the phrase. The second task is to inquire into the moral acceptability of doctors' carrying out those procedures that are appropriately labeled as PAS. It is essential to settle the conceptual task before deciding about PAS's moral acceptability. Once conceptual matters are clarified and the moral acceptability of PAS is determined, disagreements about the social consequences of legalizing PAS continue to make it an issue

on which reasonable people can take either side. However, we shall show that awareness of an alternative to PAS, namely, the refusal of food and fluids, significantly weakens the arguments in favor of legalizing PAS.

It may seem odd to claim that there is a problem in clarifying what is meant by PAS. The prototypical example of PAS, and the way it is almost always practiced, is for a doctor to provide a lethal quantity of sedating medication to a patient who subsequently ingests it and dies. Everyone agrees that the doctor who carries out such an action has engaged in PAS. The conceptual problem arises not with the prototypical example but with the conceptual analyses that some philosophers and some courts have made in commenting on whether PAS is morally justified, or is legally sanctioned or forbidden. One philosopher,

From Margaret P. Battin, Rosamond Rhodes, and Anita Silvers (eds.), *Physician-Assisted Suicide: Expanding the Debate*. Routledge, 1998, 182–202. Reproduced by permission of Taylor & Francis Group, LLC., Inc., www.taylorandfrancis.com.

for example, has claimed that there is no morally significant difference between killing a patient (voluntary, active euthanasia; VAE) and helping a patient commit suicide (PAS).[1] One circuit court has argued that performing PAS is exactly the same as withdrawing life support and rendering palliative care as a patient dies.[2] Thus PAS has been identified both as the same as killing a patient (VAE) and the same as allowing a patient to die (voluntary, passive euthanasia; VPE). We believe that the three alternatives, 1) PAS; 2) killing a patient (VAE); and 3) allowing a patient to die (VPE), are quite distinct from one another conceptually and morally.

ACTIVE AND PASSIVE EUTHANASIA

To understand how PAS, VAE, and VPE differ, it is useful to begin with the distinction between VAE and VPE. A distinction between these two has traditionally been made and accepted both by clinicians and by philosophers. VAE is killing and, even if requested by a competent patient, is illegal and has been historically prohibited by the American Medical Association. VPE is "allowing to die" and, if requested by a competent patient, it is legally permitted and morally acceptable.

None of the standard attempts to describe the conceptual distinction between VAE and VPE have gained wide acceptance. These attempts have involved the following concepts and issues: 1) acts versus omissions, 2) stopping treatment (withdrawing) versus not starting treatment (withholding), 3) ordinary care versus extraordinary care, and 4) whether the patient's death is due to an underlying malady. However none of these four ways of making the distinction has any clear moral significance and all are inadequate because they all fail to appreciate the moral significance of the *kind of decision* the patient makes, in particular whether it is a request or a refusal.[3] It is this failure that leads to the mistaken conclusion that there is no morally significant distinction between VAE and VPE.

First, a terminological matter needs to be clarified. It is perfectly standard English to use the term "request" when talking about a refusal. Thus one can say that a patient requests that a treatment (such as ventilation) be stopped. The patient is, in fact, refusing continued use of the respirator. Unfortunately, this perfectly correct and common way of talking obscures the crucial moral distinction between patients' refusals and requests. When combined with the use of the terms

"choice" and "decision," which also can be applied to both requests and refusals, the language fosters the false conclusion that all patient decisions or choices, whether refusals or requests, generate the same moral obligation for physicians.

This confusion is compounded because the most common use of the terms "decision" and "choice" with regard to a patient involves neither refusals nor requests, but rather the patient's picking one of the options that her physician has presented to her during the process of informed consent. However, when dealing with patients who want to die, this most common use of "decision" or "choice" is not relevant. Rather a patient is either 1) refusing life-sustaining treatment (VPE), or 2) requesting that the physician kill her (VAE), or 3) requesting that the physician provide the medical means for the patient to kill herself (PAS). Thus talking of a patient's decision or choice to die can be extremely ambiguous. Furthermore, refusals of treatment and requests for treatment, whether or not death is a foreseeable result, have very different moral and legal implications.[4]

• • •

REFUSAL OF TREATMENT AND THE DUTIES OF A PHYSICIAN

Overruling a competent informed patient's rational refusal of treatment, including life preserving treatment, always involves depriving the patient of freedom, and usually involves causing him pain. No impartial rational person would publicly allow these kinds of paternalistic actions and so they are morally unacceptable. Since it is morally unacceptable to overrule the rational refusal of a competent informed patient, it cannot be the duty of a physician to do so. Theoretically, the situation does not change when lack of treatment will result in the patient's death, but as a practical matter, it does make a difference. Death is such a serious harm that it is never irrational to choose any other harm in order to prevent death. Even though it is sometimes rational to choose death over other harms, choosing death may be, and often is, irrational. Further, people are usually ambivalent about choosing death, often changing their minds several times, but death is permanent, and once it occurs, no further change of mind is possible.

The seriousness of death requires physicians to make certain that patients realize that death will result from failure to receive the life sustaining treatment. It also requires physicians to make sure a patient's desire to die is not due to suffering that can be relieved by palliative care. The physician also must make certain that a patient's desire to die, and hence his request to die, is not primarily the result of a treatable depression and, more generally, that a patient's unavoidable suffering is sufficient to make it rational for him to prefer death to continuing to live. When patients have terminal diseases, however, it is generally the case that when they want to die, it is rational for them to choose death. Further, although there is often some ambivalence, in our experience, their desire to die usually remains their dominant desire. When an informed competent patient makes a rational decision to stop life-prolonging treatment, a physician cannot have a duty to overrule his refusal of treatment, even though normally a physician has a duty to prevent death.

We have shown that physicians cannot have a duty to preserve the lives of their competent patients when those patients want to die and their desires are informed and rational. When prolonging a person's life requires unjustifiably depriving him of freedom, it is morally unacceptable to do so. We have thus established that physicians do not and cannot have a duty to prolong the lives of their patients when their patients have a rational desire to die. We are not suggesting that whenever a patient with a terminal disease makes any tentative suggestion that treatment be stopped, the physician should, with no question, immediately do so. It is part of the duty of a physician to make sure both that the refusal is rational and that it is the informed, considered, and noncoerced preference of the patient. When, however, it is clear that a patient really does want to die and the refusal is rational, then it is morally unacceptable for the physician to administer life prolonging treatment.

KILLING VERSUS ALLOWING TO DIE

Having shown that a physician does not have a duty to prolong the lives of patients who rationally prefer to die, the next issue to be settled is whether not treating such patients counts as killing them. If it does count as killing them, then the conclusions of the previous section may have to be revised. In the previous section not treating was taken as simply not prolonging the life of a competent patient when he rationally refuses treatment. However, not treating is sometimes correctly regarded as killing. If a physician turns off the respirator of a competent patient who does not want to die, with the result that the patient dies, the physician has killed him. The same is true if the physician discontinues antibiotics, or

food and fluids. It may even count as killing if the physician refuses to start any of these treatments for his patient when the patient wants the treatment started and there is no medical reason for not starting it. Just as parents whose children die because of not being fed can be regarded as having killed their children, physicians who have a duty to provide life-saving treatment for their patients can be regarded as killing them if they do not provide that treatment. However, we have shown that a physician does not have a duty to provide life-saving treatment when a competent patient rationally refuses such treatment. Not treating counts as killing only when there is a duty to treat; in the absence of such a duty, not treating does not count as killing.[5]

If the patient refuses treatment and there is no duty to treat, then it does not make any moral difference whether the physician stops treating by an act, e.g., turning off the respirator, or an omission, e.g., not giving antibiotics. It also makes no moral difference whether the physician stops some treatment that has already started, e.g., turning off the respirator or discontinuing antibiotics, or simply does not start such treatment. . . .

STOPPING FOOD AND FLUIDS

. . . Since the point of dying sooner is to avoid the pain and suffering of a terminal illness, stopping only food while continuing fluids is not a good method of dying because it takes a long time, often more than a month. However, when fluids are also stopped, dying is much quicker; usually unconsciousness occurs within a week and death less than a week later. Further, contrary to what is widely assumed, dying because of lack of food and fluids is not physically unpleasant or painful if there is even minimal nursing care.[6] When there is no medical treatment keeping the patient alive, stopping food and fluids may be the best way of allowing a patient to die. It is usually painless, it takes long enough for the patient to have the opportunity to change his mind, but is short enough that significant relief from pain and suffering is gained. However, because of the psychological difficulties involved in a longer dying process, some patients may still prefer PAS to discontinuing food and fluids.

ANALYSIS OF KILLING

It may be thought that, if complying with a patient's refusal of treatment requires the physician to perform some identifiable act, e.g., turning off a respirator, which is the act that results in the patient's death, then regardless of what was said before, the doctor has killed the patient. This seems to have the support of the *Oxford English Dictionary* which says that to kill is simply to deprive of life. One may accept that a doctor is morally and legally required to turn off the respirator and thus is justified in killing her patient, but still maintain that she has killed him. Even those who accept the death penalty and hold that some prison official is morally and legally required to execute the prisoner do not deny that the official has killed the prisoner. Killing in self-defense is both morally and legally allowed, yet no one denies that it is killing. Similarly, one could agree that the doctor is doing nothing morally or legally unacceptable by turning off the respirator and even that the doctor is morally and legally required to do so, yet claim that in doing so the doctor is killing the patient.

If one accepts this analysis, then it might also seem plausible to say that an identifiable decision to omit a life-prolonging treatment, even if such an omission is morally and legally required, also counts as killing the patient. One could simply stipulate that doctors are sometimes morally and legally required to kill their patients, namely, when their action or omission is the result of a competent patient rationally refusing to start or to continue a life-prolonging treatment. Thus it would seem that the important point is that the doctor is morally and legally required to act as she does, not whether what she does is appropriately called killing. However, it is still significant whether such an action should be regarded as killing because having a too simple account of killing can cause numerous problems.

Many doctors do not want to regard themselves as killing their patients, even justifiably killing them. More importantly, all killing requires a justification or an excuse. If all the morally relevant features are the same, the justification or excuse that is not adequate for one way of killing will not be adequate for all other ways of killing either. Thus, if a justification is not publicly allowed for injecting a lethal dose of morphine, then it will not be publicly allowed for disconnecting the patient from the respirator. Since even advocates of VAE do not propose that doctors should ever be morally and legally required to kill their patients, even justifiably, doctors would not be required to comply with rational refusals of treatment by competent patients. It might even come to be thought justifiable to prohibit physicians from honoring the rational refusals of life-sustaining treatments of competent patients. Thus changing the way killing is understood (i.e., counting complying with a patient's rational refusal as killing him) would have unfortunate implications.

Those who favor legalizing VAE do not want to require doctors to kill their patients; they merely want to allow those doctors who are willing to kill, to do so. Similarly for PAS, no one has yet suggested that a doctor be required to comply with a patient's request for a lethal prescription. On the other hand, since doctors are morally and legally required to comply with a competent patient's rational refusal of life-sustaining treatment, complying with such a refusal has not been regarded as killing. Providing palliative care to a patient who refuses life-sustaining treatment is not morally controversial either. Killing a competent patient on his rational request or assisting him to commit suicide are morally controversial. No one claims that doctors are morally and legally required to do either. Thus it is clear that complying with a competent patient's rational refusal of treatment is not normally regarded as killing, nor does providing palliative care to such a patient count as assisting suicide.

Part of the problem is that insufficient attention is paid to the way in which the term "kill" is actually used. Killing is not as simple a concept as it is often taken to be. Killing is causing death, but what counts as causing death or any other harm is a complex matter. If the harm that results from one's action, or omission, needs to be justified or excused, then one is regarded as having caused that harm. Of course, causing harm often can be completely justified or excused, so that one can cause a harm and be completely free of any unfavorable moral judgment. So killing, taken as causing death, may be completely justified, perhaps even morally required.

All acts that are done in order to bring about someone's death count as causing the person's death, or killing them, for all such intentional actions need justification. Also, if the act which results in death is the kind of act which is morally unacceptable such as deceiving, breaking a promise, cheating, breaking the law, or neglecting one's duty, knowingly performing the act or omission needs justification and so counts as killing. For example, if I lie to someone, telling him that a mushroom that I know to be intensely poisonous is safe to eat, then if he eats the mushroom and dies, I have caused his death. Or if a child dies because her parents did not feed her, they have killed her, because parents have a duty to feed their children. This analysis shows why it is important to make clear that doctors have no duty to treat, or even feed, patients who refuse treatment or food. However, if one does not intend, but only knows, that one's act will result in someone's death, and the act is the kind of act that is morally acceptable, (such as giving a patient sufficient analgesia to control her severe pain) then even though this act results in the person's death, it may not count as causing his death.

When complying with the rational refusal of a competent patient, the doctor's intention is not to kill the patient, but rather to honor the patient's refusal even though she knows that the result will be that the patient dies. Even if the doctor agrees that it is best for the patient to die, her honoring that refusal does not count as intentionally causing his death. Of course, an individual doctor can want her patient to die, but her intention in these circumstances is not determined by whether she wants her patient to die. Rather, the intention is determined by what facts account for her deciding to act in one way rather than another. If she would cease treatment even if she did not want the patient to die and would not cease it if the patient had not refused such treatment, then her intention is not to kill the patient but to comply with the patient's refusal. Further, most doctors do not want to kill their patients, even if such actions were morally and legally justified, so clearly their intentions are simply to honor their patients' rational refusals. . . .

That our society does not regard death resulting from complying with a competent patient's rational refusal, even a refusal of food and fluids, as killing, is shown by the fact that almost all states have advance directives that explicitly require a physician to stop treatment, even food and fluids, if the patient has the appropriate advance directive. They also allow a presently competent patient to refuse treatment and food and fluids. None of these states allow a physician to kill a patient, under any circumstances. Most of these states do not even allow physicians to assist suicide, which strongly suggests that turning off a respirator, is not regarded even as assisting suicide when doing so is required by the rational refusal of a competent patient.

Thus, complying with a competent patient's rational refusal of treatment is not killing or assisting suicide, and it may even be misleading to say that a physician is allowing the patient to die. To talk of a physician allowing the patient to die suggests that the physician has a choice, that it is up to her to decide whether or not to save the patient's life. When a competent patient has rationally refused treatment, however, a physician has no choice. It is morally and legally prohibited to overrule the patient's refusal. The physician allows her patient to die only in the sense that it is physically possible for her to save her patient and she does not. Complying with the rational refusal of life-saving treatment by a competent patient is not merely morally acceptable, it is morally required. Overruling such a refusal is itself a morally unacceptable deprivation of freedom. . . .

IS THE REFUSAL OF LIFE-SUSTAINING TREATMENT SUICIDE?

If suicide is regarded simply as killing oneself, then the analysis of killing should apply to it in a fairly straightforward fashion. An action or an omission which is intended to result in the death of a patient and which does result in his death counts as killing. Therefore, one might argue that the refusal of treatment or of food and fluids that is intended by the patient to result in his own death and which does result in his death, should count as suicide. And if "assisting suicide" simply means doing those acts which help the person commit suicide, then physicians who provide palliative care to patients who are refusing life sustaining treatments are assisting suicide. Accepting this analysis would make providing palliative care to such patients a kind of assisted suicide.

However, it is not clear that the view that suicide is simply killing oneself should be accepted. Partly, this may be because "killing oneself" does not seem to need a justification or excuse as much as killing another person. This may be because our society, with some limitations, regards each person as allowed to do anything he wants to himself, as long as no one else is harmed. Indeed, it seems that any act which one does not intend but only knows will result in one's own death does not count as suicide. (It is only in an extended sense that someone who continues to smoke or drink or eat too much, when he knows that it may result in his death, could be said to be, slowly committing suicide.) It also seems that our society does not count as suicide any death that results from omissions, at least omissions stemming from rational decisions to omit or to stop treatment. Rather only those positive acts that are done in order to bring about one's own death immediately count as suicide, since those acts so closely resemble the paradigms of killing. Patients who take some pills to bring about their own death are committing suicide, but those who have the respirator removed or who refuse food and fluids are usually not regarded as committing suicide.[7]

This more complex analysis of suicide explains why the law has never regarded providing palliative care to those who are refusing treatment as assisting suicide. Even those states which explicitly forbid assisting suicide do not prohibit providing palliative care to those who are refusing treatment or food and fluids. Of course those who support legalizing PAS favor the simpler account of suicide because they can then claim that some PAS is already allowed, and hence that it is simply inconsistent not to allow other quicker and less painful suicides. That our society does not count refusals of treatment as suicide and hence does not count palliative care for patients who refuse treatment as assisting suicide is not intended by us as an argument against legalizing PAS. However, it does show that one argument for legalizing PAS, namely, that PAS is already allowed in the provision of palliative care for those who are refusing life-prolonging treatment, is based on a misunderstanding of how our society regards providing such palliative care.

Our argument places PAS much closer to VPE than to VAE, and so allowing PAS, one could argue, need not lead to allowing VAE. It is compatible with our analyses so far that one can either be for or against legalizing PAS. However, we believe that recognition of the option of refusing treatment or food and fluids makes much stronger the major argument against legalizing PAS, namely, that doing so will not have sufficient benefits to compensate for the risks involved. But we are also aware that different people can rank and weigh these benefits and risks differently. . . .

IS KILLING PATIENTS EVER JUSTIFIED?

Stopping food and fluids is often the best way of allowing a patient to die, but it may be claimed that killing is sometimes better. Given present knowledge and technology, one can kill a patient or allow a patient to kill herself absolutely painlessly within a matter of minutes. If patients have a rational desire to die, why wait several days or weeks for them to die; why not kill them or let them kill themselves quickly and painlessly in a matter of minutes? We have provided no argument against allowing patients to kill themselves or even killing patients who want to die that applies to an ideal world where there are never any misunderstandings between people and everyone is completely moral and trustworthy. In such a world, if one could provide a patient with pills or inject the patient with appropriate drugs so that the patient dies painlessly and almost instantaneously, there would be no need to worry about the distinction between refusals and requests, or between killing, assisting suicide, and allowing to die. But in the real world, there are misunderstandings and not everyone is completely moral and trustworthy. In the real world no one even proposes that PAS or VAE be allowed without elaborate procedural safeguards, which almost always require at least two weeks. So, on a practical level, legalizing PAS or VAE would not result in a quicker death than simply complying with a refusal of food and fluids.

On our account, VPE is complying with the rational refusal of life-saving treatment or food and fluids by a competent patient. Since there is no duty to overrule a rational refusal by a competent patient, complying with this refusal does not count as killing. Further, failing to comply with such a refusal is itself morally prohibited, for it is an unjustified deprivation of the patient's freedom. Also, in some newer codes of medical ethics, e.g., that of the American College of Physicians, respecting patients' refusals is now listed as a duty. Physicians are not merely morally allowed to practice VPE, they are morally required to do so. VAE is killing; it is complying with the rational request of a competent patient to be killed. Although PAS is not killing, it does involve active intervention by the physician that is more than merely stopping treatment. It is not simply complying with a patient's desire to be left alone; it is providing the patient with some substance that causes his death, when one has no duty to do so.

VAE is killing and so needs to be justified. This contrasts quite sharply with VPE, and even with PAS, which may not even need to be morally justified. When a patient refuses treatment or food and fluids, it is not the complying with a patient's refusal but rather the overruling of the refusal that needs to be justified. But, as noted earlier, physicians may cause pain to their patients and be completely justified, because they do so at their patients' request, or at least with their consent, and do it in order to prevent what the patient takes to be a greater harm, e.g., disability or death. VAE could be regarded as no different than any other instance of a doctor being morally justified in doing a morally unacceptable *kind of act* with regard to a patient at the patient's request, in order to prevent what the patient takes to be a greater harm. In VAE the patient takes death to be a lesser harm than suffering pain and requests that the moral rule prohibiting killing be violated with regard to himself.

If causing pain can be justified, why is killing not justified when all of the other morally relevant features are the same? The answer is that killing needs a stronger justification because of a special feature of death that distinguishes it from all of the other serious harms. The special feature is that, after death, the person killed no longer exists and so cannot protest that he did not want to be killed. All impartial rational persons would advocate that violations against causing pain be publicly allowed when the person toward whom the rule is being violated rationally prefers to suffer that pain rather than suffer some other harm, e.g., disability or death. It is uncertain how many impartial rational persons would advocate that killing be publicly allowed when the person being killed rationally prefers to be killed rather than to continue to suffer pain. This uncertainty stems from taking seriously the two features that are essential to morality, the public character of morality and the fallibility of persons.

Causing pain with valid consent can be publicly allowed without any significant anxiety being caused thereby. Patients can usually correct a mistake rather quickly by ordering a stop to the painful treatment. Also physicians have a constant incentive to be careful not to cause pain by mistake, for patients will complain if they did not really want the pain caused. Killing, even with valid consent, being publicly allowed may create significant anxiety. Patients may fear that they will be mistakenly killed and that they will have no opportunity to correct that mistake. That a patient will not be around to complain if they are mistakenly killed removes a strong safeguard against mistaken violations. But it is not merely mistakes about which a patient would not be able to complain. If a physician tries to take advantage of legalized killing and intentionally kills a patient, complaint would not be possible. Taking advantage of causing pain being publicly allowed does not pose similar problems.

Legalizing PAS might prevent some pain and suffering that could not be prevented by greater education concerning refusing food and fluids, but it would also be likely to create significant anxiety and some unwanted deaths. Impartial rational persons can therefore disagree on whether they would advocate legalizing PAS. Once it is recognized that withholding food and fluids 1) can be painless; 2) usually results in unconsciousness in one week and death in two weeks; and 3) allows for patients to change their minds, the need for PAS significantly diminishes.

Unlike others who argue against legalizing PAS, we do not claim that PAS is in itself morally unacceptable, only that it may create a serious risk of unwanted deaths. Since impartial rational persons can rank these risks as outweighing the benefits of legalization, legalizing PAS is controversial. If the goal is to allow a patient to choose her own time of dying and also dying to be accomplished relatively painlessly, there seems to be little need for PAS. If patient refusal of treatment, including refusal of food and fluids, were not sufficient for a relatively quick and painless death for the overwhelming number of terminally ill patients, then we would favor PAS, although we would still have serious objections to VAE. However, since VPE, especially when this includes refusing food and fluids, is available together with appropriate palliative care, it seems far more difficult to justify controversial methods like PAS. The harms prevented by PAS are no longer the long term suffering of patients who have no other way to die, they are only the one week of suffering that may be present while the patient is refusing food and fluids, and this suffering can be almost completely controlled by appropriate palliative care. This is an excellent example of why the presence of an alternative is a morally relevant feature.

Given the alternative of refusing food and fluids, very little additional harm seems to be prevented by PAS. The presence of an alternative is a morally relevant feature and makes it questionable whether it has sufficient benefits to justify the risks involved in legalizing it. There are good reasons for believing that the advantages of refusing food and fluids together with adequate palliative care make it preferable to legalizing PAS. This is especially true in a multicultural society where doctors and patients sometimes do not even speak the same language. There are a small number of cases in which refusal of food and fluids might be difficult, but it is necessary to weigh the benefit to this relatively small number of people against the harm that might be suffered by a great number of people by the legalizing of PAS. . . .

SUMMARY

. . . We believe that the strongest argument against PAS is that, given the alternatives available, it does not provide sufficient benefit to individual patients to justify the societal risks. Patients already have the alternative of refusing treatment and food and fluids, and of receiving palliative care while they are refusing that treatment. If physicians were to educate patients about these matters and to make clear that they will support their choices and continue to care for them if they choose to refuse treatment, there might be little, if any, call for PAS. Because of the time involved, patients seem far less likely to be pressured into refusing treatment or food and fluids than they are to avail themselves of PAS. There would also be far fewer opportunities for abuse. PAS provides less incentive to be concerned with palliative care. And finally, given the bureaucratic safeguards that most regard as necessary with PAS, death can come as soon or sooner with refusal of treatment or refusal of food and fluids than it would with PAS.[8]

A PRACTICAL PROPOSAL
FOR STATE LEGISLATORS

In order to avoid the serious societal risks of legalizing physician-assisted suicide, while still providing a method for allowing seriously ill patients to determine the timing of their deaths, we think that states should consider passing legislation based on language such as the following. This language is completely consistent with the statement of the United States Supreme Court that, "Just as a State may prohibit assisting suicide while permitting patients to refuse unwanted lifesaving treatment, it may permit palliative care related to that refusal, which may have the foreseen but unintended 'double effect' of hastening the patient's death."

If a competent patient is terminally ill or suffering from a condition involving severe chronic pain or serious permanent disability, that patient's refusal of treatment, or refusal or food and fluids, shall not count as suicide, even though the patient knows that death will result from not starting or from stopping that treatment. All physicians and other healthcare workers shall be informed that they are legally prohibited from overruling any rational refusal of a competent patient, including refusal of food and fluids, even though it is known that death will result. All patients will be informed that they are allowed to refuse any treatment, or to refuse food and fluids, even though it is known that death will result, and that physicians and other healthcare workers are legally prohibited from overruling any such rational refusal by a competent patient.

Further, there shall be no prohibition placed upon any physician who provides pain relief in any form, in order to relieve the pain and suffering of the patient who has refused treatment, or food and fluids. In particular, providing pain medication shall not be considered as assisting suicide, and there shall be no liability for the physician who provides such pain medication for the purpose of relieving pain and suffering. The physician shall not provide such medication for the purpose of hastening the time of death, but is not prohibited from providing medication which is consistent with adequate pain relief even if he knows that such medication will hasten the time of death. Physicians are required to rigorously follow the accepted standards of medical practice in determining the competence of patients who refuse any treatment, or who refuse food and fluids, when they know that death will result from complying with that refusal.

NOTES

1. Dan W. Brock, "Voluntary Active Euthanasia," *Hastings Center Report* 22 (2): 10–22 (1992).

2. *Quill v. Vacco*, the U.S. Court of Appeals for the Second Circuit.

3. See James L. Bernat, Bernard Gert, and R. Peter Mogielnicki, "Patient Refusal of Hydration and Nutrition: An Alternative to Physician Assisted Suicide or Voluntary Euthanasia," *Archives of Internal Medicine* 153: 2723–28 (December 27, 1993).

4. See Bernard Gert, James L. Bernat, and R. Peter Mogielnicki, "Distinguishing between Patients' Refusals and Requests," *The Hastings Center Report* 24 (4): 13–15 (July–August 1994).

5. See K. Danner Clouser, "Allowing or Causing: Another Look," *Annals of Internal Medicine* 87: 622–24 (1977).

6. See Kathleen M. Foley, M.D., "The Relationship of Pain and Symptom Management to Patient Requests for Physician-Assisted Suicide," *Journal of Pain and Symptom Management* 6 (5): 289–297 (July 1991).

7. This view is not held by all. Some, especially those with religious views, regard refusing treatment and especially refusing food and fluids when treatment, or food and fluids would sustain life for a long time, as committing suicide. But this is not the prevailing view, nor is it the view that governs the legal classification of the act. However, a terminally ill patient who intentionally goes into the woods in order to stop eating and drinking, does so, and thereby dies, would be regarded by most as having committed suicide. For a sensitive analysis of the difficulty of formulating a precise definition of "suicide," see Tom L. Beauchamp, "Suicide" in Tom Regan, ed., *Matters of Life and Death*, 2nd ed. (New York: Random House, 1986), pp. 77–89.

8. See K. Danner Clouser, "The Challenge for Future Debate on Euthanasia," *The Journal of Pain and Symptom Management* 6 (5): 306–311 (July 1991).

DAN W. BROCK

Physician-Assisted Suicide as a Last-Resort Option at the End of Life

Palliative care, to relieve suffering rather than to effect cure, is the standard of care when terminally ill patients find that the burdens of continued life-prolonging treatment outweigh the benefits. To better relieve suffering near the end of life, physicians need to improve their skills in palliative care and routinely discuss it with patients earlier in the course of terminal illness. In addition, access to palliative care needs to be improved, particularly for those Americans who lack health insurance. However, even the highest-quality palliative care fails or becomes unacceptable for some patients, some of whom request help hastening death. Between 10 and 50 percent of patients in programs devoted to palliative care still report significant pain one week before death. Furthermore, patients request a hastened death not principally because of unrelieved pain but because of a wide variety of unrelieved physical symptoms in combination with loss of meaning, dignity, and independence.

How should physicians respond when competent, terminally ill patients whose suffering is not relieved by palliative care request help in hastening death?[1] If the patient is receiving life-prolonging interventions, the physician should consider discontinuing them, in accordance with the patient's wishes. Some patients may voluntarily stop eating and drinking. If the patient has unrelieved pain or other symptoms and accepts sedation, the physician may legally administer terminal sedation. However, in all countries but the Netherlands and Belgium, physicians are legally prohibited from participating in physician-assisted suicide in response to such patient requests; in Switzerland, physicians and nonphysicians are permitted to participate in assisted

suicide for "altruistic motives."[2] In the United States, physician-assisted suicide is permitted only in Oregon. The U.S. Supreme Court decisions that determined that there is no constitutional right to physician-assisted suicide placed great emphasis on the importance of relieving pain and suffering near the end of life.[3] The Court acknowledged the legal acceptability of providing pain relief even to the point of hastening death, if necessary, and left open the possibility that states might choose to legalize physician-assisted suicide under some circumstances, as Oregon has done.

Voluntarily stopping eating and drinking, terminal sedation, and physician-assisted suicide are all potential interventions of last resort for competent, terminally ill patients who are suffering intolerably, in spite of intensive efforts to palliate, and desire a hastened death. Many opponents of physician-assisted suicide defend the current legal status of these options, arguing that, along with forgoing life-sustaining treatment, voluntarily stopping eating and drinking and terminal sedation constitute adequate and appropriate options for hastening death, obviating the need for legalization of physician-assisted suicide. However, in my view, the differences between these practices and physician-assisted suicide do not justify the continued prohibition of assisted suicide.

DEFINITIONS AND CLINICAL COMPARISONS

VOLUNTARILY STOPPING EATING AND DRINKING

By voluntarily stopping eating and drinking, a patient who is otherwise physically capable of taking nourishment makes an explicit decision to discontinue all oral intake and then is gradually "allowed to die," primarily of dehydration or some intervening complication. Depending on the patient's preexisting condition, the process will usually take one to three weeks; it can

From *Physician-Assisted Dying: The Case for Palliative Care and Patient Choice*, pp. 130–149, ed. Timothy E. Quill, M.D. & Margaret P. Battin, Ph.D. © 2004 The Johns Hopkins University Press.

take longer if the patient continues to take some fluids. Voluntarily stopping eating and drinking has several advantages. Many patients lose their appetites and stop eating and drinking in the final stages of many illnesses, without any intention of hastening death. Ethically and legally, the right of competent, informed patients to refuse life-prolonging interventions, including artificial hydration and nutrition, is firmly established, and voluntary cessation of "natural" eating and drinking could be considered an extension of that right. Because not eating or drinking requires considerable patient resolve, the voluntary nature of the action and the patient's settled resolve to die should be clear. Voluntarily stopping eating and drinking also protects patient privacy and independence, so much so that it potentially requires no participation by a physician.

The main disadvantages of the practice as a means to hasten death are that it may last for weeks and may initially increase suffering because the patient may experience thirst and hunger. Subtle coercion to proceed with the process, especially once it is already under way, may occur if patients are not regularly offered the opportunity to eat and drink, yet such offers may be viewed as undermining the patient's resolve or expressing disagreement with the patient's choice. Some patients, family members, or health care providers may find the notion of "dehydrating" or "starving" a patient to death to be morally repugnant. For patients whose current suffering is severe and unrelievable, the process would be unacceptable without sedation and analgesia. If physicians are not involved, palliation of symptoms may be inadequate, the decision to forgo eating and drinking may not be informed, and cases of treatable depression may be missed. Patients are likely to lose mental clarity toward the end of this process, which may undermine their sense of personal integrity and dignity or raise questions about whether the action remains voluntary. Although several articles, including a moving personal narrative, have proposed voluntarily stopping eating and drinking as an alternative to other forms of hastened death, there are no data about how frequently such decisions are made or how acceptable they are to patients, families, or health care providers.

TERMINAL SEDATION

The term *terminal sedation* refers to the administration of sedative drugs at the end of life; it is not, strictly speaking, a form of assisted death. With terminal sedation, the suffering patient is sedated to unconsciousness, if need be, usually through ongoing administration of barbiturates or benzodiazepines, and all life-sustaining interventions, including nutrition and hydration, are withheld. Generally, the patient then dies of dehydration, starvation, or some other intervening complication. Although death is inevitable, it usually does not take place for days or even weeks, depending on clinical circumstances. Because patients are deeply sedated during this terminal period, they are believed to be free of suffering.

Since sedation to relieve suffering is a long-standing and uncontroversial aim of medicine, and the subsequent withholding of life-sustaining therapy has wide legal and ethical acceptance, terminal sedation is probably legally permissible under current law.[4] The 1997 U.S. Supreme Court decisions in *Vacco v. Quill* and *Washington v. Glucksberg* gave strong support to terminal sedation, saying that pain in terminally ill patients should be treated even to the point of rendering the patient unconscious or hastening death.[5] Terminal sedation is already openly practiced by some palliative care and hospice groups in cases of unrelieved suffering, with a reported frequency from 0 to 44 percent of cases.

Terminal sedation has other practical advantages. It can be carried out in patients with severe physical limitations. The time delay between initiation of terminal sedation and death permits second-guessing and reassessment by the health care team and the family. Because the health care team must administer medications and monitor effects, physicians can ensure that the patient's decision is informed and voluntary before initiating sedation. In addition, many proponents believe that it is appropriate to use terminal sedation in patients who lack decision-making capacity but appear to be suffering intolerably, provided the patient's suffering is extreme and otherwise unrelievable and the surrogate or family agrees.

Nonetheless, terminal sedation has many of the same risks associated with physician-assisted suicide, as well as some that assisted suicide lacks. Unlike physician-assisted suicide, the final actors are the health care providers, not the patient. Terminal sedation could therefore be carried out without explicit discussions with alert patients who appear to be suffering intolerably, or even against their wishes. Some competent, terminally ill patients reject terminal sedation. They believe that their dignity will be violated if they are unconscious for a prolonged time before they die or that their families will suffer unnecessarily while waiting for them to die. Terminal sedation may not be possible for patients who wish to die in their own homes because it generally requires admission to a health care facility. In some clinical situations, it cannot relieve the patient's symptoms, as occurs when a patient is bleeding uncontrollably from an eroding lesion or a refractory coagulation disorder, cannot swallow secretions because of widespread oropharyngeal cancer, or has refractory diarrhea from AIDS. There is some controversy in the anesthesia literature about whether heavily sedated persons are actually free of suffering or are simply unable to report or remember it. Although such patients are probably not conscious of their condition once sedated, their death is unlikely to be dignified or remembered as peaceful by their families. When patients find their condition intolerable but are not in substantial pain, physicians may deem sedating them to the point of unconsciousness medically inappropriate. Finally, there may be confusion about the physician's ethical responsibility for contributing to the patient's death.[6]

With physician-assisted suicide, the physician provides the means, usually a prescription of a large dose of barbiturates, by which a patient can end his or her life. Although the physician is morally responsible for this assistance, the patient has to carry out the final act of using the means provided. Physician-assisted suicide has several advantages. Access to a lethal dose of medication may give some patients the freedom and reassurance to continue living, knowing they can escape if and when they feel the need to do so. Because patients have to ingest the drug by their own hand, their action is likely to be voluntary and done with resolve. Once the patient makes a decision in favor of death, physician-assisted suicide does not require a lingering period of days or weeks and so provides what patients and families may view as a more humane and dignified death. Physicians report being more comfortable with assisted suicide than with voluntary active euthanasia, presumably because their participation is indirect.

Opponents of physician-assisted suicide believe that it violates traditional moral and professional prohibitions against intentionally contributing to a patient's death.[7] It also has several practical disadvantages. Self-administration does not guarantee competence or voluntariness. The patient may have impaired judgment at the time of the request or of the act or may be influenced by external pressures. Since there is often a substantial period of time between the provision and use of the means for assisted suicide, and

since physicians are often not present when the means are used, there is often no evaluation and assurance of competence or voluntariness at the time of use. Physician-assisted suicide is limited to patients who are physically capable of taking the medication themselves. Because it is not always effective, families may be faced with a patient who is vomiting, aspirating, or cognitively impaired but is not dying. Patients brought to the emergency department after ineffective attempts are likely to receive unwanted life-prolonging treatment. Requiring physicians to be present when patients ingest the medication has practical difficulties and could coerce an ambivalent patient to proceed, yet their absence may leave families to respond to medical complications alone.

Although physician-assisted suicide is illegal in all states but Oregon, no physician has ever been successfully prosecuted for his or her participation.[8] Several studies have documented a secret practice of physician-assisted suicide in the United States. In Washington state, 12 percent of physicians responding to a survey had received genuine requests for assisted suicide within the year studied.[9] Twenty-four percent of requests were acceded to, and more than half of those patients died as a result. A study of Oregon physicians showed similar results.[10] Physician-assisted suicide is usually conducted covertly, without consultation, guidelines, or documentation. Public controversy about legalizing the practice continues in the United States. Although referendums to legalize physician-assisted suicide have been defeated in several states, an Oregon referendum was passed in 1994 that legalized it, subject to certain safeguards.[11] After a series of legal challenges, the Oregon referendum was resubmitted to the electorate in November 1997 and passed by a substantial margin. Several years' experience with assisted suicide in Oregon indicates that the practice largely operates within intended limits.[12] The U.S. Supreme Court ruled that laws in the states of Washington and New York prohibiting physician-assisted suicide were not unconstitutional but simultaneously encouraged public discussion and state experimentation through the legislative and referendum processes.[13]

Voluntarily stopping eating and drinking, terminal sedation, and physician-assisted suicide each have complex sets of advantages and disadvantages. For each practice, particular advantages and disadvantages may be more or less important with a specific patient seeking a hastened death. No one of these practices has a clearly superior balance of advantages over disadvantages in all cases. This implies that physician-assisted suicide should not be prohibited while voluntarily stopping eating and drinking and terminal sedation are permitted.

ETHICAL COMPARISONS BETWEEN THE PRACTICES

Many normative ethical analyses use the doctrine of double effect and the distinction between active and passive assistance to distinguish between currently permissible acts that may hasten death (forgoing life-sustaining treatment and high-dose pain medications) and physician-assisted suicide, which is generally impermissible. Using similar arguments, terminal sedation and voluntarily stopping eating and drinking have been argued to be ethically preferable alternatives to assisted suicide. However, there are more problems with the doctrine of double effect and the active-passive distinction than are often acknowledged, and terminal sedation and voluntarily stopping eating and drinking are more complex and less easily distinguished ethically from physician-assisted suicide than proponents seem to realize.

DOCTRINE OF DOUBLE EFFECT

The doctrine of double effect distinguishes between effects that a person intends (both the end sought and the means taken to the end) and consequences of the action that are foreseen but unintended. In evaluating the case at hand, as long as the physician's intentions are good and other conditions are satisfied, it is permissible for him or her to perform actions with foreseeable consequences that would be wrong to directly intend. In this view, intentionally causing death is morally impermissible, even if desired by a competent patient whose suffering could not otherwise be relieved. But if death comes unintentionally as the consequence of an otherwise well-intentioned intervention, even if foreseen with a high probability or even certainty, the physician's action can be morally acceptable. The unintended but foreseen bad effect must also be proportional to the intended good effects.

The doctrine of double effect has been important in generating acceptance of the use of sufficient pain medications to relieve suffering near the end of life. When high-dose opioids are used to treat pain, neither the patient nor the physician intends to accelerate death, but both are willing to accept the risk of unintentionally hastening death in order to relieve the pain. Recent experience suggests, however, that medications sufficient to relieve pain rarely, in fact, result in a hastened death.[14] Double effect has also been used to distinguish terminal sedation from physician-assisted suicide. Relief of suffering is intended in both options, but death is argued to be intended with assisted suicide and merely foreseen with terminal sedation. It is important to distinguish between the patient's and the physician's intentions. The patient's intention in terminal sedation and physician-assisted suicide will typically be to die. The physician's intention in terminal sedation, on the other hand, may be to relieve suffering by sedating the patient and to respect the patient's refusal of nutrition and hydration, foreseeing but not intending the patient's death. In physician-assisted suicide, as well, the physician need not intend the patient's death. He or she may only intend to relieve the patient's anxiety about dying, hoping, expecting, and intending that the patient will not use the means provided. Thus according to the doctrine of double effect, the physician's role in assisted suicide may not always be impermissible. The doctrine does not support a systematic difference between voluntarily stopping eating and drinking or terminal sedation and physician-assisted suicide.

According to the doctrine of double effect, intentionally taking innocent human life is always morally impermissible, whereas doing so foreseeably but unintentionally can be permissible when it produces a proportionate good. As applied to end-of-life medical decision making, this problematically gives more moral weight to the intentions of the physician than to the wishes and circumstances of the patient. An alternative view is that it is morally wrong to take the life of a person who wants to live, whether doing so intentionally or foreseeably. In this view, what can make terminal sedation morally permissible is that the patient gives informed consent to it, not that the physician only foresees but does not intend the patient's inevitable death. More generally, some commentators have argued that the difference between effects intended as a necessary means to a good end versus effects foreseen but unintended as necessary to reach that same end cannot bear the moral importance that the doctrine of double effect gives it. In each case, the effect of death may be unavoidable in the circumstances but judged acceptable to reach the end of relieving the patient's suffering.

The issue of intention is further complicated because the determination of what is intended by the patient or physician is often controversial and unclear and because practices that are universally accepted may involve the intention to hasten death in some cases. Death is not always intended or sought when competent patients forgo life support; sometimes patients simply do not want to continue a particular treatment but hope, nevertheless, that they can live without it. However, some patients find their circumstances so intolerable, even with the best of care, that they refuse further life support with the intent of bringing about their death. There is broad agreement that physicians must respect such refusals, even when the patient's intention is to die. Physicians may sometimes share the patient's intention when they also believe that an earlier death will be best for the patient, and then their removal of life support would be highly problematic when analyzed according to the doctrine of double effect.

THE DISTINCTION BETWEEN ACTIVE AND PASSIVE
PHYSICIAN INVOLVEMENT

According to many normative ethical analyses, active measures that hasten death are unacceptable, whereas passive or indirect measures that achieve the same ends would be permitted. The active-passive distinction is typically understood to mirror the distinction between killing and allowing to die. Passive measures that hasten death—that is, allow a patient to die—are typically believed to be justified in circumstances in which active measures—that is, killing—would not be justified. When the patient is allowed to die, the underlying disease, not the physician's action, is said to be the cause of death. However, how the distinctions between active and passive and between killing and allowing to die should be drawn, as well as how they apply to these three practices, remains controversial.[15]

Stopping life-sustaining therapies is typically considered passive assistance in dying, and the patient is said to be allowed to die of the underlying disease, no matter how proximate the physician's action and the patient's death. Physicians, however, sometimes experience their role in stopping life-sustaining interventions as very active.[16] For example, there is nothing psychologically or physically "passive" about taking someone off a mechanical ventilator if that person is incapable of breathing on his own, and some commentators have argued that these are cases of justified killing.[17] Voluntarily stopping eating and drinking is argued to be a variant of stopping life-sustaining ther-

apy, and the patient is said to die of the underlying disease.[18] However, the notion that this is passively "letting nature take its course" is unpersuasive because patients with no underlying disease would also die if they completely stopped eating and drinking. Death is the result of the patient's decision to refuse food and fluids, not a consequence of his underlying disease.

Physician-assisted suicide and terminal sedation are also challenging to evaluate according to the active-passive or kill–allow to die distinctions. Physician-assisted suicide is *active* in that the physician provides the means whereby the patient may take his or her life and thereby contributes to a cause of death that is new and different from the patient's disease. However, the physician's role in assisted suicide is *passive* or indirect in that the patient administers the lethal medication. Neither killing nor allowing to die appears clearly to apply to the physician's role in assisted suicide. In physician-assisted suicide, the patient takes his or her own life, whereas the physician only assists the patient by providing the means for doing so. The psychological and temporal distance between the prescribing and the act may also make physician-assisted suicide seem indirect. These ambiguities may allow the physician to characterize his or her actions as passive or indirect.[19]

Terminal sedation is *passive* in that the administration of sedation does not directly cause the patient's death and the withholding of artificial feedings and fluids is commonly considered passively allowing the patient to die. However, some physicians and nurses may consider it very *active* to sedate to unconsciousness someone who is seeking death and then to withhold life-prolonging interventions, including food and fluids. Furthermore, the notion that terminal sedation is merely "letting nature take its course" is problematic because often the patient dies of dehydration from the withholding of fluids, not from his or her underlying disease.

However these different interventions are properly characterized by the active-passive distinction, some commentators have challenged the moral significance of the difference.[20] If the difference lacks moral importance, then it will not be important whether a particular intervention is active or passive. The application and the moral importance of both the active-passive distinction and the doctrine of double effect are notoriously controversial and should not serve as the primary basis of determining the morality of these practices.

VOLUNTARINESS

I suggest that the patient's wishes and competent consent are more ethically important than whether the acts are categorized as active or passive or whether death is intended or unintended by the patient or physician. With competent patients, none of these acts would be morally permissible without the patient's voluntary and informed consent. Any of these actions would violate a competent patient's autonomy and would be both immoral and illegal if the patient did not understand that death was the inevitable consequence of the action or if the decision was coerced or contrary to the patient's wishes. The ethical principle of autonomy focuses on patients' rights to make important decisions about their lives, including what happens to their bodies, and may support genuinely autonomous forms of these acts. There is no systematic difference in these three practices grounded in voluntariness.

Because most of these acts require cooperation from physicians, and, in the case of terminal sedation, the health care team, the autonomy of participating medical professionals also warrants consideration. Because terminal sedation, voluntarily stopping eating and drinking, and physician-assisted suicide are not part of usual medical practice and they all result in a hastened death, health care providers should have the right to determine the nature and extent of their own participation. All physicians should respect patients' decisions to forgo life-sustaining treatment, including artificial hydration and nutrition, and provide standard palliative care, including skillful pain and symptom management. If society permits some or all of these practices (currently, terminal sedation and voluntarily stopping eating and drinking are openly tolerated), physicians who choose not to participate because of personal moral considerations should at a minimum discuss all available alternatives in the spirit of informed consent and respecting patient autonomy. Physicians are free to express their own objections to any of these practices as part of the informing process, to propose alternative approaches, and to transfer care to another physician if the patient continues to request actions to hasten death that they find unacceptable.

PROPORTIONALITY

Physicians have moral and professional obligations to promote their patients' best interests or well-being and to avoid causing unnecessary harm. The concept of proportionality requires that the risk of causing harm must bear a direct relationship to the danger and immediacy of the patient's clinical situation and the expected benefit of the intervention.[21] The greater the patient's suffering, the greater risk the physician can take of potentially contributing to the patient's death, as long as the patient understands and accepts that risk. For a patient with lung cancer who is anxious and short of breath, the risk of small doses of morphine or anxiolytics is warranted. At a later time, if the patient is near death and gasping for air, more aggressive sedation is warranted, even in doses that may well cause respiratory depression. Although proportionality is an important element of the doctrine of double effect, it can be applied independently of this doctrine. All plausible moral theories accept that, other things being equal, the benefits from our actions should where possible exceed their harms. Sometimes patients' suffering cannot be relieved despite optimal palliative care, and continuing to live offers only torment that will inevitably end in their death; in these circumstances, continued life is no longer a benefit but is now a burden to the patient.[22] Such extreme circumstances sometimes warrant extraordinary medical actions, and the forms of hastening death under consideration in this chapter may satisfy the requirement of proportionality. The requirement of proportionality, which all health care interventions should meet, does not support any principled ethical distinction between these three options.

CONFLICT OF DUTIES

Unrelievable, intolerable suffering at the end of life may create for physicians an explicit conflict between their ethical and professional duty to relieve suffering and their understanding of their ethical and professional duty not to use at least some means of deliberately hastening death. Currently, physicians who believe they should respond to such suffering by acceding to the patient's request for a hastened death may find themselves caught between their duty to the patient as a caregiver and their duty to obey the law as a citizen. Usually, though not always, solutions can be found in the intensive application of palliative care or within the currently legitimized options of forgoing life supports, voluntarily stopping eating and drinking, or terminal sedation. Situations in which these may not be adequate include terminally ill patients with uncontrolled bleeding, obstruction from nasopharyngeal cancer, and refractory AIDS diarrhea or patients who believe that spending their last days iatrogenically sedated would be meaningless, frightening, or degrading. Clearly, the physician has a moral obligation not to abandon patients with refractory suffering,[23] hence those physicians who cannot provide some or all of these options because of moral or legal reservations should search assiduously with the patient for mutually acceptable solutions or seek to transfer care to another physician willing to provide them.

SAFEGUARDS

In the United States, health care is undergoing radical reform driven more by market forces than by commitments to quality of care, and 43 million persons are currently uninsured. Capitated reimbursement could provide financial incentives to encourage terminally ill patients to hasten their deaths. Physicians' participation in hastening death by any of these methods can be justified only as a last resort when standard palliative measures are ineffective or unacceptable to the patient.

Safeguards to protect vulnerable patients from the risk of error, abuse, or coercion must be constructed for any of these practices that are ultimately accepted. These risks, which have been extensively cited in the debates about physician-assisted suicide, also exist for terminal sedation and voluntarily stopping eating and drinking and even for forgoing life-sustaining treatment. Terminal sedation and voluntarily stopping eating and drinking could be carried out without ensuring that optimal palliative care has been provided. This risk may be particularly great if voluntarily stopping eating and drinking is carried out without physician involvement. In terminal sedation, physicians who unreflectively believe that death is unintended, or that it is not their explicit purpose, may fail to acknowledge the inevitable consequences of their action as their responsibility.

The typical safeguards proposed for regulating physician-assisted suicide are intended to allow physicians to respond to unrelieved suffering while ensuring that adequate palliative measures have been attempted and that patient decisions are autonomous. These safeguards need to balance respect for patient privacy and autonomy with the protection of vulnerable patients by adequately overseeing and controlling these interventions. Similar professional safeguards should be considered for terminal sedation and voluntarily stopping eating and drinking, even if these practices are already sanctioned by the law. The challenge of safeguards is to be flexible enough to be responsive to individual patient circumstances and rigorous enough to protect vulnerable persons.

Safeguards should ensure that the following conditions have been met:

- *Palliative care has proved ineffective or is unacceptable.* Excellent palliative care must be available yet either insufficient to relieve intolerable suffering for a particular patient or unacceptable to that patient.
- *Informed consent has been given.* Patients must be competent and be fully informed about and capable of understanding their condition, the treatment alternatives, and the risks and benefits of these alternatives. Requests for a hastened death must be enduring and free of undue influence and should normally be initiated by the patient so as to avoid subtle coercion. Waiting periods must be flexible, depending on the nearness of inevitable death and the severity of immediate suffering.
- *Diagnosis and prognosis are clear.* Patients must have a clearly diagnosed disease whose prognosis, including the degree of uncertainty about outcomes and how long the patient might live, is understood.
- *An independent second opinion has been sought.* A consultant with expertise in palliative care should review the case. Specialists should also review any questions about the patient's diagnosis or prognosis. If there is uncertainty about treatable depression or about the patient's mental capacity, a psychiatrist should be consulted.
- *Accountability can be established.* Explicit processes for documentation, reporting, and review should be in place to ensure accountability.

The restriction of any of these methods to those who are terminally ill involves a trade-off. Some patients who suffer greatly from incurable but not terminal illness and are unresponsive to palliative measures will be denied access to a hastened death and forced to continue suffering against their will. Other patients whose request for a hastened death is denied will avoid a premature death because their suffering can subsequently be relieved with more intensive palliative care. Some would restrict physician-assisted suicide (and perhaps terminal sedation) to terminally ill patients because of current inequities of access, concerns about errors and abuse, and lack of experience with the process. Because of the inherent waiting period, the great resolve required, and the opportunity for reconsideration, voluntarily stopping eating and drinking might be allowed for those who are incurably ill, but not imminently dying, if they meet all other criteria. Initially restricting assisted suicide to the terminally ill would allow assessment of how realistic the risks and abuses feared by opponents are before extending the practice to patients who are not terminally ill. If any methods are extended to those who are incurably but not terminally ill, safeguards should be more stringent, including substantial waiting periods and mandatory assessment by psychiatrists and specialists, because the risk and consequences of error are increased.

The clinical, ethical, and policy differences and similarities among these three practices need to be debated openly, both publicly and within the medical profession. Some may worry that a discussion of the similarities between voluntarily stopping eating and drinking and terminal sedation, on the one hand, and physician-assisted suicide, on the other, may undermine the desired goal of optimal relief of suffering at the end of life.[24] Others may worry that a critical analysis of the principle of double effect or the active-passive distinction as applied to voluntarily stopping eating and drinking and terminal sedation may undermine efforts to improve pain relief or to ensure that patients' or surrogates' decisions to forgo unwanted life-sustaining therapy are respected.[25] However, hidden, ambiguous practices, inconsistent justifications, and failure to acknowledge the risks of accepted practices may also undermine the quality of terminal care and put patients at unwarranted risk.

Allowing a hastened death only in the context of access to good palliative care puts it in its proper perspective as a small but important facet of comprehensive care for all dying patients. Currently, terminal sedation and voluntarily stopping eating and drinking are probably legal and are widely accepted by hospice and palliative care physicians. However, they may not be readily available because some physicians may continue to have moral objections and legal fears about these options. Physician-assisted suicide is illegal in most states but may be difficult if not impossible to successfully prosecute if it is carried out at the request of an informed patient. In the United States, there is an underground, erratically available practice of assisted suicide.

Explicit public policies about which of these three practices are permissible, and under what circumstances, would have important benefits. Those who fear a bad death would face the end of their lives knowing that their physicians could respond openly if their worst fears were to materialize. For most, reassurance will be all that is needed, because good palliative care is generally effective. Explicit guidelines for the practices that are deemed permissible can also encourage clinicians to explore why a patient requests hastening of death, to search for palliative care alternatives, and to respond to those whose suffering is greatest.

I have argued that an assessment of the advantages and disadvantages of voluntarily stopping eating and drinking, terminal sedation, and physician-assisted suicide shows that no one practice is systematically better than the others and that each may be superior to the others in particular cases. In their ethical assessment, neither the doctrine of double effect nor the active-passive distinction support permitting voluntarily stopping eating and drinking and terminal sedation (as well as forgoing life support) while prohibiting physician-assisted suicide. I have argued that these are not the central issues for their ethical assessment in any case. Instead, the conditions of voluntariness and proportionality are central to ethical assessment of the practices, and they provide no basis for distinguishing voluntarily stopping eating and drinking and terminal sedation from physician-assisted suicide in public and legal policy. Physician-assisted suicide should be added to voluntarily stopping eating and drinking and terminal sedation as a permissible means of hastening death.

NOTES

1. T.E. Quill, B. Coombs Lee, and S. Nunn, "Palliative Treatments of Last Resort: Choosing the Least Harmful Alternative," *Annals of Internal Medicine* 132 (2000): 488–93.

2. S. Hurst and A. Mauron, "Assisted Suicide and Euthanasia in Switzerland: Allowing a Role for Nonphysicians," *British Medical Journal* 326 (2003): 271–73.

3. *Vacco v. Quill*, 117 S.Ct. 2293 (1997); *Washington v. Glucksberg*, 117 S.Ct. 2258 (1997).

4. T. Morita, S. Tsuneto, and Y. Shima, "Proposed Definitions for Terminal Sedation," *Lancet* 358 (2001): 335–36.

5. G. Craig, "Is Sedation without Hydration or Nourishment in Terminal Care Lawful?" *Medical Legal Journal* 62, no. 4 (1994): 198–201.

6. Brody, "Causing, Intending, and Assisting Death"; Billings, "Slow Euthanasia."

7. W. Gaylin, L.R. Kass, E.D. Pellegrino, and M. Siegler, "Doctors Must Not Kill," *New England Journal of Medicine* 259 (1988): 2319–40.

8. Quill, *Death and Dignity.*

9. Back et al., "Physician-Assisted Suicide and Euthanasia in Washington State."

10. M.A. Lee, H.D. Nelson, V.P. Tilden, L. Ganzini, T.A. Schmidt, and S.W. Tolle, "Legalizing Assisted Suicide: Views of Physicians in Oregon," *New England Journal of Medicine* 334 (1996): 310–15.

11. A. Alpers and B. Lo, "Physician-Assisted Suicide in Oregon: A Bold Experiment." *Journal of the American Medical Association* 274 (1995): 483–87.

12. K. Hedberg, D. Hopkins, and M. Kohn, "Five Years of Legal Physician-Assisted Suicide in Oregon," *New England Journal of Medicine* 348 (2003): 961–64.

13. *Vacco v. Quill; Washington v. Glucksberg; Compassion in Dying v. Washington,* 79 F.3d 790 (9th Cir. 1996); *Quill v. Vacco,* 80 F.3d 716 (2d Cir. 1996).

14. N. Sykes and A. Thomas, "Sedatives in the Last Week of Life and the Implications for End of Life Decision Making," *Archives of Internal Medicine* 163 (2003): 342–44.

15. Brody, "Causing, Intending, and Assisting Death"; Brock, "Voluntary Active Euthanasia."

16. M.J. Edwards and S.W. Tolle, "Disconnecting a Ventilator at the Request of a Patient Who Knows He Will Die: The Doctor's Anguish," *Annals of Internal Medicine* 117 (1992): 254–56.

17. Brock, "Voluntary Active Euthanasia."

18. Bernat, Gert, and Mogielnicki, "Patient Refusal of Hydration and Nutrition"; Printz, "Terminal Dehydration."

19. Brody, "Causing, Intending, and Assisting Death"; T.E. Quill, "The Ambiguity of Clinical Intentions," *New England Journal of Medicine* 329 (1993): 1039–40.

20. Brock, "Voluntary Active Euthanasia."

21. M.A.M. de Wachter, "Active Euthanasia in the Netherlands," *Journal of the American Medical Association* 262 (1989): 3316–19.

22. T.E. Quill and R.V. Brody, "You Promised Me I Wouldn't Die Like This': A Bad Death as a Medical Emergency," *Archives of Internal Medicine* 155 (1995): 1250–54.

23. T.E. Quill and C.K. Cassel, "Nonabandonment: A Central Obligation for Physicians," *Annals of Internal Medicine* 122 (1995): 368–74.

24. Teno and Lynn, "Voluntary Active Euthanasia"; Kamisar, "Against Assisted Suicide."

25. B. Mount and E.M. Flanders, "Morphine Drips, Terminal Sedation, and Slow Euthanasia: Definitions and Facts, Not Anecdotes," *Journal of Palliative Care* 12 (1996): 31–37.

Suggested Readings for Chapter 6

Angell, Marcia. "The Supreme Court and Physician-Assisted Suicide—the Ultimate Right." *New England Journal of Medicine* 336 (1997), 50–53.

Annas, George J., and Grodin, Michael, eds. *The Nazi Doctors and the Nuremberg Code.* New York: Oxford University Press, 1992.

Battin, Margaret Pabst, *Ending Life: Ethics and the Way We Die.* New York: Oxford University Press, 2005.

Battin, Margaret P., Rhodes, Rosamond, and Silvers, Anita, eds. *Physician Assisted Suicide: Expanding the Debate.* New York, NY: Routledge, 1998.

Beauchamp, Tom L., ed. *Intending Death: The Ethics of Assisted Suicide and Euthanasia.* Upper Saddle River, NJ: Prentice-Hall, 1996.

Beauchamp, Tom L., and Veatch, Robert M., eds. *Ethical Issues in Death and Dying.* Upper Saddle River, NJ: Prentice-Hall, 1997.

Beauchamp, Tom L., and Childress, James F. *Principles of Biomedical Ethics,* 5th ed. New York: Oxford University Press, 2001, chap. 4.

Brock, Dan W. "A Critique of Three Objections to Physician-Assisted Suicide." *Ethics* 109 (April 1999), 519–47.

———."Death and Dying." In Robert M. Veatch, ed. *Medical Ethics,* 2nd ed. Boston: Jones and Bartlett, 1997.

———."Medical Decisions at the End of Life." In Helga Kuhse and Peter Singer, eds. *A Companion to Bioethics.* Malden, MA: Blackwell, 1998, 231–41.

Brody, Baruch A. *Suicide and Euthanasia: Historical and Contemporary Themes.* Dordrecht, Holland: Kluwer Academic Publishers, 1989.

Callahan, Daniel. "A Case against Euthanasia," in Cohen, Andrew I. and Wellman, Christopher Heath, eds., *Contemporary Debates in Applied Ethics.* Malden, MA: Blackwell, 2005.

Cavanaugh, Thomas A. "Currently Accepted Practices That Are Known to Lead to Death, and PAS: Is There an Ethically Relevant Difference?" *Cambridge Quarterly of Healthcare Ethics* 7 (Fall 1998), 375–81.

Dowbiggin, Ian. *A Merciful End: The Euthanasia Movement in Modern America.* New York: Oxford University Press, 2003.

Dworkin, Ronald. *Life's Dominion: An Argument about Abortion, Euthanasia, and Individual Freedom.* New York: Knopf, 1993.

Dworkin, Gerald; Frey, Raymond G.; and Bok, Sissela. *Euthanasia and Physician-Assisted Suicide: For and Against.* New York: Cambridge University Press, 1998.

Emanuel, Ezekiel J. "What Is the Great Benefit of Legalizing Euthanasia or Physician-Assisted Suicide?" *Ethics* 109 (April 1999), 629–42.

Emanuel, Linda L., ed. *Regulating How We Die: The Ethical, Medical, and Legal Issues Surrounding Physician-Assisted Suicide.* Cambridge, MA: Harvard University Press, 1998.

Foley, Kathleen, and Hendin, Herbert. *The Case Against Assisted Suicide.* Baltimore: The Johns Hopkins University Press, 2002.

Gert, Bernard, Culver, Charles M., and Clouser, K. Danner, *Bioethics: A Return to Fundamentals.* New York: Oxford, 1997, chaps. 11–12.

Glover, Jonathan. *Causing Death and Saving Lives.* New York: Penguin Books, 1977.

Gostin, Lawrence O. "Deciding Life and Death in the Courtroom: From *Quinlan* to *Cruzan, Glucksberg,* and *Vacco*—A Brief History and Analysis of Constitutional Protection of the 'Right to Die.'" *Journal of the American Medical Association* 278 (November 1997), 1523–28.

Hull, Richard T. "The Case for Physician-Assisted Suicide," in Daniel, Eileen, ed. *Taking Sides: Clashing Views in Health and Society.* Dubuque, IA: McGraw Hill, 2006.

Kamm, Frances M. "Physician-Assisted Suicide, The Doctrine of Double Effect, and the Ground of Value." *Ethics* 109 (April 1999), 586–605.

Keown, John, *Euthanasia, Ethics, and Public Policy: An Argument against Legalization.* Cambridge: Cambridge University Press, 2002.

Kopelman, Loretta M., and Kenneth A. De Ville, *Physician-Assisted Suicide: What are the Issues?* Boston: Kluwer Academic, 2001.

Lifton, Robert J. *The Nazi Doctors: Medical Killing and the Psychology of Genocide.* New York: Basic Books, 1986.

Meier, Diane E., et al. "A National Survey of Physician-Assisted Suicide and Euthanasia in the United States." *New England Journal of Medicine* 338 (April 23, 1998), 1193–1201.

Meisel, Alan. *The Right to Die*, 2d ed. New York: John Wiley and Sons, 1995.

Miller, Franklin G., Fins, Joseph J., and Snyder, Lois. "Assisted Suicide Compared with Refusal of Treatment: A Valid Distinction?" *Annals of Internal Medicine* 132 (March 2000), 470–75.

New York State Task Force on Life and the Law. *When Death Is Sought: Assisted Suicide and Euthanasia in the Medical Context.* New York: New York State Task Force, 1994.

Orentlicher, David. "The Legalization of Physician Assisted Suicide: A Very Modest Revolution." *Boston College Law Review* 28 (1997), 443–75.

Pellegrino, Edmund D. "Physician-Assisted Suicide and Euthanasia: Rebuttals of Rebuttals: The Moral Prohibition Remains," *Journal of Medicine and Philosophy* 26 (2001), 93–100.

Quill, Timothy E. *Death and Dignity: Making Choices and Taking Charge.* New York: W.W. Norton, 1993.

———, and Byock, Ira R. "Responding to Intractable Terminal Suffering: The Role of Terminal Sedation and Voluntary Refusal of Food and Fluids: Position Paper." *Annals of Internal Medicine* 132 (March 2000), 408–14.

———, and Battin, Margaret P., eds., *Physician-Assisted Dying: The Case for Palliative Care and Patient Choice.* Baltimore: The Johns Hopkins University Press, 2004.

Rachels, James. "Active and Passive Euthanasia." *New England Journal of Medicine* 292 (January 9, 1975), 78–80.

———. *The End of Life: Euthanasia and Morality.* Oxford: Oxford University Press, 1986.

Rich, Ben A. "Oregon v. Ashcroft: The Battle Over the Soul of Medicine." *Cambridge Quarterly of Healthcare Ethics* 12 (2003), 310–321.

Salem, Tania. "Physician-Assisted Suicide: Promoting Autonomy—or Medicalizing Suicide?" *Hastings Center Report* 29 (May–June 1999), 30–36.

Schneider, Carl E., ed. *Law at the End of Life: The Supreme Court and Assisted Suicide.* Ann Arbor: University of Michigan Press, 2000.

Seay, Gary. "Do Physicians Have an Inviolable Duty Not to Kill?" *Journal of Medicine and Philosophy* 26 (2001), 75–91.

Shannon, Thomas A., ed. *Death and Dying.* Lanham, Md. Rowman & Littlefield Publishers, 2004.

Singer, Peter. "Voluntary Euthanasia: A Utilitarian Perspective." *Bioethics* 17 (2003), 526–41.

Snyder, Lois, and Caplan, Arthur, eds. *Assisted Suicide: Finding Common Ground.* Bloomington: Indiana University Press, 2002.

Somerville, Margaret. *Death Talk: The Case Against Euthanasia and Physician-Assisted Suicide.* Montreal: McGill-Queen's University Press, 2001.

Steinbock, Bonnie. "The Case for Physician Assisted Suicide: Not (Yet) Proven." *Journal of Medical Ethics* 31 (2005), 235–41.

ten Have, Henk, and Jos V. M. Welie, *Death and Medical Power: An Ethical Analysis of Dutch Euthanasia Practice.* New York: Open University Press: McGraw-Hill Education, 2005.

Thomasma, David C., and Graber, Glenn C. *Euthanasia: Toward an Ethical Social Policy.* New York: Continuum, 1990.

Tooley, Michael. "In Defense of Voluntary Active Euthanasia and Assisted Suicide," in Cohen, Andrew I., and Wellman, Christopher Heath, eds. *Contemporary Debates in Applied Ethics.* Malden, MA: Blackwell, 2005.

Thomson, Judith Jarvis. "Physician-Assisted Suicide: Two Moral Arguments." *Ethics* 109 (April 1999), 497–518.

Velleman, J. David. "A Right of Self-Termination?" *Ethics* 109 (April 1999), 606–28.

Wanzer, S. H., et al. "The Physician's Responsibility Toward Hopelessly Ill Patients: A Second Look." *New England Journal of Medicine* 320 (1989), 844–49.

Wellman, Carl. "A Moral Right to Physician-Assisted Suicide." *American Philosophical Quarterly* 38 (2001), 271–86.

Wolf, Susan. "Holding the Line on Euthanasia." *Hastings Center Report* 19 (1989), S13–S15.

Chapter 7
Organ Transplantation

Introduction

Organ retrieval and transplantation has raised many ethical problems since the earliest successes of transplant technologies in the late 1960s. Once organs could be successfully transplanted, questions had to be answered about how best to allocate the scarce supply of organs among the many waiting patients.

Transplantation involves the transfer of cells, tissues, or solid organs from one human to another to replace the structure or function of comparable injured or diseased body components that are defective or of inadequate function. The new abilities to transplant organs also influenced the development of a new definition of death, one that would make organ donation and transplantation after death both feasible and widely available.

Deceased donors are individuals who have died and from whom an array of organs can be taken. It is something of a misuse of consent language to refer to organs from a deceased individual as "donated," since in the majority of cases the individual never chose to donate; rather, the organs were donated by family members on his or her behalf. However, the term is commonly used this way, and it is so used in this introduction as a matter of convention.

Living donors refers to healthy individuals, usually but not always related to their recipients (by blood or marriage), who volunteer to provide either a whole, paired organ such as a kidney, or a section of an organ such as a liver or pancreas. Living donation evolved in an effort to bridge the substantial gap between the supply of available organs and the demand for them. Initially such donations were limited to people who were genetically related, but with improved drugs and medical management to combat the rejection of organs, an intimate relationship between donors and recipients has grown less important. We now see reports of donor–recipient pairs who work together, belong to the same church or community group, or whose relationship extends to nothing more than an overheard conversation in a grocery store. There are now transplant programs across the United States in which an individual can volunteer to donate a kidney to a stranger on the wait list—the epitome of an altruistic donor.

However, increased efforts to encourage organ procurement from those who have died, along with extended acceptability of living donations, have not increased the supply of organs nearly enough to satisfy the growing demand. Desperate and waiting patients often draw on whatever means and technologies are available to them. As discussed in the following pages, some patients have even solicited willing donors over the internet or through public pleas, sometimes paying questionable brokers who illegally offer organs for money.

It has been and remains a priority of the U.S. federal government to support organ transplantation and to address the increasing shortfall in supply of organs relative to demand. Programs to enhance the public's donation of organs include efforts to encourage individuals to sign donor cards, execute check boxes on their driver's licenses, or make other advance indications of their wishes, and to encourage more families to consent to donation of their loved ones' organs. The federal Organ Donation Collaborative announced in 2003 by then U.S. Secretary of Health and Human Services Tommy Thompson is an example of this priority. These federally funded efforts have had some positive effect, though adverse publicity around questionable allocation of organs damages public confidence in the transplant system and can have major negative effects on donor rates. Surveys have indicated that the public is not well informed and has reservations about organ donation in general.

The *demand* for organs, as measured by additions to the transplantation waiting list, continues to increase. It long ago outstripped the *supply* of organs. The existing supply would have to approximately double to meet the current demand, but even such large gains would likely be insufficient. Evidence suggests that a larger supply would be met with increased demand because fewer patients would die waiting for organs. Real demand seems likely to be several times the supply possible under current policies. This analysis suggests that society will continue to look to new categories of donors and new approaches to donation that might contribute significantly to supply.

This chapter examines the issues around both the sources of donated organs and the process by which they are allocated, many of which are provocative and controversial. The chosen articles sometimes reach conflicting conclusions, owing in part to the fact that transplantation is an unsettled and fast-changing area of medicine and public policy.

THE DEFINITION OF DEATH AND THE RETRIEVAL OF ORGANS

The definition of death is a fundamental problem for organ transplantation. Organs must have blood circulating through them up until the time they are removed from the body in order to be successfully used in transplant. Accordingly, the traditional "whole-body" or heart–lung definition of death—constituted by cessation of circulation—rendered organs unusable for transplant. This prompted interest in brain-based definitions of death, which could accommodate the position that a person had died when his or her brain stopped functioning by various objective measures, even though circulation was being continued through the support of mechanical ventilation.

As Robert Veatch outlines in his article in the first section of this chapter, theoretical and practical questions exist about criteria for when brain death has actually occurred. Is death constituted by an irreversible loss of the neurological capacity to integrate bodily functions such that such patients cannot be conscious and cannot survive without mechanical ventilation? Or, alternatively, is brain death better understood as the irreversible loss of some collection of higher-brain capacities making consciousness impossible? The former, whole-brain definition is more conservative in terms of who would be pronounced dead than is the higher-brain function definition. This difference has important implications for end-of-life considerations. Questions about which theory to endorse are not merely empirical and technical in nature. They have a strong value component with implications for public policy.

In particular, they have critical implications for the procurement of organs from those who have died. A practical application of any definition of death by brain criteria is that usable organs will be available for transplant. A number of policy bodies have been created to oversee the process once death has been determined and organs made available. The United Network for Organ Sharing/Organ Procurement and Transplant Network (UNOS/OPTN) is a nationwide in the U.S. effort substantially supported by federal funds and overseen through federal contract, charged with creating policies for and overseeing organ procurement and allocation from deceased donors. Organ Procurement Organizations (OPOs) are established pursuant to federal law and monitored by a federal agency (the Centers for Medicare and Medicaid Services, CMS), with the role of acting as intermediary between health care facilities where patients may be dying (and may donate organs) and the transplant teams that use the organs after they are collected from deceased donors. The Federal government connection to transplant is critical for the ability to vigorously react to reports of questionable practices or the hint of scandal in federally supervised programs or when federal funds are at stake.

In the second article in this chapter, Courtney Campbell critiques what he perceives to be an inappropriate linking of the brain death debate and discussions about organ procurement and transplantation. He focuses on the use of information collected from surveys and other assessments of public attitudes to justify what he provocatively argues are questionable policy approaches in organ transplantation. These approaches, he argues, allow the "harvesting" of organs from people who are not actually dead. No one denies the value of organ transplantation, but Campbell suggests that organ procurement policies and practices that skirt the line between life and death would greatly increase the moral and social costs of collecting and transplanting organs. Campbell is worried that society might accept such social costs as part of its understanding of "the technological imperative," a term suggesting that technological possibilities are difficult to resist and that decisions embracing technologies are made without sufficient consideration of the effects they may cause. Finally, Campbell asks whether our priorities for use of limited health care resources ought to include expensive life-extending technologies such as organ transplantation, or whether these resources could be better used in other ways. He points to the Oregon Health Plan (examined in Chapter 8) as at least one circumstance in which the public has endorsed the idea of *severely limited* public funding of organ transplantation in favor of wider availability of other health care services.

Nonetheless, evidence clearly shows that developed societies have endorsed funding schemes for at least some expensive life-saving and life-extending technologies. Many arguments have been offered for funding organ transplant procedures. For instance, the federal Task Force on Organ Transplantation (appointed by the U.S. Department of Health and Human Services (DHHS)) recommended that "a public program should be set up to cover the costs of people who are medically eligible for organ transplants but who are not covered by private insurance, Medicare, or Medicaid and who are unable to obtain an organ transplant due to the lack of funds."[1] The task force limited its proposed policy to the financially needy, grounding its recommendation on two arguments from justice. The first argument emphasizes the continuity between heart and liver transplants and other forms of medical care (including kidney transplants) that are already accepted as part of the decent minimum of health care that society should provide. The task force argued that heart and liver transplants are comparable to other funded procedures in terms of their effectiveness in saving lives and enhancing the quality of life. Under the assumption that society is committed to providing funds to meet a wide variety of health care needs, "it is arbitrary to exclude one life-saving procedure while funding others of equal life-saving potential and cost." The task force offered a second argument for the federal government's role in guaranteeing equitable access to organ transplants: Various public officials participate in efforts to increase the supply of donated organs by appealing to all citizens to donate their organs and organs from their dead relatives. These appeals are aimed at all segments of society. However, the task force argued, it is unfair and sometimes exploitative to solicit people, rich and poor alike, to donate organs if those organs are then distributed on the basis of ability to pay rather than by some equitable approach. Furthermore, it seems inconsistent to prohibit the *sale* of organs (discussed later), and then to distribute donated organs according to ability to pay.

Despite their attractive features, these arguments do not establish that justice requires the government to provide health care irrespective of its cost, or that it is arbitrary to use a reasonably structured system of rationing. Once a society has achieved a fair threshold of funding, it may select some procedures while excluding others when they are of equal life-saving potential and of equal cost, as long as it can identify relevant differences through a fair procedure involving substantial public participation.

Potential donors need to understand the limits built into the system of procurement and allocation of organs. Assuming this understanding by donors and a fair system for allocating collected organs, a government could legitimately encourage donation even if it could not pay for transplantation. In the end, recommendations about funding expensive transplants and all other expensive treatments need to be placed in the larger context of a social policy of allocation. These problems suggest that analysis of the problem of organ procurement should not be divorced from the larger health care and economic contexts in which organ transplantation is occurring.

DISTRIBUTIVE JUSTICE IN THE ALLOCATION OF ORGANS

In 2007, over 95,000 people in the United States were waiting for an organ transplant—a number that continues to grow daily. In contrast, only 29,000 transplants were performed during calendar year 2006. Evidence of the shortfall and the increasing gap between the numbers of organs available and the numbers of patients waiting for them has been apparent for decades.

The U.S. government has long been interested in alternative approaches that can be used to maximize the availability of organs from a donor without violating prevailing ethical norms governing the rights and welfare of donors. Significant ethical issues exist about how we might procure organs and how organs, once procured, should be allocated. "To allocate" here means to distribute by allotment. Such distribution does not, however, presuppose either a person or a system that rations resources. A criterion of ability to pay in a competitive market, for example, is a form of allocation. In this section, we concentrate on the question "How should organs from deceased donors be allocated?"

Efforts to answer these questions have yielded an approach in the United States that allocates organs as a shared resource to those who need them most—usually based on a combination of medical need (sickest first), time on the waiting list (longest on the list first), and geography (closest to the location of donation first). The U.S. allocation system is managed by UNOS/OPTN, which balances the sometimes competing interests involved in creating a public policy. The goal is to achieve both the best medical outcomes and equity of access to available organs.

In his article in this chapter, James Childress examines the ethical bases for just allocation of organs and the policy approaches that might follow from these bases. The shortage of organs makes it difficult to honor our sometimes conflicting values of (1) satisfying the needs of patients, (2) maximizing the likelihood of transplant successes, and (3) giving organs to those who have been waiting the longest. Childress argues that society "should seek to further specify, to weight, and to balance patient need, probable success, and waiting time through a process that involves the fullest possible and most diverse public participation." The emphasis here is on *public* participation. In addition to advocating a process that relies on a conceptual framework of justice (see Chapter 1 for discussions, especially of Rawls's approach to justice), Childress points out that political and geographical boundaries should be secondary to a theory premised on what best serves the needs of patients.

After the Childress article, David Howard provocatively proposes that we ought to pay less attention to the "rule of rescue"—by which we feel compelled to rescue identifiable individuals who are at risk of avoidable harm—in deciding how to allocate organs. This rule places a high value on saving the lives of the sickest patients in deciding who receives an organ and when they receive it. Howard argues that we need to pay more attention to efficiency (or, as some would say, utility) and less to rescue: We should allocate organs with the goal of producing the greatest benefit to the patients receiving them. By taking efficiency into account, the currently conventional approach of transplanting the sickest patients first would be reconsidered and adjusted to the standard of allocating organs *before* patients become so urgently sick that they cannot receive maximal benefit. A critical part of this proposal is that transplanting patients earlier would result in the maximal benefit from the organ, and that maximal benefit is a morally relevant, even overriding, consideration. This policy would result in transplant of different recipients, with the effect that patients eligible under the current scheme would often be denied access to life-saving treatment. But the critical claim is that patients currently not eligible would often be granted access to this life-saving technology.

But what is the value of greater efficiency without acknowledging the place of individual responsibility in a schema of the *just* allocation of scarce organs? This issue has been raised with special poignancy for patients with alcohol-related end-stage liver failure who need liver transplants. Despite dramatic increases in the number of liver transplants, livers from both deceased and living donors are still scarce, and many patients suffering from end-stage liver failure (ESLF) die before they can obtain transplants. As a result, the question arises whether patients who have alcohol-related ESLF—cirrhosis of the liver due to alcohol abuse, a major cause of ESLF—should be excluded from waiting lists for liver transplants or should be given lower priority ratings. Arguments for their lower priority or total exclusion often appeal to the probability that they will resume their alcohol abuse and destroy the transplanted liver, thereby wasting it. However, liver transplantation can be a sobering experience—quite literally—and some centers and insurers require waiting periods of a year free of alcohol consumption to show abstinence. Studies have demonstrated that patients with alcohol-related ESLF who receive a liver transplant and do abstain from alcohol do as well as patients whose ESLF resulted from other causes.[2]

Nonetheless, some in contemporary bioethics propose that patients with alcohol-related ESLF (over 50 percent of the patients with ESLF) automatically receive a lower priority ranking in the allocation of donated livers than patients who develop end-stage liver disease through no fault of their own.[3] Their argument appeals to fairness, fair opportunity, and utility. They contend that it is fair to hold people responsible for their decisions and their actions, and then to allocate organs with a view to utilitarian outcomes. Assigning lower priority to patients with alcohol-related ESLF is unfortunate, but is it unfair? Sometimes the utilitarian argument is used that public support is indispensable for liver transplantation, both for securing funds and for securing organ donations. Giving patients with alcohol-related ESLF equal priority for donated livers could reduce public support for liver transplantation, and this consequence could be devastating for transplant programs and patients needing transplants. But is this argument morally acceptable?

The issues raised by this debate will intensify when lung transplantation becomes more common and more cigarette smokers seek transplants, often in competition with patients who have lethal genetic conditions such as cystic fibrosis.

CONSENT AND SOCIAL POLICY

Any theorizing about proper allocation assumes that organs are available to be distributed. In the late 1960s and early 1970s, all states in the United States adopted the Uniform Anatomical Gift Act (UAGA).[4] This act gives individuals the right to make decisions about the donation of their organs and tissues, through a signed donor card or some other advance indication of their wishes. If the individual has not made a decision prior to death, the law authorizes the family (in a ranked ordering of members) to decide whether to donate the decedent's organs. The Act organized a system of donation, but it was not structured to encourage donation or to establish systems to encourage donations.

On the basis of opinion polls, it was expected that many individuals would sign donor cards, which would provide a sufficient supply of organs, thereby avoiding the need for living organ donors. In practice, however, few individuals made the decision to become donors in the years immediately after the UAGA was adopted, and the trend has only modestly improved over the subsequent decades. Further, donor cards or directives are sometimes improperly executed, and are rarely available at the time of death, so in practice, procurement teams virtually always check with the family (often first) even if the decedent left a valid directive. As a result, various policies have been considered and some adopted that aim to promote the common good more vigorously. Howard's theory could be taken as an example of such proposals.

The historical and the current policy toward organ donation in the United States makes it axiomatic that individuals have the right to decide whether to be organ donors, based in the principle of respect for autonomy (see Chapter 1 for further discussion of the role of autonomy). This translates into policies and practices that respect individual decisions about whether to be organ donors or, in the absence of clear directives, rely on families to make the decision about organ donation after death. This approach is distinctly different from that taken in some other countries, in which law and policy make a *presumption* toward donation. These policies—adopted in Europe for organs and in the United States for tissue transplants such as corneal transplants—are based on what has been termed "presumed consent." Such consent is inferred in a legal setting in which there are explicit rules about the right to consent and refuse, and it is assumed that persons understand that they have a right to opt out. Presumed consent laws require that organs are donated after death unless individuals opt out of donation through some form of public registration.[5]

The policy is straightforward: All legally competent persons are provided with the opportunity to refuse to donate. Any legally competent person who is a candidate for donation is presumed to have consented to donation if the person has not recorded an explicit registered refusal to donate. That is, the person's failure to register disagreement with the known public system of anatomical gifting qualifies as an authorization to retrieve organs or tissues. This policy points to a fundamental difference in perspective about how we ought to understand the status of our organs after death.

In his article in this chapter, D. Micah Hester argues that we have an obligation to give our organs to others after we die. He is proposing to rethink the idea of "donation" (which is not generally understood as an obligation) and to recast it as a duty or obligation. Hester contends that we have obligations to "do what we can to save seriously endangered lives when we can do so without risking anything of significant value to us." This argument is more consistent with programs of presumed consent (primarily in Europe) than the current practice in the United States, challenging the moral foundations of organ procurement policy. Many have argued that due to our commitment to rights and individualism, the American culture could never accommodate presumed consent. It remains to be seen whether these purported commitments are stronger than our desire to see greater numbers of available organs for transplant.

LIVING ORGAN DONATION

Among the ethical issues raised by living organ donation is that living donors are exposed to the *risks* of donation, while the medical *benefits* of the transplant go to others. Commonly, the donors and recipients are related in some way, whether through family relationships, belonging to the same community or religious groups, working together in the same office, or even after meeting in informal settings such as the grocery store. Donors are motivated at least in part by the understanding that someone they care about will benefit by their unique gift. There are important moral questions, however, about whether and under what circumstances these healthy individuals ought to be exposed to medical risk in order to benefit another person. This issue is parallel to a core moral question that arises in research on human subjects that uses healthy volunteers (see Chapter 6 for a discussion of issues in relation to the ethics of research).

In their article, Carl Elliott and Robert Crouch examine the role that family dynamics, in particular, play in living donation, and the extent to which expectations within families trump other important considerations. One possible source of insight is the way that courts have ruled when faced with questions about whether children ought to be allowed to donate organs to a member of their family. Elliott and Crouch critique the frequently invoked justification that donation is in the best interests of the donor child. They examine what such a "best interests" standard might entail in the context of family relationships, and conclude that courts and others have staked too much on the conception of best interests.

The relationship between living donors and their recipients is of increasing importance, because the numbers of living organ donations increases every year. The rise in the number of living kidney donors is so great, in fact, that since 2001 there have been more kidneys transplanted from living donors than from deceased donors. The increase has come in part from efforts to extend living donation from donations among related donors— whether by blood, marriage, or social relationship—to more tenuous "relationships," including donations by individuals who have "met" their prospective recipient on the internet.

In her article in this chapter, Lainie Friedman Ross examines the various approaches to living organ donation and their ethical acceptability. She discusses donations by total strangers to a waiting recipient they will never meet, much as a person would donate blood to a blood bank for later use for a patient in need. She also discusses so-called paired exchange, in which willing donors who are a mismatch with their proposed recipient agree to "swap" recipients. For example, suppose that a man is willing to donate one of his kidneys to his brother, but is of the wrong blood type. Similarly, suppose that a woman is willing to donate one of her kidneys to her sister, but is also a mismatch. The willing donor–recipient pairs can be matched to effectively make a trade—the man will donate his kidney to the woman's sister in return for the woman donating her kidney to the man's brother. The pairs engage in an exchange of sorts, hence the term "paired exchange."

However inventive this approach appears, it raises the specter of trading organs, which is strictly forbidden in the United States by the National Organ Transplant Act (NOTA) of 1984. This issue is one among many raised by the most novel and innovative approaches to increasing organ supply, as we will see in the final section of this chapter.

INNOVATIVE POLICIES FOR ORGAN PROCUREMENT

In spite of the efforts mentioned so far to increase the supply of organs from both deceased and living donors, there are still too few organs available to meet the demand for transplant. The shortage has prompted increasingly innovative proposals for encouraging an increased supply of organs, and brought with them increasing controversy. The most persistent, and likely most controversial, suggestion is to actively encourage the sale of organs. Such arguments are sometimes put forward by economists or those influenced by economic arguments, who say that the most efficient approaches to solving problems of shortage are to let market forces do their work. Such conditions allegedly would encourage willing vendors to sell a valuable commodity to either those willing to pay or to a central resource that would then allocate the purchased organs. There are also moral arguments in defense of this approach.

Janet Radcliffe Richards begins her article in this section of the chapter not by arguing from a commitment to free-market economics, but from the perspective that all the arguments *against* organ sales are found wanting on any close ethical analysis. She comes to the conclusion that arguments against an organ trade rely largely on feelings of repugnance rather than sound moral claims, and that prohibitions based on claims of protecting those who would sell their organs—from harm or exploitation—actually work against the welfare of those they are trying to protect.

Nancy Scheper-Hughes comes to the opposite conclusion about a trade in organs. She draws on the results of her anthropological research on what happens to organ vendors in the places in the world where organ sales occur, either clandestinely or with government support and endorsement. Her findings paint a picture of vendors who sell organs in the hope of improving their financial and social status but who find themselves worse off rather than better off than they were before they sold a kidney. They come to think that they were taken advantage of by unscrupulous kidney sellers.

There is some empirical evidence to this effect. For example, a study of 305 people who sold their kidneys in India found that the sellers were generally made worse off financially as a result of the sale, that some men forced their wives to sell a kidney, and that many sellers suffered a decline in health status.[6] This study further indicates that 96 percent of those who sell kidneys do so to pay off debts and that their poverty may be enhanced rather than reduced by a market in organs. The selling of a kidney has therefore not proved to be a solution for indigence, at least in India, debunking an idea that has formed one of the strongest supports for a market in organs. Sales of kidneys generally do not seem to function as a way to move from poverty to security, but rather function as a way of raising money to pay off high-interest loans. As is well known in even first-world countries such as the United States, high-interest loans (such as pay-day loans or automobile-title pawn loans) can prey on the poor and undereducated who are caught in a never-ending cycle of borrowing and repaying.

Desperate patients increasingly seek their own approaches to finding the lifesaving organs they need. The internet has made it possible to reach out to millions of people to make the plea for a donated organ, or to make it known that you have an organ you are willing to sell. In 1999 CNN reported that online shoppers who visited the internet auction site eBay were surprised to find a "fully functional kidney" for sale by a man giving his home as "Sunrise, Florida." He was proposing to sell one of his two kidneys. The price had been bid up to more than $5.7 million before eBay intervened and terminated the illegal auction.[7] It was never determined whether this auction was genuine, or to whom the kidney may have belonged. This auction was in public view, but a private market in kidneys would be more difficult to observe and to control.

Other entrepreneurs have created new (and legal) platforms by which to help potential donors find waiting recipients. Internet matching sites such as Matchingdonors.com create a new means by which to create donor–recipient pairs, allowing willing donors to browse the site for a recipient of their choosing, whether based on the compelling story of need, the characteristics of the person, their geographic location, or even whether they find them physically appealing or attractive. The problem is that this sort of browsing system challenges our conventional commitments to equitable allocation and central oversight of the transplant process. No longer are recipients at the mercy of UNOS/OPTN to wait for a kidney from a deceased donor. They can wait on the deceased donation list and, at the same time, try their luck, for a fee, on an internet matching site. In their articles in this section, both Robert Steinbrook and Timothy Murphy examine the ethical and policy issues in such so-called public solicitation of organs, and how they challenge our ideas about what is appropriate and acceptable when recipients are searching for organs.

What seems clear is that what was long called "the future" has arrived. The new future poses many challenges for the existing system, which is certain to be dramatically reconfigured. As organ transplant technologies evolve, approaches to procurement and allocation will evolve with them, hopefully in ways that are ethically acceptable. The challenge, then, is not only in providing organs for all who need them, but in creating processes that reflect our moral commitments as well.

J.P.K.

NOTES

1. U.S. Department of Health and Human Services, Task Force on Organ Transplantation, *Organ Transplantation: Issues and Recommendations* (Washington, DC: DHHS, 1986), p. 105.

2. T. E. Starzl, D. Van Thiel, A. G. Tzakis, et al., "Orthotopic Liver Transplantation for Alcoholic Cirrhosis," *Journal of the American Medical Association* 260 (Nov. 4, 1988): 2542–44; and A. DiMartini et al., "Outcome of Liver Transplantation in Critically Ill Patients with Alcoholic Cirrhosis: Survival According to Medical Variables and Sobriety," *Transplantation* 66 (1998): 298–302.

3. Alvin H. Moss and Mark Siegler, "Should Alcoholics Compete Equally for Liver Transplantation?" *Journal of the American Medical Association* 265 (March 13, 1991): 1295–98.

4. UAGA, 8A U.L.A. 16, 1989 (suppl).

5. British Medical Association, "Organ Donation: A System of Presumed Consent" (Nov. 2005), accessed at http://www.bma.org.uk/ap.nsf/Content/presumedconsent; March 2007.

6. M. Goyal, R. L. Mehta, L. J. Schneiderman, and A. R. Sehgal, "Economic and Health Consequences of Selling a Kidney in India," *Journal of the American Medical Association* 288 (October 2, 2002): 1589–93.

7. CNN.com (Sept. 3, 1999), "Online Shoppers Bid Millions for Human Kidney."

ROBERT M. VEATCH

The Definition of Death: Problems for Public Policy

Robert M. Veatch, Ph.D., is Professor of Medical Ethics and the former Director of the Kennedy Institute of Ethics at Georgetown University. His recent books include *The Basics of Bioethics, Case Studies in Pharmacy Ethics*, and the second editions of *Case Studies in Nursing Ethics, Cross Cultural Perspectives in Medical Ethics*, and *Transplantation Ethics*. His current research focuses on the history of professional medical ethics and its relation to philosophical and religious ethics.

At 5:41 A.M. Sunday morning, November 10, 1985, Philadelphia Flyers' hockey star Pelle Lindbergh slammed his new Porsche into a cement wall of a Somerdale, New Jersey, elementary school. The headline on the story in the newspaper the next day read, "Flyers Goalie Is Declared Brain Dead." In spite of the claim that he was "brain dead" the story went on to say that Lindbergh was listed in "critical condition" in the intensive care unit of John F. Kennedy Hospital in Stratford. . . . Flyers' team physician Edward Viner said that if Lindbergh's situation did not improve, the family would be left with a decision about how long to leave him on the respirator.

That was not the only decision they faced. If Lindbergh was dead even though some of his vital functions remained, he would be an ideal candidate to be an organ donor. His intact heart and kidneys could provide life-saving help for three other people. Possibly even his liver, lungs, pancreas, and corneas could benefit others. Suddenly it became a practical, lifesaving matter to figure out whether Pelle Lindbergh was dead or alive. The headline writer says he was "brain dead," but then the article went on to speak as if he was nevertheless still alive. The story referred to him as "near death."[1] We used to believe that persons with beating hearts were alive even though their brain function was lost irreversibly. Now we are not so sure. The way Pelle Lindbergh was treated, the decisions

his parents had to make, the behavior of the physicians and nurses, and the fate of several desperately ill human beings all hinged on figuring out whether Lindbergh was already dead or rather was in the process of dying.

The public policy discussion of the definition of death began in earnest in the late 1960s, . . . almost 20 years before Pelle Lindbergh's accident. It began in the context of a world that had in the previous decade seen the first successful transplantation of an organ from one human being to another, including the initial 1967 transplant of a human heart. It cannot be denied that this sudden infatuation with the usefulness of human organs was the stimulus for the intense discussion of the real meaning of death. What many thought would be a rather short-lived problem, resolved by the combined wisdom of the health professionals and nonscientists, . . . has lingered as an intractable morass of conflicting technical, legal, conceptual, and moral arguments. Much of this confusion can be avoided, however, by focusing exclusively on the problems for public policy.

Focusing on public policy means avoiding a full linguistic analysis of the term *death*. Although that may be an important philosophical enterprise, and many have undertaken it, this analysis is only of indirect importance for public policy questions, including organ transplant questions. . . . Likewise, we need not provide a detailed theological account of the meaning of death. Those studies are numerous but not of immediate concern in the formation of secular public policy. Nor are we concerned about the ontological question of when an entity ceases to be human. Some philosophers have tried to turn the definition of death debate into such a deep philosophical question. Most significant, a scientific description of the biological events in the brain at the time of death will not be necessary. That is of crucial importance for the science of neurology, and a vast literature is available giving such an account. The scientific, biological, and neurological description of precisely what takes place in the human body at the point of death is not a matter that need directly concern public policy makers.

THE PUBLIC POLICY QUESTION

What we are interested in is the public policy question: When should we begin treating an individual the way we treat the newly dead? Is it possible to identify a point in the course of human events at which a new set of social behaviors becomes appropriate, at which, because we say the individual has died, we may justifiably begin to treat him or her in a way that was not previously appropriate, morally or legally? In short, what we are interested in is a social system of death behaviors.

Social and cultural changes take place when we label someone as dead. Some medical treatments may be stopped when an individual is considered dead that would not be stopped if the individual were alive—even if the living individual were merely terminally ill. This of course does not imply that there are no treatments that should be stopped at other times, either before or after the time when we label somebody as dead. Many treatments are stopped before death for technical reasons. According to many there are other treatments, including some that prolong life, that may justifiably be stopped before death because the treatments are no longer appropriate, either because they no longer serve a useful purpose or because they are too burdensome. In other cases, if the newly dead body is to be used for research, education, or transplant purposes, it is possible to continue certain interventions after death has been declared. Many have held that this is morally acceptable. It appears, however, that, traditionally, at least, there have been some treatments that are stopped when and only when we decide that it is time to treat the individual as dead.

Other behaviors also have traditionally taken place at the time we consider the individual dead. We begin mourning in a pattern that is not appropriate in mere anticipatory grief. We start several social processes that are not appropriately begun before the decision is made that death behavior is appropriate. We begin the process that will lead to reading a will, to burying or otherwise disposing of what we now take to be the "mortal remains." We assume new social roles—the role of widowhood, for example. If the individual who has been labeled as dead happens to have been the president of a country or an organization, normally labeling that individual as dead leads to the assumption of the role of president by the one who was formerly vice president. Finally, and perhaps of most immediate relevance to the concern that generated the definition of death discussion, we change the procedures and justifications for obtaining organs from the body. . . . At the moment we decide to treat someone as dead, an entirely different set of procedures is called for—the procedures designated in the Uniform Anatomical Gift Act drawn up in 1968. At that point, if one agreed to posthumous donation of organs while still alive, the organs may be removed according to the terms of the donation without further consideration of the interest of the former individual or the wishes of the family members. If the deceased has not so donated, and has not expressed opposition to donation, the next of kin or other legitimate guardian in possession of the body assumes both the right and the responsibility for the disposal of the remains and may donate the organs. . . .

In short, traditionally there has been a radical shift in moral, social, and political standing when someone has been labeled as dead. Until the 1960s, there was not a great deal of controversy over exactly when such a label should be applied. There were deviant philosophical and theological positions and substantial concern about erroneous labeling of someone as dead, but very little real controversy about what it meant to be dead in this public policy sense.

Now perhaps for the first time there are matters of real public policy significance in deciding precisely what we mean when we label someone dead. In an earlier day all of the socially significant death-related behaviors were generated at the time of death pronouncement. Very little was at stake if we were not precise in sorting various indicators of the time when this behavior was appropriate. Virtually all of the plausible events related to death occurred in rapid succession, and none of the behaviors was really contingent on any greater precision.

Now matters have changed in two important ways. First, several technologies have greatly extended our capacity to prolong the dying process, making it possible to identify several different potential indicators of what we should take to be the death of the individual as a whole and making it possible to separate these points dramatically in time. Second, the usefulness of human organs and tissues for transplantation, research, and education makes precision morally imperative. . . . Of course, it is important, out of our sense of respect for persons, that we not confuse living individuals with their corpses, so in theory it has always been important that we be clear about whether someone is dead or alive. Yet traditionally the very short time frame for the entire series of events meant that there was little at stake as a matter of public policy. We could pronounce death based on the rapid succession of an inevitably linked series of bodily events: heart stoppage, stoppage of respiration, or the death of the brain.

As we extend this period of time over which these events can occur, permitting much more precision in identifying what it is in the human body that signifies that it ought to be treated as dead, we must ask the question, Can we continue to identify a single definable point at which all the social behaviors associated with death should begin? . . .

There are several plausible candidates for that critical point at which we can say the individual as a whole has died, including the time when circulatory function ceases, the time when all brain functions cease, or the time when certain important brain functions (such as mental function) cease.

The question is therefore not precisely the same as the one the philosopher asks when he or she asks the question of the endpoint of personhood or personal identity. Analyses of the concept of personhood or personal identity suggest that there may be an identifiable endpoint at which we should stop thinking of a human organism as a person. That analysis by itself, however, never tells us whether it is morally appropriate to begin treating that human the way we have traditionally treated the dead unless personhood is simply defined with reference to death behavior, which it often is not. . . .

Fortunately, for matters of public policy, if not for philosophical analysis, we need not take up the question of personhood but can confront directly the question of whether we can identify a point at which this series of death behaviors is appropriate. In this way death comes to mean, for public policy purposes,

nothing more than the condition of some group of human beings for whom death behavior is appropriate. Can we identify this point? If we can, then, for purposes of law and public policy, we shall label that point as the moment of death. The laws reformulating the definition of death do not go so far as to say they are defining death for all purposes theological, philosophical, and personal. Some explicitly limit the scope, saying that the law defines death "for all legal purposes."

This policy-oriented formulation makes clear that when we talk about death, we are talking about death of the entity as a whole. It is with reference to the entire human organism that we want to determine appropriate behavior, not some particular body part.

Unfortunately, the term *brain death* has emerged in the debate. This is unfortunate in part because we are not interested in the death of brains; we are interested in the death of organisms as integrated entities subject to particular kinds of public behavior and control. In contrast, the term *brain death* is systematically ambiguous. It has two potential meanings. The first is not controversial at all; it simply means the destruction of the brain, leaving open the question of whether people with destroyed brains should be treated as dead people. It is better to substitute the phrase "destruction of the brain" for "brain death" in this sense. It makes clear that we are referring only to the complete biological collapse of the organ or organs we call the brain. Exactly how that is measured is largely a neurological question.

Unfortunately, brain death has also taken on a second, very different, and much more controversial, meaning. It can also mean the death of the individual as a whole, based on the fact that the brain has died. The problem is illustrated in the original report of the Harvard ad hoc committee,[2] which has become the most significant technical document in the American debate. The title of that 1968 document is "A Definition of Irreversible Coma." The article sets out to define "characteristics of irreversible coma" and produces a list of technical criteria that purport to predict that an individual is in a coma that is irreversible. The name of the committee, however, is the "Ad Hoc Committee of the Harvard Medical School to Examine the Definition of Brain Death." The presumption apparently was that irreversible coma and brain death were synonymous. We now realize that this is not precisely true. An individual can apparently be in irreversible coma and still not have a completely dead brain. In any case, the title of the report and the name of the committee, taken in context of what the committee did, imply that the objective of the committee was to describe the empirical measures of a destroyed brain.

The opening sentence of the report, however, says, "Our primary purpose is to define irreversible coma as a new criterion for death."[3] It does not claim to be defining the destruction (death) of the brain but *death simpliciter*, by which everyone, including the committee members, meant death of the individual for purposes of death behaviors, clinical practice, and public policy including, of course, transplantation. . . .

Because the term *brain death* has these two radically different meanings, there is often confusion in public and professional discussion of the issues. For instance, neurologists can claim that they have real expertise on brain death—meaning, of course, expertise in measuring the destruction of the brain. Others claim, however, that brain death is exclusively a matter for public policy consideration—meaning that the question of whether we should treat an individual as dead because the brain tissue is dead is really one outside the scope of neurological expertise. A far better course would be to abandon that language entirely, substituting precise and explicit language that either refers to the destruction of the brain or to the death of the individual as a whole based on brain criteria.

PRELIMINARY ISSUES TO PUBLIC POLICY DISCUSSION

. . . One of the most crucial preliminary issues in public policy consideration of the definition of death grows out of the problem of the systematic ambiguity of the term *brain death*. Some of the questions related to the pronouncement of death based on brain-related criteria are clearly technical and scientific, whereas others are questions of morality, politics, and law. It is crucial that the two be kept separate and the public role in each of these kinds of questions be identified.

CRITERIA OF DEATH: LARGELY A SCIENTIFIC MATTER

Virtually no one holds that every body structure and function must be destroyed for the individual as a whole to be considered dead for public policy purposes. That would mean that every cell in the body would have to be determined to be dead or at least every organ would have to be destroyed. We know, however, that certain cells—fingernails and hair, for example—continue to grow for hours after what we normally think of as death occurs.

It is also generally held that those with appropriate medical skills are capable of developing tests or procedures or criteria for predicting that a particular bodily function or structure is irreversibly destroyed. For example, if heart function is determined to be important in deciding when to treat people as dead, certain measures, such as feeling the pulse or taking an electrocardiogram, are available to diagnose and predict the future status of heart function. If lower brain functions are determined to be critical, then neurologists tell us that certain reflex pathways are good predictors of the status of the lower brain. If cerebral function is determined to be critical, different tests, based on the electroencephalogram and cerebral angiography, which measures blood flow, can be useful.

The tests or procedures or criteria for determining that critical bodily structures or functions have been lost must be established by those with scientific skills in biology or medicine—that is, those with the appropriate knowledge and skill. These tests or procedures or criteria need not be incorporated into public policy or statutory law. In fact, because empirical measures of this sort are likely to change as the status of our scientific knowledge changes, many take the view that these tests should not be included in the statutory law. As a general rule, statutes that have been passed have not included any reference to any specific empirical measures or criteria.

Technically, it is not correct to treat even these criteria for measuring the death of the brain as purely scientific, completely lacking in evaluative or other public policy importance. For example, in testing to measure the destruction of the brain a judgment must be made about how often these tests are to be applied and for how long a period of time they must be satisfied before pronouncing death. . . . Deciding on the correct length of time will depend on how one assesses the moral risks of falsely considering the brain to be dead and falsely considering it still to be alive. The best neurological science can do is tell us the probabilities of each kind of error after different time periods. It cannot tell us how to trade off the two kinds of errors. That is fundamentally a moral or policy issue. . . .

THE CONCEPT OF DEATH: ESSENTIALLY A POLICY MATTER

A more obvious policy question is just which structures or functions should be tested, which changes in the body should signal the time when death-related behavior is appropriate? Should it be loss of heart function or brain function? If it is the brain, just which functions are critical? We are attempting to determine when it is appropriate to treat the organism as a whole as dead. The loss of certain essential bodily structures or functions will almost certainly signal the time when such behavior is appropriate. These potential end-points are normally called the *concepts* or *standards of death*. Picking among them, in principle, cannot be done scientifically. It is essentially a policy matter.

For example, some people take the position that the organism as a whole should be considered dead if there is irreversible cessation of spontaneous respiratory and circulatory functions. Other people take the position that the organism should be considered dead if there is irreversible loss of all spontaneous brain functions. Still others maintain that the organism should be considered dead if there is irreversible loss of certain spontaneous cerebral functions. Behind each of these formulations is some implicit view of what is essential in the human being's nature.

Although society might choose to specify precisely what that philosophical or religious understanding is, that may not be either necessary or even possible. It might turn out that different people would formulate the precise underlying concept somewhat differently but still be able to agree at the level of the standard of death that is to be specified in the law. They might be able to agree that death should be pronounced when the functions of the circulatory and respiratory system are irreversibly lost. Or they might agree that it is the functions of the entire brain that count. They might reach this agreement even though they could not agree what it was about the circulatory system or respiratory system or brain that was so important.

The selection of these basic standards of death is now generally agreed to be a task for the broader public. The only real question is the method that will be used to express public policy. Traditionally, there was such an overwhelming consensus on an apparent concept and standard of death that there was no need for explicit public policy formulation. . . .

There is in principle no scientific basis for choosing one set of standards or underlying concepts over another, although once a particular concept or standard is chosen there may be good scientific reasons for selecting a set of criteria or tests or measures that correspond to the standard or concept chosen. This does not necessarily mean, however, that the choice is entirely an arbitrary one. It is possible, in fact it is widely held, that such choices have foundations in objective reality. In deciding to make slavery or murder illegal, for example, there is no scientific proof that either of these activities is wrong. It is not even clear what a scientific proof of such a position would look like. Nevertheless, the society can feel sufficiently sure that slavery and murder are wrong that it can choose to make them illegal without any suggestion that such a decision is arbitrary or capricious. . . .

If this is true, then selecting a point when it is appropriate to treat people as dead must be a matter for public policy. In an earlier time the public judgment reflected such a wide consensus that common law was sufficient for expressing that policy judgment. Now, however, when many possible, plausible end points of life have been identified, the public policy question may have to be resolved more explicitly. For this reason many hold that the policy question should be resolved legislatively. Others see it as more appropriately derived from case law—that is, in the courts. The disadvantage of using the courts is that judges deciding many cases will potentially formulate the policy differently.

Still others appear to believe that the policy question can be resolved without any formal expression of policy. Some kind of resolution to the policy question must be reached, however. Deciding what changes in bodily structure or function justify treating an individual as dead is logically before and independent of the question of what tests, measures, or criteria should be used for determining whether those changes have taken place.

There is no need to resolve all of the philosophical problems pertaining to the definition of death to reach a public policy resolution of the question of when people are to be treated as dead. General agreements on the standards may be reached as a matter of public policy, although the philosophical disagreement remains at the most abstract conceptual level. . . .

. . . WHICH FUNCTIONS ARE CRITICAL?

We are . . . left with the most fundamental and important public policy question of which functions or structures should be identified as critical for deciding that the individual as a whole should be treated as dead. . . .

THE LATE 1960S PERIOD

The first stage of the debate began in the late 1960s, especially with the preparation of the Harvard Medical School's ad hoc committee report. At this point, virtually everyone formulated the question in terms of a struggle between two alternatives. One group believed that the critical activity that should be measured is the capacity of the heart and lungs. This seems to be included in the early common law definition of death that says that an individual shall be considered dead when there is "a total stoppage . . . of all animal and vital functions."[4]

Precisely what it was about heart and lung activity that was considered critical is not clear. . . . According to this notion, then, an individual should be considered dead when there is the irreversible loss of the capacity for the flowing of these vital fluids.

This is a rather vitalistic notion of the nature of the human being, one that sees the human as merely physico-chemical forces. It totally excludes any concern for integrated functioning or for mental processes. Yet many have apparently held that anyone who has the capacity for the flowing of these fluids ought to be treated as alive.

During this period the alternative position was that the critical loss that signaled the point at which people ought to be treated as dead was the loss of the capacities of the brain. Defenders of this position were frequently not very precise about exactly what it was in the brain that was considered critical. The empirical measures that were performed implied that the critical functions were quite diverse and inclusive. They included a large number of integrating activities, including reflex pathways in the lower brain as well as the centers that control respiration. Thus it has been suggested that holders of this view might have been taking the position at the conceptual level that people should be treated as dead when they have irreversibly lost the neurological capacity to integrate bodily activities. At this point, according to this view, the individual no longer functions as a whole and can therefore legitimately be treated as dead. . . .

THE EARLY 1970S PERIOD

In the early 1970s, however, a new and more complicated question emerged—that is, which brain functions (or structures) are so critical that their loss ought to be considered the death of the individual as a whole. Two major camps emerged in this debate. One held fast to the position that all brain function . . . must be lost.[5] The second group took the view that some functions . . . might remain intact, while it would still be appropriate to treat an individual as dead.[6] The choice was presented dramatically in two case reports by Brierley et al. in *The Lancet*.[7]

The first case was that of a 58-year-old man who had suffered cardiac arrest related to bronchospasm. He was resuscitated with cardiac massage and placed on a respirator. The electroencephalogram was flat from day 3 on. He maintained reflexes after day 1 and respired without the aid of the respirator from day 20 on. He died (based on cardiac criteria) after five months.

The second case involved a 48-year-old man who suffered a massive allergic reaction. He was resuscitated with cardiac massage and mouth-to-mouth breathing. He also had reflexes after the first day, but had a flat electroencephalogram from day 2 onward. He also died after five months (based on cardiac criteria). In both cases on examination after death it was found that tissues in the higher brain (neocortex) were dead while lower-brain centers were intact, showing slight to moderate neuronal loss. The patients at no time met the Harvard criteria purported to measure irreversible coma, yet clearly seemed to be irreversibly comatose.[8]

Once these cases are presented, they reveal that there are at least two quite different positions, each reflecting a different concept of death. Those insisting on the destruction of . . . brain function would consider these patients alive during the period when they possessed brain reflexes and unaided respiration. They breathed spontaneously. Defenders of this view probably hold fast to a concept that death is something like the irreversible loss of the capacity for bodily integration. They specifically recognize that integrated activities mediated through the lower brain, such as respiratory control mechanisms or the cough reflex, represent a level of bodily integration that would be taken as sufficient to justify treating the individual as still alive.

Others, however, have considered these patients dead. They have abandoned the whole-brain view, making it clear that a very different concept of death is operating. They focus on the activities of the higher-brain centers, including such capacities as remembering, reasoning, feeling, thinking, and the like. One underlying concept of the human's nature that might be implied is that the human is essentially a combination of mental and physical activity, both of which must be present for the individual to be alive. According to this view, a capacity for consciousness would be necessary to treat the individual as alive. . . .

A standard might be chosen that focuses on higher-brain function rather than total brain function. This standard is often articulated as the irreversible loss of total cerebral or neocortical function. The exact specification would depend on exactly what functional loss was considered crucial and where that function was localized in the brain. There is substantial debate over whether there can be any exact identification between mental functions and brain functions. Possibly we shall never be able to identify precisely which tissues are responsible for the functions often identified, such as consciousness or thinking or feeling and interacting with one's fellow humans. There is general agreement, however, that without cerebral tissue, these functions are all impossible. To the extent that is true empirically, then the standard for death according to a holder of this position would be the irreversible loss of cerebral function. Some, however, are purposely avoiding speaking of cerebral or neocortical definitions of death because they realize that some cerebral or neocortical functions may survive even if the critical functions are completely lost. They are now speaking in purposely vague language of the higher-brain definition of death. For holders of this view, in contrast with the whole-brain standard, quite clearly a different set of empirical measures or tests would be appropriate for confirming death, ones that single out these higher, presumably cerebral functions.

The emergence of the higher-brain-oriented definition of death since the 1970s has been one of the most important theoretical developments in this entire discussion. Although no nation in the world has adopted the higher-brain formulation and it therefore has little practical importance in the clinic for transplantation or any other clinical purposes, it has reshaped our theoretical understanding of what it means to be dead. . . .

SINCE THE LATE 1970S

This reformulation of the question so as to ask which brain functions are critical has begun to raise additional questions. For instance, once one has moved to a concept of death based on higher-brain function rather than total brain function, one might appropriately ask whether an individual could be considered dead even though certain higher-brain functions remain intact. . . . It is apparent that one of the dangers of the move from total brain function to higher-brain function is that there may be no obvious and clear point to stop the progression to narrower and narrower formulations. Thus there is the potential that

gradually more and more people will literally be defined out of the category of human existence. Some critics of the move to higher-brain function have opposed it not exclusively on the grounds that lower-brain activity is an essential component of life but more on the grounds that once one moves beyond total brain activity it will be impossible to find a point for a public policy at which to stop the regression. They claim that the defenders of the higher-brain positions are on a slippery slope and will not be able to avoid sliding into morally untenable positions that would treat mentally impaired but conscious humans as dead.

Defenders of the move to higher-brain-function notions of death reject this slippery slope or wedge argument. They maintain that it is possible to hold firmly to the notion that an individual should be considered dead when there is loss of consciousness but insist that no compromise be made beyond that point. In fact, I and others who defend the higher-brain formulation have recently begun to turn the slippery slope argument against those who are apparently defending the whole-brain formulations. We argue that there is no principled reason why a line can be drawn between the top of the spinal cord and the base of the brain stem. This means that the defenders of the whole-brain formulations must either acknowledge that activity of the spinal cord should be taken as a sign of life (because it provides integrated nervous system activity not distinguishable from that of the brain stem) or they must concede that some "insignificant" brain functions . . . should be discounted, thus abandoning the true whole-brain position that insists that all functions of the entire brain must be gone for a person to be dead. . . .

The concern about whether irreversible loss of mental function or consciousness can be measured may, in fact, be resolved. At least two major groups have now concluded that, at least in some cases, some irreversible loss of consciousness can be diagnosed with great accuracy.[9]

These practical and theoretical concerns with the attempt to move to a higher-brain-oriented formulation have characterized the debate since the later part of the 1970s. . . .

It is probably . . . impossible to specify clearly what it is about the human that counts as a change so significant that we ought to begin treating that human as if he or she were dead. At best we must come to some common understanding of some general area of bodily structure or function that is so significant that its destruction justifies treating the individual as dead. We may be able to agree that an individual is dead when, say, all brain function is lost even if we cannot agree on exactly what the critical function is.

The question is one that really cannot be taken any further. We must determine what bodily conditions make treating an individual as dead acceptable. It will probably be sufficient to express public policy in terms of general standards for death. Even though those standards have some concept implicit in them, it is clear that greater consensus can be reached on the standards than on the concepts themselves. The three primary candidates are those we have identified: the irreversible cessation of spontaneous respiratory and circulatory functions, the irreversible loss of all spontaneous brain functions, and the irreversible loss of all spontaneous cerebral or higher-brain functions.

The dispute among those holding these positions and the countless variants of the positions has led some of us to conclude that no single whole-brain-oriented concept of death will be able to sustain universal support. Given the countless variations on the three main types of death definitions, there may well be a collapse of the dominant consensus in favor of the whole-brain view. . . .

SOME REMAINING ISSUES

It is clear that there is and will remain controversy over which of the several plausible concepts or standards for pronouncing death ought to be adopted for public policy. Some standard or combination of standards must be chosen at least for public policy purposes.

SHOULD SAFER-COURSE ARGUMENTS PREVAIL?

This raises the question of whether, as a matter of public policy, we ought not to play it safe and choose the policy that will satisfy the most people that an individual is dead without taking a chance of calling someone dead who really should still be considered alive. Some have argued that when we are in doubt about which of several public policies to adopt, we should take the safer course, especially in matters that are literally life and death. The safer-course argument is presumably the one that will avoid treating people as dead who ought to be considered alive.

This safer-course argument might justify abandoning efforts to incorporate concepts or standards of death related exclusively to higher-brain function because many people hold that an individual can be alive even though higher-brain function is lost. There is real doubt in American society over the use of such a standard for death pronouncement. Under a safer-course argument we would move to the more conservative, now older, definition of death that requires that the whole brain be destroyed.

The problem with this safer-course argument is that we would be even safer and more inclusive were we to insist that not only the whole brain but also the heart and lung activity be irreversibly destroyed. In fact, we would be safer still if we were to insist that not only these functions be destroyed but the anatomical structures as well. If we adopted a position that all heart, lung, and brain function and structure must be destroyed, we would satisfy virtually everyone that an individual is indeed dead before being treated as such.

There are difficulties that now become apparent with the safer-course arguments. If there were no practical or theoretical problems with treating people as alive who are in fact dead, we could safely continue a policy of erring on the side of treating people as alive, but it is clear there are good reasons not to do so. There are bad consequences from treating a dead individual as alive. Some of these consequences are very practical. There are financial costs in medical care as well as human agony. There are organs and tissues that would be lost. None of these concerns about consequences would justify treating someone as dead who was really alive, but they do, at least, justify striving for precision in our social understanding of what it means to be dead. And they give us sufficient reason to avoid the extreme applications of the safer-course arguments. At the very least, this means that we can set some conservative limit on when people ought to be treated as dead. The majority of the population now seems prepared to move at least as far as the whole-brain-oriented formulations. . . .

CAN THERE BE VARIATION IN THE PUBLIC DEFINITION OF DEATH?

Because there is such disagreement among members of our society over a definition of death, many have speculated over the difficulties in reaching a policy consensus. In many cases in a pluralistic society, the resolution of this apparent problem is found in pluralism by permitting individual variation based on individual or group preferences. However, the idea of permitting such a variation in the definition of death raises serious problems, each of which should be explored. Three kinds of variation have been considered.

Variation by Expected Use of the Body First, variation might be based on the expected use of the body. Society could endorse varying definitions of death, depending, in part, on whether the body will be used for transplant, research, therapy, or other important purposes. In fact, the original law passed in the state of Kansas[10] appears to do just that. The Kansas statute includes two alternative definitions of death, one based on respiratory and cardiac function and the other based on brain function. The same alternative definitions appear in the Uniform Determination of Death Act,[11] although that law does not specifically state when a particular definition should be used. The implication, however, is that the latter should be used when transplantation is anticipated and the brain is destroyed and the heart continues to beat (because of mechanical support). Likewise, the new definition of death law in Japan permits the use of a brain-oriented definition of death only when organs are to be procured.

Critics of such a variation argue that it seems that whether one is treated as dead or alive should not be contingent on the anticipated use of the corpse. In fact, one could envision bizarre circumstances were alternative standards permitted. A transplant might be anticipated and death pronounced on that basis. But in the interim before the organ is removed from the newly deceased, the planned recipient dies suddenly, so transplant may no longer be anticipated. Or surgeons may discover that the potential donor had cancer or some other risk that excluded organ procurement. If so, there would be confusion over whether the individual continued to be dead according to the originally relevant definition or should suddenly have the other alternative definition applied for the new circumstance.

Variation Depending on the Physician's Preference Second, there is variation by physicians. The policy question is whether physicians should be required or only permitted to use brain-oriented standards when pronouncing death. Should the physician have the choice of whether to use a brain-oriented definition? As a practical matter, this reduces to the question of whether laws should say that a physician shall pronounce death or that a physician may pronounce death when all functions of the brain are irreversibly lost. A model bill by the American Medical Association (AMA), dated January 1979, says, for example, "A physician, in the exercise of his professional judgment, may declare an individual dead in accordance with accepted medical standards. . . ." The immediate bizarre implication is that a physician need not declare an individual dead in accordance with accepted medical standards. He or she might use discretion and choose some other standard. At the very least, this leads to policy confusion. Different physicians seeing the same patient could use different standards for pronouncing death. Thus a physician who sees a patient one afternoon might decide not to use brain-oriented standards, whereas another physician, seeing the patient that evening in exactly the same condition, deciding to use them, could exercise his or her option and pronounce death. In December 1979 at its Interim Meeting the AMA amended its model bill removing the term "may."

In an effort to overcome the ambiguity generated by having several different proposed statutes, the president's commission worked with the AMA, the American Bar Association, and the National Conference of Commissioners on uniform state laws to develop what is referred to as the Uniform Determination of Death Act, which all of these groups have endorsed in place of their previous proposals. It states that:

> An individual who has sustained either (1) irreversible cessation of circulatory and respiratory functions, or (2) irreversible cessation of all functions of the entire brain, including the brain stem, is dead. A determination of death must be made in accordance with accepted medical standards.[12]

As long as this proposal is interpreted as requiring that death must be pronounced if either of these conditions is met, there is no problem of variation from physician to physician. This formulation relies on "accepted medical standards," which, as we have seen, could create a problem if the consensus of the profession about the relative importance of different types of errors is significantly different from the consensus of nonprofessionals. . . .

Variation Based on the Patient's Preferences Third is the variation based on the views of individual patients or their agents. There is overwhelming evidence that citizens differ over precisely what standards should be used for pronouncing death. These differences are rooted in underlying conceptual philosophical and theological differences over the definition of death, having nothing to do with matters requiring knowledge of neurological science. It now seems clear that if any single policy is adopted, some citizens will have their personal convictions about something as basic as the meaning of life and death violated. This suggests that some limited discretion be given to individuals to exercise conscientious objection to a state's chosen definition. . . .

What is at stake is not whether a person's heart or brain has lost function. That presumably is a fact independent of the views of the individual or others. The question is when the person should be treated as dead—that is, when death behaviors become appropriate. Some limited discretion could be given to the individual or others in answering that question. Whether it should be given is, of course, another question.

It seems bizarre that the definition of death should be left to such individual discretion. We have always considered death to be an objective fact. For policy purposes, however, we are not interested in biological, or even in philosophical or theological, formulations, but rather the much more practical question of when people ought to be treated as dead. That clearly is an evaluative question where traditionally individual discretion has been tolerated within limits. The mechanics of tolerating such limited objections or basic philosophical concerns may make the option of permitting variations seem unfeasible to some, yet the alternative of insisting that all operate under the same uniform definition of death regardless of their most deeply held religious and philosophical beliefs is also alien to the American tradition. Although the president's commission recommended adopting the Uniform Determination of Death Act in all jurisdictions in the United States and specifically rejected a "conscience clause" permitting an individual (or family member where the individual is incompetent) to specify the standard to be used for determining death, it also urged ". . . those acting under the statute to apply it with sensitivity to the emotional and religious needs of those for whom the new standards mark a departure from traditional practice," implying possible physician variation in selecting standards.[13] . . .

CONCLUSION

The public policy issues raised by the definition of death are more complex than they appear. There is a growing consensus that some form of brain-oriented definition fits the religious and philosophical convictions of the majority of the population, at least of Western societies. But there is growing doubt about the present whole-brain-oriented definition that requires that literally all functions of the entire brain must be lost before death is pronounced. A minority holds religious convictions that support the traditional heart-oriented definition, whereas others favor some form of a newer higher-brain-oriented definition. The choice among the alternative definitions is fundamentally a religious or philosophical one based on personally held beliefs and values. It is for that reason that the dispute is likely to continue.

NOTES

1. David Sell, "Flyers Goalie Lindbergh Is Declared Brain Dead," *Washington Post*, Nov. 11, 1985, pp. D1, D13.

2. Harvard Medical School, "A Definition of Irreversible Coma, Report of the Ad Hoc Committee of the Harvard Medical School to Examine the Definition of Brain Death," *Journal of the American Medical Association* 205 (1968): 337–40.

3. Ibid., p. 337.

4. *Black's Law Dictionary*, 4th ed., rev. (St. Paul, MN: West, 1968), p. 488.

5. Peter M. Black, "Three Definitions of Death," *The Monist* 60 (1, 1977): 136–46; Dennis J. Horan, "Euthanasia and Brain Death: Ethical and Legal Considerations," *Linacre Quarterly* 45 (3, 1978): 284–96; "Diagnosis of Death," *Lancet* 1 (1, 8110): 261–62; D. L. Stickel, "The Brain Death Criterion of Human Death," *Ethics in Science and Medicine* 6 (Winter 1979): 177–97.

6. Bernard Haring, *Medical Ethics* (Notre Dame, IN: Fides Press, 1973), pp. 131–36; Robert M. Veatch, "The Whole-Brain-Oriented Concept of Death: An Outmoded Philosophical Formulation," *Journal of Thanatology* 3 (1975): 13–30; S. D. Olinger, "Medical Death," *Baylor Law Review* 27 (Winter 1975): 22–26; William H. Sweet, "Brain Death," *New England Journal of Medicine* 299 (1978): 410–11.

7. J. B. Brierley, J. A. H. Adam, D. I. Graham, and J. A. Simpson, "Neocortical Death After Cardiac Arrest," *Lancet* (Sept. 11, 1971): 560–65.

8. Van Till d'Aulnis de Bourouill, Adrienne. "How Dead Can You Be?" *Medical Science Law* 15 (1975): 133–47.

9. Council on Scientific Affairs and Council on Ethical and Judicial Affairs. "Persistent Vegetative State and the Decision to Withdraw or Withhold Life Support," *Journal of the American Medical Association* 263 (1990): 426–30.

10. Kansas State Ann. 77-202 (Supp. 1974).

11. President's Commission for the Study of Ethical Problems in Medicine and Biomedical and Behavioral Research. *Defining Death: Medical, Legal and Ethical Issues in the Definition of Death* (Washington, DC: U.S. Government Printing Office, 1981), p. 2.

12. Ibid.

13. S. D. Olinger, "Medical Death"; President's Commission for the Study of Ethical Problems in Medicine and Biomedical and Behavioral Research. *Defining Death: Medical, Legal and Ethical Issues in the Definition of Death* (Washington, DC: U.S. Government Printing Office, 1981), p. 43.

COURTNEY S. CAMPBELL

Harvesting the Living?: Separating "Brain Death" and Organ Transplantation

Courtney S. Campbell is Professor of Philosophy and the director of the Program for Ethics, Science, and the Environment at Oregon State University. Among his publications are two edited books, *Duties to Others* and *What Price Parenthood?*, as well as numerous professional publications on physician-assisted suicide, reproductive technologies, the status of the body in medicine, and religion and bioethics.

. . . The chronic shortage of solid organ donors has reached critical proportions with no obvious resolution in sight. . . .

What methods can be used to increase the scarce resource without violating important social and ethical values? In the past decade, arguments for commerce in organs have been debated with some frequency. . . . Other proposals have included variations on what has been termed "rewarded gifting," that is, offering potential donors and families certain financial incentives, such as compensation for funeral costs, to permit greater recovery of organs.

Still another alternative for increasing the supply of donor organs is through a reconceptualization of the understanding of "donor" and of "death." Some proposals advocate modifying or abandoning altogether the so-called "dead donor rule". . . , permitting organ retrieval from persons who have not yet met the legal standards for death. In its more dramatic version, this reconceptualization approach would increase the number of prospective donors through revision of the standards or criteria by which death is determined. In particular, leading ethicists have argued for an expanded concept of death, such that current whole-brain standards of death would be supplemented with higher-brain or neocortical criteria of death . . . or even displaced in favor of pre-mortem organ retrieval.

The data collected by Laura Siminoff, Christopher Burant, and Stuart Youngner (2004) furnishes valuable insights for the bioethics community and policymakers into public attitudes about the occurrence of death and assessments of the various options for remedying the organ shortage problem. This information can help bridge the conceptual and practical gaps between professionals, providers, and the general public. Still, I am concerned that data gathered from the public, and incorporated by bioethicists in service of an agenda to bring coherence to the definition of death debate, or to resolve the crisis in scarce organs, can be misread, or selectively used, leading to bad policy and bad ethics. I argue here that the "bridging" work the data do will not provide sufficient grounds for either revising the criteria of death or for modifying the dead donor rule; indeed, either approach will violate important social values upon which the integrity of the transplant process rests. Moreover, I contend that the chronic problem of organ scarcity should prompt bioethicists to revisit the question of the priority of organ transplants in the overall package of healthcare benefits provided to most, but not all, citizens.

PUBLIC PRECAUTIONS

Virtually every scholar who writes on the subject of organ donation contends that the public is very supportive of the practice, and indeed views it as a paradigm illustration of what is meant when one refers to the "miracles" of modern medicine. In many instances,

Reprinted with permission from *Kennedy Institute of Ethics Journal* 14:3 (September 2004), 301–318. Copyright © 2004 by Johns Hopkins University Press.

a transplant literally does rescue a person from the jaws of death. At the same time, the public is held to be somewhat confused and mystified by the process undertaken by transplant teams to recover an organ from a donor whose vital respiratory and circulatory functions are maintained by machines.

Indeed, when the recovery process is publicized, intellectual advocacy and moral commendations for donation can meet the resistance of emotional revulsion. . . . As Gaylin (1974, p. 30) put it, "After all the benefits are outlined, with the lifesaving potential clear, the humanitarian purposes obvious, the technology ready, the motives pure, and the material costs justified—how are we to reconcile our emotions?" It fell to moral philosophers, Gaylin suggested, to be attentive to these conflicts and to work out proposals to enable the use of life-saving technologies, including transplantation technologies, without simultaneously eroding our humanity and the qualities for which life is worth saving.

In the three decades since, I think it likely that the routinization of organ transplants within the medical field has provided an aura of the familiar that has diminished the revulsion. Transplants on their own seldom make it into the headline-grabbing attention of public consciousness; some other possibly scandalous association—a death-row inmate receiving a transplant, a child denied a transplant, racial stratification, or celebrity priorities—seems required for transplant policy to be deemed newsworthy. Philosophical argumentation and institutional implementation also may have had a role in resolving the moral conflict on the side of the rationality of beneficence rather than revulsion. What these influences seem not to have succeeded in doing is to eliminate the confusion over the relationship of death and organ retrieval; indeed, such confusion persists among members of the medical community who are much closer to the actual process than the public. Hence, it is entirely possible that public attitudes about transplantation are not fully clear and coherent, or at least as coherent as is assumed by bioethicists who want to appropriate public perspectives and survey responses in service of policy reform or "progress."

There is an academic or professional culture of bioethics that is somewhat disconnected from the experiences and decisions of a public that is responding to survey questions or having to face such choices as part of their personal or familial healthcare experience. As observed by Stuart Youngner, Robert Arnold, and Renie Schapiro (1999, p. xv):

Debates about the definition and determination of death have occurred almost solely among academics. By all appearances, the public has little understanding or even interest in the issue. . . . What is probably true, based on the evidence we have, is that the public cares a great deal about the actual determination of death but conceptualizes or frames the issues in a very different manner from that of academic physicians, philosophers, lawyers, and social scientists. . . .

This simply means that analysis of public attitudes on organ transplants and brain death requires substantial caution. How might bioethicists apprehend the information revealed by empirical surveys and draw out its normative implications? With no pretension to comprehensiveness, let me suggest several recurrent patterns.

1. One alternative is to support what might be called a *democratic* approach to data. Survey data may show a majority of popular preference for a particular policy, for example, the legalization of physician-assisted suicide. Arguments then can be generated to reform, or to maintain, policy in the direction preferred by the public. This approach should be inadequate for bioethicists, who will need to enquire in greater detail about not simply the conclusions, but also the rationales and values behind the public views. In addition, although the democratic approach has been influential in several venues on bioethics issues . . . bioethicists are likely to be skeptical about deriving a moral imperative or policy "ought" from an empirical fact.

2. A second approach reflects a form of intellectual *authoritarianism*. Bioethicists can be tempted to render an interpretation of public preferences that presumes reliance on their disciplinary canons of rational argumentation. In this circumstance, the professional may be advancing a claim about what the respondents ought to have said if they were thinking clearly and coherently, that is, as a professional bioethicist is supposed to have thought. This can generate moral arguments or policy proposals that are paternalistic even as they are cast in the guise of promoting the public interest.

3. A third method reflects what I think of as bioethical *hermeneutics*. It involves the selective use or appropriation of data to confirm or buttress a position that is already held on other grounds.

The method is analogous to "proof-texting" in theological discussions, in which a particular passage of sacred text is extracted from its narrative and historical context and used to advance a position on an issue like abortion or homosexuality. In both cases, the previously accepted conclusion directs selective (and arbitrary) interpretation of the data.

4. A fourth approach reflects a *pragmatist* understanding. Even though a moral position or policy might be considered not only ethically defensible, but also ethically preferable, it may be deemed impractical or unfeasible when institutional practices are examined through empirical research on public attitudes. This disparity may lead to abandonment or substantial modification of the position or policy. An illustration of this is displayed in the response of some in the bioethics community to the results of the SUPPORT study, which showed that advance directives, patient education, and caregiver communication appears to have minimal impact on the manner of dying (SUPPORT 1995). In light of these and related findings, leading scholars in bioethics seemed to abandon the use of advance directives as a feasible way to promote patient autonomy. As Arthur Caplan (1998, p. 202) asserted: "It is time to head back to the drawing board to seek new approaches to death in a technological age." Similarly, in the context of the controversy over organ procurement and the standards of death, bioethicists may mull over the chronic crisis of organ scarcity, consider public attitudes to death, and answer Robert Truog's (1997) question "Is it time to abandon brain death?" in the affirmative.

These recurrent patterns in the bioethics literature regarding interpretation of the *vox populi* warrant both caution and a greater engagement of bioethics with the social sciences, an issue I return to in the concluding section of this essay. Bioethicists need to see data about public views as illuminating, as setting the questions of bioethics in a new light. Research on public preferences provide a context for understanding how a moral problem can arise or is experienced, but the moral context does not dictate moral content: Public perceptions should not be taken to require prescriptive patterns or normative generalizations.

At the very least, there is a methodological issue to which bioethicists need to be attentive, namely, the strong possibility of differences between what the public will *say* when confronted in the abstract with a scenario laden with ethical choice, and what such individuals actually will *do* when experiencing such a dilemma in "real" life. It is entirely possible that the general attitudes expressed by the public in responding to the abstract dilemma—which is the grist for bioethical reflection—will show greater support for certain policy options deemed as more progressive than will the donating public confronted with actual decisions about the determination of death or the disposition of the organs of their (nearly) deceased relative.

The prospects of disciplinary disconnection, selective interpretation of data, or data appropriation to advance a policy proposal lead me to contend that we should avoid recommending dramatic shifts in existing policies *if* the primary rationale for such a policy shift is that of "public support." My caveat here includes proposals that address defining concepts for humanity such as the idea of "death," as well as the implications of such a shift in this boundary concept for a practice like organ transplantation. There may be other grounds, and legitimate reasons, for adoption of neocortical criteria to determine death or for modification of the dead donor rule, such as philosophical coherence or social utility, but I am not convinced such changes can be grounded in a claim that the public is "on board" with the proposals.

I think moral wisdom lies in requiring the burden of proof to be on those who advocate change from current policies to new criteria for death or for being a donor to show real and tangible, nonspeculative benefits from the changes *and* to show the anticipated benefits occur in greater proportion than the certain harms; the burden should not be on those who defend current policy to demonstrate the harms of forgoing the changes. . . .

THE PUBLIC STAKE IN "BRAIN DEATH"

The professional stake in getting the issue of "brain death" "right" was articulated long ago by Henry Beecher and the Ad Hoc Committee of the Harvard Medical School: first, avoiding the burdens—physical, emotional, financial—to patients, families, and displaced patients of maintaining the biological functions of persons who but for the mechanical interventions would be considered "dead," and second, avoiding controversy in obtaining organs for transplantation

In subsequent years, needs for practical implementation, policy formulation . . . , and philosophical justification of a "brain death" standard became additional interests of professionals involved in the definition-of-death discussion.

I suspect, by contrast, that the principal reason the concept of "brain death" has garnered public attention is due to confusion, perpetuated through media mis-statements about whether a "brain-dead" person is "really dead." Clearly, the public, no less than professionals, has an important stake in a clear and comprehensible understanding of the definition of death. Yet, the insistent need for transplantable organs is ultimately of greater interest for the public than is the discussion and potential resolution of the interesting philosophical puzzles or policy perplexities. Public interest in the "brain death" question is present because it mediates a greater interest in increasing organ procurement, or put another way, we care about the standards of death because of the hope of offering continued life to recipients.

This context is important because some scholars . . . have argued that whole-brain criteria for death are an obstacle to increased organ procurement and some of the data presented in the study by Siminoff and colleagues can be read as supporting such a position. . . . [I]n principle at least, numerous respondents seem to indicate that an *act* of organ donation is more important to them than ensuring that the patient is actually dead prior to organ retrieval.

Supportive attitudes for pre-mortem organ retrieval seem to imply that, subject to obvious limits, the "dead donor rule" may be more a construct of policymakers and academic bioethicists than an actual guiding norm for the public. Alternatively, the data might suggest that the dead donor rule could be reconstructed such that patients in a persistent vegetative condition would now be considered dead. . . .

[B]ut I have three reservations about [the public attitude's] significance as a basis for changing public policy or supporting philosophical positions. First, as John Rawls (1955) argued, it is important to distinguish between *acts* and *practices*. We may be able to justify an act in a particular circumstance as coherent with a world view and as morally permissible. The justification of a practice (or policy) is not, however, contained within the justification of a particular act. The practice or policy must be justified on its own grounds or principles. Hence, from the support of some respondents for pre-mortem organ retrieval in a

limited circumstance, it does not follow that we are warranted in concluding there is significant support for a policy instantiated in a practice in which increasing organ supplies takes preeminence over satisfying current criteria for a determination of brain death.

This leads to a second reservation. The interest in "brain death," I have claimed, resides in its door-opening role to increasing organ procurement. . . . In their responses, the public was much more supportive of both of these procurement proposals than of recovering organs from persons still considered alive. Thus, if the public interest in "brain death" really does rest on its ramifications for organ transplantation, then I think the responsibility of the bioethics community is first to explore, advocate, and argue about alternatives that involve re-envisioning notions of "consent" and "donation" rather than to engage in a reconstruction of the concept of "death."

There is a third reason to approach the apparent willingness to approve pre-mortem organ retrieval with great caution. It is one thing to contend that the public is confused in its understanding of, or inconsistent in its application of, current "brain death" criteria and that the dead donor rule replicates, and perpetuates, this confusion at the policy level. It is quite another to say that this confusion can be exploited to the point that the dead donor rule must be modified to encompass PVS patients or abandoned. It is unlikely that public confusion over "whole-brain death" can be supplanted readily by enlightened clarity regarding "neocortical death."

There may be legitimate reasons for reconstructing the dead donor rule so it expands the definition of deceased persons from whom organs can be recovered. However, those arguments already have been developed and would be advocated regardless of what the public survey data reveal or conceal. . . .

RULE OR MAXIM?

Another interpretation of the finding of some public support for pre-mortem organ recovery is possible. Perhaps the attitude reflects neither confusion over "whole-brain death" nor dissatisfaction with an inadequate rule. Moreover, the view may not represent an uninformed public that is "lagging behind" the policy and ethical discussions. On the contrary, this finding could be interpreted as populist progressivism, a public view about the priority of organ transplants as a life-saving technology that is "ahead" of even the cutting edge of both medicine and its academic commentators. This would not be without precedent: In other contexts of bioethics, such as physician-assisted suicide, public opinion has driven changes in both medical practice and in public policy. . . . In this interpretation, the dead donor rule possesses no binding or prescriptive force, but functions as a moral maxim. A maxim is a summation and generalization of the received wisdom from the past. It can provide guidance, of course, but it also can be discarded as the circumstances arise, particularly circumstances of social utility.

Treating the dead donor rule as a maxim would allow both the law and medicine to dispense with various imposed requirements that are tantamount to fictions and ritualistic charades performed for the sake of compliance with the rule. Norman Fost, among others, has long argued that these impositions impede the prospect for medical treatment and social gains from donation after "cardiac-death" protocols. . . . (Fost 1999, pp. 172–74). . . .

I do not find the pre-mortem organ retrieval proposal compelling because it does not deal adequately with the very real fact of public distrust of institutions and systems, including distrust of the medical transplant system. In the mid-1980s, the two primary reasons cited for public unwillingness to sign organ donor cards were fears that physicians might take action prematurely to obtain organs or that physicians might hasten death. . . . The image of physician as devourer of the patient, rather than rescuer of the recipient, seemed quite prominent. Given the various economic and bureaucratic incentives that have permeated medicine the last two decades, and the concomitant emergence of a *caveat emptor* ethos in medicine, as well as the general decline of trust in public institutions, I am very dubious that the level of distrust in medicine as a system has diminished.

It may be countered, however, that generalized distrust in medicine is one thing and that the particularities of transplant medicine has or can escape this diminished trust. In particular, an element of what might be called the "constituency" factor can work to mitigate the distrust. The constituency factor in medicine appears similar to that in politics: as a citizen, one can be distrustful, even contemptuous, toward "the government," but nonetheless be strongly and trustingly supportive of one's own representative. Similarly, it is possible to imagine a nearly-deceased patient and his or her family who are generally distrustful of the "system" or institution of medicine. However, when approached by their personal physician about pre-mortem organ retrieval, they may be very cooperative and compliant because of their familiarity with the physician and their long history of a professionally respectful and caring relationship. . . .

RESISTING THE TECHNOLOGICAL IMPERATIVE

There are few better examples of the technological imperative at work in contemporary medicine than in the incessant demand to increase organ procurement. There is little question that the technology is available to provide life-extension, or that it is becoming increasingly proficient. Yet, the number of persons on waiting lists for organs increases by several thousand every year, and those who die while on waiting lists by several hundred. The principal impediment in this social enterprise has been, and continues to be, the limited number of transplantable organs.

In order to comply with the technological imperative, the bioethics community is now giving serious consideration to proposals that modify the dead donor rule and/or support pre-mortem organ retrieval. That is, so compelling is the imperative of transplantation technology that leading scholars are willing to argue that society change the criteria for the determination of death again, or permit medical professionals to take the lives of those who are not dead by any standard.

Increasing organ supplies through such measures seems to me to indicate a good we want too much. The reservations of theological ethicist William F. May (1991, p. 183) seem relevant: "a tinge of the inhuman marks the humanitarianism of those who believe that social need [for organs] overrides all other considerations. . . ." I contend that the moral and social costs embedded in these procurement proposals are excessive. A revision of the dead donor rule to accommodate neocortical criteria for death presupposes an essentialist conception of the person as a disembodied consciousness. The advocacy of pre-mortem organ retrieval necessitates carving out a new exception in homicide law to the prohibition of killing in medicine. These are hardly existentially or ethically innocuous considerations, but they are morally minimized by the relentless insistence on "more" from transplantation's technology imperative.

Moreover, there is no guarantee that such proposals will solve the problem of organ scarcity, and precedent for thinking they will exacerbate that problem.

In the last two decades, the expectations that a few thousand more organs would become available each year via public educational programs and adoption of routine-inquiry protocols have not materialized, nor have these measures, as was anticipated, alleviated the problem of organ scarcity. Instead, continued refinements and successes in transplantation medicine have so increased patient expectations that the waiting list has increased four-fold from the 1980s. . . .

Although normative ethics cannot, on my view, be reduced to eliciting the preferences of individual persons or of the broader public, attentiveness and incorporation of such public views is one criterion of adequacy of a normative ethic. Moreover, bioethical theory needs to be open to revision and modification when studies provide empirical evidence of public views that run contrary to what the theory had assumed as a given. . . .

A second challenge for the bioethics community consists in examining whether the criteria for determining death are entirely socially constructed and thereby subject to ongoing evolution and manipulation in accordance with social needs. The irreversible cessation of certain biological functioning in the human organism is an occurrence that we mark by the term "death." This also signifies a shift in ontological status; the corpse of the deceased is open to medical manipulations, from organ retrieval to autopsy, that are precluded by law and ethics from being conducted on the living person, and the community engages in various rituals surrounding the disposition of the body to memorialize the person.

As noted previously, there are important social interests embedded in this question, including avoiding both premature determination of death as well as post-death assaults on the body, and in making decisions about when technologies of life extension legitimately can be terminated as well as initiated. Yet, it is also clear that social constructions of death cannot be disconnected from the underlying biological phenomenon. The dispute centers on which biological venue is socially and ontologically significant. . . . In short, the bioethics community continues to have work to do to articulate criteria for the determination of death that meet standards of philosophical defensibility, biological adequacy, and public intelligibility. . . .

A third challenge concerns the degree of continuity or extent of separation between the medical and philosophical debates about the standards for determining death and the social policy interest in increasing organ procurement. Clearly, the former has implications for the latter; a non-brain-based standard will preclude most organ retrieval and subsequent transplantation and a higher-brain standard will expand both practices substantially. What raises legitimate concern, I believe, is when the relationship is reversed and the goal of organ procurement, or its lower than desired recovery ratio, directs the standard of death that society adopts.

It is a momentous undertaking to render and reform understandings of the defining boundaries—"life" and "death"—of human existence. Reconstructing these understandings to accommodate needs for transplantable organs will permeate the transplantation process with distrust and suspicion—were these organs recovered from the living or the dead?—and infuses the philosophic discussion with arbitrariness—does it really matter how we answer the preceding question?

My contention is that the discussion of the criteria used in the determination of death needs to proceed according to its own scientific and philosophic logic, and not be driven by the pragmatic interest in procurement. There are, moreover, numerous possible alternatives to increase transplantable organs short of revising the current standard of death or of resorting to harvesting from the living. If bioethics is to be taken seriously about its rhetoric of self-determination as a critical factor in social policy, it must examine these other alternatives, seek to implement them, and evaluate their efficacy, prior to meaningful consideration of an alternative, such as pre-mortem organ retrieval, that receives the least support among the sampled public.

Finally, in concluding this essay, I return to an issue highlighted at the outset and challenge the bioethics community to have the courage to take seriously the question of the priority of organ transplants relative to other modes of healthcare. The Oregon Health Plan, now in its second decade, displays qualified acceptance by a large public constituency of a policy priority to forgo technologies of life extension, including some transplant technologies, so that more equitable access to preventive care services can be provided. Some priorities reflect a willingness to say an anguished "no" to present, identifiable patients on some matters of great expense that benefit one person in order to secure a better health future for the collective interests of the rising generation.

There are numerous philosophical arguments that contend current healthcare priorities, which emphasize rescue medicine—for which transplantation is the paradigm example—are badly misplaced. . . .

This is the social justice challenge that the bioethics community needs to take up with a vigor equal to that displayed in debates over "whole-brain death" and increasing organ procurement. A dialogue over healthcare priorities can be informed by philosophical and religious traditions about both sharing of self and about meaningful death that can give point and purpose to the practice of organ transplantation. Ultimately, the commitment to justice is a distinctive mark and sign of the ethical seriousness of bioethics.

REFERENCES

Caplan, Arthur. 1998. *Due Consideration: Controversy in the Age of Medical Miracles*. New York: John Wiley & Sons.

Childress, James F. 1997. *Practical Reasoning in Bioethics*. Bloomington: Indiana University Press.

Fost, Norman. 1999. The Unimportance of Death. In *The Definition of Death: Contemporary Controversies*, ed. Stuart J. Youngner, Robert M. Arnold, and Renie Schapiro, pp. 161–178. Baltimore, MD: Johns Hopkins University Press.

Gaylin, Willard. 1974. Harvesting the Dead. *Harpers* (September): 23–30.

Harvard Medical School Ad Hoc Committee. 1968. A Definition of Irreversible Coma. Report of the Ad Hoc Committee of the Harvard Medical School to Examine the Definition of Brain Death. *JAMA* 205: 337–40.

LifeSharers. 2003. Solicitation received from David J. Undis, Executive Director, June 5. Available at www.lifesharers.com. Accessed 9 July 2004.

May, William F. 1991. *The Patient's Ordeal*. Bloomington: Indiana University Press.

Rawls, John. 1955. Two Concepts of Rules. *Philosophical Review* 64: 3–32.

Siminoff, Laura A. 2002. Presentation at conference on Brain Death and Organ Transplantation, Case Western Reserve University, 15 November.

———; Burant, Christopher; and Youngner, Stuart J. 2004. Death and Organ Procurement: Public Beliefs and Attitudes. *Social Science & Medicine*, 59(11): 2325–34.

SUPPORT. 1995. A Controlled Trial to Improve Care for Seriously Ill Hospitalized Patients. *JAMA* 274: 1591–98.

D. MICAH HESTER

Why We Must Leave Our Organs to Others

D. Micah Hester is Assistant Professor of Medical Humanities and Pediatrics at the University of Arkansas for Medical Sciences, as well as clinical ethicist at Arkansas Children's Hospital. His book *Community As Healing* develops a pragmatist ethic for physician–patient relationship. His current research is leading toward the publication of books on end-of-life care ethics and on educating hospital ethics committees.

Organ procurement presents several ethical concerns (from what constitutes acceptable criteria for death to issues involved in specifically designating to whom an organ can be given), but none is more central than the concern for what are appropriate means for *acquiring* organs. For more than three decades now, the call

to procure organs to use in transplantation has markedly grown louder, but "supply" simply has not kept up with "demand." This fact is well known, and the statistics, although often recounted, remain quite telling. According to the United Network for Organ Sharing (UNOS) [in] 2006, approximately 92,000 patients [were] candidates for organ transplantation (e.g., more than 66,000 for kidneys alone). This is more than a 100% increase from 10 years ago. At the same time, only about 28,000 transplant operations were performed in 2005 (e.g., approximately 16,000 kidney transplants), and these numbers represent only about a 40% increase from 10 years ago (UNOS website).

In response, various strategies have been proposed to aid in the task of increasing procurement rates. . . .

However, while these . . . processes may, in fact, identify *morally* acceptable *biological* conditions for procurement, that identification provides no guarantee that patients (or their families/surrogates) will, in reality, allow organs to be made available for transplantation. Thus, rather than trying to identify such conditions, the most common and public mode of addressing the procurement issue has been through direct appeals to the populace at-large, and such strategies have traditionally taken one of two lines. The most widely accepted approach to raising the procurement rate has been an appeal to charity . . . , and this model undergirds all legally sanctioned procurement in the United States. Organ *donation* (the very term bespeaks "charity"), in this sense, has been characterized as a precious and vital *gift* to be made from one person to another. It is considered, in the language of ethics, to be supererogatory—beyond our moral obligations, but highly laudable. The metaphor has even taken root in public policy with the development of the Uniform Anatomical Gift Act (1972–1987), to encourage (and protect) donors and donations.

The most vocal alternative strategy has been one of commodification—an economic appeal or market-based model, as it were, . . . While not legally accepted in the United States, it has been argued (primarily on liberal—even libertarian—autonomy basis) that monetary incentives should be offered to potential donors. Though it eventually reversed its policy, India (as one example) has allowed for the use of monetary incentives, but the argument has never won the day in the United States. . . . Each side in this debate has put forth strong reasons why the other fails as an acceptable strategy to procure organs, but ultimately, neither puts forth sufficient support for its own position. Both sides fundamentally miss the moral point because both sides implicitly and falsely accept that organ procurement must be the result of a voluntary and supererogatory act. However, as will be argued, the call to relinquishing organs upon our deaths begins as what some would call a *prima facie* or even *ordinary* obligation, and what has also been referred to as a *de facto* obligation. As others have pointed out, charity is morally weak, and requires little of us and others. . . . This article, in

kind, argues for a stronger moral claim, one that becomes further strengthened as this *de facto* claim quickly becomes a *de jure* (i.e., moral) obligation—that is, as it becomes a "final" moral good worthy of our pursuit, in the face of no significant and comparable obligation or loss to ourselves on our deaths. . . .

The following, then, will attempt to refocus the issue away from an appeal to our charitable consciences or our pocketbooks. Instead, as intimated by Caplan (1992, 156–157) and addressed directly by Nelson (2003a), the following argues that relinquishing our organs after death in this day and age is, in fact, *obligatory* for most people. Each of us is pressed by the growing demand for our organs should we die according to acceptable procurement standards, and that desperate need has risen to such a level that not to release our organs for transplantation . . . would constitute a serious moral wrong.

The focus of this article is primarily theoretical—by which is meant that the argument contained herein relies on a moral logic. Whereas many articles on organ procurement begin with a concern about the need to increase procurement rates (and it is agreed that this is a serious practical concern), the argument that follows does not primarily aim to increase procurement. It may, in fact do so, but the central purpose of the argument is to ground our procurement practices on the surest moral footing possible. To do so, the argument begins from a basic assumption about ethical theory and the moral life—namely, that we are obligated to do what we can to save seriously endangered lives when we can do so without risking anything of significant value to us.[1] Without accepting this assumption, the argument that follows will rest insecurely within its own ethical moorings.

Granting the previous assumption about the moral life, then, the first premise is straightforward—namely, saving a life is a good which is worthy of pursuit. Unless circumstances dictate that undue harm or potential harm (whether, in the case of transplants, to the recipient or the person from whom the organ is procured) would result from life-saving measures, attempts at saving someone who would foreseeably die otherwise is a moral good.

[1]In fact, *any* viable conception of "what we owe to each other" must recognize this basic obligation. Although the phrase is from the deontologically-minded Thomas Scanlon (2000), some version of this simple moral point can be found in other deontologists such as Ross (2003), utilitarians such as Mill (1975) and Singer (1972) . . . among many others.

Second, the use of organ transplantation is a medically and ethically appropriate means to saving a life. On the whole transplants have proven to be relatively safe surgeries that extend the lives of those who have them, and transplants do so without grave harm to either the transplant patients themselves or to others. As such transplantation has demonstrated that it is not simply a case of the technological imperative running amok, but a socially positive use of ingenuity and technology in medicine.

Similarly, my third premise should be easily accepted: Namely, those who await organ transplantation *must* rely on others—physicians, nurses, benefactors, and most importantly, "donors." It may seem trivial, but it is worth emphasizing that transplant patients cannot fulfill their needs without *someone else* coming through *for* them. Also, in most cases, patients find themselves in need of a transplant through no moral failing of their own. It cannot be denied that nutrition, lifestyle and personal choice can lead to heart disease, cirrhosis and other organ-compromising disease. As such, some imply (if not claim outright) that, for example, alcoholics require liver transplants because of their moral failure to stop excessive drinking. . . . Of course, the importance of volition implied here cannot be minimized. It seems false to say that eating habits are strictly willful acts or that excessive drinking is primarily a chosen avocation. There is ample evidence, for example, that many, if not most, alcoholics develop as a consequence of genetic and environmental factors beyond their own decisive control; also, diets routinely fail even in the face of willful determination. Even if psychological and moral factors can be brought to bear to pronounce negatively on some potential recipients, surely the medical situations many patients find themselves in do not contain such morally questionable circumstances and, even when they do, genetic and biological factors at least mitigate some degree of moral responsibility. Further, many of these concerns would affect allocation, rather than procurement, decisions. Fourth, it is clear that the demand for organs is high, and those organs are vital to the patients who need them. Transplantation fulfills a basic and important good to those who receive the organs. Every year, approximately over 6,000 people on the UNOS waiting list die still waiting for a transplant. Many others wait in various stages of deteriorating health for upwards of 5 years or more. At the same time tens of thousands of kidney patients, in particular, must go through dialysis, which not only produces its own negative side-effects—both physiological and psychological . . .—but also reduces transplant success rates as well. . . .

Fifth, the most complex premise remains: Dead persons have no embodied countervailing interests that could trump the vital interests of potential transplant patients. Bodies, although significant symbols of the life once inhabiting them, have no need for the organs that remain after death. The question raised, then, is what harm could be done to now-dead persons if organs are taken without direct consent? Aristotle and others have noted that it is still possible to be harmed after one's death. The question, then, is whether any potential harms could be serious enough to affect the powerful obligation to save a life. Nelson (2003a), for one, does not think so, which follows from both "beneficence" and what Nelson calls the "easy rescue" (118–120). In a brief commentary, Nelson notes that "fastidiousness" about one's dignity, which might preclude them from consenting to life-saving acts, is not morally supportable—his argument turning on the "virtually costless" nature of certain kinds of life saving acts like organ release over-and-against the clearly beneficial nature of organ transplantation (2003b, 14).

Of course, some groups believe that the removal of organs from a dead person can itself be a form of disrespect. These claims are often made in light of larger value-systems, such as religious beliefs. For example, though most religious organizations accept donation as "charitable," none require it . . . ; at the same time some groups, such as the orthodox Jews, strict Jehovah's Witnesses, some Amish, and Confucians . . . , have particular reluctances, and still others such as the Shinto in Japan find the dead body impure and thus find procurement and transplantation inherently troubling. . . .

Such claims, however, seem difficult to support, even for long-standing religious institutions, in the face of deep moral concerns for potentially dying persons. The extent to which the body is symbolic of the person should not be discounted, but even a well-established belief system that claims that only whole-bodied persons can gain glory in an afterlife must address the question of what "shape" a body must be in and why. Does heart disease, for example, constitute an unclean bodily form, and if not, which cellular and functional apparatus must be present and which need not be? Of course, it could be claimed that even raising the question against such belief systems employs a kind of a category error that reduces bodily integrity merely to biological processes rather than utilizing spiritual language and concepts. Of course, there is a stronger argument to be made—namely, any spiritual or philosophical value system that leads to failure of ethical duties to others in your society should be held accountable for the moral weaknesses that follow. Respect and disrespect are paid to persons/moral agents, not to bodies per se. In the face of the need for healthy organs for living human beings, spiritual concepts that champion a spiritual notion of bodily integrity over helping others survive seems misguided. Instead, procurement from dead bodies should be championed as no violation of what respect is due to formerly embodied persons, but instead the fulfillment of one's moral duty.

Lastly, it may be useful to emphasize the prevailing limiting factor employed throughout this article—namely, while some demands on us would require the loss of a significant good in order to be fulfilled, relinquishing *cadaveric* organs requires no such loss. The previous argument, thus, is delimited by a practical fact—namely, the current dangers of surgery and the vital character of our organs to our own well being, weaken the force of both the second and fifth premises, leaving *live* donations as a supererogatory act. Further, as Truog (2005) has argued, cadaveric organs "should be regarded as a societal resource," not as personal property. Nelson concurs, "We ought to move closer toward seeing such organs as communal resources, and hence, as routinely retrievable" (Nelson 2005, 26). And while living donor organs may become societal resources, there is no debate that living individuals must consent to make them available to the pool of potential recipients. At the same time, though, these facts are deeply contextual, and continual protections and techniques of surgery for live donations as well as further development of the socioethical landscape may, in the future, raise the moral stakes to the level of obligation even for procurement from living individuals. Either way, concerns for surgical and general health risks, as well as legitimate morally-based property claims, do not apply in cadavers, creating a heightened moral requirement.

Thus, without need to draw out the logical conclusion, given the basic moral assumption as well as the stated premises and conditions concerning organ transplantation and procurement, each of us has a moral obligation to relinquish our organs for transplantation on our deaths.

The previous argument above makes a strong moral claim, one typically avoided (if not disparaged) in the transplantation ethics literature. However, one remaining practical matter concerns the very real existence of fear that organ procurement already occurs under questionable circumstance, and that the medical establishment supports the hastening of death *in order to* procure organs. Sociological research has already shown that such a fear exists within the current system. In particular, African-American physicians have long argued that organ "conscription" or even presumed consent policies would heighten an already complex attitude of distrust . . . within the African-American community towards medicine. . . . The particularly strong moral stance of the previous argument could be seen as ratcheting up the conditions that lead to such fear all the more with the view that if organ removal is morally required, then coercive measures to "harvest" organs might be more common, such as inappropriately withholding treatment in order to secure death sooner.

This concern, along with concerns of those who hold that organ retrieval after death is spiritually disrespectful, will strike many as a significant problem for the argument on practical/policy grounds, primarily because this society's liberal democratic valuing of autonomy and personal safety requires the use of a certain level of decisional latitude in decisions that affect us—including our bodies. Of course, strict moral logic might require a very strong policy, but important social values such as autonomy and safety might mitigate against strong policy precisely to leave room for those persons who hold the kinds of beliefs that would problematically pit organ procurement against other strongly held values. This raises the relationship between moral argument and public policy. Theory devoid of practical concerns is bound to fail, whereas practical decisions without moral grounding risk being unethical. The given argument provides careful moral reasoning concerning organ procurement; what must be taken up next is how such moral findings would be implemented given cultural conditions operative in the United States.

Thus, while the argument morally grounds the obligation to relinquish our organs after death, the concerns of those who find organ removal after death disrespectful have implications for how to deal with this moral obligation in public policy. In other words, it might seem to follow that because organ release has been shown to be an ethical obligation, we should write our laws in such a way that each of us is legally required to donate, thus matching law with morality. . . . However, that such laws should be developed is not an implication to be drawn by necessity.

And yet, while practical concerns like these are not to be ignored (and, in fact, are central to crafting ethically and medically successful public policy), the issue in this article is simply whether a *moral* case for obligatory removal can be made. Certainly, if there is a strong case for the obligation to give organs on death, then to develop ethically appropriate *means* to the implications of such an argument, there would have to be careful attention paid to the details of implementation. However, the difficulty of those details cannot be allowed to settle (by precluding) the question of whether we are morally obligated to give our organs. Thus, the moral argument for releasing our organs on death remains strong and valuable.

REFERENCES

Caplan, A. L. 1992. Requests, gifts, and obligations. In *If I were a rich man could I buy myself a pancreas?* A. L. Caplan (ed.), 145–157 Bloomington, IN: Indiana University Press.

Gundle, K. 2005. Presumed consent: an international comparison and possibilities for change in the United States. *Cambridge Quarterly of Healthcare Ethics* 14(1): 113–118.

Janssen, A., and S. Gevers. 2005. Explicit or presumed consent and organ donation post-mortem: Does it matter? *Medicine and Law* 24(3): 575–583.

Mill, J. S. 1975. *On liberty*. London, U.K.: Penguin Books.

Nelson, J. L. 2003a. *Hippocrates' maze*. New York, NY: Rowman & Littlefield.

Nelson, J. L. 2003b. Harming the dead and saving the living. *American Journal of Bioethics* 3(1): 13–15.

Nelson, J. L. 2005. Trust and transplants. *American Journal of Bioethics* 5(4): 26–28.

Ross, W. D. 2003. *The right and the good*. Oxford, UK: Oxford University Press.

Scanlon, T. M. 2000. *What we owe to each other*. Cambridge, MA: Belknap Press.

Singer, P. 1972. Famine, affluence, and morality. *Philosophy & Public Affairs* 1: 229–243.

Truog, R. 2005. Are organs personal property or a societal resource? *American Journal of Bioethics* 5(4): 14–16.

United Network for Organ Sharing (UNOS) website, www.OPTN.org. [accessed May 22, 2006]

JAMES F. CHILDRESS

Putting Patients First in Organ Allocation: An Ethical Analysis of the U.S. Debate

James F. Childress is the Hollingsworth Professor of Ethics and Professor of Medical Education at the University of Virginia, where he directs the Institute for Practical Ethics. He has written extensively on various aspects of bioethics, particularly euthanasia and access to health care. He is the author of numerous articles and several books in biomedical ethics, including *Principles of Biomedical Ethics* (with Tom L. Beauchamp), *Priorities in Biomedical Ethics, Who Should Decide? Paternalism in Health Care*, and *Practical Reasoning in Bioethics*.

INTRODUCTION

Organ allocation policy involves a mixture of ethical, scientific, medical, legal, and political factors, among others. It is thus hard, and perhaps even impossible, to identify and fully separate ethical considerations from all these other factors. Yet I will focus primarily on the ethical considerations embedded in the current debate in the United States about organ allocation policy. I will argue that it is important to *put patients first*—in the language of the title of one of the major public hearings[1]— but even then significant ethical questions will remain about exactly *how* to put patients first.

I would not characterize the current organ-allocation system in the United States as fundamentally unfair or unjust, in part because there are debates about various criteria of fairness and justice and in part because the United Network for Organ Sharing (UNOS), the national Organ Procurement and Transplantation Network (OPTN) operating under a contract with the federal government's Department of Health and Human Services (DHHS), has made substantial progress over time. However, I do believe that organ allocation policy can be further improved—largely by putting patients across the nation first, apart from particular professional and institutional interests. . . .

Reprinted with permission from *Cambridge Quarterly of Healthcare Ethics* 10 (October 2001), 365–376. Copyright © 2001 by Cambridge University Press.

DEBATES ABOUT THE COMMUNITY OF OWNERSHIP OF DONATED ORGANS

I had the good fortune to serve as vice-chair of the federal Task Force on Organ Transplantation, which in April 1986 issued its report *Organ Transplantation: Issues and Recommendations*.[2] One of this task force's major responsibilities, as mandated by the National Organ Transplant Act, was to make "recommendations for assuring equitable access by patients to organ transplantation and for assuring the equitable allocation of donated organs among transplant centers and among patients medically qualified for an organ transplant." It took me some time to discern that our debates about "equitable access" and "equitable allocation" were, in part, debates about who "owns" donated organs.

Apart from special cases of directed donation to named recipients, donated organs *belong to* the community, the public, and not to procurement and transplant teams. This fundamental conviction undergirded the Task Force's deliberations about and recommendations for equitable organ allocation: Donated organs should be viewed as scarce public resources for use for the welfare of the community. Organ procurement and transplant teams receive these donated organs as "trustees" and "stewards" on behalf of the whole community. Thus, they should not have unlimited dispositional authority over donated organs.

Over the years since the Task Force's report, the term "community" has been widely but variously used. Unfortunately, it has often been excessively narrowed. In the current debate it frequently means the "transplant community," which is sometimes limited to transplant surgeons, professionals, and their institutions, though it sometimes includes organ donors, organ recipients, transplant candidates, and their families. But even the latter interpretation of "community" is still too narrow because it fails to include the larger community, which comprises not only all these parties but all of us as *potential donors* and *potential recipients* (and relatives of potential donors and potential recipients). Policies of organ allocation should be designed *for* the public as a whole.

This view of community ownership of and dispositional authority over donated organs provides strong support for wide and diverse public participation in setting the criteria for allocating donated organs. Calls for public participation stem in part from the nature of organ procurement in the United States—it depends on voluntary, public gifts; that is, gifts by individuals and their families to the community. Indeed, there are important moral connections between policies of organ procurement and policies of organ allocation. On the one hand, the success of policies of organ procurement may reduce scarcity and hence obviate some of the difficulties in organ allocation. On the other hand, distrust is a major reason for the public's reluctance to donate organs, and policies of procurement may be ineffective if the public perceives the policies of organ allocation as unfair and thus untrustworthy. In short, public participation—for example, in the Organ Procurement and Transplantation Network (OPTN)—is very important and even indispensable to ensure actual and perceived fairness. "Organ allocation falls into the region of public decision-making," as Jeffrey Prottas insists, "not medical ethics and much less medical tradition."[3] Thus, policies of organ allocation should be designed, in part, *by* the public.

Two additional points about community ownership of donated organs and public participation in setting organ allocation criteria merit attention. First, while observing that prior to 1986 organs donated for transplantation had effectively belonged to the surgeons who removed them, Prottas contends that the fundamental philosophical shift to community ownership effected by the Task Force report both changed matters and left them the same. On the one hand, professional

dominance remains, in part because of technical expertise and medical gatekeeping. On the other hand, professional dominance is now more circumscribed and publicly accountable. With organ allocation now in the public domain, in part because transplant professionals had sought governmental assistance for transplantation, there are now more participants, particularly public participants, and the terms of the debate have changed:

Alternative allocation systems are now defended in public debate, and equity as well as efficiency must be considered and defined. Physicians dominate the debate, through knowledge as well as power, but they must justify their actions now as trustees of the public. The organs are no longer theirs.[4]

Second, some ambiguities about community ownership persist in debates in the OPTN and elsewhere about policies of organ allocation: Do donated organs belong to the national community or to regional, state, or local communities? Whereas different answers to this question may or may not lead to different policies, they certainly create different presumptions and pose different problems. Nevertheless, from either starting point, various arguments may support using organs on one geographical level rather than another. If we start from local (or state or regional) "ownership" of donated organs, then organs would be allocated first in the local community, perhaps subject to some requirements to "share" organs (e.g., a zero-antigen mismatch in kidney transplantation). If, however, the relevant community for organ distribution is the national community, as I believe it is, then that community has the right and the responsibility to allocate the organs to patients anywhere in the country according to acceptable standards and logistical constraints. Nevertheless, it may and often should allow organs to be used at the local level, if, for instance, transporting those organs would jeopardize their viability for transplantation. Such logistical problems remain especially important for heart and lung transplantation, somewhat important for liver transplantation (where the situation has improved), but only modestly important for kidney transplantation.

Although logistical problems thus remain variably important, there is nothing more than anecdotal evidence, to the best of my knowledge, to warrant the additional common claim that local allocation provides a substantial incentive for organ donation that would be lost under a national system. A truly national approach should reduce the relevance of "accidents of geography" in organ allocation and allow such geographical factors to enter only when and where they are clearly relevant for transplantation outcomes.

In short, it is now time to return to the Task Force's conception of the national community as the relevant community of dispositional authority in organ allocation and to take steps to minimize "accidents of geography"—accidents regarding where transplant candidates live or are listed—in organ allocation to the greatest extent possible with the use of the best available technologies for each type of organ. The moral point is not that the local community should "share" some organs it obtains with the larger, national community—the language of "sharing" suggests that the local community "owns" the donated organs. Rather, donated organs belong to the national community, and the "trustees" and "stewards" of those organs should allocate them according to criteria that minimize "accidents of geography" in putting patients first.

PRINCIPLES OF JUST, FAIR, AND EQUITABLE ALLOCATION

JUSTICE AND MORALLY RELEVANT AND IRRELEVANT CHARACTERISTICS

To state the last point differently, it is, in my judgment, generally *unjust* to use "accidents of geography" in organ allocation because they are not morally relevant to who should receive donated organs (unless, again, local or regional priority is required because transporting the organs would be impossible or would adversely affect their viability for transplantation). But what exactly is justice, and how should principles of justice function in organ allocation?

Justice, which may be defined as rendering to each person his or her due, includes both formal and material criteria. The *formal* criterion of justice involves similar treatment for similar cases or equal treatment for equals. Various *material* criteria of justice specify relevant similarities and dissimilarities among parties and thus determine how particular benefits and burdens will be distributed. There is debate about the *moral relevance* and *moral weight* of different material criteria, such as need, merit, societal contribution, status, and ability to pay. Different theories of justice tend to stress different material criteria. However, some material criteria may be acceptable in some areas of life, such as employment, but not in others, such as the allocation of scarce life-saving organ transplants.

Even though principles of justice permit rationing under conditions of scarcity, they rule out allocation criteria that are based on morally irrelevant characteristics, such as race or gender. However, it is much easier to agree on what is unjust, such as distribution by gender or race, than on what is just. A fundamental question concerns which material criteria satisfy the requirements of justice and are justifiable for organ allocation. As I have argued, public participation is one way—but only one way and by no means sufficient—to reduce possible biases from particular professional or institutional interests in the public process of determining which material criteria are relevant to organ allocation. In short, public participation is one way to put patients first.

JUST MATERIAL CRITERIA IN ORGAN ALLOCATION: PATIENT NEED, PROBABILITY OF SUCCESS, AND TIME ON THE WAITING LIST

There is general agreement that three material criteria are relevant, just, and justifiable in organ allocation—patient need, probability of a successful outcome, and time on the waiting list. These are recognized in UNOS policies, which attempt to balance them but which then allow local priority to produce "accidents of geography." They are also evident in the DHHS regulations, which, however, pay insufficient attention to the probability of a successful outcome, particularly in relation to the other two criteria.

The first two material criteria—patient need and probability of a successful outcome—appear at two major stages in organ allocation: (1) forming a waiting list by determining the pool of transplant candidates, and (2) allocating available organs to patients on the waiting list. The third material criterion—time on the waiting list—obviously applies only at the second stage of allocation. The difficult ethical and practical questions at each stage involve *specifying* the criteria—what exactly do they mean, how can we measure them, and so forth?—and *weighting* them in case they conflict—should one take priority over the others, should allocation policies attempt to balance them, and so forth? Even though there is little dispute about the general relevance of these three criteria, and much of that dispute focuses on waiting time rather than the other two criteria, vigorous and widespread debate occurs about how to specify and weight all three criteria.

SETTING CRITERIA FOR ADMISSION TO WAITING LISTS

There is general agreement that the waiting list of transplant candidates should be formed according to the medical criteria of need for and probability of benefiting from an organ transplant. However, consensus breaks down at the point of specification that requires determining whether to define these medical criteria broadly or narrowly, where to set the standards for need or for minimal efficacy, and which factors are relevant in determining both need and probable benefit. It also breaks down in determining which of these criteria should have priority in case of conflict.

Vigorous efforts have been undertaken, particularly through UNOS, to develop fair policies of allocating organs to patients *on* waiting lists, but it has been more difficult to ensure equitable access *to* waiting lists, perhaps in part because of transplant center discretion. And yet, decisions about who will be admitted to the waiting list appear to constitute a primary source of unequal access to organ transplants. In the absence of minimum criteria for admission to the waiting lists for organ transplants, transplant teams have had the sole authority to decide whether and when to register a patient. . . .

It is thus essential to avoid the inappropriate, unnecessary, unfair, and premature listing of transplant candidates. . . .

POINT SYSTEMS FOR ALLOCATING ORGANS

It is obviously necessary to have point systems for allocating organs across the national community. Such systems appear to provide objective, public, and impartial ways to allocate organs by reducing institutional and professional discretion and possible bias. They thereby assure the public that all patients will be treated as equals according to the standards reflected in the point system.

With the exception of time on the waiting list, the material criteria explicitly used in different point systems for organ allocation are largely medical in that they involve medical techniques used by medical personnel and arguably influence the transplant's likely success or failure. They are not, however, value free. Selecting different factors and then assigning to them various weights (points) reflect various values. The vigorous debate about how much weight each criterion should have is only partly technical and scientific (e.g., the impact of HLA matching in kidney transplantation); it is to a great extent ethical. Let me take one example: In kidney transplantation, such factors as quality of antigen match and logistical score focus on the chance of a successful outcome; both medical urgency and panel-reactive antibody in different ways

focus on patient need; and time on the waiting list introduces a nonmedical factor, even though it may overlap with panel-reactive antibody because sensitized patients tend to wait longer for transplants. The points assigned to these various factors thus reflect value judgments about the relative importance of patient need, probability of success, and waiting time. Similar observations apply to other organ transplants.

SPECIFYING AND BALANCING PATIENTS' NEEDS AND PROBABLE BENEFITS

Both patient need for a transplant and the probability of a successful transplant are ethically relevant in selecting patients for the waiting list and in selecting patients to receive a particular organ. I would argue that both the urgency of medical need and the probability of successful outcome should be used to determine which candidate should receive a particular organ, after the pool of transplant candidates has been established by the same criteria. Obviously, a patient's risk of imminent death is a strong reason for allocating an organ to that patient. But a major reason for also considering the probability of a successful outcome is to avoid wasting the gift of life. Organs are donated for effective use, and providing an organ to a patient who has only a very limited chance of success increases the probability that he or she will then need another transplant for survival, further reducing the chances for others as well as for his or her own successful transplantation.

It is important to specify as completely as possible both criteria. . . . [I]t is also necessary to try to build [an] ethical criterion of probability of success into the publicly formulated criteria of allocation rather than leaving it to medical discretion. This will be very difficult to accomplish—for instance, what counts as a success when we consider length of graft survival, length of patient survival, quality of life, rehabilitation?—and it may even be ultimately impossible. However, with both medical and public input in an open process conducted over time, we should be able to determine whether we can specify this criterion, along with status categories having to do with urgency of need. At the very least, through this process, it might be possible to set certain minimum thresholds of probable benefit. . . .

Such a public process will also need to consider how to *balance* these two morally relevant criteria of patient need and probable success. Tensions between medical urgency and probability of success may vary greatly depending on the organ in question. For instance, the category of medical urgency will probably not be as important when an artificial organ can be used as a backup (for example, dialysis for end-stage renal failure). In liver transplantation, to take another example, the dominant practice has been to give the sickest patient the highest priority (within the local area), but "medical utility" (and some would include cost-effectiveness) would often dictate placing the liver in a fitter patient to realize the greatest medical benefit (at the lowest cost). Another reason for some attention to those with a higher probability of benefit is that "as time goes on . . . the fitter patients become increasingly ill, their survivability on the waiting list declines, and their operative risk soars."[5] It is not possible to determine generally, apart from different types of organ transplants, what weights to assign to urgency of patient need and probability of success; what is needed is a public process to consider and determine their respective weights for organ-specific allocation policies.

THE MORAL RELEVANCE OF TIME ON THE WAITING LIST AND OF SEEKING TO EQUALIZE WAITING TIMES

It is fair to allocate organs according to both medical need and probability of success, but when there are no substantial differences in degree of medical need and probable benefit among various transplant candidates, it is fair to use their time on the waiting list (or queuing or first-come, first-served) to break the tie. Indeed, if two or more patients are equally good candidates for a particular organ according to the medical criteria of need and probability of success, using their different times on the waiting list may be the fairest way to make the final selection. Such an approach presupposes that there is a firm (and morally acceptable) consensus on what constitutes substantial differences in medical need and probability of success, as well as on criteria for admission to the waiting list.

Some critics charge that time on the waiting list is morally irrelevant or even morally pernicious. For example, Olga Jonasson argues that "length of time on the waiting list is the least fair, most easily manipulated, and most mindless of all methods of organ allocation."[6] She is right if this criterion is used by itself without regard to the other important criteria of urgency of need and probability of success or if it is viewed as the primary criterion. But the use of waiting time in patient selection, when medical need and probability of success are roughly equal, can be justified by various principles and values, such as fair equality of opportunity. Nevertheless, ethical and practical problems do arise in its application. For instance,

when does the transplant candidate's waiting time start—when the patient seeks medical treatment for the condition that leads to end-stage organ failure or when the patient is registered with the OPTN, to take just two possibilities? The latter has been used, but, as critics note, it is easy to manipulate, for example, by putting patients on the list as early as possible and well before their condition really merits such placement. . . .

Also, the fairness of using time on the waiting list as a criterion depends in part on background conditions. For example, some people may not seek care early because they lack insurance; others may receive inadequate medical advice about how early to seek transplantation; and so forth. . . .

CONCLUSIONS

Organ allocation poses a "tragic choice." Short of adequately increasing the supply of transplantable organs, we cannot fully realize all our values at the same time. Hence, it is morally imperative to seek the best possible balance of the whole range of relevant values, which are reflected in the material criteria of patient needs, probability of success, and waiting time.

First, we need to defuse the moral rhetoric about various organ-allocation systems. Several organ-allocation systems appear to fall within the range of ethically acceptable or relatively just and fair systems, but all of them require moral fine-tuning in the name of justice and fairness. And various participants in the debate appear to be acting in good faith, even when they seriously disagree.

Second, society should seek to further specify, to weight, and to balance patient need, probable success, and waiting time through a process that involves the fullest possible and most diverse public participation. Obviously, ethically acceptable allocation criteria cannot be formulated without the substantial input of transplant surgeons and other physicians, as well as other healthcare professionals and scientists. Nevertheless, donated organs belong to the whole community, and procurement and transplant teams receive those organs on behalf of the whole community, for which they serve as "trustees" and "stewards."

It is time to put patients first and to devise procedural and substantive criteria to protect current and future patients' rights and welfare. By putting patients first, we should be able to find common ground or reach an overlapping consensus. One way to do so is to ask, along the lines of the Golden Rule or the

Rawlsian social contract, behind the veil of ignorance, which set of criteria we would find acceptable for allocating organs to ourselves or to our families, without knowing our own or our families' precise circumstances. This is a fair way to reflect on possible material criteria for just organ allocation.

Third, the morally relevant community of ownership of, or dispositional authority over, donated organs is the national community, subject to logistical constraints that must be met in order to provide viable organs for transplantation. Thus, the allocation system should focus on patients across the country and should minimize, as much as possible, "accidents of geography." This is the main point at which I would criticize the OPTN's current system—the procedural assignment of priority to the local community in allocation, even in combination with other substantive criteria (such as medical urgency in liver allocation), results in an unacceptable patchwork of allocation and produces various inequalities across the country. The alternative is not a single, national list that ignores the potential impact, for instance, of shipping organs great distances on the probable success of the transplant. What is required is a shift in orientation—to thinking about donated organs as belonging to the national community and then to specifying and balancing allocation criteria in part according to logistical realities.

The failure to take a national perspective has now resulted in further fragmentation, as states have adopted laws that require organs donated within their boundaries to be used for patients within their boundaries and to be shared with other states only if no patient within their states could benefit from the organ. Such a result should have been anticipated by various participants in this debate over the last few years. Medical and political boundaries may not coincide. (Obviously, it is also important to consider the limitations of national boundaries, but I cannot do so here.) . . .

[Fourth], the so-called green screen is a major source of unequal access to extrarenal organ transplantation in the United States. At this time, a patient's ability to pay, either directly or through third-party coverage, is an important de facto material criterion for access to extrarenal transplants. . . . [I]n the final analysis, this issue must be addressed by the society as a whole, with the involvement of the federal and state governments.

Many of the arguments for providing funds to ensure equitable access to organ transplantation are similar to arguments for providing funds for other medical procedures. But one argument, used by the Task Force, specifically focuses on the *distinctiveness* or *uniqueness* of organ transplantation, particularly because of the social practices of procurement of organs for transplantation. This argument identifies an important moral connection between organ procurement, including organ donation, and organ distribution and allocation. In its efforts to increase the supply of organs, our society requests donations of organs from people of all socioeconomic classes—for example, through public appeals for organ donations or through state "required request" and "routine inquiry" statutes, which mandate that institutions inquire about an individual's or family's willingness to donate, or even request such a donation. However, it is unfair and even exploitative for the society to ask people, rich and poor alike, to donate organs if their own access to donated organs in cases of end-stage organ failure would be determined by their ability to pay rather than by their medical need, probability of success, and time on the waiting list.

This principled argument may be combined with an argument that focuses on the consequences of different policies. There are legitimate worries about the impact of unequal access to organ transplants (based on inability to pay) on the system of organ procurement, which includes gifts of organs from individuals and their families. There is substantial evidence that attitudes of distrust limit organ donation; this distrust appears to be directed at both organ procurement (e.g., the fear the potential donors will be declared dead prematurely) and organ distribution and allocation (e.g., the concern that potential transplant recipients from higher socioeconomic classes will receive priority). Thus, it is not at all surprising that after Oregon decided to stop providing Medicaid funds for most organ transplants "a boycott of organ donations was organized by some low-income people."[7] And cynical comments about how quickly some famous people receive scarce organ transplants reflect public suspicion of organ allocation policies.

Finally, as the previous point suggests, there are important moral connections between organ procurement; including organ donation, on the one hand, and equitable access to organ transplantation and equitable organ allocation, on the other hand. It is obvious that increasing the supply of organs would reduce some problems of organ allocation, but, perhaps less obviously, public trust in the organ allocation system also appears to be important for the public donation of organs. . . .

Our fragile system of organ transplantation depends for its very existence on public trust and thus on the public's willingness to entrust their or their relatives' organs to the trustees and stewards who will allocate them on behalf of the national community to which the organs belong.

NOTES

1. The Joint Hearing of The House Commerce Committee Subcommittee on Health and Environment and The Senate Labor and Human Resources Committee. *Putting Patients First: Resolving Allocation of Transplant Organs.* 18 Jun 1998.

2. National Task Force on Organ Transplantation. *Organ Transplantation: Issues and Recommendations.* Apr 1986.

3. Prottas JM. Nonresident aliens and access to organ transplant. *Transplantation Proceedings* 1989; 21: 3428.

4. Prottas JM. *The most useful gift: altruism and the public policy of organ transplants.* San Francisco, Calif.: Jossey-Bass Publishers, 1994: 153.

5. Jonasson O. Waiting in line. *Transplantation Proceedings* 1989; 21: 3391.

6. See note 5, Jonasson 1989: 3392.

7. Welch HG, Larson EB. Dealing with limited resources: the Oregon decision to curtail funding for organ transplantation. *New England Journal of Medicine* 1988; 319: 171–3.

DAVID H. HOWARD

Hope Versus Efficiency in Organ Allocation

David H. Howard is Associate Professor in the Rollins School of Public Health's Department of Health Policy and Management at Emory University. His research interests include economic aspects of health policy, health literacy, and organ donation. He has published numerous articles in journals including *Health Affairs*, *Health Services Research*, *Journal of Health Economics*, and *Medical Decision Making*.

The allocation system for lifesaving organs in the United States and elsewhere is based on the rule of rescue, which holds that life expectancy absent of treatment should be the primary determinant of who receives scarce medical resources. It was with this principle in mind that the Clinton administration proposed . . . to eliminate regional preferences in organ allocation and institute finer grading of patients' medical status. The proposals, particularly the former, have been the subject of intense controversy in the transplant community ever since.

Opponents of the administration have criticized national allocation on the grounds that it would direct more organs to sicker patients and hence lower aggregate success rates. For the most part, however, the debate has centered on parochial issues, and a much-needed reexamination of the rule of rescue as a basis for organ allocation has not taken place. This is unfortunate; given the continued growth of organ demand relative to supply, it is important to step back and consider whether current allocation policies, which were put into place under a very different environment and have only been modified slightly since their inception, continue to satisfy societal objectives.

Previous attempts to establish an overarching framework for rationing decisions have focused on the ethical principles of justice, fairness, and utility. This article defines three criteria—efficiency, equity, and hope—and argues that they provide a more constructive guide for structuring debates over allocation policy. Unlike the standard ethical criteria, they take into account the dynamic nature of patient health. The outcome of a given rationing policy depends not only on *who* gets treated but *when* they get treated as well. These principles, when applied to the problem of how to allocate livers, show that

Reprinted with permission from *Transplantation* 72(6) (September 2001), 1169–1173. Copyright © 2001 by Lippincott, Williams & Wilkins.

the current sickest-first policy performs well in terms of giving wait-listed patients hope, but that, by delaying transplantation, the sickest-first policy may lead transplant recipients to have poorer outcomes than if they underwent transplantation immediately after listing.

PREVIOUS ANALYSES OF ALLOCATION RULES

Arguments in favor of the sickest-first rule are typically grounded in the ethical principle of justice. Burdick et al. (1) write, "Justice might also partially explain why we might give priority to a patient for whom death was imminent without transplant." Likewise Ubel and Caplan (2) write, "Many theories of justice are based on the notion that the people in greatest need deserve special priority, even if they benefit less than other people."

Ethicists and transplant surgeons are not dogmatic in their application of justice to organ allocation; some argue that retransplantation should be curtailed based on the principle of utility (3). Nevertheless, most agree that the principle of justice dictates that patients on the waiting list be prioritized by medical urgency.

The problem with standard motivations for the sickest-first rule is they begin by assuming that patients are either "urgent" or "non-urgent"; they do not account for how patients become urgent in the first place. . . . The loss of health that patients experience on the waiting list is not an accident but rather a direct consequence of the sickest-first prioritization rule. In a dynamic setting, patient health and patient prioritization are jointly determined. A rule that assigns organs to sicker patients will cause more patients to become sick as they wait for a transplant. . . .

The loss of health that patients experience on the waiting list is a function of the scarcity of organs. In seeking universal principles of rationing, previous analyses often ignore the difference between situations of temporary treatment shortage and situations, such as the organ waiting list, where demand permanently exceeds supply. In the former, the sickest-first rule may be justified in terms of both justice and utility. When a treatment shortage is permanent, however, use of the sickest-first rule can have unintended consequences. As the waiting list grows relative to treatment supply, the percentage of patients receiving treatment in a non-urgent state will decline. Eventually, patients will receive treatment only after they have reached the sickest status category, at which point their ability to survive transplantation is diminished. . . .

DYNAMIC EVALUATION CRITERIA

ALLOCATION AS A TWO-STAGE PROCESS

Allocating organs should be viewed as a two-stage process. In the first stage rules screen out patients who are undeserving or are unlikely to receive a significant benefit from transplantation. Standard ethical approaches are ideal for addressing the questions raised in this stage, because the characteristics used to exclude patients (for example, advanced age) generally are unchanging over time. The second stage entails assigning the limited supply of organs to eligible patients. Obviously there is some connection between the first and second stages; the stringency of first-stage policies will determine the organ shortfall in the second. For reasons discussed above, however, the second stage is properly separated from the first because of the dynamic nature of patient health. Second-stage policies must not only choose between giving organs to urgent or non-urgent patients but must also try to prevent patients from reaching the most-urgent category in the first place. Below I propose three criteria that can be used to judge second-stage allocation policies. Like the standard ethical principles, they do not provide an unequivocal ranking of allocation rules. However, they are well suited for framing the trade-offs that must be faced by policymakers when choosing between alternative methods of prioritizing patients on transplant waiting lists.

EFFICIENCY

All else being equal, allocation policies should provide organs to patients when their benefit from transplantation is greatest. To illustrate, consider Figure 1, which plots the net gain from transplantation as a function of waiting time. The point of greatest benefit is probably before a patient becomes sick but may be well after his physician detects the precursors to liver failure. . . . Hence the hypothetical benefit curve is not uniformly decreasing but rather increasing after diagnosis and then declining. A policy is efficient if patients undergo transplantation at time t*, the point at which the net benefit curve reaches its maximum.

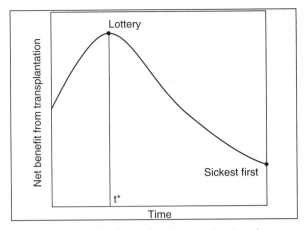

Figure 1   Net benefit of transplantation as a function of waiting time.

Note that the principle of efficiency is different from the standard ethical principle of utility. If there is one organ and two patients need a transplant, the principle of utility dictates that it should be given to the younger, healthier patient. The principle of efficiency makes no such recommendation; it only requires that whoever receives the organ get it at a point when he derives the most benefit from it.

The underlying rationale for the efficiency criteria is that no allocation policy should entail a dead weight loss. In economic terms a dead weight loss is a loss of welfare by one person that does not accrue to another. Consider an organ recipient who undergoes transplantation after his point of maximum benefit. The patient would have been made better off and no one else worse off if instead the patient had undergone transplantation a week earlier (the patient would benefit from undergoing transplantation in a healthier state, and the net loss to other patients would be zero because the patient uses one and only one organ in either case). The decline in health experienced by the patient during the week is a dead weight loss and would be prevented under an efficient policy.

EQUITY

A policy is equitable if, at the time of listing, the probability of eventually receiving a transplant is equal across patients. An inequitable policy is one under which a patient placed on the waiting list in a relatively sick state has a much lower probability of receiving a transplant than a patient placed on the waiting list in

a healthy state. This is not to say that the probability of receiving a transplant must be equal across patients after listing. Some patients will remain in their initial health status or even improve, while others will deteriorate. As long as these events are essentially random and unrelated to patients' health status at listing, however, the equity criterion is not violated.

The equity principle as defined above is based on the belief that once patients are deemed sufficiently healthy to be considered for treatment, policy should not favor one class of patients at the expense of another. To the extent that regional allocation results in differential access to transplantation, it is inequitable. In the case of patient health, patients should not be penalized for being diagnosed late in the course of their disease relative to patients diagnosed earlier. At the same time, patients' status will change for reasons that are unpredictable, and it is beyond the scope of allocation policy to try to compensate for these changes, given that organs are an indivisible good.

HOPE

Hope is formally defined as deriving pleasure or utility from a delay in the resolution of uncertainty. Practically this means that a wait-listed patient will be happier knowing that he has a chance of receiving a transplant than if he is told immediately that he will or will not get an organ. This also applies to a patient's family and society at large; we seem to place a high value on avoiding situations where an otherwise healthy individual knows with certainty that he will experience an untimely death, especially when the means exist to prevent that death. A . . . survey of public preferences for liver allocation policies found that responders were willing to allocate a portion of organs to older and sicker recipients even when they felt that, overall, the allocation system should direct organs to patients with the greatest potential to benefit (4). The value of hope is one possible explanation for this apparent contradiction. Likewise, researchers have documented preferences for hope in studies where participants were asked to choose between immediate versus future disclosure of the results of a monetary lottery (5).

Obviously there are limits to how far the concept of hope can be applied to an allocation scheme. Some patients may prefer early resolution of uncertainty to delay, especially if knowing the outcome of the allocation process changes their time horizon with respect to financial decisions. Wait-listed patients who develop conditions that render them poor candidates for transplantation should be removed from the waiting list, even if this means that they lose hope. Likewise elderly patients may be denied access to the waiting list, even if they are healthy compared to their peers.

A wait-listed patient will lose hope if his probability of receiving a transplant in the future falls below some critical level. Together equity and hope imply that all patients should start out with an equal probability of receiving an organ, regardless of initial health, and that, although the likelihood of eventually receiving a transplant may vary with patients' health levels over time, it should always be high enough to preserve hope.

OTHER PRINCIPLES

Efficiency, equity, and hope are not the only criteria that an allocation system should satisfy. Two others are legitimacy and honesty. Legitimacy holds that the public, on whose generosity the transplant system depends, should accept and understand the allocation system. Legitimacy may explain why first-come first-served queues are so often used to allocate resources, even when other mechanisms would be more efficient. Honesty implies that an allocation system should not encourage physicians to distort medical decisions or misreport information to the allocator. The current system has been criticized on both these grounds. Because hospitalized patients have a higher priority, physicians may base their site-of-care decisions on nonmedical factors. Also, physicians may overexaggerate the severity of patients' liver disease so that they can be placed on the waiting list to accumulate waiting time. Monitoring and stricter standards can help to limit gaming, but generally it is preferable to have a system that induces rather than coerces honesty.

LIVER ALLOCATION AS A CASE STUDY

Applying the principles listed above to several benchmark rationing rules for liver allocation can illustrate their usefulness and limitations. Consider an allocation system in which every patient receives a single lottery ticket upon listing and organs avail-

able on a certain day are assigned by some random mechanism to the patients who turned in their lottery ticket the day before. Assuming that individuals place a high value on life expectancy, they would redeem their lottery tickets when transplantation would do them the greatest good. This is at point t* in Figure 1. Hence, the lottery system described above, where the choice of when to enter the lottery is determined by the patient and his physician, is efficient. Also it is equitable; every patient receives one ticket. Sick patients can choose to enter the lottery as soon as they are listed, while healthy patients may prefer to wait.

The problem with a lottery system like that described above is that it is not hope-preserving. A patient who enters the lottery and loses has zero probability of receiving an organ in the future. Of course patients who value hope highly can always choose to wait to redeem their ticket right before they die, but few are likely to pursue such a strategy. Under the lottery system, the probability is constant until the patient uses the ticket at time t*. It is zero afterwards for patients who do not receive an organ at t*.

The sickest-first policy represents another extreme. Once the waiting list increases beyond a critical point, patients will receive a transplant only after they have reached the sickest health level. Hence one can think of the sickest-first policy as analogous to a lottery where patients are entered in the lottery once they become "sickest" rather than at the time of their choosing. Because the probability of receiving a transplant is always above zero, even on the last day of a patient's life, the sickest-first policy is hope-preserving. It is equitable for the same reason.

The literature on the optimal timing of transplantation does not provide a definitive answer to the question of whether the sickest-first policy is efficient. However, if faced with an unlimited supply of organs it is difficult to imagine a surgeon waiting until a patient is in an intensive care unit to perform transplantation (indeed this was not the practice in the early days of transplantation when organs were plentiful). Given the significantly lower graft success rates of patients who undergo transplantation in status 1 or 2A instead of status 3, it seems fair to conclude that optimal time for transplantation is before patients reach the sickest category . . . and that the sickest-first policy is inefficient. In choosing between the sickest-first policy and a lottery in this case, society faces a trade-off between hope and efficiency.

Although not all countries use as detailed an urgency classification system as the United States, all employ some variant of the sickest-first rule to allocate livers and other lifesaving organs. Outside of transplantation, the sickest-first rule is used to prioritize patients in crowded emergency rooms, disaster-relief shelters, and countries with nationalized health systems. Although the popular press often writes of "waiting lines" in Canada and Britain, it is usually the case that patients in dire need of treatment are moved to the head of the queue. Lotteries and other mechanisms have been used to ration treatment at various times, but the sickest-first rule seems to predominate.

That the sickest-first rule is so widely used suggests its intuitive appeal and, possibly, the value of hope in societal preferences. Can we then assume that the sickest-first rule is the right one to use for allocating organs? Not necessarily. The current organ waiting list, with its large and growing gap between organ demand and organ supply, is different from other clinical situations and from the organ waiting list a decade ago, when the sickest-first rule was first put into place. Under conditions of severe shortage, the sickest-first rule may be very inefficient, resulting in organ wastage and excessive morbidity.

Ultimately policymakers may decide that, despite its efficiency losses, the sickest-first policy is preferred over a lottery, waiting line, or any other feasible prioritization rule. If this is the case, the policy should be defended not on the grounds that it is just but rather because it preserves the hope of patients on the waiting list. It is natural to wonder, however, if there is any way to bridge the hope–efficiency trade-off. One possibility is to allow patients to choose at the time of listing between the present system and one in which they would receive a lottery ticket for an organ that could be turned in at the time of their choosing. Patients who value hope could choose the old system, while patients who value efficiency could choose the lottery. As long as organs are apportioned across systems so that the probability of eventually receiving a transplant does not depend on which scheme is chosen, this dual-system approach would be equitable while permitting greater expression of patient preferences.

REFERENCES

1. Burdick JF, Turcotte JG, Veatch RM, et al. General principles for allocating human organs and tissues. *Transplant Proc* 1992; 24: 2227.

2. Ubel PA, Caplan AL. Geographic favoritism in liver transplantation: unfortunate or unfair. *N Engl J Med* 1998; 339: 1322.

3. Ubel PA, Arnold RM, Caplan AL. Rationing failure: the ethical lessons of the retransplantation of scarce vital organs. *JAMA* 1993; 270: 2469.

4. Ratcliffe J. Public preferences for the allocation of donor liver grafts for transplantation. *Health Econ* 2000; 9: 137.

5. Chew SH, Ho JL. Hope: an empirical study of attitude toward the timing of uncertainty resolution. *J Risk Uncertainty* 1994; 8: 267.

LAINIE FRIEDMAN ROSS

The Ethical Limits in Expanding Living Donor Transplantation

Dr. Lainie Ross is a general pediatrician and a medical ethicist in the MacLean Center for Clinical Medical Ethics at the University of Chicago. Her research interests are research ethics, genetics and ethics, transplant ethics, and pediatric ethics. She recently published *Children in Medical Research: Access versus Protection* as well as professional publications on the ethics of genetic screening, organ donation, and clinical research.

The year 2001 was a watershed year: it was the first time in which there were more living than deceased kidney donors. . . . The main reasons for this trend are the failure of numerous policies designed to significantly increase the number of deceased donor organs . . . and the increased acceptance by transplant centers of the expansion of eligibility criteria for living donors. . . . The trend, however, should give one pause given that there are no potential health risks to deceased donors whereas the risks of serious morbidity and mortality to living donors, although rare, are monumental when they occur. Nevertheless, the past decade has witnessed the emergence of novel methods to increase the number of living donors. Although these programs are not likely to yield high volumes of organs, some transplant centers have gone to great lengths to establish one or more of them. The willingness to expend this type of energy and effort for small numerical gains in transplantable organs must be understood in light of both the transplant community's sincere desire to help patients and the financial incentives that fuel this creativity. In this article, I discuss some of the ethical and policy issues raised by five such programs: (1) living-paired and cascade exchanges; (2) unbalanced living-paired exchanges; (3) list-paired exchanges; (4) nondirected donors; and (5) nondirected cascade exchanges.

LIVING-PAIRED AND CASCADE EXCHANGES

In 1997, colleagues and I (Ross et al. 1997) discussed the ethics of a kidney paired exchange program between two donors who are ABO-incompatible with their intended recipients (see Figure 1).[1] In an exchange program, donor 1 is ABO-incompatible with recipient 1 but is ABO-compatible with recipient 2. Donor 2 is ABO-incompatible with recipient 2 but is ABO-compatible with recipient 1. Thus donor 1 does not give a kidney to his or her intended recipient (#1) but to recipient 2, and donor 2, in turn, gives a kidney to recipient 1 in a paired exchange. The idea had been proposed in the literature by Rapaport (1986). We advanced the idea by offering a detailed protocol that would help to ensure that the potential donors were giving voluntary consent. One major concern was that historically ABO-incompatibility served to exclude a potential donor. Although many individuals may have been disappointed that they could not help their potential intended recipients, some may have been relieved. Paired exchanges eliminate many of the medical excuses that traditionally were available to hesitant donors. As such, to ensure that the donations were voluntary, we argued that exchanges should be considered donations of last resort (Ross et al. 1997).

To ensure informed consent, it is important that the donors and recipients are aware of the risks and benefits of participating in a paired exchange. In many ways, the risks and benefits are the same as they would be for any living donor and recipient. . . .

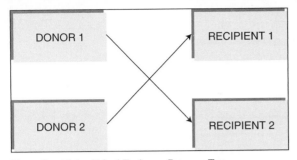

Figure 1   Living Paired Exchange Between Two Donor-Recipient Pairs.

There are other differences between donating directly versus exchanging a kidney, but their clinical significance is not known. For example, there are no data regarding the psychological impact of exchanges rather than direct donations, and whether this has any effect on compliance or graft survival. There are also no data regarding the psychological benefit or regret experienced by direct donors versus exchange donors. There is a small literature that shows that some recipients are cognitively and emotionally affected by the origin of the donated organ (Sanner 2001; Sharp 1995).

To ensure that donors have the right to renege, we suggested that donors must be offered the opportunity to opt out of the exchange up until the moment the surgery takes place. This requires that the procedures are done simultaneously (Ross et al. 1997).

Finally, we were concerned about privacy and confidentiality and the risks of identity disclosure between the pairs. This issue may be particularly acute if one donor has complications or one kidney fails. The protection of privacy and confidentiality is complicated if the two pairs are treated at one institution. Privacy and confidentiality issues are even more complicated logistically when the number of donor-recipient pairs in the exchanges increase (Figure 2 illustrates such a cascade exchange). Although I support strict privacy, data should be collected about the clinical, psychological, and emotional follow-up of the parties involved in exchanges in which identities have and have not been revealed to determine if, when, and why privacy and confidentiality are necessary.

LIMITATIONS OF LIVING-PAIRED EXCHANGES

When we conceived of living-paired exchanges, we were concerned about whether they would be legally permissible or whether they would be interpreted as a

form of barter that violates the National Organ Transplant Act (NOTA) of 1984 (P.L. 98–507 (1984)). NOTA specifically proscribes the transfer of a human organ for valuable consideration (Ross et al. 1997). We asked legal counsel, who concluded that the protocol did not violate the spirit of the law. After the publication of the living-paired exchange protocol, there was broad moral support for living-paired exchanges and concurrence that they were ethical (Park et al. 1999; Delmonico 2004; Kranenburg et al. 2004). However, Jerry Menikoff (1999) expressed concern that a "kidney swap" was a form of barter of value and a step toward for-profit transactions. He acknowledged that the restrictions we placed on the exchange program—that the only goods that can be traded are kidneys and that the exchange donors must be emotionally-related to their originally intended recipients—minimize these concerns (Menikoff 1999, p. 28). . . .

Menikoff's final objection to our protocol was its failure to provide an answer to the question, "what will be the long-term effect of allowing organ swapping on the number of organs generated by the rest of our organ donor system?" (Menikoff 1999, p. 32). Menikoff worried that exchanges might decrease altruistic donations. In fact, kidney exchanges have had minimal impact. Seven months after the publication of our article, it was pointed out that only a small number of ABO-incompatible pairs would be candidates for living-paired exchanges (Terasaki et al. 1998). Many

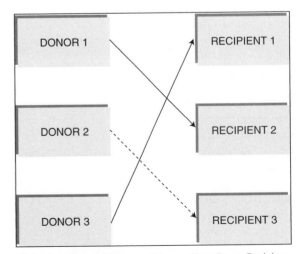

Figure 2   Cascade Exchange Between Three Donor-Recipient Pairs.

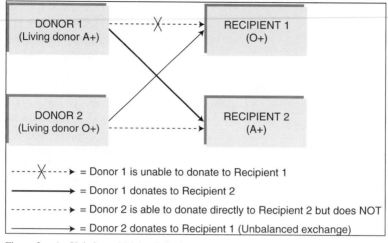

Figure 3   An Unbalanced Living Paired Exchange.

of the incompatibilities involve a donor of blood type A, B, or AB and a recipient of blood type O. However, donors of blood type O do not need to participate in an exchange—unless there is a positive crossmatch—because they are universal donors. Thus, in practice, living-paired exchanges are limited to donor-recipient pairs of blood types A and B. Not surprisingly, this has led to many fewer exchanges than we originally had hoped. A national list could help to increase the number of possible exchanges based on both blood type incompatibilities and positive crossmatches, but even here the numbers are expected to remain small.

To make any impact, then, proponents have proposed variations on living donor exchange programs. I consider here the ethical issues raised by some of these variations.

EXCHANGE VARIATIONS: UNBALANCED EXCHANGES

Because O donors rarely will need to participate in living-paired exchanges, Steve Woodle and I (Ross and Woodle 1998) considered whether it would be ethical for transplant teams to ask type O donors to participate in an exchange even though they could donate directly to their intended recipients (see Figure 3). We named this an unbalanced exchange because one donor-recipient pair cannot donate directly, but the other pair can and does not need to participate in an exchange. By agreeing to participate in an exchange, the donor who can donate directly fosters the opportunity for both donors to donate to an exchange recipient.

In many ways, the benefits and harms raised by an unbalanced exchange are the same as those raised by a balanced or paired exchange. Recipient 1 benefits from the exchange because she cannot receive a living donor organ otherwise, and this allows her to skip the wait list and to receive a kidney with a better likelihood of graft function and survival. Recipient 2 may be harmed—e.g., if donor 2 is an HLA-identical sibling because HLA-identical grafts have a slightly better rate of graft survival—or recipient 2 may benefit—e.g., if donor 1 offers a "healthier" kidney because donor 1 is younger and healthier. The unbalanced exchange again raises the questions, for which there are no data, about whether there is a different psychological reaction to receiving a kidney from a known donor than from an unknown donor and whether this has an impact on compliance.

Donor 1, the "incompatible donor" now has the opportunity to serve as a donor. Donor 1 can no longer rely on a medical excuse based on ABO-incompatibility and crossmatch sensitivity. Donor 1, then, like all donors in paired exchanges must be offered numerous opportunities to renege.

In this case, however, donor 2 is being asked to be "doubly altruistic"—not only to donate, but now to agree to donate to a stranger rather than to his intended, emotionally-related recipient. Some potential donors may be thrilled about having the possibility of saving two lives instead of one. However, if donor 2 is a sibling and HLA-identical, the decision to participate in an exchange rather than to donate directly decreases, albeit slightly, the one- and five-year graft survival for his intended recipient. He may not want to subject his sibling to such additional risks. It is also possible that the intended recipient has a preference about receiving the kidney from his or her originally intended donor.

There may, however, be some cases in which an unbalanced exchange offers the potential for greater medical benefit to both recipients than would receiving a kidney from their intended donors. Consider, for example, the case in which donor 1 is significantly younger than donor 2, and donor 2 and recipient 2 are emotionally, but not biologically, related. This means that recipient 2 is not giving up any HLA-benefits from a direct donation from donor 2, and the kidney graft from donor 1 may have a better chance for graft survival. Since recipient 1 has no choice but to participate in a living exchange or accept a deceased donor organ, recipient 1 also benefits as a kidney from an older living donor has an increased one- and five-year survival rate over a kidney from a deceased donor.

The major ethical question in all unbalanced exchanges, then, is whether a member of the transplant team morally can ask donor 2 to donate to a stranger when he or she could donate directly to the originally intended recipient. The request to participate in an exchange places donor 2 and recipient 2 in uncomfortable positions. There is no additional medical risk to donor 2, but the emotional and psychological impact may be different. Donor 2, who is dependent on the team, may find it difficult to say no, even if he calculates that the costs surpass the benefits. The transplant team is not necessarily making the request for the benefit of recipient 2, but rather to facilitate two donations rather than one. Although communitarians may laud this opportunity, it is contrary to our current system in which the transplant team has fiduciary obligations to their patients. The fiduciary obligation of the transplant team to recipient 2 may conflict with their desire to increase the number of recipients overall. This is particularly true if recipient 2 and donor 2 are genetically related and there is a slight survival advantage in a direct donation. The fiduciary obligations that may be ignored or overridden in order to increase the number of possible transplants make the request ethically troublesome.

The request by the transplant team that donor 2 and recipient 2 participate in an unbalanced exchange complicates their ability to consent because it may be difficult for them to understand the nuances that modify the benefits and risks of graft survival. The main ethical issue, however, is whether the request is too manipulative. The request forces donor 2—and recipient 2—to consider the well-being of another donor-recipient pair with whom there is no prior relationship. In no other clinical situation is a patient asked to do this. Although donor 2—and recipient 2—can refuse to participate in the exchange, many may feel obligated to accede to the request of their health care providers, even if they perceive the exchange to be contrary to their best interests. The request may threaten the voluntariness of the donation.

The ethical propriety of the request is most likely to be raised when an adverse event occurs. If an individual (donor 2) is donating to his brother (recipient 2) and the kidney develops a blood clot, both are harmed in that they suffer a setback to their goals. Imagine, however, that donor 2 donates to a stranger (recipient 1), but the kidney his brother is supposed to receive from donor 1 develops a blood clot. Although in both cases, donor 2 and recipient 2 are harmed, they might claim in the second case that they also were wronged—treated unjustly—because they did not need to participate in the exchange, but felt compelled to do so because of the request, and the compulsion invalidated their consent. . . .

The request by the transplant team to participate in an exchange when one donor can donate directly raises two additional ethical concerns. First, asking donor 2 to participate in an unbalanced exchange may make it more difficult for donor 2 to renege. Second, additional privacy issues are raised when one participates in an exchange rather than a direct donation.

In summary, exchanges raise ethical concerns that are obviated by direct donations. Individuals should not be asked to participate in an exchange unless they cannot donate directly. Thus, the transplant team cannot ethically request that donor 2 and recipient 2 participate in an unbalanced exchange.

EXCHANGE VARIATIONS: LIST-PAIRED EXCHANGE

Another variation on living-paired exchanges are list-paired exchanges, which we initially described in the literature as indirect paired exchanges (Ross and

Woodle 1998; 2000). A list-paired exchange involves an exchange between a living donor-recipient pair, a deceased donor, and a candidate on the deceased donor wait list. . . . [D]onor 1 donates a kidney electively to the deceased donor wait list (recipient 2). Afterward, recipient 1 is given highest priority for the subsequent ABO-identical deceased donor organ.

Why would donor 1 and recipient 1 want to participate in a list-paired exchange? First, it should be remembered that they are interested because a direct donation is not feasible. They would prefer a living-paired or cascade exchange. Most who are seeking a list-paired exchange do so because the recipient is blood type O and the donor is blood type A, B, or AB, which would make it highly unlikely that a living donor-recipient exchange pair could be located, particularly if living exchanges are done locally or even regionally. Remember why this is so: The paired donor would need to be of blood type O, but type O donors are universal donors and can donate to their intended recipients who have blood types A, B or AB, unless there is a positive crossmatch. Thus, the most common list-paired exchanges will be between ABO-incompatible donors and recipients. Such exchanges would result in wait-list candidates of blood type A, B, or AB getting an organ more quickly and the wait-list candidates of blood type O having their wait prolonged because the living donor's intended recipient gets priority for the next deceased donor organ of blood type O.

What are the risks and benefits of these exchanges? For the living donor, the medical risks are unchanged, and his donation allows his intended recipient to bypass the wait list. Although recipient 1 would prefer a kidney from a living donor, this is not feasible or he or she would not be in this exchange. The wait-list candidate (recipient 2) is being offered a kidney from a living donor rather than a deceased donor. This is advantageous because such kidneys have a longer expected graft survival.

The first list-paired exchanges took place in region 1 (Boston). . . . In this protocol, the living donor donates to the wait list first, and then his or her intended recipient gets first choice for the next available ABO-identical deceased organ donor. The intended recipient can and does "cherry pick," that is, he or she waits for an ideal kidney to become available. Because recipient 1 is allowed to skip the queue, a variance from the United Network of Organ Sharing (UNOS) is required because deceased donor grafts are otherwise allocated according to a strict formula. Region 1 received a variance before they began performing list-paired exchanges.

The main ethical problem raised by list-paired exchanges is that most donor-recipient pairs elect to participate in a list-paired exchange because the intended recipient is of blood type O and the living donor is of blood type A, B, or AB. In ABO-incompatible list-paired exchanges, the wait-list recipient who gets the living kidney graft (recipient 2) is a different person that the type O recipient who is skipped over because the living donor's intended recipient gets priority for the next deceased kidney graft of blood type O.

The potential harm to wait-list candidates of blood type O was raised by Ross and Woodle in 2000, before these exchanges were given a variance to proceed from UNOS, and the data from Region 1 has confirmed those fears. In the first 17 list-paired exchange transplants performed, only 1 donor was of blood type O—who had a positive crossmatch with his intended type O recipient—and only one recipient of the next appropriate deceased donor organ was not of blood type O (Delmonico et al. 2004).[2] Delmonico and colleagues realized that this would lead to an increased wait for those type O recipients on the wait list who did not have a willing living donor. . . .

Thus, even though the number of organs is increased by the list-paired exchange program, it is increased at the expense of those who are already worse off. Since candidates of blood type O already have a longer than average wait time, these exchanges further disadvantage those who are already worse off. Rawlsian justice permits inequities provided that it benefits those who are already worst off. . . . Thus, list-paired exchanges are inconsistent with a Rawlsian theory of justice.

Veatch (2000), however, argues that inequalities that do not benefit the worst off can be ethical if the least well off consent to waive the requirements of Rawlsian justice. That is, Veatch argues that disparities are ethically permissible if those who will be disadvantaged are willing to suffer minor setbacks for the greater good. That is, if wait-list candidates of blood type O supported a policy that adopted the ABO-incompatible list-paired exchange in order to increase the number of available organs, even though it meant that they might have to wait longer, then such a program would be ethical.

To determine whether blood type O wait-list candidates would consent to an incremental increase in waiting time, Paul Ackerman, Richard Thistlethwaite, and I collected data from individuals on dialysis about their attitude toward list-paired exchanges (Ackerman et al. 2006). Although 100 percent supported ABO-compatible list-paired exchanges, only 57 percent supported ABO-incompatible list-paired exchanges (p < .001) (Ackerman et al. 2006). Half of the respondents of blood type O supported ABO-incompatible list-paired exchanges even though it would increase their wait for an organ.[3] . . . Although we were surprised by the degree of altruism shown by those of blood type O, the interests of the 50 percent who stated that they would not want to wait any additional time cannot be ignored. Without their support, justice demands that ABO-incompatible list-paired exchanges should not be performed.[4] Nevertheless, our results are intriguing. Forty-one percent of our sample did not know their blood type, and they tended to be more supportive of ABO-incompatible list-paired exchanges (70%), although the difference is not statistically significant (Ackerman et al. 2006).

NONDIRECTED DONORS

The other major attempt to increase the number of living donors was the acceptance of the altruistic nondirected living donor. The concept was first presented in the literature by Arthur Matas and colleagues (2000) at which time they had been contacted by 98 persons; 18 of whom had been evaluated and 4 of whom had donated. Thus, unlike the decision at Chicago to publish our protocol before implementation (Ross et al. 1997), Minnesota described their protocol *ex post facto*. Their policy addressed many important issues, including the evaluation of the donor and recipient, the allocation, the timing of the process, and issues of privacy and confidentiality.

Before I explore the ethical issues raised by three policy decisions in their protocol, it is important to justify a nondirected program. If one assumes that it is ethical to perform living donor transplants, then a nondirected donor program can be ethically justified on the grounds of respect for autonomy. . . . Competent adults have the right to act altruistically, even if it entails some small but serious risk. Nevertheless, transplant teams are also moral agents, and they should and do refuse to accept donations if they would place the donors at significant risk. . . . Thus, the decision by Matas and colleagues (2000) to limit their nondirected program to kidneys—and not to permit nondirected liver donations, which are inherently more risky, from altruistic strangers—seems correct in principle.

The first ethical policy decision that needed to [be] made in the establishment of a nondirected donor program was whether the evaluation process should be the same for nondirected donors as it is for emotionally-related donors. The evaluation of nondirected donors by the Minnesota team included a psychosocial evaluation to rule out underl[y]ing psychiatric disorders and to ensure decisional capacity, an evaluation not included in their emotionally-related living donor program. They denied, however, that the medical criteria for nondirected donors should be different from those for emotionally-related donors (Kahn and Matas 2002). Elsewhere my colleagues and I have argued that nondirected donors should be held to stricter medical criteria because intimacy can justify greater risk-taking (Ross et al. 2002). Although the Minnesota team denies holding directed and nondirected donors to different standards, the Transplant Center (2005) performs living liver donations between emotionally-related individuals, but does not permit nondirected donations of liver grafts. This shows that, in practice, they do allow emotionally-related individuals to take greater risks.

The second policy decision concerned how to select the potential recipients. Currently, nondirected deceased organs are distributed by UNOS according to an established protocol. The protocol takes into account clinical factors, waiting time, and geography. Initially Matas and colleagues (2000) modified the UNOS algorithm for their living nondirected donors in order to maximize the probability of a successful outcome for a nondirected kidney transplant. Although they acknowledged that the modifications were arbitrary, I argued that they were not merely arbitrary but unethical (Ross 2002c). The Minnesota team now states that they use the UNOS algorithm but restrict the donations to recipients listed at their own institution (Kahn 2002).

The allocation decision also focused on what re-evaluation, if any, potential recipients should undergo. Minnesota decided that since the timing of a donation by a nondirected donor was elective, all potential recipients should undergo a re-evaluation, both to ensure that they are medically qualified and to ensure that the recipient is willing to accept a living organ under conditions of anonymity. I think this is very important. Although a living kidney graft is usually medically superior to a deceased donor graft, some candidates might not want a living person to take such risks for them. . . . In fact, the data suggest that African

Americans are more concerned about this than Caucasians. . . . One could imagine that some candidates also might be concerned about whether confidentiality and privacy would be maintained, and therefore might refuse the graft on these grounds. The follow-up data from Minnesota show that this fear is not unfounded. At least 2 donors sought out the recipients while they were still in the hospital recovering from the procedure (Jacobs et al. 2004).

The third policy decision was whether to allow the donations to be directed to a particular subgroup. Matas and colleagues were adamant that the donations should be nondirected (Matas et al. 2000; Jacobs et al. 2004). Although they acknowledged that some specific subgroups that could be defended as socially acceptable—e.g., the request to donate to a child—they chose not to enter the fray as to what constitutes a socially acceptable subgroup. They describe 5 donors who would have preferred that their kidney go to a child; 2 who wanted the kidney to be given to an African American, citing increased wait time; and 2 who wanted to designate their kidney to a single mother raising a family. All were declined and most were still willing to donate (Jacobs et al. 2004). In 2003, Aaron Spital contracted with Harris Interactive to conduct two surveys regarding the public's attitude toward directed altruistic donation. His data found that two-thirds of respondents would not allow anonymous kidney donors to direct their gifts to a member of a specific racial or religious group, but three-quarters of respondents would support kidney donation directed to children (Spital 2003).

Elsewhere, I have argued in support of permitting altruistic donors to direct their donation to particular subgroups (Ross 2002a). I argued that

. . . the decision to serve as a nondirected living donor is a charitable act. And while we have an imperfect duty to act charitably, no particular charity can demand that they have a right to our donation. Although recipients of charities prefer unrestricted gifts, they also accept restricted gifts. As such, I can donate to the general endowment of my alma mater or I can donate directly to the University's softball team. Why then, should I not be able to choose who will be the recipient of the gift of my kidney? (Ross 2002a, p. 449, citations omitted)

My argument continues by acknowledging that a transplant surgeon could refuse to accept an altruistically directed kidney if the surgeon found the restrictions ethically unacceptable, just as universities have been known to refuse restricted gifts when the terms have been unacceptable. . . .

Although in principle I continue to support the right of donors to direct their donation, the problems in practice have become clearer in light of several recent cases in which families have resorted to media appeals for both living and deceased organ donations. . . . Although directed donations are legal, the American Society of Transplant Surgeons (ASTS) issued a statement in November 2004, which it clarified in January 2005, in which it expressed its opposition "to the solicitation of organs (deceased) or organ donors (live)." ASTS (2005) argued that such solicitation and directed donation "will undermine the trust and fairness on which the system of organ transplantation depends. Society, in particular potential recipients and their families, must believe that the current organ allocation system is protected from discriminatory practices that will disadvantage certain classes of individuals." Thus, the decision to prohibit all solicitation may be the only way to ensure equity in the allocation process.

WHEN WORLDS COLLIDE: NONDIRECTED DONORS CATALYZING CASCADE EXCHANGES

In six years, the Minnesota program has only performed 22 nondirected donations despite 360 requests for information. It is clearly inefficient and will not produce the large numbers of additional organs needed to make a significant impact on the wait list.

Creativity however is never to be underestimated. At a transplant meeting on living exchanges in Chicago in March 2005, a potential case was presented in which a nondirected donor could catalyze a cascade of living donations to unintended recipients until the final donor would donate to the deceased donor wait list (see Figure 4).

The moral question is whether it is ethically permissible to use a nondirected donor as the catalyst for a cascade exchange—with individuals who have a willing but incompatible donor, see Figure 4—or whether the nondirected donor organ should be run immediately against the wait list and given to the designated recipient. From a utilitarian perspective, it makes sense to consider using the nondirected donor as a catalyst for a cascade exchange because it can maximize the number of transplants performed. The nondirected altruistic donor does not have a particular recipient in mind, so the request to donate to a cascade exchange

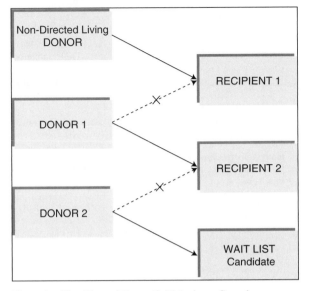

Figure 4   Non-Directed Donor Ca[t]alyzing a Cascade Exchange.

rather than directly to the wait list should not matter. If anything, the altruistic nondirected donor ought to be pleased if his or her donation leads to more than one transplant being performed.

From an egalitarian perspective it is also morally acceptable to consider using the nondirected donor as the catalyst for a cascade exchange. The danger, however, is that the donation must be viewed from the perspective of blood group equity. If the altruistic nondirected donor is of blood type O, but the cascade results in the donation of a type A kidney to the wait list, then the cascade donation encounters the same problems as those enumerated for a single list-paired exchange. Given this, I argued at the . . . meeting that it is ethical to evaluate the nondirected organ for the possibility of a cascade exchange, but the cascade exchange should be permitted only if it will not harm individuals of blood types O and B—those who are already worst off.

CONCLUSION

Paired exchanges are ethically sound but will yield only a small increase in the number of available organs. Exchange variants—unbalanced exchanges and list-paired exchanges—could increase the number of organs, but raise ethical issues that should limit their permissibility. Nondirected donations can be ethically sound. Stricter eligibility criteria for the potential

nondirected donors should be adhered to, and the kidneys should be distributed according to the criteria for the UNOS wait list. Organs from nondirected donors can be used to catalyze a cascade exchange provided that those of blood types O and B are not made worse off.

I would be remiss however if I did not emphasize that living donors should be donors of last resort. We should be sobered by the trend that more donors are living than deceased because of the risks to which living donors are exposed. If there were an alternate source of organs, one might not permit living donations, particularly between non-intimates. As I have argued elsewhere, "the ethical response to the increasing trend for live organ donation ought to be to motivate the transplant community to focus on alternate sources of organs—whether from cadavers, animal-human hybrids, or stem cells" (Ross 2002a, p. 450). I also would be remiss if I did not acknowledge that, although this article focuses on novel methods to increase the supply of kidneys for transplantation, the best solution for end-stage renal disease is not to ensure an adequate organ supply for the ever-growing demand, but rather, to focus on the prevention of organ failure in the first place.

NOTES

1. The four major blood types are A, B, AB, and O. A donor-recipient pair is ABO-compatible if the blood types of the donor and recipient permit donation. For example, a donor of blood type A is ABO-compatible with a recipient of blood type A or AB. A donor-recipient pair is ABO-incompatible if the blood types of the donor and recipient do not permit donation. Living-paired kidney exchanges are usually necessary when donor-recipient pairs are ABO-incompatible. Living-paired kidney exchanges also may be necessary when the donor-recipient pair is ABO-compatible, but the recipient has developed antibodies against the donor (positive crossmatch). These antibodies usually occur after blood transfusions or a previous transplant.

2. The Washington, DC, consortium also received a variance from UNOS. In January 2005, they published their data. All of the first 10 list-paired living donors had non-O blood types; the recipients' blood types were not reported (Gilbert et al. 2005).

3. Half of those of blood types A, B, and AB also were altruistic, arguing that ABO-incompatible list-paired exchanges should *not* be performed because no one should be asked to wait any additional time. Of those who did argue that wait-list candidates of blood type O should be willing to wait longer, most did not believe they should be asked to wait longer than an additional six months.

4. David Steinberg (2004) has suggested that the correct population to decide about whether to waive the requirements of Rawlsian justice is the population that does not know whether it will be advantaged or disadvantaged by ABO-incompatible list-paired exchanges. Those wait-list candidates who do not know their

blood type can be viewed as "behind the veil of ignorance." . . . Although we examined the perspective of this group, we argued that transplant candidates of blood group O are the appropriate group to study because they are the ones who will be harmed, and it is their consent that is necessary to waive the requirements that Rawlsian justice demands (Ackerman et al. 2006).

REFERENCES

Ackerman, Paul D.; Thistlethwaite, J. Richard, Jr.; and Ross, Lainie Friedman. 2006. Attitudes of Minority Patients with End Stage Renal Disease regarding ABO-Incompatible List-Paired Exchanges. *American Journal of Transplantation* 6: 83–88.

ASTS. American Society of Transplant Surgeons. 2005. Statement on Solicitation of Donor Organs. 20 January. Available at http://www.asts.org/donorsolicitation.cfm. Accessed 5 May 2006.

Delmonico, Francis L. 2004. Exchanging Kidneys—Advances in Living-Donor Transplantation. *New England Journal of Medicine* 350: 1812–14.

———; Morrissey, Paul E.; Lipkowitz, George S.; et al. 2004. Donor Kidney Exchanges. *American Journal of Transplantation* 4: 1628–34.

Gilbert, James C.; Brigham, Lori; Batty, D. Scott, Jr.; and Veatch, Robert M. 2005. The Nondirected Living Donor Program: A Model for Cooperative Donation, Recovery, and Allocation of Living Donor Kidneys. *American Journal of Transplantation* 5: 167–74.

Jacobs, Cheryl L.; Roman, Deborah; Garvey, Catherine; et al. 2004. Twenty-Two Nondirected Kidney Donors: An Update on a Single Center's Experience. *American Journal of Transplantation* 4: 1110–16.

Kahn, Jeffrey. 2002. Commentary: Making the Most of Strangers' Altruism. *Journal of Law, Medicine and Ethics* 30: 446–47.

———, and Matas, Arthur J. 2002. What's Special about the Ethics of Living Donors? Reply to Ross et al. *Transplantation* 74: 421–22.

Kranenburg, Leonieke W.; Visak, Tatjana; Weimar, Willem; et al. 2004. Starting a Crossover Kidney Transplantation Program in the Netherlands: Ethical and Psychological Considerations. *Transplantation* 78: 194–97.

Matas, Arthur J.; Garvey, Catherine A.; Jacobs, Cheryl L.; and Kahn, Jeffrey P. 2000. Nondirected Donation of Kidneys from Living Donors. *New England Journal of Medicine* 343: 433–36.

Menikoff, Jerry. 1999. Organ Swapping. *Hastings Center Report* 29 (6): 28–33.

Park, Kiil; Moon, Jang Il; Kim, Soon Il; and Kim, Yu Seun. 1999. Exchange-Donor Program in Kidney Transplantation. *Transplantation Proceedings* 31: 356–57.

Rapaport, F. T. 1986. The Case for a Living Emotionally Related International Kidney Donor Exchange Registry. *Transplantation Proceedings* 19 (Supplement 2): 5–9.

Ross, Lainie Friedman. 2002a. All Donations Should Not Be Treated Equally: A Response to Jeffrey Kahn's Commentary. *Journal of Law, Medicine and Ethics* 30: 448–51.

———, and Woodle E. Steve. 1998. Kidney Exchange Programs: An Expanded View of the Ethical Issues. In *Organ Allocation: Proceedings of the 30th International Conference on Transplantation and Clinical Immunology*, ed. J. L. Touraine, J. Traeger, H. Betuel, et al., pp. 285–95. Dordrecht: Kluwer Academic Publishers.

———, and Woodle, E. Steve. 2000. Ethical Issues in Increasing Living Kidney Donations by Expanding Kidney Paired Exchange Programs. *Transplantation* 69: 1539–43.

———; Glannon, Walter; Josephson, Michelle A.; and Thistlethwaite, J. Richard, Jr. 2002. Should All Living Donors Be Treated Equally? *Transplantation* 74: 418–21.

———; Rubin, David T.; Siegler, Mark; et al. 1997. Ethics of a Paired-Kidney-Exchange Program. *New England Journal of Medicine* 336: 1752–55.

Sanner, Margareta A. 2001. Exchanging Spare Parts or Becoming a New Person? People's Attitudes Toward Receiving and Donating Organs. *Social Science and Medicine* 52: 1491–99.

Sharp, Lesley A. 1995. Organ Transplantation as a Transformative Experience: Anthropological Insights into the Restructuring of the Self. *Medical Anthropology Quarterly* 9: 357–89.

Spital, Aaron. 2003. Should People Who Donate a Kidney to a Stranger Be Permitted to Choose Their Recipients? Views of the United States Public. *Transplantation* 76: 1252–56.

Steinberg, David. 2004. Exchanging Kidneys: How Much Unfairness Is Justified by an Extra Kidney and Who Decides? *American Journal of Kidney Diseases* 44: 1115–20.

Terasaki, Paul I.; Cecka, J. Michael; Gjertson, David W.; and Cho, Yong W. 1998. Spousal and Other Living Renal Donor Transplants. In *Clinical Transplants*, ed. J. Michael Cecka and Paul I. Terasaki, pp. 269–84.

Transplant Center. 2005. Living Donor, Liver. Available at http://www.fairviewtransplant.org/liver/liver_living_donor.asp. Accessed 5 May 2006.

Veatch, Robert M. 2000. *Transplantation Ethics*. Washington, DC: Georgetown University Press.

ROBERT A. CROUCH AND CARL ELLIOTT

Moral Agency and the Family: The Case of Living Related Organ Transplantation

Robert Crouch is a research assistant at the Poynter Center for the Study of Ethics and American Institutions at Indiana University Bloomington. He has interests in political philosophy, philosophy of science, and bioethics. Along with colleagues at the University of Virginia and the NIH, he edited the book, *Ethical and Regulatory Aspects of Clinical Research.*

Carl Elliott is Professor, Center for Bioethics at the University of Minnesota. He has written on the ethics of enhancement technologies, the philosophy of psychiatry, the later work of Ludwig Wittgenstein, and the novels of Walker Percy. His recent books include *Better than Well: American Medicine Meets the American Dream* and *A Philosophical Disease: Bioethics, Culture and Identity.*

INTRODUCTION

Living related organ transplantation is morally problematic for two reasons. First, it requires surgeons to perform nontherapeutic, even dangerous procedures on healthy donors—and in the case of children, without their consent. Second, the transplant donor and recipient are often intimately related to each other, as parent and child, or as siblings. These relationships challenge our conventional models of medical decisionmaking. Is there anything morally problematic about a parent allowing the interests of one child to be risked for the sake of another? What exactly are the interests of the prospective child donor whose sibling will die without an organ? Is the choice of a parent to take risks for the sake of her child truly free, or is the specter of coercion necessarily raised?

When it comes to moral decisions about the family, the tools of moral philosophy and the law have not always served us well, particularly when the question involves exposing one family member to risks for the

sake of another. This raises an obvious question: since we all have families of one sort or another, why do we find it so difficult to think clearly about them? We would like to suggest that one reason we have such difficulty thinking clearly about living related organ transplantation and the family is that we have unthinkingly imported a certain picture of moral agency into our deliberations, and this has led us ineluctably to think about these problems in the wrong way.

"Philosophy is the battle against the bewitchment of our intelligence by means of language," wrote Wittgenstein in a famous passage of his *Philosophical Investigations.*[1] Language bewitches our intelligence by suggesting to us certain ways of thinking about philosophical matters. The manner in which we ask and answer questions, use metaphors, and offer descriptions all subtly influence the way in which we think about the world. Because we do not have a clear overview of our language, we can easily be led into philosophical confusion. . . .

We want to argue that in thinking about the role of children and family members in organ transplantation, bioethics has been influenced by a certain grammatical picture of human agency. The picture is not of

Reprinted with permission from *Cambridge Quarterly of Healthcare Ethics* 8 (July 1999), 275–287. Copyright © 1999 by Cambridge University Press.

children and their parents located in a context of intimacy, but of sovereign, independent human agents free of the moral and emotional connections that typically bind family members to each other. It is a picture of human agency not unlike what Iris Murdoch (perhaps somewhat unfairly) calls the "Kantian man-God," an agent who is "free, independent, lonely, powerful, rational, responsible, brave, the hero of so many novels and books of moral philosophy."[2] We will argue that this picture, or something like it, represents a way of thinking about human agency that underlies many of the confusions that have arisen around living-related organ transplantation.

COERCION AND PARENT-TO-CHILD PARTIAL LIVER TRANSPLANTATION

In 1988 a surgical team at São Paulo Medical College Hospital and Clinics in Brazil performed the world's first living partial liver transplant, from a mother to her four-year-old child. Since that time surgical teams at a number of other universities have performed similar procedures, including a group at the University of Chicago, who in 1990 performed a mother-to-daughter partial liver transplantation for a child with biliary atresia. Because the liver ordinarily regenerates within four to six weeks after partial hepatectomy, surgeons involved in these early procedures believed that the procedure would involve no serious long-term risks to the donor. However, because of the novelty of these early procedures, the risks to the donor and the potential benefits to the recipient were at least partly unknown. Thus the ethical problem: should a transplant team offer a parent, under circumstances of uncertainty, the opportunity to donate part of her liver to her desperately ill child?

While partial liver transplantations are now more common, at the time of the early procedures many commentators objected on ethical grounds. Many of these ethical objections, rather surprisingly, appealed to notions of autonomy. Objectors argued that parents should not be offered the procedure because they will find it extremely difficult to refuse. The procedure was new and innovative, the risks uncertain, and parents, faced with the potential death of a child, may not be able to make a free choice to donate. "Does anyone really think parents can say 'No' when the option is certain death for their own son or daughter?" asked Arthur Caplan.[3] Commenting on the Chicago transplantation to the *New York Times*, George Annas said: "The parents basically can't say no."[4]

To be clear about just what these objectors are saying is important. They are not saying that parents can be pressured into donating by other family members or by the healthcare team. They are saying that parents might somehow pressure *themselves*. By virtue of their emotional ties to their child and their sense of moral obligation, parents will feel "forced" to donate. Here the more conventional image of coercion as a threat by another agent is turned inward; the threat comes not from another person but from the agent. More specifically, the threat comes from conscience and love for the child. This image of conscience as a coercive force is made explicit by Siegler and Lantos who, even while arguing that the transplantation is ethically acceptable, warn against the "internal coercion" created by guilt.[5]

Where does this argument get its persuasive force? What makes the argument so appealing to many thoughtful people? Even if the argument is misguided (as we believe it is), it does not strike most people—or at least most Westerners—as completely unreasonable. There is a sense in which a person often feels bound to act in accordance with conscience or emotional commitments, even if refusing is easy and without penalty. But without penalty for refusing, why would we say that conscience or love "forces" or "coerces" a parent to donate?

One reason may be the tension between the public and private faces of morality. Some parents may not want to donate, in fact, may not even feel morally obligated to donate, but would be ashamed to have this attitude revealed to anyone else, especially to family. The opinions of others can be powerful motivating forces; some might even call them coercive. And if public revelation of a decision can move a person to donate, through guilt or shame, then it is only a short, but misguided, step toward thinking of guilt or shame as coercive in themselves.

But perhaps a more important reason underlying the appeal of this argument is a picture of agency that identifies freedom with independence. Our language reflects this picture of agency back to us when we speak of the *bonds* of love or of being emotionally *tied* to another person. If these metaphors ring true to us, they do so because they evoke images that capture something of the actual experience of strong emotional commitments. It is true, for example, that families can be stifling, marriage confining, children limiting, divorce liberating. The attachments and commitments of the family can limit a person's independence, and if independence is identified with freedom—as it is in the American mythology of rugged frontiersmen and lonely cowboys—then these commitments will also be seen as limits on a person's freedom. The moral commitments associated with intimacy, such as loyalty and devotion, are seen as "coercive" because they motivate a person to actions that a completely independent person would not take. Thus parents who risk their own lives to donate organs to a child are not acting freely, because they are bound by moral and emotional ties to the child.

To resist this suggestion is important. Most parents make sacrifices of one sort or another for their children and do so not only freely but unhesitatingly. If we take seriously the argument that choices made for reasons of love and moral obligation are not free, we must admit that all parents who make financial sacrifices to send their children to college are somehow not making these sacrifices freely. What is more, to do so would mean that the less moral and emotional motivation a person has for donating an organ, the freer is his or her choice to donate. Thus if a child needs an organ, only strangers, not the child's parents, would be truly free to volunteer as donors.

The picture of agency underlying this concept of coercion is one that identifies the moral agent as completely free when he or she is self-interested and lacks any moral or emotional connections to other people. Morality and love are limits on freedom because they move a person to act for the sake of other people, rather than for self. Yet we have another name for agents who are self-interested and lack deep emotional attachments: we call them sociopaths. If we are ever to get straight about the nature of voluntariness, we must recognize that moral and emotional commitments are not exceptional, are not constraints on freedom, but are rather a part of ordinary human life. More specifically, they are a part of ordinary *family* life that we must take seriously if we want to understand how family members can make free choices about organ donation.

THE BEST INTERESTS STANDARD AND KIDNEY TRANSPLANTATION BETWEEN MINOR SIBLINGS

In the preceding section we have tried to show how a certain picture of human agency can distort one's thinking about parent-to-child partial liver transplantation. Now we turn to the still more vexing question whether it is ethically justifiable to use a minor as a kidney donor for a sibling. These procedures are ethically problematic because the minor donor is often incompetent to consent to the procedure, and more importantly, because the procedure is not for the child's own benefit, but for the benefit of the sibling. We will suggest that an inappropriate picture of human agency has played into how the courts have considered this issue, particularly how they have constructed the minor donor's best interests.

Because the procedure is nontherapeutic for the donor, it is not surprising that sibling-to-sibling kidney transplantations have often wound up in the courts. What is more surprising is the reasoning and willingness of U.S. courts to authorize these transplants. In many cases, both the parents of the prospective donor and the courts have reasoned that it is in a minor donor's "best interests" to serve as a kidney donor for a sibling. Given the obvious risks of donation, one might well ask: How have the courts justified their decisions?

In a word, curiously. An early case is instructive. In *Masden v. Harrison*[6] the proposed donation took place not between young children but between 19-year-old twins. However, because the age of majority in Massachusetts was 21, the donor, Leonard, could not render a legal consent. Thus although Leonard had expressed his willingness to act as a donor for his brother (Leon), and had been found by the court to be sufficiently mature to understand the consequences of his decision to donate, neither his consent nor the consent of his parents was legally sufficient to authorize the transplantation. As a result, the justice in the declaratory judgment crafted a solution to the problem by highlighting the negative psychological impact that the death of the sick brother would have on the healthy prospective donor brother:

I am satisfied from the testimony of the psychiatrist that grave emotional impact may be visited upon Leonard if the defendants refuse to perform this operation and Leon should die, as apparently he will. . . . Such emotional disturbance could well affect the health and physical well-being of Leonard for the remainder of his life. I therefore find that this operation is necessary for the continued good health and future well-being of Leonard and that in performing the operation the defendants are conferring a benefit upon Leonard as well as Leon.[7]

This construction of the problem had important consequences for later U.S. legal decisions. Two points are important. First, although the decision is written as if the donor were a minor incapable of consent, in fact he was 19 years old and probably quite capable of acting as a responsible moral agent. Second, perhaps as a result of the fact that the law did not recognize Leonard as a responsible moral agent able to consent knowingly to risks, the decision is framed in terms of Leonard's *own* interests. That is, the court suggests that donation would be not only in the interests of Leon, but also in the interests of Leonard, the donor. Satisfied that the operation would benefit both brothers, healthy and ill, the courts authorized the operation, and it was successfully carried out.

What the *Masden* court effectively did was to justify an adult's decision to donate a kidney to his brother using a decisionmaking framework more appropriate for a much younger child. Thus when later American courts followed the *Masden* court's lead, they produced rather eccentric results.[8] Consider briefly the following three examples.

First, in *Strunk v. Strunk*,[9] a Kentucky court authorized an intersibling kidney donation from Jerry Strunk, a 27-year-old institutionalized mentally incompetent person with a mental age of a six-year-old, to his dying 28-year-old brother Tommy. In reaching their conclusion, the court relied heavily upon the testimony of a court-appointed psychiatrist as well as an *amicus curiae* brief submitted by the Department of Mental Health of Kentucky. Because Tommy was Jerry's primary link to the rest of the family, and because Tommy was the only one who could understand Jerry's "defective" speech, it was felt that Tommy's continued survival was essential to Jerry's overall well-being. As the concurring justices wrote,

> it would not only be beneficial to Tommy but also beneficial to Jerry because Jerry [is] greatly dependent upon Tommy, emotionally and psychologically, and . . . his well-being would be jeopardized more severely by the loss of his brother than by the removal of a kidney.[10]

Second, consider *Hart v. Brown*,[11] a Connecticut case where a kidney donation from a seven-year-old girl to her twin sister was authorized partly on the ground that it would be in the donor child's "best interests" to donate. As part of their fact finding, the court heard from a psychiatrist who examined the prospective donor, Margaret, and testified that she had a "strong identification" with her ill sister, Kathleen. The psychiatrist testified further that the donor would be better off in a family that was happy than in a family that was distressed due to the loss of Kathleen

and, more directly, that it would be a "very great loss" to the donor if her ill sister were to die.[12]

And finally, consider the Texas case *Little v. Little*,[13] in which the courts authorized kidney donation from a 14-year-old girl with Down syndrome to her brother on the ground that it was in her best interests to do so. In reaching its decision the Texas court argued in the first instance that the dangers of the donation to Anne were "minimal," and that although Anne might be frightened by the foreign surroundings of the hospital, nonetheless evidence suggested that Anne would not suffer psychological harm as a result of her participation. Moreover, the court argued, given (1) the existence of a close relationship between Anne and Stephen, (2) a genuine concern by each child for the welfare of the other, and (3) an awareness by Anne that Stephen was ill and that she was in a position to "ameliorate Stephen's burden," a decision to permit Anne's kidney donation would prevent negative psychological effects (e.g., guilt or sadness) from occurring in the future if Stephen were to die because Anne was not permitted to help him.

What is going on in these three cases? What seems apparent is that when faced with a sick family member in need of a kidney, the courts interpreted their guiding decisionmaking principle—the best interests of the donor—as broadly as necessary in order to help the patient and her family. Equipped with the best interests standard, but confronted by a donor who would not benefit *physically* from donation, the courts used a much wider construct, one that considered potential "psychological" benefits. With these "psychological" benefits in mind, the courts argued that to donate a kidney would be in a child's "best interests."

Yet consider just what the courts are saying. They are saying that it is in the child's best interests to: (1) be exposed to the unfamiliar and frightening environment of a hospital; (2) be exposed to the risks attending the use of general anaesthetics; (3) be exposed to the potentially serious peri- and post-operative risks associated with the surgical removal of a healthy kidney; (4) be exposed to the potentially serious long-term risks associated with extended hyperperfusion of the remaining kidney, including unknown risks; (5) potentially experience the psychological trauma following a failed transplantation attempt; and finally, (6) potentially experience the "psychological benefits" following a successful transplantation attempt. As one jurist has written, the appeal to psychological benefits as a justification for authorizing donation is "pretty thin soup on which to base a decision."[14]

Why, then, have the courts used it so often? We want to suggest two reasons. First, the courts may have had in mind a picture of moral agency that identifies the agent's *interests* with *self-interests*, narrowly construed. What is clear is that the courts felt the need to justify the use of an incompetent kidney donor by showing that donating would somehow be in the donor's self-interest. And if the picture of moral agency is one of agents, sovereign, independent, and emotionally unconnected to other human beings, there will be little room for a concept of human interests that includes the interests of others. Thus the problem faced by the courts, which (apparently) wanted to approve the transplantation. Armed with this picture of the independent, rationally self-interested agent, but faced with what they implicitly realized to be beings whose interests were intimately bound up with the interests of their families, the courts quite understandably tried to construct arguments whereby a child would benefit "psychologically" by being used as an organ donor for a sibling. In effect, they said that the child could donate because to do so would be in the child's self-interest.

Now, one problem with this narrow construction—of interests *as* self-interests—is that it fails to recognize that an agent's interests (even self-interests) can include the interests of others. Joel Feinberg, for example, makes a helpful distinction between self-regarding interests and other-regarding interests.[15] Self-regarding interests are those interests that relate exclusively to the well-being of the agent himself or herself. Thus, self-regarding interests might include interest in remaining healthy or in becoming a successful writer. Other-regarding interests involve the desires that an agent has for the well-being of another person. . . .

This picture of human agency seems fairly well established in the Western tradition. To be sure, the picture drawn above would need to be filled out more in order to pass for an adequate rendition of a human agent; for example, we would have to talk about the pull that morality can exert on an agent regardless of the interests it serves, or about the intrinsic importance of the agent's autonomy—"I will act *as I want to* even if it serves no other person's interests, and even if it runs counter to my own interests," as we can imagine one saying. But the point is that a human agent can legitimately be thought of as one who acts to promote, or is at least mindful during deliberation of, self-regarding and other-regarding interests. Therefore, it is at least arguable that a prospective adult sibling donor might decide to donate a kidney because it

will promote the well-being of the sibling, but also because the donor will, among other things, benefit from being able to continue the relationship with the sibling, or benefit "psychologically" from feelings of increased happiness and self-esteem as a result of having done something of profound importance for a loved one.

But this reasoning points to the second problem in the U.S. courts' decisions. A concept of the interests an agent has in other people sounds quite reasonable *if* one is, in fact, talking about an agent—that is, about a competent adult. But is invoking agency—understood properly—reasonable in the case of a small child or a mentally incompetent adult? In many cases it is far from clear that the donor is mature and sufficiently mentally developed to have an important other-regarding interest in a sibling.

Contrast, for example, the reasoning of the *Masden* court with the court cases that followed. In the Masden case, we can reasonably assume that in making his decision to donate, the healthy brother Leonard gave consideration to what Feinberg has called other-regarding interests. We can also assume that, as a 19-year-old, Leonard was sufficiently mature to have developed interests of his own. Here to treat Leonard as an adult made sense because he *was* an adult, albeit not a *legal* adult. And although he was not a legal adult, he could reasonably be expected to experience psychological benefits from his donation experience, not only because he was emotionally mature enough for psychological benefits to be a realistic possibility, but because the act of donation could be thought of as serving Leonard's self-regarding and other-regarding interests; namely, his self-regarding interests in continuing his relationship with his brother and being spared the emotional trauma of losing him, as well as his other-regarding interest in (potentially) saving his brother's life.

Yet does this sort of construction make sense in the cases that followed? Arguably it does not, and we want to suggest that the reason has something to do with the courts' understanding of psychological best interests. Exactly what the courts mean when they refer to psychological best interests is often unclear, but the meaning seems to involve at least the following points. First, the donation can have instrumental value to the donor: in donating, the donor may save the life of a sibling and will therefore have a sibling to grow up with and to share a life with, each of which brings with it certain identifiable social and emotional benefits to the donor. Second, *ceteris paribus*, growing up in a household unaffected by the tragic loss of a sibling or child is possibly more conducive to psychological stability and general mental health than growing up in a family that has been struck by loss. Third, even if the donation is ultimately unsuccessful, the donor may receive some comfort from the recognition that everything possible was done to help the sibling, and that the role played in the medical treatment was crucial, even if unsuccessful.

The important point here is that one of the necessary preconditions of receiving what the courts call psychological benefits is that the donor have sufficient cognitive development to recognize the *social* aspect of donation; that is, the donor must be aware not merely that his or her kidney has been removed, but rather that he or she has helped the sibling *by donating* in a way that few (perhaps no) others could ever do. The distinction we are attempting to illustrate is similar to that captured by the shift in language use from "kidney extraction," or "nephrectomy"—a purely biological description—to "kidney donation"—a description of an act that takes place in a social context and carries specific meanings within that context. Thus if the donor is not mentally developed to a sufficient degree, he will not only fail to understand why he is in the hospital and why he has been physically harmed, he will also fail to understand the important role that he has played in the care of his sibling. Thus he may well *not* receive any psychological benefits as a result of his donation. Children and mentally incompetent persons are, in other words, human agents of a different sort from adults, and we must be careful about the interests that we take children or mentally incompetent persons to have. . . .

Briefly put, the problem is that *as* minors and *as* mentally incompetent persons, the prospective donors would probably *not* be able to experience the psychological benefits because of their insufficiently developed mental, emotional, and moral capacities—in short, because they are human agents in a very different sense from adults. Thus even if the courts are correct in their general identification of psychological benefits, and even if such benefits would materialize in an *adult* and outweigh the burdens associated with donation, we have reason to worry that the child or mentally incompetent person would not experience this benefit because of immaturity. Children and mentally incompetent persons simply do not fit the picture of human agency implicitly assumed in these cases.

SITUATING THE PROBLEM

The overarching point that we have attempted to make is simple: our thinking about living related organ transplantation has been affected by an implicitly assumed picture of human agency. This picture of the agent as essentially rational, independent, disengaged from others, and self-interested has, we believe, led many into error regarding either the *permissibility* of intrafamilial organ donations or the *ground* on which such donations can be authorized. We do not believe that the parent who is offered the chance to donate part of her liver to a dying child is coerced by her love for her child, or by the exhortations of her conscience; nor do we believe that the donation of a kidney by a minor child can be justified by an appeal to the donor's best interests, even when such interests include both self-regarding and other-regarding interests.

If we are to clear away the fog that has prevented us from seeing the issue clearly, we must strive to understand how our thinking about agency has influenced our thinking about living related organ transplantation. As Wittgenstein says, "A main source of our failure to understand is that we do not *command a clear view* of the use of our words."[16] We believe that the first step we must take to command a clear view is to situate the problems we have discussed squarely within the family. Once the problem is properly situated, the inadequacy of the picture of human agency that has dominated discussions of living-related organ transplantation will be put into sharper relief.

The picture of the human agent as independent and self-interested that has fueled so many errors in this context is an inadequate picture of the human agent *within the family*. To think of family members in this way is to miss what is of importance in family life and to human agency. In families, the important factor is that family members cherish each other simply for each other's sake, and that being devoted to "the family" and its members is a source of deep meaning and value in our lives and the lives of those around us. To be a member of a family is to recognize the importance of strongly "shared significances."[17] To share something in the strong sense, according to Charles Taylor, means that "the good we share in part effectively turns on our sharing; *the sharing in itself is valued*."[18] . . .

There are, we would claim, interests within families that can rightly be called "strongly valued goods," that come (to an extent, at least) from the fact that we are engaged in a shared journey. These interests include both the interests in the family *qua* family, or family in the abstract (think of the sense in which we have all, at one point or another in our lives, invoked the idea of "the family" as a reason to do, or not to do something) and the interests in the family *qua* particular individuals, or each member's love, commitment and concern for each other member. The main point here is that the concept of strongly valued goods within the family brings to expression the idea of collectivism in the family; as family members we share significances in our lives with other family members in a deeper way than we do with non-family members in our lives. . . .

Recognizing these meaningful characteristics of the family should convince us that the picture of the independent and self-interested agent is inappropriate in the context of the family. Rather, a more adequate picture of the human agent within the family would involve, we believe, a recognition that the interests of family members are often inextricably intertwined. We want to replace the discrete and separable interests of family members with a more realistic view, one that recognizes the conflict, confluence, and confusion of interests characteristic of life within the family. These interests have their origins in the intimate context of the family and lay claim to our allegiance and to our efforts. As Schoeman has revealingly said: "We *share our selves* with those with whom we are intimate and are aware that they do the same with us. Traditional moral boundaries, which give rigid shape to the self, are transparent to this kind of sharing."[19]

This richer understanding of human agency has implications for the two cases we discussed above. We do things, and should be expected to do things, for the family and for particular family members that we simply would not do for non-family members. For the most part, such burdens come with the very fact that we are bound to one another within a particular family. Thus if we view the agent's interests as being bound up with the interests of the family and its members, it should not strike one as ethically problematic that a mother might *naturally* want to donate part of her liver to her dying child. Neither love nor conscience constrains the mother's autonomy; rather, they give voice to her autonomy and say something about the kind of agent she is and the kind of family of which she is a member.

Why the use of the best interests standard may be inappropriate for thinking about kidney transplantations between minor siblings should now also be more apparent. The best interests standard is a formal and abstract framework; families are intimate and particular associations. The best interests standard is impartial; families are often partial and favoritist. Most crucially, the best interests standard is applied to an individual shorn of his or her associations; families are, or can be, intimate collectivities. The interests of more than one person are at stake. To attempt to cram a formal relation into an intimate context does violence to the morally significant aspects of the family relationship. Indeed, the traditional reliance on the best interests standard when considering the use of minors as organ donors illustrates the extent to which this reasoning has disregarded the union of family members and their interests, thus missed some of the important moral consequences that flow from the family context. What is morally important and problematic about organ transplantation is precisely that it may *not* be in the best interests of the donor.

Should living-related kidney transplantations never be done? No, but justification must rest on other grounds that take account of the fact that such transplantations are done not to advance the interests of the child donor as an individual, but for the sake of another family member, and for the sake of the family as a whole. Justification must reckon honestly with the risks to the donor, the likelihood that the procedure will succeed, the possible benefits to the recipient, and the potential alternatives. It must take account of the fact that parents have obligations not only to the child who is to donate the kidney, but to the sick child who is to receive it, whose life and welfare may be in mortal danger. And most crucially, any justification for sibling kidney transplantation must cast a critical eye on the question whether parents can legitimately expect their children to bear some burdens for the sake of family interests, even interests that the children might not yet explicitly endorse.

NOTES

1. Wittgenstein L. *Philosophical Investigations*, 3rd ed. Anscombe GEM, trans. Anscombe GEM, Rhees R, von Wright GH, eds. Oxford, UK: Basil Blackwell, 1967.

2. Murdoch I. *The Sovereignty of Good.* London: Routledge and Kegan Paul, 1970: 80.

3. Arthur Caplan's comments are taken from *Knight-Ridder Newspapers* 1989; Dec. 14.

4. George Annas' comments are taken from the *New York Times* 1989; Nov. 27.

5. Siegler M, Lantos JD. Commentary: Ethical justification for living liver donation. *Cambridge Quarterly of Healthcare Ethics* 1992; 1(4): 320–25, at p. 323.

6. No.68651 Eq., Massachusetts, 12 June 1957.

7. Quoted in Curran WJ. A problem of consent: kidney transplantation in minors. *New York University Law Review* 1959; 34: 891–98 at 893; emphasis added. *Masden*, like *Huskey v. Harrison* and *Foster v. Harrison* after it, is an unreported judgment. Therefore,

we are bound to the excerpts from the slip opinions that have been quoted in Curran's paper.

8. A clarification here is important. In both *Strunk v. Strunk* (see note 9) and *Hart v. Brown* (see note 11), unlike in *Little v. Little* (see note 13) where the best interests standard was explicitly adopted by the court, the justices in these two earlier cases held that the court's authority to authorize the minor donations rested with the common law substituted judgment doctrine. Although this is undoubtedly true as a strict matter of law, it is similarly beyond doubt that the justices would not have authorized the donations had they not found that the donation would be in the minor donor's best interests. Thus while the substituted judgment doctrine is prominent in the *language* of the courts, the point here is that the best interests standard dominates the *thinking* of the courts in all of these cases. Because of this, we will not discuss the substituted judgment doctrine here. For an excellent account of the substituted judgment doctrine in these and many other cases see Harmon L. Falling off the vine: legal fictions and the doctrine of substituted judgment. *Yale Law Journal* 1990; 100(1): 1–71.

9. *Strunk v. Strunk*, 445 S.W.2d 145 (Kentucky, 1969).

10. See note 9, *Strunk* 1969: 149.

11. *Hart v. Brown*, 289 A.2d 386 (Connecticut, 1972).

12. See note 11, *Hart* 1972: 389.

13. *Little v. Little*, 576 S.W.2d 493 (Texas, 1979).

14. In re Guardianship of Pescinski, 226 N.W.2d 180, 1975: 182.

15. Feinberg J. *Harm to Others. Volume I: The Moral Limits of the Criminal Law.* New York: Oxford University Press, 1984: 70–79. Feinberg identifies a further class of actions that are not self-interested, such as those done from principle or charity. Such acts are not done in the service of, and may be contrary to, the agent's own interests. They are mentioned here for the sake of completeness.

16. See note 1, Wittgenstein 1967: 49.

17. Taylor C. Hegel's ambiguous legacy for modern liberalism. *Cardozo Law Review* 1989; 10: 857–70 at 861.

18. See note 17, Taylor 1989: 861; emphasis added.

19. Schoeman F. Rights of children, rights of parents, and the moral basis of the family. *Ethics* 1980; 91(4): 6–19 at 8.

Innovative Policies for Organ Procurement

JANET RADCLIFFE RICHARDS

Nephrarious Goings On: Kidney Sales and Moral Arguments

Janet Radcliffe Richards is reader in bioethics at University College London, and director of its Centre for Bioethics and Philosophy of Medicine. She was formerly a member of the Department of Philosophy at the Open University, where she specialized in philosophy of science, ethics, and applied philosophy. Her books include *The Sceptical Feminist: A Philosophical Enquiry* and *Human Nature After Darwin*. She has published a wide range of academic articles on feminism, equality, and, more recently, biomedical ethics.

PART ONE—THE TRADITIONAL ARGUMENTS

I. THE SITUATION AND THE RESPONSE

When evidence of the trade in transplant organs from live vendors first filtered through to Western attention a few years ago, the most remarkable aspect of the immediate response was its unanimity. From all points of the political compass, from widely different groups who were normally hard pressed to agree about anything, there came indignant denunciations of the whole business. It was a moral outrage; a gross exploitation of the poor by the rich, who were now taking the very bodies of those from whom there was nothing else left to take, and obviously intolerable in any civilized society.

From *The Journal of Medicine and Philosophy* 21 (August 1996), 375–394 and 398–416. Copyright © 1996 by the Taylor & Francis Group. Reproduced by permission of Taylor & Francis Group, LLC., Inc., www.taylorandfrancis.com.

It is significant that this indignation was not, in the first instance, directed at the supplementary horrors of which media-fuelled rumors soon began to grow. Stories about kidneys stolen during other operations, failure afterwards to pay the agreed price, flagrant profiteering, and even abduction and murder, later inflamed the outrage, but the trade in organs from live vendors was almost universally denounced as a moral scandal quite independently of any such embellishments, and such remarkable concord must suggest that the moral case for prohibition is unequivocal.

Nevertheless, the matter is nothing like as clear as it may seem. The case has some curious features that suggest a different explanation for this unusual meeting of minds, and shows the problem of organ sales in a rather different light.

I shall limit the discussion to kidneys—which, in being both paired and non-renewable, come in some sense midway between hearts on the one hand, and livers and blood on the other—and to the problem of live vendors. Conclusions reached about laws and policies appropriate to this case will not necessarily transfer to the sale of organs or tissues of other kinds and in other circumstances, but this case raises matters of principle that are central to all, and, indeed, to most other areas of medical ethics.

II. THE BURDEN OF PROOF

Perhaps the most striking curiosity comes right at the beginning, in the way the situation is typically described. To hear the organ trade characterized in terms of the greedy rich and the exploited poor, you might think that the rich, tired of gold plating their bathrooms and surfeited with larks' tongues, had now idly turned to collecting kidneys to display with their Fabergé eggs and Leonardo drawings. But the rich in question here are *dying*, and desperately trying to save their lives; or, at the very least, to escape the crushing miseries of chronic illness and perpetual dialysis. Most critics of the trade in organs would do all they could to find similar amounts of money if private medicine offered their only chance of escaping death or disability, and would not, in doing so, expect to be regarded as paradigm cases of greed. There is, if anything, less greed involved in spending money to save your life or to achieve your freedom than in keeping it to spend on luxuries before you become ill.

And the attitude shown to the poor who are selling the organs is even odder. Consider, for instance, the case of the young Turkish father swept to everyone's television screen by the surge of outrage that followed the first revelations. He was trying to meet the expense of urgent hospital treatment for his daughter. Presumably the prospect of selling his kidney was, to say the least, no more attractive to him than it seems to us, but he nevertheless judged this to be his best available option. As we rush to intervene, therefore, saying how dreadful it is that he should be exploited in this way, we are taking away what he regards as his best option and leaving him in a situation he thinks even worse than the loss of a kidney. The same applies to other "desperate individuals" who advertise kidneys and even eyes in newspapers, or write to surgeons offering to sell them, "often for care of an ill relative". . . . The worse we think it is to sell a kidney or an eye, the worse we should think the situation in which we leave these people when we remove that option. Our indignation on behalf of the exploited poor seems to take the curious form of wanting to make them worse off still.

So, as we contemplate with satisfaction our rapid moves to thwart greed and protect the poor, we leave behind one trail of people dying who might have been saved, and another of people desperate enough to offer their organs thrust back into the wretchedness they were hoping to alleviate. And, furthermore, in a surprising contravention of our usual ideas about individual liberty, we prevent adults from entering freely into contracts from which both sides expect to benefit, and with no obvious harm to anyone else. Our intervention, in other words, seems in direct conflict with all our usual concerns for life, liberty, and the pursuit of happiness.

It is irrelevant to respond indignantly, as many people do, that no one should be in these desperate situations. Of course they should not; but even if there were any moral point in making rules for the world as we should like it to be rather than as it is, that would still provide no justification for prohibition. If we could eliminate poverty to the extent of removing all temptation for anyone to sell organs, prohibition would have nothing to do; and, conversely, as long as it has anything to do, some people must be at whatever level of desperation makes them see organ selling as their best option. Whatever the state of the world, prohibition either causes these harms or has no point at all.

Of course this is a long way from the end of the matter. The claim so far is that prohibition seems to cause various harms or to be undesirable in other ways; but a hundred times a day we make choices that have some bad aspects, because we nevertheless judge the options that involve them to be best, all things considered. To accept that some aspects of prohibition are intrinsically undesirable is compatible with claiming that it is still, all things considered, justified.

Nevertheless, when some course of action seems to involve positive harms, that does at least provide a clear direction of burden of proof. If you knew nothing more about some practice than that it involved sticking needles into children, your presumption, pending further evidence, would be that it should be stopped. You would (probably) withdraw your objections when you saw that nothing more sinister was going on than vaccination or the administration of anaesthesia, whose benefits far outweighed the intrinsic harm, but you would want the evidence first. The same applies here. Even if the conclusion can be reached that organ sales should be prohibited, the starting presumption must be the other way. Anyone wanting to forbid organ sales, therefore, must do one (or both) of two things: either show that there is something wrong with this account of the matter, and that prohibition does not involve any or all of these harms, or argue that they are outweighed by more important considerations on the other side.

It is difficult to separate these two elements in the debate, since the usual arguments against organ sales are not offered as replies to this particular challenge. Arguments that would, if successful, show that organ selling did not involve the evils alleged, are usually presented simply as arguments for prohibition. . . .

III. AUTONOMY AND CONSENT

Consider first the claim that prohibition prevents free contracts between consenting adults. Most people involved in the organs debate accept the fundamental tenet of Western liberalism that people should be allowed to control their own destinies as far as possible, but many claim that there can be no genuine, free consent to the sale of organs, and therefore (in effect) that there is no curtailment of liberty in preventing it. Since it is also claimed that genuine consent is an absolute requirement for any surgical procedure, the alleged impossibility of obtaining such consent under these circumstances is offered not merely as the removal of a *prima facie* objection to prohibition, but as a positive reason for demanding it. Several different arguments are produced to defend the claim that apparent consent to the sale of organs is not genuine. . . .

A. Incompetence through ignorance. The most obvious way to argue that would-be organ vendors are not choosing freely is to claim that there is something about the people themselves that prevents their making genuinely autonomous choices. Enlightened Westerners will hesitate to suggest that Turkish and Indian peasants must be prevented from making their own decisions just because they are poor or foreign, but they may well argue that "since paid organ donors will always be relatively poor, and may be underprivileged and undereducated, the donor's full understanding of [the] risks cannot be guaranteed" (Sells, 1993, pp. 2983–2984). The requisite informed consent is impossible, and therefore organ sales should not be allowed. . . .

In the first place, no one committed to the value of autonomy would rush to institute a prohibition that would limit the freedom of *everyone*, just on the grounds that some, or even most, of the people most likely to be involved were incapable of making autonomous choices. At the very least, the first impulse should be to try to discriminate between people, and to interfere only with the ones who really are incapable of doing so. To justify a general prohibition it would be necessary to argue both that this could not be done, and that it would be worse to risk allowing the incompetent to choose than to curtail the freedom of the competent. I am not aware of anyone's having tried to make out such a case.

Second, ignorance as such is not an irremediable state. If ignorance is the obstacle to genuine choice, anyone concerned about autonomy will try to remove the ignorance before starting to foreclose options.[1] . . .

Commitment to the intrinsic value of self-determination and fear that rational decisions about organ selling must be impossible for anyone who might be tempted by it, therefore, however unexceptionable in themselves, come nowhere near supporting the conclusion that organ sales should be prohibited. But even if the argument did work, it would still not do what is required in this context, because it would equally rule out a great many things that most objectors to organ sales have no intention of ruling out. In particular, it would preclude unpaid organ donation, at least in any population where kidney selling might be a temptation, since genuine consent would be impossible for the same reasons. Whatever moral merits there may be in the giving of an organ, it can hardly be claimed as a miraculous remover of whatever intractable ignorance would have made genuine consent to its sale impossible, let alone one that works by backward causation. . . .

B. Coercion by poverty. Arguments about ignorance and incompetence concern what might be called internalities: characteristics of agents themselves that are supposed to make them incompetent to choose properly among whatever options are open to them. The most familiar arguments about autonomy and consent in the organs debate, however, are of a different kind. Most depend on the idea that would-be vendors are coerced by external circumstances, and that a coerced choice cannot count as genuine.[2] . . .

Once again, it is easy to see how this idea gets going. The poor would not be selling organs but for their poverty, so it may be reasonable to say that the poverty is coercing them into the sale. It is also widely taken for granted that decisions and agreements made under duress should not count, and it is easy to think of cases that support this idea. If some dealer in organs kidnaps me and threatens to take out one of my kidneys in some rat-infested cellar, without anaesthetic, unless I sign a document authorizing you to do the job properly in your modern hospital, of course I sign it; but equally of course, when I am delivered already anaesthetized to your operating theatre, and you are presented with this surprising document, you rightly suspect nefarious goings on and disregard my authorization. And when you do, nobody is likely to accuse you of gratuitously interfering with my decisions about how to run my life.

Nevertheless, illustrations like this are misleading, as can be shown by a slight change of scenario. Suppose the kidnapping went as before, but you knew that if you did not perform the operation the kidnapper could easily get me back and carry out his original intention. My consent would be just as coerced as before, but it would be preposterous for you to claim that respect for my autonomy obliged you to refuse to operate and leave me to the other fate. Coercion as such, therefore, cannot justify the disregarding of stated preferences.

This may seem surprising, but the matter becomes clear if, instead of going off into the metaphysics of true consent, we ask directly what it is about coercion that makes a defender of autonomy regard it as intrinsically undesirable. Coercion is a matter of reducing the range of options there would otherwise be. Deliberate coercers come and take away options until the

best available is what they want you to choose; circumstances like poverty can, by extension, be regarded as coercive because they are also constrictors of options that make you choose what you otherwise would not. This shows what it is about the first of the kidnapping cases that makes it right for anyone concerned about autonomy to ignore the coerced choice. The relevant point is not that my original consent was coerced, but that, having got me into your hands and away from the kidnapper, you are in a position to *remove the coercion* by restoring my original range of options. In the second case, by contrast, you cannot remove the coercion because the kidnapper can get me back, and if you disregard my wishes you will (in the extended sense that allows poverty as a kind of coercion) coerce me yet further, by precluding the best option even among the horribly limited range the original coercer has left me.

This is why it is quite wrong to say that the poor should be protected from selling their kidneys, "preferably, of course, by being lifted out of poverty" (Dossetor and Manickavel, p. 63), but otherwise by the complete prevention of sales. It implies that prohibition and "lifting out of poverty" are unequally desirable variations on the same general theme, whereas the foregoing argument shows them to be, in the relevant sense, direct opposites. Protecting the poor from kidney selling by removing poverty works by increasing the options until something more attractive is available; prevention of sales, in itself, only closes a miserable range of options still further. To the coercion of poverty is added the coercion of the supposed protector, who comes and takes away (what the prospective vendor sees as) the best that poverty has left. This cannot be justified by a concern for freedom and autonomy. . . .

And, once again, even if the argument did work it could still make no distinction between sales and donations. If vendors can be said to be coerced by circumstances, then, for the same reasons, so can donors. If losing a kidney is intrinsically undesirable, it is just as undesirable for a donor as for a vendor, and chosen only because constricted circumstances have made it the best option all things considered. If coercion is a reason for not allowing organ sales, and poverty counts as a kind of coercion, coercion by threat of the death of a relative—quite a heavy kind of coercion, you would think—should equally rule out donation. The logic is the same.

C. Coercion by unrefusable offers. A different kind of argument is that tempting someone like the Turkish peasant with a payment of several hundred times his annual income amounts to making him an offer he cannot refuse, and coercing him in that way. . . .

It is once again easy to see how this idea might arise. The irresistible offer, like poverty, has the effect of making the intrinsically unattractive prospect of losing an organ part of the best all-things-considered option, and may therefore seem coercive in the same way. And, furthermore, there is a significant difference between this and coercion by poverty. You cannot improve the situation of the poor by cutting off the organ-selling option, because what needs to be removed is the poverty that is doing the coercing, not the best option poverty has left. But the irresistible offer is quite different, because it is itself the source of the alleged coercion. It may seem, therefore, that in this case ending the trade removes what is doing the coercing, and is genuinely liberating.

This argument, however, fails at a different point. The second premise is wrong: the unrefusable offer is not a form of coercion. It does indeed change the situation until the all-things-considered best option includes the intrinsically undesirable element of kidney loss, but it does so, not through the narrowing of options that is characteristic of coercion, but through a broadening of them. The original options are all still there, and if you choose the new one you presumably regard it as better, all things considered, than any you had before; and, furthermore, the more irresistible you find it, the more decisive your preference. Removing it is yet again a constriction of options, not an elimination of coercion, and therefore cannot be justified by arguments based on ideals of freedom and autonomy. . . .

IV. PROBLEMS FOR PATERNALISTS

A. Harm to the vendor. It seems to be taken for granted, in this debate, that if it is impossible to get informed, autonomous consent for nephrectomy, that is enough to rule it out. This is what underlies all the attempts to justify prohibition by way of arguments that genuine consent is unobtainable. The assumption is, however, a rather surprising one, since it is quite at odds with our usual attitudes to consent in medical contexts. If a rational agent *withholds* informed consent that is usually thought to settle the matter, but if

someone is incapable of giving consent for consent-requiring procedures such as surgery we do not automatically say that these cannot go ahead; we usually say instead that some guardian should make the decision. Even if we could show that some would-be organ vendors were incapable of deciding for themselves, therefore, that would justify only our taking the decision out of their hands. It would not, in itself, justify our deciding one way rather than another. . . .

The issue the paternalist has to settle is one of rational risk taking. The potential harm of losing a kidney must be weighed against the potential benefits of whatever payment is received, and assessed against the probabilities that these harms and benefits will actually come about. This is obviously not easy. Probabilities are difficult to estimate and differ considerably between cases, and individuals have different views about the comparative merits of different outcomes. There is also great variation in individuals' willingness to take risks.

In spite of these difficulties, however, one conclusion does seem clear. Most prospective paternalists have no hope of claiming plausibly that the poor who want to sell their kidneys are obviously wrong about what is in their interests, because they cheerfully countenance, in other contexts, the running of risks that are quite objectively much less rational than this one. The dangers of hang gliding or rock climbing, or diving from North Sea oil rigs, are much greater than those of nephrectomy; and even though it is impossible to generalize about the benefits of particular sums of money to individuals, it is plausible to say that the expected benefits will be much greater to the desperately poor, who see in selling a kidney the only hope of making anything of their wretched lives and perhaps even of surviving, than to the relatively rich. If the rich who take risks for pleasure or danger money are not misguided, it is difficult to see why the poor, who propose to take lower risks for higher returns, should be regarded as so manifestly irrational as to need saving from themselves. You might rather think, *contra* Dossetor and Manickavel, that the poorer you were the more rational it would be to risk selling a kidney.

And once again, even if we could reach the general conclusion that kidney selling was bad for the vendors, the argument would apply equally to donors. If any aspect of organ selling is against the interests of the vendor, it is not (though this obvious fact seems to be overlooked most of the time) the getting of money but the loss of a kidney, and this is in principle identical for donor and vendor. . . .

B. Harm to the purchaser. Given the way the organ selling issue is usually presented, you would expect the third claimed disadvantage of prohibition—harm to the prospective purchaser—to go uncontested. If what is complained about is the unfair advantage of the greedy rich, obviously the complainer wants to put a stop to that advantage. . . .

However, the foregoing arguments about the poor show by implication the mistakes in both these lines of argument. Even though many of the claims about exploitative and careless clinics and less than candid vendors may be true, the question here is not of whether the purchasers are less well served than they ought to be, but of whether they would be better off without the trade at all. Clearly many, if not most, would not. Even if treatment carries a significant risk of disease, the alternative for most of the patients is certain death. And, furthermore, even if the risk were not worth taking in the present circumstances, that would still be an objection only to inadequacy of control, rather than to the trade as such.

The other claim, that the purchasers have not really given voluntary consent, is yet another case in which having a narrow range of choice is confused with an inability to make a fully informed choice among the options there are. Once again, you cannot show respect for people's autonomy by preventing them from taking the best option in a range you are arguing is already too narrow. If, on the other hand, the problem is an inability to make an informed choice because of inadequate information, that is a reason for supplying the information rather than for removing the option altogether.

V. OVERRIDING OBJECTIONS

The conclusion of the arguments so far, then, is that the original account of the situation must stand. Prohibition does interfere with the choices of competent adults, and it does typically harm would-be vendors and purchasers. If the case for prohibition is to be made out, therefore, it must be shown that these intrinsic disadvantages are outweighed by considerations of greater importance. Since opponents of organ sales have not on the whole even reached the stage of recognizing that prohibition has any disadvantages, not many arguments are presented as actually setting out to do this. There are, however, several in the field that might be offered for the purpose. This section considers an assortment of the most familiar.

A. Collateral damage. The most obvious kind of objection to look for, if the vendors and purchasers themselves must on the whole be regarded as beneficiaries of the trade, is counterbalancing harm elsewhere. A first glance at possibilities, however, looks unpromising. Anecdotes and statistics are offered about harm to the principals that may have repercussions for their families; but if on the whole the principals can expect to benefit, so, typically, can their families. Help for the family is often the purpose of the sale. Increased wealth to individuals presumably also tends to benefit the surrounding community, and the process in general involves a transfer of wealth from the rich to the poor. And, indeed, *unless* the trade can be shown to be wrong—the point presently at issue—even depriving the despised middlemen and operators of clinics of their socially useful niche in lands of few opportunities must count as an unjustifiable harm. If anything, the first foray into the area of collateral harm suggests that even more harm is done by prohibition than appeared at first.

Perhaps that is why the dark predictions are usually about dangers less tangible and more amorphous, such as the corruption of sensibilities and general moral decline. Rhetoric, however, is not enough to counterbalance such positive harms as death and destitution. It is necessary to be clear about exactly which evils are threatened, what evidence there is that they would come about, and how bad it would be if they did. Most of the threats turn out to be ill equipped to withstand this kind of scrutiny.

For instance, there is the allegation that the trade is wrong because it commodifies the body. In this case the claim is clear enough—the trade involves treating parts of the body as a purchasable commodity—and since this is precisely what the trade is, rather than anything it does, the question of evidence does not arise. But so far this is just a restatement of the point at issue, not an argument for objecting to it, and the question remains of what the harm is supposed to be. "Commodification" carries derogatory overtones, of course, which is why it is used; but without further explanation the pejorative term simply begs the question. This one takes its force from our outrage at the idea of treating people themselves as commodities, but before the moral implications can be dragged over—before we approve the loaded word "commodification" in this context—we need to see whether the moral suggestion is justified; and obviously it is not. Treating people as commodities, with no say in their own destiny, is just about as different as it could be from letting them decide for themselves what to do with their own bodies, which is what is at issue here and might reasonably be regarded as the most fundamental issues of autonomy there was.

Commodification is also alleged to cause further harms. "It depreciates some of the fundamental professional and moral values of society by demeaning the dignity and autonomy of the human individual" (Abouna *et al.*, p. 170); "By commodifying the body, mutual respect for all persons will be slowly eroded" (Dossetor and Manickavel, p. 66). Those certainly sound like harms; but now there is the problem of evidence. Autonomy is not infringed by the trade, as has already been argued at length. And even though it may be degrading to be in a state where organ selling is the best option left, that does not imply that actually going through with the sale increases the degradation (as is usually thought about prostitution, for instance). On the contrary, Reddy claims that for many vendors a positive motive is given by the duties of Hindu ethics, and that respect and self-respect increase because of a duty done (Reddy, p. 176). And even in Western cultures, if some of the unemployed could get a large sum of money and start again, supporting their families instead of living on the dole, would there be anything but a huge increase in their self respect, and the respect of others? This is an empirical question, but I defy any caviller to produce any evidence the other way, or even evidence of having looked for any.

It is also said that the trade "invites social and economic corruption . . . and even criminal dealings in the acquisition of organs for profit" (Abouna *et al.*, p. 171). That too is a clear harm, but again there is the question of evidence. It is well known that when a commodity is in demand it is the illegality of trade that produces corruption, as happened during Prohibition in the United States. Many people now defend the legalization of drugs and prostitution on just these grounds.

Another idea is that the trade has adverse effects on the transplant programme itself. One claim is that if purchase is a possibility, related donors are more reluctant to come forward. But if it is being claimed as a harm of the trade that vendors rather than donors are used, that once again begs the question at issue. *Unless* there is a reason for objecting to the trade it does not matter intrinsically that organs should come from vendors rather than from donors. . . .

It is also said that if organs can be bought from living vendors there will be no incentive to overcome public resistance to a cadaver programme (Broyer, p. 199). That would indeed be a drawback, since nobody doubts that it is desirable (other things being equal) to make as much possible use of the dead before resorting to the living, but there is the question of evidence again. The availability of purchased organs is certainly not the only or main reason for the shortage of cadaver organs, since there is a shortage where they are not available. . . .

Nearly all the objections that appeal to claims about harms caused by organ selling either beg the question, or treat mere possibilities as actual, or fly in the face of positive evidence. It is still possible that trade causes collateral harms substantial enough to outweigh the harms done by prohibition, but that has yet to be shown; and in the meantime the burden of proof continues to lie against prohibition.

B. Exploitation. An objection of a different kind is that the trade must be ended because it involves exploitation. Poverty may not make people irrational, it may be agreed, but it does make them vulnerable to exploitation, and the vulnerable must be protected. The trade should therefore be stopped.

The problem about this argument lies in the way exploitation works, and, once again, in the crucial difference between coercion and inducement to do what is intrinsically unattractive. Coercion works by the removal of other options until the unattractive one is the best left; and in such cases it is possible, as already argued, to protect the victim by putting a stop to the coercer's activities. But exploitation does not take this form. It works the opposite way, by adding inducements until they just tip the balance, and the intrinsically unattractive option becomes part of a package that is, all things considered, the best available. What is bad about exploitation, and makes it different from the offering of inducements that is a normal part of buying and hiring, is that the exploiter seeks out people who are so badly off that even a tiny inducement can improve on their best option, and in that way can get away with paying less than would be necessary to someone who had more options available. (If this is exploitation, of course, it looks suspiciously like free market capitalism; there is nothing new in that idea.) But the fact remains that it works by inducement, and the logic of inducements still applies. Nobody can improve your position by removing an effective inducement, however small, because to do so is to take away your all-things-considered best option.

Once again, in other words, we have an argument with unexceptionable premises—that the poor are vulnerable to exploitation, and that they should be protected—but whose conclusion does not follow. Although we can stop the exploitation by stopping the trade, to do so would be like ending the miseries of slum dwelling by bulldozing slums, or solving the problem of ingrowing toenails by chopping off feet. We put an end to that particular evil, but only at the cost of making things even worse for the sufferers. If our aim is the protection of the poor rather than just the thwarting of the exploiters, and we lack either the will or the power to remove the poverty that makes them exploitable in the first place, the next best thing is (once again) to subject the trade to stringent controls. That is the only way of ending the exploitation that also protects the poor.

C. Altruism. Another kind of argument still is presented, like the voluntarism requirement, as a moral absolute overriding all weighings of harms and benefits. Financial inducements, it is said, are to be ruled out because they preclude altruism, and an absolute requirement of organ donation is that it should be altruistic.

Since this requirement is usually asserted rather than argued for, it is presumably taken to be self-evident. Nevertheless, it is surprising. At least the other arguments discussed so far have started with plausible moral concerns about such things as coercion and exploitation, and have foundered only in the transition between these and their conclusions. But in this case the principle itself, for all its supposed self evidence, seems positively at odds with all our usual attitudes. The world is, after all, full of transactions which the transactors see as being to their mutual benefit, and to which in principle we have not the slightest objection. We may particularly admire their one-way equivalents, when goods and services are given that would otherwise have to be bought, but it normally does not occur to us that unless some transaction can be guaranteed to be of this one-way kind it should not take place at all. It would normally be regarded as astonishing, and in the absence of explanation absurd, to claim that it would actually be better that neither side should benefit than that both should.

Even if we accepted the principle, however, it would still have the usual problem of not supporting the required conclusion. Selling is not in itself at odds

with altruism; it all depends on what the money is wanted for. It does not even matter exactly what definition of altruism is accepted. For any action that an opponent of sales would count as altruistic, it is easy to imagine a case of selling that would be altruistic by the same standards. If a father who gives a kidney to save his daughter's life is acting altruistically, then so, by the same criterion, is one who sells his kidney to pay to save his daughter's life; if it is altruistic to work long hours to earn money for your family, it is altruistic to sell your kidney for the same purpose.

And yet again, if a demand for altruism could form any part of an argument to rule out sales—if, for instance, it were claimed that organ sales should be prohibited because they *might* not be altruistic—it would rule out donations as well. . . .

D. Slavery. Another common line of objection works by appealing to other practices that most people would agree were intolerable, and attempts to derive an objection to kidney selling from a linking of the two. Slavery is the commonest of these. "It is sometimes argued that an individual should be free to sell his organs just as he sells his labor, and why should there be any objection? This argument, if taken to its conclusion, may easily be used to justify a return to allowing individuals to sell themselves into slavery, which is clearly unacceptable" (Abouna *et al.*, p. 169). Similar lines of argument suggest that if kidneys can be sold, there can be no objection to the selling of vital organs such as hearts.

Arguments like this are not always clear, and particular versions may need spelling out before detailed replies can be given. But the usual intention seems to be to produce a *reductio ad absurdum:* anyone who thinks kidney sales are acceptable is committed to thinking slavery (or, as it may be, heart selling) is also acceptable; but since slavery is manifestly wrong, kidney sales must be wrong as well.

If this is the idea, the quotation above shows by implication where this strategy goes wrong. The argument does not show that the acceptability of kidney selling entails the acceptability of slavery, but only that *one particular justification* someone might offer for condoning organ sales—that people should be free to sell whatever is theirs—also entails the acceptability of slavery. The argument therefore works only *ad hominem*, against someone who offers that particular defence. Acceptance of one practice can never, in itself, logically commit anyone to acceptance of some other: it always depends on what the reasons are. The line of argument being developed here, for instance—depending on the claim that prohibition does definite harms, and therefore that there is a presumption against it until good arguments in its favor are produced—does not depend on the principle that people have an entitlement to sell what is their own, and is immune to this particular attack.

Arguments of this kind exemplify yet again the now-familiar pattern. Most people are likely to agree that to allow slavery or the selling of hearts would obviously be wrong, but those premises are not enough to support the conclusion that kidney sales must therefore be wrong as well. And anyway, such an argument could not make the necessary distinction between sales and donations. People are not allowed to *give* themselves into slavery or give away their hearts, either, so if the argument did work we should have to conclude that the unpaid donation of kidneys should also be forbidden. . . .

PART TWO—THE IMPLICATIONS FOR MORAL ENQUIRY

VI. A SERIES OF SHOW TRIALS

The claim so far has been that the prohibition of organ sales seems to involve real harms of various sorts, and that none of the arguments offered by its defenders has succeeded in showing either that these are illusory, or that allowing the trade would cause even greater harms, or that there are overriding moral reasons of other kinds for concluding that they must be put up with. The conclusion at this stage must therefore be that there is no justification for prohibition, but only for trying to lessen whatever incidental harms are now involved in the practice.

The form the arguments have taken shows that this conclusion is only provisional. Someone may yet come along with good enough reasons to overcome the presumption in favor of organ sales; and, for what it is worth, I have a sneaking hope that this will happen, since I find the whole business as intuitively repugnant as does everybody else. But even if it does happen that will not affect the significance of the foregoing arguments, because the primary purpose of this paper is not to defend organ sales. Its purpose is to draw wider conclusions about the form of the debate; and to explain this it is necessary to go back and reconsider what has been going on so far.

A. The form of the arguments. An outsider, hearing that some essay had presented a defence of kidney selling, would probably presume that the argument was based on controversial libertarian principles about free trade and the rights of people to do what they liked with their own bodies, and—if unsympathetic—start raising moral or empirical objections to principles of that kind. But not only have the arguments offered here not depended on such principles; what is more significant is that they have not depended on controversial premises at all, either moral or empirical. They have depended almost entirely on logic and analysis, and have tried to show that the traditional arguments against organ sales fail not by the standards of some outside critic, but in their proponents' own terms. . . .

The usual run of arguments against organ sales, therefore, fails not by the standards of some external critic who is producing rival empirical claims or offering different bases for moral judgment, but in terms of the very standards recommended by the proponents of the arguments themselves. The conclusions do not follow from the principles invoked in their support, either because the logic goes wrong or because the inference depends on invented facts. And it is worth noticing that this point is relevant to the familiar, last resort, all-purpose escape route of people driven into unwelcome corners by argument, which is the claim that logic must not be placed above moral intuitions. This line of argument cannot get off the ground because what logic demonstrates in cases like these is conflicts *of intuitions* (between, for instance, the importance of autonomy and impermissibility of organ selling) which the familiar arguments try to hide by presenting them as compatible or even necessarily connected. If there really is a conflict, so that one or the other must be given up or made subordinate to the other, it is *morally essential* that this should be faced. Flailing at logic is not an appeal to a higher morality, but a refusal to attend to moral questions at all. . . .

The familiar arguments against organ sales are rationalizations, and flagrant ones at that, of something already believed for other reasons. No one starting innocently from the beginnings of these arguments could possibly arrive at the conclusions to which they are supposed to lead. They seem to work only because their proponents are already, independently, convinced of their truth.

This is also suggested by many other aspects of the debate. It appears, for instance, in the speed of public reaction to the discovery of the trade, and the terms in which it was immediately condemned. If people had really been trying to work out whether this quite new activity was justified or not, they could hardly have overlooked so completely the obvious *prima facie* harms of prohibition, and would have been agonizing over the complexities of the problem rather than rushing into action. It appears in the way every demolished argument is immediately replaced by another, with ever weaker ones recruited to the cause as the early contenders fail. If the conclusion had been reached *by means of* some argument, refutation of that argument would be recognized as removing the reasons for accepting the conclusion. It also shows in the way assorted arguments of quite different and often incompatible kinds are heaped up together, and in the flagrant invention of convenient facts. Both of these typically occur when deeply held convictions are being anxiously defended.

It is probably this deep conviction, furthermore, that underlies the ready characterization (by people who probably know nothing of the matter) of all the surgeons and clinic organizers and middlemen involved as villains. There are horror stories about all these groups; but there are horror stories about most areas of commerce, and this does not tempt us to assume that all dealers must be scoundrels or all trade profiteering, or even to express outrage (as opposed to disquiet) in other contexts where vast profits are made from the practice of medicine. If it is assumed that anything earned through organ sales must be tainted, that suggests the trade is regarded as inherently, not merely incidentally, corrupt.

The moral of these arguments, therefore, is not just that the arguments offered for prohibition do not work, though that is important in itself. What is more significant is that there obviously exists a deep intuition about the unacceptability of organ sales, quite independent of, and fuelling, the curiously bad arguments pressed into its defence. That is why, even if a good argument for prohibition does appear later, it will not undermine the significance of the failure of the familiar set. The form of that failure proves the verdict of guilty to have been pronounced in advance, and the supposed debate merely a series of show trials.

VII. REPUGNANCE AS A MORAL GUIDE

The fact that the intuitive resistance to organ sales exists quite independently of the arguments normally invoked to justify prohibition does not in itself prove that the intuition is misguided. Organ selling might still be something intrinsically evil, defying justification in terms of anything more fundamental. We do think there are such things; we must, if we think ethics is to get off the ground at all. Perhaps, then, all that can ultimately be said about the matter is caught by our rapid characterization of the whole business as *repugnant*—a word we tend to use when we are deeply averse to something, but find our feelings difficult to explain in terms of more obvious kinds of good and evil.

It is often said that such deep intuitions should be our ultimate moral authority: that "it is the emotional conviction which ultimately should determine where one makes one's stand" (Dossetor and Manickavel, p. 71). But nobody seriously believes that all strong feelings of a moral kind are reliable guides to action. We are not even tempted to think so except in the case of our own; intuitions we do not share are seen as manifestations of irrationality and bigotry. And we should have doubts even about our own when we consider how passionately people may feel about matters that detached reflection suggests must be morally neutral, such as particular forms of the treatment of the dead, or how many traditional reactions of deep repugnance to such things as interracial marriage, unfeminine women and homosexuality are now widely regarded as themselves repugnant. Mere strength of feeling cannot be taken to prove that moral bedrock has been reached.

How, then, can the moral reliability of this particular strong feeling be tested? If the idea is that whatever causes it is a fundamental evil in its own right, it is obviously irrelevant to test that claim by seeing whether it can be shown to be wrong in other terms. But anyone who is inclined to accept it as a moral guide can start by checking carefully exactly what circumstances prompt its appearance. Just as people are inclined to justify their wish to prohibit organ selling in terms of other kinds of moral concern, so, for obviously related reasons, they are inclined to explain their emotional response as arising in response to exploitation, or inequality, or some other morally plausible generator of strong feelings. To test such claims, what is needed is a series of thought experiments. Organ sales and these other causes of moral concern can be imagined away from each other, to discover what really gives rise to the feelings of disgust. When that has been identified, it will be possible to look whatever it is squarely in the eye, and see whether reflection can endorse the idea that it is a fundamental evil. . . .

We may claim to be disgusted that organs should be sacrificed for any other reason than love, or with less than complete willingness; but then we should find it no more repugnant that a father should sell his kidney to save his daughter than that he should give it to her directly, and we should feel just the same kind of repugnance at the thought that some reluctant relative should feel the heavy pressure of duty, or fear, and donate an organ without love.

We may say that what we find most repugnant about the trade is the abuse and exploitation; but in that case we should feel just as much disgust, of the same kind, about equal exploitation and abuse in other areas, and even more when these are worse (as, for instance, with the slave labor that produces cheap luxury goods for the affluent world). And, conversely, if the abuses were ended, and the trade properly regulated, the feelings of revulsion should go.

We may say that the disgust arises from the idea of cutting into, and damaging, a healthy body. If so, we should feel as much disgust about donations as about sales; and since no harm can be done by cutting into a dead body, there should be no disgust at the prospect of selling organs from the dead.

We may claim that the source of the disgust is the unfairness of distribution: "wealthy people obtaining services not available to others" (Land and Dossetor, p. 231). If so, we should feel the same repugnance about any kind of private medicine (and, indeed about state-financed triple bypasses for citizens of the rich world whose cost would save thousands of lives elsewhere), and none if public agencies were to buy organs for general distribution.

Or we may say that the disgust is aroused by the desperate situation of the poor, and their being forced by circumstances to make such terrible decisions. If so, we should feel the same kind of disgust when desperation forces them to sell their labor at appallingly low prices (and more still if they can find no one to buy at any price and cannot alleviate their situation at all), and none at the idea that some reasonably well off person from a rich society might sell a kidney to achieve some non-necessary personal project, like travelling round the world or learning to fly.

Thought experiments like these make it clear to most people that when suffering and exploitation are imagined separately from the element of selling, the *peculiar kind of horror* aroused by the trade in organs does not appear. There may be other feelings of moral outrage, but not this one. And they also make it clear that in most cases—and probably, for most people, all cases—the converse is also true. Take away these other elements that are claimed as the source of the disgust—consider organ selling in altruistic, non-exploitative, well-regulated circumstances—and the disgust obstinately remains. It really does seem to be the business of exchanging money for parts of the body, in itself and for no further reason, that catches our feelings in this distinctive way.

It is perhaps worth commenting that an indirect confirmation of this conclusion seems to lie in the only solution I have been able to think of to the mystery of the altruism requirement. There are many familiar contexts in which the contrast between giving and selling is described as between doing things for love—altruistically—and doing them for money. If this kind of contrast is (mistakenly) thought of as paradigmatic, the demand for altruism may get its apparent force from seeming to coincide with the absence of payment, while at the same time giving the appearance of offering justification because nobody doubts that altruism is a good thing. The altruism requirement, in other words, looks suspiciously like a mere restatement of the non-selling requirement, with spurious moral knobs on.

If all this is true, and the emotional reaction really is to organ sales as such, irrespective of circumstances and consequences, is it possible to endorse it as a moral guide? Can the wrongness of organ sales be accepted as a ground-level moral fact, and one of such importance as to outweigh all our usual concens about death, destitution and loss of liberty whenever they come into conflict?

When the matter is put as starkly as this it is hard to see how anyone could see it as a fundamental moral fact at all, let alone one of such overriding importance. Most people who react with repugnance to organ sales see nothing wrong in the exchange of money for goods in other circumstances, and see the donation of organs as positively commendable. Is it plausible that the combination of the two, in itself and for no further reason, can nevertheless be self-evidently and invariably evil? Can a sacrifice made with love and altruism be turned into a moral outrage just because payment comes somewhere into the matter, while an equal sacrifice made reluctantly or through vested interests is acceptable because it does not? Can the mere exchange of money transmute something inherently good into a transaction so appalling that it might even be better, as Broyer suggests (Broyer, 1991, p. 198), to risk losing genuinely unpaid donations (and allow people to die in consequence) than allow even the *possibility* that payment might be involved? Presumably the feelings of repugnance can in principle be explained, . . . but it is hard to see how anyone could endorse them as moral guides.

And as a matter of fact, it seems that nobody really does. Even if these arguments did not make it obvious that the prevention of organ selling *could* not plausibly be regarded as morally fundamental, it is nevertheless clear that it *is* not so regarded, because all the familiar arguments against organ sales try to explain its wrongness in other terms. Nobody says that it just is more important to prevent organ selling than any more obvious sort of harm, and leaves the matter there. Prohibition, it seems, must be justified, even if the only way to do it is to fudge connections and compatibilities with the very moral concerns that it overrides.

In fact, another thing that seems implied by the fragility of the familiar arguments is that the extreme strength of feeling underlying the resistance to organ sales runs with a recognition that it needs some defending. People do not resort to arguments as bad as these unless they think arguments are badly needed.

VIII. THE NEW FORM OF THE PROBLEM

The situation then is this. When states enact laws forbidding the exchange of money for organs, or professional bodies pronounce their anathemas against it, they present their conclusions as arising from plausible moral concerns about autonomy, exploitation, and the interests of the poor. If my arguments have been right, however, this is not at all what is going on. In fact there is a strong, widely held and quite independent conviction that organ sales must be wrong, into whose defence has been pressed a motley array of arguments that could not have begun to persuade anyone who was really trying to work out the rights and wrongs of the issue from scratch. The prohibition of organ sales is derived not from the principles usually invoked in its support, but from a powerful feeling of repugnance that apparently numbs ordinary moral sensitivities and anaesthetizes the intellect, making invisible the obvious harms of prohibition, giving plausibility to arguments whose inadequacy

would in less fraught contexts proclaim itself from the rooftops, and, in doing both these things, hiding the extraordinary force of its own influence. . . .

It has been shown how thoroughly the deep opposition to organ sales can distort the arguments, and how invisible its influence can be even in the relatively straightforward cases discussed earlier. In complicated arguments about risks and probabilities, or individual preferences and social policies, it is inherently difficult for even the most unprejudiced enquirer to reach objective conclusions, and therefore all too easy to go through the motions of analysis and make the conclusion come out where the emotions have already determined that they should. On the other hand, once the problem and its manifestations have been recognized, there are various ways in which the danger may be lessened.

In the first place, if the failed arguments really do involve mistakes that would not be made in neutral contexts, one remedy is to be much more critical about the analysis of arguments in general, asking firmly of any candidate what we should think of its merits if we were really starting from the premises and asking, without any preconceptions, whether they supported the conclusion. . . .

It is not only the details of the arguments, however, that have been distorted by the feelings of repugnance. More fundamentally, their influence has extended to the way the whole problem has been presented. The issue is usually seen as a "for and against" question, with two opposing sides. There is certainly an *against* side, in the sense that most of the opponents of organ sales seem to accept, as a moral absolute, the idea that organ sales are always and obviously wrong. But if you reject this idea—if you agree that the appearance of an absolute can be traced to a feeling of repugnance with highly dubious credentials—that does not mean you are *for* organ sales in the sense of supporting a corresponding absolute in favor of them, let alone in favor of an unfettered trade. To reject the absolute is, in itself, only to remove a constraint on the kind of answer that can be given to the wider question of how we can most acceptably procure organs for transplant, thereby opening the question up, and turning it (it has to be admitted) into the kind of messy calculation of pros and cons that characterizes most moral decisions about public policy. And once the problem is recognized as taking this form, it becomes clear that there is no reason to expect a single answer to it, or to think of fixed and opposing sides at all. . . .

That, as it stands, leaves entirely open the question of the permissibility of organ sales. However, the fact also remains that nothing has yet dislodged the claim that the prohibition of organ sales harms both vendors and purchasers, and involves interventions in personal liberty. Nobody setting out in an unprejudiced way to improve some situation rushes to cause harm or restrict liberty. If there are abuses and dangers in the present trade, as there certainly are, the obvious way to improve the situation is to try to remove those. Only in circumstances where that turns out to be impossible, *and* there is good reason to think that the harms of organ trading outweigh the benefits, can prohibition be justified. Since the second has not been demonstrated, or the first even tried in any systematic way, the presumption must still be against prohibition.

There is also one further, positive, reason for keeping the trade in organs, which sounds perverse but is actually offered here more than half seriously. This is the very fact that most people do find it so profoundly shocking and distressing. It certainly is shocking; it is dreadful that people should be forced by distress and destitution into selling parts of themselves. Nevertheless, the fact remains that we seem quite capable of putting up with even worse distress as long as it is not forced on our attention in this peculiarly distasteful way. Many a Turkish peasant is now presumably worse off than before we banned the trade, and the potential recipients of their kidneys may be dead; but we are not clamouring about these desperate lives and untimely deaths in the way we did about the evils of the trade. If we can be so unpleasantly reminded of the way things really are we may begin to take the despair of the poor and the dying more seriously: to make comparable outcries about the terms of third world trade, and give money to Oxfam, and leave kidneys to whoever needs them.

The sale of organs may perhaps be, as Broyer says, "a visible and intolerable symptom of the exploitation of the poor by the rich" (Broyer, 1991, p. 199), but if so that is a reason for allowing it to continue. If we are forced to suffer the intolerable symptoms, we shall less easily forget the disease.

NOTES

1. See, e.g., Broyer, 1991, p. 199: "It is far from sure that the donor would be able to understand fully the information about the sequelae of nephrectomy."

2. See also Abouna *et al.*, 1991, p. 166: "A truly voluntary and noncoerced consent is also unlikely. . . . the desperate financial need of the donor is an obvious and clear economic coercion."

REFERENCES

Abouna, G. M., Sabawi, M. M., Kumar, M. S. A., and Samhan, M.: 1991, "The negative impact of paid organ donation," in W. Land and J. B. Dossetor (eds.), *Organ Replacement Therapy: Ethics, Justice, Commerce,* Springer-Verlag, Berlin, New York, pp. 164–172.

Broyer, M.: 1991, "Living organ donation; the fight against commercialism," in W. Land and J. B. Dossetor (eds.), *Organ Replacement Therapy: Ethics, Justice, Commerce,* Springer-Verlag, Berlin, New York, pp. 197–199.

Cohen, L. R.: 1991, "The ethical virtues of a futures market in cadaveric organs," in W. Land and J. B. Dossetor (eds.), *Organ Replacement Therapy: Ethics, Justice, Commerce,* Springer-Verlag, Berlin, New York, pp. 302ff.

Dossetor, John B. and Manickavel, V.: 1992, "Commercialization: The buying and selling of kidneys," in C. M. Kjellstrand and J. B. Dossetor (eds.), *Ethical Problems in Dialysis and Transplantation,* Kluwer Academic Publishers, Dordrecht, pp. 61–71.

Kjellstrand, Carl M., and Dossetor, John B. (eds.): 1992, *Ethical Problems in Dialysis and Transplantation,* Kluwer Academic Publishers, Dordrecht.

Land, W., and Dossetor, J. B. (eds.): 1991, *Organ Replacement Therapy: Ethics, Justice, Commerce,* Springer-Verlag, Berlin, New York.

Mani, M. K.: 1992, "The argument against the unrelated live donor," in C. M. Kjellstrand and J. B. Dossetor (eds.), *Ethical Problems in Dialysis and Transplantation,* Kluwer Academic Publishers, Dordrecht, pp. 163–168.

Radcliffe Richards, J.: 1991, "From him that hath not," in W. Land and J. B. Dossetor (eds.) *Organ Replacement Therapy: Ethics, Justice, Commerce,* Springer-Verlag, Berlin, New York; reprinted in C. M. Kjellstrand and J. B. Dossetor (eds.), *Ethical Problems in Dialysis and Transplantation,* Kluwer Academic Publishers, Dordrecht, 1992, pp. 53–60.

Reddy, K. C.: 1991, "Organ donation for consideration," in W. Land and J. B. Dossetor (eds.), *Organ Replacement Therapy: Ethics, Justice, Commerce,* Springer-Verlag, Berlin, New York, pp. 173–180.

Reddy, K. C., Thiagarajan, C. M., Shunmugasundaran, D., *et al.*: 1990, Unconventional renal transplantation in India: To buy or let die. Transplant Proceedings 22: 910.

Schelling, Thomas C: 1960, 1980, *The Strategy of Conflict,* Harvard University Press, Cambridge.

Sells, R. A.: 1991, "Voluntarism of consent," in W. Land and J. B. Dossetor (eds.), *Organ Replacement Therapy: Ethics, Justice, Commerce,* Springer-Verlag, Berlin, New York, pp. 18–24.

Sells, R. A.: 1993, "Resolving the conflict in traditional ethics which arises from our demand for organs," *Transplantation Proceedings* 25 (6), December, pp. 2983–2984.

NANCY SCHEPER-HUGHES

Keeping an Eye on the Global Traffic in Human Organs

Nancy Scheper-Hughes is Professor of Medical Anthropology at the University of California, Berkeley. Her most recent research is a multi-sited ethnographic study of the global traffic in humans for their organs and is the subject of her upcoming book *The Ends of the Body: the Global Traffic in Organs*. She is co-founder and Director of Organs Watch, a medical human rights project, and is currently an advisor to the World Health Organization on issues related to global transplantation.

"If a living donor can do without an organ, why shouldn't the donor profit and medical science benefit?"

RADCLIFFE-RICHARDS J., et al.
Lancet 1998; 351:1951.

From its origins transplant surgery presented itself as a complicated problem in gift relations and gift theory, a domain to which anthropologists have contributed a great deal. Today the celebrated gift of life is under assault by the emergence of new markets in bodies and body parts to supply the needs of transplant patients. Global capitalism has distributed to all corners of the world, not only advanced medical technologies, medications, and procedures, but also new desires and expectations. These needs have spawned in their wake strange markets and occult economies.

The ideal conditions of economic globalisation have put into circulation mortally sick bodies travelling in one direction and healthy organs (encased in their human packages) in another, creating a bizarre kula ring of international trade in bodies. The emergence of the organs markets, excess capital, renegade surgeons, and local kidney hunters with links to organised crime, have stimulated the growth of a spectacularly lucrative international transplant tourism, much of it illegal and clandestine. In all, these new transplant transactions are a blend of altruism and commerce; of consent and coercion; of gifts and theft; of care and invisible sacrifice.

On the one hand, the spread of transplant technologies has given the possibility of new, extended, or improved quality of life to a select population of mobile and affluent kidney patients, from the deserts of Oman to the high rises of Toronto and Tokyo. On the other hand, these technologies have exacerbated older divisions between North and South and between haves and have-nots, spawning a new form of commodity fetishism in the increasing demands by medical consumers for a new quality product—fresh and healthy kidneys purchased from living bodies. To a great many knowledgeable transplant patients morgue organs are regarded as passé and relegated to the dustbins of medical history. In these radical exchanges of body parts, life-saving for the one demands self-mutilation on the part of the other. One person's biosociality is another person's biopiracy, dependent on whether one is speaking from a private hospital room in Quezon City, or Istanbul, or from a sewage-infested banguay (slum) in Manila or a hillside favela (shantytown) in Rio de Janeiro.

The kidney as a commodity has emerged as the gold standard in the new body trade, representing the poor person's ultimate collateral against hunger, debt, and penury. Thus, I refer to the bartered kidney as the organ of last resort. Meanwhile, transplant tourism has become a vital asset to the medical economies of poorer countries from Peru, South Africa, India, the Philippines, Iraq, China, and Russia to Turkey. In general, the circulation of kidneys follows established routes of capital from South to North, from East to West, from poorer to more affluent bodies, from black and brown bodies to white ones, and from female to male or from poor, low status men to more affluent men. Women are rarely the recipients of purchased organs anywhere in the world.

In the face of this postmodern dilemma, my colleague Lawrence Cohen and I—both medical anthropologists with wide experience and understanding of poverty and sickness in the third world—founded Organs Watch in 1999 as an independent research and medical human rights project at the University of California, Berkeley, as a stop-gap measure in the presence of an unrecognised global medical emergency, and in the absence of any other organisation of its kind. We have since undertaken original fieldwork on the changing economic and cultural context of organ transplant in 12 countries across the globe. . . .

In all, we have begun to map the routes and the international medical and financial connections that make possible the new traffic in human beings, a veritable slave trade that can bring together parties from three or more countries. In one well travelled route, small groups of Israeli transplant patients go by charter plane to Turkey where they are matched with kidney sellers from rural Moldova and Romania and are transplanted by a team of surgeons—one Israeli and one Turkish. Another network unites European and North American patients with Philippine kidney sellers in a private episcopal hospital in Manila, arranged through an independent internet broker who advertises via the web site Liver4You. Brokers in Brooklyn, New York, posing as a non-profit organisation, traffic in Russian immigrants to service foreign patients from Israel who are transplanted in some of the best medical facilities on the east coast of the USA. Wealthy Palestinians travel to Iraq where they can buy a kidney from poor Arabs coming from Jordan. The kidney sellers are housed in a special ward of the hospital that has all the appearances of a kidney motel. A Nigerian doctor/broker facilitates foreign transplants in South Africa or Boston, USA (patient's/buyer's choice), with a ready supply of poor Nigerian kidney sellers, most of them single women. The purchase agreement is notarised by a distinguished law firm in Lagos, Nigeria.

Despite widespread knowledge about these new practices and official reports made to various governing bodies, few surgeons have been investigated and none have lost their credentials. The procurement of poor people's body parts, although illegal in almost every country of the world, is not recognised as a problem about which something must be done—even less is it viewed as a medical human rights abuse. There is empathy, of course, for the many transplant patients whose needs are being partly met in this way, but there is little concern for the organ sellers who are usually transient, socially invisible, and generally assumed to be making free, informed, and self-interested choices.

From an exclusively market oriented supply and demand perspective—one that is obviously dominant today—the problem of black-markets in human organs can best be solved by regulation rather than by prohibition. The profoundly human and ethical dilemmas are thereby reduced to a simple problem in medical management. In the rational choice language of contemporary medical ethics, the conflict between non-[maleficence] (do no harm) and beneficence (the moral duty to do good acts) is increasingly resolved in favour of the libertarian and consumer-oriented principle that those able to broker or buy a human organ should not be prevented from doing so. Paying for a kidney donation is viewed as a potential win-win situation that can benefit both parties. Individual decision making and patient autonomy have become the final arbiters of medical and bioethical values. Social justice and notions of the good society hardly figure at all in these discussions.

Rational arguments for regulation are, however, out of touch with the social and medical realities pertaining in many parts of the world where kidney selling is most common. In poorer countries the medical institutions created to monitor organ harvesting and distribution are often underfunded, dysfunctional, or readily compromised by the power of organ markets, the protection supplied by criminal networks, and by the impunity of outlaw surgeons who are willing to run donor for dollars programmes, or who are merely uninterested in where the transplant organ originates.

Surgeons who themselves (or whose patients) take part in transplant tourism have denied the risks of kidney removal in the absence of any published, longitudinal studies of the effects of nephrectomy on the urban poor living in dangerous work and health conditions. Even in the best social and medical circumstances living kidney and part liver donors do sometimes die after the surgical procedure, or are themselves in need of a kidney or liver transplant at a later date. The usual risks multiply when the buyers and sellers are unrelated because the sellers are likely to be extremely poor, often in poor health, and trapped in environments in which the everyday risks to their survival are legion. Kidney sellers face exposure to urban violence, transportation and work related accidents, and infectious diseases that can compromise their remaining kidney. If and when that spare part fails, most kidney sellers we have interviewed would have no access to dialysis let alone to transplantation.

The few published studies of the social, psychological, and medical effects of nephrectomy on kidney sellers in India, Iran, the Philippines, and Moldova are unambiguous. Kidney sellers subsequently experience (for complicated medical, social, economic, and psychological reasons) chronic pain, ill health, unemployment, reduced incomes, serious depression and sense of worthlessness, family problems, and social isolation (related to the sale).

Even with such attempts as in Iran to regulate and control an official system of kidney selling, the outcomes are troubling. One of our Organs Watch researchers has reported directly from Iran that kidney sellers there are recruited from the slums by wealthy kidney activists. They are paid a pittance for their body part. After the sale (which is legal there) the sellers feel profound shame, resentment, and family stigma. In our studies of kidney sellers in India, Turkey, the Philippines, and Eastern Europe, the feelings toward the doctors who removed their kidney can only be described as hostile and, in some cases, even murderous. The disappointment, anger, resentment, and hatred for the surgeons and even for the recipients of their organs—as reported by 100 paid kidney donors in Iran—strongly suggests that kidney selling is a serious social pathology.

Kidney sellers in the Philippines and in Eastern Europe frequently face medical problems, including hypertension, and even kidney insufficiency, without having access to necessary medical care. On returning to their villages or urban shantytowns, kidney sellers are often unemployed because they are unable to sustain the demands of heavy agricultural or construction work, the only labour available to men of their skills and backgrounds. Several kidney sellers in Moldova reported spending their kidney earnings (about US$2700) to hire labourers to compensate for the heavy agricultural work they could no longer do.

Moldovan sellers are frequently alienated from their families and co-workers, excommunicated from their local Orthodox churches, and, if single, they are excluded from marriage. "No young woman in this village will marry a man with the tell-tale scar of a kidney seller", the father of a kidney seller in Mingir (Moldova) told me. Sergei, a young kidney seller from Chisinau (Moldova) said that only his mother knew the real reason for the large, sabre-like scar on his abdomen. Sergei's young wife believed his story that he had been injured in a work-related accident in Turkey. Some kidney sellers have disappeared from their families and loved ones, and one is reported to have committed suicide. "They call us prostitutes", Niculae Bardan, a 27-year-old kidney seller from the village of Mingir told me sadly. Then he added: "Actually, we are worse than prostitutes because we have sold something we can never get back. We are disgrace to our families and to our country". Their families often suffer from the stigma of association with a kidney seller. In Turkey, the children of kidney sellers are ridiculed in village schools as one-kidneys.

Despite frequent complaints of pain and weakness, none of the recent kidney sellers we interviewed in Brazil, Turkey, Moldova, and Manila had seen a doctor or been treated in the first year after their operations. Some who looked for medical attention had been turned away from the very same hospitals where their operations were done. One kidney seller from Bagon Lupa shantytown in Manila was given a consultation at the hospital where he had sold his organ, and he was given a prescription for antibiotics and painkillers that he could not afford. Because of the shame associated with their act, I had to coax young kidney sellers in Manila and Moldova to submit to a basic clinical examination and sonogram at the expense of Organs Watch. Some were ashamed to appear in a public clinic because they had tried to keep the sale (and their ruined bodies) a secret. Others were fearful of receiving a bad report because they would be unable to pay for the treatments or medications. Above all, the kidney sellers I interviewed avoided getting medical attention for fear of being seen and labelled as weak or disabled by their potential employers, their families, and their co-workers, or (for single men) by potential girl friends.

If regulation, rather than more effective prohibition, is to be the norm, how can a government set a fair price on the body parts of its poorer citizens without compromising national pride, democratic values, or ethical principles? The circulation of kidneys transcends national borders, and international markets will coexist with any national, regulated systems. National regulatory programmes—such as the Kid-Net programme (modelled after commercial blood banks), which is currently being considered in the Philippines—would still have to compete with international black markets, which adjust the local value of kidneys according to consumer prejudices. In today's global market an Indian or an African kidney fetches as little as $1000, a Filipino kidney can get $1300, a Moldovan or Romanian kidney yields $2700, whereas a Turkish or an urban Peruvian kidney can command up to $10 000 or more. Sellers in the USA can receive up to $30 000,

Putting a market price on body parts—even a fair one—exploits the desperation of the poor, the mentally weak, and dependent classes. Servants, agricultural workers, illegal workers, and prisoners are pressured by their employers and guardians to enter the kidney market. In Argentina, Organs Watch visited a large asylum for the mentally deficient that had provided blood, cornea, and kidneys to local hospitals and eye bank, until the corrupt hospital director was caught in a web of criminal intrigue that brought him to jail and the institution put under government receivership. In Tel Aviv, Israel, I encountered a mentally deficient prisoner, a common thief, who had sold one of his kidneys to his own lawyer and then tried to sue him in small claims court because he was paid half what he was promised. In Canada a businessman recently received a kidney from his domestic worker, a Philippine woman, who argued that Filipinos are a people "who are anxious to please their bosses". Finally, surgeons, whose primary responsibility is to protect and care for vulnerable bodies, should not be advocates of paid mutilation even in the interest of saving lives at the expense of others.

Bioethical arguments about the right to buy or sell an organ or other body part are based on Euro-American notions of contract and individual choice. But these create the semblance of ethical choice in an intrinsically unethical context. The choice to sell a kidney in an urban slum of Calcutta or in a Brazilian favela or a Philippine shantytown is often anything but a free and autonomous one. Consent is problematic, with the executioner—whether on death row or at the door of the slum resident—looking over one's shoulder, and when a seller has no other option left but to sell a part of himself. Asking the law to negotiate a fair price for a live human kidney goes against everything that contract theory stands for.

Although many individuals have benefited from the ability to purchase the organs they need, the social harm produced to the donors, their families, and their communities gives sufficient reason for pause. Does the life that is teased out of the body of the one and transferred into the body of the other bear any resemblance to the ethical life of the free citizen? But neither Aristotle nor Aquinas is with us. Instead, we are asked to take counsel from the new discipline of bioethics that has been finely calibrated to meet the needs of advanced biomedical technologies and the desires of postmodern medical consumers.

What goes by the wayside in these illicit transactions are not only laws and longstanding medical regulations but also the very bedrock supporting medical ethics—humanist ideas of bodily holism, integrity, and human dignity. Amidst the tensions between organ givers and organ recipients, between North and South, between the illegal and the so-called merely unethical, clarity is needed about whose values and whose notions of the body are represented. Deeply held beliefs in human dignity and bodily integrity are not solely the legacy of Western Enlightenment.

The demand side of the organ scarcity problem also needs to be confronted. Part of the shortfall in organs derives from the expansions of organ waiting lists to include the medical margins—infants, patients aged over 70 years, and the immunologically sensitive—especially those who have rejected transplanted organs after four or more attempts. Liver and kidney failure often originate in public health problems that could be preventively treated more aggressively. Ethical solutions to the chronic scarcity of human organs are not always palatable to the public, but also need to be considered. Informed presumed consent whereby all citizens are organs donors at (brain) death unless they have stipulated their refusal beforehand is a practice that preserves the value of transplantation as a social good in which no one is included or excluded on the basis of ability to pay.

Finally, in the context of an increasingly consumer-oriented world the ancient prescriptions for virtue in suffering and grace in dying appear patently absurd. But the transformation of a person into a life that must be prolonged or saved at any cost has made life itself into the ultimate commodity fetish. An insistence on the absolute value of a single life saved, enhanced, or prolonged at any cost ends all ethical inquiry and erases any possibility of a global social ethic. Meanwhile, the traffic in kidneys reduces the human content of all the lives it touches.

In his 1970 classic, *The Gift Relationship*, Richard Titmuss anticipated many of the dilemmas now raised by the global human organs market. His assessment of the negative social effects of commercialised blood markets in the USA could also be applied to the global markets in human organs and tissues: "The commercialism of blood and donor relationships represses the expression of altruism, erodes the sense of community, lowers scientific standards, limits both personal and professional freedoms, sanctions the making of profits in hospitals and clinical laboratories, legalises hostility between doctor and patient, subjects critical areas of medicine to the laws of the marketplace, places immense social costs on those least able to bear them—the poor, the sick, and the inept—increases the danger of unethical behavior in various sectors of medical science and practice, and results in situations in which proportionately more and more blood is supplied by the poor, the unskilled and the unemployed, Blacks and other low income groups".

The division of the world into organ buyers and organ sellers is a medical, social, and moral tragedy of immense and not yet fully recognised proportions.

ROBERT STEINBROOK

Public Solicitation of Organ Donors

Dr. Robert Steinbrook is a national correspondent for the *New England Journal of Medicine* and a member of its editorial board.

During the past half-century, organ donation has been fertile territory for both extraordinary compassion and complex ethical questions. As transplantation has become safer and outcomes have improved, the rules for donation and the fair allocation of organs have struggled to keep pace.

In 2004, there were about 27,000 solid-organ transplantations in the United States—nearly 1600 more than there had been in 2003. Yet the demand for organs remains far greater than the supply. As of July 2005, there were about 89,000 people on waiting lists. For the largest group—the 62,500 patients awaiting kidneys—the expectation is that only about a quarter of them will receive a transplant within the next year. Greater public awareness of the organ shortage could lead to more donations, but doubts about the safety of donation by living persons and the integrity of the allocation process can jeopardize public trust. In January 2002, a donor died after giving a portion of his liver to his brother at Mount Sinai Medical Center in New York. Subsequently, the number of liver transplantations involving living donors in the United States—which had increased from 395 in 2000 to 518 in 2001—decreased to 362 in 2002 and about 320 each in 2003 and 2004.

During the past year, a passionate controversy has developed about the public solicitation of organs, which takes place over the Internet, on billboards, and through other advertising. This is a complex matter, as discussed by Truog in [the *New England Journal of Medicine* 353, August 4, 2005], pages 444–446. Until recently, it was exceedingly rare for a kidney to be transplanted from a donor who was unknown to the recipient or whose blood or tissue was not compatible with the recipient's. Solicitation arouses concern about the potential for financial exploitation, the inequitable allocation of organs, and the subversion of the standards for donation. Federal regulations authorize directed donation, which is defined as "the

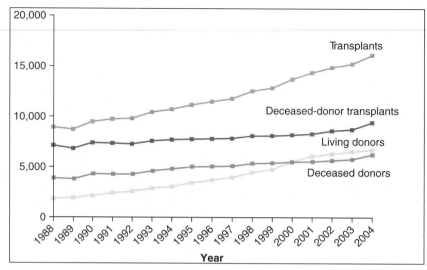

Kidney Transplantations in the United States, 1988–2004.
Data are from the Organ Procurement and Transplantation Network.

allocation of an organ to a recipient named by those authorized to make the donation." Thus, soliciting organs from a living or dead donor is not unlawful, although the National Organ Transplant Act of 1984 prohibits the transfer "of any human organ for valuable consideration for use in a human transplantation if the transfer affects interstate commerce." Reasonable payments are permitted for the costs of organ procurement and storage and for the expenses incurred by living donors—in travel, housing, and lost wages.

In August 2004, a 32-year-old Houston man with liver cancer received a directed liver donation from a deceased donor after he advertised in newspapers, on a Web site (www.toddneedsaliver.com), and on two highway billboards, and his story had been widely publicized. He died in April 2005, eight months after the transplantation. His controversial campaign might have encouraged a donation that would not have occurred otherwise—or diverted a liver from someone with a greater chance for long-term survival.

Further controversy surrounds MatchingDonors.com. On its Web site, the organization, which is based in the Boston area, describes itself as "a venue where patients and potential donors can meet and communicate, and hopefully expedite a donor agreeing to give a patient a much needed organ." It states that the organization "is a nonprofit corporation and 100% of the money paid for patient memberships is applied to running this site." Potential recipients pay a one-time fee of $595 or a monthly fee of $295 to be listed, but about 70 percent of the 65 patients with active profiles are being listed without charge, according to Dr. Jeremiah Lowney, the organization's medical director and cofounder. There is no inherent reason why it should matter whether a living donor meets his or her intended recipient at work or a place of worship, online, or in some other way. But the involvement of a commercial entity has been criticized.

Since MatchingDonors.com was launched in February 2004, it has paired about 30 living organ donors and recipients. As of July 1, 2005, 12 transplantations had taken place, all of them of kidneys. There was wide media coverage of the first of these transplantations, which occurred at a Denver hospital in October 2004. The recipient, who had been seeking a kidney for five years, said that he had not paid for the kidney but had reimbursed the donor about $5,000 for expenses. The week after the transplantation, the donor was jailed in Tennessee for failure to pay child support. In March 2005, he took—and was said to have failed—a televised polygraph test, during which he was asked if he had profited from the transplantation.[1]

Although the public solicitation of organs has been a factor in very few transplantations, the transplantation of kidneys from living donors is increasingly common. The United Network for Organ Sharing, a private, nonprofit organization based in Richmond, Virginia, operates the Organ Procurement and Transplantation Network (OPTN) under contract with the federal government. The networks share the same board of directors and are collectively known as OPTN/UNOS. At a public hearing held in Chicago in June, Dr. Francis L. Delmonico, a Boston transplantation surgeon who [was then] president of OPTN/ UNOS, noted that "anyone can be a live kidney donor who is medically and psychosocially suitable. It is no longer the case that one has to be HLA-matched. The outcome for a friend, spouse, or anonymous donor is just as good as that from a parent or child." Transplantation of a kidney from a living donor, however, remains a major surgical procedure with attendant risks and complications as discussed by Ingelfinger in [the *New England Journal of Medicine* 353, August 4, 2005 (pages 447–449).] In addition, until recently, the presence of preformed antibodies against HLA antigens or incompatibility with respect to ABO blood type has generally ruled out intended donors.[2]

Since 2000, there have been more living kidney donors than cadaveric donors in the United States, although kidneys from cadavers—because both kidneys are usually available—still account for about 60 percent of kidney transplants (see line graph). Nearly two thirds of living donors are related to their recipients by blood (see pie chart). Those without a blood relationship are most commonly spouses or others who have a previous personal relationship with the recipient that is unrelated to the person's need for a transplant. In 2004, 85 people received a kidney through anonymous donation, in which a volunteer approached a transplantation center with no knowledge of a specific recipient. In the same year, 30 people received a kidney through paired exchange, in which two donors provided a kidney to each other's intended recipients because both had been found to be incompatible with the recipient to whom they had wished to donate.

The OPTN receives the majority of its funding from a one-time computer registration fee of $459, which is assessed when a transplantation center accepts a candidate for a transplant from a deceased donor or when a person who had not been on the waiting list receives a transplant from a living donor. Historically, consistent with its federal charge, the OPTN has focused on transplants from deceased donors. Donation by living persons was less common and usually involved people who knew each other. Such donation has primarily been the responsibility of individual transplantation centers.

Now, the OPTN is taking an active role in transplantation from living donors. In October 2004, the Department of Health and Human Services directed it to develop voluntary-allocation guidelines for organ donations from living donors that are made to an anonymous pool, not to specific patients, and other voluntary policies and guidelines as "it believes necessary and

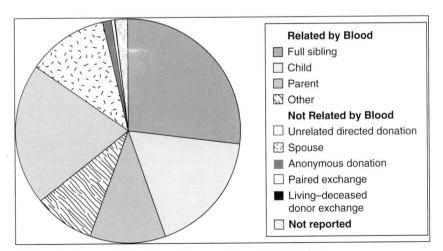

Relationships between Living Kidney Donors and Transplant Recipients in the United States, 2004.

Data are from the Organ Procurement and Transplantation Network.

appropriate to promote the safety and efficacy of living donor transplantation for the donor and the recipient."[3] The responsibilities include the development of guidelines about the public solicitation of organ donors. In November 2004, OPTN/UNOS announced its opposition to the solicitation of organs from deceased donors who had no personal or family bond with the patient.[4] According to Delmonico, such solicitations "can undermine the allocation system and prevent the best medical use of the organ."

In June 2005, OPTN/UNOS announced that it "will not participate in efforts to solicit living donors for specific transplant candidates."[5] Specifically, it will not create a Web site similar to MatchingDonors.com. OPTN/UNOS will, however, "provide comprehensive resource information to support prospective live donors, including medical criteria for who can donate and individual transplant institutions' protocols for live unrelated donation."[5]

OPTN is establishing quality criteria and guidelines for living-donor kidney and liver programs. Programs must have staff with the requisite training and expertise to evaluate donors fully, to ensure that donations are voluntary, and to perform living-donor surgery. In addition, better data about the outcomes of living donors should be forthcoming. The OPTN is also working toward requiring that transplantation centers report within 72 hours the death of a living donor or the donor's need for organ transplantation.

Finally, OPTN/UNOS will develop a nationwide mechanism for allocating organs from living donors who have not directed their donation to specific persons.[5] The principles will be similar to those for allocating organs from cadaveric donors. Eventually, there might be a registry for altruistic kidney and liver donors, such as the National Marrow Donor Program, which lists volunteer marrow donors.

The controversy over the public solicitation of organs has forced the transplantation community to address a difficult issue and to reexamine its approach to living donors. As long as there is a profound organ shortage, the challenge of trying to help patients in need of transplants while upholding the integrity of the overall allocation system will not go away.

NOTES

1. Hartman T. Donor fails lie detector test on organ transplant. Rocky Mountain News. March 11, 2005: 6A.

2. Delmonico FL. Exchanging kidneys—advances in living-donor transplantation. N Engl J Med 2004; 350: 1812–4.

3. Letter from Dr. James F. Burdick, director, Division of Transplantation, Healthcare Systems Bureau, Health Resources and Services Administration, Department of Health and Human Services, to Walter K. Graham, Executive Director, United Network for Organ Sharing, October 29, 2004.

4. OPTN/UNOS board opposes solicitation for deceased organ donation. Press release of the United Network for Organ Sharing, November 19, 2004. (Accessed July 14, 2005, at http://www.unos.org/news/newsDetail.asp?id=374.)

5. OPTN/UNOS board addresses information needs of potential living donors. Press release of the United Network for Organ Sharing, June 24, 2005. (Accessed July 14, 2005, at http://www.unos.org/news/newsDetail.asp?id=456.)

TIMOTHY F. MURPHY

Would My Story Get Me a Kidney?

Timothy F. Murphy is Professor of Philosophy in the Biomedical Sciences at the University of Illinois College of Medicine at Chicago. He conducts research and teaches primarily in the areas of genetics and ethics, assisted reproductive technologies, medicine and sexuality, and research ethics. He is the author or editor of eight books, including *Justice and the Human Genome Project* and *Gay Science: The Ethics of Sexual Orientation Research*. His most recent book is *Case Studies in Biomedical Research Ethics*.

In 2004, a businessman and a physician launched matchingdonors.com to see whether the Internet could aid people needing organ and tissue transplants. Hundreds of people now use the site to tell their stories directly to the public. Patients tell how they got sick, what it's like to be medically dependent, what a transplant would mean to them. Married people ask for organs for their spouses, and parents describe the struggles of their children. The site also features pictures of the donors and recipients it has matched.

Direct appeals to the public for an organ or tissue are not new. Over the years, families have enlisted local television stations and newspapers for help finding a donor. I usually cringe when I see this: these families appear to be cutting in front of everyone else on the waiting lists in their regions.

Yet solicited "directed donations"—donations to an identified individual—are increasingly common. The number of kidneys coming from living donors exceeds the kidneys coming from the dead, and ever more people are stepping forward to donate parts of their livers. Usually these donors want to help family members and close friends, but not always. When basketball player Alonzo Mourning needed a kidney transplant in 2003, dozens of people completely unknown to him volunteered to donate.

In 2003, former literature professor Zell Kravinsky was prepared to donate a kidney, but specifically to someone poor and black. Never mind that he didn't know anyone like this. Of course, transplant policy bars donations to groups, and for good reasons. In a 1994 case, a murder victim's family agreed to donate his organs on the condition that they go only to white people. The murder victim had been a member of the Ku Klux Klan, and, as if to add insult to injury, his murderer was black. In the soul searching that followed this case, the United Network for Organ Sharing, the federal organization overseeing organ allocation in the United States, adopted a policy barring donation to groups. For this and other reasons, several hospitals turned Mr. Kravinsky away, until an institution in New York was clever enough to introduce him to someone who met his criteria. After the introduction, the professor-turned-philanthropist was no longer donating to a group but to a woman he knew by name. Web sites make such introductions possible. Shopping the Internet for organ recipients functions like directed donation to an individual, but the process practically invites donation to groups.

What's more, recipients' stories also mark off groups. I'm not waiting for an organ transplant, but what if I were? Would anyone find my story compelling? Here's a draft: "I'm just past fifty, and my partner and I have an Australian terrier who's sweet as peaches. I have a large family: an aging Mom and

Dad, siblings, nieces, a nephew, a circle of cousins, and more. My partner's small family rounds out the domestic circle, but unfortunately no one on either side is in a position to donate. I work as a professor, acknowledge no religion, and make mosaic art in my spare time. I've been sick a long time. It's been devastating. I would be grateful beyond speech to anyone who could help." How would my story stack up against that of a sick Mom or Dad with children, someone bankrupted by medical debt, someone much younger, or someone friendlier to religion?

Ever more people are willing to face the risks of organ and tissue removal to help someone they know. Ever more will also face these risks without a direct personal connection. A few institutions in the United States now accept organs from living people who have no intended recipient; they treat the organ as if it came from a deceased donor and match it to the waiting lists. But most people still take no steps to donate their organs after death, even though that involves no medical harm whatsoever. By turning to living directed donations, we incur degrees of harm that would be virtually unnecessary if people freely donated their organs at death.

We surely need inventive ways to help donors come forward. But when it comes to Internet solicitation of organs—solicitation that benefits only a tiny fraction of the people waiting for organs—we should cringe a little bit. We need to ensure that everyone has an equal opportunity at organs, and that some groups don't gain at others' expense.

Suggested Readings for Chapter 7

GENERAL ISSUES

Caplan, Arthur. *The Ethics of Organ Transplants: The Current Debate.* Amherst, NY: Prometheus Books, 1999.

Veatch, Robert M. *Transplantation Ethics,* reprint ed., Washington, DC: Georgetown University Press, 2002.

THE DEFINITION OF DEATH AND THE RETRIEVAL OF ORGANS

Bernat, James L. "The Biophilosophical Basis of Whole-Brain Death." *Social Philosophy and Policy* 19 (2002), 324–42.

Giacomini, Mita. "A Change of Heart and a Change of Mind? Technology and the Redefinition of Death in 1968." *Social Science and Medicine* 44 (1997), 1465–82.

Kamm, F. M. "Brain Death and Spontaneous Breathing." *Philosophy & Public Affairs* 30 (2001), 297–320.

Lock, Margaret M. *Twice Dead: Organ Transplants and the Reinvention of Death.* Berkeley: University of California Press, 2002.

Potts, John T., and Herdman, Roger. *Non-Heart-Beating Organ Transplantation: Medical and Ethical Issues in Procurement.* Washington, DC: National Academies Press, 1997.

Truog, Robert D. "Organ Donation without Brain Death?" *Hastings Center Report* 35 (2005), 3.

Veatch, Robert M. "The Death of Whole-Brain Death: The Plague of the Disaggregators, Somaticists, and Mentalists." *Journal of Medicine and Philosophy* 30 (2005), 353–78.

PROCUREMENT FROM DECEASED DONORS

Childress, James. "How Can We Ethically Increase the Supply of Transplantable Organs?" *Annals of Internal Medicine* 145 (2006), 224–25.

Chouhan, P., and Draper, H. "Modified Mandated Choice for Organ Procurement." *Journal of Medical Ethics* 29 (2003), 157–62.

Etzioni, Amitai. "Organ Donation: A Communitarian Approach." *Kennedy Institute of Ethics Journal* 13 (2003), 1–18.

Gill, Michael B. "Presumed Consent, Autonomy, and Organ Donation." *Journal of Medicine and Philosophy* 29 (2004), 37–59.

Harris, John. "Organ Procurement: Dead Interests, Living Needs." *Journal of Medical Ethics* 29 (2003), 130–34.

Institute of Medicine Committee on Increasing Rates of Organ Donation, James F. Childress and Catharyn T. Liverman, eds. *Organ Donation: Opportunities for Action.* Washington, DC: National Academies Press, 2006.

Kluge, E. H. "Improving Organ Retrieval Rates: Various Proposals and Their Ethical Validity." *Health Care Analysis* 8 (2000), 279–95.

Kuczewski, Mark G. "The Gift of Life and Starfish on the Beach: The Ethics of Organ Procurement." *The American Journal of Bioethics* 2 (2002), 53–56.

Lauritzen, Paul, et al. "The Gift of Life and the Common Good: The Need for a Communal Approach to Organ Procurement." *The Hastings Center Report* 31 (2001), 29–35.

Sminoff, Laura A., and Mercer, Mary Beth. "Public Policy, Public Opinion, and Consent for Organ Donation." *Cambridge Quarterly of Healthcare Ethics* 10 (2001), 377–86.

Robertson, Christopher. "Framing the Organ System: Altruism or Cooperation?" *The American Journal of Bioethics* 4 (2004), 46–48.

Truog, Robert D. "Are Organs Personal Property or a Societal Resource?" *The American Journal of Bioethics* 5 (2005), 14–16.

JUSTICE IN THE ALLOCATION OF ORGANS

Childress, James F. "Ethics and the Allocation of Organs for Transplantation." *Kennedy Institute of Ethics Journal* 6 (1996), 397–401.

Childress, James F. "Putting Patients First in Organ Allocation: An Ethical Analysis of the U.S. debate." *CQ: Cambridge Quarterly of Healthcare Ethics* 10 (2001), 365–76.

Douglas, David D. "Should Everyone Have Equal Access to Organ Transplantation? An Argument in Favor." *Archives of Internal Medicine* 163 (2003), 1883–85.

Fung, John J. "Organ Allocation in the United States: Where Does It Stand?" *Journal of the American College of Surgeons* 192 (2001), 118–24.

Glannon, W. "Responsibility, Alcoholism, and Liver Transplantation." *The Journal of Medicine and Philosophy* 23 (1998), 31.

Howard, David H. "Hope Versus Efficiency in Organ Allocation." *Transplantation* 72 (2001), 1169–73.

Murphy, Timothy F., "Gaming the Transplant System." *The American Journal of Bioethics* 4 (2004), W28.

Murphy, Timothy F., and Veatch, Robert M. "Members First: The Ethics of Donating Organs and Tissues to Groups." *CQ: Cambridge Quarterly of Healthcare Ethics* 15 (2006), 50–59.

Neuberger, James. "Should Liver Transplantation Be Made Available to Everyone? The Case Against." *Archives of Internal Medicine* 163 (2003), 1881–83.

Piper, James B. "Organ Allocation in the United States: Where Does it Stand?" *Journal of the American College of Surgeons* 192 (2001), 124–29.

Russell, B. J. "Fair Distribution and Patients Who Receive More Than One Organ Transplant." *Journal of Clinical Ethics* 13 (2002), 40–48.

Stein, Mark S. "The Distribution of Life-Saving Medical Resources: Equality, Life Expectancy, and Choice Behind the Veil." *Social Philosophy and Policy* 19 (2002), 212–45.

Ubel, Peter A., and Caplan, Arthur L. "Geographic Favoritism in Liver Transplantation—Unfortunate or Unfair?" *New England Journal of Medicine* 339 (1998), 1322–25.

Ubel, Peter A., and Loewenstein, George. "Distributing Scarce Livers: The Moral Reasoning of the General Public." *Social Science and Medicine* 42 (1996), 1049–55.

Veatch, Robert M. "A New Basis for Allocating Livers for Transplant." *Kennedy Institute of Ethics Journal* 10 (2000), 75–80.

Zenios, Stefanos A., Woodle, E. Steve, and Ross, Lainie Friedman. "Primum Non Nocere: Avoiding Harm to Vulnerable Wait List Candidates in an Indirect Kidney Exchange." *Transplantation* 72 (2001), 648–54.

LIVING DONORS

Appel, J. M., and Fox, M. D. "Organ Solicitation on the Internet: Every Man for Himself?" *The Hastings Center Report* 35 (2005), 14–15.

Cronin, D. C., and Siegler, M. "Ethical Issues in Living Donor Transplantation." *Transplantation Proceedings* 35 (2003), 904–05.

Eghtesad, B., Jain, A. B., and Fung, J. J. "Living Donor Liver Transplantation: Ethics and Safety." *Transplantation Proceedings* 35 (2003), 51–52.

Gaston, Robert, and Eckhoff, Deven. "Whither Living Donors?" *American Journal of Transplantation* 4 (2004), 2–3.

Kaplan, Bernard, and Polise, Karen. "In Defense of Altruistic Kidney Donation by Strangers." *Pediatric Nephrology* 14 (2000), 518–22.

Mata, A. J., et al. "Nondirected Donation of Kidneys from Living Donors." *New England Journal of Medicine*, 343 (2000), 433–36.

Robertson, Christopher. "Who Is Really Hurt Anyway? The Problem of Soliciting Designated Organ Donations." *The American Journal of Bioethics* 5 (2005), 16–17.

Ross, Lainie Friedman. "Media Appeals for Directed Altruistic Living Liver Donations: Lessons from Camilo Sandoval Ewen." *Perspectives in Biology and Medicine* 45 (2002), 329–37.

Ross, Lainie Friedman. "The Ethical Limits in Expanding Living Donor Transplantation." *Kennedy Institute of Ethics Journal* 16 (2006), 151–72.

Zink, Sheldon, et al. "Living Donation: Focus on Public Concerns: Consensus Statement." *Clinical Transplantation* 19 (2005), 581–85.

INNOVATIVE POLICIES FOR ORGAN PROCUREMENT

Cherry, Mark. "Is a Market in Human Organs Necessarily Exploitative?" *Public Affairs Quarterly* 14 (2000), 337–60.

Cohen, Cynthia. "Public Policy and the Sale of Human Organs." *Kennedy Institute of Ethics* 12 (2002), 47–64.

Delmonico, Francis, et al. "Ethical Incentives—Not Payment—for Organ Donation." *New England Journal of Medicine* 346 (2002), 2002–05.

DuBois, James M. "Organ Donation and Financial Incentives: A Matter of Principle." *Health Care Ethics USA* 10 (2002), 2.

Gill, Michael B., and Sade, Robert M. "Paying for Kidneys: The Case Against Prohibition." *Kennedy Institute of Ethics* 12 (2002), 17–45.

Hippen, Benjamin E. "In Defense of a Regulated Market in Kidneys from Living Vendors." *Journal of Medicine and Philosophy* 30 (2005), 593–626.

Joralemon, Donald. "Shifting Ethics: Debating the Incentive Question in Organ Transplantation." *Journal of Medical Ethics* 27 (2001), 30–35.

Kahn, Jeffrey. "Three Views of Organ Procurement Policy: Moving Ahead or Giving Up?" *Kennedy Institute of Ethics* 13 (2003), 45–50.

Kluge, E. H. "Improving Organ Retrieval Rates: Various Proposals and Their Ethical Validity." *Health Care Analysis* 8 (2000), 279–95.

Madhav, Goyal, et al. "Economic and Health Consequences of Selling a Kidney in India," *Journal of the American Medical Association* 288 (2002), 1589–93.

Radcliffe-Richards, Janet, et al. "The Case for Allowing Kidney Sales." *The Lancet* 351 (1998), 1950–52.

Rivera-Lopez, E. "Organ Sales and Moral Distress." *Journal of Applied Philosophy* 23 (2006), 41–52.

Rothman, David J., et al. "The Bellagio Task Force Report on Transplantation, Bodily Integrity, and the International Traffic in Organs." *Transplantation Proceedings* 29 (1997), 2739–45.

Sells, Robert. "Incentives for Organ Donation: Some Ethical Issues." *Annals of Transplantation* 9 (2004), 23–24.

Veatch, Robert M. "Why Liberals Should Accept Financial Incentives for Organ Procurement." *Kennedy Institute of Ethics Journal* 13 (2003), 19–36.

Wilkinson, Stephen. "Organs for Sale" in his *Bodies for Sale*. London: Routledge, 2003.

Chapter 8
Justice and Health

Introduction

Health care costs have continued to rise dramatically for several decades. These costs have been studied by government agencies as well as scholars worldwide. Many have concluded that certain problems, including governments' own insurance schemes and payment policies, fuel unacceptable increases in expenditures for health care services. Other governments have concluded that their resources are so limited that little money can be spent on either public health or health care. The basic *economic problem* is how to control costs, maximize health benefits, and efficiently distribute resources. The basic *ethical problem* is how to structure the global order and national systems that affect health so that burdens and benefits are fairly distributed and a threshold condition of equitable levels of health and access to health care is in place. These economic and ethical objectives are intertwined in the formation of health policy, both internationally and in the policies of individual nations.

The proper role of governments in creating health policies is not the only moral consideration, but it has been and will remain at the center of these discussions. It is widely agreed that government is constituted to protect citizens against risks from the environment, risks from external invasion, risks from crime, risks from fire, risks from highway accidents, and the like. The idea that certain ways of protecting health and providing health care should be similarly provided as government services has been more controversial, especially in the United States. But even if it is agreed within a nation that its government has an obligation to protect health and to provide health care, there are severe limits to what the government can and should do. Moreover, globalization has brought a realization that problems of protecting health are international in nature and that their alleviation will require a restructuring of the global system. One abstract model for a properly constructed system is found in the opening reading in this chapter, a position statement by the United Nations, Commission on Human Rights.

THE ALLOCATION OF RESOURCES

Many problems are *allocational* in the sense that health policies allocate resources to a range of specific goals, such as purchasing ambulances and alleviating forms of poverty that affect health. Private-sector policies, such as health insurance that is provided as an employee benefit, also allocate resources. To "allocate" is to distribute goods, services, preventive measures, financial resources, and the like according to a system or principle. The distribution scheme need not be established or controlled by governments. For example, charitable organizations often distribute health care and the free market distributes health care goods and services through exchanges made by free agents acting in their own interests.

At least two primary considerations are involved in allocation decisions about promoting health and distributing health care: (1) What percentage of the total available resources should be allotted to improving health? Public health and health care must compete for funding with other social projects such as lowering energy consumption, improving educational systems, and improving highways. (2) How much that is budgeted to the various areas of public health and health care should go to each specific area? For example, how much goes to alleviation of sewage treatment facilities, to improvement of hospitals, to cancer research, to vaccination programs, to research on diseases, and to new technology for treatment facilities? A directly related problem is whether funding for *preventive* programs should take priority over funding for programs providing *health care*. The prevention of disease by improvements in unsanitary environments and childhood immunizations are often cheaper and more efficient in raising health levels and saving lives than are expensive technologies such as kidney dialysis, heart transplantation, and intensive care units. From another perspective, however, a concentrated preventive approach seems morally unsatisfactory if it leads to the neglect of sick and injured persons who could directly benefit from available resources. Many have pointed out that there is often a need to balance the two.

This chapter emphasizes issues of justice and fairness in systems and policies of allocation, starting at the global level of current injustices in the distribution of risks to health and moving to problems of rationing resources. Approaches that provide a theory or general conception of distributive justice and health policy are the focus of the first section in this chapter.

THE ROLE OF THEORIES OF DISTRIBUTIVE JUSTICE

In Chapter 1 we briefly surveyed various competing theories of justice. We will now examine the somewhat different landscape of theories or general frameworks of justice that are found in the readings in the present chapter, here dividing them into four types of theory.

Egalitarian Theory. In Chapter 1 we noted that John Rawls's *A Theory of Justice* has been a particularly influential work on social justice in the egalitarian tradition. Rawls argues that a social arrangement is a communal effort to advance the good of all in the society. Because inequalities of birth, historical circumstance, and natural endowment are undeserved, persons in a cooperative society should aim to make the unequal situation of naturally disadvantaged members more equal. Evening out disadvantage in this way, Rawls claims, is a fundamental part of our shared conception of justice. His recognition of a positive societal obligation to eliminate or reduce barriers that prevent fair opportunity and that correct or compensate for various disadvantages has clear implications for discussions of justice in health care.

Rawls's theory is fashioned for what he refers to as "the basic structure" of society. This structure is the way basic social institutions distribute fundamental rights, obligations, and burdens. Rawls does not try to fashion his principles for *all* institutions, but rather for the basic institutions in a nation-state. His theory of justice is thus confined to the rights and obligations of citizens within a nation-state. Rawls's egalitarian theory has directly influenced several articles in this chapter, most notably those by Norman Daniels, Thomas Pogge, Allen Buchanan, and Robert Veatch. Also the article by Madison Powers and Ruth Faden shares the Rawlsian idea that a theory of justice should support policies that adjust unjust social inequalities to achieve more egalitarian outcomes. From this perspective, Rawls's egalitarianism has had an enormous and continuing impact in bioethics—a deeper influence than any other theory of justice.

The second article in this chapter, by Daniels, formulates an egalitarian theory that he says extends Rawls's theory of social primary goods and justice into the domain of health and health care. Daniels addresses these questions: Is health care of special moral importance? When are health inequities unjust? How can we meet health needs fairly under reasonable limits to resources committed to the task (a process of rationing)? He also addresses questions such as "Is there a right to health care?" and "Is justice good for our health?" His theory is an account of protecting equality of opportunity by initiating health policies that will keep people close to normal (species-typical) functioning. By maintaining normal functioning, health programs protect an individual's fair share of the normal range of opportunities in society. Daniels argues that because health is affected by many social factors, theories of justice should not center entirely on access to health care, but also on the need to reduce health inequalities by improving social conditions that affect the health of societies, such as having clean water, adequate nutrition, and general sanitation. Daniels also outlines how a social system can be constructed to protect equality of opportunity and at the same time address controversial rationing problems.

Various writers interested in Rawlsian and egalitarian theory have recently pointed out that many of the considerations of justice that Rawls outlines—and those emphasized in the health arena by Daniels—apply at the international level, not merely within national states. These theories of justice are now often referred to as cosmopolitan theories. Though strongly influenced by Rawls, this model extends the theory of justice to the global stage, as Thomas Pogge does in his contribution to this chapter.

Cosmopolitan Theory. Pogge argues that Rawls's suggestion that the principles of justice are limited to specific societies (nation-states) is an ill-considered limitation on the theory of justice. For Pogge, the basic structure of society lies in the many norms and institutions that affect individuals, including those of commerce and public policy. He refuses to distinguish sharply between citizens of nations and "foreigners." He views the well-being of the worst-off members of global society as the proper starting point for a theory of justice. National citizenship seems as morally arbitrary as race, class, or gender and seems to have nothing to do with how one should be treated from the point of view of justice. Applying theories of justice only within a given nation does more to bring about vast disparaties in wealth and well-being than to alleviate the fundamental problem. Pogge insists that "we must aspire to a single, universal criterion of justice" for the global order.

Pogge is particularly concerned with the extent of poverty and inequality in the world, offering empirical evidence to support his claim that global poverty is of the highest moral importance. The consequences of extreme poverty for health are well-documented and these consequences inform his theory of basic goods and justice. He also assesses the degree to which institutional structures can be expected to fulfill the mandates of the theory. He argues that those outside a given social structure can still be affected by that social structure. The theory of justice that Pogge develops maintains that humans must have access to basic goods including housing, food, and health care. He formulates his account in terms of human rights and argues that rights to basic goods require that coercive institutions such as governments be designed to guarantee these rights to everyone.

Pogge does not seek a world government to secure the just world order he advocates. However, he does suggest that international institutions should play a larger role than they have historically: In a proper world order it might be the case that no particular governing institution, global or national, would have final and absolute sovereignty.

Capabilities Theory. A third type of theory is one framed in the language of capabilities. While in many respects egalitarian itself, this type of theory focuses on distributions intended to enable persons to reach certain functional levels. The idea is to start with an understanding of health and individual well-being and then to connect that account to capabilities for achieving levels of functioning essential to the well-being of individuals—through, for example, proper nutrition and access to health care. Amartya Sen and Martha Nussbaum are notable advocates of such a capabilities theory.

A form of capabilities theory, but one that uses a different language and develops a unique framework for health policy and public health, is found in this chapter's selection by Madison Powers and Ruth Faden, who acknowledge an "intellectual debt" to Sen and Nussbaum. They start out with a basic premise: "Social justice is concerned with human well-being," not only health but what they call six distinct and core dimensions of well-being: health, personal security, reasoning, respect, attachment, and self-determination. Each of the six dimensions is an independent concern of justice, and the "job of justice" is to secure a sufficient level of each dimension for each person. The justice of societies and of the global order can be judged by how well they effect these dimensions in their political structures and social practices.

Powers and Faden start out with a distinct focus that is less concerned with achieving equality than with reducing inequality. They begin with the world as we encounter it—a world characterized by profound inequalities in well-being and resources. They then ask the question "Which inequalities are the most unjust and the most in need of being redressed?" This focus on egregious inequalities guides their account all the way through.

While the first of the six dimensions of well-being in their account is health, Powers and Faden argue that the moral justification for health policies depends as much on the other five dimensions of well-being as it does on the dimension of health. They argue that an absence of any of the other conditions can be seriously destructive to health. A constellation of inequalities can systemically magnify and reinforce initial conditions of ill-health, creating pervasive effects that attack multiple dimensions of well-being. This is a theory of interactive effects: Poor education and lack of respect, for example, can affect core forms of reasoning as well as health status. Social structures can compound these adverse effects. The result is a "phenomenon of interactive and cascading effects" that require urgent attention from the point of view of justice. The job of justice is precisely to alleviate the social structures that cause these forms of ill-being.

Libertarian Theory. Finally, there is a fourth type of theory of justice in this chapter, found in the second section in the article by Tristram Engelhardt. This theory is almost universally referred to as "libertarian." A perennial problem concerning the distribution of health care is whether *justice requires* that societies adopt an explicit distribution plan for health care. The libertarian Robert Nozick has bluntly raised the following question about our shared conception of justice:

Hearing the term "distribution," most people presume that some thing or mechanism uses some principle or criterion to give out a supply of things. . . . So it is an open question, at least, whether *re*distribution [of resources] should take place; whether we should do again what has already been done once.[1]

---

[1]Robert Nozick, *Anarchy, State, and Utopia* (New York: Basic Books, 1974), pp. 149–50.

Proponents of the libertarian theory of justice reject the conclusion that egalitarian, cosmopolitan, or capabilities theories represent an appropriate normative ideal for distributing health care. People may be equal in many morally significant respects, libertarians say, but *justice* does not demand the collection and redistribution of economic resources that are required to fund government-distributed or international programs of health-related goods and services. For a libertarian, just distributions flow from free-market procedures of acquiring property and legitimately transferring that property. A libertarian therefore prefers a free-market system in which health care insurance is privately and voluntarily purchased by individual or group initiative as a consumer good. In fact, libertarians believe it to be an injustice when economic resources are redistributed through government programs. Accordingly, in this system no one could have property coercively extracted by the state (for example, through taxation) in order to benefit someone else.

Engelhardt relies heavily on rights of free choice, rather than on a substantive principle of justice. He rejects all principles of justice that are not voluntarily agreed to by all members of a community or nation-state. Engelhardt argues that a so-called "theory of justice" should work to protect our right not to be coerced; it should not propound a doctrine intended to distribute resources with a particular targeted outcome such as upgrading the health of the poor. Use of the tax code to effect social goals such as saving lives with advanced medical technologies is a matter of social *choice*, not social *justice*, in his view. Some disadvantages created by ill health, he argues, are very *unfortunate*, but that does not make them *unfair*. From this perspective, we should call a halt to the demands of justice at the line of the difference between the unfair (and therefore obligatory in justice to correct) and the merely unfortunate.

ACCESS TO HEALTH CARE AND THE RIGHT TO HEALTH CARE

Numerous debates about justice and fair allocation have implications for theories about a *right* to health care. If this right exists, allocations for health care would presumably be based on demands of justice, not merely on charity, compassion, or benevolence. In this context a "right" is understood as an *entitlement* to some measure of health care; rights are contrasted with privileges, ideals, and acts of charity.

In many nations there is a firmly established legal right to health care goods and services for all citizens. The legal situation in the United States, by contrast, involves entitlements for many citizens, but not for most. In 1965 Congress created Medicare and Medicaid to provide coverage for health care costs in populations that could not afford adequate coverage, especially the poor and the elderly. The programs conferred a right to health care on what were then viewed as particularly vulnerable populations. Medicare and Medicaid, as well as other publicly funded health care, such as funding for those serving in the military, subsequently stimulated discussion of whether all citizens have, or at least should have, a right to health care under similar conditions of need.

It is often asked whether moral arguments such as Daniels's (as referenced above) can support what has been called a right to a "decent minimum" of health care. Proponents of a right of this description assert that each person should have equal access to an adequate (though not maximal) level or "tier" of health care for all available types of services. The distribution proceeds on the basis of need, and needs are met by fair access to adequate services. Better services, such as luxury hospital rooms and expensive but optional services such as cosmetic dental work, can then be made available for purchase at personal expense by those who are able to and wish to do so.

Allen Buchanan (in his article in the second section of this chapter) divides the problem of a decent minimum of health care into two problems: "Is there a right to a decent minimum?" and "What comprises the decent minimum?" Buchanan understands a right as a moral entitlement that ought to be enforced by the coercive power of the state. Buchanan argues that any right to health care is weaker than a right of strong equal access, and also a right contingent on available resources and an explicit scheme of priorities (setting limits or rationing). He tries to show that it takes a combination of several theoretically well-grounded arguments to plausibly support universal rights to a decent minimum of health care.

By contrast, Engelhardt concludes that there are no rights and no social obligations of access to health care, although a society may *freely choose* to enact any policy it wishes. He grounds this view in the libertarian theory discussed previously.

The third author in this section, Robert Veatch, defends a different conclusion. Beginning with a somewhat different interpretation of Rawls and egalitarian theory, Veatch argues that those individuals who are worst off in a society (that is, are at the minimum level) should be guaranteed access to a certain level of health care. Society should improve the conditions of the least fortunate by increasing the level of care available to them. He defends a right stronger than the right to a decent *minimum*. He proposes the distribution of health care based on the individual's health care needs, by using the yardstick of an "equal right to health care." The result is that "people have a right to needed health care to provide an opportunity for a level of health equal as far as possible to the health of other people." This theory of justice and health care would result in a health care delivery system with only one class of services available, not a two-tiered system of the decent minimum and that above the decent minimum.

Even if one does not support either moral rights to health care or political obligations to supply it, one can still support legal entitlements to health care on grounds of charity, beneficence, or a sense of moral excellence in a community. Appeals other than those to moral *rights* therefore can be used to defend public distributions that confer legal rights, as Buchanan notes in his essay.

SETTING PRIORITIES AND PROBLEMS OF RATIONING

Many obstacles stand in the way of a more efficient, fair, and comprehensive system of access to health care in virtually all countries. In the United States, the problems are acute. Roughly forty-seven million U.S. citizens (including roughly 10 million children) lack any health care insurance (approximately 14 percent of the population), largely because of the high cost of health insurance and the fact that the system generally grants access through an employer-based health plan. Despite the large percentage of the gross national product spent annually for health care in the United States, the working poor and the uninsured often cannot afford or find access to adequate care.

Many U.S. citizens are uninsurable because they cannot pass physical examinations, cannot present the kind of medical histories required for insurance, or are excluded because of their occupation. In addition, many citizens are underinsured. Costs require limiting coverage even in employer-based plans (a form of rationing), and exclusionary clauses deny access for types of treatment, as well as for specific diseases, injuries, or organ systems. A few people are stuck in a cycle between having no insurance and having little insurance. They experience gaps in insurance coverage that cannot be bridged because they move quickly from job to job or suffer from temporary but lengthy layoffs. More than a million workers lose their insurance for some period of time during the year while they are unemployed, and more than one-quarter of the entire U.S. population changes insurance, with a resulting coverage gap, during the course of each year.

Most countries now face problems of undercoverage for their citizens. Each country is adjusting its system to meet the problems of health care costs and distribution, and each faces troubling issues. Many in bioethics and health policy worry that there is potentially a deep conflict between the goal of reducing costs and that of upholding the traditional ethics of medicine. Everyone lauds the elimination of waste in the system and the removal of unnecessary care, but a cost-driven system is by definition not a patient-centered system, potentially creating physicians with a divided loyalty: In these circumstances, loyalty to institutional goals of economic efficiency sometimes competes with loyalty to the patient. This divided loyalty may function to undermine patients' trust in physicians if they cannot be relied on to act in the best interests of patients.

Some systems heighten this concern through a structure of financial incentives that links remuneration or job security for physicians to efficiency and productivity. Many such practices have been outlawed or eliminated by insurers, but many remain in the system. These systems have been criticized for sloppy handling of diagnostic findings, premature discharge of hospital patients, use of cheaper but less effective drugs and devices, postponing expensive medical tests, not providing experimental treatments that constitute last-chance treatments for some patients, using less skilled physicians for some services, disallowing or discontinuing coverage for very sick patients, and the like.

Some of these problems have been described as ones of "rationing"—one of the favored terms in the article in this chapter by Peter Ubel. In the face of rising costs for health care and other social welfare needs such as education and environmental protection, it has become apparent that governments and their citizens cannot now and will never be able to afford all medically beneficial resources. It appears inevitable that limits will be placed on how much is spent on health care. That is, rationing seems inevitable. But what does it mean to ration, and how can we do so in a manner that does not discriminate against the sick and the poor?

Unfortunately, the term *rationing* has acquired more than one meaning in discussions of the allocation of health care. This term often suggests financially stringent and medically extenuating circumstances in which some persons receive care from which others are excluded. However, the original meaning of "rationing" did not suggest austerity, emergency, or exclusion. It meant a form of allowance, share, or portion, as when food is divided into rations in the military. Only recently has it been tied to limited resources, the setting of priorities in the health care budget, and the inclusion of some to the exclusion of others.

"Rationing" now has at least three meanings, all centered on the notions of *setting limits* to the use of resources and *establishing priorities* in the use of these resources. The first sense is "denial as a result of lack of resources." In a market economy, for example, many types of health care are rationed by whether a person is able to pay for a good or service. A second sense is "limited as a result of a government determination of an allowance or allotment" (i.e., some individuals are denied access to some good or service beyond an allotted amount). This ceiling is set through social policy rather than through the market. Rationing gasoline and certain types of food during a war are well-known examples, and access to health care is commonly structured in this way. A third sense combines the first two: An allowance or allotment is determined and distributed equitably, and only those who can afford additional goods are not denied access beyond the allotted amount. In this third sense, public policy fixes an allowance, but those who can afford additional units are not denied access beyond the allowance.

If poor insurance coverage and inability to pay are ways of eliminating those who are uninsured from access to health care, then much of the U.S. health care system involves rationing by level of personal resources. However, many other forms of rationing are also already in place, including forms of government reimbursement to hospitals, various forms of cost containment, restricting the elderly to certain forms of care, and methods for disseminating new medical technologies.

Many think that because rationing is inevitable, we should take steps to ensure that it be public and visible. This suggests that the kind of hidden rationing that occurs in the present system should be eliminated and replaced by a far more transparent system. The two authors in the third section of this chapter deal with these questions of fair rationing and public policy. In the first article, Peter Ubel discusses the necessity of health care rationing and the need for public policy debate on the subject. He notes that current systems of paying for health insurance encourage people to spend more than they would otherwise be willing to pay for services if they were forced to pay out of pocket. The system as a whole, therefore, is more expensive than it otherwise would be. Ubel argues that although health has a special moral priority, reasonable caps on insurance coverage plans have been and must continue to be formulated. He cautions against supposing that price reductions and waste elimination will resolve these problems of rationing. No matter the level of these reductions, rationing is still inevitable. Even if the term "rationing" generally carries a negative connotation in the United States, Ubel thinks that we must adapt to the fact that the entire structure of health protection and health care delivery involves rationing. In his broad interpretation of rationing, any explicit or implicit measure that causes or allows persons to go without beneficial health care services is a form of rationing.

In the second article in this section of the chapter, Dan Brock examines various issues that arise when cost-effectiveness standards are used to ration—that is, used for purposes of prioritizing health care resources. Because giving priority to the worst off seems intuitively the right thing to do in allocation schemes, Brock discusses several problems that arise when attempting to implement this idea, including problems in determining who qualifies for the status of "worst off." He also considers *how much* of a priority the worst off should receive. In treating these issues he assesses various egalitarian and non-egalitarian moral theories. He argues that despite the compelling needs of the worst off, there must be some balance between giving priority to them and giving priority to other compelling needs. Brock believes that work on these issues is at present significantly underdeveloped. If he is right, we are just beginning to get a good grasp on how much of preventive health and health care is now rationed and how difficult it will be to get a morally acceptable system of rationing in place.

T. L. B.

Social Justice, Health Policy, and Public Health

UNITED NATIONS OFFICE OF THE HIGH COMMISSIONER FOR HUMAN RIGHTS

The Right of Everyone to the Enjoyment of the Highest Attainable Standard of Physical and Mental Health

The Commission on Human Rights,

Reaffirming the Universal Declaration of Human Rights, the International Covenant on Economic, Social and Cultural Rights, the International Convention on the Elimination of All Forms of Racial Discrimination, the Convention on the Elimination of All Forms of Discrimination against Women and the Convention on the Rights of the Child,

Reaffirming also that the right of everyone to the enjoyment of the highest attainable standard of physical and mental health is a human right, as reflected, inter alia, in article 25, paragraph 1, of the Universal Declaration of Human Rights, article 12 of the International Covenant on Economic, Social and Cultural Rights and article 24 of the Convention on the Rights of the Child, as well as, with respect to non-discrimination, in article 5 (*e*) (iv) of the International Convention on the Elimination of All Forms of Racial Discrimination and in article 12, paragraph 1, of the Convention on the Elimination of All Forms of Discrimination against Women, and that such a right derives from the inherent dignity of the human person,

Recalling that, according to the Constitution of the World Health Organization, health is a state of complete physical, mental and social well-being and not merely the absence of disease or infirmity, . . .

Aware that, for millions of people throughout the world, the full realization of the right of everyone to the enjoyment of the highest attainable standard of physical and mental health still remains a distant goal and that, in many cases, especially for those living in poverty, this goal is becoming increasingly remote,

United Nations. Commission on Human Rights Resolution: 2004/27.

Noting with concern the lack of progress towards the targets of the General Assembly special session on HIV/AIDS highlighted in the report of the Secretary-General (A/58/184), which suggests that without stronger action those targets will not be met,

Recognizing a need for States, in cooperation with international organizations and civil society, including non-governmental organizations and the private sector, to create favourable conditions at the national, regional and international levels to ensure the full and effective realization of the right of everyone to the enjoyment of the highest attainable standard of physical and mental health, . . .

Concerned about the interrelationships between poverty and the realization of the right of everyone to the enjoyment of the highest attainable standard of physical and mental health, in particular that ill-health can be both a cause and a consequence of poverty, . . .

Considering that sexual and reproductive health are integral elements of the right of everyone to the enjoyment of the highest attainable standard of physical and mental health,

Stressing that gender equality and the empowerment of women and girls are fundamental elements in the reduction of their vulnerability to HIV/AIDS and that the advancement of women and girls is key to reversing the pandemic, and noting the importance of increasing investments in, and accelerating research on, the development of effective HIV prevention methods, including female-controlled methods and microbicides, . . .

Stressing the importance of monitoring and analysing the pharmaceutical and public health implications of relevant international agreements, including trade agreements, so that States can effectively assess and subsequently develop pharmaceutical and health policies and regulatory measures that address their concerns and priorities, and are able to maximize the positive and mitigate the negative impact of those agreements, while respecting all international obligations applicable to them,

1. *Urges* States to take steps, individually and through international assistance and cooperation, especially economic and technical, to the maximum of their available resources, with a view to achieving progressively the full realization of the right of everyone to the enjoyment of the highest attainable standard of physical and mental health, by all appropriate means, including in particular the adoption of legislative measures;

2. *Calls upon* the international community to continue to assist the developing countries in promoting the full realization of the right of everyone to the enjoyment of the highest attainable standard of physical and mental health, including through financial and technical support as well as training of personnel, while recognizing that the primary responsibility for promoting and protecting all human rights rests with States;

3. *Calls upon* States to guarantee that the right of everyone to the enjoyment of the highest attainable standard of physical and mental health will be exercised without discrimination of any kind; . . .

5. *Reaffirms* that the achievement of the highest attainable standard of physical and mental health is a most important worldwide social goal, the realization of which requires action by many other social and economic sectors in addition to the health sector;

6. *Recommends* that States establish effective mechanisms to ensure that they take due account of the realization of the right of everyone to the enjoyment of the highest attainable standard of physical and mental health in the formulation of their relevant national and international policies;

7. *Urges* all international organizations with mandates bearing upon the right of everyone to the enjoyment of the highest attainable standard of physical and mental health to take into account their members' national and international obligations related to the right of everyone to the enjoyment of the highest attainable standard of physical and mental health;

8. *Calls upon* States to pay special attention to the situation of vulnerable groups, including by the adoption of positive measures, in order to safeguard the full realization of the right of everyone to the enjoyment of the highest attainable standard of physical and mental health; . . .

52nd meeting
16 April 2004
[Adopted by a recorded vote of 52 votes to 1.]

NORMAN DANIELS

Justice, Health, and Health Care

Norman Daniels is the Mary B. Saltonstall Professor of Population Ethics at the Harvard School of Public Health. He has published in ethics, political and social philosophy, and medical ethics. Among his authored and co-authored books are *Seeking Fair Treatment: From the AIDS Epidemic to National Health Care Reform, Just Health Care,* and *Benchmarks of Fairness for Health Care Reform.*

THREE QUESTIONS OF JUSTICE

A theory of justice for health and health care should help us answer three central questions. First, is health care special? Is it morally important in ways that justify (and explain) the fact that many societies distribute health care more equally than many other social goods? Second, when are health inequalities unjust? After all, many socially controllable factors besides access to health care affect the levels of population health and the degree of health inequalities in a population. Third, how can we meet competing health-care needs fairly under reasonable resource constraints? General principles of justice that answer the first two questions do not, I argue, answer some important questions about rationing fairly. Is there instead a fair process for making rationing decisions?

About 20 years ago I answered the first question by claiming health care was special because of its impact on opportunity (Daniels, 1981, 1985). Specifically, the central function of health care is to maintain normal functioning. Disease and disability, by impairing normal functioning, restrict the range of opportunities open to individuals. Health care thus makes a distinct but limited contribution to the protection of equality of opportunity. Though I construed health care broadly to include public health as well as individual preventive, acute, and chronic care, I ignored other factors

that have a profound effect on population health. Unfortunately, focusing on just health care adds to the popular misconception that our vastly improved health in the last century is primarily the result of health care.

During the last 20 years a major literature has emerged exploring the social determinants of health. We have long known that, the richer that people are, the longer and healthier their lives. The powerful findings of the last several decades, however, have deepened our understanding of the factors at work producing these effects on population health and the distribution of health within populations. It is less tenable to believe that it is simply poverty and true deprivation that diminishes the health of some people, for there is growing evidence that the effects of race and class operate across a broad range of inequalities. Because social policies—not laws of human nature or economic development—are responsible for the social and economic inequalities that produce these health effects, we are forced to look upstream from the point of medical delivery and ask about the fairness of the distributions of these goods. John Rawls's theory of justice as fairness, quite serendipitously, contains principles that give a plausible account of the fair distribution of those determinants, thus providing an answer to the second question. . . .

During the 1980s, I became aware that my account of a just health-care system, like other general theories, failed to give specific guidance, or gave implausible answers to certain questions about rationing. . . . Though philosophers may work out middle-level principles that

From *Medicine and Social Justice: Essays on the Distribution of Health Care.* Eds. Rosamond Rhodes, Margaret P. Battin, and Anita Silvers. New York: Oxford University Press, 2002.

can supplement general accounts of distributive justice and solve these unsolved rationing problems, it is unlikely that there will be consensus on them in the foreseeable future. Distributive issues remain highly contested.

In the absence of consensus on distributive principles, we need a fair process to establish legitimacy for critical resource allocation decisions. My account of fair process for addressing these distributive issues is called "accountability for reasonableness" (Daniels and Sabin, 1997, 1998a, 2002). It is an attempt to connect views about deliberative democracy to decision making at various institutional levels, whether public or private, in our complex health systems.

My goal in this chapter is to sketch the central ideas behind my approach to all three questions and to suggest how they all fit together. Detailed arguments can be found in the references. By pushing a theory of justice toward providing answers to all three questions, and not simply the first, I hope to give a fuller demonstration that justice is good for our health.

WHAT IS THE SPECIAL MORAL IMPORTANCE OF HEALTH CARE?

For purposes of justice, the central moral importance of preventing and treating disease and disability with effective health-care services (construed broadly to include public health and environmental measures, as well as personal medical services) derives from the way in which protecting normal functioning contributes to protecting opportunity. Specifically, by keeping people close to normal functioning, health care preserves for people the ability to participate in the political, social, and economic life of their society. It sustains them as fully participating citizens— normal collaborators and competitors—in all spheres of social life.

By maintaining normal functioning, health care protects an individual's fair share of the normal range of opportunities (or plans of life) that reasonable people would choose in a given society. This normal opportunity range is societally relative, depending on various facts about its level of technological development and social organization. Individuals' fair shares of that societal normal opportunity range are the plans of life it would be reasonable for them to choose were they not ill or disabled and were their talents and skills suitably protected against misdevelopment or underdevelopment

as a result of unfair social practices and the consequences of socioeconomic inequalities. Individuals generally choose to develop only some of their talents and skills, effectively narrowing their range of opportunities. Maintaining normal functioning preserves, however, their broader, fair share of the normal opportunity range, giving them the chance to revise their plans of life over time.

This relationship between health care and the protection of opportunity suggests that the appropriate principle of distributive justice for regulating the design of a health-care system is a principle protecting equality of opportunity. Any theory of justice that supports a principle assuring equal opportunity (or giving priority to improving the opportunities of those who have the least opportunity) could thus be extended to health care. At the time I proposed this approach, the best defense of such a general principle was to be found in John Rawls's theory of justice as fairness (Rawls, 1971). One of the principles that Rawls's social contractors would choose is a principle assuring them *fair equality of opportunity* in access to jobs and offices. This principle not only prohibits discriminatory barriers to access, but requires positive social measures that correct for the negative effects on opportunity, including the underdevelopment of skills and talents, that derive from unfair social practices (e.g., a legacy of gender or race bias) or socioeconomic inequalities. Such positive measures would include among other things the provision of public education and other opportunity improving early childhood interventions.

Rawls, however, had deliberately simplified the formulation of his general theory of justice by assuming that people are fully functional over a normal life span. His social contractors thus represented people who suffered no disease or disability or premature death. By subsuming the protection of normal functioning under (a suitably adjusted version of) Rawls's principle assuring fair equality of opportunity, I showed how to drop that idealization and apply his theory to the real world (Rawls, 1993, supports this approach). In the last two decades, however, other work on egalitarianism has suggested alternative ways to connect health care to opportunity or to positive liberty or capabilities, and I shall comment on them shortly. First, I want to highlight some key elements of my approach.

The fair equality of opportunity account does not use the impact of disease or disability on welfare (desire satisfaction or happiness) or utility as a basis for thinking about distributive justice. One might have thought, for example, that what was special about health care was that good health was important for happiness. But illness and disability may not lead to unhappiness, even if they restrict the range of opportunities open to an individual. Intuitively, then, there is something attractive about locating the moral importance of meeting health-care needs in the more objective impact on opportunity than in the more subjective impact on happiness.

This analysis fits well with and extends Rawls's (1971) non-welfarist account of primary social goods. For purposes of justice, Rawls argued, we should not seek to determine what we owe each other by measuring our satisfaction or welfare, but we should measure our levels of well-being by publicly accessible measures. For Rawls this means an index of primary social goods that includes rights and liberties, powers and opportunity, income and wealth, and the social bases of self-respect. My account includes the protection of normal functioning within the scope of the primary good of opportunity. . . .

Health care is of special moral importance because it helps to preserve our status as fully functioning citizens. By itself, however, this does not distinguish health care from food, shelter, and rest, which also meet the basic needs of citizens by preserving normal functioning. Because medical needs are more unequally distributed than these other needs and can be catastrophically expensive, they are appropriately seen as the object of private or social insurance schemes. It might be argued that we can finesse the problem of talking about the medical needs we owe it to each other to meet if we assure people fair income shares from which they can purchase such insurance. We cannot, however, define a minimal but fair income share unless it is capable of meeting such needs. . . .

The account sketched here has several implications for the design of our health-care institutions and for issues of resource allocation. Perhaps most important, the account supports the provision of universal access to appropriate health care—including traditional public health and preventive measures—through public or mixed public and private insurance schemes. Health care aimed at protecting fair equality of opportunity should not be distributed according to ability to pay, and the burden of payment should not fall disproportionately on those who are ill. . . .

Properly designed universal coverage health systems will be constrained by reasonable budgets, for health care is not the only important good. Reasonable resource constraints will then require judgments about which medical needs are more important to meet than others. Both rationing and setting priorities are requirements of justice; this is because meeting health-care needs should not and need not be a bottomless pit.

The elderly might object that an opportunity-based account of a just system of health care will leave them out in the cold, for their opportunities might seem to be in the past. We can avoid this by not biasing our allocations in favor of one stage of life and instead considering the age-relative opportunity range. Still, treating people differently at different stages of life—for example, saving resources from one stage of life for use at another—does not produce inequalities across individuals in the way that differential treatment by race or gender does. We all age—though we do not change gender or race. Fairness among age groups in designing a health-care system is appropriately modeled by the idea of prudent allocation over a life span. . . . Under some conditions of scarcity, this implies that "pure" rationing by age (where age is not a proxy for other traits) is permissible. . . .

WHICH HEALTH INEQUALITIES ARE UNJUST?

Universal access to appropriate health care—health care that is just—does not break the link between social status and health that I noted earlier, a point driven home in studies of the effects on health inequality of the British National Health Service (Black et al., 1988; Acheson et al., 1998; Marmot et al., 1998) and confirmed by work in other countries as well (Kawachi et al., 1999). Our health is affected not simply by the ease with which we can see a doctor—though that surely matters—but also by our social position and the underlying inequality of our society. We cannot, of course, infer causation from these correlations between social inequality and health inequality (though later I explore some ideas about how the one might lead the other). Suffice to say that, although the exact processes are not fully understood, the evidence suggests that social determinants of health exist (Marmot, 1999).

If social factors play a large role in determining our health, then efforts to ensure greater justice in health outcomes should not focus simply on the traditional health sector. Health is produced not merely by having access to medical prevention and treatment, but also, to a measurably greater extent, by the cumulative experience of social conditions over the course of one's life. By the time a 60-year-old heart attack victim arrives at the emergency room, bodily insults have accumulated over a lifetime. For such a person, medical care is, figuratively speaking, "the ambulance waiting at the bottom of the cliff." Much contemporary discussion about reducing health inequalities by increasing access to medical care misses this point. Of course, we still want that ambulance there, but we should also be looking to improve social conditions that help to determine the health of societies.

As I noted earlier, Rawls's theory of justice as fairness was not designed to address issues of health care. Rawls assumed a completely healthy population, and he argued that a just society must assure people equal basic liberties, guarantee that the right of political participation has roughly equal value for all, provide a robust form of equal opportunity, and limit inequalities to those that benefit the least advantaged. When these requirements of justice are met, Rawls argued, we can have reasonable confidence that others are showing us the respect that is essential to our sense of self-worth. The fair terms of cooperation specified by these principles promote our social and political well-being.

The conjecture I explore is that by establishing equal liberties, robustly equal opportunity, a fair distribution of resources, and support for our self-respect—the basics of Rawlsian justice—we would go a long way in eliminating the most important injustices in health outcomes. To be sure, social justice is valuable for reasons other than its effects on health (or Rawls could not have set aside issues of health when arguing for justice as fairness). And social reform in the direction of greater justice would not eliminate the need to think hard about fair allocation of resources within the health-care system. Still, acting to promote social justice is a crucial step toward improving our health because there is this surprising convergence between what is needed for our social and political well being and for our mental and physical health.

To see the basis for this conjecture about Rawlsian principles, let us review very briefly some of the central findings in the recent literature on the social determinants of health. If we look at cross-national studies, we see that a country's prosperity is related to its health, as measured, for example, by life expectancy: In richer countries, people tend to live longer. But the relationship between per capita gross domestic product (GDPpc) and life expectancy levels off at about $8,000 to $10,000; beyond this threshold, further economic advance buys virtually no further gains in life expectancy. This leveling effect is most apparent among the advanced industrial economies. Nevertheless, even within this relationship, telling variations exist. Though Cuba and Iraq are equally poor (each has a GDPpc of about $3,100), life expectancy in Cuba exceeds that in Iraq by 17.2 years. The poor state of Kerala in India, which invested heavily in education, especially female literacy, has health outcomes far superior to the rest of India and more comparable to those in much wealthier countries. The difference between the GDPpc for Costa Rica and the United States is enormous (about $21,000), yet Costa Rica's life expectancy exceeds that of the United States (76.6 to 76.4 years).

Taken together, these observations show that the health of nations depends, in part, on factors other than wealth. Culture, social organization, and government policies also help determine population health. Variations in these factors—not fixed laws of economic development—may explain many of the differences in health outcomes among nations.

One especially important factor in explaining the health of a society is the distribution of income: The health of a population depends not just on the size of the economic pie, but on how the pie is shared. Differences in health outcomes among developed nations cannot be explained simply by the absolute deprivation associated with low economic development—lack of access to the basic material conditions necessary for health such as clean water, adequate nutrition and housing, and general sanitary living conditions. The degree of relative deprivation within a society also matters. . . .

Earlier, I cautioned that correlations between inequality and health do not necessarily imply causation. Still, there are plausible and identifiable pathways through which social inequalities appear to produce health inequalities to make a reasonable case for causation. In the United States, the states with the most unequal income distributions invest less in public education, have larger uninsured populations, and spend less on social safety nets (Kaplan et al., 1996; Kawachi and Kennedy, 1997). Studies of educational spending and educational outcomes are especially striking: Controlling for median income, income inequality explains about 40% of the variation between states in the percentage of children in the fourth grade who are below the basic reading level. Similarly strong associations are seen for high school dropout rates. It is evident from these data that educational opportunities for children in high income-inequality states are quite different from those in states with more egalitarian distributions. These effects on education have an immediate impact on health, increasing the likelihood of premature death during childhood and adolescence (as evidenced by the much higher death rates for infants and children in the high-inequality states). Later in life, they appear in the socioeconomic gradient in health.

When we compare countries, we also find that differential investment in human capital—in particular, education—is a strong predictor of health. Indeed, one of the strongest predictors of life expectancy among developing countries is adult literacy, particularly the disparity between male and female adult literacy, which explains much of the variation in health achievement among these countries after accounting for GDPpc. For example, among the 125 developing nations with a per capita GDP of less than $10,000, the difference between male and female literacy accounts for 40% of the variation in life expectancy (after factoring out the effect of GDPpc). In the United States, differences between the states in women's status—measured in terms of their economic autonomy and political participation—are strongly correlated with higher female mortality rates.

These societal mechanisms—for example, income inequality leading to educational inequality leading to health inequality—are tightly linked to the political processes that influence government policy. For instance, income inequality appears to affect health by undermining civil society. Income inequality erodes social cohesion, as measured by higher levels of social mistrust and reduced participation in civic organizations. Lack of social cohesion leads to lower participation in political activity (such as voting, serving in local government, volunteering for political campaigns). And lower participation, in turn, undermines the responsiveness of government institutions in addressing the needs of the worst-off. States with the highest income inequality, and thus lowest levels of social capital and political participation, are less likely to invest in human capital and provide far less generous social safety nets. . . .

Rawls's principles of justice thus turn out to regulate the key social determinants of health. One principle assures equal basic liberties, and specifically provides for guaranteeing *effective* rights of political participation. The fair equality of opportunity principle assures access to high-quality public education, early childhood interventions, including day care, aimed at eliminating class or race disadvantages, and universal coverage for appropriate health care. Rawls's "Difference Principle" permits inequalities in income only if the inequalities work (e.g., through incentives) to make those who are worst-off as well-off as possible. This is not a simple "trickle down" principle that tolerates any inequality as long as there is some benefit that flows down the socioeconomic ladder; it requires a maximal flow downward. It would therefore flatten socioeconomic inequalities in a robust way, assuring far more than a "decent minimum." . . . In addition, the assurances of the value of political participation and fair equality of opportunity would further constrain allowable income inequalities.

The conjecture is that a society complying with these principles of justice would probably flatten the socioeconomic gradient even more than we see in the most egalitarian welfare states of northern Europe. The implication is that we should view health inequalities that derive from social determinants as unjust unless the determinants are distributed in conformity with these robust principles. Because of the detailed attention Rawls's theory pays to the interaction of these terms of fair cooperation, it provides us—through the findings of social science—with an account of the just distribution of health.

The inequalities in the social determinants that are still permitted by this theory may still produce a socioeconomic gradient, albeit a much flatter one than we see today. Should we view these residual health inequalities as unjust and demand further redistribution of the social determinants?

I believe the theory I have described does not give a clear answer. If the Rawlsian theory insists that protecting opportunity takes priority over other matters and cannot be traded for other gains (and Rawls generally adopts this view), then residual health inequalities may be unjust. If health can be traded for other goods—and all of us make such trades when we take chances with our health to pursue other goals—then the account may be more flexible. . . . Still, Rawls's principles provide more specific guidance in thinking about the distribution of the social determinants than is provided by the fair equality of opportunity account of a just health-care system alone. . . .

WHEN ARE LIMITS TO HEALTH CARE FAIR?

Justice requires that all societies meet health-care needs fairly under reasonable resource constraints. Even a wealthy, egalitarian country with a highly efficient health-care system will have to set limits to the health care it guarantees everyone (whether or not it allows supplementary tiers for those who can afford them). Poorer countries have to make even harder choices about priorities and limits. However important, health care is not the only important social good. All societies must decide which needs should be given priority and when resources are better spent elsewhere.

How should fair decisions about such limits be made? Under what conditions should we view such decisions as a legitimate exercise of moral authority?

Answering these questions would be much simpler if people could agree on principles of distributive justice that would determine how to set fair limits to health care. If societies agreed on such principles, people could simply check social decisions and practices against the principles to determine whether they conform with them. Where decisions, practices, and institutions fail to conform, they would be unjust and people should then change them. Disagreements about the fairness of actual distributions would then be either disagreements about the interpretation of the principles or about the facts of the situation. Many societies have well-established and reliable, if imperfect, legal procedures for resolving such disputes about facts and interpretations.

Unfortunately, there is no consensus on such distributive principles for health care. Reasonable people, who have diverse moral and religious views about many matters, disagree morally about what constitutes a fair allocation of resources to meet competing health-care needs—even when they agree on other aspects of the justice of health-care systems, such as the importance of universal access to whatever services are provided. We should expect, and respect, such diversity in views about rationing health care. Nevertheless, we must arrive at acceptable social policies despite our disagreements. This moral controversy raises a distinctive problem of legitimacy: Under what conditions should we accept as legitimate the moral authority of those making rationing decisions?

I shall develop the following argument: (*1*) We have no consensus on principled solutions to a cluster of morally controversial rationing problems, and general principles of justice for health and health care fail to provide specific guidance about them. . . . (*2*) In the absence of such a consensus, we should rely on a fair process for arriving at solutions to these problems and for establishing the legitimacy of such decisions (Rawls, 1971). (*3*) A fair process that addresses issues of legitimacy will have to meet several constraints that I shall refer to as "accountability for reasonableness" (Daniels and Sabin, 1998a, 2002); these constraints tie the process to deliberative democratic procedures. . . . This issue of legitimacy and fair process arises in both public and mixed public–private health-care systems, and it must be addressed in countries at all levels of development.

To support the first step of the argument, consider a problem that has been labeled the "priorities problem": How much priority should we give to treating the sickest or most disabled patients? To start with, imagine two extreme positions. The Maximin position ("maximize the minimum") says that we should give complete priority to treating the worst-off patients. One might think that Maximin is implied by the fair equality of opportunity account (though I believe my account is only committed to giving *some* priority to the worst off, placing it in a broad family of views that leave the degree of priority unspecified). The Maximize position says that we should give priority to whatever treatment produces the greatest net health benefit (or greatest net health benefit per dollar spent) regardless of which patients we treat. . . .

Disagreement persists: A definite but very small minority are inclined to be *maximizers* and a definite but very small minority are inclined to be *maximiners*. Most people fall in between, and they vary considerably in how much benefit they are willing to sacrifice to give priority to worse off patients. . . .

If we have persistent disagreement about principles for resolving rationing problems, then we must retreat to a process all can agree is a fair way to resolve disputes about them. The "retreat to procedural justice" as a way of determining what is fair when we lack prior agreement on principles is a central feature of Rawls's account (thus "justice as [procedural] fairness"). Rather than argue for this familiar approach (the second step of my argument above), I shall move directly to characterizing the features of such a fair process.

We would take a giant step toward solving the problems of legitimacy and fairness that face public agencies and private health plans making limit-setting decisions if the following four conditions were satisfied (Daniels and Sabin, 1997):

- *Publicity condition:* Decisions regarding coverage for new technologies (and other limit-setting decisions) and their rationales must be publicly accessible.
- *Relevance condition:* The rationales for coverage decisions should aim to provide a *reasonable* construal of how the organization (or society) should provide "value for money" in meeting the varied health needs of a defined population under reasonable resource constraints. Specifically, a construal will be "reasonable" if it appeals to reasons and principles that are accepted as relevant by people who are disposed to finding terms of cooperation that are mutually justifiable.
- *Appeals condition*: There is a mechanism for challenge and dispute resolution regarding limit-setting decisions, including the opportunity for revising decisions in light of further evidence or arguments.
- *Enforcement condition:* There is either voluntary or public regulation of the process to ensure that the first three conditions are met.

The guiding idea behind the four conditions is to convert private health plan or public agency decisions into part of a larger public deliberation about how to use limited resources to protect fairly the health of a population with varied needs. The broader public deliberation envisioned here is not necessarily an organized democratic procedure, though it could include the deliberation underlying public regulation of the health-care system. Rather, it may take place in various forms in an array of institutions, spilling over into legislative politics only under some circumstances. Meeting these conditions also serves an educative function: The public is made familiar with the need for limits and appropriate ways to reason about them.

The first condition (Publicity condition) requires that rationales for decisions be publicly accessible to everyone affected by them. . . .

The Relevance condition imposes two important constraints on the rationales that are made publicly accessible. Specifically, the rationales for coverage decisions should aim to provide (a) a *reasonable* construal of (b) how the organization (or society) should provide "value for money" in meeting the varied health needs of a defined population under reasonable resource constraints. Both constraints need explanation.

We may think of the goal of meeting the varied needs of the population of patients under reasonable resource constraints as a characterization of the *common* or *public good* pursued by all engaged in the enterprise of delivering and receiving this care. Reasoning about that goal must also meet certain conditions. Specifically, a construal of the goal will be "reasonable" only if it appeals to reasons (evidence, values, and principles) that are accepted as relevant by "fair-minded" people. By "fair-minded" I mean people who seek mutually justifiable terms of cooperation. The notion is not mysterious; we encounter it all the time in sports. Fair-minded people are those who want to play by agreed-upon rules in a sport and prefer rules that are designed to bring out the best in that game. Here we are concerned with the game of delivering health care that meets population needs in a fair way. . . .

The Appeals and Enforcement conditions involve mechanisms that go beyond the publicity requirements of the first two conditions. When patients or clinicians use these procedures to challenge a decision, and the results of the challenge lead effectively to reconsideration of the decision on its merits, the decision-making process is made iterative in a way that broadens the input of information and argument. Parties that were excluded from the decision-making process, and whose views may not have been clearly heard or understood, find a voice, even if after the original fact. The dispute resolution mechanisms do not empower enrollees or clinicians to play a direct, participatory role in the actual decision-making bodies, but that does not happen in many public democratic processes as well. Still, it does empower them to play a more effective role in the larger social deliberation about the issues, including deliberation within those public institutions that can play a role in regulating private health plans or otherwise constraining their acts. The mechanisms we describe thus play a role in assuring broader accountability of private organizations to those who are affected by limit-setting decisions. The arrangements required by the four conditions provide connective tissue to, not a replacement for, broader democratic processes that ultimately have authority and responsibility for guaranteeing the fairness of limit-setting decisions.

Together these conditions hold institutions—public or private—and decision makers in them "accountable for the reasonableness" of the limits they set. All must engage in a process of establishing their credentials for fair decision making about such fundamental matters every time they make such a decision. Whether in public or mixed systems, establishing the accountability of decision makers to those affected by their decision is the only way to show, over time, that arguably fair decisions are being made and that those making them have established a procedure we should view as legitimate This is not to say that public participation is an essential ingredient of the process in either public or mixed systems, but the accountability to the public in both cases is necessary to facilitate broader democratic processes that regulate the system. . . .

CONCLUDING REMARKS

A comprehensive approach to justice, health, and health care must address all three questions I have discussed. My extension of Rawls's theory of justice to health and health care provides a way to link answers to the first and second questions. There are also three ways in which Rawls's theory also provides support for my approach to the third question. First, I propose that we use a fair process to arrive at what is fair in rationing; this is because we lack prior consensus on the relevant distributive principles. This "retreat to procedural justice" is at the heart of Rawls's own invocation of his version of a social contract. Second, Rawls places great emphasis on the importance of publicity as a constraint on theories of justice: Principles of justice and the grounds for them must be publicly acknowledged. This constraint is central to the conditions that establish accountability for reasonableness. Finally, Rawls develops the view that "public reason" must constrain the content of public deliberation and decision about fundamental matters

of justice, avoiding special considerations that might be elements of the comprehensive moral views that people hold. . . . Accountability for reasonableness pushes decision makers toward finding reasons all can agree are relevant to the goals of co-operative health-delivery schemes. In this way, accountability for reasonableness promotes the democratic deliberation that Rawls also advocates. . . .

REFERENCES

Acheson, D. (1998). *Report of the Independent Inquiry into Inequalities in Health.* London: Stationery Office.

Black, D., Morris, J. N., Smith, C., Townsend, P., and Whitehead, M. (1988). *Inequalities in Health: The Black Report: The Health Divide.* London: Penguin Group.

Daniels, N. (1981). Health-care needs and distributive justice. *Philosophy and Public Affairs* 10, 146–79.

Daniels, N. (1985). *Just Health Care.* New York: Cambridge University Press.

Daniels, N. and Sabin, J. E. (1997). Limits to health care: Fair procedures, democratic deliberation, and the legitimacy problem for insurers. *Philosophy and Public Affairs* 26, 303–50.

Daniels, N. and Sabin, J. (1998a). The ethics of accountability and the reform of managed-care organizations. *Health Affairs* 17(5), 50–69.

Daniels, N. and Sabin, J. (2002). *Setting Limits Fairly: Can We Learn to Share Medical Resources?* New York: Oxford University Press.

Kaplan, G. A., Pamuk, E. R., Lynch, J. W., Cohen, R. D., and Balfour, J. L. (1996). Inequality in income and mortality in the United States: Analysis of mortality and potential pathways. *British Medical Journal* 312, 999–1003.

Kawachi, I. and Kennedy, B. P. (1997). Health and social cohesion: Why care about income inequality? *British Medical Journal* 314, 1037–40.

Kawachi, I. and Kennedy, B. P. (1999). Income inequality and health: Pathways and mechanisms. *Health Services Research* 34, 215–27.

Marmot, M. G. (1999). *Social Causes of Social Inequalities in Health.* Harvard Center for Population and Development Studies, Working Paper Series 99.01, January 1999.

Marmot, M. G., Fuhrer, R., Ettner, S. L., Marks, N. F., Bumpass, L. L., and Ryff, C. D. (1998). Contribution of psychosocial factors to socioeconomic differences in health. *Milbank Quarterly* 76(3), 403–48.

Rawls, J. (1971). A *Theory of Justice.* Cambridge, MA: Harvard University Press.

Rawls, J. (1993). *Political Liberalism.* New York: Columbia University Press.

THOMAS POGGE

Responsibilities for Poverty-Related Ill Health

Thomas Pogge is a philosopher and Professor of Political Science at Columbia University. He has published primarily in moral and political philosophy, including work on John Rawls, Immanuel Kant, cosmopolitanism, and extreme poverty. Much of his work regards the theory and practice of human rights.

My view on justice in regard to health is distinctive in two ways. First, I hold that the strength of our moral reasons to prevent or to mitigate particular medical conditions does not depend only on what one might call distributional factors, such as how badly off the people affected by these conditions are in absolute and relative terms, how costly prevention or treatment would be, and how much patients would benefit from given treatment. Rather, it depends also on relational factors, that is, on how we are related to the medical conditions they suffer. This point is widely accepted in regard to conduct. You have, for instance, stronger moral reason to make sure that people are not harmed through your negligence than you have to ensure that they are not harmed through causes outside your control (others' negligence or their own, say, or bad weather). And your moral reason to help an accident victim is stronger if you were materially involved in causing her accident.

I assert an analogous point also in regard to any social institutions that agents are materially involved in upholding: in shaping an institutional order, we should be more concerned, morally, that it not contribute substantially to the incidence of medical conditions than we should be that it prevent medical conditions caused by other factors. Thus, we should design any institutional order so that it prioritizes the alleviation of those medical conditions it substantially contributes to. In institutional contexts as well, what is important to moral assessment is not merely the distribution of health outcomes as such, but also whether and how social factors contribute to their incidence. The latter consideration is needed to distinguish different degrees of responsibility for medical conditions and for their prevention and mitigation.

My second thesis builds on the first. It is generally believed that one's moral reason to help prevent and mitigate others' medical conditions is stronger when these others are compatriots than when they are foreigners. I reject this belief in regard to medical conditions in whose incidence one is materially involved. People can be so involved through their ordinary conduct or through their role in upholding an institutional order. In the case of ordinary interpersonal relations, for example, one's moral reasons to drive carefully and to help victims of any accident one has caused do not weaken when one is traveling abroad and among foreigners. And in institutional contexts, we ought especially to ensure that any institutional order we help impose avoids causing adverse medical conditions and makes the alleviation of any medical conditions it does cause a priority. Here my second thesis holds that this responsibility is not sensitive to whether the medical conditions at stake are suffered by foreigners or by compatriots.

Combining both theses, I hold then that foreigners' medical conditions in whose incidence we are materially involved have greater moral weight for us than compatriots' medical conditions in whose incidence we are not materially involved.

This paper is reprinted, with many updates and revisions, from *Ethics & International Affairs* 16/2 (2002), 71–79. A longer version, "Relational Conceptions of Justice: Responsibilities for Health Outcomes," appeared in Sudhir Anand, Fabienne Peter, and Amartya Sen, eds., *Public Health, Ethics, and Equity* (Oxford: Clarendon Press, 2004). The author is grateful to the editors and Blackwell Publishers for permission to reuse this material.

In interpersonal contexts, this combined thesis is not likely to be very controversial. Suppose two children have been injured by speeding drivers and money is needed to pay for an expensive medical treatment necessary to restore their health and appearance completely. In one case, the child is a foreigner and you were the driver. In the other case, the child is a compatriot and someone else was the driver. My view entails that in a situation like this you have (other things being equal) stronger moral reason to buy the expensive treatment for the foreign child; and most would probably agree.

In institutional contexts, by contrast, my view is likely to be quite controversial. It might be stated as follows: Foreigners' medical conditions, if social institutions we are materially involved in upholding substantially contribute to their incidence, have greater moral weight for us than compatriots' medical conditions in whose causation we are not materially involved. This combined thesis is radical if social institutions we are materially involved in upholding do substantially contribute to the incidence of medical conditions abroad. Is this the case?

SOCIAL INSTITUTIONS, POVERTY, AND HEALTH

Many kinds of social institutions can substantially contribute to the incidence of medical conditions. Of these, economic institutions—the basic rules governing ownership, production, use, and exchange of natural resources, goods, and services—have the greatest impact on health. This impact is mediated, for the most part, through poverty. By avoidably engendering severe poverty, economic institutions substantially contribute to the incidence of many medical conditions. And persons materially involved in upholding such economic institutions are then materially involved in the causation of such medical conditions.

In our world, poverty is highly relevant to human health. In fact, poverty is far and away the most important factor in explaining existing health deficits. Because they are poor, 830 million people are malnourished (UNDP 2006, 174), 1100 million lack access to safe drinking water and 2600 million lack access to basic sanitation (UNDP 2006, 33), 1000 million have no adequate shelter and 2000 million no electricity (UNDP 1998, 49), 2200 million lack access to essential drugs (www.fic.nih.gov/about/summary.html). Poverty-related causes account for

about one third of all human deaths, some 18 million every year (WHO 2004, 120–5) including 10.6 million children under age 5 (UNICEF 2005, inside front cover).

This massive poverty is not due to overall scarcity. At market exchange rates, the World Bank's higher ("$2/day") international poverty line corresponds today (2007) to about $280 per person per year in a typical poor country (and to $1120 in the more expensive US). The 2735 million persons living below this line, and 42 percent below it on average,[1] thus have aggregate annual income of roughly $440 billion and collectively fall short of the $2/day poverty line by about $320 billion. By contrast, the aggregate gross national incomes of the high-income countries with their 1011 million citizens amounted to $35,529 billion in 2005 (World Bank 2006, 289). However daunting the figure of 2735 million poor people may sound, global inequality is now so enormous that plausible reforms eradicating poverty worldwide solely at the expense of the high-income countries would barely be felt in the latter.[2]

It cannot be denied that the distribution of income and wealth is heavily influenced by economic institutions, which regulate the distribution of a jointly generated social product. What can be said, and is said quite often, is that the economic institutions that substantially contribute to the persistence of severe poverty in the poorer countries are *local* economic institutions in whose imposition we, citizens of the affluent countries, are not materially involved. Economists tirelessly celebrate the success stories of the Asian tigers or of Kerala (a state in India), leading us to believe that those who remain hungry have only their own institutions and governments (and hence themselves and their own compatriots) to blame. Even the philosopher Rawls feels called upon to reiterate that poverty has local explanations: "The causes of the wealth of a people and the forms it takes lie in their political culture and in the religious, philosophical, and moral traditions that support the basic structure, as well as in the industriousness and cooperative talents of its members, all supported by their political virtues. . . . Crucial also is the country's population policy" (Rawls 1999b, 108).

It is quite true, of course, that local economic institutions, and local factors more generally, play an important role in the reproduction of extreme poverty. But this fact does not show that global institutions we are materially involved in upholding play no substantial role. That the effects of flawed domestic institutions are as bad as they are is often due to global institutions—to the institution of the territorial state, for instance, which allows affluent populations to prevent the poor from migrating to where their work could earn a decent living (see Carens 1987). And health systems in poor countries fail to cope in good part because, under the TRIPS Agreement, pharmaceutical innovations must be rewarded through monopoly pricing powers, which exclude the poor from advanced medicines for the sake of incentivizing solutions to the health problems of the affluent. There are straightforward alternative ways of incentivizing pharmaceutical innovation that would not exclude the poor from its benefits.[3]

Global institutions also have a profound impact on the indigenous institutional schemes of the less developed countries. Such institutions recognize anyone holding effective power in a country—regardless of how they acquired or exercise it and to how they are regarded by the population—as entitled to sell the country's resources and to dispose of the proceeds of such sales, to borrow in the country's name and thereby to impose debt service obligations upon it, to sign treaties on the country's behalf and thus to bind its present and future population, and to use state revenues to buy the means of internal repression. By assigning such powers to any de-facto rulers, we support, reward, and encourage the undemocratic acquisition and repressive exercise of political power especially in the resource-rich poorer countries.[4]

The national institutional schemes of affluent countries, too, can have a profound influence on the national institutional schemes of poorer countries. An obvious example is that, until recently, most affluent countries (though not, after 1977, the United States) have allowed their firms to pay bribes to officials of poorer countries, and even to deduct such bribes from their taxable revenues.[5] Such authorization and moral support for bribery have greatly contributed to the now deeply entrenched culture of corruption in many less developed countries.

If the social institutions of the affluent countries and the global institutional order these countries uphold contribute substantially to the reproduction of poverty, then it is hard to deny that we citizens of affluent countries are therefore materially involved in it as well. It is true, of course, that these institutions are shaped by our politicians. But we live in reasonably democratic states where we can choose politicians and political programs from a wide range of alternatives, where we can participate in shaping political programs and debates, and where politicians and political parties must cater to the popular will if they are to be elected and reelected. If we really wanted our domestic and international institutions to be shaped so as to avoid reproducing severe poverty, politicians committed to that goal would emerge and be successful. But the vast majority of citizens of the affluent countries want national and global institutions to be shaped in the service of their own interests and therefore support politicians willing so to shape them. At least the citizens in this large majority can then be said to be materially involved in the reproduction of poverty and the associated health deficits. And they, at least, have then stronger moral reason to discontinue their support, and to help the foreign victims of current social institutions, than to help fund most services provided under ordinary health programs (such as Medicare) for the benefit of their compatriots—or so the view I have outlined would suggest.

Superficially similar conclusions are sometimes defended on cost/benefit grounds, by reference to how thousands of children in poor countries can be saved from their trivial diseases at the cost of terminal care for a single person in an affluent country.[6] My view, by contrast, turns on the different ways in which we are related to the medical conditions of others and thus may tell us to favor foreigners even if costs and benefits are equal.

This summary of my larger view on health equity was meant to be introductory, not conclusive. Seeing what is at stake, I would expect even the most commonsensical of my remarks about the explanation of global poverty to be vigorously disputed; and I certainly do not believe that this brief outline can lay such controversies to rest.

TREATING RECIPIENTS JUSTLY VERSUS PROMOTING A JUST DISTRIBUTION

The justice of iudicanda[7]—conduct, persons, and social institutions—is often thought to depend solely on the distribution of relevant goods and ills that they bring about. On such a view, alternative arrangements of a health-care system, for instance, are assessed solely on the basis of the distribution of health outcomes each would tend to produce. By focusing exclusive moral attention on those affected, such a view deploys what one might call a passive concept of justice.

An important alternative to this passive concept adds an essential place for (what I call) the *agents* of justice, for those who have or share moral responsibility for a *iudicandum*. I call it the active concept of justice, because it diverts some attention from those affected by a *iudicandum* to those who shape it. This modification is significant in several ways: for something to be unjust, there must be some identifiable agent or agents responsible for its injustice or for making it (more) just. Some agents may have responsibilities with respect to some injustice while others do not—unlike you, I may have no moral reason to seek to prevent or to remedy a minor injustice in your spouse's conduct toward your children. There may also be gradations, as when moral responsibility with regard to the injustice of some institutional order varies from agent to agent within its scope; being privileged or influential may strengthen moral responsibilities, being poor or burdened by many other responsibilities may weaken them. Furthermore, as this last thought suggests, there may be competing claims—one may have responsibilities with regard to several injustices and may then have to decide how much of an effort one ought to make with regard to each. These issues concerning responsibilities and their prioritization are crucial for giving justice a determinate role in the real world. And they tend to be overlooked from the start, or grossly oversimplified, when the topic is approached in terms of the passive concept of justice.[8]

Associated with these contrasting concepts of justice are two fundamentally different ways of understanding contemporary egalitarian liberalism. One variant sees its core in the idea that no citizen ought to be worse off on account of unchosen inequalities. This idea, duly specified, defines an ideal society in which no person is worse off than others except only as a consequence of free and informed choices this person has made. In such a society, social institutions, and perhaps all other humanly controllable factors as well, are then to be aimed at promoting such a solely choice-sensitive overall distribution of quality of life.[9] The other variant sees the core of egalitarian liberalism in the idea that a liberal society, or state, ought to treat all its citizens equally in terms of helps and hindrances. Such *equal* treatment need not be *equality-promoting* treatment. Pre-existing inequalities in, for example, genetic potentials and liabilities—however unchosen by their bearers—are not society's responsibility and not to be corrected or compensated at the expense of those favored by these inequalities.

The health equity theme provokes the most forceful clash of these two variants of egalitarian liberalism. One side seems committed to the indefinite expansion of the health-care system by using it to neutralize (through medical research, treatment, alleviation, and compensation) all handicaps, disabilities, and other medical conditions from which persons may suffer through no fault of their own. The other side seems committed to the callous (if not cruel) view that we, as a society, need do no more for persons whose health is poor through no fault of ours than for persons in good health.[10] Most contemporary theorists of justice take the purely recipient-oriented approach, though they do not explicitly consider and reject the relational alternative I propose. Much of the current debate is focused on the question of how we are to judge the justice of overall distributions or states of affairs in a comparative way.[11]

But *should* we judge the justice of conduct, people, and/or social rules solely by their impact on the quality of such overall distributions? With respect to conduct, most would reject this purely recipient-oriented mode of assessment. Abstractly considered, a situation in which everyone has at least one eye and one kidney is surely morally better than (an otherwise similar) one in which some, through no fault of their own, have no functioning eye or kidney while many others have two. But actions and persons promoting such an abstractly better distribution are nevertheless judged gravely unjust.

Cases of this kind may be used to draw the conclusion that we ought to distinguish between *treating recipients justly* and *promoting a good distribution among recipients*. With respect to social rules, a similar distinction would seem to be called for, and for similar reasons. Just social rules for the allocation of donated kidneys favor those who, through no fault of their own, have no functioning kidney over those who have one; and such rules thereby promote a better distribution of kidneys over recipients. Just social rules do not, however, mandate the forced redistribution of kidneys from those who have two to those who have none, even though doing so would likewise promote a better distribution of kidneys over recipients. Nor are just rules ones that produce a better distribution of kidneys by engendering severe poverty that compels some people to sell one of their kidneys so as to obtain basic necessities for themselves and their families.

Medical conditions that are intrinsically identical need not then be morally on a par. The moral weight of renal failures to which an institutional order avoidably gives rise depends on how patients came to be dependent on a single kidney. Was the other one forcibly taken from them through a legally authorized medical procedure (forced redistribution)? Were they obliged to sell it to obtain food? Or did it atrophy on account of a genetic defect? How important the avoidance, prevention, and mitigation of renal failures are for the justice of an institutional order depends on which of these scenarios it would exemplify. Once again, treating recipients justly does not boil down to promoting the best distribution among them—what matters is how social rules *treat*, not how they *affect*, the set of recipients.

This simple thought has been remarkably neglected in contemporary work on social justice. It is not surprising, of course, that it plays no role in consequentialist theorizing, in utilitarian thought, for example. Consequentialists, after all, hold that social rules (as well as persons and their conduct) should be judged by their impact on the overall outcome, irrespective of how they produce these effects. Consequentialists hold, that is, that the justice of social rules is determined exclusively by the quality of the overall distribution (of goods and ills, or quality of life) produced by these rules.

But it *is* remarkable that supposedly deontological approaches, such as that developed by Rawls and his followers, likewise make the justice of social rules depend exclusively on the overall distribution these rules produce. As the thought experiment of the original position makes vivid, Rawls agrees with consequentialists that the moral assessment of a social order should be based solely on what overall distribution of goods and ills it, in comparison to its feasible alternatives, tends to produce among its recipients. By judging any social order in this purely recipient-oriented way, Rawls ensures from the start that it is judged exclusively by its "output" in terms of what overall distribution of quality of life it produces among its participants—without regard to the diverse *ways* in which it affects the quality of life of these persons.[12]

RELATIONAL RESPONSIBILITIES

The most plausible alternative structure for a conception of social justice would involve weighting the impact that social institutions have on relevant quality of life according to how they have this impact. Let me illustrate this structure by distinguishing, in a preliminary fashion, six basic ways in which a social order may have an impact on the medical conditions persons suffer under it. This illustration distinguishes scenarios in which some particular medical condition suffered by certain innocent persons can be traced to the fact that they, due to how social institutions are designed, avoidably lack some vital nutrients V (the vitamins contained in fresh fruit, perhaps, which are essential to good health). The six scenarios are arranged in order of their moral weight, according to my intuitive, pre-reflective judgment[13]:

- In scenario 1, the nutritional deficit is *officially mandated*, paradigmatically by the law: legal restrictions bar certain persons from buying foodstuffs containing V.
- In scenario 2, the nutritional deficit results from *legally authorized* conduct of private persons: sellers of foodstuffs containing V lawfully refuse to sell to certain persons.
- In scenario 3, social institutions *foreseeably and avoidably engender* (but do not specifically require or authorize) the nutritional deficit through conduct they stimulate: certain persons, suffering severe poverty within an ill-conceived economic order, cannot afford to buy foodstuffs containing V.
- In scenario 4, the nutritional deficit arises from private conduct that is *legally prohibited but barely deterred*: sellers of foodstuffs containing V illegally refuse to sell to certain persons, but enforcement is lax and penalties are mild.
- In scenario 5, the nutritional deficit arises from social institutions *avoidably leaving unmitigated the effects of a natural defect*: certain persons are unable to metabolize V due to a treatable genetic defect, but they avoidably lack access to the treatment that would correct their handicap.
- In scenario 6, finally, the nutritional deficit arises from social institutions *avoidably leaving unmitigated the effects of a self-caused defect*: certain persons are unable to metabolize V due to a treatable self-caused disease—brought on, perhaps, by their maintaining a long-term smoking habit in full knowledge of the medical dangers associated with it—and avoidably lack access to the treatment that would correct their ailment.

This differentiation of six ways in which social institutions may be related to the goods and ills persons encounter is preliminary in that it fails to isolate the morally significant factors that account for the descending moral weight of the relevant medical conditions.

Lacking the space to do this here, let me merely venture the hypothesis that what matters is not merely the *causal* role of social institutions, how they figure in a complete causal explanation of the nutritional deficit in question, but also (what one might call) the implicit *attitude* of social institutions toward this deficit.[14]

My preliminary classification is surely still too simple. In some cases one will have to take account of other, perhaps underlying causes; and one may also need to recognize interdependencies among causal influences and fluid transitions between the classes.[15] Bypassing these complications here, let me emphasize once more the decisive point missed by the usual accounts of justice: to be morally plausible, a criterion of social justice must take account of—and its application thus requires information about—the particular relation between social institutions and human quality of life, which may determine whether some institutionally avoidable deficit is an injustice at all and, if so, how great an injustice it is. Such a criterion must take into account, that is, not merely the comparative impact a social order has on the distribution of quality of life, but also *how* it exerts this influence. If this is right, then it is no more true of social rules than of persons and conduct that they are just if and insofar as they promote a good overall distribution. Appraising overall distributions of goods and ills (or of quality of life) may be an engaging academic and theological pastime, but it fails to give plausible moral guidance where guidance is needed: for the assessment and reform of social rules as well as of persons and their conduct.

IN CONCLUSION

An institutional order can be said to contribute substantially to medical conditions if and only if it contributes to their genesis through scenarios 1, 2, and 3. Supposing that at least the more privileged adult citizens of affluent and reasonably democratic countries are materially involved in upholding not only the economic order of their own society but also the global economic order, we can say two things about such citizens: pursuant to my second thesis, they have equally strong moral reason to prevent and mitigate *foreigners'* medical conditions due to avoidable poverty engendered by *global* economic institutions as they have to prevent and mitigate *compatriots'* medical conditions due to avoidable poverty engendered by *domestic* economic institutions. And pursuant to my combined thesis, they have stronger moral reason to prevent and mitigate foreigners' medical conditions due to avoidable poverty engendered by global economic institutions than to prevent and mitigate compatriots' medical conditions that are not due to mandated, authorized, or engendered deficits.

In the United States, some 46 million mostly poor citizens avoidably lack adequate medical insurance (aspe.hhs.gov/health/reports/05/uninsured-cps/index.htm). Due to their lack of coverage, many of these people, at any given time, suffer medical conditions that could be cured or mitigated by treatment not in fact accessible to them. This situation is often criticized as manifesting an injustice in the country's social order. Now imagine that the poverty of the 46 million were so severe that it not only rendered them unable to gain access to the medical care they need (scenarios 5 and 6), but also exposed them to various medical conditions owing specifically to poverty-related causes (scenario 3). This additional feature, which plays a substantial role for some fraction of the 46 million, considerably aggravates the injustice—and it is central to the plight of the world's poorest populations. The global poor generally lack access to adequate care for the medical conditions they suffer, of course. But the main effect of an extra $50 or $100 of annual income for them would not be more medical care, but much less need for such care. If they were not so severely impoverished, they would not suffer in the first place most of the medical conditions for which, as things are, they also cannot obtain adequate treatment.

I have tried to lend some initial plausibility to the view that such poverty-induced medical conditions among the global poor are, for us, morally on a par with poverty-induced medical conditions among the domestic poor and of greater moral weight than not-socially-induced medical conditions among poor compatriots. In the first two cases, but not in the third, we are materially involved in upholding social institutions that contribute substantially to the incidence of medical conditions and of the countless premature deaths resulting from them.

NOTES

1. Chen and Ravallion 2004. See Reddy and Pogge 2008 for a critical assessment of the Bank's methodology.

2. This point becomes even more compelling when we consider global inequalities in wealth. In 2000, the bottom 50% of the world's adults together had 1.1% of global wealth while the top 10% had 85.1% and the top 1% had 39.9% (Davies et al. 2006, Appendix 1, Table 10a).

3. See Pogge 2005 and Pogge 2007b, chapter 9, for a fuller discussion of how pharmaceutical innovation could be incentivized without excluding the poor from its benefits.

4. See Lam and Wantchekon 1999, Wantchekon 1999, and Pogge 2007b, chapters 4 and 6.

5. Only in 1997 did the affluent states sign a *Convention on Combating Bribery of Foreign Officials in International Business Transactions* (www.oecd.org/dataoecd/4/18/38028044.pdf), which requires them to enact laws against the bribery of foreign officials. "But big multinationals continue to sidestep them with ease" (*The Economist*, 2 March 2002, pp. 63–65).

6. Representative examples of such lines of argument are Singer 1972, Rachels 1979, Kagan 1989, and Unger 1996.

7. My term, coined from the Latin: that which is to be judged/assessed.

8. Witness Rawls's generic natural duty to promote just institutions, which leaves all such more specific questions of responsibility out of account (Rawls 1999a, 99, 216, 293–94).

9. The main champion of the view that all such factors—social institutions and practices, conventions, ethics, and personal conduct—should be pressed in the service of promoting a just distribution so understood is G. A. Cohen (1989, 1992, 1997, 2000). For a detailed critique of this view, see Pogge 2000.

10. Advocates of the first view could also be accused of callousness in that the huge demands they make in behalf of persons whose health is poor through no fault of their own will, in the real world, shrink the domain of recipients, typically in line with national borders. The billions of dollars required for providing our compatriots with all the "services needed to maintain, restore, or compensate for normal species-typical functioning" (Daniels 1985, 79) would suffice to save countless millions who now die from poverty-related causes, such as malnutrition, measles, diarrhea, malaria, tuberculosis, pneumonia, and other cheaply curable but all-too-often fatal diseases. On the view I have sketched, citizens in affluent countries have stronger moral reason to prevent and mitigate most of the latter medical conditions suffered by foreigners than most of the former medical conditions suffered by compatriots.

11. Some main contributors are Sen (1982, 1992), Dworkin (1981a and 1981b, revised and expanded in 2000), Rawls (1982), Cohen (1989), and Arneson (1989). See also Galston 1980, Griffin 1986, Elster and Roemer 1991, and Pogge 1995.

12. The full story about Rawls's theory is somewhat more complicated in that he is actually offering two distinct criteria of justice. One is the public criterion by reference to which citizens are to assess and reform the basic structure of their society. For this role, Rawls proposes his two principles conjoined with the two priority rules. In justifying this proposal, Rawls appeals to the original position in which rational deliberators, each representing the higher-order interests of one citizen with unknown characteristics, are to agree on one public criterion of justice from a list of candidates. One can thus think of the original position as a meta-criterion for ranking candidate public criteria of justice. Clearly, this meta-criterion is purely recipient-oriented, attending only to information about how citizens would fare (in terms of their stipulated three higher-order interests) with various public criteria and the basic structure designs each might justify under various given conditions. And this fact biases the parties' deliberations in favor of a purely recipient-oriented public criterion, which attends only to information about how citizens would fare in terms of social primary goods. See Pogge 2007a for details.

13. Other things must be presumed to be equal here. The moral weight of the health impact declines as we go through the list. But a morally less weighty such impact may nevertheless outweigh a weightier one if the former is more severe or affects more persons or is more cheaply avoidable than the latter. In this way, an advantage in reducing scenario-4 type deficits may outweigh a much smaller disadvantage in engendering scenario-3 type deficits, for example.

14. This implicit attitude of social institutions is independent of the attitudes or intentions of the persons shaping and upholding these institutions: Only the former makes a difference to how just the institutions are—the latter only make a difference to how blameworthy persons are for their role in imposing them.

15. The case of smoking, for instance, may exemplify a fluid transition between scenarios 2 and 6 insofar as private agents (cigarette companies) are legally permitted to try to render persons addicted to nicotine.

BIBLIOGRAPHY

Arneson, Richard, 1989. "Equality and Equality of Opportunity for Welfare," *Philosophical Studies* 56, 77–93.

Carens, Joseph, 1987. "Aliens and Citizens: The Case for Open Borders," *Review of Politics* 49, 251–73.

Chen, Shaohua, and Martin Ravallion, 2004. "How Have the World's Poorest Fared since the Early 1980s?," *World Bank Research Observer* 19, 141–69.

Cohen, G. A., 1989. "On the Currency of Egalitarian Justice," *Ethics* 99, 906–44.

Cohen, G. A., 1992. "Incentives, Inequality, and Community," in Grethe Peterson, ed., *The Tanner Lectures on Human Values XIII*. Salt Lake City: University of Utah Press.

Cohen, G. A., 1997. "Where the Action Is: On the Site of Distributive Justice," *Philosophy and Public Affairs* 26, 3–30.

Cohen, G. A., 2000. *If You're an Egalitarian, How Come You're so Rich?* Cambridge, MA: Harvard University Press.

Daniels, Norman, 1985. *Just Health Care*. Cambridge: Cambridge University Press.

Davies, James B., Susanna Sandstrom, Anthony Shorrocks, and Edward N. Wolff, 2006: *The World Distribution of Household Wealth*. WIDER (www.wider.unu.edu).

Dworkin, Ronald, 1981a. "What is Equality? Part 1: Equality of Welfare," *Philosophy and Public Affairs* 10, 185–246.

Dworkin, Ronald, 1981b. "What is Equality? Part 2: Equality of Resources," *Philosophy and Public Affairs* 10, 283–345.

Dworkin, Ronald, 2000. *Sovereign Virtue*. Cambridge, MA: Harvard University Press.

Elster, Jon, and John Roemer, eds., 1991. *Interpersonal Comparisons of Well-Being*. Cambridge: Cambridge University Press.

Galston, William, 1980. *Justice and the Human Good*. Chicago: University of Chicago Press.

Griffin, James, 1986. *Well-Being*. Oxford: Clarendon Press.

Kagan, Shelly, 1989. *The Limits of Morality*. Oxford: Oxford University Press.

Lam, Ricky, and Leonard Wantchekon, 1999. 'Dictatorships as a Political Dutch Disease,' Working Paper 795, Yale University, www.library.yale.edu/socsci/egcdp795.pdf.

Pogge, Thomas, 1995. "Three Problems with Contractarian-Consequentialist Ways of Assessing Social Institutions," *Social Philosophy and Policy* 12, 241–66.

Pogge, Thomas, 2000. "On the Site of Distributive Justice: Reflections on Cohen and Murphy," *Philosophy and Public Affairs* 29, 137–69.

Pogge, Thomas, 2005. "Human Rights and Global Health," in Christian Barry and Thomas Pogge, eds., *Global Institutions and Responsibilities*. Oxford: Blackwell.

Pogge, Thomas, 2007a. *John Rawls: His Life and Theory of Justice*. New York: Oxford University Press.

Pogge, Thomas, 2007b. *World Poverty and Human Rights*, second edition. Cambridge: Polity Press.

Rachels, James, 1979. "Killing and Starving to Death," *Philosophy* 54, 159–71.

Rawls, John, 1982. "Social Unity and Primary Goods," in Amartya Sen and Bernard Williams, eds., *Utilitarianism and Beyond*. Cambridge: Cambridge University Press.

Rawls, John, 1999a [1971]. *A Theory of Justice*. Cambridge, MA: Harvard University Press.

Rawls, John, 1999b. *The Law of Peoples*. Cambridge, MA: Harvard University Press.

Reddy, Sanjay, and Thomas Pogge, 2008. "How *Not* to Count the Poor," in Sudhir Anand and Joseph Stiglitz, eds., *Measuring Global Poverty*. Oxford: Oxford University Press. Also at www.socialanalysis.org.

Sen, Amartya, 1982. "Equality of What?" in his *Choice, Welfare and Measurement*. Cambridge: Cambridge University Press.

Sen, Amartya, 1992. *Inequality Reexamined*. Cambridge MA: Harvard University Press.

Singer, Peter, 1972. "Famine, Affluence and Morality," *Philosophy and Public Affairs* 1, 229–43.

UNDP (United Nations Development Program), 1998. *Human Development Report 1998*. New York: Oxford University Press. Also at hdr.undp.org/reports/global/1998/en.

UNDP, 2006. *Human Development Report 2006*. Houndsmills: Palgrave Macmillan. Also at hdr.undp.org/hdr2006.

Unger, Peter, 1996. *Living High and Letting Die: Our Illusion of Innocence*. Oxford: Oxford University Press.

UNICEF (United Nations Children's Fund), 2005. *The State of the World's Children 2005*. New York: UNICEF. Also at www.unicef.org/sowc05/english.

Wantchekon, Leonard, 1999. 'Why do Resource Dependent Countries Have Authoritarian Governments?,' Working Paper, Yale University, www.yale.edu/leitner/pdf/1999-11.pdf.

WHO (World Health Organisation), 2004. *The World Health Report 2004*. Geneva: WHO Publications. Also at www.who.int/whr/2004.

World Bank, 2006. *World Development Report 2007*. New York: Oxford University Press.

MADISON POWERS AND RUTH FADEN

Social Justice, Inequality, and Systematic Disadvantage

Madison Powers is Director of and Senior Research Scholar at the Kennedy Institute of Ethics at Georgetown University and Professor of Philosophy at Georgetown. He is co-editor of *AIDS, Women and the Next Generation*. His research interests include political and legal philosophy, especially issues of distributive justice.

Ruth Faden is the Philip Franklin Wagley Professor of Biomedical Ethics and Executive Director of the Johns Hopkins Berman Institute of Bioethics, and also a Senior Research Scholar at the Kennedy Institute of Ethics, Georgetown University. She is co-author and editor of books on biomedical ethics that include *A History and Theory of Informed Consent; AIDS, Women and the Next Generation*; and *HIV, AIDS and Childbearing*.

INTRODUCTION

Social justice is concerned with human well-being. In our view, well-being is best understood as involving plural, irreducible dimensions, each of which represents something of independent moral significance.

From Madison Powers and Ruth Faden. *Social Justice: The Moral Foundations of Public Health and Health Policy*. New York: Oxford University Press, 2006. Used by permission.

Although an exhaustive, mutually exclusive list of the discrete elements of well-being is not our aim (and may not be possible), we build our account around six distinct dimensions of well-being, each of which merits separate attention within a theory of justice. These different dimensions offer different lenses through which the justice of political structures, social practices, and institutions can be assessed. Without attention to each dimension, something of salience goes unnoticed.

Not all dimensions of human well-being are centrally important within a theory of social justice. Some aspects of human well-being are matters of great importance to particular individuals because they are central to their specific goals and personal aspirations. Social justice, by contrast, is concerned with only those dimensions of well-being that are of special moral urgency because they matter centrally to everyone, whatever the particular life plans and aims each has.

Our theory does not require or suppose that a threshold level of each dimension of well-being identified by our theory of social justice is a *necessary* condition for a decent life. Indeed, for many of us, even this is not the case. However, we do claim that to the extent that a human life is seriously deficient in one or more of these dimensions, it is likely that an individual is not experiencing a sufficient level of well-being. . . .

ESSENTIAL DIMENSIONS OF WELL-BEING

. . . Our list contains six core dimensions: health, personal security, reasoning, respect, attachment, and self-determination. While we do not doubt that there are other theoretically appealing ways to specify the contents of the list, we think that the one we propose represents a useful set of criteria for illuminating the requirements of justice within public health and health policy and beyond. The discussion under each heading below elaborates our rationale for the inclusion of each as a separate category.

HEALTH

There are perhaps as many accounts of the concept of health as there are cultural traditions and healing professions. . . . [W]e work with what is essentially an ordinary-language understanding of physical and mental health that is intended to capture the dimension of human flourishing that is frequently expressed through the biological or organic functioning of the body. . . . [T]he absence of health refers to more than biological malfunctioning or impairments to some functional ability such as mobility, sight, or hearing. Being in pain, even if that pain does not impede proper biological functioning, is also incompatible with health. So, too, are sexual dysfunction and infertility. Health, so understood, thus reflects a moral concern with the rich and diverse set of considerations characteristic of public health and clinical medicine, including premature mortality and preventable morbidity, malnutrition, pain, loss of mobility, mental health, the biological basis of behavior, reproduction (and its control), and sexual functioning. . . .

Our approach to health . . . is quite different from the World Health Organization definition, which views health as a state of physical, mental, and social well-being (World Health Organization 1946). The problem with this otherwise noble aspiration is that it conflates virtually all elements of human development under a single rubric and thereby makes almost any deficit of well-being into a health deficit. . . .

Although health as a dimension of well-being is offered as the primary moral foundation for public health and health policy, there is no reason to suppose that every policy decision that bears on public health or medical care rests on the single moral foundation of health any more than any other intellectual discipline, profession, or social institution necessarily rests on a single moral foundation. For example, policies against female genital mutilation rest on concerns for health, the physical and psychological inviolability encompassed by the dimension we label as personal security, and self-determination. In this case, the moral foundation in justice for the policies draws upon three dimensions of well-being, none of which is reducible to the others. Each signals a separate kind of injustice produced through the mutilation.

The moral justification for health policies involving the distribution of medical services may depend as much on dimensions of well-being other than health as on health itself. For example, . . . society's obligation to ensure universal access to medical care rests not only on the effects of access on health but also on what justice requires with regard to what is necessary for being respected as a moral equal. . . . Accordingly, we argue that the concerns of any plausible theory of justice are multiple, and this plurality of concerns informs answers to questions about what justice in health policy requires.

In addition, the six general dimensions, which we put forward as a way of capturing and classifying the moral territory of social justice, are no substitute for more finely grained accounting of the many moral aspects *within* each dimension. This is perhaps particularly true of health, our primary concern, since policy makers often need to evaluate the justice of trade-offs among the various aspects of health. . . .

PERSONAL SECURITY

Many injustices involve harms to one's health, but they also involve so much more that is not reducible to the effect on health alone. Some injustices that involve harms to health involve different, additionally salient harms to other dimensions of well-being. For example, an arm broken in an unsafe workplace differs from an arm broken while being tortured. Criminal acts such as rape or battery do more than harm the body. Assault (placing another in fear of imminent bodily harm) and intimidation are invasions of personal security, even when they do not eventuate in bodily injury or pain. It is arguably extremely difficult if not impossible to live a decent life if one is in constant fear of physical or psychological abuse. Experiencing such abuse is surely a setback to well-being, regardless of who we are or what values we might otherwise have. Violations such as rape, assault, and torture are of concern to the public health community because of their impact on health, but even more so they are the objects of concern for those persons and institutions having a special focus on human rights abuses, domestic violence, crime, war, and terrorism. . . .

REASONING

Reasoning is the name given to a broad set of diverse skills and abilities, including those classified within philosophical discussions since Aristotle under the headings of practical and theoretical reason. . . .

Theoretical reasoning abilities include the basic intellectual skills and habits of mind necessary for persons to understand the natural world. Such skills include analytical ability, imagination, the ability to form beliefs based on evidence, the ability to reflect on what counts as relevant evidence for those beliefs, and the ability to weigh the probative value of each. . . .

The nature and degree of theoretical reasoning skills and abilities needed, of course, vary in historical contexts. Literacy and numeracy are vital in complex industrial and postindustrial societies and perhaps less so in primitive agrarian or hunter-gatherer societies. Nonetheless, humans need some level of ability to reason deductively and inductively. They need the ability to make logical connections and detect logical errors; to measure, count, and perform other mathematical computations; to communicate effectively with others in a culture; and to make causal inferences. Like the other categories of well-being on our list, without them, whatever other dimensions of well-being we may have, we lack something crucial to our ability to function. . . .

Certain kinds of health states are necessary for reasoning, but they are not sufficient. What further distinguishes reasoning abilities from healthy functioning of the brain is that the former also require an understanding of the world that must be *learned.*

What is learned in the first few years of life has a profound affect on our abilities to reason across the life span. In part, the impact of learning in early childhood is mediated through the brain, whose continued development throughout childhood is influenced by environmental learning. Thus, reasoning abilities are affected not only by physical well-being during childhood but also by characteristics of the social world in which childhood is experienced. . . .

RESPECT

John Rawls and many others of widely differing philosophical emphases argue that respect is an essential element of human flourishing and that it is a proper concern of justice (Rawls 1971; Sen 1992; Nussbaum 2000; J. Cohen 1989; Anderson 1999). There are many ways of putting the point, and not all highlight precisely the same set of considerations. At minimum, respect for others involves treatment of others as dignified moral beings deserving of equal moral concern. Respect for others requires an ability to see others as independent sources of moral worth and dignity and to view others as appropriate objects of sympathetic identification.

Respect for others is closely linked to self-respect as well. A capacity for self-respect involves an individual's capacity to see oneself as the moral equal of others and as an independent source of moral claims based on one's own dignity and worth.

Respect then matters to human well-being in two related ways. A life lacking in the respect of others is seriously deficient in something crucial to well-being. So, too, is a life lacking self-respect. . . .

ATTACHMENT

The formation of bonds of attachment is one of the most central dimensions of human well-being. Such bonds include both friendship and love in their most intimate expressions, as well as a sense of solidarity or fellow-feeling with others within one's community. As the philosopher Martha Nussbaum observes (with reference to what she labels "affiliation"), such bonds matter for reasons of both friendship and justice. . . .

Empirical evidence suggests there is a tight link between the ability to form bonds of attachment between children and parents and between children and others known as "authoritative communities" which are charged with the transmission of social values. When these attachments fail to take hold, the result is a lack of social connectedness that is exhibited in conduct disorders, lack of self-restraint, and antisocial levels of aggressiveness. . . . [R]espect alone is arguably lacking in the emotional depth that comes with a more robust attunement to the deepest needs and longings of others. Attachment is thus essential to justice in the same way that respect and reasoning ability are. . . .

SELF-DETERMINATION

The value of self-determination, the linchpin of liberal political theory, is a broad and encompassing category of human good. It is widely endorsed in many moral and political systems, even among those who complain that in specific cultures or concrete cases too much concern is placed on individual choices. The value of self-determination underlies many accounts of the importance of political liberty, and as we shall claim, it is a foundation for other conclusions about what a just social structure requires. . . .

Imagine a life in which the other essential dimensions of well-being are present. A person is healthy, has strong bonds of attachment, is self-respecting and enjoys the respect of others, is secure in his person, and has developed capacities for reasoning. However, from his earliest years onward, this person has been told what his path in life will be. All the elements of his life have been determined for him, including how much and what kind of schooling he will have, how he will make a living, with whom he will be friends, where he will live, whether he will have children and how, and so on. Although his life in many ways goes well, he has been denied any opportunity to shape its contours through his own choices and thus has been denied the chance to make something of his life through his own efforts. Such a life would be rich in all other respects but seriously lacking in what is required for a decent life. . . .

The successful exercise of self-determination, like the successful navigation of the helmsman, will depend also on the favorable circumstances in which other dimensions of well-being, health, personal security, attachment, respect and the exercise of reason, are present in sufficient quantity. . . . [E]ach dimension is such that a life substantially lacking in any one of these is a life seriously deficient in what it is reasonable for anyone to want, whatever else they want. Each is thus a separate indicator of a decent life which it is the job of justice to facilitate. . . .

CAPABILITIES, FUNCTIONING, AND WELL-BEING

Our theory of justice has many affinities with and owes a considerable intellectual debt to capabilities theories as developed by Amartya Sen and Martha Nussbaum. However, for a variety of reasons we prefer a somewhat different terminology and reach some considerably different conclusions about how best to characterize the central interests in human well-being. . . .

There is a crucial ambiguity between functioning and capability that has led to some measure of confusion. For many of the dimensions of well-being on our list, a central concern is for certain desirable states—being secure in our person, being healthy, being respected, and being a self-determining person. It is a stretch of language to describe them all as functionings, for example, in the case of health. . . . We think it is better to simply note that there are distinct dimensions of well-being and that, for each dimension, a part of its value lies in what states are achieved and another part often consists in our active role in bringing the states about. . . .

Sen elsewhere notes that "the central feature of well-being is the ability to achieve valuable functionings" (Sen 1985, 200). Martha Nussbaum also endorses this general conclusion, noting that the state (the city-state in Aristotle's theory) "aims at enabling people to live well" and that the "goal is a certain sort of capability—the capability to function well if one so chooses" (Nussbaum 1988, 160).

We think that even for adults, these generalizations are unwarranted, at least for the dimensions of well-being we take to be central to justice. Even for adults, our active participation in bringing about our own well-being is not definitive of our well-being. Well-being consists of being in some state or condition, such as being healthy, being respected, or leading a self-determining life. Being healthy matters to our well-being whether or not that state is achieved by our action or by the action, say, of governmental bodies that secure for us potable water. . . .

[T]he reason that our theory attends to the various elements of the social structure causally related to the development and preservation of each dimension of well-being is that such information is relevant to answering questions about which inequalities are most urgent to address. Consider two illustrative examples of when inequalities instrumentally relevant to well-being may be more urgent. One case involves circumstances in which the combined effect of two social determinants is a magnification of the adverse effects on a dimension of well-being. Neighborhoods or countries lacking proper sanitation, coupled with lack of basic primary preventive care, including the necessary immunizations, can increase both the probability and severity of communicable diseases among a population. . . .

Overlapping social determinants affecting a particular dimension of well-being, therefore, raise matters of special moral urgency when they form a constellation of inequalities that systematically magnify and reinforce the initial adverse effects. . . .

The simplest example of clusters of effects flowing from a single social determinant involves institutions and social conventions designed primarily to affect one dimension of well-being, but which simultaneously have profound and pervasive effects on other dimensions of well-being as well. For example, the effect upon health alone is not the sole criterion on our view for evaluating the justice and injustice of a health care system or public health policy. That such systems or policies result in substandard health for some is a major ground for moral concern, but so too is the impact of those systems and policies on capacities for respect for self and others, self-determination, and the ability to form bonds of attachment. . . . In these instances, clusters of effects are produced in tandem as a direct result of the design and structure of a catalytic social determinant affecting multiple dimensions of well-being simultaneously. . . .

The point is that justice, in a well-being sufficiency theory, can be achieved under such conditions either by lessening the differences in wealth and income or by lessening what can be done with wealth and income, for example, with regard to such things as financing political campaigns and causes, buying organs for transplant, and gaining entrance to elite educational institutions. If, however, circumstances are such that wealth inevitably determines how each person fares with respect to the social basis of some dimensions of well-being, then differentials in wealth and income are unjust because they cause some to fall below levels of sufficiency for multiple dimensions of well-being. . . .

There are notable examples from the social science literature on the way educational deficits and poor health display this pattern of cascading and interactive effects. Deprivations of reasoning abilities cannot help but spill over and cause or reinforce deprivations in health. Equally consequential for the prospects of developing one's reasoning capacities are deprivations in health. . . . [T]he approach described here is an interactive model, not simply a linear model in which one single causal sequence all the way down the line is assumed. The development of each dimension of well-being provides both opportunities for and constraints on the development of the other dimensions of well-being. Poor health is not just added to poor reasoning abilities. Each can be made worse by the presence of the other. Poor education not only leads to the underdevelopment of reasoning capacities but also plays a further, well-documented role in producing poor health. Not only does lack of access to health care for children undermine children's health, but the conventional public acceptance of their widespread exclusion from access to care also can adversely affect capacities for respect and affiliation for both parents and children.

There are thus instances in which social structures can compound the adverse effects on well-being in all its dimensions and mutually reinforce the probability of their production. A cascade of deprivations greater in their magnitude than each would have been in isolation is set in motion. Inequalities in such social structures are among those most urgent to address. They thus warrant a heightened level of moral scrutiny on our theory.

The phenomenon of interactive and cascading effects has some interesting implications for how we answer questions about which inequalities are most urgent to address. . . . Justice demands attention to all the dimensions of well-being. But the cascading and interactive causal model adds a twist to this logic. In some cases, it is conceivable that sufficiency of some dimensions of well-being (e.g., health) may be promoted best by attention to other dimensions (e.g., reasoning development). In such cases, the answer to which inequalities are most urgent to address may be that we should give priority to addressing inequalities in those social determinants in which the potential adverse effects on more dimensions of well-being are at stake. No simple algorithm is possible, but some additional moral guidance for public policy arises out of an awareness of how the various dimensions of well-being and the social determinants affecting them can interact. . . .

. . . In many cases, however, the inequalities that arise are not simply the consequence of unrelated instances of bad luck; they are predictable consequences of some forms of social organization that are within the power of human agency to alter. Some are likely to miss every train as a consequence of the way basic social structure is arranged. . . . The causes and effects in such situations are structural and systematic: they are artifacts of the interactive workings of the overall social structure, and the pattern of advantages and disadvantages that emerge are often the consequences of activities of numerous overlapping institutions, social practices, and individuals. . . .

One source of disadvantage, such as inequality of economic resources, can create and exacerbate deficiencies in several, if not all, dimensions of well-being. Adverse effects on any dimension of well-being can have spillover effects on other dimensions of well-being and set a cascading and interactive causal chain in motion. Poor reasoning development can contribute to poor health and vice versa. Well-being deficiencies of one sort can fuel inequalities in the social basis of other dimensions of well-being. . . .

One prominent form of systemic disadvantage is variously labeled as oppression, group domination, or subordination. Whatever the label, this particular pattern of systematic disadvantage is linked to group membership. Perhaps the most acute and most visibly manifested instances of that phenomenon are exhibited in racism, sexism, and ethnic conflict. Such patterns typically involve (a) lesser respect accorded to some persons because they are members of an identifiable group; (b) which often translates into lower respect for self and a reduced sense of personal efficacy and capacity for self-determination among members of the lower status group; and (c) members of higher status groups benefit (or believe they benefit) from a social arrangement in which members of subordinated groups are held in lower regard (Cudd 1994; Young 1990).

Domination or oppression based on shared characteristics of a group have some features in common with other forms of systematic disadvantage. Wealth, power, and opportunities may be concentrated in the hands of a few. Domination can take many forms, including political dominance, cultural dominance, intellectual dominance, market dominance, or any number of other ways in which the life prospects of some are profoundly diminished, often by virtue of the better life prospects of others within a society. . . .

Our life course model reflects the notion that much of the way our prospects are dominated by social structural conditions is not simply a matter of lack of more or better choices, but of constraints that guarantee diminished futures from an early age. Dimensions of well-being, therefore, are not reducible to what mature, autonomous, self-interested adults can choose; they refer also to the underlying unchosen conditions that determine the extent to which we are able to flourish. . . .

[W]e find much affinity with Hume's observations on justice. As we see it, the job of justice in its most pressing role demands a permanent vigilance and attention to social and economic determinants that compound and reinforce insufficiencies in a number of dimensions of well-being. For the most part, their importance is tied to a careful empirical appraisal of social institutions as a whole and their potential for profound and pervasive effects on those dimensions of well-being. What may be required by our approach is, therefore, dependent on contingent and shifting constellations of human vulnerabilities rising and falling in significance under particular forms of social organization. . . .

PUBLIC HEALTH, THE NEGATIVE POINT OF JUSTICE, AND SYSTEMATIC DISADVANTAGE

. . . [I]nequalities in health that are a part of such systematic patterns of disadvantage are the inequalities that are most morally urgent to address. Justice here demands aggressive public health intervention to document and help remedy existing patterns of systematic disadvantage and their detrimental consequences. . . .

One important implication of our theory is that whether any particular inequality in health is among those most morally pressing to address requires consideration of both how the people affected are faring with respect to the rest of their lives as well as how any public health interventions interact with other dimensions of well-being. . . .

Disadvantaged Social Groups: Disparities in health statistics take on different moral meaning when those disparities identify differences between socially dominant groups and socially disadvantaged groups. . . . [P]atterns of systematic disadvantage linked to group membership are among the most invidious, thorough going, and difficult to escape. They generally engage all the dimensions of well-being, but perhaps most centrally the dimension of respect. Group membership becomes sufficient reason for failing to treat people as dignified human beings worthy of equal moral concern. . . .

One critical moral function of public health as we see it is to monitor the health of those who are experiencing systematic disadvantage as a function of group membership, to be vigilant for evidence of inequalities relative to those in privileged social groups, and to intervene to reduce these inequalities insofar as possible. . . .

One of the most compelling recent examples of work in public health on behalf of an oppressed group involved documentation of the disastrous impact of the Taliban rule on the health of women. Research conducted by the group Physicians for Human Rights provides powerful evidence that the denial of basic human rights to women resulted not only in horrible injustices with regard to respect, affiliation, and personal security, but also with regard to health (Rasekh et al. 1998). It is not necessary, however, to point to the horror of the Taliban regime to find examples of public health research documenting the impact of oppression of women upon their health. In the developing world, as well as in some communities in the United States, the vulnerability of women to HIV is attributed in large measure to women's lack of political and social status and their dependence on men (Gollub 1999; Sanders-Phillips 2002; Buseh et al. 2002; Wyohannes 1996). Public health research has also helped direct the world's attention to the impact of violence against women on women's health (Pan American Health Organization 2003), as well as to the enormous health problems of many indigenous peoples (Pande and Yazbeck 2003; Wiseman and Jan 2000; Roubideaux 2002).

In American public health, much attention has been paid to disparities in health between white Americans and nonwhite Americans, particularly African Americans, Native Americans, and Hispanics. The implicit assumption, which we believe to be correct, is that these disparities are of particular moral concern. . . . [F]rom the standpoint of our theory of social justice, it is not necessary to establish a direct causal connection between specific health disparities and specific acts of injustice, such as overt discrimination in access to advanced medical technology or primary health care, to hold that these inequalities are of significant moral urgency. Nor are we arguing that

addressing these inequalities is of significant moral urgency as a matter of compensation for some kind of "trans-generational debt" (Loury 2002; 2003, 337). Rather, we maintain, in line with the work of Glenn Loury, that social and cultural factors that have historical roots but that remain persistent have resulted in continuing disparities in human development and flourishing. Combating overt racism and racial discrimination, although important to root out where they exist, is not sufficient to addressing this gap in well-being. Thus, for us, a different kind of causal story is required, a causal story about how a disadvantaged group's staying in relatively poorer health continues to contribute to decreased well-being overall. . . .

Poverty and Disadvantage: . . . [I]nequalities in well-being associated with severe poverty are inequalities of particular moral urgency. Those who have a proportionately tiny share of available economic resources are worse off, not simply by virtue of having a much reduced standard of living, but in having disproportionately little influence on public affairs and in the marketplace, all of which translates into their having little control over their own lives. . . . [S]ystematic patterns of disadvantage that flow from dramatic differences in material resources produce a cluster of deficiencies in well-being that makes it extremely unlikely that individuals can improve their life prospects through their own efforts. . . .

With regard to the dimension of health, perhaps the starkest indicator of the inability of all to walk the same path is found in differentials in life expectancy. Here, we live in a world of radical inequality (Pogge 1998). Despite significant improvements in life expectancy in low-income countries since 1960 (Jha et al. 2002), there is currently as much as a forty-year differential in average life expectancy between those who live in major industrial countries and those who live in southern Africa. Even if mortality in early childhood is not considered (a topic we will address shortly), in 2000, the average fifteen-year-old boy living in the United States can expect to live well into his seventies, if not beyond, while the average fifteen-year-old boy living in Uganda will be lucky to reach his fiftieth birthday. With life prospects, indeed the very prospect of living at all, so radically different, it is hard to conceive of these two youths as in any respect walking the same path. The magnitude of this source of extraordinary injustice cannot be overstated. It is estimated that each year as many as twenty million people in severe poverty in the developing world die young, by the standards of the rest of the world, from malnutrition and diseases that can be inexpensively prevented or treated. . . .

Children: . . . As a developmental matter, unless children experience a state of sufficient well-being in their young years, their capabilities as adults, and thus what they will be able to do with their lives, will be compromised. We are concerned about the actual health, reasoning abilities, and attachment of children, in part because these dimensions of well-being will develop properly, if at all, only if they are nurtured and secured in appropriate developmental stages. . . .

Perhaps the most obvious way in which compromised health in childhood forecloses options in adulthood is through child mortality. Despite significant reductions in child mortality in the 1980s and early 1990s, in 2003 more than 10 million children under the age of five years died (Gillespie et al. 2003). Almost all of these children lived in low-income countries or in poor communities in middle-income countries. Most of these deaths could have been prevented by interventions that in 2003 were available, reasonably cheap, and in widespread use (Jones et al. 2003). By any plausible account of social justice, and certainly by our own, these deaths constitute injustices of the gravest sort (Victora et al. 2003). Diarrhea, pneumonia, and malaria—the principal killers of young children, abetted by undernutrition—are all eminently treatable or preventable conditions. Among the world's poorest, many children never survive long enough for us to even begin to speak meaningfully about their capabilities, well-being, or flourishing. . . .

PUBLIC HEALTH, THE POSITIVE POINT OF JUSTICE, AND HEALTH INEQUALITIES

As we see it, the job of justice in its most pressing role looks first to conditions of the most profound disadvantage. Justice's first concern requires permanent vigilance and attention to determinants that compound and reinforce insufficiencies across multiple dimensions of well-being in ways that make it difficult if not impossible to escape. Although our theory thus concentrates the attention of public health on those gaps in well-being that are the most urgent, there is a positive as well as a negative point to our theory, one that sets aspirations for achieving a sufficient level of well-being in all of its essential dimensions for everyone. For the dimension of health, it is not possible to specify with precision what sufficiency requires, nor is it possible to establish precise numerical targets. At an outer bound,

sufficiency can be pegged to what is technologically feasible with regard to both length and health-related quality of life. The World Health Organization's Burden of Disease projects, for example, use the world's longest life expectancy, that of the Japanese, as the benchmark for measuring health burdens internationally. A less demanding account of sufficiency would require that each of us have enough health over a long enough life span to live a decent life. . . .

Note that all of our judgments about the relative urgency of inequalities in health and their relationship to the negative and positive points of justice, reflect not only the particular commitments of our theory but also the empirical particulars in which these inequalities occur. As relevant features of the world change, so too do the implications for justice and public health. While the positive aspiration of public health—to strive for all lives that are healthy and long—remains a constant, what it is possible to obtain in terms of health is ever changing. So too are the concrete demands of the negative aim of our theory for public health. Here also the moral job of public health remains constant: to document and help remedy existing patterns of disadvantage and their detrimental effects and to ensure that children achieve sufficient levels of health so that well-being in adulthood is possible. However, as patterns of social organization and systematic disadvantage alter and the greatest threats to health sufficiency and other dimensions of well-being shift, the specific moral priorities for public health also will shift. And that is as it should be.

REFERENCES

Anderson, E. 1999. What is the point of equality? *Ethics* 109: 287–337.

Buseh, A. G., L. K. Glass, and B. J. McElmurry. 2002. Cultural and gender issues related to HIV/AIDS prevention in rural Swaziland: A focus group analysis. *Health Care for Women International* 23 (2): 173–84.

Cohen, J. 1989. Democratic equality. *Ethics* 99: 727–51.

Cudd, A. 1994. Oppression by choice. *Journal of Social Philosophy* 25: 22–44.

Gillespie, D., M. Claeson, H. Mshinda, H. Troedsson, and the Bellagio Study Group on Child Survival. 2003. Knowledge into action for child survival. *The Lancet* 362: 323–27.

Gollub, E. L. 1999. Human rights is a U.S. problem, too: The case of women and HIV. *American Journal of Public Health* 89: 1479–82.

Jha, P., A. Mills, K. Hanson, L. Kumaranayake, L. Conteh, C. Kurowski, S. N. Nguyen, V. O. Cruz, K. Ranson, L. M. Vaz, S. Yu, O. Morton, and J. D. Sachs. 2002. Improving the health of the global poor. *Science* 295: 2036–39.

Jones, G., R. W. Steketee, R. E. Black, Z. A. Bhutta, S. S. Morris, and the Bellagio Child Survival Study Group. 2003. How many child deaths can we prevent this year? *The Lancet* 362: 65–71.

Loury, G. 2002. *The anatomy of racial inequality.* Cambridge, MA: Harvard University Press.

———. 2003. Racial stigma: Toward a new paradigm for discrimination theory. *American Economic Review* 93: 337.

Nussbaum, M. 1988. Nature, function, and capability: Aristotle on political distribution. In *Oxford studies in ancient philosophy, supplementary volume.* Edited by J. Annas and R. Grimm. Oxford: Clarendon Press.

———. 2000. *Women and human development.* Cambridge: Cambridge University Press.

Nussbaum, M., and A. Sen, eds. 1993. *The quality of life.* Oxford: Clarendon Press.

Pan American Health Organization. 2003. *Violence against women: The health sector responds.* Washington, D.C.: Pan American Health Organization.

Pande, R. P., and A. S. Yazbeck. 2003. What's in a country average? Wealth, gender, and regional inequalities in immunization in India. *Social Science and Medicine* 57: 2075–88.

Pogge, T. 1998. A global resources dividend. In *Ethics of consumption: The good life, justice and global stewardship.* Edited by D. A. Crocker and T. Linden. Lanham, MD: Rowman and Littlefield.

Rasekh, Z., H. M. Bauer, M. M. Manos, and V. Iacopino. 1998. Women's health and human rights in Afghanistan. *Journal of the American Medical Association* 280: 449–55.

Rawls, J. 1971. *A theory of justice.* Cambridge, MA: Harvard University Press.

Roubideaux, Y. 2002. Perspectives on American Indian health. *American Journal of Public Health* 92(9): 1401–03.

Sanders-Phillips, K. 2002. Factors influencing HIV/AIDS in women of color. *Public Health Reports* 117 (Suppl. 1): S151–6.

Sen, A. 1985. Well-being, agency, and freedom: The Dewey Lectures, 1984. *Journal of Philosophy* 82: 169–221.

———. 1992. *Inequality reexamined.* Cambridge, MA: Harvard University Press.

Victora, C. G., A. Wagstaff, J. A. Schellenberg, D. Gwatkin, M. Claeson, and J. P. Habicht. 2003. Applying an equity lens to child health and mortality: more of the same is not enough. *The Lancet* 362: 233–41.

Wiseman, V., and S. Jan. 2000. Resource allocation within Australian indigenous communities: A program for implementing vertical equity. *Health Care Analysis* 8(3): 217–33.

World Health Organization. 1946. Preamble to the constitution of the World Health Organization as adopted by the International Health Conference. New York: Official Records of the World Health Organization, no. 2, p. 100.

Wyohannes, M. 1996. Where, and why, women are at risk. Country focus: Ethiopia. *AIDS Analysis Africa* 6 (5): 9, 15.

Young, I. 1990. *Justice and the politics of difference.* Princeton, NJ: Princeton University Press.

Just Health Care and the Right to Health Care

ROBERT M. VEATCH

Justice, the Basic Social Contract, and Health Care

Robert M. Veatch is Professor of Medical Ethics and the former Director of the Kennedy Institute of Ethics at Georgetown University. His recent books include *The Basics of Bioethics, Case Studies in Pharmacy Ethics,* and the second editions of *Case Studies in Nursing Ethics, Cross Cultural Perspectives in Medical Ethics,* and *Transplant Ethics.* His current research is on the history of professional medical ethics.

The principle that each person's welfare should count equally is crucial if the community generated is to be a moral community. The moral community is one of

From *A Theory of Medical Ethics,* © 1981. Reprinted by permission of the Kennedy Institute of Ethics.

impartiality. If the community employed an impartial perspective to draw up the basic principles or practices for the society, the principles would be generated without reference to individual talents, skills, abilities, or good fortune. Another way of formulating this condition is to say that the basic principles or practices established must meet the test of reversibility. That is, they must be acceptable to one standing on either the giving or the receiving end of a transaction.[1] The general notion is that the contractors must take equal account of all persons. . . .

The most intriguing contractual theory of ethics that makes this commitment to impartiality or reversibility is that espoused by John Rawls.[2] In his version of social contract theory, Rawls asks us to envision ourselves in what he calls the original position. He does not pretend that such a position exists or ever could exist. Rather, it is a device for making "vivid to ourselves the restrictions that it seems reasonable to impose on arguments for principles of justice, and therefore on these principles themselves."[3] The restrictions on the original position are that no one should be advantaged or disadvantaged in the choice of principles either by natural fortune or social circumstances. Persons in the original position are equal. To help us imagine such a situation, he asks us to impose what he calls a "veil of ignorance," under which "no one knows his place in society, his class position or social status, nor does any one know his fortune in the distribution of natural assets and abilities, his intelligence, strength, and the like."[4]

From that position one can derive impartially a set of principles or practices that provide the moral foundations for a society. Even if we cannot discover a universal basis for ethical decisions, perhaps we can create a community that accepts rules such as respect for freedom and the impartial consideration of interests; that is, one that adopts the moral point of view and thereby provides a common foundation for deciding what is ethical. Those who take this view believe it possible to generate some commonly agreed upon principles or practices for a society. The creation of a contractual framework could then provide a basis for making medical ethical decisions that would be commonly recognized as legitimate. . . .

There is . . . a moral community constituted symbolically by the metaphor of the contract or covenant. There is a convergence between the vision of people coming together to discover a preexisting moral order—an order that takes equally into account the welfare of all—and the vision of people coming together to invent a moral order that as well takes equally into account the welfare of all. The members of the moral community thus generated are bound together by bonds of mutual loyalty and trust. There is a fundamental equality and reciprocity in the rela-

tionship, something missing in the philanthropic condescension of professional code ethics. . . .

THE MAXIMIN THEORY

Some say that reasonable people considering alternative policies or principles for a society would not opt to maximize the aggregate benefits that exist in the society. Rather, they say that at least for basic social practices that determine the welfare of members of the moral community, they would opt for a strategy that attempts to assure fundamentally that the least well off person would do as well as possible. . . .

The implication is that those having the greatest burden have some claim on the society independent of whether responding to their needs is the most efficient way of producing the greatest net aggregate benefit. Holders of this view say that the commitment of a principle of justice is to maximize not net aggregate benefit, but the position of the least advantaged members of the society. If the principle of justice is a right-making characteristic of actions, a principle that reasonable people would accept as part of the basic social contract independent of the principle of beneficence, it probably incorporated some moral notion that the distribution of benefits and burdens counts as well as the aggregate amount of them. One plausible alternative is to concentrate, insofar as we are concerned about justice, on the welfare of the least well off. This is part of those principles of justice defended by Rawls as derived from his version of social contract theory. . . .

Since Rawls's scheme is designed to provide insights into only the basic practices and social institutions, it is very hard to discern what the implications are for specific problems of resource distribution such as the allocation of health care resources. Some have argued that no direct implications can be read from the Rawlsian principles. That seems, however, to overstate the case. At the least, basic social practices and institutional arrangements must be subject to the test of the principles of justice.

It appears, then, that this view will not justify inequalities in the basic health care institutions and practices simply because they produce the greatest net aggregate benefit. Its notion of justice, concentrating on improving the lot of the least advantaged, is much more egalitarian in this sense than the utilitarian system. It would distribute health care resources to the least well off rather than just on the aggregate amount of benefit.

There is no obvious reason why our hypothetical contractors articulating the basic principles for a society would favor a principle that maximized aggregate utility any more than one that maximized minimum utility. Our contract model, as an epistemological device for discovering the basic principles, views them, after all, as committed to the moral point of view, as evaluating equally the welfare of each individual from a veil of ignorance, to use the Rawlsian language. This perspective retains the notion of individuals as identifiable, unique personalities, as noncommensurable human beings, rather than simply as components of an aggregate mass. Faced with a forced choice, it seems plausible that one would opt for maximizing the welfare of individuals, especially the least well-off individuals, rather than maximizing the aggregate.

Nevertheless, the interpretation of justice that attempts to maximize the minimum position in the society (and is hence sometimes called the "maximin" position), still permits inequalities and even labels them as just. What, for example, of basic health care institutional arrangements that systematically single out elites with unique natural talents for developing medical skill and services and gives these individuals high salaries as incentives to serve the interests of the least well off? What if a special health care system were institutionalized to make sure these people were always in the best of health, were cared for first in catastrophes, and were inconvenienced least by the normal bureaucratic nuisances of a health care system?

It is conceivable that such an institutional arrangement would be favored by reasonable people taking the moral point of view. They could justify the special gains that would come to the elites by the improved chances thus created for the rest of the population (who would not have as great a gain as the favored ones, but would at least be better off than if the elite were not so favored). The benefits, in lesser amounts, would trickle down in this plan to the consumers of health care so that all, or at least the least advantaged, would gain. The gap between the elite of the health profession and the masses could potentially increase by such a social arrangement, but at least all would be better off in absolute terms.

So it is conceivable that reasonable people considering equally both the health professionals and the masses would favor such an arrangement, but it is not obvious. Critics of the Rawlsian principles of justice say that in some cases alternative principles of distribution would be preferred. Brian Barry, for example, argues that rational choosers would look not just at the welfare of the least advantaged, but also at the average or aggregate welfare of alternative policies.[5] On the other hand, Barry and many others suggest that in some circumstances, rational choosers might opt for the principle that would maximize equality of outcome.[6] At most, considering the institutionalization of advantages for a health care elite, they would be supported as a prudent sacrifice of the demands of justice in order to serve some other justifiable moral end.

From this perspective, favoring elites with special monetary and social incentives in order to benefit the poor might be a prudent compromise.[7] It might mediate between the demands that see justice as requiring equality of outcome (subject to numerous qualifications) and the demands of the principle of beneficence requiring maximum efficiency in producing good consequences. If that is the case, though, then there is still a fourth interpretation of the principle of justice that must be considered, one that is more radically egalitarian than the maximin strategy.

THE EGALITARIAN THEORY

Those who see the maximin strategy as a compromise between the concern for justice and the concern for efficient production of good consequences must feel that justice requires a stricter focus on equality than the maximin understanding of the principle of justice. The maximin principle is concerned about the distribution of benefits. It justifies inequalities only if they benefit the least well off. But it does justify inequalities—and it does so in the name of justice.

Rawls recognizes that there is an important difference between a right action and a just or a fair action. Fairness is a principle applying to individuals along with beneficence, noninjury, mutual respect, and fidelity. The list is not far removed from the basic principles I have identified. But, given this important difference between what is right in this full, inclusive sense and what is fair, if one is convinced that incentives and advantages for medical elites are justified, why would one claim that the justification is one based on the principle of fairness? One might instead maintain that they are right on balance because they are a necessary compromise with the principle of fairness (or justice) in order to promote efficiently the welfare of a disadvantaged group. It is to be assumed, given the range of basic principles in an ethical system, that conflicts will often emerge so that one principle will be sacrificed, upon occasion, for the sake of another.

The egalitarian understanding of the principle of justice is one that sees justice as requiring (subject to certain important qualifications) equality of net welfare for individuals.[8] . . .

Everyone, according to the principle of egalitarian justice, ought to end up over a lifetime with an equal amount of net welfare (or, as we shall see shortly, a chance for that welfare). Some may have a great deal of benefit offset by large amounts of unhappiness or disutility, while others will have relatively less of both. What we would call "just" under this principle is a basic social practice or policy that contributes to the same extent to greater equality of outcome (subject to restrictions to be discussed). I am suggesting that reasonable people who are committed to a contract model for discovering, inventing, or otherwise articulating the basic principles will want to add to their list the notion that one of the right-making characteristics of a society would be the equality of welfare among the members of the moral community.

THE EQUALITY OF PERSONS

The choice of this interpretation of the principle of justice will depend upon how the contractors understand the commitment to the moral point of view—the commitment to impartiality that takes the point of view of all equally into account. We certainly are not asserting the equality of ability or even the equality of the merit of individual claims. . . .

If this is what is meant by the moral point of view, taking into account equally the individuality of each member of the community, then in addition to the right-making characteristics or principles of beneficence, promise keeping, autonomy, truth telling, and avoiding killing, the principle of justice as equality of net welfare must be added to the list. The principle might be articulated as affirming that people have a claim on having the total net welfare in their lives equal insofar as possible to the welfare in the lives of others.

Of course, no reasonable person, even an egalitarian, is going to insist upon or even desire that all the features of people's lives be identical.[9] It seems obvious that the most that anyone would want is that the total net welfare for each person be comparable. . . .

If this egalitarian understanding of the principle of justice would be acceptable to reasonable people taking the moral point of view, it provides a solution to the dilemma of the tension between focusing exclusively on the patient and opening the doors to considerations of social consequences such as in classical utilitarianism. The principle of justice provides another basis for taking into account a limited set of impacts on certain other parties. If the distribution of benefits as well as the aggregate amount is morally relevant, then certain impacts on other parties may be morally more relevant than others. A benefit that accrues to a person who is or predictably will be in a least well-off group would count as a consideration of justice while a benefit of equal size that accrued to other persons not in the least well-off group would not. The hypothetical benefits of a Nazi-type experiment would not accrue to a least well-off group (while the harms of the experiment presumably would). They are thus morally different from, in fact diametrically opposed to, a redistribution scheme that produced benefits for only the least advantaged group.

EQUALITY AND ENVY

Critics of the egalitarian view of justice have argued that the only way to account for such a position is by attributing it to a psychology of envy.[10] Freud accounted for a sense of justice in this way.[11] They feel the only conceivable reason to strive for equality is the psychological explanation that the less well off envy the better off, and they hold that contractors take that psychological fact into account. Since they believe that envy is not an adequate justification for a commitment to equal outcome, they opt instead for an alternative theory of justice. . . .

The egalitarian holds that there is something fundamentally wrong with gross inequalities, with gross differences in net welfare. The problem is encountered when people of unequal means must interact, say, when representatives of an impoverished community apply to an elite foundation for funds to support a neighborhood health program. There is no way that real communication can take place between the elites of the foundation and the members of the low-income community. It is not simply that the poor envy the foundation executives or that the executives feel resentful of the poor. Rather, as anyone who has been in such a relationship knows, the sense of community is fractured. Not only do the less well off feel that they cannot express themselves with self-respect, but the elites realize that there is no way the messages they receive can be disentangled from the status and welfare differentials. Neither can engage in any true interaction. A moral relationship is virtually impossible. . . .

THE IMPLICATIONS OF THE EGALITARIAN FORMULA

It turns out that incorporating health care into this system of total welfare will be extremely difficult. Let us begin, temporarily, therefore, by considering a simpler system dealing only with food, clothing, and shelter. Fairness could mean, according to the egalitarian formula, that each person had to have an equal amount of each of these. No reasonable person, however, would find that necessary or attractive. Rather, what the egalitarian has in mind with his concept of justice is that the net of welfare, summed across all three of these goods, be as similar as possible. We could arbitrarily fix the amount of resources in each category, but nothing seems wrong with permitting people to trade some food for clothing, or clothing for shelter. If one person preferred a large house and minimal food and could find someone with the opposite tastes, nothing seems wrong with permitting a trade. The assumption is that the need of people for food, clothing, and shelter is about the same in everybody and that marginal utilities in the trades will be about the same. If so, then permitting people to trade around would increase the welfare of each person without radically distorting the equality of net overall welfare. Up to this point, then, the egalitarian principle of justice says that it is just (though not necessarily right) to strive in social practices for equality of net welfare. . . .

For health care and education, however, the situation is much different. Here it is reasonable to assume that human needs vary enormously. Nothing could be more foolish than to distribute health care or even the money for health care equally. The result would be unequal overall well-being for those who were unfortunate in the natural lottery for health, objectively much worse off than others. If the goal of justice is to produce a chance for equal, objective net welfare, then the starting point for consideration of health care distribution should be the need for it. Education (or the resources to buy education) initially would be distributed in the same way. The amount added to the resources for food, clothing, and shelter should then be in proportion to an "unhealthiness status index" plus another amount proportional to an "educational needs index."

However, that proposal raises two additional questions: Should people be permitted to use the resources set aside for health care in some other way? And who should bear the responsibility if people have an opportunity to be healthy and do not take advantage of it?

THE CASE FOR AN EQUAL RIGHT TO HEALTH CARE

Even for the egalitarian it is not obvious why society ought to strive for an equal right to health care. Certainly it ought not to be interested in obtaining the same amount of health care for everyone. To do so would require forcing those in need of great amounts of care to go without or those who have the good fortune to be healthy to consume uselessly. But it is not even obvious that we should end up with a right to health care equal in proportion to need, though that is the conclusion that many, especially egalitarians, are reaching. . . .

Is there any reason to believe that health care is any more basic than, say, food or protection from the elements? All are absolutely essential to human survival, at least up to some minimum for subsistence. All are necessary conditions for the exercise of liberty, self-respect, or any other functioning as part of the human moral community. Furthermore, while the bare minimum of health care is as necessary as food and shelter, in all cases these may not really be "necessities" at the margin. If trades are to be tolerated between marginal food and clothing, is there any reason why someone placing relatively low value on health care should not be permitted to trade, say, his annual checkups for someone else's monthly allotment of steak dinners? Or, if we shall make trading easier by distributing money fairly rather than distributing rations of these specific goods, is there any reason why, based on an "unhealthiness index," we could not distribute a fair portion of funds for health care as well as for other necessities? Individuals could then buy the health care (or health care insurance) that they need, employing individual discretion about where their limit for health care is in comparison with steak dinners. Those at a high health risk would be charged high amounts for health care (or high premiums for insurance), but those costs would be exactly offset by the money supplement based on the index.

Perhaps we cannot make a case for equal access to health care on the basis that it is more fundamental than other goods. There may still be reasons, though, why reasonable people would structure the basic institutions of society to provide a right to equal health care in the sense I am using the term, that is a right equal in proportion to need.

Our response will depend somewhat upon whether we are planning a health care distribution for a just world or one with the present inequities in the distribution of net welfare. . . .

But obviously we do not live in a perfectly just world. The problem becomes more complex. How do we arrange the health care system, which all would agree is fundamental to human well-being at least at some basic level, in order to get as close as possible to equality of welfare as the outcome? Pragmatic considerations may, at this point, override the abstract, theoretical argument allowing trades of health care for other goods even at the margin.

Often defenders of free-market and partial free-market solutions to the allocation of health care resources assume that if fixed in-kind services such as health care are not distributed, money will be. . . .

There is a more subtle case for an equal right to health care (in proportion to need) in an unfair world. Bargaining strengths are likely to be very unequal in a world where resources are distributed unfairly. Those with great resources, perhaps because of natural talents or naturally occurring good health or both, are in an invincible position. The needy, for example those with little earning power because of congenital health problems, may be forced to use what resources they have in order to buy immediate necessities, withholding on health care investment; particularly preventive health care and health insurance, while gambling that they will be able to survive without those services.

It is not clear what our moral response should be to those forced into this position of bargainers from weakness. If the just principle of distribution were Pareto optimality (where bargains were acceptable, regardless of the weaknesses of the parties, provided all gained in the transaction), we would accept the fact that some would bargain from weakness and be forced to trade their long-term health care needs for short-term necessities. If the principle of justice that reasonable people would accept taking the moral point of view, however, is something like the maximin position or the egalitarian position, then perhaps such trades of health care should be prohibited. The answer will depend on how one should behave in planning social policies in an unjust world. The fact that resources are not distributed fairly generates pressures on the least well off (assuming they act rationally) to make choices they would not have to make in a more fair world. If unfairness in the general distribution of resources is a given, we are forced into a choice between two unattractive options: We could opt for the rule that will permit the least well off to maximize their position under the existing conditions or we could pick the rule that would arrange resources as closely as possible to the way they would be arranged in a just world. In our present, unjust society distributing health care equally is a closer approximation to the way it would be distributed in a just society than giving a general resource like money or permitting trades. . . .

I see justice not just as a way to efficiently improve the lot of the least well off by permitting them trades (even though those trades end up increasing the gap between the haves and the have-nots). That might be efficient and might preserve autonomy, but it would not be justice. If I were an original contractor I would cast my vote in favor of the egalitarian principle of justice, applying it so that there would be a right to health care equal in proportion to health care need. The principle of justice for health care could, then, be stated as follows: People have a right to needed health care to provide an opportunity for a level of health equal as far as possible to the health of other people.

The principle of justice for health care is a pragmatic derivative from the general principle of justice requiring equality of objective net welfare. The result would be a uniform health care system with one class of service available for all. Practical problems would still exist, especially at the margins. The principle, for example, does not establish what percentage of total resources would go for health care. The goal would be to arrange resources so that health care needs would, in general, be met about as well as other needs. This means that a society would rather arbitrarily set some fixed amount of the total resources for health care. Every nation currently spends somewhere between five and ten percent of its gross national product (GNP) in this area, with the wealthier societies opting for the higher percentages. Presumably the arbitrary choice would fall in that range.

With such a budget fixed, reasonable people will come together to decide what health care services can be covered under it. The task will not be as great as it seems. The vast majority of services will easily be sorted into or out of the health care system. Only a small percentage at the margin will be the cause of any real debate. The choice will at times be arbitrary, but the standard applied will at least be clear. People should have services necessary to give them a chance to be as close as possible to being as healthy as other people. Those choices will be made while striving to emulate the position of original contractors taking the moral point of view. The decision-making panels will not differ in task greatly from the decision makers who currently sort health care services in and out of insurance coverage lists. However, panels will be committed to a principle of justice and will take the moral point of view, whereas the self-interested insurers try to maximize profits or efficiency or a bargaining position against weak, unorganized consumers.

NOTES

1. Kurt Baier, *The Moral Point of View: A Rational Basis of Ethics* (New York: Random House, 1965), p. 108.

2. John Rawls, *A Theory of Justice* (Cambridge, Mass.: Harvard University Press, 1971).

3. Ibid., p. 18.

4. Ibid., p. 12; cf. pp. 136–42.

5. Brian Barry, *The Liberal Theory of Justice: A Critical Examination of the Principal Doctrines in "A Theory of Justice" by John Rawls* (Oxford: Clarendon Press, 1973), p. 109; see also Robert L. Cunningham, "Justice: Efficiency or Fairness?" *Personalist* 52 (Spring 1971): 253–81.

6. Barry, *The Liberal Theory*; idem. "Reflections on 'Justice as Fairness,'" in Justice and Equality, ed. H. Bedau (Englewood Cliffs, N.J.: Prentice-Hall, 1971), pp. 103–115; Bernard Williams, "The Idea of Equality," reprinted in Bedau, *Justice and Equality*, pp. 116–137; Christopher Ake, "Justice as Equality," *Philosophy and Public Affairs* 5 (Fall 1975): 69–89; Robert M. Veatch, "What Is 'Just' Health Care Delivery?" in *Ethics and Health Policy*, ed. R. M. Veatch and R. Branson (Cambridge, Mass.: Ballinger, 1976), pp. 127–153.

7. Barry, "Reflections," p. 113.

8. See Ake, "Justice as Equality," for a careful development of the notion.

9. Hugo A. Bedau, "Radical Egalitarianism," in *Justice and Equality,* ed. H. A. Bedau, p. 168.

10. Rawls, *A Theory of Justice*, p. 538, note 9.

11. Sigmund Freud, *Group Psychology and the Analysis of the Ego*, rev. ed., trans. James Strachey (London: Hogarth Press, 1959), pp. 51f. (as cited in Rawls, *A Theory of Justice*, p. 439).

ALLEN E. BUCHANAN

The Right to a Decent Minimum of Health Care

Allen Buchanan is Professor of Philosophy and James B. Duke Professor of Public Policy Studies at Duke University. He publishes primarily in bioethics and political philosophy. He is the author or co-author of six books, including *From Chance to Choice, Ethics, Efficiency, and the Market,* and *Deciding for Others: The Ethics of Surrogate Decision Making*.

THE ASSUMPTION THAT THERE IS A RIGHT TO A DECENT MINIMUM

A consensus that there is (at least) a right to a decent minimum of health care pervades recent policy debates and much of the philosophical literature on health care. Disagreement centers on two issues. Is there a more extensive right than the right to a decent minimum of health care? What is included in the decent minimum to which there is a right?

PRELIMINARY CLARIFICATION OF THE CONCEPT

Different theories of distributive justice may yield different answers both to the question "Is there a right to

From President's Commission, *Securing Access to Health Care,* vol. 2. Washington, DC: U.S. Government Printing Office, 1983.

a decent minimum?" and to the question "What comprises the decent minimum?" The justification a particular theory provides for the claim that there is a right to a decent minimum must at least cohere with the justifications it provides for other right-claims. Moreover, the character of this justification will determine, at least in part, the way in which the decent minimum is specified, since it will include an account of the nature and significance of health-care needs. To the extent that the concept of a decent minimum is theory-dependent, then, it would be naive to assume that a mere analysis of the concept of a decent minimum would tell us whether there is such a right and what its content is. Nonetheless, before we proceed to an examination of various theoretical attempts to ground and specify a right to a decent minimum, a preliminary analysis will be helpful.

Sometimes the notion of a decent minimum is applied not to health care but to health itself, the claim being that everyone is entitled to some minimal level, or welfare floor, of health. I shall not explore this variant of the decent minimum idea because I think its implausibility is obvious. The main difficulty is that assuring any significant level of health for all is simply not within the domain of social control. If the alleged right is understood instead as the right to everything which can be done to achieve some significant level of health for all, then the claim that there is such a right becomes implausible simply because it ignores the fact that in circumstances of scarcity the total social expenditure on health must be constrained by the need to allocate resources for other goods.

Though the concept of a right is complex and controversial, for our purposes a partial sketch will do. To say that person A has a right to something, X, is first of all to say that A is entitled to X, that X is due to him or her. This is not equivalent to saying that if A were granted X it would be a good thing, even a morally good thing, or that X is desired by or desirable for A. Second, it is usually held that valid right-claims, at least in the case of basic rights, may be backed by sanctions, including coercion if necessary (unless doing so would produce extremely great disutility or grave moral evil), and that (except in such highly exceptional circumstances) failure of an appropriate authority to apply the needed sanctions is itself an injustice. Recent rights-theorists have also emphasized a third feature of rights, or at least of basic rights or rights in the strict sense: valid right-claims "trump" appeals to what would maximize utility, whether it be the utility of the right-holder, or social utility. In other words, if A has a right to X, then the mere fact that infringing A's right would maximize overall utility or even A's utility is not itself a sufficient reason for infringing it.[1] Finally, a universal (or general) right is one which applies to all persons, not just to certain individuals or classes because of their involvement in special actions, relationships, or agreements.

The second feature—enforceability—is of crucial importance for those who assume or argue that there is a universal right to a decent minimum of health care. For, once it is granted that there is such a right and that such a right may be enforced (absent any extremely weighty reason against enforcement), the claim that there is a universal right provides the moral basis for using the coercive power of the state to assure a decent minimum for all. Indeed, the surprising absence of attempts to justify a coercively backed decent minimum policy by arguments that do *not* aim at establishing a universal right suggests the following hypothesis: advocates of a coercively backed decent minimum have operated on the assumption that such a policy must be based on a universal right to a decent minimum. The chief aim of this article is to show that this assumption is false.

I think it is fair to say that many who confidently assume there is a (universal) right to a decent minimum of health care have failed to appreciate the significance of the first feature of our sketch of the concept of a right. It is crucial to observe that the claim that there is a right to a decent minimum is much stronger than the claim that everyone *ought* to have access to such a minimum, or that if they did it would be a good thing, or that any society which is capable, without great sacrifice, of providing a decent minimum but fails to do so is deeply morally defective. None of the latter assertions implies the existence of a right, if this is understood as a moral entitlement which ought to be established by the coercive power of the state if necessary. . . .

THE ATTRACTIONS OF THE IDEA OF A DECENT MINIMUM

There are at least three features widely associated with the idea of a right to a decent minimum which, together with the facile consensus that vagueness promotes, help explain its popularity over competing conceptions of the right to health care. First, it is usually, and quite reasonably, assumed that the idea of a decent minimum is to be understood in a society-relative sense. Surely it is plausible to assume that, as with other rights to goods or services, the content of the right must depend upon the resources available in a given society and perhaps also upon a certain consensus of expectations among its members. So the first advantage of the idea of a decent minimum, as it is usually understood, is that it allows us to adjust the level of services to be provided as a matter of right to relevant social conditions and also allows for the possibility that as a society becomes more affluent the floor provided by the decent minimum should be raised.

Second, the idea of a decent minimum avoids the excesses of what has been called the strong equal access principle, while still acknowledging a substantive universal right. According to the strong equal access principle, everyone has an equal right to the best health-care services available. Aside from the weakness of the justifications offered in support of it, the most implausible feature of the strong equal access principle is that it forces us to choose between two unpalatable alternatives. We can either set the publicly guaranteed level of health care lower than the level that is technically possible or we can set it as high as is technically possible. In the former case, we shall be committed to the uncomfortable conclusion that no matter how many resources have been expended to guarantee equal access to that level, individuals are forbidden to spend any of their resources for services not available to all. Granted that individuals are allowed to spend their after-tax incomes on more frivolous items, why shouldn't they be allowed to spend it on health? If the answer is that they should be so allowed, as long as this does not interfere with the provision of an adequate package of health-care services for everyone, then we have retreated from the strong equal access principle to something very like the principle of a decent minimum. If, on the other hand, we set the level of services guaranteed for all so high as to eliminate the problem of persons seeking extra care beyond this level, this would produce a huge drain on total resources, foreclosing opportunities for producing important goods other than health care.

So both the recognition that health care must compete with other goods and the conviction that beyond some less than maximal level of publicly guaranteed services individuals should be free to purchase additional services point toward a more limited right than the strong access principle asserts. Thus, the endorsement of a right to a decent minimum may be more of a recognition of the implausibility of the stronger right to equal access than a sign of any definite position on the content of the right to health care.

A third attraction of the idea of a decent minimum is that since the right to health care must be limited in scope (to avoid the consequences of a strong equal access right), it should be limited to the "most basic" services, those normally "adequate" for health, or for a "decent" or "tolerable" life. However, although this aspect of the idea of a decent minimum is useful because it calls attention to the fact that health-care needs are heterogeneous and must be assigned some order of priority, it does not itself provide any basis for determining which are most important.

THE NEED FOR A SUPPORTING THEORY

In spite of these attractions, the concept of a right to a decent minimum of health care is inadequate as a moral basis for a coercively backed decent minimum policy in the absence of a coherent and defensible theory of justice. Indeed, when taken together they do not even imply that there is a right to a decent minimum. Rather, they only support the weaker conditional claim that if there is a right to health care, then it is one that is more limited than a right of strong equal access, and is one whose content depends upon available resources and some scheme of priorities which shows certain health services to be more basic than others. It appears, then, that a theoretical grounding for the right to a decent minimum of health care is indispensable. . . .

My suggestion is that the combined weight of arguments from special (as opposed to universal) rights to health care, harm-prevention, prudential arguments of the sort used to justify public health measures, and two arguments that show that effective charity shares features of public goods (in the technical sense) is sufficient to do the work of an alleged universal right to a decent minimum of health care.

ARGUMENTS FROM SPECIAL RIGHTS

The right-claim we have been examining (and find unsupported) has been a *universal* right-claim: one that attributes the same right to all persons. *Special* right-claims, in contrast, restrict the right in question to certain individuals or groups.

There are at least three types of arguments that can be given for special rights to health care. First, there are arguments from the requirements of rectifying past or present institutional injustices. It can be argued, for example, that American blacks and native Americans are entitled to a certain core set of health-care services owing to their history of unjust treatment by government or other social institutions, on the grounds that these injustices have directly or indirectly had detrimental effects on the health of the groups in question. Second, there are arguments from the requirements of compensation to those who have suffered unjust harm or who have been unjustly exposed to health risks by the assignable actions of private individuals or corporations—for instance, those who have suffered neurological damage from the effects of chemical pollutants.

Third, a strong moral case can be made for special rights to health care for those who have undergone exceptional sacrifices for the good of society as a whole—in particular those whose health has been adversely affected through military service. The most obvious candidates for such compensatory special rights are soldiers wounded in combat.

ARGUMENTS FROM THE PREVENTION OF HARM

The content of the right to a decent minimum is typically understood as being more extensive than those traditional public health services that are usually justified on the grounds that they are required to protect the citizenry from certain harms arising from the interactions of persons living together in large numbers. Yet such services have been a major factor—if not *the* major factor—in reducing morbidity and mortality rates. Examples include sanitation and immunization. The moral justification of such measures, which constitute an important element in a decent minimum of health care, rests upon the widely accepted Harm (Prevention) Principle, not upon a right to health care.

The Harm Prevention argument for traditional public health services, however, may be elaborated in a way that brings them closer to arguments for a universal right to health care. With some plausibility one might contend that once the case has been made for expending public resources on public health measures, there is a moral (and perhaps Constitutional) obligation to achieve some standard of *equal protection* from the harms these measures are designed to prevent. Such an argument, if it could be made out, would imply that the availability of basic public health services should not vary greatly across different racial, ethnic, or geographic groups within the country.

PRUDENTIAL ARGUMENTS

Prudent arguments for health-care services typically emphasize benefits rather than the prevention of harm. It has often been argued, in particular, that the availability of certain basic forms of health care make for a more productive labor force or improve the fitness of the citizenry for national defense. This type of argument, too, does not assume that individuals have moral rights (whether special or universal) to the services in question.

It seems very likely that the combined scope of the various special health-care rights discussed above, when taken together with harm prevention and prudential arguments for basic health services and an argument from equal protection through public health measures, would do a great deal toward satisfying the health-care needs which those who advocate a universal right to a decent minimum are most concerned

about. In other words, once the strength of a more pluralistic approach is appreciated, we may come to question the popular dogma that policy initiatives designed to achieve a decent minimum of health care for all must be grounded in a universal moral right to a decent minimum. This suggestion is worth considering because it again brings home the importance of the methodological difficulty encountered earlier. Even if, for instance, there is wide consensus on the considered judgment that the lower health prospects of inner city blacks are not only morally unacceptable but an injustice, it does not follow that this injustice consists of the infringement of a universal right to a decent minimum of health care. Instead, the injustice might lie in the failure to rectify past injustices or in the failure to achieve public health arrangements that meet a reasonable standard of equal protection for all.

TWO ARGUMENTS FOR ENFORCED BENEFICENCE

The pluralistic moral case for a legal entitlement to a decent minimum of health care (in the absence of a universal moral right) may be strengthened further by nonrights-based arguments from the principle of beneficence.[2] The possibility of making out such arguments depends upon the assumption that some principles may be justifiably enforced even if they are not principles specifying valid right-claims. There is at least one widely recognized class of such principles requiring contribution to the production of "public goods" in the technical sense (for example, tax laws requiring contribution to national defense). It is characteristic of public goods that each individual has an incentive to withhold his contribution to the collective goal even though the net result is that the goal will not be achieved. Enforcement of a principle requiring all individuals to contribute to the goal is necessary to overcome the individual's incentive to withhold contribution by imposing penalties for his own failure to contribute and by assuring him that others will contribute. There is a special subclass of principles whose enforcement is justified not only by the need to overcome the individual's incentive to withhold compliance with the principle but also to ensure that individuals' efforts are appropriately *coordinated*. For example, enforcing the rule of the road to drive only on the right not only ensures a joint effort toward the goal of safe driving but also coordinates individuals' efforts so as to make the attainment of that goal possible. Indeed, in the case of the 'rule of the road' a certain kind of coordinated joint effort is the public good whose attainment justifies enforcement. But regardless of whether the production of a public good requires the solution of a coordination problem or not, there may be no *right* that is the correlative of the coercively backed obligation specified by the principle. There are two arguments for enforced beneficence, and they each depend upon both the idea of coordination and on certain aspects of the concept of a public good.

Both arguments begin with an assumption reasonable libertarians accept: there is a basic moral obligation of charity or beneficence to those in need. In a society that has the resources and technical knowledge to improve health or at least to ameliorate important health defects, the application of this requirement of beneficence includes the provision of resources for at least certain forms of health care. If we are sincere, we will be concerned with the efficacy of our charitable or beneficent impulses. It is all well and good for the libertarian to say that voluntary giving *can* replace the existing array of government entitlement programs, but this *possibility* will be cold comfort to the needy if, for any of several reasons, voluntary giving falters.

Social critics on the left often argue that in a highly competitive acquisitive society such as ours it is naive to think that the sense of beneficence will win out over the urgent promptings of self-interest. One need not argue, however, that voluntary giving fails from weakness of the will. Instead one can argue that even if each individual recognizes a moral duty to contribute to the aid of others and is motivationally capable of acting on that duty, some important forms of beneficence will not be forthcoming because each individual will rationally conclude that he should not contribute.

Many important forms of health care, especially those involving large-scale capital investment for technology, cannot be provided except through the contributions of large numbers of persons. This is also true of the most important forms of medical research. But if so, then the beneficent individual will not be able to act effectively, in isolation. What is needed is a coordinated joint effort.

First argument. There are many ways in which I might help others in need. Granted the importance of health, providing a decent minimum of health care for all, through large-scale collective efforts, will be a more important form of beneficence than the various charitable acts A, B, and C, which I might perform *independently*, that is, whose success does not depend upon the contributions of others. Nonetheless, if I am rationally beneficent I will reason as follows: either enough others will contribute to the decent minimum project to achieve this goal, even if I do not contribute to it; or not enough others will contribute to achieve a decent minimum, even if I do contribute. In either case, my contribution will be wasted. In other words, granted the scale of the investment required and the virtually negligible size of my own contribution, I can disregard the minute possibility that my contribution might make the difference between success and failure. But if so, then the rationally beneficent thing for me to do is not to waste my contribution on the project of ensuring a decent minimum but instead to undertake an independent act of beneficence; A, B, or C—where I know my efforts will be needed and efficacious. But if everyone, or even many people, reason in this way, then what we each recognize as the most effective form of beneficence will not come about. Enforcement of a principle requiring contributions to ensuring a decent minimum is needed.

The first argument is of the same form as standard public goods arguments for enforced contributions to national defense, energy conservation, and many other goods, with this exception. In standard public goods arguments, it is usually assumed that the individual's incentive for not contributing is self-interest and that it is in his interest not to contribute because he will be able to partake of the good, if it is produced, even if he does not contribute. In the case at hand, however, the individual's incentive for not contributing to the joint effort is not self-interest, but rather his desire to maximize the good he can do for others with a given amount of his resources. Thus if he contributes but the goal of achieving a decent minimum for all would have been achieved without his contribution, then he has still failed to use his resources in a maximally beneficent way relative to the options of either contributing or not to the joint project, even though the goal of achieving a decent minimum is attained. The rationally beneficent thing to do, then, is not to contribute, even though the result of everyone's acting in a rationally beneficent way will be a relatively ineffective patchwork of small-scale individual acts of beneficence rather than a large-scale, coordinated effort.

Second argument. I believe that ensuring a decent minimum of health care for all is more important than projects A, B, or C, and I am willing to contribute to the decent minimum project, but only if I have assurance that enough others will contribute to achieve the threshold of investment necessary for success. Unless I have this assurance, I will conclude that it is less than rational—and perhaps even morally irresponsible—to contribute my resources to the decent minimum project. For my contribution will be wasted if not enough others contribute. If I lack assurance of sufficient contributions by others, the rationally beneficent thing for me to do is to expend my "beneficence budget" on some less-than-optimal project A, B, or C, whose success does not depend on the contribution of others. But without enforcement, I cannot be assured that enough others will contribute, and if others reason as I do, then what we all believe to be the most effective form of beneficence will not be forthcoming. Others may fail to contribute either because the promptings of self-interest overpower their sense of beneficence, or because they reason as I did in the First Argument, or for some other reason.

Both arguments conclude that an enforced decent minimum principle is needed to achieve coordinated joint effort. However, there is this difference. The Second Argument focuses on the *assurance problem*, while the first does not. In the Second Argument all that is needed is the assumption that rational beneficence requires assurance that enough others will contribute. In the First Argument the individual's reason for not contributing is not that he lacks assurance that enough others will contribute, but rather that it is better for him not to contribute regardless of whether others do or not.

Neither argument depends on an assumption of conflict between the individual's moral motivation of beneficence and his inclination of self-interest. Instead the difficulty is that in the absence of enforcement,

individuals who strive to make their beneficence most effective will thereby fail to benefit the needy as much as they might.

A standard response to those paradoxes of rationality known as public goods problems is to introduce a coercive mechanism which attaches penalties to noncontribution and thereby provides each individual with the assurance that enough others will reciprocate so that his contribution will not be wasted and an effective incentive for him to contribute even if he has reason to believe that enough others will contribute to achieve the goal without his contribution. My suggestion is that the same type of argument that is widely accepted as a justification for enforced principles requiring contributions toward familiar public goods provides support for a coercively backed principle specifying a certain list of health programs for the needy and requiring those who possess the needed resources to contribute to the establishment of such programs, even if the needy have no *right* to the services those programs provide. Such an arrangement would serve a dual function: it would coordinate charitable efforts by focusing them on one set of services among the indefinitely large constellation of possible expressions of beneficence, and it would ensure that the decision to allocate resources to these services will become effective.

NOTES

1. Ronald Dworkin, *Taking Rights Seriously* (Cambridge, MA: Harvard University Press, 1977), pp. 184–205.

2. For an exploration of various arguments for a duty of beneficence and an examination of the relationship between justice and beneficence, in general and in health care, see Allen E. Buchanan, "Philosophical Foundations of Beneficence," *Beneficence and Health Care*, ed. Earl E. Shelp (Dordrecht, Holland: Reidel Publishing Co., 1982).

H. TRISTRAM ENGELHARDT, JR.

Rights to Health Care, Social Justice, and Fairness in Health Care Allocations: Frustrations in the Face of Finitude

H. Tristram Engelhardt, Jr., is a Professor of Bioethics, Medicine, and Community Medicine at the Baylor College of Medicine and Professor of Philosophy, Rice University. His areas of scholarship are bioethics, philosophy of medicine, and continental philosophy. Among his books are *Foundations of Bioethics* and *Bioethics and Secular Humanism*. His most recent work is *The Foundations of Christian Bioethics*.

The imposition of a single-tier, all-encompassing health care system is morally unjustifiable. It is a coercive act of totalitarian ideological zeal, which fails to recognize the diversity of moral visions that frame interests in health care, the secular moral limits of state authority, and the authority of individuals over themselves and their own property. It is an act of secular immorality.

A basic human secular moral right to health care does not exist—not even to a "decent minimum of health care." Such rights must be created.

The difficulty with supposed right to health care, as well as with many claims regarding justice or fairness in access to health care, should be apparent. Since the secular moral authority for common action is derived from permission or consent, it is difficult (indeed, for a large-scale society, materially impossible) to gain moral legitimacy for the thoroughgoing imposition on health care of one among the many views of beneficence and justice. There are, after all, as many accounts of beneficence, justice, and fairness as there are major religions.

Most significantly, there is a tension between the foundations of general secular morality and the various particular positive claims founded in particular visions of beneficence and justice. It is materially impossible both to respect the freedom of all and to achieve their long-range best interests. . . .

Rights to health care constitute claims on services and goods. Unlike rights to forbearance, which require others to refrain from interfering, which show the unity of the authority to use others, rights to beneficence are rights grounded in particular theories or accounts of the good. For general authority, they require others to participate actively in a particular understanding of the good life or justice. Without an appeal to the principle of permission, to advance such rights is to claim that one may press others into labor or confiscate their property. Rights to health care, unless they are derived from special contractual agreements, depend on particular understandings of beneficence rather than on authorizing permission. They may therefore conflict with the decisions of individuals who may not wish to participate in, and may indeed be morally opposed to, realizing a particular system of health care. Individuals always have the secular moral authority to use their own resources in ways that collide with fashionable understandings of justice or the prevailing consensus regarding fairness.

HEALTH CARE POLICY: THE IDEOLOGY OF EQUAL, OPTIMAL CARE

It is fashionable to affirm an impossible commitment in health care delivery, as, for example, in the following four widely embraced health care policy goals, which are at loggerheads:

1. The best possible care is to be provided for all.
2. Equal care should be guaranteed.

From *Foundations of Bioethics*, 2d ed., by H. Tristram Engelhardt, Jr. Reprinted by permission of Oxford University Press, 1996.

3. Freedom of choice on the part of health care provider and consumer should be maintained.
4. Health care costs are to be contained.

One cannot provide the best possible health care for all and contain health care costs. One cannot provide equal health care for all and respect the freedom of individuals peaceably to pursue with others their own visions of health care or to use their own resources and energies as they decide. For that matter, one cannot maintain freedom in the choice of health care services while containing the costs of health care. One may also not be able to provide all with equal health care that is at the same time the very best care because of limits on the resources themselves. That few openly address these foundational moral tensions at the roots of contemporary health care policy suggests that the problems are shrouded in a collective illusion, a false consciousness, an established ideology within which certain facts are politically unacceptable.

These difficulties spring not only from a conflict between freedom and beneficence, but from a tension among competing views of what it means to pursue and achieve the good in health care (e.g., is it more important to provide equal care to all or the best possible health care to the least-well-off class?). . . .

Only a prevailing collective illusion can account for the assumption in U.S. policy that health care may be provided (1) while containing costs (2) without setting a price on saving lives and preventing suffering when using communal funds and at the same time (3) ignoring the morally unavoidable inequalities due to private resources and human freedom. This false consciousness shaped the deceptions central to the Clinton health care proposal, as it was introduced in 1994. It was advanced to support a health care system purportedly able to provide all with (1) the best of care and (2) equal care, while achieving (3) cost containment, and still (4) allowing those who wish the liberty to purchase fee-for-service health care.[1] While not acknowledging the presence of rationing, the proposal required silent rationing in order to contain costs by limiting access to high-cost, low-yield treatments that a National Health Board would exclude from the "guaranteed benefit package."[2] In addition, it advanced mechanisms to slow technological innovation so as further to reduce the visibility of rationing choices.[3] One does not have to ration that which is not available. There has been a failure to acknowledge the moral inevitability of inequalities in health care due to the

limits of secular governmental authority, human freedom, and the existence of private property, however little that may be. There was also the failure to acknowledge the need to ration health care within communal programs if costs are to be contained. It has been ideologically unacceptable to recognize these circumstances. . . .

JUSTICE, FREEDOM, AND INEQUALITY

Interests in justice as beneficence are motivated in part by inequalities and in part by needs. That some have so little while others have so much properly evokes moral concerns of beneficence. Still, . . . the moral authority to use force to set such inequalities aside is limited. These limitations are in part due to the circumstance that the resources one could use to aid those in need are already owned by other people. One must establish whether and when inequalities and needs generate rights or claims against others.

THE NATURAL AND SOCIAL LOTTERIES

"Natural lottery" is used to identify changes in fortune that result from natural forces, not directly from the actions of persons. The natural lottery shapes the distribution of both naturally and socially conditioned assets. The natural lottery contrasts with the social lottery, which is used to identify changes in fortune that are not the result of natural forces but the actions of persons. The social lottery shapes the distribution of social and natural assets. The natural and social lotteries, along with one's own free decisions, determine the distribution of natural and social assets. The social lottery is termed a lottery, though it is the outcome of personal actions, because of the complex and unpredictable interplay of personal choices and because of the unpredictable character of the outcomes, which do not conform to an ideal pattern, and because the outcomes are the results of social forces, not the immediate choices of those subject to them.

All individuals are exposed to the vicissitudes of nature. Some are born healthy and by luck remain so for a long life, free of disease and major suffering. Others are born with serious congenital or genetic diseases, others contract serious crippling fatal illnesses early in life, and yet others are injured and maimed. Those who win the natural lottery will for most of their lives not be in need of medical care. They will live full lives and die painless and peaceful deaths.

Those who lost the natural lottery will be in need of health care to blunt their sufferings and, where possible, to cure their diseases and to restore function. There will be a spectrum of losses, ranging from minor problems such as having teeth with cavities to major tragedies such as developing childhood leukemia, inheriting Huntington's chorea, or developing amyelotrophic lateral sclerosis.

These tragic outcomes are the deliverances of nature, for which no one, without some special view of accountability or responsibility, is responsible (unless, that is, one recognizes them as the results of the Fall or as divine chastisements). The circumstance that individuals are injured by hurricanes, storms, and earthquakes is often simply no one's fault. When no one is to blame, no one may be charged with the responsibility of making whole those who lose the natural lottery on the ground of accountability for the harm. One will need an argument dependent on a particular sense of fairness to show that the readers of this volume should submit to the forcible redistribution of their resources to provide health care for those injured by nature. It may very well be unfeeling, unsympathetic, or uncharitable not to provide such help. One may face eternal hellfires for failing to provide aid.[4] But it is another thing to show in general secular moral terms that individuals owe others such help in a way that would morally authorize state force to redistribute their private resources and energies or to constrain their free choices with others. To be in dire need does not by itself create a secular moral right to be rescued from that need. The natural lottery creates inequalities and places individuals at disadvantage without creating a straightforward secular moral obligation on the part of others to aid those in need.

Individuals differ in their resources not simply because of outcomes of the natural lottery, but also due to the actions of others. Some deny themselves immediate pleasures in order to accumulate wealth or to leave inheritances; through a complex web of love, affection, and mutual interest, individuals convey resources, one to another, so that those who are favored prosper and those who are ignored languish. Some as a consequence grow wealthy and others grow poor, not through anyone's malevolent actions or omissions, but simply because they were not favored by the love, friendship, collegiality, and associations through which fortunes develop and individuals prosper. In

such cases there will be neither fairness nor unfairness, but simply good and bad fortune.

In addition, some will be advantaged or disadvantaged, made rich, poor, ill, diseased, deformed, or disabled because of the malevolent and blameworthy actions and omissions of others. Such will be unfair circumstances, which just and beneficent states should try to prevent and to rectify through legitimate police protection, forced restitution, and charitable programs. Insofar as an injured party has a claim against an injurer to be made whole, not against society, the outcome is unfortunate from the perspective of society's obligations and obligations of innocent citizens to make restitution. Restitution is owed by the injurer, not society or others. There will be outcomes of the social lottery that are on the one hand blameworthy in the sense of resulting from the culpable actions of others, though on the other hand a society has no obligation to rectify them. The social lottery includes the exposure to the immoral and unjust actions of others. Again, one will need an argument dependent on a particular sense of fairness to show that the readers of this volume should submit to the forcible redistribution of their resources to provide health care to those injured by others.

When individuals come to purchase health care, some who lose the natural lottery will be able at least in part to compensate for those losses through their winnings at the social lottery. They will be able to afford expensive health care needed to restore health and to regain function. On the other hand, those who lose in both the natural and the social lottery will be in need of health care, but without the resources to acquire it.

THE RICH AND THE POOR: DIFFERENCES IN ENTITLEMENTS

If one owns property by virtue of just acquisition or just transfer, then one's title to that property will not be undercut by the tragedies and needs of others. One will simply own one's property. On the other hand, if one owns property because such ownership is justified within a system that ensures a beneficent distribution of goods (e.g., the achievement of the greatest balance of benefits over harms for the greatest number or the greatest advantage for the least-well-off class), one's ownership will be affected by the needs of others. . . . Property is in part privately owned in a strong sense that cannot be undercut by the needs of others. In addition, all have a general right to the fruits of the earth, which constitutes the basis for a form of taxation as rent to provide fungible payments to individuals, whether or not they are in need. Finally, there are likely to be resources held in common by groups that may establish bases for their distribution to meet health care concerns. The first two forms of entitlement or ownership exist unconstrained by medical or other needs. The last form of entitlement or ownership, through the decision of a community, may be conditioned by need.

The existence of any amount of private resources can be the basis for inequalities that secular moral authority may not set aside. Insofar as people own things, they will have a right to them, even if others need them. Because the presence of permission is cardinal, the test of whether one must transfer one's goods to others will not be whether such a redistribution will not prove onerous or excessive for the person subjected to the distribution, but whether the resources belong to that individual. Consider that you may be reading this book next to a person in great need. The test of whether a third person may take resources from you to help that individual in need will not be whether you will suffer from the transfer, but rather whether you have consented—at least this is the case if the principle of permission functions in general secular morality. . . . The principle of permission is the source of authority when moral strangers collaborate, because they do not share a common understanding of fairness or of the good. As a consequence, goal-oriented approaches to the just distribution of resources must be restricted to commonly owned goods, where there is authority to create programs for their use.

Therefore, one must qualify the conclusions of the 1983 American President's Commission for the Study of Ethical Problems that suggest that excessive burdens should determine the amount of tax persons should pay to sustain an adequate level of health care for those in need.[5] Further, one will have strong grounds for morally condemning systems that attempt to impose an all-encompassing health care plan that would require "equality of care [in the sense of avoiding] the creation of a tiered system [by] providing care based only on differences of need, not individual or group characteristics."[6] Those who are rich are always at secular moral liberty to purchase more and better health care.

DRAWING THE LINE BETWEEN THE UNFORTUNATE AND THE UNFAIR

How one regards the moral significance of the natural and social lotteries and the moral force of private ownership will determine how one draws the line between circumstances that are simply unfortunate and those that are unfortunate and in addition unfair in the sense of constituting a claim on the resources of others.

Life in general, and health care in particular, reveal circumstances of enormous tragedy, suffering, and deprivation. The pains and sufferings of illness, disability, and disease, as well as the limitations of deformity, call on the sympathy of all to provide aid and give comfort. Injuries, disabilities, and diseases due to the forces of nature are unfortunate. Injuries, disabilities, and diseases due to the unconsented-to actions of others are unfair. Still, outcomes of the unfair actions of others are not necessarily society's fault and are in this sense unfortunate. The horrible injuries that come every night to the emergency rooms of major hospitals may be someone's fault, even if they are not the fault of society, much less that of uninvolved citizens. Such outcomes, though unfair with regard to the relationship of the injured with the injurer, may be simply unfortunate with respect to society and other citizens (and may licitly be financially exploited). One is thus faced with distinguishing the difficult line between acts of God, as well as immoral acts of individuals that do not constitute a basis for societal retribution on the one hand, and injuries that provide such a basis on the other.

A line must be created between those losses that will be made whole through public funds and those that will not. Such a line was drawn in 1980 by Patricia Harris, the then secretary of the Department of Health, Education, and Welfare, when she ruled that heart transplantations should be considered experimental and therefore not reimbursable through Medicare.[7] To be in need of a heart transplant and not have the funds available would be an unfortunate circumstance but not unfair. One was not eligible for a heart transplant even if another person had intentionally damaged one's heart. From a moral point of view, things would have been different if the federal government had in some culpable fashion injured one's heart. So, too, if promises of treatment had been made. For example, to suffer from appendicitis or pneumonia and not as a qualifying patient receive treatment guaranteed through a particular governmental or private insurance system would be unfair, not simply unfortunate.

Drawing the line between the unfair and the unfortunate is unavoidable because it is impossible in general secular moral terms to translate all needs into rights, into claims against the resources of others. One must with care decide where the line is to be drawn. To distinguish needs from mere desires, one must endorse one among the many competing visions of morality and human flourishing. One is forced to draw a line between those needs (or desires) that constitute claims on the aid of others and those that do not. The line distinguishing unfortunate from unfair circumstances justifies by default certain social and economic inequalities in the sense of determining who, if any one, is obliged in general secular immorality to remedy such circumstances or achieve equality. Is the request of an individual to have life extended through a heart transplant at great cost, and perhaps only for a few years, a desire for an inordinate extension of life? Or is it a need to be secure against a premature death? . . . Outside a particular view of the good life, needs do not create rights to the services or goods of others.[8] Indeed, outside of a particular moral vision there is no canonical means for distinguishing desires from needs.

There is a practical difficulty in regarding major losses at the natural and social lotteries as generating claims to health care: attempts to restore health indefinitely can deplete societal resources in the pursuit of ever-more incremental extensions of life of marginal quality. A relatively limited amount of food and shelter is required to preserve the lives of individuals. But an indefinite amount of resources can in medicine be committed to the further preservation of human life, the marginal postponement of death, and the marginal alleviation of human suffering and disability. Losses at the natural lottery with regard to health can consume major resources with little return. Often one can only purchase a little relief, and that only at great costs. Still, more decisive than the problem of avoiding the possibly overwhelming costs involved in satisfying certain health care desires (e.g., postponing death for a while through the use of critical care) is the problem of selecting the correct content-full account of justice in order canonically to distinguish between needs and desires and to translate needs into rights.

BEYOND EQUALITY: AN EGALITARIANISM
OF ALTRUISM VERSUS AN EGALITARIANISM OF ENVY

The equal distribution of health care is itself problematic, a circumstance recognized in *Securing Access*

to Health Care, the 1983 report of the President's Commission.[9] The difficulties are multiple:

1. Although in theory, at least, one can envisage providing all with equal levels of decent shelter, one cannot restore all to or preserve all in an equal state of health. Many health needs cannot be satisfied in the same way one can address most needs for food and shelter.

2. If one provided all with the same amount of funds to purchase health care or the same amount of services, the amount provided would be far too much for some and much too little for others who could have benefited from more investment in treatment and research.

3. If one attempts to provide equal health care in the sense of allowing individuals to select health care only from a predetermined list of available therapies, or through some managed health care plan such as accountable (to the government) health care plans or regional health alliances, which would be provided to all so as to prevent the rich from having access to better health care than the poor, one would have immorally confiscated private property and have restricted the freedom of individuals to join in voluntary relationships and associations.

That some are fortunate in having more resources is neither more nor less arbitrary or unfair than some having better health, better looks, or more talents. In any event, the translation of unfortunate circumstances into unfair circumstances, other than with regard to violations of the principle of permission, requires the imposition of a particular vision of beneficence or justice.

The pursuit of equality faces both moral and practical difficulties. If significant restrictions were placed on the ability to purchase special treatment with one's resources, one would need not only to anticipate that a black market would inevitably develop in health care services, but also acknowledge that such a black market would be a special bastion of liberty and freedom of association justified in general secular moral terms. . . .

CONFLICTING MODELS OF JUSTICE:
FROM CONTENT TO PROCEDURE

John Rawls's *A Theory of Justice* and Robert Nozick's *Anarchy, State, and Utopia* offer contrasting understandings of what should count as justice or fairness. They sustain differing suggestions regarding the nature of justice in health care. They provide a contrast between justice as primarily structural, a pattern of distributions that is amenable to rational disclosure, versus justice as primarily procedural, a matter of fair negotiation.[10] In *A Theory of Justice* Rawls forwards an expository device of an ahistorical perspective from which to discover the proper pattern for the distribution of resources, and therefore presumably for the distribution of health care resources. In this understanding, it is assumed that societally based entitlements have moral priority. Nozick, in contrast, advances a historical account of just distributions within which justice depends on what individuals have agreed to do with and for each other. Nozick holds that individually based entitlements are morally prior to societally based entitlements. In contrast with Rawls, who argues that one can discover a proper pattern for the allocation of resources, Nozick argues that such a pattern cannot be discovered and that instead one can only identify the characteristics of a just process for fashioning rights to health care. . . .

The differences between Nozick of *Anarchy, State, and Utopia* and Rawls of *A Theory of Justice* express themselves in different accounts of entitlements and ownership, and in different understandings of nonprincipled fortune and misfortune. For Rawls, one has justifiable title to goods if such a title is part of a system that ensures the greatest benefit to the least advantaged, consistent with a just-savings principle, and with offices and positions open to all under conditions of fair equality and opportunity, and where each person has an equal right to the most extensive total system of equal basic liberties compatible with a similar system of liberty for all. In contrast, for Nozick, one simply owns things: "Things come into the world already attached to people having entitlements over them."[11] If one really owns things, there will be freedom-based limitations on principles of distributive justice. One may not use people or the property without their permission or authorization. The needs of others will not erase one's property rights. The readers of this book should consider that they may be wearing wedding rings or other jewelry not essential to their lives, which could be sold to buy antibiotics to save identifiable lives in the third world. Those who keep such baubles may in part be acting in agreement with Nozick's account and claiming that "it is my right to keep my wedding ring for myself, even though the proceeds from its sale could save the lives of individuals in dire need."

Nozick's account requires a distinction between someone's secular moral rights and what is right, good, or proper to do. At times, selling some (perhaps all) of one's property to support the health care of those in need will be the right thing to do, even though one has a secular moral right to refuse to sell. This contrast derives from the distinction Nozick makes between *freedom as a side constraint*, as the very condition for the possibility of a secular moral community, and *freedom as one value among others*. This contrast can be understood as a distinction between those claims of justice based on the very possibility of a moral community, versus those claims of justice that turn on interests in particular goods and values, albeit interests recognized in the original position. . . .

This contrast between Rawls and Nozick can be appreciated more generally as a contrast between two quite different principles of justice, each of which has strikingly different implications for the allocation of health care resources.

1. Freedom- or permission-based justice is concerned with distributions of goods made in accord with the notion of the secular moral community as a peaceable social structure binding moral strangers, members of diverse concrete moral communities. Such justice will therefore require the consent of the individuals involved in a historical nexus of justice-regarding institutions understood in conformity with the principle of permission. The principle of beneficence may be pursued only within constraints set by the principle of permission.

2. Goals-based justice is concerned with the achievement of the good of individuals in society, where the pursuit of beneficence is not constrained by a strong principle of permission, but driven by some particular understanding of morality, justice, or fairness. Such justice will vary in substance as one attempts, for example, to (a) give each person an equal share; (b) give each person what that person needs; (c) give each person a distribution as a part of a system designed to achieve the greatest balance of benefits over harms for the greatest number of persons; (d) give each person a distribution as a part of a system designed to maximize the advantage of the least-well-off class with conditions of equal liberty for all and of fair opportunity.

Allocations of health care in accord with freedom- or permission-based justice must occur within the constraint to respect the free choices of persons, including their exercise of their property rights. Allocations of health care in accord with goals-based justice will need to establish what it means to provide a just pattern of health care, and what constitutes true needs, not mere desires, and how to rank the various health goals among themselves and in comparison with non-health goals. Such approaches to justice in health care will require a way of ahistorically discovering the proper pattern for the distribution of resources.

Permission-based and goals-based approaches to justice in health care contrast because they offer competing interpretations of the maxim, "Justitia est constans et perpetua voluntas jus suum cuique tribuens" (Justice is the constant and perpetual will to render everyone his due).[12] A permission-based approach holds that justice is first and foremost giving to each the right to be respected as a free individual as the source of secular moral authority, in the disposition of personal services and private goods: that which is due (ius) to individuals is respect of their authority over themselves and their possessions. In contrast, a goals-based approach holds that justice is receiving a share of the goods, which is fair by an appeal to a set of ahistorical criteria specifying what a fair share should be, that is, what share is due to each individual. Since there are various senses of a fair share (e.g., an equal share, a share in accordance with the system that maximizes the balance of benefits over harms, etc.), there will be various competing senses of justice in health care under the rubric of goals-based justice. . . .

THE MORAL INEVITABILITY OF A MULTITIER HEALTH CARE SYSTEM

. . . In the face of unavoidable tragedies and contrary moral intuitions, a multitiered system of health care is in many respects a compromise. On the one hand, it provides some amount of health care for all, while on the other hand allowing those with resources to purchase additional or better services. It can endorse the use of communal resources for the provision of a decent minimal or basic amount of health care for all, while acknowledging the existence of private resources at the disposal of some individuals to purchase better basic as well as luxury care. While the propensity to seek more than equal treatment for oneself or loved ones is made into a vicious disposition

in an egalitarian system, a multitier system allows for the expression of individual love and the pursuit of private advantage, though still supporting a general social sympathy for those in need. Whereas an egalitarian system must suppress the widespread human inclination to devote private resources to the purchase of the best care for those whom one loves, a multitier system can recognize a legitimate place for the expression of such inclinations. A multitier system (1) should support individual providers and consumers against attempts to interfere in their free association and their use of their own resources, though (2) it may allow positive rights to health care to be created for individuals who have not been advantaged by the social lottery.

The serious task is to decide how to define and provide a decent minimum or basic level of care as a floor of support for all members of society, while allowing money and free choice to fashion special tiers of services for the affluent. In addressing this general issue of defining what is to be meant by a decent minimum basic level or a minimum adequate amount of health care, the American President's Commission in 1983 suggested that in great measure content is to be created rather than discovered by democratic processes, as well as by the forces of the market. "In a democracy, the appropriate values to be assigned to the consequences of policies must ultimately be determined by people expressing their values through social and political processes as well as in the marketplace."[13] The Commission, however, also suggested that the concept of adequacy could in part be discovered by an appeal to that amount of care that would meet the standards of sound medical practice. "Adequacy does require that everyone receive care that meets standards of sound medical practice."[14] But what one means by "sound medical practice" is itself dependent on particular understandings within particular cultures. Criteria for sound medical practice are as much created as discovered. The moral inevitability of multiple tiers of care brings with it multiple standards of proper or sound medical practice and undermines the moral plausibility of various obiter dicta concerning the centralized allocation of medical resources. . . .

Concepts of adequate care are not discoverable outside of particular views of the good life and of proper medical practice. In nations encompassing diverse moral communities, an understanding of what one will mean by an adequate level or a decent minimum of health care will need to be fashioned, if it can indeed be agreed to, through open discussion and by fair negotiation. . . .

NOTES

1. The White House Domestic Policy Council, *The President's Health Security Plan* (New York: Times Books, 1993).

2. The White House Domestic Policy Council, *The President's Health Security Plan*, p. 43.

3. Innovation would be discouraged as drug prices are subject to review as reasonable. The White House Domestic Policy Council, *The President's Health Security Plan*, p. 45.

4. In considering how to respond to the plight of the impecunious, one might consider the story Jesus tells of the rich man who fails to give alms to "a certain beggar named Lazarus, full of sores, who was laid at his gate, desiring to be fed with the crumbs which fell from the rich man's table" (Luke 16: 20–21). The rich man, who was not forthcoming with alms, was condemned eternally to a hell of excruciating torment.

5. President's Commission for the Study of Ethical Problems in Medicine and Biomedical and Behavioral Research, *Securing Access to Health Care* (Washington, D.C.: U.S. Government Printing Office, 1983), vol. 1, pp. 43–46.

6. The White House Domestic Policy Council, "Ethical Foundations of Health Reform," in *The President's Health Security Plan*, p. 11.

7. H. Newman, "Exclusion of Heart Transplantation Procedures from Medicare Coverage." *Federal Register* 45 (Aug. 6, 1980): 52296. See also H. Newman, "Medicare Program: Solicitation of Hospitals and Medical Centers to Participate in a Study of Heart Transplants," *Federal Register* 46 (Jan. 22, 1981): 7072–75.

8. The reader should understand that the author holds that almsgiving is one of the proper responses to human suffering (in addition to being an appropriate expression of repentance, an act of repentance to which surely the author is obligated). It is just that the author acknowledges the limited secular moral authority of the state to compel charity coercively.

9. President's Commission, *Securing Access to Health Care*, vol. 1, pp. 18–19.

10. John Rawls, *A Theory of Justice* (Cambridge, Mass.: Harvard University Press, 1971), and Robert Nozick, *Anarchy, State, and Utopia* (New York: Basic Books, 1974).

11. Nozick, *Anarchy, State, and Utopia*, p. 160.

12. Flavius Petrus Sabbatius Justinianus, *The Institutes of Justinian*, trans. Thomas C. Sandars (1922; repr. Westport, Conn,: Greenwood Press, 1970), 1.1, p. 5.

13. President's Commission, *Securing Access to Health Care*, vol. 1, p. 37.

14. Ibid.

Priority Setting in Health Care and Public Health

P E T E R   A .   U B E L

The Necessity of Rationing Health Care

Peter Ubel is Professor in the Department of Internal Medicine and Director at the Center for Behavioral and Decision Sciences in Medicine, at the University of Michigan Medical School. He is also staff physician at the Ann Arbor Veterans Affairs Medical Center. His research interests focus on the allocation of scarce health care resources and on the psychology of moral decision making.

Imagine you and five friends have just finished stuffing yourselves at a fancy restaurant. The waiter rolls by with a cart filled with sumptuous artery-hardening desserts: chocolate mousse, baked Alaska (at least it's not fried!), and some kind of pie cowering below six

inches of meringue. Despite having stuffed yourself, you have room in your spare "dessert stomach," and begin pondering your choices. Your waiter introduces each dessert with a pile of adjectives and . . . a six-dollar price tag!

You are crushed—your dessert stomach is simply not large enough to get six dollars of pleasure out of any of these offerings. Then, in a flash of inspiration,

From *Pricing Life: Why It's Time for Health Care Rationing* by Peter A. Ubel. Cambridge, MA: MIT Press, 2000.

you remember that you and your companions are keeping only one check for the meal, meaning the cost of your dessert will be split six ways. You are confident in your ability to get a dollar's worth of pleasure out of one of these desserts. You order the chocolate mousse and prepare to nibble at its margins, confident that it will be a dollar well spent. Unfortunately, your five dinner companions, reasoning the same way you do (your friends aren't idiots!), also order desserts. As a result, each of you ends up paying full price for a dessert that none of you would have spent six dollars on.

Health care insurance, like a single check in a restaurant, distributes expenses across many people, creating an incentive to buy health care services that cost more than they are worth, a phenomenon health economists refer to as moral hazard (Fuchs 1996; Pauly 1968; Phelps 1992). Patients respond to health insurance the same way restaurant customers respond to shared checks: they purchase more goods (Keeler et al. 1988).

Because of insurance, people often spend more money on health care than they want to. They desire a routine blood test with very little chance of benefiting them because insurance picks up most of the cost. An expensive procedure that yields small benefits compared with an inexpensive procedure is preferred by physicians, who stand to do well by doing good, and by patients, who, more often than not, do not know the relative costs and benefits of the two. Physicians and patients do not care whether a CEA [Cost-Effectiveness Analysis: analyzing how to maximize health benefits within a specific health care budget] shows that the expensive procedure costs $200,000 per QALY [Quality-Adjusted Life Year]. They only care that it is better than the less expensive one. In fact, for most people, the cost of health care and of health insurance is a mystery. Governments and employers pick up much of the cost of health insurance and deduct it from workers' salaries without their knowing its actual cost. It is almost as if health care consumers are not only splitting the check at a fancy restaurant, but are also turning the check over to their employers for reimbursement.

Health insurance increases demand for health care services, thereby promoting inflation. Fancy restaurants have little incentive to lower the price of desserts when customers split their checks and turn their receipts over to their employers (who, of course,

receive a tax deduction for the expense). Similarly, health care institutions throughout much of the developed world have little incentive to lower their prices. Insurance decreases incentives for patients and clinicians to talk to each other about the costs of services, once again promoting inflation. And insurance creates high profit margins for medical technology companies, thereby encouraging the development of newer, more expensive technologies, thereby (you guessed it) promoting inflation.

To some, the ever rising costs of providing new, beneficial technology to patients leads to the unavoidable conclusion that health care rationing is both necessary and inevitable. Daniel Callahan, cofounder of the Hastings Center, an influential bioethics think tank, maintains that health care needs are limitless. Recent decades have seen great improvements in care and in health in most industrialized countries. Yet, the demand for further improvements continues to increase (Callahan 1987, 1990). Some experts point out that the costs are driven by a technological imperative (Churchill 1987; Eddy 1994; Emanuel 1991). Perhaps the only people who demand more insistently on an increasing number of high-tech gadgets in health care than professionals are patients. Combine this limitless need and ceaseless demand with an aging population, and we have a recipe for bankruptcy.

Others counter that rationing is neither necessary nor inevitable. Some say that it is unnecessary because health care is special, therefore, it is wrong to set any limits on health care goods (Lee & Jonsen 1974). Some believe that until we eliminate wasteful health care practices, it is premature to talk about rationing (Angell 1985). Others contend that, because the need to ration is caused by the inflationary effects of health insurance, we should simply eliminate or drastically reduce the amount of the insurance so that rationing decisions can be left in the hands of consumers.

When Oregon first unveiled its plan to ration Medicaid services, many questioned whether any state in the United States had to ration health care; with the federal government spending money on B1 bombers and with citizens spending money on sport utility vehicles (or whatever they were called back then), it made no sense for Oregon to do it. If these people are right, Oregon's cost-effectiveness list was doomed to fail no matter how it ranked health care services. Indeed, in a world without a need for health care rationing, CEA is irrelevant.

But CEA is not irrelevant. We do not live in a world where health care rationing is unnecessary.

Although it is impossible to know what percentage of a country's gross domestic product (GDP) ought to go to health care, and impossible to prove that the United States, for example, is spending too much of its GDP on health care, I believe that many beneficial services that are routinely offered to patients are a poor way to spend money.

WHY HEALTH CARE RATIONING IS NECESSARY EVEN THOUGH HEALTH CARE IS SPECIAL

Some people say rationing is unnecessary because health care is special. These people are half correct. Health care *is* special. Nevertheless, it still should be rationed.

Health care is special because life is sacred, and health care is one of the few goods and services that can prevent premature death. Steel-belted radial tires and a low home mortgage rate are not much good to a dead man.

Health care is also special because health is special. Good health is necessary before people can enjoy the most basic parts of life. A mountain bike does not bring much benefit to a person with crippling arthritis, and a good conversation is difficult to have during a migraine headache. Many things we value in life, and many goods and services we value in our economy, depend on people being healthy enough to enjoy them. More important, a certain level of health is necessary for people to have fair opportunities to pursue life goals (Daniels 1985). If we do not provide glasses for them, nearsighted children will be at a disadvantage in learning how to read and, therefore, in pursuing certain types of jobs when they are done with school. Untreated congestive heart failure makes almost any pursuit more difficult. Health care, of course, cannot provide equal opportunities or equal health for everybody. Some people are blind despite the best ophthalmologic care, and many people with congestive heart failure continue to have shortness of breath despite therapy. Moreover, many factors influence health other than health care, including socioeconomic status, education, and genetics. But health care is one of the few commodities that can be vitally important to helping people achieve fair opportunity.

Because it is a special type of consumer good, people debate whether they have a right to health care. They are comfortable asserting, for example, that people have a right to basic nutrition if society can afford to give it to them. Like food, which makes life possible, health care, they insist, should be a basic

right in advanced industrialized countries. Of course, health care is more expensive than food. But life is sacred, and thus we should not put dollar values on people's lives, nor should we worry about how much of our GDP we spend on health care.

But is health care so special that we should pursue its benefits at any cost? Is life so sacred that we should extend it regardless of the price?

An answer to these questions is suggested by the way we treat certain nonhealth care products that affect health. After all, health care services are not alone in their ability to improve health and prolong life. If we spent more money on road repairs, we could reduce traffic fatalities (table 3.1; Tengs et al. 1995). If we furnished every automobile-owning family with a new Volvo, we might have a similar effect. If we established stricter environmental laws, we could probably reduce cancer deaths more effectively than by waiting until it is time for chemotherapy. Yet, we are willing, as a society, to debate how much money to spend on road repairs, automobile safety laws, and environmental protection. We ought to be equally willing to debate how much to spend on health care to promote these same ends.

Why are we willing to debate the cost-worthiness of solutions to some problems but not of health care?

Table 3.1 Life-Saving Interventions and Their Cost-Effectiveness

Intervention	Cost/Year of Life
Mandatory automobile seat belt use	$69
Mammography for 50-year-old women	$810
Beta blockers for heart attack survivors	$850
Hypertension screening for men aged 45–54	$5,200
Grooved highway pavement	$29,000
Collapsible automobile steering columns	$67,000
Hypertension screening for asymptomatic women aged 20	$87,000
Colonoscopy for routine colon cancer screening	$90,000
Automobile air bags	$120,000
Breakaway rural highway utility poles	$150,000
Annual mammography for women aged 40–49	$190,000
Home smoke detector	$210,000
Adult monitors on school buses	$4,900,000
Six (versus 5) stool guaiacs for colon cancer screening	$26,000,000

Adapted from Tengs et al.

In part, because road improvements, automobile air bags, and environmental laws improve the health of unidentifiable "statistical" people, whereas many health care interventions are targeted at specific, identifiably ill people. A fifty-year-old woman needs emergency surgery: who is going to ask how much it will cost? But an engineer develops an expensive way to reduce traffic accidents and everyone wants to know how much it will cost and how many accidents it will prevent. Rightly or wrongly, people place significantly more value on saving identifiable lives than statistical ones (Jenni & Loewenstein, 1997). . . . Since many health care interventions, especially the ones we see on television, are directed toward identifiably ill people, we mistakenly conclude that the cost of such life-saving services is irrelevant.

But of course, not all health care interventions save lives. Moreover, even some that are do not save identifiable lives but statistical lives. Blood pressure treatment reduces heart attacks and strokes. But not every patient with high blood pressure will have a heart attack or a stroke if untreated. Blood pressure control, like cholesterol reduction, Pap smears, mammograms, and exercise, helps unidentifiable, statistical lives. Similarly, new monitoring machines reduce the (already small) chance that patients undergoing surgery will have anesthesia-related complications. Hospital infection-control practices reduce the likelihood of hospital-acquired infections. But we cannot prevent all heart attacks, strokes, anesthesia complications, or hospital-acquired infections. Therefore, we should debate how much money to spend to reduce any or all of these events, and whether this money could be better spent elsewhere.

Whereas some health care services are special because of their ability to affect our longevity and our ability to pursue important goals, not all of them are special in this way. Instead, many of them offer small improvements in people's quality of life in ways that make it hard to distinguish them from a whole lot of other goods and services. Low back pain is one of the most common medical problems I encounter in my general medical practice (not to mention in my own life, which of course I have just mentioned). But relief of mild low back pain hardly rates as a service so special the we should not consider its cost. And many consumer goods and services improve quality of life more than relief of mild or moderate low back pain. I would have gladly put up with a month of low back pain for front row seats to see Michael Jordan play in a Bulls playoff game.

In fact, low back pain may be relieved as well by traditional nonhealth care consumer goods, such as well-designed office furniture and firm mattresses, as it is by health care interventions. Yet, health insurance pays for visits to physical therapists (sometimes) and for prescriptions for nonsteroidal antiinflammatory pain medications, but it rarely pays for mattresses or office chairs. Although insurance companies have to draw lines somewhere to limit expenditures for low back pain, health care is far from unique in addressing these kinds of problems. And outside of the health care market, money matters! Most of us are quite comfortable discussing how much money we are willing to spend on a mattress that might reduce our low back pain. We should be equally willing to discuss how much of our health care dollars we would spend to meet the same goal.

In summary, some health care services are special in the sense that it is unacceptable to even talk about cost-effectiveness when faced with an identifiable person in urgent need of them. But many services are not special in this way, and we ought to have an honest discussion about how much we should spend providing them.

WHY WASTE ELIMINATION AND PRICE REDUCTION WILL NOT ELIMINATE THE NEED TO RATION HEALTH CARE

Some hold that health care rationing is unnecessary because costs can be adequately contained by eliminating waste (Brook & Lohr 1986). Experts estimate that roughly one-third of health care spending in the United States goes toward wasteful and unproved services (Brook & Lohr 1986). Numerous studies demonstrate substantial geographic variation in the use of expensive procedures that do not lead to measurable differences in health outcomes. A woman's likelihood of having a hysterectomy, an elderly man's chance of prostate surgery, and a child's chance of undergoing tonsillectomy all depend in part on where these individuals live (McPherson et al. 1982; Wennberg et al. 1988). If areas performing greater amounts of surgery are not achieving greater amounts of health, we should be able to save some money by reducing unnecessary surgery.

For those who think that rationing is unnecessary, it can further be argued that health care waste can be reduced by charging less for services. Do colonoscopies have to be as expensive as they are, for example? In a colonoscopic examination, a physician inserts a fiberoptic tube into a patient's colon to look for abnormalities. The examination is proved to reduce the chance that someone will die of colon cancer, because during the procedure polyps can be removed before they become lethal (Mandel et al. 1993). But colonoscopy often costs more than $500, causing some to accuse subspecialist gastroenterologists of "scoping for dollars."

Clearly, a great deal of wasteful medical expense could be eliminated by reducing the number of unnecessary procedures or by reducing their unnecessarily high costs. But even after all this waste had been eliminated, most industrialized countries would still be spending large portions of their GDP on health care, and the rate of increase in that spending would still outpace inflation (Emanuel 1991). Because health care is a very labor intensive industry, it does not experience the type of productivity gains that could reduce the cost of its services. Unlike computer hardware, for example, which grows more powerful and less expensive every year, health care services become more powerful and *more* expensive. Many new health care technologies result from increasingly complex research and development techniques. Gene therapy and artificial hearts promise to improve many lives, but they will not be priced to compete with a laptop computer any time soon.

The ability of waste elimination to reduce the need to ration health care is limited for another reason: waste elimination itself costs money. No magic wand can be waved that will make everyone stop wasteful health care practices. Instead, research to identify waste is expensive and is not easily translated into cost savings. Identifying waste is difficult because many interventions cannot easily be categorized as effective or ineffective. Instead, they are beneficial for some patients and not for others. It is a major challenge to figure out who will benefit from what. And, once we have this information, we must create mechanisms that will direct resources to appropriate patients. This, too, costs money, and at some point it may cost more to make sure that patients receive only beneficial care than it would to let some patients receive wasteful care. . . .

Even if we successfully eliminate wasteful practices, some countries, especially the United States, would still face a major obstacle to containing costs—providing health care insurance for currently uninsured or underinsured people. To make sure everyone has a decent minimum of health care insurance would

involve an increase in health care spending. It is unlikely that waste elimination would overcome this increase. . . .

Waste elimination also has a limited ability to eliminate rationing because many beneficial services are available that even the best-insured patients are currently not receiving. Take ambulances, for example. Rapid arrival of an ambulance can be life saving; but people living in rural areas are often far away from an ambulance, much less a tertiary care hospital. Thus, their emergency care services are compromised. If improving beneficial health care regardless of cost were really the goal, even after we had eliminated wasteful, nonbeneficial services, we would have to decide when to stop building ambulances. . . .

An early CEA showed that an inexpensive screening test for colon cancer, if repeated for a sixth time in a patient whose first five tests were normal, continued to find colon cancers, but at a cost of $26 million for every year of life gained. Debates about how much of our GDP we should spend on health care are irrelevant in light of this cost. However much we spend or however much we could ultimately afford to spend on health care, we should *not* spend money this way. Even if this screening test had no harmful consequences, most people would have to agree that $26 million is an awfully high price to spend for a year of life. Those who think it is not too high have only to think about the cost of repeating the test a seventh time—it would probably take more than $100 million to save a year of life. Thus CEA teaches us that after we spend money to achieve important benefits, further benefits often come at greater and greater financial cost. At some point, we must decide to stop pursuing these incremental benefits. At some point, we must decide to ration health care.

HOW CAN WE REDUCE THE ECONOMIC IMPACT OF MORAL HAZARD?

In the opening of this chapter I explained that health insurance is a major catalyst for excessive spending because of moral hazard—the effect of sharing health care expenses through insurance on people's willingness to pay for additional services. Some may wonder whether we can avoid excessive spending, and maybe even rationing, by eliminating or reducing the economic impact of moral hazard.

ELIMINATING MORAL HAZARD BY ELIMINATING HEALTH INSURANCE

Any good waiter knows that the best way to increase how much food people order at a restaurant is to have them share their expenses on a single check. Any frugal restaurant patron (present company included) knows that the best way to reduce dining expenses is to keep separate tabs so you don't have to pay for your friend's third glass of scotch. We could similarly reduce health care expenses by eliminating health insurance, thereby requiring people (above some minimum income perhaps) to pay for their own care without anyone else's financial assistance.

In this way, patients' health care purchases would no longer be subject to moral hazard. Eliminating insurance would make patients less likely to request marginally beneficial care. It would also encourage them to examine the cost and quality of care. In theory, this would benefit patients by providing them only with services they deemed worth it. If a service is too expensive, patients will spend their money on more beneficial goods, whether they be other health care services or wall-to-wall carpeting. Eliminating health insurance would relieve society of difficult rationing decisions, because informed patients would decide whether the costs (monetary and otherwise) and benefits of their treatment options are worth while.

To be clear: eliminating health insurance would reduce health care expenditures, but it would not avoid health care rationing. Instead, it would ration according to willingness and ability to pay.

Of course, although eliminating insurance would lower costs and eliminate moral hazard, almost no one wants to eliminate insurance completely. Ability and willingness to pay are unacceptable bases for rationing many health care services. Often, these goods are not discretionary, yet purchasing them would be financially catastrophic to anyone other than Bill Gates. Some life-saving interventions, such as long stays in intensive care units, can cost hundreds of thousands of dollars, and many relatively common interventions cost more money than a typical person has available. Insurance smooths out predictable expenses, such as childbearing and prostate surgery, and distributes the expenses of unpredictable, highly expensive treatments among many people. Moreover, the mere thought of distributing some services by ability to pay is morally bankrupt. Who would ask a man with an acutely fatal condition whether he had enough money to save his life? Who would withhold a liver transplant from a dying woman simply because she did not have $400,000 in spare change? Because it is important to protect people from the often catastrophic expense of treating serious illness, we accept the economic inefficiencies of health insurance. If we want to control costs and reduce the economic impact of moral hazard, we should not do so by totally eliminating insurance.

REDUCING MORAL HAZARD BY ELIMINATING HEALTH INSURANCE FOR DISCRETIONARY SERVICES

Although it would be wrong to eliminate health insurance for all medical services, perhaps we could offer it for necessary services but eliminate it for unnecessary, or discretionary, services—the "dessert" of health care, if you will. Many health care goods are like an expensive dessert: they bring benefits, but the benefits are often not worth their financial cost.

Obstacles limit the role that out-of-pocket costs can play in the delivery of discretionary services. . . . [I]t is extremely difficult to define necessary and beneficial medical care, much less to distinguish between them. It is similarly difficult to distinguish discretionary from nondiscretionary care. Even many chronic conditions, such as diabetes and emphysema, force people to spend large sums of money to avoid serious consequences. Are insulin syringes discretionary for a patient with adult-onset diabetes? How about glucometers? Are inhalers discretionary for patients with emphysema? How about home oxygen? Without an acceptable definition, or even a list, of discretionary services, using out of pocket costs to limit them is of minimal utility. . . .

Industrialized countries, especially the United States, have to do a much better job of defining those services everyone should have access to versus those they must pay for versus those that should be unavailable to everyone. This is a very challenging task. It requires societies to define a decent minimum of health care and to make sure that this decent minimum is not eroded by allowing the middle and upper classes to purchase services it does not include. Health insurance is an important social good because it allows people to plan their lives knowing that they will not be financially crippled by the cost of receiving care for unforeseen illnesses. And many services are special goods that should not be denied simply because people do not have enough money. But health insurance, through moral hazard, drives up health care costs beyond what people would be willing to pay, and not all of the services are so special that money should be irrelevant. Therefore, society must find a way, other than by forcing people to pay out of pocket, to ration health care services.

REDUCING MORAL HAZARD AT THE TIME OF HEALTH INSURANCE ENROLLMENT

Another way some propose to reduce moral hazard is to ask people to act like rational consumers at the time they purchase health care insurance (Menzel 1990). Rather than eliminating insurance or insurance for discretionary services, this proposal asks people to choose insurance plans according to services that are covered.

Imagine a healthy person deciding between two plans. The plans are identical except that one (slightly more expensive) promises to pay for lung transplants and the other does not. The person choosing can decide how much money she is willing to pay to be assured that lung transplantation will be available if she develops lung failure. In theory, if she has information about her chances of developing lung failure in the next year and the benefits and risks of various treatments (including lung transplantation), she should be able to make a rational choice between these plans. Consequently, she will end up with a plan that reflects how she would elect to spend her dollars.

Although this proposal is appealing, it has several problems. First, it creates the opportunity for adverse selection of patients. Adverse selection occurs when patients preferentially enroll in insurance plans that cover services that they need (Buchanan & Cretin 1986; Jackson-Beeck & Kleinman 1983; Robinson, Gardner, & Luft 1993). In the example above, the prices of the two competing plans are partly based on estimates about how many people are likely to require lung transplants. But if people who predict that they will have to have a transplant preferentially enroll in the plan that covers the procedure, that insurance company will have more transplant patients than it is prepared for. Any time insurance plans distinguish themselves by the services they cover, or the copayments they have, an opportunity exists for adverse selection.

Second, this model requires patients to learn and process large amounts of information. Insurers would have to be clear and specific about what services they provide, and people would have to grasp what these differences mean to them. Many people probably do not know enough about positron emission tomographic (PET) scans, for example, to know whether they want them included in coverage. It would be staggeringly difficult to decide whether to purchase insurance that covers prostate-specific antigen (PSA) blood tests, lung transplants, PET scans for brain disease, PET scans for other diseases, or myriad other options. Even if insurance companies could be convinced to describe their benefits in sufficient detail to allow comparison, potential enrollees would be overwhelmed, they would be unlikely to comprehend the information, thus, making informed choice impossible (Hibbard et al. 1998). . . .

CEA'S ROLE IN THE NECESSARY JOB OF RATIONING HEALTH CARE

Oregon's rationing decisions in the case of Coby Howard are impossible to defend. But in its later movement toward CEA, the state seemed to be heading in the right direction. Surely, some of its Medicaid dollars must have been going toward medical services that were not worth the cost. Certainly, CEA should have been able to help it identify such services.

Although CEA seems like an ideal way to identify health care services to ration, Oregon's experience convinced many people that the analysis will never be up to the task. Many people are convinced that it simply fails to capture public rationing preferences. [However, I believe] that CEA can help us identify which health care services to ration despite its inability to capture all the values important to our rationing decisions.

REFERENCES

Angell, M. (1985). Cost containment and the physician. *Journal of the American Medical Association* 254, 1203–1207.

Brook, R. H. & K. N. Lohr. (1986). Will we need to ration effective health care? *Issues in Science and Technology* Fall, 68–77.

Brook, R. H., J. E. Ware, W. H. Rogers, et al. (1983). Does free care improve adults' health? Results from a randomized controlled trial. *New England Journal of Medicine* 309, 1426–1434.

Buchanan, J. & S. Cretin. (1986). Fee-for-service health care expenditures: Evidence of selection effects among subscribers who choose HMOs. *Medical Care* 24, 39–51.

Callahan, D. (1987). *Setting Limits: Medical Goals in an Aging Society.* New York: Simon & Schuster.

Callahan, D. (1990). *What Kind of Life: The Limits of Medical Progress.* New York: Simon & Schuster.

Churchill, L. R. (1987). *Rationing Health Care in America: Perceptions and Principles of Justice.* Notre Dame, IN: Notre Dame University Press.

Daniels, N. (1985). *Just Health Care.* Cambridge: Cambridge University Press.

Deyo, R. A., B. M. Psaty, G. Simon, et al. (1997). The messenger under attack—Intimidation of researchers by special-interest groups. *New England Journal of Medicine* 336, 1176–1180.

Eddy, D. M. (1994). Health system reform: Will controlling costs require rationing services? *Journal of the American Medical Association* 272, 324–328.

Emanuel, E. J. (1991). *The Ends of Human Life: Medical Ethics in a Liberal Polity.* Cambridge: Harvard University Press.

Fuchs, V. R. (1996). What every philosopher should know about health economics. *Health Economics* 140, 186–195.

Hibbard, J. H., J. J. Jewett, S. Engelmann, & M. Tusler. (1998). Can Medicare beneficiaries make informed choices? *Health Affairs* 17, 181–193.

Jackson-Beeck, M. & J. H. Kleinman. (1983). Evidence for self-selection among health maintenance organization enrollees. *Journal of the American Medical Association* 250, 2826–2829.

Jenni, K. E. & G. Loewenstein. (1997). Explaining the "identifiable victim" effect. *Journal of Risk and Uncertainty* 14, 235–257.

Kahneman, D. & J. Snell. (1990). Predicting utility. In R. M. Hogarth (Ed.), *Insights in Decision Making: A Tribute to Hillel J. Einhorn* (pp. 295–310). Chicago and London: University of Chicago Press.

Keeler, E. B., J. L. Buchanan, & J. E. Rolph. (1988). *The Demand for Episodes of Treatment in the Health Insurance Experiment.* Santa Monica, CA: Rand Corporation.

Lee, P. R. & A. R. Jonsen. (1974). The right to health care. *American Review of Respiratory Disease* 109, 591–592.

Lohr, K. N., R. H. Brook, C. J. Kamberg, et al. (1986). Use of medical care in the Rand health insurance experiment: Diagnosis- and service-specific analyses in a randomized controlled trial. *Medical Care* 24, S1–S87.

Mandel, J. S., J. H. Bond, M. Bradley, et al. (1993). Reducing mortality from colorectal cancer by screening for fecal occult blood. *New England Journal of Medicine* 328, 1365–1371.

McPherson, K., J. E. Wennberg, O. B. Hovind, & P. Clifford. (1982). Small-area variations in the use of common surgical procedures: An international comparison of New England, England, and Norway. *New England Journal of Medicine* 307, 1310–1314.

Menzel, P. T. (1990). *Strong Medicine: The Ethical Rationing of Health Care.* New York: Oxford University Press.

Pauly, M. V. (1968). The economics of moral hazard. *American Economic Review* 58, 231–237.

Phelps, C. E. (1992). *Health Economics.* New York: HarperCollins.

Prades, J.-L. P. (1997). Is the person trade-off a valid method for allocating health care resources? *Health Economics* 6, 71–81.

Redelmeier, D. A., P. Rozin, & D. Kahneman. (1993). Understanding patients' decisions: Cognitive and emotional perspectives. *Journal of the American Medical Association* 270, 72–76.

Robinson, J. C., L. B. Gardner, & H. S. Luft. (1993). Health plan switching in anticipation of increased medical care utilization. *Medical Care* 31, 43–51.

Tengs, T. O., M. E. Adams, J. S. Pliskin, et al. (1995). Five-hundred life-saving interventions and their cost-effectiveness. *Risk Analysis* 15, 369–390.

Wennberg, J. E., A. G. Mulley Jr., D. Hanley, et al. (1988). An assessment of prostatectomy for benign urinary tract obstruction: Geographic variations and the evaluation of medical care outcomes. *Journal of the American Medical Association* 259, 3027–3030.

DAN W. BROCK

Priority to the Worse Off in Health-Care Resource Prioritization

Dan W. Brock is the Frances Glessner Lee Professor of Medical Ethics, Department of Social Medicine, and Director of the Division of Medical Ethics at the Harvard Medical School. He also directs the Harvard Program in Ethics and Health. His books include *Life and Death: Philosophical Essays in Biomedical Ethics* and *Deciding for Others: The Ethics of Surrogate Decision Making.* His current research centers on setting priorities in health resources and rationing.

Resources available to the health-care system are and always will be scarce, however much many Americans would like to deny it. It is not possible, nor would it be rational or just, to provide all potentially beneficial

From Rosamond Rhodes, Margaret P. Battin, and Anita Silvers, eds., *Medicine and Social Justice: Essays on the Distribution of Health Care.* Oxford University Press, 2002. Used by permission of Oxford University Press.

care to everyone, no matter how small the benefits and how great the cost. As a result, use of potential resources must be given priority in a way that reflects the individual and social values at stake.

In the face of scarce resources available for health care, many will respond that such resources should be used in whatever manner will maximize the overall or aggregate health benefits for the population they serve.

Cost-effectiveness analysis using measures of benefits like quality-adjusted life-years (QALYs) is the analytic tool for comparing different health interventions and programs for their aggregate health impacts. . . . However, this utilitarian or consequentialist approach suffers from a familiar problem, which is that it looks only to the overall benefits to a population without any direct concern for how those benefits are distributed to distinct individuals. It does not matter who receives how much benefit as long as resources are used to maximize overall benefits. Distributive justice and fairness, however, concern how individuals are treated relative to other individuals—which inequalities between individuals or groups are just or unjust.

Perhaps the most common feature of different theories of justice and of the thinking of ordinary people about justice is a special concern for the worse off members of society. This is seen in popular aphorisms such as "the justice of a society can be seen in how it treats its least fortunate members." Many otherwise different religious traditions also share this concern for the worse off in their teachings and work on social justice. Concern for the worse off has a long tradition in political philosophy as well, and in more recent decades has been a central focus of the work of John Rawls and the many others he has influenced (Rawls, 1971). Rawls's well known "Difference Principle" requires that the basic social and economic institutions of society be arranged so as to maximize the expectations of the worst off representative group, though the absolute priority it gives to this group is extremely controversial. However, this principle has a specific and qualified application in Rawls's work, and he did not apply it to health care. This chapter addresses how a concern for the worse off should be reflected in health-care resource prioritization. Norman Daniels (1993) has characterized this as one of several important unsolved rationing problems.

Because the U.S. health-care system is extremely heterogeneous and complex, prioritization decisions will take different forms and will be made in different ways by different parties at different places in that system. Moreover, because our health-care system often fails clearly to assign responsibility to anyone for using available resources to meet the health needs of a population, we often lack the practical institutional and policy means for making explicit and rational resource prioritization decisions. Too often resource priorities are de facto determined by myriad decisions made by many individuals acting under a variety of often perverse incentives; it should hardly

be a surprise that the result is often both irrational and unjust.

However, a rational and just health-care system should be able to make explicit prioritization decisions such as these: a state mental health department must decide whether to use limited resources to expand services to severely and chronically mentally ill patients, or to expand treatment programs for less severely ill patients with mild to moderate obsessive compulsive disorder; a hospital must decide whether to use limited resources to expand its medical intensive care unit, which serves the most critically ill patients, or to expand its clinic serving teenage pregnant women and mothers; a health department must decide whether to use limited resources for a health-care outreach program for homeless persons or to expand hypertension screening programs for the general population. For each of these decisions, data are needed on the expected benefits and costs of the different programs, but they each raise as well, in different and complex ways, what priority, if any, should be given to the worse off.

If a cost-effectiveness standard for prioritizing health-care resources in decisions such as these is rejected in part in order to give priority to the worse off—that is, in favor of a "prioritarian" view—then we face three main sets of issues. First, why, for what reasons, should the worse off receive priority for health-care resources? Second, who are the worse off for the purposes of health-care resource prioritization? Third, how much priority should the worse off receive? These issues are complex, controversial, and unsettled in general theories of distributive justice, and so here too in theories of just or equitable health-care resource prioritization and allocation; if anything, the problem is worse in the health-care context because the issues have received less sustained attention there and so, I believe, are less well understood. This means that it will not be possible to provide anything like a precise and definitive account of what priority the worse off should receive in health-care resource prioritization, but we can at least explore some of the issues that must be resolved to develop that account.

MORAL JUSTIFICATIONS OF PRIORITY TO THE WORSE OFF

Why does justice require some priority to the worse off in health-care resource prioritization and allocation? Perhaps the most natural reason is a concern for equality. When disadvantages are undeserved, then the moral baseline would appear to be equality, for it eliminates those undeserved disadvantages. . . . Some commitment to equality is a central feature of nearly all theories of justice, with most of the dispute being in what respects should people be equal. However, whatever the relevant arguments, strong objections exist to a fundamental commitment to equality in outcomes or conditions, both in general and as the basis of a special concern for the worse off.

First, the goal of equality in outcomes is different from the goal of improving the condition of the worse off, and so equality in outcomes will not always support improving the position of the worse off. For example, consider distributions 1 and 2 for individuals *A, B,* and *C* below:

	A	*B*	*C*
1	10	20	20
2	11	15	25

Distribution 1 is more equal, whereas distribution 2 has the better outcome for the worst off. An egalitarian view is fundamentally relational—it evaluates distributions by how equal the positions of the different parties are. A prioritarian view gives greater priority to improving individuals' positions the worse off they are, without regard to whether doing so makes the overall distribution more equal.

Second, equality in outcomes or conditions is a problematic goal in its own right, even for egalitarians and even if achievable. . . . An alternative egalitarian view looks not to whether outcomes are unequal, but rather to whether inequality is brought about by unjust treatment or action. . . . However, whereas some of the conditions that make particular individuals or groups disadvantaged are the result of unjust treatment, such as discrimination against minorities, other conditions are not, such as suffering from genetically transmitted disease or from accidental injuries for which no one is at fault, and so deontic egalitarianism would not support giving priority to all the worse off in health-care or other contexts.

A more promising egalitarian appeal, especially in the health care context, might be to equality of opportunity. The most well-developed theory of justice in health care, that of Norman Daniels, focuses on the impact that disease has in limiting people's function and in turn opportunity (Daniels, 1985). Some principle of equality of opportunity is common to most theories of justice, and so they would require providing health care that prevents or restores loss of function so as to protect equality of opportunity. . . . In general, the greater the loss of function caused by illness, the more removed people will be from enjoying the normal opportunity range, and so in that respect the worse off they will be.

How this view of equality of opportunity applies to the worse off depends on how it is interpreted. The greater the loss of function that health care can prevent or restore, the greater the increase in opportunity it will produce. If equality of opportunity is given a maximizing interpretation as requiring eliminating as much as possible the aggregate reduction in opportunity from the normal range suffered by members of society, then providing health care that prevents or restores a greater loss of function and opportunity should have priority over preventing or restoring a lesser loss. This is not equivalent to maximizing opportunity, as in a consequentialist view that focuses on opportunity instead of well-being, since raising people above the normal opportunity range does not have the same moral importance as bringing people up to it. But it does not give priority to the worse off when a greater loss of function and reduction of opportunity can be prevented or restored for better-off individuals than can be achieved for others who are worse off.

The issue of priority for the worse off, however, concerns whether and to what extent we should give priority to the needs of the worse off when we could provide greater overall improvement in function and opportunity by directing resources to better-off groups—that is, whether and how much we should depart from a maximizing cost-effectiveness applied to opportunity and accept a lower level of aggregate gain in health and opportunity in order to respond to the needs of worse-off groups. To support this priority for the worse off, an equality of opportunity account must be interpreted as holding that the lower a person's level of opportunity is, the greater the moral importance of raising it. Most accounts of equality of opportunity are not clear on how they are to be interpreted in this regard. The general point then is that a shift in focus from well being to opportunity together with a commitment to equality of opportunity will not support priority to the worse off without an independent argument for the prioritarian instead of the maximizing interpretation of equality of opportunity; thus, let us pursue further how this prioritarian commitment for the worse off might be justified.

Whether in the context of equality of opportunity or more generally, we need an account of why the worse off should receive priority *because they are worse off*, not because we can often produce greater benefits by treating their greater needs. Here is how Derek Parfit states "The Priority View: Benefiting people matters more the worse off these people are" (Parfit, 1991). He characterizes the view as "weighted beneficence"; benefits have greater moral weight the worse off those who receive them are. This leaves open how much greater moral weight they have, and in particular does not commit a prioritarian adherent to a maximin position that gives absolute weight to improving the position of the worse off. How might one justify this prioritarian view? The issues are very complex and cannot be at all fully explored here, but I will at least mention three potentially promising responses especially relevant to the health-care context.

First, the worse off that people are, the greater the relative improvement a given size health benefit will provide them, and so the more the health benefit may matter to them; "mattering" could be given a subjective or objective interpretation in this context. To illustrate, suppose that on a scale of health-related quality of life like the Health Utilities Index (HUI), on which death equals 0 and full unimpaired function equals 1, person A is very seriously disabled and at level 0.20, whereas person B, who is less seriously ill and impaired, is at level 0.60; if we could use a given amount of health-care resources to move either of them up the HUI scale by 0.20—that is, produce the same size health gain for each, doing so would provide A with a 100% increase in his health-related quality of life but only a 33% increase for B. . . .

This may be what people had in mind in empirical studies in which they were offered choices between using limited resources for a treatment program that would serve a group like A or a group like B, but where those same resources would produce a larger health gain for B than for A (Nord, 1993). Most people preferred to treat the worse off group A even when doing so would produce substantially less aggregate health benefits than would have been achieved by treating group B instead. The reason many people offered for this preference was that they believed it would be more important to the more seriously ill to get treatment, even though they would receive less benefit from treatment; one reason that it could be

more important is because the worse off's relative health improvement, although not absolute, would be greater. Now, of course, giving priority to the greater relative improvement will afford only limited, not absolute, priority to the worse off: for example, if A can only be raised from 0.20 to 0.25, while B could be raised from 0.60 to 0.90. But if relative improvement is the morally important consideration, this may only reflect that the worse off should not get absolute priority no matter how large the sacrifice to better-off groups.

A different line of justification for the priority view focuses on the different strength claims generated by the different degrees of undeserved deprivation A and B suffer from their substantially different degrees of undeserved poor health relative to their being in full health. Because worse-off A's undeserved deprivation is greater, he has a greater complaint and so a stronger moral claim than does B for his deprivation to be reduced or eliminated. It is morally more important or urgent to reduce A's greater deprivation than B's just because it is the greater undeserved reduction in health-related quality of life from full health. . . .

Some line of reasoning of this sort is common in contractualist moral theories like those of Thomas Scanlon (1998) and in Thomas Nagel's work on inequality (1979, 1991). In this view, individuals' moral complaints and, in turn, their claims are determined by how well off they are in comparison with other individuals, but not other aggregates of individuals; a group of individuals with lesser claims cannot combine together to take priority over individuals with greater complaints and claims. The idea is to minimize the complaint of those with the greatest complaint, and one interpretation (there are others) of who has the greatest complaint is those worst off; if we make the position of the worst off as good as possible, we minimize the complaint they have based on their disadvantage. . . .

A similar view can be put in terms of needs, and it has a special resonance in the context of health care. Many people believe that the basic or most urgent needs of all should be met before meeting the less urgent needs or wants of any. The purpose of health care in particular should be to meet health care needs, and more urgent needs should take priority over less urgent needs. This view also requires that individual patients should confront other patients as individuals and that those with the most urgent needs should receive priority for treatment. This is a "prioritarian" view in the context of health care, though it also may be too strong in giving absolute priority to the most urgent needs.

Treating the most urgent needs first, as well as minimizing the greatest complaints, bring out the relation of the prioritarian view to the "aggregation problem"—when should greater aggregate benefits to a larger number of patients receive priority over lesser aggregate, but equal or larger individual benefits to fewer patients? . . . Consequentialists in principle accept no limits on aggregation in seeking to maximize overall benefits, and so small benefits to many individuals may in the aggregate be greater than, and so take priority over, large benefits to a few individuals. However, if we must treat the most urgent needs, or meet the strongest claims, of individuals first, we will place very strong constraints on permissible aggregation—individuals with a less urgent need or weaker claim no matter how large their number would not be treated before anyone with a more urgent need or stronger claim. This view does not rule out all aggregation, for it would not bar preferring to treat more rather than fewer patients with equally urgent needs—for example, saving more lives rather than fewer. But determining whether doing so without giving the fewer any chance to be treated is problematic. Many non-consequentialists would also permit some aggregation when needs are not equally urgent. Again, determining when to do so is a very difficult and controversial matter. . . . If always giving priority to more urgent needs or stronger claims is too strong and rules out too much aggregation, we should only give some but not absolute priority to the worse off; I return to this issue later in the chapter.

WHO ARE THE WORSE OFF FOR HEALTH RESOURCE PRIORITIZATION?

Suppose that one of these or some other line of reasoning, suitably elaborated, succeeds in establishing that it is morally more important to benefit people the worse off they are, and more specifically that it is more important to improve people's health the worse off they are. We then face the second question of who is worse off for the purposes of health-care resource prioritization and allocation. There are several parts to this question. The first is whether for purposes of health-care resource prioritization, the worse off should be understood as those who are sicker, that is, those with worse health, or as those with worse overall well-being. In a general theory of distributive justice that gives some priority to the worse off, it is overall or global well-being that is important. . . .

We could then treat health care as one among other goods whose distribution should be arranged to give priority to improving the condition of those who are overall worse off. This fits the common idea that a disadvantage in one aspect of well-being can be compensated for by an advantage in a different area; for example, the loss of rich cultural opportunities in moving from a large city may be compensated for by new outdoor recreational opportunities in the country, or a loss of income from taking a less pressured and demanding job may be compensated for by increased time to spend with one's family. One might argue, however, that health is not like these other goods in its substitutability with other aspects of well-being. To the extent that health is an all-purpose means necessary for the pursuit of nearly all people's aims and ends, its loss may not be able to be compensated for by other goods, leaving people's overall well-being intact; however, this nonsubstitutability of health, or of specific aspects of health, seems to hold only partially at most.

Applying the "prioritarian" view to overall or global well-being would have what for many are highly counterintuitive implications for health-care prioritization. For example, we would have to give lower priority to treating the rich than the poor, even when the rich are much sicker than the poor, if the overall well-being of the rich is higher despite their much worse health. If this is unacceptable, it indicates that we think of the distribution of health care as a separate sphere, subject to its own distributive principles, not simply as one aspect of overall well-being regulated by general principles of distributive justice. . . .

A "separate spheres" position, which restricts the definition of the worse off in health-care resources prioritization to those with worse health, holds that a theory of justice will apply to different spheres of goods to be distributed. Those spheres should be treated separately or independently. Thus, a concern for the worse off, for purposes of prioritizing educational resources, should look to those who are worse off with regard to education and educational opportunities, and similarly to the extent that there are other additional separate spheres. Likewise, a concern for the worse off for purposes of prioritizing health-care resources should look to those with the worse health. . . .

Even if there is good reason to restrict the concern for the worse off to those with worse health in the prioritization and allocation of health-care resources, additional issues remain. One is how to determine who has worse health. This may seem obvious and straightforward, even if there will be disagreement about close cases, but it is not. One question is whether the worse off are those with the worse overall health or those with the most serious disease now in need of treatment?

For example, suppose A has a serious disability that leaves his overall health-related quality of life as measured on the HUI at 0.5, while B's is much better at 0.9; A and B each contract the same disease, but B's case is more serious and will reduce her health-related quality of life to 0.7 without treatment, whereas A's less serious case will reduce his to 0.4 without treatment. Should a special concern or priority for the worse off favor A or B? A's overall health is worse, and will be worse than B's even if he and not B is treated, but B has the more serious illness that is now in need of treatment because her illness will have a greater adverse impact on her health-related quality of life than will A's on his; a natural description would be that B is the sickest now, but A's overall health is worse. It is doubtful that a separate sphere's argument implies that we should ignore large background differences in current health or health-related quality of life and attend only to the seriousness of the illness for which each patient now needs treatment. A case for separate spheres seeks to restrict health-care resource prioritization to considerations of patients' health, not other factors such as their economic productivity, but patients' background health state is a health consideration. And while treating B would produce the most health benefits, it would only increase the degree to which A's health is worse than B's. This question has obvious importance for the priority that should be given to treatment of patients with serious background illnesses or disabilities besides the current condition in need of treatment. . . .

Giving great weight to severity could be one explanation for the strong priority that people typically give to saving life over improving others' quality of life. Losing one's life is typically seen as losing everything, and in quantitative scales of health-related quality of life, death is the typical zero point (this leaves aside the problem of states worse than death). This supports the idea that patients with life-threatening conditions are the most severely ill and should receive priority over others less severely ill.

Another aspect of the question of who is worse off, again assuming the assessment is restricted to health, is whether only individuals' present health, or instead their health over time, including past and expected future health, is relevant. Suppose A was diagnosed with multiple sclerosis (MS) 20 years ago, has had numerous acute episodes, and has been on medications during this period, but has been left with a functional limitation in only one leg. Recently, B has been diagnosed with MS after an acute episode that leaves him with a functional limitation of one arm and one leg. A new treatment of the condition is developed that would restore the full use of their limbs to each patient, but we can only treat one of them, and no future treatment of the other will be possible. Who should be considered the worse off? Patient B's illness is more serious and results in a greater loss of function than A's, but A has suffered his lesser loss of function for 20 years while B has been healthy all his life and only now has suffered his more serious case of MS and loss of function. Patient A seems the worse off with regard to health because he has had the condition for so long, even though his condition now is less serious than B's. People's lives extend continuously over time, and our moral concern should be for the lives they lead, not simply for how good their lives are at a particular point in time, whether now or sometime in the past or the future. A concern for the worse off should reflect this concern for people's lives as a whole and so not ignore the duration of people's poor health. Moreover, in other areas besides health we often take what a person has had or suffered in the past to be relevant in distributing scarce benefits now; if one child has had little opportunity for travel in the past in comparison with her well-traveled sibling, fairness supports giving a travel opportunity to her now that can only go to one of them, even if the well-traveled sibling might enjoy and benefit from the trip more.

Differences in the duration of expected future health impairments seem relevant as well for who is worse off; for example, if both A and B contract a disease now at age 65, but A will suffer his lesser impairment for the rest of his life, while B will suffer his greater impairment only for a few years and then will regain normal function, A appears to be the worse off. In this case, if both diseases are fully treatable, what makes patient A worse off also makes treating her produce the greater benefit. Who will be worse off in the future is sometimes treated as urgency, but that concept is in fact more complex. Urgency is a function at least of how great a harm a patient will suffer if not treated, how soon a patient must be treated to prevent the harm, and how soon the patient will suffer the harm without treatment; it is a major factor in selecting candidates for transplantation of scarce organs as well as for "triaging" patients under emergency conditions. . . .

Urgency captures the aspect of who is worse off that is future directed, but ignores how well or badly off a person has been in the past. I believe that both expected and past health states are relevant to a judgment of how badly off people are, not just how bad a person's health is now.

HOW MUCH PRIORITY SHOULD THE WORSE OFF RECEIVE IN HEALTH RESOURCE PRIORITIZATION?

The third issue in developing a moral framework for determining what priority the worse off should receive in health-care resource prioritization is how much priority they should receive. The reasons for support of priority to the worse off will affect the answer. Contractualist reasoning, which requires minimizing the complaint of the person with the greatest complaint, may support maximizing the position of the worst off, or giving the worst off absolute priority. However, giving the worst off absolute priority over others for health-care resource prioritization is not plausible because it encounters what has been called the "bottomless pit" problem (Daniels, 1985). If the worst off are understood, for example, as the very severely cognitively and physically disabled who have an extremely low health-related quality of life, health interventions in the form of health care and other supportive services may provide them with only very small benefits but at very great cost. If improving their condition is given absolute priority, there may be almost no end to what could be done to provide them with minimal marginal gains consuming near limitless resources; greatly expanded medical research on their conditions, even if very unpromising and at very great cost, could also have some very small expected benefit for them. Even if some minimal threshold of significance of benefits must be met for the claim of the worst off to receive priority, great resources would be required to go to the worst off before any needs of others could be met. If we give absolute priority to the

worse off, not just the worst off, and maximize the health-related quality of life of each next most worse off group after doing everything possible for those worse off than they, few resources would remain for the important health needs of most of the population who enjoy a higher health-related quality of life.

Some balance is clearly required between giving special priority or weight to the needs of the worse off and other relevant moral considerations such as using limited resources to maximize overall health benefits and to meet the needs of those better off. Ideally, we want a principled basis or reason(s) for how much priority to give the worse off, but it is not clear what that principled basis would be. Rather, it seems that most people have independent moral concerns for the worse off and for aggregate health benefits that must be balanced, but no precise weight for the different concerns. . . . Lacking any principled basis for how much priority to give to the worse off, we could ask people, using the person trade-off methodology with various hypothetical choice scenarios, how much benefit to others they are prepared to sacrifice in order to treat the worse off. . . . Alternatively, we could turn to fair procedures, either political procedures or procedures within private health plans, to make these trade-offs. . . .

CONCLUSION

I hope it is abundantly clear by now that the question of what priority the worse off should receive in health-care resource prioritization raises a large agenda of normative issues that have received far too little attention to date. The full details and complexities of the three questions I have briefly discussed must be systematically explored: What is the moral justification for giving priority to the worse off for health-care resource prioritization? Who are the worse off for health-care resource prioritization? How much priority should the worse off receive in health-care resource prioritization?

Moreover, in applying a moral framework for priority to the worse off in health-care resource prioritization, it will likely be necessary to distinguish different contexts in which decisions are made—for example, funding different health programs versus selecting among patients for scarce treatment, and the various roles and responsibilities of different decision makers in those different contexts. I have raised many questions and issues without providing and defending solutions to many of them; in part, this is no doubt my own failing, but I believe it reflects as well the quite undeveloped state of serious work on the issues of health-care resource prioritization and allocation. Bioethicists and others of a normative bent should get to work.

REFERENCES

Daniels, N. (1985). *Just Health Care*. Cambridge: Cambridge University Press.

Daniels, N. (1993). Rationing fairly: Programmatic considerations. *Bioethics* 7(2–3), 224–33.

Nagel, T. (1979). Equality. *Mortal Questions*. Cambridge: Cambridge University Press.

Nagel, T. (1991). *Equality and Partiality*. Oxford: Oxford University Press.

Nord, E. (1993). The trade-off between severity of illness and treatment effect in cost-value analysis of health care. *Health Policy* 24, 227–38.

Parfit, D. (1991). Equality or priority? *The Lindley Lecture*. Copyright: Department of Philosophy, University of Kansas.

Rawls, J. (1971). *A Theory of Justice*. Cambridge, MA: Harvard University Press.

Scanlon, T. (1998). *What We Owe to Each Other*. Cambridge, MA: Harvard University Press.

Suggested Readings for Chapter 8

Acheson, Sir Donald, et al. *Independent Inquiry into Inequalities in Health: Report*. London: The Stationery Office, published for the Department of Health, 1998. http://www.archive.official-documents.co.uk/document/doh/ih/contents.htm (including other "Official Documents" in years following 1998).

American Journal of Bioethics 1 (Spring 2001). Special issue on "Justice, Health, and Healthcare."

Anand, Sudhir, Peter, Fabienne, and Sen, Amartya, eds. *Public Health, Ethics, and Equity*. Oxford: Oxford University Press, 2004.

Benatar, Solomon R. "Health Care Reform in the New South Africa." *New England Journal of Medicine* 336 (March 20, 1997), 891–95.

Bodenheimer, Thomas. "The Oregon Health Plan—Lessons for the Nation." *New England Journal of Medicine* 337: 9, 10 (1997), 651–56, 720–24.

Brock, Dan W. "Justice and the ADA: Does Prioritizing and Rationing Health Care Discriminate against the Disabled?" *Social Philosophy and Policy* 12 (1995), 159–85.

Buchanan, Allen. "Health-Care Delivery and Resource Allocation." In Robert M. Veatch, ed. *Medical Ethics*, 2nd ed. Boston: Jones and Bartlett, 1997, 321–61.

———. *Justice, Legitimacy, and Self-Determination: Moral Foundations for International Law*. Oxford: Oxford University Press, 2004.

———. "Managed Care: Rationing without Justice, But Not Unjustly." *Journal of Health Politics, Policy, and Law* 23 (1998), 617–34.

———. "Trust in Managed Care Organizations." *Kennedy Institute of Ethics Journal* 10 (2000), 189–212.

Callahan, Daniel. *Setting Limits: Medical Goals in an Aging Society*. New York: Simon & Schuster, 1987.

———. *What Kind of Life: The Limits of Medical Progress*. New York: Simon & Schuster, 1990.

Churchill, Larry M. *Self-Interest and Universal Health Care: Why Well-Insured Americans Should Support Coverage for Everyone*. Cambridge, MA: Harvard University Press, 1994.

Daniels, Norman. "Equity and Population Health: Toward a Broader Bioethics Agenda." *Hastings Center Report* 36: 4 (2006), 22–35.

———. "Four Unsolved Rationing Problems: A Challenge." *Hastings Center Report* 24 (July–August 1994), 27–29.

———. "Is There a Right to Health Care and, if so, What does it Encompass?" In Helga Kuhse and Peter Singer, eds. *A Companion to Bioethics*. Oxford: Blackwell Publishers, 1998.

———. *Just Health Care*. New York: Cambridge University Press, 1985.

———. *Justice and Justification: Reflective Equilibrium in Theory and Practice*. New York: Cambridge University Press, 1997.

———. "National Health-Care Reform." In Robert M. Veatch, ed., *Medical Ethics*, 2nd ed. Boston: Jones and Bartlett, 1997, 415–41.

———. "Rationing Fairly: Programmatic Considerations." *Bioethics* 7 (1993), 224–33.

Daniels, Norman, Kennedy, Bruce, and Kawachi, Ichiro. "Health and Inequality, or, Why Justice is Good for Our Health." In Anand, Peter, and Sen (above).

Daniels, Norman, Light, Donald W., and Caplan, Ronald L. *Benchmarks of Fairness for Health Care Reform*. New York: Oxford University Press, 1996.

Dougherty, Charles J. "And Still the Only Advanced Nation Without Universal Health Coverage." *Hastings Center Report* 27 (July–August 1997), 39–41.

———. *Back to Reform: Values, Markets, and the Health Care System*. New York: Oxford University Press, 1996.

Engelhardt, H. Tristram. "Freedom and Moral Diversity: The Moral Failures of Health Care in the Welfare State." *Social Philosophy & Policy* 14 (1997), 180–96.

Epstein, Richard. *Mortal Peril: Our Inalienable Right to Health Care?* Reading, MA: Addison-Wesley, 1997.

Fleck, Leonard. "Just Caring: Oregon, Health Care Rationing, and Informed Democratic Deliberation." *Journal of Medicine and Philosophy* 18 (1994), 367–88.

Goold, Susan D. "Allocating Health Care: Cost-Utility Analysis, Informed Democratic Decision Making, or the Veil of Ignorance?" *Journal of Health Politics, Policy, and Law* 21 (1996), 69–98.

Gostin, Lawrence O. "Securing Health or Just Health Care? The Effect of the Health Care System on the Health of America." *Saint Louis University Law Journal* 39 (1994), 7–43.

Hall, Mark A. *Making Medical Spending Decisions: The Law, Ethics, and Economics of Rationing Mechanisms.* New York: Oxford University Press, 1997.

Hessler, Kristen, and Buchanan, Allen. "Specifying the Content of the Human Right to Health Care." In Rosamond Rhodes, Margaret P. Battin, and Anita Silvers, eds. *Medicine and Social Justice.* New York: Oxford University Press, 2002, 84–96.

Human Rights Watch (an organization dedicated to global protection of rights). www.hrw.org/

Jones, Charles. *Global Justice: Defending Cosmopolitanism.* Oxford: Oxford University Press, 1999.

Journal of Health Politics, Policy and Law 24 (February 1999). "Special Reports from the Field on the Oregon Plan."

Journal of Medicine and Philosophy 19 (August 1994). Special issue on the "Oregon Health Plan."

Journal of Medicine and Philosophy 26 (April 2001). Special issue on "Children and a Fair Share of Health and Dental Care."

Marchand, Sarah, Wikler, Dan, and Landesman, Bruce. "Class, Health, and Justice." *Milbank Quarterly* 76 (1998), 449–67.

Mechanic, David. "Dilemmas in Rationing Health Care Services: The Case for Implicit Rationing." *British Medical Journal* 310 (1995), 1655–59.

Menzel, Paul, and Light, Donald W. "A Conservative Case for Universal Access to Health Care." *Hastings Center Report* 36: 4 (2006): 36–45.

———. *Strong Medicine: The Ethical Rationing of Health Care.* New York: Oxford University Press, 1990.

Mollendorf, Darrel. *Cosmopolitan Justice.* New York: Westview Press, 2002.

Murphy, Liam. "The Demands of Beneficence." *Philosophy and Public Affairs* 22 (Fall 1993).

———. *Moral Demands in Nonideal Theory.* Oxford: Oxford University Press, 2003.

Nord, Erik. *Cost-Value Analysis in Health Care: Making Sense out of QALYs.* Cambridge: Cambridge University Press, 1999.

———. "Concerns for the Worse Off: Fair Innings Versus Severity." *Social Science and Medicine* 60 (2005), 257–63.

———, et al. "Incorporating Societal Concerns for Fairness in Numerical Valuations of Health Programmes." *Health Economics* 8 (1999), 25–39.

Nussbaum, Martha C. "Patriotism and Cosmopolitanism." In Cohen, Joshua, ed., *For Love of Country: Debating the Limits of Patriotism.* Boston: Beacon, 1996.

———, and Sen, Amartya, eds. *The Quality of Life.* Oxford: Clarendon Press, 1993.

Pellegrino, Edmund. "Managed Care and Managed Competition: Some Ethical Reflections." *Calyx* 4 (Fall 1994), 1–5.

Pogge, Thomas W. "Cosmopolitanism and Sovereignty." *Ethics* 103 (October 1992).

———. ed. *Freedom from Poverty as a Human Right: Who Owes What to the Very Poor?* Oxford: Oxford University Press, 2007.

———. ed. *Global Justice.* London: Blackwell Publishers, 2001.

———. "Human Flourishing and Universal Justice." *Social Philosophy and Policy* 16 (1999); also in Ellen F. Paul, et al., eds. *Human Flourishing.* Cambridge: Cambridge University Press, 1999, 333–61.

———. "Human Rights and Global Health: A Research Program." *Metaphilosophy* 36 (2005), 182–209.

———. *World Poverty and Human Rights.* Cambridge: Polity Press, 2002.

Powers, Madison. "Managed Care: How Economic Incentive Reforms Went Wrong." *Kennedy Institute of Ethics Journal* 7 (1997), 353–60.

———, and Faden, Ruth. *Social Justice: The Moral Foundations of Public Health and Health Policy.* New York: Oxford University Press, 2006.

President's Commission for the Study of Ethical Problems in Medicine and Biomedical and Behavioral Research. *Securing Access to Health Care.* Vols. 1–3. Washington, DC: U.S. Government Printing Office, 1983.

Rawls, John. *The Law of Peoples.* Cambridge, MA: Harvard University Press, 1999.

Rhodes, Rosamond, Battin, Margaret P., and Silvers, Anita, eds. *Medicine and Social Justice.* New York: Oxford University Press, 2002.

Singer, Peter. *One World: The Ethics of Globalization.* New Haven: Yale University Press, 2002.

Ubel, Peter A. "The Challenge of Measuring Community Values in Ways Appropriate for Setting Health Care Priorities." *Kennedy Institute of Ethics Journal* 9 (1999), 263–84.

———. *Pricing Life: Why It's Time for Health Care Rationing.* Cambridge, MA: MIT Press, 2000.

———, and Goold, Susan Dorr. "'Rationing' Health Care: Not All Definitions Are Created Equal." *Archives of Internal Medicine* 158 (February 9, 1998), 209–14.

Unger, Peter. *Living High and Letting Die: Our Illusion of Innocence.* Oxford: Oxford University Press, 1996.

Veatch, Robert M. "Single Payers and Multiple Lists: Must Everyone Get the Same Coverage in a Universal Health Plan?" *Kennedy Institute of Ethics Journal* 7 (1997), 153–69.

World Health Organization. *The World Health Report 2006: Working Together for Health.* Geneva: World Health Organization, 2006. http://www.who.int/whr/en/

Yarborough, Mark. "The Private Health Insurance Industry: The Real Barrier to Healthcare Access?" *Cambridge Quarterly of Healthcare Ethics* 3 (1994), 99–107.

Chapter 9
Public Health

Introduction

This chapter examines emerging frameworks for public health ethics and some of the ethical issues that arise in the public health context. Specifically, this chapter discusses the foundations of public health ethics and the issues arising in the management of communicable diseases and emergency preparedness.

WHAT IS PUBLIC HEALTH?

We can point to various definitions of public health, but the Institute of Medicine has offered a concise and influential version: "Public health is what we, as a society, do collectively to assure the conditions for people to be healthy."[1] The responsibilities to assure conditions for people to be healthy fall to the public health infrastructure at the local, state, and federal government levels.

Critical functions of public health include protecting the health of communities through prevention of unhealthy conditions, injuries, and illnesses; investigation and intervention during disease outbreaks; and policymaking to prepare for and respond to issues that threaten the public health. Historically, these functions translated into efforts dedicated to sanitation, safety, infection control, and health promotion.

Public health has long had a role in assuring that clean drinking water is available and that wastewater is properly treated and disposed of, that workers are not exposed to unsafe work environments, that communicable diseases are prevented when possible and treated quickly when they arise. Helping to craft public policy that will promote safe behaviors and healthy lifestyles is also a major function. We often take these efforts for granted but we quite literally could not live without them.

With the events of September 11, 2001, and Hurricane Katrina, public health is increasingly viewed as part of the frontline protection of populations in the event of bioterrorist attack, natural disaster, or pandemic outbreak. New technologies, such as genetics, computerized databases, and global communication, are being incorporated into public health efforts, allowing for more rapid detection, treatment, and prevention of conditions that threaten the health of communities and populations.

Both the traditional and the more modern applications of public health raise ethical issues. Public health's distinctive focus on population or community interests can have the apparent effect of discounting the importance of the individual. For example, when an individual is identified as carrying a highly contagious infection, from a public health perspective the interests of the individual in autonomous decision making and privacy may be trumped by the interests of the community in preventing the spread of infection. As highlighted throughout this chapter, the community or population perspective raises significant ethical issues and tensions, many of which are unique to public health.

FOUNDATIONS OF PUBLIC HEALTH ETHICS

Those who work in public health have always faced ethical issues in the work of public health practice, research, and policy making. They have recognized that the public health perspective requires thinking about the appropriate balancing of individual rights against community and population interests.

The dominant approaches in bioethics over the latter half of the twentieth century, however, have emphasized the importance of individual rights—the right of individuals to control what is done to them, whether in medical treatment or biomedical research. Public health demands consideration of the interests of communities and populations, which can be at odds with those of individuals. Recently, Kass[2] and others[3] have convincingly argued that public health ethics deserves its own place within bioethics, and the need for an articulated ethical framework specific to public health. In the first selection of this chapter, Childress et al. examine the unique ethical and policy aspects of public health, and offer an ethics framework that explicitly acknowledges and attempts to balance the tensions between individual rights and public health goals.

One of the important aspects of public health is its global perspective, broadening considerations not only beyond individual concerns but also beyond traditional geographical and political borders. To adequately account for a global perspective, the late Jonathan Mann wrote compellingly about the importance of including a human rights perspective in any discussion of ethics and public health. One of his signature articles is included in the first section of this chapter.

The final essay in this section addresses ethical issues arising out of government initiatives to encourage healthy lifestyles. In this bioethics classic, Wikler examines the ethical tensions in public health policies that seek to reduce unhealthy behaviors, such as smoking and driving without seatbelts, through the use of incentives (smoking cessation programs), persuasion (public education campaigns), and coercion (hefty excise taxes and other penalties). His exposition of the issues translates easily into current debates over government intervention in private behavior, such as legislative initiatives focused on fast food and obesity, cellular phone use while driving, and smoking in public settings.

MANAGEMENT OF COMMUNICABLE DISEASES

Public health authorities play a critical role in preventing the spread of communicable diseases. Measures employed include assessing the scope and spread of disease through epidemiological investigation and surveillance, mandatory disease reporting by physicians and health care professionals, treating disease, and preventing disease. Prevention can be as simple as encouraging hand washing or the use of masks. It can also include vaccination, or in more extreme cases, removing the individual from public contact through the use of isolation or quarantine. The measures chosen by public health authorities to manage communicable diseases may be voluntary or mandatory depending on disease severity and transmissibility, the likelihood of individual compliance, and an assessment of the risk to the public, among other things.

Governmental authority to restrict the liberty of individuals for the benefit of public health is grounded in the law. It emanates from the police power of the state found in the U.S. Constitution, and is subject to constitutional limitations of due process, which require that a state provide an individual notice and an opportunity to be heard in response to a deprivation of liberty.

In the first essay in this section, Gostin reflects on the legacy of the classic 1905 legal case *Jacobson v. Massachusetts* and its implications for state authority to restrict individual liberty for the benefit of public health. In *Jacobson*, the city of Cambridge,

Massachusetts, issued an order (authorized by state law) requiring all adults to be vaccinated during a smallpox epidemic. The Reverend Henning Jacobson refused vaccination and was fined five dollars (valued at approximately one hundred dollars today). Though the law did not require that vaccination be forced upon Jacobson against his will, Jacobson challenged the state's exercise of police power as an unconstitutional infringement on his personal liberty. The U.S. Supreme Court held that the state had not exceeded its authority, subordinating Jacobson's liberty right to the public interest in preventing smallpox. Discussing the tension between individual liberty and the police powers of the state, the Court stated:

There is, of course, a sphere within which the individual may assert the supremacy of his own will, and rightfully dispute the authority of any human government, especially of any free government existing under a written constitution, to interfere with the exercise of that will. But it is equally true that in every well-ordered society charged with the duty of conserving the safety of its members the rights of the individual in respect of his liberty may at times, under the pressure of great dangers, be subjected to such restraint, to be enforced by reasonable regulations, as the safety of the general public may demand.[4]

Since *Jacobson*, courts have continued to defer to state powers to protect the public's health and safety in the face of health risks to third parties imposed by individual conduct. In the context of contagious diseases, this has included upholding government authority to examine individuals, isolate sick patients, quarantine healthy people exposed to contagious disease, and even treat affected individuals.

Quarantine and isolation are among the most significant restrictions on individual liberty that may be authorized in response to contagious disease, and they are infrequently invoked. In June 2007, however, the federal government in the United States detained a man with a multidrug-resistant form of tuberculosis under a federal isolation order. Tuberculosis can be spread through the air when an infected person coughs or sneezes, though transmission of the disease to another person typically requires prolonged exposure to the infected person. The man detained had known he had tuberculosis but still left the United States on vacation and potentially exposed airline passengers and others to the disease. Upon his return, the federal order was issued and the man was transported to the isolation ward of a hospital for treatment until he was no longer contagious. Before this case, it had been over forty years since the U.S. government had issued an isolation order.

In Wynia's article in this section of the chapter, he delves into the ethical justifications for quarantine. When a healthy person has been exposed to a contagious disease but is not in fact infected, he suggests that quarantine may not be fully justified by John Stuart Mill's "harm principle." Instead of preventing harm to others, Wynia argues that quarantine in this type of situation merely prevents the *risk* of harm—an insufficient justification for quarantine. Wynia further advocates attention to many of the general moral considerations and concepts discussed by Childress et al. in this chapter, including the use of least restrictive means, transparency, and accountability, among others, that must be considered when the government considers restrictions on individual liberty in the face of contagious disease.

Immunization has proven to be one of the most effective public health interventions in the prevention of infectious disease. A universal childhood immunization program has long been in effect in the United States. Support for such programs, however, is eroding. Many are no longer personally familiar with the devastating consequences of diseases that plagued childhood in the mid twentieth century. Diseases such as polio, measles, mumps, and rubella have been eliminated or significantly reduced because of immunization programs. The invisibility of the benefits of vaccination and the more visible real and perceived potential for adverse reactions from vaccination have prompted a growing number of parents (on behalf of their children) and individuals to opt out of vaccination. Indeed, most states have opt-out provisions for childhood vaccination requirements, usually based on religious belief or other principle-based objections.

For a vaccination program to be an effective prevention strategy, total coverage of the population is not required. But a certain number of immune individuals (either through vaccination or "natural" immunity gained from previous exposure) must be present to prevent the spread of the disease—a phenomenon referred to as herd immunity. Individual decisions to opt out of vaccination based on personal risk-benefit calculations potentially threaten the health of more than just the individual, and may place the health of the population at risk in the event of an outbreak of infectious disease. In the case of population-wide vaccination programs, the classic public health tension between the fair distribution of risks and benefits and respect for autonomy becomes apparent. The excerpt by Feudtner and Marcuse explores the reasons for the decline in immunization rates and advocates for consideration of ethics along with epidemiology and economics in making policy decisions about vaccination programs. They arrive at seven objectives to guide immunization policy, recognizing that decision making will require explicit or implicit value judgments and balancing of competing ethical principles. They recommend that evaluation of policy alternatives expressly recognize ethical implications of decision making. For example, a coercive immunization policy may lower individual risk and more fairly distribute the burdens of herd immunity, but may violate autonomy and place a child at risk of an adverse event.

Surveillance is another public health measure that is critical in assessing and addressing the spread of disease. Surveillance of communicable diseases involves the collection, analysis, interpretation, and dissemination of data. Data are used to detect epidemics, prompt research, develop prevention and treatment plans, and describe the disease's natural history, among other things. One method of public health surveillance is reporting of newly diagnosed cases of disease. Depending on the state, disease reporting by providers may be mandatory or voluntary. For example, providers may be required by state law to report diseases such as tuberculosis, measles, and mumps, as well as sexually transmitted diseases. Bayer and Fairchild discuss some of the ethical issues that have arisen in surveillance of one of the most devastating communicable diseases in the last 25 years, HIV/AIDS. They detail the history of HIV/AIDS reporting in the United States, particularly the debates on whether reporting should be anonymous or identify the patient by name. Reporting, especially of identifiable information, raises tension between public health goals of preventing the spread of disease to third parties and an individual's medical privacy. Anonymous reporting allows tracking of the diseases and dedication of health care resources, but does not permit early treatment of those afflicted with the disease. In the early stages of HIV/AIDS surveillance, when no treatment was available, resistance to names reporting was significant. HIV/AIDS was and is a potentially stigmatizing condition, and names reporting raised fears of partner notification without consent and even restrictions on liberty, such as quarantine. As better treatments have become available, resistance to names reporting has decreased, as those who are identified may benefit from early intervention. As Bayer and Fairchild point out, concerns about privacy and confidentiality permeate all public health surveillance efforts and require careful balancing against the public health justifications for data and information.

The discussion of communicable diseases ends with a global perspective on HIV/AIDS presented by leaders in the worldwide battle against the epidemic. Piot and colleagues discuss past and future challenges to combating the devastating impact of HIV/AIDS. In their discussion, justice concerns pervade—poverty, inequity, unequal status of women, stigma, and, more recently, barriers to treatment access. All contribute to the unrelenting spread of the disease.

EMERGENCY PREPAREDNESS

The remaining five selections in this chapter focus on public health ethics in the context of emergency preparedness, specifically addressing issues related to bioterrorism, pandemic disease, and global health effects of war and terrorism. Among the classic public health ethics issues raised are the tension between individual autonomy and protecting populations, and justice in the distribution of scarce resources.

Bioterrorism and pandemic diseases have the potential to rapidly and seriously threaten the health of large numbers of people. The threat of bioterrorism was made all the more real following the 2001 terrorist bombings of the World Trade Center in New York City. Lethal anthrax spores were mailed by an unknown source to members of the U.S. Congress and the news media. The health of all who came into contact with the letters was at risk, including postal service employees and legislative aides. These events raised questions about how to prevent risk to larger groups of the population. More recently, the outbreak of severe acute respiratory syndrome (SARS) and the threat of avian influenza turned public attention to the prospect of pandemic disease. The increasing ease of worldwide travel means that country borders are ineffective defenses against highly communicable diseases. The ability to respond to public health emergencies, such as the anthrax attack, the threat of pandemic influenza, or natural catastrophes such as Hurricane Katrina, requires intensive planning, dedication of financial and nonfinancial resources, and rapid decision making. All aspects have ethical implications.

In the first selection in this section, Wynia and Gostin identify ethical challenges to emergency preparedness within the health care system. They focus on three major roles of the health care system in addressing health care-related threats to populations, including detection (reporting and access to care), containment (preventing the spread of disease, including isolation and quarantine), and treatment (care for affected persons). They conclude that the risk to individuals and communities posed by public health emergencies requires attending to these areas and to the ethical issues raised by them.

Without appropriate planning and preparation, resources for treatment and prevention will be strained in the event of a pandemic disease. For example, the process of developing vaccines to contain the spread of disease is time-consuming and costly, requiring choices and decisions about resource allocation in an already strained health care system. Once a vaccine is developed, vaccine demand can rapidly outpace manufacturers' ability to maintain supply, requiring rationing. The U.S. Department of Health and Human Services (DHHS) produced a Pandemic Influenza Plan, excerpted in this chapter, recommending priority distribution of vaccines when supplies are limited. The Plan classifies specific populations based on job, age, or condition, and ranks them, placing priority on the need to minimize health impacts on the population. Under the Plan, the manufacturers of vaccines and certain health care workers are at the top of the list, and healthy persons aged 2 to 64 are at the bottom of the list. In contrast, Emanuel and Wertheimer arrive at an alternative ethical framework for decision making during a pandemic. Under their proposed life-cycle ranking, they place priority on maximizing life span, placing value on passing through each life stage from childhood to old age. Under the same fact scenario as used in the DHHS plan, they propose specific age distinctions and prioritize access to vaccines based on an individual's expected life years, resulting in a significantly different ranking, no longer placing healthy persons aged 2 to 64 at the bottom of the list.

Lo and Katz examine ethical dilemmas confronted at the frontlines of public health emergencies. They suggest that the traditional physician–patient relationship that emphasizes respect for patient autonomy must yield to the public's needs in an emergency, stressing throughout the differences between clinical and public health practice. They illuminate the difficulties in the role shift through two cases. In the first, a patient requests immunization during a vaccine shortage but does not meet the criteria for vaccination under public health guidelines. In the second case, a patient refuses quarantine. Physicians are advised to address the patient's needs and concerns and act in the patient's best interests *to the extent possible*, but to hold firm to the overriding responsibility to the common good.

In the final selection in this chapter, the public health implications of war and terrorism are addressed. In their article, Sidel and Levy highlight the health effects of policy decisions related to war and terrorism. They strongly argue for advocacy and action to address violations of civil liberties and human rights as well as social justice issues such as poverty and social inequity that arise as a consequence of war and terrorism.

The wide array of practices and policies that fall under the heading of public health bring with them an equally wide array of ethical issues. The articles in this chapter bring to light many of the issues and propose a range of approaches for addressing them, not in ways that are meant to provide the last word in answering them but to promote deeper reflection and thoughtful discussion of the critical questions they raise.

A.C.M.
J.P.K.

NOTES

1. Institute of Medicine, *The Future of the Public's Health in the 21st Century* (National Academy Press, Washington, DC, 2003).

2. Nancy Kass, "An Ethics Framework for Public Health," *American Journal of Public Health* 91(11): 1776–1782; November 2001.

3. Daniel Callahan and Bruce Jennings, "Ethics and Public Health: Forging a Strong Relationship," *American Journal of Public Health* 92(2): 169–176; February 2002.

4. *Jacobson v. Massachusetts*, 197 U.S. 11, 29 (1905)

Foundations of Public Health Ethics

JAMES F. CHILDRESS, RUTH FADEN, RUTH D. GAARE, LAWRENCE O. GOSTIN, JEFFREY KAHN, RICHARD J. BONNIE, NANCY E. KASS, ANNA C. MASTROIANNI, JONATHAN D. MORENO AND PHILLIP NIEBURG

Public Health Ethics: Mapping the Terrain

James F. Childress is the Hollingsworth Professor of Ethics and Professor of Medical Education at the University of Virginia.

Ruth Faden is the Philip Franklin Wagley Professor of Biomedical Ethics and Executive Director of the Phoebe R. Berman Bioethics Institute at Johns Hopkins University.

Ruth D. Gaare is executive director of the University of Virginia Institute for Practical Ethics and a core faculty member of the Medical School's Center for Biomedical Ethics.

Lawrence O. Gostin is Professor of Law at Georgetown University, Professor of Public Health at Johns Hopkins University, and the Director of the Center for Law & the Public's Health at Johns Hopkins and Georgetown Universities.

Jeffrey Kahn is Director of the Center for Bioethics and holds the Maas Family Endowed Chair in Bioethics at the University of Minnesota.

Richard J. Bonnie is Professor of Law, Professor of Psychiatric Medicine, and Director, University of Virginia Institute of Law, Psychiatry and Public Policy.

Nancy E. Kass is the Phoebe R. Berman Professor of Bioethics and Public Health in the Johns Hopkins Bloomberg School of Public Health.

Anna C. Mastroianni is Associate Professor at the University of Washington School of Law and Institute for Public Health Genetics.

Jonathan D. Moreno is David and Lyn Silfen University Professor at the University of Pennsylvania and a Senior Fellow at the Center for American Progress.

Phillip Nieburg is Senior Associate and Co-chair of the Prevention Committee on the HIV/AIDS Task Force at the Center for Strategic and International Studies.

From *Journal of Law, Medicine and Ethics* 30 (2002), 170–178.
Notes omitted.

Public health ethics, like the field of public health it addresses, traditionally has focused more on practice and particular cases than on theory, with the result that some concepts, methods, and boundaries remain largely undefined. This paper attempts to provide a rough conceptual map of the terrain of public health ethics. We begin by briefly defining public health and identifying general features of the field that are particularly relevant for a discussion of public health ethics.

Public health is primarily concerned with the health of the entire population, rather than the health of individuals. Its features include an emphasis on the promotion of health and the prevention of disease and disability; the collection and use of epidemiological data, population surveillance, and other forms of empirical quantitative assessment; a recognition of the multidimensional nature of the determinants of health; and a focus on the complex interactions of many factors—biological, behavioral, social, and environmental—in developing effective interventions.

How can we distinguish public health from medicine? While medicine focuses on the treatment and cure of individual patients, public health aims to understand and ameliorate the causes of disease and disability in a population. In addition, whereas the physician–patient relationship is at the center of medicine, public health involves interactions and relationships among many professionals and members of the community as well as agencies of government in the development, implementation, and assessment of interventions. From this starting point, we can suggest that public health systems consist of all the people and actions, including laws, policies, practices, and activities, that have the primary purpose of protecting and improving the health of the public.[1] While we need not assume that public health systems are tightly structured or centrally directed, we recognize that they include a wide range of governmental, private and non-profit organizations, as well as professionals from many disciplines, all of which (alone and together) have a stake in and an effect on a community's health. Government has a unique role in public health because of its responsibility, grounded in its police powers, to protect the public's health and welfare, because it alone can undertake certain interventions, such as regulation, taxation, and the expenditure of public funds, and because many, perhaps most, public health programs are public goods that cannot

be optimally provided if left to individuals or small groups.

The Institute of Medicine's landmark 1988 definition of public health provides additional insight: "Public health is what we, as a society, do collectively to assure the conditions in which people can be healthy."[2] The words "what we, as a society, do collectively" suggest the need for cooperative behavior and relationships built on overlapping values and trust. The words "to assure the conditions in which people can be healthy" suggest a far-reaching agenda for public health that focuses attention not only on the medical needs of individuals, but on fundamental social conditions that affect population levels of morbidity and mortality. From an ethical standpoint, public health activities are generally understood to be teleological (end-oriented) and consequentialist—the health of the public is the primary end that is sought and the primary outcome for measuring success. Defining and measuring "health" is not easy, as we will emphasize below, but, in addition, "public" is a complex concept with at least three dimensions that are important for our discussion of ethics.

First, public can be used to mean the "numerical public," i.e., the target population. In view of public health's goal of producing net health benefits for the population, this meaning of public is very important. In measurement and analysis, the "numerical public" reflects the utilitarian view that each individual counts as one and only one. In this context, ethical analysis focuses on issues in measurement, many of which raise considerations of justice. For example, how should we define a population, how should we compare gains in life expectancy with gains in health-related quality of life, and whose values should be used in making those judgments?

Second, public is what we collectively do through government and public agency—we can call this "political public." Government provides much of the funding for a vast array of public health functions, and public health professionals in governmental roles are the focal point of much collective activity. In the United States, as Lawrence Gostin notes, government "is compelled by its role as the elected representative of the community to act affirmatively to promote the health of the people," even though it "cannot unduly invade individuals' rights in the name of the communal good."[3] The government is a central player in public health because of the collective responsibility it must assume and implement. The state's use of its police powers for public health raises important ethical questions, particularly about the justification and limits of governmental coercion and about its duty to treat all citizens equally in exercising these powers. In a liberal, pluralistic democracy, the justification of coercive policies, as well as other policies, must rest on moral reasons that the public in whose name the policies are carried out could reasonably be expected to accept.

Third, public, defined as what we do collectively in a broad sense, includes all forms of social and community action affecting public health—we can call this "communal public." Ethical analysis on this level extends beyond the political public. People collectively, outside of government and with private funds, often have greater freedom to undertake public health interventions since they do not have to justify their actions to the political public. However, their actions are still subject to various moral requirements, including, for instance, respect for individual autonomy, liberty, privacy and confidentiality, and transparency in disclosure of conflicts of interest.

GENERAL MORAL CONSIDERATIONS

In providing a map of the terrain of public health ethics, we do not suggest that there is a consensus about the methods and content of public health ethics. Controversies persist about theory and method in other areas of applied or practical ethics, and it should not be surprising that variety also prevails in public health ethics. The terrain of public health ethics includes a loose set of general moral considerations—clusters of moral concepts and norms that are variously called values, principles, or rules—that are arguably relevant to public health. Public health ethics, in part, involves ongoing efforts to specify and to assign weights to these general moral considerations in the context of particular policies, practices, and actions, in order to provide concrete moral guidance.

Recognizing general moral considerations in public health ethics does not entail a commitment to any particular theory or method. What we describe and propose is compatible with several approaches. To take one major example, casuistical reasoning (examining the relevant similarities and differences between cases) is not only compatible with, but indispensable to our conception of public health ethics. Not only do—or should—public health agents examine new situations they confront in light of general moral considerations, but they should also focus on a new situation's relevant similarities to and differences from paradigm or precedent cases—cases that have gained a relatively

settled moral consensus. Whether a relatively settled moral consensus is articulated first in a general moral consideration or in precedent cases does not constitute a fundamental issue—both are relevant. Furthermore, some of the precedents may concern how general moral considerations are interpreted, specified, and balanced in some public health activity, especially where conflicts emerge.

Conceptions of morality usually recognize a formal requirement of universalizability in addition to a substantive requirement of attention to human welfare. Whatever language is used, this formal feature requires that we treat similar cases in a similar way. This requirement undergirds casuistical reasoning in morality as well as in law. In public health ethics, for example, any recommendations for an HIV screening policy must take into account both past precedents in screening for other infectious diseases and the precedents the new policy will create for, say, screening for genetic conditions. Much of the moral argument will hinge on which similarities and differences between cases are morally relevant, and that argument will often, though not always, appeal to general moral considerations. We can establish the relevance of a set of these considerations in part by looking at the kinds of moral appeals that public health agents make in deliberating about and justifying their actions as well as at debates about moral issues in public health. The relevant general moral considerations include:

- producing benefits;
- avoiding, preventing, and removing harms;
- producing the maximal balance of benefits over harms and other costs (often called utility);
- distributing benefits and burdens fairly (distributive justice) and ensuring public participation, including the participation of affected parties (procedural justice);
- respecting autonomous choices and actions, including liberty of action;
- protecting privacy and confidentiality;
- keeping promises and commitments;
- disclosing information as well as speaking honestly and truthfully (often grouped under transparency); and
- building and maintaining trust.

Several of these general moral considerations—especially benefiting others, preventing and removing harms, and utility—provide a *prima facie* warrant for many activities in pursuit of the goal of public health. It is sufficient for our purposes to note that public health activities have their grounding in general moral considerations, and that public health identifies one major broad benefit that societies and governments ought to pursue. The relation of public health to the whole set of general moral considerations is complex. Some general moral considerations support this pursuit; institutionalizing several others may be a condition for or means to public health (we address this point later when we discuss human rights and public health); and yet, in particular cases, some of the same general moral considerations may limit or constrain what may be done in pursuit of public health. Hence, conflicts may occur among these general moral considerations.

The content of these various general moral considerations can be divided and arranged in several ways—for instance, some theories may locate one or more of these concepts under others. But, whatever theory one embraces, the whole set of general moral considerations roughly captures the moral content of public health ethics. It then becomes necessary to address several practical questions. First, how can we make these general moral considerations more specific and concrete in order to guide action? Second, how can we resolve conflicts among them? Some of the conflicts will concern how much weight and significance to assign to the ends and effects of protecting and promoting public health relative to the other considerations that limit and constrain ways to pursue such outcomes. While each general moral consideration may limit and constrain public health activities in some circumstances, for our purposes, justice or fairness, respect for autonomy and liberty, and privacy and confidentiality are particularly noteworthy in this regard.

SPECIFYING AND WEIGHTING GENERAL MORAL CONSIDERATIONS

We do not present a universal public health ethic. Although arguably these general moral considerations find support in various societies and cultures, an analysis of the role of cultural context in public health ethics is beyond the scope of this paper. Instead, we focus here on public health ethics in the particular setting of the United States, with its traditions, practices, and legal and constitutional requirements, all of which set directions for and circumscribe public health

ethics. (Below we will indicate how this conception of public health ethics relates to human rights.)

General moral considerations have two major dimensions. One is their meaning and range or scope; the other is their weight or strength. The first determines the extent of conflict among them—if their range or scope is interpreted in certain ways, conflicts may be increased or reduced. The second dimension determines when different considerations yield to others in cases of conflict.

Specifying the meaning and range or scope of general moral considerations—the first dimension—provides increasingly concrete guidance in public health ethics. A common example is specifying respect for autonomy by rules of voluntary, informed consent. However, it would be a mistake to suppose that respect for autonomy requires consent in all contexts of public health or to assume that consent alone sufficiently specifies the duty to respect autonomy in public health settings. Indeed, specifying the meaning and scope of general moral considerations entails difficult moral work. Nowhere is this more evident in public health ethics than with regard to considerations of justice. Explicating the demands of justice in allocating public health resources and in setting priorities for public health policies, or in determining whom they should target, remains among the most daunting challenges in public health ethics.

The various general moral considerations are not absolute. Each may conflict with another and each may have to yield in some circumstances. At most, then, these general moral considerations identify features of actions, practices, and policies that make them *prima facie* or presumptively right or wrong, i.e., right or wrong, all other things being equal. But since any particular action, practice, or policy for the public's health may also have features that infringe one or more of these general moral considerations, it will be necessary to determine which of them has priority. Some argue for a lexical or serial ordering, in which one general moral consideration, while not generally absolute, has priority over another. For instance, one theory might hold that protecting or promoting public health always has priority over privacy, while another might hold that individual liberty always has priority over protecting or promoting public health. Neither of these priority rules is plausible, and any priority rule that is plausible will probably involve tight or narrow specifications of the relevant general moral considerations to reduce conflicts. From our standpoint, it is better to recognize the need to balance general moral considerations in particular circumstances when conflicts arise. We cannot determine their weights in advance, only in particular contexts that may affect their weights—for instance, promises may not have the same moral weights in different contexts.

RESOLVING CONFLICTS AMONG GENERAL MORAL CONSIDERATIONS

We do not believe it is possible to develop an algorithm to resolve all conflicts among general moral considerations. Such conflicts can arise in multiple ways. For example, it is common in public health practice and policy for conflicts to emerge between privacy and justice (for instance, the state collects and records private information in disease registries about individuals in order to allocate and provide access to resources for appropriate prevention and treatment services), or between different conceptions of justice (for instance, a government with a finite public health budget must decide whether to dedicate resources to vaccination or to treatment of conditions when they arise). In this paper, however, we focus on one particular permutation of conflicts among general moral considerations that has received the most attention in commentary and in law. This is the conflict between the general moral considerations that are generally taken to instantiate the goal of public health—producing benefits, preventing harms, and maximizing utility—and those that express other moral commitments. For conflicts that assume this structure, we propose five "justificatory conditions": effectiveness, proportionality, necessity, least infringement, and public justification. These conditions are intended to help determine whether promoting public health warrants overriding such values as individual liberty or justice in particular cases.

Effectiveness: It is essential to show that infringing one or more general moral considerations will probably protect public health. For instance, a policy that infringes one or more general moral considerations in the name of public health but has little chance of realizing its goal is ethically unjustified.

Proportionality: It is essential to show that the probable public health benefits outweigh the infringed general moral considerations—this condition is sometimes called proportionality. For instance, the policy may breach autonomy or privacy and have undesirable consequences. All of the positive features and benefits must be balanced against the negative features and effects.

Necessity: Not all effective and proportionate policies are necessary to realize the public health goal that is sought. The fact that a policy will infringe a general moral consideration provides a strong moral reason to seek an alternative strategy that is less morally troubling. This is the logic of a *prima facie* or presumptive general moral consideration. For instance, all other things being equal, a policy that provides incentives for persons with tuberculosis to complete their treatment until cured will have priority over a policy that forcibly detains such persons in order to ensure the completion of treatment. Proponents of the forcible strategy have the burden of moral proof. This means that the proponents must have a good faith belief, for which they can give supportable reasons, that a coercive approach is necessary. In many contexts, this condition does not require that proponents provide empirical evidence by actually trying the alternative measures and demonstrating their failure.

Least infringement: Even when a proposed policy satisfies the first three justificatory conditions—that is, it is effective, proportionate, and essential in realizing the goal of public health—public health agents should seek to minimize the infringement of general moral considerations. For instance, when a policy infringes autonomy, public health agents should seek the least restrictive alternative; when it infringes privacy, they should seek the least intrusive alternative; and when it infringes confidentiality, they should disclose only the amount and kind of information needed, and only to those necessary, to realize the goal. The justificatory condition of least infringement could plausibly be interpreted as a corollary of necessity—for instance, a proposed coercive measure must be necessary in degree as well as in kind.

Public justification: When public health agents believe that one of their actions, practices, or policies infringes one or more general moral considerations, they also have a responsibility, in our judgment, to explain and justify that infringement, whenever possible, to the relevant parties, including those affected by the infringement. In the context of what we called "political public," public health agents should offer public justification for policies in terms that fit the overall social contract in a liberal, pluralistic democracy. This transparency stems in part from the requirement to treat citizens as equals and with respect by offering moral reasons, which in principle they could find acceptable, for policies that infringe general moral considerations. Transparency is also essential to creating and maintaining public trust; and it is crucial to establishing accountability. (Below we elaborate a process-oriented approach to public accountability that goes beyond public justification to include, as an expression of justice and fairness, input from the relevant affected parties in the formulation of policy.)

SCREENING PROGRAM EXAMPLE

An extended example may illustrate how these moral justificatory conditions function in public health ethics. Let us suppose that public health agents are considering whether to implement a screening program for HIV infection, tuberculosis, another infectious or contagious disease, or a genetic condition. . . .

The relevant justificatory conditions will require public health agents to consider whether any proposed program will be likely to realize the public health goal that is sought (effectiveness), whether its probable benefits will outweigh the infringed general moral considerations (proportionality), whether the policy is essential to realize the end (necessity), whether it involves the least infringement possible consistent with realizing the goal that is sought (least infringement), and whether it can be publicly justified. These conditions will give priority to selective programs over universal ones if the selective programs will realize the goal (as we note below, questions may arise about universality within selected categories, such as pregnant women), and to voluntary programs over mandatory ones if the voluntary programs will realize the goal.

Different screening programs may fail close scrutiny in light of one or more of these conditions. For instance, neither mandatory nor voluntary universal screening for HIV infection can meet these conditions in the society as a whole. Some voluntary and some mandatory selective screening programs for HIV infection can be justified, while others cannot. Mandatory screening of donated blood, organs, sperm, and ova is easily justified, and screening of individuals may also be justified in some settings where they can expose others to bodily fluids and potential victims cannot protect themselves. The question of whether and under what conditions screening of pregnant women for HIV infection should be instituted has been particularly controversial. Evan before the advent of effective treat-

ment for HIV infection and the identification of zidovudine (AZT) as effective in reducing the rate of perinatal transmission, there were calls for mandatory screening of pregnant women, especially in "high risk" communities. These calls were defeated by sound arguments that such policies entailed unjustifiable violations of autonomy, privacy, and justice. In effect, the recommended policies failed to satisfy any of the justificatory conditions we have proposed here.

However, once it was established that zidovudine could interrupt maternal–fetal transmission of HIV, the weight of the argument shifted in the direction of instituting screening programs of some type. The focus of the debate became the tensions between the public health interests in utility and efficiency, which argued for mandatory, selective screening in high-risk communities, and considerations of liberty, privacy, and justice, which argued for voluntary, universal screening.

In many situations, the most defensible public health policy for screening and testing *expresses* community rather than *imposes* it. Imposing community involves mandating or compelling testing through coercive measures. By contrast, expressing community involves taking steps to express solidarity with individuals, to protect their interests, and to gain their trust. Expressing community may include, for example, providing communal support, disclosing adequate information, protecting privacy and confidentiality, and encouraging certain choices. This approach seeks to make testing a reasonable, and perhaps moral, choice for individuals, especially by engendering public trust, rather than making it compulsory. Several diseases that might be subjected to screening for public health reasons involve stigma, and breaches of privacy and confidentiality may put individuals' employment and insurance at risk. Expressing community is often an appropriate strategy for public health, and, *ceteris paribus*, it has priority over imposing community through coercive policies.

PROCESSES OF PUBLIC ACCOUNTABILITY

Our discussion of the fifth justificatory condition—public justification—focused on providing public reasons for policies that infringe general moral considerations; this condition is particularly applicable in the political context. While public accountability includes public justification, it is broader—it is prospective as well as retrospective. It involves soliciting input from the relevant publics (the numerical, political, and communal publics) in the process of formulating public health policies, practices, and actions, as well as justifying to the relevant publics what is being undertaken. This is especially, but not only, important when one of the other *prima facie* general moral considerations is infringed, as with coercive protective measures to prevent epidemics. At a minimum, public accountability involves transparency in openly seeking information from those affected and in honestly disclosing relevant information to the public; it is indispensable for engendering and sustaining public trust, as well as for expressing justice.

Public accountability regarding health promotion or priority-setting for public health funding additionally might involve a more developed fair process. Noting that in a pluralistic society we are likely to find disagreement about which principles should govern issues such as priority-setting in health care, Norman Daniels calls for a fair process that includes the following elements: transparency and publicity about the reasons for a decision; appeals to rationales and evidence that fair-minded parties would agree are relevant; and procedures for appealing and revising decisions in light of challenges by various stakeholders. He explains why this process can facilitate social learning: "Since we may not be able to construct principles that yield fair decisions ahead of time, we need a process that allows us to develop those reasons over time as we face real cases."[4]

Public accountability also involves acknowledging the more complex relationship between public health and the public, one that addresses fundamental issues such as those involving characterization of risk and scientific uncertainty. Because public health depends for its success on the satisfaction of deeply personal health goals of individuals and groups in the population, concepts such as "health" and "risk" cannot be understood or acted upon on the basis of *a priori*, formal definitions or scientific analysis. Public accountability recognizes that the fundamental conceptualization of these terms is a critical part of the basic formulation of public health goals and problems to be addressed. This means that the public, along with scientific experts, plays an important role in the *analysis* of public health issues, as well as in the development and assessment of appropriate *strategies* for addressing them.

Risk characterization provides a helpful example. A National Research Council report, *Understanding Risk: Informing Decisions in a Democratic Society*, concluded that risk characterization is not properly understood if defined only as a summary of scientific information; rather, it is the outcome of a complex analytic-deliberative process—"a decision-driven activity, directed toward informing choices and solving problems."[5] The report explains that scientific analysis, which uses rigorous, replicable methods, brings new information into the process, and that deliberation helps to frame analysis by posing new questions and new ways of formulating problems, with the result that risk characterization is the output of a recursive process, not a linear one, and is a decision-driven activity.

Assessment of the health risks of dioxin illustrates this process. While scientific analysis provides information about the dose–response relationship between dioxin exposure and possible human health effects, public health focuses on the placement of waste incinerators and community issues in which dioxin is only one of many hazardous chemicals involved and cancer only one of many outcomes of concern. The critical point is that good risk characterization results from a process that "not only gets the science right," but also "gets the right science."[6]

Public health accountability addresses the responsibility of public health agents to work with the public and scientific experts to identify, define, and understand at a fundamental level the threats to public health, and the risks and benefits of ways to address them. The appropriate level of public involvement in the analytic-deliberative process depends on the particular public health problem.

Public accountability requires an openness to public deliberation and imposes an obligation on decision-makers to provide honest information and justifications for their decisions. No ethical principle can eliminate the fact that individual interests must sometimes yield to collective needs. Public accountability, however, ensures that such trade-offs will be made openly, with an explicit acknowledgment that individuals' fundamental well-being and values are at stake and that reasons, grounded in ethics, will be provided to those affected by the decisions. It provides a basis for public trust, even when policies infringe or appear to infringe some general moral considerations.

PUBLIC HEALTH INTERVENTIONS VS. PATERNALISTIC INTERVENTIONS

An important empirical, conceptual, and normative issue in public health ethics is the relationship between protecting and promoting the health of individuals and protecting and promoting public health. Although public health is directed to the health of populations, the indices of population health, of course, include an aggregation of the health of individuals. But suppose the primary reason for some restrictions on the liberties of individuals is to prevent harm to those whose actions are substantially voluntary and do not affect others adversely. The ethical question then is, when can paternalistic interventions (defined as interventions designed to protect or benefit individuals themselves against their express wishes) be ethically justified if they infringe general moral considerations such as respect for autonomy, including liberty of action?

Consider the chart in Figure 1: An individual's actions may be substantially voluntary (competent, adequately informed, and free of controlling influences) or non-voluntary (incompetent, inadequately informed, or subject to controlling influences). In addition, those actions may be self-regarding (the adverse effects of the actions fall primarily on the individual himself or herself) or other-regarding (the adverse effects of the actions fall primarily on others).

Paternalism in a morally interesting and problematic sense arises in the first quadrant (marked by the number "1" in Figure 1)—where the individual's actions are both voluntary and self-regarding. According to John Stuart Mill, whose *On Liberty* has inspired this chart, other-regarding conduct not only affects others adversely, but also affects them directly and without "their free, voluntary, and undeceived consent and participation."[7] If others, in the maturity of their faculties, consent to an agent's imposition of risk, then the agent's actions are not other-regarding in Mill's sense.

Whether an agent's other-regarding conduct is voluntary or non-voluntary, the society may justifiably intervene in various ways, including the use of coercion, to reduce or prevent the imposition of serious risk on others. Societal intervention in non-voluntary self-regarding conduct is considered weak (or soft) paternalism, if it is paternalistic at all, and it is easily justified. By contrast, societal interference in voluntary self-regarding conduct would be strong (or hard) paternalism. Coercive intervention in the name of strong paternalism would be insulting and disrespectful to individuals because it would override their voluntary actions for their own benefit, even though their actions do not harm others. Such interventions are thus very difficult to justify in a liberal, pluralistic democracy.

Because of this difficulty, proponents of public health sometimes contend that the first quadrant is really a small class of cases because individuals' risky actions are, in most cases, other-regarding or non-voluntary, or both. Thus, they insist, even if we assume that strong or hard paternalism cannot be ethically justified, the real question is whether most public health interventions in personal life plans and risk budgets are paternalistic at all, at least in the morally problematic sense.

To a great extent, the question is where we draw the boundaries of the self and its actions; that is, whether various influences on agents so determine their actions that they are not voluntary, and whether the adverse effects of those actions extend beyond the agents themselves. Such boundary drawing involves empirical, conceptual, and normative questions that demand attention in public health ethics. On the one hand, it is not sufficient to show that social-cultural factors influence an individual's actions; it is necessary to show that those influences render that individual's actions; substantially non-voluntary and warrant societal interventions to protect him or her. Controversies about the strong influence of food marketing on diet and weight (and, as a result, on the risk of disease and death) illustrate the debates about this condition.

On the other hand, it is not sufficient to show that an individual's actions have some adverse effects on

		Adverse Effects of Individuals' Actions	
		Self-regarding	Other-regarding
Voluntariness of Individuals' Actions	Voluntary	1	2
	Non-voluntary	3	4

Figure 1.   Types of Individual Action.

others; it is necessary to show that those adverse effects on others are significant enough to warrant overriding the individual's liberty. Controversies about whether the state should require motorcyclists to wear helmets illustrate the debates about this condition. These controversies also show how the inclusion of the financial costs to society and the emotional costs to, say, observers and rescue squads can appear to make virtually any intervention non-paternalistic. But even if these adverse financial and emotional effects on others are morally relevant as a matter of social utility, it would still be necessary to show that they are significant enough to justify the intervention.

Either kind of attempt to reduce the sphere of autonomous, self-regarding actions, in order to warrant interventions in the name of public health, or, more broadly, social utility, can sometimes be justified, but either attempt must be subjected to careful scrutiny. Sometimes both may represent rationalization and bad faith as public health agents seek to evade the stringent demands of the general moral consideration of respect for autonomy. Requiring consistency across an array of cases may provide a safeguard against rationalization and bad faith, particularly when motives for intervention may be mixed.

Much of this debate reflects different views about whether and when strong paternalistic interventions can be ethically justified. In view of the justificatory conditions identified earlier, relevant factors will include the nature of the intervention, the degree to which it infringes an individual's fundamental values, the magnitude of the risk to the individual apart from the intervention (either in terms of harm or lost benefit), and so forth. For example, even though the authors of this paper would disagree about some cases, we agree that strong paternalistic interventions that do not threaten individuals' core values and that will probably protect them against serious risks are more easily justifiable than strong paternalistic interventions that threaten individuals' core values and that will reduce only minor risks. Of course, evaluating actual and proposed policies that infringe general moral considerations becomes very complicated when both paternalistic and public health reasons exist for, and are intertwined in, those policies.

SOCIAL JUSTICE, HUMAN RIGHTS, AND HEALTH

We have noted potential and actual conflicts between promoting the good of public health and other general moral considerations. But it is important not to exaggerate these conflicts. Indeed, the societal institutionalization of other general moral considerations in legal rights and social-cultural practices generally contributes to public health. Social injustices expressed in poverty, racism, and sexism have long been implicated in conditions of poor health. In recent years, some evidence suggests that societies that embody more egalitarian conceptions of socioeconomic justice have higher levels of health than ones that do not. Public health activity has traditionally encompassed much more than medicine and health care. Indeed, historically much of the focus of public health has been on the poor and on the impact of squalor and sanitation on health. The focus today on the social determinants of health is in keeping with this tradition. The data about social determinants are impressive even though not wholly uncontroversial. At any rate, they are strong enough to warrant close attention to the ways conditions of social justice contribute to the public's health.

Apart from social justice, some in public health argue that embodying several other general moral considerations, especially as articulated in human rights, is consistent with and may even contribute to public health. For example, Jonathan Mann contended that public health officials now have two fundamental responsibilities—protecting and promoting public health and protecting and promoting human rights. Sometimes public health programs burden human rights, but human rights violations "have adverse effects on physical, mental, and social well-being" and "promoting and protecting human rights is inextricably linked with promoting and protecting health."[8] Mann noted, and we concur, that, ultimately, "ethics and human rights derive from a set of quite similar, if not identical, core values," several of which we believe are captured in our loose set of general moral considerations.[9] Often, as we have suggested, the most effective ways to protect public health respect general moral considerations rather than violate them, employ voluntary measures rather than coercive ones, protect privacy and confidentiality, and, more generally, express rather than impose community. Recognizing that promoting health and respecting other general moral considerations or human rights may be mutually supportive can enable us to create policies that avoid or at least reduce conflicts.

While more often than not public health and human rights—or general moral considerations not expressed in human rights—do not conflict and may even be synergistic, conflicts do sometimes arise and require resolution. Sometimes, in particular cases, a society cannot simultaneously realize its commitments to public health and to certain other general moral considerations, such as liberty, privacy, and confidentiality. We have tried to provide elements of a framework for thinking through and resolving such conflicts. This process needs to be transparent in order to engender and sustain public trust.

NOTES

1. Our definition builds on the definition of health systems offered by the World Health Organization: Health systems include "all the activities whose primary purpose is to promote, restore, or maintain health." See *World Health Report 2000 Health Systems: Improving Performance* (Geneva: World Health Organization, 2000): at 5.

2. Committee for the Study of the Future of Public Health, Division of Health Care Services, Institute of Medicine, *The Future of Public Health* (Washington, D.C.: National Academy Press, 1988): at 1.

3. L. O. Gostin, *Public Health Law: Power, Duty, Restraint* Berkeley: University of California Press; New York: The Milbank Memorial Fund, 2000): at 20.

4. N. Daniels, "Accountability for Reasonableness," *British Medical Journal*, 321 (2000): 1300–01, at 1301.

5. P. C. Stern and H. V. Fineberg, eds., Committee on Risk Characterization, Commission on Behavioral and Social Sciences and Education, National Research Council, *Understanding Risk: Informing Decisions in a Democratic Society* (Washington, D.C.: National Academy Press, 1996): at 155.

6. *Id.* at 16–17, 156

7. J. S. Mill, *On Liberty*, ed. G. Himmelfarb (Harmondsworth, England: Penguin Books, 1976): at 71. For this chart, see J. F. Childress, *Who Should Decide? Paternalism in Health Care* (New York: Oxford University Press, 1982): at 193

8. J. M. Mann, "Medicine and Public Health, Ethics and Human Rights," *The Hastings Center Report*, 27 (May-June 1997): 6–13, at 11–12. Contrast Gostin, *supra* note 3, at 21.

9. Mann, *supra* note 8 at 10. Mann thought that the language of ethics could guide individual behavior, while the language of human rights could best guide societal-level analysis and response. . . . We disagree with this separation and instead note the overlap of ethics and human rights, but we endorse the essence of Mann's position on human rights.

JONATHAN M. MANN

Medicine and Public Health, Ethics and Human Rights

The late Jonathan M. Mann was dean of the Allegheny University School of Public Health. His books include *Vamps, Virgins and Victims: How Can Women Fight AIDS?* (with Robin Gorna), *Health and Human Rights: A Reader* (with Sofia Gruskin and Michael A. Grodin), and *AIDS in the World II: Global Dimensions, Social Roots, and Responses* (with Daniel J. M. Tarantola).

The relationships among medicine, public health, ethics, and human rights are now evolving rapidly, in response to a series of events, experiences, and struggles. These include the shock of the worldwide epidemic of human immunodeficiency virus and AIDS, continuing work on diverse aspects of women's health, and challenges exemplified by the complex humanitarian emergencies of Somalia, Iraq, Bosnia, Rwanda, and . . . Zaire.

From among the many impacts of these experiences, three seem particularly salient. First, human rights thinking and action have become much more closely allied to, and even integrated with, public health work. Second, the long-standing absence of an ethics of public health has been highlighted. Third, the human rights-related roles and responsibilities of physicians and other medical workers are receiving increased attention.

PUBLIC HEALTH AND MEDICINE

To explore the first of these issues—the connections between human rights and public health—it is essential to review several central elements of modern public health.

From *Hastings Center Report* 27:3 (1997), 6–13. Notes omitted.

Medicine and public health are two complementary and interacting approaches for promoting and protecting health—defined by the World Health Organization (WHO) as a state of physical, mental, and social well-being. Yet medicine and public health can, and also must be differentiated, because in several important ways they are not the same. The fundamental difference involves the population emphasis of public health, which contrasts with the essentially individual focus of medical care. Public health identifies and measures threats to the health of populations, develops governmental policies in response to these concerns, and seeks to assure certain health and related services. In contrast, medical care focuses upon individuals—diagnosis, treatment, relief of suffering, and rehabilitation.

Several specific points follow from this essential difference. For example, different instruments are called for: while public health measures population health status through epidemiological, survey, and other statistically based methods, medicine examines biophysical and psychological status using a combination of techniques, including dialogue, physical examination, and laboratory study of the individual. Public health generally values most highly (or at least is supposed to) primary prevention, that is, preventing the adverse health event in the first place, such as helping to prevent the automobile accident or the lead poisoning from happening at all. In contrast, medicine generally responds to existing health conditions, in the context of either secondary or tertiary prevention. Secondary prevention involves avoiding or delaying the adverse impact of a health condition like hypertension or diabetes. Thus, while the hypertension or insulin deficiency exists, its effects, such as heart disease, kidney failure, or blindness, can be avoided or delayed. So-called tertiary prevention involves those efforts to help sustain maximal functional and psychological capacity despite the presence of both the disease, such as hypertension, and its outcomes, heart disease, stroke, or kidney failure.

Accordingly, the skills and expertise needed in public health include epidemiology, biostatistics, policy analysis, economics, sociology, and other behavioral sciences. In contrast, medical skills and expertise center on the exploration, analysis, and response to the biophysical status of individuals, based principally on an understanding of biology, biochemistry, immunology, pharmacology, pathology, pathophysiology, anatomy, and psychology.

Naturally, the settings in which public health and medicine operate also differ: governmental organizations, large-scale public programs, and various fora associated with developing and implementing public policy are inherently part of public health, while private medical offices, clinics, and medical care facilities of varying complexity and sophistication are the settings in which medical care is generally provided.

Finally, the relationship between the profession and the people with whom it deals differs: in a sense, public health comes to you, while you go to the doctor. And expectations associated with each domain differ: from medicine, individual care and treatment are sought; from public health, protection against broad health threats like epidemic disease, unsafe water, or chemical pollution is expected.

Therefore, public health and medicine are principally distinguished by their focus on collectivities or on individuals, respectively, with a series of subsidiary differences involving methods of work, systems of analysis and measurement, emphasis on primary versus secondary or tertiary prevention, types of expertise and relevant skill, settings in which work is conducted, and client/public relationships and expectations.

Yet obviously, there is substantial overlap. Public health requires a sound biomedical basis, and involves many medical practitioners, whose services are organized in settings such as maternal and child health clinics, or immunization programs. Also, medical practice operates within a context highly influenced and governed by law and public policy. The potentially fluid relationship between public health and medicine is further suggested by recent proposals in this country that certain traditional public health functions be delegated to the private medical sector.

Despite these many differences, people equate medical care with health. Certainly, this basic confusion has informed the recent discussions of health care in the United States; and coverage of health issues in the popular press around the world reflects this perspective, in which access to medical care and the quality of that care are seen as the principal health needs of individuals and populations.

MEDICINE AND HEALTH

Yet the contribution of medicine to health, while undeniably important (and vital in certain situations), is actually quite limited. For example, it is estimated that only about one-sixth of the years of life expectancy gained in this country during this century can be attributed to the beneficial impact of medicine, medical care, and medical research. And it has been estimated that only about 10 percent of preventable premature deaths are associated with a lack of medical care. Similarly, the World Bank has estimated that a lack of essential clinical services is responsible for between 11 and 24 percent of the global burden of disease. Of course, none of these data, including also the notable decline in diseases like tuberculosis well before anti-mycobacterial therapy became available, suggest that medical care is irrelevant; rather, they suggest its limits.

In 1988, the United States' Institute of Medicine defined the mission of public health as "ensuring the conditions in which people can be healthy." This profound definition begs the most vital question for public health, namely, what are these essential conditions in which people can best achieve the highest possible level of physical, mental, and social well-being? If not medical care—its availability and quality—then what?

The vast majority of research into the health of populations identifies so-called "societal factors" as the major determinants of health status. Most of the work in this area has focused on socioeconomic status as the key variable, for it is clear, throughout history and in all societies, that the rich live generally longer and healthier lives than the poor. . . .

A major question arising from the socioeconomic status–health gradient is why there is a gradient. For example, among over 10,000 British civil servants followed for many years, health status and longevity were better for each successive category of civil servants, from lowest to highest. This raises two issues: first, while we believe we can—at least intuitively—explain poor health among the destitute when compared with the rich, associated with a lack of good food, housing, and with poor sanitary conditions, even the lowest class of British civil servants cannot be considered poor. Secondly, why should the civil servants in the next-to-highest group, living in quite comfortable circumstances, experience poorer health than the highest group?

Beyond these unanswered issues, many recent studies have pointed to the limited explanatory power of socioeconomic status, generally measured in terms of current income, years of education, and job classification. Other measures, such as the extent of socioeconomic inequality within a community, the nature, level, and temporal pattern of unemployment, societal connectedness and the extent of involvement in social networks, marital status, early childhood experiences, and exposure to dignity-denying situations have all been suggested as powerful potential components of a "black box" of societal factors whose dominant role in determining levels of preventable disease, disability, and premature death is beyond dispute.

AN ETHICS FOR PUBLIC HEALTH

Public health, although it began as a social movement, has—at least in recent years—responded relatively little to this most profound and vital knowledge about the dominant impact of society on health. To illustrate: we all know that certain behaviors have an enormous impact on health, such as cigarette smoking, excess alcohol intake, dietary choices, or levels of exercise and physical fitness. How these behaviors are conceptualized determines how they will be addressed by public health. The basic question is whether and to what extent these behaviors can be considered, and therefore responded to, as isolated individual choices.

The curve represented in Figure 1 (replicable among public health practitioners in at least three countries) reflects a strong belief that important health-related behaviors are substantially influenced by societal factors and context. Yet examining public health programs designed to address the health problems associated with these same behaviors reveals that they generally consist of activities which assume that individuals have essentially complete control over their health-related behaviors. Traditional public health seeks to provide individuals with information and education about risks associated with diet or lack of exercise, along with various clinic-based services such as counseling, or distribution of condoms and other contraceptives. However, while public health may cite, or blame, or otherwise identify the societal-level or contextual issues—which it acknowledges to be of dominant importance, both in influencing individual behavior and for determining health status more broadly—it does not deal directly with these societal factors.

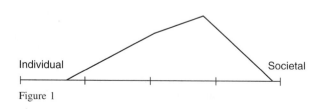

Health-Related Behaviors

Figure 1

At least three reasons for this paradoxical inaction may be proposed. First, public health has lacked a conceptual framework for identifying and analyzing the essential societal factors that represent the "conditions in which people can be healthy." Second, a related problem: public health lacks a vocabulary with which to speak about and identify commonalities among health problems experienced by very different populations. Third, there is no consensus about the nature or direction of societal change that would be necessary to address the societal conditions involved. Lacking a coherent conceptual framework, a consistent vocabulary, and consensus about societal change, public health assembles and then tries valiantly to assimilate a wide variety of disciplinary perspectives, from economists, political scientists, social and behavioral scientists, health systems analysts, and a range of medical practitioners. Yet while each of these perspectives provides some useful insight, public health becomes thereby a little bit of everything and thus not enough of anything.

With this background in mind, it would be expected that in the domains of public health and medicine, different, yet complementary languages for describing and incorporating values would be developed. For even when values are shared at a higher level of abstraction, the forms in which they are expressed, the settings in which they are evoked, and their practical application may differ widely.

Not surprisingly, medicine has chosen the language of ethics, as ethics has been developed in a context of individual relationships, and is well adapted to the nature, practice, settings, and expectations of medical care. The language of medical ethics has also been applied when medicine seeks to deal with issues such as the organization of medical care or the allocation of societal resources. However, the contribution of medical ethics to these societal issues has been less powerful when compared, for example, with its engagement in the behavior of individual medical practitioners.

Public health, at least in its contemporary form, is struggling to define and articulate its core values. In this context, the usefulness of the language and structure of ethics as we know it today has been questioned. Given its population focus, and its interest in the underlying conditions upon which health is predicated (and that these major determinants of health status are societal in nature), it seems evident that a framework which expresses fundamental values in societal terms, and a vocabulary of values which links

directly with societal structure and function, may be better adapted to the work of public health than a more individually oriented ethical framework.

For this reason, modern human rights, precisely because they were initially developed entirely outside the health domain and seek to articulate the societal preconditions for human well-being, seem a far more useful framework, vocabulary, and form of guidance for public health efforts to analyze and respond directly to the societal determinants of health than any inherited from the past biomedical or public health tradition.

PUBLIC HEALTH AND HUMAN RIGHTS

The linkage between public health and human rights can be explored further by considering three relationships. The first focuses on the potential burden on human rights created by public health policies, programs, and practices. As public health generally involves direct or indirect state action, public health officials represent the state power toward which classical human rights concerns are traditionally addressed. Thus, in the modern world, public health officials have, for the first time, two fundamental responsibilities to the public: to protect and promote public health, and to protect and promote human rights. While public health officials may be unlikely to seek deliberately to violate human rights, there is great unawareness of human rights concepts and norms among public health practitioners. . . .

Public health practice is heavily burdened by the problem of inadvertent discrimination. For example, outreach activities may "assume" that all populations are reached equally by a single, dominant-language message on television; or analysis "forgets" to include health problems uniquely relevant to certain groups, like breast cancer or sickle cell disease; or a program "ignores" the actual response capability of different population groups, as when lead poisoning warnings are given without concern for financial ability to ensure lead abatement. Indeed, inadvertent discrimination is so prevalent that all public health policies and programs should be considered discriminatory until proven otherwise, placing the burden on public health to affirm and ensure its respect for human rights.

In addition, in public health circles there is often an unspoken sense that public health and human rights concerns are inherently confrontational. At times, this has been true. In the early years of the HIV epidemic, the knee-jerk response of various public health officials to invoke mandatory testing, quarantine, and isolation did create a major clash with protectors of human rights. . . . [A]n opinion piece in the *British Medical Journal* purports that excessive respect for human rights crippled public health efforts and is therefore responsible for the intensifying and expanding AIDS epidemic.

However, while modern human rights explicitly acknowledges that public health is a legitimate reason for limiting rights, more recently the underlying complementarity rather than inherent confrontation between public health and human rights has been emphasized. Again in the context of AIDS, public health has learned that discrimination toward HIV-infected people and people with AIDS is counterproductive. Specifically, when people found to be infected were deprived of employment, education, or ability to marry and travel, participation in prevention programs diminished. Thus, recent attention has been directed to a negotiation process for optimizing both the achievement of complementary public health goals and respect for human rights norms.

A second relationship between public health and human rights derives from the observation that human rights violations have health impacts, that is, adverse effects on physical, mental, and social well-being. For some rights, such as the right not to be tortured or imprisoned under inhumane conditions, the health damage seems evident, indeed inherent in the rights violation. However, even for torture, only more recently has the extensive, life-long, family and community-wide, and transgenerational impact of torture been recognized.

For many other rights, such as the right to information, to assembly, or to association, health impacts resulting from violation may not be initially so apparent. The violation of any right has measurable impacts on physical, mental, and social well-being; yet these health effects still remain, in large part, to be discovered and documented. Yet gradually, the connection is being established.

The right to association provides a useful example of this relationship. Public health benefits substantially—even requires—involvement of people in addressing problems that affect them. Because the ability of people concerned about a health problem to get together, talk, and search for effective solutions is so essential to public health, wherever the right to association is restricted, public health suffers. Taking a positive example from the history of HIV/AIDS: needle exchange—the trading-in of needles used for drug injection for clean needles, so as to avoid needle-sharing with consequent risk of HIV transmission—was invented by a union of drug users in Amsterdam. Needle exchange was a classic example of an innovative, local response to a pressing local problem. Needle exchange was not and would have been highly unlikely to have been developed by academics, government officials, or hired consultants! Yet the creative solution of needle exchange and respect for the right of association are closely linked. Thus, in societies in which people generally, or specific population groups, cannot associate around health, or other issues, such as injection drug users in the United States, or sex workers, or gay and lesbian people in many countries, local solutions are less able to emerge or be applied and public health is correspondingly compromised.

A third relationship between health and human rights has already been suggested; namely, that promoting and protecting human rights is inextricably linked with promoting and protecting health. Once again, this is because human rights offers a societal-level framework for identifying and responding to the underlying—societal—determinants of health. It is important to emphasize that human rights are respected not only for their instrumental value in contributing to public health goals, but for themselves, as societal goods of pre-eminent importance.

For example, a cluster of rights, including the rights to health, bodily integrity, privacy, information, education, and equal rights in marriage and divorce, have been called "reproductive rights," insofar as their realization (or violation) is now understood to play a major role in determining reproductive health. From an early focus on demographic targets for population control, to an emphasis on ensuring "informed consent" of women to various contraceptive methods, a new paradigm for population policies *and* reproductive health has recently emerged. Articulated most forcefully at the United Nations Conference on Population and Development in 1994 in Cairo, the focus has shifted to ensuring that women can make and effectuate real and informed choices about reproduction. And in turn, this is widely acknowledged to depend on realization of human rights.

Similarly, in the context of HIV/AIDS, vulnerability to the epidemic has now been associated with the extent of realization of human rights. For as the HIV epidemic matures and evolves within each community and country, it focuses inexorably on those groups who, before HIV/AIDS arrived, were already discriminated against, marginalized, and stigmatized within each society. Thus, in the United States the brunt of the epidemic today is among racial and ethnic minority populations, inner city poor, injection drug users, and, especially women in these communities. In Brazil, an epidemic that started among the jet set of Rio and São Paulo with time has become a major epidemic among the slum-dwellers in the *favelas* of Brazil's cities. The French, with characteristic linguistic precision, identify the major burden of HIV/AIDS to exist among "*les exclus*," those living at the margins of society. Now that a lack of respect for human rights has been identified as a societal level risk factor for HIV/AIDS vulnerability, HIV prevention efforts—for example, for women—are starting to go beyond traditional educational and service-based efforts to address the rights issues that will be a precondition for greater progress against the epidemic.

Ultimately, ethics and human rights derive from a set of quite similar, if not identical, core values. As with medicine and public health, rather than seeing human rights and ethics as conflicting domains, it seems more appropriate to consider a continuum, in which human rights is a language most useful for guiding societal level analysis and work, while ethics is a language most useful for guiding individual behavior. From this perspective, and precisely because public health must be centrally concerned with the structure and function of society, the language of human rights is extremely useful for expressing, considering, and incorporating values into public health analysis and response.

Thus, public health work requires both ethics applicable to the individual public health practitioner and a human rights framework to guide public health in its societal analysis and response.

These relationships between medicine and public health, and between ethics and human rights, can be provisionally diagrammed as in Figure 2.

At the hypothetical extreme of individual medical care, ethics would be the most useful language. However, to the extent that the individual practitioner is cognizant of the societal forces acting upon the individual patient, societal level considerations may also be articulated in human rights terms. At the other extreme of public health, human rights is the most useful language, speaking as it does directly to the societal level determinants of well-being. Nevertheless, the ethical framework remains critical, for public health is carried out by individuals within specific professional roles and competencies. In practice, of course, positions between the hypothetical extremes of medicine and

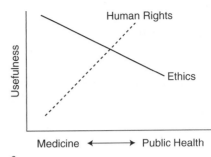

Figure 2

public health are more common, calling for mixtures of human rights and ethical concepts and language.

PROFESSIONAL ROLES AND RESPONSIBILITIES

The placement of both human rights and ethics and public health and medicine at ends of a continuum suggests also that the interest domains of individuals and organizations can be "mapped" (as in Figure 3), and areas calling for additional attention can be highlighted.

According to this mapping approach, the "French Doctors" movement can be seen as primarily medical, primarily ethics-based, yet with growing involvement in the public health dimensions of health emergencies and in human rights issues raised by these complex humanitarian crises. Similarly, many traditional, medical ethics-based institutes and centers can be placed on this map. . . . This map also suggests two major gaps in current work: on the ethics of public health, and on the relationships between medicine and human rights.

Where are the ethics of public health? In contrast to the important declarations of medical ethics such as the International Code of Medical Ethics of the

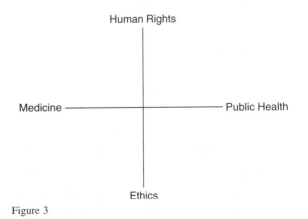

Figure 3

World Medical Association and the Nuremberg Principles, the world of public health does not have a reasonably explicit set of ethical guidelines. In part, this deficiency may stem from the broad diversity of professional identities within public health. . . . [P]ublic health cannot develop an ethics until it has achieved clarity about its own identity; technical expertise and methodology are not substitutes for conceptual coherence. . . .

To have an ethic, a profession needs clarity about central issues, including its major role and responsibilities. Two steps will be essential for public health to reach toward this analytic and definitional clarity.

First, public health must divest itself of its biomedical conceptual foundation. The language of disease, disability, and death is not the language of well-being; the vocabulary of diseases may detract from analysis and response to underlying societal conditions, of which traditional morbidity and mortality are expressions. It is clear that we do not yet know all about the universe of human suffering. Just as in the microbial world, in which new discoveries have become the norm—Ebola virus, hantavirus, toxic shock syndrome, Legionnaires' disease, AIDS—we are explorers in the larger world of human suffering and well-being. And our current maps of this universe, like world maps from sixteenth century Europe, have some very well-defined, familiar coastlines and territories and also contain large blank spaces, which beckon the explorer.

The language of biomedicine is cumbersome and ultimately perhaps of little usefulness in exploring the impacts of violations of dignity on physical, mental, and social well-being. The definition of dignity itself is complex and thus far elusive and unsatisfying. While the Universal Declaration of Human Rights starts by placing dignity first, "all people are born equal in dignity and rights," we do not yet have a vocabulary, or taxonomy, let alone an epidemiology of dignity violations.

Yet it seems we all know when our dignity is violated or impugned. Perform the following experiment: recall, in detail, an incident from your own life in which your dignity was violated, for whatever reason. If you will immerse yourself in the memory, powerful feelings will likely arise—of anger, shame, powerlessness, despair. When you connect with the power of these feelings, it seems intuitively obvious that such feelings, particularly if evoked repetitively, could have deleterious impacts on health. Yet most of us are relatively privileged, we live in a generally dignity-affirming environment, and suffer only the occasional lapse of indignity. However, many people live constantly in a dignity-impugning environment, in which affirmations of dignity may be the exceptional occurrence. An exploration of the meanings of dignity and the forms of its violation—and the impact on physical, mental, and social well-being—may help uncover a new universe of human suffering, for which the biomedical language may be inapt and even inept. After all, the power of naming, describing, and then measuring is truly enormous—child abuse did not exist in meaningful societal terms until it was named and then measured; nor did domestic violence.

A second precondition for developing an ethics of public health is the adoption and application of a human rights framework for analyzing and responding to the societal determinants of health. The human rights framework can provide the coherence and clarity required for public health to identify and work with conscious attention to its roles and responsibilities. At that point, an ethics of public health, rather than the ethics of individual constituent disciplines within public health, can emerge.

Issues of respect for autonomy, beneficence, nonmaleficence, and justice can then be articulated from within the set of goals and responsibilities called for by seeking to improve public health through the combination of traditional approaches and those that strive concretely to promote realization of human rights. This is not to replace health education, information, and clinical service-based activities of public health with an exclusive focus on human rights and dignity. Both are necessary.

For example, the challenges for public health officials in balancing the goals of promoting and protecting public health and ensuring that human rights and dignity are not violated call urgently for ethical analysis. The official nature of much public health work places public health practitioners in a complex environment, in which work to promote rights inevitably challenges the state system within which the official is employed. Ethical dimensions are highly relevant to collecting, disseminating, and acting on information about the health impacts of the entire range of human rights violations. And as public health seeks to "ensure the conditions in which people can be healthy," and as those conditions are societal, to be engaged in public health necessarily involves a commitment to societal transformation. The difficulties in assessing human rights status and in developing useful and appropriate ways to promote human rights and dignity necessarily engage ethical considerations. For example, beyond accurate diagnosis, beyond efforts to cure, and even beyond the ever-present responsibility for relief of pain, the physician agrees to accompany the patient, to stand by the patient through her suffering, even to the edge of life itself, even when the only thing the physician can offer is the fact of his or her presence. Is this not as relevant to public health? For public health must engage difficult issues even when no cure or effective instruments are yet available, and public health also must accompany, remain with, and not abandon vulnerable populations. . . .

PHYSICIANS AND HUMAN RIGHTS

Finally, turning to the third issue raised by new challenges to the domains of public health, medicine, ethics, and human rights: what about the human rights role and responsibilities of medicine and the medical professional? To what extent and in what ways are— or might, or should—medicine generally and physicians in particular be involved in human rights issues?

Physicians have developed important roles in the context of human rights work. This work generally started from a corporatist interest in the fate of fellow physicians suffering human rights abuses, and then expanded in four directions. First, physicians created the "French Doctors" movement, providing medical assistance to populations in need, across borders. This dramatic and catalyzing work, including the concept of the right to assistance and the duty to intervene, expressed—in medical terms—the same transnational, universalist impulse as the modern human rights movement. Then, groups such as Physicians for Human Rights applied medical methods and analysis to detect and document torture, executions, and other similar human rights violations. In this manner, credible documentation, necessary also for redress and prosecution, has increasingly been made available. Meanwhile, Amnesty International has been concerned with the participation of physicians in human rights violations, usually in the context of torture and imprisonment under inhumane conditions. Finally, at a global level, physicians have articulated a role in seeking to prevent health catastrophes, exemplified by the Nobel Peace Prize-winning organization, International Physicians for Prevention of Nuclear War.

These historic and often courageous engagements with human rights issues have carried physicians to the frontiers of new challenges, exemplified by complex humanitarian emergencies, efforts to identify the full range of health consequences from human rights violations, and further struggle with societal issues inextricably linked with the health dimensions of conflict, economic consumption, and the degradation of the global environment. Increased physician participation and concern with these issues will inevitably blur pre-existing boundaries between public health and medicine and create new interactive configurations between human rights and ethics.

Yet for individual medical practitioners, how is a human rights perspective relevant? Human rights and dignity will be engaged to the extent that the physician seeks to go beyond the usual, limited boundaries of medical care. Take two examples: a child with asthma, or a woman seeking emergency room care for injuries inflicted by her spouse. In each case, the limited medical perspective is vital. For the precipitating factors for asthma, and the likelihood of seeking early care as asthmatic attacks begin, lead directly to environmental conditions, economic issues, and discrimination. Similarly, domestic violence invokes, necessarily, societal issues in which the human rights framework will be useful, if not essential. Whether considering cancer, heart disease, lead poisoning, asthma, injuries, or infectious diseases, while the medical professional may start from a context dominated by individual relationships, a larger, societal set of issues will inevitably exist. The question then becomes, To what extent is the physician responsible for what happens outside the immediate context and setting of medical care? To what extent is a physician responsible for assuring access to care of marginalized populations in the community, or helping the community understand the medical implications of public policy measures, or identifying, responding to, and preventing discrimination occurring within medical institutions?

Where, that is, does the boundary of medicine end? This seems a uniquely rich context for ethical discussion, at the frontiers of human rights and public health.

Of course, for those interested in the human rights dimensions of medicine, many may accuse physicians of "meddling" in societal issues that "go far beyond" their scope or competence. Also, issues of human rights inherently and inevitably represent a challenge to power—and health professionals are often part of, or direct beneficiaries of, the societal or institutional status quo that is challenged by the claims of human rights and dignity.

In conclusion, there is more to modern health than new scientific discoveries, or development of new technologies, or emerging or re-emerging diseases, or changes in patterns of morbidity and mortality around the world. For we are living at a time of paradigm shift in thinking about health, and therefore about medicine and public health. Health as well-being, despite the World Health Organization's definition, lacks more than rudimentary definition, especially regarding its mental and societal dimensions. The universe of human suffering and its alleviation is being more fully explored. Awareness of the limits of medicine and medical care, growing recognition of the health impacts of societal structure and function, globalization and consequent interdependence, and the sometimes active, sometimes ineffectual actions of nation-states, all intersect to lead toward a new vision of health.

In the ongoing work on values and their articulation, we must acknowledge the provisional, untidy, and necessarily incomplete character of our understanding of the universe of health. In this context, medicine need not compete with public health, nor ethics with human rights; the search for meaning deserves to draw on all, as new constellations emerge and new relationships evolve.

Yet at such times of profound change, another kind of value becomes all the more vital. To build bridges—between medicine and public health, and between ethics and human rights—the critical underlying question may be, Do we believe that the world can change? Do we believe that the long chains of human suffering can be broken? Do we agree with Martin Luther King that "the arc of history is long, but it bends towards justice?" Bioethical pioneers at the frontier of human history, we affirm that the past does not inexorably determine the future—and that it is precisely through this historic effort to explore and promote values in the world for which we share responsibility, articulated in philosophy and in action—that we express confidence in our own lives, in our community, and in the future of our world.

DANIEL I. WIKLER

Persuasion and Coercion for Health: Ethical Issues in Government Efforts to Change Life-Styles

Daniel I. Wikler is Mary B. Saltonstall Professor of Population Ethics at the Harvard School of Public Health. He served as the first Staff Ethicist for the World Health Organization. He publishes on ethical issues in reproduction, transplantation, end-of-life decision making, and population and international health. His authored and co-authored publications include the book series *Studies in Philosophy and Health Policy, Population-Level Bioethics: Mapping a New Agenda*, and *From Chance to Choice: Genetics and Justice* (with Allen Buchanan, Dan W. Brock, and Norman Daniels).

What should be the government's role in promoting the kinds of personal behavior that lead to long life and good health? Smoking, overeating, and lack of exercise increase one's chances of suffering illness later in life, as do many other habits. The role played by life-style is so important that, as stated by Fuchs (1974): "The greatest current potential for improving the health of the American people is to be found in what they do and don't do for themselves." But the public has shown little spontaneous interest in reforming. If the government uses the means at its disposal to remedy the situation, it may be faced with problems of an ethical nature. Education, exhortation, and

From *Milbank Memorial Fund Quarterly/Health and Society*, 56:3 (1978), 303–338. Notes and references omitted.

other relatively mild measures may not prove effective in inducing self-destructive people to change their behavior. Attention might turn instead to other means, which, though possibly more effective, might also be intrusive or otherwise distasteful. In this essay, I seek to identify the moral principles underlying a reasoned judgment on whether stronger methods might justifiably be used, and, if so, what limits ought to be observed.

* * *

GOALS OF HEALTH BEHAVIOR REFORM

I propose to discuss three possible goals of health behavior reform with regard to their appropriateness as goals of government programs and the problems arising in their pursuit. The first goal can be simply stated: health should be valued for its own sake. Americans are likely to be healthier if they can be induced to adopt healthier habits, and this may be reason enough to try to get them to do so. The second goal is the fair distribution of the burdens caused by illness. Those who become ill because of unhealthy lifestyles may require the financial support of the more prudent, as well as the sharing of what may be scarce medical facilities. If this is seen as unfair to those who do not make themselves sick, life-style reform measures will also be seen as accomplishing distributive justice. The third goal is the maintenance and improvement of the general welfare, for the nation's health conditions have their effects on the economy, allocation of resources, and even national security.

HEALTH AS A GOAL IN ITSELF: BENEFICENCE AND PATERNALISM

Much of the present concern for the reform of unhealthy life-styles stems from concern over the health of those who live dangerously. Only a misanthrope would quarrel with this goal. There are several steps that might immediately be justified: the government could make the effects of unhealthy living habits known to those who practice them, and sponsor research to discover more of these facts. The chief concern over such efforts might be that the government would begin its urgings before the facts in question had been firmly established, thus endorsing living habits that might be useless or detrimental to good health.

Considerably more debate, however, would arise over a decision to use stronger methods. For example, a case in point might be a government "fat tax," which would require citizens to be weighed and taxed if

overweight. The surcharges thus derived would be held in trust, to be refunded with interest if and when the taxpayers brought their weight down. This pressure would, under the circumstances, be a bond imposed by the government upon its citizens, and thus can be fairly considered as coercive.

The two signal properties of this policy would be its aim of improving the welfare of obese taxpayers, and its presumed unwelcome imposition on personal freedom. . . . The first property might be called "beneficence," and it is generally a virtue. But the second property becomes paternalism, and its status as a virtue is very much in doubt. "Paternalism" is a loaded word, almost automatically a term of reprobation. But many paternalistic policies, especially when more neutrally described, attract support and even admiration. It may be useful to consider what is bad and what is good about paternalistic practices, so that we might decide whether in this case the good outweighs the bad. . . .

What is good about some paternalistic interventions is that people are helped, or saved from harm. Citizens who have to pay a fat tax, for example, may lose weight, become more attractive, and live longer. In the eyes of many, these possible advantages are more than offset by the chief fault of paternalism, its denying persons the chance to make their own choices concerning matters that affect them. Self-direction, in turn, is valued because people usually believe themselves to be the best judges of what is good for them, and because the choosing is considered a good in itself. These beliefs are codified in our ordinary morality in the form of a moral right to noninterference so long as one does not adversely affect the interests of others. This right is supposed to shield an individual's "self-regarding" actions from intervention by others, even when those acts are not socially approved ones and even when they promise to be unwise.

At the same time, the case for paternalistic intervention on at least some occasions seems compelling. There may be circumstances in which we lose, temporarily or permanently, our capacity for competent self-direction, and thereby inflict harm upon ourselves that serves little purpose. Like Ulysses approaching the Sirens, we may hope that others would then protect us from ourselves. This sort of consideration supports our imposed guardianship of children and of the mentally retarded. Although these persons often resent our paternalistic control, we reason that we are doing what they would want us to do were their autonomy not compromised. Paternalism would be a benefit under the sort of social insurance policy that a reasonable person would opt for if considered in a moment of lucidity and competence.

Does this rationale for paternalism support governmental coercion of competent adults to assure the adoption of healthy habits of living? It might seem to, at first sight. Although these adults may be generally competent, their decision-making abilities can be compromised in specific areas. Individuals may be ignorant of the consequences of their acts; they may be under the sway of social or commercial manipulation and suggestion; they may be afflicted by severe psychological stress or compulsion; or be under external constraint. If any of these conditions hold, the behavior of adults may fail to express their settled will. Those of us who disavow any intention of interfering with free and voluntary risk-taking may see cause to intervene when a person's behavior is not under his or her control.

Paternalism: Theoretical Problems. There are a number of reasons to question the general argument for paternalism in the coercive eradication of unhealthful personal practices. First, the analogy between the cases of children and the retarded, where paternalism is most clearly indicated, and of risk-taking adults is misleading. If the autonomy of adults is compromised in one or more of the ways just mentioned, it might be possible to restore that autonomy by attending to the sources of the involuntariness; the same cannot ordinarily be done with children or the retarded. Thus, adults who are destroying their health because of ignorance may be educated; adults acting under constraint may be freed. If restoration of autonomy is a realistic project, then paternalistic interference is unjustified. The two kinds of interventions are aimed at the same target, *i.e.*, harmful behavior not freely and competently chosen. But they accomplish the result differently. Paternalistic intervention blocks the harm; education and similar measures restore the choice. The state or health planners would seem obligated to use this less restrictive alternative if they can. This holds true even though the individuals might still engage in their harmful practices once autonomy is restored. This would not call for paternalistic intervention, since the risk would be voluntarily shouldered.

It remains true, however, that autonomy sometimes cannot be restored. It may be impossible to reach a given population with the information they need; or, once reached, the persons in question may prove ineducable. Psychological compulsions and social pressures may be even harder to eradicate. In these situations, the case for paternalistic interference is relatively strong, yet even here there is reason for caution. Persons who prove incapable of absorbing the facts about smoking, for example, or who abuse drugs because of compulsion or addiction, may retain a kind of second-order autonomy. They can be told that they appear unable to accept scientific truth, or that they are addicted; and they can then decide to reconsider the facts or to seek a cure. In some cases these will be decisions that the individuals are fully competent to carry out; paternalistic intervention would unjustly deny them the right to control their destinies. Coercion would be acceptable only if this second-order decision were itself constrained, compelled, or otherwise compromised—which, in the case of health-related behavior, it may often be.

A second reason for doubting the justifiability of paternalistic interference concerns the subjectivity of the notion of harm. The same experience may be seen as harmful by one person and as beneficial by another; or, even more common, the goodness (or badness) of a given eventuality may be rated very differently by different persons. Although we as individuals are often critical of the importance placed on certain events by others, we nevertheless hesitate to claim special authority in such matters. Most of us subscribe to the pluralistic ethic, for better or for worse, which has as a central tenet the proposition that there are multiple distinct, but equally valid, concepts of good and of the good life. It follows that we must use personal preferences and tastes to determine whether our health-related practices are detrimental.

Unfortunately, it is often difficult to defer the authority of others in defining harm and benefit. It is common to feel that one's own preferences reflect values that reasonable people adopt; one can hardly regard oneself as unreasonable. To the extent that government planners employ their own concepts of good in attempting to change health practices for the public's benefit, the social insurance rationale for paternalism is clearly inapplicable.

A third reason for criticism of paternalism is the vagueness of the notion of decision-making disability. The conscientious paternalist intervenes only when the self-destructive individual's autonomy is compromised. It is probably impossible, however, to specify a compromising condition. To be sure, there are cases in which the lack of autonomy is evident, such as that of a child swallowing dangerous pills in the belief that they are candy. But the sorts of practices that would be the targets of coercive campaigns to reform health-related behavior are less dramatic and their involuntary quality much less certain. Since the free and voluntary conditions of health-related practice cannot be specified in advance, there is obviously considerable potential for unwarranted interference with fully voluntary choices.

Indeed, the dangers involved in disregarding individuals' personal values and in falsely branding their behavior involuntary are closely linked. In the absence of independent criteria for decision-making disability, the paternalist may try to determine disability by seeing whether the individual is rational, *i.e.*, whether he or she competently pursues what is valuable. An absence of rationality may be reason to suspect the presence of involuntariness and hence grounds for paternalism. The problem, however, is that this test for rationality—whether the chosen means are appropriate for the individual's personal ends—is not fully adequate. Factors that deprive an individual of autonomy—such as compulsion or constraint—not only affect a person's ability to calculate means to ends but also induce ends that are in some sense foreign. Advertisements, for example, may instill desires to consume certain substances whose pleasures would ordinarily be considered trifling. Similarly, ignorance may induce people to value a certain experience because they believe it will lead to their attainment of other ends. Alcoholics, for example, may value intoxication because they think it will enhance their social acceptance. The paternalist on the lookout for non-autonomous, self-destructive behavior will be interested not only in irrational means but also uncharacteristic, unreasonable values.

The difficulty for the paternalist at this point is plain. The desire to interfere only with involuntary risk-taking leads to designating individuals for intervention whose behavior proceeds from externally-instilled values. Pluralism commits the paternalist to use the persons' own values in determining whether a health-related practice is harmful. What is needed is some way of determining individuals' "true" personal values; but if these cannot be read off from their behavior, how can they be known?

In certain individual cases, a person's characteristic preferences can be determined from wishes expressed before losing autonomy. . . . But this sort of data is hardly likely to be available to government health planners. The problem would be at least partially solved if we could identify a set of goods that is basic and appealing, and that nearly all rational persons value. Such universal valuation would justify a presumption of involuntariness should an individual's behavior put these goods in jeopardy. On what grounds would we include an item on this list? Simple popularity would suffice: if almost everyone likes something, such approval probably stems from a common human nature, shared by even those not professing to like that thing. Hence we may suspect, that, if unconstrained, they would like it also. Alternatively, there may be experiences or qualities that, while not particularly appealing in themselves, are preconditions to attaining a wide variety of goods that people idiosyncratically value. Relief from pain is an example of the first sort of good; normal-or-better intelligence is an instance of the latter.

The crucial question for health planners is whether *health* is one of these primary goods. Considered alone, it certainly is: it is valued for its own sake; and it is a means to almost all ends. Indeed, it is a necessary good. No matter how eccentric a person's values and tastes are, no matter what kinds of activities are pleasurable, it is impossible to engage in them unless alive. Most activities a person is likely to enjoy, in fact, require not only life but good health. Unless one believes in an afterlife, the rational person must rate death as an incomparable calamity, for it means the loss of everything.

But the significance of health as a primary good should not be overestimated. The health planner may attempt to argue for coercive reform of health-destructive behavior. . . . Since death, which precludes all good experience, must receive an enormously negative valuation, contemplated action that involves risk of death will also receive a substantial negative value after the good and bad consequences have been considered. And this will hold true even if the risk is small, since even low probability multiplied by a very large quantity yields a large quantity. Hence anyone who risks death by living dangerously must, on this view, be acting irrationally. This would be grounds for suspecting that the life-threatening practices were less than wholly voluntary and thus created a need for protection. Further, this case would not require the paternalistic intervenor to turn away from pluralistic ideals, for the unhealthy habits would be faulted not on the basis of deviance from paternalistic values, but on the apparent lapse in the agent's ability to understand the logic of the acts.

This argument, or something like it, may lie behind the willingness of some to endorse paternalistic regulation of the life-styles of apparently competent adults. It is, however, invalid. Its premises may sometimes be true, and so too may its conclusion, but the one does not follow from the other. Any number of considerations can suffice to show this. For example, time factors are ignored. An act performed at age 25 that risks death at age 50 does not threaten every valued activity. It simply threatens the continuation of those activities past the age of 50. The argument also overlooks an interplay between the possible courses of action: if every action that carries some risk of death or crippling illness is avoided, the enjoyment of life decreases. This makes continued life less likely to be worth the price of giving up favorite unhealthy habits. Indeed, although it may be true that death would deny one of all chances for valued experiences, the experiences that make up some people's lives have little value. The less value a person places on continued life, the more rational it is to engage in activities that may brighten it up, even if they involve the risk of ending it. Craig Claiborne (1976), food editor of *The New York Times*, gives ebullient testimony to this possibility in the conclusion of his "In Defense of Eating Rich Food":

I love hamburgers and chili con carne and hot dogs. And foie gras and sauternes and those small birds known as ortolans. I love banquettes of quail eggs with hollandaise sauce and clambakes with lobsters dipped into so much butter it dribbles down the chin. I like cheesecake and crepes filled with cream sauces and strawberries with crème fraiche . . . .

And if I am abbreviating my stay on this earth for an hour or so, I say only that I have no desire to be a Methuselah, a hundred or more years old and still alive, grace be to something that plugs into an electric outlet.

The assumption that one who is endangering one's health must be acting irrationally and involuntarily is not infrequently made by those who advocate forceful intervention in suicide attempts; and perhaps some regard unhealthy life-styles as a sort of slow suicide. The more reasonable view, even in cases of imminent suicide, seems rather to be that *some* unhealthy or self-destructive acts are less-than-fully voluntary but that others are not. Claiborne's diet certainly seems to be voluntary, and suggests that the case for paternalistic intervention in life-style cannot be made on grounds of logic alone. It remains true, however, that much of the behavior that leads to chronic illness and accidental injury is not fully under the control of the persons so acting. My thesis is merely that, first, this involuntariness must be shown (along with much else) if paternalistic intervention is to be justified; and, second, this can only be determined by case-by-case empirical study. Those who advocate coercive measures to reform life-styles, whose motives are purely beneficent, and who wish to avoid paternalism except where justified, might find such study worth undertaking.

Any such study is likely to reveal that different practitioners of a given self-destructive habit act from different causes. Perhaps one obese person overeats because of an oral fixation over which he has no control, or in a Pavlovian response to enticing television food advertisements. The diminished voluntariness of these actions lends support to paternalistic intervention. Claiborne has clearly thought matters through and decided in favor of a shorter though gastronomically happier life; to pressure him into changing so that he may live longer would be a clear imposition of values and would lack the justification provided in the other person's case.

The trouble for a government policy of life-style reform is that a given intervention is more likely to be tailored to practices and habits than to people. Although we may someday have a fat tax to combat obesity, it would be surprising indeed to find one that imposed charges only on those whose obesity was due to involuntary factors. It would be difficult to reach agreement on what constituted diminished voluntariness; harder still to measure it; and perhaps administratively impractical to make the necessary exceptions and adjustments. We may feel, after examining the merits of the cases, that intervention is justified in the compulsive eater's life-style but not in the case of Claiborne. If the intervention takes the form of a tax on obesity *per se*, we face a choice: Do we owe it to those like Claiborne *not* to enforce alien values more than we owe it to compulsive overeaters to protect them from self-destruction? The general right of epicures to answer to their own values, a presumptive right conferred by the pluralistic ethic spoken of earlier, might count for more than the need of compulsive overeaters to have health imposed on them, since the first violates a right and the second merely confers a benefit. But the situation is more complex than this. The compulsive overeater's life is at stake, and this may be of greater concern (everything else being equal) than the epicure's pleasures. Then, too, the epicure is receiving a compensating benefit in the form of longer life, even if this is not a welcome exchange. And there may be many more compulsive overeaters than there are people like Claiborne. On the other hand, the positive causal link between tax and health for either is indirect and tenuous, while the negative relation between tax and gastronomic pleasure is relatively more substantial.... Perhaps the firmest conclusion one may draw from all this is that a thoroughly reasoned moral rationale for a given kind of intervention can be very difficult to carry out.

Paternalism: Problems in Practice. .... I think it is important to note several practical problems that could arise in any attempt to design and carry out a policy of coercive life-style reform.

First, there is the distinct possibility that the government that takes over decision-making power from partially-incompetent individuals may prove even less adept at securing their interests than they would have been if left alone. Paucity of scientific data may lead to misidentification of risk factors. The primitive state of the art in health promotion and mass-scale behavior modification may render interventions ineffective or even counterproductive. And the usual run of political and administrative tempests that affect all public policy may result in the misapplication of such knowledge as is available in these fields. These factors call for recognizing a limitation on the social insurance rationale for paternalism. If rational persons doubt that the authorities who would be guiding their affairs during periods of their incompetence would themselves be particularly competent, they are unlikely to license interventions except when there is a high probability of favorable cost-benefit trade-off. This yields the strongest support for those interventions that prevent very serious injuries, and in which the danger posed is imminent ....

These reflections count against a rationale for government involvement in vigorous health promotion efforts, ... [S]tatements that smoking and similar habits are "slow suicide" and should be treated as such make a false analogy, precisely because suicide often involves certain imminent dangers of the most serious sort in situations in which there cannot be time to determine whether the act is voluntary. This is just the sort of case that the social insurance policy here described would cover; but this would not extend to the self-destruction that takes 30 years to accomplish.

Second, there is some possibility that what would be advertised as concern for the individual's welfare (as that person defines it) would turn out to be simple legal moralism, *i.e.*, an attempt to impose the society's or authorities' moral prescriptions upon those not following them. In Knowles's call for life-style reform (1976) the language is suggestive:

The next major advances in the health of the American people will result from the assumption of individual responsibility for one's own health. This will require a change in lifestyle for the majority of Americans. The cost of sloth, gluttony, alcoholic overuse, reckless driving, sexual intemperance, and smoking is now a national, not an individual responsibility.

All save the last of these practices are explicit *vices*; indeed, the first two—sloth and gluttony—use their traditional names. The intrusion of non-medical values is evidenced by the fact that of all the living habits that affect health adversely, only those that are sins (with smoking excepted) are mentioned as targets for change. Skiing and football produce injuries as surely as sloth produces heart disease.... If it is the unhealthiness of "sinful" living habits that motivates the paternalist toward reform, then ought not other acts also be targeted on occasions when persons exhibit lack of self-direction? The fact that other practices are not ordinarily pointed out in this regard provides on *argument* against paternalistic life-style reform. But those who favor pressuring the slothful to engage in physical exercise might ask themselves if they also favor pressure on habits which, though unhealthy, are not otherwise despised. If enthusiasm for paternalistic intervention slackens in these latter cases, it may be a signal for reexamination of the motives.

A third problem is that the involuntariness of some self-destructive behavior may make paternalistic reform efforts ineffective. To the extent that the unhealthy behavior is not under the control of the individual, we cannot expect the kind of financial threat involved in a "fat tax" to exert much influence. Paradoxically, the very conditions under which paternalistic intervention seems most justified are those in which many of the methods available are least likely to succeed. The result of intervention under these circumstances may be a failure to change the life-threatening behavior, and a needless (and inexcusable) addition to the individual's woes through the unpleasantness of the intervention itself. A more appropriate target for government intervention might be the commercial and/or social forces that cause or support the life-threatening behavior.

Although the discussion above has focused on the problems attendant to a paternalistic argument for coercive health promotion programs, I have implicitly outlined a positive case for such interventions as well. A campaign to reform unhealthy habits of living will be justified, in my view, so long as it does not run afoul of the problems I have mentioned. It may indeed be possible to design such a program. The relative weight of the case against paternalistic intervention can be lessened, in any case, by making adjustments for the proportion of intervention, benefit, and intrusion. Health-promotion programs that are only very mildly coercive, such as moderate increases in cigarette taxes, require very little justification; noncoercive measures such as health education require none at all. And the case for more intrusive measures would be stronger if greater and more certain benefits could be promised. Moreover, even if the paternalistic rationale for coercive reform of health-related behavior fails completely, there may be other rationales to justify the intrusion. It is to these other sorts of arguments that I now turn.

FAIR DISTRIBUTION OF BURDENS

The problem of health-related behavior is sometimes seen as a straight-forward question of collective social preference:

The individual must realize that a perpetuation of the present system of high cost, after-the-fact medicine will only result in higher costs and greater frustration . . . This is his primary critical choice: to change his personal bad habits or stop complaining. He can either remain the problem or become the solution to it; Beneficent Government cannot—indeed, should not—do it for him or to him. (Knowles, 1977)

A good deal of the controversy is due, however, not to any one person's distaste for having to choose between bad habits and high costs, but rather some people's distaste for having to accept both high costs and someone *else's* bad habits. In the view of these persons, those who indulge in self-destructive practices and present their medical bills to the public are free riders in an economy kept going by the willingness of others to stay fit and sober. Those who hold themselves back from reckless living may care little

about beneficence. When they call for curbs on the expensive health practices of others, they want the government to act as their agent primarily out of concern for their interests.

The demand for protection from the costs of calamities other people bring upon themselves involves an appeal to fairness and justice. Both the prudent person and the person with unhealthy habits, it is thought, are capable of safe and healthy living; why should the prudent have to pay for neighbors who decide to take risks? Neighbors are certainly not permitted to set fire to their houses if there is danger of its spreading. With the increasing economic and social connectedness of society, the use of coercion to discourage the unhealthy practices of others may receive the same justification. As the boundary between private and public becomes less distinct, and decisions of the most personal sort come to have marked adverse effects upon others, the state's protective function may be thought to give it jurisdiction over any health-related aspect of living.

This sort of argument presupposes a certain theory of justice; and one who wishes to take issue with the rationale for coercive intervention in health-related behavior might join the debate at the level of theory. Since this debate would be carried out at a quite general level, with only incidental reference to health practices, I will accept the argument's premise (if only for argument's sake) and comment only upon its applicability to the problem of self-destructive behavior. A number of considerations lead to the conclusion that the fairness argument as a justification of coercive intervention, despite initial appearances, is anything but straightforward. Underlying this argument is an empirical premise that may well prove untrue of at least some unhealthy habits: that those who take chances with their health *do* place a significant financial burden upon society. It is not enough to point to the costs of medical care for lung cancer and other diseases brought on by individual behavior. As Hellegers (1978) points out, one must also determine what the individual would have died of had he not engaged in the harmful practice, and subtract the cost of the care which that condition requires. There is no obvious reason to suppose that the diseases brought on by self-destructive behavior are costlier to treat than those that arise from "natural causes."

Skepticism over the burden placed on society by smokers and other risk-takers is doubly reinforced by consideration of the non-medical costs and benefits that may be involved. It may turn out, for all we know prior to investigation, that smoking tends to cause few problems during a person's productive years and then to kill the individual before the need to provide years of social security and pension payments. From this perspective, the truly burdensome individual may be the unreasonably fit senior citizen who lives on for 30 years after retirement, contributing to the bankruptcy of the social security system, and using up savings that would have reverted to the public purse via inheritance taxes had an immoderate life-style brought an early death. Taken at face value, the fairness argument would require taxes and other disincentives on *non*-smoking and other healthful personal practices which in the end would sap the resources of the healthy person's fellow citizens. Only detailed empirical inquiry can show which of these practices would be slated for discouragement were the argument from fairness accepted; but the fact that we would find penalties on healthful behavior wholly unpalatable may weaken our acceptance of the argument itself.

A second doubt concerning the claim that the burdens of unhealthy behavior are unfairly distributed also involves an unstated premise. The risk taker, according to the fairness argument, should have to suffer not only the illness that may result from the behavior but also the loss of freedom attendant to the coercive measures used in the attempt to change the behavior. What, exactly, is the cause cited by those complaining of the financial burdens placed upon society by the self-destructive? It is not simply the burden of caring and paying for care of these persons when they become sick. Many classes of persons impose such costs on the public besides the self-destructive. For example, diabetics, and others with hereditary dispositions to contract diseases, incur unusual and heavy expenses, and these are routinely paid by others. Why are these costs not resisted as well?

One answer is that there *is* resistance to these other costs, which partly explains why we do not yet have a national health insurance system. But even those willing to pay for the costs of caring for diabetics, or the medical expenses of the poor, may still bridle when faced by the needs of those who have compromised their own health. Is there a rationale for resisting the latter kinds of costs while accepting the former? One possible reason to distinguish the costs of the person with a genetic disease from those of the person with a life-style-induced disease is simply that one can be prevented and the other cannot. Health behavior change measures provide an efficient way of

reducing the overall financial burden of health care that society must shoulder, and this might be put forward as the reason why self-destructive persons may have their presumptive rights compromised while others with special medical expenses need not.

But this is not the argument we seek. The medical costs incurred by diseases caused by unhealthy lifestyles may be preventable, if our behavior-modifying methods are effective; but this fact shows only that there is a utilitarian opportunity for reducing costs and saving health-care dollars. It does *not* show that this opportunity makes it right to burden those who lead unhealthy lives with governmental intrusion. If costs must be reduced, perhaps they should be reduced some other way (*e.g.*, by lessening the quality of care provided for all); or perhaps costs should not be lowered and those feeling burdened should be made to tolerate the expense. The fact that money could be saved by intruding into the choice of life-styles of the self-destructive does not *itself* show that it would be particularly fair to do so.

If intrusion is to be justified on the grounds that unhealthy life-styles impose unfair financial burdens on others, then, something must be added to the argument. That extra element, it seems, is *fault*. Instead of the *avoidability* of the illnesses and their expenses, we point to the *responsibility* for them, which we may believe falls upon those who contract them. This responsibility, it might be supposed, makes it unfair to force others to pay the bills and makes it fair for others to take steps to prevent the behaviors that might lead to the illness, even at the cost of some of the responsible person's privacy and liberty.

The argument thus depends crucially on the premise that the person who engages in an unhealthy life-style is responsible for the costs of caring for the illness that it produces. "Responsible" has many senses, and this premise needs to be stated unambiguously. Since responsibility was brought into the argument in hopes of contrasting life-style-related diseases from others, it seems to involve the notions of choice and voluntariness. If the chronic diseases resulting from life-style were not the result of voluntary choices, then there could be no assignment of responsibility in the sense in which the term is being used. This would be the case, for example, if a person contracted lung cancer from breathing the smog in the atmosphere rather than from smoking. But what if it should turn out that even a person's smoking habit were the result of forces beyond the smoker's control? If the habit is involuntary, so is the illness; and the smoker in this instance is no more to be held liable for imposing the costs of treatment than would, say, the diabetic. Since much self-destructive behavior is the result of suggestion, constraint, compulsion, and other factors, the applicability of the fairness argument is limited.

Even if the behavior leading to illness is wholly voluntary, there is not necessarily any justification for intervention *by the state*. The only parties with rights to reform life-styles on these grounds are those who are actually being burdened by the costs involved. A wealthy man who retained his own medical facilities would not justifiably be a target of any of these interventions, and a member of a prepaid health plan would be liable to intervention primarily from others in his payments pool. He would then, of course, have the option of resigning and continuing his self-destructive ways; or he might seek out an insurance scheme designed for those who wish to take chances but who also want to limit their losses. These insured parties would join forces precisely to pool risks and remove reasons for refraining from unhealthy practices; preventive coercion would thus be out of the question. Measures undertaken by the government and applied indiscriminately to all who indulge in a given habit may thus be unfair to some (unless other justification is provided). The administrative inconvenience of restricting these interventions to the appropriate parties might make full justice on this issue too impractical to achieve.

This objection may lose force should there be a national health insurance program in which membership would be mandatory. Indeed, it might be argued that existing federal support of medical education, research, and service answers this objection now. But this only establishes another ground for disputing the responsibility of the self-destructive individual for the costs of his medical care. To state this objection, two classes of acts must be distinguished: the acts constituting the life-style that causes the disease and creates the need for care; and the acts of imposing financial shackles upon an unwilling public. Unless the acts in the first group are voluntary, the argument for imposing behavior change does not get off the ground. Even if voluntary, those acts in the second class might not be. Destructive acts affect others only because others are in financial relationships with the individual that cause the medical costs to be distributed among them. If the financial arrangement is mandatory, then the individual may not have *chosen* that his acts should have these effects on others. The situation will have been this: an individual is compelled by law to enter into financial relationships with certain others as a part of an insurance scheme; the arrangement causes the individual's acts to have effects on others that the others object to; and so they claim the right to coerce the individual into desisting from those acts. It seems difficult to assign to this individual responsibility for the distribution of financial burdens. He or she may (or may not) be responsible for getting sick, but not for having the sickness affect others adversely.

This objection has certain inherent limitations in its scope. It applies only to individuals who are brought into a mandatory insurance scheme against their wishes. Those who join the scheme gladly may perhaps be assigned responsibility for the effect they have on others once they are in it; and certainly many who will be covered in such a plan will be glad of it. Further, the burden imposed under such a plan does not occur until persons who have made themselves sick request treatment and present the bill to the public. Only if treatment is mandatory and all financing of care taken over by the public can the imposition of burden be said to be wholly involuntary.

In any case, certain adjustments could be made in a national health insurance plan or service that would disarm this objection. Two such changes are obvious: the plan could be made voluntary, rather than mandatory; and/or the public could simply accept the burdens imposed by unhealthy life-styles and refrain from attempts to modify them. The first of these may be impractical for economic reasons (in part because the plan would fill up with those in greatest need, escalating costs), and the second only ignores the problem for which it is supposed to be a solution.

There is, however, a response that would seem to have more chance of success: allowing those with unhealthy habits to pay their own way. Users of cigarettes and alcohol, for example, could be made to pay an excise tax, the proceeds of which would cover the costs of treatment for lung cancer and other resulting illnesses. Unfortunately, these costs would also be paid by users who are not abusers: those who drink only socially would be forced to pay for the excesses of alcoholics. Alternatively, only those contracting the illnesses involved could be charged; but it would be difficult to distinguish illnesses resulting from an immoderate life-style from those due to genetic or environmental causes. The best solution might be to identify persons taking risks (by tests for heavy smoking, alcohol abuse, or dangerous inactivity) and charge higher insurance premiums accordingly. This method could be used only if tests for these behaviors were developed that were non-intrusive and administratively manageable. The point would be to have those choosing self-destructive life-styles assume the true costs of their habits. I defer to economists for devising the best means to this end.

This kind of policy has its good and bad points. Chief among the favorable ones is that it allows a maximum retention of liberty in a situation in which liberty carries a price. Under such a policy, those who wished to continue their self-destructive ways without pressure could continue to do so, provided that they absorbed the true costs of their practices themselves. Should they not wish to shoulder these costs, they could submit to the efforts of the government to induce changes in their behavior. If the rationale for coercive reform is the burden the unhealthy life-styles impose on others, this option seems to meet its goals; and it does so in a way that does not require loss of liberty and immunity from intrusions. Indeed, committed immoderates might have reason to welcome the imposition of these costs. Although their expenses would be greater, they would thereby remove at one stroke the most effective device held by others to justify meddling with their "chosen" life-styles.

The negative side of this proposal stems from the fact that under its terms the only way to retain one's liberty is to pay for it. This, of course, offers very different opportunities to rich and poor. This inequality can be assessed in very different ways. From one perspective, the advantage money brings to rich people under this scheme is the freedom to ruin their own health. Although the freedom may be valued intrinsically (*i.e.*, for itself, not as a means to some other end), the resulting illness cannot; perhaps the poor, who are denied freedom but given a better chance for health, are coming off best in the transaction. From another perspective, however, it seems that such a plan simply adds to the degradation already attending to being poor. Only the poor would be forced to submit to loss of privacy, loss of freedom from pressure, and regulation aimed at behavior change. Such liberties are what make up full citizenship, and one might hold that they ought not to be made contingent on one's ability to purchase them.

The premise that illnesses caused by unhealthy habits impose financial burdens on society, then, does not automatically give cause for adopting strong measures to change the self-destructive behavior. Still, it *may* do so, if the underlying theory of justice is correct and if its application can skirt the problems mentioned here. Besides, justification for such programs may be derived from other considerations.

Indeed, there is one respect in which the combined force of the paternalistic rationale and the fairness argument is greater than the sum of its parts. The central difficulty for the fairness argument, mentioned above, is that much of the self-destructive behavior that burdens the public is not really the fault of the individual; various forces, internal and external, may conspire to produce such behavior independently of the person's will. Conversely, a problem for the paternalist is that much of the harm from which the individual would be "protected" may be the result of free, voluntary choices, and hence beyond the paternalist's purview. The best reason to be skeptical of the first rationale, then, is doubt over the *presence* of voluntariness; the best reason to doubt the second concerns the *absence* of voluntariness. Whatever weighs against the one will count for the other.

The self-destructive individual, then, is caught in a theoretical double-bind: whether the behavior is voluntary or not, there will be at least *prime facie* grounds for coercive intervention. The same holds true for partial voluntariness and involuntariness. This consideration is of considerable importance for those wanting to justify coercive reform of health-related behavior. It reduces the significance of the notion of voluntariness in the pro-intervention arguments, and so serves to lessen concern over the intractable problems of defining the notion adequately, and detecting and measuring its occurrence.

PUBLIC WELFARE

Aside from protecting the public from unfair burdens imposed by those with poor health habits, there may be social benefits to be realized by inducing immoderates to change their behavior. Health behavior change may be the most efficient way to reduce the costs of health care in this country, and the benefits derived may give reason to create some injustices. Further, life-style reform could yield some important collective benefits. A healthier work force means a stronger economy, for example, and the availability of healthy soldiers enhances national security.

There may also be benefits more directly related to health. If the supply of doctors and curative facilities should prove relatively inelastic, or if the economy would falter if too much of our resources were diverted to health care, it may be impossible to increase access to needed medical services. The social goal of adequate treatment for all would then not be realizable unless the actual need for medical care were reduced. Vigorous government efforts to change life-styles may be seen as the most promising means to this end.

The achievement of these social goals—enhanced security, improved economic functioning, and universal access to medical care—could come at the price of limits to the autonomy of that segment of society that indulges in dangerous living. If we do not claim to find fault with them, it would be unreasonable to insist that the immoderate *owed* the loss of some of their liberties to society as a part of some special debt—while continuing to exempt from special burden those with involuntary special needs due to genes or body chemistry. The reason for society to impose a loss upon the immoderate rather than upon the diabetic would be, simply, that it stood to benefit more by doing so.

Whether it is permissible to pursue social goods by extracting benefits from disadvantageously situated groups within society is a matter of political ideology and justice. Our society routinely compromises certain of its citizens' interests and privileges for the public good; others are considered inviolate. The question to be decided is whether the practices that we now know to be dangerous to health merit the protection given by the status of right. The significance of this status is that considerations of utility must be very strong before curbing the practice can be justified. Unfortunately, I see no decisive argument that shows that smoking, sloth, and other dangerous enjoyable pastimes are or are not protected by rights. . . .

MEANS OF HEALTH BEHAVIOR REFORM

Two questions arise in considering the ethics of government attempts to bring about healthier ways of living. The first question is: Should coercion, intrusion, and deprivation be used as methods for inducing change? The other question is: How do we decide whether a given health promotion program is coercive, intrusive, or inflicts deprivations? These questions are independent of each other. Two parties who agreed on the degree of coerciveness that might be justifiably employed in a given situation might still assess a proposed policy differently in this regard, and

hence reach different conclusions on whether the policy should be put into effect. . . .

HEALTH EDUCATION

Health education seems harmless. Education generally provides information and this generally increases our power, since it enhances the likelihood that our decisions will accomplish our ends. For the most part, there is no inherent ethical problem with such programs, and they do not stand in need of moral justification. Still, there are certain problems with some health education programs, and these should be mentioned.

Health education *could* be intrusive. Few could object to making information available to those who seek it out. But if "providing information" were taken to mean making sure that the public attained a high level of awareness of the message, the program might require an objectionably high level of exposure. This is primarily an esthetic issue, and is unlikely to cause concern.

Can education be coercive? Information can be used as a tool for one party to get another to do its bidding, just as threats can. But the method is different: Instead of changing the prospective consequences of available actions, which is what a threat does, education alerts one to the previously unrecognized consequences of one's acts. Educators who hope to increase healthful behavior will disseminate only information that points in that direction; they cannot be expected to point out that, in addition to causing deterioration of the liver, alcohol helps certain people feel relaxed in social settings. It is difficult to know whether to regard this selective informing as manipulative. . . . Such measures acquire more definite coercive coloration when they are combined with suppression of the other side. . . .

The main threat of coerciveness in health education programs, in my opinion, lies in the possibility that such programs may turn from providing information to manipulating attitude and motivation. . . . [W]hen health education programs are evaluated, they are not judged successful or unsuccessful in proportion to their success in *inducing belief*. Rather, evaluators look at *behavior change*, the actions which, they hope, would stem from these beliefs. If education programs are to be evaluated favorably, health educators may be led to take a wider view of their role. . . . This would include attempts to motivate the public to adopt healthy habits, and this might have to be supplied by covert appeals to other interests ("smokers are unpopular," and so on). Suggestion and manipulation may replace information as the tools used by the health educators to accomplish their purpose. . . . Indeed, health education may call for actual and deliberate *mis*information: directives may imply or even state that the scientific evidence in favor of a given health practice is unequivocal even when it is not. . . .

A fine line has been crossed in these endeavors. Manipulation and suggestion go well beyond providing information to enhance rational decision making. These measures bypass rational decision-making faculties and thereby inflict a loss of personal control. Thus, health education, except when restricted to information, requires some justification. The possible deleterious effects are so small that the justification required may be slight; but the requirement is there. Ethical concerns for this kind of practice may become more pressing as the educational techniques used to induce behavior change become more effective.

INCENTIVES, SUBSIDIES, AND TAXES

Incentive measures range from pleasantly noncoercive efforts such as offering to pay citizens if they will live prudently, to coercive measures such as threatening to fine them if they do not. Various noncoercive measures designed to facilitate healthful life-styles might include: providing jogging paths and subsidizing tennis balls. Threats might include making all forms of transportation other than bicycling difficult, and making inconvenient the purchase of food containing saturated fats.

Generally speaking, justification is required only for coercive measures, not for incentives. However, the distinction is not as clear as it first appears. Suppose, for example, that the government wants to induce the obese to lose weight, and that a mandatory national health insurance plan is about to go into effect. The government's plan threatens the obese with higher premiums unless they lose their excess weight. Before the plan is instituted, however, someone objects that the extra charges planned for eager eaters make the program coercive. No adequate justification is found. Instead of calling off the program, however, some subtle changes are made. The insurance scheme is announced with higher premiums than had been originally planned. No extra charges are imposed on anyone; instead, discounts are offered to all those who avoid overweight. Instead of coercion, the plan now uses positive incentives; and this does not require the kind of justification needed for the former plan. Hence the new program is allowed to go into effect.

The effect of the rate structure in the two plans is, of course, identical: The obese would pay the higher rate, the slender the lower one. It seems that the distinction between coercion and incentive is merely semantic. But this is the wrong conclusion. There is a real difference, upon which much ethical evaluation must rest; the problem is in stating what that difference amounts to. A partial answer is that a given measure cannot be judged coercive or non-coercive without referring to a background standard from which the measure's effects diverge favorably or unfavorably. Ultimately, I believe, the judgment required for the obesity measure would require us to decide what a fair rate would have been for the insurance; any charges above that fair rate would be coercive, and any below, incentive. . . . The rate the government plans to charge as the standard premium might not be the fair rate; and this shows that one cannot judge the coerciveness of a fee structure merely by checking it for surcharges.

Even if we are able to sort the coercive from the incentive measures, however, we may have reason to hesitate before allowing the government unlimited use of incentives. A government in a position to make offers may not necessarily coerce those it makes the offers to, but is relatively more likely to get its way; in this sense its power increases. Increased government power over life-styles would seem generally to require some justification. . . . A further problem with financial incentives is that if they are to affect the behavior of the rich they must be sizable; and this may redistribute wealth in a direction considered unjust on other grounds. . . .

Even where justifiably applied to induce behavior change, no *more* deprivation ought to be used than is necessary; but there are administrative difficulties in trying to obey this limitation. Different persons respond to different amounts of deprivation—again, the rich man will absorb costs that would deter the poor one. A disincentive set higher than that needed to induce behavior change would be unfair; a rate set too low would be ineffective. The amount of deprivation inflicted ought, then, to be tailored to the individual's wealth and psychology. This may well be administratively impossible, and injustice would result to the degree that these differences were ignored.

REGULATIVE MEASURES

The coercive measures discussed above concentrate on applying influence on individuals so that their behavior will change. A different way of effecting a reform is to deprive self-destructive individuals of the means needed to engage in their unhealthy habits. Prohibition of the sale of cigarettes would discourage smoking at least as effectively as exhortations not to smoke or insurance surcharges for habitual tobacco use. Yet, these regulative measures are surely as coercive, although they do not involve direct interaction with the individuals affected. They are merely one more way of intervening in an individual's decision to engage in habits that may cause illness. As such, they are clearly in need of the same or stronger justification as those involving threats, despite the argument that these measures are taken only to combat an unhealthy *environment*, and thus cannot be counted as coercing the persons who have unhealthy ways of living. . . . What distinguishes these "environmental" causes of illness from, say, carcinogens in the water supply, is the active connivance of the victims. "Shielding" the "victims" from these external forces must involve making them behave in a way they do not choose. This puts regulative measures in the same category as those applied directly to the self-destructive individuals.

CONCLUSIONS

I have been concerned with clarifying what sorts of justification must be given for certain kinds of government involvement in the reform of unhealthy ways of living. It is apparent that more is needed than a simple desire on the part of the government to promote health and/or reduce costs. When the measures taken are intrusive, coercive, manipulative, and/or inflict deprivations—in short, when they are of the sort many might be expected to dislike—the moral justification required may be quite complex. The principles that would be used in making a case for these interventions may have limited scope and require numerous exceptions and qualifications; it is unlikely that they can be expressed as simple slogans such as "individuals must be responsible for their own health" or "society can no longer afford self-destructiveness."

My goal has been to specify the kind of justification that would have to be provided for any coercive life-style reform measure. I have not attempted to reach a judgment of right or wrong. Either of these judgments would be foolhardy, if only in view of the diversity of health-promotion measures that have been and will be contemplated.

• • •

REFERENCES

Claiborne, C. 1976. In Defense of Eating Rich Food. *The New York Times*, December 8.

Knowles, J. H. 1976. The Struggle to Stay Healthy. Time: August 9.

———. 1977. The Responsibility of the Individual. In Knowles, J. H., ed., Doing Better and Feeling Worse. New York: W. W. Norton.

Management of Communicable Diseases

LAWRENCE O. GOSTIN

Jacobson v. Massachusetts at 100 Years: Police Power and Civil Liberties in Tension

Lawrence O. Gostin is Professor of Law at Georgetown University, Professor of Public Health at the Johns Hopkins University, and the Director of the Center for Law & the Public's Health at Johns Hopkins and Georgetown Universities. His research focuses on public health law and ethics. Professor Gostin's latest books are *Public Health Law: Power, Duty, Restraint* and *Public Health Law and Ethics: A Reader*.

Editor's note: The 1905 United States Supreme Court case *Jacobson v. Massachusetts* highlights the tension between respect for individual liberty and the common good. The Cambridge (Massachusetts) Board of Health was authorized by a state statute to mandate vaccination when it was necessary for public health or safety. The Reverend Henning Jacobson refused vaccination during a smallpox outbreak. Jacobson was convicted under the statute and fined five dollars. He appealed to the U.S. Supreme Court and lost. The Supreme Court upheld the power of the state to require smallpox vaccination during an epidemic as an exercise of the state's police power to protect public health.

Jacobson v Massachusetts (1905)[1] is often regarded as the most important judicial decision in public health. Why? Is it because of the Supreme Court's deference to public health decisionmaking? Is it because the Court enunciated a framework for the protection of individual liberties that persists today? Perhaps it is because *Jacobson* was decided during the same term as *Lochner v New York*[2]—the infamous Supreme Court case that struck down a law limiting the number of hours that bakers could work. If *Lochner* was judicial activism at its extreme for invalidating reasonable economic regulation, then *Jacobson* was judicial recognition of police power—the most important aspect of state sovereignty. There is another question that deserves attention: Would *Jacobson* be decided the same way today? It

From *American Journal of Public Health* 95:4 (April 2005), 576–581. Notes and table omitted. Reprinted with permission from the American Public Health Association.

is fitting on the 100th anniversary of *Jacobson* to examine the importance and the enduring meaning of the most famous decision in the realm of public health law.

JACOBSON IN A HISTORICAL CONTEXT: THE IMMUNIZATION DEBATES

The contention that compulsory vaccination is an infraction of personal liberty and an unconstitutional interference with the right of the individual to have the smallpox if he wants it, and to communicate it to others, has been ended [by the US Supreme Court]. . . . [This] should end the useful life of the societies of cranks formed to resist the operation of laws relative to vaccination. Their occupation is gone.[3(p6)]

Jacobson v Massachusetts was decided just a few years after a major outbreak of smallpox in Boston that resulted in 1596 cases and 270 deaths between 1901 and 1903. The outbreak reignited the smallpox immunization debate, and there was plenty of hyperbole on both sides. Antivaccinationists launched a "scathing attack"[4(p3)]: compulsory vaccination is "the greatest crime of the age," it "slaughter[s] tens of thousands of innocent children," and it "is more important than the slavery question, because it is debilitating the whole human race."[5(pF7)] The antivaccinationists gave notice that compulsory powers "will cause a riot."[6] Their influence was noticeable and resulted in a "conscience clause" from the British Parliament that exempted any parent who can "satisfy Justices in petty sessions that he conscientiously believes that vaccination would be prejudicial to the health of the child."[7(p6)]

The response of the mainstream media was equally shrill. The media characterized the debate as "a conflict between intelligence and ignorance, civilization and barbarism."[6(p4)] The *New York Times* stated, "No enemy of vaccination could ask better than to have England's compulsory vaccination law nullified by that [conscience] clause"; the paper referred to antivaccinationists as a "familiar species of crank," whose arguments are "absurdly fallacious."[7(p6)] The mainstream media continued its campaign against the "jabberings" of "hopeless cranks" for years[8(p6)] by continuing to depict them as "ignorant" and "deficient in the power to judge [science]."[9(p485)]

Before *Jacobson*, the state courts were heavily engaged in the vaccination controversy, and their judgments were markedly deferential to public health agencies: "Whether vaccination is or is not efficacious in the prevention of smallpox is a question with which the courts declare they have no concern."[10,11(p91)]

The courts routinely found school vaccination requirements constitutional. To be sure, some courts invoked a standard of "necessity," but without strong safeguards of individual liberty.[12(p854)] The courts mostly decided vaccination cases on the basis of administrative rather than constitutional law. They recognized states' police power to delegate authority to public health agencies or boards of health. In the rare instances where limits were imposed, it was because a board exceeded its statutory authority or because the courts construed that authority as requiring a state of emergency. A person's bona fide belief against vaccination was not a sufficient excuse for noncompliance; however, a person could be exempted because of a physical condition that posed a particular risk for adverse effects. The states compelled vaccination only indirectly—by imposing penalties, denying school admission, or quarantining. The courts, therefore, could avoid ruling on the constitutionality of physically requiring vaccination, because this would directly affect a person's control over his or her body.

THE MANY FACES OF *JACOBSON:* PERSONAL FREEDOM AND THE COMMON GOOD

It was within this historical context that the US Supreme Court decided *Jacobson v Massachusetts.* Justice Harlan's opinion had many faces and was, at some points, in tension. Relying on social-compact theory, Harlan displayed strong deference to public health agencies. At the same time, Harlan asserted a theory of limited government and set standards to safeguard individual freedoms. This was a classic case of reconciling individual interests in bodily integrity with collective interests in health and safety. In the 100 years since *Jacobson*, the case has been cited in 69 Supreme Court cases—most in support of police power and a minority in support of individual freedom.

SOCIAL-COMPACT THEORY: POLICE POWER AND PUBLIC HEALTH DEFERENCE

In early American jurisprudence, before *Jacobson*, the judiciary staunchly defended police powers, which Chief Justice Marshall in *Gibbons v Ogden* (1824) described as "that immense mass of legislation, [including] . . . inspection laws, quarantine laws, [and] health laws of every description."[13(p203)] In the *Slaughter-House Cases* (1873), Justice Miller asserted that police power was preeminent because "upon it depends the security of social order, the life and health of the citizen, the comfort of an existence in a thickly populated community, the enjoyment of private and social life, and the beneficial use of property."[14(p62)] The judiciary even periodically suggested that public health regulation was immune from constitutional review: "Where the police power is set in motion in its proper sphere, the courts have no jurisdiction to stay the arm of the legislative branch.[15(p532)] The core issue, of course, was to understand what was meant by the "proper legislative sphere," because it was not supposed, at least since the enactment of the 14th Amendment in 1868, that government could act in an arbitrary manner free from judicial control.

The *Jacobson* Court's use of social-compact theory to support this expansive understanding of police powers was unmistakable. Justice Harlan preferred a community-oriented philosophy where citizens have duties to one another and to society as a whole:

> [T]he liberty secured by the Constitution . . . does not import an absolute right in each person to be . . . wholly freed from restraint . . . On any other basis organized society could not exist with safety to its members. . . . [The Massachusetts Constitution] laid down as a fundamental . . . social compact that the whole people covenants with each citizen, and each citizen with the whole people, that all shall be governed by certain laws for the 'common good,' and that government is instituted 'for the protection, safety, prosperity and happiness of the people, and not for the profit, honor or private interests of any one man.[1(p26–27)]

The Court's opinion is filled with examples of the social compact that ranged from sanitary laws and animal control to quarantine and thereby demonstrated the breadth of police powers. Justice Harlan granted considerable leeway to the elected branch of government by displaying an almost unquestioning acceptance of legislative findings of scientific fact. He also was a federalist and asserted the primacy of state over federal authority in public health. The distinct tenor of the opinion was deferential to agency action.

A primary legacy of *Jacobson*, then, is its defense of social-welfare philosophy and police power regulation. Although the progressive-era appeal to collective interests no longer has currency, most of the 69 cases that have cited *Jacobson* did so in defense of police power. Post-*Jacobson* courts affirmed states' authority to (1) regulate individuals and businesses for public health and safety (8 cases), (2) limit liberty to achieve common goods (34 cases), (3) permit legislatures to delegate broad powers to public health agencies (5 cases), and (4) defer to the judgment of legislatures and agencies in the exercise of their powers (13 cases).

THEORY OF LIMITED GOVERNMENT: SAFEGUARDING INDIVIDUAL LIBERTY

Jacobson's social-compact theory was in tension with its theory of limited government. Beyond its passive acceptance of state discretion in matters of public health was the Court's first systematic statement of the constitutional limitations imposed on government. *Jacobson* established a floor of constitutional protection that consists of 4 overlapping standards: necessity, reasonable means, proportionality, and harm avoidance. These standards, while permissive of public health intervention, nevertheless required a deliberative governmental process to safeguard liberty.

NECESSITY

Justice Harlan insisted that police powers must be based on the "necessity of the case" and could not be exercised in "an arbitrary, unreasonable manner" or go "beyond what was reasonably required for the safety of the public."[1(p28)] The state must act only in the face of a demonstrable health threat.[1] Necessity requires, at a minimum, that the subject of the compulsory intervention must pose a threat to the community.

REASONABLE MEANS

Although government may act under conditions of necessity, its methods must be reasonably designed to prevent or ameliorate the threat. *Jacobson* adopted a means/ends test that requires a reasonable relationship between the public health intervention and the achievement of a legitimate public health objective. Even though the objective of the legislature may be valid and beneficent, the methods adopted must have a "real or substantial relation" to protection of the public health and cannot be "a plain, palpable invasion of rights."[1(p31)]

PROPORTIONALITY

Even under conditions of necessity and with reasonable means, a public health regulation is unconstitutional if the human burden imposed is wholly disproportionate to the expected benefit. "[T]he police power of a State," said Justice Harlan, "may be exerted in such circumstances or by regulations so arbitrary and oppressive in particular cases as to justify the interference of the courts to prevent wrong . . . and oppression."[1(p38–39)] Public health authorities have a constitutional responsibility not to overreach in ways that unnecessarily invade personal spheres of autonomy. This suggests a requirement for a reasonable balance between the public good to be achieved and the degree of personal invasion. If the intervention is gratuitously onerous or unfair, it may overstep constitutional boundaries.

HARM AVOIDANCE

Those who pose a risk to the community can be required to submit to compulsory measures for the common good. The control measure itself, however, should not pose a health risk to its subject. Justice Harlan emphasized that Henning Jacobson was a "fit person" for smallpox vaccination, but he asserted that requiring a person to be immunized who would be harmed is "cruel and inhuman in the last degree."[1(p39)] If there had been evidence that the vaccination would seriously impair Jacobson's health, he may have prevailed in this historic case. *Jacobson*-era cases reiterate the theme that public health actions must not harm subjects. Notably, courts required safe and habitable environments for persons subject to isolation or quarantine on the grounds that public health powers are designed to promote well-being and not punish the individual.

The facts in *Jacobson* did not require the court to enunciate a standard of fairness under the Equal Protection Clause of the 14th Amendment, because the vaccination requirement was generally applicable to all inhabitants of Cambridge, Mass. Nevertheless, the federal courts had already created such a standard in *Jew Ho v Williamson* in 1900. A quarantine for bubonic plague in San Francisco, Calif, was created to operate exclusively against Chinese Americans. In striking down the quarantine, the federal district court said that health authorities had acted with an "evil eye and an unequal hand."[16(p23)]

Several of these standards for protecting liberty have been discernable in cases that have cited *Jacobson* between 1905 and 2004. Some cases cited *Jacobson* for the simple, albeit important, proposition that bodily integrity is a constitutionally protected liberty interest (6 cases); others cited *Jacobson* to require that the state have an important interest (real and substantial [6 cases], compelling [1 case], or fairly balanced with individual interests [4 cases]); and still others cited *Jacobson* to prevent the state from acting arbitrarily or unreasonably (7 cases). Federalism also is used as a tool to reign in the national government, with 1 court arguing, probably incorrectly, that the federal government lacks police power.

LOCHNER V NEW YORK: THE ANTITHESIS OF GOOD JUDICIAL GOVERNANCE

Jacobson was decided during the same term as *Lochner v New York*, which was the beginning of the so-called Lochner era in constitutional law (1905–1937).[2] In *Lochner*, the Supreme Court held that a limitation on the number of hours that bakers could work violated the Due Process Clause of the 14th Amendment. The Court perceived a limitation on bakers' hours as an interference with the freedom of contract rather than as a legitimate police regulation. Yet, Justice Harlan, in a powerful dissent, said the

New York statute was expressly for the public's health. Quoting standard health treatises, Harlan observed that "[d]uring periods of epidemic diseases the bakers are generally the first to succumb to disease, and the number swept away during such periods far exceeds the number of other crafts."[2(p71)]

The *Lochner* era posed deep concerns for those who realized that much of what public health does interferes with economic freedoms that involve contracts, business relationships, the use of property, and the practice of trades and professions. *Lochner*, in the words of Justice Harlan's dissent, "would seriously cripple the inherent power of the states to care for the lives, health, and well-being of their citizens."[2(p73)] By the time of the New Deal, those who believed that individuals do not have unfettered contractual freedom and that economic transactions were naturally constrained by unequal wealth and power relationships challenged the laissez-faire philosophy that undergirded Lochnerism. It was within this political context that the Supreme Court repudiated the principles of *Lochner*. . . .

Why have legal historians viewed *Jacobson* so favorably and *Lochner* so unfavorably? *Lochner* represented an unwarranted judicial interference with democratic control over the economy to safeguard public health and the environment. *Lochner* was a form of judicial activism that was unreceptive to protective and redistributive regulation. The *Lochner* court mistakenly saw market ordering as a state of nature rather than as a legal construct. *Jacobson* was the antithesis of *Lochner*, because it granted democratically elected officials discretion to pursue innovative solutions to hard social problems.

JACOBSON AND ITS ENDURING MEANING

. . . Would *Jacobson* be decided the same way if it were presented to the Court today? The answer is indisputably *yes*, even if the style and the reasoning would differ.

The validity of *Jacobson* as a sound modern precedent seems, at first sight, almost too obvious. The federal and state courts, including the US Supreme Court, have repeatedly affirmed its holding and reasoning by describing them as "settled" doctrine.[17(p176)] The courts have upheld compulsory vaccination in particular on numerous occasions. Even the rare judicial reservations about compulsory vaccination focus on religious exemptions and do not query states' authority to create a generally applicable immunization requirement.

During the last several decades, the Supreme Court has recognized a constitutionally protected "liberty interest" in refusing unwanted medical treatment. The Court accepted the principle of bodily integrity in cases that involved the rights of persons who had terminal illnesses and mental disabilities. Outside the context of reproductive freedoms however, the Court has not viewed liberty interests in bodily integrity as "fundamental." Instead of heightened scrutiny, the Supreme Court balances a person's liberty against state interests.[2] In fact, when it adopts a balancing test, the Court usually sides with the state. The Court has held that health authorities may impose serious forms of treatment, such as antipsychotic medication, if the person poses a danger to himself or others. The treatment also must be medically appropriate. The lower courts have used a similar harm-prevention theory and have upheld compulsory physical examination and treatment of persons who have infectious diseases.

Jacobson only began a debate about the appropriate boundaries of police power that is evolving today. Americans strongly support civil liberties, but they equally demand state protection of public health and safety. The compulsory immunization controversy still swirls with flare-ups that range from childhood and school vaccinations to counterbioterrorism vaccinations for anthrax and smallpox. Despite all the discordance in public opinion, *Jacobson* endures as a reasoned

formulation of the boundaries between individual and collective interests in public health.

NOTES

1. *Jacobson v Massachussets*, 197 US 11 (1905).

2. *Lochner v New York*, 198 US 45 (1905).

3. Editorial. *New York Times*. February 22, 1905.

4. Vaccine is attacked: English lecturer denounces inoculation for smallpox. *Washington Post*. February 25, 1909.

5. Vaccination a crime: Porter Cope, of Philadelphia, claims it is the only cause of smallpox. *Washington Post*. July 29, 1905.

6. Editorial. *New York Times*. September 26, 1885.

7. The anti-vaccinationists' triumph. *New York Times*. August 18, 1898.

8. Topic of the times. *New York Times*. June 19, 1901.

9. Smallpox: vaccination and tetanus. *Curr Lit*. 1902; 32: 484–487.

10. Compulsory vaccination. *NY Law Notes*. 1901:224–228.

11. *Blue v. Beach*, 56 NE 89 (Ind 1900).

12. *Morris v City of Columbus*, 30 SE 850 (Ga1898).

13. *Gibbons v Ogden*, 22 US (1824).

14. *The Slaughter-House Cases*, 83 US [36] (1873).

15. *State ex rel Conway v Southern Pac Co*. 145 P2d 530 (Wash 1943).

16. *Jew Ho v Williamson*, 103 F 10 (CCND Calif 1900).

17. *Zucht v King*. 260 US 174 (1922).

MATTHEW K. WYNIA

Restrictions on Liberty

Matthew K. Wynia is the director of the Institute for Ethics at the American Medical Association. His research focuses on physicians' responses to utilization review and market pressures in medicine, professional ethics, and performance measures for health care ethics.

. . . As Wendy Parmet has written, "Quarantine is the most extreme form of action a government takes in the name of public health . . . Although other [restraints on

From "Ethics and Public Health Emergencies: Restrictions on Liberty," *The American Journal of Bioethics* 7:2 (2007), 1–5. Notes omitted. © 2007 Taylor & Francis. Reprinted by permission of Taylor & Francis, LLC., Inc., www.taylorandfrancis.com

liberty] raise the issue of the state's power to sacrifice an individual's rights to protect the public, quarantine poses this question in its starkest form." (Parmet 1985) So we'll use quarantine as a way to think through the ethical issues involved in restricting individual liberties to promote public health. In reality, though, quarantine would never be used alone and the Centers for Disease Control and Prevention's (CDC's) Principles of Community Containment comprise a range of coordinated strategies (Tomianovic 2006). Other impingements on liberty, such as so-called "social distancing" methods (declaring "snow days," or canceling school and other public events), surveillance and contact tracing, and making infection control measures mandatory (wearing masks, vaccination, hand washing, and so on), can also be critically important in disease control. But ethically, justifications for quarantine will subsume these less restrictive measures as well.

First, some definitions; although the terms "quarantine" and "isolation" often are used interchangeably, they are not the same. *Quarantine* refers to the separation or restriction of movement of healthy persons who have been exposed, or who might have been exposed, to an infectious disease. *Isolation* is the separation of people who already are ill and who are presumed or known to be infected. Isolation is much less controversial and it has long been used routinely for hospitalized patients with tuberculosis, chickenpox, bacterial meningitis and other infections. Not only is the rationale for isolation typically very strong (people with symptoms are often much more contagious), but people in isolation are already experiencing the indignities and suffering related to sickness. Being isolated might be the least of their worries.

By contrast, people in quarantine are healthy and many of them aren't ever going to become ill. As a result, it is not known with any certainty whether or not they are, or ever will be, contagious. For example Rothstein and his colleagues report that during the SARS epidemic in Taiwan, "131,132 people were placed under quarantine, but only 12 were found to be potential cases of SARS" (Rothstein et al. 2003, 131). Of these, they say only 2 were eventually confirmed. Another report suggested that 133 of those quarantined eventually developed SARS. . . . Even so, that means that 1,000 or so uninfected people were placed under quarantine for each person who actually was infected. And SARS cases continued to climb in both Taiwan and China after widespread quarantine was being used in both countries (Edelson 2006).

This stark fact raises the first and by far the most important dilemma related to quarantine: it entails a substantial breach of individual freedom—and it's only possible ethical justification is consequential. That is, to have any hope of being ethically acceptable, quarantine must be effective at protecting the public's health. But does it work? Is quarantine effective? If not, then any remaining notions about how to ethically justify and implement quarantine become moot.

IS QUARANTINE EFFECTIVE?

Unfortunately, there is no simple answer to this question, since the effectiveness of any particular quarantine action will depend on social characteristics (such as whether the population accepts quarantine or rebels against it), biologic/disease characteristics (such as transmissibility, duration of infectiousness, the recovery rate, and whether symptoms correlate with contagion), and even individual characteristics (such as whether or not individuals, both in and out of quarantine, adhere to infection control measures like wearing masks or avoiding public gatherings). But the absence of a uniform, clear answer doesn't mean there aren't plenty of strong opinions about the general effectiveness of quarantine.

Some have asserted, for example, that the use of quarantine for SARS was "unnecessarily harmful," if not completely ineffective (Annas 2006, 13). Quoting Benjamin Franklin, George Annas argues that, "Those who would give up an essential liberty to purchase temporary security deserve neither liberty nor security" (2006, 5). And, he rightly bemoans the effects of reorganizing public health work into a military or police model (of which quarantine is only a part), which will undermine public trust, promote fear and panic, and therefore, ultimately, backfire as a public health strategy.

To support the claim that quarantine was not worthwhile for SARS, he notes several experiences that should give pause to proponents of early and widespread involuntary quarantine as a strategy for containing disease. For instance, when a rumor spread that all of Beijing might be placed under quarantine, 245,000 migrant workers apparently fled the city. In Hong Kong's Amoy Gardens apartment complex, the site of an early outbreak, officials declared a quarantine, but when they showed up to relocate residents to the quarantine facility there was no one home in more than half of the complex's 264 apartments. . . .

These examples show that, even outside of the independence-minded United States, it is hard to enforce an involuntary quarantine. Indeed, in every country that attempted to institute quarantine for SARS, violations occurred. . . . In Singapore, one individual was arrested when his picture showed up on the front page of the paper—a beer in one hand and his quarantine order in the other. As former Senator Sam Nunn said . . . , "there is no force on earth that can make Americans do something that they do not believe is in their own best interests and that of their families" (Annas 2006, 19).

Even more concerning is that Rothstein and his colleagues note that, "officials in Taiwan now believe that its aggressive use of quarantine contributed to public panic . . ." (Rothstein et al. 2003, 131). One thing is clear from these examples and others: quarantine done poorly can induce people to mistrust and avoid the public health system—and if this happens, then quarantine is not merely ineffective, it can actually feed the spread of the disease as frightened people break quarantine, flee and disperse into the population.

On the other hand, some claim that the widespread involuntary quarantines in China "proved to be effective" (Rothstein et al. 2003, 131). Indeed, the conventional wisdom from the SARS experience is that it was the use of quarantine that ultimately broke the epidemic, since no effective therapy or vaccine was available.

In this regard, it is worth recognizing that even if quarantine weren't extremely effective, it wouldn't take much for it to surpass the effectiveness of some of the other measures taken. As a comparison, consider mass screening programs: Chinese officials screened more than 14 million travelers but found only 12 cases of SARS, and more than 1 million people had their temperatures taken at Toronto airports without identifying a single case (Edelson 2006). Now *that's* ineffective—though only in hindsight, of course. Worse yet, some clusters of cases in China were traced back to transmission that probably occurred while people were standing in line together, waiting to have their temperatures checked. . . .

In retrospect, the major key to controlling SARS was preventing transmission *after* symptoms arose and once the patient was hospitalized, since asymptomatic patients seem not to have been very infectious. . . . In other words, strict isolation was critical; quarantine of asymptomatic people probably played a relatively small part in controlling spread of the disease. Even so, that doesn't mean it was worthless, nor that quarantine wouldn't be critical in a future epidemic caused by a different organism.

For example, a recent study used mathematical models to demonstrate that even a very "leaky" quarantine could have dramatic effects on the spread and duration of a pandemic flu epidemic (Wu et al. 2006). Even if only half the people in quarantine complied,

infection rates would still be cut almost in half. This makes sense if you consider how the flu typically spreads—even very mildly symptomatic people can be contagious. So averting a single new infection early on can have huge ripple effects on subsequent infections. In addition, merely delaying infections can "smooth out" or widen the epidemic curve, giving responders more time to prepare and perhaps alleviating the strain on the health care system. . . .

Given this, it would be very helpful for policy makers to know the likely characteristics of the specific disease in question when contemplating quarantine. Since influenza is typically easy to transmit even before the infected person has severe symptoms— and given US travel patterns—it seems very unlikely that cordoning off of a region could prevent the virus from getting out. By the time symptoms are being detected among the first wave of patients, spread will already have occurred. As epidemiologic models suggest, however, home-based quarantine, or "sheltering in place," might still dramatically slow the subsequent spread of the disease, which makes the careful use of quarantine a worthwhile strategy. But policy makers should not assume that a regional quarantine would be the best approach—and it should be known that military enforcement of such an effort could easily backfire by creating public fear, mistrust and even panic, provoking attempts to escape quarantine and run.

Finally, quarantine often is used when no treatments or vaccines are available—so its effectiveness is sometimes measured against a relatively short yardstick . . . essentially doing nothing. But that's the wrong way to look at it, since quarantine should not be used alone. It would be especially helpful to assess the utility of various types of quarantine (such as at home versus in a quarantine facility), and to compare quarantine against and in combination with other detection and containment strategies (use of "snow days," screening programs, strict isolation of ill patients, and so on). Such comparisons would give policy makers better data, and would lessen over-reliance on the precautionary principle to justify early and harsh application of quarantine. I have argued for the value of the precautionary principle before (Wynia 2005), but it can also be used to justify virtually any restriction on liberty if the potential harm from failure to contain the disease is bad enough.

PUBLIC SUPPORT

Despite the uncertainty surrounding its effectiveness, the American public generally supports the use of quarantine. In a recent survey, 94% of Americans said they would comply with a 7–10 day voluntary quarantine if they were exposed to a pandemic flu (Blendon et al. 2006a). This supports Paul Edelson's comment that,

it is a canard sometimes used to justify authoritarian actions that the public responds to emergencies by losing control and panicking; indeed it is the consensus of social scientists that people in emergency situations tend to be more cooperative and more generous toward others then they may normally be (Edelson 2006, 29–30).

In short, the vast majority of Americans say that in a crisis they would be willing to sacrifice their own liberty for the good of their community.

What the public worries about, as should we, is that quarantine will be done poorly. Will those placed under quarantine be well cared for? Will they be recognized as making a sacrifice that is helping to protect the rest of the community, and for which they should receive respect, appreciation and support—or will they suffer stigma, economic losses and discrimination? Will they receive food delivery, salary replacement and job security? Will they receive rapid medical care if they become ill, or prophylaxis if it becomes available? And if they are placed under quarantine outside the home, will someone care for their children, their pets, or their parents? In a recent 4-nation survey about out-of-home quarantine, many people were concerned about overcrowding, cross-infection, and the inability to communicate with their families (Blendon et al. 2006b). Sadly, almost 25% of Americans say they could not afford to miss work for a week, and nearly 1 in 5 said their employer would probably *require* them to work while ill, even if they might infect others (Blendon et al. 2006a).

Researchers note that quarantine also places a tremendous psychological strain on the individual and the community. In one study, symptoms of post-traumatic stress disorder and depression were seen in nearly one-third of those quarantined (Hawryluck et al. 2004). Others warn that quarantine can be used in a discriminatory way (Reis 2006). History shows this is possible. . . . A court ruled in 1900, for example, that public health officials had acted with an "evil eye and an unequal hand" in placing an entire community of Chinese immigrants under quarantine in response to a plague scare (Gostin, Bayer and Fairchild 2003). While no discriminatory patterns were seen in those quarantined during the SARS outbreak in Canada, . . . caution nevertheless is warranted. Meanwhile, merely being placed under quarantine can lead to stigma. And strict medical confidentiality is almost impossible to maintain, since the reason for the quarantine is likely to be well-known.

ETHICAL JUSTIFICATIONS FOR QUARANTINE

Given these risks, and since quarantine imposes sizeable costs on individuals and communities in terms of both liberty and economic impacts, quarantine requires some ethical justification beyond mere medical effectiveness. And quarantine should always be implemented with certain ethical considerations in mind.

The basic ethical justification for quarantine—beyond the consequentialist argument—stems from our moral obligation not to harm others. Even libertarians, strict defenders of individual rights, typically find justification for at least some limited uses of quarantine on the basis of the so-called, "harm principle." As articulated by the original libertarian, John Stuart Mill in *On Liberty*, the harm principle is the notion that "the only purpose for which power can be rightfully exercised over any member of a civilised community, against his will, is to prevent harm to others" (Mill 1859). Under this basic principle, if quarantine prevents exposed people from infecting others, it can be just. Of course, this leaves a great deal open to interpretation; starting with the fact that many people in quarantine will be exposed but not infected, which means they actually pose no danger to others. So how should one decide whether to infringe liberty to prevent a mere *risk* of harm to others?

In addition, a series of widely discussed ethical principles should be borne in mind when implementing quarantine. These were succinctly captured in the "Siracusa Principles," which demand that coercive public health measures be "legitimate, legal, necessary, non-discriminatory and represent the least restrictive means appropriate to the reasonable achievement of public health goals" (United Nations 1984). In particular, note that using the "least restrictive means," suggests that any limitations on civil liberties should be proportionate and no more restrictive than is really necessary. In other words, don't use involuntary quarantine or surveillance devices such as bracelets if voluntary measures will work; don't restrict someone to one room if an entire house is available; don't preclude visitors if personal protective equipment is effective; and don't cut someone off from their work if they can do it from inside quarantine. The idea is to preserve freedom and opportunity as far as possible, while still preventing significant risk of harm to others.

Finally, a number of experts have stressed the principles of reciprocity, transparency, non-discrimination, and accountability, or the right to a due process to challenge one's quarantine (Council on Ethical and Judicial Affairs 2006; Gostin, Bayer and Fairchild 2003; Upshur 2003). Reciprocity, transparency and non-discrimination were noted already, but the last right, the right to due process, deserves a final mention.

The logistics of individualized, formal due process hearings in the setting of a mass quarantine could pose a significant challenge. But more importantly, the right to challenge one's quarantine is related to the legal notion of *habeas corpus*, . . . which has been under attack of late in response to threats against the public. . . . As a result, during an epidemic it might well be up to public health professionals, doctors and others to ensure that individual liberties are not sacrificed in vain, misguided and perhaps even counterproductive efforts to protect the public's health.

While panic among the public is rare during public health crises, the same cannot be said with any certainty of political leaders. The urge to be perceived as responding aggressively to a major problem might cause some to suggest the use of police or militarily enforced quarantines of broad populations, cities or regions, even though this would almost certainly fail to curtail most epidemics—and could make the situation much worse. Transparent communications, viewing the public as a partner, and attending to the ethical and practical issues that most concern the public are the best—and perhaps only—way to ensure Americans' compliance with quarantine in our pluralistic democracy.

REFERENCES

Annas, G. J. 2006. The statue of security: Human rights and post-9/11 epidemics. In *Ethics and Epidemics*, ed. J. Balint, S. Philpott, R. Baker, and M. Strosberg, 3–28. Amsterdam, Neth.: Elsevier Press.

Blendon, R. J., J. M. Benson, K. J. Weldon, and M. J. Herrmann. 2006a. Pandemic influenza and the public: Survey findings. Presented to the Institute of Medicine, October 26, 2006. Available online at http://www.hsph.harvard.edu/press/ releases/ press10262006.html. Accessed on November 1, 2006.

Blendon, R. J., C. M. DesRoches, M. S. Cetron, J. M. Benson, T. Meinhardt, and W. Pollard. 2006b. Attitudes toward the use of quarantine in a public health emergency in four countries. *Health Affairs* 25: W15–W25.

Council on Ethical and Judicial Affairs. 2006. *The use of quarantine and isolation as public health interventions. CEJA Opinion 1-A-06.* Chicago, IL: American Medical Association.

Edelson, P. J. 2006. Quarantine and civil liberties. In *Ethics and Epidemics*, ed. J. Balint, S. Philpott, R. Baker, and M. Strosberg, 29–42. Amsterdam, Neth.: Elsevier Press.

Gostin, L. O., R. Bayer, and A. L. Fairchild. 2003. Ethical and legal challenges posed by Severe Acute Respiratory Syndrome. *Journal of the American Medical Association* 290: 3229–3237.

Hawryluck, L., W. L. Gold, S. Robinson, S. Pogorski, S. Galea, and R. Styra. 2004. SARS control and psychological effects of quarantine, Toronto, Canada. *Emerging Infectious Diseases* 10: 1206–1212.

Mill, J. S. 1859. *On Liberty*. Available online at http://www .utilitarianism.com/ol/one.html. Accessed on November 3, 2006.

Parmet, W. E. 1985. AIDS and quarantine: The revival of an archaic doctrine. *Hofstra Law Review* 14: 53–90.

Reis, N. 2006. The 2003 SARS outbreak in Canada: Legal and ethical lessons about the use of quarantine. In *Ethics and Epidemics*, ed. J. Balint, S. Philpott, R. Baker, and M. Strosberg, 43–67. Amsterdam, Neth: Elsevier Press.

Rothstein, M. A., M. G. Alcalde, N. R. Elster, M. A. Majumder, L. I. Palmer, T. H. Stone, and R. E. Hoffman. 2003. *Quarantine and isolation: Lessons learned from SARS.* Louisville, KY: Institute for Bioethics, Health Policy and Law. Available online at http://www.louisville.edu/medschool/ibhpl/images/pdf/ SARS% 20REPORT.pdf. Accessed on October 31, 2006.

Tomianovic, D. 2006. *Quarantine: February 2006 CDC COCA conference call.* Available online at http://www.bt.cdc.gov/ coca/ppt/quarantine_020706.ppt. Accessed on October 31, 2006.

United Nations Economic and Social Council, U.N. Sub-Commission on Prevention of Discrimination and Protection of Minorities, Siracusa. 1984. *Principles on the limitation and derogation of provisions in the International Covenant on Civil and Political Rights, Annex, UN Doc E/CN.4/1984/4.* Available online at http://hei.unige.ch/~clapham/hrdoc/docs/siracusa .html. Accessed on November 3, 2006.

Upshur, R. 2003. The ethics of quarantine. *The Virtual Mentor* 5(11): n.p. Available online at http://www.ama-assn.org/ ama/pub/category/print/11535.html. Accessed on October 31, 2006.

Wu, J. T., S. Riley, C. Fraser, and G. M. Leung. 2006. Reducing the impact of the next influenza pandemic using household-based public health interventions. *PLoS Medicine* 3(9): e361.

Wynia, M. K. 2005. Public health principlism: The precautionary principle and beyond. *American Journal of Bioethics* 5(3): 3–4.

CHRIS FEUDTNER
AND EDGAR K. MARCUSE

Ethics and Immunization Policy: Promoting Dialogue to Sustain Consensus

Chris Feudtner is Assistant Professor of Pediatrics at the University of Pennsylvania. He is also the Director of Research for the Pediatric Advanced Care Team and the Integrated Care Service at The Children's Hospital of Philadelphia. He has active interests in ethics and medical history, and recently published *Bittersweet: Diabetes, Insulin, and the Transformation of Illness*.

Edgar K. Marcuse is a Professor of Pediatrics and Adjunct Professor of Epidemiology at the University of Washington and Associate Medical Director for Quality Improvement at Children's Hospital and Regional Medical Center in Seattle, Washington. His research interests in bioethics include vaccine development and immunization policy.

When Benjamin Franklin recalled, in the pages of his autobiography the death of his 4-year-old son in 1736 from smallpox, he rued his decision to forego inoculation for young Francis. Years earlier, when Boston was being ravaged by the 1721 smallpox epidemic that killed hundreds, Franklin and his older brother had lambasted the Reverend Cotton Mather and Dr Zabiel Boyleston for advocating the "mischievous" practice of variolation; but decades later the still-aggrieved father reversed his previous position and counseled parents to pursue this "safer" course of immunization.

Franklin's inner dialogue of pro and con regarding inoculation symbolizes an enduring societal debate that has embroiled immunization programs. Edward Jenner's development of "scientific" vaccination in the 1790s culminated in an 1867 British law mandating smallpox immunization, yet by 1869 organized political opposition had arisen and persisted unchecked (with children unimmunized) for decades. Louis Pasteur's immunization in 1885 of the boy Joseph Meister against rabies created an ethical uproar that turned riotous. Recent concerns about the safety of

whole-cell pertussis vaccines led to a disruption or cessation of national pertussis immunization programs and a resurgence of epidemic disease in the United Kingdom, Japan, Sweden, and West Germany. Sustained by the media, such turmoil roils while vaccination, acknowledged to be one of the most beneficial public health interventions ever, continues to prevent epidemics.

Against this historical backdrop, 3 recent trends have made decisions regarding immunization policies even more complicated. First, the broad cultural consensus that has enabled the United States' universal childhood immunization programs of the past 50 years shows signs of eroding. With most parents and many grandparents no longer personally acquainted with the morbidity and mortality of vaccine-preventable diseases, many families have shifted their focus of concern to alleged vaccine reactions. Adverse events that occur in temporal association with immunization are presumed to be causally related, leading some to oppose mandatory immunization.

Second, this questioning of mandated immunization occurs just as advances in molecular biology and immunology promise to introduce an array of novel vaccines. In the coming decade new immunizations

From *Pediatrics* 107:5 (2001), 1158–1164. Notes omitted.

will present many challenging policy and funding decisions for national committees that formulate immunization recommendations and determine federal entitlements, state legislatures that enact immunization laws and allocate some immunization program funds, and both public and private health plans that decide on coverage and payment or financing policies.

Third, for the past 2 decades the health care community has improved the methods used to evaluate medical technology and make policy decisions. Cost-effectiveness studies have weighed cost against some measure of benefit, effectiveness, or usefulness in improving health. Such analyses, however, have not formally considered ethical concerns, such as protecting individual rights or providing an equitable distribution of health care benefits. Because of this limitation, cost-effectiveness analyses, while necessary for policy decisions, are neither sufficient nor complete, because they currently do not address differences in values and perspectives that polarize our society.

These 3 trends will make immunization policy decisions more numerous and complex. Because the powers granted to public health authorities are based on the public's trust, and in democratic societies this trust is founded on broad participation in formulating policy, health care decision-makers may well feel mounting pressure to include the diverse perspectives not only of physicians and immunization experts, but also of parent groups, politicians, special-interest advocates, economists and, perhaps, ethicists. . . .

In this article we propose a systematic approach to evaluate immunization policy options. Our model combines epidemiologic, economic, and ethical concerns into a unified analytic framework, thereby helping us to understand better the tradeoffs between alternative policies, and assisting us to choose a course of action that most accords with our fundamental values. We believe that such a systematic method of deliberation would foster a more explicit and morally relevant dialogue about diverse policy considerations than do current US policy debates and analysis.

A SCENARIO OF THE PROBLEM

To illustrate our approach, imagine that we are public health officials on a distant island where the children are plagued by an endemic infection—Franklin Fever. Few children escape infection from this highly contagious virus. Most often the disease causes only a week of fever, cough, and an itchy red rash, but for ~1% it results in a prolonged course of encephalitis, and ~5%

of these children either die or suffer brain damage with long-term disability, generating substantial social costs. Through the collaborative efforts of the island's academic and industrial research communities a safe and effective Franklin Fever vaccine is now available and an expert medical committee has recommended universal immunization of the island's children, noting that the cost of immunization would be roughly comparable to total direct medical and indirect societal costs of caring for afflicted children.

As physicians with responsibility for formulating public health policy, we must choose an immunization strategy. . . .

I. CONSIDERING THE PROBLEM

The merits of particular immunization strategies can be clarified if we start by considering 3 broad domains of concerns (Table 1). First are the consequences of the disease: How much harm does it cause individual children and adults? How much does society fear these harms? Does the disease pose a substantial epidemic risk through person-to-person transmission? How much does the care of the acutely ill or subsequently disabled child cost the health care system directly as well as the family and society indirectly?

Second are vaccine considerations: How effectively does it prevent disease, both through individual and community (herd) immunity? What adverse events does the vaccine cause, how often, and how severe? Do particular immunization strategies pose other possible adverse consequences, such as altering the epidemiology of the disease and postponing infection into adult life? Might the vaccine eventually eradicate the disease, nationally or globally? Is the price of the vaccine, the costs of its administration and program implementation compatible with our valuation of other health care goods and services?

These considerations of disease, therapy, and certain aspects of cost constitute the standard focus for cost-effectiveness analysis. As public health authorities, though, we must also weigh important ethical considerations. Personal liberty—particularly the freedom to refuse medical intervention—may conflict with the right of vulnerable children to be protected from harm. This conflict requires authorities to strike a balance when specifying the degree of coercion the state should exercise to enforce a specific immunization policy. Achieving such balance is difficult when

Table 1. Policy Considerations for Immunization Programs

Considerations	Examples
Disease-related	Individual child's risk of morbidity and mortality
	For society:
	Risk of epidemic
	Fear of harm
	Cost of disease care
Immunization-related	Efficacy of disease prevention:
	Through individual immunity
	Through community (herd) immunity
	Risk of adverse vaccine-related morbidity and mortality
	Possible adverse effect of delay of disease until adulthood
	Possible other unforeseen adverse consequences
	Possible reduction in global disease burden
	Possible disease eradication
	Pricing and cost of immunization program
Policy-related Liberty	Autonomy and freedom to refuse or choose
	Vulnerability and right to be protected
	Degree of coercion needed to enforce policy
	Degree of societal consensus regarding policy
Justice	Protect due process
	Equitable distribution of benefits:
	Individual immunity
	Community (herd) immunity
	Fair distribution of burdens:
	Risk of disease
	Risk of immunization adverse event
	Cost of disease care
	Cost of immunization program
Duties of families	Protect individual child
Duties of society	Protect individual children
	Protect the community of 'healthy' children
	Protect the community of vulnerable children
	Protect future generations of children

members of society value immunization programs quite differently.

Equally important considerations involve matters of liberty and justice. Ideally the benefits of immunization—namely, protection from disease—should be equitably distributed across the population. For instance, in the United States we believe that no child should fail to benefit from a universally recommended immunization program because of limited access to care, poverty, or discrimination attributable to race or ethnicity. Ideally there should be a fair distribution of the burdens of immunization. No segment of society should be placed at heightened risk of suffering a vaccine-related adverse event or falling ill because of vaccine failure, nor disproportionately bear the costs of disease care, adverse event care, or the care provided though the immunization program as a whole. This concern for fair burden-sharing typically is posed as the question of 'free riders': should any child (or their family) be allowed to take advantage of a common good (in this case, community immunity against a disease) and potentially put that collective good at risk, even if at an individual level this course might make sense, albeit from a selfish perspective? At the same time, Americans who prize individual liberty bristle or rebel whenever any authority encroaches on personal freedom, such as occurs not only with laws requiring immunization but also statutes enforcing the use of bicycle and motorcycle helmets or automobile passenger restraints.

For childhood immunization programs and safety-promoting policies, these deeper themes of liberty and justice play out through the duties that our society entrusts to parents to promote the health and safety of their children and assigns to governmental and other agencies to safeguard the welfare of children. Acrimony often erupts when parental and societal views about these duties differ, or when parents disagree with the course of action mandated by the policy. A mandatory policy with high immunization rates, to cite a well-worn example, would protect those vulnerable children for whom immunization is contraindicated or simply fails to elicit protective immunity, but would do so by placing many individual children at a minute yet measurable risk of severe adverse vaccine events. As troubling, though less strident, is the common problem of an immunization program failing to distribute benefits equitably because of unequal access to vaccination. An optimal immunization policy process strives to minimize both the contentious conflicts and these quieter pervasive problems.

II. SPECIFYING THE OBJECTIVES

Having outlined and organized our concerns, we can now focus our thinking by transforming these concerns into the following 7 objectives for our immunization policy:

1. Minimize the deleterious consequences of the disease.
2. Minimize the deleterious consequences of the vaccine.
3. Optimize personal liberty to choose or refuse vaccination.
4. Maximize the just distribution of benefits and burdens across society.
5. Promote the duty of families to protect their child.
6. Promote the long-term duty of society to protect all children, now and in the future.
7. Use limited health care resources prudently.

Are these the only or the 'right' objectives? Certainly other worthy objectives exist. Identifying the objectives that matter most is the first of several steps required to make any policy decision. Each of these steps requires some value judgments, either explicitly or implicitly. Making these value-laden choices explicit has the virtue of facilitating debate. For example, the set of key objectives tackled by cost-effectiveness analysis typically includes only the minimization of deleterious disease and vaccine-related consequences and the prudent use of health care resources: these are not merely the most important considerations, they are the only ones. Given the incompleteness of current cost-benefit analyses, our diverse society might be well-served by debating the degree to which our final decision should be influenced by cost-benefit information to the exclusion of all other concerns.

III. ENVISIONING ALTERNATIVES

With a clearer sense of what we are seeking to accomplish with our immunization policy, we now should develop a fuller list of alternative policies. To simplify our discussion, we will consider a single characteristic of the policy—the force with which vaccination will be promoted—and envision in some detail 3 alternatives: immunization with the new Franklin Fever vaccine will either be mandatory, recommended, or elective. The mandatory system of immunization would require that all children be vaccinated against Franklin Fever on entering school; failing to do so either unwittingly or through conscious refusal would result in the unvaccinated child being excluded from school during outbreaks (which is the prevailing practice in the United States for enforcement of other mandatory immunizations). The recommended strategy would strongly encourage immunization, using public education and expert advice as the chief persuasive means of raising immunization rates. The elective policy would likewise use public education to inform parents, but make clear that the choice to immunize or not is completely at the parents' discretion.

Deciding whether the immunization policy will promote the vaccine as mandated, strongly recommended, or entirely elective is linked to other policy decisions: under each program enforcement scenario, who will pay for the vaccine: a central payer, multiple payers, or self-payment by families? Will a special fund defray costs to families unable to pay? Who will pay for vaccine-related adverse events, or for disease care among the voluntarily unimmunized? If the mandatory policy is chosen, will 'philosophical' exemptions be granted under special circumstances? If so, exactly what circumstances? Beyond exclusion from school (or even preschool child care), might this mandatory policy be enforced through restriction of welfare benefits to those families receiving public assistance, as some regions of the United States currently are doing? Alternatively, if the recommended or elective policies were selected, could immunization rates be increased through the effective use of financial incentives for providers or even parents? Would policy initiatives that enhanced access and reduced barriers to obtaining health care, or facilitated voluntary compliance with these recommended or elective vaccination guidelines suffice to raise immunization rates to desired levels?

The point of tracing out these interconnected considerations is this: as we proceed in our evaluation of these policy options, we may uncover issues that warrant our returning to this step of envisioning alternatives, developing new options, or refining and enhancing existing ones. This capacity to learn and improve our options in a reiterative manner is critical, because the quality of our ultimate decision is limited by the best alternative we create.

IV. LINKING ALTERNATIVE POLICIES TO OUTCOMES

Next, we need to assess how the 3 policy alternatives would meet, or fail to meet, our stated objectives. We can do this by gauging the impact of each immunization policy option on 5 classes of outcomes: health outcomes for individuals and the population, ethical outcomes for individuals and the community, and total net costs to society. Arraying these outcomes into a flow diagram (Fig 1) helps us to see how they are interrelated, with process-oriented ethical outcomes occurring before health-related outcomes, and the collective outcomes resulting from the aggregation of individual

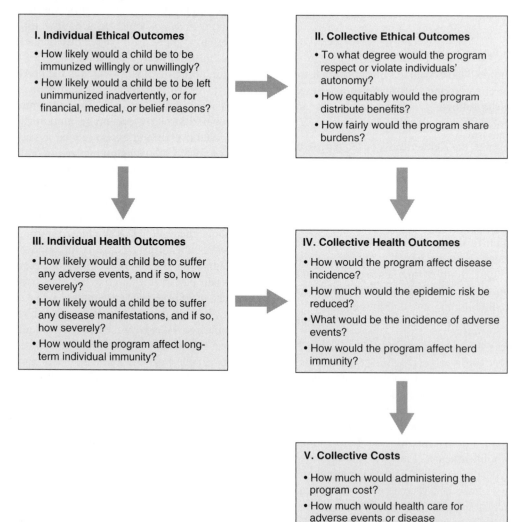

For Each Policy Option, Consider . . .

I. Individual Ethical Outcomes
- How likely would a child be to be immunized willingly or unwillingly?
- How likely would a child be to be left unimmunized inadvertently, or for financial, medical, or belief reasons?

II. Collective Ethical Outcomes
- To what degree would the program respect or violate individuals' autonomy?
- How equitably would the program distribute benefits?
- How fairly would the program share burdens?

III. Individual Health Outcomes
- How likely would a child be to suffer any adverse events, and if so, how severely?
- How likely would a child be to suffer any disease manifestations, and if so, how severely?
- How would the program affect long-term individual immunity?

IV. Collective Health Outcomes
- How would the program affect disease incidence?
- How much would the epidemic risk be reduced?
- What would be the incidence of adverse events?
- How would the program affect herd immunity?

V. Collective Costs
- How much would administering the program cost?
- How much would health care for adverse events or disease manifestations cost?

Figure 1   Schema for evaluating immunization policy options.

outcomes. For example, if under an elective enforcement policy quite a few children were left unimmunized because of financial reasons, the program would not only have failed these children ethically; it also, by allowing them to remain susceptible to disease, would have failed to distribute benefits equitably, and would have raised to some degree the risk of epidemic disease. Conversely, a mandatory immunization policy that coerced certain children to be immunized might lower their individual risk of disease and share more fairly the burdens of maintaining a protective level of herd immunity, but violate their family's autonomy and place these children at some risk of experiencing an adverse event. These health and ethical outcomes, in turn, determine much of the health care and administrative cost outcomes of alternative immunization policies. (The price of the vaccine also determines the costs, but lies beyond the scope of this article.)

For many of these outcomes, surprisingly little data exist on which to build evidence-based answers. Considering this series of process and health-oriented outcomes, however, draws our attention to how our decision would be better informed if we had reasonable estimates of how the rates of immunization were likely to differ among mandatory, recommended, and elective immunization strategies, and how the marginal differences in coverage rates would translate into beneficial and harmful outcomes. Let us illustrate this point by returning to our Franklin Fever scenario. Suppose we estimated that an immunization program promoted by recommendation would result in 80% of eligible children vaccinated, whereas a mandatory program would achieve 95% coverage. Immunizing this additional 15% of children, we might further estimate, would diminish the annual number of cases of Franklin Fever by 100 000, but compel immunization on 500 000 unwilling participants. We would then be able to ask—under these hypothetical assumptions—whether our society should choose to immunize 5 children whose families are opposed to immunization to prevent a case of disease. Such information would advance our thinking beyond simply stating qualitatively how the programs differ, enabling us to measure the amount by which they differ—a move that will help us substantially when we come subsequently to examine tradeoffs.

V. ASSIGNING VALUES

Ethical analyses of health care programs usually wrestle with how to prioritize large overarching ethical objectives, such as whether securing the greatest good for the greatest number is to be preferred over protecting the rights of all individuals. In our scheme, however, the next step is smaller and more concrete, as we assign values to particular child health and ethical outcomes. Picking several important examples, we need to ask: How do we value differently, if at all, the loss of freedom when a family cannot afford to choose to have their child immunized (as might occur under an elective system) versus the loss of freedom that occurs when an unwilling participant is coerced into being vaccinated (because of a mandatory immunization policy)? Do 'natural' illnesses caused by an infectious microbe represent the same loss of value as a precisely equivalent degree of illness caused by a vaccine-related side effect, or is the vaccine-related morbidity somehow more costly? How should we compare the value of a case of disease prevented today from one prevented a generation from now? From a societal perspective, is a dollar in immunization-generated savings that returns to the pocket of a parent of equal value to a dollar that enters an employer's corporate coffer?

Many critics decry ever assigning such values, believing the judgments required are too subjective and contentious. However, every policy decision requires us to make such evaluations; the important choice is whether these evaluations are made implicitly as they are done today or in a more transparent, explicit manner. Returning to our previous example, cost-effectiveness analyses give health status and cost full sway, but largely omit concerns for respecting family decision-making autonomy and for distributing benefits and burdens fairly. Combining the private evaluation made by different policymakers into 1 'societal' value is problematic—and in an objective formal sense perhaps even impossible. Nevertheless, every policy decision ultimately depends not just on information but also on an underlying structure of values and preferences that guide choices. Even if a ruckus ensues, we believe that a public debate about such values and their relative weights should be part of policy formulation to maintain the robust consensus required to support immunization policy.

VI. EXAMINING TRADEOFFS

We will now examine how the various policy options would or would not accomplish our objectives, constructing a table that arrays the alternatives across our objectives, then considering which alternative best addresses each objective (Table 2). Although judgments as to which options serve the various objects 'best' are

Table 2. Table of Objectives, Alternatives, and Consequences

Objectives	Policy Alternatives		
	Mandatory	Recommended	Elective
Minimize deleterious disease consequences	Best		
Minimize deleterious vaccine consequences			Best
Maximize just distribution of benefits and burdens	Best		
Optimize personal liberty to refuse or choose			Best
Promote family duty to protect child		Best	
Promote societal duty to protect children	Best		
Use health care resources prudently	Best		

debatable (and should be the subject of research and public dialogue), our major point is that this kind of table breaks down the much larger decision of 'what policy to implement' into more manageable smaller assessments, which highlight pivotal tradeoffs. Each assessment requires both factual information and value judgments. The minimization of disease-related injury versus the minimization of vaccine-related injury is 1 tradeoff dimension that at first glance has similar concerns, namely the minimization of harm. Informing the debate with numbers needed to treat for benefit and for harm might help clarify and thus promote consensus on this particular tradeoff. For each vaccine these considerations would differ, suggesting that a spectrum of policy enforcement strength is warranted, titrating the degree of coerciveness to the particular disease and vaccine-specific tradeoffs.

Underneath the debate regarding how to minimize various types of harm lies another tension, though, between promoting the just distribution of burdens and benefits and the protection of personal liberty—that is, quite specifically, for those who wish not to be immunized. Children who are left inadvertently unimmunized because of failure of poorly organized immunization programs (such as occurs under elective systems) represent instances of diminished family autonomy, not having had the chance to choose to immunize their child. Even if we wish not to call this lost opportunity a loss of freedom, certainly something of value has been lost. On the other side, compelling families to immunize their children against their wishes represents a clear loss of personal freedom. Evaluating these competing issues of justice and freedom, and striking a renewable and hence sustainable consensus, is a task as much of political dialogue as epidemiology.

These 2 levels of tension—one involving preferred health risks and the other involving civil liberties—raise

the possibility of an additional 'higher-level' tradeoff between these different levels of concern. To address this tension, we should move beyond debating general philosophical questions or arguing over which objectives we care most about, and instead concentrate on how much the differing programs enhance or compromise each particular objective. Focusing on the amounts of benefit and harm at stake when choosing between options, we can make our value judgments more relevant to the policy decision by titrating a set amount of good against varying amounts of bad. Is a single case prevented worth 10 immunized unwillingly? Or is the threshold 100 or even 1000? What if we consider, on the benefit side, disease prevention through community-wide immunity for immunocompromised children for whom vaccination may be contraindicated; does our tolerance toward immunizing children of unwilling families go up, so that we might tolerate immunizing 5000 children unwillingly to prevent a case among these vulnerable children? Conversely, if we shift to consider preventing unwilling immunization as a benefit of a recommended immunization program, how many children are we willing to see be left unimmunized inadvertently to prevent an instance of unwilling immunization? Breaking down broad tradeoffs between different categories of concerns into a comprehensible series of smaller judgments clarifies our values and facilitates the dialogue about how to think about and make these complex tradeoffs, promoting a discussion that is itself a fundamental task for a transparent policy-making process.

VII. MAKING HEALTH CARE POLICY DECISIONS

Public health programs involve more than just issues of health. In recent decades the medical literature has reflected a societal emphasis on economic considerations, but public health is also a morally-laden medical venture. Concerns for individual liberty and social equity permeate public health policy, and should be incorporated into mainstream analyses of health care programs. Outcomes research must encompass these moral and political concerns. Worry that special interest groups might manipulate or abuse such considerations is likely well-founded; omitting moral considerations, though, will not protect against such abuses. Instead, leaving moral concerns as 'gaps' in our formal analyses of such decisions merely makes the policy-making process less transparent and the abuses harder to spot. Explicitness, a virtue of clearly-stated moral considerations and how they are to be measured, would help to foster constructive debate, which, in turn, may help to sustain the consensus required for effective public health programs.

What is the ideal immunization program? Certainly, no single answer exists. Yet our society still must decide a course of action, choose a vaccination policy, and pursue it. We intended this hypothetical case study to expose more clearly our areas of confusion and genuine disagreement. We believe that this framework, straddling the interface between moral and empirical reasoning, offers several key elements of a minimally sufficient public dialogue regarding vaccine policy. Such a dialogue must involve clinicians, public health authorities, legislators and the public, and must therefore take place not only in the deliberations of national committees but in the scientific and lay press, in the electronic media, and on the Internet. We believe that a broad dialogue is essential to sustain the societal consensus that empowered the immunization initiatives of the past half-century, and that only through such continuing dialogue can we be enabled to take full advantage of new opportunities to enhance public health through immunization in the century ahead.

RONALD BAYER AND AMY FAIRCHILD

The Limits of Privacy: Surveillance and Control of Disease

Ronald Bayer is Professor at the Center for the History and Ethics of Public Health in the Department of Sociomedical Sciences at the Mailman School of Public Health, Columbia University. Dr. Bayer's research has examined ethical and policy issues in public health, with a special focus on AIDS, tuberculosis, illicit drugs, and tobacco. His recent books include *Truth and Lies in the Age of AIDS* (written with Robert Klitzman) (2003) and *Unfiltered: Conflicts over Tobacco Policy and Public Health* (edited with Eric Feldman) (2004).

Amy Fairchild is Assistant Professor of Sociomedical Sciences at Columbia University's Mailman School of Public Health. Her work focuses on the intersection of history and public health policy, and has appeared in such publications as *Science*, *The American Journal of Public Health*, and *The Bulletin of the History of Medicine*. She is currently finishing a project on the history and ethics of surveillance and launching work on the history of harm reduction and confinement for Hansen's disease, better known as leprosy.

On December 10, 1999 the Center for Disease Control made final and formal a policy it had sought to impose for some years. That new policy required of states that

From *Health Care Analysis* 10 (2002), 19–35. Notes omitted. Reprinted with permission of Springer Science and Business Media.

they adopt a system of HIV case reporting. While the CDC left open the possibility of using coded unique identifiers, it was clear that the federal health officials favored the use of names. . . . In adopting this stance the CDC brought to closure a debate that had raged for 15 years, that had pitted advocates of comprehensive public health surveillance against AIDS advocates, gay organizations, civil libertarians, and their allies in some state health departments.

What justified the Center for Disease Control's 1999 determination to require HIV case reporting? In part, it was a reflection of the triumph of tradition over privacy-focused opposition. But more it reflected a growing sense that the surveillance of the AIDS epidemic was no longer adequate to the task. The reporting of AIDS cases—universal in the United States since 1983—represented a picture of the end stage of a disease process that commenced years earlier when HIV infection occurred. If the public health required an understanding of the contours of the epidemic of HIV transmission then something very different was required. Furthermore, with the advent of the era of powerful antiretroviral therapeutics in 1995–1996 the period between infection and an AIDS diagnosis had grown. And so some believed that AIDS case reporting captured the picture of events that had occurred 10 years earlier. Only HIV case reporting could remedy the situation. The availability of powerful new therapies, then, provided an incentive for testing that might well overcome whatever the putative disincentives of HIV name reporting might be.

But why were names necessary? Why did opponents view the reporting of names with such alarm? To answer these questions requires a retelling of a history of the encounters that had occurred since the mid 1980s. With an appreciation of that history it will then be possible to locate the clash between the claims of privacy and surveillance first, in the context of the history of name based reporting; second, in the context of a range of contemporary surveillance practices; and finally it will be possible to look at the matter from an international perspective.

AIDS/HIV REPORTING: A BRIEF HISTORY

Soon after the first cases of AIDS were reported by the Center for Disease Control in June 1981, state health departments—which bear the primary responsibility for public health activities in the US—began to require physicians and hospitals to report by name each newly diagnosed case. . . . In so doing they were pursuing a course understood to be a public health tradition. They shared a common belief that the understanding and control of disease necessitated adequate surveillance data. In the epidemic's early years this entailed not

only a matter of enumeration and mapping but of investigating the commonalties among cases for which there was no etiological explanation. If gay men were so prominent among the first cases why were they? If hemophiliacs and blood transfusion recipients fell ill why was that the case? If intravenous drug users seemed at increased risk what could account for that fact? It is remarkable that given the intensity of the opposition that would emerge to HIV reporting just a few short years later that the American Association of Physicians for Human Rights—a gay and lesbian health group—would call upon local health departments to make AIDS cases reportable by name. . . .

Surveillance, in the contexts of most diseases, but not all as we will discuss below, is based on the premise that medical privacy is not an absolute. Both historically and in contemporary practice, reporting the names of those with disease to public health authorities has represented a central example of an acceptable exception to medical privacy and the confidentiality of the clinical relationship. Nevertheless, individuals whose names are placed on disease registries have a right to expect that their identities will be held in confidence, that data reported to registries would not be used in ways that pose a threat to the patient's dignity and well-being. This was done for moral as well as practical reasons. Indeed, to the extent that they do not believe that such confidentiality will prevail, they will tend to resist name-based reporting as an unacceptable intrusion on their privacy.

It was this lack of confidence that confidentiality would be respected that prevailed in the case of HIV. Once the capacity to test for the presence of the antibody to HIV became possible in 1985, it was only a matter of time before some public health official would seek to extend the reporting requirements that were in place for AIDS. The first successful effort to mandate HIV case reporting occurred in Colorado. There the health authorities presented the claims that would be made repeatedly over the next years: Reporting would alert public health officials to the presence of individuals infected with a lethal infection; would allow officials to counsel them about what they needed to do to prevent further transmission; would permit the authorities to monitor the incidence and prevalence of infection. Alert to concerns about privacy and confidentiality, Colorado health officials underscored the existence of administrative, regulatory, and statutory protections for reported names. There was no reason to believe, officials argued, that the state health department would fail to protect the identities of those with HIV when it had protected those with AIDS, tuberculosis, and other reportable infections.

To these propositions the antagonists to name-based reporting retorted that AIDS was different: social hostility and AIDS-related hysteria could lead to changes in policy, legislatively imposed, that would permit for breaches that would never occur with other conditions. And then those in registries would lose their jobs, their housing, and perhaps their liberty. The intensity of the opposition is best captured by the extent to which genocidal images were invoked. In Minnesota, which followed Colorado in making HIV reportable, one opponent declared at a public meeting, "The road to the gas chambers began with a list in Weimar Germany" (Bayer, 1989, p 131). A less extreme formulation put the issue this way: "the fear, anger, and mistrust felt by me and many other groups reflects our profound belief that the threat to our fundamental human rights posed by the existence of AIDS is an evil of equal strength to the disease itself. To ignore our feelings will only alienate the gay community thereby impeding [the health department's] often legitimate efforts to arrest this serious health problem" (Bayer, 1989).

Here then was the powerful argument against reporting that would impress many health officials in states with relatively large AIDS caseloads. Reporting would be counterproductive; it would drive people away from testing and counseling—essential control measures in the public health campaign against AIDS in the United States. It did not matter that public health departments had an exemplary record in protecting name-based reports. . . . If those most at risk for HIV had fears about what would happen to them that was all that mattered.

As therapeutic advances began to emerge in the late 1980s—as public health began to have more to offer than the perceived threat of quarantine or partner notification—fissures began to appear in the relatively broad and solid alliance against named reporting. Thus, in 1989, New York City's Health Commissioner stated that the prospects of early clinical intervention warranted "a shift toward a disease-control approach to HIV infection along the lines of classic tuberculosis practices," including the "reporting of seropositives" (Joseph, 1989). Although his proposal met with fierce and effective resistance, it is clear that his call represented part of a national trend.

At the end of November 1990, the CDC declared its support for HIV reporting, which it asserted could "enhance the ability of local, state and national agencies to project the level of required resources" for care and prevention services. . . . Within a week, the House of Delegates of the American Medical Association endorsed the reporting of names as well, thus breaking with the traditional resistance of medical practitioners to such intrusions on the physician-patient relationship. . . . In 1991, New Jersey became the first high-prevalence state to require HIV-case reporting by name. . . .

In the following years, the CDC continued to press for named reporting of HIV cases, an effort that assumed the dimensions of a campaign. During that period, it was supported by a growing number of public health officials. . . .

Nevertheless, resistance on the part of AIDS activist organizations and their political allies persisted, and as a consequence, HIV cases typically became reportable by name only in states that did not have large cosmopolitan communities with effectively organized gay constituencies or high AIDS case loads. By 1996, although 26 states had adopted HIV-case reporting, they represented jurisdictions with only 24% of reported AIDS cases (CDC, 1997). By October 1998, however, it was clear that opposition to name-based reporting was weakening: 32 states now reported cases of HIV by name, though 3 states reported only pediatric cases; Florida, with its large case load, had become a reporting state, and Texas—which together with Maryland, had experimented with a unique identifier system for HIV-case reporting as an alternative to the use of names—had come to the conclusion that such an approach was unworkable and adopted name-based reporting. . . . This trend must be seen as part of the more general move away from the exceptionalism that had placed such emphasis on the privacy and social rights of people with HIV infection and that had set AIDS policy apart from the response to other communicable conditions. . . .

Nothing more forcefully underscored the changes that occurred than the course of events in New York. In 1997, the state with the largest concentration of AIDS cases began, for the first time, to consider name reporting. Although a state health department task force charged with the responsibility of advising the commissioner of health on the matter remained bitterly divided, the lines of cleavage were stark. It was the representatives of community-based organizations who most adamantly opposed name reporting.

Public health officials on the committee and throughout the state supported HIV-case reporting by name. Objections and disagreements notwithstanding, there was significant, broad agreement on the need for HIV surveillance data to track the HIV epidemic and on the need to bring the sexual and needle-sharing contacts of individuals with HIV into testing and treatment. Yet ultimately the deadlock between community and public health officials paved the way for final action in the legislative arena. On June 19, 1998, in the waning hours of the legislative session, the Democratic-controlled assembly voted 112 to 34 for a bill that would mandate case reporting by name and a more aggressive approach to partner notification. In so doing, it joined the Republican-dominated state senate, which had already passed the bill. . . . For advocates of name reporting, the significance of the New York decision could not be overstated.

The New York decision is best understood in light of therapeutic advances on the national policy debate on name reporting. That impact was made clear in an editorial published in late 1997. Jointly authored by Larry Gostin, a well-known proponent of civil liberties, John Ward, MD, of the CDC, and Cornelius Baker, the African American President of the National Association of People With AIDS, the editorial represented a new alliance. Locating the argument for named reporting in the context of the remarkable therapeutic achievements represented by the protease inhibitors and the advent of triple-combination antiretroviral therapy, the authors declared:

We are at a defining moment of the epidemic of HIV infection and AIDS. With therapy that delays the progression to AIDS, mental illnesses, and death, HIV infection or AIDS is becoming a complex clinical disease that does not lend itself to monitoring based on end stage illness. Unless we revise our surveillance system, health authorities will not have reliable information about the prevalence of HIV infection. To correct these deficiencies, we propose that all states require HIV case reporting.

Among the additional advantages of HIV-case reporting, they asserted, was that it would give public health authorities a greater ability to "ensure timely referrals for health and social services" (Gostin et al., 1997, pp 1162–1167).

Although many, if not most, AIDS-service organizations remained adamantly opposed to name reporting, arguing instead for the use of unique identifiers,

the public health community, with the CDC in the lead, concluded that such an approach would simply impede the adoption of an effective system of surveillance. Nevertheless, marking the extent to which political factors shape decision-making in public health, the CDC, in its 1999 recommendation, opened the way to the use of unique identifiers in those states that preferred an anonymous reporting course, provided states could radically limit the error rates associated with such an approach.

It was in trying to place HIV reporting within a larger context that we came to understand that the question of public health surveillance is a much more complex issue, both in historical and contemporary practice. Indeed, it was as a result of our ongoing study of this issue that we came to recognize the need for an analysis of the broad history of public health surveillance. Without such an analysis, it becomes impossible to understand that the HIV reporting controversy was radically affected by the circumstances under which it emerged, that is, the existence of a transformed conception of the rights of privacy, constitutional limits on state authority exercised for benevolent purposes, the development of a vigorous debate about medical ethics, and the emergence of patient advocacy as a potent social force. Indeed, without underscoring similarities and differences with the histories of surveillance for other infectious diseases, vaccination, cancer, occupational diseases, and birth defects, the ability to understand the implications of the HIV debate for surveillance more generally becomes impossible.

CASE REPORTING IN HISTORICAL AND CONTEMPORARY CONTEXTS

Although the quantification of disease and concerns with health statistics have origins in the era of sanitary reform, it was not until the late nineteenth century—in the period in which the new science of bacteriology identified germs that could be transmitted from person to person as the cause of disease—that most nations began systematic reporting of infectious disease among individuals by name, often but not exclusively for the purpose of initiating quarantine, isolation, or vaccination and for epidemiological reasons, as well. . . .

The new public health practices that were linked to the bacteriological revolution, however, were also linked to a heightened public and professional concern about such practices. Notification by name for infectious diseases in many western nations followed on the heels of a period of public protest over compulsory or coercive health policies associated with the bacteriological revolution. Physicians, too, on occasion, challenged the scientific authority of public health officials to intervene in the doctor-patient relationship. In New York City for example, physician outrage over mandatory tuberculosis reporting beginning in 1897 resulted in the development of an essentially voluntary reporting system in which physicians withheld the names of their private patients and reported the names of their poor, dispensary cases. . . .

Despite such opposition and some anticipation of what might follow the extension of the reporting requirement, public health officials began to argue in the second decade of the twentieth century that "All the general arguments for complete reporting of other communicable diseases apply with equal force to venereal disease" (Snow, 1917). But they appreciated the various factors influencing the potential for venereal disease reporting. They most often opted to forego name-based notification—remaining content with an inadequate surveillance system focused on public clinics. Although it was ultimately unsuccessful, public health officials in New York requested that physicians report cases of venereal disease by code beginning in 1912. A 1911 California system, which required physicians to report cases of venereal disease by code to protect patient confidentiality, served as their model. . . . Similarly, although it ultimately opted for name reporting, Massachusetts also considered adopting a laboratory-based coded system for tracking syphilis cases in 1916. Allan Brandt has underscored the point: "Although anonymous reporting precluded rigorous case-tracing, officials hoped it would deflate the possible objections of practitioners." How opposition to name-based reporting could vary and how such opposition was often linked to the way in which reports could trigger public health interventions that could be coercive is demonstrated by the early history of polio reporting.

The New York City Department of Health declared polio a communicable disease and made it mandatory for physicians to report all cases in 1910. During 1916 the epidemic became a public affair. Newspapers reported cases amongst the most prominent in the City. The City's health commissioner published a daily tally of new cases and deaths by name and street address in local newspapers. Homes with a sick child displayed a placard warning of the presence of disease. . . .

What is astonishing is that while polio primarily struck the middle class, in sharp contrast to the history of reaction to tuberculosis reporting discussed above, reporting elicited no objection from physicians or the private patients they served in large measure due to the differential nature of departmental intervention, particularly in the case of quarantine. Families with a private toilet for the patient, separate dining facilities, and a private nurse could maintain a domestic quarantine. Children of those who lived in tenements or other types of multi-family dwellings were taken, sometimes by force, to public hospitals. Similarly, tenement homes and the children living in them were subject to unannounced inspections. As a consequence resistance to reporting and the interventions that followed has been documented only amongst poor, working class, or immigrant families. An analysis of the period recounts that during the epidemic of 1916 one mother warned that she and her child would disappear by morning if her doctor reported the case to health authorities. The Department of Health nurse assigned to inspect tenement houses received a letter promising, "If you report any more of our babies to the Board of Health we will kill you and nobody will know what happened to you. Keep off our streets and don't report our homes and we will do you no harm" (Rogers, 1992, p. 54).

The point here is to underscore the fact that opposition to name based reporting is not new. Although it is important to note that as part of the tradition of public health practice it had gone largely unquestioned in recent years—until AIDS. While infectious disease reporting represents the oldest example of public health surveillance, the creation of vaccine registries—designed to prevent infectious disease by tracking the vaccination history of children by name of the child and parents and following them across states and over time—represents the most recent effort. Development of vaccine registries began in the 1970s, but only recently have federal efforts to coordinate and link these registries begun. On January 12, 1999, in response to sporadic disease outbreaks, poor coverage in urban, inner-city communities, increasingly complex vaccine schedules, family mobility, and poor provider and patient awareness of immunization coverage levels, the National Vaccine Advisory Committee (NVAC), as part of the federal Initiative on Immunization Registries, recommended creation of a nationwide network of state and community immunization registries. . . .

The federal initiative to register immunization coverage put a premium on community participation and cooperation, principally because of the fears of immigrant communities (worried that registry information would be a means of alerting the Immigration and Naturalization Service to their status), parents (those who opposed vaccination for their children feared that they would be harassed and discriminated against), and providers (those with low immunization rates were concerned that they would be "punished" in some fashion).

Central to the recommendations of the National Vaccine Advisory Committee was the protection of patient confidentiality. Registry developers were to give careful consideration to privacy and confidentiality issues in a way that reflected the values and special needs of the communities they served. The committee's analysis of confidentiality highlighted the fact that a tension existed between a need for the completeness of data and risks of unacceptable disclosure. The committee thus adopted as a guiding principle a commitment to direct, active parental notification that the registry exists and to parental choice in participation: "Parents," said NVAC, "must be given the option to decide whether or not their children will participate in a registry." Remarkably, despite these recommendations, the most recent survey of immunization registries has found that 35 rely on implied consent to participation in registries and that 12 states did not notify parents of their child's participation.

Cancer registries in the United States provide the primary example of a surveillance regime that has not produced ethical or political controversy. . . . Nevertheless such registries, by their very definition, represent an ongoing intrusion on privacy and confidentiality. . . . Cancer registries have been in existence for 60 years and, outside of infectious disease reporting, represent one of the most substantial efforts of the public health and medical communities to trace patterns of morbidity and mortality and evaluate therapeutic interventions. In 1971 the National Cancer Act mandated that collection and analysis of data on cancer be undertaken to assist in the prevention, treatment, and diagnosis of cancer. The Surveillance, Epidemiology, and End Results program at the National Cancer Institute was organized to take advantage of cancer data already being collected at several population-based tumor registries. Some 20 years later, Congress enacted the Cancer Registries Amendment Act (1992), which authorized the CDC to establish a national program in support of cancer registries. The goal of the program

was to enhance existing registries and to help establish new ones so that all states would have registries that met minimum standards for completeness, timeliness, and quality.

Despite the wide array of medical information to which cancer registries are linked or linkable and the duration of surveillance for each case—from the first pathology report through death—few patients are ever told that they will be reported and followed over time.

Although cancer is historically a highly stigmatized disease and registration of cases in Western Europe has in recent years been the subject of strict regulation, the necessity for reporting and tracking those with cancer without consent has almost never been challenged in the United States. For example, in Rhode Island there is an exception to the confidentiality statute, which permits reporting of health care information on an individual to the state's central cancer registry. . . . While professionals often note the importance of preserving patient confidentiality, the focus of their concern has been on enhancing the reliability and usability of the registries as part of follow-up research. . . .

When issues of privacy and confidentiality have been addressed, those most committed to cancer registries have argued strongly for the necessity of using names as the basis for linking records, grounding their arguments in the demands of surveillance accuracy. For example, researchers assert, "The incontrovertible fact is that linkage of individual records is essential if cancer is to be measured accurately, the causes ascertained at minimum expense, and the effect of control measures assessed. This is an issue that has to be faced squarely: one cannot have both absolute secrecy and rational cancer control" (Muir et al., 1985, p. 21). The North American Association of Central Cancer Registries has declared, "The public health surveillance system must be exempted from restrictions on collection and retention of personal identifying information in medical privacy legislation. Personal identifiers . . . must be collected . . . without individual consent" (North American Association of Central Cancer Registries, 1999).

In a climate where privacy and confidentiality concerns have become so salient, the status and function of cancer registries has become a matter of consternation. In 1999 the National Cancer Institute (NCI) noted, "Unfortunately, in the current concern about confidentiality protections, the needs of clinical research are not often explicitly addressed. Some of the contemplated or actual legal remedies, or their interpretation, seriously threaten the conduct of important medical research."

The NCI explained, "One of the difficulties in the formation of policy to cover a broad and complex area like health care is that laws or regulations designed to protect against worst-case scenarios may exert unintended and highly adverse consequences on the conduct of medical research, which depends on access to and exchange of information" (National Cancer Institute, http://www.nci.nih.gov/confidentiality.html).

It was not however only public health agencies that were concerned with how privacy standards could effect registries. In sharp contrast to the events that surrounded AIDS, breast cancer advocates urged the maintenance of reporting requirements. The National Breast Cancer Coalition, in their February 2001 "Position Statement on Medical Privacy" (NBCC, http://www.natlbcc.org/bin/index.htm) stressed, "The fundamental right to privacy must include the right to keep one's health information confidential and control the flow of and access to this information," but noted, "Privacy protections should ensure that health information remains private but should not impede the progress of medical research." The statement continued, "Specific authorization to disclose health care information should be required for uses that are not directly related to treatment, payment, or health care operations. A trustworthy system with a proper informed consent process should create an environment where most people would not object to sharing health care information for the purpose of research. With large studies," the NBCC noted, "there are legitimate and serious questions about the feasibility of seeking individual authorizations, because sometimes the research involves thousands of individuals. In cases where it is not possible or feasible to obtain individual consent, there should be clear, consistent and transparent criteria for determining when individual authorization should be waived." The statement acknowledged, "While data can be encrypted, researchers need to link this data back to individuals in order to generate meaningful conclusions." This commitment to research was put to the test in Massachusetts, where an effort to make cancer registration voluntary was opposed by breast cancer advocates who declared: "To have that kind of requirement would certainly undermine 100 percent ascertainment" (NBCC, 2001, http://www. natlbcc.org/bin/ index. htm). This encounter underscores the fact that there are occasions when those whose privacy will be compromised view such limits not as a burden but as serving their interests. This pattern could also be seen in the context of occupational disease reporting.

Although sixty thousand people die each year of occupational diseases and the federal government has borne primary responsibility for the surveillance of occupational diseases and injuries, advocates of workers' health argue that such diseases and injuries are under-recognized. . . . Advocates have accordingly urged that occupational diseases be made reportable for purposes of epidemiological surveillance and, significantly, intervention to protect workers' health.

It was the relative inadequacy of existing reporting mechanisms that ultimately led the National Institute for Occupational Safety and Health (NIOSH) to develop the Sentinel Event Notification System for Occupational Risks in 1987 (SENSOR). SENSOR helps 20 state programs expand their reporting capacity and develop standardized case definitions. The program initially focused on six targeted conditions (silicosis, occupational asthma, pesticide poisoning, lead poisoning, carpal tunnel syndrome, and noise-induced hearing loss) and has since expanded to include accidental amputation, work-related dermatitis, and injuries to minors. But the full range of occupational disease surveillance supported by NIOSH is much broader.

Infectious disease surveillance and its role in guiding public health efforts have also served as a model for those concerned about birth defects. In 2000, the Pew Environmental Health Commission declared, "The United States has an adequate network to capture data on infectious disease in order to spot dangerous outbreaks before they spread. Certainly, we know how to build an effective mechanism that provides the consistency of reporting data and privacy protections." What is needed, however, "is a national policy to guide state implementation of a comprehensive, modern tracking program that will help identify environmental and other preventable factors that contribute to birth defects and other disabilities and chronic diseases" (Pew Environmental Health Commission, 2000).

Although New Jersey required the reporting of birth defects in 1928, the modern era of birth defects registries did not begin until the 1960s, when the Thalidomide disaster and growing concern over addressing environmental and teratogenic hazards to the fetus in utero sparked new interest in surveillance. . . . The Metropolitan Atlanta Congenital Defects Program was the first new state-based registry, established in 1967. The pace of development was slow, however. The

CDC began its own Birth Defects Monitoring Program using hospital discharge data in 1974 and became the largest source of birth defects information in the nation. But by 1978, only two states (Nebraska and Florida) had established registries. As of the mid-1980s, 14 additional states had developed registries. By the year 2000, 42 states had done so. In 1999, following a congressional mandate to develop a clearing house of birth defects surveillance, the CDC was given appropriations to establish or improve state-based surveillance.

Advocates for birth defects reporting note the importance of using names. For instance, CDC states, "the use of personal identifiers facilitates follow-up studies and allows investigators to link infant, maternal, and paternal records" (Lynberg and Edmonds, 1992).

This brief historical and contemporary review has sought to demonstrate that the move toward HIV name-based reporting must be viewed as entailing an effort to integrate HIV/AIDS into the broad system of public health surveillance in the United States, to end the exceptionalism that had characterized AIDS policy in the epidemic's formative period.

Nonetheless it is instructive to note that with its emphasis on name reporting, the United States sets itself apart from the practice common in Europe. In February 1998, a meeting of European experts convened under the auspices of the European Centre for the Epidemiological Monitoring of AIDS concluded:

At the European level AIDS case reporting, introduced in 1984, has been the principal means of monitoring the epidemic. . . . However, in the changing epidemiological context [AIDS case reporting] is no longer sufficient. HIV case reporting is a key element for HIV surveillance. . . . It should be continued where it exists and, where necessary, developed. At a country level, confidentiality should be guaranteed and elimination of duplicate reports should be ensured. HIV case reports should be linkable with AIDS case reports (Hammers, 1998, p. 51).

All of this, the experts concluded, could be achieved without the use of names. The commitment to linkable records without the use of names reflected the professional concerns of epidemiologists troubled by the existence of reporting systems that failed to meet the highest statistical standards or accurate surveillance.

These recommendations reflected current practice regarding HIV reporting in Europe. A 1998 study found that 36 countries, including 9 European Union countries, had nationwide HIV reporting systems. Reporting was mandatory in 27. Notification was by name in 10 countries, by code in 20, and without unique identifiers in 6. Strikingly, the use of names was almost exclusively restricted to the former Communist nations. As in the United States, AIDS-related organizations in Europe have tended to support coded HIV reporting but oppose the use of names as a threat to privacy and human rights. Thus, in Spain, which approved a national anonymous registry of people with HIV using a 15-digit code, the Movimiento Cuidado Antisida supported the new registry, but expressed its opposition to the name-based approach adopted in the region of Asturias. "We do not agree with a [name-containing] registry since names of persons have nothing to do with the epidemiologic knowledge of the infection and, in addition, may seriously harm the confidentiality of a given person" (Bosch, 1999, p. 977).

CONCLUSION

The central ethical question posed by HIV name reporting indeed of all disease reporting is: When do the claims of public health legitimately trump the claims of privacy and confidentiality in the context of disease surveillance? A subsidiary question is: Do the claims of privacy carry sufficient weight to make reporting systems that are less accurate, but that are nevertheless adequate more compatible with ethical standards?

While these questions have, in some way, been at the heart of disease reporting for more than a century, with the exception of HIV/AIDS, despite almost three decades of systematic discussion of the ethics of human subjects research, no sustained discussion of the ethics of public health reporting has been undertaken. In the 1970s, Leon Gordis, Alexander Capron, and others began to discuss whether the emerging rules and regulations for human subjects research would apply to epidemiological studies, whether the principle of informed consent for the use of records was necessary, and whether such requirements would render epidemiological research virtually impossible. . . .

Yet that discussion has not extended to public health surveillance. While research, including epidemiological research, has been the subject of IRB review, public health surveillance has not been subject to similar oversight. Indeed, dispute exists over the boundary distinguishing research—that must be subject to review—from public health practice—such as case identification and treatment. . . .

Surveillance, undertaken for public health purposes rather than epidemiological research, carries the risk, however small, that information might be inadvertently disclosed despite the best efforts to keep it confidential. It also may trigger public health intrusions, such as, in the case of HIV/AIDS, partner notification. Notifying the sexual partners of people with HIV may place them at risk of domestic violence, of losing housing, or of losing employment. Yet the consequences and risks change over time. As we have seen in the prior discussion, they vary by both the nature of the disease in question and the social perception of it. They also vary in terms of those who bear the burden of disease and their own sense of social vulnerability. Thus, as we noted, breast cancer advocates have proven adamantly opposed to the notion of requiring informed consent for registration of cases.

The case of HIV dramatically underscores the limits of considering ethical questions regarding surveillance out of political and social context, in a way that does not account for the characteristics of the people affected by disease including their agency and vulnerability, the cultural perception of the disease in question, and the public health consequences of disease. Fairness requires that equals be treated equally. It also requires that where morally relevant differences exist, they be taken into account. In short, we must begin to account for those factors—such as race, gender, and class that clinical medical ethics needed to elide to prevent researchers from capitalizing on social or political vulnerability in designing and conducting studies—in a systematic yet not rigid fashion.

What then can be said about how the confrontation over the limits of privacy and confidentiality should have gone forward in the case of HIV and should go forward in other instances of surveillance? What standards should govern decision-making? The following might serve as principles worthy of consideration.

1. Wherever the state seeks to breach confidentiality for purposes of the surveillance it bears the burden of demonstrating that such an intrusion on privacy is critical for the ends of protecting the public health.
2. When the state breaches confidentiality in the name of surveillance it must demonstrate that it

has taken all necessary steps to protect the confidentiality of the names it will collect; that it has in place mechanisms that will preclude the possibility or unwarranted intrusions upon its records; that it has promulgated regulations and laws that will penalize unwarranted intrusions.
3. When those whose names are to be reported express fears about how they will suffer as a consequence of notification the state must seek to address their concerns directly and respectfully in a process of an open consultation.

But, though officials and even some advocates may prize the demands of public health over those of privacy, in the end it is clear that there is an inherent tension between public health and the claims of privacy, though the response to the tension may vary over time and place. What we have a right to expect is that the balance struck will be fair, judicious, and carefully wrought. To believe, however, that we can escape the tension is a dangerous illusion.

REFERENCES

Bayer R. (1989) *Private Acts Social Consequences: Aids and the Politics of Public Health.* New Brunswick: Rutgers University Press.

Bosch. (1999) Confidential Spanish Registry of HIV-infected Individuals. *JAMA* 281, 977.

CDC (1997) HIV/AIDS Surveillance Report. Atlanta: CDC 8.

Gostin L., Ward J. and Baker C. (1997) National HIV case reporting for the United States: a defining moment in the history of the epidemic. *N Engl J Med.* 337, 1162–1167.

Hammers F. (1998) Recommendations for HIV Surveillance in Europe. *Eurosurveillance* 3, 5, 51.

Joseph S. (1989) Remarks at the 5th International Conference on AIDS. (June 5) mimeo.

Lynberg M. and Edmonds L. (1992) Surveillance of Birth Defects. In: W. Halperin and E. L. Baker (Eds.). *Public Health Surveillance.* New York: Nostrand Reinhold, pp. 157–177.

Muir C., Demaret E. and Boyle P. (1985) The Cancer Registry in Cancer Control: An Overview. *The Role of the Registry in Cancer Control.* IARC Scientific Publications, 21.

North American Association of Central Cancer Registries (1997). Policy Statement 99–01: Confidentiality. November 17.

Pew Environmental Health Commission (2000) Healthy, from the Start: Why America Needs a Better System to Track and Understand Birth Defects and the Environment.

Rogers N. (1992) *Dirt and Disease: Polio Before FDR* (pp. 54). New Brunswick: Rutgers University Press.

Snow W. (1917) Public Health Measures in "Relation to Venereal Diseases." *Proceedings of the Second Pan American Scientific Congress,* 1915–1916, Section 8, Part I (Washington, D.C.) 9: 491.

PETER PIOT, RICHARD G. A. FEACHEM, LEE JONG-WOOK AND JAMES D. WOLFENSOHN

A Global Response to AIDS: Lessons Learned, Next Steps

Peter Piot is the executive director of the Joint United Nations Programme on HIV/AIDS and Under-Secretary-General of the United Nations. Under his leadership, UNAIDS has become the chief advocate for worldwide action against AIDS. He is the author of 16 books and more than 500 scientific articles.

Richard G. A. Feachem is Under-Secretary-General of the United Nations and Executive Director of the Global Fund to Fight AIDS, Tuberculosis and Malaria. His research interests include health policy, health and economic development, international health, environmental health, and epidemiology.

The late Lee Jong-wook was the director-general of the World Health Organization.

James D. Wolfensohn is president of the World Bank Group, Washington, DC, USA.

Every 2 years, the scientific community working on AIDS is joined by activists, health officials, and government leaders to take stock of the AIDS epidemic and to share the latest findings. Since the last International AIDS Conference in Barcelona, some 10 million people have been infected with HIV and just under 6 million people have died from AIDS. Projections now suggest that some countries in sub-Saharan Africa will face economic collapse unless they bring their epidemics under control. AIDS weakens and kills adults in their prime. AIDS-impacted countries are losing teachers, nurses, and civil servants at a faster rate than they can educate new ones. An estimated 14 million children have lost one or both parents, stretching the capacities of families and local communities.

In 2002 alone, there were 1 million new infections in the Asia Pacific region. Asia has provided the world with models for tackling the AIDS epidemic, from Thailand, Cambodia, and elsewhere. We've seen striking leadership emerge in China. But the window of opportunity is closing. Inequity, poverty, unequal status of women, stigma against people living with HIV, and cultural myths about sex contribute to an explosive epidemic. The risk of the epidemic's spreading in India raises grave concerns. Already 10% of the world's HIV-positive population lives in India—more than 4 million people. In 6 years, 10 million Chinese could be living with HIV unless infection rates are slowed.

Eastern Europe and Central Asia are also at the center of rapidly expanding AIDS epidemics that affect more than 1 million people, compared with only 30,000 in 1990. In Eastern Europe, young people make up 40% of the population and are at particular risk.

Globally, women make up nearly half of all people infected with HIV. Yet, they lack prevention, care, and support services.

From *Science* 304 (25 June 2004), 1909–1910. Notes omitted. Reprinted with permission from AAAS.

We have the science, the technical capacity, and the know-how, yet investments still have not begun to yield substantial and lasting impact on the AIDS epidemic. It is too easy to assign blame: Some countries have been too slow to recognize the scope of their epidemics, and some countries with emerging epidemics have wasted precious time by not preventing localized infections from spreading into the general population. Moreover, some AIDS programs have been developed in isolation by well-intentioned donors, UN agencies, and nongovernmental organizations (NGOs) and so have duplicated demands on struggling nations. Often responses have been so locally focused that they have not strengthened systems on the national level.

Yet there is room for optimism. . . . The campaign for access to treatment for all who need it is driving a much wider and deeper understanding of the AIDS epidemic in many countries. This, together with a better realization of the economic and social impact of the epidemic, has pushed up development assistance for fighting HIV/AIDS.

Substantial progress has been made in understanding the relation between prevention and treatment, as well as how important reduction of stigma is to make people willing to be tested and to seek treatment. . . . [T]he World Health Organization (WHO) has developed a simplified set of antiretroviral drug regimens, testing, and treatment guidelines[1] that are consistent with the highest standards of quality of care. The guidelines are intended to be used at all levels of the health system, including the community, to monitor and promote adherence to treatment. Because these regimens make it possible for even the poorest areas to start treating those who need them, they ensure that rollout of treatment programs can be done equitably.

A growing number of countries have shown that increasing access to treatment is both possible and effective. Brazil has the most advanced national HIV/AIDS treatment program in the developing world—it is estimated that between 1994 and 2002, almost 100,000 deaths have been averted (a 50% drop in mortality) through the introduction of antiretroviral therapy (ART). As a result of the program, hospital admissions have declined significantly, and cost savings in reduced hospital admissions and opportunistic infections are estimated at more than US$1 billion[2]. The program has also been effective in reducing the rates of tuberculosis and other opportunistic infections.

Access to drugs is a central element in any effective strategy to fight HIV-AIDS. In affirming that the Agreement on Trade-Related Aspects of Intellectual Property Rights (TRIPS Agreement) should be interpreted and implemented so as to protect public health and to promote access to medicines, the Doha Declaration on the TRIPS Agreement and Public Health[3] has ensured that international trade rules and intellectual property rights protection support the efforts of developing countries to secure such access. It is crucial to ensure that all countries adhere to the Doha Declaration as TRIPS comes into effect in 2005.

To provide treatment to those who need it safely and effectively, we need to develop simplified drug treatments, based on fixed-dose combinations and copackaging. We have affordable and effective first-line drugs to treat AIDS, but second-line drugs are still too expensive and out of reach for most countries. Affordable second-line regimens are needed. To treat AIDS in children, effective pediatric formulations are desperately needed.

A STRENGTHENED APPROACH

The Joint U.N. Programme on HIV/AIDS (UNAIDS) brings nine United Nations system agencies together, providing technical assistance to countries across a wide range of disciplines. It is the central point of reference on what works in responding to AIDS, and it leads the world's advocacy on AIDS. HIV/AIDS is a priority for the World Bank, which has committed US$1.6 billion to the cause through the Multicountry HIV/AIDS Programs (MAP) in Africa and the Caribbean and other AIDS work, including grants to the poorest countries. The Global Fund to Fight AIDS, TB, and Malaria provides substantial new resources for country-designed and driven HIV/AIDS prevention and treatment programs. WHO develops and sets standards in (for example) prevention and treatment protocols; provides countries with technical assistance to strengthen health systems and to design and implement their programs; and assists countries in choosing and procuring affordable, high-quality drugs and other commodities through its prequalification process. UNAIDS, WHO, the World Bank, and the Global Fund have reexamined our relations to make sure that we have forged the strongest possible alliance.

We are working to ensure that the resources are spent wisely to help countries mount sustainable and effective AIDS strategies. We recognize the importance of streamlining and focusing our work in every country. This is why we and other governments and donors, including the United States and the United Kingdom, are jointly promoting the principle of the "Three Ones"[4]: one agreed-upon HIV/AIDS action framework that provides the basis for coordinating the work of all partners; one national AIDS coordinating authority, with a broad-based mandate; and one agreed-upon country-level monitoring and evaluation system.

To that end, the Global Fund, the World Bank, WHO, UNAIDS, and other partners have agreed on a monitoring and evaluation toolkit[5], for use by all partners and governments. This is based on global consensus, and we are working with partners such as the U.S. President's Emergency Plan for AIDS Relief to harmonize indicators, data collection, and technical support.

KEY CHALLENGES

As a contribution to a constructive debate in Bangkok, we outline below what we believe to be the three key challenges for the fight against HIV/AIDS.

Increasing human capacity and global funding. As drug prices fall and resources become increasingly available, lack of human resources will become the main brake on a scale-up of HIV/AIDS interventions, in particular for a roll-out of treatment. In Africa alone, WHO estimates that around 100,000 health workers are missing, because they have died from the disease, have emigrated, or have left for better-paid work. Essential work to tackle personnel crisis ranges from giving health workers priority in receiving ART to continue helping others to compensating for extensive brain-drain created by rich countries' demand for doctors and nurses.

Involvement of communities is also essential to the success of integrated prevention and treatment programs. Motivating communities to know their HIV status in a context of access to ART is encouraging greater openness and helping a community-based response to reduce the stigma and denial that have enabled the virus to spread so disastrously.

Substantial new financial resources are becoming available to fight HIV/AIDS. Even so, we are still far from the level of $20 billion, which will be needed every year. This is a challenge both to donor countries and developing countries. Domestic expenditure needs to increase substantially, and it could do so in a number of middle-income countries.

It is unrealistic for the majority of developing countries to be able to cover all or even most of the funding needed to counter the spread of HIV/AIDS with domestic resources over the coming 10 or 15 years. We must acknowledge that some countries will need the support of the international community for decades.

Ensuring prevention and treatment. We can now leave simplistic discussions of prevention versus treatment behind. Growing scientific evidence supports common sense in arguing that new HIV infections will only be substantially reduced when broad access to treatment is combined with strengthened prevention efforts.

To reach those in need, we must develop much more effective systems to offer routine testing universally without losing the important principles of free choice and support through counseling and, increasingly, offers of treatment.

Scaling-up testing and counseling is a lynchpin of prevention, particularly for high-risk and vulnerable groups, including youth, sex workers, and injecting drug users, as well as for people with tuberculosis and pregnant women. Nonetheless, we must not underestimate the challenge posed by the stigma and discrimination faced by people living with HIV[6]. Combatting them has to be central to any prevention and treatment strategy.

The debate has also matured to a level where we now should be able to agree that national prevention strategies need to be based on a combination of universal access to tools that enable individuals to protect themselves from infection and individual and collective behavior change. The tools include condoms, clean needles, and effective blood screening, as well as factual, uninhibited knowledge about how people can reduce risk of HIV transmission. Behavior change should focus not only on abstinence and a reduction in the number of sexual partners, but also on economic and social practices that promote the spread of HIV, such as labor structures that split families for extended periods of time and violence against women. We must intensify research in new technologies, particularly those that will help women, such as microbicides.

National preparedness and ownership. At the heart of every national success story against HIV/AIDS is strong and visible national commitment and leadership. Direction from the top is essential to break public taboos and to forge a genuinely multi-sector response both within government and in the broader society.

Governments must engage health service deliverers that function outside the public heath system. In several developing countries, NGOs, faith-based organizations, and private commercial entities provide well over half of all health services. These sectors need to be mobilized in a coordinated and unified manner, within a coherent national strategy of open stewardship.

National leadership is also needed to set priorities. It is essential that donors respect and adhere to guidelines and requirements set out by the national authorities, in particular relating to treatment protocols. It is also crucial that countries receive the newest data and best possible technical advice to enable them to make these decisions. The Global Fund is designed specifically to respond to a country-driven process, and it is adjusting its practices to better serve its grantees. This is a model that should also guide other donor programs.

The flip-side of this process is a focus on results. Donors have a right to expect that their funding leads to measurable, long-term impact. To achieve this, programs need to be drawn up against specific targets, and future funding should be contingent on showing realistic progress toward these targets through simple, widely shared monitoring and evaluation systems.

The international community can and must support local efforts by providing funding, guidance, and technical support to governments and partners and by encouraging involvement by civil society. Ultimately, the most critical element of a sustained global response to AIDS is the willingness and ability of nations to take ownership of the problem.

We are gaining experience of what works. Although no one size fits all, we cannot wait for the perfect solution. We must learn by doing and ensure better coordination and use of resources.

NOTES

1. "Scaling up antiretroviral therapy in resource-limited settings: Treatment guidelines for a public health approach" (Department of HIV/AIDS, WHO, Geneva, 2003); available at http://whqlibdoc.who.int/hq/2004/9241591552.pdf

2. Ministry of Health of Brazil, "National AIDS Drug Policy" (Ministry of Health of Brazil, Brasilia, 2002).

3. See www.wto.org/english/tratop_e/dda_e/dohaexplained_e.htm

4. Commitments to Principles for Concerted AIDS Action at Country Level (UNAIDS, Geneva, 25 April 2004).

5. "Monitoring and Evaluation Toolkit" (Global Fund to Fight AIDS, TB, and Malaria; UNAIDS; WHO, draft 14 January 2004); available at http://www.theglobalfund.org/pdf/4_pp_me_toolkit_4_en.pdf

6. "Report on the Global HIV/AIDS Epidemic" (UNAIDS, Geneva, July 2002).

MATTHEW K. WYNIA AND LAWRENCE O. GOSTIN

Ethical Challenges in Preparing for Bioterrorism

Matthew K. Wynia is the director of the Institute for Ethics at the American Medical Association. His research focuses on physicians' responses to utilization review and market pressures in medicine, professional ethics, and performance measures for health care ethics.

Lawrence O. Gostin is Professor of Law at Georgetown University, Professor of Public Health at Johns Hopkins University, and the Director of the Center for Law & the Public's Health at Johns Hopkins and Georgetown Universities. His research focuses on public health law and ethics. Professor Gostin's latest books are *Public Health Law: Power, Duty, Restraint* and *Public Health Law and Ethics: A Reader*.

The intentional dispersal of anthrax spores in the United States demonstrates the need for preparedness for bioterrorism, and the . . . outbreak of severe acute respiratory syndrome (SARS) has renewed fears of unintentional or naturally occurring infectious epidemics. In responding to these threats, the public health system has rightfully garnered much of the attention, after decades in which government has starved public health agencies of needed resources. However, an effective response also will require the health care system to fulfill critical roles. By the term *health care system*, we mean those professionals (e.g., physicians and nurses) and institutions (e.g., hospitals and health plans) obliged to diagnose, treat, and care for individuals exposed to or infected with contagious diseases. We specify *contagious* diseases because although anthrax is not transmissible from person to person, many experts reserve their deepest fears for transmissible agents such as smallpox, plague, hemorrhagic fevers (e.g., the Ebola, Marburg, Lassa, and Crimean-Congo hemorrhagic fever viruses), and new (e.g., SARS) or designer viruses and bacteria.

Thinking systematically, what are the obligations of the health care system in handling contagious diseases?

From *American Journal of Public Health* 94:7 (July 2004), 1096–1102. Notes omitted. Reprinted with permission from the American Public Health Association.

The health care system should rapidly identify threats, help to prevent the spread of disease in the population, and care for infected patients. These 3 tasks—detection, containment, and treatment—are vital to the efficient handling of contagious epidemics. To prepare for each task, policymakers have emphasized training, clarification of public health quarantine powers, facilities improvements, and pharmaceutical stockpiling. Although these steps are important, we wish to draw attention to several challenges related to medical ethics and professionalism that might hinder detection, containment, and treatment and that have been much less discussed. Ours is not an exhaustive compilation of the many ethical issues associated with bioterrorism, but the issues we raise have received relatively little attention recently and are at risk of being lost in the highly publicized debates over, for example, the ethics of smallpox vaccination. These issues also illustrate that contagious diseases raise critical questions about the ethical relationship between medicine and public health.

DETECTION: REPORTING AND ACCESS TO CARE

In some bioterror scenarios, such as an aerosol release into a crowd, simultaneous widespread infections would mark an attack; if this were the case, then limiting the outbreak through early detection might provide little benefit (though early recognition and treatment of the illness might still save lives). But smaller-scale attacks are potentially much easier for terrorist organizations to organize, finance, and carry out. As the anthrax mailings of October 2001 demonstrated, even relatively small attacks can provoke widespread anxiety and disruption. In a stealth attack, early detection becomes critically important, as it is in stemming naturally occurring outbreaks.

To improve detection, the United States is expanding the public health system's capacity for surveillance. However, public health surveillance relies largely on reports from health care professionals. Persons with symptoms arrive first in physician's offices, clinics, or hospital emergency departments. For this system to work, therefore, patients must first have access to the health care system, and their illnesses must then be reported to the public health system.

The health care system must improve its reporting performance. Many physicians are unaware of reporting requirements, complain of the administrative burden of reporting, do not see reporting as important to patient care, or are unconvinced that reporting is of value. Reporting must be made easier (or even automatic, through electronic links), and physicians should be given feedback on how their reports are used to safeguard public health, reinforcing the value of the physician–public health partnership. Examination of the physician's role in reporting contagious illnesses should be included in new curricula on professionalism in the context of exploring the social roles of the medical profession. . . .

In the area of patient access to health care, more challenging dilemmas arise. Strong ethical reasons have long been recognized as supporting universal access to a decent minimal set of health care services, yet our nation has been unable or unwilling to accomplish this. Perhaps if policymakers understand that inadequate access to care poses a threat to national security, progress can be made. In the United States, more than 40 million Americans lack health insurance, and this number is rising. Although some uninsured individuals use emergency rooms to obtain care when they are acutely ill, many of the uninsured and underinsured avoid the health care system for as long as possible. Some have argued that bioterror-related illnesses are so severe that anyone affected would surely seek care. But uninsured patients discriminate poorly between appropriate and inappropriate care and tend to avoid both equally. Numerous studies demonstrate that the uninsured are more likely to present in an

advanced stage of illness, and many die without ever being evaluated.[1–3]

Terrorists undoubtedly recognize that even a small-scale release of an infectious agent into a community with a high rate of uninsurance might be devastatingly effective. Because most of the uninsured are employed and working throughout cities, suburbs, and rural areas, starting an outbreak in such a community—using a low-tech approach, such as an infected "martyr"—would reduce the likelihood of early detection and raise the odds of broad spread of the disease. Unfortunately, this scenario is not mere speculation: "natural experiments" that simulate such an attack have demonstrated the vulnerability of poor, especially uninsured immigrant, populations and their ability to spread disease throughout the population. Many naturally occurring infectious diseases, including tuberculosis, food-borne illnesses, and HIV/AIDS, disproportionately burden the uninsured and subsequently spread to the community at large.

Maintaining barriers to accessing health care in the face of today's threats should be unacceptable, morally and politically. In the aftermath of the September 11 attacks, New York ordered its health care system to provide care to all possible victims and the state health commissioner, Antonio Coello Novello, declared to providers: "Thou shalt not ask who will pay for this."[4] Over the next 4 months. New York's special Disaster Relief Medicaid program enrolled and cared for almost 400 000 people New York dramatically streamlined the application process for Medicaid and obtained additional funding for the state pool for the uninsured. The public, government, and the medical community widely approved these actions as appropriate, given the threat.

Learning from this experience, federal and state officials should make clear that individuals with symptoms that suggest infection with a contagious illness should present for evaluation and ensure that those who do can be treated without prejudice. Funding must be provided to cover screening and treatment of patients with contagious illnesses; in particular, funding for hospital emergency departments that see large volumes of uninsured patients must be increased. Because patients cannot be expected to know in advance whether their illness is infectious, programs can be targeted toward contagious illness but ultimately, they will need to be broad based. Finally, funding alone might not guarantee ready access to care for certain populations, especially recent immigrants and those who mistrust the health care system.

The current policy focus on addressing racial and ethnic health disparities should be used to build a culturally sensitive primary care system in which all patients feel welcome.

CONTAINMENT: ISOLATION BEFORE QUARANTINE

In late October 2001, the secretary of the US Department of Health and Human Services asked the states to increase their legal preparedness for potential epidemics Twenty-two states and the District of Columbia have since enacted laws based on the Model State Emergency Health Powers Act, drafted by the Center for Law and the Public's Health at the request of the Centers for Disease Control and Prevention. These laws seek to ensure that when facing a clear emergency, the public health system can carry out screening, vaccination, quarantine, and treatment. Even with these powers, however, the public health system cannot contain an outbreak as rapidly as might health care professionals who are willing and empowered to use short-term involuntary isolation when needed.

Of course, most contagious patients will comply voluntarily with an isolation request; but recent bioterror training scenarios assume that not everyone will cooperate with treatment and quarantines, and this assumption is borne out in experiences with SARS. Illness and fear can hinder clear thinking. Physicians should know this and be prepared to intervene if necessary. Under what legal authority might health care professionals isolate a potentially contagious patient *in advance* of a public health quarantine? Health care professionals have a general obligation to prevent patients from harming themselves or others and may use compulsion when necessary. The most common application of this power might be to "hold" psychiatric patients thought to pose a suicide or homicide risk. Such short-term physician holds usually require judicial review within 24 to 48 hours, but this kind of short-term legal authority could serve as an early stop to an outbreak in the event that one or more patients decline necessary interventions before the public health authority enforces quarantine.

In general, public health officers, not one's physician, should declare quarantine, because separation of these roles allows physicians to attend to individual patients' interests. Indeed, using professional powers to hold patients involuntarily poses a fundamental ethical challenge for physicians, because it entails overriding an individual patient's wishes in deference to the community's needs—balancing respect for patient autonomy against public health benefit. Challenging though it may be, however, mediating the tension between individual and community needs is integral to the role of the medical profession in society—and demonstrates why the profession must maintain some independence from both the state and patient interests.

There are significant risks in physicians' acting as agents of the state, yet attention to civic obligations is as ancient a part of professionalism as is attention to patients' interests. Plato bluntly recognized this balancing act when he wrote that physicians are "statesmen" who are to do what "is best for the patients *and* for the state."[5(p6)] More recently, Creuss and Creuss noted that during the 19th century

legal measures for the first time granted medicine a broad monopoly over health care–along with both individual and collective autonomy–with the clear understanding that in return medicine would concern itself with the health problems of the society it served and would place the welfare of society above its own.[6(p943)]

The original 1847 Code of Medical Ethics of the American Medical Association noted that a physician's skills "are qualities which he holds in trust for the general good,"[7(p318)] and one of its 3 chapters—entitled. "Of the Duties of the Profession to the Public, and of the Obligations of the Public to the Profession"—dealt explicitly with physicians' social duties.[7(p333)]

In the era after 1955, however, medicine began to move away from balancing social obligations, tilting toward a more restricted advocacy position. Obligations regarding public health were minimized, and physicians were eventually urged to ignore civic considerations altogether and to think only of the welfare of the patient before them. In 1984, Norman Levinsky wrote that "physicians are required to do everything that they believe may benefit each patient, without regard to costs or other societal considerations."[8(p1574)] This statement reflected the domination of medical ethics by respect for patient autonomy and the loss of a cardinal feature of professionalism: mediation between private and community interests. But, bereft of its role as a social protector, medicine was left with only technical expertise to support its claims to professional prerogatives, which are granted by society and have since steadily eroded. Recognizing this chain of events, recent scholars of the medical profession are returning to a civic understanding of professionalism as necessary to maintaining public trust and, with it, professional privileges. Dr. William Sullivan wrote of this return to a classic role for the professions in society: "Historically, the legitimacy, authority, and legal privileges of the most prestigious professions have depended heavily on their claims (and finally their demonstration) of civic performance, especially social leadership in the public interest."[9(p11)]

Ethically, therefore, when time is limited, physicians should be empowered and willing to use short-term holds to prevent immediate spread of disease, because physicians' professional duty sometimes should tilt toward protecting the public—although not incidentally, of course, most individuals will also benefit from enforced isolation and treatment. Some physicians and patients, raised on the medical ethics of the last 50 years, will chafe at the paternalism of this statement, but we find that professionalism requires meaningful attention to civic duties such as protecting the public health. Because the power to hold patients involuntarily can be abused constraints such as requiring 2 physicians to concur, ensuring the short-term nature of the hold (24 hours or less), and ensuring rapid judicial review, should be applied. Legally, in jurisdictions where it is not clear whether physicians' authority to hold patients for dangerousness applies outside the psychiatric setting, clarification is required. Bioterror training should reinforce physicians' ethical obligations regarding isolation of dangerously infectious patients, and there should be open debates on appropriate limits to this power, as well as to address practical considerations regarding quarantine, such as when public health authorities should enforce community quarantine and how to respectfully care for those under quarantine.

TREATMENT: THE DUTY TO TREAT

Recent discussions of treatment barriers during bioterror-related outbreaks tend to focus on potential shortages of antibiotics and vaccines. But stockpiles can be calculated with reasonable certainty and increased as needed. More challenging in these scenarios is that 1 treatment variable is critically important yet very difficult to estimate: how many health care professionals will fail to show up for work because they fear contracting the illness?

It is almost certain that some will not willingly face the risk. At least 1 hospital in China had difficulty maintaining services because of absenteeism in the face of SARS. Some hospitals in New York have announced they will not care for victims of bioterror attacks. Physician performance during epidemics,

from the black plague to the HIV epidemic, has been notoriously spotty. And relatively few physicians have volunteered to receive smallpox vaccination, despite high-level government requests.

There is legitimate reason for trepidation on the part of health professionals. More than one third of health care personnel treating patients after the sarin gas attack in Tokyo became ill from cross-contamination. Health care workers are common second-wave victims of Ebola and SARS. In the United States, there are 56 documented cases of health care workers' becoming infected with HIV due to needle-stick injuries,[10] and countless more have contracted hepatitis B or C, tuberculosis, and other potentially deadly infections. Into the 1950s, exposure to and infection with tuberculosis was a near-ubiquitous medical training experience, especially for pulmonologists.

Several ethical and practical bases for a "duty to treat" have been proposed that taken together provide a strong justification for its reaffirmation today. Health care professionals receive special training, which increases the general obligation to render aid to others in need, because it increases the value of the aid and may reduce the risk associated with providing it. Physicians have long subscribed to explicit codes of ethics that demand the duty to treat, codes that the public assumes to be binding. In 1991, despite recent interprofessional wrangling over the treatment of patients with HIV, 72% of the public agreed with the statement that physicians are obligated to "treat all sick people."[11] Physicians also receive social standing and trust as part of a social contract, which includes an obligation to place the welfare of patients above self-interest.

When professional associations last confronted this issue, in the early years of the AIDS epidemic, early wavering gave way to consensus that a duty to treat still exists. According to the Infectious Diseases Society of America and the American College of Physicians, health care professionals "must provide high-quality nonjudgmental care to their patients, even at the risk of contracting a patient's disease.[12(p576)] The American Medical Association's recently (December 2001) adopted Declaration of Professional Responsibility states that physicians must "treat the sick and injured with competence and compassion and without prejudice," and "apply our knowledge and skills when needed, though doing so may put us at risk."[13]

Two steps should be taken to reinforce this obligation. First, language in professional codes of ethics addressing treatment during epidemics was largely removed in the 1970s, at a time when epidemics appeared to be on the wane. Subsequent statements focused almost exclusively on HIV/AIDS and often were framed in terms of antidiscrimination principles rather than professional obligations. Professional associations should make clear their current stances on physicians' obligations to care for patients during epidemics. Ideally, the inspiring spirit and language of the early American Medical Association Code of Medical Ethics should be reaffirmed today: "When an epidemic prevails, a physician must continue his labors for the alleviation of suffering people, without regard to the risk to his own health or to financial return."[14(p354)]

Second, to justify and strengthen this obligation, special efforts should be made to ensure that health care professionals receive all reasonable preventive and treatment measures in the event of an outbreak, such as vaccines, prophylactic therapies, and safety training. Such preferential treatment makes practical sense, because only healthy practitioners will be of value in responding to any ongoing threat. Ethically, when health care professionals tend to patients in epidemics, healthy people place themselves (and often their families) at risk to benefit the common good. The state must recognize that this burden, in some manner, should be shared by the community as a whole. This value was implicitly recognized in policy discussions regarding early smallpox vaccination for health care workers. However, beyond smallpox, health care workers should be assured that in the event of an attack, all that is possible will be done to protect them— and their families. Local stockpiles of vaccines and other therapies should be set aside for health care workers, ensuring that those who may be at greatest risk will receive early and effective protection. In addition, the families of health care workers who perish in epidemics should receive predictable compensation. By offering fair compensation, the government can further spread the burden of pursuing the public interest.

CONCLUSIONS

Defense against bioterror and naturally occurring infectious epidemics requires a strong public health system. But the public health system cannot function without an effective health care system to detect, contain, and treat infectious diseases. Hence our national defense against bioterrorism must ensure universal rapid access to knowledgeable and compassionate health care professionals who in turn can and will evaluate and care for potentially contagious patients. When ethical barriers in the health care system stand in the way of detection, containment, and treatment, they must be confronted and resolved, because undiagnosed, unconfined, and untreated infections pose a risk to individuals and the community.

NOTES

1. Schroeder SA. The American paradox: lack of health insurance in a land of plenty. In: *Americans Without Health Insurance: Myths and Realities*. Princeton, NJ: Robert Wood Johnson Foundation; 1999. Robert Wood Johnson Foundation Annual Report 1999.

2. Institute of Medicine. *Care Without Coverage: Too Little, Too Late*. Washington. DC: National Academy Press; 2002.

3. American College of Physicians—American Society of Internal Medicine. No health insurance: it's enough to make you sick–scientific research linking the lack of health coverage to poor health. November 30, 1999. Available at: http://www.acponline.org/uninsured/lack-paper.pdf. Accessed October 22, 2003.

4. Novello A. APHA response to acts of terrorism. In: Proceedings of the 129th Annual Meeting and Exposition of the American Public Health Association; October 22, 2001; Atlanta, Ga. Executive Board Special Session: Session 3099.1.

5. Plato. *Republic*. Book III. Quoted in: Jonsen AR. *A Short History of Medical Ethics*. New York, NY: Oxford University Press; 2000.

6. Creuss RL. Creuss SR. Teaching medicine as a profession in the service of healing. *Acad Med*. 1997; 72: 941–952.

7. Bell J. Hayes I. Appendix C: Code of Ethics (1847). In: Baker RB, Caplan AL. Emanuel LL, Latham SR, eds. *The American Medical Ethics Revolution*. Baltimore, Md: Johns Hopkins University Press; 1999.

8. Levinsky N. The doctor's master. *N Engl J Med*. 1984; 311: 1573–1575.

9. Sullivan WM. What is left of professionalism after managed care? *Hastings Center Rep*. 1999; 29: 7–13.

10. Centers for Disease Control and Prevention. Update: US Public Health Service guidelines for the management of occupational exposures to HBV. HCV, and HIV and recommendations for post-exposure prophylaxis. *MMWR CDC Surveill Sumon*. 2001; 50(RR-11): 1–52.

11. Roper Survey Research Associates. *Great American TV Poll No. 4*. Vol. 2002. Princeton, NJ: Princeton Survey Research Associates; 1991. Available at:http://headlines.kff.org/healthpollreport/templates/reference.php?page=16_1991_02&feature=feature2. Accessed June 1, 2004.

12. Health and Public Policy Committee. American College of Physicians, and the Infectious Diseases Society of America. Position paper: acquired immune deficiency syndrome. *Ann Intern Med*. 1986; 104: 575–581.

13. American Medical Association Declaration of professional responsibility: medicine's social contract with humanity. December 4, 2001. Available at: http://www.ama-assn.org/go/declaration. Accessed October 22, 2003.

14. 1912 Code of Medical Ethics of the American Medical Association. In: Baker RB, Caplan AL. Emannel LE. Latham SR, eds. *The American Medical Ethics Revolution*. Baltimore, Md: Johns Hopkins University Press; 1999.

U.S. DEPARTMENT OF HEALTH AND HUMAN SERVICES

Pandemic Influenza Plan

An influenza pandemic has the potential to cause more death and illness than any other public health threat. If a pandemic influenza virus with similar virulence to the 1918 strain emerged today, in the absence of intervention, it is estimated that 1.9 million Americans could die and almost 10 million could be hospitalized over the course of the pandemic, which may evolve over a year or more. Although the timing, nature and severity of the next pandemic cannot be predicted with any certainty, preparedness planning is imperative to lessen the impact of a pandemic. The unique characteristics and events of a pandemic will strain local, state, and federal resources. It is unlikely that there will be sufficient personnel, equipment, and supplies to respond adequately to multiple areas of the country for a sustained period of time. Therefore, minimizing social and economic disruption will require a coordinated response. Governments, communities, and other public and private sector stakeholders will need to anticipate and prepare for a pandemic by defining roles and responsibilities and developing continuity of operations plans.

[T]he HHS Pandemic Influenza Plan serves as a blueprint for all HHS pandemic influenza preparedness and response planning. . . .

THE PANDEMIC INFLUENZA THREAT

A pandemic occurs when a novel influenza virus emerges that can infect and be efficiently transmitted among individuals because of a lack of pre-existing immunity in the population. The extent and severity of a pandemic depends on the specific characteristics of the virus. . . .

From U.S. Department of Health and Human Services, HHS Pandemic Influenza Plan (November 2005), 4-8; D-10; D-12 to D-18.

PANDEMIC PLANNING ASSUMPTIONS

. . . Characteristics of an influenza pandemic that must be considered in strategic planning include:

- The ability of the virus to spread rapidly worldwide;
- The fact that people may be asymptomatic while infectious;
- Simultaneous or near-simultaneous outbreaks in communities across the U.S., thereby limiting the ability of any jurisdiction to provide support and assistance to other areas;
- Enormous demands on the healthcare system;
- Delays and shortages in the availability of vaccines and antiviral drugs; and
- Potential disruption of national and community infrastructures including transportation, commerce, utilities and public safety due to widespread illness and death among workers and their families and concern about on-going exposure to the virus.

DOCTRINE FOR HHS PANDEMIC INFLUENZA PLANNING AND RESPONSE

. . . In addition to the characteristics of a pandemic noted above, HHS' preparedness planning and response activities are guided by the following principles:

1. Preparedness will require coordination among federal, state and local government and partners in the private sector.
2. An informed and responsive public is essential to minimizing the health effects of a pandemic and the resulting consequences to society.
3. Domestic vaccine production capacity sufficient to provide vaccine for the entire U.S. population is critical, as is development of vaccine against each circulating influenza virus with pandemic

potential and acquisition of sufficient quantities to help protect first responders and other critical personnel at the onset of a pandemic.

4. Quantities of antiviral drugs sufficient to treat 25% of the U.S. population should be stockpiled.
5. Sustained human-to-human transmission anywhere in the world will be the triggering event to initiate a pandemic response by the United States.
6. When possible and appropriate, protective public health measures will be employed to attempt to reduce person-to-person viral transmission and prevent or delay influenza outbreaks.
7. At the onset of a pandemic, vaccine, which will initially be in short supply, will be procured by HHS and distributed to state and local health departments for immunization of predetermined priority groups.
8. At the onset of a pandemic, antiviral drugs from public stockpiles will be distributed to health care providers for administration to predetermined priority groups.

KEY PANDEMIC RESPONSE ELEMENTS AND CAPABILITIES FOR EFFECTIVE IMPLEMENTATION

The nature of the HHS response will be guided by the epidemiologic features of the virus and the course of the pandemic. An influenza pandemic will place extraordinary and sustained demands not only on public health and health care providers, but also on providers of essential services across the United States and around the globe. Realizing that pandemic influenza preparedness is a process, not an isolated event, to most effectively implement key pandemic response actions, specific capabilities must be developed through preparedness activities implemented before the pandemic occurs. . . . [K]ey actions for an effective pandemic response [involve] surveillance, investigation, protective public health measures; vaccines and antiviral drug production; healthcare and emergency response; and communications and public outreach. . . .

Once sustained human infection is documented, early in a pandemic, especially before a vaccine is available or during a period of limited supply, HHS may implement travel-related and community-based public health strategies in order to impede the spread of the virus and reduce the number of people infected. In particular, travel advisories and precautions, screening of persons arriving from affected areas, closing schools, restricting public gatherings, quarantine of exposed persons and isolation of infected persons may be implemented with the intent of slowing introduction and transmission of the virus. The use and continuation of these interventions will be determined by assessments of their effectiveness.

VACCINES AND ANTIVIRAL DRUGS

Vaccines and antiviral drugs have the potential to significantly reduce morbidity and mortality during a pandemic. In addition, vaccines and antiviral drugs may also limit viral spread. Although antiviral drugs can be stockpiled, a pandemic vaccine can only be made once the pandemic virus is identified. . . .

At the onset of a pandemic, HHS will accelerate its ongoing work with industry to facilitate the production and distribution of antiviral drugs and pandemic vaccines. HHS will continue to monitor antiviral drug and pandemic vaccine distribution effectiveness, and adverse events. Since vaccine and antiviral drugs are likely to be in short supply at the onset of an influenza pandemic, identification of predefined groups in which these medications will be used will be discussed as part of federal planning activities. HHS will work with state and local governments to develop guidelines and operational plans for the distribution of available supplies of a pandemic vaccine and antiviral drugs.

• • •

[NVAC/ACIP RECOMMENDATIONS FOR PRIORITIZATION OF PANDEMIC INFLUENZA VACCINE]

Two federal advisory committees, the Advisory Committee on Immunization Practices (ACIP) and the National Vaccine Advisory Committee (NVAC), provided recommendations to the Department of Health and Human Services on the use of vaccines . . . in an influenza pandemic. . . .

The primary goal of a pandemic response considered was to decrease health impacts including severe morbidity and death; secondary pandemic response goals included minimizing societal and economic impacts. However, as other sectors are increasingly engaged in pandemic planning, additional considerations may arise. The advisory committee reports explicitly acknowledge the importance of this, for example highlighting the priority for protecting critical components of the military. . . .

On July 19, 2005, ACIP and NVAC voted unanimously in favor of the vaccine priority recommendations summarized in Table D-1. These votes followed deliberations of a joint Working Group of the two committees, which included as consultants representatives of public and private sector stakeholder organizations and academic experts. There was limited staff level participation from [federal government agencies]. Several ethicists also served as consultants to the Working Group.

to 5 million 15µg doses per week with 3 to 6 months needed before the first doses are produced. Two doses per person were assumed to be required for protection. . . .

B. DEFINITIONS AND RATIONALES FOR PRIORITY GROUPS

1. *Healthcare workers and essential healthcare support staff*

a) Definition Healthcare workers (HCW) with direct patient contact (including acute-care hospitals, nursing homes, skilled nursing facilities, urgent care centers, physician's offices, clinics, home care, blood collection centers, and EMS) and a proportion of persons working in essential healthcare support services needed to maintain healthcare services (e.g. dietary, housekeeping, admissions, blood collection center staff, etc.). Also included are healthcare workers in public health with direct patient contact, including those who may administer vaccine or distribute influenza antiviral medications, and essential public health support staff for these workers.

b) Rationale The pandemic is expected to have substantial impact on the healthcare system with large increases in demand for healthcare services placed on top of existing demand. HCW will be treating influenza-infected patients and will be at risk of repeated exposures. Further, surge capacity in this sector is low. To encourage continued work in a high-exposure setting and to help lessen the risk of healthcare workers transmitting influenza to other patients and HCW family members, this group was highly prioritized. In addition, increases in bed/nurse ratios have been associated with increases in overall patient mortality. Thus, substantial absenteeism may affect overall patient care and outcomes.

2. *Groups at high risk of influenza complications*

a) Definition Persons 2–64 years with a medical condition for which influenza vaccine is recommended and all persons 6–23 months and 65 years and older. Excludes nursing home residents and severely immunocompromised persons who would not be expected to respond well to vaccination.

b) Rationale These groups were prioritized based on their risk of influenza-related hospitalization and death and also their likelihood of vaccine response.

A. CRITICAL ASSUMPTIONS

The recommendations summarized in Table D-1 were based on the following critical assumptions:

- *Morbidity and mortality.* The greatest risk of hospitalization and death—as during the 1957 and 1968 pandemics and annual influenza—will be in infants, the elderly, and those with underlying health conditions. In the 1918 pandemic, most deaths occurred in young adults, highlighting the need to reconsider the recommendations at the time of the pandemic based on the epidemiology of disease.
- *Healthcare system.* The healthcare system will be severely taxed if not overwhelmed due to the large number of illnesses and complications from influenza requiring hospitalization and critical care. CDC models estimate increases in hospitalization and intensive care unit demand of more than 25% even in a moderate pandemic.
- *Workforce.* During a pandemic wave in a community, between 25% and 30% of persons will become ill during a 6 to 8 week outbreak. Among working-aged adults, illness attack rates will be lower than in the community as a whole. A CDC model suggests that at the peak of pandemic disease, about 10% of the workforce will be absent due to illness or caring for an ill family member. Impacts will likely vary between communities and work sites and may be greater if significant absenteeism occurs because persons stay home due to fear of becoming infected.
- *Critical infrastructure.* Only limited information was available from which to assess potential impacts on critical infrastructure sectors such as transportation and utility services. Because of changes in business practices and the complexity of networks, information from prior pandemics was not considered applicable.
- *Vaccine production capacity.* The U.S.-based vaccine production capacity was assumed at 3

Table D-1: Vaccine Priority Group Recommendations

Tier	Subtier	Population	Rationale
1	A	• Vaccine and antiviral manufacturers and others essential to manufacturing and critical support (~40,000) • Medical workers and public health workers who are involved in direct patient contact, other support services essential for direct patient care, and vaccinators (8–9 million)	• Need to assure maximum production of vaccine and antiviral drugs • Healthcare workers are required for quality medical care (studies show outcome is associated with staff-to-patient ratios). There is little surge capacity among healthcare sector personnel to meet increased demand.
	B	• Persons ≥ 65 years with 1 or more influenza high-risk conditions, not including essential hypertension (approximately 18.2 million) • Persons 6 months to 64 years with 2 or more influenza high-risk conditions, not including essential hypertension (approximately 6.9 million) • Persons 6 months or older with history of hospitalization for pneumonia or influenza or other influenza high-risk condition in the past year (740,000)	• These groups are at high risk of hospitalization and death. Excludes elderly in nursing homes and those who are immunocompromised and would not likely be protected by vaccination
	C	• Pregnant women (approximately 3.0 million) • Household contacts of severely immunocompromised persons who would not be vaccinated due to likely poor response to vaccine (1.95 million with transplants, AIDS, and incident cancer × 1.4 household contacts per person = 2.7 million persons) • Household contacts of children <6 month olds (5.0 million)	• In past pandemics and for annual influenza, pregnant women have been at high risk; vaccination will also protect the infant who cannot receive vaccine • Vaccination of household contacts of immunocompromised and young infants will decrease risk of exposure and infection among those who cannot be directly protected by vaccination.
	D	• Public health emergency response workers critical to pandemic response (assumed one-third of estimated public health workforce = 150,000) • Key government leaders	• Critical to implement pandemic response such as providing vaccinations and managing/monitoring response activities • Preserving decision-making capacity also critical for managing and implementing a response
2	A	• Healthy 65 years and older (17.7 million) • 6 months to 64 years with 1 high-risk condition (35.8 million) • 6–23 months old, healthy (5.6 million)	• Groups that are also at increased risk but not as high risk as population in Tier 1B
	B	• Other public health emergency responders (300,000 = remaining two-thirds of public health work force) • Public safety workers including police, fire, 911 dispatchers, and correctional facility staff (2.99 million) • Utility workers essential for maintenance of power, water, and sewage system functioning (364,000)	• Includes critical infrastructure groups that have impact on maintaining health (e.g., public safety or transportation of medical supplies and food); implementing a pandemic response; and on maintaining societal functions

Tier	Subtier	Population	Rationale
		• Transportation workers transporting fuel, water, food, and medical supplies as well as public ground public transportation (3.8 million)	
		• Telecommunications/IT for essential network operations and maintenance (1.08 million)	
3		• Other key government health decision-makers (estimated number not yet determined)	• Other important societal groups for a pandemic response but of lower priority
		• Funeral directors/embalmers (62,000)	
4		• Healthy persons 2–64 years not included in above categories (179.3 million)	• All persons not included in other groups based on objective to vaccinate all those who want protection

*The committee focused its deliberations on the U.S. civilian population. ACIP and NVAC recognize that Department of Defense needs should be highly prioritized. DoD Health Affairs indicates that 1.5 million service members would require immunization to continue current combat operations and preserve critical components of the military medical system. Should the military be called upon to support civil authorities domestically, immunization of a greater proportion of the total force will become necessary. These factors should be considered in the designation of a proportion of the initial vaccine supply for the military.

Other groups also were not explicitly considered in these deliberations on prioritization. These include American citizens living overseas, non-citizens in the U.S., and other groups providing national security services such as the border patrol and customs service.

Information from prior pandemics was used whenever possible, but information from interpandemic years was also considered. Nursing home residents and severely immunocompromised persons would be prioritized for antiviral treatment and/or prophylaxis and vaccination of healthcare workers and household contacts who are most likely to transmit influenza to these high risk groups.

3. Critical infrastructure

a) Definitions and rationale Those critical infrastructure sectors that fulfill one or more of the following criteria: have increased demand placed on them during a pandemic, directly support reduction in deaths and hospitalization; function is critical to support the healthcare sector and other emergency services, and/or supply basic necessities and services critical to support of life and healthcare or emergency services. Groups included in critical infrastructure are needed to respond to a pandemic and to minimize morbidity and mortality, and include the following sectors:

- Persons directly involved with influenza vaccine and antiviral medication manufacturing and distribution and essential support services and suppliers (e.g., growers of pathogen-free eggs for growth of vaccine virus) production activities.

- Key government leaders and health decision-makers who will be needed to quickly move policy forward on pandemic prevention and control efforts
- Public safety workers (firefighters, police, and correctional facility staff, including dispatchers) are critical to maintaining social functioning and order and will contribute to a pandemic response, for example by ensuring order at vaccination clinics and responding to medical emergencies
- Utility service workers (water, power, and sewage management) are prioritized as the services they provide are also essential to the healthcare system as well as to preventing additional illnesses from lack of these services unrelated to a pandemic.
- Transportation workers who maintain critical supplies of food, water, fuel, and medical equipment and who provide public transportation, which is essential for provision of medical care and transportation of healthcare workers to work and transportation of ill persons for care
- Telecommunication and information technology services critical for maintenance and repairs of these systems are also essential as these systems are now critical for accessing and delivering medical care and in support of all other critical infrastructure.

- Mortuary services will be substantially impacted due to the increased numbers of deaths from a pandemic and the fact that impact will be high in the elderly, a growing segment of the population.

4. Public health emergency response workers

a) Definition This group includes persons who do not have direct patient care duties, but who are essential for surveillance for influenza, assessment of the pandemic impact, allocation of public health resources for the pandemic response, development and implementation of public health policy as part of the response, and development of guidance as the pandemic progresses.

b) Rationale Persons in this sector have been critical for past influenza vaccine pandemics and influenza vaccine shortages and little surge capacity may be available during a public health emergency such as a pandemic.

5. Persons in skilled nursing facilities

a) Definition Patients residing in skilled nursing facilities. Not included in this group are persons in other residential settings (e.g., assisted living) who are more likely to be mobile, in a setting that is less closed, and have decentralized healthcare.

b) Rationale This group was not prioritized for vaccine because of the medical literature finding poor response to vaccination and occurrence of outbreaks even in the setting of high vaccination rates. Other studies have suggested that vaccination of healthcare workers may be a more effective strategy to prevent influenza in this group. Further, surveillance for influenza can be conducted in this group and antiviral medications used widely for prophylaxis and treatment. Ill visitors and staff should also be restricted from visiting nursing home facilities during outbreaks of pandemic influenza.

This strategy for pandemic influenza vaccine differs from the interpandemic vaccination strategy of aggressively vaccinating nursing home residents. The rationale considers several factors: 1) these populations are less likely to benefit from vaccine than other groups who are also at high risk; 2) other prevention strategies feasible for this group are not possible among other high-risk groups; 3) the overall morbidity and mortality from pandemic is likely to severely impact other groups of persons who would be expected to have a better response to the vaccine; and 4) a more severe shortage of vaccine is anticipated.

6. Severely immunocompromised persons

a) Definition Persons who are undergoing or who have recently undergone bone marrow transplantation and others with severe immunodeficiency (e.g., AIDS patients with CD4 counts <50, children with SCID syndrome, recent bone marrow transplant patients). The numbers of persons in these categories is likely much smaller than the anticipated number assumed in tiering above, but sources for more specific estimates have not been identified.

b) Rationale These groups have a lower likelihood of responding to influenza vaccination. Thus, strategies to prevent severe influenza illness in this group should include vaccination of healthcare workers and household contacts of severely immunocompromised persons and use of antiviral medications. Consideration should be given to prophylaxis of severely immunocompromised persons with influenza antivirals and early antiviral treatment should they become infected.

7. Children <6 months of age

a) Rationale Influenza vaccine is poorly immunogenic in children <6 months and the vaccine is currently not recommended for this group. In addition, influenza antiviral medications are not FDA-approved for use in children <1 year old. Thus, vaccination of household contacts and out-of-home caregivers of children <6 months is recommended to protect this high-risk group.

C. OTHER DISCUSSION

There was substantial discussion on priority for children. Four potential reasons were raised for making vaccination of children a priority:

- At the public engagement session, many participants felt that children should have high priority for vaccination.
- Children play a major role in transmitting infection, and vaccinating this group could slow the spread of disease and indirectly protect others.
- Children have strong immune systems and will respond well to vaccine whereas vaccination of the elderly and those with illnesses may be less effective.

- Some ethical frameworks would support a pediatric priority.

ACIP and NVAC did not make children a priority (other than those included in tiers, because of their underlying diseases [Tiers 1B and 2A] or as contacts of high-risk persons [Tier 1C] for several reasons:

- Healthy children have been at low risk for hospitalization and death in prior pandemics and during annual influenza seasons.
- It is uncertain whether vaccination of children will decrease transmission and indirectly protect others.

- Studies that show this impact or mathematical models that predict it rely on high vaccination coverage that may not be possible to achieve given limited supplies in a pandemic.
- The committees recognize that this is an area for further scientific work; that children may be a good target population for live-attenuated influenza vaccine (FluMist®) if it is available; and that education of the public will be needed to provide the rationale for the recommendations.

EZEKIEL J. EMANUEL AND ALAN WERTHEIMER

Who Should Get Influenza Vaccine When Not All Can?

Ezekiel J. Emanuel is Chair of the Department of Clinical Bioethics at the Warren G. Magnuson Clinical Center at the National Institutes of Health (NIH). He has published widely on the ethics of clinical research, health care reform, international research ethics, end-of-life care issues, euthanasia, the ethics of managed care, and the physician–patient relationship. Dr. Emanuel's books include *The Ends of Human Life: Medical Ethics in a Liberal Polity* and *No Margin, No Mission: Health-Care Organizations and the Quest for Ethical Excellence*.

Alan Wertheimer is John G. McCullough Professor of Political Science at the University of Vermont. His research focuses on political theory, law, and ethics. He is the author of several books, including *Coercion and Exploitation*, and *Consent to Sexual Relations*, and numerous articles.

The potential threat of pandemic influenza is staggering: 1.9 million deaths, 90 million people sick, and nearly 10 million people hospitalized, with almost 1.5 million requiring intensive-care units (ICUs) in the United States (1). The National Vaccine Advisory Committee (NVAC) and the Advisory Committee on Immunization Policy (ACIP) have jointly recommended a prioritization scheme that places vaccine workers, health-care providers, and the ill elderly at the top, and healthy people aged 2 to 64 at the very

bottom, even under embalmers (1) (see table). The primary goal informing the recommendation was to "decrease health impacts including severe morbidity and death"; a secondary goal was minimizing societal and economic impacts (1). As the NVAC and ACIP acknowledge, such important policy decisions require broad national discussion. In this spirit, we believe an alternative ethical framework should be considered.

THE INESCAPABILITY OF RATIONING

Because of current uncertainty of its value, only "a limited amount of avian influenza A (H5N1) vaccine is being stockpiled"[1]. Furthermore, it will take at least

From *Science* 312 (12 May 2006), 854–855. Notes omitted.

4 months from identification of a candidate vaccine strain until production of the very first vaccine (*1*). At present, there are few production facilities worldwide that make influenza vaccine, and only one completely in the USA. Global capacity for influenza vaccine production is just 425 million doses per annum, if all available factories would run at full capacity after a vaccine was developed. Under currently existing capabilities for manufacturing vaccine, it is likely that more than 90% of the U.S. population will not be vaccinated in the first year (*1*). Distributing the limited supply will require determining priority groups.

Who will be at highest risk? Our experience with three influenza pandemics presents a complex picture. The mortality profile of a future pandemic could be U-shaped, as it was in the mild-to-moderate pandemics of 1957 and 1968 and interpandemic influenza seasons, in which the very young and the old are at highest risk. Or, the mortality profile could be an attenuated W shape, as it was during the devastating 1918 pandemic, in which the highest risk occurred among people between 20 and 40 years of age, while the elderly were not at high excess risk. Even during pandemics, the elderly appear to be at no higher risk than during interpandemic influenza seasons.

Clear ethical justification for vaccine priorities is essential to the acceptability of the priority ranking and any modifications during the pandemic. With limited vaccine supply, uncertainty over who will be at highest risk of infection and complications, and questions about which historic pandemic experience is most applicable, society faces a fundamental ethical dilemma: Who should get the vaccine first?

THE NVAC AND ACIP PRIORITY RANKINGS

Many potential ethical principles for rationing health care have been proposed. "Save the most lives" is commonly used in emergencies, such as burning buildings, although "women and children first" played a role on the Titanic. "First come, first served" operates in other emergencies and in ICUs when admitted patients retain beds despite the presentation of another patient who is equally or even more sick; "Save the most quality life years" is central to cost-effectiveness rationing. "Save the worst-off" plays a role in allocating organs for transplantation. "Reciprocity"— giving priority to people willing to donate their own organs—has been proposed. "Save those most likely to fully recover" guided priorities for giving penicillin to soldiers with syphilis in World War II. Save those "instrumental in making society flourish" through economic productivity or by "contributing to the well-being of others" has been proposed by Murray and others.[2, 3]

The save-the-most-lives principle was invoked by NVAC and ACIP. It justifies giving top priority to workers engaged in vaccine production and distribution and health-care workers. They get higher priority not because they are intrinsically more valuable people or of greater "social worth," but because giving them first priority ensures that maximal life-saving vaccine is produced and so that health care is provided to the sick. Consequently, it values all human life equally, giving every person equal consideration in who gets priority regardless of age, disability, social class, or employment. After these groups, the save-the-most-lives principle justifies priority for those predicted to be at highest risk of hospitalization and dying. We disagree with this prioritization.

LIFE-CYCLE PRINCIPLE

The save-the-most-lives principle may be justified in some emergencies when decision urgency makes it infeasible to deliberate about priority rankings and impractical to categorize individuals into priority groups. We believe that a life-cycle allocation principle (see table) based on the idea that each person should have an opportunity to live through all the stages of life is more appropriate for a pandemic. There is great value in being able to pass through each life stage—to be a child, a young adult, and to then develop a career and family, and to grow old—and to enjoy a wide range of the opportunities during each stage.

Multiple considerations and intuitions support this ethical principle. Most people endorse this principle for themselves. We would prioritize our own resources to ensure we could live past the illnesses of childhood and young adulthood and would allocate fewer resources to living ever longer once we reached old age. People strongly prefer maximizing the chance of living until a ripe old age, rather than being struck down as a young person.

Death seems more tragic when a child or young adult dies than an elderly person—not because the lives of older people are less valuable, but because the younger person has not had the opportunity to live and develop through all stages of life. Although the life-cycle principle favors some ages, it is also intrinsically egalitarian. Unlike being productive or contributing to

Priorities for Distribution of Influenza Vaccine

Tier*	NVAC and ACIP recommendations (subtier)†	Life-cycle principle (LCP)	Investment refinement of LCP including public order
1	Vaccine production and distribution workers	Vaccine production and distribution workers	Vaccine production and distribution workers
	Frontline health-care workers	Frontline health-care workers	Frontline health-care workers
	People 6 months to 64 years old with ≥2 high-risk conditions or history of hospitalization for pneumonia or influenza		
	Pregnant women		
	Household contacts of severely immunocompromised people		
	Household contacts of children ≤6 months of age		
	Public health and emergency response workers		
	Key government leaders		
2	Healthy people ≥65 years old	Healthy 6-month-olds	People 13 to 40 years old with <2 high-risk conditions, with priority to key government leaders; public health, military, police, and fire workers; utility and transportation workers; telecommunications and IT workers; funeral directors
	People 6 months to 64 years old with 1 or more high-risk conditions	**Healthy 1-year-olds**	
	Healthy children 6 months to 23 months old	Healthy 2-year-olds	
	Other public health workers, emergency responders, public safety workers (police and fire), utility workers, transportation workers, telecommunications and IT workers	**Healthy 3-year-olds** etc.	**People 7 to 12 years old and 41 to 50 years old with <2 high-risk conditions with priority as above**
			People 6 months to 6 years old and 51 to 64 years old with <2 high-risk conditions, with priority as above‡
			People ≥65 years old with <2 high-risk conditions
3	Other health decision–makers in government	People with life-limiting morbidities or disabilities, prioritized according to expected life years	People 6 months to 64 years old with ≥2 high-risk conditions
	Funeral directors		
4	Healthy people 2 to 64 years old		People ≥65 years old with ≥2 high-risk conditions

*Tiers determine priority ranking for the distribution of vaccine if limited in supply. †Subtiers in [bold] text establish who gets priority within the tier (starting from the top of the tier) if limited vaccine cannot cover everyone in the tier; prioritization may occur within subtiers as well. ‡Children 6 months to <13 years would not receive vaccine if they can be effectively confined to home or otherwise isolated.

others' well-being, every person will live to be older unless their life is cut short.

THE INVESTMENT REFINEMENT

A pure version of the life-cycle principle would grant priority to 6-month-olds over 1-year-olds who have priority over 2-year-olds, and on. An alternative, the investment refinement, emphasizes gradations within a life span. It gives priority to people between early adolescence and middle age on the basis of the amount the person invested in his or her life balanced by the amount left to live. Within this framework, 20-year-olds are valued more than 1-year-olds because the older individuals have more developed interests, hopes, and plans but have not had an opportunity to realize them. Although these groupings could be modified, they indicate ethically defensible distinctions among groups that can inform rationing priorities.

One other ethical principle relevant for priority ranking of influenza vaccine during a pandemic is public order. It focuses on the value of ensuring safety and the provision of necessities, such as food and fuel. We believe the investment refinement combined with the public-order principle (IRPOP) should be the ultimate objective of all pandemic response measures, including priority ranking for vaccines and interventions to limit the course of the pandemic, such as closing schools and confining people to homes. These two principles should inform decisions at the start of an epidemic when the shape of the risk curves for morbidity and mortality are largely uncertain.

Like the NVAC and ACIP ranking, the IRPOP ranking would give high priority to vaccine production and distribution workers, as well as health-care and public health workers with direct patient contact. However, contrary to the NVAC and ACIP prioritization for the sick elderly and infants, IRPOP emphasize people between 13 and 40 years of age. The NVAC and ACIP priority ranking comports well with those groups at risk during the mild-to-moderate 1957 and 1968 pandemics. IRPOP prioritizes those age cohorts at highest risk during the devastating 1918 pandemic. Depending on patterns of flu spread, some mathematical models suggest that following IRPOP priority ranking could save the most lives overall.

CONCLUSIONS

The life-cycle ranking is meant to apply to the situation in the United States. During a global pandemic, there will be fundamental questions about sharing vaccines and other interventions with other countries. This raises fundamental issues of global rationing that are too complex to address here.

Fortunately, even though we are worried about an influenza pandemic, it is not upon us. . . . This gives us time both to build vaccine production capacity to minimize the need for rationing and to rationally assess policy and ethical issues about the distribution of vaccines.

NOTES

1. U. S. Department of Health and Human Services (HHS), *HHS Pandemic Influenza Plan* (HHS, Washington, DC, 2005), supplement E at (www.hhs.gov/pandemicflu/plan/) (accessed 29 March 2006).

2. C. J. L. Murray, A. D. Lopez, Eds., *The Global Burden of Disease* (World Health Organization, Geneva, 1996).

3. C. J. L. Murray, A. K. Acharya, *J. Health Econ.* 16, 710 (1997).

BERNARD LO AND MITCHELL H. KATZ

Clinical Decision Making During Public Health Emergencies: Ethical Considerations

Bernard Lo is Professor of Medicine and Director of the Program in Medical Ethics at University of California-San Francisco. He served as a member of President Clinton's National Bioethics Advisory Commission. He has published extensively in many areas of bioethics, including medical decisionmaking, HIV infection, human subjects research, and stem cell research. His publications include *Resolving Ethical Dilemmas: A Guide for Clinicians*.

Mitchell H. Katz is the Director of Health for the City and County of San Francisco. He is also Professor of Medicine, Epidemiology, and Biostatistics at the University of California, San Francisco. He has published extensively in the scientific and public health literature.

Recent public health emergencies involving anthrax, the severe acute respiratory syndrome (SARS), and shortages of influenza vaccine have dramatized the need for such public health measures as outbreak investigations, contact tracing, quarantine, isolation, and rationing. On the public policy level, the justifications for restrictive public health measures have been discussed extensively. However, less attention has been given to clinical dilemmas that front-line physicians will face during public health emergencies when patients disagree with public health measures. Two different scenarios may arise: Patients might request interventions that are not recommended or for which they are not eligible, or they might object to public health measures. Clinicians need to consider how they would respond to such scenarios in future public health emergencies.

In this paper, we analyze 2 hypothetical cases that illustrate such disagreements. In both, the physician's primary responsibility is to the public rather than the individual patient. We recommend that in public health emergencies, physicians address the patient's needs and concerns, recognize their changed roles, work closely with public health officials, and act in the best interests of patients to the extent possible. Physicians can still work on behalf of patients by advocating for exceptions and changes in policies and by mitigating the adverse consequences of public health measures.

HOW DOES PUBLIC HEALTH DIFFER FROM CLINICAL MEDICINE?

In clinical medicine, physicians promote the best interests of individual patients and respect their autonomy. In contrast, public health focuses on the best interests of the population as a whole rather than on the interests of the individual patient. Under some circumstances, the liberty and autonomy of the individual patient may be overridden for the good of the public. In response to a serious, probable threat to the public, it may be appropriate for public health officials to impose mandatory testing, treatment, vaccination, quarantine, or isolation. In addition, public health officials may restrict access to vaccines or drugs that are in short supply.

Recent treatises and articles have set forth criteria that must be satisfied to justify compulsory public

From *Annals of Internal Medicine* 143:7 (October 4, 2005), Health Module, 493–498. Notes omitted. American Public Health Association.

health interventions (1–5). The intervention must be *necessary and effective*; that is, the public health threat must be serious and likely, and there must be a sound scientific basis for the intervention. The intervention should be the *least restrictive alternative* that will effectively respond to the threat. There should be *procedural due process* that offers persons deprived of their freedom the right to appeal. Furthermore, the benefits and burdens of intervention should be *fairly distributed* in society, consistent with the epidemiologic features of the threat. Even the perception that some groups are being treated unfairly or are receiving preferential treatment will undermine public support for compulsory measures. Finally, there should be *transparency*. Public health officials should make decisions in an open and accountable manner.

Public health policies in an emergency fall within the authority of public health officials, not individual clinicians. If doctors have questions or disagreements, they should raise their concerns to public health officials instead of taking it upon themselves to override guidelines. Generally, public health officials welcome input from front-line clinicians, particularly with new threats for which knowledge and policies are evolving.

Although public health officials have police powers to enforce public health regulations, they generally prefer voluntary measures and resort to mandatory ones only as a last resort. Full compliance with public health measures usually is not necessary to control an outbreak. Moreover, mandatory measures have costs and adverse consequences. They may divert limited resources, cause confrontation with patients, and undermine public cooperation. Public health investigations require the cooperation of affected persons to identify contacts and provide information. Voluntary measures generally promote cooperation more than do mandatory ones.

From the perspective of clinicians, strict enforcement of public health measures may also be problematic. In routine public health practice, mandatory reporting of certain diseases, such as seizures and AIDS, may not be strictly enforced. Reporting to public health officials by physicians may compromise the physician–patient relationship, particularly if reporting is controversial or leads to restrictions on the patient's freedom, such as the right to drive. Fears about such public health measures may deter patients from seeking needed care or returning for follow-up.

REQUESTS FOR INTERVENTIONS NOT RECOMMENDED IN PUBLIC HEALTH GUIDELINES

CASE 1: PATIENT WHO REQUESTS IMMUNIZATION

During the fall of 2004, a 58-year-old man with no chronic medical condition requests an influenza immunization, as he does every year. However, this year there is a severe shortage of vaccine because of the closure of a major manufacturing plant. The physician explains that only patients at highest risk for complications from influenza are eligible for vaccination this year. The patient responds, "Every year you tell me I should get a flu shot. Even with the shot, I usually get a bad case of bronchitis that puts me at home for a week. I worry that if I get a bad case of the flu, I could die. Can't you just say that I have chronic lung disease, so I can get the shot?"

This case dramatizes how public health emergencies differ from ordinary clinical practice. In this case, the patient requests an intervention that is recommended by evidence-based practice guidelines. However, because of a severe shortage of vaccine, the Centers for Disease Control and Prevention and local health departments established prioritization criteria to ensure that patients at greatest risk received the limited supply (6). Patients who ordinarily would be urged to get immunized, such as healthy persons older than 50 years of age, were not eligible. Moreover, no alternatives were available for season-long prophylaxis; intranasal live attenuated influenza vaccine is not approved by the U.S. Food and Drug Administration for persons older than 50 years of age. Thus, individual patients were denied an effective and cost-effective intervention in order to help persons at greater risk. California and other jurisdictions declared a public health emergency and ordered health care providers to limit vaccinations to patients in designated high-priority categories (7,8). Under such an emergency declaration, public health officials have the authority to buy unused stocks of vaccine or to seize vaccines from providers who vaccinated persons who were not in the high-priority groups.

In ordinary clinical practice, physicians work as advocates for individual patients, helping them to obtain interventions that are in their best interests. In clinical practice, care to 1 patient usually only indirectly affects third parties—for example, through increased health care costs. In contrast, during a public health emergency, it may not be appropriate or feasible to provide beneficial interventions to persons outside the guidelines.

As in any disagreement with patients, physicians should first elicit and address the patient's concerns and needs. Anxiety, anger, fear, and a feeling of loss of control are natural reactions to an emergency. Furthermore, physicians should acknowledge the uncertainty inherent in a situation in which knowledge is evolving. Doctors can use empathic comments to encourage patients to explore their emotions and to normalize them. Trying to reassure patients simply by telling them not to worry is unlikely to be effective. It is reasonable for someone to be worried about not receiving a beneficial medical intervention. Patients may be more willing to consider the public health implications of their decision after their own concerns are acknowledged.

PROTECT THE PUBLIC HEALTH

In public health emergencies, physicians' responsibilities to the common good supersede responsibilities to individual patients. Unlike in ordinary clinical practice, making a decision for one patient may significantly affect the spread of an epidemic, public trust, and perceptions of fairness. Case 1 involved an absolute shortage of vaccine rather than merely concerns about cost. Providing immunizations to persons at low priority might make them unavailable to those at greatest risk. Furthermore, in an emergency, exceptions to guidelines are likely to be publicized, leading to a perception that the guidelines are being unfairly implemented or that the threat differs from what officials acknowledge. As a result, trust in public health officials and policies may be undermined.

ACT IN THE BEST INTERESTS OF THE PATIENT TO THE EXTENT POSSIBLE

In a public health emergency, physicians should maintain their usual role of acting in the best interests of the patient to the extent possible. Physicians can build on their experience with other disagreements with patients and other public health situations.

Maintain the Physician–Patient Relationship Ongoing contact with patients is particularly important during a public health emergency. As more knowledge is gained about the epidemic, recommendations for prevention and treatment may be modified. Criteria for immunization were broadened several times after existing supplies of vaccine were not fully used by high-priority groups, and additional vaccine was obtained.

In case 1, the patient may be reassured if he knows he will be recontacted if vaccine becomes available.

After acknowledging the patient's personal concerns, the doctor can then explain why the patient has a personal stake in a fair distribution system—as do all members of the public. The patient's family or friends may be in groups recommended to receive the vaccine.

Set Limits Clearly Physicians should tell patients if they have no discretion over public health orders. In case 1, the physician should state clearly that she and other providers cannot give the vaccine as requested this year.

To circumvent limits, some patients may ask doctors to misrepresent their condition. For instance, the patient in case 1 requests that the doctor say he has a chronic condition to justify the immunization. Some physicians may believe that it is acceptable to misrepresent a patient's condition to a health insurance plan to obtain coverage for needed services. However, it is ethically problematic for doctors to deceive third parties on behalf of patients. If doctors use deception in one situation, neither their own patients nor the public can trust them to be truthful in other situations. In public health emergencies, the public needs to trust that doctors accept public health measures and are implementing them fairly. Furthermore, one deception is likely to create a web of complications that might necessitate further deception. If the doctor says that the patient has a chronic medical condition, she could be asked to name the condition or provide documentation.

REFUSAL OF PUBLIC HEALTH INTERVENTIONS

CASE 2: PATIENT WHO REJECTS QUARANTINE

During the SARS epidemic in 2002, a 48-year-old businessman presents with fever, cough, and malaise. Five days earlier, he returned from a trip to a country where SARS cases have been reported, but he was not near any SARS-affected areas. He says his symptoms are no different from what he commonly experiences after such long travel. Because SARS cases have been reported in your city, public health officials are requiring physicians to report such cases for consideration of home quarantine. He objects strongly. "If I had known that, I wouldn't have come in. I have a lot of meetings that I can't do over the phone. My business would go down the tubes if I were quarantined."

In clinical practice, when patients refuse recommended interventions, their informed wishes are respected. However, in public health emergencies, individual autonomy is not paramount. Compulsory measures such as quarantine and isolation may be imposed to prevent transmission to others and to control an outbreak of a serious infection.

ADDRESS THE PATIENT'S NEEDS AND CONCERNS

Physicians should acknowledge that quarantine or isolation entails hardships. Persons in home isolation and quarantine experience difficulties with shopping for food and other necessities; inability to care for children and other dependents; economic setbacks from lost income; and emotions such as anxiety, anger, fear, loss of control, and loneliness.

PROTECT THE PUBLIC HEALTH

The starting presumption in public health emergencies is that physicians should follow public health guidelines. Exceptions need to be carefully justified, as we later discuss. Inconsistent implementation of public health guidelines fosters perceptions of unfairness and suggests that the threat is not as serious as officials claim.

SET LIMITS CLEARLY

Physicians need to be clear about the limits of their discretion. In an emergency, doctors need to report cases to public health officials despite the patient's objections. Infections may be reported directly by hospitals or clinical laboratories rather than individual physicians. In some situations, isolation and quarantine may be voluntary rather than mandatory; if this is true in case 2, physicians may use their discretion.

ESTABLISH COMMON GROUND WITH PATIENTS

Most patients who reject public health measures do not want to infect others. In addition, businesspeople may harm their reputation and business relationships if they refuse public health measures and others are infected as a result. Furthermore, cooperating with public health officials may provide access to special tests that are not otherwise available.

Advocate on Behalf of Patients   Doctors should advocate on behalf of patients for changes in guidelines or exceptions that they believe are justified. In an emergency, public health recommendations are made under uncertainty and time constraints. Public health officials cannot foresee all pertinent considerations and all situations. Guidelines will change over time as knowledge about the outbreak grows and its trajectory becomes clear. Hence, a particular case may be a justified exception to public health policies or may show that a policy should be modified. For example, quarantine of all symptomatic persons who have traveled to a particular country may not be justified if cases of the disease have been reported only from a well-defined area of a large country. Of course, the details of the patient's travel history and current symptoms would also be pertinent.

Advocacy does not mean trying to obtain whatever the patient wants. Instead, physicians should seek an exception or change in guidelines only when there are principled reasons to support it. The ethical principle of justice requires that similar cases be treated similarly, while cases that differ in ethically pertinent ways should be treated differently. Physicians who urge an exception for a particular patient should also be willing to support an exception for other similar patients. If such a widespread exception would not be feasible or justified, it would be unfair to make an exception for an individual patient. Only ethically pertinent considerations should be taken into account; the risk for disease is certainly relevant, but economic hardships are not. It would not be ethically persuasive to argue that patients who might suffer great economic losses should be exempted from home quarantine.

Mitigate the Adverse Consequences of Public Health Restrictions   As previously noted, persons in isolation or quarantine experience a range of economic and practical problems. Although most of these problems fall outside the physician's expertise and control, the doctor can help patients obtain needed services by referring them to appropriate social service agencies. The doctor can also advocate for programs to address such needs. Furthermore, the physician can provide emotional support to these patients through telephone or e-mail conversations. In other situations, patients appreciate that their physician is present for them, even though the doctor cannot change the objective situation.

Although it is impossible to predict what specific disagreements may occur with future emergency public health measures, several general principles should help physicians resolve them (Figure).

BUILD ON CLINICAL EXPERIENCE AND SKILLS

The traditional tools of the physician–patient relationship—eliciting and responding to patient concerns, providing ongoing care, listening with empathy, and simply being available—can be therapeutic because patients feel that someone understands them and cares about them. Doctors can help patients to cope with the emergency even if they cannot fulfill the patient's requests or change the underlying situation.

RECOGNIZE THE CHANGED ROLE OF PHYSICIANS IN PUBLIC HEALTH EMERGENCIES

Although caring for patients in public health emergencies is similar to ordinary patient care in many ways, there are also crucial differences. As noted, physicians' primary ethical responsibility in a public health emergency is the well-being of the public, not the interests of the individual patient. Physicians need to be clear in their own minds about their altered responsibilities, the heightened public scrutiny of their decisions, and the importance of perceptions of fairness. In addition, physicians also need to explain to patients both the changes and continuities in their role. Front-line physicians play an important role in conveying to the public that emergency public health measures are necessary and fair.

WORK CLOSELY WITH PUBLIC HEALTH OFFICIALS

Although public health officials and practicing physicians have different perspectives and roles, they can and should work closely during public health emergencies (Figure). Physicians in practice should seek advice from public health officials when they cannot persuade patients to accept public health guidelines. Often, experienced public health officers can offer constructive suggestions on how to talk with nonadherent patients. In some cases, public health officials may take over discussions with patients who refuse emergency public health measures or may decide to enforce public health guidelines using police powers.

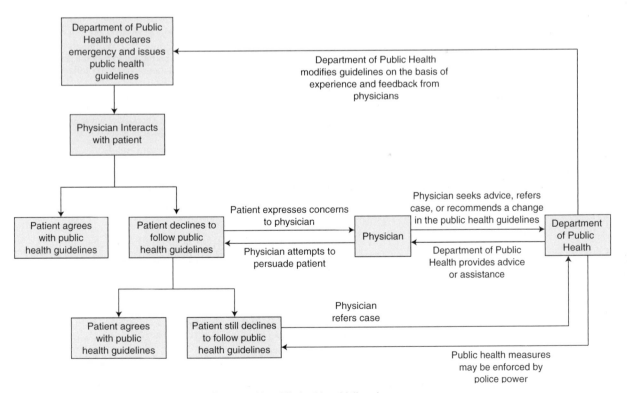

Figure.   Physician responses when patients disagree with public health guidelines in an emergency.

Officials also may be able to provide social services to patients subjected to public health measures such as quarantine.

Officials can enforce restrictive public health measures in ways that support the physician–patient relationship. If SARS is diagnosed in a hospitalized patient, responsibility for reporting the case can be placed on the hospital, not the patient's personal physician. From a public health perspective, it may suffice to enforce reporting only of hospital-based cases. Stringent reporting of office-based possible cases may be low-yield and may be taxing on physician–patient relationships. In an emergency, public health officials should promulgate only restrictive measures that are essential to public health objectives and that they will vigorously enforce.

Public health officials also should give a clear public message that the situation is a true emergency and that compliance with public health restrictions is needed. They also can acknowledge the hardships of restrictive measures, assure that the least restrictive measures are being used, and appeal to a sense of civic responsibility. Officials can take advantage of the intense media exposure that occurs during public health emergencies.

The questions, concerns, and objections of practicing physicians should be of great interest to public health officials. These officials have the responsibility for making timely policy decisions but may not address particular situations. Hearing from front-line physicians may help them improve or change existing policies. Ideally, there should be some mechanism for officials to communicate regularly with physicians on the front lines of the epidemic—for example, through meetings with the local medical society board.

CONCLUSION

In public health emergencies, the time for physicians to deliberate about a particular case may be limited. Before a crisis occurs, physicians should think through how they will respond to dilemmas arising when patients disagree with public health recommendations or requirements. Physicians can still act in the best interests of their patients within the limits posed by emergency public health orders.

REFERENCES

1. Childress J. F., Faden R. R., Gaare R. D., Gostin L. O., Kahn J., Bonnie R. J., et al. Public health ethics: mapping the terrain. J Law Med Ethics. 2002;30:170–8.

2. Gostin L. O., Public Health Law: Power, Duty, Restraint. Berkeley, CA: Univ of California Pr; 2000.

3. Gostin, L. O., Public health law in an age of terrorism: rethinking individual rights and common goods. Health Aff (Millwood). 2002;21:79–93.

4. Gostin L. O., Sapsin J. W., Teret S. P., Burris S., Mair J. S., Hodge J. G. Jr, et al. The Model State Emergency Health Powers Act: planning for and response to bioterrorism and naturally occurring infectious diseases. JAMA. 2002;288:622–8.

5. Gostin L. O., Bayer R., Fairchild A. L., Ethical and legal challenges posed by severe acute respiratory syndrome: implications for the control of severe infectious disease threats. JAMA. 2003;290:3229–37.

6. Updated interim influenza vaccination recommendations—2004–05 influenza season. MMWR Morb Mortal Wkly Rep. 2004; 53:1183–4.

7. Centers for Disease Control and Prevention. Interim influenza vaccination recommendations—2004–05 influenza season. MMWR. 2004;53:923–4.

8. California Department of Health Services. State public health officer orders healthcare providers to limit flu shots to high risk individuals. 8 October 2004. Accessed at www.applications.dhs.ca.gov/pressreleases/store/PressReleases/04-64.html on 13 January 2005.

VICTOR W. SIDEL AND BARRY S. LEVY

Global Challenges to Public Health: War, Terrorism, and Public Health

Victor W. Sidel is Distinguished University Professor of Social Medicine, Montefiore Medical Center and Albert Einstein College of Medicine and Adjunct Professor of Public Health at the Weill Medical College of Cornell University. He has spoken and published widely on the economic, social, environmental, and health consequences of the arms race, on the risks posed by the proliferation of nuclear, chemical, and biological weapons and on the diversion of resources and the curtailment of human rights entailed in responses to the threat of bioterrorism. Dr. Sidel is coeditor with Dr. Barry Levy of *War and Public Health* and of *Terrorism and Public Health*.

Barry S. Levy is Immediate Past President of the American Public Health Association. Dr. Levy has written more than 100 published articles and book chapters and edited 14 books and monographs, including three editions of a textbook on work-related disease and its prevention; a book on international perspectives on environment, development, and health; and, most recently, the book *War and Public Health*.

War and terrorism have profound effects on health, on health services, on ethics, and on law. This paper explores elements of these impacts and suggests what health workers, policy-makers, and the people they serve can do to help prevent war and terrorism and, if they cannot be prevented, to minimize their health consequences.

First, some definitions are in order, "War" is conventionally defined as armed conflict conducted by nation-states. The term is also used to denote armed conflicts within nations ("civil wars" or "wars of liberation") and armed actions by clandestine groups against governments or occupying forces ("guerilla wars" or "intifadas"). The word "war" is used in many other contexts, such as "war on cancer," "war on evil," and "Christian soldiers marching as to war." The concept of "just war" is important in ethics, law and medicine.

"Terrorism" is often defined in a partisan fashion: those called "terrorists" by one side in a conflict may be viewed as "patriots," "freedom fighters," or "servants of God" by the other. We have defined "terrorism" as "politically motivated violence or the threat of violence, especially against civilians, with the intent to instill fear." The meanings of "terrorism" have considerable overlap with the meanings of "war" and many actions conducted during war fit our definition of terrorism.

There are also many definitions of the term "public health." We prefer the definition used in *The Future of Public Health* report, published by the Institute of Medicine in 1988: Public health is "what we, as a society, do collectively to assure the conditions in which people can be healthy.[1] War and terrorism are generally anathema to public health, and present serious challenges to law, medicine, and ethics.

WAR AND PUBLIC HEALTH

War has an enormous and tragic impact on people's lives. War accounts for more death and disability than many major diseases. War destroys families,

From *Journal of Law, Medicine and Ethics* 31 (2003), 516–523. Notes omitted.

communities, and sometimes entire nations and cultures. War siphons limited resources away from health and other human services and damages the infrastructure that supports these services. War violates human rights. The mindset of war—that violence is the best way to resolve conflicts—contributes to domestic violence, street crime, and many other kinds of violence in the world. War damages the environment. In sum, war threatens not only the people's health but also the very fabric of our civilization.

Some of the impacts of war on public health are obvious, while others are not. The direct impact of war on mortality and morbidity is apparent. Many people, including an increasing percentage of civilians, are killed or injured during war. An estimated 191 million people died directly or indirectly as a result of conflict during the 20th century, more than half of whom were civilians. The exact figures are unknowable because of generally poor recordkeeping in many countries and its disruption in times of conflict. During some wars in the 1990s, approximately 90 percent of the people killed were noncombatants.[2] Many of them were innocent bystanders, caught in the crossfire of opposing armies: others were civilians who were specifically targeted during wars. During each year of the past decade, there have been approximately 20 wars, mainly civil wars that are infrequently reported by the news media in the United States. For example, more than 3.3 million people have died during the civil war in Congo in the past several years. As another example, over 30 years of civil war in Ethiopia have led to the deaths of one million people, about half of whom were civilians.[3]

Many people survive wars, only to be physically scarred for life. Millions of survivors are chronically disabled from injuries sustained during wars or the immediate aftermath of wars. Landmines are a particular threat. For example, in Cambodia, one in 236 people is an amputee as a result of a landmine explosion.[4] Approximately one-third of the soldiers who survived the civil war in Ethiopia were injured or disabled and at least 40,000 individuals lost one or more limbs during the war.[5]

Millions more are psychologically impaired from wars, during which they have been physically or sexually assaulted; forced to serve as soldiers against their will; witnessed the death of family members; or experienced the destruction of their communities or entire nations. Psychological trauma may be demonstrated in disturbed and antisocial behavior, such as aggression toward others, including family members. Many soldiers suffer from post-traumatic stress disorder (PTSD) on return from military action.

Rape has been used as a weapon in many wars—in Korea, Bangladesh, Algeria, India, Indonesia, Liberia, Rwanda, Uganda, the former Yugoslavia, and elsewhere. As acts of humiliation and revenge, soldiers have raped the female family members of their enemies. For example, at least 10,000 women were raped by military personnel during the war in Bosnia and Herzegovina.[6] The social chaos brought about by war also creates situations and conditions for sexual violence.

Children are particularly vulnerable during and after wars. Many die as a result of malnutrition, disease, or military attacks. Many are physically or psychologically injured. Many are forced to become soldiers or sexual salves to military officers. Their health suffers in many other ways as well, as reflected by increased infant and young-child mortality rates and decreased rates of immunization coverage.

The infrastructure that supports social well-being and health is destroyed during many wars, so that many civilians do not have access to food, clean water, medical care, or public health services. For example, during Gulf War I in 1991 and in the 12 years of economic sanctions that followed, it is estimated that more than 350,000 children died, with most of these deaths due to inadequate nutrition, contaminated water, and shortages of medicines. All of these deaths may be indirectly related to destruction of the infrastructure of civilian society, including health-care facilities, electricity-generating plants, food-supply systems, water-treatment and sanitation facilities, and transportation and communication systems.[7] The 2003 attack on Iraq by the United States and United Kingdom left much of what was left of the infrastructure damaged.

In addition, many civilians during wartime flee to other countries as refugees or become internally displaced persons within their own countries, where it may be difficult for them to maintain their health and safety. Refugees and internally displaced persons are vulnerable to malnutrition, infectious diseases, injuries, and criminal and military attacks. A substantial number of the approximately 20 million refugees and internally displaced persons in the world today were forced to leave their homes because of war or the threat of war.

In addition to the direct effects of war, three categories of indirect and less obvious and indirect impacts on health of war and preparation for war: diversion of resources; domestic and community violence; and damage to the environment.

War and the preparation for war divert huge amounts of resources from health and human services and other productive societal endeavors. This is true in many countries, including the United States, which ranks first among nations in military expenditures and arms exports, but 27th among nations in infant mortality. In some less-developed countries, national governments spend $10 to $20 per capita on military expenditures, but only $1 per capita on all health-related expenditures. The same type of distorted priorities also exist in more-developed countries. For example, in early 2003, at a time when federal, state, and local governments in the United States were experiencing substantial budgetary shortfalls and it was difficult for them to find monies to maintain adequate health and human services, the U.S. Congress allocated more than $70 billion for the war in Iraq. The U.S. occupation of Iraq, which continues as this article is published, is estimated to cost $4 billion per month.

War often creates a cycle of violence, increasing domestic and community violence in the countries engaged in war. War teaches people that violence is an acceptable method for settling conflicts. Children growing up in environments in which violence is an established way of settling conflicts often choose violence to settle conflicts in their own lives. Teenage gangs mirror the activity of military forces. Men, sometimes former military servicemen who have been trained to use violence, commit acts of violence against women, sometimes murdering their wives on return from the battlefield.

Finally, war and the preparation for war have profound impacts on the environment. The disastrous consequences of war for the environment are often clear. Examples include: bomb craters in Vietnam that have filled with water and provide breeding areas for mosquitoes that spread malaria and other diseases; destruction of urban environments by aerial carpet bombing of major cities in Europe and Japan during World War II; and the more than 600 oil-well fires in Kuwait that were ignited by retreating Iraqi troops in 1991 and had a devastating effect on the ecology of the affected areas and caused acute respiratory symptoms among those exposed, sometimes many miles away. Less obvious are the environmental impacts of the preparation for war, such as the huge amounts of nonrenewable fossil fuels used by the military before (as well as during and after) wars and the environmental hazards of toxic and radioactive wastes, which can contaminate air, soil, and both surface water and groundwater. For example, much of the area in and around Chelyabinsk, Russia, site of a major nuclear-weapons production facility, has been determined to be highly radioactive and residents there have been evacuated.

In the early 21st century, new geopolitical, tactical, and technological issues concerning war are arising that have an impact on health, law and ethics. These issues include use of new weapons, the increasing use in guerilla warfare (and terrorism) of suicide, or "homicide," bombers: the use of drone (unmanned) aircraft and high-altitude bombers: and newly-adopted United States policies on "pre-emptive" wars and on "usable" of nuclear weapons. . . .

TERRORISM AND PUBLIC HEALTH

Like war, terrorism has direct and indirect consequences for public health services and the health of populations. Terrorist attacks, most obviously, can cause fatal as well as nonfatal injuries and diseases. While much current attention is focused on biologic, chemical, and nuclear and other radiologic ("dirty-bomb") weapons, most terrorist acts are committed with small arms, explosives, and incendiaries. The examples of use of lethal chemical weapons in recent years are few in number, including use against the Kurds in Iraq in the 1980s and in subways in Japan in 1994 and 1995. Biological weapons have also been rarely used, including a cult's contamination of salad bars with Salmonella bacteria in Oregon in 1985 and dissemination of an anthrax spores through the U.S. mail in 2001. Nuclear weapons have repeatedly been tested but have not been used since 1945, although enormous stockpiles of nuclear weapons and fissile materials exist. There is understandable and appropriate concern regarding use of these "weapons of mass destruction" (WMD), given the feasibility of terrorists gaining access to them and the many people who might be affected by them. Indeed, fear of their possession of WMD was one of the reasons given for the attack on Iraq in 2003.

The possibility of future terrorist threats and terrorist attacks has led to an increased focus in the United States and elsewhere on preparedness and the improvement of societal capability of preventing and responding to threats and attacks. In our view, however, terrorism preparedness requires a balance between protection of the population from hazards of terrorism and protection of the population from the consequences, or "collateral damage," of preparedness. These consequences, especially in the case of "preparedness against bioterrorism" that involves medical and public health organizations, facilities, and personnel include the following: the risk of adverse consequences of inappropriate warnings, hazardous immunizations, inappropriate use of antibiotics, and inappropriate isolation and quarantine of individuals or populations. Non-specific warnings, often using color codes, have been frequently given since September 11, 2001, with disruptive consequences. Hazardous immunizations for anthrax and for smallpox have been given with little or no justification, at times leading to major side effects. Antibiotics were inappropriately used in many instances as prophylaxis against anthrax after the dissemination of anthrax spores.

Restriction of federal grants to state and local health departments for bioterrorism preparedness, rather than "dual-use" purposes, would enable state and local health departments to improve their capabilities more broadly at a time of severe budget shortfalls. Much of the use of federal grants to state and local health departments for bioterrorism preparedness (in 2002, $1.1 billion; in 2003, $940 million) is restricted and may require health departments to shift deployment of personnel and other resources in dysfunctional ways.

This funding diverts state and local health departments from urgent public health work on such widespread problems as tobacco dependence, alcohol and substance abuse, firearm-related injuries and fatalities. AIDS and other serious infectious diseases, and chronic diseases, such as heart disease, stroke, cancer, and diabetes. Funds are also being diverted from protection against existing chemical risks, such as spills, leaks, and explosions. In Seattle, for example, the local health department has been forced to become the first line of defense against bioterrorism. This diversion of attention and a shrinking health department budget have contributed to Seattle's worst tuberculosis outbreak in 30 years. At the federal level, more than $200 million in AIDS research grants are being

cut to divert monies to the development of new vaccines against anthrax. The campaign to vaccinate 500,000 medical personnel against smallpox was a failure, with only 38,297 people vaccinated and most of the vaccine wasted.[8]

Diversion of resources from urgent international public health work, in which even small investments in prevention can lead to major reductions in disease occurrence and mortality can have disastrous results. In India in 1999, there were two million new cases of tuberculosis, causing about 450,000 deaths. Effective treatment of tuberculosis in India costs about US$15 per person treated. The United Nations has estimated that about US$10 billion invested in safe water supplies could reduce by one-third the current 4 billion annual cases of diarrhea that result in 2.2 million deaths.

Constraints on civil rights and human rights in the United States related to terrorism and bioterrorism preparedness and prevention have been threatened or have already occurred. These have been imposed by adoption by states of elements of the Model State Emergency Health Powers Act [and other federal statutes].

The Model State Emergency Health Powers Act is a "model" for legislation that has been proposed for adoption by state legislatures in the United States, since public health is viewed as a responsibility of the states rather than the federal government. The model act, which is generally viewed as less Draconian than the federal acts, was drafted at Georgetown University Law Center and is being promulgated by the Centers for Disease Control and Prevention for the attention of all state legislatures. If adopted by a state, the governor and/or the health commissioner of the state would have the power to declare a state public health emergency and to impose quarantines, to require immunizations and to conduct surveillance. Although legal protections have been built into the model, the model act has been widely criticized as too broad in the powers it grants and very few states have adopted any part of it.[9] . . .

MAJOR ISSUES FOR ADVOCACY AND ACTION

ADDRESSING VIOLATIONS OF CIVIL LIBERTIES AND HUMAN RIGHTS

These violations include abrogations of civil liberties in the United States and violations of human rights of people outside the United States, such as the rights of soldiers captured during the war in Afghanistan who have been imprisoned by the United States at Guantanamo Bay in Cuba. In these cases, in which the United States has the primary responsibility for the violations, the United States must act to end them. Amnesty International has criticized the U.S. occupation of Iraq for violations of accepted legal procedures. In the United States, the new rules for trials of alleged terrorists are so constrictive that they may deter lawyers from representing the defendants.

More broadly, instead of acting militarily, the United States should strengthen international law to deal with criminal acts. . . .

ADDRESSING THE UNDERLYING CAUSES OF WAR AND TERRORISM

These problems include poverty, social inequities, adverse effects of globalization and shame and humiliation. The Carnegie Commission on Preventing Deadly Conflict has identified the following factors that put nations at risk of violent conflict, including.[10]

- Lack of democratic processes and unequal access to power, particularly in situations where power arises from religious or ethnic identity, and leaders are repressive or abusive of human rights.
- Social inequality characterized by markedly unequal distribution of resources and access to these resources, especially where the economy is in decline and there is, as a result, more social inequality and more competition for resources.
- Control by one group of valuable natural resources, such as oil, timber, drugs, or gems.
- Demographic changes that are so fast that they outstrip the capability of the nation to provide basic necessary services and opportunities for employment.

The United States and other nations must increase funding for humanitarian and sustainable development programs which address the root causes of terrorism such as hunger, illiteracy, and unemployment.

PREVENTING WAR AND CONTROLLING WEAPONS OF MASS DESTRUCTION

Health professionals, lawyers, and others are already playing a major role to prevent war and to control or outlaw weapons of mass destruction. The International Physicians for the Prevention of Nuclear War was awarded the 1985 Nobel Peace Prize for its work and the work of its affiliates, such as Physicians for Social Responsibility in the United States, to prevent use of nuclear weapons and to ban their production, testing, and transfer. Similar efforts have been made by health professionals and others to strengthen the Biological Weapons Convention and the Chemical Weapons Convention. . . .

Overall, the United States must change priorities to reflect real security needs, by eliminating military spending for wasteful Pentagon programs and investing those resources in urgent domestic needs for health care, education, and jobs; by providing new investments in renewable energy alternatives to reduce U.S. dependencies on foreign oil; and by providing adequate peacekeeping funding to nations, such as Afghanistan, Liberia, and the Congo, that would secure peace and stability.

RESTORING RESOURCES AND SETTING APPROPRIATE PRIORITIES

It is relatively easy for national leaders to convince the people of a nation to make war on an "enemy.". . . It is much harder to convince people to work for peace and justice.

Health professionals, lawyers, ethicists, and others must stress bringing public attention and financial resources to protect and promote social services and health care where they are needed most. In the United States, these include provision of health and other human services for those in need, provision of preventive and public-health programs to address major problems, such as use of tobacco, alcohol, violence, AIDS, chronic diseases, and occupational and environmental health problems. In less-developed countries, priorities should first focus on providing resources to meet basic needs, to provide essential health services, and to promote maternal and child health.

NOTES

1. Institute of Medicine, Committee for the Study of Public Health. *The Future of Public Health* (Washington, DC: National Academy of Sciences 1988)

2. R. M. Garfield and A. I. Neugut, "The Human Consequences of War", in B. S. Levy and V. W. Sidel, eds., *War and Public Health*, [(New York: Oxford University Press, 1997).]

3. H. Kloos, "Health Impacts of War in Ethiopia." *Disasters*, 16 (1992): 347–354.

4. E. Stover *et al.,* "The Medical and Social Consequences of Land Mines in Cambodia." *JAMA*, 272 (1994): 331–336.

5. H. Kloos, *supra* note 3.

6. M. W. Ashford and Y. Huet-Vaughn. "The Impact of War on Women," in B. S. Levy and V. W. Sidel, eds., *War and Public Health, supra note* 3: 186–196.

7. E. Hoskins. "Public Health and the Persian Gulf War," in B. S. Levy and V. W. Sidel, eds., *War and Public Health, supra* note 3: 254–278.

8. S. Smith, "With Demand Weakening, Smallpox Vaccine Expiring." *Boston Globe*, August 23, 2003.

9. G. J. Annas, "Bioterrorism. Public Health. And Human Rights." Health Affairs 11. no. 6 (2002): 94–97: G. J. Annas, "Bioterrorism, Public Health, and Civil Liberties," NEJM, 346 (2002): 1337–1342: G. J. Annas, "Terrorism and Human Rights," in J. D. Moreno, ed., *In the Wake of Terror: Medicine and Morality in a Time of Crisis* (Cambridge, Mass: MIT Press. 2003).

10. Carnegie Commission on Preventing Deadly Conflict. *Preventing Deadly Conflict: Final Report* (New York: Carnegie Corporation, 1997).

Suggested Readings for Chapter 9

FOUNDATIONS OF PUBLIC HEALTH ETHICS

Bard, Jennifer. "Standing Together: How Bioethics and Public Health Can Join Forces to Provide Equitable Health Care." *The American Journal of Bioethics* 5 (2005), W20–W21.

Bayer, Ronald, and Fairchild, Amy. "The Genesis of Public Health Ethics." *Bioethics* 18 (2004), 473–92.

Bayer, Ronald, and Moreno, Jonathan D. "Health Promotion: Ethical and Social Dilemmas of Government Policy." *Health Affairs* 5 (1986), 72–85.

Beauchamp, Dan E. "Community: The Neglected Tradition of Public Health." *The Hastings Center Report* 15 (1985), 28–36.

Boylan, Michael. "Gun Control And Public Health." In Michael Boylan, ed. *Public Health Policy and Ethics*. Boston, MA: Kluwer Academic Publishers, 2004, 119–134.

Callahan, Daniel, and Jennings, Bruce. "Ethics and Public Health: Forging a Strong Relationship." *American Journal of Public Health* 92 (2002), 169–76.

Häyry, M. "Public Health and Human Values." *Journal of Medicine and Ethics* 32 (2006), 519–21.

Jones, Marian Moser, and Bayer, Ronald. "Paternalism & Its Discontents: Motorcycle Helmet Laws, Libertarian Values, and Public Health." *American Journal of Public Health* 97 (2007), 208–17.

Kass, Nancy E. "An Ethics Framework for Public Health." *American Journal of Public Health* 91 (2001), 1776–82.

Mello, Michelle M., Studdert, David M., and Brennan, Troyen A. "Obesity—The New Frontier of Public Health Law." *New England Journal of Medicine* 354 (2006), 2601–10.

Moreno, Jonathan D. "In the Wake of Katrina: Has 'Bioethics' Failed?" *The American Journal of Bioethics* 5 (2005), W18–W19.

Moreno, Jonathan D., and Bayer, Ronald. "The Limits of the Ledger in Public Health Promotion." *The Hastings Center Report 15* (1985), 37–41.

O'Neill, Onora. "Informed Consent and Public Health." *Philosophical Transactions of the Royal Society London B* 359 (2004), 1133–36.

———. "Public Health or Clinical Ethics: Thinking Beyond Borders." *Ethics & International Affairs* 16 (2002), 35–45.

Pellegrino, Edmund N., and Thomasma, David C. "The Good of Patients and the Good of Society: Striking a Moral Balance." In Michael Boylan, ed. *Public Health Policy and Ethics*. Boston, MA: Kluwer Academic Publishers, 2004, 17–37.

Teays, Wanda. "From Fear to Eternity: Violence and Public Health." In Michael Boylan, ed. *Public Health Policy and Ethics*. Boston, MA: Kluwer Academic Publishers, 2004, 135–65.

Tong, Rosemarie. "Taking On 'Big Fat': The Relative Risks And Benefits Of The War Against Obesity." In Michael Boylan, ed. *Public Health Policy and Ethics*. Boston, MA: Kluwer Academic Publishers, 2004, 39–58.

Wikler, Daniel, and Brock, Dan W. "Population-Level Bioethics: Mapping a New Agenda." In Angus Dawson and Marcel Verweij, eds. *Ethics, Prevention and Public Health*. Oxford: Clarendon Press, 2007, 79–94.

MANAGEMENT OF COMMUNICABLE DISEASES

Annas, George J. "Control of Tuberculosis—the Law and the Public's Health." *New England Journal of Medicine* 328 (1993), 585–88.

Bayer, Ronald. "AIDS and the Making of an Ethics of Public Health." In Ronald O. Valdiserri, ed. *Dawning Answers: How the HIV/AIDS Epidemic Has Helped to Strengthen Public Health*. Oxford: Oxford University Press, 2003, 135–54.

Bryan, Charles S. "HIV/AIDS and Bioethics: Historical Perspective, Personal Retrospective." *Health Care Analysis* 10 (2002), 5–18.

Colgrove, James. "The Ethics and Politics of Compulsory HPV Vaccination." *New England Journal of Medicine* 355 (2006), 2389–91.

Colgrove, James, and Bayer, Ronald. "Manifold Restraints: Liberty, Public Health, and the Legacy of Jacobson v Massachusetts." *American Journal of Public Health* 95 (2005): 571–76.

Fairchild, Amy L., and Bayer, Ronald. "Ethics and the Conduct of Public Health Surveillance." *Science* 303 (2004), 631–32.

Frieden, Thomas R. et al. "Applying Public Health Principles to the HIV Epidemic." *New England Journal of Medicine* 353 (2005), 2397–402.

Gostin, Lawrence O. "HIV Screening in Health Care Settings: Public Health and Civil Liberties in Conflict?" *Journal of the American Medical Association* 296 (2006), 2023–25.

———. "Rights and Duties of HIV Infected Health Care Professionals." *Health Care Analysis* 10 (2002), 67–85.

Mariner, Wendy K., Annas, George J., and Glantz, Leonard H. "*Jacobson v Massachusetts*: It's Not Your Great-Great-Grandfather's Public Health Law." *American Journal of Public Health* 95 (2005), 581–90.

Parmet, Wendy E., Goodman, Richard A., and Farber, Amy. "Individual Rights versus the Public's Health—100 Years after *Jacobson v. Massachusetts*." *New England Journal of Medicine* 352 (2005), 652–54.

Sade, Robert M. "HIV/AIDS as an Epidemic: Ethical Issues at the 20th Anniversary." *Health Care Analysis* 10 (2002), 1–4.

Smith, Charles B. et al. "Are There Characteristics of Infectious Diseases That Raise Special Ethical Issues?" *Developing World Bioethics* 4 (2004), 1–16.

Verma, Geetika et al. "Critical Reflections on Evidence, Ethics and Effectiveness in the Management of Tuberculosis: Public Health and Global Perspectives." *BMC Medical Ethics* 5:2 (2004).

Wynia, Matthew K. "Ethics and Public Health Emergencies: Rationing Vaccines." *The American Journal of Bioethics* 6 (2006), 4–7.

EMERGENCY PREPAREDNESS

Annas, George J. "Bioterrorism, Public Health, and Civil Liberties." *New England Journal of Medicine* 346 (2002), 1337–42.

———. "Bioterrorism, Public Health, and Human Rights." *Health Affairs* 21 (2002), 94–97.

Bayer, Ronald, and Colgrove, James. "Rights and Dangers: Bioterrorism and the Ideologies and Public Health." In Jonathan D. Moreno, ed. *In the Wake of Terror: Medicine and Morality in a Time of Crisis.* Cambridge, MA: MIT Press, 2003, 51–74.

———. "Bioterrorism, Public Health, and the Law." *Health Affairs* 21 (2002), 98–101.

Childress, James F. "Triage in Response to a Bioterrorist Attack." In Jonathan D. Moreno, ed. *In the Wake of Terror: Medicine and Morality in a Time of Crisis.* Cambridge, MA: MIT Press, 2003, 77–94.

Etzioni, Amitai. "Public Health Law: A Communitarian Perspective." *Health Affairs* 21 (2002), 102–04.

Gostin, Lawrence O. "Public Health Law in an Age of Terrorism: Rethinking Individual Rights and Common Goods." *Health Affairs* 21 (2002), 79–93.

———. "Pandemic Influenza: Public Health Preparedness for the Next Global Health Emergency." *Journal of Law, Medicine & Ethics* 32 (2004), 565–73.

Gostin, Lawrence O. "Law and Ethics in a Public Health Emergency." *The Hastings Center Report* 32 (2002), 9.

Gray, George M., and Ropeik, David P. "Dealing With the Dangers of Fear: The Role of Risk Communication." *Health Affairs* 21 (2002), 106–16.

Hodge, Jr., James G., and Gostin, Lawrence O. "Protecting the Public's Health in an Era of Bioterrorism." In Jonathan D. Moreno, ed. *In the Wake of Terror: Medicine and Morality in a Time of Crisis.* Cambridge, MA: MIT Press, 2003, 17–32.

King, Nicholas B. "The Ethics of Biodefense." *Bioethics* 19 (2005), 432–46.

Kotalik, Jaro. "Preparing for an Influenza Pandemic: Ethical Issues." *Bioethics* 19 (2005), 422–31.

Rhodes, Rosamond. "Justice In Allocations For Terrorism, Biological Warfare, And Public Health." In Michael Boylan, ed. *Public Health Policy and Ethics.* Boston, MA: Kluwer Academic Publishers, 2004, 73–90.

Ruderman, Carly et al. "On Pandemics and the Duty to Care: Whose Duty? Who Cares?" *BMC Medical Ethics* 7:5 (2006).

Singer, Peter A. et al. "Ethics and SARS: Lessons from Toronto." *British Medical Journal* 327 (2003), 1342–44.

Thompson, Alison K. et al. "Pandemic Influenza Preparedness: An Ethical Framework to Guide Decision-making." *BMC Medical Ethics* 7:12 (2006).

Trotter, Griffin. "Of Terrorism and Healthcare: Jolting the Old Habits." *Cambridge Quarterly of Healthcare Ethics* 11 (2002), 411–14.

Veatch, Robert M. "Disaster Preparedness and Triage: Justice and the Common Good." *The Mount Sinai Journal of Medicine* 72 (2005), 236–41.

Introduction

The pace of biotechnology and bioscience research over the last few decades has brought remarkable discoveries in areas as diverse as human embryonic stem cell biology, genetic modification of plants and animals, nanotechnology, neurosciences, and synthetic biology. This research has brought important information about fundamental questions of human developmental biology, applications to agriculture, medicine, consumer products, and even national defense. But these discoveries don't come without numerous costs. Major financial investment over many years, from both the public and private sectors, are required in new areas of science before advancements can be realized. More important for this chapter, new areas of science often bring controversy along with their promise.

HUMAN EMBRYONIC STEM CELL RESEARCH

The ability to isolate human embryonic stem cells is an important step toward solving one of the important tenets of human developmental biology: understanding how every cell in the body can start from a single egg fertilized by a single sperm. Somehow, as the embryo divides, cells are programmed to become heart, liver, skin, hair, eyes, and the multitude of other body parts it takes to become a fully formed human. Embryonic stem cells have the potential to become any of these so-called differentiated cells, a quality known as pleuripotency. Because of this quality they are extremely valuable in understanding what makes cells become one type instead of another, and also for the therapeutic potential that could come with controlling that process. Once cell control is harnessed, researchers may be able to grow colonies of particular cell types to treat organ failure, and treat diseases in wholly new ways. But researchers argue that such applications will likely require a sufficient supply and variety of stem cells.

The first isolation of human embryonic stem cells (hESCs) was in 1998, by a group at the University of Wisconsin led by developmental biologist Jamie Thomson. This breakthrough led to great interest in the scientific community, as well as interest on behalf of the Clinton administration in funding the research through federal funding sources such as the National Institutes of Health (NIH). But the administration faced a policy roadblock going back to the early 1980s, when a ban was instituted on federal funding for research that would harm or destroy human embryos.[1] The ban did not make such research illegal, but it prevented the use of federal dollars to support it. In its interest in funding hESC research, the Clinton administration requested a legal ruling from the NIH General Counsel about whether funding of research involving embryonic stem cells would violate the existing ban on human embryo research funding. The ruling was that research on the cells themselves would not violate the ban, as long as federal funding was not used to collect the cells from embryos. The distinction in the NIH ruling created the possibility of a private market for supplying stem cells for publicly funded research, and though the Clinton administration proposed to fund research proposals that adhered to this distinction, no funding was granted before President Clinton left office. For those who object to the destruction of embryos for stem cell research, this represented an unacceptable end run around the intent of the original research ban. In practice, the embryos used in the collection of stem cells were left over from attempts to assist reproduction—donated by couples who used in vitro fertilization. There are hundreds of thousands of frozen embryos throughout the world awaiting decisions about what should be done with them, the vast majority of which will either remain frozen indefinitely or be discarded. Proponents of embryonic stem cell research ask why not allow them to be donated for research purposes, while opponents of such research find it morally objectionable to destroy what they contend is a nascent human life.

President George W. Bush provided his administration's answer to the question of whether hESC should be permitted with federal funds in a primetime televised national address to the nation on August 9, 2001. In his speech that night he laid out a middle-ground position, saying he favored funding of stem cell research so long as the cell lines used were created before the date and time of his address. In this way, federally funded hESC research could go forward, but without requiring the further destruction of embryos. Over sixty such hESC lines were identified as existing around the world, each of which relied on the destruction of a single embryo in order to create a dividing colony of stem cells. In defense of their use, the President argued that the "life and death decision has already been taken" about those sixty-plus embryos, but pledged that no additional embryos would be destroyed in federally funded hESC research. By issuing an Executive Order, President Bush limited the expenditure of federal dollars to those stem cell lines. But in a classic example of the checks and balances of the U.S. system, the President did not have the power to go further and order the same for private funds—that would have amounted to his making law, which is the prerogative of the Congress or state legislatures. In fact, some in the State of California saw the limitations on federal funding as an opportunity to invest, and worked to place a proposition on the ballot that not only would allow state monies to be used in a wide array of hESC research, but dedicated $3 billion over ten years solely to support hESC research. Proposition 71 was passed by California's voters in November 2004 by a wide majority, and after numerous unsuccessful court challenges, the necessary infrastructure is being built and initial research grants are beginning to be awarded. The U.S. Congress has passed bills relaxing federal restrictions on hESC research on two separate occasions, first in 2006 and again in 2007. Both were vetoed by President Bush.

Among the interesting features of the hESC policy debate in the United States is that there is little disagreement about the legality of hESC research or even of embryo research more generally. Instead it has focused on the appropriate limits on the use of public dollars, in the form of federal funding, for what some people take to be morally unacceptable research. An important byproduct of a ban on federal funding for the creation and use of new hESC lines is that it pushed such research outside the reach of government control and oversight, as well as away from public scrutiny—just the opposite of what many believe is most needed for controversial research.

The moral controversy over human embryonic stem cell research comes from the source of the cells. Two different sources have been successfully used to collect these cells so far, and both raise ethical issues. One technique uses discarded fetal tissue, and the other uses embryos created in fertility clinics and donated by couples who no longer need or want to use them. Each source raises important moral questions. Fetal tissue comes from either miscarriages or therapeutic abortions, and so some activists have argued that research on embryonic stem cells will create new demand for fetal tissue and incentives for abortions. This seems unlikely given the ample ongoing supply of fetal tissue, and the important prohibition in federal policy against paying donors for the tissue so as not to create financial incentives for abortion. Others argue that the use of fetal tissue for research is unacceptable because it takes advantage of an immoral act, making the researcher and subsequent research finding complicit in the moral wrong of abortion. As a matter of public policy, so long as abortions are carried out in ways that are consistent with law and policy, the use of fetal tissue is acceptable. Of course for those who defend abortion on moral grounds, the use of fetal tissue does not raise moral concerns. The use of human embryos in research, on the other hand, challenges us to confront their moral status, whether they are embryos that were created for infertile couples who no longer need them, or are created expressly for research uses. Does the intention for which the embryos were created matter? Do embryos deserve special respect because of what they are and the potential they represent? These and other issues are addressed by Rebecca Dresser in her article in this chapter.

Embryos created *in vitro* (outside the body, as in the laboratory) can only survive for about fourteen days after fertilization, before they must be either frozen for some later use or implanted into a woman's body. Hence one potential supply of embryos for research is the many infertility clinics across the United States and around the world. These clinics create embryos for use in in-vitro fertilization (IVF), many of which are never used (estimated at more than 400,000 stored excess embryos in the United States alone)[2] and are frozen in clinics, waiting for a decision about their disposition. Couples for whom embryos were created for reproductive purposes control what will happen to them if they are not needed, and the default in the United States has been to allow the embryos to remain frozen indefinitely, which has led to the large excess of stored embryos. Couples can decide to use the embryos to try to have children in the future, or they can donate them to other couples for reproduction—this is sometimes termed "embryo adoption," though this is a somewhat loaded term. Couples who decide not to use stored embryos for reproductive purposes can decide to discard them or donate them for research such as human embryonic stem cell research.

While they offer the greatest supply for hESC research, frozen embryos have limited uses. For instance, a likely approach for therapeutic uses would be cells that are immunologically matched to their recipient. Researchers suggest that the best matched cells could come from an embryo cloned from the patient's own cells. This is termed somatic cell nuclear transplant (SCNT) and is the same technique used to create Dolly the sheep. Many in the hESC debate prefer to distinguish SCNT-created embryos used for the purpose of extracting stem cells (sometimes called "research cloning") from SCNT embryos used for the purpose of reproduction ("reproductive cloning").

For some, the ethics of the two sources of embryos for hESC research are different. Using spare embryos that were created with the intention of trying to have a child but have become unnecessary for that purpose is deemed morally different from creating embryos with the intention of extracting their stem cells. The motivation or intention in one case is reproduction, with some embryos left over after the process. In the other case, the intention is to create embryos for the purpose of using them in research. In either case the outcome for the embryo is the same. Whether intention or outcome is morally more important is a matter of perspective on whether means or ends has greater moral importance—as discussed in Chapter 1. It turns out that much of the public opinion data in the United States shows that the majority of Americans endorse the use of excess IVF embryos in federally funded hESC research but object to creating embryos expressly for such research.[3]

Interestingly, the range of answers as to the use of embryos in research does not track perfectly with views on abortion. The most apparent differences between abortion and hESC research are that (1) abortion is a procedure that takes place substantially later in development, well after the 10–14 day window for embryo research, and (2) abortion terminates a pregnancy, necessarily within a woman's body, while hESC research relies on embryos created in the laboratory and never implanted into a woman's body. For some, a pregnancy represents a nascent human life in a way that an embryo *in vitro* never will. It is this justification that allows Senator Orrin G. Hatch (R-UT), a staunch abortion opponent, to support hESC research without contradiction.[4]

The debate on the use of human embryos in research seems to become more strident when more is at stake. In the early 1980s, when restrictions on federal funding of embryo research were first implemented in the United States by President Ronald Reagan, the science was far less compelling than it is in the twenty-first century. As tangible, if prospective, benefits of hESC research come into focus, the major policy questions going forward will be about how well the principles articulated nearly three decades ago can stand in the face of the pressures and promise of research. Some of the prospective approaches are outlined and discussed in this chapter, including by Greene and colleagues in their article on the grafting of human neural (nervous system) cells into non-human primates. As the remainder of this chapter will illustrate, stem cell research is far from the only controversial area of bioscience and biotechnology facing society in the twenty-first century.

ETHICS AND GENETICALLY MODIFIED ORGANISMS

Genetic technologies were controversial even before the first recombinant DNA technologies were developed. Scholars, pundits, legislators, and scientists themselves saw the potential for both the promise and peril of technologies that would allow predictive genetic testing (discussed in Chapter 4), as well as genetic modification of plants, animals, and humans. In this section of the chapter, articles by Comstock, and Engelhardt and Jotterand examine the ethical issues arising in the creation and use of genetically modified organisms (GMOs), and the policy approaches for dealing with them. It is estimated that over a quarter of all crop acreage planted in the world contains genetically modified (GM) plants, and the United States accounts for nearly two-thirds of all so-called biotechnology crops planted globally, mostly corn, soybeans, and cotton.[5] GM crops are a major part of the U.S. and global agriculture, and a significant part of the food supply and textile industries.

While GM crops and products made from them are nearly ubiquitous, there is great unease among the public about their effects on humans and our environment. A popular response as a policy option is to engage what has been termed "the precautionary principle" in which the burden of proof is placed on those who propose adoption of new technologies to show or produce evidence that there will no harm caused by the technologies. This is in comparison to the traditional, and opposite, policy approach in which new technologies are presumed to be allowed to go forward unless it can be shown that they will cause harm. Engelhardt and Jotterand argue that the precautionary principle needs reconsideration and is deeply flawed as a policy approach. The adoption, use, and oversight of GMOs are a crucial social issue, and signal the beginnings of larger questions about oversight of technologies related to modification, enhancement, and other applications of cutting-edge technologies.

GENETIC ENHANCEMENT, NEUROSCIENCE, AND NANOTECHNOLOGY

In addition to bioscience applications to modify organisms for human use, there are a number of technologies aimed at modifying humans themselves—often with the intent to enhance existing properties or characteristics. The success of the Human Genome Project led to predictions and concerns about the use of genetic technologies to "engineer" human beings in ways that might change our expectations of "normal" human behavior, undermine our notion of humanity, and even be put to nefarious purposes. None of these have come to pass, of course, but their prospect still looms large over the future uses of genetic technologies. These prospects are not limited to genetic technologies, however, and new understandings of neuroscience and nanotechnology make their human applications more likely. Jonathan Glover's article is carried over from the previous edition, with insights as applicable today as they were when it first appeared. Glover's perspective stands in contrast to the article by Langdon Winner, who makes a compelling argument that human-affecting technologies cannot and should not be avoided but must be embraced. The leading edge applications of such technologies must be neuroscience, whose applications may not only help us better understand the workings of the brain, but may also lead to the ability to change the very workings of the brain itself. Martha Farah and her colleagues provide an examination of both what sorts of changes neuroscience may bring, and how far we should go in using them.

SYNTHETIC BIOLOGY AND BIOSECURITY

Finally, it may well be the case that the true frontiers of bioscience go past the "mere" modification of existing organisms to creating organisms from the building blocks of life. Much as synthetic chemistry builds molecules using chemical components, the goal of synthetic biology is to build living organisms from their molecular building blocks. This is science engaged in the creation of life, with all its interesting and important implications. As is often the case in frontier science, it is difficult to envision where the research will lead and therefore difficult to predict its impact and foresee its implications. The final section of the chapter attempts to map out some possible directions for synthetic biology and their implications, with the article by Tucker and Zalinskas examining the "promises and perils" of a new area of science, including the national and international security implications of the creation of novel organisms. The good news is that prospective policy analysis is occurring alongside prospective science, and the excerpt from a larger report by Fischer exemplifies attempts to wrestle with how best to foster the benefits of bioscience while exerting appropriate controls over it.

Many have said that we are living in the bioscience century, and it is difficult to argue with that assertion. It is the responsibility of those working in cutting-edge science areas to consider its implications carefully, of those engaged in policy making to carefully consider both the benefits and burdens of new applications of science, and of all members of society to better understand the issues we will face collectively as twenty-first century science unfolds.

J. P. K.

NOTES

1. The ban eventually became known as the "Dickey Amendment," as it was an amendment attached to one of the federal budget appropriations acts annually since 1996.

2. D. I. Hoffman, G. L. Zellman, C. C. Fair, J. F. Mayer, et al., "Cryopreserved Embryos in the United States and Their Availability for Research," *Fertility and Sterility* 79 (May 2003): 1063–69.

3. M. C. Nisbet, "Public Opinion about Stem Cell Research and Cloning," *Public Opinion Quarterly* 68 (2004): 131–54.

4. "Hatch Urges Senate Action on Stem Cell Bill," Press Release from the Office of Senator Orrin G. Hatch, May 25, 2005, accessed at http://hatch.senate.gov/index.cfm?FuseAction=PressReleases.View& PressRelease_id=1353.

5. Pew Initiative on Food and Biotechnology, "Fact Sheet: Genetically Modified Crops in the United States," August 2004, accessed at http://pewagbiotech.org/resources/factsheets/display.php3?FactsheetID=2.

REBECCA DRESSER

Stem Cell Research: The Bigger Picture

Rebecca Dresser is the Daniel Noyes Kirby Professor of Law and Professor of Ethics in Medicine at Washington University in St. Louis. Since 1983, she has taught medical and law students about legal and ethical issues in end-of-life care, biomedical research, genetics, assisted reproduction, and related topics. Her book *When Science Offers Salvation: Patient Advocacy and Research Ethics* was published in 2001. She is a co-author of *The Human Use of Animals: Case Studies in Ethical Choice* and *Bioethics and Law: Cases, Materials and Problems*.

In 1998, a team led by Wisconsin researcher James Thomson created the first line of human embryonic stem cells. Since then, stem cells have rarely left the headlines. Not since Asilomar and the genetic engineering controversy has a basic science topic generated so much press and political discussion. Why? What accounts for the preoccupation and the passion?

Part of the explanation lies in the compelling moral claims made on both sides of the debate. Also at work is an unprecedented level of advocacy, not just from the usual suspects—researchers, scientific organizations, and pro-life groups—but from patients, families, and celebrities, too.

Research using human embryonic stem cells raises an array of complex ethical issues, including, but by no means limited to, the moral status of developing human life. Unfortunately, much of the public discussion fails to take into account this complexity. Advocacy for liberal and conservative positions on human embryonic stem cell research can be simplistic and misleading. This research will always be controversial, but a richer public debate could clarify the issues and point to more thoughtful policy approaches to the stem cell question. . . .

I focus on different possibilities for implementing an approach incorporating the position that human embryos have an intermediate moral status. I also call

attention to important but neglected considerations that should be part of the debate over federal support for human embryonic stem cell research.

MORAL STATUS AND DEVELOPING HUMAN LIFE

Stem cells themselves are not human embryos, but they must be derived from embryos. To derive stem cells, scientists must destroy a human embryo. Is this morally permissible? Each individual's position on this issue is affected by that individual's view of the early embryo's moral status.

Some people believe that embryos have the moral status of persons, based on the view that conception is the point that a person begins. . . . *OBJECTION*

For people who share this belief, possible knowledge gains cannot justify stem cell or any other research that requires embryo destruction. This belief underlies President Bush's decision to limit federal funding for human embryonic stem cell research. According to the decision, the National Institutes of Health (NIH) may support only projects using stem cells from lines developed before August 2001, when the President made his announcement. This time limit for NIH funding was imposed to keep government research support from becoming an incentive for further embryo destruction (Bush 2001).

Of course, many people disagree with the position that human embryos have the same moral status as children and adults. People who see the embryo as something less than a full person note that early

Reprinted with permission from *Perspectives in Biology and Medicine* 48:2 (2005), 181–194. © 2005 by The Johns Hopkins University Press.

embryos lack many characteristics that make persons morally significant, such as the ability to think and feel pain and pleasure. In early embryos, the beginning of nervous system, the primitive streak, hasn't yet formed. At the point that stem cells are derived, which is about five days after conception, embryos are not even clear individuals—twinning can occur after that point. . . .

The location of the embryos also matters to some people. For example, Jewish law has been interpreted to hold that the embryo has no status outside a woman's body. . . . Similarly, abortion opponent Senator Orrin Hatch supports embryonic stem cell research because "human life requires and begins in a mother's nurturing womb" (Hatch 2002). According to this view, the human embryo's ability to develop depends on being in the right environment. When embryos are created in the laboratory, through either in vitro fertilization (IVF) or cloning, they cannot move beyond the embryonic stage unless a human actor transfers them to a woman's uterus. For people holding this view, embryos fertilized in the laboratory lack their ordinary developmental capacity and, as a result, lack the moral status of embryos fertilized in the usual way.

The embryos' location separates the stem cell controversy from the abortion debate, too. Rather than a clash between preserving early human life and protecting a woman's control over her body, stem cell research pits embryonic life against the social value of advancing knowledge. Although people in the United States are enthusiastic about promoting scientific research, this activity has not received the same constitutional and common law protection as have the individual bodily integrity interests at stake in decisions about pregnancy. . . .

Whatever the ethical justification for their position, people who fail to see embryos as morally equivalent to persons usually adopt a developmental approach to moral status, in which prenatal life gains increased moral status over time. . . .

Those taking [this] position . . . must answer a further question, however. If early embryos aren't persons, are they just objects or property? Can *anything* be done with them? Some people do take this position. . . .

But many people rejecting the embryos as persons view reject [this] position, too. People in this group think that embryos should be treated with "special respect" because they have the potential to become persons. Several advisory groups considering the ethics of embryo research have endorsed this view, as has at least one court resolving a divorcing couple's dispute over how to dispose of frozen embryos (Davis v. Davis 1992; DHEW Ethics Advisory Board 1979; NBAC 1999; NIH 1994).

Simply saying that embryos should be treated with special respect fails to resolve the stem cell research question, however. Anyone holding this view must decide what special respect means in the research context. Is it possible to show special respect to an organism while at the same time allowing it to be used in destructive research to advance the interests of others?

EXAMINING SPECIAL RESPECT

A few policy proposals seek to put the special respect position into practice. A relatively popular idea is to allow embryos remaining after infertility treatment to be used in research, but to forbid creating embryos purely for research. People holding this view think that using unwanted IVF embryos to advance medical knowledge is more ethical than discarding them or storing them indefinitely. . . . Research embryos are expected to come from fertility patients who don't want to donate them for reproduction, . . . because they don't want someone else raising their genetic children. If these individuals can't donate for research, their embryos will be destroyed or left in storage, where they could eventually lose viability.

Many people think that it would be better to permit embryos that would otherwise be discarded to be used in research that might help future patients. At the same time, some of these people also see significant moral differences between studying donated IVF embryos and producing embryos purely for research purposes. They object to the latter activity because it treats embryos as products to be manufactured for utilitarian reasons. . . .

Yet this position has its challengers, too. . . . [I]n both cases embryos are created for worthwhile activities—helping infertile couples have children and generating knowledge that might help future patients.

What is different, though, is intent. In one situation, scientists purposely create embryos to be destroyed so that stem cells may be obtained. In the other situation, embryos are created with the hope that they will develop into children, a goal more consistent with respecting embryos as potential persons. When embryos are created in the clinic, prospective parents and the medical professionals assisting them do not know whether all of the embryos will be needed for infertility treatment. And they do not know whether the couple will eventually choose to donate or destroy any embryos that might remain once the treatment effort is finished.

Sandel argues that the difference in intent is insufficient to create a legitimate moral difference between the two practices. If creating embryos for research "is exploitative and fails to accord embryos the respect they are due," he declares, then so are fertility clinic practices that create excess embryos that are likely to be destroyed (through research or discard). Moral consistency requires either allowing embryos to be created for research or changing IVF clinic practices so that no excess embryos are created (Sandel 2002).

Moral and legal analysts often distinguish acts performed with the explicit aim of producing a problematic result and those done with awareness of a risk that the problematic result will materialize, and one could argue that such a distinction should be drawn here. . . . Also, . . . even if IVF practice changed so that no more excess embryos were created, we would still need to address the permissible disposition of embryos now stored in clinic freezers. . . . According to clinicians, many of those embryos would not be suitable for implantation, because they are abnormal in ways that would hamper healthy fetal development. As a result, such embryos ought not be adopted for reproduction. Are they thus permissible sources of stem cells for research?

At the same time, Sandel's arguments, as well as scientific claims that certain studies can be done only with specially created research embryos, make it imperative to evaluate the morality of creating embryos purely for research. In the stem cell context, the debate centers on whether it would be permissible to create an embryo by cloning a living person's cell for biomedical research purposes. This procedure, often called "therapeutic cloning," is promoted as a means to avoid immune system rejection of transplanted stem cells in patients who need replacement tissue. In theory, researchers could create an early embryo by combining the nucleus of a patient's somatic cell with an enucleated human egg cell. After allowing the embryo to develop for a few days, they would attempt to harvest the resulting embryonic stem cells and establish a cell line for transplantation into the patient. . . .

Such cloned embryos could also be valuable in basic research investigating the origins of various diseases. . . .

Research cloning critics argue that deliberate creation of potential human life purely to serve as a research tool treats human embryos too much like objects. Besides undermining the special respect position, they say, it could lessen respect for other forms of human life. In the words of one such critic, . . . "The very act of creating embryos for the sole purpose of exploiting and then destroying them will ultimately predispose us to a ruthless utilitarianism about human life itself" (Krauthammer 2002, p. 325).

A related set of objections focuses on risks to women providing the eggs necessary to create research embryos. Women supplying eggs must take high doses of hormones and undergo numerous tests and procedures. The process is known to carry a small risk of serious injury and, rarely, death. . . . Some experts also worry that it might contribute to health and fertility problems later in life. . . . A further problem is that the process seems to enlist women in the manufacturing of research tools—to regard their bodies as a means of production. And to obtain an adequate supply of eggs, researchers would probably have to pay women, which again makes it look as though embryos are being manufactured as if they were objects or property. There is concern as well about the quality of decisions to donate eggs for research. Monetary incentives to provide eggs raise concerns about undue inducement, especially among students and low-income women.

Of course, several of the same problems apply when women supply eggs to help infertile people have children, and some embryo research critics oppose this practice, too. Others say that providing eggs for infertility treatment is more respectful of women and embryos, because the aim is to create children who will be loved and valued as persons, rather than to produce a useful item for research. Moreover, because a limited number of women are willing to undergo the demanding hormone regimen and egg retrieval procedure, there is a shortage of eggs available for infertility treatment. In some areas of the country, clinics engage in "bidding wars," offering higher payments to attract women to their programs. . . . Increased demand for eggs in research could exacerbate the competition for donors, intensifying worries about commodification and undue inducement. These worries have led some women's health advocates to call for a moratorium on research cloning, at least until there is more animal research demonstrating the distinct value of stem cells from cloned embryos. . . .

TOWARD A RESEARCH POLICY BASED ON SPECIAL RESPECT

I see the disagreement on these matters as part of a struggle to work out what special respect for early human life should mean in the research context. Given that this is a relatively new ethical, social, and policy question, it is not surprising that we lack consensus at this point.

The inquiry is also part of a broader moral examination, one that concerns research conducted with what might be called "moral intermediates." This is research that involves the destructive study of organisms generally viewed as having appreciable moral significance, but not the moral worth of a fully developed human being. Such intermediates include human embryos and fetuses, as well as nonhuman mammals and perhaps some other species. There is heated debate over the general moral responsibilities we have toward these organisms, and over the circumstances in which it is morally permissible to use them to produce scientific knowledge. These questions are among the primary moral challenges we face today. The controversy over the appropriate conduct of human embryonic stem cell research occurs in this broader moral context.

As we have seen, some who support the special respect view argue that we should prohibit the creation of embryos purely for research. There are additional ideas for putting the special respect position into policy, though they have received less attention in the public debate over stem cell research. In an essay called "On The Elusive Nature of Respect," theologian Karen Lebacqz (2001) explored the moral basis for one such policy approach. Lebacqz applied the concept of respect to persons, to sentient beings, and to the natural world. Then she considered what respect might mean in the context of human embryonic stem cell research. According to Lebacqz, it is possible to treat embryos with "awe or reverence," to regard them as having "incredible value; as something precious that cannot be replaced with any other [embryo], whose existence is to be celebrated and whose loss is to be grieved," and at the same time, to allow them to be used and killed in limited circumstances, when necessity is established. As an analogy, she cited traditional Native American attitudes toward killing animals for food.

Lebacqz's reflections suggest that at the very least, decisions about stem cell research should incorporate a careful analysis of the justification for embryo use. Two tasks are essential to this analysis. One is to assess the value of a proposed study's objectives, which requires us to rank the good of various research ends. Embryonic stem cell research could advance a variety of human interests, such as improved health,

extension of the average life span, economic interests, career advancement, and satisfaction of scientific curiosity. Which of these interests, if any, is important enough to warrant creation and destruction of human embryos and the other potential harms, such as injury to women providing eggs, that could accompany the research?

Besides evaluating the importance of a proposed project's goal, we must also consider how essential embryo use is to attaining that goal. Thus, the second dimension of the justification assessment involves probability and prediction: what is the likelihood that a proposed embryo study will advance important human interests? To what extent could the human interests at stake be satisfied by an alternative approach?

Certain substantive limits on human embryonic stem cell research could be justified under this approach. For example, some scientists think that it will not be necessary to use stem cells from cloned embryos to avoid the immune rejection problem. Alternatives, such as a bank of stem cells with a range of genetic characteristics, might avoid the need to create cloned embryos purely for research. . . . Alternatives may also prove more feasible and cost-effective, for the evolving view seems to be that cloning an embryo for each patient would be too expensive and complicated to constitute a practical therapeutic alternative. . . . So-called adult stem cells, which are present in the tissues of adults and children, may be adequate alternatives to embryonic stem cells in certain types of research; stem cells from donated umbilical cords and fetal cadavers could also be adequate for some scientific investigations. . . .

Determining whether there is adequate scientific and moral justification for embryo creation and destruction will inevitably be an imperfect process. Nevertheless, some level of advance screening is reasonably attainable and, under the special respect view, ethically warranted. The review process for making research funding decisions provides a partial model for decisions on the justification for human embryo use. In the funding context, scarce monetary resources are awarded on the basis of predictions about the potential contributions that could come from competing projects. Reviewers make judgments about the likelihood of success and the value of project objectives, despite the unavoidable flaws characterizing this process. Similarly, human embryos may be viewed as organisms of extraordinary moral value, to be reserved for the most promising and worthwhile projects that could contribute to benefits unavailable through other means.

The integrity of such a review process will also depend on the quality and commitment of those conducting the review. Study proposals should be considered by a review group that is more diverse than the scientific panels that make research funding decisions. The difficult moral judgments central to the evaluation should be made by individuals with wide-ranging expertise, including philosophers, theologians, and other nonscientists. Reviewers should also have different views on the moral issues raised by creating and destroying human embryos for research. In short, the review process should not be designed to promote easy consensus. Instead, it should be designed to generate the lively and serious exchanges one would expect from a policy incorporating the special respect position on scientific uses of early human life.

Policy decisions on stem cell research should also take into account the line-drawing issues. Three years ago, researchers at a biotech company reported that they had created tissue that formed functioning kidney-like organs in cows. To achieve this, they first cloned an embryo from one cow's cell and implanted that embryo into another cow's uterus. They let the embryo develop to the early fetal stage, removed it and harvested the tissue, then implanted that tissue into the first cow. . . . In this instance, producing tissue for cell therapy involved not only the creation of a cloned embryo, but also the gestation and destruction of a cloned fetus.

Would the prospect of benefits to patients lead us to permit this in humans? At what point would we say that no benefit to others could justify the instrumental creation and destruction of developing human life? Because there is likely to be pressure to allow destructive research on developing humans past the point at which stem cells can be retrieved, we need to establish a strong moral and policy basis for drawing the line at a particular point, a line that will prevent a slide down the slippery slope and enable us to stand firm against the allure of achievements that could come from permitting research that destroys human life at later stages of development.

PROBLEMS WITH THE PUBLIC DEBATE

Responses to the line-drawing issue are one problem with the public debate over stem cell research. Many debate participants, as well as journalists reporting on the debate, have failed to promote informed public discussion. Some research cloning opponents have exaggerated the slippery-slope threats. For example, President Bush has said that a government willingness to allow cloning for biomedical research would inevitably lead to "human beings . . . grown for spare body parts" (Goldstein 2002). On the other hand, research supporters downplay the slippery-slope challenges. Some of them would accept a rule prohibiting embryo destruction after 14 days of development, but others would permit destruction later than that point. For example, a majority of the NIH Human Embryo Research Panel (1994) favored extending the limit to 21 days, citing the valuable knowledge that might be gained from such research. In a world where vulnerable humans have often been seen as resources for experimentation to benefit the powerful, it would be dangerous to dismiss the line-drawing challenges implicit in policy making about research that destroys developing human life.

A second problem with the public debate is exaggeration about potential cures and therapies from stem cell research. This research is at an early stage, but certain members of Congress, patient advocates, scientists, and scholars paint quite a different picture. According to these individuals, anything less than wholehearted support for embryonic stem cell research is equivalent to denying effective treatment to patients with Parkinson's, Alzheimer's, diabetes, and other devastating illnesses. . . .

This charge conflates the goal of biomedical research, which is to advance knowledge, with the goals of established medical care, which are to heal and prevent disease. . . . Embryonic stem cells are a new tool for basic research, not a sure cure for serious illness. Research proponents portray stem cells as a source of miracle treatments in order to attract support that would be less forthcoming if they acknowledged the potential barriers to devising effective therapies. A graphic example of this strategy comes from Senator Ted Kennedy, who reportedly declared that research cloning will allow officials "to empty three-quarters of the nursing home beds in Massachusetts" (Holden 2002).

Use of certain terms also represents an effort to conflate research and therapy. Research supporters use the term "therapeutic cloning" to refer to creation of cloned embryos for research. . . . And the blending of early-stage research with proven beneficial therapy occurs on both sides of the stem cell debate. Opponents of human embryonic stem cell research exaggerate the promise of adult stem cell research, while embryo research supporters do the same for human embryonic stem cell studies.

Portraying any kind of stem cell research as therapeutic is highly misleading. A few scientists openly admit that the prospects for stem cell therapies have been inflated. For example, James Thomson, the scientist whose team first isolated human embryonic stem cells, has said, "we've raised a lot of false hope for quick fixes and that's not going to happen" (Holden and Vogel 2002). When pressed to assess the state of the science, reputable scientists recognize that many obstacles could thwart efforts to develop effective therapies. Researchers must devise ways to coax stem cells to turn into properly functioning tissues. They must learn how to prevent the cells from causing cancer. There is also the problem of immune rejection. . . . In November 2003, a group of distinguished experts in science, law, and philosophy described the numerous safety questions that must be investigated in animal studies before stem cell–based interventions are tried in humans (Dawson et al. 2003). It is entirely possible that stem cells will go the way of other highly publicized but disappointing technologies, such as gene therapy, the artificial heart, and fetal tissue transplants.

Speakers who exaggerate (to put it kindly—one could say misrepresent) the speed with which stem cell therapies could become available do patients no service. Unrealistic optimism can reinforce patients' and families' hopes for a miracle cure and then exacerbate their disappointment when they realize that clinical applications are nonexistent. Such unrealistic predictions are also bad for science—they risk a loss of public and congressional support if stem cell research fails to generate therapies quickly. . . .

A third problem with the public debate is a failure on all sides to consider the distributive justice implications of stem cell research. Much stem cell research targets diseases of aging. Of course, it would be wonderful to prevent or delay conditions like Alzheimer's and heart disease. . . . Thus, the debate over stem cell research should consider questions such as: what value should be assigned to the "regenerative medicine" that supporters claim will come from stem cell research? Should the ability to extend the average U.S. life span be a priority in biomedical research? Is it defensible for wealthy countries to devote substantial funds to research on diseases of aging, while allo-

cating relatively little for the study of malaria, TB, and other diseases responsible for high rates of premature death worldwide?

We should also consider stem cell research in the context of access to health care. Health debates in this country place a disproportionate emphasis on stem cell research, research cloning, and other exotic investigational interventions. Indeed, support for stem cell research has become an effective yet undemanding strategy for politicians and other public figures seeking to show concern for suffering patients. Meanwhile, millions of people in this country lack access to quality health care. Many, many patients cannot obtain existing therapies that could extend and improve their lives. And the situation is much worse in developing nations. The desire to develop better treatments for future patients is understandable, but we should not forget that people today are often denied the benefits of past research breakthroughs. Thus, to advance the general goal of helping patients, we should not allow the stem cell issue to divert our elected leaders from this nation's deepening health care crisis.

Public and policy discussion should also acknowledge the challenge of supplying patients with any stem cell treatments that might emerge, treatments that would probably be expensive. Would stem cell therapies be available solely to the wealthy? If not, would already strapped managed care, Medicare, and Medicaid programs be required to cover these therapies? Of course, these are questions that arise with many other biomedical innovations. But because helping patients is the ultimate ethical justification for conducting stem cell research, access to potential therapies should be part of the national discussion.

The final problem with the public debate over stem cell research is that it sometimes lacks civility. Partisans in the debate too often dismiss the concerns of those who disagree, and they dismiss as well the idea that deliberation, accommodation, and compromise might be warranted. For example, in an essay in *The Nation*, bioethicist Arthur Caplan portrayed research cloning opponents as a "bizarre alliance of antiabortion religious zealots and technophobic neoconservatives along with a smattering of scientifically befuddled anti-biotech progressives [who are] pushing hard to insure that the Senate accords more moral concern to cloned embryos in dishes than it does to kids who can't walk and grandmothers who can't hold a fork or breathe" (Caplan 2002, p. 5).

Other troubling remarks come from Irving Weissman, chairman of a National Academy of Sciences panel that endorsed research cloning. Writing in the *New England Journal of Medicine*, Weissman praised his panel for withholding judgment until "all the relevant data and information had been received and discussed." In contrast, he criticized the President's Council on Bioethics, which recommended a four-year moratorium on cloning, for being insufficiently informed and receptive to arguments that conflicted with members' preconceived notions (Weissman 2002, p. 1578).

Such charges are disturbing and raise questions about our country's ability to cope with the many moral and policy issues that science and biotechnology will bring in the coming years. As political scientists Dennis Thompson and Amy Gutmann have observed, bioethics controversies are increasingly debated in institutional settings, where theories of deliberative democracy become relevant. According to these writers, deliberative democracy has at its core "the idea that citizens and officials must justify any demands for collective action by giving reasons that can be accepted by those who are bound by the action. When citizens morally disagree about public policy, they . . . should deliberate with one another, seeking moral agreement when they can and maintaining mutual respect when they cannot" (Thompson and Gutmann 1997, p. 38).

Thompson and Gutmann's advice should guide future policy work on stem cell research. Currently, few government restrictions apply to embryonic stem cell research conducted with funds from the private sector (some states strictly limit embryo research, but others have laws promoting research with embryonic stem cells). Moreover, scientific and patient advocacy organizations are engaged in intense lobbying to expand the embryonic cell lines eligible for government support. . . .

At the same time, Congress has refused since the mid-1990s to permit federal funding for any research that destroys a human embryo. . . . As long as this prohibition remains in force, NIH dollars will be unavailable to researchers seeking to develop new embryonic cell lines. Furthermore, even the relatively liberal Clinton administration's stem cell research policy prohibited federal support for studies with cells from embryos created for research through either cloning or IVF. . . . This suggests that producing human embryos purely for research purposes troubles people on different parts of the political spectrum.

Amid the questions about moral status, special respect, and whether stem cells will eventually yield safe and effective therapies, one thing is certain.

Arguments over federal research policy will be resolved through the democratic process. People dissatisfied with the current situation, whether it is unhappiness with the absence of constraints on embryo research supported with private funds or unhappiness with limits on federal support for embryonic stem cell research, must accept that change will require working with others who do not share their precise views. Individuals on all sides of the debate may insist that policy incorporate their specific positions and possibly achieve nothing, or they may grant the legitimacy of competing views and try to craft points of agreement. Research proponents unwilling to seek common ground and an oversight system acceptable to those with differing views could end-up hindering the very advances in knowledge they champion.

REFERENCES

Bush, G. W. 2001. Remarks by President George W. Bush on stem cell research. In President's Council 2004, 183–87.

Caplan, A. L. 2002. Attack of the anti-cloners. *The Nation*, June 17, 5–6.

Davis v. Davis. 1992. 842 S. W.2d 588 (Tenn. Sup. Ct.).

Dawson, L., et al. 2003. Safety issues in cell-based intervention trials. *Fertil Steril* 8: 1077–85.

Department of Health, Education and Welfare (DHEW) Ethics Advisory Board. 1979. *Report and conclusions: HEW support of research involving human in vitro fertilization and embryo transfer.* Washington, DC: U.S. GPO. http://bioethics.gov/reports/past_commisions/index/html.

Goldstein, A. 2002. President presses senate to ban all human cloning. *Washington Post*, April 11.

Hatch, O. 2002. The pro-life case for cloning. *NY Times*, May 2.

Holden, C. 2002. Battle heats up over cloning. *Science* 295: 2009.

Holden C., and G. Vogel. 2002. Plasticity: Time for a reappraisal? *Science* 296: 2126–29.

Lebacqz, K. 2001. On the elusive nature of respect. In *The human embryonic stem cell debate: Science, ethics, and public policy*, ed. S. Holland, K. Lebacqz, and L. Zoloth, 149–62. Cambridge: MIT Press.

Malakoff, D. 2002. Moratorium replaces ban as U.S. target. *Science* 296: 2117.

National Bioethics Advisory Commission (NBAC). 1999. *Ethical issues in human stem cell research. Vol. 1, Report and recommendations.* http://bioethics.georgetown.edu/nbac.

National Institutes of Health (NIH) Ad Hoc Group of Consultants to the Advisory Committee to the Director. 1994. *Report of the human embryo research panel*, vol. 1. http://ospp.od.nih.gov/policy.

Sandel, M. 2002. The anti-cloning conundrum. *NY Times*, May 28.

Thompson, D. E., and Gutmann, A. 1997. Deliberating about bioethics. *Hastings Cent Rep* 27(3): 38–41.

Weissman, I. L. 2002. Stem cells: Scientific, medical, and political issues. *N Engl J Med* 346: 1576–79.

INTERNATIONAL SOCIETY FOR STEM CELL RESEARCH (ISSCR)

Guidelines for the Conduct of Human Embryonic Stem Cell Research

International Society for Stem Cell Research (ISSCR)

1) JUSTIFICATION FOR STEM CELL RESEARCH AND GOALS

1.1) Stem cell research, with foundations in the fields of cell and developmental biology and genetics, seeks to answer basic questions about the nature of tissue formation and maintenance. The first stem cells to be isolated were from developed tissues and organs, and are now used in tissue and organ regeneration experimentally and clinically.

1.2) The rapid growth of the field of stem cell research follows numerous recent seminal discoveries, including the isolation of human embryonic stem cells and stem cells of various types that have the potential to generate many different cells and tissues.

1.3) Stem cell research encompasses new approaches for the elucidation of disease mechanisms, offers promise for discovery of novel drugs that act on stem cells, and may yield cell replacement therapies for a multitude of devastating and widespread genetic, malignant, and degenerative diseases that are currently untreatable. Stem cell research is certain to advance fundamental knowledge and to have a profound impact on medicine. The goals of stem cell research are widely accepted in the biomedical research community and endorsed by diverse scientific societies worldwide. Long-term goals include improvements in human health and the relief of disease, infirmity, and human suffering through advances in knowledge and new clinical tools that can be made available and affordable throughout the world.

1.4) The International Society for Stem Cell Research (ISSCR) endorses the goals of stem cell scientists and exists to promote innovation in research, education, and the free exchange of scientific ideas and research materials.

2) MISSION OF TASK FORCE

2.1) Scientific, cultural, religious, ethical, and legal differences across international borders affect how early stages of human development are viewed, and how research on human embryos and embryonic stem cells is conducted. ISSCR calls for due consideration and appropriate oversight of human stem cell research to ensure transparent, ethical, and responsible performance of scientific experiments.

2.2) The ISSCR Task Force is charged with formulating guidelines that articulate ethical principles and rules of behavior for the performance of human stem cell research.

2.3) These Guidelines are meant to emphasize the responsibility of scientists to ensure that human stem cell research is carried out according to rigorous standards of research ethics, and to encourage uniform research practices that should be followed by all human stem cell scientists globally. . . .

4) SCOPE OF GUIDELINES

4.1) . . . This Guideline document focuses on issues unique to stem cell research that involves pre-implantation stages of human development, research on the derivation or use of human pluripotent stem cell lines, and on the range of experiments whereby such cells might be incorporated into animal hosts.

4.2) These Guidelines pertain to the procurement, derivation, banking, distribution, and use of cells and tissues taken from preimplantation stages of human development; to procurements of gametes and somatic tissues for stem cell research; and to the use of human totipotent or pluripotent cells or human pluripotent stem cell lines.

4.3) These Guidelines assert that researchers involved in human stem cell research must adhere to ethical and transparent practices for performing research and sharing research materials.

4.4) These Guidelines assign criteria for defining categories of research that are non-permissible, that are permissible under currently mandated review processes, and research that is permissible yet should be subjected to an added level of oversight. These Guidelines prescribe the nature of regulatory review and oversight for each of the permissible research categories.

4.5) These Guidelines do not pertain to research on animal stem cells, or on classes of human somatic stem cells that remain restricted in tissue potential and are not known to possess totipotent or pluripotent potential. Research pertaining to these classes of stem cells does not raise the same sets of issues as dealt with in these Guidelines.

4.6) In their current form, these Guidelines are incomplete in their potential application to various types of fetal stem cells, which raise a unique set of issues around their procurement. Future revised versions of the Guidelines may incorporate more specific information pertinent to fetal stem cells.

5) RESPONSIBILITY FOR CONDUCT

5.1) International scientific collaboration and mutual trust among researchers are vital to the success and advancement of science and should be encouraged. Collaborations between scientists in different jurisdictions will raise issues due to the differences in the laws and regulations that govern stem cell research. An underlying principle of these guidelines is that any and all stem cell research shall be conducted in accordance with any applicable laws and regulations of the country or region where such research takes place, recognizing and respecting that certain laws and regulations may be applicable to individual researchers, regardless of where the research will take place.

5.2) Researchers must assume the responsibility for compliance with local statutes and adherence to guidelines. Institutions sponsoring stem cell research must take steps to ensure that education and appropriate training takes place to make researchers aware of regulations and professional guidelines. If warranted, institutions should obtain legal opinions on any issues of concern on behalf of their researchers.

5.3) Scientists and clinicians must be transparent and truthful about issues relating to human stem cell research and its potential to advance medicine. To guard against the creation of unrealistic expectations of success and to safeguard patients from serving prematurely as experimental subjects in human stem cell research, scientists and clinicians must clearly articulate the distinct goals of basic research, preclinical studies, and clinical trials. Investigators must assume the responsibility to educate the public about the many steps required to garner the scientific and clinical evidence to establish treatments as safe and effective.

5.4) Scientific trainees and technical staff who have a conscientious objection to aspects of stem cell research should not be required to participate in research, and should be free of retribution or undue discrimination in assessments of professional performance. Clinical personnel who have a conscientious objection to stem cell research should not be required to participate in providing donor information or securing donor consent for research use of embryos, gametes, or somatic cells; that privilege should not extend to the clinical care of a donor.

6) STATEMENT ON REPRODUCTIVE CLONING

6.1) Human reproductive cloning is defined as the act of seeking to establish either a pregnancy or the birth of a child by gestating or transfering into a uterus human embryos that have been derived in vitro by nuclear transfer or nuclear reprogramming. Given current scientific and medical safety concerns, attempts at human reproductive cloning should be prohibited.

7) ISSUES PERTINENT TO INTERNATIONAL COLLABORATIONS AND THE ROLE OF ISSCR

7.1) In the context of international collaborations, issues will arise that relate to ownership and custodianship of intellectual property. As a general principle, the ISSCR stands for the open exchange of scientific ideas and materials to maximize exploration, to promote innovation and to increase the probability of public benefit through affordable advances made possible by human stem cell research. Given the need to respect the varying laws and regulations of different jurisdictions that may apply to any international collaboration, intellectual property issues are best left to be negotiated among the collaborating parties, taking into consideration the protection regimes or other relevant laws and regulations of their respective jurisdictions. Nonetheless, we endorse in the strongest possible terms the principle that research with human materials is valuable to all, and that the proper practice of science requires unhindered distribution of research materials to all qualified investigators engaged in non-commercial research and the dissemination of its benefits to humanity at large on just and reasonable terms.

7.2) Pluripotent human stem cell lines are important tools for research and replication of experimental data and scientific collaboration are vital to scientific advancement. The ISSCR recommends that institutions engaged in human stem cell research, whether public or private, academic or otherwise, develop procedures whereby research scientists are granted, without undue financial constraints or bureaucratic impediment, unhindered access to these research materials for scientifically sound and ethical purposes, as determined under these Guidelines and applicable laws. The ISSCR urges such institutions, when arranging for disposition of intellectual property to commercial entities, to take all possible care to preserve nonexclusive access for the research community, and to promote public benefit as their primary objective. The ISSCR endorses the principle that as a prerequisite for being granted the privilege of engaging in human stem cell research, researchers must agree to make the materials readily accessible to the biomedical research community for non-commercial research. Administrative costs such as shipping and handling should be borne by the receiving party so as not to pose a severe financial burden on the researcher providing the cells.

7.3) The ISSCR encourages scientists conducting human stem cell research to submit any human stem cell lines they derive to national or international depositories that allow open distribution in order to facilitate the wider dissemination of these valuable research tools across national boundaries. Scientists and stem cell bio-banks should endeavor to work together to harmonize standard operating procedures to facilitate international collaboration.

7.4) The process of identifying international ethical standards and practices for the conduct of human stem cell research should include concerted efforts to engage people throughout the world in honest and realistic conversations about the science and ethics of stem cell research and its emerging applications.

8) RECOMMENDATIONS FOR OVERSIGHT

8.1) All experiments pertinent to human embryonic stem cell research that involve pre-implantation stages of human development, human embryos or embryonic cells, or that entail incorporating human totipotent or pluripotent cells into animal chimeras, shall be subject to review, approval and ongoing monitoring by a special oversight mechanism or body equipped to evaluate the unique aspects of the science. Investigators should seek approval through a process of Stem Cell Research Oversight (SCRO).

8.2) Review can be performed by an oversight mechanism or body at the institutional, local, regional, national, or international level, or by some coordinated combination of those elements provided that the review as a whole occurs effectively, impartially and rigorously. Multi-institutional arrangements for coordinated review, which involve delegation of specific parts of this review, shall be permitted as long as they meet that standard. A single review rather than redundant review is preferable as long as the review is through and pertains to the uniquely sensitive elements of human stem cell research. Unless the review is specifically designed to be comprehensive, the SCRO process shall not replace other mandated reviews such as institutional reviews that assess the participation of human subjects in research, or the oversight for animal care, biosafety, or the like. Institutions engaged in stem cell research must establish procedures to ensure that research conducted under their auspices have been subject to appropriate review.

8.3) Review must include assessment of:

  i) *Scientific rationale and merit of proposal.* Research with human embryonic material, or totipotent or pluripotent cells requires that scientific goals and methods be scrutinized to ensure scientific rigor. Appropriate scientific justification for performing the research using the specified materials is required.
  ii) *Relevant expertise of investigators.* Appropriate expertise and/or training of the investigators to perform the stated experiments must be ascertained in order to ensure the optimal use of precious research materials. For derivation

of new human cell lines or experiments that involve use of human embryonic materials, relevant expertise would include prior experience with embryonic stem cell derivation in animal systems and competence in the culture and maintenance of human embryonic stem cells.

iii) *Ethical permissibility and justification.* Research goals must be assessed within an ethical framework to ensure that research proceeds in a transparent and responsible manner. The project proposal should include a discussion of alternative methods, and provide a rationale for employing the requested human materials, the proposed methodology and for performing the experiments in a human rather than animal model system.

8.4) The mechanism or body that provides SCRO function is responsible for interpreting Guidelines, defining research practices, and monitoring compliance.

8.4a) The SCRO function should assume responsibility for monitoring and periodic review and re-approval of ongoing research proposals.

8.4b) The SCRO function has the responsibility for defining whether a research proposal constitutes permissible or non-permissible research.

8.5) Recommendations for composition of participants to be engaged in providing SCRO function; appropriate expertise, objectivity and responsibility.

8.5a) Scientists and/or physicians with relevant expertise, including representation from scientists that are not directly engaged in the research under consideration. Relevant expertise includes areas of stem cell biology, assisted reproduction, developmental biology, and clinical medicine.

8.5b) Ethicists with ability to interpret the moral justifications and implications of the research under consideration.

8.5c) Members or advisors familiar with relevant local legal statutes governing the research.

8.5d) Community members, unaffiliated with the institution through employment or other remunerative relationships, who are impartial and reasonably familiar with the views and needs of research subjects, patients and patient communities who could be benefited by stem cell research, and community standards.

8.5e) Those responsible for formulating the mechanism or body to provide SCRO function must be cognizant of the potential for conflicts of interest that might compromise the integrity of the review process, and attempt to eliminate such conflicts. Potential participants in the SCRO process should be selected based on the capacity for impartiality and freedom from political influence.

8.6) Each institution, academic or commercial, that engages in human stem cell research shall determine an appropriate SCRO procedure, either internal or external, by which their researchers will be subject to review, approval, and monitoring of their human stem cell research activities.

9) MECHANISMS FOR ENFORCEMENT

9.1) The development of consensus in ethical standards and practices in human stem cell research through thoughtful and transparent dialogue is a critical catalyst for international collaboration to proceed with confidence, and for research from anywhere in the world to be accepted as valid by the scientific community. These standards and practices should be incorporated in a comprehensive code of conduct applicable to all researchers in the field. Senior or corresponding authors of scientific publications should specifically be charged with the responsibility of ensuring that the code of conduct is adhered to in the course of conducting human stem cell research and of supervising junior investigators that work in their respective organizations or projects. Institutions where such research is undertaken shall strive to provide to researchers working on any such projects under their auspices, particularly junior investigators, with up-to-date information on such standards and practices on an ongoing basis.

9.2) Journal editors should require a statement of compliance with the ISSCR 'Guidelines for the Conduct of Human Embryonic Stem Cell Research' or adherence to an equivalent set of guidelines or applicable regulations, and a statement that the research was performed after obtaining approvals following a suitable SCRO process.

9.3) Grant applicants, in particular the individual scientists undertaking the research, should undertake to provide funding bodies with sufficient documentation to demonstrate that the research for which funding is requested is ethically and legally in accordance with relevant local and national regulations and also in compliance with the ISSCR 'Guidelines for the Conduct of Human Embryonic Stem Cell Research.' Funding organizations should pledge to comply with these Guidelines or their equivalent and require entities whose research is funded by such organizations to do the same.

9.4) In order to facilitate the adoption of uniform standards and practice of human stem cell research, the ISSCR will make available for download on the ISSCR website examples of informed consent documents for obtaining human materials for stem cell research (gametes, embryos, somatic tissues), and a Material Transfer Agreement for the sharing and distribution of materials. . . .

10) CATEGORIES OF RESEARCH

To ensure that stem cell research is proceeding with due consideration, to ensure consistency of research practices among scientists globally and to specify the nature of scientific projects that should be subject to SCRO review, we propose specific categories of research.

10.1) Category 1: Experiments that are permissible after review under existing mandates and by existing local committees, and are determined to be exempt from full SCRO review. These will include experiments with pre-existing human embryonic stem cell lines that are confined to cell culture or involve routine and standard research practice, such as assays of teratoma formation in immune-deficient mice. We recommend that all institutions pursuing such research establish a mechanism capable of determining that a) these projects can be adequately reviewed by committees with jurisdiction over research on human tissues, animals, biosafety, radiation, etc. and b) that full review by a SCRO mechanism or body is not required. This mechanism should include a determination that the provenance of the human embryonic stem cell lines to be used has been scrutinized and deemed acceptable according to the principles outlined in this document, and that such research is in compliance with scientific, legal and ethical norms.

10.2) Category 2: Forms of research that are permissible only after additional and comprehensive review by a specialized mechanism or body established to address the issues pertinent to stem cell research (i.e., the SCRO function). Such forms of research will require provision of greater levels of scientific justification, consideration of social and ethical aspects of the research and justification for not pursuing alternative methods to address the same experimental goals. If the research requires obtaining informed consent from human subjects, the research will require review to ensure that treatment of human subjects is consistent with international norms and local laws, and any other applicable regulations or guidelines. Review of such forms of research should consider the protection of genetic and medical privacy of donors; such a review is typically done by a local institutional review board or its equivalent, but could also be performed as part of the SCRO process, with the SCRO exercising due regard for the authority of the institutional review board and avoiding duplication of its functions.

10.2a) Forms of research that involve the derivation of new human pluripotent cell lines by any means.

10.2b) Forms of research in which the identity of the donors of blastocysts, gametes, or somatic cells from which totipotent or pluripotent cells are derived is readily ascertainable or might become known to the investigator.

10.2c) Forms of research in which human totipotent cells or pluripotent stem cells are mixed with pre-implantation human embryos. In no case shall such experiments be allowed to progress for more than 14 days of development in vitro, or past the point of primitive streak formation, whichever is first.

10.2d) Clinical research in which cells of totipotent or pluripotent human origin are transplanted into living human subjects.

10.2e) Forms of research that generate chimeric animals using human cells. Examples of such forms of research include, but are not limited to introducing totipotent or pluripotent human stem cells into non-human animals at any stage of post-fertilization, fetal, or postnatal development.

i) We note that chimeric animal research has a long history and has been a scientifically essential and valid procedure for understanding cellular, tissue, and organ function, and has also served as a key pre-clinical stage of research in the evaluation of therapeutics.

ii) There are two main points of concern with chimeric animals containing human cells: the degree of the resulting chimerism and the type of tissues that are chimerized. The earlier that human cells are introduced during animal development, the greater the potential for their widespread integration during development. Introduction of a greater number of cells later in development may have an equivalent effect. In general, chimerism of the cerebral cortex or the germ-line are of greatest concern.

iii) In reviewing forms of research of this type, the SCRO mechanism or body should communicate with the appropriate mechanism or body that oversees research involving animal subjects, and give special attention to a number of issues including: A) the probable pattern and effects of differentiation and integration of the human cells into the non-human animal tissues: and B) the species of the animal, with particular scrutiny given to experiments involving non-human primates. Experiments that generate chimerism of the cerebral cortex or germ-line should be subjected to especially careful review. Although it is highly unlikely that any viable fertilization event of an animal gamete by a human gamete generated in an animal would occur, chimeric animals should typically not be allowed to produce offspring, whether by natural or artificial means. If there is a very strong scientific rationale for deriving offspring from such animals, then review committees should consider whether such an experiment might be appropriate to pursue. In any case, interbreeding of such chimeras should not be allowed, to preclude the possibility of inadvertent human-human fertilization events.

10.3) Category 3: Research that should not be pursued at this time because of broad international consensus that such experiments lack a compelling scientific rationale or raise strong ethical concerns. Such forms of research include:

10.3a) *In vitro* culture of any post-fertilization human embryos or organized cellular structures that might manifest human organismal potential, regardless of derivation method, for longer than 14 days or until formation of the primitive streak begins, whichever occurs first.

10.3b) Research in which any products of research involving human totipotent or pluripotent cells are implanted into a human or non-human primate uterus.

10.3c) Research in which animal chimeras incorporating human cells with the potential to form gametes are bred to each other.

11) PROCUREMENT OF MATERIALS

The procurement of human gametes, pre-implantation embryos, and somatic cells are integral to the conduct of human stem cell research. The international community of professional scientists conducting human stem cell research must ensure that human biological materials are procured in a manner according to globally accepted principles of research ethics. Chief among the ethical principles applicable to the conduct of human stem cell research are that persons should be empowered to make voluntary and informed decisions to participate or to refuse to participate in research. In the case of human embryonic stem cell research, the public participates by providing necessary human biological materials. Persons should be afforded a fair opportunity to participate in research, and they must be treated justly and equitably. Furthermore, privacy and confidentiality of personal information should be protected with the utmost care. Caution must also be taken to ensure that persons are not exploited during the procurement process, especially individuals who are vulnerable due to their dependent status or their compromised ability to offer fully voluntary consent. Consistent with well-established principles of justice in human subject research, there must be a reasonable relationship between those from whom such materials are received and the populations most likely to benefit from the research. Finally, the voluntary nature of the consent process must not be undermined by undue inducements or other undue influences to participate in research.

11.1) Institutional review for procurement of materials: Rigorous review, whether at the local institutional, regional, or national level, must be performed prior to the procurement of all gametes, embryos, or somatic cells that are destined for use in stem cell research. This will include the procurement of oocytes and embryos in excess of clinical need from infertility clinics, fertilized oocytes and embryos generated by IVF specifically for research purposes, and oocytes, sperm, or somatic cells donated for development of totipotent cells or pluripotent stem cell lines by parthenogenesis, androgenesis, nuclear transfer or other means of somatic cell reprogramming. Review at all levels must ensure that vulnerable populations are not exploited due to their dependent status or their compromised ability to offer fully voluntary consent, and that consent is voluntary and informed, and that there are no undue inducements or other undue influences for the provision of human materials.

11.2) Contemporaneous consent for donation: Consent for donation of materials for research should be obtained at the time of proposed transfer of materials to the research team. Only after a rigorous review by a SCRO mechanism or body can permission be granted to use materials for which prior consent exists but for which re-consent is prohibitively difficult. Consent must be obtained from all gamete donors for use of embryos in research. Donors should be informed that they retain the right to withdraw consent until the materials are actually used in research.

11.3) Informed consent: Researchers should exercise care in communicating the concept of "informed consent" to ensure that such consent has actually been obtained. The informed consent process should take into account language barriers and the educational level of the subjects themselves. In order to facilitate the adoption of sound and uniform standards of informed consent for the procurement of materials for human stem cell research, the ISSCR has made sample documents available to researchers by download from the ISSCR website (http://www.isscr.org). The samples will need to be customized for use in specific research studies.

11.3a) The informed consent document and process should cover, at a minimum, the following statements (adapted to the particular research project):

i) that the materials will be used in the derivation of totipotent or pluripotent cells for research.

ii) that the materials will be destroyed during the process of deriving totipotent or pluripotent cells for research (unless the specific research protocol aims to preserve the integrity of the research material, as in the case of embryo biopsy for procurement of blastomeres for human embryonic stem cell generation. In this circumstance, disclosure that the materials "may be destroyed" rather than "will be destroyed" would be appropriate).

iii) that derived cells and/or cell lines might be kept for many years and used for future studies, many of which may not be predictable at this time.

iv) that cells and/or cell lines might be used in research involving genetic manipulation of the cells or the generation of human-animal chimeras (resulting from the mixing of human and non-human cells in animal models).

v) that the donation is made without any restriction or direction regarding who may be the recipient of transplants of the cells derived, except in the case of autologous transplantation.

vi) whether the donation is limited to specific research purposes and not others or is for broadly stated purposes, including research not presently anticipated, in which case the consent shall notify donors, if applicable under governing law, of the possibility that permission for broader uses may later be granted and consent waived under appropriate circumstances by an ethical or institutional review board. The consent process should explore whether donors have objections to the specific forms of research outlined in the research protocol.

vii) disclosure of what donor medical or other information and what potential donor identifiers will be retained; specific steps taken to protect donor privacy and the confidentiality of retained information; and whether the identity of the donor will be readily ascertainable to those who derive or work with the resulting stem cell lines, or any other entity or person, including specifically any oversight bodies and government agencies.

viii) disclosure of the possibility that any resulting cells or cell lines may have commercial potential, and whether the donor will or will not receive financial benefits from any future commercial development.

ix) disclosure of any present or potential future financial benefits to the investigator and the institution related to or arising from proposed research.

x) that the research is not intended to provide direct medical benefit to anyone including the donor, except in the sense that research advances may benefit everyone.

xi) that neither consenting nor refusing to donate materials for research will affect the quality of care provided to potential donors.

xii) that there are alternatives to donating human materials for research, and an explanation of what these alternatives are (e.g. donation for fertility treatment, discard, etc.).

xiii) (for donation of embryos) that the embryos will not be used to produce a pregnancy, and will not be allowed to develop in culture in vitro for longer than 14 days from conception.

xiv) (for experiments in embryonic stem cell derivation, somatic cell nuclear transfer, somatic cell reprogramming, parthenogenesis, or androgenesis) that the resulting cells or stem cell lines derived would carry some or all of the DNA of the donor and therefore be partially or completely genetically matched to the donor.

11.4) Separation of informed consent for research donation from clinical treatment. To facilitate free and voluntary choice, decisions related to the donation of gametes or creation of embryos for fertility treatment should be free of the influence of investigators who propose to derive or use human embryonic stem cells in research. Wherever possible, the treating physician or infertility clinician should not also be the investigator who is proposing to perform research on the donated materials.

11.5) Additional guidelines for procurement of specific research materials:

11.5a) *For donating embryos or gametes generated in the course of clinical treatment.* Except when specifically authorized by the SCRO process, no reimbursement of direct expenses or financial considerations of any kind may be provided for donating embryos or gametes that have been generated in the course of clinical treatment and are in excess of clinical need or deemed of insufficient quality for clinical use. Researchers may not request that members of the infertility treatment team generate more embryos or harvest more oocytes than necessary for the optimal chance of reproductive success. People who elect to donate stored materials for research should not be reimbursed for the costs of storage prior to the decision to donate. Reimbursement for direct expenses incurred by donors as a consequence of the consent process may be determined during the SCRO process.

11.5b) *For provision of oocytes for research, when oocytes are collected outside the course of clinical treatment.* In locales where oocyte donation for stem cell research is allowed, the SCRO mechanism or body is responsible for conducting rigorous review of any protocol to ensure the safety and the free and informed choice of oocyte providers, according to the following principles:

i) There must be monitoring of recruitment practices to ensure that no vulnerable populations, for example, economically disadvantaged women, are disproportionately encouraged to participate as oocyte providers for research.

ii) In locales where reimbursement for research participation is allowed, there must be a detailed and rigorous review to ensure that reimbursement of direct expenses or financial considerations of any kind do not constitute an undue inducement.

iii) At no time should financial considerations of any kind be given for the number or quality of the oocytes themselves that are to be provided for research.

iv) Oocyte procurement must be performed only by medically qualified and experienced physicians, and non-aggressive hormone stimulation cycles and frequent monitoring must be used to reduce the risk of ovarian hyperstimulation syndrome (OHSS).

v) Due to the unknown long-term effects of ovulation induction, women should not undergo an excessive number of hormonally induced ovarian stimulation cycles in a lifetime, regardless of whether they are induced for research or assisted reproduction. The limits should be determined by thoughtful review during the SCRO process, which should be informed by the latest available scientific information about the health risks.

vi) There should be a provision to pay for the cost of any medical care required as a direct and proximate result of a woman's provision of oocytes for research.

vii) An infertility clinic or other third party responsible for obtaining consent or collecting materials should not be paid specifically for the material obtained, but rather for specifically defined cost-based reimbursements and payments for professional services.

11.5c) *For provision of sperm for research.* Reimbursement for direct expenses incurred by donors as a consequence of the consent process may be determined during the SCRO process.

11.5d) *For provision of somatic cells for research.* Reimbursement for direct expenses incurred by donors as a consequence of the consent process may be determined during the SCRO process.

i) In the case that the somatic cell donor is a child or a decisionally incapacitated adult, consent must be provided by a legal parent or guardian or other person authorized under applicable law.

ii) Contemporaneous consent is not necessary if researchers procure somatic cells from a tissue bank. However, somatic cells may be procured from a tissue bank only if the tissue bank's informed consent documents specifically designate nuclear transfer or other reprogramming methods for stem cell research as one of the possible uses of the donor's tissues, and only if researchers use somatic cells from tissue samples whose donors have clearly consented to this possible use.

11.6) Steps to enhance the procurement process: Attempts should be made to improve the informed consent process for human materials procurement. The informed consent document is but one aspect of this process. The purpose of the informed consent document is to record that all the ethically relevant information has been discussed. The informed consent document alone can never take the place of an interactive dialogue between research staff and providers of human materials. Researchers are thus encouraged to focus on enriching the informed consent process itself, in addition to ensuring that the informed consent document includes all of the ethically relevant information. The informed consent process can be enhanced in the following ways:

i) Whenever possible, the person conducting the informed consent dialogue should have no vested interest in the research protocol. If members of the research team participate in the informed consent process, their role must be disclosed and care must be taken to ensure that information is provided in a transparent and accurate manner.

ii) Empirical research has shown that informed consent is most effective as a dynamic, interactive, and evolving process as opposed to a static, one-time disclosure event. Thus, researchers should provide ample opportunities for providers of human materials to discuss their involvement in the research protocol.

iii) Counseling services should be made available upon request to any providers of human materials prior to procurement.

iv) Procurement procedures should be revised in light of a) ongoing studies of the long-term risks associated with oocyte retrieval; and b) research on informed consent for all types of human biological materials procurement.

v) Researchers should consider on a regular basis, subject to annual review, the possible use of alternatives to hormonally induced oocytes procured solely for stem cell research, such as oocytes derived from pluripotent stem cells, in vitro maturation of oocytes from ovariectomy samples, and egg sharing programs offered through infertility clinics.

12) PRINCIPLES FOR DERIVATION, BANKING, AND DISTRIBUTION OF HUMAN PLURIPOTENT STEM CELL LINES

Proposals for derivations of new human pluripotent stem cell lines should be scientifically justified and executed by scientists with appropriate expertise. Hand-in-hand with the privilege to perform derivations is the obligation to distribute the cell lines to the research community. A clear, detailed outline for banking and open access to the new lines should be incorporated into derivation proposals. New pluripotent stem cell lines should be made generally available as soon as possible following derivation and first publication. The ISSCR encourages researchers to deposit lines early into centralized repositories where the lines will be held for release and distribution upon publication.

12.1) Derivation of new lines

12.1a) Proposals to attempt derivation of new totipotent cells or pluripotent stem cell lines from donated pre-implantation human embryos, embryonic cells, or via nuclear reprogramming must be approved by a SCRO process. New derivations by necessity involve procurement of materials from human subjects and, therefore, will need to be approved by institutional oversight bodies with specific responsibility for protection of human subjects, as well as by the SCRO process. In some jurisdictions, the SCRO process will be formulated in a manner that encompasses all human subjects and stem cell oversight responsibilities.

12.1b) The scientific rationale for the need to derive new totipotent cells or pluripotent stem cell lines must be provided by the researcher, with justification of the numbers of pre-implantation embryos to be used. For proposals that incorporate nuclear transfer or reprogramming, an explicit scientific justification is needed and the numbers of trials to be attempted must be justified.

12.1c) Researchers must demonstrate appropriate expertise or training in the culture and maintenance of existing human embryonic stem cell lines and expertise or training in the derivation of pluripotent non-human stem cell lines before being granted permission for attempts at derivations of new human stem cell lines.

12.1d) Investigators performing derivations should have a detailed, documented plan for characterization, storage, banking and distribution of new lines.

12.1e) Embryos made via nuclear transfer, parthenogenesis, androgenesis, or other in vitro mean of embryo production shall not be transferred to a human or non-human uterus or cultured in vitro intact as embryos for longer than 14 days or until formation of the primitive streak, whichever occurs first.

12.1f) Investigators performing derivations should propose a plan to safeguard the privacy of donor information.

12.2) Banking of stem cell lines: The ISSCR encourages the establishment of national and international repositories, which are expected to accept deposits of newly derived stem cell lines and to distribute them on an international scale. In order to facilitate easy exchange and dissemination of stem cell lines, repositories should strive to form and adhere to common methods and standards; at a minimum, each repository must establish its own clear guidelines and make those available to the public. Repositories must have a clear, easily accessible material transfer agreement (MTA). . . . Each repository may have its own criteria for distribution. The repository has right of refusal if a cell line does not meet its standards. . . .

12.3) Provenance of stem cell lines: Owing to the nature of the materials involved in the generation of human stem cell lines, appropriate safeguards should be used to protect the privacy of donors and donor information. In order for the stem cell lines to be as useful as possible and so as not to preclude future potential therapeutic applications, as much donor information as possible should be maintained along with the cell line, including, but not limited to: ethnic background, medical history, and infectious disease screening. Subject to local laws, donor samples and cell lines should be de-identified (anonymized) and coded using internationally accepted standards for maintaining privacy. Informed consent and donor information will be gathered and maintained by the repository, including whatever reimbursement of direct expenses or financial considerations of any kind were provided in the course of the procurement. Documentation of the provenance of the cell lines is critical if the cell lines are to be widely employed in the research community, and the provenance must be easily verified by access to the relevant documents.

12.4) Maintenance of a database of human stem cell lines and verification of provenance: The ISSCR will curate and maintain a website listing of human stem cell lines that testifies to independent validation of the provenance of the cell lines. It will become the responsibility of the ISSCR Standards Committee to scrutinize the

documents relevant to the derivation of stem cell lines to vouch for the provenance of the cell lines, according to the principles laid out in these Guidelines.

13) DISPUTE RESOLUTION

Any conflicts of interest or other conflicts or disputes that may arise in the course of any international collaboration, for example, disagreements or difference of opinions between researchers from different countries involved in common projects, may be resolved in accordance with an agreed-upon dispute resolution mechanism in a forum with international representation from countries doing research and clinical trials in human stem cells. Members of the forum will, as appropriate, seek guidance from experts in the fields of science, ethics, law and medicine from different national, social and religious backgrounds. It is recommended that all international collaboration agreements incorporate a dispute resolution provision providing that any disputes or differences shall be settled through mediation or arbitration by international forum, and this provision shall stipulate whether or not any decision made by the forum will be binding on the relevant parties. . . .

THE PRESIDENT'S COUNCIL ON BIOETHICS

Human Cloning and Human Dignity: An Ethical Inquiry

The President's Bioethics Council was created by President George W. Bush in 2001 to "advise the President on bioethical issues that may emerge as a consequence of advances in biomedical science and technology."

THE MORAL CASE AGAINST CLONING-FOR-BIOMEDICAL-RESEARCH

Our colleagues who joined . . . in making the case for cloning-for-biomedical-research began their analysis

by describing the medical promise of such research. Those of us who maintain—for both principled and prudential reasons—that cloning-for-biomedical-research *should not* be pursued similarly begin by acknowledging that substantial human goods might be gained from this research. Although it would be wrong to speak in ways that encourage false hope in those who

Reprinted from The President's Council on Bioethics, *Human Cloning and Human Dignity: An Ethical Inquiry* (Washington, DC: 2002), chapter 6.

are ill, as if a cure were likely in the near future, we who oppose such research take seriously its potential for one day yielding substantial (and perhaps unique) medical benefits. Even apart from more distant possibilities for advances in regenerative medicine, there are more immediate possibilities for progress in basic research and for developing models to study different diseases. All of us whose lives benefit enormously from medical advances that began with basic research know how great is our collective stake in continued scientific investigations. Only for very serious reasons—to avoid moral wrongdoing, to avoid harm to society, and to avoid foolish or unnecessary risks—should progress toward increased knowledge and advances that might relieve suffering or cure disease be slowed.

We also observe, however, that the realization of these medical benefits—like all speculative research and all wagers about the future—remains uncertain. There are grounds for questioning whether the proposed benefits of cloning-for-biomedical-research will be realized. And there may be other morally unproblematic ways to achieve similar scientific results and medical benefits. For example, promising results in research with nonembryonic and adult stem cells suggest that scientists may be able to make progress in regenerative medicine without engaging in cloning-for-biomedical-research. We can move forward with other, more developed forms of human stem cell research and . . . with animal cloning. We can explore other routes for solving the immune rejection problem or to finding valuable cellular models of human disease. Where such morally innocent alternatives exist, one could argue that the burden of persuasion lies on proponents to show not only that cloned embryo research is promising or desirable but that it is *necessary* to gain the sought-for medical benefits. Indeed, the Nuremberg Code of research ethics enunciates precisely this principle—that experimentation should be "such as to yield fruitful results for the good of society, *unprocurable by other methods or means of study.*" Because of all the scientific uncertainties— and the many possible avenues of research—that burden cannot at present be met.

But, we readily concede, these same uncertainties mean that no one—not the scientists, not the moralists, and not the patients whose suffering we all hope to ameliorate—can know for certain which avenues of research will prove most successful. Research using cloned embryos may in fact, as we said above, yield knowledge and benefits unobtainable by any other means.

With such possible benefits in view, what reasons could we have for saying "no" to cloning-for-biomedical-research? Why not leave this possible avenue of medical progress open? . . .

To see the moral reality of cloning-for-biomedical-research differently, move beyond questions of immediately evident benefits or harms alone toward deeper questions about what an ongoing program of cloning-for-biomedical-research would mean. In part, this approach compels us to think about embryo research generally, but cloning (even for research purposes alone) raises its own special concerns, since only cloned embryos could one day become cloned children. . . .

Our analysis proceeds along three pathways: what we owe to the embryo; what we owe to society; and what we owe to the suffering. . . . [W]e all agree that *moral objections to the research itself* and *prudential considerations about where it is likely to lead* suggest that we should oppose cloning-for-biomedical-research, albeit with regret.

A. WHAT WE OWE TO THE EMBRYO

The embryo is, and perhaps will always be, something of a puzzle to us. In its rudimentary beginnings, it is so unlike the human beings we know and live with that it hardly seems to be one of us; yet, the fact of our own embryonic origin evokes in us respect for the wonder of emerging new human life. Even in the midst of much that is puzzling and uncertain, we would not want to lose that respect or ignore what we owe to the embryo. The cell synthesized by somatic cell nuclear transfer, no less than the fertilized egg, is a human organism in its germinal stage. It is not just a "clump of cells" but an integrated, self-developing whole, capable (if all goes well) of the continued organic development characteristic of human beings. To be sure, the embryo does not yet have, except in potential, the full range of characteristics that distinguish the human species from others, but one need not have those characteristics in evidence in order to belong to the species. And of course human beings at some other stages of development—early in life, late in life, at any stage of life if severely disabled—do not forfeit their humanity simply for want of these distinguishing characteristics. We may observe different points in the life story of any human being—a beginning filled mostly with potential, a zenith at which the organism is in full flower, a decline in which only a residue remains of what is most distinctively human. But none of these points is itself the human being. That being is, rather, an organism with a continuous history. From zygote to irreversible coma, each human life is a single personal history.

But this fact still leaves unanswered the question of whether all stages of a human being's life have equal moral standing. Might there be sound biological or moral reasons for according the early-stage embryo only *partial* human worth or even none at all? If so, should such embryos be made available or even explicitly created for research that necessarily requires their destruction—especially if very real human good might come form it? Some of us who oppose cloning-for-biomedical-research hold that efforts to assign to the embryo a merely intermediate and developing moral status—that is, more humanly significant than other human cells, but less deserving of respect and protection than a human fetus or infant—are both biologically and morally unsustainable, and that the embryo is in fact fully "one of us": a human life in process, an equal member of the species *Homo sapiens* in the embryonic stage of his or her natural development. All of us who oppose going forward with cloning-for-biomedical-research believe that it is incoherent and self-contradictory for our colleagues . . . to claim that human embryos deserve "special respect" and to endorse nonetheless research that requires the creation, use, and destruction of these organisms, *especially when done routinely and on a large scale*. The case for treating the early-stage embryo as simply the moral equivalent of all other human cells . . . is entirely unconvincing: it denies the continuous history of human individuals from zygote to fetus to infant to child; it misunderstands the meaning of potentiality—and, specifically, the difference between a "being-on-the-way" (such as a developing human embryo) and a "pile of raw materials," which has no definite potential and which might become anything at all; and it ignores the hazardous moral precedent that the routinized creation, use, and destruction of nascent human life would establish for other areas of scientific research and social life.

The more serious questions are raised—about individuality, potentiality, and "special respect"—by those who assign an intermediate and developing moral status to the human embryo, and who believe that cloned embryos can be used (and destroyed) for biomedical research while still according them special human worth. . . . But the arguments for this position—both biological and moral—are not convincing. For attempts to ground the special respect owed to a maturing embryo in certain of its developmental features do not succeed. And the invoking of a "special respect" owed to nascent human life seems to have little or no operative meaning once one sees what those who take this position are willing to countenance. We are not persuaded by the argument that fourteen days marks a significant difference in moral status. Because the embryo's human and individual genetic identity is present from the start, nothing that happens later during the continuous development that follows—at fourteen days or any other time—is responsible for suddenly conferring a novel human individuality or identity. The scientific evidence suggests that the fourteen-day marker does not represent a biological event of moral significance; rather, changes that occur at fourteen days are merely the visibly evident culmination of more subtle changes that have taken place earlier and that are driving the organism toward maturity. Indeed, many advocates of cloning-for-biomedical-research implicitly recognize the arbitrariness of the fourteen-day line. The medical benefits to be gained by conducting research beyond the fourteen-day line are widely appreciated, and some people have already hinted that this supposed moral and biological boundary can be moved should the medical benefits warrant doing so. . . .

There are also problems with the claim that its capacity for "twinning" proves that the early embryo is not yet an individual or that the embryo's moral status is more significant after the capacity for twinning is gone. There is the obvious rejoinder that if one locus of moral status can become two, its moral standing does not thereby diminish but rather increases. More specifically, the possibility of twinning does not rebut the individuality of the early embryo from its beginning. The fact that where "John" alone once was there are now both "John" and "Jim" does not call into question the presence of "John" at the outset. Hence, we need not doubt that even the earliest cloned embryo is an individual human organism in its germinal stage. Its capacity for twinning may simply be one of the characteristic capacities of an individual human organism at that particular stage of development, just as the capacity for crawling, walking, and running, or cooing, babbling, and speaking are capacities that are also unique to particular stages of human development. Alternatively, from a developmental science perspective, twinning may not turn out to be an intrinsic process within embryogenesis. Rather, it may be a response to a disruption of normal development from which the embryo recovers and then forms two. Twinning would thus be a testament to the resilience of self-regulation and compensatory repair within early life, not the lack of individuation in the early embryo. From this perspective, twinning is further testimony to the potency of the individual (in this case two) to fullness of form.

We are also not persuaded by the claim that in vitro embryos (whether created through IVF or cloning) have a lesser moral status than embryos that have been implanted into a woman's uterus, because they cannot develop without further human assistance. The suggestion that extra-corporeal embryos are not yet individual human organisms-on-the-way, but rather special human cells that acquire only through implantation the potential to become individual human organisms-on-the-way, rests on a misunderstanding of the meaning and significance of potentiality. An embryo is, by definition and by its nature, potentially a fully developed human person; its potential for maturation is a characteristic it *actually* has, and from the start. The fact that embryos have been created outside their natural environment—which is to say, outside the woman's body—and are therefore limited in their ability to realize their natural capacities, does not affect either the potential or the moral status of the beings themselves. A bird forced to live in a cage its entire life may never learn to fly. But this does not mean it is less of a bird, or that it lacks the immanent potentiality to fly on feathered wings. It means only that a caged bird—like an in vitro human embryo—has been deprived of its proper environment. There may, of course, be good human reasons to create embryos outside their natural environments—most obviously, to aid infertile couples. But doing so does not obliterate the moral status of the embryos themselves.

As we have noted, many proponents of cloning-for-biomedical-research (and for embryo research more generally) do not deny that we owe the human embryo special moral respect. Indeed, they have wanted positively to affirm it. But we do not understand what it means to claim that one is treating cloned embryos with special respect when one decides to create them intentionally for research that necessarily leads to their destruction. This respect is allegedly demonstrated by limiting such research—and therefore limiting the numbers of embryos that may be created, used, and destroyed—to only the most serious purposes: namely, scientific investigations that hold out the potential for curing diseases or relieving suffering. But this self-

limitation shows only that our purposes are steadfastly high-minded; it does not show that the *means* of pursuing these purposes are *respectful of the cloned embryos* that are necessarily violated, exploited, and destroyed in the process. To the contrary, a true respect for a being would nurture and encourage it toward its own flourishing. It is, of course, possible to have reverence for a life that one kills. This is memorably displayed, for example, by the fisherman Santiago in Ernest Hemingway's *The Old Man and the Sea*, who wonders whether it is a sin to kill fish even if doing so would feed hungry people. But it seems difficult to claim—even in theory but especially in practice—the presence of reverence once we run a stockyard or raise calves for veal—that is, once we treat the animals we kill (as we often do) simply as resources or commodities. In a similar way, we find it difficult to imagine that bio-technology companies or scientists who routinely engaged in cloning-for-biomedical-research would evince solemn respect for human life each time a cloned embryo was used and destroyed. Things we exploit even occasionally tend to lose their special value. It seems scarcely possible to preserve a spirit of humility and solemnity while engaging in routinized (and in many cases corporately competitive) research that creates, uses, and destroys them.

The mystery that surrounds the human embryo is undeniable. But so is the fact that each human person began as an embryo, and that this embryo, once formed, had the unique potential to become a unique human person. This is the meaning of our bodied condition and the biology that describes it. If we add to this description a commitment to equal treatment—the moral principle that every human life deserves our equal respect—we begin to see how difficult it must be to suggest that a human embryo, even in its most undeveloped and germinal stage, could simply be used for the good of others and then destroyed. Justifying our intention of using (and destroying) human embryos for the purpose of biomedical research would force us either to ignore the truth of our own continuing personal histories from their beginning in embryonic life or to weaken the commitment to human equality that has been so slowly and laboriously developed in our cultural history.

Equal treatment of human beings does not, of course, mean identical treatment, as all parents know who have more than one child. And from one perspective, the fact that the embryo seems to amount to so little—seems to be little more than a clump of cells—invites us to suppose that its claims upon us can also not amount to much. We are, many have noted, likely to grieve the death of an embryo less than the death of a newborn child. But, then, we are also likely to grieve the death of an eighty-five-year-old father less than the death of a forty-five-year-old father. Perhaps, even, we may grieve the death of a newborn child less than the death of a twelve-year-old. We might grieve differently at the death of a healthy eighty-year-old than at the death of a severely demented eighty-year-old. Put differently, we might note how even the researcher in the laboratory may react with excitement and anticipation as cell division begins. Thus, reproductive physiologist Robert Edwards, who, together with Dr. Patrick Steptoe, helped produce Louise Brown, the first "test-tube baby," said of her: "The last time I saw her, she was just eight cells in a test-tube. She was beautiful then, and she's still beautiful now." The embryo seems to amount to little; yet it has the capacity to become what to all of us seems very much indeed. There is a trajectory to the life story of human beings, and it is inevitable—and appropriate—that our emotional responses should be different at different points in that trajectory. Nevertheless, these emotions, quite naturally and appropriately different, would be misused if we calibrated the degree of respect we owe each other on the basis of such responses. In fact, we are obligated to try to shape and form our emotional responses—and our moral sentiments—so that they are more in accord with the moral respect we owe to those whose capacities are least developed (or those whom society may have wrongly defined as "nonpersons" or "nonentities").

In short, how we respond to the weakest among us, to those who are nowhere near the zenith of human flourishing, says much about our willingness to envision the boundaries of humanity expansively and inclusively. It challenges—in the face of what we can know and what we cannot know about the human embryo—the depth of our commitment to equality. If from one perspective the fact that the embryo seems to amount to little may invite a weakening of our respect, from another perspective its seeming insignificance should awaken in us a sense of shared humanity. This was once our own condition. From origins that seem so little came our kin, our friends, our fellow citizens, and all human beings,

whether known to us or not. In fact, precisely because the embryo seems to amount to so little, our responsibility to respect and protect its life correspondingly increases. . . .

B. WHAT WE OWE TO SOCIETY

Having acknowledged all that, we would miss something if we stopped with what is owed to the embryo—with the language of respect, claims, or rights. An embryo may seem to amount to little or nothing, but that very insignificance tests not the embryo's humanity but our own. Even those who are uncertain about the precise moral status of the human embryo—indeed, even those who believe that it has only intermediate and developing status—have sound ethical-prudential reasons to refrain from using embryos for utilitarian purposes. Moreover, when the embryos to be used have been produced by cloning, there are additional moral dilemmas that go beyond the ethics of embryo research alone. There are principled reasons why people who *accept* research on leftover IVF embryos created initially for reproductive purposes should *oppose* the creation and use of cloned embryos explicitly for research. And there are powerful reasons to worry about where this research will lead us. All these objections have their ground not only in the embryo's character but also in our own, and in concern not only for the fate of nascent human life but for the moral well-being of society as a whole. *One need not believe the embryo is fully human to object vigorously to cloning-for-biomedical-research.*

We are concerned especially about three ways in which giving our moral approval to such research would harm the character of our common life and the way of life we want to transmit to future generations: (i) by crossing the boundary from sexual to asexual reproduction, in the process approving, whether recognized or not, genetic manipulation and control of nascent human life; (ii) by allowing and endorsing the complete instrumentalization of human embryos; and (iii) by opening the door to other—for some of us, far greater—moral hazards, such as cloning-to-produce-children or research on later-stage human embryos and fetuses.

1. ASEXUAL REPRODUCTION AND THE GENETIC MANIPULATION OF EMBRYOS

It is worth noting that human cloning—including cloning-for-biomedical-research itself and not simply cloning-to-produce-children—would cross a natural boundary between sexual and asexual reproduction, reducing the likelihood that we could either retrace our steps or keep from taking further steps. Cloning-for-biomedical-research and cloning-to-produce-children both begin with the same act of cloning: the production of a human embryo that is genetically virtually identical to its progenitor. The cloned embryo would therefore be the first human organism with a single genetic "parent" and, equally important, with a genetic constitution that is known and selected in advance. Both uses of cloning mark a significant leap in human power and human control over our genetic origins. Both involve deliberate genetic manipulation of nascent human life. It is, of course, precisely this genetic control that makes cloned embryos uniquely appealing and perhaps uniquely useful to those who seek to conduct research on them. But we should not be deceived about what we are agreeing to if we agree to start to clone: saying yes to cloned embryos in laboratories means saying yes *in principle* to an ever-expanding genetic mastery of one generation over the next.

2. THE COMPLETE INSTRUMENTALIZATION OF NASCENT HUMAN LIFE

By approving the production of cloned embryos for the sole purpose of research, society would transgress yet another moral boundary: that separating the different ways in which embryos might become available for human experimentation. It is one thing, as some have argued, to conduct research on leftover embryos from IVF procedures, which were created in attempts to have a child and, once no longer needed or wanted, are "destined" for destruction in any case. It is quite another to create embryos *solely* for research that will unavoidably and necessarily destroy them. Thus, for example, the National Bioethics Advisory Commission (in its report on stem cell research) reasoned that in circumstances where embryos were going to be discarded anyway, it did not undermine the moral respect owed to them if they were destroyed in one way (through research) rather than another (by being discarded when no longer wanted for IVF). By contrast, the Commission reasoned that it was much harder to embrace the language of respect for the embryo if it were produced solely for purposes of research and, having been used, then destroyed. This argument maintained the following moral and practical distinction: that embryos created for reproduction but no longer desired could, with proper consent, be used as research subjects, but that embryos ought not be produced solely in order to be used as research subjects. So long as we

oppose morally and may perhaps one day prohibit legally the production of cloned children, it is in the very nature of the case that cloned human embryos will not be acquirable as "spare" embryos left over from attempts at reproduction. To the contrary, they will have to be produced solely and explicitly for the purpose of biomedical research, with no other end in view.

Some have argued that there is no significant moral difference between creating excess IVF embryos for reproduction *knowing in advance* that some will be discarded and creating cloned embryos for research *that leads necessarily* to their destruction. Because in both cases embryos are wittingly destroyed, there is, so the argument goes, no moral difference here.

When viewed simply in terms of the fates of embryos once they are created, the distinction between using leftover embryos and creating embryos solely for research may indeed be morally insignificant. But when viewed in terms of the different effects these two activities might have on the moral fabric of society— and the different moral dispositions of those who decide to produce embryos for these different purposes—the issue is more complex. In the eyes of those who create IVF embryos to produce a child, *every embryo*, at the moment of its creation, is *a potential child*. Even though more eggs are fertilized than will be transferred to a woman, each embryo is brought into being as an end in itself, not simply as a means to other ends. Precisely because one cannot tell which IVF embryo is going to reach the blastocyst stage, implant itself in the uterine wall, and develop into a child, the embryo "wastage" in IVF is more analogous to the embryo wastage in natural sexual intercourse practiced by a couple trying to get pregnant than it is to the creation and use of embryos that requires (without exception) their destruction.

Those who minimize or deny this distinction— between producing embryos hoping that one of them will become a child and producing embryos so that they can be used (and destroyed) in research—demonstrate the very problem we are worried about. Having become comfortable with seeing embryos as a means to noble ends (be it having a child or conducting biomedical research), they have lost sight of the fact that the embryos that we create as potential children are not means at all. Even those who remain agnostic about whether the human embryo is fully one of us should see the ways in which conducting such research would make us a different society: less humble toward that which we cannot fully understand, less willing to extend the boundaries of human respect ever outward, and more willing to transgress moral boundaries that we have, ourselves, so recently established, once it appears to be in our own interests to do so. We find it disquieting, even somewhat ignoble, to treat what are in fact seeds of the next generation as mere raw material for satisfying the needs of our own. Doing so would undermine the very prudence and humility to which defenders of limited embryo research often appeal: the idea that, while a human embryo may not be fully one of us, it is not humanly nothing and therefore should not be treated as a resource alone. But that is precisely what cloning-for-biomedical-research would do.

3. OPENING THE DOOR TO OTHER MORAL HAZARDS

This leads directly to our third concern—that the cloning of human embryos for research will open the door to additional (and to some of us, far greater) moral hazards. Human suffering from horrible diseases never comes to an end, and, likewise, our willingness to use embryonic life in the cause of research, once permitted, is also unlikely to find any natural stopping point. To set foot on this slope is to tempt ourselves to become people for whom the use of nascent human life as research material becomes routinized and everyday. That much is inherent in the very logic of what we would do in cloning-for-biomedical-research. In addition, the reasons justifying production of cloned embryos for research can be predicted to expand. Today, the demand is for stem cells; tomorrow it may be for embryonic and fetal organs. The recent experiments with cloned cow embryos implanted in a cow's uterus already suggest that there may be greater therapeutic potential using differentiated tissues (for example, kidney primordia) harvested from early fetuses than using undifferentiated stem cells taken from the very early embryo. Should this prove to be the case, pressure will increase to grow cloned human blastocysts to later stages—either in the uteruses of suitably prepared animal hosts or (eventually) using artificial placenta-like structures in the laboratory—in order to obtain the more useful tissues. One can even imagine without difficulty how a mother might be willing to receive into her womb as a temporary resident the embryonic clone of her desperately ill child, in order to harvest for that child life-saving organs or tissues. In such ways the coarsening of our moral sensibilities can be the fruit of understandable desires.

Indeed, to refuse such further steps in the name of moral wisdom might come to seem increasingly sentimental, and, even if we were reluctant to give our approval, we might be hard-pressed to say why.

We should not be self-deceived about our ability to set limits on the exploitation of nascent life. What disturbs us today we quickly or eventually get used to; yesterday's repugnance gives way to tomorrow's endorsement. A society that already tolerates the destruction of fetuses in the second and third trimesters will hardly be horrified by embryo and fetus farming (including in animal wombs), if this should turn out to be helpful in the cure of dreaded diseases.

We realize, of course, that many proponents of cloning-for-biomedical-research will recommend regulations designed to prevent just such abuses (that is, the expansion of research to later-stage cloned embryos and fetuses). Refusing to erect a red light to stop research cloning, they will propose various yellow lights intended to assure ourselves that we are proceeding with caution, limits, or tears. Paradoxically, however, the effect might actually be to encourage us to continue proceeding with new (or more hazardous) avenues of research; for, believing that we are being cautious, we have a good conscience about what we do, and we are unable to imagine ourselves as people who could take a morally disastrous next step. We are neither wise enough nor good enough to live without clear limits.

Cloning-for-biomedical-research could require thousands of human eggs and would, as presently contemplated, give rise, as we have said, to a new industry of embryo manufacture. This industry would depend on eggs procured from women, themselves participants in the research, who would need to take drugs stimulating ovulation and to submit to the egg retrieval procedure.

One might wonder whether their informed consent is sufficient to permit this in circumstances where, in the very nature of the case, the research is so preliminary that it cannot possibly provide effective therapies for patients. We might also worry lest women who are potential donors (because, for example, they have sought in vitro fertilization) might be vulnerable to pressure to participate in this research or financial inducements to do so. Even if such pressure does not rise to the level of coercion, we should acknowledge that there are inducements a just society would not offer and risks it would not ask potential research subjects—themselves vulnerable for a variety of reasons—to accept. To get around the shortage of human eggs and the ethical dilemmas it could produce, scientists are exploring the possibility of substituting animal eggs in the initial cloning step of SCNT. Experiments creating animal-human hybrid-embryos, produced by inserting human DNA into enucleated rabbit oocytes, have already been conducted in China, with development up to the blastocyst stage. Yet far from solving our ethical dilemma, the use of animal eggs raises new concerns about animal-human hybrids. We have no idea where these and later interspecies experiments might lead. Yet the creation of such chimeras, even in embryonic form, shows how ready we seem to be to blur further the boundary—biological and moral—between human being and animal.

Finally, if we accept even limited uses of cloning-for-biomedical-research, we significantly increase the likelihood of cloning-to-produce-children. The technique will gradually be perfected and the cloned embryos will become available, and those who would be interested in producing cloned children will find it much easier to do so. The only way to prevent this from happening would be to prohibit, by law, the implantation of cloned embryos for the purpose of producing children. To do so, however, the government would find itself in the unsavory position of designating a class of embryos that it would be a felony not to destroy. It would *require*, not just permit, the destruction of cloned embryos—which seems to us the very opposite of showing such cloned embryos "special respect."

4. CONCLUSION: WHAT PRUDENCE REQUIRES

As history so often demonstrates, powers gained for one purpose are often used for other, less noble ones. We are about to harness powers over our own (human) nature to be used for our own well-intentioned purposes. But the knowledge that provides this power does not teach us how to use it. And given our fallibility, that should give us pause. We should consider, in making our moral judgment about cloning-for-biomedical-research, not simply the origin of these cells, but their possible uses (and misuses), as well as their place in the larger story of our increasing technological powers. We must keep in mind not simply where we took these cells from, but where they might take us, and what might be done with them.

In light of these moral and prudential dangers—namely, the crossing of the boundary from sexual to asexual reproduction; the possible misuse of our new genetic powers over embryonic life; the reduction of human embryos to nothing more than a resource and the coarsening of our moral sensibilities that would

come with it, the prospect of a law that would mandate the destruction of nascent human life; and the prospect of other (greater) harms down the road, most notably the production of cloned children, research on later-stage fetuses, or genetic engineering of future generations—we must take pause and resist. In trying to discern where a wise and prudent boundary must be drawn—to protect those beings who are humanly inviolable, to prevent the dangers that most tempt us, and to protect the moral fabric of society—we hold that the boundary must be drawn by prohibiting the production and use of cloned embryos. To cross this boundary or to set it further down the road—that is, "with limits"—is to invite (and perhaps ensure) that some (or all) of the dehumanizing possibilities described above will come to pass.

C. WHAT WE OWE TO THE SUFFERING

The final question to be considered is what we owe to the suffering. Like our colleagues who endorse cloning-for-biomedical-research, we believe it would be less than human to turn a blind eye to those who suffer and need relief, or to stand silent in the face (especially) of suffering and premature death. In saying "no" to cloning-for-biomedical-research, we are not closing the door on medical progress—not in principle and not in practice. We are simply acknowledging that, for very strong moral reasons, progress must come by means that do not involve the production, use, and destruction of cloned embryos and that do not reduce nascent human life to a resource for our exploitation. This does mean, of course, that advances in basic research and progress in the cure of disease, though not halted, might be slowed (though, as described above, this is far from certain on scientific grounds). It is possible that some might suffer in the future because research proceeded more slowly. We cannot suppose that the moral life comes without cost. And honesty compels us not to offer guarantees where our human limits—and the unpredictable nature of the future—ensure that no such assurances are possible.

There may be occasions in life when the only means available for achieving a desired end is a means that it would be wrong to employ. This is especially true in circumstances such as those considered here; for to give our initial approval to cloning-for-biomedical-research is to set foot on a path whose deepest implications can scarcely be calculated. People sometimes imagine that human beings are responsible for all the harms they could prevent but do not; yet, this cannot be true. When we refuse to achieve a good outcome by doing what is wrong, and thereby perhaps accept some suffering that might have been avoided, we are not guilty of causing that suffering. To say otherwise would mean that sufficiently evil men could always hold us morally hostage. In order to obligate us to do an evil deed, they need only credibly threaten to do great harm unless we comply. Were we actually responsible for all the harm we might have prevented but did not, they would have us in their moral power. If our duty to prevent harm and suffering were always overriding, if it always held moral trump, we could not live nobly and justly.

We are not deaf to the voices of those who desperately want biomedical research to proceed. Indeed, we can feel the force of that desire ourselves, for all of us—and those we love most—are or could one day be patients desperate for a cure. But we are not only patients or potential patients. We are human beings and citizens, and we know that relief of suffering, though a great good, is not the greatest good. As highly as we value health and longer life, we know that life itself loses its value if we care only for *how long* we live, and not also for *how* we live.

Suppose, then, that we refrain from such research and that future sufferers say to us: "You might have helped us by approving cloning for research, but you declined to do so." What could we say to them? Something like the following: "Yes, perhaps so. But we could have done so only by destroying, in the present, the sort of world in which both we and you want to live—a world in which, as best we can, we respect human life and human individuals, the weak and the strong. To have done it would have meant stepping across boundaries that are essential to our humanity. And, although we very much want to leave to our children a world in which suffering can be more effectively relieved, that is not all we want to leave them. We want to bequeath to them a world that honors moral limits, a world in which the good of some human lives is not entirely subordinated to the good of others, a world in which we seek to respect, as best we can, the time each human being has and the place each fills."

This understanding of what commitment to our shared humanity requires is not alien to the efforts of scientific researchers to make progress in the cure of disease and relief of suffering. Theirs is, after all, a moral mission, which serves us all and which we all support. But if history teaches anything, it is the danger of assuming that, because our motives are praiseworthy and our hope is to heal, our actions cannot possibly violate or diminish human well-being. Indeed, we may be least likely to see the dangers when we are most confident of the goodness of our cause. Scientists already accept important moral boundaries in research on human subjects, and they do not regard such boundaries as unwarranted restrictions on the freedom of scientific research. More generally, the scientific enterprise is a moral one not only because of the goals scientists seek but also because of the limits they honor. Indeed, it is precisely the acceptance of limits that stimulates creative advance that forces scientists to conceive of new and morally acceptable ways of conducting research. Surely, therefore, before society takes a step that cannot be undone, it should ponder soberly the moral implications of accepting cloning, even for research. . . .

When we consider what we owe to the embryo, to our society, and to the suffering, we can see it more clearly and can, perhaps, acquire the wisdom and even the courage not to put this cup to our lips.

CONCLUSION

In this chapter, Council Members have presented as best we can the moral cases for and against cloning-for-biomedical-research, seen in the contexts of efforts to heal the sick; present and projected developments in reproductive, developmental, and genetic biotechnology; and the moral concerns for nascent life and the moral well-being of American society. Our different moral outlooks and judgments have been preserved and, we hope, clarified. We are now ready to move from ethics to public policy, in search of the best course of action regarding human cloning.

MARK GREENE, ET AL. [1]

Moral Issues of Human–Non-Human Primate Neural Grafting

Mark Greene is Assistant Professor of Philosophy at the University of Delaware. Originally trained in veterinary science, he has a doctoral degree in philosophy and post-graduate training in bioethics. His philosophical work centers on bioethics, with interests also in ethical theory, philosophy of biology, and philosophy of language and metaphysics.

If human neural stem cells were implanted into the brains of other primates what might this do to the mind of the recipient? Could such grafting teach us anything of value for treatment of neurological injury and disease? Could we change the capacities of the engrafted animal in a way that leads us to reexamine its moral status? These questions have gained significance since publication of research involving grafting human neural stem cells into the brains of fetal monkeys. . . .

[1]This paper is the product of the Working Group on Interspecific Chimeric Brains, a collaboration of scientists, philosophers, physicians, and lawyers drawn from multiple universities addressing the scientific and moral implications of stem cell research with non-human primates, deriving from a funded project at the Phoebe R. Berman Bioethics Institute, Johns Hopkins University, and supported by a grant from the Greenwall Foundation. Other members of the Working Group, who were also co-authors on this article, included Kathryn E. Schill (Johns Hopkins University), Shoji Takahashi (Johns Hopkins University), Alison S. Bateman-House (Johns Hopkins University), Tom Beauchamp (Georgetown University), Hilary Bok (Johns Hopkins University), Dorothy Cheney (University of Pennsylvania), Joseph T. Coyle Harvard University), Terrence Deacon University of California, Berkeley), Daniel C. Dennett (Tufts University), Peter Donovan (University of California, Irvine), Owen Flanagan (Duke University), Steven Goldman (University of Rochester), Henry Greely (Stanford University), Lee Martin (Johns Hopkins University), Earl Miller (Massachusetts Institute of Technology), Dawn Mueller (University of Maryland, Baltimore), Andrew Siegel (Johns Hopkins University), Davor Solter (Max Planck Institute of Immunobiology), John Gearhart (Johns Hopkins University), Guy McKhann (Johns Hopkins University), and Ruth R. Faden (Johns Hopkins University).

Some group members have serious ethical concerns over *any* use of nonhuman primates in invasive research. However, we set aside broader controversies to focus on ethical challenges specific to human–to–non-human primate (H-NHP) neural grafting. . . .

There is considerable controversy . . . over the likely value of interspecies stem cell work for progress toward therapies. We cannot graft human neural stem cells into human beings solely for experimental purposes, even if they will lead to human therapies. Group members arguing for the value of research on human cells in NHPs pointed out that, because the aim is to learn about human neural stem cells, it makes most sense to use human lines. The fact that available NHP lines are few and poorly characterized is an additional reason to use human lines. Another consideration is the need to assess candidate human cell lines for viability, potential to differentiate, and safety with regard to such possibilities as tumor formation. NHPs may be appropriate for in vivo screening.

Skeptics argued that differences between humans and NHPs could render results uninterpretable and that the preferred path for many questions is to study NHP neural stem cells in NHPs. Assessments of the scientific merit of the research must form and develop along with the field itself.

We unanimously rejected ethical objections grounded on unnaturalness or crossing species boundaries. Whether it is possible to draw a meaningful distinction between the natural and the unnatural is a matter of dispute. However, stipulating that research is "unnatural" says nothing about its ethics. Much of modern medical practice involves tools, materials, and behaviors that cannot be found in nature but are not unethical as a consequence

Another concern is that H-NHP neural grafting is wrong because it transgresses species boundaries. However, . . . the notion that there are fixed species boundaries is not well supported in science or philosophy. Moreover, human–nonhuman chimerism has already occurred through xenografting. For example, the safety and efficacy of engrafting fetal pig cells has been studied in people with Parkinson's disease and Huntington's disease without moral objection. Indeed, some have suggested that porcine sources may be less morally contentious than the use of human fetal tissue. Merely because something has been done does not prove it right. However, we, like the National Academy, see "no new ethical or regulatory issues regarding chimeras themselves."[1]

The central challenge is whether introducing human cells into NHP brains raises questions about moral status. A variety of reasons have been given for according different moral standing to humans and NHPs. . . .

Many of the most plausible and widely accepted candidates for determining moral status involve mental capacities such as the ability to feel pleasure and pain, language, rationality, and richness of relationships. To the extent that a NHP attains those capacities, that creature must be held in correspondingly high moral standing. There are those . . . who believe that we already overestimate differences in relevant mental capacities, and thus of moral status between humans and NHPs. But the issue here is the extent to which human/NHP neural grafting might change capacities in a way that changes moral status.

Although we cannot assess altered capacities by experiencing an animal's mental life from within, we can assess its performance on cognitive tasks and observe its behavior. Establishing whether and in what ways engrafted animals undergo cognitive or behavioral changes requires an understanding of what the normal range is for a particular NHP species. Unfortunately, our understanding of NHP cognitive capacities is patchy, data are tricky to gather and difficult to interpret. . . . Thus, even if we observe what appear to be more humanlike capacities in an engrafted animal, we may be unable either to establish whether the capacities are outside of the normal range for that species, or to interpret the moral meaning of observed changes.

One conceivable result of H-NHP neural grafting is that the resulting creature will develop humanlike cognitive capacities relevant to moral status. H-NHP neural grafting may not be unique in having the potential to alter the capacities of NHPs. Chimps reared with humans behave in a more humanlike way than chimps reared by chimps. Transfer between species of predispositions relating to auditory perception was found after transplantation of already formed portions of brain tissue. Introduction of human neural progenitor cells into developing mouse brains resulted in widespread incorporation of human neural progenitor cells; but behavioral alterations were not reported. Although such results are not reasons to think it likely, one unanimous conclusion of our group is that we are unable to rule out the possibility of effects on cognition of the sort that matter to moral status.

One option is to treat any development of more humanlike cognitive capacities as a risk to avoid. Alternatively, it might be argued that the challenge is less to avoid a direct ethical ill and more to understand the mental capacities of engrafted animals and to treat them in a manner appropriate to their moral status. Indeed, it might even be argued that such changes constitute a potential benefit to the engrafted animal, insofar as the changes are viewed as enhancements of the sort we value for ourselves. However, these more humanlike capacities might also confer greater capacity for suffering that would add to existing concerns about the harms caused by inadequate conditions for NHPs in research.

We propose six factors that research oversight committees and other review groups should use as a starting framework. They are (i) proportion of engrafted human cells, (ii) neural development, (iii) NHP species, (iv) brain size, (v) site of integration, and (vi) brain pathology.

Though even a few engrafted cells may affect neural activity, we expect that a higher proportion of engrafted human cells relative to host cells will increase the prospect of more humanlike neural function and, thus, of more humanlike cognitive capacities. High proportions of engrafted cells are more likely to be achieved by implantation early in neural development.

We also expect that the potential for engrafted cells to have significant functional influence will be markedly greater for engraftment at very early stages of development than for engraftment into the established architecture of adult brains. Although neural progenitor cells engrafted into the neonatal primate brain disseminate widely and integrate throughout the brain, the mature primate brain tends to resist incorporation of engrafted cells.

MARK GREENE ET AL.   751

A graft recipient's degree of relatedness to our own species may matter for several reasons. Genetics contribute to brain structure by providing the protein building blocks that shape neurons and their interconnections. Factors such as cell surface markers and the mechanisms of cellular signaling are more similar in our closer relations. Also, although the picture is complicated by lifestyle similarities that cut across phylogenetic groups, our closest relatives among NHPs tend to show greater neuroanatomic similarities to human brain structures.

Also related to recipient species is brain size. It is unlikely that the structural complexity needed for any significant degree of humanlike mental capacity can be achieved under tight size limitations. However, brain size influences the size of the developing cranium, an effect seen naturally in hydrocephalus. Thus, a fetal marmoset engrafted with human neural cells might, to some extent, develop a larger brain than is typical for the species.

The specific sites into which the human neural cells become integrated within the recipient brain is also of potential significance. Functional integration into the cerebrum, which is associated with higher brain functions, seems more likely to affect cognitive capacities than does integration into the cerebellum; although engrafted neural cells may migrate and project to disparate brain areas.

Overall, we think it unlikely that the grafting of human cells into healthy adult NHPs will result in significant changes in morally relevant mental capacities. However, in the case of NHP models of human neurological disease and injury, adult recipients of human neural cells may have extensive disruption to their neural structures that might allow greater scope for engrafted human neural cells to affect cognitive capacities. We do not consider this a strong possibility, because diseased or injured brains will be starting from an impaired state from which even a return to species' normal functional levels is unlikely. However, the therapeutic point is to reinstate lost function, and we cannot be certain that this will be the only functional result of interspecies neural grafting. Furthermore, some of the disorders likely to be of interest (such as Alzheimer's) involve higher-level cognitive capacities.

There is no simple relation between these factors and, thus, no formula for making evaluative judgments.

Considering issues of moral status that go beyond the ethical challenges attending any invasive NHP work, our framework suggests that experiments of greatest concern are those in which human neural stem cells are engrafted into the developing brains of great apes and constitute a large proportion of the engrafted brain. On the basis of this concern, and on doubts about scientific merit, some of us believe that engraftment of human neural cells into great apes should not be permitted, particularly early in neural development. Others argue against outright prohibition on grounds that scientific justifications might be forthcoming as the field progresses. For example, if a useful great ape model of a neurological disease is developed, and a promising human neural stem cell line is ready for use, there might be reason to proceed with human–great ape work, rather than waiting to develop great ape lines. Our framework suggests that experiments involving engraftment into healthy adult brains of our most distant monkey relations, especially when the proportion of engrafted cells is small relative to host cells, are the least likely to raise concerns about significant cognitive effects. However, especially as we consider experiments involving implantation of relatively large numbers of human cells early in development, there is no present empirical basis on which to rule out changes that might implicate moral status, whether the engrafted NHPs are great apes or monkeys.

In view of the challenges arising from moral status, we support the National Academy's recommendation that H-NHP neural grafting experiments be subject to special review. We agree that such review should complement, not replace, current review by animal-use panels and institutional review boards. We further recommend that experiments involving H-NHP neural grafting be required, wherever possible, to look for and report changes in cognitive function. Explicit data collection on cognition and behavior will help to ensure that ethical guidelines can be developed appropriately as the field advances.

NOTE

1. Committee on Guidelines for Human Embryonic Stem Cell Research, "Guidelines for Human Embryonic Stem Cell Research" (National Research Council, National Academy of Science, Washington. DC. 2005); 33.

GARY COMSTOCK

Ethics and Genetically Modified Foods

Gary Comstock is Professor of Philosophy and Director of the Research and Professional Ethics Program at North Carolina State University. Professor Comstock's most recent book is *Vexing Nature? On the Ethical Case Against Agricultural Biotechnology.* His current work focuses on the central dogma of the humanities, that humans are *singular* among earthly life forms.

Much of the food consumed in the United States is genetically modified (GM). GM food derives from microorganisms, plants, or animals manipulated at the molecular level to have traits that farmers or consumers desire. These foods often have been produced by techniques in which "foreign" genes are inserted into the microorganisms, plants, or animals. Foreign genes are genes taken from sources other than the organism's natural parents. In other words, GM plants contain genes they would not have contained if researchers had used only traditional plant breeding methods.

Some consumer advocates object to GM foods, and sometimes they object on ethical grounds. When people oppose GM foods on ethical grounds, they typically have some reason for their opposition. . . .

Ethically justifiable conclusions inevitably rest on two types of claims: (i) empirical claims, or factual assertions about how the world *is*, claims ideally based on the best available scientific observations, principles, and theories; and (ii) normative claims, or value-laden assertions about how the world *ought to be*, claims ideally based on the best available moral judgments, principles, and theories.

Is it ethically justifiable to pursue GM crops and foods? There is an objective answer to this question, and we will try here to figure out what it is. But we must begin with a proper, heavy dose of epistemic humility, acknowledging that few ethicists at the moment seem to think they know the final answer.

Should the law allow GM foods to be grown and marketed? The answer to this, and every, public policy question rests ultimately with us, citizens who will in the voting booth and shopping market decide the answer. To make up our minds, we will use feelings, intuitions, conscience, and reason. However, as we citizens are, by and large, not scientists, we must, to one degree or other, rest our factual understanding of the matter on the opinions of scientific experts.

Therefore, ethical responsibility in the decision devolves heavily on scientists engaged in the new GM technology.

ETHICAL RESPONSIBILITIES OF SCIENTISTS

Science is a communal process devoted to the discovery of knowledge and to open and honest communication of knowledge. Its success, therefore, rests on two different kinds of values.

Epistemological values are values by which scientists determine which knowledge claims are better than others. The values include clarity, objectivity, capacity to explain a range of observations, and ability to generate accurate predictions. Claims that are internally inconsistent are jettisoned in favor of claims that are consistent and fit with established theories. (At times, anomalous claims turn out to be justifiable, and an established theory is overthrown, but these occasions are rare in the history of science.) Epistemological values in science also include fecundity, the ability to generate useful new hypotheses; simplicity, the ability to explain observations with the fewest number of additional assumptions or qualifications; and elegance.

Personal values, including honesty and responsibility, are a second class of values—values that allow scientists to trust their peers' knowledge claims. If scientists are dishonest, untruthful, fraudulent, or excessively self-interested, the free flow of accurate information so essential to science will be thwarted. . . .

The very institution of scientific discovery is supported—indeed, permeated—with values. Scientists have a variety of goals and functions in society, so it should be no surprise that they face different challenges. . . .

At its core, science is an expression of some of our most cherished values. The public largely trusts scientists, and scientists must in turn act as good stewards of this trust. . . .

ETHICAL ISSUES INVOLVED IN THE USE OF GENETIC TECHNOLOGY IN AGRICULTURE

Discussions of the ethical dimensions of agricultural biotechnology are sometimes confused by a conflation of two quite different sorts of objections to GM technology: intrinsic and extrinsic. It is critical not only that we distinguish these two classes but that we keep them distinct throughout the ensuing discussion of ethics.

Extrinsic objections focus on the potential harms consequent upon the adoption of GM organisms (GMOs). Extrinsic objections hold that GM technology should not be pursued because of its anticipated results. Briefly stated, the extrinsic objections go as follows. GMOs may have disastrous effects on animals, ecosystems, and humans. Possible harms to humans include perpetuation of social inequities in modern agriculture, decreased food security for women and children on subsistence farms in developing countries, a growing gap between well-capitalized economies in the northern hemisphere and less capitalized peasant economies in the South, risks to the food security of future generations, and the promotion of reductionistic and exploitative science. Potential harms to ecosystems include possible environmental catastrophe; inevitable narrowing of germplasm diversity; and irreversible loss or degradation of air, soils, and waters. Potential harms to animals include unjustified pain to individuals used in research and production.

These are valid concerns, and nation-states must have in place testing mechanisms and regulatory agencies to assess the likelihood, scope, and distribution of potential harms through a rigorous and well-funded risk assessment procedure. It is for this reason that I said above that GM technology must be developed responsibly and with appropriate caution. However, these extrinsic objections cannot by themselves justify a moratorium, much less a permanent ban, on GM technology, because they admit the possibility that the harms may be minimal and outweighed by the benefits. How can one decide whether the potential harms outweigh potential benefits unless one conducts the research, field tests, and data analysis necessary to make a scientifically informed assessment?

In sum, extrinsic objections to GMOs raise important questions about GMOs, and each country using GMOs ought to have in place the organizations and research structures necessary to ensure their safe use.

There is, however, an entirely different sort of objection to GM technology, a sort of objection that, if it is sound, would justify a permanent ban.

Intrinsic objections allege that the process of making GMOs is objectionable *in itself*. This belief is defended in several ways, but almost all the formulations are related to one central claim, the unnaturalness objection:

It is unnatural to genetically engineer plants, animals, and foods (**UE**).

If **UE** is true, then we ought not to engage in bioengineering, however unfortunate may be the consequences of halting the technology. Were a nation to accept **UE** as the conclusion of a sound argument, then much agricultural research would have to be terminated and potentially significant benefits from the technology sacrificed. A great deal is at stake.

[There are] 14 ways in which **UE** has been defended. For present purposes, those 14 objections can be summarized as follows:

(i) To engage in ag biotech is to *play God*.
(ii) To engage in ag biotech is to *invent world-changing technology*.
(iii) To engage in ag biotech is *illegitimately to cross species boundaries*.
(iv) To engage in ag biotech is to *commodify life*.

Let us consider each claim in turn.

(i) To engage in ag biotech is to *play God*.

In a western theological framework, humans are creatures, subjects of the Lord of the Universe, and it would be impious for them to arrogate to themselves roles and powers appropriate only for the Creator. Shifting genes around between individuals and species is taking on a task not appropriate for us, subordinate beings. Therefore, to engage in bioengineering is to play God.

There are several problems with this argument. First, there are different interpretations of God. Absent the guidance of any specific religious tradition, it is logically possible that God could be a Being who wants to turn over to us all divine prerogatives, or explicitly wants to turn over to us at least the prerogative of engineering plants, or who doesn't care what we do. If God is any of these beings, then the argument fails because playing God in this instance is not a bad thing.

The argument seems to assume, however, that God is not like any of the gods just described. Assume that the orthodox Jewish and Christian view of God is correct, that God is the only personal, perfect, necessarily existing, all-loving, all-knowing, and all-powerful being. On this traditional western theistic view, finite humans should not aspire to infinite knowledge and power. To the extent that bioengineering is an attempt to control nature itself, the argument would go, bioengineering would be an unacceptable attempt to usurp God's dominion.

The problem with this argument is that not all traditional Jews and Christians think this God would rule out genetic engineering . . . tradition[ally]. God is thought to endorse creativity and scientific and technological development, including genetic improvement. Other traditions have similar views. In the mystical writings of the Jewish Kabbalah, God is understood as One who expects humans to be co-creators, technicians working with God to improve the world. At least one Jewish philosopher, Baruch Brody, has suggested that biotechnology may be a vehicle ordained by God for the perfection of nature.

I personally hesitate to think that humans can perfect nature. However, I have become convinced that GM might help humans to rectify some of the damage we have already done to nature. And I believe God may endorse such an aim. For humans are made in the divine image. God desires that we exercise the spark of divinity within us. Inquisitiveness in science is part of our nature. Creative impulses are not found only in the literary, musical, and plastic arts. They are part of molecular biology, cellular theory, ecology, and evo-

lutionary genetics, too. It is unclear why the desire to investigate and manipulate the chemical bases of life should not be considered as much a manifestation of our god-like nature as the writing of poetry and the composition of sonatas. As a way of providing theological content for **UE**, then, argument (i) is unsatisfactory because it is ambiguous and contentious.

> (ii) To engage in ag biotech is to *invent world-changing technology*, an activity that should be reserved to God alone.

Let us consider (ii) in conjunction with a similar objection (iia).

> (iia) To engage in ag biotech is to *arrogate historically unprecedented power* to ourselves.

The argument here is not the strong one, that biotech gives us divine power, but the more modest one, that it gives us a power we have not had previously. But it would be counterintuitive to judge an action wrong simply because it has never been performed. On this view, it would have been wrong to prescribe a new herbal remedy for menstrual cramps or to administer a new anesthetic. But that seems absurd. More argumentation is needed to call historically unprecedented actions morally wrong. What is needed is to know *to what extent* our new powers will transform society, whether we have witnessed prior transformations of this sort, and whether those transitions are morally acceptable.

We do not know how extensive the ag biotech revolution will be, but let us assume that it will be as dramatic as its greatest proponents assert. Have we ever witnessed comparable transitions?

The change from hunting and gathering to agriculture was an astonishing transformation. With agriculture came not only an increase in the number of humans on the globe but the first appearance of complex cultural activities: writing, philosophy, government, music, the arts, and architecture. What sort of power did people arrogate to themselves when they moved from hunting and gathering to agriculture? The power of civilization itself.

Ag biotech is often oversold by its proponents. But suppose they are right, that ag biotech brings us historically unprecedented powers. Is this a reason to oppose it? Not if we accept agriculture and its accompanying advances, for when we accepted agriculture we arrogated to ourselves historically unprecedented powers.

In sum, the objections stated in (ii) and (iia) are not convincing.

(iii) To engage in ag biotech is *illegitimately to cross species boundaries.*

The problems with this argument are both theological and scientific. I will leave it to others to argue the scientific case that nature gives ample evidence of generally fluid boundaries between species. The argument assumes that species boundaries are distinct, rigid, and unchanging, but, in fact, species now appear to be messy, plastic, and mutable. To proscribe the crossing of species borders on the grounds that it is unnatural seems scientifically indefensible. . . .

In conclusion, it is difficult to find a persuasive defense of (iii). . . .

(iv) To engage in ag biotech is to *commodify life.*

The argument here is that genetic engineering treats life in a reductionistic manner, reducing living organisms to little more than machines. Life is sacred and not to be treated as a good of commercial value only to be bought and sold to the highest bidder.

Could we apply this principle uniformly? Would not objecting to the products of GM technology on these grounds also require that we object to the products of ordinary agriculture on the same grounds? Is not the very act of bartering or exchanging crops and animals for cash vivid testimony to the fact that every culture on earth has engaged in the commodification of life for centuries? If one accepts commercial trafficking in non-GM wheat and pigs, then why object to commercial trafficking in GM wheat and GM pigs? Why should it be wrong to treat DNA the way we have previously treated animals, plants, and viruses?

Although (iv) may be true, it is not a sufficient reason to object to GM technology because our values and economic institutions have long accepted the commodification of life. Now, one might object that various religious traditions have never accepted commodi- fication and that genetic engineering presents us with an opportunity to resist, to reverse course. Kass[1] for example, has argued that we have gone too far down the road of dehumanizing ourselves and treating nature as a machine and that we should pay attention to our emotional reactions against practices such as human cloning. Even if we cannot defend these feelings in rational terms, our revulsion at the very idea of cloning humans should carry great weight. Midgley[2] has argued that moving genes across species boundaries is not only "yukky" but, perhaps, a monstrous idea, a form of playing God.

Kass and Midgley have eloquently defended the relevance of our emotional reactions to genetic engineering but, as both admit, we cannot simply allow our emotions to carry the day. . . . But as much hinges on the reasoning as on the emotions.

Are the intrinsic objections sound? Are they clear, consistent, and logical? Do they rely on principles we are willing to apply uniformly to other parts of our lives? Might they lead to counterintuitive results? . . .

If a moral rule or principle leads to counterintuitive results, then we have a strong reason to reject it. For example, consider the following moral principle, which we might call the doctrine of naive consequentialism (NC):

Always improve the welfare of the most people (NC).

Were we to adopt NC, then we would be not only permitted but required to sacrifice one healthy person if by doing so we could save many others. If six people need organ transplants (two need kidneys, one needs a liver, one needs a heart, and two need lungs) then NC instructs us to sacrifice the life of the healthy person to transplant six organs to the other six. But this result, that we are *obliged* to sacrifice innocent people to save strangers, is wildly counterintuitive. This result gives us a strong reason to reject NC.

I have argued that the four formulations of the unnaturalness objection considered above are unsound insofar as they lead to counterintuitive results. I do not take this position lightly. Twelve years ago, I wrote "The Case Against bGH," an article, I have been told, that "was one of the first papers by a philosopher to object to ag biotech on explicitly ethical grounds." I then wrote a series of other articles objecting to GM herbicide-resistant crops, transgenic animals, and, indeed, all of ag biotech.[3] I am acquainted with worries about GM foods. But, for reasons that include the weakness of the intrinsic objections, I have changed my mind. The sympathetic feelings on which my anti-GMO worldview was based did not survive the stirring up of reasoning.

WHY ARE WE CAREFUL WITH GM FOODS?

I do not pretend to know anything like the full answer to this question, but I would like to be permitted the luxury of a brief speculation about it. The reason may have to do with a natural, completely understandable, and wholly rational tendency to take precautions with what goes into our mouths. When we are in good health and happy with the foods available to us, we have little to gain from experimenting with new food and no reason to take a chance on a potentially unsafe food. We may think of this disposition as the precautionary response.

When faced with two contrasting opinions about issues related to food safety, consumers place great emphasis on negative information. The precautionary response is particularly strong when a consumer sees little to gain from a new food technology. When a given food is plentiful, it is rational to place extra weight on negative information about any particular piece of that food. It is rational to do so, . . . even when the source of the negative information is known to be biased.

There are several reasons for us to take a precautionary approach to new foods. First, under conditions in which nutritious tasty food is plentiful, we have nothing to gain from trying a new food if, from our perspective, it is in other respects identical to our current foods. Suppose on a rack in front of me there are 18 dozen maple-frosted Krispy Kreme doughnuts, all baked to a golden brown, all weighing three ounces. If I am invited to take one of them, I have no reason to favor one over the other.

Suppose, however, that a naked man runs into the room with wild-hair flying behind him yelling that the sky is falling. He approaches the rack and points at the third doughnut from the left on the fourth shelf from the bottom. He exclaims, "This doughnut will cause cancer! Avoid it at all costs, or die!" There is no reason to believe this man's claim and yet, because there are so many doughnuts freely available, why should we take any chances? It is rational to select other doughnuts, because all are alike. Now, perhaps one of us is a mountain climber who loves taking risks and might be tempted to say, "Heck, I'll try that doughnut." In order to focus on the right question here, the risk takers should ask themselves whether they would select the tainted doughnut to take home to feed to their 2-year-old daughter. Why impose any risk on your loved ones when there is no reason to do so?

The Krispy Kreme example is meant to suggest that food tainting is both a powerful and an extraordinarily easy social act. It is powerful because it virtually determines consumer behavior. It is easy, because the tainter does not have to offer any evidence of the food's danger. Under conditions of food plenty, rational consumers do and should take pre-

cautions, avoiding tainted food no matter how untrustworthy the tainter.

Our tendency to take precautions with our food suggests that a single person with a negative view about GM foods will be much more influential than many people with a positive view. The following experiment lends credibility to this hypothesis. In a willingness-to-pay experiment, Hayes and colleagues paid 87 primary food shoppers $40 each.[4] Each participant was assigned to a group ranging in size from a half-dozen to a dozen members. Each group was then seated at a table at lunchtime and given one pork sandwich. In the middle of each table was one additional food item, an irradiated pork sandwich. Each group of participants was given one of three different treatments: (i) the *pro-irradiation* treatment; (ii) the *anti-irradiation* treatment; and (iii) the *balanced* treatment.

Each treatment began with all the participants at a table receiving the same, so-called "neutral" description of an irradiated pork sandwich. The description read, in part, like this:

> The U.S. FDA has recently approved the use of ionizing radiation to control Trichinella in pork products. This process results in a 10,000-fold reduction in Trichinella organisms in meat. The process does not induce measurable radioactivity in food.

After the participants read this description, they conducted a silent bid to purchase the right to exchange their nonirradiated sandwich for the irradiated sandwich. Whoever bid the highest price would be able to buy the sandwich for the price bid by the second-highest bidder. To provide participants with information about the opinions of the others at their table so that they could factor this information into their future bids, the lowest and highest bids of each round were announced before the next round of bidding began. At the end of the experiment, 1 of the 10 bidding rounds was selected at random, and the person bidding the highest amount in that round had to pay the second-highest price bid during that round for the sandwich.

After five rounds of bidding, the second-highest bids in all three groups settled rather quickly at an equilibrium point, roughly 20 cents. That is, someone at every table was willing to pay 20 cents for the irradiated pork sandwich, but no one in any group would pay more than 20 cents. The bidding was repeated five times in order to give participants the opportunity to respond to information they were getting from others at the table and to ensure the robustness of the price.

After five rounds of bidding, each group was given additional information. Group a, the so-called *pro* group, was provided with a description of the sandwich that read, in part:

Each year, 9000 people die in the United States from food-borne illness. Some die from Trichinella in pork. Millions of others suffer short-term illness. Irradiated pork is a safe and reliable way to eliminate this pathogen. The process has been used successfully in 20 countries since 1950.

The *pro*-group participants were informed that the author of this positive description was a pro-irradiation food industry group. After the description was read, five more rounds of bidding began. The price of the irradiated sandwich quickly shot upward, reaching 80 cents by the end of round 10. A ceiling price was not reached, however, as the bids in every round, including the last, were significantly higher than in the preceding round. The price, that is, was still going up when the experiment was stopped.

After its first five rounds of bidding, group b was provided with a different description. It read, in part:

In food irradiation, pork is exposed to radioactive materials. It receives 300,000 rads of radiation—the equivalent of 30 million chest x-rays. This process results in radiolytic products in food. Some radiolytic products are carcinogens and linked to birth defects. The process was developed in the 1950s by the Atomic Energy Commission.

The source of this description was identified to the bidders as "Food and Water," an anti-irradiation activist group in England. After group b read this description, it began five more rounds of bidding. The bid went down, quickly reaching zero. After the first five rounds produced a value of 20 cents in group b for the pork sandwich described in a "neutral" way, *no one* in this group would pay a penny for the irradiated sandwich described in a "negative" way. This result obtained even though the description was clearly identified as coming from an activist, nonscientific group.

After five rounds of bidding on the neutral description, the third group, group c, received *both* the positive and negative descriptions. One might expect this group's response to be highly variable, with some participants scared off by the negative description and others discounting it for its unscientific source. Some participants might be expected to bid nothing while others would continue to bid highly.

However, the price of the sandwich in the third, so-called *balanced* group, also fell quickly. Indeed, the price reached zero almost as quickly as it did in group b, the negative group. That is, even though the third group had both the neutral and the positive description in front of them, no one exposed to the negative description would pay 2 cents for the irradiated sandwich.

Hayes' study illuminates the precautionary response and carries implications for the GM debate. These implications are that, given neutral or positive descriptions of GM foods, consumers initially will *pay more* for them. Given negative descriptions of GM foods, consumers initially will *not* pay more for them. Finally, and this is the surprising result, given *both* positive and negative descriptions of GM foods, consumers initially will *not* pay more for them. Both sides in the GM food debate should be scrupulous in providing reasons for all their claims. But especially for their negative claims.

In a worldwide context, the precautionary response of those facing food abundance in developed countries may lead us to be insensitive to the conditions of those in less fortunate situations. Indeed, we may find ourselves in the following ethical dilemma.

For purposes of argument, make the following three assumptions. (I do not believe any of the assumptions is implausible.) First, assume that GM food is safe. Second, assume that some GM "orphan" foods, such as rice enhanced with iron or vitamin A, or virus-resistant cassava, or aluminum-tolerant sweet potato, may be of great potential benefit to millions of poor children. Third, assume that widespread anti-GM information and sentiment, no matter how unreliable on scientific grounds, could shut down the GM infrastructure in the developed world.

Under these assumptions, consider the possibility that, by tainting GM foods in the countries best suited to conduct GM research safely, anti-GM activists could bring to a halt the range of money-making GM foods marketed by multinational corporations. This result might be a good or a bad thing. However, an unintended side effect of this consequence would be that the new GM orphan crops mentioned above might not be forthcoming, assuming that the development and commercialization of these orphan crops depends on the answering of fundamental questions in plant science and molecular biology that will be answered only if the research agendas of private industry are allowed to go forward along with the research agendas of public research institutions.

Our precautionary response to new food may put us in an uncomfortable position. On the one hand, we want to tell "both sides" of the GM story, letting people know about the benefits and the risks of the technology. On the other hand, some of the people touting the benefits of the technology make outlandish claims that it will feed the world and some of the people decrying the technology make unsupported claims that it will ruin the world. In that situation, however, those with unsupported negative stories to tell carry greater weight than those with unsupported positive stories. Our precautionary response, then, may well lead, in the short term at least, to the rejection of GM technology. Yet, the rejection of GM technology could indirectly harm those children most in need, those who need what I have called the orphan crops.

Are we being forced to choose between two fundamental values, the value of free speech versus the value of children's lives?

On the one hand, open conversation and transparent decision-making processes are critical to the foundations of a liberal democratic society. We must reach out to include everyone in the debate and allow people to state their opinions about GM foods, whatever their opinion happens to be, whatever their level of acquaintance with the science and technology happens to be. Free speech is a value not to be compromised lightly.

On the other hand, stating some opinions about GM food can clearly have a tainting effect, a powerful and extraordinarily easy consequence of free speech. Tainting the technology might result in the loss of this potentially useful tool. Should we, then, draw some boundaries around the conversation, insisting that each contributor bring some measure of scientific data to the table, especially when negative claims are being made? Or are we collectively prepared to leave the conversation wide open? That is, in the name of protecting free speech, are we prepared to risk losing an opportunity to help some of the world's most vulnerable?

THE PRECAUTIONARY PRINCIPLE

. . . Now, as mad cow disease grips the European imagination, concerned observers transfer fears to genetically modified foods, advising: "Take precaution!" Is this a valuable observation that can guide specific public policy decisions, or well-intentioned but ultimately unhelpful advice?

As formulated in the 1992 Rio Declaration on Environment and Development, the precautionary principle states that ". . . lack of full scientific certainty shall not be used as a reason for postponing cost-effective measures to prevent environmental degradation." The precautionary approach has led many countries to declare a moratorium on GM crops on the supposition that developing GM crops might lead to environmental degradation. The countries are correct that this is an implication of the principle. But is it the only implication?

Suppose global warming intensifies and comes, as some now darkly predict, to interfere dramatically with food production and distribution. Massive dislocations in international trade and corresponding political power follow global food shortages, affecting all regions and nations.

In desperate attempts to feed themselves, billions begin to pillage game animals, clear-cut forests to plant crops, cultivate previously non-productive lands, apply fertilizers and pesticides at higher than recommended rates, kill and eat endangered and previously non-endangered species.

Perhaps not a likely scenario, but not entirely implausible, either. GM crops could help to prevent it, by providing hardier versions of traditional lines capable of growing in drought conditions, or in saline soils, or under unusual climactic stresses in previously temperate zones, or in zones in which we have no prior agronomic experience.

On the supposition that we might need the tools of genetic engineering to avert future episodes of crushing human attacks on what Aldo Leopold called "the land," the precautionary principle requires that we develop GM crops. Yes, we lack full scientific certainty that developing GM crops will prevent environmental degradation. True, we do not know what the final financial price of GM research and development will be. But if GM technology were to help save the land, few would not deem that price cost-effective. So, according to the precautionary principle, lack of full scientific certainty that GM crops will prevent environmental degradation shall not be used as a reason for postponing this potentially cost-effective measure.

The precautionary principle commits us to each of the following propositions:

(1) We must not develop GM crops.
(2) We must develop GM crops.

As (1) and (2) are plainly contradictory, however, defenders of the principle should explain, why its implications are not incoherent.

Much more helpful than the precautionary principle would be detailed case-by-case recommendations crafted upon the basis of a wide review of nonindustry-sponsored field tests conducted by objective scientists expert in the construction and interpretation of ecological and medical data. Without such a basis for judging this use acceptable and that use unacceptable, we may as well advise people in the GM area to go crazy. It would be just as helpful as "Take precaution!" . . .

MINORITY VIEWS

When in a pluralistic society the views of a particular minority come into genuine conflict with the views of the majority, we must ask a number of questions: How deep is the conflict? How has the minority been treated in the past? If the minority has been exploited, have reparations been made? If the conflict is so deep that honoring the minority's views would entail overriding the majority's views, then we have a difficult decision to make. In such cases, the conclusions of the state must be just, taking into account the question of past exploitation and subsequent reparations or lack thereof. This is a question of justice. . . .

[S]hould the minority cite past oppression as the reason their values ought to predominate over the majority's, then a different question must be addressed. Here, the relevant issues have to do with the nature of past exploitation, its scope and depth, and the sufficiency of efforts, have there been any, to rectify the injustice and compensate victims. If the problem is long-standing and has not been addressed, then imposing the will of the majority would seem a sign of an unjust society insensitive to its past misdeeds. If, on the other hand, the problem has been carefully ad-dressed by both sides and, for example, just treaties arrived at through fair procedures have been put in place, are being enforced, are rectifying past wrongs, and are preventing new forms of exploitation, then the minority's arguments would seem to be far weaker. This conclusion would be especially compelling if it could be shown that the lives of *other* disadvantaged peoples might be put at risk by honoring a particular minority's wish to ban GMOs.

CONCLUSION

Earlier I [mentioned that] I personally came to change my mind about the moral acceptability of GM crops. My opinion changed as I took full account of three considerations: (i) the rights of people in various countries to choose to adopt GM technology (a consideration falling under the human rights principle); (ii) the balance of likely benefits over harms to consumers and the environment from GM technology (a utilitarian consideration); and (iii) the wisdom of encouraging discovery, innovation, and careful regulation of GM technology. . . .

NOTES

1. L. Kass, *Toward a More Natural Science: Biology and Human Affairs* (Free Press, 1988).

2. M. Midgley, Biotechnology and monstrosity. Why we should pay attention to the 'yuk factor,' *Hastings Center Report* 30(5), 7–15 (2000).

3. G. Comstock. The case against bGH. *Agric. Hum. Values* 5, 36–52 (1988).

4. D. Hayes, J. Fox, J. Shogren. Consumer preferences for food irradiation: how favorable and unfavorable descriptions affect preferences for irradiated pork in experimental auctions, *J. Risk Uncertainty* 24(1), 75–95 (2002).

H. TRISTRAM ENGELHARDT, JR., AND FABRICE JOTTERAND

The Precautionary Principle: A Dialectical Reconsideration

H. Tristram Engelhardt, Jr. holds full professorships at Baylor College of Medicine and Rice University and is a member of the Center for Medical Ethics and Health Policy. Engelhardt has authored over two hundred fifty articles and chapters of books in addition to numerous book reviews and other publications. He most recently edited *Global Bioethics: The Collapse of Consensus* (2006).

Fabrice Jotterand is Assistant Professor in Center for Values in Medicine, Science & Technology at the University of Texas at Dallas. His research interests include medical professionalism, research ethics and ethics aspects of nanotechnology. He recently co-edited (with H. T. Engelhardt, Jr.) the forthcoming *The Philosophy of Medicine Reborn: A Pellegrino Reader.*

I. PRUDENT RISK-TAKING

The so-called precautionary principle raises a cluster of questions about how prudently to engage in risk-taking. All human activities involve risks. The development of new technologies is no exception. However, given a not-implausible account of the human situation, the unavailability of at least some biomedical technologies may itself count as a risk to continued human survival. This essay will examine an overlooked element of the precautionary principle: a prudent assessment of the long-range or remote catastrophes possibly associated with technological development must include the catastrophes that may take place because of the absence of such technologies. In short, this brief essay will attempt to turn the precautionary principle on its head by arguing that, (1) if the long-term survival of any life form is precarious, and if the survival of the current human population is particularly precarious, especially given contemporary urban population densities, and (2) if

technological innovation and progress are necessary in order rapidly to adapt humans to meet environmental threats that would otherwise be catastrophic on a large scale (e.g., pandemics of highly lethal diseases), then (3) the development of biomedical technologies in many forms (some, such as human reproductive cloning or embryo research may be prohibited on moral grounds), . . . but in particular including human germ-line genetic engineering, may be required by the precautionary principle, given the prospect of the obliteration of humans in the absence of such enhanced biotechnology. The precautionary principle thus properly understood requires an ethos that should generally support technological innovation, at least in particular areas of biotechnology.

II. PUTTING THE PRECAUTIONARY PRINCIPLE IN CONTEXT

There are a number of difficulties in making prudent assessments of risk. To begin with, intuitions vary widely about how to compare risks appropriately. There are some who regard a one-hour commercial flight with greater apprehension than a four-hour automobile journey to the same city. This is the case even though in general the risks are greater from the

From *Journal of Medicine and Philosophy* 29(3) (June 2004), 301–312. Copyright © 2004 Taylor & Francis. Reprinted by permission of Taylor & Francis, Inc., www.routledge-ny.com.

latter than the former. In part, this perception is grounded in the difference in psycho-social impact of learning about the death of 200 passengers in an airline crash versus learning of 200 automobile accidents in a year's time, each involving one fatality. The same number of people dying or being disabled at the same time usually has a more dramatic psycho-social impact than the same number being disabled or dying over a more extended period of time. So, too, were it the case that the number of individuals likely to be disabled or killed by nuclear power plant accidents were no greater than the number of persons likely to be disabled or killed by the generation of the same amount of electric power from the use of fossil fuels, the socially disruptive character of all of the deaths happening at once appears to give this mass tragedy a weight greater than the sum of all the individual tragedies. Intuitions that favor giving greater weight to concerns regarding airplane crashes and nuclear power plant accidents may contribute to the intuitions that are invoked to support the precautionary principle.

In this essay, the precautionary principle is understood as the rule that one should never engage in a technological development or application unless it can be shown that this will not lead to large-scale disasters or catastrophes. The possibility of a large-scale disaster or catastrophe is regarded as sufficient to prohibit the application of new technologies that offer considerable benefit to humans. In this sense, the precautionary principle is a variation of a principle of risk-aversiveness, so that one takes maximal regard of possible large-scale or catastrophic disasters, however remote and despite the benefits that might accrue from the technology. This understanding of the precautionary principle would constrain one to accept the likelihood of a number of deaths in order to avoid the remote possibility of even greater catastrophes.

For example, the precautionary principle has been invoked to prohibit the introduction of genetically modified organisms, until one can with a very high degree of certainty rule out the possibility of catastrophic outcomes. Those who embrace the precautionary principle would accept the starvation of millions in third-world countries who could be fed by genetically modified grains, rather than assume a very remote and very unlikely interruption of the ecological balance as a result of unexpected or unforeseen genetic effects as a result of genetically modified organisms.

Although the availability of genetically modified foodstuffs might aid the starving, this very important good would be seen to be outweighed by a possible, albeit unlikely, ecological catastrophe. New technologies are thus held to be guilty until proven innocent. . . . In this vein, Goklany acknowledges that in order to meet food demands additional deforestation of millions of hectares will be required. In 1997, according to the Food and Agricultural Organization, it was estimated that already 1,510 million hectares were devoted to cropland and by 2050 an additional 1,600 million hectares of habitat land would be lost. . . . He also notes that an annual increase of productivity of 2% (through the use of genetically modified crops) would be translated into at least 422 million hectares of cropland currently under plow that could be returned to nature or made available for habitat or other human uses, thus increasing environmental benefits. . . .

Because of the difficulty of proving that new technologies will not involve unanticipated catastrophic outcomes, the precautionary principle if interpreted strictly, as shown from the example of policy responses regarding food from genetically modified crops, would seem to place an unjustifiable burden on all technological progress. It would not only appear to forbid anything but the most gradual introduction of most new technologies, but also give equal grounds for the suspension of technological interventions for which there has not been ample time to assess unforeseen risks. For instance, one might hypothesize that a wide range of current pharmaceutical agents may carry with them unforeseen consequences for the development of senile dementia, etc. With a sufficiently active imagination one could bring much of contemporary biotechnology under suspicion without a ready ability to lift the cloud of uncertainty.

The concern to give proper weight to possible catastrophic outcomes is further augmented by discounting particular benefits, especially possible economic benefits. Among many of the proponents of the precautionary principles, there is a view either that it is improper to give any weight to economic benefits or that the importance of such benefits has been improperly inflated. Nancy Myers, for instance, claims that the World Trade Organization and the North American Free Trade Agreement "institutionalized . . . the ascendancy of commerce over environmental and public health concerns" and hence cost-benefit assessments, it is argued, dictate that products or technological innovations outweigh the costs of possible environmental harms (Myers, 2002, p. 214). If all consideration of economic benefits were removed from cost-benefit calculations, a considerable burden would have been placed on the development of promising new technologies. This criticism of the weight to be given to economic benefits opens the larger issue of how to compare different genre of benefits and harms.

Finally, one must note the precautionary principle is often interpreted so as to give equal if not greater weight to concerns with the environment in and of itself, not simply as harms to the environment may have indirect impacts on human welfare. Here the question is not simply of comparing benefits and harms, but the question of whose harms and benefits should be compared and in what way. That is, how is one to compare the possibility of harm to animals, ecosystems, and the environment with the possibility of harms and benefits to humans? This weighting of the environment, especially ecosystems in and of themselves, is noted by Alston Chase who asserts that the precautionary principle reflects concerns regarding benefits and harms that are biocentric rather than humanistic or human-centered. As he puts it, "biocentrism is the fundamental value conveyed in most treaties or protocols promoting the Precautionary Principle" (Chase, 1997, p. 5). In these terms one can justify the starvation of millions of people for the sake of the well-being of the ecosystem.

The assessment of risks to the environment requires an account of how to compare harms and benefits to humans as well as to other living organisms and the environment generally. Such comparisons would require a complex account differentiating diverse benefits and harms as these have impact on humans, animals, ecosystems, and the environment in itself. Such rankings of goods and harms fall beyond a factual description of the consequences of particular technological interventions. It requires choosing one among a number of competing moral visions. . . .

However one sorts out the proper assessment of harms and benefits, the cultural force of the precautionary principle would seem to place the burden of suspicion on technological innovation and progress, in that all innovative technological interventions carry with them an unassessable prospect of an unanticipated, large-scale, catastrophic side effect. This conclusion would seem to follow, given intuitions that give a greater weight to possible significant catastrophic outcomes over equal but less catastrophic

costs in human lives and suffering. This conclusion is further fortified by discounting economic benefits and adding a biocentric accent to the calculation of benefits and harms. All of this seems to lead to regarding the precautionary principle as hostile to biotechnological progress. This conclusion will now be brought into question.

III. THE NEED FOR RAPID RE-ADAPTATION OF HUMANS TO AN EVER-CHANGING AND OFTEN THREATENING ENVIRONMENT

Without addressing the issue of how to compare harms and benefits, one can bring into question the putative conclusion that the precautionary principle will under all circumstances place a burden against technological progress. The arguments developed below show that the precautionary principle, if properly understood, should support at least certain areas of biotechnological innovation, rather than constitute an impediment. In what follows, the focus is given to human welfare. With a few changes, the focus could be brought to bear on ecosystems as well. As developed, the argument does take into account concerns with the ecosystems insofar as they would constitute a threat to the long-range survival of the human species.

The long-range survival of humans depends on the capacity of humans to withstand threats from an environment often significantly hostile to the survival of humans, indeed, to the long-range survival of any species of organisms. Among those threatening elements are new viruses, new variations of old viruses, and bacteria that have become altered so as to be drug-resistant and/or toxic to humans in new ways. Similar threats to human survival can be envisaged in terms of viruses and other life forms that might threaten the human food supply and the environment. Given the network of rapid global travel, quarantine over any significant period of time is likely to be ineffective without a near total paralysis of international trade. . . . From Ebola and AIDS to new forms of influenza and SARS, recent history has provided numerous possibilities for environmental confrontations that could lead to large-scale, indeed catastrophic, loss of human life.

The protean possibilities for future threats of a large-scale, indeed catastrophic magnitude, given a reasonable interpretation of the precautionary principle, would require the vigorous development of a biotechnology sufficient to produce not simply new antimicrobials and new vaccines, but able genetically to modify humans as well as the organisms that serve as foodstuffs for humans. Given the prospect of a catastrophic development of a hyper-virulent microbe threatening either humans or their foodstuffs, the human ability both to kill such threatening microbes as well as rapidly to readapt humans and their foodstuffs to resist such threats would be obligatory under the precautionary principle. The precautionary principle should require vigorously supporting technological and scientific progress.

This result is an important acknowledgement. There are two sides or dimensions of the precautionary principle. On the one hand, the precautionary principle requires considering the untoward consequences of new technological innovation. On the other hand, the precautionary principle requires considering the untoward consequences of not supporting technological innovation. In short, one must not only fear catastrophes that will flow from a technology, but also the catastrophes that will flow from its absence.

The question then is how to compare the two sides or dimensions of the precautionary principle. Which set of unforeseen, large-scale, and catastrophic consequences should be given greater weight and why? Possible catastrophes frame technology or frame its absence. To begin with, there are factual considerations. Given the recorded history of disastrous epidemics when communication among humans was less global than today, one might very well have grounds to tilt the balance in favor of giving greater weight to the unforeseen consequences likely to flow from the failure to accelerate biotechnological progress and encourage biotechnological innovation. Should such reflections on the history of the hostility of environments to organisms in general and to humans in particular be credible, then there would be a strong moral argument grounded in the precautionary principle in favor of sustaining a bias in favor of biotechnological progress and innovation. In this circumstance, the precautionary principle would need to be reinterpreted in order to be understood as substantively technology-friendly.

The greater the plausibility of bioenvironmental threats, the greater the obligation will be to encourage the development of an appreciation of biomedicine and the biomedical technologies as core to the human enterprise. When the precautionary principle is combined with any moral vision that gives weight to obligations to future generations, then the biomedical technologies will be core to the human endeavor of ensuring the survival of the human species. In short, a more balanced appreciation of the precautionary principle should transform the principle from being central to an anti-technological ethos to a principle that when rightly understood is a cardinal foundation of an ethos supportive of biotechnological innovation. In addition, insofar as such innovation turns out as a fact of the matter to be enhanced by larger-than-usual profit-margins in the pharmaceutical and medical device industries, then one will wish to avoid forms of cost containment, tort liability, and tax policies that encumber profitability in this industry. In short, a more balanced consideration of the principle may shed important light on a broader range of risks associated with biotechnology, namely, those connected with a failure wholeheartedly to support it.

IV. THE ARGUMENT FROM IGNORANCE GOES BOTH WAYS

At the very least, this dialectical exploration of the precautionary principle shows its other side and excluded dimension, thus indicating one of the major difficulties involved with arguments from ignorance. Evenly applied, the precautionary principle invites us to give at least as much weight to the catastrophes we may face from not developing a certain technology as from developing the technology. Were one of the opinion that the historical record of devastating epidemics and other environmental changes was not sufficient to tip the balance vigorously in favor of technological innovation on the basis of the precautionary principle, then both appeals to ignorance would simply cancel each other out. In that case, the precautionary principle would be devoid of force.

It must be acknowledged that this analysis of the precautionary principle focuses on its application only in areas where it would bear on technologies whose unavailability could foreseeably lead to catastrophic human harms. Thus, there may be some (surely not these authors) who might be of the view that the precautionary principle should preclude the use of cell phones until the magnetic waves involved had been tested on primates for a sufficiently long period so as to assess the possibility of long-range adverse outcomes. Were the precautionary principle to be employed to block the further use of cell phones, this concern might not be as easily outweighed by the health risks from the unavailability of cell phones.

This brief reflection leaves us with two conclusions, at least for some. First, a balanced appreciation of the precautionary principle leads to any unanticipated result: rather than setting cautionary blocks to biotechnological development, the principle should, given a number of plausible empirical assumptions, encourage biotechnological development. Second, if the factual assumptions necessary to tip the balance in favor of the precautionary principle as supporting biotechnological innovation are brought into question, then the default position will be to deprive the principle of any credible force, at least in a significant range of biotechnologies. Either the precautionary principle means something that most have not anticipated (i.e., it is technology-friendly), or, at least in many areas, it is rendered void by the possibility of contrary catastrophic possibilities.

REFERENCES

Chase, A. (1997). Some cautionary remarks about the precautionary principle. 'Countdown to Kyoto': The consequences of the mandatory global carbon dioxide emissions reductions, Australian APEC Study Center, Canberra, 19–21 August 1997.

Myers, N. (2002). The precautionary principle puts values first. Bulletin of Science, Technology and Society, 22, 210–219.

Ethics and Enhancement

JONATHAN GLOVER

Questions about Some Uses of Genetic Engineering

Jonathan Glover is Professor of Ethics at King's College, University of London, and Director of the college's Centre of Medical Law and Ethics. He has published several books on ethics, including *Choosing Children: The Ethical Dilemmas of Genetic Intervention* (2006), *Humanity: A Moral History of the Twentieth Century* (1999), *What Sort of People Should There Be?* (1984), and *Causing Death and Saving Lives* (1977). He chaired a European Commission Working Party on Assisted Reproduction, which issued *The Glover Report* in 1989. His current research interests include global ethics and ethical issues in psychiatry.

There is a widespread view that any project for the genetic improvement of the human race ought to be ruled out: that there are fundamental objections of principle. The aim of this discussion is to sort out some of the main objections. It will be argued that our resistance is based on a complex of different values and reasons, none of which is, when examined, adequate to rule out in principle this use of genetic engineering. The debate on human genetic engineering should become like the debate on nuclear power: one in which large possible benefits have to be weighed against big problems and the risk of great disasters. The discussion has not reached this point, partly because the techniques have not yet been developed. But it is also partly because of the blurred vision which fuses together many separate risks and doubts into a fuzzy-outlined opposition in principle.

1. AVOIDING THE DEBATE ABOUT GENES AND THE ENVIRONMENT

In discussing the question of genetic engineering, there is everything to be said for not muddling the issue up with the debate over the relative importance of genes and environment in the development of such characteristics as intelligence. One reason for avoiding that debate is that it arouses even stronger passions than genetic engineering, and so is filled with as much acrimony as argument. But, apart from this fastidiousness, there are other reasons.

The nature-nurture dispute is generally seen as an argument about the relative weight the two factors have in causing differences within the human species: "IQ is 80 per cent hereditary and 20 per cent environmental" versus "IQ is 80 per cent environmental and 20 per cent hereditary." No doubt there is some approximate truth of this type to be found if we consider variations within a given population at a particular time. But it is highly unlikely that there is any such statement which is simply true of human nature regardless of context. To take the extreme case, if we could iron out all environmental differences, any residual variations would be 100 per cent genetic. It is only if we make the highly artificial assumption that different groups at different times all have an identical spread of relevant environmental differences that we can expect to find statements of this kind applying to human nature in general. To say this is not to argue that studies on the question should not be conducted, or are bound to fail. It may well be possible, and useful, to find out the relative weights of the two kinds of factor for a given characteristic among a certain group at a particular time. The point is that any such conclusions lose relevance, not only when environmental differences are stretched out or compressed, but also when genetic differences are. And this last case is what we are considering.

We can avoid this dispute because of its irrelevance. Suppose the genetic engineering proposal were to try to make people less aggressive. On a superficial view, the proposal might be shown to be unrealistic if there were evidence to show that variation in aggressiveness is hardly genetic at all: that it is 95 per cent environmental. (Let us grant, most implausibly, that such a figure turned out to be true for the whole of humanity, regardless of social context.) But all this would show is that, within our species, the distribution of genes relevant to aggression is very uniform. It would show nothing about the likely effects on aggression if we use genetic engineering to give people a different set of genes from those they now have.

In other words, to take genetic engineering seriously, we need take no stand on the relative importance or unimportance of genetic factors in the explanation of the present range of individual differences found in people. We need only the minimal assumption that different genes could give us different characteristics. To deny *that* assumption you need to be the sort of person who thinks it is only living in kennels which make dogs different from cats.

2. METHODS OF CHANGING THE GENETIC COMPOSITION OF FUTURE GENERATIONS

There are essentially three ways of altering the genetic composition of future generations. The first is by environmental changes. Discoveries in medicine, the institution of a National Health Service, schemes for poverty relief, agricultural changes, or alterations in the tax position of large families, all alter the selective pressure on genes.[1] It is hard to think of any social change which does not make some difference to who survives or who is born.

The second method is to use eugenic policies aimed at altering breeding patterns or patterns of survival of people with different genes. Eugenic methods are "environmental" too: the difference is only that the genetic impact is intended. Possible strategies range from various kinds of compulsion (to have more children, fewer children, or no children, or even compulsion over the choice of sexual partner) to the completely voluntary (our present genetic counselling practice of giving prospective parents information about probabilities of their children having various abnormalities).

The third method is genetic engineering: using enzymes to add to or subtract from a stretch of DNA.

Most people are unworried by the fact that a side-effect of an environmental change is to alter the gene pool, at least where the alteration is not for the worse. And even in cases where environmental factors increase the proportion of undesirable genes in the pool, we often accept this. Few people oppose the National Health Service, although setting it up meant that some people with genetic defects, who would have died, have had treatment enabling them to survive and reproduce. On the whole, we accept without qualms that much of what we do has genetic impact. Controversy starts when we think of aiming deliberately at genetic changes, by eugenics or genetic engineering. I want to make some brief remarks about eugenic policies, before suggesting that policies of deliberate intervention are best considered in the context of genetic engineering.

Scepticism has been expressed about whether eugenic policies have any practical chance of success.

Medawar has pointed out the importance of genetic polymorphism: the persistence of genetically different types in a population.[2] (Our different blood groups are a familiar example.) For many characteristics, people get a different gene from each parent. So children do not simply repeat parental characteristics. Any simple picture of producing an improved type of person, and then letting the improvement be passed on unchanged, collapses.

But, although polymorphism is a problem for this crudely utopian form of eugenics, it does not show that more modest schemes of improvement must fail. Suppose the best individuals for some quality (say, colour vision) are heterozygous, so that they inherit a gene A from one parent, and a gene B from the other. These ABs will have AAs and BBs among their children, who will be less good than they are. But AAs and BBs may still be better than ACs or ADs, and perhaps much better than CCs or CDs. If this were so, overall improvement could still be brought about by encouraging people whose genes included an A or B to have more children than those who had only Cs or Ds. The point of taking a quality like colour vision is that it may be genetically fairly simple. Qualities like kindness or intelligence are more likely to depend on the interaction of many genes, but a similar point can be made at a higher level of complexity.

Polymorphism raises a doubt about whether the off-spring of the three "exceptionally intelligent women" fertilized by Dr. Shockley or other Nobel prize-winners will have the same IQ as the parents, even apart from environmental variation. But it does not show the inevitable failure of any large-scale attempts to alter human characteristics by varying the relative numbers of children different kinds of people have. Yet any attempt, say, to raise the level of intelligence, would be a very slow affair, taking many generations to make much of an impact. This is no reason for preferring to discuss genetic engineering. For the genetic engineering of human improvements, if it becomes possible, will have an immediate effect, so we will not be guessing which qualities will be desirable dozens of generations later.

There is the view that the genetic-engineering techniques requires will not become a practical possibility. Sir MacFarlane Burnet, writing in 1971 about using genetic engineering to cure disorders in people already born, dismissed the possibility of using a virus to carry a new gene to replace a faulty one in cells throughout the body: "I should be willing to state in any company that the chance of doing this will remain infinitely small to the last syllable of recorded time."[3] Unless engineering at the stage of sperm cell and egg is easier, this seems a confident dismissal of the topic to be discussed here. More recent work casts doubt on this confidence.[4] So, having mentioned this skepticism, I shall disregard it. We will assume that genetic engineering of people may become possible, and that it is worth discussing. (Sir MacFarlane Burnet's view has not yet been falsified as totally as Rutherford's view about atomic energy. But I hope that the last syllable of recorded time is still some way off.)

The main reason for casting the discussion in terms of genetic engineering rather than eugenics is not a practical one. Many eugenic policies are open to fairly straightforward moral objections, which hide the deeper theoretical issues. Such policies as compulsory sterilization, compulsory abortion, compelling people to pair off in certain ways, or compelling people to have more or fewer children than they would otherwise have, are all open to objection on grounds of overriding people's autonomy. Some are open to objection on grounds of damage to the institution of the family. And the use of discriminatory tax- and child-benefit policies is an intolerable step towards a society of different genetic castes.

Genetic engineering need not involve overriding anyone's autonomy. It need not be forced on parents against their wishes, and the future person being engineered has no views to be overridden. (The view that despite this, it is still objectionable to have one's genetic characteristics decided by others, will be considered later.) Genetic engineering will not damage the family in the obvious ways that compulsory eugenic policies would. Nor need it be encouraged by incentives which create inequalities. Because it avoids these highly visible moral objections, genetic engineering allows us to focus more clearly on other values that are involved.

(To avoid a possible misunderstanding, one point should be added before leaving the topic of eugenics. Saying that some eugenic policies are open to obvious moral objections does not commit me to disapproval of all eugenic policies. In particular, I do not want to be taken to be opposing two kinds of policy. One is genetic counselling: warning people of risks in having children, and perhaps advising them against having them. The other is the introduction of screening-programmes to detect foetal abnormalities, followed by giving the mother the option of abortion where serious defects emerge.)

Let us now turn to the question of what, if anything, we should do in the field of human genetic engineering.

3. THE POSITIVE-NEGATIVE DISTINCTION

We are not yet able to cure disorders by genetic engineering. But we do sometimes respond to disorders by adopting eugenic policies, at least in voluntary form. Genetic counselling is one instance, as applied to those thought likely to have such disorders as Huntington's chorea. This is a particularly appalling inherited disorder, involving brain degeneration, leading to mental decline and lack of control over movement. It does not normally come on until middle age, by which time many of its victims would in the normal course of things have had children. Huntington's chorea is caused by a dominant gene, so those who find that one of the parents has it have themselves a 50 per cent chance of developing it. If they do have it, each of their children will in turn have a 50 per cent chance of the disease. The risks are so high and the disorder so bad that the potential parents often decide not to have children, and are often given advice to this effect by doctors and others.

Another eugenic response to disorders is involved in screening-programmes for pregnant women. When tests pick up such defects as Down's syndrome (mongolism) or spina bifida, the mother is given the possibility of an abortion. The screening-programmes are eugenic because part of their point is to reduce the incidence of severe genetic abnormality in the population.

These two eugenic policies come in at different stages: before conception and during pregnancy. For this reason the screening-programme is more controversial, because it raises the issue of abortion. Those who are sympathetic to abortion, and who think it would be good to eliminate these disorders will be sympathetic to the programme. Those who think abortion is no different from killing a fully developed human are obviously likely to oppose the programme. But they are likely to feel that elimination of the disorders would be a good thing, even if not an adequate justification for killing. Unless they also disapprove of contraception, they are likely to support the genetic-counselling policy in the case of Huntington's chorea.

Few people object to the use of eugenic policies to eliminate disorders, unless those policies have additional features which are objectionable. Most of us are resistant to the use of compulsion, and those who oppose abortion will object to screening-programmes.

But apart from these other moral objections, we do not object to the use of eugenic policies against disease. We do not object to advising those likely to have Huntington's chorea not to have children, as neither compulsion nor killing is involved. Those of us who take this view have no objection to altering the genetic composition of the next generation, where this alteration consists in reducing the incidence of defects.

If it were possible to use genetic engineering to correct defects, say at the foetal stage, it is hard to see how those of us who are prepared to use the eugenic measure just mentioned could object. In both cases, it would be pure gain. The couple, one of whom may develop Huntington's chorea, can have a child if they want, knowing that any abnormality will be eliminated. Those sympathetic to abortion will agree that cure is preferable. And those opposed to abortion prefer babies to be born without handicap. It is hard to think of any objection to using genetic engineering to eliminate defects, and there is a clear and strong case for its use.

But accepting the case for eliminating genetic mistakes does not entail accepting other uses of genetic engineering. The elimination of defects is often called "negative" genetic engineering. Going beyond this, to bring about improvements in normal people, is by contrast "positive" engineering. (The same distinction can be made for eugenics.)

The positive-negative distinction is not in all cases completely sharp. Some conditions are genetic disorders whose identification raises little problem. Huntington's chorea or spina bifida are genetic "mistakes" in a way that cannot seriously be disputed. But with other conditions, the boundary between a defective state and normality may be more blurred. If there is a genetic disposition towards depressive illness, this seems a defect, whose elimination would be part of negative genetic engineering. Suppose the genetic disposition to depression involves the production of lower levels of an enzyme than are produced in normal people. The negative programme is to correct the genetic fault so that the enzyme level is within the range found in normal people. But suppose that within "normal" people also, there are variations in the enzyme level, which correlate with ordinary differences in [the] tendency to be cheerful or depressed. Is there a sharp boundary between "clinical" depression and the depression sometimes felt by those diagnosed as "normal"? Is it clear that a sharp distinction can be drawn between raising someone's enzyme level so that it falls within the normal range and raising someone else's level from the bottom of the normal range to the top?

The positive-negative distinction is sometimes a blurred one, but often we can at least roughly see where it should be drawn. If there is a rough and ready distinction, the question is: how important is it? Should we go on from accepting negative engineering to accepting positive programmes, or should we say that the line between the two is the limit of what is morally acceptable?

There is no doubt that positive programmes arouse the strongest feelings on both sides. On the one hand, many respond to positive genetic engineering or positive eugenics with Professor Tinbergen's though: "I find it morally reprehensible and presumptuous for anybody to put himself forward as a judge of the qualities for which we should breed" [*Guardian*, 5 March, 1980].

But other people have held just as strongly that positive policies are the way to make the future of mankind better than the past. Many years ago H. J. Muller expressed this hope:

And so we foresee the history of life divided into three main phases. In the long preparatory phase it was the helpless creature of its environment, and natural selection gradually ground it into human shape. In the second—our own short transitional phase—it reaches out at the immediate environment, shaking, shaping and grinding to suit the form, the requirements, the wishes, and the whims of man. And in the long third phase, it will reach down into the secret places of the great universe of its own nature, and by aid of its ever growing intelligence and cooperation, shape itself into an increasingly sublime creation—a being beside which the mythical divinities of the past will seem more and more ridiculous, and which setting its own marvellous inner powers against the brute Goliath of the suns and the planets, challenges them to contest.[5]

The case for positive engineering is not helped by adopting the tones of the mad scientist in a horror film. But behind the rhetoric is a serious point. If we decide on a positive programme to change our nature, this will be a central moment in our history, and the transformation might be beneficial to a degree we can now scarcely imagine. The question is: how are we to weigh this possibility against Tinbergen's objection, and against other objections and doubts?

For the rest of this discussion, I shall assume that, subject to adequate safeguards against things going

wrong, negative genetic engineering is acceptable. The issue is positive engineering. I shall also assume that we can ignore problems about whether positive engineering will be technically possible. Suppose we have the power to choose people's genetic characteristics. Once we have eliminated genetic defects, what, if anything, should we do with this power? . . .

4. THE VIEW THAT OVERALL IMPROVEMENT IS UNLIKELY OR IMPOSSIBLE

There is one doubt about the workability of schemes of genetic improvement which is so widespread that it would be perverse to ignore it. This is the view that, in any genetic alteration, there are no gains without compensating losses. On this view, if we bring about a genetically based improvement, such as higher intelligence, we are bound to pay a price somewhere else: perhaps the more intelligent people will have less resistance to disease, or will be less physically agile. If correct, this might so undermine the practicability of applying eugenics or genetic engineering that it would be hardly worth discussing the values involved in such programmes.

This view perhaps depends on some idea that natural selection is so efficient that, in terms of gene survival, we must already be as efficient as it is possible to be. If it were possible to push up intelligence without weakening some other part of the system, natural selection would already have done so. But this is a naive version of evolutionary theory. In real evolutionary theory, far from the genetic status quo always being the best possible for a given environment, some mutations turn out to be advantageous, and this is the origin of evolutionary progress. If natural mutations can be beneficial without a compensating loss, why should artificially induced ones not be so too?

It should also be noticed that there are two different ideas of what counts as a gain or a loss. From the point of view of evolutionary progress, gains and losses are simply advantages and disadvantages from the point of view of gene survival. But we are not compelled to take this view. If we could engineer a genetic change in some people which would have the effect of making them musical prodigies but also sterile, this would be a hopeless gene in terms of survival, but this need not force us, or the musical prodigies themselves, to think of the changes as for the worse. It depends on how we rate musical ability as against having children, and evolutionary survival does not dictate priorities here.

The view that gains and losses are tied up with each other need not depend on the dogma that natural selection *must* have created the best of all possible sets of genes. A more cautiously empirical version of the claim says there is a tendency for gains to be accompanied by losses. John Maynard Smith, in his paper on "Eugenics and Utopia,"[6] takes this kind of "broad balance" view and runs it the other way, suggesting, as an argument in defence of medicine, that any loss of genetic resistance to disease is likely to be a good thing: "The reason for this is that in evolution, as in other fields, one seldom gets something for nothing. Genes which confer disease-resistance are likely to have harmful effects in other ways: this is certainly true of the gene for sickle-cell anaemia and may be a general rule. If so, absence of selection in favour of disease-resistance may be eugenic."

It is important that different characteristics may turn out to be genetically linked in ways we do not yet realize. In our present state of knowledge, engineering for some improvement might easily bring some unpredicted but genetically linked disadvantage. But we do not have to accept that there will in general be a broad balance, so that there is a presumption that any gain will be accompanied by a compensating loss (or Maynard Smith's version that we can expect a compensating gain for any loss). The reason is that what counts as a gain or loss varies in different contexts. Take Maynard Smith's example of sickle-cell anaemia. The reason why sickle-cell anaemia is widespread in Africa is that it is genetically linked with resistance to malaria. Those who are heterozygous (who inherit one sickle-cell gene and one normal gene) are resistant to malaria, while those who are homozygous (whose genes are both sickle-cell) get sickle-cell anaemia. If we use genetic engineering to knock out sickle-cell anaemia where malaria is common, we will pay the price of having more malaria. But when we eradicate malaria, the gain will not involve this loss. Because losses are relative to context, any generalization about the impossibility of overall improvements is dubious.

5. THE FAMILY AND OUR DESCENDANTS

Unlike various compulsory eugenic policies, genetic engineering need not involve any interference with decision by couples to have children together, or with their decisions about how many children to have. And let us suppose that genetically engineered babies grow in the mother's womb in the normal way, so that her relationship to the child is not threatened in the way it might be if the laboratory or the hospital were substituted for the womb. The cruder threats to family relationships are eliminated.

It may be suggested that there is a more subtle threat. Parents like to identify with their children. We are often pleased to see some of our own characteristics in our children. Perhaps this is partly a kind of vanity, and no doubt sometimes we project on to our children similarities that are not really there. But, when the similarities do exist, they help the parents and children to understand and sympathize with each other. If genetic engineering resulted in children fairly different from their parents, this might make their relationship have problems.

There is something to this objection, but it is easy to exaggerate. Obviously, children who were like Midwich cuckoos, or comic-book Martians, would not be easy to identify with. But genetic engineering need not move in such sudden jerks. The changes would have to be detectable to be worth bringing about, but there seems no reason why large changes in appearance, or an unbridgeable psychological gulf, should be created in any one generation. We bring about environmental changes which make children different from their parents, as when the first generation of children in a remote place are given schooling and made literate. This may cause some problems in families, but it is not usually thought a decisive objection. It is not clear that genetically induced changes of similar magnitude are any more objectionable.

A related objection concerns our attitude to our remoter descendants. We like to think of our descendants stretching on for many generations. Perhaps this is in part an immortality substitute. We hope they will to some extent be like us, and that, if they think of us, they will do so with sympathy and approval. Perhaps these hopes about the future of mankind are relatively unimportant to us. But, even if we mind about them a lot, they are unrealistic in the very long term. Genetic engineering would make our descendants less like us, but this would only speed up the natural rate of change. Natural mutations and selective pressures make it unlikely that in a few million years our descendants will be physically or mentally much like us. So what genetic engineering threatens here is probably doomed anyway. . . .

6. RISKS AND MISTAKES

Although mixing different species and cloning are often prominent in people's thoughts about genetic engineering, they are relatively marginal issues. This is partly because there may be no strong reasons in favour of either. Our purposes might be realized more readily by improvements to a single species, whether another or our own, or by the creation of quite new types of organism, than by mixing different species. And it is not clear what advantage cloning batches of people might have, to outweigh the drawbacks. This is not to be dogmatic that species mixing and cloning could never be useful, but to say that the likelihood of other techniques being much more prominent makes it a pity to become fixated on the issues raised by these ones. And some of the most serious objections to positive genetic engineering have wider application than to these rather special cases. One of these wider objections is that serious risks may be involved.

Some of the risks are already part of the public debate because of current work on recombinant DNA. The danger is of producing harmful organisms that would escape from our control. The work obviously should take place, if at all, only with adequate safeguards against such a disaster. The problem is deciding what we should count as adequate safeguards. I have nothing to contribute to this problem here. If it can be dealt with satisfactorily, we will perhaps move on to genetic engineering of people. And this introduces another dimension of risk. We may produce unintended results, either because our techniques turn out to be less finely tuned than we thought, or because different characteristics are found to be genetically linked in unexpected ways.

If we produce a group of people who turn out worse than expected, we will have to live with them. Perhaps we would aim for producing people who were especially imaginative and creative, and only too late find we had produced people who were also very violent and aggressive. This kind of mistake might not only be disastrous, but also very hard to "correct" in subsequent generations. For when we suggested sterilization to the people we had produced, or else corrective genetic engineering for *their* offspring, we might find them hard to persuade. They might like the way they were, and reject, in characteristically violent fashion, our explanation that they were a mistake.

The possibility of an irreversible disaster is a strong deterrent. It is enough to make some people think we should rule out genetic engineering altogether, and to make others think that, while negative engineering is perhaps acceptable, we should rule out positive engineering. The thought behind this second position is that the benefits from negative engineering are clearer, and that, because its aims are more modest, disastrous mistakes are less likely.

The risk of disasters provides at least a reason for saying that, if we do adopt a policy of human genetic engineering, we ought to do so with extreme caution. We should alter genes only where we have strong reasons for thinking the risk of disaster is very small, and where the benefit is great enough to justify the risk. (The problems of deciding when this is so are familiar from the nuclear power debate.) This "principle of caution" is less strong than one ruling out all positive engineering, and allows room for the possibility that the dangers may turn out to be very remote, or that greater risks of a different kind are involved in *not* using positive engineering. These possibilities correspond to one view of the facts in the nuclear power debate. Unless with genetic engineering we think we can already rule out such possibilities, the argument from risk provides more justification for the principle of caution than for the stronger ban on all positive engineering. . . .

DECISIONS

Some of the strongest objections to positive engineering are not about specialized applications or about risks. They are about the decisions involved. The central line of thought is that we should not start playing God by redesigning the human race. The suggestion is that there is no group (such as scientists, doctors, public officials, or politicians) who can be entrusted with decisions about what sort of people there should be. And it is also doubted whether we could have any adequate grounds for basing such decisions on one set of values rather than another. . . .

1. NOT PLAYING GOD

Suppose we could use genetic engineering to raise the average IQ by fifteen points. (I mention, only to ignore, the boring objection that the average IQ is always by definition 100.) Should we do this? Objectors to positive engineering say we should not. This is not because the present average is preferable to a higher one. We do not think that, if it were naturally fifteen points higher, we ought to bring it down to the present level. The objection is to our playing God by deciding what the level should be.

On one view of the world, the objection is relatively straightforward. On this view, there really is a God, who has a plan for the world which will be disrupted if we stray outside the boundaries assigned to us. (It is *relatively* straightforward: there would still be the problem of knowing where the boundaries came. If genetic engineering disrupts the programme, how do we know that medicine and education do not?)

The objection to playing God has a much wider appeal than to those who literally believe in a divine plan. But, outside such a context, it is unclear what the objection comes to. If we have a Darwinian view, according to which features of our nature have been selected for their contribution to gene survival, it is not blasphemous, or obviously disastrous, to start to control the process in the light of our own values. We may value other qualities in people, in preference to those which have been most conducive to gene survival.

The prohibition on playing God is obscure. If it tells us not to interfere with natural selection at all, this rules out medicine, and most other environmental and social changes. If it only forbids interference with natural selection by the direct alteration of genes, this rules out negative as well as positive genetic engineering. If these interpretations are too restrictive, the ban on positive engineering seems to need some explanation. If we can make positive changes at the environmental level, and negative changes at the genetic level, why should we not make positive changes at the genetic level? What makes this policy, but not the others, objectionably God-like?

Perhaps the most plausible reply to these questions rests on a general objection to any group of people trying to plan too closely what human life should be like. Even if it is hard to distinguish in principle between the use of genetic and environmental means, genetic changes are likely to differ in degree from most environmental ones. Genetic alterations may be more drastic or less reversible, and so they can be seen as the extreme case of an objectionably God-like policy by which some people set out to plan the lives of others.

This objection can be reinforced by imagining the possible results of a programme of positive engineering, where the decisions about the desired improvements were taken by scientists. Judging by the literature written by scientists on this topic, great prominence would be given to intelligence. But can we be sure that enough weight would be given to other desirable qualities? And do things seem better if for scientists we substitute doctors, politicians or civil servants? Or some committee containing businessmen, trade unionists, academics, lawyers and a clergyman?

What seems worrying here is the circumscribing of potential human development. The present genetic lottery throws up a vast range of characteristics, good and bad, in all sorts of combinations. The group of people controlling a positive engineering policy would inevitably have limited horizons, and we are right to worry that the limitations of their outlook might become the boundaries of human variety. The drawbacks would be like those of town-planning or dog-breeding, but with more important consequences.

When the objection to playing God is separated from the idea that intervening in this aspect of the natural world is a kind of blasphemy, it is a protest against a particular group of people, necessarily fallible and limited, taking decisions so important to our future. This protest may be on grounds of the bad consequences, such as loss of variety of people, that would come from the imaginative limits of those taking the decisions. Or it may be an expression of opposition to such concentration of power, perhaps with the thought: 'What right have *they* to decide what kinds of people there should be?' Can these problems be side-stepped?

2. THE GENETIC SUPERMARKET

Robert Nozick is critical of the assumption that positive engineering has to involve any centralized decision about desirable qualities: "Many biologists tend to think the problem is one of *design*, of specifying the best types of persons so that biologists can proceed to produce them. Thus they worry over what sort(s) of person there is to be and who will control this process. They do not tend to think, perhaps because it diminishes the importance of their role, of a system in which they run a "genetic supermarket," meeting the individual specifications (within certain moral limits) of prospective parents. Nor do they think of seeing what limited number of types of persons people's choices would converge upon, if indeed there would be any such convergence. This supermarket system has the great virtue that it involves no centralized decision fixing the future human type(s)."[7]

This idea of letting parents choose their children's characteristics is in many ways an improvement on decisions being taken by some centralized body. It seems less likely to reduce human variety, and could even increase it, if genetic engineering makes new combinations of characteristics available. (But we should be cautious here. Parental choice is not a guarantee of genetic variety, as the influence of fashion or of shared values might make for a small number of types on which choices would converge.)

To those sympathetic to one kind of liberalism, Nozick's proposal will seem more attractive than centralized decisions. On this approach to politics, it is wrong for the authorities to institutionalize any religious or other outlook as the official one of the society. To a liberal of this kind, a good society is one which tolerates and encourages a wide diversity of ideals of the good life. Anyone with these sympathies will be suspicious of centralized decisions about what sort of people should form the next generation. But some parental decisions would be disturbing. If parents chose characteristics likely to make their children unhappy, or likely to reduce their abilities, we might feel that the children should be protected against this. (Imagine parents belonging to some extreme religious sect, who wanted their children to have a religious symbol as a physical mark on their face, and who wanted them to be unable to read, as a protection against their faith being corrupted.) Those of us who support restrictions protecting children from parental harm after birth (laws against cruelty, and compulsion on parents to allow their children to be educated and to have necessary medical treatment) are likely to support protecting children from being harmed by their parents' genetic choices.

No doubt the boundaries here will be difficult to draw. We already find it difficult to strike a satisfactory balance between protection of children and parental freedom to choose the kind of upbringing their children should have. But it is hard to accept that society should set no limits to the genetic choices parents can make for their children. Nozick recognizes this when he says the genetic supermarket should meet the specifications of parents "within certain moral limits." So, if the supermarket came into existence, some centralized policy, even if only the restrictive one of ruling out certain choices harmful to the children, should exist. It would be a political decision where the limits should be set.

There may also be a case for other centralized restrictions on parental choice, as well as those aimed at preventing harm to the individual people being designed. The genetic supermarket might have more oblique bad effects. An imbalance in the ratio between the sexes could result. Or parents might think their children would be more successful if they were more thrusting, competitive and selfish. If enough parents acted on this thought, other parents with different values might feel forced into making similar choices to prevent their own children being too greatly disadvantaged. Unregulated individual decisions could lead to shifts of this kind, with outcomes unwanted by most of those who contribute to them. If a majority favour a roughly equal ratio between the sexes, or a population of relatively uncompetitive people, they may feel justified in supporting restrictions on what parents can choose. (This is an application to the case of genetic engineering of a point familiar in other contexts, that unrestricted individual choices can add up to a total outcome which most people think worse than what would result from some regulation.)

Nozick recognizes that there may be cases of this sort. He considers the case of avoiding a sexual imbalance and says that "a government could require that genetic manipulation be carried on so as to fit a certain ratio."[8] He clearly prefers to avoid governmental intervention of this kind, and, while admitting that the desired result would be harder to obtain in a purely libertarian system, suggests possible strategies for doing so. He says: "Either parents would subscribe to an information service monitoring the recent births and so know which sex was in shorter supply (and hence would be more in demand in later life), thus adjusting their activities, or interested individuals would contribute to a charity that offers bonuses to maintain the ratios, or the ratio would leave 1:1, with new family and social patterns developing." The proposals for avoiding the sexual imbalance without central regulation are not reassuring. Information about likely prospects for marriage or sexual partnership might not be decisive for parents' choices. And, since those most likely to be "interested individuals" would be in the age group being genetically engineered, it is not clear that the charity would be given donations adequate for its job.[9]

If the libertarian methods failed, we would have the choice between allowing a sexual imbalance or imposing some system of social regulation. Those who dislike central decisions favouring one sort of person over others might accept regulation here, on the grounds that neither sex is being given preference: the aim is rough equality of numbers.

But what about the other sort of case, where the working of the genetic supermarket leads to a general change unwelcome to those who contribute to it? Can we defend regulation to prevent a shift towards a more selfish and competitive population as merely being the preservation of a certain ratio between characteristics? Or have we crossed the boundary, and allowed a centralized decision favouring some characteristics over others? The location of the boundary is obscure. One view would be that the sex-ratio case is acceptable because the desired ratio is equality of numbers. On another view, the acceptability derives from the fact that the present ratio is to be preserved. (In this second view, preserving altruism would be acceptable, so long as no attempt was made to raise the proportion of altruistic people in the population. But is *this* boundary an easy one to defend?)

If positive genetic engineering does become a reality, we may be unable to avoid some of the decisions being taken at a social level. Or rather, we could avoid this, but only at what seems an unacceptable cost, either to the particular people being designed, or to their generation as a whole. And, even if the social decisions are only restrictive, it is implausible to claim that they are all quite free of any taint of preference for some characteristics over others. But, although this suggests that we should not be doctrinaire in our support of the liberal view, it does not show that the view has to be abandoned altogether. We may still think that social decisions in favour of one type of person rather than another should be few, even if the consequences of excluding them altogether are unacceptable. A genetic supermarket, modified by some central regulation, may still be better than a system of purely central decisions. The liberal value is not obliterated because it may sometimes be compromised for the sake of other things we care about.

3. A MIXED SYSTEM

The genetic supermarket provides a partial answer to the objection about the limited outlook of those who would take the decisions. The choices need not be concentrated in the hands of a small number of people. The genetic supermarket should not operate in a completely unregulated way, and so some centralized decisions would have to be taken about the restrictions that should be imposed. One system that would answer many of the anxieties about centralized decision-making would be to limit the power of the decision-makers to one of veto. They would then only check departures from the natural genetic lottery, and so the power to bring about changes would not be given to them, but spread through the whole population of

potential parents. Let us call this combination of parental initiative and central veto a "mixed system." If positive genetic engineering does come about, we can imagine the argument between supporters of a mixed system and supporters of other decision-making systems being central to the political theory of the twenty-first century, parallel to the place occupied in the nineteenth and twentieth centuries by the debate over control of the economy.[10]

My own sympathies are with the view that, if positive genetic engineering is introduced, this mixed system is in general likely to be the best one for making decisions. I do not want to argue for an absolutely inviolable commitment to this, as it could be that some centralized decision for genetic change was the only way of securing a huge benefit or avoiding a great catastrophe. But, subject to this reservation, the dangers of concentrating the decision-making create a strong presumption in favour of a mixed system rather than one in which initiatives come from the centre. And, if a mixed system was introduced, there would have to be a great deal of political argument over what kinds of restrictions on the supermarket should be imposed. Twenty-first-century elections may be about issues rather deeper than economics.

If this mixed system eliminates the anxiety about genetic changes being introduced by a few powerful people with limited horizons, there is a more general unease which it does not remove. May not the limitations of one generation of parents also prove disastrous? And, underlying this, is the problem of what values parents should appeal to in making their choices. How can we be confident that it is better for one sort of person to be born than another?

4. VALUES

The dangers of such decisions, even spread through all prospective parents, seem to me very real. We are swayed by fashion. We do not know the limitations of our own outlook. There are human qualities whose value we may not appreciate. A generation of parents might opt heavily for their children having physical or intellectual abilities and skills. We might leave out a sense of humour. Or we might not notice how important to us is some other quality, such as emotional warmth. So we might not be disturbed in advance by the possible impact of the genetic changes on such a quality. And, without really wanting to do so, we might stumble into producing people with a deep coldness. This possibility seems one of the worst imaginable. It is just one of the many horrors that could be blundered into by our lack of foresight in operating the mixed system. Because such disasters are a real danger, there is a case against positive genetic engineering, even when the changes do not result from centralized decisions. But this case, resting as it does on the risk of disaster, supports a principle of caution rather than a total ban. We have to ask the question whether there are benefits sufficiently great and sufficiently probable to outweigh the risks.

But perhaps the deepest resistance, even to a mixed system, is not based on risks, but on a more general problem about values. Could the parents ever be justified in choosing, according to some set of values, to create one sort of person rather than another?

Is it sometimes better for us to create one sort of person rather than another? We say "yes" when it is a question of eliminating genetic defects. And we say "yes" if we think that encouraging some qualities rather than others should be an aim of the upbringing and education we give our children. Any inclination to say "no" in the context of positive genetic engineering must lay great stress on the two relevant boundaries. The positive-negative boundary is needed to mark off the supposedly unacceptable positive policies from the acceptable elimination of defects. And

the genes-environment boundary is needed to mark off positive engineering from acceptable positive aims of educational policies. But it is not clear that confidence in the importance of these boundaries is justified. . . .

NOTES

1. Chris Graham has suggested to me that it is misleading to say this without emphasizing the painful slowness of this way of changing gene frequencies.

2. *The Future of Man* (The Reith Lectures, 1959), London, 1960, chapter 3; and in "The Genetic Improvement of Man," in *The Hope of Progress*, London, 1972.

3. *Genes, Dreams and Realities*, London, 1971, p. 81.

4. "Already they have pushed Cline's results further, obtaining transfer between rabbit and mouse, for example, and good expression of the foreign gene in its new host. Some, by transferring the genes into the developing eggs, have managed to get the new genes into every cell in the mouse, including the sex cells; those mice have fathered offspring who also contain the foreign gene." Jeremy Cherfas: *Man Made Life*, Oxford, 1982, pp. 229–30.

5. *Out of the Night*, New York, 1935. To find a distinguished geneticist talking like this after the Nazi period is not easy.

6. John Maynard Smith: *On Evolution*, Edinburgh, 1972; the article is reprinted from the issue on "Utopia" of *Daedalus, Journal of the American Academy of Arts and Sciences*, 1965.

7. *Anarchy, State and Utopia*, New York, 1974, p. 315.

8. Op. cit., p. 315.

9. This kind of unworldly innocence is part of the engaging charm of Nozick's dotty and brilliant book.

10. Decision-taking by a central committee (perhaps of a dozen elderly men) can be thought of as a "Russian" model. The genetic supermarket (perhaps with genotypes being sold by TV commercials) can be thought of as an "American" model. The mixed system may appeal to Western European social democrats.

MARTHA J. FARAH, ET AL.[1]

Neurocognitive Enhancement: What Can We Do and What Should We Do?

Martha J. Farah is the Walter H. Annenberg Professor of Natural Sciences and the Director of the Center for Cognitive Neuroscience at the University of Pennsylvania. Her current research interests include the effects of socioeconomic adversity on children's brain development and emerging social and ethical issues in neuroscience. She has published widely in neuroethics, neuroscience, and psychology, including her recent books *The Cognitive Neuroscience of Vision* (2000) and *Visual Agnosia: Second Edition* (2004).

Many are predicting that the twenty-first century will be the century of neuroscience. Humanity's ability to alter its own brain function might well shape history as powerfully as the development of metallurgy in the Iron Age, mechanization in the Industrial Revolution or genetics in the second half of the twentieth century. This possibility calls for an examination of the benefits and dangers of neuroscience-based technology, or "neurotechnology," and consideration of whether, when and how society might intervene to limit its uses.

At the turn of the century, neurotechnology spans a wide range of methods and stages of development. Brain–machine interfaces that allow direct two-way interaction between neural tissue and electronic transducers remain in the "proof of concept" stage, but show substantial promise. Neurosurgery is increasingly considered as a treatment for mental illnesses and an array of new procedures are under development, including the implantation of devices and tissue. Non-invasive transcranial magnetic stimulation (TMS) of targeted brain areas is the basis of promising new treatments for depression and other psychopathology.

On the leading edge of neurotechnology is psychopharmacology. Our ability to achieve specific psychological changes by targeted neurochemical interventions, which began through a process of serendipity and trial and error in the mid-twentieth century, is evolving into the science of rational drug design. The psychopharmacopia of the early twenty-first century encompasses both familiar, and in some cases highly effective, drugs, and a new generation of more selective drugs that target the specific molecular events that underlie cognition and emotion. For the most part, these drugs are used to treat neurological and psychiatric illnesses, and there is relatively little controversy surrounding this use. However, psychopharmacology is also increasingly used for "enhancement"—that is, for improving the pscychological function of individuals who are not ill.

The enhancement of normal neurocognitive function by pharmacological means is already a fact of life for many people in our society, from elementary school children to ageing baby boomers. In some school districts in the United States the proportion of boys taking methylphenidate exceeds the highest estimates of the prevalence of attention deficit–hyperactivity disorder (ADHD), implying

[1] This paper is based, in part, on a meeting held at the New York Academy of Sciences in June 2003, supported by a grant from the National Science Foundation. Attendees at the meeting and co-authors on this article included Judy Illes (Stanford University), Robert Cook-Deegan Duke University), Howard Gardner (Harvard University), Eric Kandel (Columbia University), Patricia King (Georgetown University), Erik Parens (The Hastings Center), Barbara Sahakian (Cambridge University), and Paul Root Wolpe (University of Pennsylvania).

that normal childhood boisterousness and distractibility are being targeted for pharmacological intervention. . . . Sales of nutritional supplements that promise improved memory in middle age and beyond have reached a billion dollars annually in the United States alone, despite mixed evidence of effectiveness. In contrast to the other neurotechnologies mentioned earlier, whose potential use for enhancement is still hypothetical, pharmacological enhancement has already begun.

WHAT CAN WE DO?

Many aspects of psychological function are potential targets for pharmacological enhancement, including memory, executive function, mood, appetite, libido and sleep. We will use the first two of these, memory and executive function, as examples to show the state of the art in psychopharmaceutical enhancement, the ethical issues raised by such enhancement and the policy implications of these ethical issues. . . .

Memory enhancement. Memory enhancement is of interest primarily to older adults. The ability to encode new memories declines measurably from the third decade of life onwards, and by the fourth decade the decline can become noticeable and bothersome to normal healthy individuals. Memory difficulties in middle or old age are not necessarily a harbinger of future dementia but can be part of the normal pattern of cognitive ageing, which does not make it any less inconvenient when we misplace our glasses or forget the name of a recent acquaintance. What can current and imminent neurotechnologies offer us by way of help?

The changes that underlie normal age-related declines in memory probably differ from those that underlie Alzheimer's disease, indicating that the optimal pharmacological approaches to therapy and enhancement might also differ. . . . Recent advances in the molecular biology of memory have presented drug designers with many entry points through which to influence the specific processes of memory formation, potentially redressing the changes that underlie both normal and pathological declines in memory. Most of the candidate drugs fall into one of two categories: those that target the initial induction of long-term potentiation and those that target the later stages of memory consolidation. . . .

The pursuit of mastery over our own memories includes erasing undesirable memories as well as retaining desirable ones. Traumatic events can cause lifelong suffering by the intrusive memories of post-traumatic stress disorder (PTSD), and methods are being sought to prevent the consolidation of such memories by pharmacological intervention immediately after the trauma. Drugs whose primary purpose is to block memories are also being developed by the pharmaceutical industry. Extending these methods beyond the victims of trauma, to anyone who wishes to avoid remembering an unpleasant event, is another way in which the neural bases of memory could be altered to enhance normal function.

Enhancement of executive function. Executive function refers to abilities that enable flexible, task-appropriate responses in the face of irrelevant competing inputs or more habitual but inappropriate response patterns. These include the overlapping constructs of attention, working memory and inhibitory control. Drugs that target the dopamine and noradrenaline neurotransmitter systems are effective at improving deficient executive function, for example in ADHD, and have recently been shown to improve normal executive function as well. . . .

[I]t is possible that some drugs would compress the normal range of performance in both directions. One of the authors (M.J.F.) found that the dopamine agonist bromocriptine improved performance on various executive function tasks for individuals with lower-than-average working memory capacity, but lowered the performance of those with the highest working memory capacities. Whether enhancement can boost the performance of already high-performing individuals must be determined empirically for each drug and for each type of cognitive ability.

Newer drugs might improve executive function in different ways, influencing different underlying processes and interacting in different ways with individual differences (for example, in working memory capacity) and states (such as restedness). . . .

WHAT SHOULD WE DO?

Ethical problems and policy solutions. Neurocognitive enhancement raises ethical issues for many different constituencies. These include academic and industry scientists who are developing enhancers, and physicians who will be the gatekeepers to them, at least initially. Also included are individuals who must choose to use or not to use neurocognitive enhancers themselves, and parents who must choose to give them or not to give them to their children. With the advent of widespread neurocognitive enhancement, employers and educators will also face new challenges in the management and evaluation of people who might be unenhanced or enhanced (for example, decisions to recommend enhancement, to prefer natural over enhanced performance or vice versa, and to request disclosure of enhancement). Regulatory agencies might find their responsibilities expanding into considerations of 'lifestyle' benefits and the definition of acceptable risk in exchange for such benefits. Finally, legislators and the public will need to decide whether current regulatory frameworks are adequate for the regulation of neurocognitive enhancement, or whether new laws must be written and new agencies commissioned.

To focus our discussion, we will dispense with some ethical issues that are important but not specific to neurocognitive enhancement. The first such issue is research ethics. Research on neurocognitive enhancement, as opposed to therapy, raises special considerations mainly insofar as the potential benefits can be viewed as smaller, and acceptable levels of risk to research subjects would be accordingly lower. This consideration is largely academic for those neurocognitive enhancers that come to market first as therapies for recognized medical conditions, which includes all of the substances that are now available for enhancement, although this might not be true in the future. Another important ethical issue concerns the use of neurocognitive enhancement in the criminal justice system, in which a large proportion of offenders fall in the lower range of cognitive ability in general and executive inhibitory control in particular. Although neurocognitive enhancement brings with it the potential for subtle coercion in the office or classroom, 'neurocorrection' is more explicitly coercive and raises special issues of privacy and liberty that will not be discussed here. Finally, the ethical problems that are involved in parental decision-making on behalf of minor children are complex and enter into the ethics of neurocognitive enhancement in school children, but will not be discussed here.

The remaining issues can be classified and enumerated in various ways. Four general categories will be used here to organize our discussion of the ethical challenges of neurocognitive enhancement and possible societal responses.

Safety. The idea of neurocognitive enhancement evokes unease in many people, and one source of the unease is concern about safety. Safety is a concern with all medications and procedures, but our tolerance for risk is smallest when the treatment is purely elective. Furthermore, in comparison to other comparably elective treatments such as cosmetic surgery, neurocognitive enhancement involves intervening in a far more complex system, and we are therefore at greater risk of unanticipated problems. Would endowing learners with super-memory interfere with their ability to understand what they have learned and relate it to other knowledge? Might today's Ritalin users face an old age of premature cognitive decline? The possibility of hidden costs of neurocognitive enhancement might be especially salient because of our mistrust of unearned rewards, and the sense that such opportunities can have Faustian results.

With any drug, whether for therapy or enhancement, we can never be absolutely certain about the potential for subtle, rare or long-term side effects. Instead, our regulatory agencies determine what constitutes a sufficiently careful search for side effects and what side effects are acceptable in view of a drug's benefits. Although consensus will have to be developed on these issues in connection with neurocognitive enhancement, we see no reason that the same approach cannot be applied here.

Coercion. If neurocognitive enhancement becomes widespread, there will inevitably be situations in which people are pressured to enhance their cognitive abilities. Employers will recognize the benefits of a more attentive and less forgetful workforce; teachers will find enhanced pupils more receptive to learning. What if keeping one's job or remaining in one's school depends on practicing neurocognitive enhancement? Such dilemmas are difficult but are not without useful legal precedent. . . .

Of course, coercion need not be explicit. Merely competing against enhanced coworkers or students exerts an incentive to use neurocognitive enhancement, and it is harder to identify any existing legal framework for protecting people against such incentives to compete. But would we even want to? The straightforward legislative approach of outlawing or restricting the use of neurocognitive enhancement in the workplace or in school is itself also coercive. It denies people the freedom to practice a safe means of self-improvement, just to eliminate any negative consequences of the (freely taken) choice not to enhance.

Distributive justice. It is likely that neurocognitive enhancement, like most other things, will not be fairly distributed. Ritalin use by normal healthy people is highest among college students, an overwhelmingly middle-class and privileged segment of the population. There will undoubtedly be cost barriers to legal neurocognitive enhancement and possibly social barriers as well for certain groups. Such barriers could compound the disadvantages that are already faced by people of low socioeconomic status in education and employment. Of course, our society is already full of such inequities, and few would restrict advances in health or quality of life because of the potential for inequitable distribution. Unequal access is generally not grounds for prohibiting neurocognitive enhancement, any more than it is grounds for prohibiting other types of enhancement, such as private tutoring or cosmetic surgery, that are enjoyed mainly by the wealthy. Indeed, in principle there is no reason that neurocognitive enhancement could not help to equalize opportunity in our society. In comparison with other forms of enhancement that contribute to gaps in socioeconomic achievement, from good nutrition to high-quality schools, neurocognitive enhancement could prove easier to distribute equitably.

Personhood and intangible values. Enhancing psychological function by brain intervention is in some ways like improving a car's performance by making adjustments to the engine. In both cases the goal is to improve function, and to the extent that we succeed without compromising safety, freedom of choice or fairness we can view the result as good. But in other ways the two are very different, because modifying brains, unlike engines, affects persons. The fourth category of ethical issue encompasses the many ways in which neurocognitive enhancement intersects with our understanding of what it means to be a person, to be healthy and whole, to do meaningful work, and to value human life in all its imperfection. . . .

Attempts to derive policies from these considerations must contend with the contradictory ways in which different values are both challenged and affirmed by neurocognitive enhancement. For example, we generally view self-improvement as a laudable goal. At the same time, improving our natural endowments for traits such as attention span runs the risk of commodifying them. We generally encourage innovations that save time and effort, because they enable us to be more productive and to direct our efforts towards potentially more worthy goals. However, when we improve our productivity by taking a pill, we might also be undermining the value and dignity of hard work, medicalizing human effort and pathologizing a normal attention span. The self-transformation that we effect by neurocognitive intervention can be seen as self-actualizing, or as eroding our personal identity. Neither the benefits nor the dangers of neurocognitive enhancement are trivial.

In weighing the dangers of neurocognitive enhancement against its benefits, it is important to note the many ways in which similar tradeoffs are already present in our society. For example, the commodification of human talent is not unique to Ritalin-enhanced executive ability. It is probably more baldly on display in books and classes that are designed to prepare preschoolers for precocious reading, music or foreign language skills, but many loving parents seek out such enrichment for their children. Americans admire the effort that was expended in Abraham Lincoln's legendary four-mile walk to school every day, but no-one would do that (or want their child to do that) if a bus ride were available. Medicalization has accompanied many improvements in human life, including improved nutrition and family planning. And if we are not the same person on Ritalin as off, neither are we the same person after a glass of wine as before, or on vacation as before an exam. As these examples show, many of our lifestyle decisions end up on the right side of one value and the wrong side of another, but this does not necessarily mean that these decisions are wrong.

Disentangling moral principle and empirical fact. Since pre-Socratic times, philosophers have sought ways of systematizing our ethical intuitions, to identify a set of guiding principles that could be applied in any situation to dictate the right course of action. All of us have ethical intuitions about most situations; one goal of ethics is to replace case-by-case intuitions with principled decisions. A practical social advantage of ethical principles is that they can provide guidance when intuitions are unclear or inconsistent from person to person. The success of an ethical discussion depends on the discussants' ability to articulate the relevant principles as well as the relevant facts about a situation to which the principles apply.

In the ethics of neurocognitive enhancement we are still feeling our way towards the relevant principles and we still have much to learn about the relevant facts. Is it a matter of principle that "medicalization" is bad, or that hard work confers 'dignity'? Or are these moral heuristics, rules of thumb that might be contradicted in some cases? And is it a matter of fact that Ritalin reduces our opportunities to learn self-discipline, or could it in fact have no effect or even help us in some way? Until we have disentangled the *a priori* from the empirical claims, and evaluated the empirical claims more thoroughly, we are at risk of making wrong choices.

When not to decide is to decide. Neurocognitive enhancement is already a fact of life for many people. Market demand, as measured by sales of nutritional supplements that promise cognitive enhancement, and ongoing progress in psychopharmacology portend a growing number of people practicing neurocognitive enhancement in the coming years. In terms of policy, we will soon reach the point where not to decide is to decide. Continuing our current *laissez-faire* approach, with individuals relying on their physicians or illegal suppliers for neurocognitive enhancement, risks running afoul of public opinion, drug laws and physicians' codes of ethics. The question is therefore not whether we need policies to govern neurocognitive enhancement, but rather what kind of policies we need. The choices range from minimal measures, such as raising public awareness of the potential practical and moral difficulties of neurocognitive enhancement, to the wholesale enacting of new laws and the creation of new regulatory agencies. In between these extremes lie a host of other options, for example the inclusion of neurocognitive enhancement policies in codes of ethics of the professional organizations of physicians, scientists, human resource managers and educators, and short-term moratoria on neurocognitive enhancement.

Francis Fukuyama has argued for new legislation to control the use of neurocognitive enhancement, among other biotechnologies. He characterizes the work of groups such as the President's Council on Bioethics in the USA and the European Group on Ethics in Science and New Technology as the "intellectual spade work of thinking through the moral and social implications of biomedical research," and suggests that "it is time to move from thinking to acting, from recommending

to legislating. We need institutions with real enforcement powers."

We admit to being less certain about the right course of action. With respect to the first three categories of issue, concerning safety, freedom and fairness, current laws and customs already go a long way towards protecting society. With respect to the fourth category of issue, we believe that there is much more 'spade work' (in Fukuyama's words) to be done in sorting out the moral and social implications of neurocognitive enhancement before we move from recommendations to legislation. . . .

The need for more discussion of the issues is a predictable conclusion for an article like this one, but nevertheless a valid one. One urgent topic for discussion is the role of physicians in neurocognitive enhancement. Although western medicine has traditionally focused on therapy rather than enhancement, exceptions are well established. Cosmetic surgery is the most obvious example, but dermatology, sports medicine and fertility treatments also include enhancement among their goals. Enabling a young woman to bank her eggs to allow later childbearing, for example, is not therapeutic but enhancing. Will neurocognitive enhancement join these practices? If so, will it be provided by specialists or family practitioners? What responsibility will physicians take for the social and psychological impact of the enhancements they prescribe, and by what means (for example, informal or formal psychological screening as used by cosmetic surgeons or fertility specialists)?

Beyond these immediate practical issues, we must clarify the intangible ethical issues that apply to neurocognitive enhancement. This requires interdisciplinary discussion, with neuroscientists available to identify the factual assumptions that are implicit in the arguments for and against different positions, and ethicists available to articulate the fundamental moral principles that apply. As a society we are far from understanding the facts and identifying the relevant principles. With many of our college students already using stimulants to enhance executive function and the pharmaceutical industry soon to be offering an array of new memory-enhancing drugs, the time to begin this discussion is now.

LANGDON WINNER

Resistance Is Futile: The Posthuman Condition and Its Advocates

Langdon Winner is Thomas Phelan Professor of Humanities and Social Sciences at Rensselaer Polytechnic Institute. Langdon Winner is a political theorist who focuses on social and political issues that surround modern technological change. He is the author of *Autonomous Technology*, a study of the idea of "technology-out-of-control" in modern social thought, *The Whale and The Reactor: A Search for Limits in an Age of High Technology*, and editor of *Democracy in a Technological Society*.

Twentieth-century philosophers skeptical about "progress" have sometimes argued that the quest to dominate nature for the benefit of humanity was likely to backfire. Eventually, the same techniques and powers used to dam the rivers, split the atom, and adapt plants and animals for our consumption would be focused on human beings themselves, leading to a thorough modification and, perhaps, the elimination of the human altogether. This prospect was sometimes upheld as the ultimate horror involved in the thoughtless proliferation of sciences and technologies in modern society—an impression echoed in hundreds of science-fiction novels and motion pictures from the 1950s to the present.

Concerns of this kind appear in the concluding pages of two notable works that explore the deeper roots and broader prospects of our civilization. In the final chapter of *The Technological Society*, French sociologist and theologian Jacques Ellul ponders the future of what he describes as "the monolithic technical world that is coming to be." "The new order," he writes, "was meant to be a buffer between man and nature. Unfortunately, it has evolved autonomously in such a way that man has lost all contact with his natural framework and has to do only with the organized technical intermediary which sustains relations both

with the world of life and the world of brute matter." Ultimately, Ellul believes, this will lead to "a new dismembering and a complete reconstitution of the human being so that he can at last become the objective (and also the total object) of techniques."[1]

Similar musings appear at the end of Lewis Mumford's last great work, *The Myth of the Machine: The Pentagon of Power*. The book explores several centuries of philosophical, scientific, technical, industrial, and military developments that have gone into the making of what he calls "the megamachine." Trying to anticipate the future trajectory of a system that had given the world Hiroshima, the Apollo program, and the Vietnam War, Mumford observes, "On the terms imposed by technocratic society, there is no hope for mankind except by 'going with' its plans for accelerated technological progress, even though man's vital organs will all be cannibalized in order to prolong the megamachine's meaningless existence."[2]

In light of these bleak, seemingly overwrought warnings from decades ago, it is astonishing to see that in our time, the nightmare of the philosophers is now widely embraced as a fascinating, plausible, desirable, and perhaps even necessary project in biotechnology and information technology. For many of our contemporaries, the "abolition of the human" is no longer regarded as a distasteful possibility, much less a manifestation of evil. As the new millennium begins, projects in this genre—variously called posthuman, metahuman, transhuman, ultrahuman, or cyborg—are widely cherished as a marvelous intellectual challenge, a path to future profits, an opportunity for artistic fulfillment, and an occasion for exquisite personal transcendence. Although sentiments of this kind are increasingly common in writings about science, technology, and humanity, they remain minority views among intellectuals and within the world's populace. Nevertheless, they may signal the emergence of a climate of opinion that could influence policy choices in years to come. This climate, much like a weather front moving in from the west, stands in contrast to the elaborate, detailed arguments about the ethics of biotechnology and other policy debates about possible modifications to the human species. Yet it may be that a shift in the overall climate of prevailing views, a long-term change in the weather of beliefs, will prove more decisive than the outcome of particular debates in moral philosophy and public policy.

SCIENTIFIC ENTHUSIASTS OF POSTHUMANISM

One does not have to look far to find statements by those who are either engaged in speculation about prospects for the creation of posthumans or who propose programs of research to advance the cause. A number of prominent scientists and publicists for science are willing to lend their imprimatur to this quest. In his flamboyant essay *Metaman: The Merging of Humans and Machines into a Global Superorganism*, Gregory Stock presents a series of brash claims.

Both society and the natural environment have previously undergone tumultuous changes, but the essence of being human has remained the same. Metaman, however, is on the verge of significantly altering human form and capacity.

As the nature of human beings begins to change, so too will concepts of what it means to be human. One day humans will be composite beings: part biological, part mechanical, part electronic. By applying biological techniques to embryos and then to the reproductive process itself, Metaman will take control of human evolution.

No one can know what humans will become, but whether it is a matter of fifty years or five hundred years, humans will eventually undergo radical biological change.[3]

Stock's PhD in biophysics from Johns Hopkins University as well as an MBA from Harvard have helped give him a clear-eyed view of what lies ahead. As director of the Center for the Study of Evolution and the Origin of Life at the University of California at Los Angeles, Stock has outlined the changes he believes the future holds in store, including the conquest of aging. "The human species," he remarks, "is moving out of its childhood. It is time for us to acknowledge our growing powers and begin to take responsibility for them. We have little choice in this, for we have begun to play god in so many of life's intimate realms that we probably could not turn back if we tried."[4] In Stock's hyperinflated burlesque of ethical reasoning, taking "responsibility" involves recognizing the "inevitability" of Metaman and seizing each opportunity to use genetic engineering to move the human organism beyond what he depicts as its present decrepit condition. While he acknowledges that such developments will generate "stresses within society," he argues that moral deliberation and decisions about public policy are irrelevant. "But whether such changes are 'wise' or 'desirable' misses the essential point that they are largely not a matter of choice; they are the unavoidable product of the technological advance intrinsic to Metaman."[5]

Another colorful spokesperson for the posthuman future in the scientific community is molecular biologist Lee Silver. His book *Remaking Eden: Cloning and Beyond in a Brave New World* surveys near and distant prospects for biotechnology in various fields of medicine, especially those involved with control of human reproduction. In his view, ongoing developments in scientific laboratories will produce a revolution in society, an upheaval whose consequences will include the radical division of the species into superior and inferior genetic classes. Imagining conditions that he believes will characterize the United States in the year 2350, he writes:

The GenRich—who account for 10 percent of the American population—all carry synthetic genes. . . . The GenRich are a modern-day hereditary class of genetic aristocrats.

All aspects of the economy, the media, the entertainment industry, and the knowledge industry are controlled by members of the GenRich class. . . . In contrast, Naturals work as low-paid service providers or as laborers.[6]

Silver speculates that by the end of the third millennium, the two groups will have become "entirely separate species with no ability to cross-breed, and with as much romantic interest in each other as a current human would have for a chimpanzee."[7] For those who think his vision of the future resembles a bizarre sci-fi screenplay, Silver notes that his scenario "is based on straightforward extrapolations from our current knowledge base." It is "inevitable" that the use of repro-genetic technologies will change the species in fundamental ways. "There is no doubt about it. For better *and* worse, a new age is upon us."[8]

When statements of a similar sort were made in earlier decades, the horrified response would often be: "Aren't the scientists preparing to 'play God'?" And until recently, the common tendency among scientists was to reassure the public by saying, in effect, "No, we do not intend to play God at all. What we're actually doing is far more modest." Today, however, it appears that a number of scientists—not just zealots like Stock and Silver but also figures central to the development of biotechnology—are willing to own up to the godlike implications of their proposals for human bioengineering. Thus, James Watson, codiscoverer of the DNA double helix, announced at a scholarly symposium in 1998: "And another thing, because no one has the guts to say it, if we could make better human beings by knowing how to add genes, why shouldn't we do it? What's wrong with it?"[9] Addressing members of the British Parliament in May 2000, Watson exclaimed, "But then, in all honesty, if scientists don't play God, who will?"[10]

Scientific advocates for the radical retailoring of the human species and "progress" toward a posthuman successor species are not limited to the field of biotechnology. With his familiar eloquence, physicist Freeman Dyson has written about the branching of humanity into several distinct, deliberately created new varieties, some of which are superior to existing humans and destined to live on the moons of Jupiter and other homes in outer space. The fields of computer science and robotics have spawned a number of posthuman visionaries including Marvin Minsky, Raymond Kurzweil, Hans Moravec, and Kevin Warwick. In their projections of where research and development in information technology will lead, thinkers of this stripe make it clear that humans are no longer the ultimate beneficiaries of technological development and are probably destined to obsolescence. In the larger picture, "progress" in the hot fields of computer science and robotics is truly *for* something else. . . .

Moravec sees the eventual replacement of humans as foreshadowed by ongoing innovations in the business world—changes propelled by the quest for better service at lower prices. Phone calls are handled by intelligent systems of voice mail; automated teller machines take care of much of the work of banking;

automated factories increasingly handle the work of production as the contribution of human labor subsides. He expects developments of this variety to spread, absorbing all significant areas of economic activity before long. Even the belief that the owners of the means of production are the ones who will guide these changes and benefit from them is, in Moravec's view, woefully mistaken. Before long, he argues, "owners will be pushed out of capital markets by much cheaper and better robotic decision makers."

Moravec imagines generations of robots in the distant future that look less like the clunky machines we see today, and more like artificial, self-reproducing organisms. One has the shape of "the basket starfish"; another model, "the Bush Robot," features a stem, treelike branches, balls attached to its limbs like fruit, and microscopic fingers that "might be able to build a copy of itself in about ten hours." Eventually, superintelligent creatures of this kind, "Ex-humans" or "Exes," would grow weary of the limitations of Earth, seeking their fortunes elsewhere in the universe. The question of what will become of ordinary humans in this brave new world is for Moravec of little concern. It is clear that his sympathies lie with the smarter, more resourceful, more powerful successors to our pathetically weak and incompetent species. At one point, he suggests that . . . robots [will] end up producing all foods and manufactured goods. . . . In the longer term, however, this pattern is likely to prove unstable. . . . He speculates that generations of robots who leave Earth may eventually return with aggressive intentions. "An entity that fails to keep up with its neighbors is likely to be *eaten*, its space, materials, energy, and useful thoughts reorganized to serve another's goals. Such a fate may be routine for humans who dally too long on slow Earth before going Ex."[11]

Unstated in visions of this kind, but clearly implied by the drift of discussion, is the conviction that God's original creation was inadequate. With the knowledge available to them now and in the future, scientists can do better than the Creator, that bumbling old fool, who gave us such a terribly inadequate world and equipped us with such a decrepit physique (especially the brain). Surely, we the enlightened can do far better, designing new beings and new worlds based on the power of rapidly advancing technologies. If one prefers a story that sidesteps the theological dimensions and relies on theories of evolution, a common prediction among posthumanists is that science will create the means to channel evolution along marvelous new paths, ones that will, alas, eventually lead to human extinction.

In either context, though, the belief that somehow progress is "for us" needs to be discarded; at this juncture it is merely an outmoded prejudice.

ENTHUSIASTS OF POSTHUMANISM IN POPULAR CULTURE

What is it that attracts people to speculations about the creation of posthumans and to projects that seem to lead in that direction? Clearly, there are many motives at work. For some contemporary scientists, the goal of "improving" or transcending humanity is appealing simply because it is there to be done. Why not use the same knowledge and techniques that we apply to the cloning of Dolly and Polly the sheep or the creation of genetically modified foods and apply them to our own species? Why not produce generations of superartifacts that expand intelligence far beyond anything mere humans could ever hope to achieve? Because it is possible to accomplish powerful, unprecedented effects, the impulse for doing so seems irresistible to some people. Indeed, the default setting on the moral compass of technological choice in our time seems to be, "Hell, why not?" As a science undergraduate in a colleague's philosophy class recently explained, "If I had the opportunity to make the first cloned human, would I do it? Hell yeah!"

Even projects in this genre that have little likelihood of success may seem highly appealing because they hold our possibilities of great wealth and instant fame. Support from venture capital in Silicon Valley and other centers of high technology already awaits biotech entrepreneurs who can spin plausible tales about the eventual payoff of cutting-edge research. Expectations of enormous profits surround corporations jockeying for position in the emerging field of genomics. Meanwhile, the prospect that someone might actually achieve results worthy of mention in the *Guinness Book of Records* inspires a good many to give it a shot. Each morning I read the newspaper, expecting to find the headline "Science Clones First Human Being" or perhaps "Science Clones First Bioethicist." That story has not appeared yet, but I'm told it's just a matter of months. . . .

For the time being, the posthumanist, transhumanist movement is fairly small—a few hundred to a few thousand internationally at most—comprised of colorful, publicity-seeking artists and visionaries and their followers who have had good luck winning the attention of journalists and radio talk show hosts. In Marina del Mar, California, the Extropy Institute, headed by Max More and Natasha Vita-More, regularly organizes conferences and workshops to promote the Extropian vision. "We're at the early transhuman stage now," Vita-More told a reporter for *L. A. Weekly*. "Then we'll get to the mid-transhuman stage, where we start shedding more and more of our biology, start interfacing more and more with machines, prosthetics, implants, and transplants. It's a process, and it's becoming more rapid all the time."[12]

Perhaps an extreme reflection of the California desire to remain forever young in the sun, the Extropians are obsessed with the quest for perpetual beauty, longevity, and the avoidance of death. As Max More observes, "I think people will look back on the twentieth century and think, 'Why didn't more people see that there was a possibility now of actually doing something about aging and death, and why didn't people do something.'"[13] His wife is even more explicit about the elements of transhumanism that derive from upper-middle-class consumerism and hedonism. "I love fashion," Vita-More asserts. "Our bodies will be the next fashion statement; we will design them in all sorts of interesting combinations of texture, colors, tones, and luminosity."[14] . . .

Another group in the vanguard of posthuman publicity is the Raelian movement, a cult founded by French journalist Claude Villion, who calls himself Rael. Its several hundred members in Canada and the United States are attracted by a message Rael received from a friendly extraterrestrial in 1973—the revelation that intelligent life on Earth had been created long ago by a visit from space aliens. In the Raelian view, it is now the duty of humankind to continue the work of those beneficent forebears, improving the species through cloning, genetic manipulation, and other techniques. To that end, the Raelians have organized Clonaid, Inc., "the first human cloning company." Based in the Bahamas where cloning is still legal, the firm hopes to make a variety of reproductive services, including human reproductive cloning, available to the market. Spokespeople for the Clonaid company indicate that some one hundred women have offered to help produce the first artificially cloned child, a result they expect to accomplish very soon.

Of course, one can dismiss groups like the Extropians and Raelians as fringe movements whose ideas cannot be taken seriously. But when the U.S. Congress took up the question of whether to allow or ban human cloning in the United States in hearings held in March 2001, among the first witnesses called were none other than Rael himself and the "scientific director" of Clonaid, Brigitte Boisselier. "They say we're a cult," Rael told reporters before testifying. "But we're not a religion. Our God is science." Several Congresspeople who heard their testimony appeared shocked by the claims of Rael, Boisselier, and other witnesses who promised they were well on the way to cloning humans. Rael explained that the long-term goal was to enable adults to make clones of themselves just before their deaths. . . . As the hearings ended, the chair of the Committee on Energy and Commerce, Rep. Billy Tauzin, promised legislation to ban the practice altogether. While lobbying by the likes of Rael and Boisselier may generate negative reactions in the short term, today's posthumanists may be remembered as bold opinion leaders of a movement in which the combined fascination with UFOs, alien abductions, cyborg fashions, age-old yearnings for transcendence, and the promise of life-enhancing biomedical breakthroughs began to seem like an entirely reasonable, highly marketable package.

FROM TOOLMAKING ANIMAL TO CYBORG

Beyond the extravagant pronouncements of zealots from the community of scientists and the dreams of posthuman publicists, one finds that ideas that are at least highly compatible with projects of posthumanism are now very much in vogue in the social sciences and the humanities. Among prominent scholars and writers, the view that humans are stable, coherent natural entities has gone out of fashion. At the same time, the once commonsense view that there is an important distinction to be drawn between human beings and the technical implements they use has begun to fade, replaced by the conclusion that humans and their tools have finally merged.

The rise of this way of thinking can be traced through a sequence of three perspectives on humans and technology that have focused scholarly debates in recent decades. One persuasion widely endorsed by educated people in the middle of the twentieth century held that humans are toolmaking animals. This conception, formulated by Benjamin Franklin and creatively expanded by Karl Marx, took on renewed significance with twentieth-century archaeological evidence of protohumans and their evolution. Thus, anthropologist Sherwood Washburn, among others, argued that the chance discovery or haphazard creation of sharpened stones used in hunting enabled

Australopithecus to increase the amount of animal protein in its diet, and this in turn led to the evolution of a larger brain and more robust physical features. In this view, toolmaking and tool use, especially the ability to perfect tools over time, was the ability that distinguished humans from other species and established their dominance. From this foundation, the complex structures of social organization and cultural life arose as a consequence of the toolmaking, tool-using abilities of Homo sapiens.

A common moral and political lesson from the homo faber, "toolmaking animal," theory was that the projects of modern technology—including nuclear weapons, the space program, and computers—were manifestations of humanity's most basic urges. As celebrated in numerous World's Fair exhibits, television documentaries, and the famous ape scene in Stanley Kubrick's movie *2001: A Space Odyssey*, tools make us who we are. So prominent was this point of view in the 1950s and 1960s that the skeptical Lewis Mumford chose to attack it directly in the first volume of *The Myth of the Machine*, subtitled *Technics and Human Development*.[15] Mumford argued that the development of symbols, language, and ritual both preceded the contribution of material tools and was far more influential in generating the intellectual, economic, and political accomplishments of human beings in prehistoric and historical times than anything tools had made possible. The myth of the machine, in his view, was the worshipful obsession with technology, a pathological obsession that deflects people from recognizing other, more hopeful dimensions of human creativity.

Although toolmaking animal conceptions stress the centrality of technology in human evolution and history, the underlying assumption is that humans are still distinct from the tools they fabricate and employ. Our instruments are available to us, ready to be used when needed. And certainly, the conditions of their use changes the activities and productivity of individuals and social groups, affecting how different populations flourish and how power is distributed among them. But this viewpoint takes for granted that a firm, reliable boundary exists between humans as organisms and tools regarded as material aids to their activity.

A second idea that has often been used to frame discussions of humans and artificial means—one that is greeted in some quarters as an important advance beyond simple notions about tools and humans—is the claim that technologies are powerful extensions of human organs. Although it had been suggested by earlier thinkers, this perspective attracted considerable attention in the late 1960s and early 1970s as the writings of Marshall McLuhan gained a widespread audience. An obvious appeal of the extensionist position is that it finds power for individuals within the very complexes of electronic media and other sophisticated technologies of modern life that might otherwise seem overwhelming. Thus, the telephone extends a person's ability to hear and speak; television extends the effective perceptual range of one's eyes and ears; automobiles, trains, ships, airplanes, and so forth, are an extension of the mobility provided by human legs. The happy lesson that the extensionist vision inspires is that enormous technological systems developed for corporate and military purposes eventually come to benefit everyday folks. During the so-called space age and era of multimedia spectacles, many found it thrilling to imagine themselves enlarged and augmented by guided missiles and satellite communications. For many, this was good news because it suggested individuals could overcome the limitations of biological forms and abilities received at birth. Hence, during the era of Richard Nixon, Gerald Ford, and Jimmy Carter, McLuhanesque fantasies of the "global village" along with dreams of the colonization of space gave hope to technophiles, especially in the United States. By the 1990s, such dreams had by and large shifted to a new technical template, the Internet.

But despite the insistence that "technology is humanity extended," despite the growing sense that humans and technical systems are intimately connected, extensionist renderings of the story still assume that electronic and other technologies are to a considerable degree distinct from the human organism itself. Yes, one frequently attaches new media to one's limbs and sense organs. But these devices are not in themselves regarded as intrinsic features of human beings; they are long links that could at any moment be disconnected and replaced with extensions of another variety, or by none at all. It remained for another turn in thinking about the relationship between humanity and technology to take a further step, affirming that there is actually no meaningful boundary between humans and technology at all.

Within prominent fields of social theory today— science studies and cultural studies, for example— commonly used categories point to a continual, pervasive blending of nature and artifice. Among the more popular names for these blended entities are "hybrid," "quasi-object," and "cyborg," with events that bring such creations into being called "implosions" and "boundary crossings." The initial stimulus for notions of this kind came from a growing sense that the objects studied by social scientists and humanists should be regarded as social and cultural constructions. Rejecting positivist notions that science obtains knowledge through neutral observation of what happens in nature, many scholars assert that knowledge is to a large extent constructed rather than "discovered." From this belief it becomes possible to reexamine or "interrogate" objects in the world once regarded as purely natural, and find them to be intricate combinations of cultural, social, and physical features. An eagerness to identify and interpret social constructs and blended entities now extends to the names of the activities and institutions once called "science and technology," but now renamed "technoscience" to acknowledge that, if one looks carefully, the two realms continually flow into and through each other.

There are a number of ways in which terms like hybrid and cyborg, and the intellectual strategies associated with them, have been useful to scholars. This terminology and perspective makes it possible to account for the interactions of scientific knowledge, technological change, and social practice in ways not limited by conceptions of nature and society inherited from earlier times. Thus, discussions of power and how it works—including power derived from natural sources—can be depicted in a new light, as a set of hybrid creations whose description enables us to propose new strategies for dealing with sources of power. Similarly, discussions of various knowledge claims about the natural realm need not commit us to judgments that naturalize things that are better regarded as social and cultural constructions, as the history of biological taxonomy and medical definition of various diseases, to cite two examples, clearly reveals. By looking at products, institutions, and living inhabitants of modern society as hybrids, elaborate mixes of elements from culture and nature, social theorists sidestep the badly mistaken identifications and explanations inherited from earlier generations.

Approaches of this kind have played a significant and, in my view, largely positive role in helping historians, philosophers, and social scientists reexamine the concepts, theories, research programs, political ideologies, and social policies that have surrounded science and technology in modern society. There have been many fruitful debates about when and how distinctions among animals/humans/machines have been drawn, and about the practices involved in drawing them. Inquiries in this vein also have interesting political implications, for it is evident that projects in Western science and technology frequently have imposed categories on groups of people and natural things that contained highly suspect, often flagrantly unjust assumptions, ones frequently implicated in relationships of domination. A positive first step is to call into question these inherited categories and to rethink the beings and situations involved. In this way, a wide variety of prejudices can be dispelled, opening the way (in theory at least) for renegotiation of who and what has standing, and which practical steps are most promising. Thus, science studies and cultural studies about technoscience sometimes present themselves as radical, not just in an intellectual sense, but also as a force for progressive political change. . . .

Even more explicit as an advocate of ideas about the condition of humanity as thoroughly infused with the projects and products on contemporary technoscience is Donna J. Haraway, whose writings have inspired a vast literature on cyborgs and what she calls "promising monsters." Humans, in her view, are merely one of a vast range of entities that have finally been removed from anything resembling their original biological condition and are now subject to powerful, intellectually challenging acts of "transgressive border-crossing." Her category "cyborg" includes much more than the human/machine creations described in cold war research documents and depicted in sci-fi films such as *Terminator*. Haraway writes that "cyborg figures—such as the end-of-the-millennium seed, chip, gene, database, bomb, fetus, race, brain, and ecosystem—are the offspring of implosions of subjects and objects and of the natural and artificial."[16] Needed today, in Haraway's grand narrative (which she terms a "modest-witness"), are wide-ranging, feminist deconstructions that reveal the character of these "implosions" and give us ways of thinking about their products unbiased by benighted programs of scientific and philosophical discourse received from previous generations.

To focus on cyborgs and their histories, in Haraway's view, is merely to recognize things that already exist and/or are rapidly coming to be. Yes, their features sometimes strike many people as grotesque. But rather than recoil in horror at even the most unsettling hybrids produced by contemporary technoscience, one must seek to find kinship with the cascade of synthesized, recombinant entities and creatures that increasingly populate the world. She asks, "Who are my kin in this odd world of promising monsters, vampires, surrogates, living tools, and aliens? What kinds of crosses and offspring count as legitimate and illegitimate, to whom and at what cost?" One of the beings she recognizes as kin, for example, is the genetically modified OncoMouse—bred explicitly for research that seeks cures for cancer—a creature she calls "my sister." "Whether I agree to her existence and use or not, s/he suffers, physically, repeatedly, and profoundly, that I and my sisters may live."[17]

In Haraway's elusive, endlessly beguiling way of writing, the methodological commitments of contemporary science studies and cultural studies begin to generate a collection of moral sentiments—ones offered as interpretive insights, but never fully argued as explicit ethical commitments. Thus, her expressions of kinship with cyborgs and hybrids stem from the view that "technoscience as cultural practice and practical culture, . . . requires attention to all the meanings, identities, materialities, and accountabilities of the subjects and objects in play. That is what kinship is about in my 'ethnographic' fugue."[18] An important consequence of this approach is to discredit beliefs that things in nature have distinctive integrity, wholeness of being, or harmony with their surroundings that deserve emphasis in considerations about where technoscience and global corporations can properly move. In Haraway's view, beliefs of this kind predicate a world that no longer exists, if indeed it ever did. What we must focus on now are the circumstances in which a culturally created nature confronts us with things that are only partly identifiable by origins and conditions that existed prior to the arrival of modern civilization. . . .

One can, however, appeal to the weird, the transgressive, and the disharmonious. In her vision of the world, nature is reduced to a kind of comic puzzle. The category that now merits our attention, indeed our awe, is technoscience, the new buzzword of science studies, which she continually reifies in all of its colorful, shape-shifting perversity.

One of Haraway's concerns, a legitimate one, is that the names and the theories produced by science in the past have helped inspire and justify racist policies and institutions in both the North and the South. Using her methods to witness "implosions of nature and culture" and undermine racist strategies and their rhetorics of "purity," she feels she must also dismiss contemporary arguments that applications of biotechnology violate the natural order, for ideas of that kind have gotten us into trouble in the past. She recognizes that, unfortunately, this stance puts her at odds with many of her colleagues in progressive movements around the globe that deploy arguments about purity and danger to resist forceful intrusions of global capitalism. She laments, "Perhaps it is perverse for me to hear the dangers of racism in the *opposition* to genetic engineering and especially transgenics at just the moment when national and international coalitions of indigenous, consumer, feminist, environmental, and development nongovernmental organizations have formed to oppose 'patenting, commercialization and expropriation of human, animal and plant genetic materials.' "[19] But this is a perversity that Haraway decides she can live with. She opposes the patenting of many life-forms, including human genes, because the practice commodifies genetic resources and also excludes the participation of indigenous people, who have a right to decide how these resources are used. But she rejects all contentions that affirm the need to protect species boundaries as a primary good, for such policies are at odds with her belief that the primary responsibility of feminist theory and the new science studies is to call all such boundaries into question, and to deconstruct and thereby reject all claims about wholeness.

Many of Haraway's personal political commitments are laudable ones. She hopes that her work will support efforts by a host of local groups to make "claims rooted in a finally amodern, reinvented desire for justice and democratically crafted and lived well-being." But her approach forbids producing arguments that could make these "claims" evident as coherent and persuasive positions to illuminate personal and policy choices. What she calls for instead are ongoing "contestations"—"contestations for possible, maybe even liveable, worlds of globalized technoscience."[20] In a world in which many of the plans and strategies of global corporations are hatched in secret with little public awareness or debate, one can only hope that such contestations spread and flourish. But Haraway's perspectives on these matters offer little in the way of guidance for those with specific causes to advance or battles to carry to those in power. "We must cast our lot with some ways of living on this planet, and not with others," she suggests.[21] Yet other than observing that ways of living are endlessly contestable (which they certainly are), her writings offer no tangible suggestions about where, when, how, and in which direc-

tion particular lots ought to be cast. In Haraway's postmodernism/posthumanism, moral and ethical sentiments are always emotive and personal, expressed on the fly rather than rigorously argued. In an odd way, the philosophy of science in this mode echoes the prejudices of the logical positivists decades earlier for whom moral judgments were little more than expressions of personal taste.

In the end, as Haraway describes the ongoing mergers of natural and artificial things, she clearly sides with the artificial. Her books and writings take delight in depicting and deconstructing the projects and products of corporate technoscience, modestly witnessing a flow of laboratory and corporate concoctions that will leave indelible marks on the future. At the same time, she derides attempts by others to uphold some things as "natural" as a risible blunder. Indeed, the valence of her writings lends support to the radical restructurings of natural creatures and their habitats, including measures that involve obvious acts of violence. A similar disposition seems to have taken hold within the new subdisciplines of science studies, cultural studies, and technology studies: a kind of bemused indifference when confronted with a world filled with artificial devices, artificial systems, and now, artificially produced living beings. Scholars began with a methodological affirmation that the world for us is composed of social and cultural constructs. Perhaps it is no surprise that they ended up embracing things that most clearly are constructs, hybrid entities that are the products of engineering broadly conceived. In this way, the new scholarship meshes nicely with the work of radical reconstruction and recapitalization at stake in today's technical and corporate realms. In fact, many scholars enjoy the work of ethnography and theory that places them elbow to elbow with the scientific researchers and business leaders who move and shake with initiatives in globalization. Overlooked in this approach is a haunting memory: that most of the world still consists of things and creatures that neither scientists, business people, nor social theorists had any hand in making.

CONCLUSION

Will the prevailing winds in the three arenas of discussion I have described eventually come together to produce a change in climate in society's view of the prospects for posthumanism? It is too soon to tell.

There are signs, however, that the borders between theory in the social sciences and the humanities and the advocacy of scientific zealots and posthumanist social movements has begun to blur. Haraway's writings, for example, are often cited not only as aids in thinking about the world of cyborgs and posthumans but also as a justification for plowing ahead in that direction as rapidly as possible. Thus, James Hughes's manifesto for the radical modification of the human species, "Embracing Change with All Four Arms: A Post-Humanist Defense of Genetic Engineering," cites Haraway as "the principal touchpoint for posthumanism." From now on, Hughes contends, true social progress depends on "faith in the potential unlimited improvability of human nature and expansion of human powers far more satisfying than a resignation to our current limits."[22]

As the old millennium drew to a close, enthusiastic speculation about cyborgs and their ways of living became a popular topic of discussion among supposedly radical voices in the U.S. and European academy. . . .

The vogue of posthumanism reflects a basic disagreement in modern political philosophy about what radical, progressive thinking involves. One understanding of its purpose seeks freedom and social justice for all human beings, with people regarded as being fundamentally equal. During the past two centuries, thinkers who began from that standpoint saw the key challenge as that of justifying and working to realize the social, economic, and political conditions that would foster human liberation. Always key to these efforts was the elimination of oppressive institutions and the creation of better ones. Approaches of this kind are to be found in the writings of a host of reformers and revolutionaries from the eighteenth century to the present day—such as Jean-Jacques Rousseau, Thomas Jefferson, the utopian socialists, Marx, John Dewey, and the like.

A quite different path for radicalism, however—one characteristic of some nineteenth-century romantic visionaries, twentieth-century sci-fi novelists, and today's prophets of posthumanism—is one that aspires to the transcendence of the human shell in quest of more exquisite ways of being. The possibility that fascinates many here, is that a vastly improved person, a Nietzschean *Übermensch* or other superior creature, is an accomplishment well worth seeking. Hence, the focus of revolutionary aspirations no longer rests on cumbersome institutions so notoriously difficult to change, but rather on the physical composition of the body one inhabits. The recent shift in social theory away from concerns about justice and the retailoring of human institutions toward narcissistic concerns about achieving a revolution in the body points to a definite weariness about the strategies for change advocated in earlier decades—organizing unions and resistance movements, for example. In its place is a renewed willingness to affirm the transformative powers of science and technology while overlooking the sometimes unsavory workings of the complex of institutions recently dubbed technoscience.

Whether they intend to or not, social theorists fascinated with hybrids and cyborgs could end up playing a significant role in upcoming debates about practical initiatives to achieve posthuman dreams in tangible form. More eloquently than the scientists who have embraced posthumanist projects, they express a weariness about identifying oneself as merely human at all. That label and all it implies seems to many thinkers so badly outmoded or so badly stained by histories of violence and injustice that it would be just as well to renounce it altogether. Rather than persist in the failed project called humanity, let's find something new and improved. In fact, let's junk this worn-out theme, the human, altogether and come up with a better trope. Much of contemporary social theory has this message as an explicit subtext. Such sentiments dovetail nicely with visions like that of cyberneticist Kevin Warwick, a British scientist who now implants computer chips in his own body as a way to augment his nervous system and who often proclaims his fervent desire to become a cyborg. "I was born human," he wrote in *Wired*. "But this was an accident of fate—a condition merely of time and place. I believe it is something we have the power to change."[23]

For anyone who wanted to argue that there exist fundamental boundaries that should not be crossed in biotechnology, robotics, and other engineering projects, the response of cyborg social theorists is perfectly clear: Face it, folks, the relevant boundaries have already been breached. Thousands of ingenious boundary crossings are already evident in the creation of hybrids of every conceivable description. Mixes of things formerly given in nature along with new things from laboratories, design shops, and marketing agencies have already filled our world. How can anyone suggest this should not continue as it already has for some time now? At the very least, no one can claim any longer that such boundary crossings and their progeny are unprecedented.

As should be clear from the tone of my observations so far, I find the themes and projects of posthumanism a bizarre way of imagining the choices we face. Within three prominent domains of contemporary posthumanism—the natural sciences, social movements, and social theory—one finds levels of self-indulgence and megalomania that are simply off the charts. The greatest puzzle about this fin de siècle fad is how tawdry notions could have attracted such a large audience at all.

Fortunately, there is an appealing alternative to today's frenzy about cyborgs, hybrids, transhumans, extropians, and the like—rethinking what it means to be human in the first place. Far from being an exhausted concept or failed project, being human is a question whose possibilities are very much open to intellectual inquiry and practical realization. The relevant category, in my view, is perhaps less that of "human nature" than of the "human condition." To face this condition squarely involves, for example, the recognition of mortality as a basic fact of human existence. It also entails acknowledging that we are creatures whose history and prospects for survival are indelibly rooted in the circumstances of a blue planet that revolves around the Sun. Yes, it is possible to rebel against fundamental conditions of this kind, for instance, by seeking a vastly extended longevity or by rocketing away from Earth into cold, inhospitable corners of the universe. But such attempts are haunted by the question, Why would anyone want to take such steps other than as an expression of sheer hubris?

It is perfectly true that our ways of being human in the modern world are deeply connected to scientific knowledge and technological devices of all kinds. As I proofread this paper, I am helplessly dependent on the eyeglasses that help me see. But pondering this situation, does one emphasize the glasses or the person viewing, the package of technical equipment in the mix or the distinctive organism that puts it to use? The penchant for placing the technical hardware before the human (and it has come to that in much of contemporary thinking) is to my mind a terrible blunder, the perfect operational definition of a condition long feared in modern society—dehumanization.

One serious consequence of the move to abandon a vital concern for humans and their condition and to search for more exotic, posthuman ways of being is to remove the foundations on which some crucial moral and political agreements can be sought—an appeal to our common humanity. Thus, at the beginning of World War II, Franklin Delano Roosevelt argued that the central issue in the conflict was not merely the victory of the United States and its allies over the Fascists but the victory of democracy and its "simple principles of common decency and humanity." From this simple but persuasive standpoint, Roosevelt announced that "the objective of smashing the militarism imposed by war lords upon their enslaved peoples; the objective of liberating the subjugated nations; the objective of establishing and securing freedom of speech, freedom of religion, freedom from want, and freedom from fear everywhere in the world."[24] The creation of the United Nations after the war and the affirmation of the Universal Declaration of Human Rights by the UN General Assembly offered hope that the principles of "common decency and humanity" might be realized. And while it is obvious that practice has fallen far short of this idealistic affirmation, the concern for a shared humanity and the desire to alleviate the suffering of one's fellow humans remains perhaps the most powerful anchor for ethical conduct and wise policy in global politics, even among those who disagree on specific steps. Are there similar anchors in today's inflated rhetoric about posthumans—moral lessons derived from "our common cyborgity" perhaps? I think not. Indeed, most of the benefit from such discourse appears to be career development for well-heeled intellectuals in Paris, Santa Cruz, Cambridge, and other R & D hubs.

What can one say about the actual condition of the humans living on Earth at present? For anyone who cares to examine them, the data are chilling. According to the 2001 edition of the UN *Human Development Report*, 1.2 billion people on the planet suffer in extreme poverty, surviving on less than $1 a day, while a total of 2.8 billion (roughly half the world's population) live on less than $2 a day. Some 2.4 billion people are without access to basic sanitation. Of the world's children, 325 million are out of school at the primary and secondary levels. For children under the age of five, 11 million die annually from preventable causes. Perhaps those now enthralled with cyborgs, hybrids, extropians, and posthumans will find such information insufficiently novel or thrilling to deflect their ambitious philosophical and research agendas. But the rest of us should take notice.

It is interesting to imagine what humanity as a whole might become if the best of moral understandings, personal sympathies, and practices of democracy were universally applied. One promising approach has never been tried—evening out the wealth available to human individuals, including redistributing worldwide much of the wealth now commanded by the most prosperous states of Europe and North America. If undertaken with sufficient concern for the health of the world's ecosystems and the diverse species that coinhabit the planet with us, this seems a far more promising policy than that of breeding exotic posthuman hybrids. In fact, it is well overdue for scientists and intellectuals in the North to focus strongly on all present and future members of human species, seeking to improve understandings of and connections with them—matters that have, by all accounts, remained woefully underappreciated with the creation of a modern, industrial society and today's global economy. To set aside this effort may be simply the latest stage of colonization, even among those who label themselves postcolonialist thinkers. Yet many seem eager to announce to persons living on less than one dollar a day that their bodies, abilities, and identities have been superseded by new products, new hybrids, produced in European and U.S. high-tech labs and social theory seminars.

In the decades ahead, a climate of opinion centering on posthumanism could well emerge to inform debates about crucial points of departure in public policy. Within this mood, initiatives of bioengineering will be regarded as perfectly normal and endlessly fascinating. By the same token, any resistance to innovations in human reproductive cloning and human germ line modification could appear regressive, reactionary, and outmoded. Within this "forward-looking," "progressive" climate of opinion, one might still debate which specific models of cyborgs, posthumans, transhumans, and the like should be engineered. These are the matters that we can "interrogate,"— matters that are still wonderfully "contestable." But to deny that any such projects should be launched at all will likely be rejected as simply out of touch with contemporary trends. For you see, dear friends, the boundaries have already been breached, the precedents established, the work of innovation set in motion, and the "promising monsters" all introduced at the cyborg-feminist/science studies debutante ball. What fascinates us now is the lovely and, oh, so wonderfully frightening dance of "transgressions" performed to the currently fashionable "ethnographic fugue."

Hence, as we look forward to pending discussions on the posthuman prospect, contemporary social the-

orists may have something consequential to add. For those who propose that it would be a grand idea to erase biological boundaries and embark on a wide range of radical and untested adventures in the reengineering of humankind, scholars in "the humanities" can happily say, "Haven't you heard? It's already well under way!"

NOTES

1. Jacques Ellul, *The Technological Society*, trans. John Wilkinson (New York: Alfred A. Knopf, 1965), 428, 431.

2. Lewis Mumford, *The Myth of the Machine: The Pentagon of Power* (New York: Harcourt Brace Jovanovich, 1970), 435.

3. Gregory Stock, *Metaman: The Merging of Humans and Machines into a Global Superorganism* (New York: Simon and Schuster, 1993), 150, 152, 164, 168.

4. Gregory Stock, "Human Germline Engineering: Implications for Science and Society," Introduction, http://research.mednet.ulca.edu/pmts/Germline/bhwf.htm.

5. Stock, *Metaman*, 168.

6. Lee M. Silver, *Remaking Eden: Cloning and Beyond in A Brave New World* (New York: Avon Books, 1997), 4, 6.

7. Ibid., 7.

8. Ibid, 11.

9. James Watson, cited in Gregory Stock and John Campbell, ed., *Engineering the Human Germline: An Exploration of the Science and Ethics of Altering the Genes We Pass to Our Children* (New York: Oxford University Press, 2000), 79.

10. James Watson, cited in Steven Connor, "Nobel Scientist Happy to 'Play God' with DNA," *Independent*, May 7, 2000, 7.

11. Hans Moravec, *Robot: Mere Machine to Transcendent Mind* (New York: Oxford University Press, 1999), 146.

12. Natasha Vita-More, cited in Brendan Bernhard, "The Transhumanists," *L.A. Weekly*, January, 19–25 2001, 3.

13. Max More, cited in ibid., 6.

14. Natasha Vita-More, cited in Brian Alexander, "Don't Die, Stay Pretty: Introducing the Ultrahuman Makeover," *Wired* 8, no. 1 (January 2000) 6.

15. Lewis Mumford, *The Myth of the Machine: Technics and Human Development* (New York: Harcourt Brace Jovanovich, 1967).

16. Donna J. Haraway, *Modest_Witness@Second_Millennium: FemaleMan©_Meets_OncoMouse^{TM}: Feminism and Technoscience* (New York: Routledge, 1996), 12.

17. Ibid., 52, 79.

18. Ibid., 82.

19. Ibid.

20. Ibid., 267, 270.

21. Ibid., 270.

22. James Hughes, "Embracing Change with All Four Arms: A Post-Humanist Defense of Genetic Engineering," *Eubios: Journal of Asian and International Bioethics* 6.4 (1996): 94–101.

23. Kevin Warwick, "Cyborg 1.0," *Wired* 8, no. 2, (February 2000) 1. See also Kevin Warwick, "I Want to Be a Cyborg," *Guardian*, January 26, 2000, www.guardian.co.uk/comment/story/0,3604,238778,00.html (accessed January 20, 2004).

24. Franklin Delano Roosevelt, "Annual Message to Congress," January 6, 1942, in *The Public Papers and Addresses of Franklin D. Roosevelt*, 1942, ed. Samuel I. Rosenman (New York: Harper and Brothers Publishers, 1950) 32–42.

Ethics and Bioscience

JONATHAN B. TUCKER
AND RAYMOND A. ZILINSKAS

The Promise and Perils of Synthetic Biology

Jonathan B. Tucker is a Senior Fellow in the Washington, D.C. office of The Center for Nonproliferation Studies at the Monterey Institute of International Studies where he specializes in chemical and biological weapons issues. He is the editor of *Toxic Terror: Assessing Terrorist Use of Chemical and Biological Weapons* (2000) and the author of *Scourge: The Once and Future Threat of Smallpox* (2001) and *War of Nerves: Chemical Warfare from World War I to Al-Qaeda* (2006).

Dr. Raymond A. Zilinskas directs the Chemical and Biological Weapons Nonproliferation Program at The Center for Nonproliferation Studies at the Monterey Institute of International Studies. His research focuses on achieving effective biological arms control, the proliferation potential of the former Soviet Union's biological warfare program, and meeting the threat of bioterrorism. Dr. Zilinskas's book, *Biological Warfare: Modern Offense and Defense,* was published in 1999. He also is coeditor of the *Encyclopedia of Bioterrorism Defense,* published in 2005.

Over the past fifty years, several pivotal advances have transformed the life sciences, including the discovery of the structure of DNA, the deciphering of the genetic code, the development of recombinant DNA technology, and the mapping of the human genome. Synthetic biology is another transformative innovation that will make it possible to build living machines from off-the-shelf chemical ingredients, employing many of the same strategies that electrical engineers use to make computer chips. Drawing upon a set of powerful techniques for the automated synthesis of DNA molecules and their assembly into genes and microbial genomes, synthetic biology envisions the redesign of natural biological systems for greater efficiency, as well as the construction of functional "genetic circuits" and metabolic pathways for practical purposes.

Among the potential applications of this new field is the creation of bioengineered microorganisms (and possibly other life forms) that can produce pharmaceuticals, detect toxic chemicals, break down pollutants, repair defective genes, destroy cancer cells, and generate hydrogen for the post-petroleum economy. Although synthetic biology is chiefly an engineering discipline, the ability to design and construct simplified biological systems offers life scientists a useful way to test their understanding of the complex functional networks of genes and biomolecules that mediate life processes.

Today, synthetic biology is at roughly the same level of development as molecular genetics was in the mid- to late 1970s, some five years after the invention of recombinant-DNA technology. In June 2004, the first international conference devoted to the new field, "Synthetic Biology 1.0," was held at the Massachusetts Institute of Technology (M.I.T.). The organizers claimed to have "brought together, for the first time, researchers who are working to: (1) design and build

From *The New Atlantis* 12 (Spring 2006), 25–45. Reprinted with permission. For more information, see www.TheNewAtlantis.com.

biological parts, devices, and integrated biological systems, (2) develop technologies that enable such work, and (3) place this scientific and engineering research within its current and future social context." In addition to technical presentations, policy analysts addressed the security, safety, and ethical issues associated with synthetic biology. . . . Meanwhile, at M.I.T. and several other universities, synthetic biology has become a powerful catalyst for interdisciplinary research and teaching that bridges the life sciences and engineering, attracting the interest of undergraduates, graduate students, and faculty members from a wide variety of fields.

Many of the enabling technologies for synthetic biology have existed for several years. The metabolic engineering of bacteria for natural product synthesis was first achieved in the early 1970s, and engineered bacterial plasmids for biotechnology were developed during the 1980s. Genetically modified organisms with relatively sophisticated systems for gene expression and containment have been around for nearly as long. The main difference between genetic engineering and synthetic biology is that whereas the former involves the transfer of individual genes from one species to another, the latter envisions the assembly of novel microbial genomes from a set of standardized genetic parts. These components may be natural genes that are being applied for a new purpose, natural genes that have been redesigned to function more efficiently, or artificial genes that have been designed and synthesized from scratch.

Although much of the current work on synthetic biology is taking place in the United States, research groups are also active in Europe, Israel, and Japan, and the technology will surely spread to other countries. Over the next decade, synthetic biology is likely to enter a phase of exponential growth. . . .

If the history of molecular biology is any guide, synthetic biology research will generate a vast amount of new information about life processes—from the role of specific genes to the metabolism of whole organisms—as well as numerous applications in medicine, agriculture, industry, bioremediation, and energy. And as with any powerful new technology, synthetic biology is likely to create new risks for society, including possible unintended harmful consequences for human health or the environment, or deliberate misuse for hostile purposes. . . .

RESEARCH OBSTACLES AND POTENTIAL RISKS

Although synthetic biologists have accomplished a great deal in a short time, major obstacles remain to be overcome before the practical applications of the technology can be realized. One problem is that the behavior of bioengineered systems remains "noisy" and unpredictable. Genetic circuits also tend to mutate rapidly and become nonfunctional. Drew Endy of M.I.T., one of the pioneers in the field, believes that synthetic biology will not achieve its potential until scientists can predict accurately how a new genetic circuit will behave inside a living cell. He argues that the engineering of biological systems remains expensive, unreliable, and ad hoc because scientists do not understand the molecular processes of cells well enough to manipulate them reliably.

Writing in *Nature* in late 2005, Endy suggested three strategies for overcoming these obstacles. The first, *standardization*, refers to the "promulgation of standards that support the definition, description and characterization of the basic biological parts, as well as standard conditions that support the use of parts in combination and overall system operation." The M.I.T. Registry of Standard Biological Parts is a first step toward that end. The second, *decoupling*, is the effort to "separate a complicated problem into many simpler problems that can be worked on independently, such that the resulting work can eventually be combined to produce a functioning whole." Finally, *abstraction* is a method for organizing information describing biological functions into "hierarchies" that operate at different levels of complexity. Following these strategies, Endy writes, "would help make routine the engineering of synthetic biological systems that behave as expected."

An assessment of the risks involved in synthetic biology research must begin with two obvious points. First, because engineered microorganisms are self-replicating and capable of evolution, they belong in a different risk category than toxic chemicals or radioactive materials. Second, some of the risks of synthetic biology are simply indefinable at present—that is, there may be risks that we cannot anticipate with any degree of precision at this early stage in the development of the field.

That said, we can use history as a guide—particularly the history of recombinant DNA technology—to discern three main areas of risk in synthetic biology. First, synthetic microorganisms might escape from a research laboratory or containment facility, proliferate out of control, and cause environmental damage or threaten public health. Second, a synthetic microorganism developed for some applied purpose might cause harmful side effects after being deliberately released into the open environment. Third, outlaw states, terrorist organizations, or individuals might exploit synthetic biology for hostile or malicious purposes.

THE RISK OF ACCIDENTAL RELEASE

The history of the risks and safeguards involved in recombinant DNA research, which involves the cutting and splicing of genes from different species, is instructive for understanding the risks associated with synthetic biology. The first people to voice concerns about the potential risks of recombinant DNA research were the scientists doing the work. During the summer of 1975, the leading investigators in the field met at the Asilomar Conference Center in Pacific Grove, California, to discuss the hazards associated with the new technology. They concluded that although most gene transfers posed a low level of risk, a few types of experiments, such as the insertion of toxin genes and virulence factors into bacteria, could entail significant dangers. In response, the National Institutes of Health (NIH) established a Recombinant DNA Advisory Committee (RAC) to develop biosafety guidelines and a process for institutional oversight that would apply to all NIH-funded research projects.

Under the NIH Guidelines, which were adopted in 1976, the most dangerous experiments were banned and others were subjected to a thorough risk assessment. The guidelines specify the level of laboratory biocontainment required for different types of gene-transfer experiments. Many scientists considered the NIH Guidelines overly restrictive when they were first introduced, but over the past thirty years, the guidelines have gradually evolved in response to experience: Because of the excellent safety record of gene-splicing research and development, the RAC has since downgraded the biosafety requirements for most types of recombinant DNA experiments.

Despite the fact that no accidental release of a genetically-engineered microorganism (GEM) from a laboratory has been reported, it is possible that such releases have occurred but that the effects were so unremarkable that they remained undetected. GEMs generally appear to be less "fit" than their natural counterparts and hence would probably die off rapidly in the environment. Nevertheless, given their potential to replicate and evolve, special precautions are warranted. To reduce the probability that GEMs could proliferate outside a containment facility, the NIH Guidelines require that scientists build safeguards into the host microbes that receive foreign DNA. For example, researchers have developed bacterial strains that are metabolically deficient and thus require special nutrients that are not available in nature, so that the bacteria can survive and propagate only under artificial laboratory conditions.

The main lesson for synthetic biology from the regulation of recombinant DNA research concerns the extent of the researcher's familiarity with the host microbe that is being genetically modified. Because the microorganisms used for genetic engineering, such as the bacterium *E. coli* and the yeast *S. cerevisiae*, are well understood by scientists, the transfer of one or two foreign genes is unlikely to change the characteristics of the host in a dramatic, unpredictable way.

To what extent would the risks associated with a synthetic microorganism differ from those of a genetically engineered one? At least for the near future, the vast majority of synthetic biological systems will be engineered by transferring small genetic circuits into a well-understood bacterial host, limiting the level of risk. A decade from now, however, synthetic genomes may be assembled from BioBricks that have been redesigned or are entirely artificial, having been created *de novo*. If a synthetic microorganism is built by combining these genetic elements in a new way, it will lack a clear genetic pedigree and could have "emergent properties" arising from the complex interactions of its constituent genes. Accordingly, the risks attending the accidental release of such an organism from the laboratory would be extremely difficult to assess in advance, including its possible spread into new ecological niches and the evolution of novel and potentially harmful characteristics.

During the process of laboratory research, animal testing in a contained facility may suggest whether or not a synthetic microorganism is pathogenic. Nevertheless, no animal model can predict infallibly how a novel microbe will behave in a human host, and there is no reliable way to measure its possible impact on complex ecosystems. It is also unclear whether or not the standard techniques used to prevent GEMs from proliferating outside the laboratory will be effective for synthetic microbes. As a result, future research involving the creation of synthetic microorganisms will pose major challenges for assessing and managing biosafety risks. It is not too early to begin thinking about this problem, which is likely to be quite difficult to solve.

To the extent that synthetic microorganisms lack a natural genetic pedigree, regulators may insist on developing new biosafety guidelines or regulations to prevent their accidental release into the environment. At present, it is unclear if these rules would resemble the NIH Guidelines or would be specific to synthetic biology. One approach to reducing the possible risks associated with synthetic microorganisms would be to ensure that they are inherently incapable of surviving and replicating outside the laboratory. For example, synthetic bacteria might be endowed with a redesigned genetic code and unnatural amino acids so that even if the engineered genes were taken up by natural cells or viruses, they could not be expressed. Scientists may also build into a synthetic microbe a "self-destruct" mechanism that is triggered by a high density of microorganisms, a specified number of cell divisions, or an external chemical signal. Nevertheless, such built-in control mechanisms may not be foolproof. If, for example, a synthetic microorganism is accidentally released into the environment, it might conceivably mutate or exchange genetic material with indigenous natural microorganisms in a way that makes the built-in controls ineffectual.

Given these uncertainties, it would be prudent to adopt the "precautionary principle" and treat synthetic microorganisms as dangerous until proven harmless. According to this approach, all organisms containing assemblies of BioBricks would have to be studied under a high level of biocontainment (Biosafety Level 3 or even 4) until their safety could be demonstrated in a definitive manner. As George Church argued in *Nature* in 2005, "Learning from gene therapy, we should imagine worst-case scenarios and protect against them. For example, full physical isolation and confined lab experiments on human and agricultural pathogens should continue until we have data on a greater number of potential consequences—ecological and medical—of engineering such systems."

THE RISK OF TESTING IN THE OPEN ENVIRONMENT

By definition, some of the proposed applications of synthetic biology, such as biosensing, agriculture, and biore-

mediation (for example, cleaning up soil contaminated with toxic chemicals), would involve the use of synthetic microorganisms in the open environment. To date, only a small number of GEMs have been developed for applications outside of the laboratory or containment facility. According to the U.S. Department of Agriculture's Animal and Plant Health Inspection Service, GEMs may be developed and used for agricultural purposes, such as enriching soil, without a permit if the "recipient microorganisms . . . are not plant pests and . . . result from the addition of genetic material containing only noncoding regulatory regions."

With respect to bioremediation, the Environmental Protection Agency requires a stringent risk assessment before it will approve the release into the environment of a GEM that can break down specific pollutants. Although few GEMs have been developed for this purpose, including genetically modified strains of the common soil bacterium *Pseudomonas putida*, they have been tested only in the laboratory and in one field test carried out in 1996 under tightly controlled conditions. In that experiment, Gary Sayler and his colleagues at the University of Tennessee's Center for Environmental Biotechnology used soil lysimeters, steel-lined tanks measuring eight feet in diameter and filled with a large volume of soil, to monitor bioengineered bacteria as they degraded a toxic chemical. Because of the uncertain ecological impacts of conducting such experiments in the open environment, however, no GEMs developed for bioremediation are currently in the regulatory pipeline.

Theoretically, three types of negative effects could result from releasing a synthetic microorganism into the environment. First, the organism could disrupt local biota or fauna through competition or infection that, in the worst case, could lead to the extinction of one or more wild species. Second, once a synthetic organism has successfully colonized a locale, it might become endemic and thus impossible to eliminate. Third, the synthetic organism might damage or disrupt some aspect of the habitat into which it was introduced, upsetting the natural balance and leading to the degradation or destruction of the local environment.

U.S. government agencies, foreign governments, and intergovernmental organizations all take different approaches to assessing the risks associated with the deliberate release of a GEM into the open environment. Generally speaking, though, an inventor seeking permission to release a GEM must answer five questions in detail:

1. Are you thoroughly familiar with the microorganism donating the genetic material?
2. Are you thoroughly familiar with the microorganism receiving the genetic material?
3. Are you thoroughly familiar with the environment of the site into which the genetically engineered microorganism will be introduced?
4. Will you be able to contain the introduced organism to the designated site of introduction?
5. Should containment fail, do you know the damage that the escaped microorganism would cause to human health and/or the environment?

Based on the answers to these five questions, a regulatory agency can perform an objective risk assessment of the proposed release of a GEM. It is by no means clear, however, that one could answer these questions for a synthetic microorganism. Because a microbe constructed from BioBricks would not contain genetic material transferred from another species, Questions 1 and 2 are not relevant as stated, although the "familiarity" criterion is key. Could the inventor of a synthetic microorganism be said to be truly "familiar" with it? On the one hand, the inventor would know every BioBrick making up the genetic circuitry of the organism. On the other hand, he or she would have little understanding of the organism's emergent properties, including how the synthetic microbe will interact with other living entities after its release into the ecosystem. Assuming that the answer to Question 3 (familiarity with the environment) is "yes," the answer to Question 4 must inevitably be "no" when dealing with self-replicating synthetic microorganisms. Thus, the answer to Question 5 is critical. Because of a lack of empirical evidence, the inventor of a synthetic microorganism could not predict the effects of its release on human health and the environment with any degree of confidence.

Given these uncertainties, scientists seeking to develop synthetic microorganisms for applications outside a containment facility will need to develop new ways to assess their impact on the environment. One approach is to perform systematic testing in an experimental ecosystem that has been designed and constructed by biologists to analyze ecological dynamics. There are two types of model ecosystems: a "microcosm," which varies in size from a few milliliters to 15 cubic meters, and a "mesocosm," which is larger than 15 cubic meters. These model systems consist of elements of a natural ecosystem, such as soil, vegetation, lake water, and sediment, which are brought together in a container such as an aquarium, an earth-lined pond, or a PVC tank, and allowed to equilibrate. (The soil lysimeter described above is a type of mesocosm.) Ideally, a model ecosystem should be sufficiently realistic and reproducible to serve as a bridge between the laboratory and a field test in the open environment.

Microcosm and mesocosm studies have been useful in several environmental applications, such as measuring the stress placed on various types of ecosystems by synthetic chemicals, natural microorganisms, and GEMs. In addition, model ecosystems have served to estimate the extent to which the foreign genetic material introduced into a GEM can be transferred to other organisms or can persist by itself in the environment. However, some scientists and regulatory agencies have rejected data from microcosm and mesocosm studies because of a lack of consistency in the way the experiments were performed and the results interpreted. With this problem in mind, it may be necessary for the synthetic biology community to develop a standardized methodology for testing the environmental impact of its inventions.

One of the lessons from the history of recombinant DNA research is that the *products* made by genetically engineered microbes are no more hazardous than those manufactured by more traditional methods. Thus, for drugs and proteins made by synthetic microorganisms (such as the artemisinin precursor produced in yeast), U.S. regulators will probably focus on the safety of the final product rather than the method of production. In contrast, countries in Western Europe and other parts of the world have taken a more restrictive approach to genetically modified foods and may likewise be inclined to discriminate against drugs and other items manufactured by synthetic microorganisms.

THE RISK OF DELIBERATE MISUSE

The 1972 Biological and Toxin Weapons Convention (BWC) bans the development, production, stockpiling, and transfer of "microbial or other biological agents, or toxins whatever their origin or method of production, of types and in quantities that have no justification for prophylactic, protective or other peaceful purposes." Thus, the BWC implicitly prohibits the synthesis of known or novel microorganisms for hostile purposes. Moreover, if synthetic organisms were designed to produce toxins, then the development and production of these poisons for weapons purposes would be prohibited by both the BWC and the 1993 Chemical Weapons Convention. Nevertheless, because the BWC has not been signed and ratified by every country, lacks formal verification mechanisms, and does not bind non-state entities such as terrorist organizations, it does little to prevent the deliberate misuse of synthetic biology for hostile purposes.

One potential misuse of synthetic biology would be to recreate known pathogens (such as the Ebola virus) in the laboratory as a means of circumventing the legal and physical controls on access to "select agents" that pose a bioterrorism risk. Indeed, the feasibility of assembling an entire, infectious viral genome from a set of synthetic oligonucleotides has already been demonstrated for poliovirus and the Spanish influenza virus. As DNA synthesis technology improves, the assembly of even larger viruses (such as variola, the causative agent of smallpox) may eventually become feasible. J. Craig Venter noted, in testimony before a Senate subcommittee in 2005, that although a bioterrorist could use synthetic genomics to make a pathogenic virus, "the number of pathogens that can be synthesized today is small and limited to those with sequenced genomes. And for many of these the DNA is not infective on its own and poses little actual threat. Our concern is what the technology might enable decades from now."

Indeed, projecting a decade or more into the future, some analysts have made dire predictions about the potential misuse of synthetic biology techniques for the development of more lethal or militarily effective biological warfare agents. In November 2003, for example, an expert panel set up by the U.S. Central Intelligence Agency released a short white paper that concludes, "Growing understanding of the complex biochemical pathways that underlie life processes has the potential to enable a class of new, more virulent biological agents engineered to attack distinct biochemical pathways and elicit specific effects." This unclassified report provides no details concerning the expertise, equipment, and facilities that would be required to develop such engineered biowarfare agents, nor a time estimate for how long the development process might take.

In a similar effort at prediction, Mark Wheelis, a microbiologist at the University of California, Davis,

painted a frightening picture of synthetic biology twenty years or more into the future. Among his predictions in a 2004 *Arms Control Today* article: "Living synthetic cells will likely be made in the next decade; synthetic pathogens more effective than wild or genetically engineered natural pathogens will be possible sometime thereafter. . . . Such synthetic cellular pathogens could be designed to be contagious or noncontagious, lethal or disabling, acute or persistent."

How should one assess these predictions about the potential misuse of synthetic biology for hostile purposes? At present, the primary threat of misuse appears to come from state-level biological warfare programs, some of which probably exploit advanced molecular biology techniques. It is known that Soviet weapons scientists conducted genetic engineering research with dangerous pathogens, such as those that cause anthrax, plague, and tularemia. Could scientists possessing this expertise employ synthetic biology to design and construct an entirely artificial pathogen that is significantly more deadly and robust than those that already exist in nature?

In fact, such a scenario is extremely unlikely. To create such an artificial pathogen, a capable synthetic biologist would need to assemble complexes of genes that, working in unison, enable a microbe to infect a human host and cause illness and death. Designing the organism to be contagious, or capable of spreading from person to person, would be even more difficult. A synthetic pathogen would also have to be equipped with mechanisms to block the immunological defenses of the host, characteristics that natural pathogens have acquired over eons of evolution. Given these daunting technical obstacles, the threat of a synthetic "super-pathogen" appears exaggerated, at least for the foreseeable future.

The most likely misapplication of synthetic biology for hostile purposes involves the recreation of *known* pathogenic viruses in the laboratory. Contrary to popular belief, however, a biological weapon is not merely an infectious agent but a complex system consisting of (1) a supply of pathogen, either produced in the form of a wet slurry or dried and milled into a dry powder; (2) a complex "formulation" of chemical additives that is mixed with the agent to stabilize it and preserve its infectivity and virulence during storage; (3) a container to store and transport the formulated agent; and (4) an efficient dispersal mechanism to disseminate the formulated agent as a fine-particle aerosol that can infect the targeted personnel through the lungs. Finally, the aerosol cloud must be released under optimal atmospheric and meteorological conditions if it is to inflict casualties over a large area. Given the major technical hurdles associated with weaponization and delivery, the advent of synthetic biology is unlikely to cause a dramatic increase in the threat of bioterrorism.

Nevertheless, two possible scenarios for the deliberate misuse of synthetic biology provide some grounds for concern. The first involves a "lone operator," such as a highly trained molecular biologist who develops an obsessive grudge against certain individuals or groups (or society as a whole). If Theodore Kaczynski, the "Unabomber," had been a microbiologist instead of a mathematician, he might have fit this profile; perhaps the perpetrator of the 2001 anthrax-letter attacks does fit it. So-called "lone wolf" terrorists have proven very innovative and difficult to locate; if armed with a weapon of mass destruction, such a lone operator could cause as much damage as an organized group.

How likely is this lone operator scenario? In any large population of professionals, a small minority may be prepared to use their skills for illicit purposes. Thus, the growing synthetic biology community can be expected to include a few individuals with access to laboratory equipment and supplies who are highly intelligent and well-trained but also deeply disgruntled, have sociopathic tendencies, or wish to prove something to the world. Such an individual might work alone to synthesize a natural pathogen or one incorporating foreign virulence factors. Possible motivations might include inflicting harm on a former or current employer, lover, or a hated ethnic group, profiting from blackmail, eliminating rivals, obtaining perverse pleasure from overcoming technical challenges, or demonstrating scientific and technical superiority.

A lone operator with expertise in synthetic biology would also have a number of characteristics that would pose special difficulties for those seeking to prevent or defend against terrorist attacks. He would not be restricted in his actions by group decision-making and could purchase dual-use equipment and materials for a DNA synthesis laboratory, none of which would provide an obvious tip-off of illicit activity. And precisely because he would be working solo, a lone operator would be unlikely to be discovered by the intelligence community or the police before he strikes.

The pool of people capable of misusing synthetic biology is currently limited to the small number of undergraduates, graduate students, and senior scientists who constitute the research community—probably fewer than 500 people in early 2006. In the future, however, the number of capable individuals will grow rapidly as researchers are drawn to this exciting and dynamic field.

The second scenario of concern is that of a "biohacker," an individual who does not necessarily have malicious intent but seeks to create bioengineered organisms out of curiosity or to demonstrate his technical prowess—a common motivation of many designers of computer viruses. The reagents and tools used in synthetic biology will eventually be converted into commercial kits, making it easier for biohackers to acquire them. Moreover, as synthetic-biology training becomes increasingly available to students at the college and possibly even high-school levels, a "hacker culture" may emerge, increasing the risk of reckless or malevolent experimentation.

MITIGATING THE RISKS

The risks of inadvertent or deliberate harm from synthetic biology clearly warrant a policy response. Although some scientists consider it premature to consider ways of regulating the field at such an early stage in its development, prudence suggests that it is better to start addressing the problem early, rather than having to react after an unanticipated mishap or disaster has provoked a political backlash.

Returning to the historical record, more than three decades of experience have shown that the NIH Guidelines governing recombinant DNA research have functioned reasonably well to protect scientists and the public from potential hazards, while allowing science to advance relatively unhindered. The main concerns about the possible hazards from GEMs have shifted over the years from laboratory research to field testing and use. Nevertheless, public suspicions persist, particularly in Western Europe, about the safety of genetically engineered foods. It is therefore important to consider how the public will respond to the commercial applications of synthetic biology. Although the first such products will not appear for several years, one can imagine the impact of a news report that a team of scientists has created an entirely new life form that is busily replicating itself in a laboratory. Fear of the unknown, whether rational or irrational, might lead to a hasty or inappropriate response, one that unnecessarily impedes scientific progress or ineffectively protects the public good.

Yet it also seems likely that, given the difficulty of anticipating and assessing the risks associated with synthetic organisms, synthetic biology will require a new approach to regulation that differs significantly from the NIH Guidelines on recombinant DNA. Accordingly, it would be useful to bring several leading practitioners of synthetic biology together with biosafety experts, social scientists, ethicists, and legal scholars to brainstorm about reasonable approaches for the oversight and control of such research. The following elements of a regulatory regime might be considered:

Screening of oligonucleotide orders. At present, it is possible to place orders for oligonucleotides and genes over the Internet to custom supply houses, which synthesize any DNA sequence upon request and keep the transaction confidential. As University of Washington biotechnology analyst Rob Carlson has noted, oligonucleotide producers have emerged in several countries around the world, including nations such as China and Iran. A U.S. gene-synthesis company, Blue Heron Biotechnology, voluntarily uses special software to screen all oligonucleotide and gene orders for the presence of DNA sequences from "select agents" of bioterrorism concern. When such a sequence is detected, the request is denied, although there is currently no procedure for reporting such incidents to U.S. government authorities. Nevertheless, suppliers are currently under no legal obligation to screen their orders, and because many clients value confidentiality, companies might put themselves at a competitive disadvantage by doing so. There are two possible solutions to this problem. First, Congress could pass a law requiring U.S. suppliers to screen all oligonucleotide and gene orders for pathogenic DNA sequences. Alternatively, suppliers could agree among themselves to screen orders voluntarily, or legitimate researchers could choose to patronize only those companies that do so. Because the trade involves several countries, however, an effective regulatory regime would have to be international in scope.

Ecological modeling of synthetic microorganisms. Given the difficulty of predicting the risks to public health and the environment posed by synthetic microorganisms, it will be essential to study the ecological behavior of such agents in enclosed microcosms or mesocosms that model as accurately as possible the ecosystem into which the organism will be released. Such studies should examine the extent to which the genetic material from a synthetic microorganism is transferred to other organisms or persists intact in the environment. In the event that the uncertainties associated with the liberation of synthetic microbes prove to be irreducible, it may be necessary to ban all uses in the open environment until a robust risk assessment can be conducted for each proposed application.

Oversight of research. Research in synthetic biology may generate "dual-use" findings that could enable proliferators or terrorists to develop biological warfare agents that are more lethal, easier to manufacture, or of greater military utility than today's bioweapons. In rare cases, it may be necessary to halt a proposed research project at the funding stage or, if unexpectedly sensitive results emerge that could threaten public health or national security, to place constraints on publication. Relevant guidelines for the oversight of "dual-use" research are currently being developed by the U.S. government's National Scientific Advisory Board for Biosecurity and should eventually be "harmonized" internationally.

Public outreach and education. Because of the potential for intense controversy surrounding synthetic biology, public outreach and education are needed even at this early stage in the field's development. Although it is often difficult to persuade scientists to leave the laboratory for even a few hours to participate in a public discussion of their work and its implications for society, such efforts should be encouraged because they generate good will and may help to prevent a future political backlash that could cripple the emerging field of synthetic biology.

SYNTHETIC BIOLOGY AND THE PUBLIC GOOD

At present, synthetic biology's myriad implications can be glimpsed only dimly. The field clearly has the potential to bring about epochal changes in medicine, agriculture, industry, ethics, and politics, and a few decades from now it may have a profound influence on the definition of life, including what it means to be human. Some critics consider the idea of creating artificial organisms in the laboratory to be a frightening example of scientific hubris, evocative of Faust or Dr. Frankenstein. Yet given the momentum and international character of research in synthetic biology, it is already too late to impose a moratorium, if indeed one was ever contemplated.

Instead, practitioners and policy analysts should begin a wide-ranging debate about how best to guide synthetic biology in a safe and socially useful direction without smothering it in the cradle. In so doing, it will be useful to hark back to the enlightened group of biologists who met at Asilomar in 1975 to discuss another exciting new technology—recombinant DNA—that appeared to offer great benefits and unknown dangers.

Their deliberations led to the decision to proceed with caution, subjecting potentially dangerous experiments to careful risk assessment and oversight. That approach, which has since proven remarkably successful, bears emulating today. In the process, however, we may discover that synthetic biology poses novel regulatory and ethical challenges as scientists learn how to manipulate the most basic elements of living systems.

JULIE E. FISCHER

Stewardship or Censorship? Balancing Biosecurity, the Public's Health, and the Benefits of Scientific Openness

Dr. Julie E. Fischer leads the Henry L. Stimson Center's Global Health Security program. Dr. Fischer is a former Council on Foreign Relations International Affairs Fellow (2003–04) and American Association for the Advancement of Science Congressional Fellow (2000–01). She served as a senior research fellow at the University of Washington/Seattle Biomedical Research Institute, and an independent consultant to a Thai-U.S. collaboration aimed at strengthening Thai capacity to identify and control emerging infections of regional and global significance.

. . . A culture of fear may breed compliance, but does little to engage bioscientists in a culture of responsibility based on shared values and consensus. At the same time, it deliberately casts scientists, law enforcement, and security professionals in an adversarial relationship. Any biosecurity regulatory framework destined to endure as a part of daily research life will do so only with "buy-in" from the research community. A snapshot of the current culture suggests that a small percentage of scientists have embraced the government's biosecurity paradigm fully—in some cases so enthusiastically that they question the stringency of the self-regulation adopted by scientific journals and urge tighter controls on dual-use materials and infor-

mation. The majority has demonstrated ambivalence, with some concern about the possibility of a biological attack but a sense of mild skepticism about the need for or effectiveness of controls outside of securing "high-risk" pathogens. Although no community-wide surveys exist to bolster anecdotal observations, few scientists who conduct research with select agents or other pathogens appear to feel engaged in the policy-making process underlying either biodefense or biosecurity paradigms. In general, sensitivity to dual-use technologies as potential threats appears even lower in fields where biodefense funding has made little impact and select agent concerns have required few changes in laboratory practices. At the other extreme, a fraction of scientists have regarded the movement toward increased biosecurity cynically, pointing to the polemics surrounding all issues related to "weapons of mass destruction," the technical obstacles to making any biotechnologies or pathogens into

Reprinted with permission from *Stewardship or Censorship? Balancing Biosecurity, the Public's Health, and the Benefits of Scientific Openness* (Washington, DC: Stimson Center, 2006) Chapter 9, pp. 76–92. Copyright © 2006 The Henry L. Stimson Center.

such weapons, and the channeling of resources into protection against unlikely scenarios. As articulated by Dr. Gerald Epstein: "[As] a basic requirement for anything to work, it's got to be fully supported by the people who are going to be subject to it, and the people who are going to be implementing it. So, that's again the notion that dialogue between the research community and the security community—the people who can identify the problems, the people who know what the consequences of that policy approach are going to be—is absolutely essential."[1] . . .

First, is there a real threat to be countered? If the answer is yes, what can be done to engage the entire biosciences community—not just the fraction most affected by select agents research, or seeking biodefense funding—in a productive dialogue to help the security community define the threats of high-risk pathogens and dual-use technologies accurately? By the same token, how can we arrive at a reasonable biosecurity strategy that matches the most appropriate solutions to the potential problems and fosters a biodefense agenda that can prove dual-use in the sense of approaching both man-made and natural threats to human, agricultural, and environmental health?

DEFINING THE THREAT, SEEKING SOLUTIONS

Does the current biosecurity regime represent a satisfactory, if occasionally annoying, solution to a serious threat of pathogen diversion in domestic laboratories, or an exaggerated response to a hypothetical problem? Similarly, does the current U.S. paradigm for biodefense research go too far in dedicating public health resources to a handful of pathogens that could be used as weapons, or not far enough in preparing for a deliberate epidemic? The answer to both questions is an unsatisfactory, "it depends who you ask," as there is continuing discord within the bioscience community's leadership as well as between experts in biological security. The only way to arrive at a better answer is to strengthen channels of communication between the broader biosciences community and those charged with overseeing national security, a prospect hampered not only by mistrust and cultural differences but by the simple dearth of a strong forum. Several formal and informal channels exist to provide technical advice to stakeholders in the national biological security policy process, but a lack of shared

vocabulary and the dissociation of the larger biosciences community from policy decision-making processes present challenges to establishing buy-in from both sides. Embarrassing gaffes in the last few years, including a minor fracas over whether the report on an unclassified session for microbiologists to discuss scientific openness with the intelligence community would itself be classified, have done little to build trust.

The alternative to developing a stronger relationship between the bioscience and security communities would probably prove more painful for the former. Many scientists remain unconvinced of the necessity to pursue more stringent biosecurity regulations and adopt greater controls on open sharing of scientific information—not unreasonably, as many of the warnings from the security and policy analysis communities have taken the form of dire portents that seem technically far-fetched. Nonetheless, on the other side of the argument, the consensus about a real threat seems firm. To help evaluate real threats accurately and define acceptable costs for mitigating them, the biosciences community as a whole must openly and thoughtfully consider assumptions advanced by security analysts about the possible misuse of scientific information. Otherwise, the broader biosciences community risks being excluded from ongoing discussions of biosecurity regimes deliberately, rather than through simple neglect. As emphasized by George Poste, chair of the Bioterrorism Task Force for the Defense Science Board of the office of the U.S. Secretary of Defense, between the security and science communities there continues to be "a very profound climate of distrust, which just cannot be dismissed as merely the ramblings of non-scientific Philistines. This is a potential collision course that we are on, and I would submit that denial of this risk or obfuscation by the science and technology community would not only damage credibility with political leadership, but also the public, and, thus, predispose us to what several people have said would be well-intentioned but nonetheless flawed policies to control access to information and materials."[2] . . .

BUILDING PUBLIC TRUST

That public trust in science and scientists oscillates through periods of profound misgivings hardly qualifies as news. Since the anthrax assaults engendered a sudden awareness of bioterrorism in an already fragile national psyche, stories of potentially mishandled clinical trials, conflicts of interest, and emotionally charged cloning and stem cell questions have joined the ongoing debate about genetically modified organisms in the news headlines. Biodefense strategies have raised concerns of their own, first with the announcement that the government would dramatically expand the amount of Biosafety Level 3 and 4 laboratory space available in the United States in the next few years. News that one of three new Biosafety Level 4 containment laboratories had been awarded to Boston University provoked local dissent, within the scientific community as well as the general public, and in other states awarded funding to expand lower-level facilities, citizens' groups objected to the proliferation of the Orwellian-sounding "biosafety laboratories." A spate of laboratory incidents involving select agents fanned such anxieties. In one case, a laboratory worker was exposed to Ebola virus at Fort Detrick. In another, a failure to inactivate a *Bacillus anthracis* culture inadvertently exposed seven California researchers to anthrax. Meanwhile, three Boston University laboratory workers were alleged to have contracted tularemia, and three SARS incidents were reported in Asian laboratories.

Any biosecurity regulatory framework, and particularly one based on self-regulation, must do more than just satisfy science and security professionals: It must engage the public's trust. Abigail Salyers, former president of ASM, explains it this way:

Although scientists themselves are well aware of the importance of the free exchange of information within the research community, a community that transcends national boundaries, the public may not necessarily be convinced that scientists can be trusted to this extent. There remains an undercurrent of public discomfort with what is seen by some, however wrongly, as freedom without responsibility. This generalized discomfort has been evident during the debates on the safety of genetically modified foods and the ethics of stem cell research. All of us in the scientific community, either individually or through our professional societies, must be prepared to make a strong and well-documented case for the importance of the free flow of information if such a defense becomes necessary. It is no longer sufficient to tell the public: "Trust us, we know what is good for you." We need to be able to explain why our position is in the public interest.[3]

Policymakers will respond to public concerns, and a public that fears the consequences of open scientific communication will support draconian safety measures if less stringent schemes appear ineffective. Professional societies that have already taken steps toward self-governance in publishing must keep the public apprised of such decisions and their implications.

WHERE ARE THE REASONABLE COMPROMISES?

. . . The effectiveness of the still-new system of self-regulation in biosciences publishing, with assessment built into the peer-review process, has already been scrutinized during the publication of the 1918 Spanish flu manuscripts—undoubtedly not the last time that this will happen—and NSABB will apparently be expected to advise relevant federal agencies on dual-use publication policies while participating directly in the publication process.

Ronald Atlas notes: "Review for 'sensitive' information is difficult and complicated. There is no common definition of what is dangerous or sensitive information and no individual is empowered to decide what is potentially dangerous knowledge."[4] Questions about the real costs of short delays or partial censorship have not been answered clearly by the research community any more than the exact nature of extant threats has been explained by the security community. Specific proposals from some security experts have included registration schemes for access to scientific publications as well as genome databases, with publicly available versions of articles omitting technical details from materials and methods sections that would be available to registered institutional users. Others have suggested a stalling tactic. In this stratagem, where the open and rapid publication of research results "will improve the hands-on 'know how' of how to handle dangerous pathogens, or may help a terrorist organization or proliferant state to avoid long and costly dead-end lines of research, or overcome other technical obstacles, a *modest* delay before communication for the purposes of security review would not be inappropriate."[5]

While continuing the current plan of primarily self-regulation in biosciences publishing, the broader biomedical research community should thoughtfully evaluate the arguments for stricter limits on scientific communication and either develop well-articulated, supported counterarguments, or decide what points can be conceded without violating the integrity of the scientific process. For example, a decision to restrict detailed materials and methods sections to institutional subscribers would clearly contradict the principles of open access, and affect collaborators in developing nations disproportionately, but specific examples of how this might affect research productivity, collaborations, or public health emergencies would provide a more compelling case than objections based in philosophical argument.

INTERNATIONAL HARMONIZATION

The Fink Report pointed out that any efforts to reduce the potential risks of dual-use research "must ultimately be international in scope, because the technologies that could be misused are available and being developed throughout the globe."[6] From 1988 to 2001, the number of internationally co-authored papers (with authors representing institutions in more than one country) more than doubled from 8 to 18%, with U.S. authors represented in 44% of these in 2001. In that year, the United States accounted for about one-third of all published science and engineering articles—the largest percentage of any single nation, but no monopoly. Whether self-imposed or developed with government guidance in the future, consistent application of a U.S. standard for "sensitive information" to manuscripts from nations with discordant security requirements would undoubtedly have an impact on international collegiality, and not inconceivably on publishing patterns.

Biosecurity regulations that constrain the open sharing of scientific information by U.S. researchers and journals in the context of an increasingly global research enterprise would "certainly adversely impact biomedical research in the United States. Whether it could help deter bioterrorism is far from clear."[7]

The lack of international harmonization presents very practical problems for infectious diseases researchers. The mousepox paper cited above illustrates part of the dilemma. Although published in a U.S. journal, the research in question was conducted in Australia. Procedurally, then, decisions about whether this line of inquiry represents contentious research that should be carefully reviewed for risks and benefits prior to advancing would depend upon another nation's review system, and only the decision to publish or reject the manuscript would be left to U.S. journals. In the past few years, other high-output research nations (including the United Kingdom, France, Germany, Japan, Israel, and Canada) have passed domestic laboratory biosecurity legislation, and the European Union issued a 2003 directive calling for best practices to help guide national legislation for controlling access to pathogens and toxins. Thus far, the current Administration has resisted any multilateral efforts to negotiate international biosecurity guidelines on the basis that these might "water down the U.S. standards." However, the lack of a single best-practices model could result in a "patchwork of inconsistent regulations," leading to problematic international collaborations at best and venue-shopping for weak regulatory frameworks at worst. The former has already become apparent. The announcement that foreign researchers working with U.S. researchers on federally funded select agent projects will have to meet the equivalent of U.S. biosecurity standards could pressure resource-poor collaborators "to serve as mere sample exporters." Sharp disparities in biosecurity requirements and available resources can exaggerate the burdens of compliance for all laboratories and researchers involved. No additional funding resources have been made available to help individual U.S. laboratories bring their foreign collaborators' laboratories up to U.S. physical and personnel security standards.

At the same time, three separate laboratory-based outbreaks leading to at least nine cases of SARS infections in China, Taiwan, and Singapore have drawn attention to variable compliance with specific biosafety guidelines issued by the WHO, let alone general suggestions that laboratories should incorporate biosecurity risk assessments. . . . A realistic risk matrix that integrates biosecurity and biosafety strategies more closely could prove as valuable for providing common ground for international harmonization efforts as it could for optimizing risk-benefit in U.S. domestic biosecurity regulations. The institutional review model for biosafety, for example, has been widely adopted internationally, not because the United States imposed its template upon the WHO or other nations but because it provides a practical model for relatively unobtrusive and cost-effective regulation of experiments that might pose a hazard to researchers or the public. . . .

While reaching international consensus is daunting, forcing the U.S. select agent list and guidelines on researchers in other nations seems an equally unlikely model for success. First, perceptions of high-risk pathogens differ based on nations' varying epidemic and endemic diseases profiles. Second, such demands—focusing largely on the personnel and physical security emphasized by the select agent rules—may be seen as ranging from wildly impractical to imperialistic. Finally, until the United States has demonstrated that the benefits of the select agent rules and the evolving dual-use biotechnology regulatory paradigm outweigh the costs to the satisfaction of its own research community, convincing other nations will remain challenging.

CODES OF CONDUCT

Codes of conduct have been proposed as both an educational tool to explain risks to individual researchers and a compact between those scientists and society by the Fink Report and other analyses. A template code flexible enough to incorporate national practices, but universal enough to capture a shared ethos, could provide one method for "bottom-up" international harmonization of biosecurity practices. The NSABB has been charged with developing a code of conduct for biosecurity, but this can and should involve an iterative process with input from professional societies, institutions, and individual scientists. Many questions remain about the type of code to be adopted (with models of aspirational, educational, and enforceable codes to be considered), as well as how to make such codes relevant to life sciences researchers. If the true strategy of the biosecurity regulatory framework lies in developing a culture of responsibility that transcends national law, individual scientists must feel ownership in, as well as necessity for, vital codes of conduct or ethics.

TIME FOR ANOTHER ASILOMAR—OR TWO?

The biosciences community cannot simply wait for the NSABB to fill all of its potential roles, especially as the committee will probably stagger under its considerable workload for some time to come. The National Academies and policy analysis organizations have facilitated meetings between scientists, science policy analysts, security and intelligence professionals, and policymakers that should continue despite previous misunderstandings—and even in the absence of a recent bioterrorism event. Professional societies, especially those whose members do not gravitate naturally toward select agents or pathogens issues, can also play a role by convening discussion sessions at national meetings, developing educational curricula on the issues at hand, and creating policies on a range of scientific openness issues that can be shared with the NSABB and directly with policymakers. In partnership, professional societies and

policy organizations can also play a key role in developing realistic case studies that examine the consequences of delayed or restricted research publications objectively, as a matter for serious analysis, rather than simply asserting the desirability of open scientific communications.

Some leaders in the field of biodefense have called for a second Asilomar, a reincarnation of the 1975 conference that outlined the current working system for biosafety and gave rise to the institutional review system. Such a meeting could provide a manageable forum for addressing the many issues raised above: defining the real risks, identifying short-term goals and long-term strategies for dealing with those risks in the context of responsible self-regulation where possible, and determining how these would affect both individual researchers and the overall state of scientific communication in biological and biomedical research. Like the first Asilomar Conference, such a program would have to engage stakeholders from beyond the most directly affected community of researchers, involving the public through media coverage and participation by stakeholders from various community and policy sectors. Building on lessons learned in the last three decades, such a conference should also include discussions of ethical, legal, and social issues, in addition to the technical issues of concern.

Asilomar may not provide exactly the right model, as the hazards of biodefense research have been debated publicly now for several years, by-passing the opportunity to engage in thoughtful scientific debate about the perceived risks before broaching the subject with the general public and policymakers. However, a summit for interested members of the biosciences community to focus on the entire range of issues related to open scientific communication, including public trust, remains desperately needed. Due to the scope of community involvement required, the correct answer might be a series of Asilomars, or meetings repeated with an identical agenda, distributed either by geography or held after the regular conferences of various large professional societies. Such a series would provide a means through which the newly selected members of the NSABB might judge the current interests and needs of bioscientists from various disciplines or institutions. Regardless of whether this community-wide summit takes place as a single conference or a series of meeting, a venue for addressing the whole range of concerns that surround issues of biodefense, biosecurity, and open scientific communication might offer an opportunity to explore divisions within the biosciences community, as well as to improve public understanding.

THE ROLE OF THE INDIVIDUAL

As in every community, the involvement of individual scientists in political and policy issues ranges from intense involvement in advocacy issues to almost complete disengagement apart from paying annual dues to a professional society. Following the anthrax assaults and the subsequently imposed biosecurity regulations, several scientists have become articulate advocates for scientific openness and related issues. However, many assumptions about the impact of current and proposed regulatory measures stem from the observations of those vocal few, or from limited surveys inherently biased through self-selection. Stronger channels for feedback from individual scientists on specific biosecurity and biosafety issues—designed to avoid professional repercussions and maximize responses—would help decision-makers, professional organizations, and institutions perform the kind of evaluations necessary to foster a successful and sustainable biosecurity framework.

Although federal workshops occasionally allow individuals to address such issues, few researchers have the time or resources to travel to Washington, DC-area meetings solely to provide comments on national policies. Professional societies and institutions will most likely provide the most appropriate conduit for conveying individual concerns to the NSABB or other appropriate forums at the federal level. They could provide an inestimable service through the joint development of a more active, standardized mechanism for monitoring scientists' awareness of and response to biosecurity issues than can be generated by researchers in a single study. Such information could at least establish a true baseline for understanding the impact of the current biosecurity regulatory framework.

The science community must rely on individual scientists to engage the issue, learning as much as possible about the policy and political aspects of the biosecurity debate. An educated researcher steeped in these details as well as the technical facets of the biosecurity regulation challenge can serve as a far more effective advocate for reasonable approaches to understanding and averting the threat of dual-use technologies. The security community does not take the "right to research" for granted. Neither can scientists.

NOTES

1. Epstein, Gerald L. "Panel Discussion: Preventing the Misuse of Biotechnology." 15 Nov. 2002. Carnegie International Non-Proliferation Conference. 1 Feb. 2005. <http://www.ceip.org/files/projects/npp/pdf/conference/lottmantranscripts/Epstein.pdf>.

2. Poste, George. Remarks to the *Scientific Openness and National Security Workshop*. Washington, DC: National Research Council, 2003. 1 Feb. 2005. <http://www.csis.org/tech/ssi/sonsw/>.

3. Salyers, Abigail. "Science, Censorship, and Public Health." *Science* 296.5568 (2002): 617.

4. Atlas, Ronald M. Testimony before the House Science Committee.

5. Wallerstein, Mitchel B. "Remarks at Scientific Openness and National Security Workshop," 9 Jan. 2003. National Research Council. 1 Feb. 2005. <http:// www.csis.org/tech/ssi/sonsw/>.

6. *Biotechnology Research in an Age of Terrorism*, 124.

7. Atlas, "National Security and the Biological Research Community," 754.

Suggested Readings for Chapter 10

HUMAN EMBRYONIC STEM CELL RESEARCH

Cynthia, Cohen B. *Renewing the Stuff of Life: Stem Cells, Ethics, and Public Policy.* New York: Oxford University Press, 2007.

Committee on Guidelines for Human Embryonic Stem Cell Research, National Research Council. *Guidelines for Human Embryonic Stem Cell Research.* Washington, DC: National Academies Press, 2005.

Greely, Henry T. "Moving Human Embryonic Stem Cells from Legislature to Lab: Remaining Legal and Ethical Questions." *PLoS Medicine* 3 (2006), e143.

Gruen, Lori. "Oocytes For Sale?" *Metaphilosophy* 38 (2007), 285–308.

Herder, Matthew. "Proliferating Patent Problems with Human Embryonic Stem Cell Research?" *Bioethical Inquiry* 3 (2006), 69–79.

Karpowicz, Phillip, Cynthia, Cohen B., and van der Kooy, Derek. "It Is Ethical to Transplant Human Stem Cells into Nonhuman Embryos." *Nature Medicine* 10 (2004), 331–35.

Karpowicz, Phillip, Cynthia, Cohen B., and van der Kooy, Derek. "Developing Human–Nonhuman Chimeras in Human Stem Cell Research: Ethical Issues and Boundaries." *Kennedy Institute of Ethics Journal* 15 (2005), 107–34.

Lo, Bernard, et al. "A New Era in the Ethics of Human Embryonic Stem Cell Research." *Stem Cells* 23 (2005), 1454–59.

Loring, Jeanne F., and Campbell, Cathryn. "Science And Law: Intellectual Property and Human Embryonic Stem Cell Research." *Science* 311 (2006), 1716–17.

Magnus, David, and Cho, Mildred K. "Issues in Oocyte Donation For Stem Cell Research." *Science* 308 (2005), 1747–48.

Meissner, A., and Jaenisch, R. "Mammalian Nuclear Transfer." *Developmental Dynamics* 235 (2006), 2460–69.

Robert, Jason S. "The Science and Ethics of Making Part-Human Animals in Stem Cell Biology." *The FASEB Journal* 20 (2006), 838–45.

Robert, Jason S., and Baylis, Francoise. "Crossing Species Boundaries." *The American Journal of Bioethics* 3 (2003), 1–13.

Robertson, J. A. "Human Embryonic Stem Cell Research: Ethical and Legal Issues." *Nature Review Genetics* 2 (2001), 74–78.

Streiffer, Robert. "At the Edge of Humanity: Human Stem Cells, Chimeras, and Moral Status." *Kennedy Institute of Ethics Journal* 15 (2005), 347–70.

ETHICS AND GENETICALLY MODIFIED ORGANISMS

Almond, Brenda. "Commodifying Animals: Ethical Issues in Genetic Engineering of Animals." *Health, Risk & Society* 2 (2000), 95–105.

Comstock, Gary L. *Vexing Nature? On the Ethical Case Against Agricultural Biotechnology.* Boston, MA: Kluwer, 2000.

Cooley, D. R. "Who's Afraid of Frankenstein Food?" *Journal of Social Philosophy* 33 (2002), 442–63.

Loftis, J. Robert. "Germ-Line Enhancement of Humans and Nonhumans." *Kennedy Institute of Ethics Journal* 15 (2005), 57–76.

Maienschein, Jane. *Whose View of Life? Embryos, Cloning, and Stem Cells.* Cambridge MA: Harvard University Press, 2003.

Rollin, Bernard E. "Bad Ethics, Good Ethics and the Genetic Engineering of Animals in Agriculture." *Journal of Animal Science* 74 (1996), 535–41.

Shrader-Frechette, Kristin. "Property Rights and Genetic Engineering: Developing Nations at Risk." *Science and Engineering Ethics* 11 (2005), 137–49.

Soule, Ed. "The Precautionary Principle and the Regulation of U.S. Food and Drug Safety." *Journal of Medicine and Philosophy* 29: 3 (2004), 333–50.

Thompson, Paul B. "Science Policy and Moral Purity: The Case of Animal Biotechnology." *Agriculture and Human Values* 14 (1997), 11–27.

Thompson, Paul B. "Ethical Issues in Livestock Cloning." *Journal of Agricultural and Environmental Ethics* 11 (1997), 197–217.

Thompson, Paul B. "Value Judgments and Risk Comparisons. The Case of Genetically Engineered Crops." *Plant Physiology* 132 (2003), 10–16.

Torgersen, Helge. "The Real and Perceived Risks of Genetically Modified Organisms." *EMBO Reports* 5 (2004), S17–S21.

GENETIC ENHANCEMENT, NEUROSCIENCE, AND NANOTECHNOLOGY

Daniels, Norman. "Normal Functioning and the Treatment Enhancement Distinction." *Cambridge Quarterly of Healthcare Ethics* 9 (2000), 309–22.

Farah, Martha J. "Neuroethics: The Practical and the Philosophical." *Trends in Cognitive Science* 9 (2005), 34–40.

Gardner, William. "Can Human Genetic Enhancement Be Prohibited?" *Journal of Medicine and Philosophy* 20 (1995), 65–84.

Gazzaniga, Michael S. *The Ethical Brain.* Washington, DC: Dana Press, 2005.

Juengst, Eric T. "Can Enhancement Be Distinguished from Prevention in Genetic Medicine?" *Journal of Medicine and Philosophy* 22 (1997), 125–42.

McKenny, Gerald. "Human Enhancement Uses of Biotechnology, Ethics, Therapy vs. Enhancement." In Thomas H. Murray and Maxwell J. Mehlman, eds. *Encyclopedia of Ethical, Legal, and Policy Issues in Biotechnology.* 2 vols. New York: John Wiley & Sons, 2000, 507–15.

Mehlman, Maxwell J. "Human Enhancement Uses of Biotechnology, Law, Genetic Enhancement, and the Regulation of the Acquired Genetic Advantages." In Thomas H. Murray and Maxwell J. Mehlman, eds. *Encyclopedia of Ethical, Legal, and Policy Issues in Biotechnology.* 2 vols. New York: John Wiley & Sons, 2000, 515–27.

Mnyusiwalla, Anisa, Daar, Abdallah S., and Singer, Peter A. ' "Mind the Gap': Science and Ethics in Nanotechnology." *Nanotechnology* 14 (2003), R9–R13.

Moreno, Jonathan D. "Neuroethics: An Agenda for Neuroscience and Society." *Nature Reviews Neuroscience*, 4 (2003), 149–53.

Muller, Hermann J. "The Guidance of Human Evolution." *Perspectives in Biology and Medicine* 3 (1959), 1–43.

Parens, Erik, ed. *Enhancing Human Traits: Ethical and Social Implications.* Washington, DC: Georgetown University Press, 1998.

Resnik, David B. "The Moral Significance of the Therapy Enhancement Distinction in Human Genetics." *Cambridge Quarterly of Healthcare Ethics* 9 (2000), 365–77.

Scully, Jackie Leach, and Rehmann-Sutter, Christoph. "When Norms Normalize: The Case of Genetic 'Enhancement.'" *Human Gene Therapy* 12 (2001), 87–95.

Shapiro, Michael H. "Human Enhancement Uses of Biotechnology, Policy, Technological Enhancement, and Human Equality." In Thomas H. Murray and Maxwell J. Mehlman, eds. *Encyclopedia of Ethical, Legal, and Policy Issues in Biotechnology.* 2 vols. New York: John Wiley & Sons, 2000, 527–48.

Stock, Gregory. *Redesigning Humans: Our Inevitable Genetic Future.* Boston, MA: Houghton Mifflin, 2002.

Wachbroit, Robert. "Human Enhancement Uses of Biotechnology: Overview." In Thomas H. Murray and Maxwell J. Mehlman, eds. *Encyclopedia of Ethical, Legal, and Policy Issues in Biotechnology.* 2 vols. New York: John Wiley & Sons, 2000, 549–52.

Weil, Vivian. "Zeroing In on Ethical Issues in Nanotechnology." *Proceedings of the IEEE* 91 (2003), 1976–79.

Whitehouse, Peter J., and Marling, Cynthia R. "Human Enhancement Uses of Biotechnology, Ethics, Cognitive Enhancement." In Thomas H. Murray and Maxwell J. Mehlman, eds. *Encyclopedia of Ethical, Legal, and Policy Issues in*

Biotechnology. 2 vols. New York: John Wiley & Sons, 2000, 485–91.

SYNTHETIC BIOLOGY AND BIOSECURITY

Bhutkar, Arjun. "Synthetic Biology: Navigating the Challenges Ahead." *Journal of Biolaw & Business* 8 (2005), 19–29.

Cho, Mildred, Magnus, David, Caplan, Arthur, McGee, Daniel, and the Ethics of Genomics Group. "Ethical Considerations in Synthesizing a Minimal Genome." *Science* 286 (1999), 2087–90.

Committee on Research Standards and Practices to Prevent the Destructive Application of Biotechnology, *National Research Council Biotechnology Research in an Age of Terrorism.* Washington, DC: National Academies Press, 2004.

Falkow, S., and Kennedy, D. "Letters: Science Publishing and Security Concerns." *Science* 300 (2003), 737–39.

Green, Shane K., Taub, Sara, Morin, Karine, and Higginson, Daniel for The Council On Ethical And Judicial Affairs Of The American Medical Association. "Guidelines to Prevent Malevolent Use of Biomedical Research." *Cambridge Quarterly of Healthcare Ethics* 15 (2006), 432–47.

Keel, B. A. "Protecting America's Secrets While Maintaining Academic Freedom." *Academic Medicine* 79 (2004), 333–42.

Kelley, M. "Infectious Disease Research and Dual Use Risk." *Virtual Mentor* 8 (2006), 230–34.

King, Nicholas B. "The Ethics of Biodefense." *Bioethics* 19 (2005), 432–46.

Moreno, Jonathan D. "Bioethics and the National Security State." *Journal of Law, Medicine & Ethics* 32 (2004), 198–208.

Tucker, J. B., and Hopper, C. "Protein Engineering: Security Implications." *EMBO Reports* 7 (2006), S14–S17.

Rai, A., and Boyle, J. "Synthetic Biology: Caught Between Property Rights, the Public Domain, and the Commons." *PLoS Biology* 5 (2007), e58.

Relman, David A. "Bioterrorism—Preparing to Fight the Next War." *New England Journal of Medicine* 354 (2006), 113–15.

Tucker, Jonathan B. "Preventing the Misuse of Biology: Lessons from the Oversight of Smallpox Virus Research." *International Security* 31 (2006), 116–50.